Twentieth-Century Literary Criticism

Topics Volume

Guide to Gale Literary Criticism Series

For criticism on	Consult these Gale series
Authors now living or who died after December 31, 1999	*CONTEMPORARY LITERARY CRITICISM (CLC)*
Authors who died between 1900 and 1999	*TWENTIETH-CENTURY LITERARY CRITICISM (TCLC)*
Authors who died between 1800 and 1899	*NINETEENTH-CENTURY LITERATURE CRITICISM (NCLC)*
Authors who died between 1400 and 1799	*LITERATURE CRITICISM FROM 1400 TO 1800 (LC)* *SHAKESPEAREAN CRITICISM (SC)*
Authors who died before 1400	*CLASSICAL AND MEDIEVAL LITERATURE CRITICISM (CMLC)*
Authors of books for children and young adults	*CHILDREN'S LITERATURE REVIEW (CLR)*
Dramatists	*DRAMA CRITICISM (DC)*
Poets	*POETRY CRITICISM (PC)*
Short story writers	*SHORT STORY CRITICISM (SSC)*
Black writers of the past two hundred years	*BLACK LITERATURE CRITICISM (BLC)* *BLACK LITERATURE CRITICISM SUPPLEMENT (BLCS)*
Hispanic writers of the late nineteenth and twentieth centuries	*HISPANIC LITERATURE CRITICISM (HLC)* *HISPANIC LITERATURE CRITICISM SUPPLEMENT (HLCS)*
Native North American writers and orators of the eighteenth, nineteenth, and twentieth centuries	*NATIVE NORTH AMERICAN LITERATURE (NNAL)*
Major authors from the Renaissance to the present	*WORLD LITERATURE CRITICISM, 1500 TO THE PRESENT (WLC)* *WORLD LITERATURE CRITICISM SUPPLEMENT (WLCS)*

ISSN 0276-8178

Volume 118

Twentieth-Century Literary Criticism

Topics Volume

**Criticism of Various Topics
in Twentieth-Century Literature, including Literary
and Critical Movements, Prominent Themes and
Genres, Anniversary Celebrations, and Surveys
of National Literatures**

Janet Witalec
Project Editor

GALE®

THOMSON

GALE

Detroit • New York • San Diego • San Francisco • Cleveland • New Haven, Conn. • Waterville, Maine • London • Munich

Twentieth-Century Literary Criticism, Vol. 118

Project Editor
Janet Witalec

Editorial
Jenny Cromie, Scott Darga, Kathy D. Darrow,
Julie Keppen, Ellen McGeagh, Ron Morelli,
Linda Pavlovski

Research
Nicodemus Ford, Sarah Genik, Tamara C. Nott,
Tracie A. Richardson

Permissions
Debra Freitas

Imaging and Multimedia
Lezlie Light, Kelly A. Quin, Luke Rademacher

Product Design
Michael Logusz

Composition and Electronic Capture
Carolyn Roney

Manufacturing
Stacy L. Melson

LIBRARY OF CONGRESS CATALOG CARD NUMBER 76-46132

ISBN 0-7876-5862-6
ISSN 0276-8178

Printed in the United States of America
10 9 8 7 6 5 4 3 2 1

Contents

Preface

Since its inception more than fifteen years ago, *Twentieth-Century Literary Criticism* (*TCLC*) has been purchased and used by nearly 10,000 school, public, and college or university libraries. *TCLC* has covered more than 500 authors, representing 58 nationalities and over 25,000 titles. No other reference source has surveyed the critical response to twentieth-century authors and literature as thoroughly as *TCLC*. In the words of one reviewer, "there is nothing comparable available." *TCLC* "is a gold mine of information—dates, pseudonyms, biographical information, and criticism from books and periodicals—which many librarians would have difficulty assembling on their own."

Scope of the Series

TCLC is designed to serve as an introduction to authors who died between 1900 and 1999 and to the most significant interpretations of these author's works. Volumes published from 1978 through 1999 included authors who died between 1900 and 1960. The great poets, novelists, short story writers, playwrights, and philosophers of the period are frequently studied in high school and college literature courses. In organizing and reprinting the vast amount of critical material written on these authors, *TCLC* helps students develop valuable insight into literary history, promotes a better understanding of the texts, and sparks ideas for papers and assignments. Each entry in *TCLC* presents a comprehensive survey on an author's career or an individual work of literature and provides the user with a multiplicity of interpretations and assessments. Such variety allows students to pursue their own interests; furthermore, it fosters an awareness that literature is dynamic and responsive to many different opinions.

Every fourth volume of *TCLC* is devoted to literary topics. These topics widen the focus of the series from the individual authors to such broader subjects as literary movements, prominent themes in twentieth-century literature, literary reaction to political and historical events, significant eras in literary history, prominent literary anniversaries, and the literatures of cultures that are often overlooked by English-speaking readers.

TCLC is designed as a companion series to Gale's *Contemporary Literary Criticism,* (*CLC*) which reprints commentary on authors who died after 1999. Because of the different time periods under consideration, there is no duplication of material between *CLC* and *TCLC*.

Organization of the Book

A *TCLC* entry consists of the following elements:

- The **Author Heading** cites the name under which the author most commonly wrote, followed by birth and death dates. Also located here are any name variations under which an author wrote, including transliterated forms for authors whose native languages use nonroman alphabets. If the author wrote consistently under a pseudonym, the pseudonym will be listed in the author heading and the author's actual name given in parenthesis on the first line of the biographical and critical information. Uncertain birth or death dates are indicated by question marks. Single-work entries are preceded by a heading that consists of the most common form of the title in English translation (if applicable) and the original date of composition.

- A **Portrait of the Author** is included when available.

- The **Introduction** contains background information that introduces the reader to the author, work, or topic that is the subject of the entry.

- The list of **Principal Works** is ordered chronologically by date of first publication and lists the most important works by the author. The genre and publication date of each work is given. In the case of foreign authors whose works have been translated into English, the English-language version of the title follows in brackets. Unless otherwise indicated, dramas are dated by first performance, not first publication.

- Reprinted **Criticism** is arranged chronologically in each entry to provide a useful perspective on changes in critical evaluation over time. The critic's name and the date of composition or publication of the critical work are given at the beginning of each piece of criticism. Unsigned criticism is preceded by the title of the source in which it appeared. All titles by the author featured in the text are printed in boldface type. Footnotes are reprinted at the end of each essay or excerpt. In the case of excerpted criticism, only those footnotes that pertain to the excerpted texts are included.

- A complete **Bibliographical Citation** of the original essay or book precedes each piece of criticism.

- Critical essays are prefaced by brief **Annotations** explicating each piece.

- An annotated bibliography of **Further Reading** appears at the end of each entry and suggests resources for additional study. In some cases, significant essays for which the editors could not obtain reprint rights are included here. Boxed material following the further reading list provides references to other biographical and critical sources on the author in series published by Gale.

Indexes

A **Cumulative Author Index** lists all of the authors that appear in a wide variety of reference sources published by the Gale Group, including *TCLC*. A complete list of these sources is found facing the first page of the Author Index. The index also includes birth and death dates and cross references between pseudonyms and actual names.

A **Cumulative Nationality Index** lists all authors featured in *TCLC* by nationality, followed by the number of the *TCLC* volume in which their entry appears.

A **Cumulative Topic Index** lists the literary themes and topics treated in the series as well as in *Classical and Medieval Literature Criticism, Literature Criticism from 1400 to 1800, Nineteenth-Century Literature Criticism,* and the *Contemporary Literary Criticism* Yearbook, which was discontinued in 1998.

An alphabetical **Title Index** accompanies each volume of *TCLC*. Listings of titles by authors covered in the given volume are followed by the author's name and the corresponding page numbers where the titles are discussed. English translations of foreign titles and variations of titles are cross-referenced to the title under which a work was originally published. Titles of novels, dramas, nonfiction books, and poetry, short story, or essay collections are printed in italics, while individual poems, short stories, and essays are printed in roman type within quotation marks.

In response to numerous suggestions from librarians, Gale also produces an annual paperbound edition of the *TCLC* cumulative title index. This annual cumulation, which alphabetically lists all titles reviewed in the series, is available to all customers. Additional copies of this index are available upon request. Librarians and patrons will welcome this separate index; it saves shelf space, is easy to use, and is recyclable upon receipt of the next edition.

Citing *Twentieth-Century Literary Criticism*

When writing papers, students who quote directly from any volume in the Literary Criticism Series may use the following general format to footnote reprinted criticism. The first example pertains to material drawn from periodicals, the second to material reprinted from books.

George Orwell, "Reflections on Gandhi," *Partisan Review* 6 (Winter 1949): 85-92; reprinted in *Twentieth-Century Literary Criticism,* vol. 59, ed. Jennifer Gariepy (Detroit: The Gale Group, 1995), 40-3.

William H. Slavick, "Going to School to DuBose Heyward," *The Harlem Renaissance Re-examined,* ed. Victor A. Kramer (AMS, 1987), 65- 91; reprinted in *Twentieth-Century Literary Criticism,* vol. 59, ed. Jennifer Gariepy (Detroit: The Gale Group, 1995), 94-105.

Suggestions are Welcome

Readers who wish to suggest new features, topics, or authors to appear in future volumes, or who have other suggestions or comments are cordially invited to call, write, or fax the Managing Editor:

Managing Editor, Literary Criticism Series
The Gale Group
27500 Drake Road
Farmington Hills, MI 48331-3535
1-800-347-4253 (GALE)
Fax: 248-699-8054

Acknowledgments

The editors wish to thank the copyright holders of the excerpted criticism included in this volume and the permissions managers of many book and magazine publishing companies for assisting us in securing reproduction rights. We are also grateful to the staffs of the Detroit Public Library, the Library of Congress, the University of Detroit Mercy Library, Wayne State University Purdy/Kresge Library Complex, and the University of Michigan Libraries for making their resources available to us. Following is a list of the copyright holders who have granted us permission to reproduce material in this volume of *TCLC*. Every effort has been made to trace copyright, but if omissions have been made, please let us know.

COPYRIGHTED MATERIAL IN *TCLC*, VOLUME 118, WAS REPRODUCED FROM THE FOLLOWING PERIODICALS:

COPYRIGHTED MATERIAL IN *TCLC*, VOLUME 118, WAS REPRODUCED FROM THE FOLLOWING BOOKS:

Literary Criticism Series Advisory Board

The members of the Gale Group Literary Criticism Series Advisory Board—reference librarians and subject specialists from public, academic, and school library systems—represent a cross-section of our customer base and offer a variety of informed perspectives on both the presentation and content of our literature criticism products. Advisory board members assess and define such quality issues as the relevance, currency, and usefulness of the author coverage, critical content, and literary topics included in our series; evaluate the layout, presentation, and general quality of our printed volumes; provide feedback on the criteria used for selecting authors and topics covered in our series; provide suggestions for potential enhancements to our series; identify any gaps in our coverage of authors or literary topics, recommending authors or topics for inclusion; analyze the appropriateness of our content and presentation for various user audiences, such as high school students, undergraduates, graduate students, librarians, and educators; and offer feedback on any proposed changes/enhancements to our series. We wish to thank the following advisors for their advice throughout the year.

Hard-Boiled Fiction

INTRODUCTION

Although the genre of crime fiction has existed in continental and American literature since at least the nineteenth century, the particular form of it known as "hard-boiled" fiction reached its greatest popularity during the period of the 1920s through the 1960s. Critics point out that authors who shaped the genre during this era—especially Dashiell Hammett, Raymond Chandler, and Ross McDonald—reinvented the crime fiction style popularized by such predecessors as Sir Arthur Conan Doyle and Dorothy L. Sayers in several key ways. They placed their crime stories not in a rural setting, as was typical of earlier crime fiction, but in a sinister and forbidding urban environment. Perhaps most importantly, they introduced the figure of the tough-talking, brave, but also disillusioned and alienated private eye, who contrasted markedly with the intellectual type of detective exemplified by Sherlock Holmes. On the thematic level, hard-boiled fiction focused on the secrets, mental depravity, and human weakness that lead to crime, rather than on the swift restoration of law and order. Neither high literature nor pulp fiction, hard-boiled fiction was crafted to be accessible to the common reader, yet it also incorporated modernist themes and techniques. While some critics have denigrated hard-boiled fiction as nothing more than a lengthy puzzle, others have written about the genre as a tool for social commentary and as a vehicle for discussing changing notions about justice, morality, and personal and civic virtues.

In novels such as Hammett's *The Maltese Falcon* (1930), Chandler's *The Big Sleep* (1939), James M. Cain's *The Postman always Rings Twice* (1934), Mickey Spillane's *I, the Jury* (1947) and *Kiss Me, Deadly* (1952), the hard-boiled detective emerged as the major point of interest in the work. The individual detectives—Sam Spade, Philip Marlowe, Lew Archer, Spenser, and Travis McGee, respectively—became as famous as the authors themselves, and their personal journeys toward solving the crime in question took on more importance than the resolution of the plot. The hard-boiled detective's main traits were cynicism, toughness in difficult situations, and a wise-cracking sense of humor, but also a strong sense of morality, the desire to see justice done, and the willingness to be physically or emotionally wounded. Scholars have traced the evolution of this character type in later hard-boiled novels, such as those of Jules Feiffer, Richard Brautigan, and Thomas Berger. These later authors present a more complex view of evil, with lines sometimes blurred between victim and criminal, and with a private eye who is less certain of the justice of his or her mission or of the system he or she serves. Still, many common elements remain in later hard-boiled fiction: violent crime, an intricate and exciting plot, and a brave but vulnerable private eye in the center of the action.

There has been much critical interest in the hard-boiled novel since its beginnings, but especially from the 1970s onward. Critics John G. Cawelti, Larry E. Grimes, and Gary Levisi have examined the characteristics, development, and central role of the hero in hard-boiled fiction. The theme of evil in hard-boiled fiction is the subject of studies by James F. Maxfield and Frederick Isaac. Studies of the hard-boiled novel's stylistic elements have also been popular, including Isaac's examination of humor, Scott R. Christianson's study of the influence of modernism, and Michael Pettengell's discussion of naturalistic elements. Many critics of the 1980s and 1990s have focused on women in hard-boiled fiction, both as authors and as protagonists. Studies by Robert Sandels, Timothy Shuker-Haines, Martha M. Umphrey, Priscilla L. Walton, and Manina Jones have probed the ways in which hard-boiled fiction has been influenced by the emergence of such private eyes as Sue Grafton's Kinsey Millhone and Sara Paretsky's V. I. Warshawski.

REPRESENTATIVE WORKS

Dwight V. Babcock
The Gorgeous Ghoul (novel) 1941
A Homicide for Hannah (novel) 1941
Hannah Says Foul Play (novel) 1946

Thomas Berger
Who Is Teddy Villanova? (novel) 1977

Andrew Bergman
The Big Kiss-Off of 1944 (novel) 1974

Richard Brautigan
Dreaming of Babylon: A Private Eye Novel (novel) 1942

James M. Cain
The Postman always Rings Twice (novel) 1934

Raymond Chandler
The Big Sleep (novel) 1939
Farewell, My Lovely (novel) 1940
The High Window (novel) 1943
The Lady in the Lake (novel) 1944
The Little Sister (novel) 1949

The Long Goodbye (novel) 1954
Playback (novel) 1958

Sir Arthur Conan Doyle
The Valley of Fear (novel) 1915

Harlan Ellison
Web of the City (novel) 1958
Spider Kiss (novel) 1961
Mefisto in Onyx (novel) 1993

Jules Feiffer
Ackroyd (novel) 1977

Sue Grafton
F Is for Fugitive (novel) 1989
H Is for Homicide (novel) 1991

Dashiell Hammett
Red Harvest (novel) 1929
The Maltese Falcon (novel) 1930
The Glass Key (novel) 1931
The Thin Man (novel) 1934

Stuart Kaminsky
Murder on the Yellow Brick Road (novel) 1977
You Bet Your Life (novel) 1979
Catch a Falling Clown (novel) 1982

Jonathan Latimer
The Lady in the Morgue (novel) 1936

Ross McDonald
The Wycherley Woman (novel) 1963

Sara Paretsky
Indemnity Only (novel) 1982
Deadlock (novel) 1984
Killing Orders (novel) 1985
Bitter Medicine (novel) 1987
Blood Shot (novel) 1988; also published as *Toxic Shock*, 1988

Robert Parker
God Save the Child (novel) 1974
The Godwulf Manuscript (novel) 1974
Mortal Stakes (novel) 1975
Early Autumn (novel) 1981

Bill Pronzini
The Snatch (novel) 1975
Scattershot (novel) 1982

Roger Simon
The Big Fix (novel) 1973
Wild Turkey (novel) 1975

Mickey Spillane
I, the Jury (novel) 1947
Kiss Me, Deadly (novel) 1952

Rex Stout
The Black Mountain (novel) 1954
Champagne for One (novel) 1958

OVERVIEWS AND GENERAL STUDIES

John G. Cawelti (essay date fall 1975)

SOURCE: Cawelti, John G. "The Gunfighter and the Hard-Boiled Dick." *American Studies* 16, no. 2 (fall 1975): 49-64.

[*In the following essay, Cawelti compares the image of the hero inherent in hard-boiled detective fiction with that found in Western fiction and films. He notes that the hard-boiled hero embodies a darker, more violent, and more anarchic view of the world than his Western counterpart.*]

The thriving little frontier settlement is suddenly beset with outlaws. Coming out of nowhere they viciously attack, beating the citizens and killing the old sheriff. Desperately the citizens gather in the church. After prayer for divine guidance, a debate breaks out between those who would leave the town to the outlaws, and those who think they should tough it out. The braver element prevails and the townspeople determine to stay. They petition the governor for a new sheriff. In the nick of time, a heroic figure, beautifully dressed in fringed buckskin and riding a magnificent stallion rides out of the desert. With his help the townspeople successfully defend themselves against the outlaw bands until, in a final confrontation, the hero exposes, tracks down and outshoots the corrupt politician who has tried to drive the people out and take over their land. With law and order restored, the hero leaves a grateful townsfolk behind and rides off into the desert (and the sunset) with his faithful partner.

Sound familiar? It should, since with minor changes this could be a plot description of any of a hundred Western films ranging from an episode of the Lone Ranger, through John Ford's *My Darling Clementine*, George Steven's *Shane* and Fred Zinneman's *High Noon* to Clint Eastwood's *High Plains Drifter*. Actually the film I was more or less following in this summary is Mel Brooks' total send-up of the Western, *Blazing Saddles*. The hilarious effectiveness of *Blazing Saddles* depends to a considerable extent on the way in which it follows through the Hollywood archetype of the Western hero, with certain incongruous details that enable Brooks to keep his audience in stitches while he reduces the great myth of the Western gunfighter to a shambles.

The fact that the new sheriff in *Blazing Saddles* is black constitutes the most pervasive burlesque of the mythic tradition. Though there have been a few black heroes in Western films, particularly of more recent vintage, the heroic lawman of the Hollywood myth has traditionally been white in more than his hat. However, Brooks did not create the satire of *Blazing Saddles* simply by setting a black man in a traditionally white heroic role. It is not just his blackness, but his style that makes Cleavon Little's portrayal of the new sheriff so incongruous with the tradition. The external characteristic of blackness and Little's more subtle qualities of manner, attitude and gesture expose to our sense of the ridiculous certain basic assumptions that have always dominated the portrayal of the Western lawman-hero in American films.

First of all, there is the fact that the Western lawman is almost never presented to us as a man of law. Though the vast majority of Western films work toward that climactic moment in which a heroic figure redeems the law by destroying the outlaws who would deny it, this character is rarely a man *of* the law by profession on career. In *Blazing Saddles* this convention is burlesqued by making the new sheriff a black railroad worker who is dragooned into serving as sheriff in order to save his skin. Even in *High Noon*, one of the few films in which a professional sheriff plays the role of hero, the action takes place after the sheriff has determined to retire from office. In most Westerns, the heroic lawbringer is not a sheriff or marshal at all, but a cowboy, a reformed outlaw or a mysterious gunfighter. In the list of 106 representative Western films from 1903-1966 which I assembled for the appendix of *The Six-Gun Mystique*,[1] only eleven clearly and unmistakably have professional sheriffs or marshals as heroic protagonists, and in several of these the hero is not a sheriff at the beginning or ending of the film. Most Westerns do have a sheriff or marshal present as a minor character, but he is likely to be old and helpless, confused or corrupt; often enough he has been suborned by the outlaws or by the evil tycoon.

The hero's ambiguous relationship to law embodies, among other things, a traditional American notion of individualism. The Western hero acts out the myth that society and its organized processes of law, however necessary, are incapable of bringing about true justice. Society and law exist, not as a fountainhead of what is just, but as a set of rules controlling the action of individuals who are the true source of morality and justice as well as of injustice. Because the law is only a set of shifting rules it can readily be bent by those who are strong or unscrupulous enough to do so. Thus, for Americans, the individual who can mold society and the law to his own ends is as much admired as condemned. There seems a slight edge of contempt in our attitude toward the conscientious and law-abiding citizen as if there were some weakness or impotence that prevented him from acting aggressively for himself.[2] On the other hand, Americans are clearly not prepared to extend this view of individualism to its logical conclusion of a war of all against all, for there are other, different values which are also important to us, in particular the ideals of equality and community. These, too, must somehow come into play if justice is to be accomplished. The grasping tycoon, the egocentric rancher, or the lawless outlaw—favorite Western villains—may be partly justified in their ignoring of the law, but when their aggressions threaten the community or harm the innocent farmers, something must be done. The community must be redeemed and the unjust individualist purged. In the Western, society's law cannot do this, since it has not yet been established, or has broken down. At this point, the hero must appear, and he must have the same aggressive force and skill in violence that the villain commands. To carry out his mission, he must be a lawman, not a man of society's law which is useless in such situations, but obedient to an inner code of his own—"a man's got to do what a man's got to do"[3]—which happens to coincide with the need of the community. Thus his act of aggressive violence is legitimated, the excessive individualist threat to the community is purged and the ultimate harmony between individualism and justice is mythically reaffirmed.

These considerations indicate why the sheriff-hero of *Blazing Saddles* comically exposes the Hollywood myth of the lawman not only through his blackness but through his style. The black sheriff of *Blazing Saddles* is a supercool dude; he is elegant and urbane, a connoisseur of fine wines and good food; he is sensuous and erotic and something of a dandy; he prefers trickery to an open fight; most shocking of all he is even—perhaps—just a wee bit gay in his inclinations. These characteristics of style, so antithetical to the tight-lipped austere dignity and puritanical rigor of Gary Cooper or John Wayne, provide a mocking commentary on the traditional myth of the lawman. But why does the supercool style undercut the myth so effectively? I think because it exposes the degree to which the role of heroic lawbringer as portrayed in the Western is a construction of fantasy, and thereby self-contradictory and even absurd. Because of his function as a superior man of violence, capable of purging whole bands of outlaws, the mythical lawman has to be a heroic outsider like the Lone Ranger; after all, if we felt it appropriate for the community to do the job through its duly constituted legal agencies, there would be no need for the myth in the first place. However, having invented this potently aggressive hero to symbolize the ideal individualist, we also need to be assured that he is using his force in a just and moral fashion for the benefit of we, the people. Consequently, though he is trained and dedicated to killing, the heroic lawman must also be a man of great restraint and morality, even gentleness. He must be an outsider, but also in a very deep sense one of us. This, I think, is why the blackness of the sheriff in *Blazing Saddles* constitutes such a comic shock. The hero must be wonderfully potent, but also ascetic and pure in his habits; he must avoid erotic entanglements in order to put his whole force into his moment of violent redemption. In comic contrast to this image of Western heroism, Mel Brooks' sheriff is richly sensuous and obviously interested in sex. Finally, though the Hollywood lawman is characterized by his austerity toward the opposite sex, there must never be the slightest question of his total and unquestioned masculinity. Even if he prefers the company of men and horses, and is something of a dandy, we must never see a hint of effeminacy or homoeroticism. This, too, becomes an object of mockery in the running commentary of gay gestures and jokes in *Blazing Saddles*.

That the heroic Western marshal was so ripe and hilarious an object of parody in *Blazing Saddles* suggests how important he has been as a figure in the American imagination.[4] In fact, we can probably go so far as to say that, at least in the period of his peak popularity—the late fifties and early sixties—the Western hero was considered by many to be the archetypal American. Unfortunately, the more archetypal a heroic figure becomes, the more he is likely to mean a great variety of things. In a complex, pluralistic society, popular heroes and their myths probably perform an important integrative role by providing common objects of vicarious identification and admiration for people with very diverse attitudes and backgrounds. However, for the mythical hero to function in this way, he must be susceptible to many different kinds of interpretation; he must be, in effect, a container into which various meanings can be poured without breaking or changing the basic shape of the container. The Western hero is clearly a figure of this sort, since he has been the inspiration not only of a great variety of interpretations, but of a number of different versions.[5] For example, in his recent book on the subject, Philip French suggests that the Westerns of the last two decades can be classified into fairly distinctive "Kennedy," "Johnson," "Goldwater" and "Buckley" versions of the basic Western story.[6] Whether or not one agrees with this particular anatomy, the Western obviously encompasses a considerable ideological range and, depending on the perspective of the viewer, can be seen as expressive of either conservative or liberal attitudes, sometimes simultaneously. Indeed, the doughty John Wayne, survivor of so many imaginary gunfights, has managed in recent years to become something of a cult figure among young radical movie fans without changing in any significant degree the reactionary stance he has taken on most public issues. This is presumably because in his various roles as Western hero he transcends political controversy and embodies something that is at once vaguer and more archetypal.

Because of this archetypal or mythical dimension, the Western is extremely difficult to interpret in specific ideological terms. One reads the various critics who have attempted such interpretations and tends to agree with all or none of them. Each interpreter makes a more or less persuasive account of what the Western is all about, but it seems very difficult to demonstrate that one interpretation is more correct than another except in the case of individual works. We can more or less arrive at a consensus about which lines of interpretation are relevant to Owen Wister's *The Virginian*, Jack Schaefer's *Shane* or Thomas Berger's *Little Big Man*, but when it comes to the Western

myth as a whole, which somehow includes these three very different works along with several thousand others, it is increasingly difficult to be specific about just what it means. The more versions of the Western myth our inquiry includes the more difficult it is to state what political or social attitudes if any are implied by its popularity. One solution to this problem is to take a broad structural approach to the analysis of the myth, seeking to define those basic elements and relations that are invariably present in all versions of the Western. This is the method I attempted in *The Six-Gun Mystique* where I tried to describe the basic opposition of pioneers and outlaw-savages mediated in some fashion by the hero which permeates all instances of the Western I am familiar with. However, while this did provide a useful framework for viewing the Western as a popular artistic genre, and also suggested some interesting speculations about the cultural meaning of the Western myth, the treatment remained at a high level of generality, and I was never fully satisfied that I had clearly established the cultural significance of the basic structural elements. In particular, I found it difficult to separate the cultural and artistic imperatives involved in the creation of Westerns, to be sure which themes were present because they embodied important cultural meanings and which were simply part of the conventional artistic structure.

In this paper, I propose to approach the inquiry into the cultural significance of the Western in a slightly different way by attempting to sort out the most important cultural themes of the Western as they relate to another genre of contemporaneous popularity. My basic assumption is that those elements or patterns which we find in two or more related but different popular genres reflect basic cultural themes. In other words, when a certain kind of character, or situation or pattern of action appears in more than one mythical structure, we have grounds for believing that this pattern is of basic cultural importance and not simply the reflection of the attitudes of a particular creator. I have chosen for this purpose the popular genre commonly known as the hard-boiled detective or private eye story.[7]

Many previous scholars and critics have noted the relationship between the hard-boiled detective and the Western hero. Lewis Jacobs, in his *Rise of the American Film*, comments on the gangster cycle of the 1930s—which is one type of the hard-boiled story—as an urban version of the Western. Robert Warshow, in his two brilliant essays "The Gangster as Tragic Hero," and "The Westerner," draws similar comparisons. But neither of these writers, nor anyone else so far as I am aware, has attempted to make a systematic comparison between these two genres as a basis for discovering the cultural themes which they may embody. That is the purpose of the following discussion. The results, as the reader will doubtless note, cannot be considered definitive. Even when one has established common patterns between two popular genres, it is difficult to be sure of their relationship to popular attitudes. Moreover, when two literary genres have much in common, it seems likely that the artistic imperatives of a certain kind of story are as influential in shaping similarities in character and theme as the expression of cultural attitudes. Thus, the results of our comparison remain in the area of the speculative and the possible. Nonetheless, I would argue that there are enough differences between the hard-boiled detective story and the Western to suggest that the similarities are at least in part the result of a cultural need to represent the same fantasy in different garb. In addition, there is much to be said for the point that when a culture creates and consumes so much literary material of the same fundamental sort, it is expressing something about itself. Tentative as they are, the results of this comparison suggest the existence of a tradition in American popular culture which is worth further investigation.

At first glance, there are a number of striking differences between the hard-boiled detective story and the Western. For example, the setting of the two genres is almost antithetical. The Western takes place on the edge of the wilderness or in a frontier settlement and with the exception of a distinctive subgenre in the present time—such films as *Lonely Are the Brave, The Misfits* and *Bad Day at Black Rock*—represents a historic moment in the past. The private-eye genre is almost always set in the city and takes place in the present. In line with this difference in setting, the cast of characters in the two story types seems at first to bear little relationship to one another. The Western centers upon the sort of people likely to be found in the rural West: ranchers, small-town merchants and farmers, a banker, possibly a doctor and a newspaper editor, the sheriff, the schoolmarm, the dancehall girl, the boys down at the saloon and, of course, a complement of outlaws or Indians to generate the excitement and danger of the plot. The hard-boiled detective, on the other hand, typically has to thread his way through the manifold social levels and complexities of a modern city: rich businessmen, mobsters and their gangs, the district attorney and the police, the middle-class and, sometimes, bejewelled glamour girls and women of the night. For example, within the first few chapters of Raymond Chandler's *The Big Sleep* private investigator Philip Marlowe encounters the millionaire General Sternwood and his two wild and beautiful daughters, a pornographer named Arthur Gwynn Geiger, a cheap hoodlum and his moll, a seductive bookstore salesgirl, an old friend from the district attorney's office and a miscellaneous cast of policemen and grifters. Such a variety of types is impossible in the simpler environment of the Western. The pattern of action also differs from genre to genre. The hard-boiled detective is, above all, involved in the investigation of a crime, and the climactic point in his story usually revolves around the unmasking of a criminal or a conspiracy, while the Western is generally a tale of conflict—between townspeople and outlaws, ranchers and rustlers, cattlemen and farmers, or pioneers and Indians—leading to a shootout between the hero and the antagonist which resolves the conflict, usually through the destruction of the antagonist. Beyond these contrasts in setting, character and action, the Western and hard-boiled detective genres have innumerable differences in symbolic detail: horses vs. cars; six-shooters and winchesters vs. .45 automatics and tommy guns; boots, spurs and chaps vs. busi-

ness suits; smoke signals vs. telephones, etc. Finally, there is frequently a contrast in narrative structure between these two genres. The hard-boiled story is usually a first-person narrative, told to us by the detective-hero, while the Western almost never adopts this form of story-telling.

Underneath these many differences, however, there are certain fundamental patterns which the Western and hard-boiled detective stories have in common, which, if our initial assumption is correct, embody important American cultural themes. First of all, the two heroes have very similar characteristics. Each is a skilled professional man of violence, and, while the hard-boiled detective story ends less often in a shoot-out than the Western, the hero is always prepared for this eventuality. However reluctant he may be to use them, he is skilled with guns and fists. This connection between hard-boiled detective and Western heroes becomes even more obvious when we compare the American detective with his English counterparts like Sherlock Holmes, Hercule Poirot, Lord Peter Wimsey or Mr. Campion, who possess great powers of inference and deduction, but are almost never called upon to engage in violent confrontations with guns. In America, even the relatively pacifistic Lew Archer knows how and when to handle a gun, while the more vehement and vengeful Mike Hammer usually climaxes his investigations by shooting the criminal. This readiness for violence is one important common characteristic of hard-boiled detective and Western heroes, but they also share another aspect of their persona: reluctance to use their skills in violence, which is often related to a sense of ambiguity about their involvement in the situation in which they find themselves. These are typically heroes who do not initiate their heroic actions. Instead, they are forced into them.[8]

The hero's reluctance seemingly results from two aspects of his situation. First, as a skillful man of violence his actions are likely to bring about someone's death. Consequently, his involvements cannot be entered into lightly. Secondly, the hero has a penchant for becoming committed to other persons in such a deep emotional and moral fashion that his actions not only affect the lives of others, but have a deep impact on himself. The model of these circumstances is the situation of Sam Spade in *The Maltese Falcon*. Sam is initially drawn into the case when a woman asks him to investigate the disappearance of her supposedly missing, but actually fictitious sister. This has become a favorite opening for the hard-boiled detective story. For example, the recent film *Chinatown* begins when a woman impersonating the wife of an important Los Angeles official asks the detective to secure evidence of the official's supposed liaison with a younger woman. As in the case of Sam Spade, this initial mission is purely a matter of business for the detective. He has no personal interest or concern in the outcome of the case, except as a matter of doing his job. However, this apparently insignificant initial mission is soon revealed to be a cover for much more serious and dangerous complications which gradually draw the detective into a web of emotional and moral commitments. Sam Spade finds himself falling in love with the woman whom he must, in the end, expose as a vicious killer. Something of the same sort happens to Polanski's J. J. Gittes as he moves from a purely businesslike connection with the case to a deeply personal involvement with his client. The same sort of commitment typically occurs in the case of hard-boiled heroes as different as Philip Marlowe and Mike Hammer.

This is one of the structural features which most sharply differentiates the American hard-boiled hero from the English ratiocinative detective protagonist. Sherlock Holmes, Hercule Poirot and Dr. Gideon Fell who typify this brand of detective story generally retain a rather cool detachment from their clients, focusing their energies on the unravelling of intricate puzzles through inference and deduction from clues. The private eye, on the other hand, either becomes more personally interested in the crime or has such an interest from the very beginning. In Mickey Spillane's *I, the Jury* one of the detective's friends is murdered while Raymond Chandler's *The Long Goodbye* begins with a friend as one of the prime suspects. In this respect, the private eye resembles the Western hero much more than the classical detective. Though the Westerner is only tangentially involved in detection, he is characteristically caught up in a violent action through personal involvement that he cannot escape. One of the common motives ascribed to Western heroes is revenge. Just as Mickey Spillane's Mike Hammer sets out to avenge the murder of a close friend, John Ford's Wyatt Earp in *My Darling Clementine* accepts the job of marshal in Tombstone in order to avenge the murder of his younger brother. In other instances, like Jack Schaefer's *Shane* or Anthony Mann's *The Far Country,* the hero is reluctantly drawn into violence to protect a group of people for whom he feels a moral responsibility.

Whatever the specific motives may be, and these can range from a desire for revenge to a feeling of moral obligation toward a particular group or community, the hard-boiled and Western heroes are usually characterized as having a personal code of morality which transcends both the written law and the conventional morality of society. This code appears to be both a matter of style and of moral behavior. In terms of style, the most obvious similarity between Westerner and private eye is their laconic, understated and tough manner of speech. These heroes are men of few words. Above all, they rarely attempt to justify or explain in words the morality of their actions, as if prepared to stand or fall by actions alone. Or to put it another way, these heroes are so unwilling to submit their behavior to the judgment of others that they refuse to give any explanation or justification for what they do. Only those who themselves participate in the code really understand why the hero does what he does, and these do not need to put it into words. Sometimes, on climactic occasions, the hero is forced to explain himself, as when the heroine of Wister's *The Virginian* threatens to leave the hero forever if he fights the villain Trampas, or when Sam Spade feels he must explain to Brigid O'Shaughnessy why he is going to turn her into the police. But, even in these circumstances, the hero usually finds that words are not very satisfactory

and finally resorts to gnomic generalization like "A man's got to do what a man's got to do," or "I won't play the sap for anybody."

Even when, as is generally the case with the hard-boiled detective genre, the story is told to us by the hero, we still retain the impression of a man of few words, who is willing to tell only the smallest portion of what he knows and feels. The narrative tells us with great precision what the detective does and where he goes and, in the case of skillful writers like Dashiell Hammett and Raymond Chandler, is studded with humorous and lyrical observations about the people he encounters and the places he visits. But he rarely comments directly on his feelings, his motives and his moral judgments. Even Mickey Spillane's Mike Hammer, the crudest and most overtly moralistic of the private eyes, tends toward a style of tough, if garish, understatement, while in the case of more sophisticated writers like Raymond Chandler, the detective's narrative style holds so much back that we are often unclear through the middle of his stories just why he is carrying on his investigation in the way he is. No doubt this is partly a result of the need for mystification about the detective's inquiry which characterizes any mystery story, but in the hard-boiled story the enigma extends beyond keeping the reader in the dark about the facts of the crime to the point where he is also forced to guess at the motives and morality of the detective, a situation that rarely arises in the classical detective story.

Because the hero's code is so personal, it is difficult to analyze it into component elements. Like all heroic codes, it places strong emphasis on a concept of honor. Yet this is not the traditional aristocratic conception of honor, or the epic principle of glory, both of which require a social validation. For the epic hero it is of primary importance that his deeds become part of the legend of the tribe so that the memory of his glory will be preserved from generation to generation. For the aristocrat, honor involves preserving and adding to the greatness of his family name. However, hard-boiled and Western heroes are preeminently private persons, as is perhaps appropriate for the heroic archetype of a democratic society. They spring from no noble lineage, but are, in effect, self-made men. Instead of seeking publicity for their deeds, they seem more inclined to resent even the temporary local fame their acts inspire. Here we see another dimension of the laconic, tight-lipped style. Where the Homeric hero loves to tell of his feats of valor, this American figure seems to seek instead the deepest recesses of individual privacy. Like the Lone Ranger, once he has accomplished his mission, he prefers to ride off as quietly as possible. It should be noted, that in this, as in a number of other respects, there are important differences between earlier and more recent avatars of the Western hero. Wister's Virginian parlays his heroic accomplishments into a position of importance in society, as do many other Western protagonists of the early twentieth century. However, since the development of the hard-boiled hero in the early thirties, the Western hero has become increasingly alienated from the society for whose sake he performs his deeds, just as the hard-boiled detective is more commonly criticized than applauded by the society in which he operates. Thus, the concept of honor espoused by hard-boiled detective and Western gunfighter is a very personal and private thing. He fights, as Robert Warshow puts it, to maintain the purity of his image of himself, rather than to gain social prestige or status.[9]

Other aspects of the hard-boiled and Western hero's code include great physical courage and endurance as well as highly-developed skills in the use of guns and in hand-to-hand combat. These heroes are extremely tough and dangerous men, a toughness that they frequently manifest as much in their ability to endure physical punishment as to shoot quickly and with great accuracy. The hard-boiled detective is knocked out and beaten up regularly before he arrives at the solution to the mystery. Similarly, a bruising fist fight is almost *de rigeur* for the Western hero, though he usually accomplishes the final shootout through his skill at the fast draw. In fact, it has become increasingly common in Westerns to subjct the hero to an extended ordeal and even, on occasion, a considerable humiliation, before he finally defeats his antagonists. The tough-guy hero, then, must always be prepared for violence, because this is what he expects of his world.

The hero's code cannot be considered in complete isolation from the world which he inhabits. We noted earlier that the Western and hard-boiled detective genres had quite different settings, one usually taking place in the contemporary city and the other on a past frontier. However, beneath the surface these settings have two fundamental characteristics in common. They are on the edge of anarchy, and within their societies, legitimate authority tends to be weak and corrupt. The wildness of the Western town is obvious enough, since it is typically on the edge of a wilderness where there is nothing but savage Indians and outlaws. At any time an Indian attack, an outlaw raid or a gunfight down at the saloon may erupt and it is far from certain that law and legitimate social authority will suffice to restore order and bring about justice. This is the conventional Western situation which *Blazing Saddles* burlesques because it is the archetypal moment of our Western fantasies. But essentially the same situation exists in the hard-boiled detective story despite its more recent urban setting. For the hard-boiled detective confronts a situation in which as, Raymond Chandler puts it:

> Gangsters can rule nations and almost rule cities . . . a world where . . . the mayor of your town may have condoned murder as an instrument of money-making, where no man can walk down a dark street in safety because law and order are things we talk about but refrain from practising.[10]

For Indians and outlaws the hard-boiled detective story substitutes gangsters; for the frontier, the dark and dangerous streets where no man or woman can go in safety. Legitimate social authority is even more obviously weak and corrupt in the typical hard-boiled detective story, for it usually turns out that the rich and respectable pillars of society are implicated with the criminal underworld, while in relation to this corrupt alliance of wealth and criminal power, the police and the courts are either weakly incompetent or actively on the take. In Westerns this corrupt alliance is sometimes represented as a tie between an overbearing and tyrannical rancher who hires outlaws to run out the homesteaders, between a greedy Indian agent and a group of militant warriors, or between a dishonest banker or railroad tycoon who uses hired killers to take away an honest farmer's land. Occasionally, as in *High Noon*, the entire town is too cowardly or avaricious to confront the outlaw gang. In other cases, there is a basic conflict between the good townspeople and the saloon crowd who favor a wide-open and lawless society. But despite these variations, the Western town and the city of the hard-boiled detective story are places of lawlessness, violence and inadequate social authority. Indeed, the kinship between the two genres was clear from the very beginning of the hard-boiled detective story, since Dashiell Hammett's first major hard-boiled novel, *Red Harvest* was actually set in a Western city not far removed in time from its days as a frontier mining settlement.[11] Moreover, in terms of the characterization of the hero and the portrayal of the weakness and corruption of social authority, the Western and the hard-boiled detective story have been growing more similar in recent decades. In his style and manner, in his cynicism and the moral ambiguity of his conduct, the western hero played by Clint Eastwood in so many recent films bears a far greater resemblance to Dashiell Hammett's Sam Spade than he does to Tom Mix and W. S. Hart.

Against the lurid background of a savage and corrupt society, the hero's code stands out as a beacon of disinterested morality. Because of his readiness for violence, his skepticism and his unwillingness to play the sap for anybody, the hard-boiled hero is a figure capable of moving freely "down these mean streets" and surviving.[12] Yet as a man with a profoundly personal sense of honor and feeling of obligation to his role, this figure is never content with remaining a mere survivor. Reluctantly, but inexorably, he finds himself drawn into the quest for justice.

When the hero becomes committed to the cause of some other individual or group, the problem of his moral relationship to his code and to society becomes more complex and ambiguous. Because society is presented as wild and corrupt, its law and police machinery are at best inadequate and at worst unjust. The hero's code, however, rests primarily on a personal sense of honor and rightness which is outside both law and conventional morality and, being primarily concerned with the individual's own image, does not contain a clear conception of the social virtue of justice. Thus, the hero appears in the rather paradoxical position of one who acts outside the law in order, supposedly, to more fully uphold it by bringing a just retribution to those society is unable to expose and punish. This paradoxical and ambiguous act—the stepping outside of the law in order to make manifest a more perfect justice—is, I should say, the central myth shared by the Western and hard-boiled detective genres, and, as such, suggests the existence of deep-lying moral and cultural patterns in American society.

One of the most striking things to me about this myth of the hard-boiled, bitter and reluctant hero moving through a corrupt and chaotic society is the degree to which it seems, at first, to be at odds with the generally optimistic, moralistic and progressive tone of the mainstream of American popular culture. Where do Sam Spade, Mike Hammer and Shane fit in the procession of Horatio Algerish self-made men of nineteenth century popular novels and plays, or the noble, dedicated and problem-solving doctors, lawyers and teachers who provide much of what passes for heroic action on our television screens? How does the corrupt and decaying society of the hard-boiled hero relate to that sense of the "smiling aspects of life" and the faith in progressive individual and collective betterment which seemingly characterized the popular vision of America at least until the 1960's? Of course, scholars like Leslie Fiedler have long argued that the mainstream of American literary creation has been more dominated by a pervasive gothic pessimism and an overpowering sense of evil than by optimism and a sense of boundless American potentiality for good.[13] Still earlier, D. H. Lawrence argued from his reading of Cooper that the true American soul was not the dauntless civilization-bringing pioneer but a bitter, alienated hunter—"hard, stoic, isolate, and a killer."[14] But such a vision of America has seemed more characteristic of major writers like Hawthorne and Melville or of alienated intellectuals such as Henry Adams than of our popular mythology.

It is possible that the hard-boiled detective and the more recent Western gunfighter represent something new in American popular mythology. The hard-boiled detective story, the gangster saga and the new tougher style of Western hero exemplified by the gunfighters of the 1940's and 1950's developed around the time of the depression and World War II. If, as most historians believe, the depression created large-scale disillusion and skepticism about American society, while World War II and the atomic bomb generated a still deeper global sense of insecurity and anxiety, it probably makes sense to see in the hard-boiled protagonist a collective fantasy of a heroic figure who is defined by the world of violence, corruption and anarchy he inhabits, capable not only of personal survival but of imposing at least a modicum of his sense of rightness and order on that world. Thus, one might see the emergence of the hard-boiled hero as the adaptation into popular formulas of the more ambiguous vision of the world developed earlier by writers in the pessimistic and critical literary tradition of naturalism. That the early stories of Hemingway seem to be one major source of the style and ethos of the hard-boiled detective writers does argue for this view, suggesting that with the impact of depression and war, the more despairing naturalistic view of life so brilliantly articulated by Hemingway came to seem more plausible and exciting to the general public than the optimistic religious and moralistic vision which characterized most nineteenth century popular genres.

Yet the special power of the hard-boiled hero may also depend on deeper sources in the American past then the particular anxieties and doubts of the twentieth century. The theme of the violent hero and the quest for salvation through violence certainly reaches back through American history to the seventeenth century myths of Indian captivity. As Richard Slotkin has recently demonstrated in *Regeneration through Violence,*[15] the sense of an evil and corrupt culture (the Indians) tempting the individual to throw over the austere morality of his code (Christian civilization) was a threat felt so deeply and ambiguously in the Puritan imagination that it could be resolved only in fantasies, or actualities, of destructive violence. Perhaps the deepest source of the twentieth century fantasy of the hard-boiled detective lies in the Puritan sense of pervasive evil to be overcome only by the most sustained and austere self-discipline, and, in the final sense, by an act of violence. In this connection, the Puritan's extreme embodiment, or perhaps perversion would be a better word, was in the act of detection, both in sniffing out his own sins and in the hunting and destruction of witches, which might be viewed as one historical prototype of the hard-boiled detective story. Like Sam Spade, such witchhunters as Cotton Mather ruthlessly pursued the tiniest clues until they had uncovered and proven the guilt of the evil women who had become the chief source of sin through their trafficking with the devil. Many of the most striking hard-boiled villainesses—Brigid O'Shaughnessy of *The Maltese Falcon,* Carmen Sternwood of *The Big Sleep* and Charlotte Manning of *I, the Jury,* for example—have a witchlike aura and must be captured or destroyed by the detective to prevent the corruption of others.[16] Moreover, the witch hunt situation also contains in embryo another social theme of the hard-boiled hero saga—the failure of a secularized law to cope with pervasive evil and corruption. In the Puritan community in its earlier phases, moral, religious and secular law were one and the same. In the twentieth century Western and hard-boiled detective story, this is, of course, not the case. The secular law has become separated from the moral law and the function of the detective or gunfighter is to enforce the moral law in the face of the weakness and corruption of the secular law. The difficulty of moralizing the law is one major source of the isolation, loneliness and frustration of the hard-boiled hero and in this, he differs from the witchhunter, who, like the vigilante, was not a lone individual but the agent of an aroused community.

Possibly, then, the Puritan witchhunter was the first example of that image of the ruthless pursuer of transcendant crimes who would later develop into the hard-boiled private eye and the gunfighter. In any case as this figure developed in the nineteenth century, he no longer had the explicit religious overtones of the witchhunter. Cooper's Leatherstocking and the Daniel Boone legends on which he was based added a number of new dimensions to the conception of an American hero. The Leatherstocking hero was more completely separated from society; he was of obscure origins; and he possessed great skills in violence and woodcraft. One particularly haunting version of the

Western hero—the Indian-hater who so fascinated major writers like Melville and Hawthorne—seems in his peculiar isolation and despair, as well as in the obsessive nature of his commitment to the destruction of evil, to be even closer in spirit to the contemporary hard-boiled detective than the more benevolent Leatherstocking.

By the later nineteenth century, the myth of the heroic tracker and hunter, able to move through a corrupt and chaotic world without being sullied by that corruption, had evidently become part of the legend of the American city, for the occasional memoirs of later nineteenth century police detectives often include characterizations of the detective which bear a striking resemblance to the later fictional figures of Hammett, Chandler and Spillane. For example, George S. McWatters, a New York police detective from 1858 to 1870 remarks in his memoirs that

> [the detective] is as bad in these days as was his prototype, St. Paul in his, 'all things to all men' but like him he is defensible, in that his rogueries and villainies are practiced for other people's salvation or security; and aside from the fact that the detective, in his calling, is often degraded to a sort of watchman or ordinary policeman, to help the big thieves, the merchants, etc. protect themselves from the small thieves, who are not able to keep places of business . . . his calling is a very noble one, and a singularly blessed one, inasmuch as it is the only one which I call to mind, by which hypocrisy is elevated into a really useful and beneficent art.[17]

Such a statement seems to imply that the mythos of the heroic tough-guy, who is prepared to use all the dirty tricks and amoral and lawless skills he knows to accomplish justice in a corrupt society, was already well developed by the 1880s. I would speculate further that this hard-boiled ethos had very important cultural consequences at the end of the nineteenth century by providing a dramatic self-image for a number of the muckrakers. Lincoln Steffens, in particular, not only tells us that he learned his new view of the basic corruption of American society from his association with police detectives, but until his later conversion to socialism, Steffens' conception of the heroic muckraking reproter seems to be another version of the lone hunter who prowls the mean streets of the corrupt city and immerses himself in its evil ways in order to expose the deeper crimes which the law prefers to ignore. It certainly seems no accident that the world through which the fictional detectives of Hammett, Chandler and Spillane hunt their evil prey seems very close to the shameful cities of the muck-rakers with their corrupt alliances of business, politics and crime.

Thus, the particular resonance which the myth of the hard-boiled hero carries for our time, may well have an even deeper source than the special anxieties of the twentieth century. If, as I suspect. the hard-boiled hero, the gun-fighter and their worlds of evil and corruption are contemporary versions of a myth of the isolated hero in a pervasively corrupt society, these images underline a strain of pessimism and despair in the American tradition which has been a part of our popular as well as intellectual culture. This strain is certainly a different one than the complex of ideology and feeling ordinarily associated with the popular vision of the American Dream and it suggests that there may have always been doubts about the American Dream among the public as well as among more sceptical intellectuals. Indeed, one of the most perceptive observers of American life in the early nineteenth century, de Tocqueville, gave a striking characterization of

> that strange melancholy which often haunts the inhabitants of democratic countries in the midst of their abundance, and that disgust at life which sometimes seizes upon them in the midst of calm and easy circumstances. . . . In democratic times enjoyments are more intense than in the ages of aristocracy, and the number of those who partake in them is vastly larger; but, on the other hand, it must be admitted that man's hopes and desires are often blasted, the soul is more stricken and perturbed, and care itself more keen.[18]

Further analysis of these contemporary genres and their relation to earlier expressions of similar mythical patterns may reveal to us more precisely some of the ways in which Americans have tried to articulate and fantasize about feelings at odds with the public celebration of the American dream of continual social progress and self-improvement.

Notes

1. J. Cawelti, *The Six-Gun Mystique* (Bowling Green, Ohio, 1971), 110-113.

2. Every Western has its contingent of decent law-abiding citizens who eschew violence and depend on the law to secure justice. They are nice, but foolish, and they invariably need the violent hero. The same thing is true of the hard-boiled detective story. Even in the situation comedy, the kind of foolish terror which the good citizen feels when confronted with the law is a perennial source of comedy, as if those who accept the rule of law are somehow ridiculous. One discovers, I think, the same sort of attitude in the ambiguity which American parents so often demonstrate when confronted with that classic situation of the bullied child. Should the child be advised to use violence on his oppressor or to turn the other cheek or to seek justice either from his peers or an authority such as the teacher. Most parents seem to feel their child is a little foolish and even contemptuous if he refuses to "stand up," i.e. to use violence, in pursuit of his interests.

3. The *locus classicus* of this Western cliche is Owen Wister's *The Virginian* where the hero asks his genteel law-abiding schoolmarm sweetheart "Can't yo' see how it must be about a man?" *The Virginian* (1902). In the Houghton-Mifflin edition (Boston, 1968), 288.

4. It may also suggest that he is a little past his prime, though this is not necessarily the case, since parody

and burlesque do not invariably indicate a loss of power in the object or figure being satirized. The Western hero was richly burlesqued by Bret Harte and Mark Twain in the later nineteenth century, long before he became one of the central figures of twentieth century film and television.

5. Some indication of the diversity of interpretations the Western myth has inspired can be found in Jack Nachbar, ed. *Focus on the Western* (Englewood Cliffs, N.Y., 1974).

6. Philip French, *Westerns* (New York, 1974), 28-42.

7. The hard-boiled detective story has not received as much attention as the Western until recently, but there are a number of useful studies including the essays on the hard-boiled genre in David Madden, ed., *Tough-Guy Writers of the Thirties* (Carbondale, Ill., 1968), George Grella, "Murder and the Mean Streets: The Hard-boiled Detective Novel," *Contempora,* I (March 1970), 6-15; John Paterson, "A Cosmic View of the Private Eye," *Saturday Review of Literature,* 36 (August 22, 1953) 7-8; Philip Durham, *Down These Mean Streets a Man Must Go* (Chapel Hill, 1966); William F. Nolan, *Dashiell Hammett: A Casebook* (Santa Barbara, California: McNally and Lofton, 1969); and most recently William Ruehlmann, *Saint with a Gun: The Unlawful American Private Eye* (New York, 1975). I have also profited from a recent University of Chicago doctoral dissertation on Ross Macdonald by Ms. Johnnine Hazard and from the essays by Raymond Chandler, "The Simple Art of Murder," Ross Macdonald, "The Writer as Detective Hero," and Dashiell Hammett, "Memoirs of a Private Detective" which have been reprinted in a number of places.

8. Some qualification of this generalization needs to be made. Spillane's Mike Hammer and his more recent descendants such as "The Enforcer," "The Destroyer" and "The Butcher" are far less reluctant with their violence than Philip Marlowe, Lew Archer and the Continental Op. Similarly, in the case of the Western, there are heroes with little of the gentleness and reluctance displayed by Gary Cooper in *The Virginian, Man of the West* and *High Noon*; Alan Ladd in *Shane*; James Stewart in *Destry Rides Again, The Man from Laramie* or *Winchester 73*. In general, the less sophisticated a version of the myth, the less ambiguity there is about the hero's violence. Undoubtedly, this reflects some difference in the level or segment of the public at which a particular version of the myth is directed. It probably also reflects differences in meaning of the myth for different subgroups within the culture but we need more information about the social and psychological makeup of audience groupings to deal adequately with these differences.

9. Robert Warshow, "The Westerner," in *The Immediate Experience* (Garden City, N.Y., 1964), 89-106. Warshow also deals brilliantly with some of the central themes of the present essay: the hero's reluctance; the sense of melancholy and defeat that accompany his deeds; the peculiar concept of honor.

10. Chandler, "The Simple Art of Murder," in Howard Haycraft, ed., *The Art of the Mystery Story* (New York, 1946), 236.

11. The television series "Have Gun: Will Travel" was an interesting reversal of the *Red Harvest* situation. There, a Western hero showed all the characteristics of a hard-boiled detective. Still more recently, in the film *Coogan's Bluff* and its television spinoff "McCloud," a cowboy lawman is translated from the West into New York City where he encounters a typical hard-boiled social setting. Such variations suggest that the Western and the hard-boiled detective genre may evolve into some kind of a synthesis, though at the present time they still retain a fairly distinct generic differentiation.

12. The quotation is from Chandler's essay "The Simple Art of Murder."

13. Cf. Leslie Fiedler, *Love and Death in the American Novel* (New York, 1966).

14. D. H. Lawrence, *Studies in Classic American Literature* (Garden City, N.Y., 1951), 72. The original hardcover edition was published by Viking in 1923.

15. (Middletown, Conn., 1973).

16. This figure of the *femme fatale* or bitch-villainess, so common to the hard-boiled detective story, rarely appears in the Western. This may reflect both a generic difference and a difference in mythic tradition which appeals to slightly different audiences.

17. George S. McWatters, *Knots United: Or Ways and By-Ways in the Hidden Life of an American Detective* (Hartford: Burns and Hyde, 1873) as quoted in an unpublished paper "Beneficent Roguery: The Detective in the Capitalist City," by John M. Reilly of the State University of New York at Albany, to whom I am indebted for this and other related quotations.

18. Alexis de Tocqueville, *Democracy in America* (New York: Vintage Books, 1954) II, 147.

David J. Geherin (essay date 1978)

SOURCE: Geherin, David J. "The Hard-Boiled Detective Hero in the 1970s: Some New Candidates." *Armchair Detective* 11, no. 1 (1978): 49-51.

[*In the following essay, Geherin presents a survey of detective fiction from the 1970s, finding writers Robert Parker Spenser, Roger Simon, and Andrew Bergman faithful to the hard-boiled tradition.*]

The hard-boiled detective hero has had a long and illustrious career in American detective fiction: Sam Spade, Philip

Marlowe, and Lew Archer are the most famous examples of the type and, taken together, illustrate the gradual development of the hard-boiled private eye over the past fifty years. But Ross Macdonald has now had the stage pretty much to himself for the last two decades and a question arises—Is the hard-boiled detective novel written out, an anachronism in the 1970s, or are there young writers with skill enough to carry on the tradition and to invite favorable comparisons with Dashiell Hammett, Raymond Chandler, and Ross Macdonald?

It is obvious that any writer who attempts to write in this genre faces a particularly difficult task. To receive attention, he almost has to be better than his predecessors, with whom he will be inevitably compared, usually to his disadvantage. Also, he must be faithful to the conventions of the genre without becoming slavishly imitative. Any private eye who has to work in the shadow of Sam Spade, Philip Marlowe, and Lew Archer might never be able to establish his own identity.

Nevertheless, no challenge is too tough, especially for writers of tough guy fiction, and there are currently several pretenders to the throne, at least three of whom have an excellent chance of stamping their own identities on the form. These three—Robert B. Parker, Roger L. Simon, and Andrew Bergman—are the new breed and their novels illustrate three possible approaches available to writers working in a genre so well-established as the hard-boiled detective novel: Parker imitates, Simon updates, and Bergman parodies.

Robert Parker's Spenser, the thirty-seven-year-old private eye hero of *The Godwulf Manuscript* (1973), *God Save the Child* (1974), *Mortal Stakes* (1975), and *Promised Land* (1976), comes closest to fitting snugly into the Spade-Marlowe-Archer mold. Like them, Spenser is a loner, an excop whose personality, independence, and conscience have led him to a private pursuit of justice; he explains his mode of operation this way: "I handle the problems I choose; that's why I'm freelance. It gives me the luxury to worry about justice." He too is both cynical and tough (he can trade wise-cracks with the best of them) yet sympathetic and understanding. He, too, is a romantic whose scorn for the absurdities and excesses of modern America matches his predecessors at their darkest moments. And like Marlowe and, especially, Archer, he becomes personally involved in the lives of his clients and turns the solution of the crime into a moral issue.

For example, in *The Godwulf Manuscript* he continues on the case after the missing manuscript is found in order to prove the innocence of a young girl falsely accused of murder. In *Mortal Stakes,* he is hired by an official of the Boston Red Sox to find out if his star pitcher is shaving points. Spenser discovers he is but, because he is a decent kid who is being blackmailed because of his wife's shady past, he transfers his allegiance to the pitcher, protecting him from discovery. The Red Sox official never learns the truth. In both cases, something besides money is the moti-

vating factor; like his predecessors, Spenser's sympathy for the innocent victim will never allow him the luxury of becoming wealthy.

But just as Marlowe is not another Spade, nor Archer another Marlowe, Spenser is no mere carbon copy of the earlier private eyes. For one thing, his territory is Boston rather than Southern California; it is his shrewd choice of setting which may provide Parker with the most effective way of distinguishing Spenser's identity from Marlowe's and Archer's. Boston provides an urban setting that is vivid, fresh and, with the exception of George Higgins' novels, relatively untapped. For another thing, Spenser is allowed to enjoy himself from time to time, even to the extent of carrying on an affair with one of the characters in *God Save the Child* and continuing it in *Mortal Stakes.* He is, furthermore, a gourmet cook who often interrupts his narratives to reveal a favorite recipe, an ex-boxer, and an artist who does wood carvings. He keeps himself so busy, he simply does not have as much time on his hands to become as world-weary and *angst*-stricken as some of his fictional colleagues.

Parker's novels are fast-paced and well-written and show the same feeling for character, mood, and atmosphere as those of Hammett, Chandler, and Macdonald. It is not surprising, then, to learn that Parker wrote his doctoral dissertation on Hammett and Chandler; the alert reader will find echoes of both writers in his books. For example, Spenser has an affair with a woman named Brenda Loring; this is an echo of Linda Loring, the name of the woman Philip Marlowe marries in Chandler's unfinished final novel, *The Poodle Springs Story.* But despite these similarities, Spenser is his own man, an interesting and complex character who appears to have enough substance to support a long series of novels and to survive a comparison with the famous private eyes who preceded him.

Rather than avoiding the Hollywood setting, as Parker does, Roger Simon confronts it directly, setting his two novels, *The Big Fix* (1973) and *Wild Turkey* (1975) in Southern California. Simon's hard-boiled hero is Moses Wine, a thirty-one-year-old law school dropout and ex-Berkeley activist whose social conscience has led him into detective work. Simon is the most original and innovative of the new writers in that he is striving to dust off the old form, to modernize the private eye and bring him from the forties into the seventies. Although the Lew Archer novels are still being written today, there is a timeless quality about them. Perhaps Macdonald's obsession with mythic overtones and archetypal patterns results in his lack of emphasis on specific time. In contrast to this, Simon reminds us on every page that Moses Wine lives *now*: references to Patty Hearst, Sly Stone, Haldeman, Ehrlichmann, and the White House Tapes, to contemporary songs and singers locate Wine in the immediate and recognizable present. Of course Simon runs the risk of writing novels that may become as stale as yesterday's newspaper, but he takes the chance in order to achieve a very contemporary atmosphere.

"A stoned Sam Spade" is how one character refers to Wine and the remark serves to remind the reader of the many similarities between Wine and the classical hard-boiled private eyes; he is strong, heroic, tough-talking, cynical (especially about politicians), burdened with a strong sense of morality and a nagging social conscience. But, like Parker's Spenser, he is his own man. Instead of bourbon and beer, Wine uses grass and hash to anaesthetize himself. Although a loner, his daily life is enlivened in ways foreign to the traditional private eye: he has custody of his two pre-school children. Whereas Lew Archer always seems to be searching for the sons he never had, Wine finds himself often searching simply for someone to take his sons off his hands long enough to work a bit on solving his cases. (Worse still, his youngest isn't even toilet trained. Changing a diaper is something Sam Spade never had to do.) Like Marlowe and Archer, Wine's turf is Southern California, but not the glamorous California of the nostalgic past. Wine's California is one of massage parlors, Sexual Freedom Leagues, nude encounter groups on the one hand, and random violence and terrorist bombings on the other. How much out of place in that world Marlowe would feel is vividly suggested in Robert Altman's recent film version of *The Long Goodbye.*

Simon's novels feature two elements which also figure prominently in Andrew Bergman's novels: corrupt politics and an ethnic hero. Both Moses Wine and Bergman's Jack LeVine (born Jacob Levine) are Jewish. Since his inception, the American private eye has been predominantly, if not exclusively, WASP-ish. By introducing an ethnic element into their characterizations, Simon and Bergman add a dash of color and flavor long absent from the traditional hard-boiled novel. And in this regard, the detective novel parallels the new ethnicity of contemporary TV: the home screen is filled with such sleuths as Columbo, Kojak, Baretta, Starsky, and the like.

A more significant parallel, however, is the emphasis on politics in the new novels. In Simon's *The Big Fix,* Wine is hired by a Presidential candidate to find out who is behind an attempt to rig the California primary in order to collect on a $10,000,000 bet. In *Wild Turkey,* Wine's investigations reveal that the California attorney general, noted for his strict morality and a popular crusade against porno theatres and sex shops, is the secret owner of several such prosperous establishments. Wine's conclusion: "Once you begin to place your trust in a politician, you were something of a fool."

Political themes loom even larger in Andrew Bergman's novels. *The Big Kiss-Off of 1944* (1974) involves a variety of schemes and counterschemes designed to influence the outcome of the Roosevelt-Dewey election in 1944. *Hollywood and LeVine* (1975) deals with the infamous blacklisting of Hollywood writers suspected of Communist leanings in the late forties. But neither of these is a typical historical novel. *The Big Kiss-Off* is almost a High Camp parody of the Philip Marlowe novels, a witty exploitation of the current nostalgia craze. Bergman's hero Jack Le-

Vine is a fat, bald, thirty-eight-year-old detective who lives in Queens and works out of a shabby Broadway office. LeVine sounds like an old radio show: sarcastic, disillusioned, quick with a witty quip—LeVine has the patter down perfectly. But where Simon recreates the now, Bergman is more interested in the then, capturing the atmosphere of the forties very effectively: Esther Williams, Betty Grable, The Pepsodent Show, Stromberg-Carlson radios, H. V. Kaltenborn, gas rationing—there is something in the novel to warm the heart of every nostalgia buff.

Unfortunately, simply returning to the forties does not automatically guarantee a successful reincarnation of Sam Spade or Philip Marlowe. The problem with *The Big Kiss-Off* is that Bergman wants to have it too many ways: he aims for humor by parodying the excesses of his predecessors (that he co-authored *Blazing Saddles* with Mel Brooks indicates his lack of subtlety); he appeals to mystery readers by capitalizing on the traditions of the hard-boiled novel; and he wraps it all up in a serious attempt to draw parallels between the political chicanery of the forties and the Watergate scandals of the seventies. Politics, parody, and private eyes make strange and uncomfortable bedfellows.

Bergman's second Jack LeVine novel, *Hollywood and LeVine,* on the other hand, is much more successful. Parody of a genre like the hard-boiled detective novel is a dead end; having done it once, where does one go? Happily, Bergman seems to have understood this limitation and eliminates most traces of parody from *Hollywood and LeVine.* By toning down the witty exchanges and by making LeVine more attractive (he is no longer fat and although still bald, bald has become beautiful), Bergman sacrifices humor for substance. By combining historical characters and situations with fictional characters and events, he evokes a new perspective on events of the past. In *The Big Kiss-Off,* LeVine meets Thomas Dewey, who thanks him for his efforts in trying to discover who is attempting to sabotage his campaign. In *Hollywood and LeVine* he gets lectured on the dangers of Communism by young Congressman Richard M. Nixon, rubs shoulders with Spencer Tracy, Ava Gardner, and Gregory Peck at a Hollywood cocktail party, and enlists the aid of Humphrey Bogart in capturing the bad guys. What a dream team! Jack LeVine and Hollywood's version of *both* Sam Spade and Philip Marlowe. Parker may be the most faithful in carrying on the tradition of the hard-boiled novel and Simon the most contemporary in atmosphere, but Bergman is the most innovative in conception. His attempts to recreate the past from the perspective of the present suggest parallels with such other contemporary novels as John Fowles' *French Lieutenant's Woman,* E. L. Doctorow's *Ragtime,* Ishmael Reed's *Mumbo Jumbo,* and, most interesting of all, Joe Gores' *Hammett,* a detective novel whose hero, Dashiell Hammett, is a San Francisco private investigator who, in 1928, begins a part-time career as a mystery writer.

All in all, the situation of the hard-boiled novel is very healthy. Devoted readers of Hammett, Chandler, and Macdonald will find echoes of their favorite private eyes in all of these books. And although they will not find another Sam Spade or Philip Marlowe or Lew Archer, they won't be disappointed, for they will discover private eyes who are interesting characters in their own ways. Parker, Simon, and Bergman demonstrate in their books the capacity of the hard-boiled detective novel to adapt to the changing times while remaining faithful to the spirit of the form which continues as one of the most popular genres in American fiction.

Larry E. Grimes (essay date autumn 1983)

SOURCE: Grimes, Larry E. "Stepsons of Sam: Re-Visions of the Hard-Boiled Detective Formula in Recent American Fiction." *MFS: Modern Fiction Studies* 29, no. 3 (autumn 1983): 535-44.

[*In the following essay, Grimes explores three modern novels as "revisions" of Raymond Chandler's hard-boiled detective formula that increasingly focus on the role of the imagination in detection.*]

During the past decade, a small industry has developed, using American hard-boiled detective stories as its primary raw material. Both films and fiction have been made from this well-established formula. A partial list includes such successful films as *Chinatown, The Late Show, Foul Play, Play It Again, Sam,* and *Murder by Death.* Joe Gores' *Hammett,* Roger Simon's Moses Wine books, the le Vine novels of Andrew Bergman, and Andrew Fenady's *The Man with Bogart's Face* are representative of the wide range of popular detective novels (serious, upbeat, comic, nostalgic) derived from the formula.[1] Indeed, interest in the formula has spilled over into the world of serious fiction in recent years. It is the purpose of this paper to examine the effect of that spill-over on the formula. To do so, I will examine re-visions of the formula in novels by three nondetective writers of some literary repute. The works I will discuss are Jules Feiffer's *Ackroyd,* Richard Brautigan's *Dreaming of Babylon,* and Thomas Berger's *Who Is Teddy Villanova?*[2]

I have chosen to hyphenate "re-vision" quite deliberately, for something more radical than "revision" has taken place in the novels at hand. The relation of these works to the hard-boiled formula is complex. They are not blood descendants of the Hammett-Chandler school. Rather, it seems that these novels were reared in minds full of Freud, Kafka, Jewish New York, Ionesco, Joyce, Nabokov, and, in the instance of Brautigan, Algerian hashish. They were certainly more than toddlers when they were brought into the family and formula of Marlowe, Spade, and Archer. Nevertheless, their authors present them to us as members of the hard-boiled clan. Hence the tag of "stepsons."

To determine the nature and significance of these recent re-visions, it is necessary that I set forth the original for-

mula. That hard-boiled formula, to be properly understood, must be seen against the backdrop of the classical detective novel. Fortunately, John Cawelti has delineated the essentials of the hard-boiled formula and has done so while noting its relation to the formula as set forth in classical detective fiction. Cawelti makes it clear that in hard-boiled detective stories, as in so-called classical ones, the formula "moves from the introduction of the detective and the presentation of the crime, through the investigation, to a solution and apprehension of the criminal."[3] What stands the two detective formulas apart is setting and resolution. According to Cawelti, the city has the air of a new Arabian Nights in the classical detective novel, whereas in hard-boiled fiction it stands forth as "empty modernity, corruption and death."[4] Against their respective backdrops, the two formulas are drawn toward very different resolutions. As Cawelti puts it, the hard-boiled detective's investigation becomes "not simply a matter of determining who the guilty person was but of defining his own moral position."[5] In the process of defining his own moral position, the hard-boiled detective reveals himself to be a "marginal professional" who "must reject the public ideals and values of society to seek to create his own personal code of ethics and his own set of values."[6]

The resolution of action in the classical detective formula is achieved by an act of mind. It is reached in hard-boiled fiction by an act of will. Accordingly, with the advent of the hard-boiled detective, the mystery novel takes a turn toward subjectivity. Before Hammett's operative came on the scene, the formula presupposed that order begets order. It assumed that there was an objective order, if often obscured, in the chain of events that led up to and away from any incident. Consequently, an objective and orderly examination of events would allow one to understand and to reconstruct any incident. Solution was resolution according to the classical formula. Solution, however, is hardly resolution in a work such as *The Maltese Falcon.* Sam Spade does find out who killed his partner. But the tensions in the story are heightened and not relieved by that discovery. Spade has allowed himself to become emotionally involved with the murderer. So for him the real problem is not who-did-it but what to do about the fact that she did it. Sam is not allowed to be a detective only; he is forced to be judge and jury as well. The hard-boiled detective becomes, then, as Robert Edenbaum notes, a "daemonic hero." And in order for him to function in this capacity, he must be "free of sentiment, of the fear of death, of the temptation of money and sex."[7]. In the final analysis, ethical attributes set the hard-boiled hero apart from lesser mortals. Raymond Chandler has described this hero best:

> Down these mean streets a man must go who is not himself mean, who is neither tarnished nor afraid. . . . He is the hero; he is everything. . . . He must be the best man in his world and a good man for any world. . . . The story is the man's adventure in search of a hidden truth, and it would be no adventure if it did not happen to a man fit for adventure. He has a range of awareness that startles you, but it belongs to him by

right, because it belongs to the world he lives in. If there were enough like him, the world would be a very safe place to live in, without becoming too dull to be worth living in.[8]

So emerges the face and formula of hard-boiled detection. But what of the stepsons of Sam? What of the re-vision of the formula?

There can be no doubt about the fact that "subjectivity" reigns triumphant in Jules Feiffer's *Ackroyd,* for the novel is presented as a series of diary entries that recount the activities of one Robert Hollister, a.k.a. Roger Ackroyd. Feiffer makes effective use of this form, letting it function as a detective's log, a novelist's notebook, a psychiatrist's casebook, and a personal dairy.

The novel records Hollister-Ackroyd's quest for personal identity, hence the subtitle—*A Mystery of Identity.* It amplifies, as I have noted, the subjectivity inherent in the hard-boiled formula with which Ackroyd identifies. Ackroyd admits that he "went into business to be Sam Spade."[9] Later, pretty partner in tow, he plays Nick and Nora Charles as he is led from Holiday Inn to Holiday Inn by Oscar Plante, the chief subject of his investigation, his constant antagonist, and his client. Ackroyd is not, however, a simple 1960s version of the hard-boiled detective. In fact, he takes issue with the hard-boiled tradition: "Philip Marlowe does not take divorce cases. Well, I will. It isn't my business to impose judgments on clients" (p. 3).

This departure from the formula is, of course, a major one. Ackroyd's refusal to "impose judgments on clients" is a refusal to exert his will, a refusal to cease being just a detective and to become judge and jury. Ackroyd refuses to assume the ethical attributes essential to the hard-boiled hero. He refuses because (1) he must find himself before he can assert himself and because (2) the only self attainable in the world he inhabits must, of necessity, exist in such a fragile shape as to preclude hard-boiled moral assertion. The novel is the proof and elaboration of this claim.

In the first instance, there is never any doubt in the narrative but that Ackroyd is a self in flux. He states at the outset that he has deliberately become another self, "changing names, going into the detective business" (p. 3). As a detective, he finds that professional duty requires him to assume yet other identities. And finally he leaves the detective business, becomes an army officer and then a speaker and writer who retrieves his real name, Robert Hollister—if we dare to believe him. His ever-changing identity is paralleled in the book by the protean shape of Plante, a.k.a. Logan Jessup. As Ackroyd's alter ego and father substitute, as well as his client and antagonist, Plante affords the younger Ackroyd a model of how one adapts to life as a shifting self.

As the novel moves from absurdist mystery (the case of the missing parakeet) to more complicated investigations

centering around missing notebooks and Byzantine relationships, it becomes apparent that Ackroyd must have a clue, a model, or a guide capable of making known to him the secret of how to live in a world of flux. Plante, as said above, provides that model, but not immediately. First Ackroyd must become part of the life-fiction of Oscar Plante and run the risk of self-loss. The matter of parakeets and notebooks brings him into Plante's world and under Plante's influence. By midbook Ackroyd is aware of the magnetism of Plante's life-fiction and resolves to release himself from its pull. At this point, his detection becomes completely subjective. He plans to release himself by

> taking [himself] as a client. My assignment is to build a dossier of the authentic Plante, check out his past and his present with friends, enemies, and, eventually, if I think I am up to it, the subject himself. Once I have a book on the flesh and blood Plante there is a very good chance that the Plante in my head will not be able to stand up to it. It will be like daylight in a haunted head—I meant to write "house," but let it stand.
>
> (p. 151)

Ackroyd becomes more forceful, more self-assured, as a result of this decision. Shortly after he has made this decision, he reclaims his old name and tells himself,

> I am confident for the first that there is an enormous difference between Roger Ackroyd and Robert Hollister; I am not making it up. Ackroyd served his purpose as a transitional figure but, thank God, he's dead and buried and Plante's insideous influence is buried with him.
>
> (p. 186)

Of course, life in the world of flux is not that simple. Plante's influence is not so easily put behind. Ackroyd-Hollister soon finds himself in need of Plante. Plante is a successful sports writer and novelist. Hollister, after his break with Ackroyd and as a result of his tour of duty in the army, has become an antiwar celebrity. As a celebrity, he is expected to put his Vietnam experience into book form. This he has difficulty doing. Enter Plante. Plante begins to revise the book and slowly takes it (Hollister-Ackroyd's autobiographical work) over. As Ackroyd puts it, Plante becomes his "ghost" (p. 213).

That being the case, there is nothing left for Ackroyd to do but to attempt to exorcise the spirit. But, as he notes, his detective's license has expired (p. 226). He must, then, try to get to the heart of the mystery without benefit of a bona fide private eye. (It would seem that one can't even trust oneself with a case anymore.) Ackroyd proceeds as he had planned earlier in the adventure. He goes back to Plante's boyhood home and tries to reconstruct the truth about Plante's life. What Ackroyd finally unravels is the mystery of identity in modern America. He discovers that "[Plante] invented himself from scratch. . . . that's the wonderous part of it, the psychic embodiment of the American Dream—he didn't merely raise himself by his bootstraps, he materialized himself from nonexistence. Small wonder he haunts my soul" (pp. 255-256).

The mystery of Plante revealed, Ackroyd is able to come to grips with the mystery of his own identity. He is free, as he puts it, to "come up with a clue to what . . . to make myself" (p. 309).

In *Ackroyd,* Feiffer has so revised the formula as to "unboil" the hard-boiled detective. Ackroyd drops the defining and insular code of the hard-boiled self in favor of fictive life. In *Ackroyd,* theme (the successful self as the fictive self) becomes form: Ackroyd's diary is the novel we are reading. Living becomes synonymous with story-telling, and the only meaningful mode of detection open to Ackroyd at the end of the book does not require a license. For the whole diary is not case record but autobiography—self-detection, the pursuit of the ever-changing mystery of identity.

Like Feiffer, Brautigan makes formula fiction the playground of the fictive self. Hardly a novice to the art of re-visioning formula fiction, Brautigan had tinkered with the historical romance (*The Abortion*), the gothic novel and the western (*The Hawkline Monster*), and the mystery story (*Willard and His Bowling Trophies*) prior to *Dreaming of Babylon*. And like its predecessors, *Dreaming* is a spacey, comic tribute to its original.

Brautigan always touches base before he runs. *Dreaming* opens as should all good hard-boiled novels—with the private eye down at the heels of his gumshoes. A good news-bad news joke begins this first-person circular narrative. The good news is that on this day, 2 January 1942, C. Card, private eye, has been declared 4-F. The bad news is that he'd "gotten a case that [he] needed a gun for but [he] was fresh out of bullets."[10] He is also fresh out of money and just about out of shelter. He is behind on his rent, and previously he has been forced to sell his car and to fire his secretary. As Card puts it (he usually talks in exaggerated hard-boiled similes),

> here I was with no bullets for my gun and no money to get any and nothing left to pawn. I was sitting in my cheap little apartment on Leavenworth Street in San Francisco thinking this over when suddenly hunger started working my stomach over like Joe Louis. Three good right hooks to my gut and I was on my way to the refrigerator.
>
> (p. 4)

Card's problems do not get particularly worse, although his similes do. We have to put up with them as Card wanders from police station to mortuary in his search for free bullets to fill his gun. His quest for bullets and the slow turn of the clock toward his scheduled rendezvous with his client are all we are given to keep us going (speaking of hunger) for the first 114 pages, slightly more than half of the book. That and, of course, Babylon.

Not only is Card a detective; he is also a dreamer. Beginning with a fastball to the head, which ended his attempt to become a big league player, Card has been subject to sudden "head trips" to ancient Babylon. There Card is a baseball hero named Samson Ruth. There he is the author of a private eye serial featuring villain Dr. Abdul Forsythe and detective Ace Stag. Ace is replaced later by detective Smith Smith in such classics as "Smith Smith Versus the Shadow Robots."

Meanwhile, back in San Francisco, action intensifies and becomes both absurd and morbid in the second half of the novel. Card meets his client, a petite, beer guzzling blonde woman who never takes a piss. The blonde offers Card $1,000 to steal the corpse of a hooker from the morgue. She tells Card she has picked him for the job, rather than any one of a number of better known detectives, because "you're the only one we could trust to steal a body for us. . . . The other detectives might have some scruples. You don't have any" (p. 130). Card acknowledges that she is right and that he isn't offended by the charge. So much for the ethical attributes of the hard-boiled hero.

Card has considerable difficulty stealing the body because a pair of body-snatchers has been hired by the same lady to compete with him. Morbid humor and hard-boiled perversity dominate the scenes at the morgue as Card watches his cop friend, Rink, interrogate the bungling body-snatchers. Even Card has difficulty finding similes to fire the scene: "There are no words to describe the expression on the hood's face when Sergeant Rink pulled him out of the refrigerator. He opened it up just a crack at first. You could only see the guy's eyes. They looked as if Edgar Allan Poe had given them both hotfoots" (p. 171).

There is violence, absurdity, and adventure enough in the last forty pages of the novel. Card is chased around town by angry blacks who threaten to make him into stew meat. He is forced to hide the abducted corpse in his refrigerator. And, although he keeps vigil, he is unable to retain his $1,000. Even worse, at the cemetery he is caught by his mother and upbraided by her for causing the death of his father. In retrospect, Card concludes his narrative of 2 January 1942 with this observation: "I was right back where I started, the only difference being that when I woke up this morning, I didn't have a dead body in my refrigerator" (p. 220).

The effect of *Dreaming in Babylon* on the hard-boiled formula is, as I have suggested already, similar to the one *Ackroyd* has. But significantly different are mode and tone. *Ackroyd* is, basically, a serious novel, even when it is absurd. *Dreaming* is a comic work that parodies the formula even as it reshapes it.

Both form and theme in *Dreaming* stretch the formula beyond its usual shape by making it clear that there is a tension between the facts of life and the meaning of life. Facts include no bullets for one's gun and a corpse in one's refrigerator. They have no intrinsic meaning. But Babylon has. It exists only because it is an active extension of mind. Meaning, then, is connected with Babylon, with the pure imagination, and not with objective fact. The implication for the formula is clear. According to Brautigan, nothing meaningful is gained by taking murder out of the drawing room and placing it in the streets. The real and the meaningful are not synonyms. This is the case because, at least in *Dreaming,* the world of facts is patently absurd—guns but no bullets, refrigerators stocked with corpses.

So the world turns, accumulating facts but not revealing patterns. That being the case, a rich imagination, a lush fantasy life, is to be preferred to a life of adherence to objective facts of objectified codes. Card agrees. He is not, once you get past the marginality and the similes, a very hard-boiled hero. He is, rather, an unembroiled hero—detached from the world, narcissistic. Card. Smith Smith. Ace Stag. Call him what you will. He is more protean than daemonic. The fictive hero strikes again.

From *Little Big Man* through *Arthur Rex* and *Neighbors* Thomas Berger, like Brautigan, has been writing revisions of formula fiction. *Who Is Teddy Villanova?,* Berger's re-vision of hard-boiled detective fiction, is the best of the lot under discussion here. As Hemingway might put it, Berger works close to the horns. *Teddy Villanova* is quite recognizably a hard-boiled detective novel, not a parody of or an invention from one. The hard-boiled formula is the skeleton that gives shape to both plot and character. Indeed, Berger's borrowings are quite extensive; plots and characters from Hammett and Chandler abound. *The Maltese Falcon,* in particular, is raided, yielding up a trio of crooks (Bakewell, Washburn, and Natalie) who are brought together by their mutual lust for a figurine—the Sforaza figurine. Or at least so it appears on the surface.

But, debts admitted, *Teddy Villanova* is, nevertheless, a re-visioning of the hard-boiled novel. Berger's re-vision is subtle, and it is achieved against the backdrop of full adherence to the formula. For example, he employs standard tough-guy language complete with simile. After a beating, Berger's detective says, "Sam's image registered on my retinas as if I were staring through lenses of lemon-lime Jell-O in which banana rounds were embedded."[11] Elsewhere he observes, "If he was not as dead as the cold lasagna on which the tomato sauce has begun to darken, I was a Dutchman" (p. 20). Berger also includes the requisite social commentary: "Just as a tissue of clichés did not, these days, rule out a Harvard education, his Roman numeral was not necessarily a suggestion of good birth" (p. 16). Later he offers extended commentary:

> The cuckold is, or once was, at least, a stock character in the farces of France and Italy, but in America he has always played a dreary role, because seldom even for native Catholics has marriage been considered seriously sacramental; thus whatever pain comes from its miscarriages is merely private, with no references to social arrangements designed in heaven. Perhaps this explains why I, a student of traditional cultures, have never wed.
>
> (p. 58)

This long quotation prepares us for a brief comment later: "Having no sense of where it was that I had begun my fight, I feared I might, Vico-like, be on a course of mere recirculation" (p. 125).

Obviously the beads above add up to more than a string of hard-boiled pearls. In fact, the balanced sentence suggests the parlors of Johnson's London and not the streets of the Op's San Francisco.

Then there are the references to "traditional cultures" and to "Vico-like recirculation." These betray more than a smattering of book learning. In fact, hard-boiled similes prove to be but a pinch of salt in the richer style that gives shape to the sensibility of Berger's narrator. It is through that narrative sensibility that Berger re-visions the formula. And it is both natural and not surprising that Berger has provided us with a detective, Russel Wren, who held a job as an English instructor until he was declared redundant.

Berger's mystery, like those of Feiffer and Brautigan, needs all the help it can get from the literary profession. His novel, too, is set in the world of shifting fictive selves. Wren slowly learns that the case he is trying to solve is a live drama. Indeed it is a series of live dramas featuring one Bakewell who is first a client, then an assailant, then a corpse, then missing, then alive and well again; featuring cops named Zwingli, Calvin, and Knox who are really actors who are really cops who are doing a fictional autobiography of their careers called "The Reformers"; featuring a sex-pot stewardness who turns out to be a lesbian Treasury Agent.

At least all of this is true in the drama being directed by Wren's landlord, Sam Polidor. It may not, however, be true in the simultaneous but different drama (same cast) directed by Boris Stavrogin. Boris, unlike Polidor, deals directly with Wren. Polidor refuses to recognize Wren as a definite self and constantly calls him by names such as Run, Ram, Ran, Rind, and Rain. When possible, in fact, Polidor tries to deal with Wren through an intermediary. And a confusion resulting from indirect communication is the cause of the drama Polidor directs. Once the confusion is cleared up, Wren is able to extricate himself from Polidor's play.

Wren is not so successful with the sinister and mysterious Boris. Wren is attracted to this perverse man and is considering a trip to Bavaria to visit Boris at the end of the novel. Still under the spell of Boris, Wren admits that he knows that "by no means have all the *bizarreries* of the past twenty-four hours been explained" (p. 247). This admission by Wren testifies to an important departure from formula that exists in *Teddy Villanova*. According to the formula, the hard-boiled detective is pushed beyond the role of detective to that of judge and jury. But in *Teddy Villanova,* as in *Ackroyd* and *Dreaming* (though the matter was not discussed in relation to those books), the detective is pushed beyond the role of detective, not in order that he may become judge and jury but in order that he may pursue the mystery of life-in-process.

Two other signs of Berger's re-vision of the formula are also evident, in spite of the fact that the formula itself is so carefully integrated into his re-vision. First, and I have already examined this, Berger's style keeps bursting the bonds of concretion, keeps fraternizing with abstraction. Second, the matter of the ending. Absurdist elements in the plot prevent final resolution of action and, therefore, of acting. Wren is not left with enough earth beneath his feet to take the kind of ethical stand required of the truly hard-boiled hero.

Nor does Wren attempt such a stand. According to the drama directed by Boris, the Sforaza figurine exists and is of considerable worth. Should Wren go to visit Boris in Bavaria, he would be departing drastically from the formula and the ways of Sam Spade. Because the story of Wren is parallel to the story of Spade, Wren's visit to Bavaria would be the equivalent of Spade joining Gutmann in search of the falcon. Wren, unlike Spade, is sorely tempted by the mysterious quest. True mystery and not the moral self, ontology and not ethics, most concern Berger and Wren. A re-vision of the formula indeed.

An overview of this literary study shows that the re-visions of the hard-boiled formula undertaken by these various hands have much in common. First, although urban setting has been preserved, it now signifies a reality different from that in the hard-boiled formula. If the hard-boiled formula converted the city from "object of wonder" in classical detective fiction into an image of modernity, corruption, and death, then these recent revisions have given the screw another turn and have exchanged the existential vision of the hard-boiled formula for an absurdist view of the city. In these novels the city has become a stage for absurdist activity and theater. The city and its inhabitants serve as catalysts for actions that are unpredictable and ever changing.

The plot of the hard-boiled formula has been modified accordingly. Significant causes for action are hard to locate in these novels, or when located turn quickly to absurdist mist and mirth. The result is a plot of infinitely incomplete action. The formula's demand that the detective become more than a detective is put to the service of plot at this point. As I noted in the study of *Teddy Villanova*, detectives are pushed beyond detection in these re-visions too. But they become writers or dreamers and not moral selves as a result of the push.

Of course, the effects of the re-visions are most striking when we turn to character. The novels examined here suggest that a third stage in the evolution of the detective hero has begun: from rational man to daemonic-code hero to protean hero and fictive self. Clearly, all three authors agree that their characters cannot live effectively in their surroundings as adherents of a code, even a personal one. A personal code presumes a definite sense of personhood.

The central characters in the three novels I have examined are all better understood as "works in progress" than as "code personalities." The phrasing is deliberate, for another distinguishing trait in the re-visions is the substitution of style for morals. Imagination and not integrity is the ingredient essential to a meaningful life in the world of the hard-boiled formula revisioned. Or, to build around Chandler's vision of the hard-boiled hero, once it was said that down these dark streets a man may go if bright reason is by his side. Then it was said that down these mean streets a knight must go who is not himself mean, who is neither tarnished nor afraid. But now it is written that through strange and ever-changing streets a man must twist and turn, slip and slide.

Notes

1. See Andrew Bergman, *Hollywood and le Vine* (New York: Ballantine, 1975); Andrew J. Fenady, *The Man With Bogart's Face* (New York: Avon, 1977); Joe Gores, *Hammett* (New York: Ballantine, 1975); and Roger Simon, *Wild Turkey* (New York: Pocket Books, 1975).

2. Thomas Berger, *Who Is Teddy Villanova?* (New York: Delta Books, 1977); Richard Brautigan, *Dreaming of Babylon: A Private Eye Novel 1942* (New York: Delacorte Press, 1977); and Jules Feiffer, *Ackroyd A Mystery of Identity* (New York: Avon, 1977).

3. John G. Cawelti, *Adventure, Mystery, and Romance: Formula Stories as Art and Popular Culture* (Chicago, IL: University of Chicago Press, 1976), p. 142.

4. Cawelti, p. 141.

5. Cawelti, p. 146.

6. Cawelti, p. 161.

7. Robert I. Edenbaum, "The Poetics of the Private Eye: The Novels of Dashiell Hammett," in *The Mystery Writer's Art*, ed. Francis M. Nevis, Jr. (Bowling Green, OH: Bowling Green State University Popular Press, 1970), p. 99.

8. Raymond Chandler, *The Simple Art of Murder* (New York: Ballantine, 1972), pp. 20-21.

9. Feiffer, p. 53. Further references will be included parenthetically within the text.

10. Brautigan, p. 2. Further references will be included parenthetically within the text.

11. Berger, p. 14. Further references will be included parenthetically within the text.

Frederick Isaac (essay date 1987)

SOURCE: Isaac, Frederick. "Laughing with the Corpses: Hard-Boiled Humor." In *Comic Crime*, edited by Earl F. Bargainnier, pp. 23-43. Bowling Green: Bowling Green State University Popular Press, 1987.

[*In the following essay, Isaac presents an overview of the various forms of humor to be found in hard-boiled detec-*

tive fiction, emphasizing humor in description, characterization, action, and relationships.]

> I first heard Personville called Poisonville by a red-haired mucker named Hickey Dewey in the Big Ship in Butte. He also called his shirt a shoit. I didn't think anything of what he had done to the city's name. Later I heard men who could manage their r's give it the same pronunciation. I still didn't see anything in it but the meaningless sort of humor that used to make rich-ardsnary the thieves' word for dictionary. A few years later I went to Personville and learned better.[1]

It would be interesting to eavesdrop on a reader opening Dashiell Hammett's first novel on its release in 1929. What is this first paragraph supposed to say, anyway? Is it a simple linguistic joke, played by a sly author trying to unsettle an sophisticated reader? Or is it a swipe taken by the narrator toward his opponents, as yet unseen? It is, of course, hard to tell at this point, before the speaker has even introduced himself to his audience. The real point of the story, that the Continental Op is telling nothing but the truth, is the final irony in Hammett's pattern; the funny anecdote is not, in the end, funny at all, but grimly predictive. With this in mind it would not be surprising to have our reader of sixty years ago throw the book across the room in frustration, vowing never to read another crime novel as long as he lived.

Max Eastman begins his *The Enjoyment of Laughter* with the following caveat:

> I must warn you, reader, that it is not the purpose of this book to make you laugh. As you know, nothing kills the laugh quicker than to explain a joke. I intend to explain all jokes, and the proper and logical outcome will be, not only that you will not laugh now, but that you will never laugh again. So prepare for the descending gloom.[2]

Luckily, I have no such designs for the readers of this essay. What I propose is that there is an underlying and generally agreed principle for much of the humor in hard-boiled detective fiction; it is something like the misdirection of a good magician. While there are instances of many types of humor and the comic in the hard boiled, they rely to a large extent on the use of exaggeration and comparisons of incompatible objects for laughs.

I have taken some of my understanding of humor from John Morreall and his book *Taking Laughter Seriously*. Morreall posits that much of what we consider humorous "results from a pleasant psychological shift."[3] Morreall subsumes within this definition three major theoretical constructs: that there is a psychological change within the person, for one of a number of reasons (superiority, release of tension, or perceptual); that the change is abrupt; and that it is pleasant. Morreall utilizes his theory to analyze the work of such comics as Woody Allen, whose best work deals with the logic behind apparently incompatible groupings.[4] While I agree with much of his reasoning and analysis, I believe that Hard-boiled humor deals more fre-

quently in what he terms "the incongruity theory."[5] This sub-division, which Morreall employs as a part of his completed pattern, may best be described using examples. In one case, the entire range of cartoons by Rube Goldberg suggests the extent to which incongruous objects may be joined. Goldberg's humor derives from the utilization of outlandish and complex schemes to accomplish simple tasks. This is far from the *New Yorker* cartoons of Peter Arno, with his sophisticated and witty social comments. But as Max Eastman shows, they both present the world from alternate points of view, each of which is congruent from a particular perspective. It is in fact the discovery of these unapparent likenesses that creates humor in Hard-boiled fiction.

From its beginnings in the 1920s, the private eye story has always had a sense of humor, though the fact is frequently missed by its detractors. The common view of the form by its enemies is somewhat akin to letting a mad dog (the detective) loose in a rat- (villain-) infested alley (Raymond Chandler's "mean streets" are often cited as the best description). The expectation of the reader is that the hero will crush his enemies, thus allowing society to go about its business. The story is viewed as singularly unfunny, little more than murder followed by mayhem, a series of bloody episodes punctuated by gunfire and brawling. Wherein the hero interrupts his massacre of the bad guys only to take a drink or six, and to bed one or another of the beautiful dames he has met along the way. The solution of the original plot is immaterial, so long as there is lots of action.

In fact, there is plenty of fun to be found in the hard-boiled novel. From my perspective, the special joy of the hard-boiled is in its inversion of logic, making things that ought not to work together seem plausible. My reading in the form has uncovered many examples of intended humor, particularly in the work of Dashiell Hammett and Raymond Chandler but also in the writings of all of its best practitioners. There are also elements of the hard-boiled in some books not easily classifiable.

1. HUMOR IN DESCRIPTION

Much of the humor in hard-boiled fiction is descriptive. One of the best examples is at the top of this essay. It is easy to see the humor precisely in the way Hammett talks about the town. When the Continental Op arrives, he is struck at once by the grit that not only fills the air but has also seemingly invaded the people. The portrait is not merely sad, and not quite vicious. Somehow the reader is persuaded to smile at the Continental Op's growing comprehension, even as the complete corruption of Personville is made visually apparent:

> The city wasn't pretty. Most of its builders had gone in for gaudiness. Maybe they had been successful at first. Since then the smelters whose brick stacks stuck up tall against a gloomy mountain to the south had yellow-smoked everything into uniform dinginess. The result was an ugly city of forty thousand people, set in an

ugly notch between two ugly mountains that had been all dirtied up by mining. Spread over this was a grimy sky that looked as if it had come out of the smelters' stacks.

The first policeman I saw needed a shave. The second had a couple of buttons off his shabby uniform. The third stood in the center of the city's main intersection—Broadway and Union Street—directing traffic, with a cigar in one corner of his mouth. After that I stopped checking them up.[6]

This description takes us into Personville for a first-hand look at the Continental Op's job. It is, in a very real way, extremely funny. The repetition of "ugly" joins with the imagery to create a sharp picture of the town. The inclusion of the police, the guardians (supposedly) of the townspeople, suggests that at best they do not care about their appearance. At worst (and we will of course find out that this is the case) it points to the evil that pervades the entire town.

The Hard-boiled often uses humor as mocking commentary on what the detective sees. In his first appearance, Philip Marlowe describes the weather and his clothes, and only then goes on to talk about the job. "I was neat, clean, shaved and sober, and I didn't care who knew it. I was everything the well-dressed private detective ought to be. I was calling on four million dollars."[7] This use of self-deprecation includes a second, more biting comment in the dehumanization of the Sternwoods, and wealth in general. The replacement of people, unknown to the detective, by a simple certainty, in this case wealth, is a striking case of humor that is used frequently by Hard-boiled writers.

The exaggerated situation and the overstated description have become trademarks of the private eye story. When done well, however, they leave the reader with a very definite impression. Marlowe first describes Chris Lavery, the man his client says his wife has run away from at the beginning of *The Lady in the Lake* as "Six feet of a standard type of homewrecker. Arms to hold you close and all his brains in his face."[8] It is a quick notation, but every reader will identify Lavery from that point with a man of his or her acquaintance. The smile is one of recognition, and it is the juxtaposition, the incongruity of the patterns that allows us to make the connection so quickly.

2. THE HUMOROUS CHARACTER

Perhaps even more commonly recognized than humorous description, though not necessarily more important to its development, is the humorous character. Wilmer Cook, the young gunman in Hammett's *The Maltese Falcon,* is an obvious sort of humorous character. Wilmer is funny because of his actions. He isn't supposed to be, and shouldn't be, but in order to convince the gang hunting the black bird that he is serious, Spade forces Wilmer into making bad choices and then humiliates him. In chapter 13, after disarming Wilmer on the way to see the Fat Man, Spade tells an obvious lie which further disgraces the gunsel in front of his employer:

Gutman opened the door. A glad smile lighted his fat face. He held out a hand and said: Ah, come in, sir! Thank you for coming. "Come in."

Spade shook the hand and entered. The boy went in behind him. The fat man shut the door. Spade took the boy's pistols from his pockets and held them out to Gutman. "Here. You shouldn't let him run around with these. He'll get himself hurt."

The fat man laughed merrily and took the pistols. "Well, Well," he said, "What's this?" He looked from Spade to the boy.

Spade said: "A crippled newsie took them away from him, but I made him give them back."

The white-faced boy took the pistols out of Gutman's hands and pocketed them. The boy did not speak.

Gutman laughed again. "By Gad, sir," he told Spade, "You're a chap worth knowing, an amazing character.[9]

It is worth noting that John Huston's classic movie retained the entire scene intact, with Elisha Cook grimly scowling at Bogart. Both the menace and the laughter are clear for the viewer. The result is a feeling of superiority on Spade's part, which will assist him later in the novel. For us, though, Wilmer becomes an impotent character, only good for a laugh. Earlier in the book Spade warns Joel Cairo that "if he gets to be a nuisance I may have to hurt him."[10] This occurs even before we know that both men are working for Gutman.

Cairo himself can be seen as humorous, though in a far more complex and menacing way. His first appearance (which Huston also kept) features the turning of the hunter on the hunted and then back, within a very few pages.[11] When we see Cairo in later scenes we understand that his place is not comic relief, or the need for an extra body (the place filled by Wilmer) but as one of the key players in the game. The balance has been tipped to the other side, and though he retains a bit of the ludicrous for us, we also understand that in the end he did win his encounter with Spade.

There is also Chandler's classic image of Moose Molloy at the beginning of *Farewell, My Lovely,* gazing from Central Avenue at the place where his "little Velma" used to work:

He was looking up at the dusty windows with a sort of ecstatic fixity of expression, like a hunky immigrant catching his first sight of the Statue of Liberty. He was a big man, but not more than six feet five inches tall and not wider than a beer truck . . .

He wore a shaggy borsalino hat, a rough grey sports coat with white golf balls on it for buttons, a brown shirt, a yellow tie, pleated grey flannel slacks and alligator shoes with white explosions on the toes. From his outer breast pocket cascaded a show handkerchief of the same brilliant yellow as his tie. There were a couple of colored feathers tucked into the band of his hat, but he didn't really need them. Even on Central Avenue, not the quietest dressed street in the world, he looked about as inconspicuous as a tarantula on a slice of angel food.[12]

From that point on Moose is etched in the reader's mind. He becomes central to the plot of the book, even though he only returns on the final few pages. And our realization of his importance is only enhanced when, midway through the novel, the police *think* they have found Moose, but have only mistaken somebody else for him. How, we may wonder, can anybody, especially the police, not only not find such a distinctive man, but think another guy who is merely big their quarry. The very possibility reinforces our impression of Moose's special-ness, and the humor of the situation.

It is difficult at times to differentiate between the humorous character and the character described in humorous fashion. The Hard-boiled contains more than its share of wisecracks, and many of them are used in the description of its people. In *The High Window* Marlowe describes Lois Magic, Alex Morny's wife, in terms that indicate both her style and the vapidity that it is supposed to hide:

> From thirty feet away she looked like a lot of class. From ten feet away she looked like something made up to be seen from thirty feet away. Her mouth was too wide, her eyes were too blue, her makeup was too vivid, the thin arch of her eyebrows was almost fantastic in its curve and spread, and the mascara was so thick on her eyelashes that they looked like miniature iron railings.[13]

From another angle he describes Mrs. Florian, who used to employ Moose Molloy's girl Velma, to Det. Nulty:

> She's a charming middle-aged lady with a face like a bucket of mud, and if she has washed her hair since Coolidge's second term, I'll eat my spare tire, rim and all. . . . She is a girl who will take a drink if she has to knock you down to get the bottle.[14]

While neither of these descriptions are meant to flatter the women involved, they are also not meant to move beyond the physical. The result is that the characters are not comical, but their facades have been removed. Exposing the differences between the superficial, public faces which people show, and their underlying realities is a major element of the humor to be found in the best Hard-boiled. What is common to them as well is the juxtaposition of unlike elements in order to create an effect that is both humorous and immediately apprehended by the reader.

In all of these cases, whether the character is intended to be humorous in whole or is merely described in an off-handed manner in order to put the reader at ease, the repeated element is the seemingly unforced use of overstatement or the development of a sensible mental picture from obviously unlike elements. It should be noted that, in the case of Lois Magic, and in many more descriptions throughout the form, the humorous commentary is used to make a negative statement. There is beneath much hard-

boiled humor a realization that the world is a difficult place, and that in order to make it more livable the people who rule it must be stripped of their power and beauty. In talking about Mrs. Florian, Marlowe sees her degradation, and comments on it. His reaction to her, though, differs markedly from his impression of Lois. There is a tinge of regret mixed with his anger at the old woman's alcoholism, but no second thoughts involved with the gangster's wife. The difference between the emotion-engaging and the denigrating effects of humor must be identified and recognized in order to understand the detective's feelings and the author's intent in employing laughter.

3. HUMOR IN ACTION

A third humorous element comes with the humorous situation, a scene or occasionally a series of scenes, that contain comic elements. We have already noted that the scene early in *The Maltese Falcon* between Spade and Joel Cairo can be used to portray Cairo as at least partially a humorous character. The scene itself is a funny one, though, no matter who takes part, because of the shifting points of danger and the clear understanding that the story is only just beginning. When Cairo points his gun at Spade for the second time and says "earnestly" "You will please keep your hands on the top of the desk. I intend to search your offices", Spade laughs. And so should we, if only in amazement.

It is frequently the abruptness of an act that makes us laugh. Even though we think we are ready for whatever may come, especially in a hard-boiled story, we want to be surprised, and can even be disappointed when we are not. Surprise, as Morreall and others have noted, can be the cause of laughter all by itself, even—or perhaps especially when—the event is far from funny.

Take the example of Nick and Nora Charles, one of the first couples to star in a mystery. In Ch. 8 of *The Thin Man* Shep Morelli is holding a gun on the pair in their hotel bedroom. As they talk and Morelli tries to convince Nick that he has nothing to do with the case, somebody "drummed on the corridor door, three times, sharply . . .":

> The knuckles hit the door again, and a deep voice called:
>
> "Open up. Police."
>
> Morelli's lower lip crawled up to lap the upper, and the whites of his eyes began to show under the irises. "You son of a bitch," he said slowly, almost as if he were sorry for me. He moved his feet the least bit, flattening them against the floor.
>
> A key touched the outer lock.
>
> I hit Nora with my left hand, knocking her down across the room. The pillow I chucked with my right hand at Morelli's gun seemed to have no weight; it drifted slow as a piece of tissue paper. No noise in the world, before or after, was ever as loud as Morelli's gun going off. Something pushed my left side as I sprawled across the floor. I caught one of his ankles and rolled over

with it, bringing him down on me, and he clubbed my back with the gun until I got a hand free and began to hit him as low in the body as I could.

Men came in and dragged us apart.

It took us five minutes to bring Nora to.

She sat up holding her cheek and looked around the room until she saw Morelli, nippers on one wrist, standing between two detectives. Morelli's face was a mess: the coppers had worked him over a little just for the fun of it. Nora glared at me. "You damned fool," she said, "you didn't have to knock me cold. I knew you'd take him, but I wanted to see it."

One of the coppers laughed. "Jesus," he said admiringly, "there's a woman with hair on her chest."

She smiled at him and stood up.[15]

What strikes us about this short scene is the rapidity of the incongruous events, which combine to create a comic effect. That the man would slug his wife is not in itself humorous. Her first words on being revived, though, show Nora to be more than a spectator. She wants to see Nick subdue Morelli. She is aggrieved that she has lost the chance. The finale is given by the cop. It is a case of continual surprises, and the reader isn't sure which is the last one. (Like Huston's *Maltese Falcon,* the movie version of *The Thin Man* starring William Powell and Myrna Loy was surprisingly faithful to Hammett's book. This may have helped convince MGM to continue the characters as a series, though none of the sequels matched the original.)

In a different way Jonathan Latimer writes humor into his masterpiece, *The Lady in the Morgue.* The very concept of a body disappearing from the coroner's office may be ridiculous to some people, but Latimer invests the plot with so many twists that the tale becomes more menacing because of its unpredictability. The things Bill Crane must do to solve the crime and unravel the many situations surrounding it lead to some bizarre and exciting scenes. In chapter 3 he cases the dead woman's room, but is interrupted by the police. He climbs out the window and into the next room, where a couple is asleep. He ties the woman up, carries the man (who is drunk) into the bathroom, and then turns the cops and the night clerk away by acting drunk himself. The chapter carries its share of danger, but Crane pulls it off with aplomb.

4. Irony vs. Cynicism. When Being Funny Isn't Fun.

The hard-boiled novel has frequently been accused of brutality, the belief that the style contains a narrow and nasty view of life itself. Life is so cheap, say those who dislike the form, that the detectives themselves have no sense of its goodness. The nearness and the graphic depiction of death signifies a callousness that these people equate with an uncaring spirit on the part of the heroes. Alternatively, the stories can be seen as life viewed through eyes slightly askew, using humor rather than fury. The genre's finest work is filled with twists of vision and understanding, as

we have already seen. In such presentations the detectives establish and repeat the need to observe life's problems from a distance.

Probably the most consistent use of the ironic tone in Hard-boiled fiction is related to the police. As the guardians of the public welfare cops must, as a rule, be obeyed. Yet when they are not the heroes, the traditional detective story makes them the enemies of the protagonist. From Holmes' battles with Lestrade through Agatha Christie's simple dismissal to S. S. Van Dine's gratuitous insults and bullying, the police most often are seen as non-entities, without the mental skill to capture the criminals in the stories. Yet few of these writers comment on the fact. They allow their work, with its lack of mention of the law, to make the point.

In the Hard-boiled, though, the cops are treated differently, if on the surface not much better than before. It is very much worth noting that Sam Spade respects—if he doesn't always trust—his friend Tom Polhaus. And while he has no love for Lt. Dundy, Polhaus' partner, Spade never crosses him. Also significant is the amount of truth Spade gives the cops. He doesn't tell everything he knows, but he only lies when he feels there is no alternative, and only as much as he must. There is no spinning of yarns in order to put the police off. Spade knows the limits. This wariness has continued to characterize the relation between the hard-boiled detective and the police for the past fifty-five years. The detectives are always cautious, noting the subtlety of the interaction, using wit and wry comments to soften the antagonism.

As with many aspects of the style, Raymond Chandler uses both humor and serious commentary in describing the police. In *The Little Sister* he paints this portrait:

They had the eyes they always have, cloudy and gray like freezing water. The firm set mouth, the hard little wrinkles at the corner of the eyes, the hard hollow meaningless stare, not quite cruel and a thousand miles from kind. The dull ready-made clothes, worn without style, with a sort of contempt; the look of men who are poor and yet proud of their power, watching always for ways to make it felt, to shove it into you and twist it and grin and watch you squirm, ruthless without malice, cruel and not always unkind. What would you expect them to be? Civilization had no meaning for them. All they saw of it was the failures, the dirt, the dregs, the aberrations and the disgust.[16]

Like much of Chandler's best writing, this passage is neither sympathetic nor pleasant, but it makes several vital points. It notes the utter sadness of the men, and the unhappiness of their condition. At the same time it introduces a true distance between Marlowe and the cops. Finally, it has just a touch of irony, suggesting that Marlowe understands his position, and that this knowledge will protect the law from his most damaging sarcasm. That there is no mockery, no anger but a bleak recognition of the reality of the situation, indicates further Marlowe's awareness that the difference between himself and the cops is tenuous.

Other practitioners have included the slightly mocking tone toward the police in their work. John D. Macdonald has at times turned Travis McGee into more of a vigilante than a "salvage consultant" because of the unhelpful attitude the police have put forward. Robert B. Parker's Quirk and Belsen, Bill Pronzini's Eberhardt, and other present-day cops are not as lax as the bums in Personville, but they cannot be counted on when the detective is in a real fix, even though they may wish to do so. The distinction may be subtle, but it is unquestionably implicit in the work of all hard-boiled detective writers. As we shall see, though, this lack of complete confidence is far from a lack of awareness; the smile is not a sneer.

The best practitioner of the ironic view is Ross Macdonald, whose Lew Archer always found ways to separate himself from his clients and their troubles, while maintaining a steady pace toward the resolution of the problems he has been given. This ability to establish a distance from his surroundings is especially noticeable in Archer's sense of humor. Unlike the directness which we associate with Hammett and Chandler, however, Macdonald has a sly, wry way to make his points. In *The Wycherly Woman,* for instance, Archer silently comments on the doctor in Sacramento, asking "if the Sacramento River ran alcohol instead of Water."[17] Later, he stops a woman he has been following:

> She backed away from me with her fist at her chin. "What are *you* doing here?"
>
> "Waiting for Godot."
>
> "Is that supposed to be funny?"
>
> "Tragicomic. Where do you want to go?"[18]

By constantly interjecting such comments, Archer may judge from a distance the things he sees and is thus better able to comprehend their meanings and the connections they make.

Archer's use of humor is not just wry, however; frequently it has edges to it, making clear his wary nature. At such times his narrative voice contains small sad smiles, sometimes sardonic, and occasionally weary, as of a man who senses that his own quests are doomed to fail. At the same time Archer sees and recognizes his weakness, and knows that others are even less competent to deal with trouble. As a result, he is willing for them to lean on him until they can find their bearings.

I do not know anyone who laughs aloud at Ross Macdonald's humor. There are very few large gestures, and both the issues treated and the tragic resolution, especially of the later books, are frequently too bleak for even a smile. At the same time I doubt that any serious reader can deal with Archer's ironic texture without acknowledging it as a major aspect of the work.

When there is no complexity, though, there can be no humor. Take Mickey Spillane and the writers who have fol-

lowed him over the past forty years. In his work Spillane employs many of the locutions we have discussed thus far. Yet the tone of the books imparts a different feeling. When, for example, Chandler describes Moose Molloy, there is an impression not of danger but of the comic. After Marlowe sees Moose tear up the club, he is hardly inclined to laugh; but the aura of humor, rather than horror, remains with the reader. This is true for much of the side commentary in hard-boiled humor, especially that of Chandler and Ross Macdonald. The authors wish to keep the reader off-guard. The world is a rough place, they seem to say, and men can be menacing, even dangerous. Do not be put off or deceived by appearances, though. Even amid the grimness of reality, there is something to smile or laugh about. Without this we would all sink to the level of the gangsters and the punks. Spillance goes much farther in his warning. His understanding of the world, as passed through the exploits of Mike Hammer, is that we will *always* be caught by the bad guys. We must constantly keep ahead of the game, always know what is going on. This comprehension of the world carries through the violent action in the books and includes Spillane's attempts at humor. He has no room for weakness or subtle meanings, nor does he hide his feelings behind contrived screens of sarcasm. His smile is permanently grim, and the attitude toward the world uniformly aggressive. The result is a singularly bleak and unblinking view of society. Spillane seldom uses humor on Hammer's friends or clients; instead, the "comedy" is directed toward his enemies, as if the hero's hatred alone could destroy them. In some ways Spillane corresponds to H. C. McNiele and Sidney Horler, who directed their own fury toward England's enemies and their own during the 1920s and 1930s.[19]

The primary use of irony for most hard-boiled writers is as a covering for any fear on the part of the detective, or any uncertainty at the possibilities for success. Spillane, however, over-steps the bounds of this convention by imposing humor beyond the bounds of the reasonable. Hammer despises the criminals he seeks (they are routinely called "slime," "vermin," or other disgusting names) and lets few opportunities to demean them pass unused. The result is an almost unhealthy disdain for the subtleties of society. Where Spillane sends Hammer there is no quarter asked or given. Even humor is no longer funny.

5. RELATIONSHIPS: PAIRS AS ALTERNATIVE VIEWS OF REALITY

One of the easiest ways to get a laugh is to put two unlike things together. The very premise behind crime fiction as a form is the juxtaposition of men who uphold the moral law and others who would do away with it, either in individual cases or more broadly. The idea of putting unlike people together in detection is of course not new. The joining of Holmes and Watson surely is one of Conan Doyle's greatest gifts to the genre. The humor was not uncovered until 1936, when Rex Stout gave his famous speech to the Baker Street Irregulars proving once and for all time that "Watson was a Woman."[20] Stout's own writing also proved him a genius at the integration of different types. The team of Nero Wolfe and Archie Goodwin brought forth in its forty years many instances of humor allied with serious detecting. Wolfe's delicate orchids and the masterful cookery have given rise to much admiring comment from readers. What seems to have escaped our notice, or—more likely—has been so obvious as not to need attention, is Archie's role as a hard-boiled detective, and its effect on the series as a whole.

Wolfe's life-style, in fact, is unthinkable without Archie. Who will go out to the store on Sunday when they have had to flee the Brownstone and the police in *The Mother Hunt*? Who is constantly lectured to about various aspects of current events or history? And, above all, who goes out to interview the suspects, make deals, and occasionally get his head knocked on Wolfe's behalf? Archie, of course! The incongruity of the pair creates a dynamic that is by its very nature a comic one. Readers who have only read the later novels may sense this, but in the early books Archie is clearly a young cousin of Marlowe. And while he becomes less brash and more sophisticated over the years, he is always in contact and therefore in contrast with Wolfe, the quintessential armchair detective. Archie knows the streets, Wolfe knows the mind; together, but only together, they outwit the police.

In fact, Archie;s role as a hard-boiled detective can best be viewed in his interactions with the various levels of police in the books. He constantly challenges Inspector Cramer, both at Wolfe's behest and on his own. In fact, in two instructive scenes Wolfe reminds Archie of the need for good relations with the law.

> I have sometimes been high-handed in dealing with . . . the officers of the law. . . . But I have never flouted their rightful authority, nor tried to usurp their rightful powers.[21]

> To bedevil Mr. Cramer for a purpose is one thing; to do so merely for pastime is another.[22]

But while Cramer is treated carefully and somewhat respectfully by the pair, his underlings are not. Archie's relationship with Purley Stebbins indicates his origins in the Hard-boiled; the difference appears because Archie has no compunctions about using Wolfe as a cover when necessary. Further down the line, Archie makes it clear to Lt. George Rowcliffe that he is vastly superior to the ordinary policeman, and drives the point home several times. The result of these relationships is to introduce both tension and humor in the books, as relief from the tiring didacticism and absolute superiority which Wolfe represents.

More ordinary as a pair are John D. Macdonald's Travis McGee and his friend and occasional partner Meyer. McGee has come to be viewed by many readers as the sensitive macho detective. His mixture of two-fisted action blends well with his tenderness (often ending in bed) toward the women who seek his help. Meyer, though, has become personally involved in some adventures, and has

been vital to Travis in dealing with financial matters on a regular basis. Macdonald makes the two men's interaction more powerful through humor. Most striking is McGee's own feelings of inadequacy when speaking of Meyer's success at attracting the pretty young girls on the Fort Lauderdale beaches. (A particularly revealing and completely unexpected explanation is contained in the opening pages of *Deadly Shade of Gold*). While McGee is usually prone to think of such situations as cute, rather than threatening to his own sexual prowess, the idea that Meyer is attractive to these women presents Travis with a problem of merging the serious side of his friend with the playful one. When the pair goes out together on an "operation," Meyer and McGee again make a study in contrasts that has its comic elements. In one respect, they are directly opposed to the inter-action between Archie and Wolfe. Here Meyer is the front for McGee's experienced investigative sense, while McGee resolves the problems by allowing people to believe that he is less important than Meyer. This aspect of their cases has few examples of surface humor; once they begin, McGee becomes focussed on his quarry. Even so, the inclusion of Meyer, with his educated air and clear grasp of financial information, is by itself a use of embedded humor in the series. Without him, the books lose a measure of their humanity.

Many people consider Robert B. Parker's Spenser novels the best series developed in recent years. His use of Boston and the seriousness of his plots make him a major force in the genre today. While Spenser may not be able to cook like Nero Wolfe, or become as well-off as Travis McGee, Parker has given him a certain amount of the same humorous content as the other heroes have. Spenser is the central element in a trio whose interaction simultaneously heightens and dispels tension.

Spenser's first encounter in print with Hawk occurs early in *Promised Land*. Later in the book, Hawk meets Susan Silverman in an encounter that establishes the three of them as among the best humorous relationships in all of detective fiction. After the opening encounters have established the two men as nearly equals, they continue their banter as Hawk drives along Cape Cod:

> "I have explained to the people that employ me about how you are. I don't expect to frighten you away, and I don't expect to bribe you, but my employer would like to compensate you for any loss if you were to withdraw from this case."

> "Hawk," I said. "All this time I never could figure out why sometimes you talk like an account exec from Merrill Lynch and sometimes you talk like Br'er Bear."

> "Ah is the product of a ghetto education." He pronounced both t's in ghetto. "Sometimes my heritage keep popping up."

> "Lawdy me, yes," I said. "What part of the ghetto you living in now?"

> Hawk grinned at Susan. "Beacon Hill," he said.[23]

From this time on the two men (both with Susan and in her absence) continue the skirmishing through the series, sometimes goading each other, occasionally just to relieve the tension of the ordinary world.

As much as Hawk and Spenser enjoy each other's company and the male bonding, the books would not be the same without Susan Silverman. She and Spenser meet in an early novel, and she becomes his conscience and his partner in thought. Along with the serious work, however, there is a lightness of touch to this couple that many readers have come to take for granted. Their love affair contains a good deal of sexual innuendo that is clearly intended as fun. This sense of joy and excitement travels into the other aspects of their lives together, and we know their commitment to each other because of Spenser's desolation after she decides to leave him in *Valediction*. Both that book and its successor, *A Catskill Eagle*, contain a level of seriousness that is foreign to Spenser's earlier adventures, and Susan's departure is the direct cause of Spenser's change. These two novels, with only small exceptions, are as dark and void of lightness as much of Spillane's work.

Hawk's interactions with Susan are humorous precisely to the extent that they combine the man's brutality with a precise awareness of the formulae of correct behavior. Hawk is always solicitous toward Susan, courteous to a fault; even so, his evil side is evident to anyone who knows his other attributes. This proper relationship, hinted at in the quotation, acts as a contrast to his "massa an' slavey" relationship with Spenser. For her part, Susan defers to Hawk, both out of respect for his own care in her regard and for his physical presence and prowess. The author's ability to move between the three of them and maintain the integrity of each is a mark of his own deftness.

6. INNER-DIRECTED HUMOR: OR, EVEN THE BEST DETECTIVE CAN HAVE A ROTTEN DAY

> The bumper sticker said: Jogging is for Jerks. I stood there in my brand-new blue jogging suit, panting and dripping sweat on the sidewalk, and I thought: Amen, brother.[24]

Much of the humor in detective stories and novels appears to be directed outward from the protagonist. With a few well-known exceptions, such as Joyce Porter's Dover and Donald Westlake's Dortmunder, the hero is almost always painted as a paragon rather than a chump. Because for the most part we see ourselves performing the deeds we read about, it would not do for the author to create a character through whom we cannot win all of our battles. From the days when Hammett's Continental Op cleaned up Poisonville, the identification factor in the genre has been significant, and almost complete. The detective is a superior man, and I become the detective by virtue of the use of the first person narrative: Therefore, ipso facto, Zowie-zap, I am the same superior man I read about. In fact, I am even better than my alter ego because I can see where he goes wrong. I can therefore escape into the easy and successful world of crime, where everything is tied up neatly at the end. Bill Pronzini's Nameless detective is directly accused by a woman of being in the business precisely because he wants to be like the private eyes in his extensive collection of old pulp magazines.[25]

Here, most readers would agree, is at least one level of association we make with the mysteries we read. In this idealized existence the detective may make jokes about other men and women, but it is at best unusual for them to reciprocate. Carmen Sternwood's verbal posturing toward Marlowe is used by Chandler to develop her character. When we finally find out her secret, we are less surprised than we might be precisely because of her unpredictable behavior. Susan Silverman attacks Spenser throughout their relationship, but we understand that her position is that of a lover. And when Nero Wolfe chides Archie for some dubious word or other malefaction, we put that under the category of employee relations.

Less frequent still is the self-deprecation we think we see hidden within much of the hard-boiled personality. Occasionally there is a self-doubt, but it is almost inevitably swept away. In *The Lady in the Lake* Marlowe comments on his propensity for discovering bodies:

> Nobody yelled or ran out of the door. Nobody blew a police whistle. Everything was quiet and sunny and calm. No cause for excitement whatever. It's only Marlowe, finding another body. He does it rather well by now. Murder-a-day Marlowe, they call him. They have the meat wagon following him around to follow up on the business he finds.
>
> A nice enough fellow, in an ingenious sort of way.[26]

Or take Travis McGee's comments about his friend Meyer, and McGee's complaints about his own efficacy as a lover. They may appear serious at the time, but in fact the situation is a set-up by the author. The story will probably conclude with McGee lounging on the Busted Flush somewhere in the Caribbean making love to the woman he has recently rescued and has taken as his latest "salvage reclamation project." As much as we want to believe him, old Trav always comes out all right in the end.

So what are we to make of Bill Pronzini's detective? He is over fifty, only moderately successful (what he wouldn't give for some of McGee's "early retirement" between jobs), and as we can see, more than a bit overweight. In fact, his life really can be considered quite sad. He has had one serious scare because of a lesion on one lung, and when he went to the mountains to escape he found that an old friend had become very distant. His best friend is a cop who will have to quit the force. And his love life is something short of a complete success.

What Pronzini does in *Scattershot* is to suggest that the old adage "cheer up, things could be worse" is true. Things do get worse throughout this book, and all we can do is smile. *Scattershot* is an expansion of three short stories. Together they tell us that even when things go well for the detective, they really can be getting worse. He goes to a wedding and one of the presents is stolen from a locked room that he is guarding. Even though he has no key, he is accused and almost arrested. Another case finds him trying to deliver a summons to a woman; he discovers her dead. In the third, a woman wants him to destroy her husband; in searching for evidence, however, he finds himself siding with his quarry, instead of his client. At the end of the book he has solved all of the crimes but has been suspended. Now not only can he point to his unbroken success in these jobs; he knows that the police feel the same way. Rotten.

It is not for us to say in this context that Pronzini's detective messes up the cases, as the author himself has claimed.[27] The point to be made here is that the character becomes aware of his lacks and sees them unblinkingly. This entire book recounts the trials of a man who understands his limitations, but who may be unable to change his life. When he sees himself as the hero of one of the pulp magazines he collects, the detective finds not satisfaction, but problems.

Marcia Muller and other women writing currently in the hard-boiled style have taken additional steps to assure their heroines that they are not superior. In *Edwin of the Iron Shoes* Sharon McCone is constantly made aware of her inferiority by police detective Greg Marcus. And in *Ask the Cards a Question* she is interrupted after returning from tailing a suspect:

> "I was in my office, sewing up the rip in the seat of my pants, when Hank barged in. He scratched furiously at his head and muttered, "Oh, you're not dressed.""
>
> "No, I'm not." I draped the pants over my bare legs. "Why don't you come back in about five minutes."
>
> "Uh, sure." He backed out the door, his eyes bemused as he tried to act as if finding me half-naked in my office were an everyday event.[28]

Here and elsewhere in the hard-boiled world, the focus is not on the possibility of sexism or of lacks in the make-up of the detective. Rather, it should suggest that these writers know their characters' quirks, the things that make the fictitious people uneasy, and use them to good advantage. One could hardly say the same of Mike Hammer. What would he do if a client found him with a needle and thread in his hand? Operate on sealing the intruder's lips—for good?

7. THE OUTLANDISH AND THE ODDBALL

We have seen in the above discussions many of the uses to which humor is put in hard-boiled fiction by its best practitioners. We have also noted that there are cross-over elements which allow the detectives to comment on their environments and for them to see themselves in ways that make us smile. For the most part this occurs through misdirection by the writer, the use of incongruous parts to create a humorous effect.

What remains is to examine quickly other writers whose work makes us smile. Some of these write unashamedly comic mysteries; others are far more ambiguous. The result, though, is always the same. As we read their books, we smile. Sometimes this is because of the writing style, as in the case of Robert L. Bellem and his short stories. Bill Pronzini points to Bellem in his book *Gun in Cheek* as "an awesome figure," and continues:

> Those of us in the contemporary world who have read Bellem's work might also be inclined to run screaming into the streets but with laughter, not anguish. Anyone whose sense of humor leans toward the ribald, the outrageous, the utterly absurd is liable to find himself convulsed by the antics and colloquialisms of Dan Turner, Bellem's immortal "private skulk."[29]

It is in fact impossible to read a Bellem story with a straight face. His attraction to—at best unlikely—twists of speech ought to gain him serious consideration for the Humorists' hall of fame.

> I grinned at Mitzi Madison. "Nix, hon. I've been a private gumshoe here in Hollywood too many years to go for a corny gag like that. It wears whiskers."
>
> Mitzi was a gorgeous little taffy-haired morsel, dainty as a Dresden doll in a combed wool ensemble. It was about ten-thirty at night when she ankled into my apartment, making with the moans regarding an alleged fortune in sparklers which she said had been glommed from her dressing bungalow on the Supertone lot.[30]

The piling of unlikely bits of Hollywood jargon of the 1940s into what ought to be complete nonsense is funny in itself. The realization that the hero is serious, and that the speech is totally comprehensible stuns us for a moment. Finally, when we realize that the character is a rough private shamus just like Marlowe, we cannot help but giggle a bit.

In the 1970s Ross Spencer brought his twisted sense of humor into the form, in the shape of the Chance Purdue novels. From their wonderfully improbable titles—*The Abu Wahab Caper* is my personal favorite—to the idiosyncratic style, these books have a bizarre sort of charm. And while Pronzini is correct in condemning them for their utter simplicity (simple-mindedness may be a more appropriate term), they add a new and unexpected twist to the concept of the one-liner.

Two novelists whose work in the Hard-boiled field suggests that its humorous capacity may not have been reached are Richard Brautigan and Thomas Berger. Both wrote single books featuring private eyes, and each uses the form in ways that explore the meaning—and at times meaninglessness—of the conventions readers take for granted. Brautigan's *Dreaming of Babylon* stars a downtrodden schmoo named C. Chance, who has been clobbered on the noggin several times too often. If he doesn't tend strictly to business, his mind wanders off to an ongoing movie he creates in his head that takes place in Babylon (yes, the ancient land, that's the one) and features Card himself. In the single day encompassed by the short novel just about everything happens, nothing is resolved, and Card floats through it oblivious. It is, in a way, as curious a work as anything Bellem ever created.

In much the same way he questions suburban life in *Neighbors* and medieval legends in *Arthur Rex,* Thomas Berger makes mincement of the hard-boiled detective in *Who Is Teddy Villanova.* From the first page the book follows Russel Wren through a Hammett-and-Chandleresque adventure as seen through a funhouse mirror. Nothing is as it seems, and nothing is as it doesn't seem. Every way you try to turn, Berger has magically altered your position. The result is a comic work that owes everything to the masters of private eye fiction, but is totally unlike anything they could have come up with.

Frederic Brown is characterized as "paradoxical" by Newton Baird[31] and that can be taken as a summation of his work. Yet it is hard to stop at that single word when such curiosities as *Night of the Jabberwock* are available. Jabberwock is not a hard-boiled story; it is more of a dream sequence, a nightmarish charade perpetrated on Doc Stoeger, editor of the Carmel City *Clarion* one night. The cast includes a mysterious stranger who quotes *Alice in Wonderland* at will, a group of inept but determined bank robbers, and a quiet town that will never really understand what went on. As in the best literary dreams, none of our questions as readers are answered; we merely catch hold of the onrushing narrative and ride it to the end of the line.

I have left the most serious of the contemporary humorists for last. Stuart Kaminsky and his stories about 1940's Hollywood detective Toby Peters, can be seen as simple throwbacks. In the same way Andrew Bergman puts his Jack LeVine into wartime Los Angeles and New York, Kaminsky has Toby acting in a special time and place. What separates this series from most other historical detection is the depth of the author's research. This extends beyond knowing the basic events of the time, as any good writer should. It includes knowing the details of life as ordinary people lived it. Toby's breakfast cereal box has been noted, as have some of the songs on the radio. The verisimilitude of such details allows readers to enter the character's life.

There are of course unique people in Toby's world; Gunther Werthmann, a midget who was accused of murder while working as one of the munchkins in *The Wizard of Oz*; Shelly Minck, the world's least professional dentist; and Jeremy Butler, professional wrestler turned sensitive poet. They could turn the books into a complete parody of the genre; in fact, they are deftly used to complement and assist Toby in solving the peculiar cases he acquires.

In addition to the fictional characters who people Kaminsky's work, there are the real "names." We see Bela Lugosi, trapped in his role as Dracula (*Never Trust a Vampire*), and Emmett Kelly working the tent circus (*Catch a Falling Clown*). Kaminsky has his people in their accustomed places, doing not only what we think of them as doing, but doing what they really were doing at the time. In *You Bet Your Life* Toby's clients are the Marx brothers: Groucho is loud and obnoxious; Chico is gambling and then running out on the debts, and Harpo is quiet and watchful. For anybody who knows about the trio, the vision is as true as anything in their biographies and much easier to follow than any of the movies. *Murder on the Yellow Brick Road* contains several scenes with Toby and Raymond Chandler, who is doing the research that will help him create Marlowe as he should be. As in other instances, the specificity of detail turns absurdity into comedy, ridicule into humor.

There are ludicrous aspects to Toby and his continuing saga. He has been slugged so often on the head one wonders whether he really can think any more. His relationship with his brother Phil, the typical stupid cop with brains in his fists, leaves much to be desired. Last, the queer logic that puts the biggest names in Hollywood in touch with an unknown like him is compelling at the same time that it borders on farce. Through it all, Toby perseveres, and with his motley crew of cohorts, has given us some of the best laughs in all of the hard-boiled.

8. CONCLUSION

As we have seen, there are several ways in which the hard-boiled detective story can make us smile, chuckle, or laugh aloud. The very thought of Moose Molloy can bring a grin (but if Moose himself saw it he might well break both of our arms). Joel Cairo's persistence with Spade is a moment of high comedy that John Huston transferred whole to the screen. And more recently some of the scenes featuring Susan Silverman and Hawk should leave a lasting impression on lovers of fictional counterpoint.

Whatever one thinks of mystery fiction, its very premise is so grim that humor is a necessary element. While some writers have used assistants, such as the ordinary Dr. Watson, to set off the heroes, the Hard-boiled has not. The writers and novels we have been examining have created marvelous comic effects by allowing the incongruity of reality to emerge. While the other definitions of what makes us laugh (discomfort, superiority, and the rest) have their place in Hammett, the Macdonalds and the others, what we find funny here is the focus on simple details. At first they may seem displaced, but on consideration they all have two purposes. On one hand they make us look twice at what they show. Pronzini's hero can't really have a week like this one, for instance. But he does! At the same moment they heighten our awareness and force us to analyze what they are telling us; the world really is like this.

The realization of the doubling, and the simultaneous knowledge that it has forced us to think twice about everything we see, creates precisely the pleasant psychological shift that Morreall has identified. But it is the juxtaposition, and results through repetition within the stories, which allows the shift to take place, relaxing us in anticipation of the author's next twist. At the end the very grimness of the stories is incongruous with the humorous images through which it is presented. And therein lies the greatest fun of all.

Notes

1. Dashiell Hammett, *Red Harvest,* in *The Novels of Dashiell Hammett* (New York: Knopf, 1965), p. 1. This volume contains all four of Dashiell Hammett's novels: *Red Harvest, The Maltese Falcon, The Glass Key,* and *The Thin Man.* All references to Hammett come from this volume.

2. Max Eastman, *The Enjoyment of Laughter* (New York: Simon & Schuster, 1937), p. xv.

3. John Morreall, *Taking Laughter Seriously* (Albany, N.Y.: State University of New York Press, 1983), p. 39.

4. Allen's movies "Play it Again, Sam" and to an even greater extent "The Purple Rose of Cairo" are based on the entirely plausible effects of ludicrous events.

5. Morreall, ch. 3. pp. 15-19.

6. Hammett, *Red Harvest,* p. 1.

7. Raymond Chandler, *The Big Sleep,* in *The Omnibus Raymond Chandler,* New York: Knopf, 1964. p. 1. This volume contains four novels: *The Big Sleep, Farewell, My Lovely, The High Window,* and *The Lady in the Lake.* Unless otherwise noted, all references to these novels are from this volume.

8. Raymond Chandler, *The Lady in the Lake,* p. 527.

9. Dashiell Hammett, *The Maltese Falcon,* p. 375.

10. Hammett, *The Maltese Falcon,* p. 329.

11. Hammett, *The Maltese Falcon,* pp. 323-27.

12. Raymond Chandler, *Farewell, My Lovely,* pp. 159-160. 15.

13. Chandler, *The High Window,* p. 380.

14. Chandler, *Farewell, My Lovely,* p. 182.

15. Hammett, *The Thin Man,* p. 609.

16. Raymond Chandler, *The Little Sister* (New York: Pocket Books, 1951), p. 140.

17. Ross Macdonald, *The Wycherly Woman* (New York: Bantam, 1963); p. 108.

18. Ross Macdonald, *The Wycherly Woman,* p. 175.

19. LeRoy L. Panek, *The Special Branch: The British spy novel, 1890-1980* (Bowling Green, Ohio: Popular Press, 1981). Panek discusses both McNeile (as "Sapper," his original pseudonym) and Horler in separate chapters. See also Bill Pronzini, *Gun in Cheek* (New York: Coward, McCann & Geoghegan, 1982) for an extended analysis of Horler's viciousness (pp. 120-130). Pronzini says that "he was sui generis" (p. 122.)

20. Howard Haycraft, ed. *The Art of the Mystery Story* (New York: Grosset & Dunlap, 1946), pp. 311-318.

21. Rex Stout, *The Black Mountain* (New York: Viking, 1954), p. 153.

22. Rex Stout, *Champagne for One,* (New York: Viking, 1958), p. 50.

23. Robert B. Parker, *Promised Land,* (New York: Dell, 1983), pp. 85-86.

24. Bill Pronzini, *Scattershot* (New York: St. Martin's, 1982), p. 1.

25. Bill Pronzini, *The Snatch* (London: Sphere Books, 1975), p. 81-82.

26. Raymond Chandler, *The Lady in the Lake,* p. 596.

27. Frederick Isaac, "Nameless and Friend: an afternoon with Bill Pronzini, *Clues,* vol. 4, #1, p. 42.

28. Marcia Muller, *Ask the Cards a Question* (New York: St. Martin's Press, 1982), p. 103.

29. Pronzini, *Gun in cheek,* p. 229.

30. Robert Leslie Bellem, "Diamonds of Death" in *The Arbor House Treasury of Detective and Mystery Stories from the Great Pulps.* Compiled by Bill Pronzini (New York: Arbor House, 1983), p. 290.

31. *Twentieth Century Crime and Mystery Writers,* Second Edition, ed. John M. Reilly (New York: St. Martin's Press, 1985) p. 113.

Scott R. Christianson (essay date 1990)

SOURCE: Christianson, Scott R. "A Heap of Broken Images: Hardboiled Detective Fiction and the Discourse(s) of Modernity." In *The Cunning Craft: Original Essays on Detective Fiction and Contemporary Literary Theory,* edited by Ronald G. Walker and June M. Frazer, pp. 135-48. Macomb, IL: Western Illinois University, 1990.

[*In the following essay, Christianson examines hard-boiled fiction in the context of modern literature. He argues that, like, for example, T. S. Eliot's* The Wasteland, *hard-boiled fiction presents an "oppositional" stance toward the world, while at the same time upholding many of its values.*]

First of all, this paper will attempt to problematize the study of popular culture—more specifically popular literature, and in particular detective fiction, avoiding in the process the reductive methodology of adversarial approaches to "mass culture" (from both the right and the left) as well as the "euphoric celebration" (Polan 169) of popular literature to which writing about detective fiction has been peculiarly susceptible. Beyond merely problematizing, the paper will take the position that "mass art may be a potentially contradictory cultural form, blending progressive and regressive elements.'"[1] I will employ, to use Tony Bennett's words, "a critical strategy aimed at deconstructing the category of Literature . . . in short, the canonized tradition" (237-38), as part of an attempt "to legitimize the critical study of *all* forms of writing" (Humm 15). Moving toward perceiving all writing as rhetorically significant because of its inherently political or ideological nature (Eagleton 194-217) reflects my increasing concern that literary study contribute to social change[2] and seems to me to be the broad imperative of literary scholarship, theory, and study in the classroom today.

As numerous recent writers have noted, the question of popular culture—as of "knowledge" or "culture" more generally—is a question of power relations.[3] However, it is not simply a matter either of power exercised over the masses by an all-powerful culture industry, or of "power to the people" expressed through popular/populist culture forms. The former attitude—like its counterpart in the elitist critique of mass culture from the right—has led to political quietism (more on that later); the latter fosters an inane idealism and optimism unjustified by successful action for change in the world.

More specifically, this paper will situate hardboiled detective fiction *within,* rather than outside or in opposition to, the culture of modernity, a complex web of "enlightenment"—as it was initially named and continues to be called by Jürgen Habermas—or "disenchantment," a term which seems to be expressive of the "modernist" transformations of the culture of modernity.[4] The specific moment of "modernism" is a discourse which has been in conflict yet also deeply implicated with other movements and discourses within that culture, or meta-discourse, of modernity. This paper will challenge the simple dichotomy between modernism and mass culture by tracing close connections between the literature of modernism and of hardboiled detective fiction.

This way of reading popular texts alongside modernist texts adheres to the principles espoused by the editors of *Popular Fiction: Essays in Literature and History,* who, in addition to denying the "factitious distinction between high and low culture," demand that popular fictions "be read and analyzed not as some kind of sugar-coated sociology, but as narratives which negotiate, *no less than* the classic texts, the connection between 'writing, history, and ideology'"; the editors remind us that popular fictions "receive very 'close reading' from those who buy or borrow them" (Humm 2). Like the articles of *Popular Fiction,* this paper may tend to "concentrate on the formal structures of the written text rather than the social structures in which those texts are produced and read"—not at the expense of history, but so that it can "resist patronizing generalizations about the reading habits of those (unlike ourselves) who live and read outside the academy" (Humm 3).

FALSE DICHOTOMIES

One of the more confusing areas of discussion in twentieth-century criticism has been that involving "modernity" and "modernism." Students or scholars of literature tend to talk exclusively about the latter, whereas critical theorists, philosophers, and sociologists prefer the former, seeing "modernism" as subsumed beneath "the modern" or "modernity." It amounts, really, to a matter of perspective (in both time and space): those who write about "modernism" typically do so from an exclusively twentieth-century frame of reference (time), and in relation only to literature and the arts (space, or area of knowledge or endeavor). Thus, in 1986 we get C. K. Stead's book entitled *Pound, Yeats, Eliot and the Modernist Movement,* which perceives Modernism (he always capitalizes it) as a distinctly literary *period*: "We stand now in relation to the Pound and Eliot of those early years of Modernism roughly as Arnold did to the English Romantics . . ." (5). As another example, *A Genealogy of Modernism,* by Michael H. Levenson, is subtitled *A Study of English Literary Doctrine 1908-1922.*[5] Contrast these with the revised *Five Faces of Modernity: Modernism, Avant-Garde, Decadence, Kitsch, Postmodernism,* by Matei Calinescu, which situates "modernism" within the culture or metadiscourse of "modernity," with attention paid, as well, to the history of modernity prior to the twentieth century. For the purposes of this paper, we will consider the term "modernity" in its philosophical/sociological sense of the modern period in human history dating from the "Enlightenment" (late 17th Century/early 18th Century). "Modernism" is a late 19th- and 20th-century manifestation within the culture of modernity characterized—as we shall see in the discussion of *The Waste Land* (1922), below—by a self-conscious sense of crisis and apocalyptic change.

Most scholars could live with these distinctions. However, while they might agree that the discourse of modernism is *different* from other "modern" discourses, they would probably dispute its *relation* to those discourses. In *After the Great Divide,* Andreas Huyssen contends that a "great divide" in modern culture has been perceived, not between "modernism" and "postmodernism," but between "high art and mass culture" (vii). This Great Divide represents a "volatile relationship" which "has remained amazingly resilient over the decades" because "Modernism constituted itself through a conscious strategy of exclusion, an anxiety of contamination by its other: an increasingly consuming and engulfing mass culture" (vii). This "anxiety of contamination" has appeared throughout the history of "modernism"

> in the l'art pour l'art movements of the turn of the century (symbolism, aestheticism, art nouveau) . . . in the privileging of experimental writing, and in the official canonization of "high modernism" in literature and literary criticism, in critical theory and the museum.
>
> (vii)

Huyssen's analysis both borrows and departs from the critique of mass culture known as the Frankfurt School, offering a reading of that school "in reverse" or "against the grain": he deconstructs the theory of the culture industry (forwarded most notably by Theodor Adorno) which perceives modernist art to be the only (yet doomed) force of resistance to the commodification of culture which has produced a mindless and mind-controlling mass culture. Huyssen deconstructs critical theory of the Frankfurt School because its main thesis "can only lead to resignation or moralizing about universal manipulation and domination" (18-19).

While Huyssen perceives a problematic dichotomy between "high art and mass culture," between "modernism" and its "other," it is clear that he remains within the Frankfurt School perspective of critical theory.[6] Yet Huyssen correctly observes that some notion of a "Great Divide" between "high art and mass culture" continues to figure in most discussions of popular culture and literature. In his recent study of intellectuals and popular culture Andrew Ross observes, "There has long been, and still is, an unlikely consensus among certain voices from the right and the left about the intrinsic evils of new technologies and the monstrous mass cultures to which they give birth" (209). Ross is referring to the battle against mass culture waged by the right wing of twentieth-century modernism as well as the critique of the culture industry posited by the critical theorists of the Frankfurt School.[7] Diane Raymond offers a recent, concise formulation:

> Ironically, the conservative and radical critics of popular culture agree on the criticism, but where the conservative finds the problem in the masses the radical maintains that the problem is in the hegemonic culture which seeks to manipulate and exploit the masses.
>
> (103)[8]

The foregoing is only a brief overview of what Huyssen calls the Great Divide. It is related to another binary opposition and false dichotomy: between critics who study "mass culture" (for the most part inheritors of the Frankfurt School critique of the culture industry, though some are neoconservatives still touting the virtues of "high modernism")[9] and those who study "popular culture" (an often overly enthusiastic group distinguished by their substitution of the more friendly word "popular" for "mass"). As Tania Modleski states,

> If the problem with some of the work of the Frankfurt School was that its members were too far outside the culture they examined, critics today seem to have the opposite problem: immersed in their culture, half in love with their subject, they sometimes seem unable to achieve the proper critical distance from it. As a result, they may unwittingly wind up writing apologias for mass culture and embracing its ideology.
>
> (xi)

Modleski is being much kinder in her comment about critics of popular culture than Polan, writing in the same volume (*Studies in Entertainment*); Polan refers to "the euphoric sort of celebration of popular culture to be found in *The Journal of Popular Culture*" which, like the "scapegoating mechanism" by which the heirs of the Frankfurt School have made mass culture one of the "most recurrent

Others" of cultural studies, exalts "cases of popular culture only when the mythic, spiritual, transcendental values usually attributed to high culture can also be projected onto them."[10]

One may resist Polan's hostile definition of "popular culture studies" and yet still feel uncomfortable—especially within the narrower field of detective fiction studies—with the uncritical (if meticulously researched) efforts to study the popular. The history of detective fiction criticism outside of critical theory or "cultural studies" has been an almost unbroken narrative of unmitigated praise (until recently broken only by passionate defense when someone like Edmund Wilson asks, "Who Cares Who Killed Roger Ackroyd?").[11]

Recent decades have seen the critical methodologies of structuralism and post-structuralism applied to detective fiction. Such approaches tend to avoid the "euphoric celebration" of detective fiction enthusiasts, as well as the doom-and-gloom perspective of the critics of mass culture. However, with few exceptions—and however "positively" they treat detective fiction—such approaches tend to dichotomize "high art and mass culture"—"serious literature" and "detective fiction"—as outlined generally, above.

In *The Pursuit of Crime*, Dennis Porter borrows from structuralist and post-structuralist critics, such as the Russian Formalists and Roland Barthes, to produce an interesting "reader-response" approach to the specific genre or formula of detective fiction. In the fourth chapter of his book, Porter extends his "battery of critical concepts" for analyzing detective fiction to include Roland Barthes' "opposition between *le lisible* and *le scriptible*"—which, in Porter's own translation of Barthes becomes "readable" and "writable" texts (83). Paraphrasing Barthes, Porter explains the distinction:

> A text is writable to the extent that it does not exist as a work of narrative to be read in a traditional sense. It has rather the character of a pre-text, of a work in which the reader is required to acknowledge and participate in the writing process. . . .
>
> (83)

Readable texts, in contrast to writable ones, are "the great mass of novels with which we are all familiar"; and the characteristic of readable texts is that they "deliberately limit the play of significance as a consequence of the familiar narrative conventions they employ" (83). The phrase "familiar narrative conventions" applies closely to formulas like detective fiction; and indeed, Porter has already made his position clear in his title for the chapter: "The Detective Novel as Readable Text."

While Porter insists on the "readability" and formulaic nature of detective fiction, he takes care to point out that the emphasis on the use of language in American hardboiled detective fiction turns these novels into Barthes' *text de plaisir,* rather than the *texte de desir* of pure plot entertainment. Porter says that "the best novels in the genre are like all the novels we most admire" (107). This is in direct contradiction to the earlier theorizing on detective fiction by Tzvetan Todorov, who insists that "to 'improve upon' detective fiction is to write 'literature,' not detective fiction," and that the "whodunit par excellence is not the one which transgresses the rules of the genre, but the one which conforms to them . . ." (*Poetics* 43).

A recent collection of essays, Most and Stowe's *The Poetics of Murder*, confirms a general theoretical development suggested by Porter's observations about "the best novels in the genre" of detective fiction: a willingness to read some American detective fiction as "writable" texts—texts which, like works within the so-called canon of English Literature, seriously engage the reader in the process of making meaning. The trend continues in an even-more-recent collection, Rader and Zettler's *The Sleuth and the Scholar.* Yet in nearly all of the essays, some kind of generic distinction or dichotomy is enforced between detective fiction and "serious literature,"[12] a dichotomy summed up in the following comparison by Most:

> Measured against the novels of early twentieth-century modernism, let alone against those of more recent movements like the French "new novel," detective stories could come to seem increasingly artificial and distant from the very social realities they often purported to analyze.
>
> ("Elmore Leonard" 108-09)

The dichotomy—which this paper contends to be false— between "serious literature" and detective fiction, persists. Tania Modleski contends "that many postmodernists [such as Barthes] do in fact engage in the same kind of oppositional thinking about mass culture that characterized the work of the Frankfurt School" (156). Moreover, Modleski also perceives a link between contemporary critics and the right wing of the mass culture critique promoting "the older modernists ideas about art," in which—to cite her example—Barthes' *The Pleasure of the Text* is "caught up" (157). Modernists and Postmodernists, neo-conservatives and Marxian critical theorists alike are "caught up" in the false dichotomy between "high art and mass culture," between "serious literature" and detective fiction.

MODERNISM, DETECTIVE FICTION, AND THE BATTLE OF THE SEXES

Before exploring an approach to detective fiction which links it formally with modernism and which situates both within the culture of modernity, it is necessary to pull together some scattered commentary on a specific aspect of the false dichotomizing outlined above. The commentary has to do with notions of "the other"—which, with "difference" (and Derrida's *différance*) and "sexual/textual politics," represents an important constellation of contemporary concerns. Polan has called mass culture "one of culture studies' most recurrent Others—a repository and a stereotypic cause of all the social ills of life under capitalism" (169). Shumway insists that, "just as popular culture

is scapegoated by high culturists," so "[h]igh or elite culture is the Other for popular culturists" (166). When those "popular culturists" are also academics (often the case), Shumway insists, both elite and popular culture figure as "other," because academics "are participants in an academic culture which is not identical with any of the cultures they study" (167).

For his part, Huyssen offers an interesting conceptualization of "the other" aspect of popular culture (44-62). In "Mass Culture as Woman: Modernism's Other," Huyssen refers to the relationship between "the powerful masculinist mystique which is explicit" in certain of the modernists and "the persistent gendering of mass culture as feminine and inferior" by those same modernists (55). Modleski, in her overview of Huyssen's essay, observes,

> Once it is recognized that a misogynistic attitude lies at the very core of the high culture/mass culture opposition, the need for new ways of thinking and new theoretical paradigms becomes obvious.
>
> (xiv)

I would agree with "many of the other contributors" to Modleski's book, that "the critical view that can provide genuinely new insights into mass culture is a feminist one" (xiii). The well-known misogyny of hardboiled detective fiction links the discourse closely with the texts of modernism in a united front against women in what Leslie Fiedler and Sandra Gilbert and Susan Gubar have called "the battle of the sexes."

Leslie Fiedler writes that "The struggle of High Art and low has . . . been perceived as a battle of the sexes." He reminds us that Nathaniel Hawthorne inveighed against the "horde of damned female scribblers"; writers like Hawthorne—"those writers who aspired to critical acclaim and an eternal place in libraries"—have had to "struggle for their very existence against the authors of 'best sellers,' whom they secretly envy and publicly despise." He also reminds us that before men took to writing in the genre of the novel—which, after all, is the main form for popular fiction of all kinds—women had established themselves as successful practitioners. Fiedler proffers the interesting irony that "the authors of monumental, long-lasting popular successes have continued to come from the sex which thinks of itself as otherwise exploited, oppressed, dominated in a patriarchal society" (28-29).

Fiedler's point about the "battle of the sexes" is taken up in an important way by Gilbert and Gubar, the whole of whose *The War of the Words,* the first volume of *No Man's Land,* seeks to discover how modernism "is differently inflected for male and female writers." Gilbert and Gubar find that, in the "words and works" of both men and women, modernism acts out a "battle of the sexes" (xii); they assert that T. S. Eliot, in particular, often concentrated "with virtually sadistic fervor on the war between the sexes," and created women characters in his poetry "whose breaking of nature . . . also threatens to break the grounds of culture" (30-31). Alternatively, Eliot produced women characters who insistently voice female "hysteria," and whose hysterical language "embodies 'the horror, the horror,' that the poet spells from an impotent sibyl's leaves and leavings": "For ultimately, like Joyce, Eliot transcribes female language in order to transcend it, thus justifying Joyce's claim that *The Waste Land* ended the 'idea of poetry for ladies'" (236).

The masculinism and misogyny of modernist literature by men is paralleled by the same features in hardboiled detective fiction. In fact, it is the misogyny of the latter that goes without saying, and the recognition of sexism in the "serious" texts of modernism that affords the link between them and hardboiled detective fiction. It should not be necessary to detail this feature in hardboiled fiction. The connection, however, needs to be emphasized: in a cultural context in which modernism perceives its "other"—its primary antagonist—to be both female and popular, it is surely significant that a popular genre adopts an important part of that attitude. Within the discourse or culture of modernity, the literature of modernism and of hardboiled detective fiction share a "reaction-formation" regarding the perceived "feminization of culture." This is to asseverate what Polan suggests: "[t]hat mass art may be a potentially contradictory cultural form, blending progressive and regressive elements." Clearly, anti-feminism or misogyny is one of the "regressive elements" in hardboiled detective fiction. Just as clearly, however, we have deconstructed the notion of mass culture—in its specific case of hardboiled detective fiction—as modernism's "other," and further demonstrated the falseness of the dichotomy between "serious literature" and hardboiled detective fiction.

THE HARDBOILED DICK IN THE WASTE LAND

Generally, in the hardboiled American detective novels of Hammett, Chandler, and Macdonald, we get an urban environment not unlike that of *The Waste Land*. Both Porter and Cawelti have noted that that environment resembles Lincoln Steffens' *The Shame of the Cities*, a muckraking text of the early 20th Century; and Cawelti draws a comparison between that work and Eliot's vision of the modern waste land:

> The setting of the hard-boiled detective story resembles nothing so much as a world born out of a curious marriage between the muckraking of Lincoln Steffens and the lyrical sterility of T. S. Eliot's "Waste Land," shading off at times into the glamorous high life of *Playboy* or its earlier avatar, *Esquire*. It is a world of lurking dangers but also a fast-moving, frenetic scene appropriate to the furious pace for which most hard-boiled writers strive.[13]

Through extending the analogy with Eliot's poem, this section will try to demonstrate that hardboiled detective fiction proceeded from a world-view enunciated most prominently by that poem, and—more importantly—that the two share similarities of form and language which produce similar effects for readers. The texts by Chandler and

other hardboiled detective fiction writers would thereby be recognized as an integral part of the "discourse of modernity," related specifically to "modernism" in literature, a movement which derived from and was most infamously represented by Eliot's poetry.

The Waste Land has been a literary emblem, even a "formula," of the "modernist" approach to literature. In that poem, and in earlier poetry like "The Love Song of J. Alfred Prufrock," Eliot outlines a vision of modern experience which is nihilistic and fragmented; and his own symbol for this chaos is the "unreal city," which is London and all modern industrial cities. Eliot evokes this city and the whole of modern experience in uniquely metaphorical language which combines the "literary" with the "tough-minded" and colloquial in a way that critics have likened to the "metaphysical" poetry of the seventeenth century—but which seems to me to be even more closely related to the "tough guy" style of hardboiled fiction.

The Waste Land is fragmented and obscure, in form logically discontinuous, demanding that the reader participate in making meaning. The words don't "add up" in a neat linear or logical fashion to "tell" something; rather, they "show" things, in terms of detail and spatial arrangement, and leave it to the reader to make inferences and interpretations. Barthes would call it a very "writerly" text. In brief, it has five sections, each with a cryptic title like the puzzle or mystery element in detective fiction. After the five-part sequence of diverse and disconnected episodes, the final vision in the poem presents the poet or protagonist (related to Tiresias, the blind prophet of classical mythology) sitting on a shore, fishing, with the arid plain behind him and amid a welter of literary detail and allusion, asking, "Shall I at least set my lands in order?" At the very end he responds to his own question, "These fragments I have shored against my ruins."

"These fragments" refers, I would suggest, to the poem itself. That fragmentary structure, and what I will call the "Tiresian posture" of the poet/hero sitting on a heap of broken images, constitute important parts of *The Waste Land*'s "formula." The poem also details an heroic quest for the Holy Grail, several sordid episodes in the life of the modern city, a variety of modern characters speaking in the full range of the modern vernacular, with a witty interplay of slang, metaphor, and simile. All that should begin to sound familiar in conjunction with hardboiled detective fiction: the "formula" elements of Eliot's poem are also important elements in works by Hammett, Chandler, Macdonald, and others.

The fragments of Eliot's poem are analogous to the episodes in hardboiled detective fiction—episodes strung loosely over a mystery or "whodunit" plot, as the episodes of Eliot's poem are strung loosely over a dramatic five-part structure. The Tiresian posture of the poet/hero of *The Waste Land*—the isolated modern hero sitting before a spectacle of modern chaos and trying to make sense of it all—is the posture of the autonomous and lonely hard-boiled detective. The attempt of the poet/hero to order that experience, at the same time that he remains true to its futility, describes the linguistic efforts of the hardboiled narrator. And the colloquial language of Eliot's poem—"O O O O that Shakespeherian Rag—/It's so elegant/So intelligent"—combines with imaginative metaphor and simile to present a complex attitude to modern experience. All these language elements are directly analogous to the tough talk, wisecracks, hardboiled similes, and dialogue of American detective fiction. In general, both *The Waste Land* and the works of hardboiled novelists project an attitude of disgruntled alienation toward a distinctively *modern* civilization.

To develop the parallel, let us consider the works of Raymond Chandler. By the end of Chandler's novels, Philip Marlowe has come to the end of a series of episodic experiences; he has also realized—and proceeds to offer—some explanation of the mysteries and problems he has encountered. He details "whodunit." But the image of modern chaos and corruption revealed in the course of his "case" overwhelms any mere solution to "whodunit," because the world is in such disorder, and the reasons for that are so very complex. Moreover, in the evolution of Chandler's fiction, from *The Big Sleep* (1939) to *Playback* (1958), Marlowe's attitude toward the civilization of modern California and the city-scape of Los Angeles changes from one of savvy-if-critical comfort in the milieu to unmitigated disgust and disillusionment. As Geoffrey O'Brien remarks about "the extended arias of *The Little Sister* [1949] and *The Long Goodbye* [1954]," Marlowe "collides with an ultimate sense of the void" (78).

Consider the basic structure of Chandler's novels: Marlowe proceeds almost blindly, at the mercy of disparate and unconnected experiences, now hitting upon something which might be a clue to some part of the mysteries he has encountered, then getting beaten up, shot full of "dope," kidnapped and imprisoned, at once helped and hindered by the nefarious characters he encounters. *Farewell, My Lovely* (1940) is paradigmatic in this respect, with Marlowe's sojourn in the cultish asylum and his various violent encounters with Moose Malloy and others of his ilk. Like Hamlet, the only thing Marlowe knows is that there is something rotten in the state of Denmark—or rather, California. Like Prufrock, however, Marlowe knows he is "not Prince Hamlet, nor was meant to be"; while he is the protagonist in his own story, he's just a bit player in the social drama of the L.A. underworld. The "denouement" in Chandler's novels offers only the return of the detective to the same place he began. As in *The Big Sleep,* he is always Doghouse Reilly living Eliot's dictum that "in my end is my beginning"; in that novel, the reader will recall, one of the first characters Marlowe encounters—Carmen Sternwood—is revealed at the end to be the murderer. In a pattern repeated throughout the novels, Marlowe is no richer and has no fuller understanding of the world except for a wider experience of its discontinuity and futility.

All Marlowe can do is wait for the next case—and attempt to convey his experiences through language. And he can only convey; he cannot order that experience, except in a series of fragments or episodes. But more importantly, he can only attempt to "set his own lands in order"—which, as the course of his text reveals, has been an attempt at least to achieve some self-control, and control over his perceptions of the world, through tough talk, wisecracks, and hardboiled conceits that convey his complex sensibility. Marlowe's posture is the "Tiresian posture" of the poet at the end of *The Waste Land.*

Like the speaker of Eliot's poem, Marlowe strives to order his experience in a narrative. Chandler has Marlowe fill in more of the gaps between the fragmented episodes and experiences he narrates than Eliot's speaker does, but that just means that Chandler makes more explicit or literal the function Marlowe shares with Tiresias. As Eliot writes in the notes to *The Waste Land,* "Tiresias, although a mere spectator and not indeed a 'character,' is yet the most important personage in the poem, uniting all the rest." I take that to mean that Tiresias is the narrator, and is not a "character" in the sense that he is not described from the outside like Madame Sosostris or the "young man carbuncular." Marlowe serves the same function, as he also actively participates in the narrative's action.

The real thing Marlowe shares with Tiresias is the way they both "make meaning." As the speaker of Eliot's poem, Tiresias faithfully depicts the chaotic and fragmented quality of modern experience; so does Marlowe. While Marlowe talks more to the reader between fragments and episodes—a talk trying to make sense of what happens—the effect of Marlowe's narrative is very similar to the logically discontinuous quality of Tiresias'. Both end up not with a neat and tidy ordering of experience, but a faithful record of that experience's disorder—that is, a faithful rendering of experience, which is as much as either can hope for.

In that rendering of experience, Marlowe and Tiresias have recourse to similar uses of language. Both narrators skillfully exploit colloquial language to show, or reveal, modern characters: Eliot in the pub scene with Lil, Marlowe in the language of the mean streets, the tough talk of Marlowe himself and of other tough guys. Furthermore, through highly metaphorical language permeating the poem, Eliot/Tiresias conveys a complex sensibility toward modern experience: in "A Game of Chess," the male companion to the neurotic, nagging woman responds to her question, "What are you thinking of," by saying—not aloud, but to himself—"I think we are in rats' alley/Where the dead men lost their bones." Similarly, Marlowe reveals his own complex sensibility through frequent and startling hardboiled metaphors and similes, such as "face like a collapsed lung," or "a mouth like a wilted lettuce"—readers will recognize this frequent type of rhetorical figure as distinctive of Chandler.

PROBLEMATIZING HARDBOILED DETECTIVE FICTION

With the hardboiled dick in the Waste Land, what do we really have? On the one hand, we have another *modernist* attempt to arrive at personal autonomy, a unity of self-presence which has been the goal of Western metaphysics since Descartes, and which the various literary discourses of modernity have attempted to achieve through the autonomy of the literary text—the autonomy of art. The individual may be "lost in the cosmos," as the late Walker Percy suggests, and not in control of his own experience, but he can control his destiny through language—the last real refuge of saints and scoundrels alike.

Frank Lentricchia sums up the efforts of the critics and theorists of modernism—the so-called New Critics—to assert the autonomy of art as "a continuing urge to essentialize literary discourse by making it a unique kind of language" (*After the New Criticism* xiii). Modernist art and hardboiled detective fiction are deeply conflicted—which is to say that they are both ripe for deconstruction. Both testify to the fragmentation and meaninglessness of the modern condition, and its concomitant disintegration of the self, at the same time that they seek to make sense of that world and the resultant self through the literary text. Yet they also "defamiliarize" the very reality they depict through formal disorientation and linguistic experimentation.

For a time, as noted earlier, critics from both the right and the left perceived this "difficult" modernist art as the only hope for a doomed age. Lentricchia points out, however, that the "ironic vision that declares the inability of literature to declare, refer, or have a message"—"this so-called humane enlightenment . . . would, in its 'wise' counsel of resignation' and 'fear,' uphold the status quo" (*Criticism and Social Change* 65). The discourse of modernism, finally, from both right and left, promotes political quietism. The only posture that makes any sense is a self-conscious, critical, but detached irony which acknowledges that modern existence is confined in Weber's 'iron cage.'

Can the same be said of the discourse of hardboiled detective fiction? This is where the study of a popular culture form becomes problematical. Hardboiled detective fiction was, unlike *The Waste Land* and *Ulysses* (1922) and other modernist classics, genuinely popular. It was consumed widely in throwaway pulp magazines in the twenties and thirties, and even more widely in the throwaway paperbacks of the forties and fifties; and as Geoffrey O'Brien insists, "a society's routine throw-aways become a reflection of that society, and a teacher to those who approach it from outside" (9). O'Brien reminds us that exploitation of a mass market was largely on the minds of the publishers of hardboiled detective fiction; yet the publishers based the books' appeal—as O'Brien's brilliant "reading" of their lurid covers demonstrates—on an inherently "subversive longing for all that is not nice" (13, 11). O'Brien reminds us, further, that governments and regimes, from democratic to totalitarian, have censored the kind of vio-

lent melodrama found in hardboiled detective fiction: the Nazis outlawed gangster films, and Mao's China prohibited the reading of detective stories because they extolled the prowess of the individual, not the collective (12). So, O'Brien observes, the genre seems to have an overall subversive effect, which he also ties into the message of the meaninglessness of modern life. This operated, says O'Brien, as "an antidote to an equally prevalent American penchant for bombast and self-glorification"; we are "cautioned again and again to beware of the forked tongues of politicians, preachers, lawyers, and movie producers . . ." (15). Yet (another reversal) O'Brien wryly notes that the same genre that enabled Dashiell Hammett to conduct his critique of capitalist America allowed Mickey Spillane to exercise his "ferocious sadism" against women and Commie subversives (12).

As I am trying to do, O'Brien points up the complex—the "problematical"—nature of hardboiled detective fiction. It seems to promote the subversion of, or resistance to, modern culture at the same time that it props up that culture. In the matter of its misogyny, hardboiled detective fiction undergirds the whole system of Western patriarchy. Yet writers like Chandler and Hammett, especially, have used the genre to criticize vehemently a system which is rotten to the core.

John Fiske acknowledges the difficulty of answering the question of the effect of any given popular culture form: "Evaluating the potential progressiveness of popular culture is beyond us at the present state of our understanding, and may well remain so" (189). Far from sidestepping the issue of popular culture's political effects, however, Fiske chooses to speculate on those features which assert themselves against cultural hegemony. While Fiske does not specifically address hardboiled detective fiction, he does discuss the violence of much popular culture—and, by extension, of hardboiled fiction. According to Fiske,

> Violence is popular because it is a concrete representation of social domination and subordination, and therefore because it represents resistance to that subordination.
>
> (136)

Without falling into the dichotomizing of Barthes, he adapts that critic's terminology (used also by Porter) to delineate the innate "producerly" (as opposed to "writerly") nature of popular texts: such texts, though not difficult to read, involve "consumers" in complex acts of production and appropriation for their own needs and ends (103-06). Based on this understanding of popular texts (which I have grossly oversimplified), Fiske is able to conclude as follows:

> Popular pleasures must be those of the oppressed, they must contain elements of the oppositional, the evasive, the scandalous, the offensive, the vulgar, the resistant. The pleasures offered by ideological conformity are muted and are hegemonic; they are not popular pleasures and work in opposition to them.
>
> (127)

According to this definition, hardboiled detective fiction represents what Fiske would consider to be the genuinely popular, and thereby the subversive and resistant.

As part of the culture of modernity, as a discourse sharing important similarities with literary modernism, hardboiled detective fiction possesses features which are discernibly quietistic, politically and socially: it almost always promotes the anti-feminist cause in the battle of the sexes, and thereby is guilty of fostering the subjection of women; it buys into a metaphysics which seeks to find a lost self-presence, an autonomous identity, in the metaphysical contradictions of modernist aesthetics; it even seems to acknowledge the meaninglessness of everything, of every human endeavor, each text sado-masochistically exposing the rotten underbelly of modern civilization. Yet hardboiled detective fiction is also identifiably subversive and oppositional: the hardboiled dick bucks the system; he goes down the mean streets, a man "who is not himself mean, who is neither tarnished nor afraid" (Chandler, "Simple Art" 20)—which may be mere posturing, or even an outright lie, but which is also oppositional, resistant. Against the good taste and breeding of hegemonic, dominant culture, the hardboiled private eye is scandalous, indecorous, vulgar, offensive—and violent. He speaks the tough vernacular the average man speaks in his heart—or after the fact, when he has had a chance to formulate the perfect wisecrack which he was not able to come up with when the occasion demanded it.

Perhaps much of the immediately preceding should have been written in the past tense, because this paper has focused on the modernist and hardboiled detective literature primarily of the first half of this century. Recent developments in detective fiction have blown the usual categories wide open: there are feminist hardboiled male detectives and female private eyes; there are intellectual detectives who do more than find bodies in libraries; and there is a host of "postmodernist" literature which borrows from detective fiction and other popular genres to evoke the "postmodern condition" or experience. Yet the impetus of much contemporary hardboiled fiction—Sue Grafton and Sara Paretsky, Robert B. Parker and Andrew Vachss, and even Norman Mailer's *Tough Guys Don't Dance* (1984)—is still an attempt to make sense through language of our modern experience. As someone said of Eliot (Pound, I think), they have looked into the abyss and never forgotten what they saw. And if Fiske is right about popular culture and its effects, we can take heart from the "micropolitical" potential of a popular culture which affords the imaginative space for opposition and resistance:

> The preservation of fantasy as an interior place beyond the reach of ideological colonization, and the ability to imagine oneself acting differently in different circumstances, may not in itself result in social action, whether at the micro or macro level, but it does constitute the ground upon which any such action must occur.

(Fiske 190)

Fiske, indeed, cites research evidence suggesting that, on the micro level at least, popular culture has effected empowerment that has enabled or encouraged progressive social action (192). It may be impossible to ascertain precisely the social effect of the hardboiled detective novels which rubbed shoulders—and eventually book-jackets—with the literary texts of modernism.[14] But there are strong reasons to believe that they have kept alive, at least in readers' imaginations, the struggle against oppression and domination.

Notes

1. Polan 170; see also John Fiske, *Understanding Popular Culture,* especially the chapter "The Jeaning of America," 1-21; Kaja Silverman's discussion of fashion, "Fragments of a Fashionable Discourse"; Bernard Gendron's problematization of the analysis of popular music in "Theodor Adorno Meets the Cadillacs"; Andrew Ross, *No Respect,* 3-6; Tony Bennett, "Marxism and Popular Fiction," 250-51. See also Geoffrey O'Brien's neglected study, *Hardboiled America,* 8; contrary to its title this is a serious, critical, and sound study interweaving critical analyses of texts with audience analysis based upon sales figures and upon the impact of the lurid covers on paperback editions of hardboiled novels.

2. This is a goal or preoccupation evident from Arnold, Eliot, and Leavis, to Lentricchia, Habermas, and many other contemporary critics and theorists: e.g., McDiarmid, Giroux and Simon, Giroux and McLaren, Fiske, Ross, Huyseen, Modleski, and Humm.

3. Ross 5; see also Susan Easton et al, *Disorder and Discipline,* 22. "Knowledge and Power" has been a popular formulation since Michel Foucault, though Kenneth Burke talked about it much earlier.

4. See Morris Berman's "semipopular book" (his phrase, 1), *The Reenchantment of the World* and the discussion later in the paper.

5. The subtitle, however, could be seen as the author's purposeful definition or focus of his topic; although Levenson discusses only the literary doctrine of modernism, he explicitly acknowledges the limits of his topic.

6. Huyssen says, after all, that the dichotomy between high art and mass culture "was culturally and politically valid" during the time of the "historical avant-garde," but that the "postmodern condition" has changed all that (ix). He elaborates on the importance of postmodernism—in terms strongly similar to the Frankfurt School's extolling of modernism—in the third section of his book.

7. Ross 209; Ross's discussion of this two-pronged attack on mass culture is within the context of the Cold War—see 50-55.

8. Diane Raymond 103; see also Michael Real, "Marxism and Popular Culture," 147, 150, 151, and espe-

cially 155; David R. Shumway, "Post-Structuralism and Popular Culture," 166; Modleski ix; and Bennett 249.

9. On the former, see Shumway 166; among the latter, see Cantor.

10. Polan 169. In fairness to the "popular culture movement," so-called by Ray B. Browne who founded and edits *The Journal of Popular Culture,* published by the Popular Press, Polan's remarks are cited at length—and not so they can be attacked—in a chapter of *Symbiosis,* also published by the Popular Press and edited by Browne.

11. Haycraft (*Art*), Winks, Allen and Chacko, Geherin (*Sons*), Geherin (*American*), Nolan, and Baker and Nietzel. The subtitle used by Baker and Nietzel (*One Hundred and One Knights*) announces its stance, as does the first sentence in the book (by Bill Pronzini): "The private eye story, that acclaimed (and sometimes unfairly vilified) sub-genre of crime fiction, is important for the contributions of its best writers and for its influences on other aspects of popular culture . . ." (vii).

12. This is evidenced in two titles: "Hard-Boiled Virgil: Early Nineteenth-Century Beginnings of a Popular Literary Formula" (note persistence of notion of "formula"); and "The Hard-Boiled Detective Story: From the Open Range to the Mean Streets" (persistence of "frontier literature" genealogy of detective fiction, which underscores its "popularity," as opposed to its "seriousness").

13. Porter 162, 172; John G. Cawelti, *Adventure, Mystery, and Romance,* 154. Cawelti's work is famous, as its title indicates, for establishing the formulaic analysis of popular literature; the book does much to alter the notion that "popular" literature, *because* of its formulaic nature, is inferior to "serious" literature, but it does insist on a difference of *type.* Similarly, Humm, Stigant, and Widdowson write that "'Formula' and 'genre' *are* important to the study of popular fiction, but not because these notions serve to distinguish it from 'Literature,' rather because they draw attention to the ways in which readers go about their reading" (10).

14. A concluding acknowledgment must be made, that one idea treated so seriously in this paper—the affinity between *The Waste Land* and hardboiled detective fiction—has been explored with imagination and humor in Martin Rowson's cartoon parody, *The Waste Land,* which begins, "It was April, the cruellest month, according to the poet, and I guess he ought to know. . . ." I discovered this book, published only this year, at the annual convention of the Popular Culture Association in Toronto in March, mere hours before delivering a much compressed version of this paper. I refer anyone unconvinced by my analysis to Rowson's wonderful and wicked creation.

Michael Pettengell (essay date spring 1991)

SOURCE: Pettengell, Michael. "The Expanding Darkness: Naturalistic Motifs in Hard-Boiled Detective Fiction and the Film Noir." *Clues* 12, no. 1 (spring 1991): 43-55.

[*In the following essay, Pettengell contends that hard-boiled detective fiction is part of the Naturalistic literary movement in American literature because it emphasizes common experiences and everyday life.*]

Although Naturalism as a literary type of American fiction is defined by the work of a relatively small group of writers spanning a short period of time; the influences and implications of the movement branched out (much like Norris' "Octopus") into almost every artistic endeavor of the twentieth century.

It is not surprising that the ideas of these, for the most part, elite writers filtered down into popular art. It is again no surprise that these ideas which dealt with the realistic squalor of life, the unexplainable violence of man-against-man, the unforeseeable hand of fate, and the unimportance of man in the universe should surface roughly ten years after the demise of the elite movement in popular literature. As these ideas began to take hold within the popular consciousness, they were fictionally resurrected in the form of hard-boiled detective fiction which seemed to belch forth like steam out of a sewer. Years later, when Americans were experiencing the pessimism of a World War, Naturalism again crept into mass consciousness (though it had hardly been lying dormant) in the form of Film Noir.

Hard-boiled detective fiction was born in December 1922 when Carroll John Daly's "The False Burton Combs" was published in *Black Mask.* As an offspring, it is far from perfect. And as is most often the case with a new species, it had evolved—in this case, from a mutant strain of adventure story which had been appearing for some time in the pages of the *Black Mask* pulp. If the origins of hard-boiled fiction are not as glorious as some would have hoped, the movement would soon reach fruition in the writings of Dashiell Hammett. Because Hammett is proclaimed by those who followed him as the crown prince of the tarnished city, it is necessary to consider his accomplishments and their relevance to Naturalism; however, even before Hammett took control of the form, this new type of writing was affecting a revolution with the printed word much like that attempted by the Naturalistic writers.

Pulp magazines had been flourishing since the turn of the century and would continue to gain readers until complications arose during World War II. The critical attitude towards these magazines was, as might be expected, negative. Margaret MacMullen wrote in *Harper's* (July 1937): "The steady reader of this kind of fiction is interested in and stirred by the same things that would interest and stir a savage" (qtd. O'brien 45). This description fits in nicely with both the philosophy of the Naturalists and the world-view of the hard-boiled writers. These popular artists were rebelling not only against the elite aesthetics of so-called literary "high brows" but against the rather lifeless fiction found in many of the middle-class monthlies. Frank Norris is quoted as stating that literature of the genteel tradition is as "safe as a graveyard, decorous as a church, as devoid of immorality as an epitaph. . . . They can be safely placed in the hands of any young girl in the country" (qtd. Cowley). Writers like Hammett were similarly anti-genteel. Raymond Chandler describes Hammett as "giv[ing] murder back to the kind of people that commit it for reasons . . . and with the means at hand, not hand-wrought dueling pistols, curare and tropical fish" ("Simple" 16). Hammett took crime out of the drawing room and put it on the "mean streets" and gave a glimpse of the world for what it was, a corrupt and danger-infested place where, in the tradition of Darwin's teachings, only the fittest survive. Immediately there is a connection between what the Naturalists were attempting to do and the raging manifesto of the hard-boilers.

Within this new code of ethics there is one addition to a basically very Naturalistic point-of-view. There was never a hero like Sam Spade or Phillip Marlowe in the Naturalism school. Perhaps the dog, Buck, from *Call of the Wild*, would be his closest relative in that they both need to understand their environment and adapt to it in order to survive. Neither Spade nor Marlowe pretend to right the wrongs of the world, but both place a high value upon honor. The pulp magazine *Black Aces* describes the detective hero in animalistic terms:

> Since the first mists of time the man who ran out of the pack has been a front page story. . . . He is the Lone Wolf. Beyond the temptation of money or place he meets the criminal on even terms.

Although he is uncharacteristically moral, the force that derives him is considerably naturalistic. The detective must use violent means to be successful. These actions, and the knowledge that these actions are inevitable, work to metamorphasize the hero from human to animal. In a world which functions according to the rules of Darwin, it is this adaptability which both saves and condemns. In the *Maltese Falcon,* a book which uses description sparingly, Sam Spade is repeatedly described as wolfish. In the first paragraph his face is described: "his chin a jutting V under the more flexible V of his mouth. . . . His yellow-grey eyes were horizontal" (3). The brute force which the hero must utilize for his survival brings with it animal passion, or in Freudian terms, the Id. A prime example can be found in James M. Cain's *The Postman Always Rings Twice*:

> I took her in my arms and mashed my mouth up against hers. . . . "Bite me! Bite me!"
>
> I bit her. I sunk my teeth into her lips so deep I could feel the blood spurt into my mouth. It was running down her neck when I carried her upstairs.
>
> (15)

As in *Postman,* this passion leads the characters to their destruction.

Raymond Chandler, in his famous essay "The Simple Art of Murder," describes the detective hero rather poetically: "Down these mean streets a man must go who is not himself mean, who is neither tarnished nor afraid" (20). This popular notion of heroic morality is somewhat overly romantic, in that in order to survive in his world, the hero must become a part of that world—to embody enough grime to function effectively in a dirty society. Although he could not endure the pages of a purely Naturalistic novel (if there is such a creature), the hero's potentially opposite characteristics of Romance and Realism fuse together, a trait which is acceptable within Naturalism. It is just such a combination which makes him both "saint" and "satan" and endears him to generations of detective fiction readers.

Although the detective hero may represent a break with Naturalism in terms of his morality, the environment in which he acts and the world within which he must make his moral decisions is firmly grounded in the Dreiser/Norris tradition. The *Maltese Falcon,* for instance, is based primarily on historically accurate sights. The hard-boiled writers saw the city as a mirror of the post WW I American soul. It is a clouded reflection of corruption and evil which can be found within the marrow of the highest political official and the lowest bowery bum. Mickey Spillane may have described it best two decades later in his book *Kiss Me, Deadly*:

> I sat there for a while, staring at the multicolored reflections of the city that made my window a living, moving kaleidoscope. The voice of the monster outside the glass was a constant drone, but when you listened long enough it became a flat, sarcastic sneer that pushed ten million people into bigger and better troubles, and then the sneer was heard for what it was, a derisive laugh that thought blood running from an open wound was funny, and death was the biggest joke of all.
>
> (33)

The prominence of the cityscape (both thematically and physically) marked a definite split between Hard-boiled and Golden Age (popularized by Doyle, Christie, Sayers, and others) fiction. No longer is the setting a perfectly ordered universe where the detective hero acts as savior. In the world of Hammett, Chandler, Cain, and others society is a cancer whose temporary remedy is violence. Like many Naturalistic writers, they chose to tell their story in a place much like the dark alley Maggie listlessly stumbles down in Crane's fatalistic novel.

The detective's world of violence and passion is mirrored in the style and jargon of the text. Like the Naturalistic writers, hard-boilers used a unique blend of gothicism and common language to tell their tale. Shocking and grotesque scenes became even more effective, as in Chandler's *The Lady in the Lake*:

The thing rolled over once more and an arm flapped up barely above the skin of the water and the arm ended in a bloated hand that was the hand of a freak. Then the face came. A swollen pulpy gray white mass without features, without eyes, without mouth. A blotch of gray dough, a nightmare with human hair on it.

(40)

In this clipped yet imaginative wording, the detective/narrator's words rivet the reader like machinegun fire. Common language elevates the detective's pessimistic worldview to high tragedy as it fuels the narrative flame, as in Chandler's *The Big Sleep*:

What did it matter where you lay once you were dead? In a dirty sump or in a marble tower on top of a high hill? You were dead, you were sleeping the big sleep, you were not bothered by things like that. Oil and water were the same as wind and air to you. You just slept the big sleep, not caring about the nastiness of how you died or where you fell. Me, I was part of the nastiness now. . . .

(38)

This dark attitude toward life, which leaves the hero down and out and staring into a half-empty liquor bottle at the conclusion of most hard-boiled novels, is yet another connection between the Naturalist elitists and these popular fiction works.

The social climate following WW I, like that of every war, was one of disillusionment. The "war for democracy" accomplished very little, and so artists, both popular and otherwise, began to question major American beliefs and values, such as material success and individualism. In short, the "Roaring Twenties" decade saw the American dream as a distorted perversion. For a time, hope was drained out of the American wishing well leaving only a couple of slimy pennies. Chance and Fate loomed over the individual while Alger's "Pluck and Luck" shivered in the shadows. The importance of Chance is evident in three specific works of the period, Hammett's "Bodies Pile Up" and *Maltese Falcon* and Chandler's "Red Wind."

"Bodies Pile Up," first published in *Black Mask* in 1923, is a story which illustrates the importance of chance in the hard-boiled canon. The Continental Op (the first nameless detective—and an interesting comment upon American individualism) is assigned a job by chance; two men are killed not because they are criminals, but because of a chance mistake made by a gangster seeking revenge. The tragedy of this story, and of much of the work which follows it, is that the crime is solved but the corruption continues to engulf society. *The Maltese Falcon,* perhaps the most well-known hard-boiled detective novel is another pessimistic portrait of American life. The characters search in vain for an object which may or may not exist. Romantic love—a crucial myth of American society—is revealed also to be unobtainable, and even though Sam Spade has learned by his experience, his life profits very little because of this knowledge.

Chandler's "Red Wind" is interesting in that the hot, dry, lifeless wind which permeates the story defines the inner qualities of the characters. This element of environmental determinism, found frequently within the canon of Naturalistic literature, portrays Nature as a controlling and unaltering force among the characters in the story. Again, the ideal love is proven to be worthless, and the most important crime in the story (the murder in the bar) is revealed as happenstance.

Like many of the Naturalistic writers, Hammett and other hard-boilers were interested in social matters—many becoming involved in the socialist movement in America, Hammett being jailed in 1951 for refusing to name names for the HUAC committee. This concern for society at large is dealt with in their writing, although at times a sense of nihilism engulfs the story, as in Cornell Woolrich's *Night Has a Thousand Eyes*:

Death has begun. Darkness has begun, there in the full jonquil-blaze of the dinner-table candles. Darkness. A spot no bigger at first than that spilled drop of consomme. Growing, steadily growing, by the days, by the weeks, by the months, until it has blotted out everything else. Until all is darkness. Until there is nothing but darkness. Darkness and fear and pain, doom and death.

(qtd. O'brien 91)

Although he did not publish again after 1934, Hammett had started a revolution in detective fiction. His work was published by the prestigious press of Alfred A. Knopf and soon after made it into the cinema. Although it may have softened a bit over the years, hard-boiled fiction and its influence is still prominent in the fiction market today in writers like Stuart Kaminsky and Kinky Friedman. It is no surprise that the energy and freshness of such writing would interest filmakers in Hollywood, especially during and following WW II when disillusionment would again run high. The movement which most keenly felt the sharp prod of hard-boiled fiction and which would magnify those sensibilities shared by the Naturalists—exposing them to the world on the giant motion picture screen—was Film Noir.

The term "film noir" is French for "black film" and refers to films made in America roughly between 1941 and 1957. The storyline of these films is characteristically dark in plot as well as in physical texture. The setting, like the hard-boiled school of fiction is the city—an environment where possible danger and/or death lurks behind every corner. The characters lie, deceive, and even kill in a struggle to avoid their fate, which is usually brought about by a chance occurrence and biological drives. As in Naturalism, the characters seem to walk in a world they have no control over. They create a pattern from which there is no escape. First written about by Nino Frank in 1954 (he was attempting to critically come to grips with the influx of American films coming into France after WW II), Film Noir is not a genre but a type of film. Although most of the films in this category deal with law enforcement or crime as a central theme, noir films have shown up as screw-ball comedies and Westerns. In crossing this genre line, they are very similar to Naturalistic novels. Norris could write about the railroad, Dreiser about big business, and London about conflicts within nature—but the ideological basis is labeled as Naturalism. The defining aspects of Film Noir are much the same. Foster Hirsch describes the typical noir film as incorporating a harsh, "dog-eat-dog" world where stories of obsession and self-destruction are enacted in a kind of vacuum—a sealed off environment of airless rooms, and of threatening, lonely streets (9). Whether they take place on the open plains, the confined space of a cluttered office, or between towering skyscrapers, the camera angles, use of setting, and abundance of shadows create a sense of claustrophobia on film.

Clearly, the hard-boiled writers were an influence on those directors who created Film Noir, but there were other major influences worth noting. Filmakers in Berlin in the 1920s were developing a style they had borrowed from earlier German theatre called "expressionism." The aim of this technique was to distort reality and suggest the psychological state of the characters through manipulating sets and acting styles. A film like *The Cabinet of Dr. Caligari* (1919) uses sets created at odd angles to reflect the nightmarish deeds of the sinister sonambulist. *Nosferatu* (1922) makes use of shadows to develop the fiendishness of the first feature vampire on film. As Hitler began to gain power in Germany, many expressionistic directors emigrated to America. Among them were Fritz Lang, who had recently directed Peter Lorre's screen debut in "M" (the German title being, *The Murderer among Us*) and would go on to feature Edward G. Robinson in two ground-breaking noir films, *Scarlet Street* and *The Woman in the Window*; Otto Preminger, perhaps most noted for directing *The Man with the Golden Arm,* a film starring Frank Sinatra showing detailed footage of drug addiction; Billy Wilder, who would team up with Raymond Chandler in creating the film version of Cain's *Double Indemnity*; and the cult figure, Edgar G. Ulmer, who was able to make artistic films with almost no budget and in a matter of days, his masterpiece being the noirish *Detour* (1945).

The second major foreign influence on the emergence of Film Noir was Italian Neorealism. After WW II the studios in Italy were found to be destroyed beyond use. The Italian filmakers took to the streets to make their pictures. This added a documentary feel to the films which had been absent before. Also, this association with real people and events had been developing since the Naturalistic writers had first dealt with the "dirtiness" of life and living. Location shooting of this type would show up in films like *D.O.A.* (1949) and Phil Karlson's *Pheonix City Story* (1955), the latter being a violent crime drama based on an actual occurrence and even including interviews with those involved.

Although the foreign influences were important, earlier American films were also influential in establishing the noir trend. Gangster and horror films from the 1930s helped solidify character roles and filming techniques. The fated protagonist of the gangster film and his perverted rise to riches comes close to noir sentiments (represented in Naturalism by Drieser's monomaniacal Cowperwood), while the gothic shadows and desolate castles found in many early horror films need just a touch of imagination before they become the treacherous cityscapes of the 40s and 50s films. This rich heritage of film noir is interesting in itself, but one of the greatest differences between these films and those of the pre-war studio years is the highly unconventional male and female lead roles.

The protagonist in Film Noir is either a tortured heroic figure, like Sam Spade with his Flitcraftian insight, or a sensitive and frightened victim, like Chris Cross, unable to find his niche in American society. He is, indeed, at the mercy of his environment, much like the hero of the Naturalistic novel. Often it is this normal "Joe's" momentary laps of control over the Id (i.e. passion) which leads him to destruction. In *Double Indemnity,* Walter Neff is an insurance salesman who because he drops by a client's house when the wife is alone, and because he sees her wearing nothing but a towel (and an anklet with her name on it which "cuts" into her leg), he gets involved with a scheme that leads him "right down the line . . . to the cemetery." Perhaps Tom Neal said it best in Ulmer's *Detour,* "That's life. . . . sometimes, for no reason at all, Fate sticks out its foot to trip you."

Of course, the protagonist might just survive unscathed if not for that sinister black widow of a woman, the Noir Female. These "bitch goddesses" are emissaries of Fate who use sex as a lure. Phyllis Dietrichson (Barbara Stanwyck) in *Double Indemnity* entangles Neff into killing her husband; she had earlier murdered the husband's first wife by leaving the poor, sick woman in front of an open window during a particularly cold, wintery night. Joan Bennett in *Scarlet Street* not only signs her name to Robinson's paintings after bleeding him dry of available cash, she laughingly tells him how ugly and repulsive he is to her. Of course, she does meet with a rather gruesome encounter with an ice pick, but even then continues to haunt the protagonist to the point of suicide. These characters may well reflect society's fear of the sexually aggressive and free woman which developed during the war and then was expected to return to the kitchen immediately afterwards. This view of female breaks the normal Hollywood stereotype and attempts to bring real life motivations to the screen, in a sense, another attack of the genteel.

Both of these character types interact in a world confined within the menacing city. At times the protagonist may attempt to rid himself of the grime and filth of his environment, but this action is usually unsuccessful and leads to the character's death. A good example of this can be found in *The Asphalt Jungle* (1950) where Sterling Hayden, a good natured hoodlum, makes it back to "Hickory Ranch" but dies in the pasture of a bullet wound. There are those who argue that it is necessary in Film Noir to have an unhappy ending, but there are a number of ambiguous closing scenes which may be at odds with the typical Hollywood finale and still offer some solace to the hero. *On Dangerous Ground* (1951) is a case in point. Robert Ryan becomes contaminated by the city in his job as police-detective and leaves the violent and corrupt environment to get away from the "garbage"; "How do you do it? How do you live with yourself?" he asks his partner. In the country he meets the rural equivalent of himself in Ward Bond—perhaps enabling him to see more clearly his savage shadow self. Through the care of a blind woman he is given insight into himself. It is not, however, the country that saves him; there is no mythical, rural land free from corruption. The scenes are dreamlike studies of mud and snow, poverty and ignorance. As in Naturalism, the "dirt" is exposed and the myth and accompanying value system is deflated. By seeing into the darkness—the darkness of the blind woman and the darkness trapped within him—and adapting to it, Ryan is able to survive. This may seem rather hopeful, but before the movie ends the blind woman's brother (a mentally ill killer for whom the men are searching) commits suicide. Whether the woman's blindness will eventually be cured remains unanswered.

Film Noir as a movement died out around 1958 because Hollywood began to rely on the epic spectacle films to regain the audience television was stealing from them. The obsoletism of the "B" movie and the advent of color helped hasten its demise. Also, many of the writers, directors, and actors who had been working in Film Noir were blacklisted during the same HUAC sessions that imprisoned Hammett. Movies returned momentarily to an overly optimistic and sentimental view of the world. In summing up the real nucleus of meaning which worked to weave together the movement as a whole, Jon Tuska states that

> Film Noir is a darkling vision of the world, a view from the underside, born of fundamental disillusionment perhaps, but also invariably the result, no matter how timid, of a confrontation with nihilism.
>
> (135)

In summation, it is possible to see that attitudes, ideas, and objectives of the Naturalistic school in literature reflected and expanded in the popular fiction and motion pictures that followed it. Both attempted to get at the essence of life through the common experience. The naturalists' view of language was certainly similar to that of the hard-boiled writers. Seeing the world as violent and uncaring, and life as potentially beyond one's control is continually emphasized both in the fiction and in Film Noir. The exploitation of the common man by a society eaten through with corruption is as much as a concern of the noir director John Huston as it is with Hammett, Dreiser, and Zola. What is different is that hard-boiled fiction and Film Noir were products of artistic content that were appreciated by much of the population. Where the earlier writers had somehow failed to gain mass appeal, Hammett, Chandler, and the Noir movement succeeded.

Works Cited

Cain, James M. *The Postman Always Rings Twice.* New York: Grosset, 1934.

Chandler, Raymond. *The Lady in the Lake.* (1943) New York: Vintage, 1976.

———. *The Simple Art of Murder.* (1950) New York: Vintage, 1972.

Goulart, Ron. *The Dime Detectives: A Comprehensive History of the Detective Pulps.* New York: Mysterious Press, 1988.

Gregory, Sinda. *Private Investigations: The Novels of Dashiell Hammett.* Edwardsville: Southern Illinois UP, 1985.

Hamilton, Cynthia S. *Western and Hard-Boiled Detective Fiction in America: From High Noon To Midnight.* Iowa City: University of Iowa Press, 1987.

Hammett, Dashiell. "Bodies Pile Up." (1923) Reprinted in William F. Nolan *The Black Mask Boys: Masters in the Hard-Boiled School of Detective Fiction.* New York: Mysterious Press, 1985.

———. *The Maltese Falcon.* (1929) San Francisco: North Point Press, 1984.

Hirsch, Foster. *Film Noir: The Dark Side of the Screen.* New York: Da Capo Press, 1981.

Johnson, Diane. *Dashiell Hammett: A Life.* New York: Random House, 1983.

Layman, Richard. *Shadow Man: The Life of Dashiell Hammett.* New York: Harcourt Brace, 1981.

Nachbar, Jack. "Film Noir," in *Handbook of American Genres.* Ed. by Wes D. Gehring. New York: Greenwood Press, 1988.

O'brien, Geoffrey. *Hardboiled America: The Lurid Years of Paperbacks.* New York: Van Nostrand, 1981.

Selby, Spencer. *Dark City: The Film Noir.* Jefferson, NC: McFarland, 1984.

Spillane, Mickey. *Kiss Me, Deadly.* New York: Signet, 1952.

Tuska, Jon. *Dark Cinema: American Film Noir in Cultural Perspective.* New York: Greenwood Press, 1984.

———. *In Manors and Alleys: A Casebook on the American Detective Film.* New York: Greenwood Press, 1988.

MAJOR AUTHORS

E. R. Hagemann (essay date 1979)

SOURCE: Hagemann, E. R. "Introducing Paul Cain and his *Fast One*: A Forgotten Hard-Boiled Writer, a Forgotten Gangster Novel." *Armchair Detective* 12, no. 1 (1979): 72-76.

[*In the following essay, Hagemann presents an overview of the career of hard-boiled writer Paul Cain, author of the novel* Fast One—*"the best of its kind ever to appear," according to Hagemann.*]

I. Career

During his professional writing career, 1932-1948, he used Paul Cain for his fiction and Peter Ruric for his movie work, passing off the latter as his real name; yet he was born George Sims in Iowa, 30 May 1902. Nothing is known of his personal life and little of his professional life either before or after he broke into print in March 1932.

In a discarded Introduction (ca. 1946) to *The Hard-Boiled Omnibus,* Joseph T. Shaw, its editor known for his supervision of *Black Mask,* cites Ruric's "recollections of his boyhood experiences in Chicago where [he] saw something of life in its toughest phases. We suspect that Peter drew from these first-hand glimpses for his first published work, a book-length Black Mask serial titled *Fast One.*"[1]

And it is for *Fast One,* and *Fast One* alone, his only novel, that Cain should be remembered but inexplicably has not been.

Having accepted Cain's Chicago youth (on Shaw's testimony alone), we next find that he came to Los Angeles in 1918 and entered the movie industry in 1923. He lays claim to have worked with Josef von Sternberg in 1925 on *Salvation Hunters* but there is no proof. Indeed, much of Cain's/Ruric's assertions for movies, books, etc., absolutely cannot be verified, either by title, publisher, or name—any one of his three names.

This much is known: In 1933 he was residing at 6650 Franklin Avenue, Hollywood. This was the Montecito Hotel Apartments, Franklin and Cherokee, situated on a steep hill and facing the hills to the north and overlooking Holywood to the south. It had opened in 1931 and is still in operation, but seedy and shabby. However, in 1932 it was a fine place to live (the entrance is a classic bit of Art Deco) and to work.

And work Cain did, in fiction and on screenplays for sixteen years. His (verifiable) fiction career began in March 1932 in *Black Mask,* the only magazine to print him, with "Fast One," the first installment of the serialization. Page 26 of the issue advertises "Lead Party," by Paul Cain, "another fast story around several of these same characters in *April Black Mask.*" Further back, page 120, editor Shaw speculates about "if and when 'Fast One,' 'Lead Party,' and their subsequent stories . . . are moulded into shape for book publication and brought out as one book."

There were five installments.[2] In May, "Black," Cain's first short story, was published. Black, first-person narrator, moves into a corrupt town to avenge successfully a murder committed over rum-running and to start trouble successfully among those who run the town. An average pulp piece, it reminds one, faintly, of Dashiell Hammett's *Red Harvest,* but it is nowhere as good. The second interlude was "Parlor Trick" in July, a brutal little tale which although damaged by some cheap coincidences is one of his better contributions. In December, Cain published "Red

71," his best (although marred) story. "'Am I a swell dick—or am I a swell dick?' asks Dick Shane. He is swell all right. He operates just beyond the fringes of the New York underworld and solves the murder of gambler Charley Rigas who ran a joint known as Red 71. The ending is ambiguous, to say the least, and the plotting is complicated.[3]

Ruric's precise work in the movies is open to dispute.

His first (verifiable) credit was as author (story) of a Paramount flick starring Cary Grant and Benita Hume called *Gambling Ship.* Released 29 June 1933 and directed by Max Marcin, it was "derived" from the *Black Mask* version of "Fast One." But this is absurd; all that remains is a gambling ship with another name. Glenda Farrell and Jack LaRue, two Golden Oldies, were in the cast. The critic Abel in *Variety,* 18 July 1933, called it a fair job. "Of the gangster meller genera. . . . Film doesn't drag, save in negligible moments, but in toto it's a familiar formula of mob vs. mob."[4]

Ruric's first solo credit was his screenplay of *The Black Cat* (Universal), released 4 May 1934, with Boris Karloff and Bela Lugosi in the leads. Edgar G. Ulmer was the director; Carl Laemmle, Jr., the producer. Edgar Allan Poe was billed as the "author"—another absurdity. *Film Daily,* 19 May, said: "Horror pix has two great exponents of the school, Karloff and Lugosi, doing grand thrill job. . . . It takes its place in the same category with *Frankenstein* and *Dracula,* and this brings them together for the first time. . . ."[5] About a week later *Affairs of a Gentleman* came out of the Universal lot. Ruric and Cyril Hume shared screenplay credits; Paul Lukas and Leila Hyams, two other Golden Oldies, shared top billing. *Film Daily,* 23 June, declared it "a fair drama of many loves given unconvincing treatment with Paul Lukas holding it up with good work."

So far, Ruric had hardly knocked them dead in the studios.

Marginally more successful was the publication of *Fast One* by Doubleday, Doran on 25 October 1933. Cain claimed it was written "on a bet." It tells complexly—fantastically so—the rapid rise and obliteration of tough-guy hoodlum Gerry Kells (not quite "kills") and his dipso lover, S. Granquist (she is graced with no prename, but she is a grand twist!), as they take over, or try to, Los Angeles in 1932.[6] The publisher worked hard to peddle it in the abyss of The Great Depression and dispatched paperbound advance copies with a hard-driving front- and back-cover blurb:

> You've read *The Maltese Falcon*[,] *Green Ice*[,] *Iron Man*[,] hard, fast stories all, but now comes the hardest, toughest, swiftest novel of them all FAST ONE[.] Two hours of sheer terror, written with a clipped violence, hypnotic in its power. The author is Paul Cain whom we consider the greatest discovery in his field in many years. Not a detective story, not a mystery, *Fast One* is a brutal novel of passion and death. Kells, the hero; Granquist, the heroine, are two of the strangest

figures in contemporary fiction. They will be talked about; their bullet-spattered love will arouse new emotions in the hearts of thousands of readers looking for something fresh, different, gripping. Read this special advance copy . . . see if you yourself can escape from the nightmare spell of these pages.[7]

I am not one to praise blurbs but this one, with pardonable hyperbole, is right on; it is a shame that neither it nor the novel attracted "thousands." Reviewers didn't help much. "The Criminal Record" in *Saturday Review of Literature* called it "the hardest-boiled yarn of a decade. So h.-b. it gets funny. But it moves like a machine-gun. Zowie!"[8] *The New York Times Book Review,* under the head, "Gangsters Gone Mad," attacked it, after acknowledging the blurb, as "a ceaseless welter of bloodshed and frenzy, a sustained bedlam of killing and fiendishness, told in terse staccato style." It concluded: ". . . There is no minute's let-up in the saturnalia of 'black-and-blue passion, bloodlust, death.'"[9] Los Angeles book critics shied away from it for the most part. There was enough real-life corruption in The City of the Angels. But one did take a shot at it. "Well! Well! *Fast One,* Paul Cain's tale of crime in Los Angeles . . . is the toughest, hardest, most ruthless crime story they have ever published, they tell me. However, it is only fair to state that *Kells,* the hero, is a thief and a murderer who hails from the Middle West!"[10]

In England *Fast One* was issued by Constable in March 1936 and given a reprint in a cheap edition in March 1937. *TLS,* 18 April 1936, had a review which is worth quoting in full:

> The jacket declares that this novel "has in America the reputation of being the most genuine gangster novel ever written" and although this may be a matter of opinion it is interesting to speculate on how the author gains such remarkable effects of verisimilitude in a story which, on recollection, seems so far from normal experience with its hundred-mile-an-hour speed, its baker's dozen of murders, its blackmailings, double-crossings and tortures.
>
> Kells was a "muscle-man" and he went West to enjoy a holiday and to "play" for a few years. He is rapidly dragged into a whirl of political jobbery in a gangridden city, and for those who can keep pace with the changing motives the book will not be easy to put aside. None of the familiar tricks of suspense or the clichés of characterization seem in evidence, and it is only when the book is finished that the reader will realize how completely the mannered style has bemused him into thinking the story real for a moment. American writers are becoming increasingly adept at this method of hypnotism and this author has obviously learned the various passes thoroughly.[11]

A decade later, Cain, in a letter to Shaw, advised that *Fast One* enjoyed "a spectacular critical reception [sic] but was not so hot at the box-office. In England, however[,] where he [Cain] didn't think they'd be able to give it away, it sold like sixty or seventy. Literary gents like Torquemada and James Agate waxed practically ecstatic." Where, he

does not say—or when.[12] And "sixty or seventy" is exaggeration; yet a second edition is more than he managed over here.

However, in late 1944 or early 1945, there appeared a 25-cent paperback reprint, with some textual changes, by the Shaw Press, a subsidiary of The Saint Enterprises in Hollywood.[13] An epigram by The Saint, with his logo, says: "Never have I seen so many one-way tickets to the hereafter; there must be a convention in Hell." Of more interest is the blurb, and I quote in part: "This novel . . . is the hardest, toughest, fastest moving yarn of the entire gangster era. It is a killer story to end all killer stories."[14]

In 1938, Peter Ruric had a hand in doctoring the script of an awful movie, *Dark Sands,* starring Paul Robeson, Henry Wilcoxon, and Wallace Ford, and distributed in England in late summer. He shared "original story" credit with Garret Fort, a well-known writer of gangster and prison movies, in 1939, for *Twelve Crowded Hours,* an RKO-Radio release with Richard Dix and Lucille Ball—yes, Lucy! *Film Daily,* 1 March, said, "It is all rather involved and the action is not very clear-cut nor productive of thrills carrying much tension." Shortly before World War II, Ruric wrote the screenplay for a low-budget little B-movie called *Grand Central Murders* released 24 April 1942. *Film Daily* liked it. Van Heflin was one of the leads.

In January 1943, Ruric went to MGM on a six-months' term-contract; from there he moved over to RKO again to collaborate with Joseph Mischel on the script of *Mademoiselle Fifi,* derived from tales by De Maupassant. The now respected (and deservedly so) Robert Wise directed; the now legendary (and deservedly so) Val Lewton produced it. Remember Simone Simon? She played the laundress. This was Ruric's movie highpoint when one considers the company he kept. From then on it was all downhill. His last credit was as author of something called *Alias a Gentleman* out of MGM in Culver City in 1948.[15]

To backtrack just a bit. From New York, on 29 November 1945, Shaw wrote Ruric in Los Angeles: "For the Black Mask anthology [*The Hard Boiled Omnibus*] . . . your RED 71 has been selected. . . . You mentioned this story and I agree that it is one of the best you did at that time."[16] In another letter on the matter, 10 January 1946, Shaw wrote: "In the forthcoming anthology they [Simon and Schuster] ask me to write some brief introduction on each story, so will you please give me a little background material. . . ."[17] Ruric's reply was in the third person and odd.

> Before "Fast One" Cain-Ruric had swung with roughly annual irregularity between the vast extremes of writing motion-pictures for large sums in gold, or writing privately printed "extra-surrealistic" novels, and stories, poems, articles for "advanced" European magazines, for nothing. His productive activities have followed the same spotty and obtuse pattern ever since—he has not, as yet, learned the "wondrous secret of writing what I want to write, for a living."
>
> He is the author of "Hypersensualism, A Practical Philosophy for Acrobats"; "Syncopaen"; "The Naked

Man"; "Advertisement for Death"; "Broad"; "The Cock-Eyed Angel"; "Seven Men Named Caesar" and "The Ecstasy Department," a play to be produced in the Fall of '46-a couple of dozen films, here and abroad, and, under the Paul Cain *nom de shocker*, twenty odd short stories and novelettes. . . .

He has traveled extensively in Central and South America, the West Indies, Europe, Northern Africa and the Near East, been a bo's'ns mate on tramps, a (successful, yet!) Dada painter, a professional gambler, editor, consulting gynocologist [sic], and balloonist. He is, at this writing, dividing his time between three plays, a definitive work on the sexual implications of Oncidium Fuchsias, and Warner Brothers.[18]

What is one to make of this jumble? The only "autobiographical" statement Cain-Ruric ever wrote? Allowing Ruric his fun, something he did not display in his fiction, we are still faced with absurd titles and dreamland achievements, not one of them to be vouched for. Allowing Ruric his parodying of the bio-bib headnote, we are still faced with a bewildering array of activities, not one of them to be confirmed, his fiction and film work excepted although he magnifies the output. The play, by the way, was not produced on Broadway.

In a P.S., Ruric asked that "Red 71" be sent to him for "p-reading and slight editing before inclusion in anth."; Shaw obliged and he emended oaths and profanity, etc. On 8 November Shaw sent him a check for $50. Meanwhile, Cain had been collecting seven of his *Mask* stories for a paperback called *Seven Slayers*, published by The Saint Enterprises.[19]

His career was ended two years later with the *Gentleman* movie. He died in obscurity on 23 June 1966 in Los Angeles of cancer. His death certificate stated that he had been a resident of the city on the ocean for forty-eight years and that he had been a writer for forty-three years.[20] This latter claim would put him back around the time he said he worked for Von Sternberg on *Salvation Hunters* and we are returned to our starting point. Intentionally or unintentionally, Cain-Ruric-Sims had effectively blocked all efforts to learn anything about him.[21] Ignorant of his birthname, Joe Shaw once mused:

> Why Peter chose a pseudonym at all, why he hit upon "Paul Cain"—before another Cain came into literary prominence—is a secret of Peter's. Being of a modest nature, we suspect that therein lay its cause, unsure because untried, hence reluctant to prevision success.[22]

Thus: Paul Cain-Peter Ruric-George Sims. Together as one "they" exploded in one flash of near genius—*Fast One*.

II. AUTOPSY

Why was *Fast One* so quickly forgotten after publication? And, basically, has remained forgotten since 1952?

It had waited for over a year for publication since its final installment in the September 1932 *Mask*. Therefore, the

book appeared near the end of an "era" (commencing early in 1929) which had been studded with gangster novels, hard-boiled private-eye novels, gangster movies, *et al.* Preceding it had been Hammett's four great novels: *Red Harvest* (February 1929), *The Dain Curse* (July 1929), *The Maltese Falcon* (February 1930), and *The Glass Key* (April 1931); Raoul Whitfield's three fine hard-boiled pieces: *Green Ice* (July 1930), *Death in a Bowl* (March 1931), and *The Virgin Kills* (February 1932); W. R. Burnett's *Little Caesar* (June 1929), Donald Henderson Clarke's *Louis Beretti* (October 1929), and Armitage Trail's popular but terrible *Scarface* (March 1930).

Then came the figurative deluge of gangster-racketeer movies: *Little Caesar* (January 1931), *The Public Enemy* (May 1931), and *Scarface: The Shame of a Nation* (March 1932), the classic though unintended trilogy. Edward G. Robinson, James Cagney, and Paul Muni were large on the screen and large in the Public Eye; they *were* gangsters to thousands of Americans, as were William Powell (*Street of Chance,* February 1930), Edmund Lowe (*Born Reckless,* May 1930; derived from Clarke's *Louis Beretti*), Lew Ayres (*The Doorway to Hell,* October 1930), Gary Cooper (*City Streets,* April 1931; script by Hammett), Walter Huston (*The Ruling Voice,* Oct. 1931), Jean Hersholt (*The Beast of the City,* February 1932), Warren William (*The Mouthpiece,* May 1932), and many more; but, truth to tell, the gangster genre was pretty well petered out by late 1933.

So it is quite likely that when *Fast One* made the shops in October 1933, many people were bored with the sight of yet another gangster novel. But *Fast One* was not just another; it was the best of its kind ever to appear. Sad to state: the best is often more difficult to sell than the worst. In his cast-aside *Omnibus* introduction, Shaw keenly appraised Cain's situation:

> At the time of its writing, Peter was a close associate of Raoul Whitfield and Dashiell Hammett, who were then in full stride, and found himself, indeed, in fast company. However, it has been said that, in the matter of grim hardness, while Raoul and Dash paused on the threshhold, Peter went all the way in *Fast One*.[23]

Judging by the reviewers' reactions, he went too far, too fast; readers were not yet prepared for the brutality Cain roistered in.

Finally, I must observe that no writer, except under extraordinary circumstances, finds reputation and fame with one novel. Cain stopped writing fiction in 1936. Memories are short. Competition, fierce and unending, came to Cain from other quarters and writers and not merely from his own kind. Perry Mason debuted in *The Case of the Velvet Claws* in March 1933 and returned in *The Case of the Sulky Girl* in September. He was an instant success. The Ellery Queen-Barnaby Ross duo (quartet?) published four novels in 1933, the fourth, *The Siamese Twin Mystery,* on 13 November. A condensation of Hammett's *The Thin Man* was in *The Redbook Magazine* in December and in book form in January 1934. Perry Mason was back (*Lucky Legs*) in February.

Then, on 19 February, came the other Cain—James M.—with *The Postman Always Rings Twice.* Two Cains meant trouble for Paul and one reviewer in Los Angeles, Wilbur Needham, was confused in his review of *Postman*:

> James M. Cain—who is, we believe, that mysterious bearded gentleman who wrote "A Fast One" [sic] under the name of Paul Cain last season—has a terse, savage and dynamic style. . . . [T]he speed of the narrative . . . spills the characters out into a smashing and bloody climax, not unlike that in Paul Cain's "A Fast One."[24]

So *Fast One* was forgotten. But not by everyone. Shaw, admitting (erroneously, now) that the novel was dated, felt it was "a story to be shuddered at and not easily forgotten." Raymond Chandler, who once met Cain and did not particularly like him, had nothing but applause for the novel:

> . . . His book *Fast One,* composed of four [sic] novelettes published in the *Black Mask,* is some kind of high point in the ultra hard-boiled manner. And the last episode in it is about as murderous and at the same time poignant as anything in that manner that has ever been written.[25]

And not forgotten by Southern Illinois Press which in September 1978 reissued *Fast One* as a part of the Lost American Fiction series under the general editorship of Professor Matthew J. Bruccoli.[26]

III. Afterword

I like to imagine Paul Cain in his elegant Montecito apartment on Franklin Avenue writing the episodes of *Fast One* for Shaw's *Black Mask,* bringing to life and to my memory (always) Gerry Kells and S. Granquist, evoking Los Angeles of a long-gone time as no other writer ever has. Maybe, through his windows, now and then he saw the Lido Apartments (6500 Yucca, at Wilcox), Musso and Frank Grill (6669 Hollywood Boulevard, near Cherokee), the Brown Derby on Vine (between Selma and the Boulevard), the Hollywood Knickerbocker Hotel (at 1714 Ivar, just north of the Boulevard), and the Hollywood Division Police Station (1358 North Wilcox, at De Longpré). They all figure in the novel and only the station is gone, abandoned and demolished in November 1976. Hell! In those beautiful days every setting in The City of the Angels was a postcard come alive, and Cain could easily have seen the Ambassador Hotel down at 3400 Wilshire where Kells had a suite with a built-in bar, when it was one of the best hotels anywhere.

You could see *far* then—in 1932. And you could get killed, too, out there on the old Coast Highway on the way to Ventura in the treacherous night rain, like Kells and Granquist.

He kissed Granquist's cold mouth and turned and crawled through the mud away from the light, away from the voices.

He wanted to be alone in the darkness; he wanted the light to please go away. . . .

There, after a little while, life went away from him.

Notes

1. From the Joseph T. Shaw Correspondence file, Special Collections, University of California, Los Angeles. Permission to quote was kindly given by Mr. Brooke Whiting. I wish to thank Mrs. Hilda Bohem and Mrs. Kayla Siegel, and the staff as well, for their generous help.

2. "Fast One" (March), "Lead Party" (April), "Velvet" (June), "The Heat" (August), and "The Dark" (September).

3. Cain wrote twelve stories for *Black Mask*; in addition to those mentioned, they were "One, Two, Three," May 1933; "Murder Done in Blue," June 1933; "Pigeon Blood," November 1933; "Hunch," March 1934; "Trouble-Chaser," April 1934; "Chinaman's Chance," September 1935; "Death Song," January 1936; "Pineapple," March 1936; and "Dutch Treat," December 1936, which terminated his fictional efforts.

4. All quotations from reviews of Ruric's movies with one exception are from the files in the Margaret Herrick Library, Academy of Motion Picture Arts and Sciences, Beverly Hills, California. I extend my thanks to the staff for making my sojourn there so profitable.

5. One latter-day film historian supports *Film Daily.* Rose London, *Cinema of Mystery* (New York, 1975), pp. 36-38, calls it "the extraordinary Lugosi and Karloff film of 1934"; unfortunately she fails to mention Ruric!

6. I have refrained from a long plotting of the story; the novel needs a careful critical analysis and I am engaged on same.

   The first edition of *Fast One* is a rarity in the book trade. The dedicatee was actress Gertrude Michael who managed to make for herself a reputation in the 1930's in Hollywood, chiefly in B-movies. Her best known part was Sophie Lang, a lady jewel thief.

7. From the copy in the Guymon Collection of Detective and Mystery Fiction, Special Collections Room, Library, Occidental College, Los Angeles. I wish to acknowledge, with gratitude, the liberal help given me by Mr. Michael Sutherland, Head, Special Collections.

8. 10 (28 October 1933), 222.

9. 29 October 1933, p. 21. The review appears in the "Latest Works of Fiction" section. Perhaps this is

what Doubleday, Doran preferred, for the firm published *Fast One* under its own name and not under The Crime Club. These two reviews are the only ones I have been able to find in major publications; Will Cuppy ignored it in *The New York Herald Tribune Books*.

The first paperback reprint prints extracts from three newspaper reviews: *Philadelphia Ledger* ("a nervous novel full of fire and fever"), *Los Angeles Times* ("its short staccato sentences jet from the pages like black sparks"), and the *Cincinnati Times* ("all the sinister silence of Faulkner, the cryptic dialogue of Hemingway"). I searched diligently but never found the *Los Angeles Times* review.

10. "Book Stuff," *Rob Wagner's Script* (Beverly Hills), 10 (18 November 1933), 17; signed by a Mrs. Jack Vallely.

11. P. 335. *The Manchester Guardian* refused to notice it.

12. TLS, 13 January 1946; Shaw Correspondence file, UCLA. Cain possibly may have been referring to the London *Daily Mirror* or the *Irish Press* (Dublin) where the novel is known to have been reviewed.

13. A Bonded Mystery, No. 10; 144 pp., no date. The verso of the half title page says: "This edition is published by special arrangement with Doubleday Doran & Co. Inc[.] This is a War Time Book[.]" Does The Shaw Press suggest Joe Shaw himself? I don't know.

14. Such strenuous efforts produced few sales, for this edition is now scarce indeed. I purchased a copy some twenty-five years ago and consider myself fortunate to own it, tattered as it is. The textual changes, minor and few in number yet intriguing, indicate that Cain made them.

Avon Publishing Co. reprinted it "by Special Arrangement with the Author" in 1948 in paperback, 189 pp. This, too, is rare. I own a 1952 imprint; so there was another printing. Its title page advertises Cain as the author of "'Seven Slayers.'"

15. As I have said before, Ruric's movie work is disputable. In the Academy of Motion Pictures Arts and Sciences library there is mention of his having contributed to treatments of six scripts, 1934-1940. None went before the cameras. Records at MGM show that he labored on seven scripts, 1940-1942, but only one, *Grand Central Murders,* carried his name.

16. Shaw Correspondence file, UCLA.

17. *Ibid.*

18. *Ibid.,* 13 January 1946. See n. 12. As it turned out, Shaw wisely did not use any of this material in *Omnibus.* There was one Introduction wherein he stressed the importance of the hard-boiled style as developed in *Mask.*

19. *Ibid.* In the Shaw file, UCLA, are tear-sheets of eight stories by Cain from *Mask* with corrections, etc., in

pencil and the name changed to Peter Ruric on each title page, a change not observed. From this came *Seven Slayers.* It was reprinted in 1950 by Avon, No. 268, and is practically unobtainable on the market.

20. I am indebted to Mr. Cliff McCarty, owner of the Boulevard Bookshop, Los Angeles, for these data. A close perusal of the *Los Angeles Times,* 23-30 June 1966, did not turn up an obituary or a news item. By a coincidence, on 24 June, when his death might have been noted, the *Times* was occupied with the memorial services for recently dead Ed Wynn, the comic.

21. In the summer of 1976, I visited and pestered both the Writers' Guild of America West, Inc., 8955 Beverly Boulevard, and the Guild's pension office up the street on San Vicente Boulevard in Los Angeles, hoping to find some information. Neither organization had any record of him.

22. Discarded introduction to *The Hard Boiled Omnibus,* Shaw Correspondence file, UCLA.

23. *Ibid.*

24. *Saturday Night* (Los Angeles), 14 (17 February 1934), 10; the publication was a decent enough Pasadena ballyhoo sheet; Needham was the best reviewer in the Southland, next to Paul Jordan Smith of the *Times.* He remained confused about the identity of the two Cains for some time. In a review of P.J. Wolfson's *Is My Flesh of Brass?,* he comments on its "crashing climax, exactly like so many of these melodramatic finales in hard-boiled novels. Paul Cain, James M. Cain (twins?) and half a dozen others have carried their characters out of the story by automobile wrecks. . . ." *Ibid.,* 14 (7 July 1934), 10.

25. RC to James M. Sandoe; TLS; 4 February 1953; quoted by permission of Special Collections, UCLA.

26. Too bad, but the advertisement of *Fast One* by SIU Press in its catalogue, Fall-Winter Books, 1978-79, contains errors and questionable statements, e.g., the novel was *not* published in 1932 by Doubleday, etc. The Afterword by Irvin Faust is so-so.

James Naremore (essay date 1983)

SOURCE: Naremore, James. "Dashiell Hammett and the Poetics of Hard-Boiled Detection." In *Art in Crime Writing: Essays on Detective Fiction,* edited by Bernard Benstock, pp. 49-72. New York: St. Martin's Press, 1983.

[*In the following essay, Naremore discusses style, characterization, and themes in the novels of Dashiell Hammett, praising his handling of language and placing his works in historical context.*]

I

Dashiell Hammett is a profoundly romantic figure, and the most important writer of detective fiction in America after

Edgar Allan Poe. During the years when he was doing his best work—chiefly the late 1920s—he managed to reconcile some of the deepest contradictions in his culture. He was a man of action and a man of sensibility, an ex-private-eye who looked like an aristocrat; he wrote five novels and a few dozen stories which provided material for scores of film, radio and television adaptations, but at the same time he evolved one of the most subtle and influential prose styles of his generation. Unfortunately Hammett was an alcoholic in an era when alcoholic authors were glamorous, and this helped cut his work short. In other ways, too, he was a deeply symptomatic writer of the twenties, and his career seems to have ended with the historical conditions that had sustained it. Afterwards, according to Stephen Marcus, 'His politics go in one direction; the way he made his living went in another—he became a hack writer, and then finally no writer at all.'[1]

There is, however, an admirable integrity about Hammett's behaviour in those later years. He worked in Hollywood for a while, but he did not neurotically dramatise himself in the manner of Fitzgerald, nor did he try to write a Hollywood novel. He was not suicidal like Hemingway (whom he resembles in so many other ways), and when a doctor told him he would have to quit drinking or die, he quit. In the fifties he was imprisoned and then blacklisted for his Marxist political sympathies, but unlike many others he did not complain publicly and refused to make himself a martyr. *Tulip,* the unfinished autobiographical novel he worked on when he left prison, is touchingly pastoral and a fascinating account of his attitude towards his work: 'When you write,' his protagonist says at one point,

> you want fame, fortune and personal satisfaction. You want to write what you want to write and to feel it's good, and you want this to go on for hundreds of years. You're not likely ever to get all these things, and you're not likely to give up writing and commit suicide if you don't, but that is—and should be—your goal. Anything else is kind of piddling.[2]

Such behaviour indicates that Hammett was probably as strong as any of his heroes, who are all to some extent like him. The Continental Op has a job similar to the one Hammett once had with the Pinkerton Detective Agency; Sam Spade has Hammett's first name (Samuel Dashiell Hammett); Ned Beaumont resembles Hammett physically; and Nick Charles's life with Nora is based on the one Hammett shared with Lillian Hellman in the early thirties. More importantly, all these characters speak with what might be called the Hammett voice, which can be heard in the passage quoted above. Its diction is homely; its syntax mainly declarative statements strung together with conjunctions. It has a fine rhythm which depends on the rather calculated run-on syntax, the driving repetition of certain words and the variation between long and short periods; nevertheless, this rhythm is meant to seem more instinctive than eloquent. It is a transparent language, of the sort that wants to cut through the crap and get down to truths so basic to the culture that they seem like natural laws. It sometimes makes an appeal to commonplace notions of

behaviour, trying to sweep away lies and rationalisations. For example, here is Ned Beaumont speaking to Janet Henry in *The Glass Key* (1931), when she tells him about one of her dreams: 'I think you made that up. It starts out to be a nightmare and ends up something else and all the dreams I ever had about food ended before I ever got a chance to do any actual eating.'[3] And here is Nick Charles telling Nora what will happen to all the characters in *The Thin Man* (1938) after the murder has been solved: 'Nothing new. They'll go on being Mimi and Dorothy and Gilbert just as you and I will go on being us and the Quinns will go on being the Quinns. Murder doesn't round out anybody's life except the murdered's and sometimes the murderer's.'[4]

This less deceived language is always placed in the dialogue of the detective or in his first-person narration, rather than in the neutral, third-person descriptions, where Hammett's prose is much more ambiguous and stylised. It is a dramatised voice, taking the form of a virile man talking to women, children or mendacious crooks. It isn't quite the voice of Reason, as with Dupin or Holmes, because it has less to do with solving puzzles than with exposing various kinds of falsehood or naïveté. Nor is it quite the voice of Metaphysics or Morality, as with Father Brown (even though in a general sense any fictional detective becomes the story's omniscient narrator and hence a type of God), because Hammett is sceptical of absolutes and his heroes are not virtuous. It is more like the voice of Male Experience, and it usually speaks with brutal frankness after a period of reticence or silent knowingness. In *Red Harvest* (1929), when the ageing capitalist tells the Continental Op that he wants a 'man' to 'clean this pigsty of a Poisonville for me, and to smoke out the rats, little and big', the Op replies, 'What's the use of getting poetic about it? If you've got a fairly honest piece of work to be done in my line, and you want to pay a decent price, maybe I'll take it on.'[5] In *The Maltese Falcon* (1929), when Brigid argues that Spade can't turn her over to the police because he loves her, he comments, 'But I don't know what that amounts to. Does anyone ever? But suppose I do? What of it? Maybe next month I won't. . . . Then I'll think I played the sap.'[6] Clearly it is a voice which cannot be taken in by abstract appeals to morality or even love, and while it situates itself on the right side of the law, it is too honest to give the usual reasons for being there. As Ned Beaumont says, 'I don't believe in anything.'

The sceptical, unpretentious honesty of Hammett's various spokesmen is one of the things that marks him as a writer with serious aspirations. But because he is a writer of detective stories, and because he is such a classic instance of the literary tough guy, he presents special problems for the critic who wants to take him seriously. His fiction is a rare combination of light entertainment and radical intelligence. He challenges the easy distinctions between popular and high art, and the critical language that normally sustains those divisions; any critical approach to him is likely to go awry if it becomes too serious, too sociological or too frivolous. A much greater problem is that the toughness of his characteristic voice is sexualised, linked to fantasies of male power, and nowadays especially it invites an easy clinical interpretation. Even Neil Simon has been able to joke about Sam Spade, in *Murder by Death*, where the private eye is revealed as a closet gay. Hence the sexual case against Hammett needs to be acknowledged at the outset, in order to get at the complexities beyond it.

The pen may not always be a substitute penis, but with Hammett it often seems to be. His best prose has a Parnassian hardness, a lack of 'feminine' adornment, and many of his titles have a phallic quality. He writes about strong, silent men who have an acute sense of discipline, and about predatory women who have to be sent off to prison. His detectives are usually bachelors, but unlike their nineteenth-century predecessors they are loners, eating meals in various restaurants or hotel rooms, living as far from domesticity as a frontier scout. They are somewhat homophobic—see, for example, the Continental Op's reaction to Burke Pangborn in 'The Girl with the Silver Eyes', or Sam Spade's reaction to Cairo and Wilmer in *The Maltese Falcon*—and although they are attracted to the sexy females they encounter, the only women they trust are the ones who behave like boy scouts. Thus Nora Charles is described by a veteran cop as a lady with 'hair on her chest', and Sam Spade compliments Effie Perine, his 'boyish' secretary, by saying 'You're a damned good man, sister.' Of course Hammett wrote charmingly about married life in *The Thin Man,* but Nick and Nora Charles are only buddies compared to Ned Beaumont and Paul Madvig, the male couple of *The Glass Key,* who have an intense, passionate, sometimes violent relationship that feels more like love.

Hammett was fond of blood sports and military camaraderie, and he wrote fiction in which women are always 'other' to a central male consciousness. It would be meaningless to call him a latent homosexual because everyone is always potentially another sex; nevertheless his work speaks a masculine ideology, generally portraying women as naïve students of male wisdom or as dangerously amoral creatures. What redeems Hammett is that his protagonists never become proto-fascist supermen of the James Bond variety. His novels are written in an impersonal, detached style that sometimes allows the male ethos to undermine itself, and his readers are not allowed to settle into a comfortable identification with characters like Sam Spade. The sparse autobiographical evidence indicates that Hammett *was* tough, in a way that goes far deeper than braggadocio or sportsmanship. His temperament was egalitarian, and his later work, no doubt tempered by his relationship with Lillian Hellman, shows that he was somewhat dissatisfied with the figure of the phallic detective; the autobiographical protagonist of *Tulip* even jokes about homophobic 'he-men'. In any case, a properly useful analysis of Hammett's sexual politics should avoid glib ego-psychology; it should focus on Hammett's language rather than his 'personality', partly because he was always deeply concerned with problems of literary form, and partly because his style was an historical phenomenon.

American literature of the twenties was generally hardboiled, and if Hammett had not become the 'father' of the tough detective, someone else probably would have. Actually his attraction to the detective story is as much a sign of his aestheticism as of his love of male action. Like Chandler, he began by writing verse, and like the other aesthetes of his period he found his true vocation by reacting against the genteel, prettified, vaguely homosexual tone of the nineties. (Dupin and Holmes were of course nineteenth-century aesthetic types.) In the teens the manner of Pater and Wilde had given way to the manner of T. E. Hulme, and metaphors of sculpture began to replace metaphors of music in poetic theory. Pound, Yeats and the early Imagists had tried to purge poetic language of 'rhetoric' and beauty, a project later supported by the writers who experienced the first world war. The 'little magazine' became a vehicle for most of these authors, but Hammett's distinction is that he applied the new literary sensibility to the pulps, attacking bourgeois values from below rather than from above. In fact, *Black Mask,* where his hard-boiled stories first appeared, was begun by H. L. Menken as a way of supporting *The Smart Set,* a little magazine which published some of the early modernists. Hammett was therefore very much a part of the literary atmosphere of his period, and it is no accident that he and Hemingway became popular at virtually the same moment.

Hammett's writing, like Hemingway's, is an especially clear instance of the irony and suspicion of noble language which can be found everywhere in post-war literature, a phenomenon admirably documented by Paul Fussell in *The Great War and Modern Memory.*[7] Indeed Hammett was a veteran of the war, which left him with a serious respiratory ailment, and all his life he was fascinated with combat. Among the other extra-literary influences on his work, his experience as a Pinkerton agent in the years before and after the war is obviously of major importance. San Francisco, where he worked in the early twenties, was the most aesthetically pleasing of American cities, but it was also the home of the Hearst Press, the Barbary Coast and the most famous of Chinatowns. It had some of the feel of the wild west, and Hammett lived there during one of the most brutal phases of the national history—a period of unrestrained capitalism and vicious labour struggles, of official corruption in the White House and of legal hypocrisies spawned by Prohibition. In America in those days, as Sam Spade says, you could 'take the lid off' life, in much the same way as the war had taken the lid off European civilisation. Nevertheless, the Depression had not yet arrived, and it was still possible to view it all in terms of rather detached, cynical adventure stories. Hammett was in a good position to become the Flaubert of detective fiction.

II

The reputation Hammett ultimately achieved is succinctly stated by his current paperback publishers, who describe him as the 'creator of the modern, realistic crime novel'.[8]

We should remember, however, that the origin of any literary form is impossible to establish, and as Hammett's protagonist in *Tulip* says, 'Realistic is one of those words when it comes up in conversation sensible people put on their hats and go home.' Hammett's work seems real in the sense that it constructs a relevant model of his society, but also in the sense that it never departs truly from the realist conventions of the nineteenth century. He was a key practitioner of what was immediately named a 'modern' style, but much of his early work was geared to the demands of pulp fantasy. Before examining some of the more unusual aspects of his fiction, therefore, it may be useful to emphasise the typical fantasies he offers his readers.

One of his stories, 'The Gutting of Couffignal', has an amusing self-reflexive moment which alludes to his function as an entertainer. The Continental Op has been hired to guard some expensive wedding presents at a reception on the island of Couffignal, just off the California coast. After the guests have left and the owners of the house have gone up to bed, he pulls up a chair beside the mound of gifts and decides to pass the time by burning a few Fatimas and reading a book:

> The book was called *The Lord of the Sea,* and it had to do with a strong, tough, and violent fellow named Hogarth, whose modest plan was to hold the world in one hand. There were plots and counterplots, kidnappings, murders, prison-breakings, forgeries and burglaries, diamonds large as hats and floating forts larger than Couffignal. It sounds dizzy here, but in the book it was as real as a dime.

With a few qualifications, this is a good description of the story Hammett is writing, which suddenly turns into a tale of bombings, burglaries and conspiracies, peopled with Russian emigré crooks, a femme fatale, and assorted thugs who plan to loot the entire island. Like all of Hammett's work, the story contains elements of mystery, including an ending in which the detective uncovers a killer we had not expected. Nevertheless, Hammett is writing adventures as much as puzzles, so he keeps his detective in physical danger, transforming the intellectual quest into an actual chase, with bullets flying through the air. The audience for *Black Mask* seems to have expected such plots, and Hammett gave them true thrillers, stories that are still interesting for the way they subordinate everything to flat, paratactic statements of action.[9]

But if, as Graham Greene once suggested, the key to the modern thriller lies in the formula, 'adventure happening to unadventurous men', then Hammett's work is more modern than *The Lord of the Sea*. Certainly his hero is no Hogarth. All his early fiction concerns a short, fat, fortyish man with no name and no life beyond his job with the San Francisco branch of the Continental Detective Agency. He is an unglamorous and hence 'realistic' creation who, in terms of his general social status, probably resembles the majority of Hammett's first readers. There is in fact a potentially Walter-Mittyesque comedy (which Hammett takes care not to exploit) in the disparity between the Op's appearance and his physical powers. For example, in a quasi-Western story called 'Corkscrew', involving murder in an Arizona mining town, the Op rides a bucking bronco which tosses him four times; on the last try he punches out a cowboy who wants to restrain him from remounting. A bit later in the same story, the Op has a street fight with an ex-boxer, who breaks his fist on the Op's jaw. In *Red Harvest* he spends all night drinking gin with a blonde, takes a cold bath, and has a fight with a killer, whom he overpowers and hauls to the police; he then takes another cold bath and has another battle with *two* killers, knocking one out and beating the other to the draw; finally, having been grazed on the wrist with a stray bullet, and without even the benefit of another cold bath, he captures an escaped convict in a dark alley and solves a murder mystery that has had the local police fooled for years.

True, during all this the Op complains about being old and out of shape, and after the events in *Red Harvest* he needs a good twelve hours of sleep. Nevertheless, to borrow one of Hammett's similes, he is as tough as a bag of nails. He resembles the other great detective heroes in being improbably heroic and a bit eccentric—outwardly the quintessential company man, he seems to love his rough life for its own sake. He is an effective instrument of fantasy precisely because he does not encourage readers to imagine that they are handsomer, younger or richer (W. H. Auden's test for 'escapist' literature); instead he encourages the notion that such things do not matter, given courage, stamina and a certain hard-edged view of life.

The Op needs these last qualities because he inhabits a world of almost cataclysmic violence; some of his longer adventures have as much action as a Keystone cops film and more corpses than an Elizabethan revenge tragedy. It is difficult to keep count of the dead in 'The Big Knockover', '$106,000 Blood Money', 'Corkscrew', *Red Harvest* and *The Dain Curse* (1929), all of which have plots that leap from one killing to another and scenes of pitched battle that portray a society literally at war. Hammett published this longer fiction serially in *Black Mask,* making each instalment build to a violent climax or to the solution of a mystery, then having the story continue because the ultimate resolution was not at hand. Even granting the demands of their form, however, the Op stories contain an extraordinary amount of death and destruction. In 'The Big Knockover', an army of crooks invades the San Francisco financial district, loots the two largest banks and has a shoot-out with the entire police department; they escape with the bank money, but their greed makes them begin killing one another, so that the Op's pursuit of them leads to whole rooms full of dead bodies. A comment the Op makes during one of the brawls in the story is an apt description of Hammett's work as a whole during this period:

> Swing right, swing left, kick, swing right, swing left, kick. Don't hesitate, don't look for targets. God will see that there's always a mug there for your gun or blackjack to sock, a belly for your foot.

Sometimes this delirious violence freezes into a tableau, as if Hammett were providing material for the pulp illustrations. In *Red Harvest* a prize-fighter wins a match, and as his hand is raised in victory a knife comes whistling out of the audience, its 'silvery streak' ending as the blade plunges into the fighter's neck. In *The Dain Curse* the crazed leader of a religious cult attempts ritual murder on a crystal altar illuminated by a beam of blue light, his carving knife poised over the body of a semi-nude woman who is bound head and foot. In 'The Girl with the Silver Eyes', a crook named Porky Grout stands in the middle of a roadway, 'the dull metal of an automatic in each hand', and blasts away at an automobile which is rushing towards him like a 'metal comet'. In 'Dead Yellow Women' the Op is trapped on a stairway in the secret passageway of a house in Chinatown; below him is a beautiful girl with a 'red flower of a mouth' and four Tong-warriors reaching for their automatics; above him is a big Chinese wrestler with a 'foot of thin steel in his paw'.

It is difficult to tell how much burlesque is intended in these over-heated visions—although Hammett seems to me to have a greater sense of humour in the Op stories than is usually recognised. The Op recounts everything in deadpan fashion, as if he were making raw reports under pressure. The style gives him a plausible character, and it suggests that Hammett himself has the same values as his protagonist, doing a quick professional job in a relatively disreputable but adventurous trade, with a minimum of fuss and a single-minded determination to get the story told. In a sense, the plainness of the language contributes to the illusion of realism and honesty, especially when Hammett combines the spectacular events with documentary detail or accounts of the more quotidian aspects of the Op's job. He fills the stories with precise, almost city-map-style references to San Francisco street and place names, and he likes to include bits of information about the 'inside' of professional detective work. In this regard it is worth noting that the self-reflexive passage quoted earlier from 'The Gutting of Couffignal' has a double function: at the same time that it declares an affinity between Hammett and the traditional romancers, it also contrasts the Op's workaday world with that of literature. Hammett may have been writing melodramas, but he knew how to make them as real as a dime.

III

Hammett soon abandoned the Op and began to write more subtle, complex fictions, but even at the first it was clear that his work was as much about language as about toughness and mystery. Although much of his early prose seems to have been hastily composed, it inevitably contains moments of wordplay and lapidary stylisation. Sometimes the clipped, stark language seems pushed toward a kind of self-parody. Here, for example, is an except from the opening of a piece called 'The Farewell Murder':

> I was the only one who left the train at Farewell.
>
> A man came through the rain from the passenger shed.

He was a small man. His face was dark and flat. He wore a gray waterproof cap and a gray coat cut in military style.

He didn't look at me. He looked at the valise and gladstone bag in my hands. He came forward quickly, walking with short, choppy steps.

He didn't say anything when he took the bags from me. I asked:

'Kavalov's?'

He had already turned his back to me and was carrying my bags towards a tan Stutz coach that stood in the roadway beside the gravel station platform. In answer to my question he bowed twice at the Stutz without looking around or checking his jerky half-trot.

I followed him to the car.

Three minutes of riding carried us through the village. We took a road that climbed westward into the hills. The road looked like a seal's back in the rain. . . .

Presently we left the shiny black road for a paler one curving south to run along a hill's wooded crest. Now and then this road, for a hundred feet or more at a stretch, was turned into a tunnel by tall trees' heavily leafed boughs interlocking overhead. . . .

The flat-faced man switched on the lights, and increased our speed.

He sat rigidly erect at the wheel. I sat behind him. Above his military collar, among the hairs that were clipped short on the nape of his neck, globules of moisture made tiny shining points. The moisture could have been rain. It could have been sweat.

We were in the middle of one of the tunnels.

The flat-faced man's head jerked to the left, and he screamed.

In terms of 'content' this is nothing more than the ordinary paraphernalia of Gothic melodrama. The language, however, is more interesting. There is first the play on the name 'Farewell', which suggests that Hammett is interested in something more than pure representation. Then there is the narrator's style, which is so curt that it vaguely resembles free verse, given a kind of significance by all the empty white space around the lines. The language is radically simple, but it can't be described as telegraphic because it contains several deliberate repetitions, little jerking points of emphasis which create a nervous rhythm in keeping with the chauffeur's 'short, choppy' steps: 'A man came through the rain from the passenger shed. He was a small man'; 'He didn't look at me. He looked at the valise and gladstone bag.' Everything has been reduced to a series of bald, brief statements, so that even the simplest figures of speech or variations of syntax are foregrounded. For example, once the car speeds away from the station and into the woods, a complex, alliterative cadence asserts itself: the road 'was turned into a tunnel by tall trees' heavily leafed boughs interlocking overhead'. The imagery works along similar lines, confining itself to a few notes of colour or references to the chauffeur's 'flat face',[10] until a single, vivid simile appears: 'The road looked like a seal's back in the rain.'

In keeping with the demands of a journal like *Black Mask,* the opening of 'The Farewell Murder' is designed to get the story underway as quickly as possible, without windy exposition or authorial promises of dangers to come, offering what the pulp writers used to call narrative 'hooks' to keep the reader turning pages. Hammett conveys everything in dramatic form, but even though he tells everything from the Op's point of view, he has been selective about how much subjectivity he allows us to see. The Op is a sort of *camera obscura*; if he is fatigued by his journey, baffled by his reception, fearful of the speed of the car or the sudden scream, he does not say so. This was a style much admired by the French existentialists in the forties and fifties, who gave it a sort of philosophic interpretation; to them it was a 'zero degree' prose suggesting a mind living completely in the present, in touch with an imminent reality. The cerebral French in those days had a tendency to romanticise the physical Americans, but there is some truth to what they believed. One of the deepest pleasures of reading Hammett may come from the illusion he creates of a mind which never seems alienated, uncertain or even seriously troubled. It isn't a primitive consciousness because it registers things with a certain aesthetic grace; if the world it describes is violent, it responds to that violence by simply attending to the business at hand.

Hammett's later novels use an even more neutral technique, a third-person narration which presents everything from the detective's point of view without ever telling us what the detective is thinking. The narrator stands outside the character, like a camera watching an actor, describing only his movements. But it is typical of Hammett that this language of pure action sometimes calls attention to itself *as* language. Here, for example, is a scene from *The Maltese Falcon,* just after Spade has received a phone call telling him that his partner has been murdered:

> Spade's thick fingers made a cigarette with deliberate care, sifting a measured quantity of tan flakes down into curved paper, spreading the flakes so that they lay equal at the ends with a slight depression in the middle, thumbs rolling the paper's inner edge down and up under the outer edge as forefingers pressed it over, thumbs and fingers sliding to the paper cylinder's ends to hold it even while tongue licked the flap, left forefinger and thumb pinching their end while right forefinger and thumb smoothed the damp seam, right forefinger and thumb twisting their end and lifting the other to Spade's mouth. He picked up the pigskin and nickel lighter that had fallen to the floor, manipulated it, and with the cigarette burning in a corner of his mouth stood up. He took off his pyjamas. The smooth thickness of his arms, legs, and body, the sag of his big rounded shoulders, made his body like a bear's. It was like a shaved bear's: his chest was hairless. His skin was childishly soft and pink.

In part, this technique serves the interest of the mystery story, characterising Spade in terms of the objects around him, but keeping his chain of thought a secret until he solves the crime. By withholding information, Hammett gives the plot tension, investing the simplest movements with the importance that gunshots and fistfights had in the earlier fiction. As in the Op stories, the method suggests a world where actions are more important than thoughts; it portrays Spade as a sort of latter-day cowboy, rolling a cigarette while he ponders his next move. In other ways, however, the technique is less 'organic'. Except for the phrase, 'made a cigarette with deliberate care', the description of Spade rolling a cigarette is almost as defamiliarised as the pseudo-scientific account of Bloom returning home in the penultimate chapter of *Ulysses*. It makes Spade a technician, brooding on the fine points of a problem, but it also displaces the traditional ratiocinative values of detective fiction in favour of another quality that was always inherent in the form—a representation of the surfaces of things. Detective stories are the most fetishistic of literary genres because the trivial objects of the investigation—the 'clues'—function like the overdetermined symbols of dreams. But in Hammett's work this overdetermination extends to everything: the reader, confronted with impersonality and a cool, objective description, is invited to interpret the meaning of images. At one point the narrator himself seems almost surprised, or perhaps hypnotised, by these ambiguous surfaces, so that he repeats himself: 'like a bear's. It was like a shaved bear's.'

This is a very different style from Raymond Chandler's, and I think it is closer to the spirit of literary modernism. I make this point because Chandler is normally regarded as a man who polished Hammett's relatively crude innovations, bringing them to their full literary potential. But consider this play with the word order of a descriptive sentence in *The Glass Key*:

> He found and lit a cigar then and, with it between his teeth burning, stood by the table and squinted down through smoke at the front page of the *Observer* lying there.

Again the effect is rather Joycean, and it is the opposite of Chandler, who played syntactical tricks only with the dialogue.[11] Hammett now and then makes the third-person narration rather strange, calling attention to his artifice in a more basic way.

Of course Hammett was conservative in other respects, and was easily adapted to the movies. Hollywood never accurately reproduced the trenchant social observation or the moral ambiguity of his best work, but they took the melodrama and much of the dialogue straight from his pages. A brilliant dramatist, Hammett wrote effective speeches for his characters, but like a film-maker he also used what I have described as a *camera obscura* narration, and he paid close attention to clothing and décor. His most specialised vocabulary refers to colours and fabrics, and he carefully documents popular tunes, slang and hair styles.[12] Sometimes it is hard to tell how much he influenced the movies and how much he was influenced by them. Notice, for example, this description of Janet Henry in *The Glass Key*:

She turned on a lamp beside the piano and sat down there with her back to the keyboard, her head between Ned Beaumont and the lamp. Her blond hair caught lamplight and held it in a nimbus around her head. Her black gown was of some suedelike material that reflected no light and she wore no jewellery.

The passage seems to have come straight from a Hollywood photographer of the period, complete with backlighting and black-and-white composition—although it suggests that Janet herself has been watching movies and has arranged her own lighting. In any case it shows how much Hammett's prose sometimes aspired to the condition of cinema, and why his novels made some of the best American films.

IV

Hammett was no avant-gardist, but the impersonal, ironic technique of his novels grows out of a deeply critical and sceptical attitude towards American society, a view of life that affects the form of his fiction in other important ways. The endings of his novels are always bleak, even in the early work where there is somewhat less emphasis on characterisation: in *Red Harvest* the Op solves the mysteries in a technical sense, but nothing has fundamentally changed at the conclusion, and the Op himself has barely survived with his job intact. In *The Dain Curse* the killer Fitzstephan is captured, but he spends only a year in an insane asylum before being set free; most of his body has been destroyed by one of his own bombs, and Hammett's understated description of his insane egotism haunts the end of the story, like an evil that cannot be exorcised. Always Hammett threatens to undermine the authority of the detective and the neat closure of the typical mystery plot; even the tough-guy ideology and the love of adventure which defines his heroes show signs of strain. The following brief review of his later work should indicate the delicate balance he sustained between popular forms and the deep questioning of those forms.

From the first Hammett was admired by critics who did not particularly like the detective-story formula, because in his novels the crimes were messy, the chase circuitous, the solution to the murder less important than the depiction of a *milieu*. To slightly revise Edmund Wilson's famous question, Who cares who killed Miles Archer? In one sense nobody, and that is the whole point of *The Maltese Falcon*. Archer's murder has a crucial function in the plot, and is part of a whole chain of enigmas; nevertheless, we and Spade soon become distracted by the search for the falcon, and one of Hammett's deepest ironies is that Spade himself has a possible motive and the right temperament to have committed the crime. Archer is an unpleasant fellow whom we meet only once, when he crudely looks Brigid up and down and pockets her money. He has been cheating on his wife, who in turn has been having an affair with Spade, and he is not particularly clever or trustworthy as a detective. Spade thinks he is a 'louse' and has been planning to sever the partnership anyway, by legal means. He tells Brigid that she has done him a kind of

favour by killing Archer, and when he turns her over to the police the seven reasons he gives have nothing to do with revenge, justice or law and order. Commentators on his long speech usually claim that it shows a 'code' which sustains Hammett's heroes; looked at closely, however, the speech is about nothing more than self-preservation. Spade knows that somebody has to 'take the fall' for the murder, and that Brigid is likely to get a 'better break' from the police. 'When a man's partner is killed', he says, 'he's supposed to do something about it'; in other words he is *expected* to do something about it, and if he did not obey the conventional social ethic, his business would suffer. People would assume he is either incompetent or a killer himself. At the level of Nature rather than Culture, Spade says that he is instinctively a hunter, and that letting his quarry go wouldn't be the 'natural thing'. He admits that this rule has its exceptions, but in this case too much is at stake: his entire position has been compromised by the death of his partner. Brigid obviously can't be trusted anyway, and if he did not turn her over he would have no job or anything else.

Spade's climactic speech indicates that Hammett isn't writing about guilt or innocence, or even about professional ethics, but about what he regards as a bewildering, predatory struggle beneath civilisation. Civilisation makes everyone, including the detective, an impostor. 'Don't be too sure I'm as crooked as I'm supposed to be', Spade tells Brigid. 'That kind of reputation might be good for business.' This remark may serve to reassure the reader about Spade's intentions, but it is a more ambiguous reassurance than we are usually given. It tends to mock the idea of a 'just solution' to murder, just as the Maltese Falcon itself mocks the idea of ownership or private property. Born out of a colossal hypocrisy—a 'Holy War' which, as Gutman says, 'was largely a matter of loot', the Falcon does not rightly belong to anyone. To quote Gutman again, 'An article of that value passed from hand to hand by such means is clearly the property of whoever can get hold of it.' The final irony, as Stephen Marcus has pointed out, is that the *rara avis* turns out to be as bogus as everyone else; a disguised (but rather phallic) signifier, it is supposed to have value beneath its skin, giving a meaning to the frantic, violent activity of the novel.[13] But when the skin is peeled away, there is only a lead shape, an empty object of exchange.

Spade is the hero of this potentially anarchistic world, but he is a hero of an unusual kind. Morally he is hardly any better than his dead partner, and there is nothing particularly likeable about him. Physically and emotionally he is somewhat frightening, a very different character from the one created by Humphrey Bogart in John Huston's film version of the novel.[14] Spade is a big 'bear' of a man with thick fingers and a face described in the first paragraph as 'rather pleasantly like a blond Satan'. He has a nasty temper and an animal quality which Hammett repeatedly emphasises ('Spade grinned wolfishly, showing the edges of his teeth far back in his jaw'). His 'glowing' eyes are contrasted with Brigid's 'velvet' gaze, and this contrast is given meaning by one of his own similes: 'expecting me to run criminals down and then let them go free is like asking a dog to catch a rabbit and let it go.' He seems as potentially cruel as any of his adversaries—particularly so in the scene where the dying Captain Jacobi delivers him the Falcon: in one hand Spade grasps the statuary, his fingers showing 'ownership in their curving'; with his free arm he grips Effie Perine so strongly that she cries out in pain; and with his left foot he inadvertently steps on the dead Jacobi's hand, 'pinching a quarter-inch of flesh at a side of the palm between heel and floor'.

The novel makes us respect Spade in a complex, qualified way, chiefly because of his intelligence and ability to master his own sometimes ugly instincts. His behaviour suggests that he has a heightened sense of the danger lying in wait for him should he try to join Brigid or Gutman. In the first chapter he is vividly contrasted with Archer, who serves as his foil. Spade has a suspicion of easy sex and money, a reserve that ultimately keeps him alive. He tells Brigid that life is not a 'clean orderly sane responsible affair', and what is especially interesting about this philosophy is that it means that he might as well be a crook as a cop. At some point he has become neither, operating a private practice in a legally indeterminate region between. Ultimately he serves the interests of official society, but not out of any faith in its justice. His job satisfies his taste for hunting and adventure, and he can survive best on the right side of the law.

It is almost a rule of Hammett's novels that at some point the detective's ambiguous position must be tested by a bribe. If he passes this test, his victory is mainly personal, a kind of survival of the fittest. There is no question of returning the society to some kind of order; if decent people exist in that society, they are always rather naïve, like Effie Perine and her family, or like the 'liberal' Donald Willsson, the first murder victim in *Red Harvest*. The only alternative to such innocence is the stoic, isolated intelligence of the detective, who is affected in various ways by the world he investigates. Thus another rule of Hammett's novels is that the detective is always personally involved in some basic betrayal of trust. In *Red Harvest* the Op complains that the violence of Personville (the most obviously symbolic of Hammett's names) is making him 'blood simple', and he feels vaguely responsible for the murder of Dinah Brand, the amoral lady who has been a sort of friend to him; in fact at one point he thinks he might have stabbed her while he was drunk or drugged. In *The Dain Curse* the Op's friend and only confidant turns out to be the killer. In *The Maltese Falcon* Spade must betray Brigid, just as she has betrayed him, and just as he has betrayed his partner and his partner's wife. In *The Glass Key* Ned Beaumont spends the entire novel trying to save his closest friend, only to end up leaving town with the woman his friend loves. In *The Thin Man* the killer is revealed to be an old wartime companion of Nick Charles, a man whose life Charles once saved in the trenches in Europe.

The best example of this troubling, pessimistic quality of Hammett's work is *The Glass Key*, which gives such a detached, accurate picture of the politics of a moderately large American city that the detective story elements—a set of clues involving a hat and a fancy walking stick, a denouement in which an amateur detective forces a confession out of a killer—become somewhat obtrusive. To his credit, however, Hammett treats these elements ironically and makes them thematically functional. For example, the clue of the hat, emphasised throughout, is finally dismissed as 'unimportant'. The detective doesn't believe the confession, calling it a 'campaign speech' and leaving us in doubt as to what actually happened. As in *Falcon,* the victim deserved to die, and the detective says that the killer performed a 'favour'. Also as in *Falcon,* the only truly innocent characters are naïve females who live under the protection of corrupt men. Paul Madvig, the wrongly accused suspect, is a political boss who collects graft and intimidates the nominal leaders of the community into following his orders. He is a likeable enough fellow, with a sweet old mother and a certain working-class directness, and Ned Beaumont says he 'never had anybody killed'; nevertheless he is as crooked as anyone else.

The murder in the novel is interesting, given the city's strongman politics. It is an Oedipal anxiety made real; a state senator murders his own son—with a walking stick, no less—in order to preserve his reputation and rule. This phallic imagery is carried over into the book's title; the glass key is identified ultimately as a symbol from Janet Henry's dream—a key which unlocks a door and then breaks, releasing chaos. At one level the symbol describes Hammett's ironic solution to the murder story: there is a 'key' to the mystery, but its discovery results in an end to the friendship between Beaumont and Madvig. At other levels the failed key is an appropriate image for a novel that seems preoccupied with symbolic castrations—for example, Ned Beaumont coolly seduces a newspaper publisher's wife, thus driving the publisher to suicide. In the last scene, Paul Madvig suffers one of these castrations, losing the woman he loves to his best friend. It is as though the tough-guy ethos were unleashing a horror, even though the novel as a whole makes toughness a value.

In keeping with this atmosphere, *The Glass Key* contains Hammett's darkest treatment of violence and sexuality, particularly in the extended, sado-masochistic torture scenes of chapter 4, where the thug Jeff keeps calling Beaumont 'sweetheart', and where the symbolic castrations threaten to become real:

> 'I got something to try.' He scooped Ned Beaumont's legs and tumbled them on the bed. He leaned over Ned Beaumont, his hands busy on Ned Beaumont's body.
>
> Ned Beaumont's body and arms and legs jerked convulsively and three times he groaned. After that he lay still.

Even conventional relations between men and women are ambivalent—as between Beaumont and Janet Henry—or drained of passion. For example, here is a scene describing the aftermath of a night at a speakeasy:

The remaining girl took Ned Beaumont, who called her Fednik, to an apartment on Seventy-third Street. The apartment was very warm. When she opened the door warm air came out to meet them. When she was three steps inside the living-room she sighed and fell down on the floor.

Ned Beaumont shut the door and tried to awaken her, but she would not wake. He carried and dragged her difficulty into the next room and put her on a chintz-covered day-bed. He took off part of her clothing and opened a window. Then he went into the bathroom and was sick. After that he returned to the living-room, lay down on the sofa in all his clothes, and went to sleep.

Such prose resembles Hemingway at his best, but *The Glass Key* is better described as Hammett's *The Waste Land*. He had been reading Eliot at about the time he wrote the novel (Lillian Hellman says that she and Hammett discussed the poet for hours when they first met in 1930),[15] and he has named one of the streets in his fictional city 'upper Thames Street' (cf. *The Waste Land*, line 260). Ned Beaumont, the professional gambler momentarily turned detective, is vaguely implicated in the corruption of the city, but he has aristocratic looks and a certain sensibility that suggests an Eliot-like cultural nostalgia. His rooms are decorated 'in the old manner, high of ceiling and wide of window', and when Janet Henry first sees them she remarks, 'I didn't think there could be any of these left in a city as horribly up to date as ours has become.' She thinks Beaumont is a 'gentleman', although he sneers at the word, knowing that Janet's father, the other gentleman of the novel, is capable of any crime.

Actually *The Glass Key* has a good deal in common with modernist literature in general, chiefly because it refuses to give the reader any comfortable position from which to judge the events it depicts. The crooked politicians, the sadistic gangsters, the criminally naïve females, the cruelly detached gambler—detective are all recognisable stereotypes from familiar cultural or literary 'texts', but they are presented without any narrative commentary and without any character (like Chandler's Marlowe) who could act as a moral norm. *The Glass Key* has all the adventure and heroics of a normal melodrama and much of the social detail of a muck-raking naturalist novel, but it presents this material neutrally What, finally, are we to think of Beaumont and Madvig? How are we to judge the city without feeling like the 'respectable element' of comfortable bourgeois citizens whom Beaumont mocks? Perhaps the deepest reason why we feel Hammett is tough is that his commonplace, clear language is destructive of any liberal complacency.

After this impressive novel, however, Hammett seems to have become cautious. *The Thin Man,* written two years later when he was out of money, strongly resembles the classic detective story form. Nick Charles, the hero, is a retired detective who has married a rich young woman; she becomes his Watson, eager to go slumming in the New York underworld. The murder plot is elaborately complicated and more like a puzzle than Hammett's other

work. The setting is a glamorous one, and the tone is largely comic—perfect and harmless escapism for the years of the Depression. Even so, Hammett's attitude is much more satiric than the immensely popular series of *Thin Man* films derived from the book:[16]

> We went into the living room for a drink. Some more people came in. I spoke to them. Harrison Quinn left the sofa where he had been sitting with Margot Innes and said: 'Now ping-pong.' Asta jumped up and punched me in the belly with her front feet. I shut off the radio and poured a cocktail. The man whose name I had not caught was saying: 'Comes the revolution and we'll all be lined up against the wall—first thing'. He seemed to think it was a good idea.

Clearly this is a dark, absurd comedy, and Nick Charles seems to be using liquor mainly as an anaesthetic. In fact his alcoholism becomes the sign of a man who feels slightly guilty and emasculated. Much as he and Nora like one another, he is a potential *Doppelgänger* of Jorgenson, the gigolo who has married Mimi Wynant, and the only point when he briefly stops drinking is when he becomes a detective again.

With only a slight turn of the screw *The Thin Man* could have been as unsettling as any of Hammett's other works. The chief metaphor of the novel is cannibalism, established in the long quotation from Duke's *Criminal Cases of America* in chapter 13.[17] And like the previous books, it returns us at the end to a world where nothing has fundamentally changed—as the Continental Op says to his client in *Red Harvest,* the city is 'all nice and clean and ready to go to the dogs again'. Hammett again calls the solution to the crime into slight question: in the last chapter Nick explains everything to Nora, acting the role of the typical omniscient detective. Normally in such scenes the detective is a privileged narrator, but this novel is comic and Nora Charles is no passive Watson. Her questions continually upset our expectations by exposing the holes in Nick's story. 'But this is just a theory, isn't it?' she asks. Nick says he is only trying to describe what is most probable, and reaches for a drink. At the end Nora complains, 'it's all pretty unsatisfactory.'

Of course Nora's words actually function as Hammett's defence; by satirising his form he allows it to work. Nevertheless, it is interesting that these are his last words as a novelist, and it may be significant that he gave them to a woman.

No one can say exactly why Hammett stopped writing, but there is a theory, as tentative as Nick Charles's account of a crime, that offers one reason: the detective novel had become unsatisfactory to him. During his long silence he once complained, 'it is impossible to write anything without taking some sort of stand on political issues.'[18] Throughout the 'committed' thirties Hammett was too good a writer not to realise that the form of writing is itself political; he seems to have been reluctant to use language in a completely transparent, authoritarian way, and the reactionary fifties silenced him altogether. He could not become a demagogue or a party hack, and his one surviving fragment is *Tulip,* a novel about the problem of writing a novel. This problem is not expressed as a matter of content, but as a matter of form. 'Where in the name of God', says his exasperated protagonist at one point, invoking the name that stands behind most of the supposedly 'realistic' uses of language, 'do you get the notion that writers go around looking for things to write about? Organising material is the problem, not getting it.'

In the long view, and given the particular historical context of Hammett's work, this emphasis on the problem of form has important political implications. It suggests that Hammett had become philosophical about the relation between language and ideology. Thus his central character in *Tulip* has been experimenting with the sort of language games that would appeal to the post-Wittgenstein theorists—including writing a story on paper shaped into a Möbius strip, in such a way that the reader can start at any point. He is critical of any philosophy of language or science that is based on a notion of ultimate reality or metaphysical presence, and he wonders 'what arrangements would be necessary in mathematics if one, the unit, the single item, were not considered a number at all, except perhaps as a convenience in calculating'. He tries to write a story about a friend named Tulip, who represents a facet of himself:

> His being a side of me was all right, of course, since everybody is in some degree an aspect of everybody else or how would anybody ever hope to understand anything about anybody else? But representations seemed to me—at least they seem now . . . devices of the old and tired . . . like conscious symbolism, or graven images. If you are old and tired you ought to rest, I think, and not try to fool yourself or your customers with coloured bubbles.

Hammett never solved his problem, but his attempt was leading him in characteristically radical directions. He could no longer figure out a way to be a popular writer, and, as he says, he was feeling old and tired. In any case the novels he did write need no apology. They are a remarkable achievement, a moment when melodrama becomes indistinguishable from literature.

Notes

1. Stephen Marcus, 'Introduction' to the *The Continental Op,* by Dashiell Hammett (Random House, 1974), p. xxviii. After 1930 Hammett worked mainly as a screenwriter, and until more research is done into this period, it may be an exaggeration to call him a 'hack'. His best-known scripts are *City Streets* (1933), for which he is credited as the author of the 'original story', and *Watch on the Rhine* (1943), an adaptation of Lillian Hellman's play, which won him an academy award nomination.

2. *The Big Knockover* (New York: Vintage Books, Random House, 1956).

3. *The Glass Key* (New York: Vintage Books, Random House, 1972).

4. *The Thin Man* (New York: Vintage Books, Random House, 1972).

5. *Red Harvest* (London: Pan Books, 1975).

6. *The Maltese Falcon* (New York: Vintage Books, Random House, 1957).

7. (New York: Oxford University Press, 1975).

8. *The Thin Man.*

9. A brief history of *Black Mask* and its publishers is in Frank MacShane's *The Life of Raymond Chandler* (New York: E. P. Dutton, 1976), pp. 44-50.

10. Hammett liked to describe his crooks in terms of some simple deformity, and in the Op stories he sometimes creates the feeling of a cartoon. In 'The Big Knockover', the Op walks into a speakeasy full of thugs: 'Men—rat-faced men, hatchet-faced men, square-jawed men, slack-chinned men, pale men, scrawny men, funny-looking men'.

11. See *The Life of Raymond Chandler,* p. 58. Chandler's brilliant essay, 'The Simple Art of Murder', originally published in *The Atlantic Monthly,* Dec. 1944, may be chiefly responsible for Hammett's reputation as a kind of primitive. Chandler also implicitly argued that Hammett never showed a world of official corruption, where 'gangsters could rule cities'. This is an odd notion, given *Red Harvest* and *The Glass Key.*

12. The slang in Hammett's work is interesting because so much of it is no longer in use, and it is difficult to say how accurate it might be. Some of his characters like to speak in Pig-Latin, as in 'the big umpchay', or 'unkdray'. Sometimes they sound like Jazz-Age college boys: 'What's the proposish', or 'What's the diffugalty?' Other terms, especially in the Op stories, are more obscure. 'To get a rear out of' means to enjoy. 'Let's screw' means let's get out of here. 'Give me your sig' means give me your signature. 'For fair' means for sure. 'Swing the play' means do the job. I am uncertain what 'It's one underdish' might mean.

13. 'Introduction' to *The Continental Op,* p. xxv. See also Roland Barthes's commentary, 'From Sculpture to Painting', in *S/Z* (New York: Hill & Wang, 1974) pp. 207-8.

14. See James Naremore, 'John Huston and *The Maltese Falcon*', *Literature/Film Quarterly,* Summer, 1973, pp. 239-49.

15. 'Introduction' to *The Big Knochover.*

16. The thin man in the novel is of course the victim, not the detective popularised by the series of films. However, I cannot resist praising William Powell's beautiful performance as an elegant, graceful drunkard.

17. This book, published in San Francisco by J. H. Barry Publishers, 1910, appears to have been a personal favourite of Hammett's. My thanks to Chris Anderson for locating bibliographic information about the book for me.

18. Quoted by Martin Seymour-Smith, *Who's Who in Twentieth-Century Literature* (New York: McGraw-Hill, 1977), p. 148.

James F. Maxfield (essay date spring 1985)

SOURCE: Maxfield, James F. "Hard-Boiled Dicks and Dangerous Females: Sex and Love in the Detective Fiction of Dashiell Hammett." *Clues* 6, no. 1 (spring 1985): 107-23.

[*In the following essay, Maxfield focuses on Dashiell Hammett's* The Glass Key, *suggesting that the author's seemingly straightforward, objective style contrasts with the ambiguous, self-contradictory characterizations in the novel.*]

The Glass Key is perhaps the most controversial and problematic of Dashiell Hammett's five novels. Julian Symons gives the novel his highest praise: "*The Glass Key* is the peak of Hammett's achievement, which is to say the peak of the crime writer's art in the twentieth century"; in Robert I. Edenbaum's judgment, "*The Glass Key* is Hammett's least satisfactory novel."[1] Edenbaum supplies clearer reasons for his negative assessment than does Symons for his laudation. Edenbaum sees the novel's central weakness as Hammett's failure (or perhaps refusal) to clarify the motives of his protagonist: ". . . it is impossible to tell what is under Ned Beaumont's mask."[2] As a result, crucial actions of the novel's hero are left ambiguous. The effect of this ambiguity, Peter Wolfe suggests, is to deprive Hammett's characters of any depth: "The book's dark glimmering surface reveals characters who resemble silhouettes or sheet-tin cutouts."[3]

The causes of the ambiguity are inherent in the stylistic method Hammett chose for his final three novels. He employs a completely objective approach, merely reporting the conversations and describing the surface actions of his characters, never directly presenting their thoughts and feelings. The author's method is aptly summed up by Nick Charles, the detective hero of Hammett's last novel, *The Thin Man*: "'I just tell you what happens; I don't explain it'" (Chapter 20).[4] This objective style enables Sam Spade in *The Maltese Falcon* for nearly the entire novel to conceal from both the other characters and the reader the fact that he has possessed the solution to his partner's murder from the moment he heard of the circumstances of the killing. Ned Beaumont similarly hides from the reader and Janet Henry his suspicions of her father. But more troublesome—since it is not unusual for the hero of a detective novel to hold back the solution to the mystery until the last possible moment—is the fact that the reader can only speculate on Ned Beaumont's motives for agreeing to take Janet Henry with him to New York at the end of the book. While Ned may be in love with Janet, he certainly never says that he is; and as we shall see later, the novel allows a very different interpretation of his motivation.

The result of the obscurity of Ned Beaumont's motivations, Robert Edenbaum says, "is not the richness of fruitful ambiguity but the fuzziness of inner contradictions."[5] Yet for an unsophisticated reader imbued with the conventions of popular fiction such ambiguity or fuzziness probably does not exist. Ned Beaumont is the hero of the book (the detective who solves the murder); Janet Henry is the heroine (the beautiful girl who aided the detective in finding the solution). If they go off together at the conclusion, the reason is that they love each other—as heroes and heroines of popular fiction normally do. Ned Beaumont does not need to say he loves Janet; it can simply be assumed.

In making this undoubtedly naive assumption, the conventional-minded reader is likely correct because the preponderance of evidence in the novel supports it. The reason a sophisticated critic like Edenbaum finds it difficult to make the same assumption is that he is considering Ned Beaumont as merely a variation on the detective heroes of Hammett's earlier fiction, the Continental Op and Sam Spade, both of whom resolutely resisted emotional commitments or romantic entanglements. Although he shares a number of traits with Spade and Op, Ned Beaumont is ultimately a different person and a different kind of hero. The reasons why he is willing to make the kind of emotional commitment they are not willing to make can best be understood through an examination of both the ways in which Ned Beaumont resembles the Op and Spade and the crucial ways in which he deviates from their behavior patterns.

One thing Hammett's heroes have in common is that, according to Karen Horney's formulations, they are all neurotics of a certain type. Horney argues that one of the defining characteristics of neurosis is the individual's shifting of his energies "from developing the given potentials of the real self to developing the fictitious potentials of the idealized self."[6] The heroes of detective fiction are virtually all neurotics of the type whose idealized self is that of the master or dominator. They seek to "actualize" their idealized self by mastering life through the exercise of "intelligence and will power" (p. 192). Such an individual has to believe that he is in control at all times: he feels "he should be able to master the adversities of fate, the difficulties of a situation, the intricacies of intellectual problems, the resistances of other people, conflicts in himself" (p. 92). Almost every fictional detective's concept of self-worth collapses when he appears unable to solve a crime or bring a criminal to justice—in short when he fails to assert his mastery.

The hard-boiled detective—for which Hammett's Op and Sam Spade established the archetype—is also a neurotic of the "arrogant-vindictive type." In real life the origins of this neurosis typically lie in an abused childhood. (Hammett never tells us anything about the childhoods of his heroes. Ned Beaumont's remark, "'I never told anybody where I came from'" (p. 2), holds true in the broadest sense for all of them. The Hammett hero refuses to be the victim of anyone or anything—including his past.) As a result of being treated harshly as a child, the arrogant-vindictive personality "has a need to retaliate for all injuries and to prove his superiority to all rivals. . . . He trusts no one, avoids emotional involvement, and seeks to exploit others in order to enhance his own feelings of mastery."[7] What better profession for a person who distrusts others and needs to feel superior to them than that of the detective? Because he deals with known criminals and in the course of an investigation may have reason to suspect everyone, the detective has license to be "openly arrogant, often rude and offensive . . . (p. 199). Active aggressiveness seems the only rational stance to the detective who sees life as a battle, "a merciless struggle of all against all" (p. 204). For the detective "to have invincible strength and to be inviolable . . . appear . . . not only desirable but indispensible" (p. 204). Hammett's heroes take their greatest pride "in being above hurts and suffering" (p. 205). As Edenbaum puts it, the Hammett hero aspires to (and within the limits of most of the stories achieves) "a godlike immunity and independence, beyond the power of his enemies."[8]

One way in which the hero's immunity is displayed is in his ability to bear physical pain. Much in the same manner as Dostoyevsky's Stavrogin, Sam Spade is able to receive a blow in the face from a policeman and through sheer will power suppress his impulse to strike back (Chapter 8). (After the policeman leaves his apartment, Spade curses "for five minutes without break" to relieve his pent-up rage, then announces complacently that taking the punch was "a cheap enough price to pay for *winning*"—Chapter 9, italics added). Sapped and dumped into the middle of San Francisco Bay, the Op swims seemingly for hours until he is finally rescued by a passing boat just as he loses consciousness; upon reviving he refuses to be taken to the hospital, cures his chill by drinking "half a pint of whiskey" and rubbing himself "with a coarse towel," then goes off to confront the villains ("The Tenth Clew"). After receiving a "long but shallow" knife wound down the side of his spine, the Op is back at his office the following day merely "sitting forward in [his] chair to spare [his] back" ("$106,000 Blood Money"). The worst physical punishment endured by any Hammet hero, however, is Ned Beaumont's savage beating in Chapter 4 of *The Glass Key*. In this case the hero's immunity is not only physical but also moral. Despite repeated pummeling from Shad O'Rory's thugs, Beaumont refuses to betray his friend (O'Rory's political and criminal rival) Paul Madvig and continues to attempt to escape until he finally succeeds. Even if the speaker intends them ironically, the comments of the thug Jeff Gardner regarding his victim seem to be Hammett's tribute to the courage of Ned Beaumont: "'You can't croak him. He's tough. He's a tough baby'" (p. 3). Because

toughness is a quality of Hammett's heroes value in themselves, they tend to admire it even when it is manifested by the criminals they oppose; the Op shows respect for a dying gangster in *Red Harvest* when he says, "He meant to die as he lived, inside the same tough shell. . . . He was Reno Starkey who could take anything in the world without batting an eye, and he would play it out that way to the end" (Chapter 27). In the same way, Ned Beaumont is affirming a sort of creed when he says, "'I can stand anything I've got to stand'" (1,2).

There are, however, more subtle threats to the Hammett hero's invulnerabilty than that posed by physical pain. Emotional vulnerability is a far greater menace than physical vulnerability. The Continental Op is on guard against feeling pity for any of the criminals he encounters, lest that feeling deflect him from the performance of his duty. Often when the Op shows apparent sympathy for another character, he stresses in his first person narrative that he is merely feigning the emotion he expresses. For instance, in "$106,000 Blood Money" when he asks Angel Grace Cardigan why she has attempted to commit suicide, he says in an aside to the reader, "I was surprised at the fatherly tone I achieved." Despite her criminal activities, Angel Grace may strike the reader as a woman of integrity (it is a matter of honor to her not to inform on her criminal companions) who truly deserves pity (her lover has been killed); but the Op not only denies the genuineness of his sympathy for her, when she won't tell him what he wants to know, he has her thrown in jail to see if that method will work any better. If the Op is less sympathetic to Angel Grace than the reader is likely to be, perhaps that is because she shares one quality with a number of other women the Op sends to prison: she is physically attractive to him.

Sexual desire is possibly the greatest threat to the Hammett hero's invulnerability. In story after story the Op encounters a beautiful but thoroughly unscrupulous female who seeks to tempt him from the performance of his duty.[9] Of Elvira (alias Jean Delano) in "The House in Turk Street" and "The Girl With the Silver Eyes" the Op says, "She was as beautiful as the devil, and twice as dangerous." He describes Ines Almed in "The Whosis Kid" as "appealing, and pathetic, and anything else you like—including dangerous." The Op recognizes his potential vulnerability to the temptation these women present. When he sees Elvira manipulating one of her fellow crooks in "The House on Turk Street," he comments, "In his place I might have believed her myself—all of us have fallen for that sort of thing at one time or another. . . ." And when Ines cuddles up against him, he tells the reader, "I'd be a liar if I didn't admit that she had me stirred up inside. . . ."

The Op's chief defense against the temptation posed by the attractive female criminal is his role as detective. With Ines he reminds himself, "when the last gong rings I'm going to be leading this baby . . . to the city prison. That is an excellent reason—among a dozen others I could think of—why I shouldn't get mushy with her." In "The

Gutting of Couffignal" when the beautiful Russian Princess, who has masterminded the robbery of the wealthy residents of the island, attempts to bribe the Op not only with a share of the loot but also with her body, he tells her that his instincts as a detective make acceptance of her offer impossible: "'You think I'm a man and you're a woman. That's wrong. I'm a manhunter and you're something that has been running in front of me. . . . You might just as well expect a hound to play tiddly-winks with a fox he's caught!'" In effect the Op is saying that in committing himself to his role as detective he has significantly reduced the range of his humanity—and with it the extent of his human vulnerability. The single instinct, that of the manhunter, overrides all other instincts—like sexual desire—that might interfere with it.

But sometimes overriding the sexual instinct requires a greater effort than at other times. In the two linked novellas "The Big Knockover" and "$106,000 Blood Money," the Op is plainly attracted to Ann Newhall alias Nancy Regan. The first time he sees her he sums up his impression of her by saying, "Without getting steamed up over the details, she was nice." The next time he encounters her he does tend to get steamed up over the details, discovering that her smile and voice are also "nice" and "the cocky little blue hat that hid all her hair didn't handicap her niceness any. . . ." When at the end of the second story he arrests her for harboring the mastermind of a massive bank robbery, the Op is upset by the effect she has on him: "It annoyed me to find I was staring into the girl's eyes as fixedly as she into mine, and that when I wanted to take my gaze away it wasn't easily done." Although Ann Newhall, a millionaire's daughter, has been guilty of little more than irresponsibility and bad judgment in her involvement with the criminals, the Op insists on turning her in to the police, whereas in the story "The Scorched Face" he covered for his client's daughter, Myra Banbrock, allowing her to get away scot-free after committing a more or less justifiable homicide. Though she would likely have been acquitted, the Op wanted to spare Myra the humiliation of standing trial. However, he righteously tells Ann, "'You can't run around with a mob of cutthroats, get yourself tied up in a flock of crimes, and then when you're tripped say, "excuse it, please," and go free'." Perhaps he is more merciful to Myra simply because she is his client while Ann is not, but another possibility is that he can afford (in terms of preserving the concept of his idealized self) to be merciful to Myra, who doesn't attract him, whereas mercy to Ann, who does, would be a sign of his vulnerability.

At the end of "$106,000 Blood Money" the Op causes the death of Jack Counihan, a young Continental operative who has betrayed the organization by collaborating with the bank robbers. The Op's ostensible motive for setting up Counihan's shooting is that bringing legal charges against the young man would give the Continental agency a black eye, while letting him go unpunished would be unacceptable. But a stronger motive for the act is implicit in the Op's summary of Counihan's motive for putting in

with the robbers: "'You met the girl [Ann Newhall] and were too soft to turn her in. But your vanity—your pride in looking at yourself as a pretty cold proposition—wouldn't let you admit it even to yourself'." So Counihan succumbed to the temptation to play a role—"a super-gentleman crook"—to deceive not only the world but himself about his sentimental motives. When the Op sets Counihan up for the kill, he is destroying his double, the embodiment of his own susceptibility to the girl's beauty and charm—and possibly of his fear that *his* toughness also may be no more than a mere facade. In killing Counihan he is trying to obliterate his own weakness.

In the sixteen collected stories and two novels in which he appears, the Op only opens up emotionally to a single female character—and she dies within a few hours of receiving his revelations. In Chapter 20 of *Red Harvest* the Op confesses to Dinah Brand his fear that he is "going blood-simple" as a result of playing the mobsters of "Poisonville" off against each other so that they will solve the city's crime problem by slaughtering one another. Dinah suggests he forget his anxiety by consuming a mixture of gin and laudanum. Following her advice, the Op passes out and wakes up the following morning to find himself clutching the handle of an ice pick plunged deep into Dinah's breast. This rude awakening is preceded by two extremely significant dreams.

In the first he sees a woman wearing a veil and realizes she is someone he knows, "someone important to" him although he can't remember who she is. She runs away, and he pursues her through "half the streets in the United States" until finally, when he is tired and discouraged and resting in a train station, she gets off an in-coming train and comes over and begins kissing him. His response is one of embarrassment because people are looking at him and the woman and laughing. In the second dream the Op is hunting, with an open knife in his pocket, for a man he hates—"a small brown man" wearing an "immense sombrero." He chases the little brown man to the top of a tall building; and as he grabs the man's head ("a smooth round head no larger than a large egg") and tries to pull the knife from his pocket, they plunge together off the edge of the roof, dropping "giddily down toward the millions of upturned faces in the plaza, miles down" (Chapter 21).

Both dreams offer numerous possibilities for psychological interpretation, but the ones I wish to stress are Jungian.[10] The woman in the first dream is the Op's "anima," the feminine, intuitive side of his nature. Because in his chosen role of tough, rationalistic thief-catcher he has rigorously suppressed this side of his personality, he does not consciously recognize her—it is veiled from him. He yearns to be united with this lost part of his being; yet when it comes forth to embrace him, to make him complete, he is made "uncomfortable"; for the new self violates the hard masculine image which he has long striven to present to others. To publicly embrace a real woman, link his life to hers would similarly violate his chosen image, so the dream is also about the Op's yearning for but unwillingness to accept love. Again in Jungian terms, the little brown man in the second dream is the Op's "shadow"—the primitive, destructive impulses within him.[11] The pursuit takes place on a Sunday morning when "Church bells are ringing"; perhaps the Op perceives his task as a moral or divinely sanctioned one—that of eradicating evil. But to seek to destroy evil by an act of violence (as the Op is doing in Poisonville) is to become evil oneself. In the act of destroying the "shadow" the Op becomes united with it and destroys himself as well.

When the two dreams are put together, the implication is that the Op has replaced the pursuit of the anima with the pursuit of the shadow—seeking not the consummation of love (productive of life) but the consummation of violence (productive of death). Although the plot of the novel reveals that the Op has not killed Dinah Brand, the two dreams clearly indicate that he is psychologically disposed to be her murderer. (The true killer, Reno Starkey with his "tough shell," is merely a criminal surrogate for the Op.) If the Op has not murdered Dinah, he has surely slain both the possibility of love in his life and the "feminine" potentialities of his self.

Sam Spade, the most intense arrogant-vindictive neurotic of Hammett's heroes, is quite careful to select sexual partners who are unsuitable for long-term relationships because they fail to possess the kind of characteristics that would deserve respect or admiration from him. The only "decent" woman in *The Maltese Falcon* is Spade's secretary, Effie Perine, and his way of praising her positive qualities is also his way of declaring her off-limits for his sexual attentions: "'You're a damned good man, sister'" (Chapter 16). By sexually involving himself only with women he dislikes (Iva Archer, the wife of his partner) and/or distrusts (Iva and Brigid O'Shaughnessy), Spade feels totally justified in treating them in the classic manner of the arrogant-vindictive neurotic who exploits "women for the satisfaction of his sexual needs with utter disregard for their feelings" (Horney, p. 199).

Spade's great fear, moreover, seems to be that someday he will meet a woman who will use him as callously as he has treated other women. Although he itemizes seven different reasons why he has to turn Brigid O'Shaughnessy over to the police for having killed his partner Miles Archer, it is clear from the way he obsessively repeats a certain phrase that one reason predominates over all the others. Seven times in less than four pages he repeats with only slight variation the statement: "'I won't play the sap for you'." (One additional time he substitutes "sucker" for "sap.") His true enemy is not even Brigid; it is his emotional susceptibility which makes him potentially vulnerable to her. His ultimate reason for turning her in is his need to resist the desire to let her go: "'I won't [let you go] because all of me wants to . . . because—God damn you—you've counted on that with me the same as you counted on that with the others'" (Chapter 20). Perhaps Brigid's greatest sin in Spade's eyes is that she has considered him a mere mortal man—like all the "others"—

and failed to realize that he, not she, was properly cast in the godlike role (unmoved mover) in their relationship.

Where the Op, in an almost monk-like way, withholds himself from intimate sexual relationships and Spade's involvements with women are purely exploitative (and neither character seems to have a close friend of the same sex), from the beginning of *The Glass Key*, it is clear that Ned Beaumont is capable of human commitments. Paul Madvig is his friend and Ned is concerned enough about Paul's welfare to give him the sort of candid advice ("'I'm warning you to sew your shirt on when you go to see [Senator Henry and his daughter], or you'll come away without it, because to them you're a lower form of animal life and none of the rules apply'"—1,2) that a mere hanger-on would never have the nerve to offer. To be sure, there are both material advantages and considerable ego gratification for Beaumont in his relationship with Madvig. When he is losing at craps at the outset of the novel, all Beaumont has to do is ask Madvig for a "couple hundred" and he is given the money with no more difficulty than a faint admonition that he ought to consider "laying off" when his luck is "sour" (1,2).

Although political boss Paul Madvig possesses the money and the power in Beaumont's milieu, the younger man is clearly the superior in terms of knowledge and judgment. He freely advises Madvig on subjects ranging from gang warfare (he says Madvig should have left Shad O'Rory "'an out, a line of retreat. You shouldn't have got him with his back to the wall'"—3,7) to courtship etiquette ("'You're not supposed to give people things unless you're sure they'd like to get them from you'"—1,2), to proper apparel ("'You oughtn't to wear silk socks with tweeds'"—3,5). While giving such advice clearly allows Beaumont to feel superior, it also seems intended to promote his friend's welfare. When Beaumont judges that Madvig is embarked on a self-destructive course of action, the gambler plans to leave town, completely abandoning the financial benefits of their connection. Although Hammett's objective style makes it impossible for the reader to know Beaumont's exact motive when he is preparing to leave for New York at the end of Chapter 3, the most likely possibilities seem to be a desire not to witness Madvig's downfall or through the threat of his leaving to shock the politician into re-evaluating his course of action. That Beaumont's motivation is not a selfish desire to desert a sinking ship but a genuine concern for his friend is indicated by the gambler's decision to stay after he and Madvig have fought and made up (3,7).

A crucial difference between Beaumont and the two detective heroes who preceded him is that detection is not Beaumont's profession. Spade and the Op endeavor to bring criminals to justice because it is their job to do so. Their conception of themselves as man- (or woman-) hunters rules out any possibility of their not carrying an investigation through to its logical and just conclusion. In an image both Spade and the Op use, the hunting dog can't let his prey go after he catches it. But as a gambler and close associate of a corrupt politician, Beaumont has his true allegiance with the foxes rather than the hounds; his motives for involving himself in the investigation of Taylor Henry's murder are personal rather than professional. Although Spade and the Op try to rule out or suppress feelings in their investigations, Beaumont only solves the murder in *The Glass Key* because of his feelings first for Paul Madvig then for Janet Henry.

To be sure, Beaumont does sometimes share with the Op and Sam Spade a willingness to exploit others ruthlessly. He humiliates the newspaper publisher H. K. Mathews in his own home in front of his young wife and then, after the older man has gone upstairs to bed, drinks and necks with the girl. When Mathews comes to the head of the stairs to plead first with his wife to come up to him and then, when she makes no move, with Beaumont to send her up, the younger man merely turns toward the older "a face cruelly placid" (6,5). When Mathews responds to his wife's betrayal by shooting himself, Beaumont wastes no time on remorse; he simply steals and destroys Mathews' last will so that the publisher will have died intestate, enabling a Madvig-controlled judge to appoint an administrator of the estate who will see that Mathews' newspaper *The Observer* ceases its attacks on Paul (6,6). Although Eloise Mathews is apparently at least half right when she accuses Beaumont of being responsible for her husband's death, he never shows the faintest sign of regret for what he has done to either husband or wife. His overriding concern for the welfare of a single individual—Madvig—seems to preclude Beaumont's feeling the slightest sympathy for anyone who has to be sacrificed for Paul's benefit.

In the last four chapters of the novel it may seem that Beaumont is using Janet Henry in much the same way he used Eloise Mathews. He allows her to think that he is gathering information that may prove Madvig to be the killer of her brother, but actually he is laying a trap for her father whom he suspects of the murder. Even after the quarrel that effectively ends their friendship—Ned has told Paul that Janet hates him, and Paul has responded by accusing Ned of coveting Janet for himself—Beaumont's feelings toward Madvig can be considered his primary motivation. Clearing Paul of Taylor Henry's murder becomes a way not only of saving Paul but of getting revenge on him—by showing him that the Henrys have used him ruthlessly all the time. By taking Janet Henry away with him at the end of the novel, Beaumont deprives his former friend of the thing Paul himself said he wanted "'more than [he] ever wanted anything in [his] life'" (8,1). What better revenge on the man who rejected his friendship than to confirm Paul's accusation that he (Ned) wanted Janet for himself? Beaumont's final act in the novel is to tell Madvig, "'Janet is going away with me'" (10,3); and it is possible to conclude that Ned is simply using Janet at this point to hurt Paul—who remains, as he has throughout the novel, the only other important person in Ned's life.

But Hammett's objective style allows us to draw other conclusions. It is just as likely, for instance, that Ned tells Paul about Janet because it seems to him the honorable thing to do. In their final conversation Paul feels that he has wronged Ned, that he has turned his friend against him by lying to him. When Ned says he has to leave town, Paul replies, "'Well, it serves me right'." By asking Janet to come out of the bedroom so Paul may see her, Beaumont is revealing that his motive for leaving is not so simple or self-righteous. He and Paul can no longer be friends because Ned is taking the woman Paul loves. Nor is it illogical to conclude that the reason Ned is taking her is that he loves her too.

The preponderant evidence of the latter part of the novel indicates that Janet Henry is much more to Beaumont than the mere instrument of his revenge on Madvig. Beaumont's relationship with Janet Henry is very different from the one with Eloise Mathews. Because Eloise was clearly using Beaumont to hurt her husband, the gambler felt no compunction about using her for his own motives. Although Janet and Ned use each other too, they do so much more openly and honestly. After Janet admits that she has written the anonymous letters pointing the finger of suspicion at Paul, she is completely open with Ned concerning her intentions. Beaumont does suppress his suspicions of Senator Henry from both Janet and the reader, but he consistently tells her that he is carrying out the investigation to help Paul rather than harm him. More importantly the two characters are open with each other concerning their feelings—even feelings likely to be unacceptable to the other person. Janet admits her hatred of Madvig and her passionate desire for vengeance on him, and Ned frankly tells her, "'The part of you that's tricked Paul and is trying to trick him is my enemy'" (7,3). Later he tells her of a dream of his which symbolizes his doubts about her (he caught an enormous rainbow trout and she "threw it back in the water") and admits "'I'm not sure of you'" (8,4).

Janet responds to Ned's fish dream by telling him a dream of her own—although she suppresses its true ending until just before the end of the novel. The dream, which supplies the book with its title, sums up one of Hammett's major themes and, in its final form, shows that Beaumont and Henry ultimately share the same vision of life. In the dream Janet and Ned are lost in a forest; exhausted and hungry, they come to a small house, through the windows of which they see a "great big table piled high with all imaginable food." But when they find a key and open the door, they discover the floor of the house is covered with "hundreds and hundreds of snakes." In Janet's first version of the dream she and Ned slam the door on the snakes, then climb up on the roof of the house, open the door again to allow the snakes to slither away, and go inside to eat the food after locking the door behind them (8,4). Later she admits that in the true ending, "'the key was glass and shattered in our hands just as we got the door open. . . . We couldn't lock the snakes in and they came out all over us and I woke up screaming'" (10,3).

The dream offers a wide range of interpretive possibilities, particularly psychosexual (with both the key and the snakes being standard phallic symbols), but its basic meaning is relatively simple: it shows what happens when we seek to obtain our desires. Throughout the novel intense desire leads to disaster. Shad O'Rory wants to seize power from Madvig—and winds up dead. Senator Henry's desire to be re-elected, to maintain his political power, causes him to kill his son and ultimately lose his power. Madvig's desire for Janet leads him to cover up for the Senator and seriously jeopardize his political career. Janet's passion to gain vengeance on Madvig in the end destroys her father, her respect for him, and whatever security she formerly gained from their relationship. (At one point Beaumont ironically warned her about seeking vengeance for her brother's death: "'I hope you like it when you get it'"—8,4). Even Beaumont's more altruistic desire to help his friend Madvig culminates in the destruction of their relationship. Again and again the message seems to be, to seek the food your soul desires is to release the serpents of destruction.

Janet in her first, altered version of the dream tries to deny the tragic perception her unconscious has revealed to her. She constructs a happy, wish-fulfillment ending in which it is possible to have and enjoy what you want and evade the dangers attendant on it. Ned, with his more consciously tragic perception of reality, doubts the truth of this version immediately upon hearing it ("'I think you made that up'"). By the end of the novel Janet accepts both his and her own realization of the truth of the message the dream conveys.

While it may be helpful for a man and a woman who link their lives together to share the same vision of life, it would seem something of a disadvantage for that vision to be one which holds all desire—including their desire for each other—to be ultimately destructive. As Robert Edenbaum puts it, the logical interpretation of Janet's dream is that "to get at the heart's need is to open a Pandora's box. . . . It would seem that the only safety is in not letting down your guard in the first place: do without the food and you escape the snakes."[12] Yet in running off together Janet and Ned are in effect choosing to go after the food. How can they make such a decision which goes against both reason and the promptings of the unconscious?

Janet asks similar questions when she considers her feelings about Madvig and Beaumont after her father's exposure. Of Paul she says, "'I hated him . . . and I wronged him and I still hate him'." To Ned she says, "'And you . . . tricked me and made a fool of me and brought this on me and I don't hate you'." When she asks Ned how she can feel in such illogical ways, he only replies that her questions are "riddles" (10,2). Feelings are not rational. Janet asks Beaumont to take her away with him not because she has any good reason to believe that pursuing her desire for him will turn out any better than her pursuit of vengeance, but simply because she nevertheless *does* want him.

Ned's response to her request indicates that his motivation is basically the same: "'Do you really want to go or are

you just being hysterical?. . . . it doesn't make any difference. I'll take you if you want to go'." In essence he is saying that it doesn't matter to him whether she is motivated by love or hysteria—he still wants her. Neither the Op nor Sam Spade would have gone off with Janet, for as detectives they both strove to be ruled as much as possible by reason. But Beaumont is a gambler instead of a detective—a man used to taking risks. Just as he continues to bet while he is on a losing streak, he is willing to make another kind of wager on Janet—despite the great odds of the relationship ending badly.[13] Because he is willing to accept the risks that human commitments entail, Beaumont is, if not Hammett's ideal hero, his most completely human hero.

Notes

1. Julian Symons, *Mortal Consequences* (1972; rpt. New York: Schocken Books, 1973), p. 139; Robert I. Edenbaum, "The Poetics of the Private Eye: The Novels of Dashiell Hammett," in *Tough Guy Writers of the Thirties,* ed. David Madden (Carbondale: Southern Illinois Univ. Press, 1968), p. 99.

2. Edenbaum, p. 99.

3. *Falling Beams: The Art of Dashiell Hammett* (Bowling Green, OH: Popular Press, 1980), p. 139.

4. Because Hammett's novels are available in a wide variety of hardcover and paperback editions, quotations will be located by chapter or—in the case of *The Glass Key*—chapter and section-numbers.

5. Edenbaum, p. 101.

6. *Neurosis and Human Growth* (New York: Norton, 1950), p. 192. Further references to this work will be located by page numbers in my text.

7. Bernard J. Paris, "Third Force Psychology and the Study of Literature, Biography, Criticism and Culture," *The Literary Review,* 24 (1981), 193.

8. Edenbaum, p. 81.

9. William Marling in "The Hammett Succubus," *Clues: A Journal of Detection* 3:2 (1982), 66-75, argues that Hammett's depictions of dangerous females draw upon the convention of "the succubus, a female demon who has sex with sleeping, helpless men" (67). Marling rightly identifies the means by which the Hammett hero defends himself: "the succubus allures the hero with her sexual beauty, which hides an evil that the hero . . . can only recognize by cool reason. Emotional response must be put aside" (68).

10. For alternate but perhaps equally valid interpretations of these dreams see Wolfe, p. 88, and John S. Whitley, "Stirring Things Up: Dashiell Hammett's Continental Op," *Journal of American Studies,* 14 (1980), 447.

11. More specifically Jung calls the shadow "that hidden, repressed, for the most part inferior and guilt laden

personality whose ultimate ramifications reach back into the realm of our animal ancestors. . . ." *Memories, Dreams, Reflections* (New York: Vintage-Random House, 1965), p. 399. Perhaps Jung's reference to "animal ancestors" helps explain why the Op's "small brown man" has a rather monkey-like aspect.

12. Edenbaum, p. 101.

13. Hammett's biographer Richard Layman points out that *The Glass Key* is dedicated to Nell Martin, the woman Hammett took with him to New York when he left San Francisco in 1929—*Shadow Man: The Life of Dashiell Hammett* (New York: Harcourt, Brace, Jovanovich, 1981), pp. 114, 121. By the time the novel was published they had broken up, but who can judge the value of the relationship while it lasted?

David Wilt (essay date 1991)

SOURCE: Wilt, David. "Dwight V. Babcock." In *Hardboiled in Hollywood*, pp. 121-47. Bowling Green, OH: Bowling Green State University Popular Press, 1991.

[*In the following excerpt, Wilt recounts the varied career of hard-boiled writer Dwight V. Babcock, evaluating his achievements in the fields of the novel, pulp fiction, screenwriting, and television work.*]

Dwight V. Babcock's writing career spanned more than 25 years, and included numerous short stories, several novels, and many motion picture and television scripts. From 1934 to 1939 he was one of the more popular and prolific writers for *Black Mask,* considered the apex of detective/mystery fiction pulp magazines. After authoring several well-received mystery novels, Babcock turned his back on public acclaim and entered the ranks of screenwriters, a largely unsung lot.

Currently, many of the works of Dwight Babcock are hard to locate for reexamination. Babcock was not a prolific writer, especially when compared to wordsmiths like Erle Stanley Gardner, a fellow *Black Mask* alumni. Babcock's pulp stories have never been reprinted, and his novels are likewise long out of print (the paperback versions are probably scarcer than the hardcover originals). The films he wrote were virtually all "B" pictures, generally ignored by film scholars and certainly not discussed in terms of their scripts; and television has a tradition of being an almost certain ticket to obscurity for a writer.

While one should not expect to discover an unheralded genius in Dwight V. Babcock, his work is consistently professional, and his short stories and novels are particularly entertaining rediscoveries. Even the least of his work bears examination within the context of his career as a crime/mystery writer.

. . . . .

Dwight Vincent Babcock was born on February 19, 1909 in Oak Grove, Iowa. However, he was raised in California,

and was educated at Modesto (California) Junior College. After school, according to the dustjacket copy on his first novel, *A Homicide for Hannah,* Babcock "was by turns piano tuner, vice-president of a grape-juice concern, and owner of a service station before he decided to become a writer."[1] He broke into the ranks of *Black Mask* writers one month before his twenty-fifth birthday.[2]

"At the Bottom of Every Mess" appeared in the January 1934 issue of *Black Mask,* and was the first of two stories featuring a private detective named Maguire. With only one exception, all of Babcock's 21 stories in *Black Mask* would be series entries with continuing characters. This first story would also set the pattern for most of his fiction, with its California locale. "At the Bottom of Every Mess" is written in the hard-boiled pulp style, although if anything, Babcock's style in this first story is somewhat overdetailed. Each movement the characters make is described; the opening paragraph is a good example of this:

> Maguire sizzled the coal of his cigarette in the dark coffee that had slopped over into his saucer, found his meal check, donned his new Panama and crossed the tile floor of the drugstore to the cigar counter where Mary, the pert little cashier, reigned.[3]

The story has the traditional components: Maguire, the hard-boiled dick; Jerry Lane, his "newshound" pal; Lt. Higgins, the chief detective; and Schmidt, Higgins' irascible, fat assistant. During a gunfight, several stray bullets kill Mary, the cashier. Maguire tracks down the gangsters responsible:

> "Why didn't you give Mary a break? You two killed her, damn your dirty hides!" Maguire rolled a harsh laugh between closed teeth. "Now you're going to swing for it! How do you like that?"[4]

Over the next six years, Babcock would continue to sell stories regularly to *Black Mask*: four stories appeared in 1935 and five in 1936, his writing style improving noticeably as time passed. "Death's Ransom" (April 1935) was the last of three stories about "Al," a former private detective now working as a bodyguard for a young woman named Hildred Kyle (in the first story of the trio, Al is hired by her uncle, who is then murdered). Despite the awkward first-person present-tense narration, and a predictable plot about insurance swindles, the story is quite good. One choice bit of hard-boiled verbiage deserves reprinting:

> He socks me a couple on the kisser that make my lights shimmy but they don't go out.[5]

The first of seven stories about FBI agent Chuck Thompson appeared in 1935. Thompson's last appearance was also perhaps his finest, the 38-page lead story in the July 1937 issue entitled "Flight at Sunrise."[6] Reverting to standard third-person style, Babcock devised a somewhat topical plot as Thompson is assigned to guard the prototype of a new pursuit aircraft. There are references to the war in China, the Spanish Civil War, and revolutions in Central

America. A bit of sex creeps in: Thompson hides in the bedroom closet of a spy, Nadja Poteska, and she enters and partially disrobes before realizing he is watching. One other point of particular interest is the inclusion of a black FBI agent named (unfortunately) "Jigaboo" Jones. Jones is extremely favorably portrayed: he has a law degree, is considered a good agent, speaks in black dialect only as a disguise, and dies bravely in the line of duty. For popular literature of the period, this is an unusually fair-minded racial portrayal. Only Jones' tactless nickname (ostensibly used in a friendly manner) mars Babcock's otherwise commendable work.

After completing Chuck Thompson's adventures, Babcock switched to writing about Dave Beeker (aka Beek), a former San Francisco newspaperman. This final series of eight stories (the first, "Murder on the Side" appeared in December 1936; the second didn't appear until January 1938) represents Babcock's best work to that time. The character of Beek develops from story to story, and the series has a lighter overall tone than the Chuck Thompson tales. Babcock commented:

> I was tired of writing stories about overly-heroic heroes who took themselves too seriously, and it was a pleasant relief to do a yarn about a lead character I considered an ordinary human being with a normal urge for self-preservation.[7]

The Beek stories were all "novelettes" by *Black Mask* standards (more than 20 pages long), including two in the lead position in the issue (March and October 1939). Although not a detective, Beek travels around the country (mostly California and nearby areas of the West) and usually becomes involved in a crime of some sort. In several stories he is assisted by a reformed crook named Adelbert "Mac" McGillicuddy. The final Beek story, "Blood on the Snow" (December 1939) was also Babcock's last *Black Mask* work.[8]

Just over a year later, Babcock joined Alfred A. Knopf's stable of crime and mystery novelists, which at various times included Raymond Chandler, George Harmon Coxe, James M. Cain, and Eric Ambler. *A Homicide for Hannah* (published 21 January 1941) was the first of two hardback mystery novels featuring Joe Kirby, erstwhile custom-car salesman, and Hannah Van Doren, beautiful writer of "true-crime" stories.[9] Both books are well-written, filled with outre' characters and situations, and contain some entertainingly arch dialogue and prose.

Babcock's first novel is dedicated to his wife, Ruth Babcock. The Babcocks were among a group of pulp/mystery novel/film writers resident in Southern California during these years, and a social gathering might include such luminaries as Raymond Chandler, Craig Rice, Cleve Adams, Erle Stanley Gardner, W. T. Ballard, John K. Butler, and their respective friends or spouses.[10]

A Homicide for Hannah takes place just after Christmas in Southern California. Joe finds a nude, badly-beaten red-

head in an alley and takes her home. When he returns later that night, the woman is gone but the body of one of Joe's acquaintances is on the floor, dead. More murders follow. Joe runs afoul of a subversive organization called "True Americans," and meets Hannah. Her father, a police detective, had been killed in the line of duty and she now writes true-crime stories for a living. Joe and Hannah team up to solve the case and become friends, although Joe's attempt to advance their relationship earns him a jujitsu lesson from the petite blonde:

> 'A girl alone in the world has to learn how to take care of herself, by fair means or foul.'
>
> 'I was only trying to get better acquainted,' he explained in a hurt tone of voice. 'You can't blame a guy for trying. How was I to know you'd turn out to be a female Strangler Lewis?'
>
> 'When I want you to rape me, I'll let you know.'
>
> 'Thanks. I wish you would. Now I know what Engel meant when he said he was worried about what might happen to me, being left alone with you. He must have been speaking from bitter experience.'[11]

The mystery is properly mysterious, and everything is happily resolved at the end. Babcock's strength lies not in constructing a mystery plot or depicting a hard-boiled milieu, but in his writing style, particularly his characterizations: the minor characters are often sketchily drawn, but are memorable nonetheless.

Reviews for Babcock's first novel were generally good. A sequel, *The Gorgeous Ghoul,* was published eight months later. Joe and Hannah believe they have found the lost nephew of eccentric Sybil Peabody, who has posted a large reward for his return. The young man is heavily bandaged due to an accident, and has lost his memory, so they drive him to the Peabody home in northern California. Once more Joe takes his share of the lumps while Hannah utilizes her angelic charms to uncover clues to the various murders which ensue. Again, Babcock creates a cast of unusual characters, including a fat mastermind with a sidekick named Dopey, a crooked private eye, a dwarf, a young mechanical genius, a feuding county sheriff and town police chief, and so on. If anything, *The Gorgeous Ghoul* is even more farcical than Babcock's first novel. And again, the writing style provides considerable entertainment:

> 'Sure, but I can't very well do much toward finding Ted in this weakened condition,' Kirby pointed out plaintively, '—dying from starvation. Look, I'm practically drooling, just thinking of food.' He made slobbering noises, pointing at his mouth. But she didn't look. He began to suspect that he was back in the dog-house again.[12]

The Gorgeous Ghoul was even more enthusiastically reviewed than Babcock's first novel. The *Saturday Review of Literature* called it "a well thought-out and forthrightly written yarn with stunning finish. Tops—in its class."[13] Will Cuppy, reviewing the novel in *Books,* remarked:

"There's plenty of action and some real excitement . . . with rigorous blue-pencilling, Dwight V. Babcock ought to be an item for the carriage trade."[14]

Although Babcock's first two novels are extremely pleasant pieces of work, their long unavailability (each was reprinted twice by Avon in paperback, but the most recent edition was 1951) has led to their current obscurity. Babcock wrote one more Hannah Van Doren/Joe Kirby novel, _Hannah Says Foul Play_ (1946), published only in paperback as part of the Avon Murder Mystery Monthly series. He also wrote an occasional short story, such as "The Black Rose," which appeared in _Street & Smith's Detective Story Magazine_ in 1944, but would generally confine his writing to the more ephemeral media of motion pictures and television for the next two decades.

. . . . .

Dwight Babcock joined the writing staff of Universal Pictures in November 1943.[15] He may have received only the standard six-month contract given to relative unknowns, since by the following fall he was working at Republic Pictures. Despite a relatively short tenure at the studio, Babcock received nine credits from Universal, on films released up to three years after his arrival at the studio.

His first credit came on _Dead Man's Eyes,_ shot in March and April 1944, and released that November. _Dead Man's Eyes_ was the third of six "Inner Sanctum" series films made by Universal between 1943 and 1946. The studio had bought the rights to the name "Inner Sanctum" from Simon & Schuster in June 1943. The popular series of novels and the related radio show were selling points for the movie versions, although—unlike the earlier "Crime Club" series Universal had produced in 1937-38—the "Inner Sanctum" films were generally _not_ based on novels or radio shows. All six of the films starred Universal's resident horror star, Lon Chaney Jr. _Calling Dr. Death_ (1943), an original script, was followed by _Weird Woman_ (1944), based on Fritz Leiber Jr.'s novel _Conjure Wife._ Babcock's first screenplay was thus the third in the series and the second original script. Some consider the film the best of a rather poor lot.

Artist David Stuart (Chaney) loves Heather Hayden (Jean Parker), which makes his current model Tanya (Acquanetta) jealous. Tanya accidentally switches a bottle of acid with David's eyewash, causing him to go blind. He is embittered, but Heather's father promises his own corneas for transplantation after the older man's demise. Shortly afterward, Heather finds David standing blindly over her father's body. Captain Drury suspects Nick, one of Heather's former boyfriends, as well as Alan Bittaker, a psychiatrist who loves Tanya. After the operation, David claims he is still blind. Tanya, acting as David's nurse, tries to expose the murderer but is killed herself. David identifies a small nail he found near Dad Hayden's body as coming from Alan's walking stick. Alan attempts to kill him, but David had concealed the success of the operation: his eyesight restored, the artist escapes death and the killer is arrested.

Constructed along traditional mystery lines, including a wide variety of suspects with sufficient motive and opportunity, _Dead Man's Eyes_ is a competent little program picture. The cornea-transplant gimmick is treated matter-of-factly, with no supernatural overtones, but is rather interesting nonetheless. The identity of the murderer hinges on a single physical clue—the nail—a plot device used by Babcock in several later films, including _Road to Alcatraz_ and _The Jungle Captive._ The film is unique in that it is the only solo screenplay credit Babcock was to receive during his career. This may not be as unusual as it seems at first glance: solo writing credits were far from numerous during the years of the Hollywood studio system, when contract writers were always available for rewrites and revisions. Some films went to the other extreme: _A Yank at Oxford_ (1938) gives screen credit to eight writers, with two more working uncredited!

Babcock's second assignment was _The Mummy's Curse,_ shot during the first two weeks of August 1944, although it wasn't released until February 1945. _Curse_ was the fourth and final Universal Mummy film of the Forties (in order, they were _Hand, Tomb, Ghost,_ and _Curse_), with Lon Chaney Jr. the nominal star of the final three, replacing Tom Tyler. Attempts were made, as in the "Frankenstein" series, to connect each film with the previous entry. _The Mummy's Hand_ (1940), although not a sequel to _The Mummy_ (1932), uses stock footage from the earlier film. _The Mummy's Tomb_ (1942) uses extensive footage from _Hand,_ and three of the principal players repeat their _Hand_ roles. _The Mummy's Ghost_ features George Zucco for the third time, although the narrative string is broken somewhat. _The Mummy's Curse_ is a direct sequel to _Ghost,_ ostensibly taking place 25 years after the previous film (which is sort of foolish, since both pictures are obviously set in 1940s America). The locale also mysteriously changes from a New England village (in _Tomb_ and _Ghost_) to the Louisiana bayou country. Footage from _The Mummy's Hand_ is used once more, with Tom Tyler very visible as Kharis in his pre-Mummy days.[16]

Dwight Babcock and Leon Abrams shared screen story and adaptation credit, with screenplay credit going to Bernard Schubert. At the end of _Ghost,_ the Mummy had sunk into quicksand carrying Amina, the reincarnation of his lost love. _Curse_ begins as a government project drains the swamp. First the Mummy is uncovered and revived by a sinister Egyptian priest (Peter Coe, a poor substitute for series predecessors George Zucco and John Carradine), then Amina is unearthed. However, when she revives she has no memory of her previous existence (she's played by a different actress, which might explain it). The Mummy spends the rest of the film chasing her (how anyone ever gets caught by the Mummy, who moves at a snail's pace and is very clumsy besides, is one of the great mysteries of the movies). Eventually, the Mummy is "killed" by the collapse of an abandoned monastery, and Amina reverts to her aged, mummified state, which doesn't seem quite fair.

In 1945, although Babcock had since left Universal Pictures, he received credit on five films at the studio, including shared story credit (with Jack Natteford) on a 13-chapter serial, *The Master Key.* Nazi spies, out to steal a process for extracting gold from sea water, are opposed by Federal agents and a plucky female reporter. Serial scripting was a rather specialized field, and relatively few men wrote a majority of the sound serials: George Plympton (who co-scripted *The Master Key* with Joseph O'Donnell and Ande Lamb) had 49 serial credits, for example, Ronald Davidson 41, Sol Shor 22, and so on. *The Master Key* had been announced as early as February 1944; after serials supervisor Henry Macrae died, Ray Taylor and Morgan Cox took over the production chores in October.

The Jungle Captive was released in 1945. Babcock received sole story credit and shared screenplay credit with M. Coates Webster. *The Jungle Captive* followed *Captive Wild Woman* ('43) and *Jungle Woman* ('44) in the adventures of "Paula Dupree," a woman created from a gorilla, unlikely as this may sound. The first film was an ingenious attempt to establish a female Wolfman character (with obvious resemblances to RKO's *Cat People* as well), and use large segments of footage from a 10-year old Clyde Beatty circus picture, *The Big Cage.* The exotic Aquanetta portrayed the ape-girl, and the whole affair was rather successful. *Jungle Woman* brought her back, with stock footage from *The Big Cage* now appearing *third*-hand, in addition to flashbacks from *Captive Wild Woman.* *The Jungle Captive* was shot in September 1944, and released the following June.

The Jungle Captive introduces and scientist Stendahl (Otto Kruger), who has discovered a method of reviving the dead, using blood transfusions and an electric needle inserted in the heart of the corpse. Stendahl's brutish assistant Moloch (Rondo Hatton) steals Paula Dupree's body from the morgue. The police suspect Don, Stendahl's young medical student-assistant, because a medical smock was found near the hearse which transported the body. Stendahl uses blood from his secretary Ann to restore Paula to life, and then intends to transplant Ann's brain into the ape-girl's body. In town, Don spots Moloch wearing a fraternity pin which had been given to Ann by Don. Following Moloch to the farm, Don is captured. He incites Moloch to revolt against Stendahl's plan to remove Ann's brain. Stendahl kills Moloch but is in turn killed by Paula, who has reverted to ape form. The police arrive and kill the ape-girl.

This film was the first written by Babcock to feature Rondo Hatton. Hatton, who suffered from a glandular condition called acromegaly, was briefly used by Universal as a "monster" in the mid-Forties: he played a secondary menace role (similar to Moloch) in *The Spider Woman Strikes Back,* and was billed as "the Creeper" in three films (*House of Horrors, The Pearl of Death,* and *The Brute Man*), before dying of heart trouble early in 1946.

Road to Alcatraz was Babcock's first screenplay credit away from Universal. He shared script honors with Jerry Sackheim, based on a story entitled "Murder Stole My Missing Hours," by Francis K. Allen. Babcock and Sackheim wrote the screenplay in the fall of 1944 and it was filmed by Republic Pictures in January 1945. *Road to Alcatraz* is a straight whodunit, with no supernatural or science-fiction overtones.

Young attorney John Norton awakes from a sleepwalking episode with a pistol in his pocket. He discovers his partner, Charles Cantrell, has been murdered. Cantrell's death benefits not only Norton, but two other men, Angreet and Payne. Norton recalls seeing Angreet's spectacles cord in Cantrell's apartment; when he goes there to search for evidence, he is forced to use the dumbwaiter to elude the police. In the dumbwaiter, he cuts his hand on a fraternity pin (shades of *Jungle Captive*), which identifies Payne as the killer.

Although Babcock had left Universal in 1944, films bearing his name were still being released in the fall of 1945. *River Gang* was the next, adapted by Babcock from a story by producers Charles David and Hugh Gray, with final screenplay credit going to Leslie Charteris, creator of "The Saint." As an idea of the sort of timetable involved in film production at the major studios during the 1940s, producer David was signed to a Universal contract in June 1944, and "Fairy Tale Murder" (the working title of *River Gang*) was announced at that time as his first assignment.[17] Shooting began in September 1944, but it was a year before the picture was released.

River Gang features Gloria Jean, a young girl Universal was trying to develop into another Deanna Durbin. She portrays Wendy, who lives with her uncle Bill in his pawnshop. A mysterious man pawns a violin, which leads to a murder. A gang of neighborhood boys helps Wendy solve the crime, which turns out to have been masterminded by Uncle Bill.

The final "Inner Sanctum" series release was also Babcock's last Universal credit of 1945. *Pillow of Death,* with a script by George Bricker based on Babcock's screen story, followed *Strange Confession* and *The Frozen Ghost,* the fourth and fifth films in the series. *Pillow of Death* is unusual among the "Inner Sanctum" pictures for several reasons. First, Lon Chaney Jr. turns out to be the real murderer, instead of a suspect or red herring, as in the previous films. Also, the plot gives some indication of actual supernatural activity, a very unusual occurrence in the "Inner Sanctum" films and radio show. The existence of the "ghost" in *Pillow of Death* is not clearly explained away, although there is contradictory evidence which would support an explanation of fakery by the film's medium, or hallucinations on Chaney's part.

Wayne Fletcher (Chaney) loves his secretary, Donna Kincaid, but before he can ask his wife Vivian for a divorce, she is suffocated. Donna's aunts Belle and Amelia engage psychic Julian to conduct a seance in an attempt to prove Wayne's guilt. During the seance, Vivian's voice accuses her husband of murder. He denies this, but later that night he sees and hears Vivian's ghost (the audience hears her voice on all occasions, but she is never visible, an example of the ambiguity in the film). Wayne finds her crypt empty. Sam Kincaid, Donna's uncle, is found dead the next morning, suffocated. Belle later dies in the same way. Wayne agrees to stay at Donna's house to protect her, but after she has retired for the night, he hears Vivian again. His dead wife urges him to reenact Sam's murder, and Wayne does, also confessing to the murders of Belle and Vivian. He then tries to kill Donna, but she is saved by the intervention of Bruce, a neighbor. Wayne, once more following his dead wife's orders, leaps to his death through a window.

Pillow of Death is a little confusing, but the real identity of the murder is well concealed, in part because Chaney was hardly ever the killer in the "Inner Sanctum" films. The final reconciliation of Donna with Bruce is poorly done, however: throughout the whole film she has been nasty to Bruce, who is convinced of Wayne's guilt. Once Wayne is exposed as the killer, she fairly leaps into Bruce's arms.

As mentioned above, the supernatural element is deliberately obscured, with only a tiny hint that Julian the psychic has been working with the police to trap Wayne. However, even this couldn't explain *all* the manifestations of Vivian's ghost. There's one good line at the climax: Vivian's ghost tells Wayne, "At last [Donna] realizes that you are a psych-o-path-ic killer!" (It's the way she says "psychopathic").

Pillow of Death was the first of six films Babcock wrote in collaboration with George Bricker. *House of Horrors* united them again, Bricker once more scripting from Babcock's screen story. Sculptor Marcel DeLange (Martin Kosleck) lives in poverty because the art establishment ridicules his avant-garde work. DeLange saves a man from drowning, not knowing he is the killer known as the Creeper (Rondo Hatton). Marcel sees him only as a model for a bust of "the perfect Neanderthal man." The next night, the Creeper goes out and kills a streetwalker. Marcel begins to suspect his guest is not exactly normal:

MARCEL:

> I've often wondered why a man would want to snap a woman's spine.

THE CREEPER:

> (*deadpan*) She screamed.

Marcel drops a hint that critic Harmon is keeping him poor (Creeper: "You don't like the guy?"). That night, newspaper writer Joan Medford (Virginia Grey) visits Harmon, who criticizes the one-man show of Steve Morrow (Harmon: "The morons wallow in a sea of girls, girls, unbelievably well-proportioned girls.") Joan leaves, the Creeper kills Harmon: the police suspect Steve. Marcel reads about the death of his enemy in the paper (Creeper: "You glad? Good, everybody happy."), and is visited by

Joan, who peeks at the bust he is sculpting. The police convince art critic Ormiston to criticize Steve's work, but Ormiston makes the mistake of comparing Steve to DeLange, which brings the wrath of the Creeper down on him. Marcel is happy: "Soon every critic will recognize my genius." The Creeper: "They'd better." Joan steals Marcel's sketch of the Creeper, and takes it to her newspaper. When she tries to sneak it back, Marcel says he'll kill her and turn the Creeper over to the cops to take the rap. This makes the Creeper mad, and he kills Marcel. The police and Steve arrive in time to save Joan and kill the Creeper.

House of Horrors is not a great film, but it has its moments. Hatton is hardly what one would call a dynamic presence, but the script does manage to work up some sympathy for him, as the Creeper expresses his pathetic gratitude to DeLange the only way he knows—murder (this is amplified upon in *The Brute Man* later). Hatton's delivery makes his lines chillingly humorous at times, and even a little touching at others: Marcel asks him what he thinks of the monstrous bust and the Creeper replies "It's pretty."

It is interesting to note that the "Creeper" character was deliberately conceived as a Universal monster character in the Wolfman/Mummy/Dracula mode. A trade paper notice in November 1944 indicates that producer Ben Pivar of the B-film unit had been assigned to develop new series characters, and the "Creeper" was the first (and only one, as it turned out). Rondo Hatton was signed for the continuing role in December, although he may have been in Pivar's mind all along.[18]

She Wolf of London was another collaboration between Babcock and Bricker, although "collaboration" doesn't necessarily mean the two men worked together on the script. As noted above, Babcock may have written a large number of screen stories for Universal in a relatively short period of time; these stories may have been stockpiled until needed, and then converted into scripts by Bricker, or Bricker may also have done a lot of writing quickly, and then the completed scripts were put on ice. *She Wolf of London* is one example: the title turns up in a production announcement as early as June 1944, but the film wasn't shot until December 1945. Babcock certainly wasn't at the studio at this time, and Bricker was probably also gone.

The film begins in London "at the turn of the century." A man claims he was attacked in a park by a *female* werewolf. As the attacks continue, Phyllis Allenby (June Lockhart) begins to believe she becomes a werewolf as a result of the Allenby Curse. Her fiance Barry Lanfield doesn't believe in the curse, but her "aunt" Martha (actually the longtime housekeeper) and "cousin" Carol aren't so sure. Carol loves artist Dwight Severn but her mother prefers Barry as a possible mate. Eventually, Martha is exposed as the killer, and is killed by falling on a knife she planned to use on Phyllis.

She-Wolf of London is one of the most perfunctory B-pictures ever made. The Universal standing sets make it *look* good, but no attempt is ever made to actually suggest a real werewolf: the plot is transparent from very early on. There are a few bits of inside humor worth mentioning. Carol's boyfriend is named "Dwight," obviously an inside joke. He's played by Martin Kosleck, usually a villain (as in *House of Horrors,* where he also played an artist) but here in a very small role as a good guy. The maid in the Allenby house is named "Hannah" (as in "Hannah van Doren"?). Barry Lanfield says he's in law practice with his father, and a policeman says "Not Sir Sidney Lanfield?" (director Sidney Lanfield directed the 1939 version of *The Hound of the Baskervilles*). And June Lockhart, later a regular on the *Lassie* TV series, has one scene where a huge dog snarls viciously at her, which is funny in retrospect, at least.

. . . . .

In late 1946, Babcock received belated credit for one more film from his brief tenure at Universal. As it developed, Universal's merger with International Pictures in 1946 caused the cessation of the type of films Babcock had written for the company anyway: all B pictures including Westerns, horror movies, serials and films running less than 70 minutes in length were dropped, and a number of production personnel were laid off as a result.

The last release of the nine Universal films to bear Babcock's name is unusual for a number of reasons. *The Brute Man* was shot in mid-December 1945 (star Rondo Hatton died a few months later, in February 1946), but the film was not released until October 1946. And the releasing company was not Universal, the production company—it was Producer's Releasing Corporation (PRC). Sometime between the completion of the film and its release, the film was sold by Universal to PRC. On October 23, 1946, *Variety* reported the deal had been consummated "about 10 weeks ago." However, the announcement was not made until October, when PRC showed the film to the trade press. The sale price was about $125,000, representing Universal's negative cost plus interest.[19] The information in the copyright files at the Library of Congress has "Universal Pictures" crossed out and the new claimant, "Pathe Industries" (PRC's corporate body) written on the sheet in pencil! Even the enclosed pressbook advertisements bear the Universal logo.

The instance of one studio selling a completed film to another was not totally unknown—MGM bought *Hitler's Madman* from PRC in 1942, but this was actually the case of an independently-produced film being sold by one releasing organization to another; it happened again in 1944, when PRC sold *Voice in the Wind* to United Artists—but it was certainly not the usual circumstance. Universal's new policy of no B pictures instigated the sale: two Jon Hall films were also considered for such disposal, but since they were in Cinecolor, the new administration at Universal-International decided to keep them.

Rondo Hatton was once again dubbed "The Creeper," although his character was not the same as in *House of Hor-*

rors; Tom Neal portrayed a murder victim, and Jane Adams a blind pianist (she had previously been cast as a hunchbacked nurse in *House of Frankenstein,* 1945, making one wonder if she had an enemy in the casting office). Babcock wrote the screen story, and M. Coates Webster and George Bricker split screenplay credit.

The Brute Man begins with the Creeper committing a murder and escaping from the police. Hiding briefly in Helen's room, he is gratified when she doesn't give his presence away. Helen is blind, although he doesn't know this at first. Later, the Creeper kills a delivery boy delivering supplies to the shack where he is hiding. After he flees, the police discover his hideout and find an old photograph of three people: Hal Moffatt, Clifford Scott, and Virginia. The police question Scott (now married to Virginia), and the story of the Creeper's origin is revealed (in a long flashback sequence):

> The year is 1930, and Hal is star of the college football team. Both he and Scott are in love with Virginia. Scott gives Hal the wrong answers to a chemistry quiz, and the athlete is required to stay after class and work on an experiment. The experiment backfires and Hal is horribly disfigured. He disappears from their lives.

> Now, in 1945, he is the Creeper, seeking revenge. However, he has one weak spot: Helen. Stealing a butterfly pin from a pawnshop, and killing the proprietor in the process, the Creeper gives it to Helen. She tells him she has a chance to regain her sight, but needs an expensive operation. The Creeper tries to get the money from Scott, and a fight ensues, in which Scott is killed and the Creeper wounded. He escapes with some of Virginia's jewelry. Helen is caught when she unwittingly takes the stolen loot to be appraised. Told of the Creeper's real character, she helps the police trap him.

The Brute Man goes a step further than *House of Horrors* in its attempt to humanize the character of the Creeper. Aside from the dubious taste of using Hatton's real-life medical condition as the basis for a horror character, the script does more to elicit sympathy for him than the "heavy" roles in *The Jungle Captive,* et al. The relationship with the blind Helen undoubtedly owes a strong debt to *The Bride of Frankenstein* and Chaplin's *City Lights.* Taken as a whole, *The Brute Man*'s tidy little revenge-motive plot is certainly as good or better than the plots of the other Universal horror films of the mid-1940s.

But by the time *The Brute Man* hit the theatres, Babcock had been away from Universal and employed at Columbia Pictures for some time.[20]

His first two assignments were on films in the short-lived "I Love a Mystery" series. "I Love a Mystery" was a popular radio serial created by Carlton E. Morse, and in 1944 Columbia added it to their already crowded list of mystery series, which at the time included "The Whistler," "The Crime Doctor," and "Boston Blackie." Morse signed a contract in May 1944 for 10 films: two films a year for five years, at $25,000 per film. However, only three were actually made. The first film in the new series was entitled *I Love a Mystery* (1945) and included one member of the radio cast, Barton Yarbrough, in his radio role of "Doc Long." Jim Bannon played "Jack Packard," while the third member of the radio series' heroic trio, "Reggie" (Tony Randall had this role for a time on the radio), was dropped. The second "ILAM" film, *The Devil's Mask,* was the first for Babcock, who was credited with additional dialogue. The picture, originally announced as "The Head" in October 1945, was shot in February 1946. Loosely based on the radio episodes entitled "The Decapitation of Jefferson Monk," the film concerns an "extra" shrunken head in a collection. It turns out to be the head of a murdered explorer. A crazed taxidermist killed him because the explorer had killed so many animals! The murderer is slain by his pet leopard, Diablo. Charles O'Neal received screenplay credit.

The Unknown was the third and last "I Love a Mystery" adaptation of the Forties (there was a one-shot TV movie, made in 1967 but not aired until 1973). Dwight Babcock and Charles O'Neal received screen credit as adaptors (probably from the ILAM radio story called "The Thing That Cries in the Night"), while Malcolm Stuart Boylan and Julian Harmon wrote the screenplay. The film was shot under the title "The Coffin" in April, 1946. Young Rachel Martin informs her parents of her secret marriage to Richard Arnold. Richard argues with Rachel's father, and the old man is accidentally killed. Phoebe Martin buries her husband's body behind the fireplace and swears the family to secrecy. Years later, Rachel's daughter Nina returns to the old house, accompanied by Jack and Doc. Phoebe has died, and Rachel, who has been mentally unbalanced for years, lives in the house with her two brothers. The reading of Phoebe's will is the scheduled big event, but Richard also returns after an absence of many years, Phoebe appears alive (and then dies for real), and a mysterious figure tries to entomb Jack and Doc alive. Finally, one of Nina's uncles is revealed as the killer. Rachel regains her sanity and is reunited with Richard; Nina plans to marry the lawyer who was to read the will.

Babcock's third Columbia credit of 1946 (although the film was shot in December 1945, prior to either of his "I Love a Mystery" films) was *So Dark the Night,* a picture that *Variety* said "barely misses the 'A' tag."[21] Joseph H. Lewis, a talented visual stylist, had had a minor success the previous year with *My Name is Julia Ross,* although his best work was to come in 1949, with the excellent *Gun Crazy.*

Babcock shared screenplay credit on *So Dark the Night* with Martin Berkeley, based on a screen story by Aubrey Wisberg. Interestingly enough, Columbia had purchased the story from Wisberg in March 1945 with the intention of making it the fifth in the "Whistler" series.[22] Upon reflection, one can see how easily the story would have fit in this series (although the setting probably would have been contemporary America), but the decision was made to shoot the film as a non-series picture, and "The Whistler"

#5 was instead the superb *Mysterious Intruder,* written by Eric Taylor, q.v.

So Dark the Night received good critical marks, but the non-star cast (Steven Geray had the leading role: he was usually cast in supporting roles, such as "Uncle Pio" in *Gilda,* made the same year at Columbia) kept the film from really breaking out of its budget-imposed class. *Variety* also blamed script deficiencies:

> The pic's failure lies in the decisive province of the screenplay [because] the scripters . . . solve the case through an unfitting and totally mechanical foray into the realm of psychopathology.[23]

The film is set in pre-WWII France. Henri Cassin, ace detective of the Paris Surete, takes a vacation in the rural village of St. Margot. The local innkeeper's wife decides that her daughter, Nanette, would make a good match for the middle-aged but eminent civil servant. Michaux, the innkeeper, isn't so sure about this, nor is Nanette's farmer boyfriend, Leon. Leon tells Nanette: "I saw the way he looked at you, like a hungry dog begging for a favor. And you loved it." When Nanette claims she still loves only Leon, he replies "If I can't have you, I'd kill you rather than lose you to anyone else." Despite Nanette's protestations of faithfulness, she and the detective soon become engaged. At the engagement party, Leon storms out angrily and Nanette runs after him. By the next day, neither has returned. Cassin is despondent: "I knew it was too good to be true. That much happiness just wasn't meant for me." However, Nanette's body turns up in the river, and suspicion falls on Leon. Cassin and the local gendarmes search Leon's farm and find him dead, with a bottle of acid in his hand. Cassin proves it was not, as it appears, suicide. He makes a plaster cast of the killer's footprint. Later, Cassin receives a note stating "Another will die." Mme. Michaux, the innkeeper's wife, is murdered. Cassin returns to Paris, admitting failure, but when he describes the killer's general appearance to the police sketch artist, the portrait comes out looking like him! His footprint fits the plaster cast, and his handwriting (left-handed) matches the notes. Cassin says he must be the killer, although he remembers nothing. Cassin escapes and returns to St. Margot, where he attacks Michaux. They struggle, but the police arrive and kill Cassin.

The idea of a killer being unaware of his crime (due to a mental disorder) is also the pivotal point of the plot of *Pillow of Death,* which Babcock had also co-written. This is a connection no one seems to have previously drawn. These two films, made a year apart at different studios, both deal with a protagonist striving to solve the murder of a woman (a wife in *Pillow of Death,* fiancée in *So Dark the Night*), only to learn in the end that *he* is the killer. To complicate matters even further, consider the plot of *The Power of the Whistler* (Columbia, 1945), script by Aubrey Wisberg—author of the screen story of *So Dark the Night* (which was originally bought as a "Whistler" film story!). In this picture, Richard Dix plays a man with amnesia as the result of an automobile accident. He and a woman friend try to discover his true identity, but when Dix's memory returns, he learns he is an escapee from a mental hospital, and he intends to murder the head of the asylum and the judge who sent him there! Once again, an abrupt switch, with the star/protagonist revealed to the audience (and to himself) as a killer. Certainly each of these three films has its own unique aspects, but the ideas behind them are remarkably similar.[24]

After six screen credits in 1946 (although some of this work had been written much earlier), Babcock's output dropped off considerably. In fact, it would take seven more years for him to earn another six film credits, although this may be partially explained by his move into TV writing in the early 1950s. The last of Babcock's four Columbia films was released in 1947. *The Corpse Came C.O.D.* is perhaps closest in tone to Babcock's novels, although in fact it is based on a novel by Jimmy Starr, a Hollywood columnist. Starr wrote three novels featuring reporter Joe Medford, of which *The Corpse Came C.O.D.* (1944) was the first.[25] Starr assigned the movie rights to agent Frank Orsatti in October 1944, and there was talk of producing the film independently, with Lloyd Bacon as director.[26] For one reason or another, this project fell through and Columbia picked up the property in 1946. The script was probably written in the summer of that year, Babcock and George Bricker collaborating on their fifth picture together. The film was scheduled to begin shooting in December, but was postponed until early 1947 due to the illness of star George Brent. The national release date was June.

The Corpse Came C.O.D. is set in the studios of "Palisades Pictures" (the Columbia studios serving as the "sets"). As the film opens, a crime movie is being shot (the director instructs the actors—"Please gentlemen, show a little more life when you die!") Palisades star Mona Harrison receives a crate containing the dead body of costume designer Hector Rose. Mona calls Joe Medford (Brent), a reporter friend, who in turn notifies detective Mark Wilson. Joe sees Mona hide a bolt of dress material from the crate, but forgets about it in his rush to solve the crime before Rosemary Durant (Joan Blondell), a rival reporter. Next to die is the publicity director of Palisades Pictures. Joe learns that the cloth Mona stole contains diamonds. Mona tells him that Wilson, Rose and the publicity man were part of a gem-smuggling ring, and that Wilson is really her ex-husband. The police arrive and save Joe, Rosemary and Mona before Wilson can kill them.

Brent and Blondell, both former Warner Brothers stars of the 1930s, were on the downward path in their careers but were still capable of turning in good performances (they were also teamed in the 1947 United Artists release *Christmas Eve*). The relationship between Joe and Rosemary is in the familiar screwball-comedy love/hate/rivalry mold: Joe locks Rosemary in a closet, she steals his photos, he steals them back, and so on. At one point Joe is knocked unconscious; waking up in the hospital and spotting Rosemary, he remarks—"This can't be heaven: you're here."

The other film credit for Dwight Babcock in 1947 came on an Eagle-Lion film. Eagle-Lion had absorbed the PRC studio and product (the owners of Eagle-Lion later took over Film Classics, and in 1951 bought United Artists). Ben Pivar, former production head of the "B" picture unit at Universal where Babcock got his start in the industry (and who had been fired—along with a number of other executives—in July 1946 when the Universal-International merger came about), reunited Babcock and June Lockhart (from *She Wolf of London*) for *Bury Me Dead*. The screenplay was written by Babcock and Karen DeWolf, who had credits on a number of "Blondie" features but worked on few non-comedy films. Radio actress Irene Winston wrote the screen story: desirous of breaking into the film business, she wrote a 25-page original story with the leading role tailored to her own acting talents. She approached Eagle-Lion in late 1946, only to be told that the story was salable but *she* wasn't right for the part! Apparently deciding half a loaf was better than none, Winston sold the story and stayed in radio.[27] The film was shot in April 1947 and released in October.

A fire breaks out in the stables of the Corlin estate, and Rod Corlin identifies the body of a woman found in the ruins as his wife Barbara (Lockhart). But Barbara shows up at her own funeral, revealing herself to Mike, the family lawyer. Whoever died in the stable had been murdered. There are a number of flashbacks in the film as the convoluted relationships between Barbara, her sister Rusty, Rod, their friend Helen, and others are described. Eventually the body is identified as Helen, and Mike is exposed as the murderer.

In its brief existence, Eagle-Lion was responsible for a number of very interesting mystery and crime films from various producers, including memorable *films noir* such as *T-Men, He Walked by Night, Raw Deal, Ruthless,* and *Port of New York*. *Bury Me Dead* isn't quite a classic, but is rather unjustly forgotten today.

13 Lead Soldiers was Babcock's sole screen credit for 1948. Produced by Edward Small's Reliance Pictures and released through 20th Century Fox, it was one of two "Bulldog Drummond" films that year. Drummond, who first appeared in novels in 1920, was incarnated in films many times over the next four decades. Ronald Colman, Ray Milland, John Lodge, and John Howard all appeared as the British sleuth, with Howard essaying the role in seven Paramount films between 1937-39. Columbia Pictures took over the character for two 1947 releases, and in 1948 it was Fox's turn.

Bernard Small, who co-produced the two Columbia efforts, teamed with Ben Pivar for the Fox films, *The Challenge* and *13 Lead Soldiers*. Ron Randell, Columbia's most recent Bulldog Drummond, was replaced by former film "Falcon" Tom Conway. John Newland played assistant Algy in conventional silly-ass Britisher style.

Based on a short story by "Sapper" (H. C. McNeile), *13 Lead Soldiers* was adapted by Babcock and scripted by Irving Elman, who had co-written *The Challenge* with

Frank Gruber. The plot bears a resemblance to "The Six Napoleons," a Sherlock Holmes story filmed as *The Pearl of Death*. Instead of murders being committed for plaster busts of Napoleon (or music boxes, as in another Holmes film, *Dressed to Kill*, coincidentally adapted by Gruber), the criminals are after the 13 toy soldiers of the title. They are the key to a royal treasure, hidden by King Harold before the Battle of Hastings.

Dwight Babcock received no screen credits in either 1949 or 1950, but in 1951 he co-wrote *F.B.I. Girl* with Richard Landau, for low-budget clearinghouse Lippert Pictures (the PRC of the Fifties). Based on a story by Rupert Hughes (whose nephew Howard had recently purchased RKO Radio Pictures), *F.B.I. Girl* is a good, if little-known, example of the documentary-style crime features of the period. Copyrighted by "Jedgar Productions" (get it?), the film was produced and directed by William Berke. Cesar Romero, a Lippert stalwart, shared star billing with George Brent (Gene Evans was originally announced for one of the leads), with Audrey Totter in the eponymous role of an FBI fingerprint clerk. Raymond Burr added another to his long list of villainous, pre-Perry Mason parts.

The film concerns Shirley, whose boyfriend is a lobbyist in the pay of Blake, the power behind the governor of a nearby state (possibly Virginia). The governor—rather improbably—has a criminal record under his real name. Blake tries to retrieve the governor's files from the FBI, first by blackmailing the brother of one clerk, then by pressuring Shirley through her boyfriend. In the end justice triumphs and even Shirley's week-kneed boyfriend seems forgiven.

Babcock's motion picture writing diminished significantly in the late 1940s and early 1950s, probably due his increased television duties. This aspect of his career will be briefly discussed at the end of the chapter, but it should be noted that, chronologically, he began to concentrate on television at this point.

Savage Frontier (Republic, 1953) is unique among Babcock's screen credits, as his only film Western (he shared screenplay credit with veteran Western scripter Gerald Geraghty). The feature is one of the final four "B" Westerns starring Allan "Rocky" Lane. The Lane films weren't spectacular, but they maintained a steady level of quality.

Rocky Lane, U.S. Marshal, is trailing three outlaws wanted for murder. One of them, the Cherokee Kid, visits dentist/town marshal Nugget Clark for treatment of a toothache, and is arrested by Rocky while still dizzy from the laughing gas Nugget administered. Reformed outlaw Sam Webb (Bob Steele) is framed for the Kid's subsequent escape by Oakes, secret head of the gang. While pursuing the outlaws, Rocky is blamed for shooting Sam, but with the help of Nugget he exposes Oakes and captures the gang.

Babcock and George Bricker collaborated for one final time on a crime script entitled "Off the Record," which was revised by Warren Douglas and released as *Loophole* (Allied Artists, 1954).[28] Douglas, who was also the associate producer, co-wrote *Cry Vengeance* that same year with Bricker.

Herman Tate robs a bank of $50,000 by posing as a bank examiner. Teller Mike Donovan (Barry Sullivan) is at first suspected of the crime, but manages to convince the police of his innocence. However, bonding company investigator Gus Slavin (Charles McGraw) believes Mike assisted in the robbery. He arranges for Mike to lose his job. Each time Mike finds a new job, Slavin gets him fired. Finally, the former teller takes a job as a cab driver and begins to rebuild his life. One day Mike spots Tate working as a teller in another bank and demands the stolen money. Tate's girlfriend Vera wants to murder Mike, but Gus arrives and accuses them of being partners. The trio eludes Gus. Vera shoots Tate after he refuses to kill Mike, and the police arrest her. Mike is cleared and returns to his bank job, but as the film ends Slavin is still lurking in the background.

Although shot in a flat, near-documentary style (there is even voice over narration a la *Dragnet*: "The story you are about to see actually happened"), *Loophole* contains plot elements reminiscent of *film noir*. Mike Donovan has a happy marriage, a small house, a responsible, steady job and yet he sees his life crumble due to circumstances beyond his control. He goes from job to job, has to move into a small apartment, and his wife must work to help pay the bills. The monomaniacal Slavin constantly trails him, waiting for him to make a slip. On several occasions Mike almost runs into Tate: once Tate and his girlfriend get into his cab but leave before Mike recognizes them; several times Mike just misses Tate at the bank where Mike and his wife have their account; Mike inspects photos of bank tellers in the bonding company's files, but misses Tate's card when Slavin annoys him. Each time, fate intervenes and Tate gets away. Mike finally comes face to face with the man who (unintentionally) ruined his life (Tate didn't set out to frame Mike; it was actually Slavin's persecution that cost Mike his job). Tate himself is a nondescript man lured into crime by desire for a younger woman. Vera rejects him at the end: "With a few bucks I could stand you. Without it, you're just a broken-down, middle-aged bank clerk." Even when Mike's life was at its worst, *he* still had his loyal wife—Tate had to buy Vera's affection, and even that is denied him at the end. Mike eventually regains his former standing, but Tate loses the money, the woman, and his life.

Babcock's career as a motion picture scripter came to an end in 1955 with two films for producer Sam Katzman. *Devil Goddess* and *Jungle Moon Men*, released by Columbia, were the last gasps of the "Jungle Jim" series. With the final three entries in the series (beginning with *Cannibal Attack* in 1954), star Johnny Weissmuller played "Johnny Weissmuller" rather than "Jungle Jim," but otherwise the films were indistinguishable from their predecessors. The budgets were low, Weissmuller looked bored, and the "African" natives were played by white actors. Black actors were cast in some of the earlier features in the series, but by and large the "natives" were played by people like Rick Vallin, John Dehner and other Caucasians, dressed in costumes suggesting the South Seas rather than the Dark Continent. The series occasionally had some points of interest: *Captive Girl* (1950) features another former Tarzan, Buster Crabbe, along with the beautiful Anita Lhoest (as a female Tarzan-type). Mostly, though, the films are watchable only for the unintentional humor which may be garnered from the wretched production values.

Devil Goddess was scripted by George Plympton from Babcock's screen story. A scientist and his daughter travel to the forbidden land of the fire worshipers in search of a missing friend, and run afoul of bad guys who steal the natives' treasure. *Jungle Moon Men* had slightly more entertainment value (the title alone is worth something). A tribe of (white, naturally) pygmies worships a "She"-like white goddess (Helen Stanton). Jo Pagano and Babcock scripted from Pagano's screen story.

Although these two films were the last Babcock wrote, his name does appear on the credits of one final feature. *The Trouble with Girls* (MGM, 1969), was based on a 1960 novel written by "Dwight Vincent" and Day Keene entitled *Chautauqua*.[29]

According to the jacket copy, Babcock and Keene had known each other for 30 years prior to their collaboration on the novel.[30] Keene, author of numerous stories, paperback novels and radio dramas, had worked with Babcock on TV scripts, and together they took a story by Mauri Grashin (a screenwriter, novelist, and author's agent) and expanded it to novel length. *Chautauqua* was the result.

The book is well-written and very readable, obviously influenced by the phenomenal success of *Peyton Place* in its depiction of small-town lust. Set in Radford Center, Iowa in 1921 (Babcock, one recalls, was born in Iowa), the novel is full of authentic period touches: not only the fascinating details of the Chautauqua tent shows, but even the smaller aspects of small town life are carefully depicted.

Nita Bixby is, unknown to her husband, the town prostitute, though she does it only because she hates the small town and needs enough money to flee with her young daughter. She doesn't know her husband, dying of a war injury, is driving himself relentlessly to make money to give them when he expires. Betty Wagner, a nymphomaniac, is engaged to the son of the town banker, who also hates Radford Center and wants to become an aviator. He falls in love with a Chautauqua woman. Betty becomes pregnant by a traveling film salesman. Walter Hale, manager of the Chautauqua show, meets a woman he had loved and lost years before, now living in Radford Center. And so on. The town druggist is murdered by Nita Bixby, although her husband confesses to the crime.

The novel must have seemed like a sure bet for the movies, once again recalling the success of the *Peyton Place*

adaptation. The book was probably purchased by MGM shortly after publication, but sat around in the studio's files until it was unearthed as a change of pace for Elvis Presley. In any event, the resultant film was extremely poor. The script used only random characters and events from the novel (the date was changed for no particular reason to 1927), dropping the character of Ira Bixby entirely and many of the other sub-plots. *The Trouble with Girls* fails as a drama, comedy, period piece or Elvis Presley musical (he does have one good song). It also contains some bad acting of epic proportions (Sheree North stands out in this regard). What MGM had in mind is beyond comprehension; what they got was a real failure.

But by 1969, Dwight Babcock had been involved in the fourth phase of his writing career for nearly two decades. His television work eventually supplanted his film writing, just as pulp stories were replaced by novels, and novels by movie scripts. Though it is known Babcock wrote over 100 TV shows, the particular titles and episodes are difficult to pinpoint.

Around 1951, Babcock went to work for Apex Films, which produced commercials, TV shows, and sponsored films. He had moved to Screen Gems by 1955, and in 1956 he was hired by Walt Disney Productions for their TV productions. Among verified scripts done by Dwight Babcock are "King for a Day" (*Superman,* 1954), "Lost River Roundup," "Storm the Pass," and "Underground Ambush" (1957 episodes of *Sgt. Preston of the Yukon*). He also worked on episodes of *Sky King, Kit Carson, Chevron Theatre, Photocrime, Roy Rogers, Dick Tracy, Lux Video Theatre, The Adventures of Ellery Queen,* and *Hawaiian Eye,* among others.[31]

Babcock's television work indirectly led to another screen credit, similar to Eric Taylor's posthumous credit on *White Goddess. The Yellow-Haired Kid,* released in 1952 by Monogram Pictures, was actually two episodes of the "Wild Bill Hickok" television series spliced together. Dwight Babcock and Maurice Tombragel were given script credit. As with most such films, the domestic release was negligible.

· · · · ·

Dwight Babcock died in 1979, leaving behind a large and varied body of work. His career is rather difficult to characterize, since he worked in so many different areas. His pulp writing is certainly competent but not especially memorable; his novels, on the other hand, are very entertaining but too few in number and too long out of print to have much impact on his reputation. As a screenwriter Babcock was not prolific and his credits came mostly on lower-case efforts. And finally his television work—as noted earlier—is difficult to evaluate (or even locate).

What may be said about Babcock is this: his work was consistently interesting, sometimes above average and sometimes mediocre (although his film work particularly is clouded by the contributions of collaborators). His "Hannah van Doren" novels stand out as probably Babcock's finest work; his film and TV careers cannot be discounted, although only occasionally did his work here approach the quality of his prose.

Notes

1. Dwight Babcock, *A Homicide for Hannah* (New York: Knopf, 1941). More information on Babcock's life—with especial detail on his pulp career—may be found in James L. Traylor's excellent article "Murder Up His Sleeve," *The Armchair Detective* 23 (Winter 1990) 56-73. This was published well after my research on Babcock was complete, but I managed to incorporate some of Traylor's biographical information into this chapter. Traylor does not go into detail on Babcock's film career.

2. Actually, Babcock had sold this story to *Black Mask* during the summer of 1933. Traylor 57.

3. Dwight V. Babcock, "At the Bottom of Every Mess," *Black Mask,* January 1934: 84.

4. "At the Bottom of Every Mess": 93.

5. Babcock, "Death's Ransom," *Black Mask* April 1935: 94-95.

6. This title had earlier been used by Horace McCoy for a story appearing in the May 1934 issue of *Black Mask.*

7. Babcock, "Behind the Black Mask," *Black Mask* March 1939: 31.

8. Babcock's first pulp sale had been to *Black Mask,* but during his career he also sold to numerous other magazines, including *All Detective, Dime Detective, The Shadow Magazine, Super Detective, Thrilling Detective, Complete Stories, Popular Detective, Double Detective,* and *Ten Detective Aces.* After leaving *Black Mask,* former editor Joseph T. Shaw became an author's agent and represented Babcock for many years. Traylor 67, 73.

9. A 1935 Chuck Thompson adventure, "Death Goes Free," featured a female criminal named "Hard Hannah" Dorne. She is Hannah Van Doren's predecessor in name only.

10. Frank MacShane, *The Life of Raymond Chandler* (New York: Penguin Books, 1978) 74-75.

11. Babcock, *A Homicide for Hannah* 89.

12. Babcock, *The Gorgeous Ghoul* (New York: Knopf, 1941) 63-64.

13. *Saturday Review of Literature* 1 November 1941: 19.

14. Will Cuppy, *Books* 7 December 1941: 36.

15. According to Traylor, Gerald Drayson Adams contacted Babcock in 1937 (when he was also representing Eric Taylor), and negotiated a sale of film rights to Babcock's story "Hide-Out" to Monogram Pic-

tures. The story was apparently never used as the basis for a film. Traylor 67.

16. Oddly enough, Chaney never appears without makeup in his three Mummy films; indeed, how much work was actually done by Chaney and how much was done by various stunt doubles such as Eddie Parker is debatable. Chaney was completely unrecognizable under the makeup, and Universal could conceivably have gotten away with having someone else play the monster in *all* of the scenes.

17. *Variety,* 7 June 1944: 6.

18. Motion Picture Herald 18 November 1944: 41 and 16 December 1944: 35.

19. *Variety* 23 October 1946: 7.

20. Babcock went to Columbia "early in 1945" on a recommendation from his agent, Joseph T. Shaw. Traylor 72-73.

21. *Variety* 18 September 1946: 16.

22. *Motion Picture Herald* 10 March 1945: 38.

23. *Variety* 18 September 1946: 16.

24. To further complicate matters, a 1935 film written by Karen DeWolf—*Condemned to Live*—features Ralph Morgan as a kindly doctor who becomes a murderous vampire at night without knowing it.

25. In 1942, PRC Pictures released *Night for Crime,* based on a story by Starr. In this film, "Joe Powell," publicity agent for "Sunset Studios" teams up with "Susan Cooper," newspaper reporter, to solve the murder of a Hollywood extra during a blackout. Mona Harrison, the studio's biggest star, has also disappeared. At the climax, it is revealed that Mona's twin sister murdered her and tried to take her place as a movie star. The film was scripted by Arthur St. Claire and Sherman Lowe.

26. *Variety* 4 October 1944: 9.

27. *Variety* 11 December 1946: 1, 49.

28. Traylor indicates this was Babcock's favorite of the films he wrote. Traylor 73.

29. On the credits of *The Trouble with Girls,* Babcock was identified by his full name. Why *Chautauqua* was published under his first and middle names only is not known.

30. Traylor's article contains a photograph of a "Fictioneers" dinner from 1946, where Babcock and Keene are both present. Also in the picture are W. T. Ballard and Robert Leslie Bellem, among others. Traylor 72.

31. Traylor 73.

Geoff Mayer (essay date 1993)

SOURCE: Mayer, Geoff. "A Hard-Boiled World: *Goodbye Paradise* and *The Empty Beach*." *Literature/Film Quarterly* 21, no. 2 (1993): 112-19.

[*In the following essay, Mayer discusses film adaptations of Raymond Chandler's works, commenting on ways in which Chandler's style becomes altered in the screen realizations of his novels.*]

> In anything that can be called art there is a quality of redemption. It may be pure tragedy, . . . and it may be pity and irony, and it may be the raucous laughter of the strong man. But down these mean streets a man must go who is not himself mean, who is neither tarnished nor afraid. . . . He must be, to use a rather weathered phrase, a man of honor, by instinct, by inevitability, without thought of it, and certainly without saying it. He must be the best man in his world and a good enough man for any world.[1]

This passage from Raymond Chandler's 1946 essay, "The Simple Art of Murder," established a crucial difference between his conception of the hard-boiled genre and the paradigm largely established by Dashiell Hammett and Carroll John Daly in the pages of *Black Mask* magazine in the early 1920s. Although Chandler freely acknowledged his debt to Hammett, the arbitrary world assumed within Hammett's fiction was rarely duplicated in Chandler's novels. Chandler, on the other hand, emphasised the ethical protagonist living in a debased world. His novels clearly recognised a moral universe, even if it was rapidly fading into the past, and the tension and sadness found in his work resulted from the alienation of this man who "is neither tarnished nor afraid . . . a man of honor."

An essential difference between Chandler and Hammett is summarized by the Flitcraft parable in Hammett's *The Maltese Falcon*. In this four-page story Spade tells of a man who suddenly disappears from his middle-class existence for no apparent reason. When the detective finds him five years later the man, Flitcraft, tells Spade that, on the day he decided to leave, a building beam crashed into the pavement right next to him and he "felt like somebody had taken the lid off life and let him look at the works."[2] Up to this point Flitcraft was a model citizen, husband and father, and the "life he knew was a clean, orderly, sane responsible affair. Now a falling beam had shown him that life was fundamentally none of these things."[3] He leaves his home town, works at a variety of jobs, and eventually resumes an identical life style. As Spade explains, Flitcraft "adjusted himself to beams falling, and then no more fell, and he adjusted himself to them not falling."[4]

The arbitrary nature of Flitcraft's—and Spade's—world is evident. A "moral" life counts for nothing when a falling beam can suddenly destroy existence and the parable reveals, as Steven Marcus points out, the "ethical irrationality of existence, the ethical unintelligibility of the world."[5] Chandler, on the other hand, assumes an ethical center to

the universe, even if he cannot find much evidence of it in the world. In 1950 he wrote in the *Saturday Review* that most of the characters of the pulp magazines lived in a world gone wrong:

> . . . a world in which, long before the atom bomb, civilization had created the machinery for its own destruction and was learning to use it with all of the moronic delight of a gangster trying out his first machinegun. The law was something to be manipulated for profit and power. The streets were dark with something more than the night.[6]

The "emotional basis of the hard-boiled story," according to Chandler, was based on the premise that only a "very determined individual"[7] could restore some degree of criminal and moral justice in such a world. This perception of the world produced the characteristic mixture of sadness and indignation in Chandler's fiction, a characteristic that was evident in many of his thirties short stories. *Red Wind,* for example, closes not just with the "solution" to the crime but with the sense of pain and disgust felt by private detective John Dalmas, Marlowe's predecessor, as he walks away from a married woman he is attracted to, after protecting the memory of her dead lover:

> I went out of the bar without looking back at her, got into my car and drove west on Sunset and down all the way to the Coast Highway. Everywhere along the way gardens were full of withered and blackened leaves and flowers which the hot wind had burned.

The sense of futility gradually intensified in Chandler's novels and by 1953, with the publication of *The Long Goodbye,* the surface action and murder-mystery conventions were pushed even further than usual into the background as Chandler concentrates on this "strange corrupt world we live in, and how any man who tried to be honest looks in the end either sentimental or foolish." At the end of the novel Marlowe refuses to renew his friendship with Terry Lennox because Lennox had let a good man die. When Lennox walks away Marlowe watches the door close and listens to the sound of his friend's footsteps:

> After a while they got faint, then they got silent. I kept on listening anyway. What for? Did I want him to stop suddenly and turn and come back and talk me out of the way I felt? Well, he didn't. That was the last I saw of him.

Chandler's detective, and his world of "withered and blackened leaves," has its dramatic roots in the polarised world of melodrama. His detective's perpetual quest for what he calls the "hidden truth" is a journey to reveal the "true" moral condition (expressed through the detective). Chandler's "hidden truth" is similar, in the way it determines the discursive basis of the drama, to the desire in melodrama to recognize and articulate the underlying "moral occult," a term used by Peter Brooks to describe the "domain of operative spiritual values." Brooks argues that the "moral occult" is "both indicated and masked by the surface of reality" and the essential function of this dramatic mode is to establish where guilt and innocence lie. Chandler's fiction shares the same concern, a desire to make the "world morally legible, spelling out its ethical forces and imperatives in large and bold characters."

Goodbye Paradise was initially conceived by scriptwriter Denny Lawrence as a transformation of Raymond Chandler's world to Surfer's Paradise in Queensland. The script by Lawrence and Bob Ellis was filmed in Surfer's Paradise, and surrounding locations, on a budget of $1.1 million in the middle of 1981 under the direction of Carl Schultz. The film clearly shares Chandler's fascination, and disgust, with the glitter and "false" values of the big city, a theme that was particularly evident in Chandler's novel *The Little Sister* (1949) which was partly motivated by his disillusionment with Hollywood following his period as a scriptwriter in the mid-1940s. In *Goodbye Paradise* this is expressed in the film's contempt for politicians, doctors, police, and the alternative cults feeding off the gullible inhabitants of the Gold Coast.

The film also shares Chandler's sense of an inward-looking drama, a drama that is less concerned with the "outer narrative core," the mystery and "whodunit," and more with the personal anxieties and attitudes of the central character. The casting of Australian actor Ray Barrett was a crucial element in shifting the emphasis in this direction. Although there were some initial reservations that he was too old, Barrett's characterisation does not resemble any of the forties productions of Chandler's novels, with Humphrey Bogart, George Montgomery, or Robert Montgomery as Philip Marlowe, or the 1975 American version of *Farewell, My Lovely,* scripted by David Zelag Goodman and directed by Dick Richards. Compare, for example, the opening narration in both films. *Farewell, My Lovely* begins with Marlowe (Robert Mitchum), with a drink in his hand, looking out of a hotel window lined with the characteristic *film noir* outline of a flashing neon light:

> This past Spring was the first I had felt tired and realised I was growing old. Maybe it was the rotten weather we had been having in L.A. . . . Or maybe it was the plain fact that I am tired and growing old. The only real pleasure I'd had at all was following Joe DiMaggio belting the apple at an incredible clip for the New York Yankees.

The tired, disillusioned protagonist, beaten down but not out by a corrupt world, is also evident in the opening scene in *Goodbye Paradise* as an incongruous figure in a shabby white suit, Michael Francis Xavier Stacey, O.B.E., walks along the distinctive Surfer's Paradise beach where the sea quickly gives way to high rise apartments:

> The winter sun was going down on Surfer's Paradise. It was my ninety-eight day on the wagon and it didn't feel any better than my ninety-seventh. I miss my hip flask of Johnny Walker, my ex-wife Jean, my pet dog Samarri and my exorbitant salary as Deputy Commissioner of Police. . . . I wanted to be twelve years old again and the best spin bowler in Southport High. I

wanted a lot of things [the voice-over is interrupted by his landlady's voice]. And so did my landlady, including the rent.

Stacey returns to his old vices when he learns that his publisher has decided not to publish his exposé of the corruption in the Queensland police force. During a night-long drinking binge Stacey encounters old friends, including Kate (Robyn Nevin), his lover from a time "when the world was young," a crooner "who sounded like two old cheese graters fornicating in an iron tank" and Senator Les McCredie (Don Pascoe), a childhood friend and now a local member of Parliament. Stacey finally collapses at an all-male revue in the company of a prostitute (Kris McQuade).

Next morning he receives an invitation to visit McCredie from a couple of his "associates," and Stacey's narration during the speedboat journey to McCredie's house in the film smoothly transforms a familiar convention of the hard-boiled genre. The detective's initial ironic reaction to the material extravagance and decadence in, for example, *The Big Sleep* and *Farewell, My Lovely* becomes a sardonic commentary on the "new rich" waiting to die in the sunshine of the Gold Coast:

> We went up river from the Isle of Capri, past bungalow after bungalow of rich men waiting for the eternal boatman on their summer lawns, avoided the Rialto, turned right at Sorrento, and went on past the portals of Orion into the Shangri-La Estate.

This transformation of recognisable conventions is a feature of *Goodbye Paradise*. Situations, characterisations and setting are reinterpreted through reference to distinctive Australian imagery. For example, a corrupt doctor, a recurring character in Chandler's novels (see, for example, *Farewell My, Lovely* and *The Lady in the Lake*), tells Stacey that "this town [Surfer's Paradise] is what Australians have instead of an after-life . . . they come like Christmas Beetles crawling down the wall to die within the smell of the sea." Similarly, at McCredie's house, Stacey encounters another familiar icon of the hard-boiled fiction and its film noir counterpart, the femme fatale. Stacey's reaction, through his first-person narration, reaffirms the existence of stereotype while appropriating it to an Australian context: McCredie's wife (Kate Fitzpatrick) "looked ten years younger since her hysterectomy and meaner than a beachful of blue bottle."

When McCredie hires Stacey to find his "wild" daughter Cathy, who has absconded with the family Drysdale painting, the film reminds the viewer that it must be read within the context of a specific genre (see *The Big Sleep*). Thus, as expected, the initial investigation proves to be a red herring as the investigator strips away the layers of deceit to uncover the main crime, a right wing attempt to separate the Gold Coast from the rest of Queensland. This, however, merely provides the motivation for the "real" crime, Stacey's personal betrayal by two old friends, a familiar "inward" narrative movement found also in Chandler's novels.

Unfortunately the strong build-up throughout *Goodbye Paradise* is dissipated by a shift in the film's dramatic tone at the climax to the story. While there has been a certain gentle mocking of the hard-boiled conventions throughout the film, *Goodbye Paradise* remains firmly within its generic context, except for the final section when Stacey wanders through a military battle between the rebels and the Australian Army in an alcoholic haze. This sudden shift into an absurdist mode, similar to that used by Robert Altman in *The Long Goodbye* (1973), subverts all expectations established in the body of the film.

A key difference between *Goodbye Paradise* and Altman's *The Long Goodbye* is the consistent attempt in the latter film to present Marlowe as a man completely out of touch with his world and as a complete loser. *Goodbye Paradise*, on the other hand, presents Stacey as a man with certain abilities and, although circumstances and personal weakness have diminished his effectiveness, he is normally able to operate within this corrupt society. He only becomes the fool in the final section. The 1975 version of *Farewell, My Lovely*, on the other hand, includes a similar scene when Marlowe wanders from a brothel in a drug-induced state. Yet this occurs in the middle of the film, thus allowing the detective time to regain his dignity and some sense of control in the climax. Unfortunately Stacey's impotence is presented at the end of the film, a recurring characteristic in Australian films in the 1980s which regularly conclude with a sense of defeat or alienation.

It is not just the farcical nature of the ending, where characters Stacey had encountered during his investigation, such as Kris McQuade's prostitute, now in a military uniform, suddenly reappear, but its failure to fulfill expectations carefully established in the body of the film. For example, when Stacey learns that his former friends had inadvertently killed Kate, the most sympathetic character in the film, with a car bomb meant for him, the melodramatic desire for confrontation and revenge is intense, particularly as his former friends have also kidnapped McCredie's daughter Cathy.

The film, however, subverts these expectations by transforming Stacey into an impotent fool. It is at this point that the film indicates its refusal to acknowledge the detective as saviour hero, a convention expressed in the motif of the knight-errant and hinted at by the name (Mallory) used by Marlowe's predecessor in Chandler's first short story ("Blackmailers Don't Shoot"), derived from Sir Thomas Malory's *Le Morte D'Arthur*. Instead of showing the knight-errant saving the damsel in distress, *Goodbye Paradise* presents the fool, as Stacey travels to Cathy's rescue in a large tourist bus with the words "Midnight Cowboy" written across the side.

Yet the epilogue attempts to re-establish Stacey's dignity and morality. After farewelling Cathy, the film concludes with an affectionate, and undeniably romantic presentation, of Stacey walking along the beach at dawn, with his dog:

> Cathy and I met and talked and parted, the way I knew we had to and she knew too now. And I raised my milkshake to her and wished her good luck and imagined her naked and kindly to my old age one last time and took my bones off into the dawn.
>
> I thought about homes and families and Kate, and everything I'd loved and lost and tasted once and been afraid of ever since I was a schoolboy here in this strange town. I wasn't sadder, or wiser, or perceptibly older, but I knew how old I was. And that was good too, in its own way.

This wistful quality, an approximation of Marlowe's mixture of regret and alienation, is a recurring motif in *Goodbye Paradise* and frequently surfaces in Stacey's desire to recapture the city of his youth:

> I drove past a green and clean Pacific, not yet choked and corrupted with oil, and I thought about things in general, like Arabs and the Americans, and the profit motive and the CIA-backed revolutions and how close they were getting to my home town.

Goodbye Paradise also retains the dual narrative structure that characterises Chandler's novels as the outer narrative structure gradually yields to an inner structure and this inner structure normally contains the central concerns of the work. Thus, while the outer structure provides the initial narrative impetus, and involves the investigator with gangsters, crime, corruption, and victims, the inner structure gradually assumes prominence through the "betraying, personally threatening force" directed at the investigator's private self.

The basis of this inner structure is established early in *Goodbye Paradise* through Stacey's long-running chess game with Quiney (Guy Doleman), a former military colleague, and close friend, in Malaya. Stacey's investigation also leads him to another old friend, Bill Todd (John Clayton), from their days fighting the communists in Malaya. The reunion between Stacey, Quiney and Todd takes place on an empty beach at dawn in front of a giant chess board. The overt link to Chandler is clear at this point as chess is also Philip Marlowe's hobby. When Quiney and Todd ask Stacey to join their coup he declines:

> I've got a bad liver. I'm a shandy off the horrors even on my good days. My old friends are dying off like flies, my wife is on with my lawyer. I'm a tired man.

After receiving their word that neither he nor Cathy will be harmed, Stacey leaves with a promise that he will send them a post card from the "People's Republic of North Victoria" if they are victorious. However the "reunion" is a ruse as Stacey's "friends" place a bomb in his car, the bomb that kills Kate. This betrayal forms the emotional centre of the film and it is particularly disappointing when the subsequent scenes fail to meet the expectations established by this scene, as Stacey never receives the chance to confront his two old friends—Quiney merely disappears off the screen during the final battle and Todd is killed by the army.

This disappointment is not based on the premise that Chandler and the hard-boiled formula is static and somehow inviolable. Instead the objection emanates from the inconsistency of the narrative shift at the end of the film. A recurring feature of the Australian cinema throughout the late 1970s and 1980s is the failure, or lack of desire, to complete the "third act," to fulfil the physical and/or emotional expectations generated in the body of the film. The "non-ending," the muted climax, the emotional estrangement or sense of isolation is a regular feature of this cinema. This, in itself, is not necessarily a weakness, although the chosen dramatic context, melodrama, normally demands a strong, cathartic climax that removes all the obstacles and blockages to desire. Whilst the re-establishment of a moral universe is not always possible in a hard-boiled world, the story normally clarifies the ethical basis of this world through the actions of the detective ("It is not a very fragrant world, but it is the world you live in").

Except for the vital lapse at the climax of the film, *Goodbye Paradise* reworks the genre, and its melodramatic basis, into an effective evocation of a confused society caught between the dubious values of the past and the corrupt values of the future. The past is represented by Stacey and Quiney, the military leader of the coup—at once both repressive and idealistic, fighting in their different ways to retain the past. Todd, on the other hand, is associated with the superficial values of the present and future (represented in a parodic form in a religious cult and alternative culture). The present is also represented by an all-male revue, prostitution, scheming wives (Mrs. McCredie who wants to be leader of the breakaway Gold Coast), corrupt police and opportunistic politicians: the film was produced when Premier Jo Bjelke-Petersen's National Party controlled Queensland. No wonder Stacey merely wants to walk along the beach with his dog whilst dreaming of being the best spin bowler at Southport High.

Three years after *Goodbye Paradise,* another Australian film based on the conventions of the hard-boiled detective genre, was released. *The Empty Beach* (1985), based on the fourth Cliff Hardy novel written by Australia's best exponent of the genre, Peter Corris, did not utilise the characteristic first-person narration. Although there have been a number of fine detective films that have ignored this expressive technique (including *The Big Sleep* and *Chinatown*), it is an effective way of establishing an imaginative bond between the detective and the audience, particularly as his point of view is a crucial element in the presentation. His narration normally contains not only descriptions of character, setting and events, but also a distinctively alienated, ironic world view.

This loss is apparent in the opening minutes of the film. The novel begins with Hardy's reaction to the people surfing in front of the Regal Hotel in Bondi:

> They looked frail, as if the sea was playing around with them rather than the other way around. Any

minute, it seemed, the water could rise up and obliterate them. But the sun was shining and the sand glowed; some of the pale people were turning pink and it was no time for glum thoughts. I took two lungfuls of the ozone and still wanted a cigarette.

Whilst the film presents the basic action, Hardy's arrival at the Regal Hotel, without this narration, fails to communicate the detective's reaction to the people on the beach and appears more like a travelogue or television commercial as Hardy wanders amongst the bronze bodies. More important, the smell of fear ("it seemed, the water could rise up and obliterate them"), and the detective's alienation ("I took two lungfuls of the ozone and still wanted a cigarette") is absent from this presentation.

The division between the detective's public and private voice, as Stephen Knight points out, is extremely important in Chandler's work. Marlowe's meditations are shared only with the audience, not the other characters, and are "both subtle and ironic":

> When speaking to the reader his sensitive humanity shows through, however much he ironically protects it. But to the people he meets in the action he is uniformly tough and insensitive: to them he is witty in ways that are aggressive, clipped, unimaginative, even relentless. In fact a lot of the time Marlowe says little; he just responds with an ironic grin and lets the other person flounder.

The same is true of the film. Without the use of voice-over, Cliff Hardy (Bryan Brown) comes across as an introverted observer intermittently delivering smart remarks and pseudo-tough threats.

This decision also weakens the presentation of the special relationship between the detective and his world, the large, threatening, impersonal city. While Roman Polanski in *Chinatown* and Howard Hawks in *The Big Sleep* compensate for the lack of first-person narration by suggesting a hostile world through a combination of music, imagery and performances, the film version of *The Empty Beach* fails to match Corris's expressive description of the "mean streets." For example, when Hardy follows a lead to a building in Clovelly, the film cuts from the man providing the information to a long shot of a solitary building at night, accompanied by a couple of ominous chords on the soundtrack. The imagery created by the novel, on the other hand, reinforces the detective's sense of threat and alienation:

> Clovelly is a headland tucked in south of Bronte and east of Randwick. It's a bit like those two suburbs, but down market on both of them. The flats are a bit meaner, the house fronts and the streets narrower. Monk Lane was thin, twisted and a dead end. . . . A sheer rock wall with some creeper clinging to it rose up behind the house, which was three storeys high, heavy ungracious.

> . . . It was a forbidding pile.

Causality, and a smooth narrative flow, was never Chandler's strong point. His well-documented habit of "cannibalising" material from his short stories for his novels often resulted in strong atmospheric individual scenes and a certain looseness in the over-all narrative structure together with a vague sense of time. The same comment is essentially true of Corris's novel. The "mystery" as to whether a man who supposedly drowned is still alive is merely a premise to explore character interaction and contemporary attitudes within a generic framework. Yet there is also a dramatic logic in Corris's story as Hardy's investigation exposes political corruption, welfare fraud and organised crime in Sydney. Yet, like Chandler, Corris constantly moves the story from the action, the outer structure, to the inner, personal, structure.

The film, on the other hand, stays with the surface or outer structure of Hardy's world through its emphasis on the action, not reaction of the detective. This is reinforced by addition to the film of a plot concerning a missing audio tape linking "respectable" members of the community with underworld figures. This, in turn, deflects attention from the detective and his personal reaction to the action set-pieces involving a surfboard killing and a car chase, neither of which is in the novel.

A comparison between the way in which both present the first murder in the film illustrates the essential difference between the novel and the film. Hardy's investigation into the disappearance of underworld figure John Singer takes him to "The Punk Palace of Fun," a pinball parlour. Outside of the parlour Hardy is rescued from a beating by Bruce Henneberry, a freelance journalist, and the detective forms a brief relationship with the journalist. This is subsequently severed by the latter's death and, whilst the film transforms the incident into an emotionally bland piece of action as Henneberry is stabbed whilst surfing, the novel shifts the emphasis from the action, the killing, to Hardy's reaction to Henneberry's mutilated body. Sickened, Hardy walks into the dead man's bathroom to wash the blood off his hands:

> I looked at my face in the mirror. I'd been sweating and my hair flopped down lankly onto my forehead. I was blinking convulsively and the search had given me a fixed, long-faced look, like a wax dummy. If someone had walked in, put a knife in my hand and said, "He did it," I'd have believed it.

The film further weakens the narrative logic, and dramatic impact, of the novel by reversing two set-pieces in the story, the kidnapping of Hardy and his imprisonment in the Monk Lane building. In the novel, Hardy is kidnapped and taken to a criminal's rural property at Camden. He eventually escapes and later in the story he comes across a scheme whereby pensioners are imprisoned in a large house in Monk Lane, where they are drugged, fed on pet food and robbed of their pension cheques. Corris's gothic description of the house, with sickness and insanity in every room and bodies buried in the back garden, provides a powerful climax to one of the central narrative strands in

the book. The film, on the other hand, reverses this order and presents the Monk Lane episode before the abduction to Camden and this removes an effective emotional climax to the story. In its place is a predictable action piece involving the detective's escape from Camden.

The novel's inner structure culminates in the revelation that Hardy's client, Singer's wife, has used the detective to destroy her criminal rivals so that she can control the gambling and other illicit activities in Sydney. This is achieved in the climax to the story when Hardy orchestrates a shoot-out between Ward and McLeary, Marion Singer's underworld competitors. Whilst the emphasis in the film is on the shoot-out, the novel is more concerned with the betrayal. When she offers Hardy $50,000 to investigate a story that her husband was seen in Bangkok with a woman, the novel concludes with the detective expressing his personal morality and his indignation ("No, I said") in the final line.

The film's attempt to present the moral superiority of the detective is conveyed through a romantic subplot between Hardy and Ann Winter, a university student working amongst the prostitutes, alcoholics, and drug addicts in the Bondi area. Whereas the novel maintains the ambiguity and sexual tension between the two characters through to an inconclusive ending, the film closes on the characteristic (at least in terms of the Australian cinema) hostility and estrangement between the sexes. Similarly the motivation for this falling out is poorly developed in the film, except for a brief scene where Winter refuses to release the mysterious tape because of her father's involvement. At the end of the film, after rejecting Marion Singer's offer, Hardy walks past Winter and virtually ignores her except for a cold comment ("enjoy your lunch"). Again this is poorly motivated as Winter has demonstrated her goodwill by releasing the tapes. Instead of reinforcing the detective's moral code, Hardy appears merely petulant.

A superficial study of the Australian cinema in the 1980s may conclude, based on the enormous commercial success of *Crocodile Dundee* and, to a lesser extent, *The Man from Snowy River,* that an optimistic, populist strain was the norm. In quantitative terms at least, both films, and their sequels, are aberrations, especially in terms of their optimistic, clear-cut endings. In fact the Australian cinema, at least since *Picnic At Hanging Rock,* has frequently tried to assimilate the characteristic ambiguity and "open" endings of the "art cinema" with the basic appeal of the classical narrative form.

This is largely a result of the desire to assert the independence and "difference" of Australian films from those associated with Hollywood. However, *Goodbye Paradise* is a clear demonstration that popular genres and melodrama are available to all film cultures and need not produce a compromised work. Although *Goodbye Paradise* is far more successful than *The Empty Beach* in transforming Chandler's dual narrative structure, by utilising the outer structure, the right wing conspiracy, as a way of exploring aspects of contemporary Australian culture, neither film could be accurately accused of perpetuating the dreaded "mid-Atlantic" model, the pseudo-American prototype that periodically infects the local industry (see, for example, *Color Me Dead*, 1970, *Sidecar Racers*, 1975, and *The Return of Captain Invincible*, 1982).

A significant difference between the Australian films and Chandler resides in the recurring assumption, or hope, of redemption in the latter. This is a much less significant factor in the Australian films, although it may simply be explained by the fact that Chandler was writing forty years earlier as this aspect is not as prominent in contemporary America's authors working within this tradition today, such as Stephen Greenleaf and Robert Parker. Nevertheless, Chandler's strong sense of alienation and cynicism complements the Australian cinema of the 1980s, although the power of the individual to combat this immoral condition appears to be significantly reduced as the "knight" is increasingly tarnished by the world around him.

Notes

1. Raymond Chandler, *The Simple Art of Murder* (London: Hamish Hamilton, 1950) 14.

2. Dashiell Hammett, *The Maltese Falcon* (London: Pan Books, 1975) 59.

3. Ibid 59.

4. Ibid 60.

5. Stephen Marcus, "Introduction," *The Continental Op* (London: Pan Books, 1977) 14.

6. Reprinted in Raymond Chandler, *Pearls Are a Nuisance* (Harmondsworth: Penguin Books, 1973) 7.

7. Ibid 8.

WOMEN AND HARD-BOILED FICTION

Robert Sandels (essay date fall 1989)

SOURCE: Sandels, Robert. "It Was a Man's World." *Armchair Detective* 22, no. 4 (fall 1989): 388-96.

[*In the following essay, Sandels explores the characterization of Sara Paretsky's V. I. Warshawski in several of her novels, noting that, despite Warshawski's feminist tendencies, she has much in common with her male counterparts.*]

Contemporary writers such as Sara Paretsky, Sue Grafton, and Marcia Muller are only a few of the growing number of female authors who have developed female private eye characters in recent years. Lady detectives are, of course,

nothing new. Nor is the feminism implicit in their choice of profession new. What is new, of course, is the imitation of the violent and cynical male hardboiled detective. Dorothy Sayers, Agatha Christie, and Amanda Cross represent a more genteel tradition of female detection which stretches back into the nineteenth century and the writing of Anna Katherine Green. That tradition reminds us, however, of the limitations which culture and the market have always placed upon the feminism of those intellectual puzzle mysteries and places now on the contemporary tough-guy adventures of female private eyes.[1]

To become a sleuth at all is to impose oneself upon the world. Successful detection alters the course of social events, forcing courts and police to bow to the superior art of the detective. For the female sleuth, therefore, detection offers possibilities for her advancement toward full equality. Typically, however, female writers have restrained the feminism of their characters within the acceptable gender boundaries of their times. Thus, during mystery fiction's Golden Age, the female sleuth might be the busybody spinster—hardly a powerful feminist model. Somehow the absurdity of aging spinsters or sixteen-year-old girls in blue roadsters solving murders never mattered much to readers of Miss Marple or Nancy Drew. And that is probably because these books were absurd in a manner which was in harmony with the roles assigned to women. Indeed, it seems clear that the idea of a woman as sleuth in the fashion of Miss Marple was itself a deeply sexist one inasmuch as she succeeded because the crimes she unraveled were those that only someone regarded as a "fluffy and dithery octogenarian"[2] could solve. These were not real crimes anyway, we would say, but playacting be villages full of characters produced especially for the deprived and hallucinatory mind of lonely or obsessed women. How convenient that in Christie's *What Mrs. McGillicuddy Saw!* the body tossed from the train lands practically at the doorstep of the nearly infirm Miss Marple, that the case is soluble only with a knowledge of maps and train schedules, and that Miss Marple has a nephew with British Railways and an acquaintance who is deeply into maps.

Far from flinging herself upon the world in a way which would alter its perceptions of women, Miss Marple confirms women's marginality to the world. Everything about her antique and cluttered tearoom adventures suggests stasis and limits—the physical and spiritual imprisonment of the sleuth within the very puzzle she attempts to solve. Much of the mystery fiction of the Golden Age, whether featuring male or female sleuths, was constructed along similar lines. After all, who is a better example of the aging spinster detective than Hercule Poirot himself?

Even some contemporary women writers offering feminist perspectives have not flung themselves upon a male-built world. In the exquisitely crafted novels of Amanda Cross, for example, Kate Fansler and her circle are literate people at literary play. Fansler's feminist message seems faint because it refers to a nonexistent world in which everyone has read James Joyce.

If P. D. James's characters found detection an unsuitable job for Cordelia Gray, it was certainly not because there were no precedents in genteel lady sleuths but because Cordelia Gray proposed to work in the "real" world of crime. For a woman to do "real" detection would mean that she must uproot herself from the garden of the country home and invade the world with the same direct power and recklessness that men employ.

The development of the hardboiled school, therefore, had the effect of virtually excluding female detectives for the first time in the history of the genre. E. R. Hagemann's index to *Black Mask*³ shows no women series characters in the magazine's 31-year history.⁴ The solution to crimes of the real world did not yet depend on some vaguely laughable faculty of the mysterious and irrelevant mind of the rooted female. The disorderly world of the hardboiled detective was far removed from railway-timetable crimes.

If the hardboiled school represents a masculine search for order through violent struggle, then a female detective venturing into it must either adopt those methods—thus effectively cancelling out any feminist alternative—or she must re-create the genre in her own image. Feminist writers can avoid both difficulties by having their female sleuths rely upon a man to take over when her powers of detection fail. In *Gaudy Night*, Dorothy Sayers's strong-willed and independent Harriet Vane flounders about at Shrewsbury College, unable to make headway in the case of the nasty letters. In desperation, she sends for Lord Peter Wimsey: "I wish to God you were here and could tell me what to do." Abject capitulation like this will not be seen in Sara Paretsky's female private eye, V. I. Warshawski.⁵ After many encounters with thugs and gangsters in *Indemnity Only*, she visits her lover in the hospital, where he is recovering from a bullet wound he never would have received had he listened to her. "I've been falling in love with you," he says, "but you don't need me." V. I. and the reader agree with him, and so ends the relationship.

V. I. Warshawski's toughness—indeed, her very presence in the world of "real" crime—invites us to wonder if she too has not abandoned any feminist alternative to the masculine, hardboiled world.

Lawrence Block has observed that the private eye should be a cynical loner, a man at odds with society and its values:

> That's not something women normally relate to. Women aren't cynical loners. . . . [I]f they want to go into the profession seriously, women writers will have to change the myth itself, instead of trying to fit themselves into it.⁶

What sets writers like Paretsky apart from the Christie-Sayers tradition is their attempt to adopt the trappings of the conventional detective-hero myth and alter it at the same time. Paretsky writes self-consciously within the hardboiled tradition—so much so that in her first two books she comes close to parody. Her books are littered

with such conventions as the fight ended by a blow to the head stoically endured by the detective and the "ride" to confront the underworld boss whom she defies with brave jests. In the 261 pages of the paperback edition of *Deadlock,* there are fifty mentions of drink or drinking and thirty mentions of cars or driving. To cement the kinship with the male private eyes, V. I. works out of a downtown Chicago office in the execrable Pulteney building, with its tired elevators and pitted marble walls. In *Deadlock,* V. I. takes a minor character all the way downtown for a five-minute conversation for no other purpose than to permit us to see the female detective in the ancient male habitat and to watch the neon sign across the street blink on and off. Paretsky has borrowed all her symbols of professional authenticity from a male myth, updated to allow for Warshawski's jogging, her reading of the *Wall Street Journal,* and her brand-name consumerism. After a corpse has been taken away in *Deadlock,* Warshawski offers the bereaved widow of the murdered man a ride in her car—a miserable Mercury Lynx—and tells us, as an aside, that she would love to have "something really wonderful, like an Audi Quarto."

All this invites the reader to dismiss V. I. as a Frankenstein's monster put together from the bodies of male detectives long dead and a few female shoppers. Why employ the remnants of a thoroughly masculine myth so often used by detectives of the past? Paretsky's purpose, it appears, is to transfer the still usable values of the old male private eye to a female detective: his suspicion of the rich and privileged, his reliance on proletarian simplicity, his directness of speech, his sense of personal calling. "I can't try explaining to you tonight," says V. I., "why this is my job—but please believe me that it is my job and that I can't give it to the police and run away." A more direct paraphrasing of this heroic cliché might be: "There are some things a woman just has got to do." Even the traditional resolution through violence remains. Though Warshawski does not employ violence as the chief method of investigation, so commonly used by her contemporary, Robert B. Parker's Spenser, she manages to maneuver events so that other forces kill villains for her.

An example of how Paretsky alters the male myth can be found in *Deadlock.* The chief villain is a rich, powerful, sexist male. But she discovers that two others are guilty of crimes for which the law has no punishment—and both are women. Mrs. Phillips and her sister, Paige Carrington, have used their sexuality to drive men to crime and to their deaths. Here women seem to be up to their old tricks, for Mr. Phillips commits crimes to keep his wife and daughter well clothed in designer garments. In devising so hideous a female criminal, Paretsky has first established her detective both as a feminist and as a tough private detective. Warshawski is free to accuse men of ruthlessly seeking power and to accuse women of the parallel crime of ruthlessly pursuing vanity. Paretsky's women are not innocent any more than were Mickey Spillane's men. Paretsky's guilty women commit their "crimes" out of precisely the same set of supposed, almost mythical, feminine weaknesses so often found in the writings of the founding fathers of hardboiled fiction.

In her study of the professional female private detective, Kathleen Gregory Klein notes that Paretsky's detective is not a cynical loner at all and that her chief feminist contribution is to reveal the "secrets which the [masculine] system would keep hidden . . . to share information with those who have been systematically uninformed."[7] Whether or not the acquisition of self-awareness has the healing or revolutionary effect which Freud and Marx claimed for it, is open to debate. But, no matter how much Warshawski peels back the layers of greed or corruption in the various institutions she approaches, she never quite confronts those institutions. Warshawski often exposes the crimes of powerful men, but nothing she does is subversive and threatening to the system. While she solves corporate crimes from deep within the system, she does not suggest that crime is characteristically endemic to that system but specific to the individuals working in it. The institutions themselves seem morally neutral instruments, susceptible to criminal manipulation whether in the hands of men or women.

In each of her cases, as Klein has pointed out, Warshawski pries into male-dominated institutions: banking, shipping, organized religion, and medicine.[8] In sharp contrast to the female snoops of the puzzle mystery, who confined themselves to safe inquiries around the edges of their "gardens," we find V. I. entering the forbidden chambers of male power as though seeking its sexual sources. We find her gazing at the files of business executives and descending into the engine room of a grain freighter—where, by ancient custom, no woman must go. In one book, she looks for an archbishop's dark secrets in his monastic cell and hides under his bed. When V. I. beats up that same archbishop and kills a business magnate on his own motorboat, we know that we are witnessing a counterattack on male power and privilege made possible by a Promethean theft of its exalted and mystifying knowledge. It is not the street criminal, after all, that Warshawski chases. She is an investigator of business crimes that take place on the thirteenth floor.

The intriguing thing about this kind of feminist exploration within the male world is that it offers the opportunity to go beyond the world-weary cynicism of the traditional male private eye who knew nothing at all except that everybody is corrupt. While male private eyes long before had understood that crime existed within the legitimate order itself, they generally applied their intelligence to the streets, confident that little could be done to eradicate crime from the places of power. Even wiping out the gangsters who controlled an entire city gave the Continental Op little satisfaction in Dashiell Hammett's *Red Harvest*, for he knew that nothing he did had cured Personville of its sickness. The Op knew how the mind of the cheap crook worked. Warshawski, by contrast, seizes documentary knowledge of how the ruling institutions of society work.

Yet there is a curious absence of criticism of the institutions with which Warshawski's criminals are associated

and which are the sources of their malevolent power. The greedy shipping magnate is balanced off by a rival of opposite tendencies. The crimes of one doctor are contrasted with the selfless dedication of another. The corrupt hospital is contrasted with an honest one. The establishment criminals whom V. I. tracks down are generally money manipulators doing what they do out of greed for the same kinds of material goods which Warshawski covets in smaller quantities. Bankers want more money, shipping magnates want more ships, and so forth. Yet their power to do mischief comes from the same male-dominated institutions which Warshawski, armed with her knowledge, presumably must attack if she is to do any good.

V. I.'s feminist messages then, are not addressed to these great centers of institutionalized male power. They take a more subtle form than harangues against the agencies and instruments of patriarchy. The institution with which V. I. seems most concerned is not the male-dominated Catholic Church or bank but the family—the one established institution which in the 1980s cannot properly be considered patriarchal.

The mean streets of the hardboiled city lead into the living rooms of its suburbs, where men such as Dr. Paciorek in *Killing Orders* become wealthy providers and absent husbands and fathers; where women like Mrs. Paciorek turn away from both domesticity and career to embrace remote causes. "I should have spent more time at home," observes Mr. Paciorek, and Mrs. Paciorek "should have had her own career."

Warshawski does not find "true guilt" within the great institutions of the partiarchal monster but within the men and women who commit the invisible crimes of everyday existence. The murderers go off to prison, leaving V. I. to decide what is to be done with such people as Paige Carrington, whose fear of being seen in old dresses has led to murder.

The family is a "myth" to V. I. Few people, she observes, "live like an advertisement, with golden harmony, and enough money. . . . I'm feeling a longing for a myth, not the reality." The "real" families in Paretsky's novels are usually depressing caricatures. Thayer, the crooked banker in *Indemnity Only*, has spawned a nest of vipers. McGraw, the crooked union leader, has contributed to the death of his daughter's lover. The wives are no better, as we have seen in the example of Mrs. Phillips, whose discontent with her husband's $90,000-a-year salary drove him into crime. In *Bitter Medicine*, V. I. meets Mrs. Alvarado, a "passive woman who runs her guilt-filled bus over the nearest passerby." The woman's daughter, Consuelo, probably would not have gotten pregnant by a tragically wrong man, V. I. thinks, nor died in childbirth, "if she hadn't had an earful of 'Thank God your father died instead of living to see you do x or y or z.'" Every Paretsky novel has its wounded family, and V. I. throws herself into its private nightmares even though she is never hired to do so.

What lies at the heart of V. I.'s job is as much family therapy as it is traditional detection. She offers herself as surrogate mother, sister, or daughter to those in need of one. She takes fourteen-year-old Jill Thayer out of her parents' destructive household in *Indemnity Only,* so that she and her own surrogate mother, a physician friend, Lotty, can create a loving, artificial family.

Indeed, V. I. is a troubled daughter herself, and we are made to feel that her detection is motivated by a wish to discover the sources of her own family's guilt. In the first three novels, her relationship to her dead mother, Gabriella, is a strong sub-theme and emerges in *Killing Orders* as a more interesting story than the somewhat contrived plot concerning clergymen, gangsters, and missing bonds. *Killing Orders* begins with her visit to a detested aunt whom she would never see but for her mother's deathbed request. It ends with the revelation from the lips of the aunt, driven crazy by years of rage, that her husband had killed himself after an affair with Gabriella. *Killing Orders* is an exploration of residual guilt within the detective's own family: the aunt's guilt for turning V. I.'s mother—a young immigrant—out into the Chicago winter with no money and no English; Gabriella's guilt over the affair and suicide; V. I.'s guilt for her hatred and hostility, which contributed in no small measure to her aunt's madness.

Paretsky's novels seem less social than familial, less subversive than confessional. Her detective seems more concerned with emotional perfection and material satisfaction than with raising questions about the structures of society which her villains inhabit. In these things, she has much in common with contemporary male writers. Charles Nicol points out the similarity in Paretsky, Robert B. Parker, John D. MacDonald, and other writers whose detectives share an interest in physical fitness, in consumption of approved consumer goods, and in a ceaseless search for personal growth and emotional enrichment. Contemporary detectives—male and female—he makes clear, are not the same as the hardboiled prototypes of the 1930s. The hardboiled detective, says Nicol, "is a reflection of America and America itself has changed. Our current concerns are ourselves and our families, which are in pretty bad shape."[9]

In her most recent adventure (*Blood Shot,* 1988), Warshawski sets out to find the unknown father of a childhood friend whose mother is dying after years of toil in a South Chicago chemical plant. V. I. explores industrial toxins and corporate culpability, and these are linked to the toxins of the family and family culpability. By now she has all but given up the studied hardboiled manner of *Indemnity Only*—hardly setting foot in the classical detective office these days. That environment clashes too much with V. I.'s evolving concern with relationships and emotional states.

The industrial villains she tries to expose are mirrored by the quiet crimes of monstrous parents who nearly wreck their daughter's life, condemning her for a teen pregnancy while condoning the behavior of the mystery father. In *Blood Shot,* V. I.'s client is part of the growing Warshawski extended "family." Although still a paper trail P.I. with a business-world clientele, she seems headed for a specialty in family practice. Sorting out who fathered whom, she helps her client discover her own identity in life while strengthening their sisterly ties. Along the way, she pries a spinster loose from sixty years with a pathetically weak yet domineering brother. Embarked at last on a new life, the elderly woman tells V. I., "You're the one who made it possible, showing me how a woman can live an independent life."

Just as feminist writers of the puzzle mystery tradition stayed close to the thinking of their time, current feminist writers of detective fiction reflect what has already become acceptable. The female private eye has not so much feminized the detective business as she has secured an equal-opportunity position in a literary genre already infused with her values. It must be axiomatic that no detective is employed to upset a social order that has not already begun to collapse—that all detectives are essentially conservative. We must not expect them to radically change society with fundamental attacks on "the system." Order—not the detective as subversive—is what one sees reflected in detective fiction.

Notes

1. See Patricia Craig and Mary Cadogan, *The Lady Investigates: Women Detectives and Spies in Fiction* (New York: St. Martin's Press, 1981); Michele B. Slung, ed., *Crime on Her Mind: Fifteen Stories of Female Sleuths from the Victorian Age to the Forties* (New York: Pantheon, 1975); Bobbie Ann Mason, *The Girl Sleuth: A Feminist Guide* (Old Westbury, N.Y.: The Feminist Press, 1975).

2. Agatha Christie's description of Miss Marple in *What Mrs. McGillicuddy Saw!*

3. E. R. Hagemann, *A Comprehensive Index to "Black Mask," 1920-1951* (Bowling Green, Ohio: Bowling Green State University Popular Press, 1982).

4. Cited in Marcia Muller's preface to Bernard Drew, ed., *Hard-Boiled Dames* (New York: St. Martin's Press, 1986), p. xiii.

5. Sara Paretsky, *Indemnity Only* (Dial, 1982; Ballantine, 1983) *Deadlock* (Dial, 1984; Ballantine, 1985) *Killing Orders* (Dial, 1985; Ballantine, 1986) *Bitter Medicine* (Morrow, 1987).

6. Quoted in Marilyn Stasio, "Lady Gumshoes: Boiled Less Hard," *New York Times Book Review,* April 28, 1985.

7. Kathleen Gregory Klein, unpublished manuscript, pp. 324, 325. I wish to thank Professor Klein for letting me read this section of her forthcoming book.

8. *Ibid.*

9. Charles Nicol, "The Hard-Boiled Go To Brunch," *Harper's Magazine,* October 1987, p. 62.

Timothy Shuker-Haines and Martha M. Umphrey (essay date 1998)

SOURCE: Shuker-Haines, Timothy and Martha M. Umphrey. "Gender (De)Mystified: Resistance and Recuperation in Hard-Boiled Female Detective Fiction." In *The Detective in American Fiction, Film, and Television*, edited by Jerome H. Delamater and Ruth Prigozy, pp. 71-82. Westport, CT: Greenwood Press, 1998.

[*In the following essay, Shuker-Haines and Umphrey explore the respective characterizations of Sara Paretsky's V. I. Warshawski and Sue Grafton's Kinsey Millhone, drawing some conclusions about the general attributes of feminist hard-boiled fiction.*]

What should we make of the recent emergence of the female hard-boiled detective? In a literary-historical sense she is an oxymoron, standing outside the gendered traditions of both the classic female detective and the tough-guy dick. The classic archetype, a Miss Marple or a Jessica Fletcher, generally operates within the domestic sphere, solving drawing-room crimes and reestablishing harmony through a combination of skillful listening, good sense, and intuitive judgment about character.[1] She uses her social knowledge and skills to identify the criminal and thus locate the source of social disruption, purifying and restabilizing society. The hard-boiled detective stands in stark opposition to this female figure. His locale is not the drawing room but the liminal zone of the criminal underworld, and his qualities are not intuition and social knowledge but violence and a personal code of honor. Whereas the classic detective novel presents a stable social order with an isolated crime, hard-boiled fiction presents a world filled with corruption, destabilized by the dangerous allure of female sexuality. With his strict code of honor and renunciation, the hard-boiled hero embodies a vision of righteousness and justice.[2]

The hard-boiled detective would thus appear to be a necessarily male figure, defined by his emphasis on violence, individuation, and horror of female sexuality. David Glover (1989) has argued that the hard-boiled tradition was developed as a masculine reclaiming of the detective novel, which was seen as overly feminized, dominated by detectives who were female (Miss Marple, Harriet Vane) or insufficiently masculine (Hercule Poirot, Peter Wimsey). Thus, the gender confusion inherent in the female hard-boiled detective has the potential to destabilize radically this gendered opposition between classic and hard-boiled detective fiction by problematizing both the construction of the detective and the socially restorative function of detection.

Yet these potentials are not consistently realized when the detective's sex is changed, as a comparison of Sue Grafton's *"F" Is for Fugitive* and Sara Paretsky's *Blood Shot* reveals. Each novel foregrounds gender as central to both the construction of the detective and the development of the narrative. Yet each writer uses gender differently.

Grafton's Kinsey Millhone undermines the relation between gender and biological sex, emphasizing gender's performative nature, but she does so by leaving intact masculinity and feminity—and their hierarchical relation. Paretsky's V. I. Warshawski, on the other hand, presents a valorized female self that enables her to reject both traditional feminine and masculine positions and to offer a critique of male power formations from a feminist perspective, opening up the utopian possibility of community without gender hierarchy. Yet this very utopian vision is based on an uncritical acceptance of the concept of a unified "woman's" identity and community.

Gender relates to the figure of the female hard-boiled detective in complicated and contradictory ways. Initially, both Millhone and Warshawski identify themselves as autonomous and ungendered, and their names reflect this identity metonymically. "Kinsey," Millhone's mother's last name, is ambiguous in gender. "V. I.," on the other hand, stands for "Victoria Iphigenia," an explicitly feminized name that echoes V. I.'s Italian mother's side; yet V. I. rejects that name, allowing her friends to call her, if anything, "Vic." In contrast, hostile acquaintances who want her to circumscribe her activities and behave more like a proper woman (for example, Sergeant Mallory, an old family friend) call her "Vicki." Both "Kinsey" and "Vic" thus operate as ungendered and single-word identifiers that circulate as de facto masculine signifiers in a tough world off-limits to femininity.

At the same time, though, both Millhone and Warshawski identify themselves relationally, either positively or negatively, in a way that accords more with "the feminine" as socially defined.[3] Millhone describes herself in the opening pages of *"F" Is for Fugitive* as "thirty-two years old, twice married, no kids, currently unattached and likely to remain so given my disposition, which is cautious at best" (FF [*"F" Is for Fugitive*] 3).[4] This description both assumes the primacy of the relational (the male hard-boiled dick could omit his marital status because his bachelorhood would be taken for granted) and rejects it so as to emphasize autonomy.

Warshawski opens her narrative with memories—memories of her childhood in South Chicago and of the people who lived next door while she grew up, the mother-daughter family of Djiaks. Throughout the book she thinks of herself in terms of this former context, especially as it evokes memories of her mother, Gabriella, who once defended the unmarried and pregnant Louisa Djiak from the righteous wrath of her neighbors. Thus, while not explicitly gendering herself, Warshawski is gendered feminine twice over: once as she is constituted in relation to others rather than as contextless and unbound, and again as she reads her identity through the lens of a female community.

In other words, both Millhone and Warshawski remain inscribed to some extent within categories of masculinity and femininity as they are socially constructed. Yet, the strategies mobilized by each to grapple with this gendering differ: Millhone operates independently and remains within a binary heterosexual economy, oscillating between masculine and feminine subject positions; Warshawski uses a mediating, homosocial network of female friends and family to redefine the paradigm of "femininity" via an implicit feminist critique. And just as Warshawski ruptures the heterosexual binary that Millhone caricatures but leaves intact, *Blood Shot* challenges the socially reconstitutive role of detective fiction that *"F" Is for Fugitive* ultimately accepts.

Kinsey Millhone's persona is gendered substantially as masculine. A woman who has few friends and lives for her work, she is self-consciously, almost parodically male-defined, as, for example, when she describes her tendency to amuse herself with the abridged California Penal code and textbooks on auto theft (FF 209) rather than engaging in the teatime gossip of a Miss Marple. This masculine stylization and thus her identification with male hard-boiled dicks are perhaps clearest in relation to her gun: "I sat at the kitchen table, loaded seven cartridges in the clip and smacked it home. This was my new handgun. A Davis .32 chrome and walnut with a five-and-a-quarter inch barrel. . . . This one weighed a tidy twenty-two ounces and already felt like an old friend" (FF 149). The gun, described here in such loving detail, becomes a fetishized "old friend" with clear phallic overtones. Millhone's strong identification with her male precursors is further reinforced in this scene by the setting—vapor street-lights filtering through the window, the neon vacancy sign sputtering red light into the room—which has become associated with the hard-boiled tradition through film noir's visual conventions (Place and Peterson 1976; Schrader 1986; Hirsch 1981).

Yet, crucial to Millhone's construction is the psychological mutability of gender, its discontinuity and oscillation. "There was something enormously appealing," she remarks early in the book, "in the idea of setting one persona aside and constructing a second to take its place" (FF 19). She ably plays the feminine role when appropriate, particularly in the context of the heterosexual romance. When she and Dwight Shales, a potential suspect, have dinner for example, they discuss their leisure activities (his is backpacking, hers the penal code); but as the scene grows more intimate she quickly shifts gears: "I listened with both eyes and one ear trying to discern what was really going on. . . . While his mouth made noises . . . his eyes said something else. I disconnected my brain and fine-tuned my receiver, picking up his code. This man was emotionally available" (FF 209). Most notable about this passage is the extremity of the gender switch: She disconnects the "male" logic of her brain so as to engage her "female" sexual intuition; she moves from the penal code to sexual dalliance.[5] Thus, even as she refuses the biological "naturalness" of gender identity in this oscillation, she remains caught within a heterosexual economy that posits two distinct genders (so distinct as to be parodic), unwilling to escape or reimagine the gender roles that define them.

Just as Millhone's character is grounded in the heterosexual binary, so too is the narrative of *"F" Is for Fugitive*, which centers on the psychic dramas of two groups: Daughters yearning for paternal love and patriarchs succumbing to the temptations of illicit sex. Millhone is called into a small town to investigate the murder of Jean Timberlake, the promiscuous, illegitimate daughter of Shana Timberlake, "the town roundheel." The town's leading citizens (men, of course) come under suspicion as Millhone discovers that each was sexually involved with either Jean or Shana. Doctor Dunne, the town physician, turns out to have been Jean's father. Reverend Haws, the minister at the town's only church, had sex with Jean every week in his office before choir practice. Shales, the high school principal, had gotten Jean pregnant just before her death. With the pillars of society thus implicated in a young girl's demise, the way is open for a critique of the sexual oppression and abuse of women.

Yet, rather than condemning the men's behavior, Millhone forgives it. All these men had wives with failing bodies or minds—Mrs. Dunne had paranoid schizophrenia; Mrs. Shales, multiple sclerosis; Mrs. Haws, a serious skin condition. Millhone views these women as do their husbands—with pity, contempt, and revulsion. By pathologizing the female body, Millhone identifies with and forgives the men driven by such extreme circumstances to extra-marital sex.

Male innocence is further reinforced by the overwhelming power of female promiscuity and sexual aggression. Millhone describes Shana, for example, as "exhibitionistic" when she dances in the local bar and notes how Shana has "no modesty at all" (FF 128). Jean is seen as the instigator in her affairs with both Haws and Shales and is described as "insatiable," driven by "a need to dominate." "We were at her mercy," one of her high school paramours says, "because we wanted her so much" (FF 118). This focus on Jean's sexual power leads to the extraordinary implication that a high school principal's sexual affair with a student is a function not of his power, but of hers. There is no correlation between the social power of the men involved and their sexual activities; in the face of the dangerous and disruptive sexuality of Shana and Jean, they are helpless.

Here we find ourselves back in the traditional dynamics of the detective novel; female sexuality is a disruptive force that threatens the social order and must be punished.[6] This is hard-boiled with a twist, for at least the traditional femmes fatales—Brigid O'Shaughnessy in *The Maltese Falcon*, Phyllis Dietrichson in *Double Indemnity*—offered a thrilling vision of transforming their sexual charisma into material and personal power. Shana and Jean Timberlake, on the other hand, remain merely disruptive, reaping no such benefits.

This patriarchal vision of female desire as dangerous ties the revelations of social scandal to the family romance at the heart of the narrative. Millhone, originally hired by Royce Fowler to free his son Bailey, discovers that the murderer was neither Bailey nor any of the men sexually involved with Jean, but Ann Fowler, Bailey's sister. Ann, obsessively in love with Shales, kills Jean to prevent her pregnancy from ruining him and kills Shana because she believes, incorrectly, that Shana is involved with him.

Thus, the murders of the sexually dangerous women are tied not to men protecting their social standing, but to a jealous woman. The incestuous nature of Ann's jealousy is revealed by her third murder: that of her own mother. Deprived of the love of her stern father, who is interested only in his son Bailey, she both frames Bailey and kills her mother to claim her father's love. It thus becomes clear that Ann's desire for Shales was tied to his paternal function; he was the principal at the school where she was a counselor. Just as Shales's affair with his young student Jean had incestuous overtones, Ann's murder of Jean is meant to open a space she can occupy as the beloved of Shales, the father substitute.

Ultimately, the daughter's yearning for the father implicates Millhone, evoking memories of her sense of loss at the death of her own father when she was five. In the end, Millhone muses on her links with both Jean (who, before she died, was searching for her father) and Ann: "None of us had survived the wounds our fathers inflicted all those years ago. Did he love us? How would we ever know? He was gone and he'd never again be what he was to us in all his haunting perfection" (FF 306).

Yet, the book implies that women can, through self-denial, win a shred of this paternal love. When Ann shoots off her foot after struggling with her father over a gun, she cries, "You were never there for me. . . . You were never there" (FF 305); but at that moment she ends up in his arms. Both shooting off her foot and giving up the gun act as symbolic castrations; Ann relinquishes her claims to phallic power by handing the gun over to her father, and she cripples herself as a form of punishment. Rendered helpless and dependent, she finally gains the paternal embrace. Millhone takes this lesson to heart. While the book opens with Millhone's complaints that her elderly landlord, Henry Pitts, is too doting and threatens her independence, it closes with her determination to treasure him. "He may," she says, "be the closest thing to a father I'll ever have" (FF 307).

The book locates the source of disruption in the daughter's unreciprocated love for the father. The danger of incest, its threat to the patriarchal order, lies in the desires of the daughter and can be overcome only by curbing female desire and independence: Just as all the men must be protected or exonerated, so the women must be killed or imprisoned. On the one hand, Millhone could never identify with this threatening version of femininity and thus ensures that the women are punished and stability is restored; on the other, Millhone as daughter accepts her subordination within the father/daughter dyad. Thus, her primary identification with masculinity not only maintains gender as gender difference but also, in a contradictory and narratively conservative way, reinscribes gender as gender hierarchy. Even as she plays with gender difference by parodying both masculinity and (to a lesser extent) femininity, such playfulness fails as a disruptive strategy in the final analysis.

Where *"F" Is for Fugitive* defines gender in terms of individual psychology, *Blood Shot* locates it in social formations and resists rather than reinscribes gender hierarchy. The oppressive function of gender categories is clear in the way Warshawski is constructed by others—particularly the men she pursues—as an unnaturally unfeminine woman, a "bitch": mongrel bitch, cold-blooded bitch, meddlesome bitch. Such an epithet signals a need to reinforce femininity ("bitch" only applies to women) even as Warshawski's detective activities transgress the boundaries of proper femininity: Compliance, subservience, submission to the wills of men. It forcefully reinscribes Warshawski as female Other to the masculine Self, reasserting female inferiority through metaphors of animality even as the female detective acts to subvert and usurp male power.

Warshawski resists such constructions by locating an authentic and valorized female "Self" through her relations with strong female characters. Gabriella, Warshawski's deceased mother, exists in her memories as an accomplished opera singer and exemplary parent. Lotty, Warshawski's closest friend and mother-surrogate, is a renowned doctor who runs a family clinic for impoverished women and children. And Ms. Chigwell is a seventy-eight-year-old, fearless woman whose medical career was blocked by her gender but who becomes Warshawski's partner in a daring rescue.

These women, whose strength is *not* represented as traditionally "masculine," function as a community, homosocial in character and intensity, that mediates Warshawski's relationship to a tough world in which femaleness can be, if not a liability, then certainly an anomaly—a world in which she must rely on deception in order to succeed. Warshawski relates to each of them without deception or bravado, describing Lotty, for example, as "the one person I never lie to. She's—not my conscience—the person who helps me see who I really am, I guess" (BS [*Blood Shot*] 339). This authentic Self, constructed as female but not feminine within Warshawski's community, in turn enables her to defy the psychologized heterosexual binary that condemns feminity in *"F" Is for Fugitive*. Such a community, a crucial departure from the radically individualist male hard-boiled tradition, empowers Warshawski on a social level as she attacks the abuses of male power.

Paretsky, as opposed to Grafton, views incest within this political frame of male power. For Paretsky, incest signifies not a female desire that threatens the social order, but a male desire that constitutes it. Paretsky makes this argument structurally by overlaying two narratives—the search for Caroline Djiak's father and an investigation of industrial poisoning. Originally hired by Caroline, a childhood friend, to discover the identity of her father, Warshawski tries to trace some friends of Caroline's mother Louisa, who used to work at the Xerxes solvent plant. But these friends had died as a result of the chemical's toxicity, and Warshawski finds herself investigating a massive corporate cover-up.

This investigation leads to three powerful men—Humboldt, wealthy financier and owner of Xerxes; Dresberg, an organized crime boss; and Jurshak, a corrupt South Chicago politician. These three figures represent bastions of power, and Warshawski topples them all. She also discovers that Jurshak is the father of Caroline, whose mother Louisa was Jurshak's niece. Whereas the symbolically incestuous acts in Grafton are blamed on the daughters, here Jurshak is clearly responsible for the rape of his niece, part of a systematic pattern of abuse begun with Louisa's older sister.

The theme of the powerful abusing the powerless unites these stories of incest and corporate greed. By superimposing a crime of gender and a crime of class, Paretsky brings together the tales of two rapes: The rape of the girl's body by her uncle and the rape of workers' bodies by their employer. Both are performed by leading citizens who veil their culpability by allowing their victims to be blamed for their suffering: The pregnant Louisa was thrown out of the house to avoid scandal while the workers' illnesses were attributed to their smoking rather than their work environment.

Warshawski uncovers the truth behind these lies. This truth-bearing function is, of course, a central part of the traditional detective story, but here that function is radicalized. Classic detective narratives cleanse society by locating the source of disorder in specific deviant individuals who can be identified and purged, with the truth acting simultaneously to expose the criminal and to clear society as a whole (Cawelti 1976, 80-105; Taylor 1989). Paretsky's novels locate society's evils not on the margins but in its most central, stable figures. Her villains make up the pantheon of a male elite—politicians, corporate executives, bankers, union bosses, religious leaders. Nor are these villains deranged. Their motivations are inevitably financial, and their movement into crime is simply an extension of the logic of business.

This corrupt power lies not only in the public realm of business and politics but also in the private realm of the family. Thus, Warshawski physically or financially ruins Dresberg, Jurshak, and Humboldt; she also confronts Louisa's parents about disowning her. When Louisa's mother finally acknowledges the incest, her husband slaps her. Warshawski punches him in return, initiating a full-scale fight. "I stood over him panting from fury, my gun in my hand barrel-first, ready to smash it into him if he started to get up. His face was glazed—none of his women-folk had ever fought back against him" (BS 273).

Most significant here is not that Warshawski gets into a fight, a standard trope in hard-boiled fiction, but that she

fights on behalf of women. The gun, barrel-first, is no longer Millhone's fetishized phallus, but a threatening bludgeon. Warshawski fights not so much like a man as like a fury, an avenging spirit striking out against malevolent uses of male power; and with such a gesture she transforms detection into political resistance. Grafton, accepting both gender opposition and hierarchy, offers no such social model; her individualism leads to a maintenance of the gendered status quo rather than social transformation. Paretsky, on the other hand, rethinks the detective's inscription in both social and gender hierarchies and offers a utopian social model grounded in values of authenticity and egalitarianism, a model in which women (and some men) emerge as a unified political force with a single, clear response to women's oppression.

She does so, however, at the expense of a critical examination of the construction of Warshawski's identity. Just as Warshawski's political utopia is a fiction, so too is any sense of authentic and unified "selfhood." Yet both fictions are necessary in the politics of Paretsky's work, which posits a feminist Archimedean point from which Warshawski can critique male power formations.

In this light, Grafton's epistemology of performance may be more politically useful in the long run, since her play with gender categories offers the possibility of their symbolic deconstruction. More recent works, Grafton's *"H" Is for Homicide* and the movie *V. I. Warshawski,* exhibit both the potential and the limitations of this more playful approach to gender.

Like *"F" Is for Fugitive, V. I. Warshawski,* a Disney film loosely based on two of Paretsky's novels, parodies gender categories and thus subverts Paretsky's more trenchant critiques of male power. In this film, Warshawski is firmly embedded in the heterosexual binary, her toughness treated as a cross-dressing joke. We first see her as she wakes up in her filthy apartment and sniffs her running clothes before putting them on; we then cut from the morning's jogging shoes to the evening's high heels. Clearly she occupies both masculine and feminine positions, but the borderline never blurs. The movie dispenses with Warshawski's female community while playing up her heterosexual attachments. Lottie is marginalized, while Murray Ryerson, Warshawski's reporter friend, becomes both central and romantic; and the narrative is set in motion when she picks up a man in a bar who is later murdered.

The plot of the film reinforces a conservative rather than an alternative social and familial vision. Warshawski seduces Boom-Boom Grafalk, a hockey star and part owner of a threatened shipping business; when he is murdered, she both takes care of his daughter Kat and investigates his death. The ultimate villain is Boom-Boom's ex-wife, now married to his dissolute brother. Identified by her loose morality (promiscuity, drug and alcohol dependency), she ultimately attempts to kill her own daughter to gain her inheritance. Warshawski thus is positioned on the side of the paternal bond against the bad mother, just as she is positioned on the side of corporate stability and inherited wealth against hedonistic criminals. Finally, Warshawski is established here on the side of mystification over truth. After killing Kat's mother, who is trying to drown her daughter, Warshawski asks Murray to print the report that the mother died trying to protect Kat. "You wouldn't want her growing up thinking her mother tried to kill her." In stark contrast to her decision to tell Caroline of her incestuous parentage, the filmic Warshawski lies to reinforce the ideology of the nuclear family. The film ends with the rebellious female detective reinserted in the family, as she and Murray take the place of Kat's now-dead parents.

Thus the film flips pronouns but ultimately maintains the structure and generic rules of the traditional thriller. Its gender switch acts as a joke, easily laughed off as one returns to the comfortable position of the nuclear family by the end. Yet, this bifurcation between stable opposites, this fragmentation of gender subjectivity, however regressive in the film and in *"F" Is for Fugitive,* has the potential to open a conceptual space for destabilizing "femininity" as such. *"H" Is for Homicide,* one of Grafton's later novels, suggests (despite its use of class and ethnic stereotypes) the possibility—however fragile—of a politics that binds rather than divides women, a politics dependent upon the instability of bourgeois ideological constructions of "femininity." "Woman" becomes pluralized into "women," differentiated by ethnicity and class but linked by shifting alliances born of the performative quality of gender.

One first encounters Millhone as she returns from Los Angeles in her VW bug at 3:00 A.M. to her cozy home, recently rebuilt by her landlord Henry Pitts. "Life was good," Millhone muses. "I was female, single, with money in my pocket and enough gas to get home. I had nobody to answer to and no ties to speak of" (HH [*"H" Is for Homicide*] 3). Soon, however, this self-assured Millhone goes under cover for most of the book as "Hannah Moore"—skintight pants, ratted hair, inexpert makeup, and cheap perfume abounding. "What a vamp . . . what a tramp!" Millhone chirps. "I didn't know I had it in me" (HH 48). This literal performance, this parodic persona of the trashy woman, complicates Grafton's already-destabilized gender categories as class becomes a marker of difference *within* "femininity."

"Hannah Moore" accompanies Bibianna Diaz, a woman Millhone's been tailing for auto insurance fraud, back to Los Angeles. Both are more or less abducted by Raymond Maldonado, a kingpin in the fraud industry and Diaz's viciously self-appointed fiance. In her initial interactions with Maldonado, Millhone experiences a kind of exhilaration at the freedoms of her newfound persona. "I was making up Hannah's character as I went along, and it was liberating as hell. She was short-tempered, sarcastic, outspoken and crude. I could get used to this. License to misbehave" (HH 125). This impertinent femininity allies her across class lines with Diaz, whom she tries to protect from Maldonado's advances and abuses.

But Hannah Moore's exaggerated femininity shifts as the book progresses from sass and trash to the vulnerability that also marks Diaz's relationship with Maldonado. As she finds herself trapped in a rundown apartment, making dubious friends with a pit bull, guarded constantly by one of Maldonado's men, no gun and no telephone to call for help, such discursive freedom feels hollow. This disempowered feminine position vis-à-vis male violence provokes a rupture in the text, an intense moment of homesickness. "I felt a squeezing in my stomach," she says, "not an ache, but some process that was almost like grief" (HH 212). Her thoughts slip back to childhood and a child's memories of the horrors of the first moments away from home at summer camp.

This return to home, the safe and comfortable space of the bourgeois, signifies both Millhone's need to escape the suffocation of a specifically gendered class position that she has come dangerously close to adopting and the conventional detective story's need for closure. The return is thus a gesture that provides haven for the individual while leaving unequal social relations intact: Millhone has an out, while Diaz may not. Still, in spite of the conservatism of the resolution, "Hannah Moore's" friendship with Diaz suggests the utopian possibilities of a postmodern approach to identity. Gender in this scheme cannot be contained within stable binary oppositions (masculine and feminine) based on either biology or equally shared oppression; gender categories are themselves decentered, creating the possibility of alliance by exposing the fictionality of a unity based on the erasure of ethnic and class difference.

Complicated questions thus arise about the implications of the gender strategies employed by Paretsky and Grafton. Is Paretsky's vision of authentic truth and justice a function of the epistemology of the detective story, which is built around the masculine paradigm of uncovering the single truth and achieving closure? Does Grafton's post-structuralist destabilization of gender categories have the potential to break out of those narrative conventions? Or is some form of realist epistemology an essential foundation for any substantive political critique and ultimately more powerful than a focus on discursive instability?

The academic paper, like the detective novel, is conventionally structured around the search for evidence, the weighing of hypotheses, the investigation of causation. And like the detective novel, the academic paper climaxes with the privileged understanding, the story that makes all the details fall into place. This paper does not conclude that way. Instead of suppressing the contradictory moments in collaborative writing, we wish to foreground them by breaking into our individual voices for a final commentary:

Timothy Shuker-Haines: While acknowledging the tremendous power of post-structuralist critiques of representation, I want to defend Paretsky's project and ultimately the very concept of closure. Any social critique, including feminism, that is going to remain politically substantive and generative must ground itself, at least implicitly, on a vision of what the world is and what it should be. An exclusive focus on strategies of representation would condemn feminism to academicism, aestheticism, and marginality. To critique oppression we must believe in an alternative justice; to critique falsehood, we must believe in some form of an alternative truth. Such concepts as truth and justice sound hopelessly bourgeois and masculine and are clearly potentially oppressive, but I think we implicitly believe in them; and we are shackling ourselves if we do not articulate them, offer a critique of them, and ultimately fight for them. I see this as Paretsky's project; I think it's a noble one.

Martha Umphrey: Yet it seems to me that, in the realm of fiction, politics and representational strategies are inseparable. Warshawski's sense of identity (at least Paretsky's version of it) is the vehicle for and epistemologically equatable with the sense of closure and catharsis offered in the detective story's generic structure. Thus, it may well be that the conservative ideology of form inhering in the detective story serves to contain as much as to liberate Paretsky's feminist politics. One key insight in current feminist theory, informed by post-structuralism and, I think, more importantly by critiques of "mainstream" feminism offered by women of color, is that just as subjectivity itself is multiple and fragmented, so too is the category of "woman." Closing down the play of meaning by fixing it in the unproblematized identity of a single woman, a female detective, appears in that light as potentially regressive; and thus Grafton's strategies for destabilizing subjectivity appear at least potentially more promising as a means of politicizing the genre than Paretsky's. It's possible, as Gertrude Stein wrote of her own mystery *Blood on the Dining Room Floor,* that "on the whole a detective story does have to have an ending" (Stein 1982, 88) (and, one might add, a detective); but if so, then to perform feminist cultural work that is potentially liberating for all women, the very form of the detective narrative may have to dissolve, as has this essay, into nonresolution.

Notes

1. This figure is not the only type of classic female detective, but she remains one of the best known. For surveys of female detectives, see Kline (1988), Craig and Cadogan (1981), and Reddy (1988).

2. Cawelti (1986) remains a crucial work in analyzing classic and hard-boiled detective fiction.

3. For the most popularized, although problematic because potentially essentializing, analysis of femininity as relational, see Gilligan (1982).

4. Quotations from the novels are cited in the text using the following abbreviations:

    FF: Sue Grafton's *"F" Is for Fugitive* (1990)

    HH: Sue Grafton's *"H" Is for Homicide* (1991)

    BS: Sara Paretsky's *Blood Shot* (1988).

5. For an extended theoretical discussion of gender as performative, see Butler (1990).

6. For a summary of theory on the disruptiveness of female sexuality, see E. Ann Kaplan (1980).

References

Butler, Judith. *Gender Trouble: Feminism and the Subversion of Identity.* New York: Routledge, 1990.

Cawelti, John. *Adventure, Mystery, and Romance: Formula Stories as Art and Popular Culture.* Chicago: University of Chicago Press, 1976.

Craig, Patricia, and Mary Cadogan. *The Lady Investigates: Women Detectives and Spies in Fiction.* London: Victor Gollancz, 1981.

Gilligan, Carol. *In a Different Voice: Psychological Theory and Women's Development.* Cambridge, MA: Harvard University Press, 1982.

Glover, David. "The Stuff That Dreams Are Made of: Masculinity, Femininity and the Thriller." In *Gender, Genre, and Narrative Pleasure,* edited by Derek Longhurst, 67-83. London: Unwin Hyman, 1989.

Grafton, Sue. *"F" Is for Fugitive.* New York: Henry Holt and Company, 1989. Reprint. New York: Bantam, 1990.

————. *"H" Is for Homicide.* New York: Henry Holt and Company, 1991.

Hirsch, Foster. *The Dark Side of the Screen: Film Noir.* San Diego, CA: A. S. Barnes, 1981.

Kaplan, E. Ann. "Introduction." In *Women in Film Noir,* edited by E. Ann Kaplan, 1-5. London: British Film Institute Publishing, 1980.

Kline, Kathleen. *The Woman Detective: Gender and Genre.* Urbana: University of Illinois Press, 1988.

Paretsky, Sara. *Blood Shot.* New York: Delacorte, 1988. Reprint. New York: Dell, 1989.

Place, J. A., and L. S. Peterson. "Some Visual Motifs of Film Noir." In *Movies and Methods: An Anthology,* edited by Bill Nichols, 325-38. Berkeley: University of California Press, 1976.

Reddy, Maureen. *Sisters in Crime: Feminism and the Crime Novel.* New York: Continuum, 1988.

Schrader, Paul. "Notes on Film Noir." In *Film Genre Reader,* edited by Barry Keith Grant, 169-82. Austin: University of Texas Press, 1986.

Stein, Gertrude. *Blood on the Dining Room Floor.* Alice B. Toklas, 1948. Reprint. Berkeley, CA: Creative Arts Book Company, 1982.

Taylor, Barry. "*Gorky Park*: American Dreams in Siberia." In *Gender, Genre, and Narrative Pleasure,* edited by Derek Longhurst, 136-56. London: Unwin Hyman, 1989.

Priscilla L. Walton and Manina Jones (essay date 1999)

SOURCE: Walton, Priscilla L. and Manina Jones. "Does She or Doesn't She?: The Problematics of Feminist Detection." In *Detective Agency: Women Rewriting the Hard-Boiled Tradition*, pp. 86-117. Berkeley: University of California Press, 1999.

[*In the following essay, Walton and Jones discuss some ways in which various hard-boiled detective novels written by women, and featuring a female detective, transform the hard-boiled genre by questioning elements of the tradition.*]

> If feminism is now an uncomfortable part of the thriller's cultural repertoire, it is one which necessarily calls the achievements of Hammett and Chandler into question. Down these mean streets no easy male/female transpositions are possible.
>
> David Glover, "The Stuff That Dreams Are Made Of"

Negotiating the Generic Contract

Many feminist scholars of detective fiction have been skeptical about the potential of women's practice of the hard-boiled detective novel to negotiate resistance, critique, or change within in a literary genre typically aligned with oppressive masculinity. While some critics applaud the feminist potential of the form in the hands of women writers, many others contend that any such potential gets lost in translation—that feminist political aims are necessarily negated by the inherently conservative demands of the genre. These scholars see "detective agency" as a contradiction in terms. We argue, on the contrary, that feminist agency is possible not just within the confines of or despite the conventions of the genre, but *through* those very conventions. The feminist appropriation of the hard-boiled mode can redefine textual and cultural boundaries precisely because it comes into intimate contact with them. In other words, such practices make it possible to renegotiate the "generic contract" between industry, authors, audiences, and texts. The ability of women's hard-boiled fiction to perform this task is made possible by its threefold character: it is a *practical* application of *political* tenets expressed through a *popular* form. This chapter looks at the critical controversy over women's appropriation of the hard-boiled novel in order to address the ways in which feminist politics and fictive practice may be brought together in the reading and writing of the genre.

In *The Woman Detective*, the most extensive study of female detectives to date, Kathleen Gregory Klein outlines her interpretation of the "woman questions" at issue when women take up the conventions of the professional investigator novel. She sees such novels as a struggle between gender and genre in which the conventional private eye formula inevitably achieves primacy over feminist ideology:

> The predictable formula of detective fiction is based on a world whose sex/gender valuations reinforce male hegemony. Taking male behavior as the norm, the genre defines its parameters to exclude female characters, confidently rejecting them as inadequate women or inadequate detectives. A detective novel with a professional woman detective is, then, a contradiction in terms. The existence of the one effectively eliminates the other.
>
> (223)

The use of the hard-boiled mode by contemporary authors like Sue Grafton, Marcia Muller, and Susan Steiner, she contends, "falsely seems to signal a change in the genre," for such works simply reproduce patterns Klein sees as repeating themselves over and over since the first female sleuths appeared in the nineteenth century (221). Klein argues that because mass-mediated culture in general, and the detective genre in particular, serves the interests of a relatively small elite power structure, it necessarily confronts authors with a compromise in which "either feminism or the formula is at risk" (202). Thus, while Klein's most recent work suggests that some versions of women's crime writing do successfully challenge and reformulate both the detective formula and gender norms, she does not find these innovations in mainstream popular fiction (see "*Habeas Corpus*").

Rosalind Coward and Linda Semple, in their article "Tracking Down the Past," also see the conventions of hard-boiled writing as inhospitable to feminism. Like Klein, these critics do praise some mystery novels written by women as explicitly feminist in their aims and effects (especially those published by alternative presses), but they see the hard-boiled mode as particularly unaccommodating: "Given the extreme individualism, violence and outrageous social attitudes towards women and other minority groups which writers like Mickey Spillane, Dashiell Hammett and Raymond Chandler often display, it is hard to imagine a form less susceptible to a feminist interpretation." Despite "the sympathetic, independent heroines and politically satisfying plots" (46) in the work of such writers as Paretsky and Grafton, the genre is highly problematic, they argue, particularly because it offers little or no criticism of the violence of the traditional gumshoe novels. We take up the question of violence and the female body in chapter 5; here we note only that for Coward and Semple, as for Klein, gender and genre are necessarily at odds, and feminist intentions (however well-placed and sympathetic) simply cannot resist the hard-boiled genre's traditional power as a misogynist mode.[1] Australian fiction writer Finola Moorehead echoes this judgment when she insists that her book *Still Murder* "is not a genre novel. It can't be, because it has a women-identified central reality" (99). To gain the acceptance that is necessary for popularity, she submits, "the formula must be fundamentally male—even though it is written by women" (102).

Like popular culture itself, however, genres are neither simply subversive nor intrinsically conservative. Genre, rather, serves as a relational, conventional, and contradictory location that tends to complicate in practice any simple either/or categorization. For example, the original exemplars of the hard-boiled detective mode reconsidered some of the class constructions that had become a conventional element of the British mystery story, and thus have often been seen (particularly in light of their American origins) as revolutionizing the genre, both politically and linguistically. At the same time, the genre dramatized some of the conservative fears and anxieties arising from changes in traditional class and gender structures in the United States during the 1920s and 1930s. Thus the iconic characterization of the femme fatale in these stories dramatized the powerful allure (and mystery) of a refractory woman in control of her own desires, at the same time as the conventional narrative structure of hard-boiled novels regulated the legitimacy of that power in her inevitable incrimination, death, or confinement at the end of the story. In his discussion of the possibility of "Radical Thrillers," Stephen Knight asks, "Is the genre completely tainted with conservatism?" (186). He answers, in part, by offering a historical argument demonstrating that the political orientations of writers within the traditional genre, including Hammett and Chandler, differ substantially (179). Knight argues that if popular culture is a significant site of ideological production, then it is "a crucial force-field into which the left must enter" (186). We argue, similarly, that if the popular hard-boiled genre is a significant regulatory site for gender roles and behaviors, then co-opting such a form is an extremely important revisionary gesture that may work to alter the paradigms of both genre and gender.

In their introduction to *Killing Women*, a collection of essays by Australian women detective writers and critics, Delys Bird and Brenda Walker acknowledge the heterogeneity of the "mainstream" audience, as well as the potential agency of writers and readers to produce culturally resistant readings through popular culture itself:

> That popular writing is not simply (or at all) an opiate, but represents the tastes and values of many and is capable itself of political activity, means it can no longer be regarded as always innocently and conventionally reproducing dominant mass-consumer-directed ideologies. Women writers of crime fiction, then, working in a male preserve with a genre always considered definitively masculine despite its numerous very well-known female practitioners, might now use the genre in a way that confronted and challenged its maleness. Women readers too could identify with these challenges, or construct their own through re-readings of earlier "pre-feminist" writers.
>
> (12)

Bird and Walker configure a compelling legal scenario regarding feminist crime fiction when they observe that there is more than one way of responding to the misogyny of conventional crime writing: "Crime fiction invites classification and investigation not from the point of view of a narrow feminist prosecution, as a kind of class action, but rather as part of the forensics of sexuality and narrative structure" (11).

Their point is well taken. The notion of a "class action" is, nevertheless, an appealing one, for it can represent the collective challenge posed by the development of a sub*genre* (as opposed to a singular challenge from any individual author), as well as the audience's participation in that development. The term also evokes the popular "democratization" of American literature essayed by the original hard-boiled writers (a *class* action), now including women in that democracy. And it suggests the possibility of both authorial and readerly response (a class *action*), in the sense not just of legal action *against* but of agency *through* prescribed generic conditions. Bird and Walker's choice of words implies that the writing of the novel itself might be a "forensic" gesture, producing writing that goes beyond *describing* a legal case to, at some level, effectively *making* a case for or against some set of principles.

Like Bird and Walker, Barbara Godard recognizes that the rewriting of genre "reveals women's engagement with narrative as a critical strategy." Godard suggests the radical potential of such generic "border/play," since it works "to expose the positioning of woman as silent other on whose mutilated body the narrative is constructed in dominant discourse and to posit alternative positionings for women as subjects producing themselves in/by language" (45). Godard also underscores the importance of the popular audience to the political value of crime fiction. Indeed, Godard argues that feminist detective fiction is effective precisely because it constructs as criminal (and thus questions) the ideological formations in which readers are implicated, effecting a "double transformation" in which "the text is transformed from a work of suspense fiction to a political fiction and the practice of the novel is changed from one of mystification and revelation to one of investigation and transformation" (49). In Godard's analysis, both mainstream and avant garde fiction fall on a continuum of generic practices that "turn dominant discourses inside out" (45).

Maureen Reddy's work, in her book *Sisters in Crime* and elsewhere, begins to account for the dialogic, responsive qualities of formula fiction previously left largely unaddressed. Reddy situates the development of the genre as coincident and analogous with the modern women's movement: "Feminist literary criticism, feminism as a social movement, and feminist crime novels have grown up together, so to speak. Just as feminist literary criticism challenges the traditional assumptions of the discipline of literary studies, so too does the feminist crime novel challenge the conventions of crime fiction" ("Feminist Counter-Tradition" 174). She concludes, "Feminist crime novels are best understood as constituting a new genre, less part of an existing tradition than a distinct countertradition" (174). Reddy's parallels between feminist literary criticism and literary practice are insightful, but her notion of "a distinct counter-tradition" might be interpreted as a strategic evasion of the problematics of generic revision, one that defuses important questions of reversal and resistance. It also ignores the ways in which women's writings are not "caught" in the prescriptions of genre but are necessarily always already inscribed in its discursive formulations, just as subjects are always already inscribed in the discursive formulations of gender.

Although Reddy conceives of the dialogic potential of the feminist countertradition she identifies, she still insists on labeling the genre itself (as distinguished from its feminist practice) as "basically monologic in form" (*Sisters in Crime* 6). For Klein, similarly, it is only feminist (mainstream) detective fiction that offers a "double-voiced discourse" (*Woman Detective* 57). That is, it offers two sets of contradictory meanings to readers differentiated by gender: Women, she submits, are offered the fantasy of freedom and independence, while "men's fear of a reality in which women can become the dominant group is assuaged by the persistent fantasy of women who fail. . . . Reading the same novels, they can read altogether different stories" (*Woman Detective* 170). While the insight that readers may read the same texts in conflicting ways is essential, the conservative and progressive elements of generic conflict are unlikely simply to split readers into separate gendered camps. Rather, generic texts function much more equivocally for any given reader, offering both reassurances and reformative possibilities—in this case, potential for both identification and difference, as we noted in the reader responses cited in chapter 2. Moreover, Klein's theory fails to explain why certain readers prefer certain generic types and how readers distinguish among subgenres of detective fiction with some skill: those who harbor genuine fears about women's power, or who are uncomfortable exploring a subjectivity or ideology *significantly* different from their own, are likely to choose to read a variant of the genre that does not challenge their preconceptions.

REVISING THE SCRIPT

Klein's observations about the way genre can accommodate conflict might be modified and extended by taking into account an effect of what Michel Foucault refers to as "reverse discourse," or a discourse that repeats and inverts the ideological imperatives of the dominant discourse in order to authorize those marginalized by it.[2] If the feminist hard-boiled novel is perceived as a reverse rather than a double discourse, then it can be read as producing a critique of the formula by reproducing it with strategic differences, thus redirecting the trajectory of dominant discourse. In isolation, a reverse discourse does not change or reconfigure anything; its efficacy depends on the reader's recognition of differential intertextual relationships. It also depends on genre's ability to signify in alternative ways, to accommodate ideologically contradictory practices without ceasing to be recognizable. The reverse discourse employed by gay rights activists provides an example outside genre: the pink triangle (originally used to identify gay men in Nazi concentration camps) has been co-opted to symbolize gay pride.

As Linda Grant puts it of her own practice as a detective writer, "I thought, 'Gee, the private investigator is such a male archetype, wouldn't it be fun to see what would happen if you put a woman in that role?' because when you take an archetype and stand it on its head, interesting stuff drops out." *Simple* gender role reversal, however, is not

effective—or even possible: Sara Paretsky has described her initial experiments with the genre as a parody of the "Raymond Chandler-type" novel: "I had my detective, her name was Minerva Daniels, and she was in this sleazy office, down to her last two dollars, and this guy comes in—slim hips, broad shoulders—and he was going to be my main bad guy. But it wasn't working: there are too many things you have to keep in mind if you're doing role reversal" (qtd. in Shapiro, "Sara Paretsky" 67). "It occurred to me," Paretsky adds elsewhere, "that what I really wanted was not a stereotype, but someone who was like me and my friends" (qtd. in Shepherdson 38).

Feminist detective fiction constitutes a reverse discourse exploring positions of resistance and agency that were offered by previous practices but that were inaccessible to women. Reinscribing those discourses refuses stereotypical structures at the same time as it reveals their contradictions. For example, in Paretsky's experiment the hard-boiled convention of female sexuality as dangerous and even evil conflicts with the heroic status of the detective, and simple parody doesn't quite work. However, reinscribing and revising prior discourses does, potentially, allow a space for *differential* practice—this, perhaps, is the "interesting stuff" that drops out when you turn an archetype on its head. As Foucault has argued, a reverse discourse is an alternative discourse of power:

> Discourses are not once and for all subservient to power or raised up against it, any more than silences are. We must make allowance for the complex and unstable process whereby discourse can be both an instrument and an effect of power, but also a hindrance, a stumbling-block, a point of resistance and a starting point for an opposing strategy. Discourse transmits and produces power; it reinforces it, but it also undermines and exposes it, renders it fragile and makes it possible to thwart it.
>
> (100-101)

The power of the reverse movement is apparent in the ways in which it employs the constructions of the dominant discourse in order to foreground (and transpose) the ideological imperatives that motivate it. To invert Klein's assertion: with reverse discourse, neither feminism nor the formula is necessarily at risk.

Reverse discourse is not in itself a subversive gesture—it can also be used strategically to suppress marginal voices. As Susan Faludi demonstrates in her study *Backlash,* the rhetoric of "women's liberation" has been used by its detractors during the 1980s and 1990s to discredit the movement (e.g., in "backlash films" such as *Fatal Attraction* and *Disclosure*). Indeed, in chapter 7 we read the "adaptation" of Sara Paretsky's detective V. I. Warshawski novels to film as one instance of this backlash strategy. Because discourses are not stable or simple, their cultural contexts and effects need to be analyzed. As Foucault argues, "Discourses are tactical elements or blocks operating in the field of force relations; there can exist different and even contradictory discourses within the same strategy; they can, on the contrary, circulate without changing their form from one strategy to another, opposing strategy" (101-2).

"MARLOWE'S KISS MEANT EITHER DEATH OR JAIL"

Women writers of detective fiction strategically talk back to a genre that has often demeaned, trivialized, and even demonized women. The genre itself, however, offers an attractive position from which to investigate agency. Equally important, even traditional examples of the hard-boiled genre have recognized the power of female subjectivity and desire in the figure of the femme fatale. Both Katherine V. Forrest and Sparkle Hayter have commented on the complex female characterizations developed by hard-boiled novels as one of the features of the genre they find most appealing. Hayter affirms that while she loves to read classic hard-boiled fiction, "I always wish I could also read the story as told by one of its women characters." In some ways Hayter's Robin Hudson novels undertake this reading by telling a (comic) story in which the central role of subjectivity and agency is female. Linda Grant identifies the importance of the figure somewhat differently. The femme fatale is, in effect, the victim of the hard-boiled detective's struggle to achieve a kind of macho independence by criminalizing feminine influences: "The tradition," she comments, "emphasized autonomy at the cost of intimacy. Marlowe's kiss meant either death or jail. Think about it: any time he got involved with a women she's either dead or off to jail. These were guys for whom any sign of emotional intimacy was dangerous. And the Lone Wolf is just the far end of autonomy." In her character Catherine Sayler, Grant capitalizes on the generic autonomy of the detective character because women, "at least in my generation, we're not raised to be very autonomous"; but she reverses the genre in her characterization of intimacy.

Female detective writers routinely draw attention to the ways they have used the conventions of the hard-boiled mode to engender agency in their female characters. Linda Barnes, author of the Carlotta Carlyle series, lists male hard-boiled writers of the past and their male descendants of the present among her literary influences, and points to the ways in which these authors function for her as a negative example:

> [T]he Dashiell Hammett, Ross Macdonald group [are among the authors who influenced my writings]. I mean even John D. [MacDonald] has been an influence on me, in that I don't kill all the women in my books, as he infuriated me by using a woman in each book, and disposing of her as easily as he possibly could so his hero could spend the rest of the book avenging this disposable female. And the "disposable female syndrome" is one of the things that I really get after the current guys for.

Barnes's description actually casts such narrative strategies as criminal: "no one ever kept a body count on John D. MacDonald as he killed them all, after [his character had finished] sleeping with them. I mean, that man was a serial killer."

Sara Paretsky diagnoses an extreme version of this very convention as it extends to contemporary crime fiction, reading it as a symptom of fears about women's social power:

> Since the passage of the initial Civil Rights Act, the emergence of women in significant numbers into the professions that had previously been mostly closed to them is resolved and OK for some men, but for others, it's a terrifying, emasculating experience. And when you feel terrified and helpless, your response is great anger toward the people you perceive as causing it. And this is being played out in what has become increasingly more graphic and furious material about the destruction of women—through rape, dismemberment, snuff films, etc.
>
> ("What Do Women Really Want?" 13)

Paretsky sees her own writing and that of others like her as a version of the crime genre that is in competition for audience sympathy: "I don't know which trend will come out on top in the end" (13). Far from being passive victims trapped in generic conventions, writers such as Paretsky, Grafton, Barnes, and the others under study here engage with them in order to counter them, and thus are able to exercise agency not in spite of their status as genre writers, but because of it.

The effects of reverse discourse depend on the reader's ability to recognize difference between *this* particular performance of the genre and those it both repeats and counters. Women writers frequently reflexively play on that recognition by alluding to hard-boiled conventions and writers. In Marele Day's *Case of the Chinese Boxes,* for instance, her detective Claudia Valentine encounters a man whose name is Joel Cairo: "If you're looking for the Maltese Falcon, you've come to the wrong place," she quips (43). The remark might also be read as directed to the reader of *The Case of the Chinese Boxes*: if you're looking for *The Maltese Falcon,* you'll find this place familiar—but also recognize its strategic difference from that literary norm. Lesley Grant-Adamson alludes to and mocks the individualistic heroism characteristic of hard-boiled novels through her characterization of detective Laura Flynn. Laura relaxes by reading a novel about a detective hero who succeeds where the police fail, addressing the reader with this aside: "You know the type: a courageous figure, a lone ranger operating outside society, untrammelled by friends and family and any consideration but Getting His Man and Seeing Justice Done. I like a little fantasy before I fall asleep" (14). Similarly, Sarah Dunant often writes self-consciously about hard-boiled iconography, both defining her character by it and distancing her from it. In *Fatlands,* for example, Hannah Wolfe comments that the clients who come into the office aren't "glamorous women with skirts slit to the thighs who tell their story through lazy curls of cigarette smoke while the light casts film noir shadows on the wall" (43). In *Under My Skin,* Hannah is surprised by a suspect's reference to *The Big Sleep*: "I mean for me Raymond Chandler is just part of the myth, the kind of thing PI's read instead of fairy-tales, but I don't expect others to be so well versed" (89).

When Wendi Lee's Angela Matelli decides to leave the military to become a professional investigator, she muses, "I had no illusions about the private eye business. I'd read a few detective novels and had really enjoyed them, but my reasons for being in the investigation field had more to do with my limited job skills than with romantic fantasies involving tough guys with names like Spade, Marlowe, or Hammer" (*Good Daughter* 3). Val McDermind's Kate Brannigan also reminds readers of the fictional "text books" on which her role is based—and her difference from them: "It's a piece of cake, being a lawyer or a doctor or a computer systems analyst or an accountant. Libraries are full of books telling you how to do it. The only text books for private eyes are on the fiction shelves, and I don't remember ever reading one that told me how to interrogate an eight-year-old without feeling like I was auditioning for the Gestapo" (*Crack Down* 120). In Sue Grafton's novels, Kinsey Millhone frequently points to the differences between the actions of her hero and those of her male counterparts. In *"F" Is for Fugitive,* the PI laments: "I felt like I'd spent half my time on this case washing dirty dishes. How come Magnum, PI, never had to do stuff like this?" (159). The distinction is just as great between her and her "real" male peers; when Kinsey discovers, in *"I" Is for Innocent,* that the male PI on the case before her had charged $50 an hour, she queries wryly, "Morley was getting fifty? I couldn't believe it. Either men are outrageous or women are fools. Guess which, I thought. My standard fee has always been thirty bucks an hour plus mileage" (23). S. J. Rozan's Chinese American PI Lydia Chin makes a similar comment in *China Trade* about a male PI with whom she occasionally works, in an ironic addendum on the contingencies of economic (and iconic) difference: "He's a solo p.i., a one-person shop with a varied caseload, just like me. Only he's older, taller, and tougher looking—oh, and a male white person—which means he doesn't go as long between cases as I sometimes do" (13).

Grafton further shifts the mode's conventions by suggesting that the job of the detective was always one suited to women, but that those "feminine" aspects of detection have been strategically elided in traditional conceptions of the tough guy PI. Kinsey's comments, for example, often recuperate the domestic sphere into professional space, a gesture that makes women central to (rather than alienated from) the investigative process: "It had not been a very satisfying day but then most of my days are the same: checking and cross-checking, filling in blanks, detail work that was absolutely essential to the job but scarcely dramatic stuff. The basic characteristics of any good investigator are a plodding nature and infinite patience. Society has inadvertently been grooming women to this end for years" (*"A" Is for Alibi* 27). The author makes a similar gesture in *"B" Is for Burglar* when Kinsey emphasizes the importance of detail work again: "I was going to have to

check it out item by item. . . . There's no place in a PI's life for impatience, faintheartedness, or sloppiness. I understand the same qualifications apply for housewives" (33).

RECASTING THE DICK

Despite such practical subversions of gender roles, critiques of women's practices of hard-boiled writing often condemn these novels as "drag performances," in effect using the language of "queerness" to discredit them. Susan Geeson, for example, sums up her criticism of writers such as Paretsky, Grafton, Barbara Wilson, and Liza Cody with the line, "You could say that the feminist PI's are Philip Marlowe in drag" (116). Ann Wilson is more moderate, suggesting that "drag" is a tactical problem involved in negotiating gender and genre performance: "The problem is one of having the heroine occupy a male subject position—the role of the hard-boiled detective—without making her seem as if she is a man in drag. The negotiations of gender and sexuality in Grafton, Muller, and Paretsky are deft attempts to remain faithful to the tradition of tough-guy detective fiction while disrupting its gender codes" (148). Alison Littler raises important questions about the "tactical production" of the hard-boiled mode—or the types of knowledge and power it promotes. In condemning its practices she inadvertently indicates its political potential:

> How the term "feminist" is defined, of course, will be crucial to the kind of answers that are offered. If, for example, "feminist" is used in a liberal-humanist-independent-career-woman-in-control-of-her-own-life sense, then most certainly the recent series of women private eyes are feminist. If, however, "feminist" refers to a woman deconstructing phallocentric ideologies wherever they are naturalized and structured into social, cultural and political practices, then a feminist private eye is a contradiction in terms. She is a man in woman's clothing—or is it a woman in man's clothing?
>
> (133)

Littler's final unresolved question—is she a man in woman's clothing or a woman in man's clothing?—points to the ways that feminist hard-boiled novels, conceived as a complex performance of gender and genre, may destabilize and denaturalize the very gender categories inherent to the phallocentric ideologies. The "liberal humanist" and "deconstructive" feminist modes, while theoretically in conflict, may operate simultaneously in practice.

As Littler suggests, how the term "feminist" is defined is an important criterion of assessment. In *Murder by the Book?* Sally Munt organizes women's detective fiction into categories that correspond to different schools of feminism. She sees hard-boiled writing correlating with liberal feminist theory, an association made by Littler as well. And also like Littler, Munt resorts to conventionalized gender positions in her analyses of the form. While Munt does point out that different readers might respond to characters in different ways, she also reverts to gender stereotyping when she comments at some length on V. I. Warshawski's frequent clothing changes in Paretsky's novels:

> for the heterosexual male reader, or the lesbian reader, she may function as a glamorous spectacle (the outfits are often silk and almost always are expensive); for the heterosexual female reader the function may be more aspirational, her style metonymically suggesting a bourgeois fantasy of empowerment. As a fantasy of empowerment, Warshawski's style reassures the female reader that "dressing up" enables you to do the job.
>
> (47)

Offering several interpretations of this "curious feature," Munt contends: "The fetishization of clothes in Paretsky's work implies the 'draggish' imperative of femininity, signalling its artifice" (47). Munt closes off the radical potential of gender-bending in such novels, implicitly aligning the clothing changes with eating disorders ("female excess always exacts a price"; 47). While she does draw attention elsewhere in her study to the possibility of gender play she restricts that play to lesbian practice, thus failing to take into account the ways in which gender is "performed" by heterosexual subjects too.

The references to drag in these critical assessments point to the ways in which gender is subtly rehearsed in feminist hard-boiled novels. As B. Ruby Rich notes in "The Lady Dicks," feminist hard-boiled protagonists are involved in "crisscrossing the borders of sex and gender" (24). Theorist Teresa de Lauretis's argument, in *The Practice of Love*, foregrounds how the operation of clothing and fantasy contributes to political agency: "Foucault's term '*reverse*' *discourse* actually suggests something of the process by which a representation in the external world is subjectively assumed, reworked through fantasy, in the internal world and then returned to the external world resignified, rearticulated discursively and/or performatively in the subject's self-representation—in speech, gesture, costume, body stance, and so forth." Expanding on her point, de Lauretis stresses "the importance that fashion and social performance have, in all cultures and cultural (self-)representations, for the normative sexual identity of their subjects" (308). Thus fantasy and costume can disrupt normative gender and sexual representations. In Sue Grafton's novels, for example, clothing is often the subject of the narrator's ironic commentary. Kinsey, who wears jeans and turtleneck sweaters, has an "all-purpose black dress," adaptable to any situation requiring more conventionally feminine attire: "black with long sleeves, in some exotic blend of polyester you could bury for a year without generating a crease" (*"I" Is for Innocent* 216). The dress, in fact, becomes a kind of running joke in the series that may even signify the embattled status of conventions of femininity in Grafton's novels: it has survived immersion in an irrigation ditch (*"G" Is for Gumshoe*) and a bomb explosion (*"E" Is for Evidence*). The large frame of Linda Barnes's Carlotta Carlyle also resists feminine norms, literally prohibiting her from fitting into most female fashions: "I go barefoot a lot because I'm six one and I wear size 11

shoes. You may not realize this, but for all practical purposes, women's shoes stop dead at size 10," she confides to the reader (*A Trouble of Fools* 4).

Grafton actually makes a point of representing—and making a comic spectacle of—garments "unmentionable" in polite discourse. Trapped in a hotel room in *"G" Is for Gumshoe*, Kinsey is forced to listen to the avid lovemaking of her neighbors through the wall. Ever adaptable, the detective "stuffed a sock in each cup of my bra and tied it across my head like earmuffs, with the ends knotted under my chin. Didn't help much. I lay there, a cone over each ear like an alien, wondering at the peculiarities of human sex practices. I would have much to report when I returned to my planet" (87). Indeed, the bra itself might be seen as one of the peculiarities of human sex practices, and Grafton here defamiliarizes—and de-eroticizes—its use, employing at the same time a turn on the trope of the detective as (alien) outsider. Sparkle Hayter effects a slightly different process of comic defamiliarization in her parody of the iconic image of the pistol-packing male investigator. Hayter deliberately feminizes not just her protagonist, but her protagonist's weapons: Robin carries not a gun but "a bottle of cheap spray cologne spiked with cayenne pepper to approximate Mace and a battery-operated Epilady, which I realized after one use was a better offensive weapon than feminine aid" (*What's a Girl Gotta Do?* 22). Hayter thus also highlights the masochist devices that are conventionally used by women against themselves, in order to "produce" femininity.

The play on/with/of gender that is manifested by a female character assuming a conventionally male position works to destabilize and denaturalize norms established through behavior and dress. By shifting the signification of clothing and the bodies that clothing mediates, the feminist hard-boiled genre *performs* gender. And as Judith Butler's work demonstrates, performative gender can intervene in the reproduction of power relations. It complements reverse discourse, since it too depends on repetition with difference: "Performativity," Butler argues, "cannot be understood outside of a process of iterability, a regularized and constrained repetition of norms. And this repetition is not performed *by* a subject; this repetition is what enables a subject and constitutes the temporal condition for the subject. This iterability implies that 'performance' is not a singular 'act' or event, but a ritualized production" (*Bodies That Matter* 95). And it is a ritualized production analogous with genre itself. Butler's analysis applies well to the problematics of female hard-boiled writers, who work within—and against—a patriarchal literary and cultural tradition. These writers counter the utopian notion that one can work outside the patriarchal structure of Western society, at the same time that they make possible an understanding of gender as a set of regulating discourses that can be disrupted in practice. As Butler puts it, such performativity establishes "a kind of political contestation that is not a 'pure' opposition,' a 'transcendence' of contemporary relations of power, but a difficult labor of forging a future from resources inevitably impure" (241).

Reverse discourse and the notion of performative gender are concepts more frequently used by queer theorists than by theorists of heterosexuality, perhaps because the potential of the reverse most obviously speaks to the refashioning of gender enacted by gay and lesbian discourse. Yet it is in the interest of all gender critics to problematize and shift conventional gender constructions. Here, too, Butler's work is extremely useful. As Dennis W. Allen points out in "Mistaken Identities," "Although Butler's point is precisely that heterosexual identities are also constituted in the same way [as other identities], the tendency in the culture at large to dematerialize the heterosexual into a transcendental ground for discussion strongly counters a recognition of Butler's point while at the same time overdetermining the materiality of lesbians and gays." Allen asserts the need for a popular recognition of the fact that "the gender and sexuality of straight men such as Jesse Helms are also performative" (138-39). Butler's theories help to conceptualize heterosexual femininity as itself an "impure," unstable category.

REORIENTATIONS

Rebecca Pope sees Paretsky's novels evoking the possibility of deep, affectionate bonds between women outside the heterosexual romance plot, most notably in their development of the ongoing relationship between V. I. and her friend Dr. Lotty Herschel (159). To Pope, this and other explorations of lesbian themes suggest that V. I.'s "desire is more various and fluid than her practice" (166). Such desires are difficult to name in the terms available to conventional hard-boiled narratives in the masculine tradition. Their representation in Paretsky's novels is thus foregrounded, not least because her work does not simply recapitulate the homosocial unease characteristic of those earlier narratives. Gender role instability is even more overtly thematized in Nevada Barr's *Track of the Cat*, Mercedes Lambert's *Dogtown*, and Sarah Dunant's *Under My Skin*, all novels in which ostensibly heterosexual detectives reflect on their sexual orientation, thereby making an investigation of the nature of sexual desire a central component of the narrative.

In Barr's novel, park ranger Anna Pigeon finds herself powerfully attracted to a lesbian colleague. When Anna articulates her feelings to her psychiatrist sister Molly, Molly considers alternate ways of explaining Anna's situation: "Maybe you're overwhelmed that this woman was warm and kind and female. Maybe you're gun-shy of attachment since Zach left you. . . . Maybe you are turning gay. That's well and good. I just wanted to give you some other things to think about. Powerful need for affection, identification—all that underrated and over-exploited sisterhood stuff—is visceral. Feels almost sexual to those not in touch with themselves" (83-84). While Anna finally decides that she is heterosexual, the text highlights the permeability of heterosexual-homosexual desires. Lambert's novel confronts the theme more overtly, when investigating attorney Whitney Logan's attraction to another woman leads her to question her sexual orientation; the text im-

plies that with the solving of the mystery, a dis-solving of rigid heterosexuality has taken place.

In *Under My Skin,* Dunant links lesbian desire to the resistant reading by women of the film noir figure of the femme fatale, a reading that reconfigures the vicious trajectory of heterosexual desire in such films. In an interview, Hannah Wolfe is told about a woman who was in love with Lauren Bacall's character in the film *The Big Sleep*: "In love with Lauren Bacall, eh?" Hannah muses to herself, "She wasn't the only one" (89). In the course of an assignment at a women's health club, Hannah discovers the pleasure of another woman's sexual touch, an extension of a health massage:

> "Oh, that's good," I said slightly breathlessly. Because I wanted her to feel secure and because it was. Flesh. This story was all about flesh and how important it was to make sure somebody else loves it. And when you come to think of it, I had something to learn from that too.
>
> So I let her play around my upper thighs for a while, caressing, suggesting, exciting, until with an expert little flick her fingers slid under and in, into the mouth of me, where no one had been for what felt like such a long time.
>
> (234)

Though this pleasure is ultimately regulated by Hannah's role as an investigator of the club and the masseuse, and though Hannah's desire is finally recovered into a heterosexual dynamic at the end of the novel by a possible relationship with a man, these pat solutions do not fully recuperate either the language of pleasure or the fact that another woman has literally and figuratively gotten under her skin.

The female dick, in effect, signifies difference. This in-between locus can counter dominant constructions of gender and sexuality by placing in question the clear-cut and essentialized character of the norms established by previous practices of the hard-boiled mode. And mainstream formula fiction offers a controlled space that enables a wide audience to explore the borders of established categories and conventions. Thus, as John Cawelti contends, formula narratives may assist in the process of altering cultural norms on a broad scale, absorbing new possibilities while contributing to cultural continuity ("Study of Literary Formulas" 143).

This power of a popular genre is perhaps most evident in the recent growth of the lesbian detective novel, a development we identified in chapter 1. Until recently, however, Sandra Scoppettone, who features an "out" lesbian investigator in her Lauren Laurano series (the first, *Everything You Have Is Mine,* was published by Ballantine in 1991), was alone in her exploration of lesbian detection in the mainstream.[3] Almost all lesbian novels appeared in alternative press publications: since the 1970s, feminist presses such as Naiad, Seal, and Virago offered their readers lesbian investigators, including Sarah Dreher's Stoner McTavish, Katherine V. Forrest's Kate Delafield, J. M. Redmann's Mickey Knight, Mary Wings's Emma Victor, and Barbara Wilson's Pam Nilsen (in the United States); Eve Zaremba's Helen Keremos and Lauren Wright Douglas's Caitlin Reece (in Canada); Claire McNab's Carol Ashton (in Australia); and Val McDermid's Lindsay Gordon (in the United Kingdom). Such alternative publishing houses can produce novels that fall outside the purview of purely profit-driven mainstream publishers (presumably because they were perceived as "small-market" texts). For example, Susan Brown argues that

> [Barbara] Wilson, unlike say, Grafton or Sara Paretsky, who publish with major publishers, has much greater freedom to the extent that, as co-publisher of Seal Press, she controls her immediate mode of literary production. The fact that Seal is an avowedly feminist press which views books not solely as means to create profits but as "essential tools in stirring up debate and contributing much-needed facts and analysis," and is committed to "publishing books that are fun as well as empowering" (catalogue blurb), means that Wilson writes within a much different set of constraints than more mainstream detective novelists.
>
> (8)

While Brown's point is an important one, the crossover of a number of lesbian writers from small press to mainstream is evidence of the potential continuity of the two markets—that lesbian readers may be "mainstream readers" too. It also points to the possibility that once small press authors have adapted mainstream genres, they can gain access to other publishing outlets and audiences through the appeal of genre. As Scoppettone comments of her lesbian detective series, her readers "are predominantly lesbian but there are some gay men and a lot more heterosexuals than you, than I, ever expected. It does seem to have crossed over in the mystery field. I don't think there are a lot of . . . non-mystery readers, reading it. But there are a lot of heterosexuals that don't have a problem with it, or more than *do* have a problem." Since the early 1990s, it has become much more common for narratives featuring openly lesbian detectives to be published by mainstream presses.

It is worth recalling Cawelti's argument that "allowing for a certain degree of inertia in the process, the production of formulas is largely dependent on audience response" ("Study of Literary Formulas" 34). According to Katherine V. Forrest (who, as well as being a writer, is also an editor for Naiad Press), it was reader demand for her novels that generated a shift in publishers' conception of the mainstream audience itself:

> Initially, most of us [lesbian writers] went to small presses because the major presses simply wouldn't publish us. They had no notion of any sort of audience out there. There just wasn't that much interest in the kind of books we wrote, and so that gave rise to all of these small lesbian and feminist presses, which are still flourishing. And I think that what the small presses have

proven is that there *is* an audience out there for these books, that it's sizable, it's literate, it's affluent, and it's significant.

Forrest perceives her novels as "crossover" texts; in them, genre makes possible the convergence of different readerships. While affirming that she writes for a lesbian audience, Forrest observes: "A wider audience has found these books. But I think they're finding them because people who like good mysteries like good mysteries." One of the reasons she decided to shift from Naiad to Putnam is that reviewers tend to overlook small press publications, which results in less audience awareness. Forrest affirms the importance of being "heard" by lesbian and straight readers, reiterating Dutton editor Carole DeSanti's observation that lesbians' "are the only untold stories." Thus, for Forrest, moving to a mainstream press is a "dream . . . come true." Her character, Kate Delafield "is in a high-visibility, high-profile, very high-pressure job," which allows the author to explore "how that impacted on her as a lesbian and her lesbian identity." The relationship between professional and sexual identity has become "a crucial dynamic in the series." And Forrest adamantly asserts that she has not been asked by Putnam to downplay or soften her character's lesbianism. Forrest's *Murder at the Nightwood Bar* is now gaining further public exposure: it is being made into a Hollywood film.[4]

Both Phyllis Knight and Laurie R. King began publishing their lesbian detective series with mainstream houses, and a number of other authors have shifted from alternative to commercial publishing houses, including J. M. Redmann and Mary Wings. The change in mainstream publishers' responses to lesbian authors is evident in Knight's explanation of how her lesbian detective Lil Ritchie's "coming out" evolved as part of a process that involved author, agent and editor:

> I hadn't made it at all obvious that Lil was a gay woman and the agent that I sent it to said, "you know, obviously, Lil's a gay woman." I was just going to try to ignore it because I thought I'd never get published by a mainstream press, and then when my agent sent it to St. Martin's, the editor there . . . said to me, "I'm going to take it anyway, but, you know she's obviously a gay woman." So when he sent me back my manuscript the first time with changes, at the end I had her dancing with a stranger and he said, "I put a woman in there, tell me if it's not all right." I didn't have the courage to do it, and so to have a publisher insist was sort of interesting.

COLORING OUTSIDE THE LINES

Racial and ethnic boundaries have been similarly challenged through the agency of genre convention. This is not simply, as Sally Munt would argue, a "literary equal opportunity" approach or a "positive images" strategy engineered by mainstream white feminist authors in which the traditional alignment of white skin with good and black skin with bad is reversed, and in which (as Munt argues of Sara Paretsky's novels) all conflicts and differences are effaced (90). While Munt accurately observes that alternative presses have made and continue to make efforts to publish female detectives of color, her argument assumes that race and racism are concerns that can be addressed only from marginal positions of literary production (i.e., works having non-"mainstream" authors, publishers, and audiences). She overlooks the ways that mainstream presses may extend the process she attributes to small presses, making the perspectives they offer accessible to a wide audience. Mass audience publications can and do work both to complicate racial categories and to subvert (rather than merely inverting) the racially linked moral absolutes of traditional detective fiction. They may also use the marginal position of the private detective and the popular genre itself to interpellate a heterogeneous audience that other publishing venues cannot reach.

A number of mainstream press writers—including Valerie Wilson Wesley, Eleanor Taylor Bland, and Chassie West, who feature African American protagonists; Dana Stabenow, whose central character is an Aleut; and Gloria White, whose detective is half-Latina—have made racial issues central to their narratives of investigation. These writers use the generic figure of the detective as outsider to explore the subjectivity of racial categories that fall "outside the law," a strategy we will examine at further length in chapter 6. In so doing, they use the rules of genre to explore the cultural regulations that define outsider status.

For example, Valerie Wilson Wesley uses the detective novel to expose the crimes of racism within law enforcement. Wesley's protagonist Tamara Hayle is a former cop who quits the force. In *When Death Comes Stealing,* she inquires into the death of a young African American man whom the police have routinely written off as a junkie. The victim of crime has been elided with the criminal, a situation Tamara aims to rectify: "Some lazy cop, tired at the end of the day or late for lunch, had proclaimed that Terrence Curtis had lived and died a junkie, and there was no more to be said about it. But I know different now. If he'd died of crack, he hadn't been an addict, and I was hot for a minute, angry again at the bullshit so many cops put down when it comes to black folks—the official incompetence, the easy way out" (36).

In Gloria White's novels, her half-Latina protagonist, Ronnie Ventana, often confronts racism. In *Charged with Guilt,* Ronnie's inquiries lead her to San Francisco's Hispanic underworld, an underworld that has erected its own system of justice because it has been written off by the police. Ronnie must request assistance from an old friend of her father's, and her ability to "translate" between the cultures is central to her ability to open doors literally and figuratively to the information that circulates in different communities:

> Santiago Rosales had decided to set up his bar on Ellis Street. Not that it was really a bar. It was an exchange. People went to El Ratón Podrido for information, to make connections, to score goods and weapons. They went there for things they couldn't get anyplace else. And Santiago never turned anybody away. . . .

> I reached the bar and, when the bartender ambled over, I said, "I need to see Santiago."

> He raised his eyebrows and lowered his eyelids. He didn't need to say a word. It was obvious he needed to hear more before he'd consider letting me through.

> "Ronnie Ventana," I said.

> His surly face broke into an unexpected grin. "Ah, *sí.* 'Cisco's daughter. *Cómo no! Pase, pase. Por aquí.*"

> (283-85)

In Chassie West's *Sunrise,* police detective Leigh Ann Warren is so tired of the pressures placed on her by the Washington police force that she returns to her hometown in North Carolina for respite. While there she helps ensure that a proposed mall does not recklessly destroy an old African American cemetery. Eleanor Taylor Bland's *Dead Time* dramatizes the way the signifiers "black," "woman," and "police detective" can be read in contradictory ways, thus compromising Marti MacAlister's ability to be recognized as "representative" of official law enforcement. Called to a crime scene, Marti overhears how onlookers respond to her presence:

> "Well, *she* certainly isn't a police officer. I thought they were only letting in people on official business."

> A tiny dark-skinned woman with at least five slips hanging below a short, fuzzy blue robe answered.

> "Hah. Got cop written all over her. Now ain't that a sight, Betty? Black and a woman and not wearin' a uniform."

> (21)

Novelists often use the detective narrative and the subjectivity that focalizes it to investigate race and ethnicity—including white authors, who complicate the concept of homogeneous whiteness. For example, in Rochelle Majer Krich's *Angel of Death* and April Smith's *North of Montana,* a narrative of identity parallels the narrative of investigation, and the protagonist of each novel learns that her ethnicity is not as homogeneous as she thought it was. As these novels demonstrate, the texts of white writers as well as those of writers of color can serve as sites from which dominant perceptions of race and ethnicity may be interrogated. One of the earliest exemplars of the female PI, Marcia Muller's Sharon McCone is part Shoshone, a feature often overlooked in critical discussions of Muller's work. Linda Barnes's novels almost invariably begin by establishing her character's ethnic and religious hybridity (she is Irish-Jewish). Consider, for example, the opening paragraph of *Snapshot*:

> Every April my mother used to host her own version of the traditional Passover seder. A mishmash of Hebrew, Yiddish, English, and Russian, it involved all Mom's union pals—Jews, Christians, Muslims, and pagans— who'd give rapid-fire thanks for the release of the ancient Hebrews from Egyptian bondage, and then launch into pre-chicken-soup tirades against General Motors,

J. Edgar Hoover, and the FBI. I grew up thinking they were part of the religion.

(1)

Even Paretsky's mainstream hero, whom Munt cites as a perpetrator of simplistic "liberalist pluralism," has complex class and ethnic identifications. The child of a Polish father and an Italian immigrant mother, V. I.'s first-generation, "new" world status is central to her position as investigator, and the character frequently calls attention to her cultural background and the dis/position it establishes: "I guess my ideals died the hardest. It's often that way with the children of immigrants. We need to buy the dream so bad we sometimes can't wake up" (*Killing Orders* 86-87). Her comment here also calls attention to the attraction of the liberal humanist democratic ideal as one possible (though not the only) source of agency. V. I.'s position creates a potential point of identification in the novels with more marginalized positions, one also opened up to readers. For instance, in *Bitter Medicine* V. I. perceives the institutional marginalization of Philippa Barnes, an African American woman who works for the Department of Environment and Human Resources. Barnes tells V. I., "The bureaucracy in a place like this just about kills you. If I had charge of the whole program, instead of just a piece of it—' She folded her lips, cutting off the sentence." In a moment of recognition that the reader shares, V. I. realizes, "We all . . . knew that having a sex-change operation—and perhaps dyeing her skin—was the only way that would happen" (165-66).

Feminist hard-boiled detective novels provide their readers with fictional narratives that have repercussions beyond their immediate textual performances. It is therefore important not to belittle the liberal feminist "fantasy of empowerment" that Sally Munt describes so disparagingly; writers and readers may use this fantasy as a point of departure, a site of agency and change. As we saw in chapter 2, letters to Sara Paretsky demonstrate that a fictional problem-solving heroine sometimes helps readers feel as if they can solve their own problems. In "Surviving Rape," an essay in *Theorizing Black Feminisms,* Andrea Rushing describes the pleasure and affirmation she experienced in reading "books about new-style U.S. women detectives" after she had been sexually assaulted:

> Week after week I gulp, as if drowningly desperate for air, their plain-spoken stories about acid-tongued, fast-thinking, single and self-employed women who not only dare to live alone, but scoff, sneer, seethe when men try to put them in their "weaker sex" place. Parched and starved, I read and reread Sue Grafton's alphabet adventures, but Sara Paretsky's books became my favourites because her Chicago-based private investigator is even more bodacious and sassy than my pre-rape self. And, in stark contrast to television and movie renditions of women as powerless victims of men, she both withstands and metes out physical violence in every single book. Murder mysteries restore order to worlds thrown out of balance.

(137)

Murder mysteries also offer alternative readings about just what constitutes "order" and "balance." And even if they do not always fully restore order, they repeatedly dramatize, address, and renegotiate fantasies, fears, and conflicts in the lives of their readers. Through reverse discourse, with its performative gender possibilities, these texts can both inscribe an empowered female subject and rework the conventions of subjectivity that make that position problematic.

"WELCOME TO MASS CULTURE"

Some novels even address explicitly their status as popular culture fantasies, offering a version of reverse discourse that relates to their own fictional practice. Lia Matera's *Face Value* and Mary Willis Walker's *Red Scream* both thematize the very system of popular culture that makes them possible. Matera's *Face Value* is, among other things, an unusually self-conscious example of the apparently contradictory way an author can use the popular cultural form of the detective novel to look beyond the "face value" of popular culture itself, foregrounding how its discourses (popular fiction, film, television, journalism) construct a sense of "the real" that embodies powerful ideological messages. Matera's detective, lawyer Laura Di Palma, explains how she rose to fame on a defense tactic, used in a murder case, that came to be known as the "television syndrome" defense: she argued "that television creates a reality more powerful than personal experience" (14). The defendant shot two U.S. senators, under the influence of Clint Eastwood and Charles Bronson movies: he "had been inundated with television images of lone-wolf, take-the-law-in-their-own-hands good guys" (155). Those images might well be related to the tough guy detectives of the hard-boiled literary tradition; and in evoking the extreme example of a man who kills because of the models they provide, Matera's novel dramatizes how rhetorically powerful such fictional representations can be. On a less extreme note, the novel may also make readers more self-conscious about the ways in which popular cultural forms shape our sense of reality, even as it *uses* the popular form of the novel of private investigation to posit alternative possibilities for being and acting. The novel repeatedly suggests the ways in which "real" identities are repeatedly performed—for example, in the fashion, grooming, and (profitable) public spectacles of the high-powered female lawyer, the stripper, the New Age guru, and even Miss America. Contemplating the pervasive societal need for "something real," Laura wryly comments, "Welcome to mass culture" (16).

The narrative of *Face Value* involves Laura's investigation of a quasireligious cult's practice of taping, visually modifying, and then marketing—without permission of the participants—the sexual consciousness-raising sessions that are part of its "therapy." Having viewed some of these tapes, Laura comments, "Like other 'erotic' films I'd seen, these tracked lowest-common-denominator fantasies featuring people who, for the most part, might have stepped off a television set. They left me feeling as if I'd watched a particularly embarrassing episode of 'The Newlywed Game.' They made me want to distance myself from mass culture, to flee into the artistic refinement of classical novels and old jazz" (30). Laura does not retreat, however. Indeed, she has no choice, since she is already implicated in the performances that make her own subjectivity and sexuality possible. Nor does Matera attempt to escape mass culture, though she does appropriate and redirect it in order to investigate the implications of different forms of popular "visual manipulation," both of images and audiences.

Walker's *Red Scream* uses the narrative of investigation to inquire into the ways in which crime writing controls the legitimating discourses that make "truths" about crime and criminality public currency. *Red Scream*'s investigative reporter Molly Cates has published a "true crime" book, *Sweating Blood,* that focuses on the motivations and actions of convicted serial killer Louie Bronk. During the writing of the book, Molly "had wrestled with the problem inherent in writing a book for entertainment which was based on other people's private disasters" (4). Yet as a writer she also gets a great deal of satisfaction from the way the final product lives up to the generic—and profit-generating—standards of the "true crime" genre:

> From the minute her publisher had first showed her the cover art, she had loved it because it was so attention-grabbing. The painting depicted a lonely stretch of highway with a woman's body lying in a ditch alongside; from the body blood flowed and surrounded the entire cover, front and back, with a shiny vivid red. She had recognized immediately that it would sell books. It was commercial, yes, sensational even. But that was the nature of true crime books and she wasn't going to apologize for it.
>
> (4)

Molly must confront her own complicity in sensationalizing the murders when *Sweating Blood* focuses unwanted attention on the family of Tiny McFarland, for whose murder Bronk has received the death penalty. Molly is also forced to consider the possibility that her book might be responsible for generating a copycat murder, reenacting its representation: "what if some maniac read her account of Tiny McFarland's murder and decided to do the same thing? . . . She felt a flush of hot confusion, like waking panicked from a nightmare not knowing what was real and what wasn't" (69).

Questions of what is "real" and what is "fiction" pervade this narrative, since Molly's "true crime" account is thrown into doubt when she visits Bronk on death row and is informed by the convict that in their initial interviews, his representation of events was not true but was what he believed she wanted to hear. At this meeting, Bronk contends that he is not responsible for Tiny's murder (though there is no question that he committed the others for which he has been jailed), and Molly must now deal with her own conflicting inclinations. Her first response is to disbelieve Bronk, because his latest statement threatens the generic claims of her "true crime" book: "If Louis didn't do it, then *Sweating Blood* was largely fiction" (191). Molly's second response is to conduct a supplementary investigation of the killings, over the course of which she becomes convinced that Louie's new narrative may be the "real" narrative—a narrative that is now impossible to verify, because much of the evidence has disappeared. When Molly realizes that she cannot sufficiently establish that Louis is not guilty of Tiny's murder, she tries to obtain a stay of execution by convincing the governor that Louie is now telling the truth.

Although the governor denies Molly's request, she does offer Molly advice about an alternative (legitimate) perspective for crime writing: "'I have a suggestion for you: how about writing more about crime from the victim's point of view? I reckon serial murderers sell books, but where are the stories of the [victims] of the world? People who survive the unimaginable and go on cheerfully—the stuff of real heroes'" (274). The "true crime" account of *Sweating Blood* has left the stories of the murder victims untold. And it has also potentially made Louie Bronk both criminal in and victim of its narrative, since it has shaped public opinion of him. Unable to stop the legal proceedings, Molly attends the execution and watches Bronk die for a murder he did not commit. *Red Scream* concludes with yet another story, an article in the *Lone Star Monthly* in which Molly corrects previous accounts and expresses her anger at the justice system and at herself for her complicity in Bronk's death:

> No one tried to stop [the execution]. Not one of us. I knew he was innocent, but I did nothing. I didn't object or cry bloody murder, or give in to the red scream—that shriek of terror and rage death-row inmates talk about. I just stood and watched—a passive witness.
>
> But no more.
>
> Here is my red scream. . . .
>
> (324, her ellipsis)

Molly's "true crime" account is embedded in a crime *fiction* that allows Walker to leave the reader with questions about how stories are constructed and what kinds of truths they produce, as well as about the legitimating power of the crime writer.

There are no easy answers to such questions—indeed, in a characteristic gesture, the narrative of *Red Scream* produces structural closure (we learn whodunit) but leaves its readers with a profound sense that other issues remain to be resolved. These include the legitimating function of the popular culture text itself—its ability to mediate alternative and often contradictory constructions of the real—and the related question of the connection between language, genre, and power. In chapter 4, we turn to the conventional language of hard-boiled fiction, which its American innovators saw as a uniquely truthful and powerful way of representing the sensational world of crime and criminals.

Women writing in the hard-boiled tradition question their progenitors by drawing on the interrogative power of tough talk itself.

Notes

1. The debate over contemporary avant-garde writing—postmodern theory and fiction—casts an interesting light on arguments over finding feminist agency in detective fiction. Because postmodern literature often undertakes a decentering of the individual subject, many of its critics doubt its ability to convey subversive messages. In her theoretical writings, Nancy K. Miller engages with the postmodern celebration of subject fragmentation (or the critique of the self-contained and coherent thinking, knowing being) by asserting that "only those who have it [subjectivity] can play with not having it" (53). While postmodern novels are frequently attacked for fracturing the subject and thereby displacing political potential by abrogating boundaries, critics of the feminist hard-boiled novel often condemn the mode for insufficiently questioning traditional liberal formations of subjectivity. For example, in appraising Anna Lee, Liza Cody's character, Sally Munt notes that the professional PI functions as "the self-determining agent of liberal fantasy, reinstating the quintessentially liberal myth of independence" (52). Munt inadvertently draws attention to a catch-22 faced by the woman writer: to some extent she's damned if she does, and damned if she doesn't. For a more extended discussion of the debate over poststructuralist and postmodern theory, see Butler and Scott's collection, *Feminists Theorize the Political*, and Hutcheon's *Politics of Postmodernism*.

2. Munt notes in passing that lesbian fiction constitutes a reverse discourse in action (126), but she does not extend her argument to explore the ways in which feminist revisions of the hard-boiled mode function similarly.

3. As we observed in chapter 1, the first installment of Eve Zaremba's lesbian detective series was published by a mainstream press, but this was "an aberration" (Zaremba, "A Canadian Speaks" 45).

4. Sandra Scoppettone describes her sense that the film and television industry lags behind popular novels in its representation of lesbians by about ten years. Scoppettone had her own brief encounter with Hollywood when actress Cybill Shepherd optioned her books: "She approached all the networks. Nobody would do it." Perhaps in return for Shepherd's enthusiasm for the project, Scoppettone makes her a "guest" character in *My Sweet Untraceable You*. Scoppettone relates that she was contacted by a prospective film producer just after her Lauren Laurano series first appeared; "We love everything you have," he said, "We think it's great, but is the lesbian thing important?"

Works Cited

Allen, Dennis W. "Mistaken Identities: Re-Defining Lesbian and Gay Studies." *Canadian Review of Comparative Literature* 21 (1994): 133-48.

Bird, Delys, and Brenda Walker. Introduction to Bird, *Killing Women* 1-61.

Butler, Judith. *Gender Trouble: Feminism and the Subversion of Identity.* New York: Routledge, 1990.

Coward, Rosalind, and Linda Semple. "Tracking Down the Past: Women and Detective Fiction." In *Genre and Women's Writing in the Postmodern World,* edited by Helen Carr, 39-57. London: Pandora, 1989.

Geeson, Susan. "Ain't Misbehavin'." In Bird, *Killing Women* 111-23.

Godard, Barbara. "Sleuthing: Feminist Re/writing the Detective Novel." *Signature* 1 (summer 1989): 45-70.

Klein, Kathleen Gregory. *Great Women Mystery Writers: A Biocritical Dictionary.* Westport, Conn.: Greenwood, 1994.

Knight, Stephen. *Form and Ideology in Crime Fiction.* Bloomington: Indian University Press, 1980.

Littler, Alison. "Marele Day's 'Cold Hard Bitch': The Masculinist Imperatives of the Private-Eye Genre." *Journal of Narrative Technique* 21 (1991): 121-35.

Munt, Sally R. *Murder by the Book?: Feminism and the Crime Novel.* London: Routledge, 1994.

Reddy, Maureen T. *Sisters in Crime: Feminism and the Crime Novel.* New York: Continuum, 1988.

Rich, B. Ruby. "The Lady Dicks: Genre Benders Take the Case." *Voice Literary Supplement,* June 1990, 24-27.

Rushing, Andrea. "Surviving Rape." In *Theorizing Black Feminisms,* edited by Stanlie M. James and Abena P. A. Busia, 129-42. London: Routledge, 1993.

Priscilla L. Walton and Manina Jones (essay date 1999)

SOURCE: Walton, Priscilla L. and Manina Jones. "The Text as Evidence: Linguistic Subversions." In *Detective Agency: Women Rewriting the Hard-Boiled Tradition,* pp. 118-48. Berkeley: University of California Press, 1999.

[In the following excerpt, Walton and Jones focus on the use of language in hard-boiled fiction written by women, pointing out that these female authors both appropriate and transform the tough language of the traditional detective.]

"If it's that delicate," I said, "maybe you need a lady detective."

"Goodness, I didn't know there were any." Pause. "But I don't think a lady detective would do at all. You see,

Orrin was living in a very tough neighborhood, Mr. Marlowe. At least, I thought it was tough. The manager of the rooming house is a most unpleasant person. He smelled of liquor. Do you drink, Mr. Marlowe?"

"Well, now that you mention it—"

"I don't think I'd care to employ a detective that uses liquor in any form. I don't even approve of tobacco."

"Would it be all right if I peeled an orange?"

I caught the sharp intake of breath at the far end of the line. "You might at least talk like a gentleman," she said.

"Better try the University Club," I told her. "I heard they had a couple left over there, but I'm not sure they'll let you handle them." I hung up.

Raymond Chandler, *The Little Sister*

TOUGH GUYS/TOUGH TALK

Ross Macdonald once observed, "The Chandler-Marlowe prose is a highly charged blend of laconic wit and imagistic poetry set to breakneck rhythms. Its strong colloquial vein reaffirms the fact that the *Black Mask* revolution was a revolution in language as well as in subject matter" ("The Writer" 183). Chandler himself read the innovations of his predecessor Dashiell Hammett as part of a "rather revolutionary debunking" not just of the material of fiction, but of its *language*; he traces this movement back to poet Walt Whitman and to novelists of the naturalist school, associating it with an American vernacular strain of literary practice ("Simple Art" 233). Hard-boiled writers saw their work as part of a revolution that made it possible to represent a more authentic version of reality with a different kind of literary "lingo." More specifically, they launched a rebellion against what they thought of as the artificial formal restrictions of the popular British cozy tradition, with its stylized techniques of characterization, its confining ratiocinative plot structures and modes of narration, and, perhaps most important, its conventionalized literary language. The Golden Age mystery was popular precisely because of its ingeniousness and artificiality: as one critic put it, "the charm of the pure detective story is its utter un-reality" (Nicolson 117-18). Hard-boiled writers such as Chandler were clearly unmoved by this charm, judging it phony and pretentious. Chandler concludes in "The Simple Art of Murder" that the kind of writing practiced by Dorothy L. Sayers "was an arid formula which could not even satisfy its own implications" (232), and Macdonald affirms that the *Black Mask* writers felt the formula "had lost contact with contemporary life and language" ("The Writer" 181).

The Golden Age murder mystery of the interwar period was stereotypically identified not just with the British, but especially with the female novelists who established its popularity, including Sayers, Agatha Christie, Marjorie Allingham, Josephine Tey, and Ngaio Marsh. As Alice Yaeger Kaplan perceives (27), it is both a British and a feminized current in mystery writing that Chandler denounces

in "The Simple Art of Murder." Moreover, it is a tradition frequently associated with its extensive audience of female *readers,* whom Chandler's famous essay parodies as old ladies jostling at the mystery bookshelf for titles like *The Triple Petunia Murder Case* or *Inspector Pinchbottle to the Rescue* (224). The vulgarity of wisecracking hard-boiled speech was indeed shocking and subversive of conventional literary decorum; it was precisely the kind of language not to be used in the company of ladies, much less be used by the ladies themselves. In describing the present-day version of the classical mystery (the mystery that features an amateur detective), novelist Nancy Pickard once again relates this sense of decorum to a feminine audience of delicate sensibility, advising aspiring writers that in composing such mysteries "you generally can't use as much *bad language,* violence, sex or gore as you could in some other types of mysteries. And isn't *that* a relief? And isn't your mother grateful?" (65, first emphasis added). Sue Grafton, incidentally, wittily revises this stereotype of the fragile sensitive old woman reader of cozies in her novel *"B" Is for Burglar.* When Grafton's detective conscripts an elderly woman to help with her investigation, the woman eagerly responds by offering to learn the language of hard-boiled detection: "I'm going to start reading Mickey Spillane just to get in shape," she says; "I don't know a lot of rude words, you know" (103).[1] The character creates an analogy between her active participation in the case (she has to "get in shape") and a repertoire of hard-boiled linguistic "moves."

The hard-boiled stylistic revolution should also be read as running counter to the "high literary" avant-garde antirealist experimentations of modernist writers such as James Joyce and Virginia Woolf; in particular, detective fiction is in part defined by its mass-market appeal, while this form of literary modernism, typically characterized as elitist and academic "high culture," is seen as somehow exempt from the exigencies of the literary marketplace (see chapter 2). Such definition by contrast occurred during the Golden Age of detective fiction itself. In a 1929 article, for example, Marjorie Nicolson remarked on the academic reader's fondness for formal mysteries, which she claimed had developed as a kind of reader "revolt" against the "formlessness" and general decadence of contemporary literature (113, 114). Writing before women writers of Golden Age fiction had achieved their ascendancy Nicolson saw the detective genre not simply as "a man's novel" but as a more generally masculine endeavor, since its writers were able to engineer an "escape from a school of fiction which is becoming too feminized" (123).[2]

JUST THE FACTS, MA'AM

Hard-boiled writing was, as Julian Symons notes, an "American revolution" (153) in crime fiction, and this was specifically a stylistic revolution in that it validated the vernacular of the urban United States as its legitimate linguistic territory. It was at the same time a self-consciously populist "democratic" revolution that countered the inaccessible, anti-realist prose of modernism with its new brand of popular "vernacular realism." It is no coincidence that the forms of writing against which the hard-boiled style is defined are routinely constructed as simultaneously artificial, elitist, and *feminine*. As Dennis Porter puts it, "the new ethos of hard-boiled detective fiction was not only anti-English and anti-elitist, it was also antifeminist" (184). Intimately related to the popular, realist, and American "revolution" in novelistic language is hard-boiled writing's development of a self-consciously masculine style, a style that would act as an antidote to the perceived effeminacy of other approaches. When Chandler considered how Hammett's writing recovers and reshapes "the speech of common men," the gender specificity of his noun needed no emphasis ("Simple Art" 234). It is not surprising, therefore, that the modern literary stylist with whom hard-boiled writing is most often associated is Ernest Hemingway. Although critics have never really decided whether Hemingway was an influence on Hammett, or vice versa (see Chandler, "Simple Art" 233; Symons 157; Worpole 36), critics of both writers almost always use terms associated with masculinity to describe their innovations in narrative style (Worpole 39). Porter extends this notion of a masculine vernacular style to the formal innovations of a whole line of canonical American literature:

> Those stylists who from Mark Twain to Hemingway, Faulkner, and Norman Mailer created the idiom of the American literary mainstream also conspired to ensure that the voice of American fiction should be an aggressively male voice. At least until Erica Jong there has been no vernacular for women outside quotation marks. Bad grammar, slang, and even a strong regional accent, like cussing, blaspheming, hard drinking, and tomcatting, were the prerogatives of men and boys, defensive reactions against the encroachments of civilizing womankind and the tyranny of hearth and home. A linguistic double standard operated, making such language in a female mouth the sign of a bumpkin or a fallen woman.
>
> (184)[3]

The stylistic originality of hard-boiled writing included what Walker Gibson identifies as the rhetorical strategies of "tough talk." His description of these strategies, based on an analysis of the opening paragraph of Hemingway's *Farewell to Arms* (1929) (and later extended in a modified form to the discussion of Chandler's work), makes clear the degree to which the efficacy of the tough-talking narrator depends on his "plain-spoken" demeanor, on his anti-"literary" idiom, and on an implicit, fraternal bond with the reader. Gibson's use of gender pronouns stipulates that the narrator—and by extension the author—and assumed reader are by definition male:

> [The tough talker's] rhetoric, like his personality, shows his limitations openly: short sentences, "crude" repetitions of words, simple grammatical structures with little subordinating (I have no use for elegant variation, for the worn-out gentilities of traditional prose). His tense intimacy with his assumed reader, another man who has been around, is implied by colloquial patterns from oral speech and by a high frequency of the definite ar-

ticle. He lets his reader make logical and other connections between elements (You know what I mean; I don't have to spell it all out for *you*). He prefers naming things to describing them, and avoids modification, especially when he is self-conscious about his language—even about language generally.

> (41)

Despite the almost exclusive use of the "subjective" point of view in hard-boiled stories and the implicit intimacy between narrative speaker and reader, the flat, tough-talking voice denotes a certain sense of distance from its subject matter; its bluntness and often cynical tone give a feeling of straightforwardness and authenticity. The tough-talker's language tells us that he shoots straight from the hip, both literally and figuratively. And taciturn narrators such as Philip Marlowe or Mike Hammer give the impression of objectivity—their reticence implies a refusal to engage with and thus become implicated in the corrupt world that surrounds them. Hammett's description of Sam Spade as observing a room with the "detached air of a disinterested spectator" well characterizes the hard-boiled narrative voice (*Maltese Falcon* 74).

David Glover identifies another rhetorical effect of the tough-talking narrator: the repositioning of women as readers, which, he contends, contributed to a gendered segregation of the popular fiction market from the 1930s onward. As Tania Modleski points out, a second "Gothic revival" of fiction marketed to women occurred at the same time that hard-boiled detective novels were generating an unprecedented audience of male readers (*Loving with a Vengeance* 21).[4] Glover argues in addition that the hard-boiled "masculinization of crime fiction" repositions women as fictional characters as it simultaneously excludes them as authors (74). The estrangement of women as readers, authors, and characters is thus a product of what Bethany Ogodon calls the "'hard-boiled' collectivity (readers, writers, detective-heroes)," a closed masculine circle formed by the genre that encourages an antagonistic "us against them" structure (84).

We need to extend these observations in order also to recognize the way the "vernacular style" validated the common *man*'s language and experience, universalizing the masculine perspective and in effect alienating women from the very language it designates as realistic, despite its self-styled democratic aims. For example, Ross Macdonald commented in an interview, "I think the American 'hard-boiled' detective novel was invented to reflect American society, which is essentially an equalitarian [*sic*] society" ("Interview" 183). It is perhaps no coincidence that at a moment in American history when women had just been accorded full voting rights (the Nineteenth Amendment was passed in 1920), they were implicitly excepted from the development of this uniquely American, "democratic" revolutionary literary genre. Although hard-boiled authors relied on a formulaic narrative of investigation, and although they developed their own easily recognizable (and highly artificial) protocols of style, these writers affirmed again and again their privileged access to the average American's real life (see, for example, Chandler, "Simple Art"; Macdonald, "Interview").

Kenneth Worpole recognizes how the kind of life they represent might alienate women readers, but he insists that "it is still important to defend, critically, vernacular realism because of its narrative strength and popular accessibility to the language of everyday life" (47). Yet it is also important to understand that the language of vernacular realism suggested that "everyday life"—in effect, reality itself—was a masculine space. Contemporary women writers in the hard-boiled mode seem to be acting on Worpole's injunction: they implicitly defend vernacular realism by employing recognizable (if modified) versions of hard-boiled "tough talk" and by self-consciously appropriating strategies of narrative and description from the hard-boiled repertoire. In so doing they gesture toward a reclamation of the territory of "the real" from which such writing had tacitly estranged women writers and readers. At the same time, they also draw on the strength of the hard-boiled detective narrative in order to be recognizable and accessible to a popular audience of both men and women. But they defend that reclaimed territory *critically,* appropriating popular culture as a viable (if limited) locus of feminist analysis and making the hard-boiled narrative of investigation available as an instrument of literary and social critique. And the formal and stylistic characteristics of their fiction are themselves elements of that critique. In fact, in appropriating and reversing the discourse of earlier novels, these works may be read as an investigation of the nature and power of hard-boiled language itself.

Talking Back

Peter Rabinowitz's analysis of the conclusion of Sue Grafton's first novel, *"A" Is for Alibi,* helps to illuminate how this early work cleverly forecasts the subversive potential of women's appropriation of hard-boiled generic conventions. Grafton's detective narrative reaches its climax when her detective, Kinsey Millhone, chased by the killer, Charlie, conceals herself in a large metal garbage container, clutching her gun. Charlie tracks her to this hiding place. Grafton ends the main narrative:

> He lifted the lid. The beams from his headlights shone against his golden cheek. He glanced over at me. In his right hand was a butcher knife with a ten-inch blade.
>
> I blew him away.
>
> (214)

As Rabinowitz argues, ultimately Kinsey's position "serves to remind us that even the trashiest literature can, if taken over and remade, serve as a site of empowerment" ("Reader, I Blew Him Away" 333). Grafton's language in this passage and elsewhere self-consciously evokes the attributes of the tough-talking hard-boiled narrator: the direct matter-of-fact descriptive voice; the short, simple words and sentences; the repetitive structures; the use of the definite article and material details; and an understated

concluding punch line. That language becomes a point of departure for Grafton, a kind of sanction for her own ability to speak as a popular writer and a way of designating the tradition which she both emulates and contradicts. Thus, Scott Christianson observes, "Grafton appropriates hard-boiled language for feminist purposes as an exercise of language as power; in Foucauldian terms, she seizes the 'rules of formation' for the 'discourse' of hard-boiled fiction, thereby occupying a space or 'subject position,' formerly reserved for men only, from which she may speak with power as a woman" ("Talkin' Trash" 136). It enables her, in other words, to talk back to the masculine tradition on—or in—its own terms.

The ending of *"A" Is for Alibi* is also an implicit reconsideration of the formulaic narrative structure of many hard-boiled novels. As Kinsey's lover-turned-betrayer, Charlie is a male version of the hard-boiled femme fatale—he is an *homme fatal,* if we may coin a term. The final paragraph is therefore a self-conscious gender reversal of the hard-boiled narrative convention—one almost wants to call it the literary cleansing ritual—that involves achieving a sense of closure by violently eliminating (and in doing so silencing) the betraying woman, who epitomizes the threat to the narrator's moral authority.[5] In particular, it echoes the language and violent finales of many Mickey Spillane novels. Grafton's "I blew him away" evokes the blunt, pithy ending of Spillane's *I, the Jury* in which Hammer remorselessly guns down the femme fatale as he recounts, "The roar of the .45 shook the room": "How c-could you?" she gasps, realizing she is mortally wounded, and Hammer responds, "I only had a moment before talking to a corpse, but I got it in. 'It was easy,' I said."[6] Grafton's novel allows much more ambivalent readings. For example, unlike *I, the Jury, "A" Is for Alibi* ends with an epilogue that cannot quite contain the implications of the final killing. Kinsey's ambivalence about it is especially pronounced since she must acknowledge that her actions were part of a job from which she profited and which she continues to practice: "All together, I was paid $2978.25 for services rendered in the course of the sixteen days and I suppose it was fair enough. The shooting disturbs me still. It has moved me into the same camp with soldiers and maniacs. . . . I'll recover, of course. I'll be ready for business again in a week or two, but I'll never be the same" (214). Read at another level, Kinsey's admission might also cue readers to the necessarily ambivalent position in which Grafton too is placed, as one who uses her hard-boiled series to capitalize professionally on the powerful conservative conventions of the hard-boiled tradition (a choice that moves her, after all, into the same camp with the likes of Spillane), at the same time that she turns them to revisionist ends.

"You Know What I Mean; I Don't Have To Spell It Out For You" (Walker Gibson)

One of the central rhetorical strategies of "tough talk" involves its interpellation of readers; it cements a familiar bond with them. From their inception, hard-boiled stories used a direct appeal to the audience in the style of the dramatic aside to reinforce an identification between narrator and reader. In fact, what is arguably the first hard-boiled story, "Three Gun Terry," published in *Black Mask* on May 15, 1923, and featuring Carroll John Daly's detective Terry Mack, began:

> My life is my own, and the opinions of others don't interest me; so don't form any, or if you do, keep them to yourself. If you want to sneer at my tactics, why go ahead; but do it behind the pages—you'll find that healthier.
>
> So for my line. I have a little office which says "Terry Mack, Private Investigator," on the door; which means whatever you wish to think it. I ain't a crook, and I ain't a dick; I play the game on the level, in my own way. I'm in the center of a triangle; between the crook and the police and the victim. The police have had an eye on me for some time, but only an eye, never a hand; they don't get my lay at all. The crooks; well, some is on, and some ain't; most of them don't know what to think, until I've put the hooks in them. Sometimes they gun for me, but that ain't a one-sided affair. When it comes to shooting, I don't have to waste time cleaning my gun. A little windy that; but you get my game.
>
> (43-44)

Detective novels authored by women, using a similar formal strategy, often both call attention to and frustrate the exclusive nature of the male bonding that such asides manufacture. The gesture accomplishes at least two functions in this context: it develops an intimate bond of identification between the narrator and a differently constituted readership, and it throws the techniques of male hard-boiled fiction into (often comic) relief.

Whether explicitly or implicitly, narratives *always* construct a "you" that is addressed by the narration. Women's hard-boiled novels tend to highlight women's traditional alienation from that "you," offering the woman reader a privileged, self-conscious place in the narrative. For example, Carlotta Carlyle's initial address to her readers in the opening pages of Barnes's *Trouble of Fools* stands in stark contrast with the adventure-style beginning of Daly's story: "The vacuum cleaner hummed pleasantly. If you've ever considered your Hoover's voice soothing, you've probably been shoving it across a high-pile carpet. From the right distance, propelled by other hands—in this case the paint-smeared hands of Roz, my tenant cum new-wave artist cum sometime assistant—vacuum cleaner buzz could make the lullaby obsolete" (1). As noted in chapter 3, Kinsey Millhone contrasts her routines with those of male counterparts in interrogative asides to the reader that, like Carlotta's aside, de-romanticize the macho myth of the detective through associations with women's domestic work. Sara Dunant's Hannah Wolfe mysteries often directly address the reader, and sometimes humorously develop a sly kind of female bonding through that address. For instance, in *Fatlands,* after having consumed too much coffee, the detective remarks, "Of course, feminism has given us girls

the confidence to pee anywhere, but it had been a long time since breakfast and if I was going to stop I might as well make it work for me" (100). When she admits to having to ask for directions twice in one day, she solicits the reader to take her side and keep the information from her male partner: "I won't tell Frank if you don't" (100).

DISRUPTING THE GAG ORDER

Strategies that encourage an identification between narrator and reader are central to how tough talk and especially wisecracks function in women's hard-boiled writing. The narrator of hard-boiled stories speaks not just *to* but *for* the reader. In his article on detective fiction and the discourses of modernity, Scott Christianson recognizes the ways traditional hard-boiled wisecracks are defined against acceptable codes of literary and social decorum. The acting out represented by the wisecrack offers a vicarious thrill for the reader: "Against the good taste and breeding of hegemonic, dominant culture, the hard-boiled private eye is scandalous, indecorous, vulgar, offensive—and violent" ("Heap of Broken Images" 146). J. M. Redmann's detective Micky Knight uses the scandalous, indecorous, vulgar, and offensive nature of the wisecrack as a defensive device against a man who uses sexual obscenities to threaten her over the telephone. Micky puts the phone down until he is done speaking, then picks it up again and responds: "Sorry, Joey, my tampon was bleeding over and I could feel the blood running down my legs. I had to pull it out—it was covered with big, dripping clots. What were you saying?" (104). Her remark draws attention to the socially constructed nature of women's bodies as excessive, "monstrous," and even obscene—when they are not subject to masculine sexual control: Micky's uncontrollable status as a lesbian in her relationship to Joey has "provoked" his attempt to subordinate her by evoking a pornographic verbal scenario.

A similarly defensive "vulgar" gesture is enacted by Karen Kijewski's detective Kat Colorado, who casually picks her nose when she is taken captive, in defiance of her male captor's sense of propriety and, significantly, as a means of verbally shifting the balance of power between them:

> Picking one's nose is a small, but a crude and disgusting thing. It is repellent to most of us, to our sense of manners and presumably to our romantic and sexual sensibilities. Blackford looked astounded and repulsed. I smiled.
>
> "How very unladylike!"
>
> "I don't pretend to be a lady."
>
> "Just a private investigator," he said scornfully as he handed me my wine. I wiped my hand on the chair arm before I took the wine and watched him wince.
>
> "Exactly."
>
> The control had shifted. I no longer felt remotely like a captive or a whore and he no longer saw me as one.
>
> (*Katwalk* 212)

Kat's "unladylike" demeanor resists subordination. Through it, she refuses to be captive to rules that govern the role of "lady"—a role that here is antithetical to Kat's performance as a private investigator.

D. B. Borton's private eye Cat Caliban is a grandmother who, on the first page of the first novel in the series, explains both her genre-altering difference from the stereotype of the detective and her penchant for swearing as a means of making herself heard:

> "You don't look like no 'tectives on TV, Granny," Ben had announced at his first opportunity to comment on my new career. He'd stuck one pudgy digit up his nose and pointed another one at me accusingly. "None o' them gots white hair."
>
> "Stick around for a few seasons, kid. They will," I'd answered.
>
> What the hell. I was used to skepticism. Any veteran mother that isn't has her goddam ears stuffed with kumquats.
>
> Swearing was a habit I'd picked up when Fred was alive. One day I got the impression that Fred hadn't been listening to me for a while. Say, twenty years. So I thought I'd try a little verbal variety to see if he'd notice.
>
> *(One for the Money* 1)

Above all, the wisecrack provides the potential for discursive resistance. When in Chandler's *Big Sleep* General Sternwood suggests that detective Philip Marlowe disliked working for the district attorney, Marlowe replies, "I was fired. For insubordination. I test very high on insubordination, General" (10). Wisecracks are a method of wittily scoring through language; they are an instance of verbal insubordination. Lew Archer, for example, uses the wisecrack both as an insult and as a way of verbally resisting a police officer. Indeed, his remarks jokingly call attention to the disruption of his very patterns of language when he is mistreated by authority. Asked "who the hell are you, anyway," he provides identification and adds, "Now ask me what the hell I'm doing here. Unfortunately my chronic aphasia has taken a bad turn for the worse. It always goes like that when a dumb cop takes a shot at me" (Macdonald, *Drowning Pool* 59). This dynamic of insubordination is extended and developed in significant ways in private eye novels in which the investigator is a woman. These works often emphasize the role of gender in the relationship between language and power.

In Sandra West Prowell's *By Evil Means,* the sexual power dynamic of the verbal response is made obvious when private detective Phoebe Siegel is leered at by Crank, a character who was bitten in the crotch by dogs. Her response to his aggressive visual advance draws attention, and, metaphorically at least, contributes to his (sexual) impotence:

> As soon as I approached, he looked me up and down with one of those looks that made me wish I was wearing a shroud. His eyes settled on my chest.

> "I hear you're a dick," he said.
>
> "I hear you're not."
>
> His mouth dropped open, and his face turned a deep crimson.
>
> (110)

For female private eyes, the wisecrack is a means of opposing conventional codes of feminine conduct. Such deflection takes place when characters "crack wise" within such novels; it also occurs when authors use tough talk to respond to the hard-boiled tradition itself. Talking back to masculine authority traditionally has been viewed as inappropriate behavior for women: it is a mode of resistance more plausible and ethical—and potentially subversive—than, say, physical violence. As a *Newsweek* reviewer once quipped of "the new breed of mystery heroines," "they're more apt to shoot from the lip than the hip" (Ames and Sawhill 66). Indeed, when Dunant's Hannah Wolfe faces a physical assault, she uses language: "My words were my weapons, sharp little knives slicing through the air, whistling ever closer to that smooth skin" (*Fatlands* 198).

Liza Cody's second Anna Lee mystery, *Bad Company,* is a particularly interesting example of the use of tough talk as resistance. The novel is, in an odd way, a hard-boiled version of the classic "locked room" mystery—but here it is the detective herself who is abducted by motorcycle gang members and locked in a tiny room with Verity, the young girl she tries to protect. The problem of the novel is one of agency: what does the detective do when the physical limitations are so constricted that she is denied almost all possibilities of action? As far as her movements are concerned, the plot is extraordinarily static: Anna is locked in the room for 185 of the novel's 287 pages. While her co-captive remains fearful and submissive, Anna resists their three male captors in the only way she can—verbally. Greeting them with such comments as, "Well, if it isn't Shake, Rattle, and Roll. . . . What kept you?" (109), she incessantly mocks them and cajoles them into providing adequate conditions for the captives. For example, when one of them grabs Verity, Anna comments "Oh, very clever. . . . Gestapo tactics on little girls. Pity there aren't any kittens for you to drown. You'd like that too" (110).

Verity worries that Anna is only provoking the men, who have all the power: "It isn't safe to talk back and cheek to them," she says. Anna replies, however, that the authority of their captors is the very thing that makes her verbal resistance necessary: "It might be even more dangerous to let them walk all over us. They've got too much of an edge already. We can't let them take more" (135). The child's compliance results in her perverse identification with her assailants and against Anna. At one point, Anna explains to Verity the principle behind her own antagonism, significantly incorporating an explanation of the way little girls are culturally conditioned to submission: "Listen, I know you're a well-brought-up girl, and you probably do what you're told at school too, but there are times when you've got to make trouble. It may be hard for you to believe, but some people don't deserve respect or good manners. And there are times when being polite and passive and timid only gets your rear-end kicked" (134). Anna feels "the danger of acquiescing very keenly indeed," but her resistance holds off her captors from "further liberties" (210).

The exercise of tough talk as reverse discourse is framed comically in Linda Grant's *Woman's Place* when Catherine Sayler is patted on the behind by a male co-worker at the office. She responds in kind: "I'd reached over and returned the compliment, commenting, 'Not bad. A little time at the gym would tone that right up'" (7). Her gesture, of course, repeats and parodies that of her male "admirer," revealing that his presumptuous touch was anything but a compliment. In Sandra West Prowell's *Killing of Monday Brown*, private investigator Phoebe Siegel admonishes a police officer for cruelly lifting a young Native American boy by the belt loops on his pants; "I love seeing law enforcement at work, and that snuggie hold is nothing short of brilliant. Glad to see you guys have been trained in testicle tactics," she whispers ironically in his ear (35). After smart-mouthing a police officer, Val McDermid's private detective Kate Brannigan muses to herself and readers that her insubordination seems to be provoked by the authority of the police (much like Lew Archer's): "I can't help myself, I swear. Every time I run up against a copper who thinks he's in the last days of his apprenticeship to God, I get one on me" (*Dead Beat* 157).

STAND-UP COMEDY

An *Entertainment Weekly* reviewer put his finger on Karen Kijewski's character's combination of hard-boiled cynicism and comedic feminist fractiousness, as well as that of her generic counterparts, when he described Kat Colorado as "tough, single, beautiful, early 30s, hard-bitten, and, in prose style, the illegitimate child of Raymond Chandler and Roseanne Arnold (check the mystery shelves of your local bookstore—she has half a dozen identical sisters who practice under different names)" (Harris 58). Margaret Atwood expressed similar sentiments, observing that Eve Zaremba's lesbian detective Helen Keremos is "a cross between Lily Tomlin and Philip Marlowe" (qtd. in Skene-Melvin 18). Sparkle Hayter, author of the Robin Hudson series, is herself both a stand-up comedian and an experienced journalist. Her television journalist character's career is on the downslide because of her literal inability to keep her mouth shut: she belched during a live broadcast of a White House news conference, sometimes asks indelicate questions of interviewees, and often makes infelicitous comments to co-workers: "I always say," says Robin, "it takes seven major muscle groups just to hold my tongue" (*Nice Girls Finish Last* 4). When one of her companions reminds her that "as the old saying goes, you get more flies with honey than with vinegar," Robin responds, "Well, if you *really* want flies, you ought to try bullshit. . . . It's an old folk remedy" (*What's a Girl Gotta Do?* 52). Hayter's writing is a veritable *tour de farce* of comedic hard-boiled conceits.[7] At a network cock-

tail party, for example, she uses a version of the hard-boiled simile to describe one of her senior colleagues whose routine sexual harassment she describes wryly as "this little problem relating to women": "When he's sober and he comes face to face with a woman in a social setting, he tends to become focused on her breasts and can't look her in the eye. If she moves from side to side, his head moves from side to side too, *like a dog watching a tennis ball*" (*What's a Girl Gotta Do?* 16, emphasis added).[8]

The role of humor is crucial for several reasons. First, it allows the expression of sentiments that in any other form would be socially unacceptable, even "unspeakable"—or at the very least unpalatable in an entertainment genre. Sandra Scoppettone, like many of these authors, recognizes its utility: "I try not to preach. . . . Anything I do that is connected to a social issue or a comment on society I try to do with humor." Second, the detective's wisecracking use of humor represents the appropriation both of a certain kind of language and of the dominant speaking position. It thereby epitomizes the author's appropriation of the hard-boiled mode itself, which uses tough talk in order to talk back to and alter the ideological trajectory of traditional literature. As Susan Purdie remarks in her study of the power politics of humor, "Because discourse is potent, its control yields power; because joking intrinsically constructs a mastery of discourse, it always has unambiguous political effects which are produced on the back of its psychic operations" (125).

The detective is thus "the figure for the reader in the text"—not just in the classical sense, to which Glenn Most points, that both are intellectually engaged in solving the mystery (349), or even in the sense that the reader gets a vicarious thrill from the detective's exploration of the borders between the permitted and the forbidden, as John Cawelti argues (*Adventure* 35-36), but in her discursive positioning as one who is both able and permitted (in the space of the novel) to talk back to authority. This sense of vindication is clearly represented in J. M. Redmann's *Intersection of Law and Desire* when lesbian detective Micky Knight verbally lashes out at one of her interrogators for his homophobia during a police interview: though he is a criminologist, he confuses homosexuality with criminal child abuse. Micky's friend, a lesbian assistant district attorney who remains in the closet to protect her career, later approaches Micky, hugs her, and says, "You do give the best fireworks show. . . . I wanted to say something, but I get so caught up in what it'll cost me and what'll I gain." Micky responds, "He wouldn't hire me and I wouldn't work for him, so I have nothing to lose. As long as you've got me to mouth off, you don't have to" (299).

THE PRIVATE EAR: LISTENING IN ON LANGUAGE

Sandra Scoppettone engages in a more generalized version of reverse discourse in her novel *I'll Be Leaving You Always* by having her detective effectively talk back to language itself. The inquiry of Scoppettone's private detective Lauren Laurano into the death of her oldest friend

Meg is as much an investigation into the social signification of everyday realist language as it is the investigation of a murder. Lauren, whose friends jokingly call her "Lobes Laurano, private dick" (5), is in fact identified as a kind of "private ear" who solves her cases by forcing herself to *listen* to words—not just because she is an obsessive eavesdropper (though she is), but because she is attentive to the voices of others and their linguistic subtleties. The epigraph to the novel, "My lifetime listens to yours" ([vii]), identifies issues of receptivity as a central concern of *I'll Be Leaving You Always,* though they are often developed obliquely. At one point in the story, for example, having been subjected to the "sonorous soliloquy" of a long-winded taxi driver, Lauren comments, "I confess, I don't understand people who love to hear the sound of their own voice. I already know what *I* know, so I find it much more interesting to hear what others think" (69). This attentiveness to other voices is presumably what makes her an effective detective. Perhaps it is also what makes Scoppettone an effective detective writer.

Lauren listens not just to what people say but to how they say it, and to what their linguistic choices signify. In one sense, *I'll Be Leaving You Always* is an investigation into the language of death, a language that is *always* at the center of detective fiction. Nevertheless, it is very seldom taken up as a subject of discussion—partly because the genre is to some extent realist, and realist language by definition is language that does not call attention to its own functioning: it pretends to be neutral and transparent. This is a rule that Scoppettone's work creatively bends by making language the frequent subject of her narrator's contemplation, setting realism against reflexivity. The metalinguistic commentary is integrated into the narrative, troubling—without actually breaking—its realist surface and placing the "real world" of the story in question. For example, in a gesture often used in her work, Scoppettone uses italics and the rhetorical strategy of reification—the figurative depiction of an abstraction as if it were a concrete thing—to transform ordinary language into something that the reader must reexamine. Indeed, Scoppettone makes words into clues in the investigation: "*Dead, murdered, killed, death.* The words rattle round in my head like alien beings" (16). This novel is at some level about coming to *terms* with death, and as such it is not just a "private" but a personal investigation that conflates the narrative of detection with the process of mourning.

As part of both processes, Scoppettone evokes and violates the kind of narratorial distance that is a convention of hard-boiled writing. For example, Lauren must confront the reality that her formerly vital, living, breathing friend has been reduced to a corpse, and that confrontation is represented as mediated through language. When a police officer, Cecchi, tells her that the authorities will release the body, she responds:

> *Body.* It takes me by surprise. This is Meg's body Cecchi is referring to and I'm not ready to accept her as a body.
>
> "You made the arrangements?"

"No." I remind him about Blythe's not showing up.

"So where's it gonna go?"

It. I have the impulse to ask Cecchi to stop talking about Meg this way, but I curb that because I don't want to appear timorous or he might stop confiding in me.

(85)

The violent narratives of hard-boiled fiction rely precisely on the treatment of death as a flat, material, unemotional fact and the representation of the body—particularly the female body—as an object. The original hard-boiled writers may have taken the body out of the library and put it onto the mean streets, but the voice of the tough-talking narrator ensured that it was invested with little emotional weight. For instance, having viewed the murdered body of his partner Miles Archer, Sam Spade is clearly unmoved. Even when a police officer offers the sympathetic observation that "Miles had his faults same as the rest of us, but I guess he must've had some good points too," the detective's reaction is curt: "'I guess so,' Spade agreed in a tone that was utterly meaningless, and went out of the alley" (Hammett, *Maltese Falcon* 16).

Lauren, in contrast, attends to the material details of her friend's death, arranging for the transfer of the body and for the funeral. In the course of these activities, she meditates on the way polite euphemisms can be used in an effort to distance a speaker and defamiliarize—or perhaps even disguise—distressing subjects. When the funeral director refers to the casket as a "container," Lauren muses, "No one says what anything really is anymore. Missions become *sorties,* handicapped are *physically challenged,* pets are *animal companions,* instead of a mistake, *friendly fire.* And now a coffin is a goddamn *container.* It's as if sanitizing the language will ease the pain of reality. It doesn't work" (*I'll Be Leaving You Always* 35). Everyday language is thus denaturalized, its shaping of reality exposed. Later in Scoppettone's novel, Lauren catches herself practicing the euphemistic tactic when she refers to the grim task of looking through the dead woman's apartment after her death as "the business at hand:" "*The business at hand?*" she repeats to herself, "Have I become a master at euphemisms? Am I such a coward I can no longer be direct, honest, candid even with myself? I'm disgusted" (115). Part of the detective's heroism involves facing up to the realities of language itself.

It is not just the polite language of euphemism that is emphasized by the prose of the novel but the more vulgar, hard-boiled terminology surrounding death. While tough talk may *seem* to confront reality more directly than more "refined" language, Scoppettone's novel recognizes both as capable of their own varieties of euphemism. In response to Lauren's questions, a suspect explodes, "You think *I* wasted Meg?" and Lauren is prompted to muse, "Here it is again. The only thing that ever changes is the verb: wasted; murdered; killed; offed; punched her/his ticket" (101). S. J. Rozan's detective Lydia Chin similarly observes how much it bothers her when cops talk about death using "words like stiff, whacked, burned. It always throws me, but I try not to show it" (66). Scoppettone's character realizes how thoroughly she has absorbed this kind of language as a tool of the private investigation trade when she is caught using it in order to detach herself from her emotions. Lauren speculates to her lover Kip on why Meg was killed: "Here's the thing: if Meg was about to blow the whistle, whoever dealt with the store owners probably knew about it and had some mechanic take her out" (239). Her language here draws on the very kind of slang that became a signature of hard-boiled writing. One example is Lew Archer's report in Ross Macdonald's *Drowning Pool* of a character's assassination and immolation: "They knocked me out. Then they ventilated Reavis with a dozen slugs and gave him a gasoline barbecue" (132). In Scoppettone's novel, however, the distancing effect of such elaborate figurative language is countered when Kip reprimands Lauren for offhandedly referring to a professional killing as being "taken out" by a "mechanic." Lauren responds,

> "That's what hit men are called."
>
> "You do it so you don't have to feel anything."
>
> I ignore this because it's true.
>
> (238)

Paretsky's V. I. Warshawski has a similar illuminating moment regarding hard-boiled language when she responds to a friend's inquiries "with a Sam Spade toughness I was far from feeling. . . . It sounded good, but it didn't mean anything" (*Bitter Medicine* 69). Such gestures in *I'll Be Leaving You Always* and elsewhere offer a kind of illocutionary analysis of vernacular realism, a critique of its functions and effects. At the same time, this analysis is delivered in the realistic manner that readers demand.

The narrative of Scoppettone's novel also documents Lauren's experience as a lesbian, not only because it is a central issue of the character's identity but also because the murder victim was a childhood friend who helped Lauren come to recognize and name her sexual orientation (Meg herself was heterosexual). When, as a teenager, Meg confronts Lauren with the idea that Lauren is not sexually attracted to men, Lauren denies it, as she has always denied it to herself, but Meg insists on the truth of her observation and assures her friend that it makes no difference to their relationship. "But Meg, I'm a freak," Lauren says. Meg replies,

> "No you're not. You're just a lesbian."
>
> The word ricocheted round the room, puncturing me in several places while it made its tour. *Lesbian.* It was ugly, degrading, and embarrassing.
>
> "I hate that word," I whispered, staring at the flowered carpet in her room.
>
> "You like *dyke* better?"
>
> "Ugh." I started to cry.
>
> (11)

Once again, a word is figuratively represented as if it were a substantial object—in this case a stock object of crime fiction violence, the ricocheting bullet. This description subtly brings the reader's attention to bear not just on the language of violence (which is an iconic element of hard-boiled narratives) but on the *violence of language itself*, the power of words to do harm. Valerie Wilson Wesley makes just this point in *When Death Comes Stealing* when a suspect being interviewed by private investigator Tamara Hayle uses the word "nigger":

> I couldn't believe what she'd just said! *Who you calling a nigger, white girl?* I hadn't heard a white person say that word since I'd left the [Police] Department and heard it every day. My reaction was pure reflex: I pushed the anger down to that place inside me where I'd always put it when I'd been on the force. Nigger bitch. Nigger whore. Nigger bastard. Nigger son of a bitch. I'd heard it so much it had lost its meaning. Just another word.
>
> (87)

Tamara's theory that the word has lost its meaning is belied, however, both by her initial reaction and by her realization that the woman who spoke the word with such contempt actually feels it applies to herself and her son, both of whose lives and self-esteem are in a shambles: "*Maybe that's your problem. Maybe that's why your son is so messed up,* I thought, but didn't say" (87).

Whereas in traditional hard-boiled novels language's force often originates in its referential and promissory power, in the guaranteed correspondence between spoken threat and physical action (the hard-boiled private eye is, in this sense, "a man of his word"), it is here and elsewhere exposed as powerful in itself. In *I'll Be Leaving You Always,* the young Lauren and her friend consider "queer" as an alternative to other homophobic labels for homosexuality, but finally arrive at the conclusion that "there's no good word" (12). The available names are not transparent, neutral terms; they constitute a kind of social value judgment. Using them, nevertheless, becomes a significant act of recognition for Lauren: it constitutes the first stage in her coming out.

Later in *I'll Be Leaving You Always,* when an altercation breaks out in the line of a New York delicatessen, Lauren hears the language of homosexuality used as a form of vicious insult: "Listen, fag," says the man at the counter to the customer who has angered him, "'I ain't givin' you nothin'. Get outta here" (90). The exchange deteriorates into a succession of jibes that vilify homosexual sex and that figuratively dismember and objectify the body. The novel creates an analogy between insult and assault; and as violent linguistic exchange mirrors a physical struggle, aggressive masculine sexuality is parodied: "There ensues a scuffle, and the words *cock* and *dick* are thrown back and forth as if there are no two other words in the language" (91). Lauren's own confrontation with the man behind the counter, interestingly, deals with the issue first in decorous, elevated "literary" language, and then in a wisecracking hard-boiled response that proudly reappropriates and affirms the term "dyke" as a defensive tactic. Lauren realizes that she cannot order from a man who has used such "distasteful" language:

> I say to him, "Sir, you have a childlike grasp of the English language, you're homophobic and one of the dumbest people I've ever encountered." I turn to leave.
>
> "Fucking dyke," he yells after me.
>
> "Absolutely," I say. "As much as I can."
>
> (91)

On the one hand, this is a retake of the hard-boiled smart-ass retort. On the other, it is a far cry from Sam Spade's snide references to "the gooseberry lay" or Mike Hammer's virulent homophobic rhetoric. Scoppettone's novel even emphasizes the offensiveness of the language of prejudice by associating it with criminal offenses. In the course of her investigation, Lauren discovers that she may not have known her friend Meg as well as she thought, for Meg may have been involved in criminal activity. She is also wounded to learn that Meg had referred to Lauren disparagingly as a "dyke" behind her back: "Which is worse," Lauren reflects, "that Meg might have been involved in something illegal, that she called me a dyke, or that she wasn't who I thought she was?" (77).

I'll Be Leaving You Always is remarkable for its extended, self-conscious investigation of language as a clue to a broader social text, but it is certainly not unique in making the power of words the subject of investigation. Indeed, a key strategy of feminist detective fiction in general is to incorporate metalinguistic implications into the texture of the realistic narrative. Nancy Baker Jacobs's detective Devon MacDonald, for example, often gets into linguistic wrangles with her older, more traditional partner Sam, who sometimes baits her by using language that might be seen as a misogynist relic of his hard-boiled professional role. Their friendly sparring—which Jacobs refers to as a "loving battle"—is often used to evoke the political aspects of language. "It's sort of a game that they play," says Jacobs, "and yet I'm hoping that through the game there are some points that might be made to the reader about the conditions women live in." When Sam makes an offensive reference, Devon thinks to herself, "If I could simply ignore Sam's bigoted terminology, he'd probably clean it up. I tried that technique often with third graders who used profanity to get my attention and it worked on them. But Sam isn't a third grader and he usually manages to push just past the point where I can hold my tongue. He needs to liberalize this thinking; I need more patience" (*Turquoise Tattoo* 16). Earlier, she explains that "One of Sam's favorite ways of needling me is to call me a 'girl,' but today I refused to rise to his bait. Sometimes dealing with Sam Sherman feels like being back in my third grade classroom" (10). Devon's musings strikingly reverse the symbolic age difference constructed by the word "girl," making *his* behavior seem infantile.

It has become what might be seen as a generic tic for detectives to flag the use of the diminutive word "girls" (and similar terms) to describe women, whether designating a detective or a victim. These may seem like small linguistic gestures, but Sara Paretsky offers insight into the importance of such offhand references in colloquial language:

> the way that we [women] are defined is part of this insisting on a system of subordination, and calling a woman a girl is fundamental to it, because a girl *is* a child. A girl is not a fully realized human being. And the fact that it's integral to the culture and the use of language doesn't mean that that isn't the case. It means that it's so very much the case that we now have internalized the idea that we are not fully adult human beings.
>
> (interview by Richler)

Surely one of the central effects of the private 'I' of the female detective is the representation of a woman's performance of an empowering speaking position made available by the genre. The subjective point of view of the traditional hard-boiled detective novel is thus supplemented by an insistence on language that constructs and reinforces that position. For example, Paretsky's own V. I. Warshawski, asked by her host, "Now, you're not one of those modern girls who only drinks white wine, are you?" asserts her hard-boiled persona, insisting on a tough guy's iconic drink and a tough *woman's* appellation: "No, I'm a modern woman, and I drink neat whisky. Black Label, if you have it" (*Guardian Angel* 195). Sarah Dunant's detective Hannah Wolfe expresses sentiments very like V. I.'s when she corrects a character who has called her "a very smart girl": "'Woman, please,' I said. 'It's deeply patronizing to be called a girl'" (*Fatlands* 200). In an interview with a Chinese gang boss, S. J. Rozan's Asian American detective Lydia Chin is identified by her ethnicity and gender: the man snidely remarks, "you smart for ABC girl." Lydia implicitly accepts the ethnic identification but strategically rejects the designation "girl": "ABC, that's American-Born Chinese. Girl, that's not me" (29). In a conversation in Judith Van Gieson's *North of the Border,* investigator Neil Hamel anticipates the resolution of a sexual joke that a man is in the course of telling, thus disturbing the verbal power dynamic implicit in the joke's rhetoric. Instead of feigning ignorance, she supplies the punch line, *literally* punching her interlocutor in the shoulder and adopting the masculine voice (7). The stranger responds, "Not bad. . . . Not bad for a girl," but Neil insists on her adult professional status: "I'm not a girl; I'm a lawyer" (7). When an acquaintance flippantly addresses Karen Kijewski's detective as "baby," Kat Colorado muses, "Baby? I thought about it as I hung up. Baby? What kind of a name was that for a thirty-three-year-old PI? Dumb, that's what" (*Kat's Cradle* 189).

The analysis is not restricted to references to the private eye herself; it is often extended in order to call attention to the ways victim positions are *verbally* constructed and reinforced. In Lia Matera's *Face Value,* Laura Di Palma interviews a man who had been acquainted with several murder victims, to whom he refers offhandedly as "girls," and Laura detects in this diminutive term a sign of his lack of respect: "There was little sympathy in his manner," she observes, "little acknowledgment that people—not just 'girls'—had died" (122). In Michelle Spring's *Every Breath You Take,* detective Laura Principal makes a similar gesture, responding to police officer Neill's reference to "the dead girl" with an insistence on her proper name (65). This refusal to "have her reduced by Neill to 'that dead girl'" is part of the humanizing function of her investigation, which, her partner observes, is "to breathe life into 'this dead girl.' . . . I understand: you're going to make her real" (80). In a sense, Spring's realist narrative reverses the male murderer's sexual assault, linguistically reviving the victim by asserting her humanity. Similarly, Wendy Hornsby's Maggie MacGowan, in conversation with her police detective lover, catches him offhandedly using the word "girls" in a dismissive story about police "groupies." Maggie insists that he call them "women," but Mike responds, "Back then, we were pigs, they were girls. You gotta know the language of the times or you're not going to get this story at all" (*Bad Intent* 267). Nevertheless, Maggie later corrects him again: "She wasn't a *girl,* for chrissake, Mike, she was a human being with a big problem" (268).

The Semantics of Crime

Many works integrate an extended linguistic analysis into the texture of their narratives. In Karen Kijewski's *Copy Kat,* for instance, Kat must convince another character of the criminal nature of his sexual behavior, engaging in what amounts to a "semantic" argument that "I took her" and "I *made* her love me" or "I gave her 'payback'" all function as synonyms—or, rather, as euphemisms—for "rape" (306-8). The title of Sara Paretsky's *Bitter Medicine* might well be read as referring to the damaging linguistic "prescriptions" of patriarchal discourse, in particular those that underpin the American privatized corporate medical institution and the right-wing Christian antiabortion movement, which are linked in the novel's narrative. Paretsky's book is a particularly interesting example because it, like Scoppettone's *I'll Be Leaving You Always,* implicitly inquires into the language of mortality, the language on which detective fiction is founded but which it must generally naturalize in order to sustain its realistic effects. As Barbara Godard observes, while conventional murder mysteries ignore "the sexual politics of death," the feminist detective novel evinces a commitment to "the spying out of ideological discourses and the social practices they define" (49). For Paretsky, the definition of "murder" often becomes a profoundly political semantic issue. For instance, the death that propels the narrative of *Bitter Medicine* is that of a family friend of V. I., Consuelo Hernandez, who dies during childbirth at a private health care facility. This death, while not technically a murder, is the result of medical mismanagement, which originates in racial prejudice as well as the for-profit medical establishment's greater concern for protecting revenues than for attending to the needs of its patients—especially, it is implied, its female patients.

Although Consuelo's death results from medical malpractice rather than legally defined murderous intent, the narra-

tive of the novel involves the "solution" of her death as if it were a murder—a process that entails attributing responsibility not simply to an individual but to a medical system that in various ways made proper treatment inaccessible to Consuelo. From the start, the hospital staff's use of language demonstrates little concern for Consuelo's humanity. The nurses refer to her as "number 108," transforming her linguistically from a person to a "case" (8). Because Consuelo is Hispanic, she is almost instantly stereotyped as indigent by the hospital staff, and the quality of her care is thus compromised: "She's some Mexican girl who got sick on the premises," says the nurse, "We do not run a charity ward here. We're going to have to move this girl to a public hospital" (10). Because of this misidentification, her treatment is delayed. When V. I. discovers the form the nurse had been completing, she comments cynically on its description—or rather construction—of Consuelo: "The only items completed were sex—they'd hazarded a guess there—and source of payment, which a second guess had led them to list as 'Indigent'—euphemism for the dirty four-letter word poor. Americans have never been very understanding of poverty, but since Reagan was elected it's become a crime almost as bad as child-molesting" (11). V. I.'s sardonic commentary is a good example of Paretsky's signature use of the detached hard-boiled narrative voice to provide offhand political and linguistic commentary: the character's observations highlight how language is used to categorize and evaluate—in a way that is ultimately implicated in Consuelo's death. In this case, the pregnant woman is deprived of all identity save her sex and the prejudicial label "Indigent," which is based on her racial appearance. The degree to which the novel judges such categorizations as both political and perverse is suggested in the last sentence of the quotation above, in which the government under Reagan is shown to have inverted the distinction between victim and crime. The narrator insinuates that language that effects such an inversion is itself, despite—or rather because of—its euphemisms, obscene.

Much of the narrative of *Bitter Medicine* centers on the Chicago women's health clinic that V. I.'s friend Dr. Lotty Herschel helps operate. The clinic is targeted by an antiabortion group whose demonstration against it finally erupts into a riot. The protesters are so threatening in part because of their appropriation of the language of crime to describe activities at the clinic, which include therapeutic abortions: they call the doctor "a murderer" (93). Once again, the definition of "murder" is a matter of interpretation, and the body in question, the novel emphasizes, is the female body as a site of contested power. Murder, it suggests, is a women's health issue. The antiabortion protesters borrow from the lexicon not just of crime but of crimes against humanity. They invoke the Holocaust, shouting "Murderers! Nazis!" (94); their news-letter calls the clinic "a DEATH camp more hideous than Auschwitz" (129). This perspective, however, is reversed by the novel's structure, which opposes Lotty's cooperative women's health clinic to the unhealthy practices of mainstream patriarchal medicine and religion. It is also resituated by Lotty, a Jewish woman, who reinvokes the language used by the protesters in order to tell V. I. how much their mentality frightens her, and how it threatens the American democratic ethos: "There was a night in Vienna when a Nazi mob gathered in front of our house. They looked just like this—animals, oozing hate. They broke all the windows. My parents and my brother and I fled through the garden and hid at a neighbor's and watched them burn our house to the ground. Never did I expect to feel that same fear in America" (95). Evoking the language of fascism is one of the ways that *Bitter Medicine* suggests the political operations of language. It also implicitly contrasts the conventionally individualized murders of mystery fiction with a historical instance of genocide. It is a book as much concerned with uncovering the institutional discourses—legal, medical, political—that have the power to define and control women's bodies as it is with the individualized bodies of the murder victims that are part of its more conventional detective plot. Or rather, it portrays the life-and-death fate of any individual body *as* a political body.

In so doing, the novel provides a discursive diagnosis, a forensic inquiry into the language of crime and the crimes of language. When women writers renegotiate the conventions of the hard-boiled tradition, they engage in a dialogue with detective novels of the past, interpreting them collectively as a body of evidence. Consequently, the (legal, medical, political) discourses that constitute them are subject to investigation. In his analysis of "tough talk," Walker Gibson describes the tough-talking narrator as taciturn and self-conscious about his use of language: "He is close-lipped, he watches his words" (41). Like the traditional terse hard-boiled narrator, the woman detective also carefully watches her words, using them strategically to readdress and redress power imbalances. Equally important, the woman writer of detective fiction engages with both patriarchal language and the masculine hard-boiled tradition, appropriating and shifting their formal strategies. In other words, she watches *his* words too. Her text is evidence of this.

Notes

1. As an example of the broad age spectrum that female PI novels reach, one eighty-five-year-old reader responded to our inquiries by observing that Sara Paretsky is her favorite author and that she "regularly reads" Linda Barnes, Sue Grafton, and Karen Kijewski. Grafton herself commented in an interview that "I get notes from little old ladies who complain about my language. I write back and we have chats about the F-word. It's fun" ("G Is for (Sue) Grafton" 12).

2. In granting permission to reprint her essay in *The Art of the Mystery Story,* Nicolson noted,

   I hope it may be possible for you to call the attention of your readers to the fact that this essay was published in 1929. The only part of the essay which I think is now seriously out-of-date is my statement that women do not write good detective stories. In 1929 Agatha Christie's *The Murder of Roger Ackroyd* was well known, but as I indicated in the essay, it was written as a tour de force. In 1929, Dorothy Sayers was comparatively

little known in America. Ngaio Marsh was still in her (literary) cradle. Other women like Mignon Eberhart and Leslie Ford were just beginning to appear on the horizon. As a matter of fact, so many of the best detective stories of the last decade have been written by women that my statement sounds either naïve or uncritical. Since these women are among my favourite mystery authors, I should not like readers to feel that I do not admire their works. Therefore if you can call the readers' attention to the fact, you will relieve my conscience and I won't feel that I have sold the ladies down the river!

   (111)

3. It is important to note that hard-boiled language did not necessarily come "naturally" even to its male practitioners. As Fredric Jameson has observed, Chandler himself, because he was educated in England, came to the American idiom secondhand: "even those clichés and commonplaces which for the native speaker are not really words at all, but instant communication, take on outlandish resonance in his mouth, *are used between quotation marks,* as you would delicately expose some interesting specimen" (124, emphasis added); the same argument has been used of Ross Macdonald, whose origins were Canadian (Knight 141).

4. Modleski sees a similar split in film production occurring around the same time:

   In the forties, a new movie genre derived from Gothic novels appeared around the time that hard-boiled detective fiction was being transformed by the medium into what movie critics currently call "film noir." . . . Beginning with Alfred Hitchcock's 1940 movie version of *Rebecca* and continuing through and beyond George Cukor's *Gaslight* in 1944, the gaslight films may be seen to reflect *women's* fears about losing their unprecedented freedoms and being forced back into the homes after the men returned from fighting to take over the jobs and assume control of their families.

   (*Loving with a Vengeance* 21)

5. Catherine Belsey defines closure in the "classic realist" text:

   Among the commonest sources of disorder at the level of plot in classic realism are murder, war, a journey or love. But the story moves inevitably towards *closure* which is also disclosure, the dissolution of enigma through the re-establishment of order, recognizable as a reinstatement or development of the order which is understood to have preceded the events of the story itself.

   The moment of closure is the point at which the events of the story become fully intelligible to the reader. The most obvious instance is the detective story where, in the final pages, the murderer is revealed and the motive made plain.

   (70)

6. Rabinowitz also notes this echo ("Reader, I Blew Him Away" 333).

7. Scott Christianson describes the hard-boiled conceit as "a particularly pointed or extended metaphor or simile which is usually serious, and which is spoken to the reader directly to convey the detective/narrator's complex sensibility" ("Talkin' Trash" 133).

8. Some writers, like Dana Stabenow, use the hard-boiled simile as a marker not of gender but of cultural difference. Stabenow's Aleut investigator Kate Shugak describes an oil pipeline whose outer metal layer is peeling off: "big chunks of the second, foam-like layer were gouged out seemingly at random and a green plastic subderma hung in strips like velvet from a caribou rack" (*Cold-Blooded Business* 56).

Works Cited

Ames, Katrine, and Ray Sawhill. "Murder Most Foul and Fair." *Newsweek,* May 14, 1990, 66-69.

Cawelti, John. *Adventure, Mystery, and Romance: Formula Stories as Art and Popular Culture.* Chicago: University of Chicago Press, 1976.

———. "The Simple Art of Murder." In *The Art of the Mystery Story,* edited by Howard Haycraft, 222-37. New York: Grosset and Dunlap, 1946.

Christianson, Scott R. "A Heap of Broken Images: Hard-boiled Detective Fiction and the Discourse(s) of Modernity." In *The Cunning Craft: Original Essays on Detective Fiction and Contemporary Literary Theory,* edited by Ronald G. Walker and June M. Frazer, 135-48. Macomb: Western Illinois University Press, 1990.

———. "Talkin' Trash and Kickin' Butt: Sue Grafton's Hard-boiled Feminism." In Irons, *Feminism in Women's Detective Fiction* 127-47.

Gibson, Walker W. *Tough, Sweet, and Stuffy: An Essay on Modern American Prose Styles.* Bloomington: Indiana University Press, 1966.

Glover, David. "The Stuff That Dreams Are Made Of: Masculinity, Femininity, and the Thriller." In *Gender, Genre, and Narrative Pleasure,* edited by Derek Longhurst, 67-83. London: Unwin Hyman, 1989.

Grafton, Sue, ed. *Writing Mysteries: A Handbook by the Mystery Writers of America.* Cincinnati: Writer's Digest Books, 1992.

Modleski, Tania. *Loving with a Vengeance: Mass-Produced Fantasies for Women.* New York: Routledge, 1982.

Most, Glenn W., and William W. Stowe, eds. *The Poetics of Murder: Detective Fiction and Literary Theory.* San Diego: Harcourt Brace Jovanovich, 1983.

Nicolson, Marjorie. "The Professor and the Detective." In *The Art of the Mystery Story,* edited by Howard Haycraft, 110-27. New York: Grosset and Dunlap, 1946.

Pickard, Nancy. "The Amateur Sleuth." In Grafton, *Writing Mysteries* 61-66.

Porter, Dennis. *The Pursuit of Crime: Art and Ideology in Detective Fiction.* New Haven: Yale University Press, 1981.

Purdie, Susan. *Comedy: The Mastery of Discourse.* Toronto: University of Toronto Press, 1993.

Rabinowitz, Peter J. "'Reader, I Blew Him Away': Convention and Transgression in Sue Grafton." In *Famous Last Words: Changes in Gender and Narrative Closure,* edited by Alison Booth, 326-46. Charlottesville: University Press of Virginia, 1993.

Symons, Julian. *Bloody Murder: From the Detective Story to the Crime Novel: A History.* London: Pan, 1972.

Worpole, Ken. *Dockers and Detectives.* London: Verso, 1983.

FURTHER READING

Bibliographies

Conquest, John. *Trouble Is Their Business: Private Eyes in Fiction, Film, and Television, 1927-1988.* New York: Garland Publishing, 1990, 497 p.

> A comprehensive reference guide to authors, works, genres, and numerous other aspects of the private eye tradition.

Skinner, Robert E. *The Hard-Boiled Explicator: A Guide to the Study of Dashiell Hammett, Raymond Chandler, and Ross Macdonald.* Metuchen, NJ: The Scarecrow Press, Inc., 1985, 125 p.

> A bibliographic guide to literary criticism and various other materials on the works of Hammett, Chandler, and Macdonald.

Criticism

McCann, Sean. *Gumshoe America: Hard-Boiled Crime Fiction and the Rise and Fall of New Deal Liberalism.* Durham, NC: Duke University Press, 2000, 370 p.

> Examines the ways in which hard-boiled fiction reflected and commented on the political climate in the United States between 1930 and 1960.

Nyman, Jopi. *Men Alone: Masculinity, Individualism, and Hard-Boiled Fiction.* Amsterdam, The Netherlands: Rodopi, 1997, 384 p.

> Explores the image of masculinity projected in hard-boiled fiction and discusses its stylistic, thematic, and social implications.

O'Brien, Geoffrey. "Juno Was a Man; or, the Case of the Hardboiled Homophobes." *Armchair Detective* 18, no. 3 (summer 1985): 248-57.

> Discusses the treatment of homosexuals and lesbians in hard-boiled fiction from the 1920s onward.

Hollywood and Literature

INTRODUCTION

The advent of cinema in the early 1900s rapidly led to a link between film and literature, the confluence of both medium becoming especially significant during the early 1930s, a period that is often referred to as the classic cinematic period. These years saw the adaptation of several classic works of literature for film, including such titles as *Anna Karenina* (1875), *Jane Eyre* (1847), and *Wuthering Heights* (1847). Although the relationship between film and fiction has been largely beneficial, often resulting in increased recognition for novels that were previously unpopular, critical study of the convergence has frequently focused on the drawbacks of this adaptive and interpretive partnering. In recent years, the tie-in between literature and cinema has seen an intense and sustained revival, but discussion continues among critics and reviewers regarding the credibility of film adaptations from texts of fiction.

Studying the relationship between film and fiction, critics have noted the value and limitation of each medium. A major point of discussion among scholars is the ability of the written word to convey multiple layers of meaning and consciousness, in contrast to the usually linear progression of events portrayed in film. In fact, some theorize that because of the sheer depth and intensity of novel-length narratives, the novella or short story are more often the right length for adaptation to feature film. Yet, there are examples of several successful adaptations of epics to cinema, including such classics as *Gone with the Wind* (1936) and *The Grapes of Wrath* (1939). Although controversy surrounds the adaptive methods employed by the screenwriters for both texts, there is consensus about the success of both the text and film versions of these works. In his essay discussing the relationship between works of literature and their adapted screenplays, John Orr notes that adaptations work best when the director and author share a historical framework of meaning, and also when they are part of the same culture.

Focusing in particular on Hollywood's efforts at adapting works of fiction for the screen, Mark Axelrod points out that audiences and readers most often compare character renditions and the progression of a realistic storyline. In order to ensure financial success, Axelrod notes, Hollywood has tended to stress and follow the traditional Aristotelian narrative, with a clear beginning, middle, and end to the stories told on screen. Therefore, linear narratives such as E. M. Forster's *Howard's End* (1910), have worked best for adaptation to film. Certain texts are periodically re-filmed for this reason alone, including several works by Charles Dickens. Axelrod also notes, as do others, that this propensity for linear narratives, often leads adaptations of works of literature to ignore the posture of the original text. For example, in a work like *The French Lieutenant's Woman* (1969), what gets adapted more readily is the realistic narrative storyline, but not the stylistic essence of the work. This inability of film to translate all the nuances of the written narrative to screen has led many authors to disassociate themselves from the screenwriting of their own texts. This is especially true of authors with extremely popular works of fiction, who are often unwilling to participate in the abridgement of a much-loved work of literature. A famous example of this reticence, explains Alan David Vertrees in his essay on the screenwriting process for the script of *Gone with the Wind,* was author Margaret Mitchell, who refused to participate in the venture until well after the motion picture was released.

Regardless of the controversy surrounding adaptations, cinema continues to adapt fiction for the screen. In recent years, the trend has grown especially strong, with modern-day interpretations of several Shakespearean classics, as well as the novels of Jane Austen becoming increasingly available. Many critics have noted the importance of technological advancements for the renewed interest and success of adaptive works on screen. For example, Linda Troost and Sayre Greenfield state that although Austen's works have always been popular candidates for adaptation on screen and stage, globalization of culture and the ease of cross-Atlantic marketing practices have made recent adaptations of the author's works much more accessible to audiences in the United States and England. Troost and Sayre also point out that the themes Austen explores in her works continue to be of interest to modern audiences while "the characters in her works present a realistic balance of recognizable types and individuals with complex motivations and idiosyncratic personalities."

Born at the height of the industrial and social revolutions of the late nineteenth and early twentieth centuries, cinema became an early means of cheap entertainment for masses of people who were able to afford little else by way of leisure activity. This was especially true in the United States, where in addition to presenting idealized versions of reality, the movies also came to reflect the dreams, values, and fears of the American people. In that sense, films became significant not only as a commercial force and a new craft, but also as a powerful new medium that both reflected and affected social culture. Additionally, films also became a way for audiences to project themselves into a realm of sentiment and nostalgia that took them beyond the humdrum reality of their own lives. Early on, then, there was a split between such critically acclaimed film adaptations as *The Grapes of Wrath,* which received overwhelming critical preference, versus such nostalgic works as *Gone with the Wind.* Despite the intense debate about critical acclaim versus audience approval, Hollywood continues to adapt fiction that reflects both American dreams and ideals as well as themes of social and political concern. And despite the debate surrounding acceptable methods of adaptation, the relationship between film and fiction remains strong.

REPRESENTATIVE WORKS

Jane Austen
Sense and Sensibility (novel) 1811
Pride and Prejudice (novel) 1813
Emma (novel) 1816
Persuasion (novel) 1818

Lynne Reid Banks
The Indian in the Cupboard (novel) 1980

Alan Bennett
The Madness of George III (play) 1991

Charlotte Brontë
Jane Eyre (novel) 1847

Emily Brontë
Wuthering Heights (novel) 1847

William S. Burroughs
Naked Lunch (novel) 1959

E. M. Forster
A Room with a View (novel) 1908
Howard's End (novel) 1910
A Passage to India (novel) 1924

John Fowles
The French Lieutenant's Woman (novel) 1969

Norman Mailer
The Naked and the Dead (novel) 1958
An American Dream (novel) 1966
Tough Guys Don't Dance (novel) 1984

David Mamet
Sexual Perversity in Chicago (play) 1975

Margaret Mitchell
Gone with the Wind (novel) 1936

John Steinbeck
The Grapes of Wrath (novel) 1939

Leo Tolstoy
Anna Karenina (novel) 1875

Edward Lewis Wallant
The Pawnbroker (novel) 1961

Tennessee Williams
The Glass Menagerie (play) 1945
A Streetcar Named Desire (play) 1947
The Rose Tattoo (play) 1951
Cat on a Hot Tin Roof (play) 1955
Sweet Bird of Youth (play) 1959

OVERVIEWS AND GENERAL STUDIES

John Orr (essay date 1992)

SOURCE: Orr, John. "Introduction: Proust, the Movie." In *Cinema and Fiction: New Modes of Adapting, 1950-1990,* edited by John Orr and Colin Nicholson, pp. 1-9. Edinburgh: Edinburgh University Press, 1992.

[*In the following essay, Orr compares literature and film, characterizing the relationship between the two mediums as somewhat symbiotic and usually mutually beneficial.*]

In film history from 1930 onwards cinema and fiction have always closely intertwined, not only in the United States but throughout Europe and the rest of the world. Hollywood produced a set of classic adaptations in its classic period—*Anna Karenin, Madame Bovary, Jane Eyre, Wuthering Heights,* and in Europe Josef von Sternberg adapted Heinrich Mann, Jean Renoir adapted Zola and David Lean adapted Dickens. Hollywood now adapts Stephen King, Mario Puzo and Thomas Harris for global audiences, and trans-national co-productions of the eighties have brought Proust, García Marquez, Fowles, Kundera and other major novelists to the contemporary screen. On a more modest scale, film and fiction can now clearly work to their mutual advantage as in Bill Forsyth's recent adaptation of Marilynne Robinson's *Housekeeping.* The fidelity of Forsyth's version to the original novel not only allows his film great passages of visual imagination; it has also stimulated interest in a remarkable but previously underrated American novel. If the book was essential to the picture, the picture, in turn, has been vital to the creation of a wider audience for the book.

It is not just with the classics, the popular genre or the major author that adaptation has taken place. Literary adaptation has occurred at all levels, using short stories as well as full-length novels, resurrecting writers from obscurity as well as adapting best-selling authors of the moment. Literary and dramatic input has also worked in other ways. Screenwriters have been drawn from fiction and from the theatre to produce original screenplays, many of them working in close collaboration with the film's directors. Such is the current intensity of the tie-in, the intertextuality of the written word and the visual image in our electronic culture, that one is tempted to speak, as John Izod does convincingly in this volume, of 'literary and cinematic *fictions*' as the shared property of the book and the screen. On the other hand, a common mode of addressing the adaptation, the 'picture-book' as we shall call it, is to assess how far the film can be seen as a credible or faithful rendering of the text. Does it do justice to the book or does it 'betray' its literary antecedent: that is, how is the question repeatedly framed by critics and viewers? Less often, but just as important, is whether we can speak of a picture-book *improving* on the literary text, even transforming it out of all recognition. Such an example is the celebrated anecdote of Howard Hawks and William Faulkner deciding to adapt the worst, in their opinion, of Hemingway's novels, *To Have and Have Not,* for the screen. They regarded it as not the best of his work, but as the greater challenge. An equally striking example is Luis Buñuel's decision to adapt *Tristana* from what he regarded as the worst story of his favourite novelist, Benito Pérez Galdós.

The picture-book is always a tempting project because film and fiction have two things in common. They are both narrative forms, and both are referential. Both produce stories which work through temporal succession. Both refer to, or connote, pre-existent materials. Fiction works through a pre-existent language, film through the raw data of the physical world which its cameras record.[1] In both cases, words and images give off associations which go beyond the immediacy of their language or their physical objects. For different groups of readers and viewers words and images may well connote many different things. But there are vital differences too between the picture and the book. In fiction, narrative language is used to describe consciousness, but the camera has no analogous convention for rendering thought. Consequently, although both use dialogue, the narrative language of feeling, attitude, and judgement in the novel often becomes more ambiguous and problematic when rendered through the image. It is also, some critics would argue, more limited. Film relies more on visual gesture and expression but cannot hope to replicate the complex fictive language of feeling purely through the look. Moreover the camera largely works from a series of fixed viewpoints. Though this can be changed with rapid cutting or tracking, none the less the fluid interchangeability of the point of view which is a feature of the classic novel up to Henry James is less easy. Although the techniques of voice-over can be used very effectively, as film noir shows by rendering sonically the hard-boiled prose of private-eye fiction, there is often no defining narrative voice.

For the picture-book, we thus find a major dilemma. The camera is not omniscient like the nineteenth-century narrator nor is its powerful intimacy as subjective as a stream-of-consciousness narrative. In short, the cinema cannot be Tolstoy and it cannot be Joyce. It does not deal well with a multitude of major characters or a panoramic view of the social world. Conversely, it cannot dissect the subterranean life of thought in all its verbal intricacies. It works best in a scaled-down milieu, in the close connecting links between the personal and the social. Moreover, it cannot usually absorb the sheer density of text which the full-length novel seems to demand as the price of fidelity to narrative. The novella and the short story are more often the right length for a two-hour feature film. The truly epic picture-book of the cinema is not the American or Soviet versions of *War and Peace* but Luchino Visconti's adaptation of Giuseppe di Lampedusa's *The Leopard* which takes a historical novel of the mid-twentieth century and transposes its modest length of two hundred pages to three very full hours of cinema.

The Leopard is illuminating in another way. Between its director and its author there is a shared historical frame of meaning. The picture-book is at its best when film and text are part of the same culture, part of the same age, yet also when some time has elapsed between book and film, when the picture-book is also a retrospective rendering of the text. Lampedusa and Visconti share, in the middle of the twentieth century, a retrospective of a part of the previous century's history in Italy. It is an achievement repeated, in a slightly narrower time band, by Bernardo Bertolucci's picture-book of Alberto Moravio's novel of Fascist Italy, *The Conformist.* The dates here are instructive. Lampedusa's novel was published in 1938, Visconti's film made in 1964. Moravia's novel was published in 1952, Bertolucci's film made in 1969. Orson Welles' picture-book of Kafka's *The Trial* is an example of extreme distance of this shared frame of meaning. The novel of 1912, a tragic fable highly prophetic of the police states, tyrannical bureaucracies and genocide in the Europe of this century, is transposed by Welles to a central Europe of 1960 which has 'come out the other side' of world war and entered the age of the nuclear bomb and the computer. In a similar vein, 1984 seemed an appropriate year for Mike Radford, the British film-maker, to adapt Orwell's futuristic novel of 1948, *Nineteen Eighty-Four,* to a vision of Britain mediated by contemporary experience.

At this point, perhaps, we ought to look further at the aesthetic objections to the picture-book, especially Alain Resnais' powerful reason for refusing to adapt literary texts. For Resnais, the written fiction brings a pre-existent weight to the cinema which burdens the process of film-making. His own solution, as one of the most literary of modern film-makers, was to opt for the original screenplay commissioned from major contemporary writers such as Marguerite Duras, Alain Robbe-Grillet, Jean Cayrol and David Mercer. As the writers concerned have testified, working with Resnais was a highly successful form of collaboration, one which linked their own developments in writing to innovations in film-making. Many critics have noted the close and fertile connection in France between the *nouveau roman* and the *nouvelle vague.* Thus Resnais' undisputed triumph as a film-maker of the literary screenplay not only shows the close relationship of cinema and fiction but also constitutes a challenge for the advocate of the picture-book. Is not the picture-book on this plane clearly redundant? We have major directors like Antonioni and Buñuel who have used gifted *literary* screenwriters such as Tonino Guerra or Jean-Claude Carrière. We have others like Welles, Bergman or Herzog who are gifted enough to write their own screenplays. All of them work from original screenplays which are later published as literary texts. Is not the picture-book by comparison simply a secondary offshoot of the cinema's tie-in with other forms of culture? Is it not a convenient shortcut, a flight from originality?

At one level, the answer must be yes, the picture-book often is secondary and derivative. At another level, the answer must be no. The culture of the picture-book cannot genuinely be separated from that of the literary screenplay, or of the current interpenetration of written and electronic media, the increasing symbiosis of different cultural forms. Moreover, it shows us what is all too often forgotten, the organic historical connections of word and image, of verbal and visual literacy which at their most basic, in television and newspapers, are both forms of collage.[2] All modern fiction, from Joyce, Kafka and Faulkner to Kundera and Pynchon, is a form of writing which has an awareness of the power of the moving image at this basic level. Conversely, the picture-book at its best transforms the important narrative text into an enduring cinematic image. At its most powerful, it illustrates the power of the text by persuading us to read it if we have not already done so. If we have, it graphically reminds us of textual power. On the other hand, the text chosen can be fairly marginal to its genre or to its author's work in general. For the film-maker it may not be a text at all, but merely an idea, a fragment, a treatment, an inspiration. It may remind us simply that all stories come from somewhere and have always been in circulation, in some form or other.

Despite the various crises—financial, artistic, political—in contemporary cinema, the picture-book remains a cogent force. *The Leopard, The Trial* and *The Conformist* were among the most powerful films of the sixties, itself one of the most important decades in film history. In the last decade two of the most outstanding films to be considered for any top-ten listing have been adaptations. The first is the Francesco Rosi/Tonino Guerra picture-book of the novel by Gabriel García Marquez *Chronicle of a Death Foretold* and the second the adaptation of Milan Kundera's *The Unbearable Lightness of Being* by Philip Kaufman and Jean-Claude Carrière, analysed here by Catherine Fellowes. Moreover fiction by John Fowles, William Styron, Margaret Atwood, Doris Lessing, Angela Carter, Ian MacEwan, Robert Stone and many other current writers has been adapted in the last decade. In addition, the new or revitalised genres of popular fiction, horror, crime thrillers, science fiction have fed directly into the American cinema either to provide obvious tie ins, as in the case of Stephen King or Thomas Harris. Such fictions can also be a source of new experiments in genre, as in the case of Jim Thompson's novels, *The Grifters* and *The Kill-Off,* or Stanley Kubrick's picture-book of King's *The Shining,* discussed here in an essay by John Brown.

The recent 'discovery' of Jim Thompson, who wrote his best novels in the fifties and significantly worked on the screenplays of two of Kubrick's best movies, *The Killing* and *Paths of Glory,* is an interesting match of popular genre and picture-book, showing the importance of shared meaning in the context of American modes of adapting. During the reign of the Hollywood studio code and its creed of compensating moral value for the graphic depiction of evil, Thompson's novels, with their terse lacerating ironies, were too challenging to become obvious screen properties. Indeed, as critics have noted, the total absence of a moral centre makes Raymond Chandler at times look sentimental. Thompson was a prophetic writer, a visionary of pure amoralism, an observer viewing criminality as the bedrock of modern American life and witnessing the moral paralysis it induces. The film-makers who have used him— Sam Peckinpah and Walter Hill, Stephen Frears, Maggie Greenwald—have responded both to the America of the present where crime is a mere fact of life and to its recent past, updating him and yet trying to retain that sense of continuity with an earlier, less frantic age. Yet reading Thompson and pondering his profound sense of the contradictions of criminality, it is those film-makers working at the limits of genre, not his movie-adaptors, who seem to match that Nietzschean irony and amoralism which strikes a raw American nerve.

Terence Malick's *Badlands* shot in 1974 but set in 1958, with its formal etiquette, its ironised literary voice-over, its casual juxtaposition of everyday pleasantries and psychopathic killing, is much closer to *The Getaway* than Thompson's adaptors. David Lynch's *Blue Velvet* more than matches the chilling eruptions of suburban menace in *The Kill-Off* as a horrifying present with past echoes. The fake nostalgia of fifties hit-records is uncanny in its casual power, while Maggie Greenwald's recent film version of *The Kill-Off* is in turn clearly influenced by Lynch's landmark picture. Lynch's more recent *Wild at Heart* has strong echoes of *The Getaway* and *The Grifters* and Lynch's *mise-en-scène* has uncanny parallels with Thompson's narrative prose. Lynch's return to the composed framing of classic studio melodrama, his self-conscious reverence for the spoken word as opposed to multi-layered sound track *à la* Robert Altmann, the demise of the zoom, his intense neo-Expressionist focus on the clinching gesture within the single shot; all these give us a stylistics of the recent past of the cinema haunting the American present. Just as Lynch recycles the classic stylistics of obvious meaning for a completely heretical purpose, namely to frame actions which are *inexplicable,* so for the nineties reader Thompson's narrative line with its formal proprieties and gentle dialogue constantly disrupted by existential terror correlates 'then' with 'now', a specific history repeating itself as the perpetual present.

Within the conventions of film noir, there are similar drawbacks and ambiguities over adapting. *Ossessione,* Visconti's 1942 unofficial picture-book of James Cain's *The Postman Always Rings Twice,* is far superior to Tay Garnett's official Hollywood version of 1946 with John Garfield and

Lana Turner. Visconti's feel for exterior location, the un-bridled and fluid sensuality of his camera-work, his unerr-ing ability to render obsession at a visceral level contrast with a clumsily-framed Hollywood movie which is hide-bound by the censorship code of the Hays Office and clearly ill at ease with exterior locations—the latter film in effect fails to get out of the studio. But the 1982 remake of the film by Bob Rafelson after the death of the code at the Hays Office, is little better. The challenge, of course, is to use exteriors more effectively, and to make sexually ex-plicit the erotic encounter which the original film version could only fudge. But Rafelson's film has no sense of pe-riod and equally, no sense of love or obsession, which it merely replaces with kitchen table scenes of copulation. For a film which unerringly links eros, adultery, money and power into an unbreakable chain, as in Cain's novel, we have to look at Lawrence Kasdan's *Body Heat,* filmed from Kasdan's original screenplay. Set in contemporary Florida, Kasdan's highly erotic movie has self-conscious echoes of the whole noir history and uncannily evokes the forties at every juncture. Yet its sexual and financial mores are clearly those of its own period—the eighties. Thus, like the films of Lynch and Malick, it comes closer to fic-tion by not adapting it, and closer to the past by engaging the present.

II

Another problem with the picture-book lies in its form. If it is to succeed, it has to be a work of transposition, yet if it is a work of transposition, does it not violate the nature of the original? The problem has been exposed recently by the lure of one of the great modern masterpieces of fiction, *In Remembrance of Things Past.* Is it at all conceivable to make Proust, the movie? Two assaults by the cinema on the Proustian edifice tell us much about the inherent risks of the picture-book. The first, *Swann in Love,* by Volker Schlöndorff, whose film version of *The Tin Drum* is dis-cussed in this volume by Richard Kilborn, went for the modest task of adapting the first volume, *Swann's Way.* Scripted by Jean-Claude Carrière, Peter Brook and Marie-Hélène Estienne with a high degree of fidelity to narrative and dialogue, the film clearly shows why Schlöndorff pre-fers the first volume. It contains the one part of the novel where the presence of the Narrator is minimal, where he exists largely as a voice, a mere commentator. It thus be-comes possible to eliminate him as a character from the film. The film turns to Swann instead, dissecting his erotic passion for Odette, a Parisian courtesan. Swann's passion is to be matched later in the novel by the Narrator's own for Gilberte and Albertine, but ends here in a happiness the Narrator can never attain. Swann's jealous obsession with Odette culminates in a marriage whose mutual advan-tages are social rather than personal. Odette gains status through her new position while Swann gains a social con-fidence from his marriage to offset the ethnic disadvan-tages of his Jewishness. Though Proust's narrative of Swann's life, as opposed to the life of his Narrator, works chronologically, the film version reverses the author's nar-rative sequence by starting with the climax to Swann's suspicions of Odette's liaisons with both men and women,

and then tracing the early blossoming of their affair through flashback.

Yet there is a problem of reflexive narrative which Schlön-dorff cannot resolve. In Proust's text, his Narrator, a per-sona of Proust himself, can exorcise the sufferings of sexual betrayal by transforming memory into an artwork, into a fictional narrative of his biography. For Swann, there is no such artistic fallback, and the reflexive Prous-tian quality of narrative is lost. The film cannot render memory as recollection, judgement, because Swann's per-sona is not outside the film, not part of the process of making it, while the narrator, as a literary device, has dis-appeared. The film cannot make up for it. Swann has no narrative voice, so that much depends on the iconography of the gaze. The face of the anguished Swann (Jeremy Irons) is pale and melancholy, at times desperate, at times diffuse, always passively haunted. That of Odette (Ornella Muti) is alert, composed, razor sharp, always focused on the tangible and the specific. We see things through Swann's eyes but see him through hers. It is a composed and balanced procedure, but also a romantic convention. The film as a commodified vehicle also forsakes fidelity of appearance to film stardom. Jeremy Irons is a photogenic Keatsian hero, not the carrot-haired eczematic Jew whom Proust describes in the novel. In a way Irons is made too passive a figure for film narrative, which is why for the audience the more gripping scenes are the appearances of de Charlus (a virtuoso performance by Alain Delon) as he mocks his own sexual predation.

The litmus test of Proust, the movie, comes however, with the movie which was never made but whose screenplay is preserved as a literary text in its own right. Harold Pint-er's screenplay for Joseph Losey, a project of the early seventies, runs to 166 pages and contains 455 separate shots.[3] The ambitious project was never made because the massive financial backing needed never materialised. But the text remains a literary document rather than a technical shooting script, asking perhaps to be judged in the place of the images which it never engendered. It is a picture-book without a picture, stranded between novel and film. But it clearly shows the dilemma of Proust, the movie. Pinter rightly centres the narrative on the Narrator, whom he calls Marcel. His strategy is to start with the memories of Marcel in the last volume of the novel, *Time Regained,* written by Proust directly after *Swann's Way,* as Marcel visits the house of the Prince de Guermantes in 1921. It then reverts directly to the first volume, rendering Mar-cel's childhood at Combray and proceeding in largely chronological manner through the novel, now and again using flashback or repetition.

There is no voice-over, no obvious strategy of asserting narrative presence, of searching for a facsimile. As writ-ten, the screenplay narrative is imagistic and fragmented, a mosaic of remembrances which evolves gradually into an icy geometry of sexual betrayal. Pinter thus opts for no half-measures. Acknowledging that there is no way of rep-licating the narrative presence of Marcel, he chooses to objectify him instead, to make him a figure in a mosaic of sexual and social hypocrisies, a naive, gullible obsessive around whom hypocrites circle until some form of belated recognition dawns. Pinter's Marcel is at best a passive centre, overshadowed, like Swann in Schlöndorff's film, by de Charlus who is not only the central predator but also the central commentator on betrayal and rapacity in general. It is difficult to envisage Marcel on screen as anything other than a figure to whom things happen, and a figure who remains on the outside, an observer for whom screen presence would be very difficult to create. In the novel, acts of reflecting and recollecting, the narrator's retroactive imposition of a desperate reason upon the volatility of the emotions, is what gives the narrative its power. The power of first-person narrative, intimate yet discursive, and the Proustian epiphanies of memory are the magic gifts which atone for inaction, obsession, betrayal.

The narrative problematic also takes us back to the vexed question of a shared frame of meaning between author and screenwriter. Here of course, there is little shared frame of meaning. The problem which confronts Pinter here is the one posed by L. P. Hartley in *The Go-Between,* which Pinter also adapted for Joseph Losey, the past as 'another country'. What atones for this hiatus in Pinter's Proust screenplay, as it does in Christopher Hampton's adaptation of *Les Liaisons Dangereuses* are the complex cynicisms of seduction whose rites in this case, span classes, nations and epochs. The success of Hampton's adaptations, as both theatre and cinema, lies precisely in this appeal. In Stephen Frears' picture-book, Hampton dispenses with accurate social etiquette, while Frears uses his American stars, Glenn Close, John Malkovich and Michele Pfeiffer to give his themes a more contemporary appeal, making a deliberate pitch for anachronism. The sexual and moral vices of the French aristocracy are now, Pinter and Hampton imply, those of the Western middle-classes in general who have shed their puritanical heritage. In the age of consumer capitalism bourgeois audiences can now share vicariously in ritualised, costume versions of their own sexual and political cynicism. Even the historical picture-book is a product of its own age but it works best when it does not self-consciously parade its anachronism. Thus a literary device, an omniscient narrator of the twentieth century commenting on the mores of the nineteenth, which works well for John Fowles in *The French Lieutenant's Woman,* is largely lost in Karel Reisz's picture-book equivalent. Pinter's ingenious doubling of the love affair between Charles and Sarah as an affair between the two film actors who are playing them is a parallel plot, a film within a film, which stands in for the omniscient narrator that cinema can scarcely render. But as a stand-in device, it is a secondary and rather contrived surrogate.

In Fowles' novel, the first-person Fowlesian narrator is too distant with his sharp anachronisms from his nineteenth century characters to be truly cinematic. On the other hand, Proust's first-person Narrator is too singular, obsessive, all-encompassing, locked into memory. Kafka is perhaps unique among the great modern writers in using a

narrative structure, as opposed to single imagistic epiphanies, which suggests direct filmic potential. In *The Trial* his character-narrator has no omniscient knowledge and we see the world much as he does. Certainly we see things in the novel from no one else's point of view. Yet K is an objectified presence, a third person character-narrator whom we also observe, dispassionately, from the outside. As Citati puts it: 'Kafka adopted the paradoxical condition of totally accepting the character's viewpoint—but at the same time he created a glass wall between himself and Joseph K.'[4] The camera in Welles' picture-book gives a genuinely Kafkaesque narrative because it taps the unique properties of the novel which correspond more vitally to the nature of cinema itself. So it is that we begin with *The Trial.*

Notes

1. For a fuller discussion of this problem see David Cohen *Film and Fiction: The Dynamics of Exchange,* New Haven: Yale University Press, 1979, p. 80: also Geoffrey Wagner *The Novel and the Cinema,* London: The Tantivy Press, 1975.

2. See Anthony Giddens *Modernity and Self-Identity,* Cambridge: Polity Press, 1991, p. 25.

3. Harold Pinter *The Proust Screenplay: 'A la recherche du temps perdu',* London: Eyre Methuen, 1978.

4. Pietro Citati *Kafka,* London: Minerva, 1991, p. 108.

Mark Axelrod (essay date 1996)

SOURCE: Axelrod, Mark. "Once Upon a Time in Hollywood; or, The Commodification of Form in the Adaptation of Fictional Texts to the Hollywood Cinema." *Literature/Film Quarterly* 24, no. 2 (1996): 201-08.

[*In the following essay, Axelrod states that Hollywood adaptations of works of literature tend to ignore the stylistic nuances of the written word in favor of linear development of the characters and storyline.*]

When I once asked a film composer friend if he had seen the remake of *Les Liaisons Dangereuses* he responded with the comment, "No, but I heard the soundtrack." It was, of course, an ironic response, but as an ironic response it makes an implicit statement on the relationship between cinematic and literary forms as well as cinematic and musical ones. The usual response to the query "have you read such-and-such a novel?" is often "No, but I've seen the movie," or vice versa, both of which imply an equivalence of art forms, so that the relationship between what one reads and what one sees, based on the same material, is somehow equal as well. However, another response that "I saw the movie and it's better than the book," or vice versa, somehow implies an inequivalence. In other words, there is something integrally superior in one that is apparently inferior in the other. Caught in between the art forms as either being equivalent or not, one is also left foundering between whether the art forms are equal or not. Obviously, they are not, but for someone to think that in some way they are equal, or may be or could be, implies a method of adaptation that is generally incumbent upon the target material adapted, which is usually, though not always, fiction. Though in fact original screenplays can be "novelized," that, in itself, is a purely commercial process of "reverse adaptation" in which the commodification is nothing more than the unmitigated attempt to expand a 120-page screenplay into a "novel-like" form of between 180 and 240 pages by merely expanding the linear narrative and the preexisting dialogue; but what we're interested in is how fiction is "cinematized."

What is in question is how a work of fiction is adapted to the screen in such a way that a reader/viewer can postulate it is or isn't as good as the original text. What is a reader/viewer comparing? Metaphor? Irony? Style? Is it something that is fundamentally rooted within the structure of the text that is being compared or is it something else? Is it the symphony of the sentence, its rhythm, the ability of the writer to master his/her material that is translated for the reader/viewer to synthesize? Is it, perhaps, the power and expression of the dialogue? Or is it merely the beauty of the written word? Actually, it is none of these. What reader/viewers tend to compare consciously or unconsciously are the veritable cornerstones of traditional "Realistic" fiction; that is, story line and character, and how these fictional idioms are conveyed; namely, through a linear narrative that has the correct proportions of agitation and resolution coupled with a dialogue that propels the story line toward its inevitable, and usually obvious, conclusion. In other words, how the story is told and with what efficacy the characters are realistically presented become the standards on which the work is evaluated. This form of adapting material often tends to undermine the effusive nature of a work of fiction by transforming it, transfiguring it, into a linear narrative that pays homage to the "state of realism," or the "state of storytelling" that was founded upon the principles of narration doubtlessly begun with Aesop, if not Moses, and polished by Walter Scott and Balzac.

But the question still lingers: "Why is this aspect of Aristotelian poetics, of telling a story in a particular manner, so appealing to Hollywood?" Presumably, it is because that particular movement is familiar to the public. Of all the elements Aristotle analyzes in the *Poetics,* plot "holds first place" and plot, "in its fullest sense is the artistic equivalent of 'action in real life'" (Butcher 334). In other words audiences are shown a film the plot structure of which somehow resembles stories they have been told in the past, which has an element of action, mainly external, that propels the plot forward. It is not that the story itself is similar in content (though Hollywood thrives on the iterative), but the manner in which it is told is familiar. But Hollywood has not stopped with appropriating certain Aristotelian notions of story line, it has appropriated Joseph Campbell as well, whose studies in myth have been keenly applied on a structural level. A study of many action-adventure-Western hero-dominated Hollywood films will show that their story structure and resolution owe a great deal to Campbell's multifaced hero whose evolution can be stylized along any one of a number of preordained story typologies in which the twelve stages of a hero's quest and the three stages of the journey (i.e., separation, initiation, return) respond to the Hollywood thirst for a satisfying and leisure-intensive structure. This structure, which clearly establishes the linear process the hero must travel in order to resolve his/her conflicts, has been used quite effectively by Hollywood "script doctors" who are called in when the original structure of a particular script is "not working." The resemblance is in the form in which the tale is told and the commodification of that form is the manner in which the Hollywood film industry has co-opted the original material in order to make it adhere to the principles of formulaic commercial filmmaking. Such a commodification gives new "meaning" to the notion of a "master narrative."

If we can return to one of the primers of novel criticism, *Wayne Booth is The Rhetoric of Fiction,* it states that narratives should be realistic, dramatic, and "that the choice of evocative 'situations and chains of events is the writer's most important gift'—or, as Aristotle put a similar point, the 'most important of all is the structure of incidents'" (97). And the structure of incidents, especially in a proper order, is of paramount importance in Hollywood filmmaking. And that structure is unquestionably a structure with a well-defined beginning, middle, and end. In that order. Of course, Booth has his own biases since he mentions Beckett and Butor only once each and doesn't mention any Latin American writers at all, while Henry James is cited no fewer than 200 times; however, Booth's biases are not the exception, but the rule. In Philip Stevick's *The Theory of the Novel,* Phyllis Bentley writes in the "Art of the Narrative" vis-à-vis Thackeray's *Vanity Fair* (filmed in 1932 and 1935) "and so it goes on through this and every other English novel written between 1719 and 1919: scene, summary, description, scene, summary. The blend of scene, summary and description is—or was between 1719 and 1919 (Defoe and Woolf)—the novelist's medium, his fictitious prose narrative; through and by this he must present his material; through and by this he must portray characters and actions representative of reality in a story line of more or less complexity; through and by this he must give us that patterned impression of dynamic life which is the purpose of all art" (57). Of course, in this theory of the novel, as in most, the novel begins and ends in England and the virtuosity of anything occurring farther north than Berwick-on-Tweed (condolences to Alasdair Gray) or farther south than Cornwall (unless one includes the Malvinas as England's lands-end) doesn't gain much credence, but Bentley's dogma does account for the fact that in those 200 years of devotion to a standardized, linear narrative garnished by scenes, summaries, and descriptions, readers and, by extension, viewers have absorbed a particular way of realizing the world and that realization has become the sine qua non of the screen adapter's craft.

But in addition to the fixtures of scene, summary, and description, the narrative, linear as it may be, in order to fulfill the substantive quota of narrative elements, must also include a "strong" story line and "relatable" characters since story line and character are needed to "tell a good tale." Norman Friedman's essay "Forms of the Plot" explains that, "These, then, are the three variables we must consider in defining and understanding the central change around which story lines are built: the protagonist's state of mind, his character and behavior, and his situation with regard to the external environment" (Stevick 151). Friedman then goes on to talk about several kinds of story lines beginning with "The Action Plot" about which Friedman writes that it is "the first and most primitive type of plot also, I daresay, the most common in terms of the reading public as a whole. The primary, and often the sole, interest lies in 'what happens next, and the characters and their thought are portrayed minimally in terms of the bare necessities required to forward the action. That is to say, we rarely, if ever, become involved here in any serious moral or intellectual issue; nor does the outcome have any far-reaching consequences for the fortune, character, or thought of the protagonist, leaving him free to start all over again, it may be, in a sequel; and the pleasures we experience are wholly those of suspense, expectation, and surprise, the plot being organized around a basic puzzle and solution cycle" (Stevick 157-58). Friedman continues by categorizing these types as being adventure, detective, western, or science-fiction/fantasy stories. What is revealing about this statement is that it not only validates the "normal" criteria for narrative storytelling, but substantiates the genres which Friedman indicates are the genres which are or have been the most popular among film audiences. Though some of these genres are cross-overs (e.g., *Star Wars* as a science-fiction/Western or *Indiana Jones* as a science-fiction/adventure) they constitute the lowest common denominator in the arsenal of Hollywood fabrication. The Hollywood trade magazine *Variety* annually reports the financial figures for the top grossing films of all time which validates that as well. *Batman, Jurassic Park, Star Wars, The Empire Strikes Back, Superman, Close Encounters of the Third Kind, ET, Return of the Jedi, Star Trek, Raiders of the Lost Ark, Indiana Jones and the Temple of Doom, Indiana Jones and the Last Crusade* all have grossed in excess of $100 million each. These figures could hardly go unnoticed by the moguls who run the Hollywood film factories. As Adorno has written in *The Culture Industry: Enlightenment as Mass Deception*, "movies and radio need no longer pretend to be art. The truth that they are just business is made into an ideology to justify the rubbish they deliberately produce" (121). Though one may argue whether these films are "artistic" or not, one cannot argue against them being commodities and it is difficult to exist within a market economy without becoming a commodity oneself. Even Brecht opined about writing in Hollywood that "If Arthur Koestler can make money writing pornography, I can do it writing films" (Lyon 46). Just as certain Hollywood screenwriters become commodified as being "hot properties" so too are the expressions of their craft: the scripts. This commodification applies not only to

content, but to length and even typeface. A script of fewer than 100 pages or more than 130 becomes an economic liability and a script printed in something other than courier becomes a typographic "postmodern" alien.

Paralleling the element of story line is the element of character and in speaking of character Forster pleads "that we shall no longer expect them (characters) to coincide as a whole with daily life, only to parallel it" (65). Forster then proceeds to divide characters into the "flat" group and the "round" group. The former "are constructed round a single idea or quality; when there is more than one in them, we get the beginning of the curve towards the round" (67). Flat characters, for Forster, are like Dickens's Mrs. Micawber or Proust's Princess of Parma. Round characters are those which are capable of "surprising in a convincing way" like all the main characters in *War and Peace,* all of Dostoevsky's characters, Madame Bovary, Tom Jones. In Hollywood terms, what makes these characters "round" is their ability to be "life like" or "relatable" or "heroic." Flat characters are not profitable in Hollywood. Round characters are. Butch and Sundance, Thelma and Louise, Rocky and Rambo, Dirty Harry are characters around whom story lines develop, around whom the narrative begins, middles, and ends. The flat characters are "supporting" characters and, like their cinematic counterparts, exist solely to act in counterpoint to the main character(s). Round characters are memorable; flat ones, unless they look like Michael J. Pollard or act like Christopher Lloyd, generally are not. So these items of story line and character, conveyed in a linear narrative that is framed by description, scene, and summary are what make a novel—at least a traditional, Realistic novel, novel—and which lend themselves to adaptability, a verisimilitude that appeases the financial mandates of the Hollywood film industry. The irony here is that Forster, whose major works (*A Passage to India, Maurice, A Room with a View, Howards End*) have all been adapted to the screen because of their clear structural suitability and because they are stories that have "a narrative of events arranged in a time sequence" (30), despised the cinema and speculated on the "novel being killed" by it (171). Were he alive he would certainly have relished the revitalization of his work Merchant-Ivory has given it and the fact that *A Passage to India* and *A Room with a View* both have grossed in excess of $12 million each. Perhaps his estate is grateful.

It would appear then that particular texts are preferable for standardization and exploitation within the Hollywood film industry because of the way they are written while other texts that appear to be "radical" (if they are adapted) are reduced to a kind of cinematic homogenization that precludes any formalized comparison between what's read in the text and what's seen on the screen. As we might expect, the works that generally tend to be adapted are the type that easily lend themselves to adaptability in both story line and character. They are the kind of texts that one would find presented as a mini-series on *Masterpiece Theatre.* In other words, they are simplified linear narratives, with well-constructed story lines, and rounded characters; they are easy to open, easy to close, and easily understood. Balzac's *Le Père Goriot*, Zola's *Thérèse Raquin*, or Waugh's *Brideshead Revisited* would be preferable to Beckett's *Watt* or Cortázar's *Hopscotch* or Calvino's *if on a winter's night a traveler* or Sarduy's *Cobra*. In other words, works that have a linear story line and can be reduced to a formulated and formalized prescription tend to have more "market appeal" than those that do not and, for that reason, tend to be the works chosen for adaptation. One need only recall non-Hollywood adaptations of Cortázar's short story "Las Babas del Diablo," which became the basis for Antonioni's *Blow Up*, Borges's short short story "Theme of the Hero and the Traitor" which became the basis for Bertolucci's *Spider's Stratagem*, and Garcia Márquez's melange of fictions which became the basis for Eréndira to see that Hollywood is not very interested in adapting those tales that have an "aberrant structure" to begin with.

One may think that's coincidental, that the selection of a work doesn't really depend on the kind of work adapted for the screen, but on the work itself. But Hollywood cinema history proves otherwise. Between 1932-65, Edgar Wallace, a master of mystery writing, had 34 of his novels made into feature films. In comparison, Agatha Christie had only 21 between 1945-85 (not including televised dramatizations) and Ian Fleming had 16 between 1964-91. Given Friedman's dictum, it is not coincidental that Wallace, Christie, and Fleming (all mystery/adventure writers) would have been, and are, some of the most adapted writers. Add to that list Robert Ludlum, John LeCarré, and Stephen King and one has cornered a sizable market. In that same period of time, there have been no feature films produced of novels written by Butor or Pinget or Christine Brooke-Rose or Flann O'Brien or, closer to Hollywood, authors such as Robert Coover or Donald Barthelme. John Barth's novel *The End of the Road* was, in comparison to his more textually convoluted works (e.g., *Lost in the Funhouse* and *Giles Goat Boy*), a "straight-up" narrative worthy of easy adaptation, as was done in 1969. Nothing of his has been done since. Likewise, Huston's making of *Under the Volcano* barely scratched the surface of that rich tapestry and his skills were better suited to something more "realistic" like *The Dead*, which was "adapted" almost word for word, while Kubrick's *Lolita*, though it captured Sellers capturing Quilty, captured neither Humbert's voice nor Nabokov's wit.

Neil Sinyard, in his *Filming Literature: The Art of Screen Adaptation*, summed up the problem quite effectively by stating that "the legacy of the nineteenth-century novel is the twentieth-century film. One of cinema's most immediate effects was to supplant the novel as the foremost art form of narrative realism" (vii). And narrative realism is the genre which is most appealing to those who tend to finance films not only as original works, but as adaptations and as remakes. Certain texts are so preferred to others that they are periodically refilmed under the same or different title. Dickens's work alone appears as a partial listing of what's been refilmed: *A Christmas Carol* has been

filmed fourteen times since 1908 including the classi[c] 1992 Muppet adaptation; *David Copperfield*, six times be[tween] 1911-84; *Dombey and Son*, three times since 193[1]; *Great Expectations*, three times since 1934; *Nicholas Nick[le]by*, four times since 1912; *Oliver Twist*, nine times sinc[e] 1909; *Pickwick Papers*, three times since 1912; and *Ta[le] of Two Cities*, seven times since 1911. With Dickens, ther[e] is no such thing as going to the well too often and mor[e] than likely there will be no end to the number of remake[s] and perennial restagings of Dickens's work. Likewis[e] Hemingway's *To Have and Have Not* was produced unde[r] that title in 1944 (script cowritten by Faulkner), refilme[d] in 1950 as *The Breaking Point*, and refilmed again in 195[8] under the title *The Gun Runners*. *The Maltese Falcon* wa[s] refilmed at least five times between 1932-91 (and once fo[r] *Masterpiece Theatre*) and both Maugham's *Of Huma[n] Bondage* and *The Razor's Edge* have been remade thre[e] times each since 1934. One may argue (for differen[t] reasons) that Dickens, Hemingway, Hammett, Flauber[t] and Maugham were all literary artists, but one would b[e] hard pressed to argue that those particular works wer[e] much less adaptable to film than Machado de Assis's *Th[e] Posthumous Memoirs of Braz Cubas* or Flann O'Brien['s] *The Third Policeman* or Biely's *St. Petersburg*.

John Fowles once said that, "for a novelist in the positio[n] of having his work adapted to the screen, the director t[o] fear is the one who swears absolute fidelity to every word[ ]" (Sinyard 135). That feeling was based on the malignmen[t] of Fowles's novel *The Magus*, but not every author feel[s] the same about non-allegiance to words and their adapta[-] tion. Huston's *The Dead*, for example. But Sinyard feel[s] the "cardinal rule" of screen adaptation is "Fidelity not t[o] the letter of the source, but to the spirit" (x), a rule whic[h] Beckett would have been one of the first to break sinc[e] even when a text is allegedly adapted in spirit what ofte[n] results is a work totally lacking in anything which eve[n] approaches the original. For example, David Mamet fe[lt] that his *Sexual Perversity in Chicago* was so brutally de[-] stroyed in TriStar's *About Last Night*, he walked off th[e] set. The "bastardization" of Paddy Chayefsky's *Altere[d] States* prompted him to remove his name from the fil[m] credits, and when asked what Isaac Bashevis Singe[r] thought about Barbra Streisand's adaptation of *Yentl* th[e] master politely replied that one should not try to do every[-] thing there is to do in a film by oneself. Politic indee[d] Fowles's *The French Lieutenant's Woman* was filmed in a[ ] conservative attempt to take advantage of the popularity o[f] the novel. According to Sinyard, "it was felt that the pres[-] ence of an invisible or even visible narrator (Peter Usti[-] nov, perhaps) could be used to approximate Fowles's in[-] terventions in his novel and narrate the author's moder[n] reflections on the historical events he invents and de[-] scribes. But this would probably have seemed irritating[ ] and artificial" (135). Instead, they solved the "problem" i[n] an "ingenious" way: a film within a film. The problem, a[s] Sinyard sees it, and as most producers would probably se[e] it, is that the text was too convoluted, too self-conscious[,] too "postmodern" to be played the way it was, so they de[-] cided to create not one, but two "realistic" narratives. It is[ ] hardly doing justice to the "spirit" of the text if a present-day narrator is commenting on a Victorian love story through asides, flash-forwards, multiple endings, footnotes, epigraphs, and scenes that include the author himself. To say that using a visible or invisible narrator would have seemed "irritating and artificial" misses the point. The difference is that the use of two rather conventional story lines within a single film gave the pretense of doing something "radical" while only perpetuating and reinforcing an industrialized form. To help commercially, they also chose Harold Pinter to write the script, Karel Reisz to direct, and Meryl Streep and Jeremy Irons to perform. In other words, the producers tried to hedge their investment even while creating a "radical" script.

At this time one may ask, "But what about the director? the alleged auteur? Doesn't s/he have an appropriate vision of the final product?" The answer is a profound "kind of," but within certain parameters and the parameters, as far as the script is concerned, are generally followed by the directors. At least Hollywood directors. At least Hollywood directors who want their films funded. The myth that directors are somehow in control of the entire project (one generally fomented by academicians who've never worked as extras) has been perpetuated to the same degree that the quest of Joseph Campbell's hero has and in terms of screen adaptations the director's ability to run amok is even more limited, given the "scriptural" liabilities of adapted works.

Adaptations of such texts as *The French Lieutenant's Woman* or *Les Liaisons Dangereuses,* though both fundamentally well-crafted films in Hollywood terms, tend to ignore the posture of the text. That is to say, what tends to get adapted is not the stylistic essence of the text, or its spirit, but the linear narrative within the text. A work like Laclos's *Les Liaisons Dangereuses* was an exceptional epistolary novel, due mainly to Laclos's extraordinary handling of voice within the context of the letters. The letters are dated and arranged so that the narrative is held within bounds of passing days and weeks; correspondence is written because circumstances require it and the content expresses individual character through thought, feeling, and style. The brevity of some letters allows separate versions of a particular event, or a fresh view of a character, to emerge as the story line unfolds. The letters contain scenes which are described with enough concrete detail for them to be visualized easily and no lengthy descriptions of appearance, bearing, and facial expression are needed to get a sense of who the characters are. Yet in the film, screenwriter Christopher Hampton, a playwright by practice, a French scholar by education, ignored the epistolary virtues of the form and opted instead for the time-tested virtues of Hollywood cinema production: story line and character. In a way, Hampton Hollywoodized Laclos by gerrymandering the text and transmogrifying epistolary Paris into a kind of Dallas replete with fashionable costumes, North American accents, and McDonald's table manners.

What seems to be apparent, at least in the Hollywood film industry, is that certain works lend themselves more naturally to the economic function of the screen than others and those that don't are modified for the sake of profitability. Though this entire notion eventually leads to the inkwell of screenwriting commodification, what needs to be understood is that the Hollywood film industry is regulated by a profitability digest that virtually consumes the essence of even its own most-popular journals *Variety* and *The Hollywood Reporter.* Each year *Variety*'s Cannes Edition lists the "All-Time Film Rental Champs." This section is particularly telling since it never offers a listing of "All-Time Critically Acclaimed Films" or "All-Time Most Unprofitable Films." No, these are film rental champions. But without going into a tedious deconstruction of the phrase "all-time" or the word "champion," it's particularly interesting to see which most-successful films were adapted from novels and what those novels were.

In 1926, *The Birth of a Nation* made $10 million and *Ben Hur* grossed $4.5 million. The former was based on Thomas Dixon's *The Clansman* and *The Leopard's Spots* and the latter on the Lew Wallace novel. In 1939, *Gone with the Wind* grossed over $77 million. In 1959, a remake of *Ben Hur* grossed almost $37 million. In 1965, *The Sound of Music,* based on the *Story of the Trapp Family Singers,* grossed over $79 million and the film adaptation of Pasternak's *Dr. Zhivago* grossed over $47 million. In 1975, Peter Benchley's *Jaws* grossed over $129 million, W. P. Blatty's *The Exorcist* over $89 million, and Mario Puzo's *The Godfather* over $86 million. In 1983, Larry McMurtry's *Terms of Endearment* grossed over $50 million, Alice Walker's *The Color Purple* (minus the lesbian overtones) over $48 million, and Isak Denisen's *Out of Africa* over $43 million. Granted, much of the success of these films must be attributed to the star system in Hollywood, since Edmund O'Brien as Rhett Butler, Dom Deluise as the Godfather, Roseanne Barr as Isak Dinesen, and Wallace Shawn as Batman would, no doubt, have made major monetary dents in their respective films. But star systems notwithstanding, what is common to all of these films, with or without special effects, is that each of them inculcates the traditional notion of story telling. The story telling structure is imperative if one is to understand the tenor of the Hollywood film industry. The query "What's it about?" begs a demarcation. The bromide in Hollywood is that if a screenwriter can pitch what a story is about in three lines or ten seconds (whichever is shorter) s/he is a genius. So much for Joyce or Cervantes. That's one of the reasons Fitzgerald failed as a screenwriter.

No matter how the text starts out, inevitably what becomes adapted in a Hollywood film is a story line with rounded characters and linear story development. Something that perpetuates an answer to the inevitable question "What's next?" It is not puzzling that Edgar Wallace, Agatha Christie, and Ian Fleming (dead or alive) have held such popular appeal with Hollywood producers. As we have seen, traditional mysteries and thrillers are perfectly formulated for adaptation since they are full of action and character and story line. They tantalize the senses and invigorate interest. Nor is it puzzling to see scads of "how to write screenplay" manuals which constantly repeat the same structures of beginning, middle, and end, plus the obligatory pair of story line points that propel the story line forward. As a matter of fact, each year the Academy of Motion Picture Arts and Sciences sponsors a national contest for new screenwriters. In the rules that accompany the application there is a section titled "A few words of advice" in which they write, "Significant problems and conflicts need to surface near the beginning of your story, not in the last act. Introduce characters and problems in the first 20-30 pages, escalate those conflicts over the next 60 pages, then draw the tale to a climax and conclusion." And so the perpetuation of an industrialized form continues in spite of Christian Metz's option that a "scriptwriter's cinema" actually exists or may have.

One often hears the statement that film is literature or film should be like literature, but literature, as I understand it, is dynamic in its form as well as its content primarily because the evolution of fiction has been a dynamic process in form as well as content. The novel from Scott to García Márquez, the short story from Chekhov to Borges has not been static. Literary (as opposed to commercial) fiction has not become commodified. But Hollywood film, to a great measure, has. And not just Hollywood film. The "formula" has become so pervasive that even cinematic "renegades" like Terry Gilliam have been "victimized" by the commodification process. For adaptations genuinely to reflect the spirit of the original, the isolation of one or two elements will not suffice. As Adorno has written, "The whole world is made to pass through the filter of the culture industry. The old experience of the movie-goer, who sees the world outside as an extension of the film he has just left (because the latter is intent upon reproducing the world of everyday perceptions) is now the producer's guideline. The more intensely and flawlessly his techniques duplicate empirical objects, the easier it is today for the illusion to prevail that the outside world is the straightforward continuation of that presented on the screen" (Adorno 126). It is not that there aren't artists capable of utilizing innovations in writing for film, it is just that the Hollywood film industry has had an opportunity to follow either Lumière or Méliès and has chosen the former as the shining path to the silver dollar, often at the expense of any other artistic or social reality. And political implications in the broad stroke, both implicit and explicit, are often written out of a script if they may be perceived as having negative box-office appeal. This would include, but not be limited to, issues of homosexuality, of homelessness, and of attacks on the mother of all social issues, capitalism. But regardless of issues of content, the form remains an ideological tool in the arsenal of Hollywood production which must be adhered to, if not sanctified, if one is to become a maker of feature films.

Quoting Georges Duhamel's *Scènes de la vie future* (1930) Walter Benjamin writes that movies were "a pastime for helots, a diversion for the uneducated, wretched, worn-out

creatures who are consumed by their worries, a spectacl[e] which requires no concentration and presupposes no inte[l]ligence, which kindles no light in the heart and awaken[s] no hope other than the ridiculous one of someday becom[]ing a 'star in Los Angeles'" (239). Six decades later Ho[l]lywood has yet to dispel the notion and the commodifica[]tion of film form which lives on in the hearts and minds [of] producers who are or who wish to be. The sociologica[l] and psychological implications on the register of percep[]tions becomes of paramount importance since it is con[]ceivable that if an industry can manipulate the way on[e] perceives the world and that industry has global influenc[e] the inevitable result is the homogenization of a world vie[w] that is predicated on the sanctity of cost effectiveness.

Works Cited

Adorno, Theodor, and Max Horkheimer. *Dialectic of En[]lightenment.* New York: Continuum Publishing, 1991.

Aristotle. *Theory of Poetry and Fine Art.* Trans. S. H[.] Butcher. New York: Dover Publications, 1951.

Benjamin, Walter. *Illuminations.* Trans. by Harry Zohn[.] New York: Schocken Books, 1969.

Booth, Wayne. *The Rhetoric of Fiction.* Chicago: U o[f] Chicago P, 1961.

Forster, E. M. *Aspects of the Novel.* New York: Harcourt[,] Brace, Jovanovich, 1955.

Lyon, James K. *Bertolt Brecht in America.* Princeton, NJ[:] Princeton UP, 1980.

Stevick, Philip, ed. *The Theory of the Novel.* New York[:] The Free Press, 1967.

Sinyard, Neil. *Filming Literature: The Art of Screen Adap[]tation.* London: Croom Helm, 1986.

ADAPTATIONS

Barry H. Leeds (essay date 1994)

SOURCE: Leeds, Barry H. "*Tough Guy* Goes to Hollywood." In *Take Two: Adapting the Contemporary American Novel to Film,* edited by Barbara Tepa Lupack, pp. 154-68. Bowling Green: Bowling Green State University Popular Press, 1994.

[*In the following essay, Leeds discusses the film adaptation of Norman Mailer's 1984 novel,* Tough Guys Don't Dance, *characterizing the cinematic version of this work [as] an artistically superior work to the original.*]

Norman Mailer's relationship with the world of film has grown throughout his career from passive and distant t[o] active and quite intimate.

The earliest adaptations of his work—the movie versions of *The Naked and the Dead* (1958) and *An American Dream* (1966)—are quite awful. While both films have many weaknesses, the primary failure in each case lies in the respective conclusions, which dramatically reverse Mailer's intended vision.

In *The Naked and the Dead* (1948), Mailer's celebrated first novel, the liberal, Harvard-educated Lieutenant Hearn struggles politically and metaphysically with the conservative General Cummings, while the malevolent Sergeant Croft plots to regain control of Hearn's platoon. One of Mailer's primary thematic messages in the novel involves the collusion of Croft with Martinez to withhold information which ultimately results in Hearn's death. Thus, on an allegorical level, Mailer forcefully suggests that postwar American liberalism will be destroyed by the uneasy alliance of the upper and lower classes in their affinity for reactionary political views. In the movie version of *The Naked and the Dead,* however, Sergeant Croft (played by Aldo Ray) is killed by Japanese fire, while Lieutenant Hearn (Cliff Robertson) is wounded, but carried safely back to headquarters by the enlisted men of his platoon, notably "a Baptist preacher and a wandering Jew," thus thwarting the tyrannical fascist General Cummings (Raymond Massey). In fact, in the screenplay by Denis and Terry Sanders, Robertson's Hearn triumphantly announces to Massey's Cummings, "There is a spirit in man that will survive . . . godlike, eternal, indestructible."

In Mailer's *An American Dream* (1965), the existential and ultimately hopeful vision of the novel is implicit in the fact that Stephen Richards Rojack survives the horrific American experience, aided by the sacrificial deaths of his lover Cherry and her ex-lover, the black jazz musician Shago Martin. In the movie (whose title in British release was *See You in Hell, Darling*), Rojack (Stuart Whitman) is killed by mobsters after being betrayed by Cherry (Janet Leigh), who thus saves herself. The last line in the movie is her solitary murmur: "What did you expect from a whore?" Shago (Paul Mantee) is present for only a brief moment. Thus, Mailer's indictment of the flaws and hypocrisies endemic in American society, coupled with existential hope and expressed so powerfully in the novel, is replaced in the film by a general sense of purposeless cynicism; and the novel's allegorical implication that what is potentially fine in the American character can best be realized by an alliance with downtrodden groups like blacks and women is completely lost on the screen.

During the late 1960s, Mailer's relationship with Hollywood took a new turn: he produced, directed and starred in three feature-length films: *Wild 90* (1967), the story of three gangsters in hiding; *Beyond the Law* (1968), set in a police station during a series of interrogations; and most notoriously, *Maidstone* (1970), a mystery involving an assassination attempt upon a presidential candidate/film director, Norman T. Kingsley (played by Norman Kingsley Mailer). Made with no script, no retakes, and no continuity ("Everything . . . is created as he cuts," noted Sally

Beauman) (Mailer, *Maidstone* 9), these unconventional productions were critical and financial failures, though Mailer demonstrated a gathering understanding and control of cinematic technique with each one. When *Maidstone* was issued as a paperback book in 1971, Mailer added an essay on filmmaking (in which, among other things, he contemplated the difficulty of "transporting a novelist's vision of life over to a film" [143] and concluded that, since the coherence of the original novel is "cremated and strewn" by the process of adaptation, it is "no wonder great novels invariably make the most disappointing movies . . . and modest novels . . . sometimes make very good movies" [144]). A decade later, in 1981, he returned to Hollywood in yet another role: a cameo appearance as Stanford White in the movie version of E. L. Doctorow's *Ragtime*.

Also in 1981, Mailer wrote the screenplay for the 1982 NBC Television Network miniseries based on his 1979 "true life novel," *The Executioner's Song,* which was later shown on cable premium channels and seen in theaters in Europe. Mailer was nominated for an Emmy award for the screenplay, and Tommy Lee Jones won one (Outstanding Actor in a Drama Special) for his starring role as Gary Gilmore, the first man to be executed in America in ten years. So eager was Mailer to write this screenplay himself that he took the unusual step of writing on speculation. The fact that this was clearly a labor of love shows in the vitality of the production, which garnered generally strong reviews. Subsequently, Mailer explained: "I thought no one could do 'The Executioner's Song' as well as I could. Part of the problem is that it's a very long book with over 200 characters, and a job of digestion had to be done. I wrote that book, so I'd already done that digesting" (Harmetz).

But the most important film of Mailer's career to date is unquestionably *Tough Guys Don't Dance,* based on his 1984 novel of the same title, for which Mailer wrote the screenplay and also directed. *Tough Guys* is the story of Tim Madden—ex-con, ex-amateur fighter, and unsuccessful writer—who wakes up with a hangover one morning to discover a new tattoo on his arm, a fresh blood stain on his car seat, and a severed head in his marijuana stash. Although Tim has only vague memories of his activities during the previous night, he begins to fear his complicity in the various murders which are soon revealed; and he tries to reconstruct the events so that he can prove his innocence, to himself and to others who suspect him.

For Mailer, the novel was like "an illegitimate baby. It was written in two months, therefore born out of wedlock" (Bowden 40-44). In fact, he was surprised by the fact that the event even took place, since—though he had been drawing an advance—he had not written a word for months. "[I]f I didn't write it," he remarked after *Tough Guys'* publication, "with all that I owed the IRS and my old publisher, I'd have to begin cheating Random House [publisher of *Tough Guys*] immediately" (40).[1]

Nevertheless, the form which Mailer adopted in the novel was one to which he had been drawn for some time. "I'd been thinking of doing [a murder mystery] for many years. And I've always loved Hammett and Chandler. Whenever I get tired of writing, I go and read them. I read them five times, eight times. Every one of their books. This is over many years, over 40 years. They're a tonic. So, I've always wanted to write a murder mystery and I've always been curious as to how it would turn out" (Bowden 44).

Tough Guys Don't Dance turned out to be a relatively insignificant novel, clearly overshadowed by Mailer's substantial body of work, particularly by *Ancient Evenings* (1983), which it most immediately follows, and *An American Dream* (1965), which it most closely resembles. But its similarities to the latter are particularly interesting. For, while *Tough Guys* suffers by comparison to the earlier novel, it does represent a return to themes and situations first developed in *An American Dream,* including many of the significant and symbolic preoccupations that have governed Mailer's work for decades: a highly personal vision of American existentialism, an obsessive preoccupation with cancer as a symbol of moral failure, and, above all, a Manichaean vision of the universe.

Moreover, many of the plot details in the two novels are similar. Again, an estranged wife is murdered, possibly by her husband, the first-person narrator. Again, the existential will of the protagonist is tested by the danger of falling from heights, by a hostile police investigator, and by various other adversaries from the demi-monde. Again, cancer figures prominently, supernatural omens abound, and potential salvation is offered through a regenerative heterosexual love. Even the circumstances of the composition of the novels were much the same: *American Dream* was written hurriedly against monthly deadlines for publication in *Esquire* (January through August, 1964); *Tough Guys* was completed in sixty days, and two long sections from it were published in *Vanity Fair.*

In *An American Dream,* two primary structural patterns lend coherence to Mailer's thematic preoccupations. One is the sense of a pilgrimage by Stephen Richards Rojack from imminent alcoholism, madness and damnation to sanity and salvation. In a modern analogue of *Pilgrim's Progress,* he confronts a series of adversaries, defeating them and the weaknesses in himself that they represent, and in the process absorbing their strengths. The second is a pattern of sexual connections among the characters, with Rojack at its hub. These structural patterns are replicated in both versions of *Tough Guys Don't Dance.*

In *Cannibals and Christians* (1966), Mailer writes of James Baldwin's *Another Country:*

> There is a chain of fornication which is all but complete. . . . With the exception of Rufus Scott, who does not go to bed with his sister, everybody else in the book is connected by their skin to another character who is connected to still another. . . . All the sex in the book is displaced, whites with blacks, men with men, women with homosexuals; the sex is funky to suffocation, rich but claustrophobic, sensual but airless.

Baldwin understands the existential abyss of love. In a world of Negroes and whites, nuclear fallout, marijuana, bennies, inversion, insomnia, and tapering off with beer at four in the morning, one no longer falls in love—one has to take a brave leap over the wall of one's impacted rage and cowardice. And nobody makes it, not quite. . . . They cannot find the juice to break out of their hatred into the other country of love.

(114)

In *Tough Guys Don't Dance,* as in *An American Dream,* Mailer presents a series of characters as promiscuously connected to one another sexually as those who people Baldwin's book. But while the sexual world of Mailer's characters is as dark as Baldwin's, it is in the realm of sexual love that Mailer offers his statement of hope for salvation; for Tim Madden and Madeleine Falco (like Rojack and Cherry in *American Dream*) are ultimately able, in both versions of *Tough Guys,* to take the "brave leap over the wall of . . . impacted rage and cowardice." . . .

Ironically, *Tough Guys,* a far less ambitious novel than *American Dream,* becomes in Mailer's hands a far more artistically successful film. As both screenwriter and director, Mailer manages to translate to the screen much of the tonal ambience of the novel's fictive voice, as integral to his work as Fitzgerald's finely styled narrative is to *The Great Gatsby.* But whereas *Gatsby's* tonal resonance is lost and the awkwardness of the bald plot made prominent (despite Nick Carraway's verbatim voice-over in the third film adaptation), Mailer as director is able to evoke even more fully than he did in the novel the bleakness of his Provincetown winter; and while his adaptation of *Tough Guys* still highlights (as in the *Gatsby* films) the excesses of the murder mystery plot, they are ameliorated to some degree by a pervasive tone of black humor.

Mailer's protagonist in the film *Tough Guys Don't Dance,* the aspiring novelist Tim Madden (surprisingly well-evoked in his seedy alcoholism by Ryan O'Neal), lies at the center of a complex round of sexual connections. Just as Rojack in *American Dream* is linked to his satanic adversary, Barney Oswald Kelly, by the fact that each has had affairs with Deborah, Ruta and Cherry, Tim Madden in *Tough Guys* is connected to his former colleague, multi-millionaire Meeks Wardley Hilby III (called Wardley Meeks III in the film and played by John Bedford Lloyd) through Tim's estranged wife Patty Lareine (Debra Sandlund), and to Meeks' associate, Lonnie Pangborn (R. Patrick Sullivan) through Jessica Pond (Frances Fisher), whom Tim meets—and sleeps with—on the fateful night he does not fully recall. But Madden's most significant connection is to Alvin Luther Regency (Wings Hauser), the Acting Chief of Police of Provincetown, who, like Madden, has been intimate with Patty Lareine and Jessica Pond and who is married to Tim's former lover, Madeleine Falco (Isabella Rossellini).

Wings Hauser is quite effective at portraying Regency's intense rectitude (echoed in his middle name, "Luther") as well as his criminal venality, his sexual rapacity and his borderline madness. (He sometimes looks as if he is about to rotate his head 360° and vomit pea soup.) In fact, he tells Tim and his father, Dougy, that he has two sides, "the enforcer and the maniac." In both novel and film, the primary antagonist and the police investigator become one, as Madden finds himself unwittingly participating in a wife-swap with Regency. Unlike the relatively simple, deceptively innocent swap twelve years earlier in which Madden met Patty Lareine (then married to her first husband, the football coach-preacher-chiropractor called "Big Stoop") and ultimately lost his real love, Madeleine, this one has life and death stakes.

These geometric sexual patterns in turn are part of a series of shifting criminal alliances and betrayals which lead in the book to five murders and two suicides (six and one in the film), and two postmortem beheadings, treated with a more disarming black humor in the film's conclusion than in the novel. Yet the most significant relationship in both versions is that between Tim and his forceful father Dougy (powerfully portrayed by Lawrence Tierney, an actor who in life had a history of drunken brawling similar to that of his character).[2] . . . It is Dougy who provides Tim with the veritable Zen koan which forms the book's title (although the boxing anecdote is omitted from the film); it is Dougy who, despite being ravaged by cancer, remains the tough guy (though—as he confesses—the spirits now hover around him at night and taunt him, telling him it is time for him to dance); and it is Dougy who performs the dirtier responsibilities, such as disposing of the severed heads, which Tim cannot. (In a nice symmetry at the end of the film, however, Dougy—made a little less tough by his illness—and Tim—made a little more tough by his recent experience—work together to clean up the week's terrible mess when they sail out at night and dispose of the bodies.) It is no wonder, then, that of the animal imagery so pervasive in the novel, the most positive has been reserved for Dougy. He has "tiger's balls" and is as "powerful as a Kodiak bear," descriptions which emphasize his massive size and courage and his large role as a moral paradigm for his son (Mailer, *Tough Guys* 254, 88). (Tim, by contrast, is more diminutive, feeling "like a cat trapped for six days in a tree" [99] when he cannot complete the climb up the Provincetown monument and "like a puppy in a new house" [75], soiled by panic in fear of his unseen adversaries.)[3]

In the film as in the book, no one and nothing is as it appears to be. Regency, the top police officer, is actually a criminal. Tim, the apparent murderer, is the only entirely innocent character. Patty Lareine, the "murdered" wife, is actually a murderess until she herself is murdered. Both homosexuals, Wardley and Pangborn, become temporarily heterosexual. The menacing Bolo Green (a.k.a. "Mr. Black"), Patty's chauffeur and lover, acts amicably toward Tim (who had been Patty's chauffeur and lover when she was married to Wardley). Even Tim's Black Labrador, Stunts (so named because he knows none), performs one surprising and heroic act by taking in his heart the knife intended for Tim.

A series of minor *Doppelgängers* populates both versions of *Tough Guys,* echoing the Tim/Regency connection. Patty and Jessica are so interchangeable as blonde sex objects that when Tim finds the first severed head in his marijuana stash he is confused as to whose head it actually is. (This confusion is somewhat deemphasized in the film.) Wardley and Pangborn have parallel anomalous sexual relationships with Patty and Jessica, respectively, in which they are replaced by Tim Madden, and ultimately in the book they shoot themselves with matching pistols. (In the movie, however, Pangborn is shot by Jessica, who wields the pistol he has handed over to her.)

Similarly, in the novel, Tim Madden is connected to a seemingly unlikely counterpart, the sordid and unsavory Hank "Spider" Nissen. Like Tim, Spider is an unsuccessful writer (Mailer, *Tough Guys* 102); like Tim, he is supported by the woman with whom he lives (though Spider and Beth's circumstances are more modest than Tim and Patty's); and, like Tim (who was kept from completing his climb by the overhang near the top), he made an abortive attempt to scale the Provincetown Monument. While Tim's attempt, made many years earlier, is beneficial to his soul and his nerve, Spider's attempt serves less purpose. Rather than any existential reserve, it merely provides Spider with a parallel which he happily emphasizes. "[Spider] would look at me," says Tim, "and give me a giggle as if we had both had a girl together, and each took turns sitting on her head" (101). (The parallels, however, are omitted from the movie; only the suggestion that Spider is supported by Beth remains.)

But if Spider, in his pinched venality, his vicious treachery, is an unlikely alter ego for Tim, Wardley is even more so. Wardley was, incredibly, a classmate of Tim's at Exeter. Both were expelled on the same day, for different reasons. They were, too, "classmates" at a school of harder knocks: a Florida penitentiary. Further, both have been married to Patty Lareine (Wardley being the rich man Patty marries after leaving "Big Stoop" and becoming a stewardess, an intention she announced to Tim the day after the wife-swap a decade earlier).

But as in *An American Dream,* the differences between these parallel lives are far more important than their similarities. Wardley is a homosexual by eager and early choice; Tim resists successfully even the enforced homosexuality of the prison power structure. ("They called me Iron Jaw" [Mailer, *Tough Guys* 254], he tells Dougy in the novel; in the film his declaration becomes, "I did three years in the slammer standing up. Nobody made a punk out of me.") And two instances of appearance masking reality serve finally to define these men. In the book, the one redemptive act of courage ever committed by Wardley, the daring creep along a ledge from one window to another of his father's house (though committed in the service of a venal blackmail scheme), has always elicited from Tim a certain admiration. Tim claims, in fact, that it was this image in his mind that stayed his hand when Patty Lareine asked him to kill Wardley (before she realized that divorce was almost as lucrative as murder). Near the book's conclusion, Wardley admits with glee that the story is pure fabrication. Again, where Tim suspects himself of being Patty's murderer, Wardley admits that *he* is responsible. Finally, while Tim goes on to a redemptive new life and love with Madeleine Falco Regency, Wardley shoots himself (after threatening to kill Tim and then dying in his arms). Meanwhile, Spider, the other dubious brother of the heights, is revealed as the other half of the Patty-head crime: after Wardley killed her, Spider beheaded her. (In both novel and film, Wardley in turn kills Spider and buries him near the two headless women.)

Many of the differences between the film and the novel versions of *Tough Guys Don't Dance* are implicit in the respective strengths and limitations of the two media. It is obvious that Mailer was obliged to telescope various events and limit or omit scenes or characters in order to fit the several hundred pages into two hours. Examples include the omission of minor characters like the eccentric local Harpo, nicknamed for his desire to "harpoon" women; in the novel Harpo does Tim's new tattoo, while in the movie that task falls to Spider's accomplice, Stoodie. Bolo Green (played by Clarence Williams III of *Mod Squad* infamy) disappears after the first scene, and the plot is altered so that his murder of Stoodie is committed by Wardley. The motives for most of the murders and beheadings are ascribed almost entirely to greed over a proposed cocaine deal, with dashes of lust and jealousy (notably in Patty Lareine's murder of Jessica Pond), whereas in the novel much of the plot involves a real estate scam.

While all of the aforementioned changes are explicable, even expected, there are two striking alterations—in point of view and in the film's conclusion—which profoundly alter the thematic message of the work. The loss of Tim Madden's first person narrative and his concomitant internal cerebrations weaken the film somewhat, since Tim's existential struggles with his own fears (as in the case of the climb up the Provincetown monument) are omitted or less effectively evoked. This is evident at its most awkward in the scene when Tim, confronted by Madeleine's note informing him that her husband Regency and Tim's wife Patty are having an affair, repeats the seemingly interminable litany, "Oh God, Oh man," as the sky wheels about him.

Mailer addressed the issue of point of view directly in an interview with Dinitia Smith for *New York* magazine:

> It's difficult not entering Madden's head. There's no offscreen narration. Narration in a film is a confession of weakness. Offscreen narration ruined *Sunset Boulevard* and *Apocalypse Now*. The more sardonic aspects of Madden's character can hardly be captured.

Mailer does, however, bring the illusion and flavor of the first person narrative into the early stages of the movie by the common and simple expedient of having Tim relate the story to date to his father: awakening on the twenty-eighth day of Patty's "decampment" to find Dougy seated at the table in his dining room, Tim recounts the strange happenings of the last week.

And Mailer does succeed in bringing some of the central novelistic themes into the film. In *An American Dream*, cancer (in Deborah, the mafioso Eddie Gannucci, and others) was perceived as a metaphor for moral failure. In *Tough Guys Don't Dance*, Patty Lareine speaks disdainfully of middle class kids "Trying to get vengeance on their folks for giving them cancer!" (Mailer, *Tough Guys* 106). More significantly, Dougy Madden presents a cohesive vision of life in which cancer is the eventual consequence of a major failure of will. Ultimately, he forces his own disease into remission through a crucial act of selfless courage on behalf of his son: sinking the severed heads of Patty and Jessica at sea. In a scene near the end of the film, which echoes a conversation occurring earlier in the novel, Dougy again remarks on the high (moral) cost of curing cancer.

In the film *Tough Guys* as in the novel, God and the devil are again embattled in a Manichaean struggle over the best and worst in the human soul.[4] Just as Rojack's journey through the New York night, and later through the artifice of Las Vegas, is seen as infernal, Tim's drive to his marijuana stash where the *heads* are secreted (Mailer may be punning here) smacks of a trip into hell and provokes an equivalent dread in him. His salvation ultimately must lie in overcoming his visceral terror. This internal struggle, though, is far less evident in the camera's eye than in Tim's narrative in the book.

But perhaps the greatest difference between the two versions of *Tough Guys*—and the greatest difference between *Tough Guys* and *American Dream*—is in the endings. The numerous murders and beheadings, for instance, when revealed in the novel, are reminiscent of Elizabethan blood tragedy. Stated in bald outline, they seem almost silly. The seven deaths and two postmortem decapitations, perpetrated by nine different culprits, suggest that Mailer is just having fun with the reader, toying with the genre. In *An American Dream,* Mailer took a cliché (as indicated by his title) and made of it a sophisticated allegorical indictment of American society. In *Tough Guys Don't Dance,* he takes a potentially serious popular form and, in a good-natured and unpretentious, if bloody manner, makes an ultimate cliché of it.

Yet whereas *An American Dream* ends on a sophisticated series of controlled ambiguities, with a resolution of Rojack's existential quest but no simple final solutions to the various mysteries presented in the course of it (nuances which are omitted in the film)—e.g., What was Jack Kennedy's true connection to Barney Oswald Kelly? Was Deborah really a spy, or even a double agent? What was the nature of the "work" Cherry did for Detective Roberts?—*Tough Guys* ends on a lengthy series of elaborate, often forced explanations of how the nine culprits and an additional supporting cast did away with the seven victims. There are solutions in abundance, but no true *resolution.*

Perhaps Tim's return to Madeleine, a pallid echo of Rojack's discovery of love with Cherry, may serve as a metaphor for Mailer's return to his old love for the mystery novel in an attempt to replicate his daring success in *An American Dream*. But as Mailer said of *Barbary Shore* (1951) in *Advertisements for Myself* (91-92), *Tough Guys Don't Dance* collapses in its last hundred pages, and never recovers (94).

In the novel, after a series of somewhat improbable resolutions (or simple solutions) to the involved plot, Tim and Madeleine move to Key West, living modestly both in terms of finances and hopes:

> Madeleine and I went out to Colorado for a while, and now we inhabit Key West. I try to write, and we live on the money that comes from her work as a hostess in a local restaurant and mine as a part-time bartender in a hole across the street from her place. Once in a while we wait for a knock on the door, but I am not so sure it will ever come.
>
> (Mailer, *Tough Guys* 367)

Thus, Tim and Madeleine find themselves in similar, if slightly more modest and certainly more satisfying, circumstances to those they lived in at the beginning of their affair years earlier.

In the screenplay, however, Madeleine surprises Tim with a house, presumably in Key West, purchased with the two million dollars from the aborted coke deal which precipitates most of the murders, money which she found in a briefcase in Regency's closet. Her final line—and the final line in the film—is, "Carry me across the threshold, you dummy." In terms of verisimilitude, it may be remarked that two people appearing so suddenly and acquiring their home so mysteriously would seem quite obtrusive. But Mailer's intent here may be part of the borderline parody and consequent black humor of the film's concluding messages, which makes the film's ending superior to the book's: we have just witnessed Dougy and Tim sinking six bodies at sea, while "Pomp and Circumstance" plays in the background and they discuss cancer and schizophrenia as mutual cures for each other. In the novel, Mailer writes, "Doubtless I am in danger of writing an Irish comedy, so I will not describe the gusto with which Dougy now made his preparations to take Alvin Luther to the watery rest . . ." (*Tough Guys* 367). In the movie, he makes us witnesses to the act itself. Perhaps because of this disarming shift to black humor, the film's excesses are more acceptable than those of the novel, since the audience's expectations of verisimilitude are lowered.

Mailer apparently enjoyed bringing his novel to the screen. He spent six months on the screenplay (compared to only two months for the writing of the book on which it is based); and, as he remarked to me and to other interviewers, he liked the excitement involved in directing, especially after decades of writing in isolation:

> I enjoyed it a lot. The trouble is, I like making movies more than writing now. I'm tired of writing. I've been doing it for forty years, and there's not much fun left.
>
> (Leeds 359-77)

Furthermore, in addition to directing the film, throughout the production he engaged himself personally in other ways: it is his Provincetown home—radically redecorated, with white lacquer and pastel colors in keeping with Patty Lareine's social aspirations—which serves as Tim and Patty's Provincetown residence; and Mailer even co-authored the lyrics to one of the film's songs, "You'll Come Back (You Always Do)." There was also a special kinship with some of the actors: Ryan O'Neal was an old sparring buddy, whose reputation for bellicosity rivals Mailer's. And Mailer's fifth wife, Carol Stevens, played the voice of one of the witches.

The film *Tough Guys Don't Dance* was met with sometimes negative or hostile reviews. But despite the criticism, Mailer in his first foray as director of a major commercial film shows his growth and virtuosity as an artist, and presents us with precisely what he described in *Maidstone*: a good movie made from a modest novel.

Notes

1. By contrast, Mailer's ambitions for many of his other novels were far less modest. As Joan Didion forcefully wrote in "I Want to Go Ahead and Do It," rev. of *The Executioner's Song* by Norman Mailer, *The New York Times Book Review* 7 Oct. 1979: 1,

   > It is one of those testimonies to the tenacity of self-regard in the literary life that large numbers of people remain persuaded that Norman Mailer is no better than their reading of him. They condescend to him, they dismiss his most original work in favor of the more literal and predictable rhythms of *The Armies of the Night*; they regard *The Naked and the Dead* as a promise later broken and every book since as a quick turn for his creditors, a stalling action, a spangled substitute, tarted up to deceive, for the "big book" he cannot write. In fact, he has written this "big book" at least three times now. He wrote it the first time in 1955 with *The Deer Park* and he wrote it a second time in 1965 with *An American Dream* and he wrote it a third time in 1967 with *Why Are We in Vietnam?* and now, with *The Executioner's Song,* he has probably written it a fourth.

2. Tierney's drinking kept him unemployable for many years. Tierney maintains in Gerald Peary, "Medium-Boiled Mailer," *Sight & Sound International Film Quarterly* Spring 1987: 104-07, that his career was sabotaged by gossip columnist Hedda Hopper, who would "print terrible lies" about him. Most of Tierney's early roles were as criminals in 1940s B-movies, including *Dillinger* (1945) and *Born to Kill* (1947). He also played Jesse James in *Badman's Territory* (1946) and *Best of the Badmen* (1951), and the villain who "derailed the circus train in Cecil B. DeMille's *The Greatest Show on Earth* (1952)." After Tierney quit drinking, he played in *Prizzi's Honor* (1985) and appeared in episodes of *Hill Street Blues* as, ironically, a police sergeant.

3. If courage, the capacity to steel oneself and rise above immediate fear, is here (as throughout Mailer's work) perceived as the noblest expression of the *human* will, many of the characters are described in pointedly animal terms. Other animal imagery in the novel includes the moment when, facing a new challenge, Tim feels "a descent from man to dog" (97) before he musters the will to go on. Yet, ironically, the attributes of the true dog are shown to be positive when Tim's Labrador Retriever, Stunts, demonstrates courage, sacrifice and loyalty by giving his life for Tim, dying with Spider's knife in his heart. (Although this scene is incorporated into the movie, Stunts's appearance in the plot is sudden and unexpected.) The truly negative animal metaphors are reserved for Spider Nissen, in his hideous nickname, his "crablike mouth" (103) and Tim's observation that "he had a touch of the hyena . . . that same we-eat-tainted-meat-together intimacy that burns out of a hyena's eyes behind the bars of his cage" (101). John Snyder's portrayal of Spider in the film evokes a palpable distaste in the viewer, but this animality is only vaguely implied.

4. This is clearly another echo of *An American Dream* (New York: Dial, 1965), in which Mailer posits the existence of a cohesive cosmic order, "An Architecture to Eternity," within which Mailer's Manichaean God and Devil struggle for men's souls:

> No, men were afraid of murder, but not from a terror of justice so much as the knowledge that a killer attracted the attention of the gods; then your mind was not your own, your anxiety ceased to be neurotic, your dread was real. Omens were as tangible as bread. There was an architecture to eternity which housed us as we dreamed, and when there was a murder, a cry went through the market places of sleep. Eternity had been deprived of a room. Somewhere the divine rage met a fury.
>
> (204)

Works Cited

Bowden, Mark. "Norman Mailer: The Prisoner of Celebrity." *Philadelphia Inquirer Sunday Magazine* 2 December 1984: 40-44.

Harmetz, Aljean. "Tracy Wynn Fighting to Get TV-Series Credit." *The New York Times* 15 January 1982: C8.

Leeds, Barry H. "A Conversation with Norman Mailer." *Connecticut Review* 10.2 (Spring 1988): 6-7. Rpt. in *Conversations with Norman Mailer.* Ed. J. Michael Lennon. Jackson: University of Mississippi, 1988. 359-77.

Mailer, Norman. *Advertisements for Myself.* New York: Putnam's, 1959.

———. *Cannibals and Christians.* New York: Dial, 1966.

———. *Maidstone: A Mystery.* New York: NAL, 1971.

———. *Tough Guys Don't Dance.* 1984. New York: Ballantine, 1985.

Smith, Dinitia. "Tough Guys Make Movie." *New York* 12 January 1987: 32-35.

Alan David Vertrees (essay date 1997)

SOURCE: Vertrees, Alan David. "Sidney Howard and the Screenwriting of *Gone with the Wind*." In *Gone with the Wind and Hollywood Filmmaking: Selznick's Vision*, pp. 21-53. Austin: University Press of Texas, 1997.

[*In the following essay, Vertrees presents a detailed history and analysis of the screenwriting process for Margaret Mitchell's novel about the American Civil War,* Gone with the Wind.]

A commonplace in film history asserts that motion pictures are only as good as the scripts upon which they are based. In fact, this truism is informed by a fundamental relationship that developed between the scenario and the screen. Preparation of a detailed filmscript had become a pre-production requirement of the American film industry as early as 1914 in order for its studios to ensure both quality of product and efficiency of operation. According to Janet Staiger in *The Classical Hollywood Cinema*, the "continuity script," in which each shot of a picture was prescribed and enumerated in advance of filming, served as the "blueprint from which all other work was organized."[1] She also proposed that, concurrently with the development of this shooting script, the organization of the film industry evolved from a director-unit system of production to an arrangement controlled by a central manager or producer.

Although the director continued to exercise authority over the filming of a motion picture, he was accountable no longer for all aspects of production but instead served, in Staiger's words, as a sort of "technical expert" who specialized in directing talent and crew during shooting. Staiger explained: "The producer chose a director from that department just as he would select a writer or designer or cameraman to be combined with a story and cast. In shooting, the director topped the hierarchy of workers, but the producer took over coordinating production decisions."[2]

This hierarchical arrangement continued with the development of the producer-unit system, a mode of film production that was championed in the early 1930s by Selznick himself. Under the "unit" system, studio-employed producers personally supervised the making of a limited number of films, monitoring and influencing their development from conception to completion. The "blueprint" by which all production work was organized often became subject to the variable element that was described by Robert Sklar in *Movie-made America* as the "manipulative style of producer control." According to Sklar, "some producers had a genuine talent for conceiving effective or popular film stories and for marshaling the resources—the right writer, director and players—to realize their conception." He cited Irving Thalberg as the progenitor of this type of producer, and identified David O. Selznick and Darryl F. Zanuck as Thalberg's most noteworthy successors.

> The manipulation of writers therefore became as essential a part of the producers' power game as the manipulation of stars. They aimed at developing a script that belonged more to them than to any of the writers who worked on it. Often a similar assignment was given to more than one writer; writers were asked to rewrite the work of others; different writers were assigned separate segments of the same script. When the shooting script was ready, the only steady hand that guided it along the way was more likely than not the producer's: he was the "author" whose conception the director was to put into visual images, and he retained authority to revise the director's work, whether by ordering changes after seeing the daily rushes, or by taking control of the final cutting and assembling of the picture.[3]

In the 1920s and the early 1930s, Thalberg, Selznick, and Zanuck served as production chiefs of MGM, RKO, and Warner Bros., respectively, and as such wielded enormous power as central producers over their studio's output. Subsequent positions as "prestige unit" producers at MGM between 1933 and 1935 allowed Thalberg and Selznick the time to exert even greater control over the motion pictures that were developed and realized under their supervisory authority. By the time he established Selznick International Pictures (SIP) in 1935 and arranged for distribution through United Artists as an independent production company, Selznick had grown to believe that greater rewards could be achieved by undertaking fewer, albeit grander, productions per annum. "There are two kinds of merchandise that can be made profitably in this business: either the very cheap pictures or the very expensive pictures," Selznick declared, stating his own preference for producing the latter kind. Of equal importance to his own vision of filmmaking was his belief that "in the making of good pictures [it was] essential for a producer to collaborate on every inch of the script, to be available for every conference, and to go over all details of production."[4]

Selznick's reputation for monitoring very closely the progress of screenwriters employed on the films that he produced and of editing their work personally was established early in his career. According to legend, the director William Wellman approached Selznick's table at the Academy Awards banquet of 1938 and offered the producer the Oscar statuette presented to Wellman himself for his part in the creation of the scenario of *A Star is Born,* with the remark, "Here, you deserve this, you wrote more of it than I did." The invariable course of Selznick's interaction in the development of his films' scripts led to his receiving formal credit as screenwriter of *Since You Went Away* (1944), *Duel in the Sun* (1946), and *The Paradine Case* (1947).

Selznick's supervision of the screenwriting process in his adaptation of *Gone with the Wind* is examined in this chap-

ter. Although many commentators have described this producer's interaction with the filmscript as counterproductive and unjustified, a review of the successive versions of the screenplay preserved in the Selznick archives reveals that Howard's initial drafts are disappointing with respect to exploitation of many of the dramatic and spectacular features of Margaret Mitchell's novel and that Selznick's insistence upon revision was a critical factor in the film's success. Too often, in his efforts to condense the story line to a standard length for theatrical exhibition, Howard resorted to employing conventions that were characteristic of literary adaptations developed more for the stage than for the cinema. Howard also was inclined to invent scenes and dialogue that deviated markedly from the original novel's narrative.

Although Selznick objected to the latter tendency, he valued his screenwriter's literary reputation (both Mitchell and Howard had been awarded the Pulitzer Prize, in the respective categories of fiction and drama). During the lengthy time in which problems associated with the film's casting were resolved, Selznick hoped that a satisfactory collaboration might be effected between producer and scenarist and that a faithful transcription of the book might be written. Howard objected to Selznick's editorial role in the filmscript's revision and to his demand for fidelity to the novel, and he temporarily withdrew from the project. In spite of the number of other writers employed during his absence, Howard remained the only one to be credited for the task of screenwriting. Skeptical that the film could replicate both the story and the celebrity of her novel, Mitchell herself refused to participate in the enterprise despite Selznick's entreaties and, until the motion picture was released and its success was assured, she privately disparaged his attempt to adapt her work.

READ THE BOOK, VISUALIZE THE MOVIE:
ADAPTING A BESTSELLER

Selznick acquired the screen rights to *Gone with the Wind* on July 30, 1936, one month after the novel's publication and after much encouragement by John Hay Whitney and Katharine ("Kay") Brown, SIP's chairman of the board of directors and New York story editor, respectively. By this time, copies of Margaret Mitchell's novel had begun to sell at a remarkable rate. "A first novel does well if it sells five thousand copies in a lifetime," observed Edwin Granberry, who praised the book in a review for the *New York Sun.* "*Gone with the Wind* has run up such unprecedented sales as fifty thousand copies in a single day, a half-million in less than one hundred days, more than a million copies in six months." He also noted that Allen Hervey's *Anthony Adverse,* which he described as "its nearest rival in the history of publishing" to that date, had sold less than 400,000 copies in its first year (1933).[5]

Two million copies of Mitchell's novel had been sold by the time the film adaptation was released and to date the total has surpassed twenty-eight million. The $50,000 that Selznick agreed to pay for the screen rights may appear to have been a modest figure in view both of this novel's spectacular commercial history and of the publisher's original asking price of $100,000, but most commentators have maintained that Selznick's offer was a relatively generous one. At the time, the highest price paid for the screen rights for a first novel had been the $40,000 paid by Warner Bros. for *Anthony Adverse* (released as a film in 1936). Selznick also paid $50,000 in 1938 for the screen rights to *Rebecca,* which was written by a previously published author (Daphne du Maurier) and which became the second best-selling book on the market. Moreover, it is less commonly known that Whitney and Selznick later offered Mitchell an additional $50,000 as a measure of goodwill and as an investment in maintaining the author's approval of their work.[6]

Determined to mount a spectacular Civil War epic, Selznick had entertained remaking *The Birth of a Nation* at the time of his formation of SIP (before the publication of *Gone with the Wind* was brought to his attention), but had dismissed this idea because of the racial controversy which had become inseparable from the reputation of Griffith's film.[7] Selznick's decision to undertake the adaptation of Mitchell's book undoubtedly was influenced by the fact that it was breaking records as a bestseller, as well as by the fact that it had been lauded in the *New York Times Book Review* as "one of the most remarkable first novels produced by an American writer" and as the "best Civil War novel that has yet been written"[8]—in spite of the film industry's superstition surrounding stories set in this period and its prejudice against using them. The otherwise perspicacious Irving Thalberg purportedly cautioned Louis B. Mayer against MGM's purchasing the rights to Mitchell's work. "Forget it, Louis," Thalberg reputedly declared, "no one ever made a dime on Civil War pictures."[9] "[SIP] was less than a year old when David asked me if I wanted to see a movie of a Civil War story. Of course I didn't. *He* didn't. No one did, not conceivably," Irene Mayer Selznick, Selznick's first wife, confessed in her autobiography, *A Private View.* "It was a first novel, carrying a stiff price and a terrible title," she argued. "All that and the Civil War besides."[10]

Selznick himself telegraphed words of caution to Katharine Brown on May 25, 1936, concerning acquisition of film rights to *Gone with the Wind.* "I feel . . . that its background is very strongly against it, as witness *So Red the Rose* [the popular romance by Stark Young, published in 1934] which also threatened to have tremendous sale and which in some particulars was in same category and which failed miserably as a picture." In particular, a sympathetic view of the plight of landowning Southern families during the time of the War Between the States and disapproval of the Union's emancipation of the slaves impaired the marketing of Paramount's 1935 adaptation of Young's novel. The *New York Times*'s reviewer of this film concluded: "It is difficult in this turbulent day to subscribe to the film's point of view or to share its rage against the uncouth legions of Mr. Lincoln as they dash about the lovely Southern landscape putting crazy notions in the heads of the

plantation slaves. By presenting the alien forces which destroyed this civilization as cruel and vulgar intrusions instead of inevitable realities, *So Red the Rose* cheats itself of contemporary meaning."[11]

In contrast, it is apparent to anyone familiar with Margaret Mitchell's novel that *Gone with the Wind* is more than a "story of the Old South" (as the book itself was subtitled)—or, more accurately, is more than a story of the periods of the American Civil War and Reconstruction, which provide a historical backdrop for the melodrama presented by its characters. "This book is really magnificent," wrote Charles W. Everett, a professor of English and American literature at Columbia University who also served as a reader for Macmillan, which published the novel upon his recommendation. "Its human qualities would make it good against any background, and when they are shown on the stage of the Civil War and Reconstruction the effect is breathtaking." Everett specifically praised as an "admirable" choice the "device of using an unsympathetic character to arouse sympathetic emotions."[12] What most appeals to the novel's readership even today is the story of this same main protagonist, Scarlett O'Hara, who not only survives this cataclysmic time for Southerners but prospers through her wiles, drive, and courage. "If the novel has a theme, the theme is that of survival," Mitchell herself wrote shortly after the book's publication, revealing a contemporary, personal relevance for many of its readers. She continued:

> What makes some people able to come through catastrophes and others, apparently just as able, strong, and brave, go under? We've seen it in the present Depression. . . . Some people survive; others don't. What qualities are in those who fight their way through triumphantly that are lacking in those who go under? What was it that made some of our Southern people able to come through a War, a Reconstruction, and a complete wrecking of the social and economic system? I don't know. I only know that the survivors used to call that quality "gumption." So I wrote about the people who had gumption and the people who didn't.[13]

The fact that the lives of many of this novel's initial readers had been affected by the stockmarket crash of October 1929 and by subsequent events during the years of the Depression undoubtedly accounts for much of the identification with Scarlett's straits. Equally important was the recent entry into the workforce of great numbers of women who were readers and members of film audiences. In fact, female interest was crucial to the success of both book and film. In his history of American filmmaking in the thirties, Tino Balio recognized that because the "era's most successful [motion picture] production was targeted at women and employed a women's perspective . . . *Gone with the Wind* . . . should be more accurately classified as a prestige 'woman's picture'"—a genre in which Selznick specialized as a film producer.[14]

The novel relates the career of Scarlett O'Hara, a wealthy Georgia planter's attractive and willful daughter, whose infatuation with their neighbor's son, Ashley Wilkes, is not abated by the young man's marriage to his cousin, Melanie Hamilton, nor by Scarlett's own series of sudden—albeit shrewd—marital alliances. To spite Ashley and to become a member of his bride's family, Scarlett accepts the brash proposal of Melanie's brother, Charles, who marries her after enlisting in the Confederate Army and who shortly afterward dies. Widowed with a newborn son, Scarlett moves to Charleston to join Melanie's household and to maintain contact with Ashley during his infrequent furloughs; there, Scarlett experiences most of the Civil War's destructive trajectory over the South, as it arcs through states of optimism and braggadocio, of inflation and deprivation, and of invasion and collapse. In Ashley's absence, she assists in the delivery of Melanie's baby hours before fleeing the city with them during its evacuation on the eve of the Yankee onslaught; returning to Tara, she finds the plantation plundered by the invading army, her mother dead, and her father mad from grief. Combating starvation, as well as fending off marauders and tax collectors in her new role as the family's matriarch, Scarlett elicits a proposal from, and marries, her sister's fiancé, Frank Kennedy, to prevent foreclosure on Tara and, as a store-owner's wife, to benefit from the postwar boom in business and building in Atlanta.

Left with another child, Scarlett survives her second husband's premature demise and marries Rhett Butler, one of the richest men of the "New South," who amassed his wealth during the war as a speculator and blockade runner and afterward is rumored to have augmented this fortune with the bullion from the Confederate Treasury placed in his own care. Scarlett and Rhett have been acquainted with one another since early on in the narrative, when he introduced himself to her at a party in the Wilkes's plantation home after revealing that he inadvertently overheard her passionately pleading with Ashley to abandon his engagement with Melanie in favor of a romantic relationship with herself. ("Sir, you are no gentleman!" she reprimands Butler for having eavesdropped, to which he "airily" replies, "And, you, Miss, are no lady.")[15] Their sparring during his pursuit of her affection is in fact the true course of the novel. Rhett also assists Scarlett in one or two emergencies; for example, her evacuation from Atlanta with Melanie and the children during the war is expedited by his escort. Sadly, their marriage does not survive their own child's accidental death. The book concludes with Rhett departing their home in Atlanta, having requested a divorce after hearing news of Melanie's death. Tragically, Scarlett becomes aware of the profundity of her husband's love—now lost—only minutes before their separation and cannot prevent his exit. Still she refuses to accept defeat, deferring concern to the next day, when she plans to return to Tara for recuperation; she ultimately concludes, "Tomorrow is another day"—a truism that was also the book's original title.

PRELIMINARY SCREEN TREATMENT AND
DIFFERENCES OF OPINION ON ADAPTATION

Selznick's correspondence with Brown indicates as early as September 25, 1936, his interest in Ben Hecht and Sidney Howard as candidates for screenwriter of *Gone with the Wind*. Both writers were appealing to the producer for not being tied contractually to another studio, and were considered—in Selznick's words—to have been "rare in that you don't have to cook up every situation for them and write half of the dialogue." Hecht had achieved fame on Broadway as co-author with Charles MacArthur of *The Front Page* (1928) and *Twentieth Century* (1932) and had received an Academy Award for his screenplay of *Underworld* (1927), as well as an Oscar nomination for his filmscript of *Viva Villa!* (1934), which Selznick produced for MGM. He was described by Richard Corliss in *Talking Pictures* not only as the definitive Hollywood screenwriter but as a "personification of Hollywood itself."[16]

However, Hecht's oeuvre may not have appeared sufficiently representative of *belles lettres* to promote the adaptation of *Gone with the Wind*. Instead, Selznick secured Howard for this job, and expressed his pleasure at having done so to Brown on October 8, 1936, although he regretted that the writer would not undertake the work in California but preferred to write the initial draft on his farm in the Berkshires in Massachusetts. "I have never had much success leaving a writer alone to do a script without almost daily collaboration with myself and usually the director," the producer admitted.

Howard was certainly an attractive candidate, and his theatrical and literary prestige specifically appealed to Selznick. Highly respected by the press as the adaptor of Sinclair Lewis's novel *Dodsworth* for the stage in 1934, and as the author of the 1925 drama *They Knew What They Wanted,* for which he was awarded a Pulitzer Prize, Howard had been lauded in *Time* magazine as "one of the half dozen ablest playwrights in the U.S." and as a "better theatrical craftsman" than Eugene O'Neill.[17] Moreover, his screen adaptations for Samuel Goldwyn were highly successful. *Arrowsmith* (1931)—one of Goldwyn's most critically acclaimed films of the 1930s—had been proposed as a project to the producer by Howard himself, who subsequently adapted Lewis's Nobel Prize-winning novel and received an Academy Award nomination after the film's release—as did the motion picture itself, in the best picture category.

Lewis, too, had been pleased by the cinematic presentation of *Arrowsmith* and had proposed that Howard undertake the dramatic adaptation of *Dodsworth,* which the playwright produced on Broadway and afterward sold to Goldwyn for film production. Howard's collaboration with the novelist involved numerous conferences in New York and on Lewis's farm in Vermont, during which fourteen "master scenes" evolved from a complete rewriting of the original work. Howard's term for the procedure was "dramatizing by equivalent"; it was a procedure that Lewis greatly admired, and was described by both writers separately in prefaces to the play's text, published in 1934.

Theoretically, Howard's method of adaptation entailed invention of scenes that were not presented in the book but which manifested ideas that were suggested in the original text. He himself confessed that the "filmed novel bears no more relationship to the real thing than any other variety of illustration." He also wrote:

> The truth of the matter is that no dramatization can do justice to any but a pretty completely inadequate novel. The road to happiness in dramatization begins, I am certain, with a lean novel, a novel deficient in both characters and incident, a novel which has attracted no readers to speak of.

He concluded his "Postscript on Dramatization" with the announcement that he would attempt no more adaptations in the future. "Works of art are best left in the form their creators selected for them," he explained and aphorized that "old books lose something when art shoppes cut their innards out to make cigarette boxes of them."[18]

Ironically, according to a biographer, Hollywood provided Howard (who, in a diatribe published in 1932 in the *New Republic,* parodied it also as the "Golgonda of the entertainment racket") with the "crowning accomplishment to his career" via his tenure on Selznick's production of *Gone with the Wind.*[19] The East Coast elements of classical American film production were distinguished from the Hollywood community not only in terms of studio ownership—the financial offices of the major film companies being located in Manhattan—but also by the superior, literary pose of many of the screenwriters, some of whose dramatic works had been produced on Broadway. Howard was among the most notable of these writers; although honored by an Academy Award for his script of *Gone with the Wind,* he persistently deprecated the work in his correspondence.

Howard's cynicism may have been aggravated by the indifference exhibited by the novel's author toward the task of adaptation. Margaret Mitchell had been resistant to leave her home in Atlanta in order to participate in the editing of her manuscript in New York and adamantly refused to journey to Hollywood after selling the screen rights to Selznick. "Of course, I would love to help out in any way I can but I have no ideas at all about changes and could be of no help whatsoever in such a matter," the novelist responded on October 16, 1936 to Brown's entreaty that she agree to assist members of the company in making "changes of continuity" in her work. "Besides, if news got out that I was in even the slightest way responsible for any deviations from the book, then my life wouldn't be worth living," the author also explained. "You see . . . each and every reader feels that he has part ownership in it and they are determined that nothing shall be changed."[20]

Mitchell was pleased to learn that Selznick had hired Howard for the task of adapting her novel for the screen, and she expressed knowledge of and admiration for the playwright's work in a letter to the producer on October 19, 1936. Nevertheless, she refused to cooperate in any part of her novel's dramatization.[21] Her reaction surprised Howard, who had written to her for assistance the follow-

ing month when Selznick's publicity chief, Russell Birdwell, began to arrange a visit to Atlanta by Katharine Brown, George Cukor (who had been contracted as director), and set designer Hobe Erwin (with whom Cukor had worked on *Little Women*) for the purpose of scouting locations for filming and for generating publicity and eliciting goodwill from the region. Birdwell also had hoped to suggest to the public the novelist's participation in the film enterprise by her association with this group.

"You know you have given me more story than I can compress into the two hours a picture is, at the outside, permitted," Howard remarked in his letter of November 18, 1936 to Mitchell. "Some things will have to go because nothing is less adequate than a picture which tries to cover too much ground and so covers none of it properly." He asked Mitchell to examine his drafts and explained that this was the procedure followed successfully with Sinclair Lewis. "When I sold the book to Selznick Company, I made it very plain that I should have nothing whatsoever to do with the picture," she responded by letter on November 21. "I know just as much about Sanskrit as I do about writing for movies." The novelist also felt that she lacked the necessary time—not surprisingly, given that even the fan letters in her daily mail were answered without secretarial assistance. Most of all, she was discouraged by the fear of being held accountable for the film's abridgment of her narrative.[22]

Howard explained in his reply on November 25 that the purpose of his earlier letter "was chiefly to assure you—in so far as it is in my power to assure you—that you would have all possible measure of approval or criticism of your picture before it reaches the irrevocable stage of celluloid." "I know you must have thought my abrupt letter the height of discourtesy," the novelist responded on December 1. "The truth of the matter is, as I wrote you before, that I haven't the time to work on the picture; I haven't the inclination; I haven't the experience—and moreover, I do not want to let myself in for a lot of grief." On December 5 Mitchell also informed Birdwell more bluntly, "I'll be very glad to meet Mr. Howard, for whom I have a vast admiration, but I will not read a line of the script."[23]

The task of adaptation remained entirely Selznick's responsibility. Bob Thomas wrote in his biography of the producer that, immediately after purchasing the rights to the property during the summer of 1936 and while on vacation in Hawaii with his wife, Selznick brought along his own copy of Mitchell's novel and "made elaborate notes in the margins, indicating what scenes and characters might be cut and what should be retained." Thomas also wrote that this same copy was loaned to Howard.[24] Both Howard and Selznick's initial impressions of the novel's story line may have been influenced, too, by the fifty-page synopsis prepared by Franclien Macconnell, a story-department employee. While Macconnell also summarized each of the book's chapters as a separate undertaking, her retelling of the general narrative provided not simply a denser reduction but was the first attempt to abridge the novel in a faithful manner but with a cinematic orientation.

Dividing her summary of the book into four sections, Macconnell opened the story not at Tara but with the bombardment of Fort Sumter by the Confederates; the first section concluded at the point in the story toward the end of the war when Rhett Butler leaves Scarlett O'Hara on the road to Tara, having escorted her safely from a besieged and burning Atlanta. The ensuing events at Tara open the second section, which concludes when Scarlett fashions a new dress from her late mother's parlor curtains and prepares to return to Atlanta in order to present Rhett with her offer of concubinage in order to raise money for the tax due on Tara. Beginning with Rhett's rejection of this offer, Macconnell's penultimate section concludes with his earnest proposal of marriage to Scarlett following the death of her second husband, Frank Kennedy, who himself had provided the money that was needed for the tax payment. Her final section summarized the remainder of the novel.

Notwithstanding the diligence of her rendition, Macconnell did not recognize that the five original divisions of Mitchell's novel signaled distinct stages in the story line—namely, Scarlett's departure for Atlanta to live with Ashley Wilkes's in-laws in order to continue her quest for his affection; the news of Ashley's imprisonment in the North; Ashley's return to Tara and to the arms of his wife, Melanie; Scarlett's marriage to Rhett Butler; and, finally, Melanie's death and Rhett's departure. In contrast to the conclusions of these five parts of the novel, in which triangular tension is maintained between Scarlett and Ashley and Rhett, those of Macconnell's four sections suggest that her synopsis exploited a simpler conflict between Scarlett and Rhett. In Mitchell's novel, Ashley Wilkes is allowed to motivate the conclusions of the first three parts, after which Rhett attempts to command Scarlett and the story line; Macconnell, on the other hand, relegated Ashley's part to a supporting role by her structural reorganization of the narrative.

The five parts of Mitchell's novel also bear a structural resemblance to classical tragedy. Scarlett is presented as an attractive, albeit flawed, protagonist who, in spite of enormous historical and environmental pressure, is responsible for her own misfortune by forsaking the love of Rhett Butler until it is too late, suffering instead from an extended infatuation with Ashley Wilkes, who is married to another. The novel's divisions recall the five acts prescribed for tragic drama by Horace in *Ars poetica,* and which were elaborated in pyramidal form, as a series of stages and crises, by Gustav Freytag in *Die Technik des Dramas,* published originally in 1863.

Specifically—and with respect to the pyramidal structure formulated in Freytag's treatise, which is claimed to have influenced the education of several previous generations of American playwrights—the novel's first part, which is set at Tara and at Twelve Oaks, serves to introduce the characters and their situations. The first crisis—Scarlett's discovery that she has lost Ashley to Melanie in marriage—initiates the rising movement which continues into the second part, in which Scarlett infiltrates the Hamiltons'

home in Atlanta as Melanie's bereaved sister-in-law, following Ashley's departure to war. This action precedes a climax (*Hohenpunkt,* in Freytag's terminology), in which Scarlett assists in the delivery of the Wilkes's child and afterward, with Rhett's assistance, evacuates the besieged city, retreating in the company of Melanie and their children to Tara, which has been desolated by the war and where she is informed of her mother's death. This second crisis, or tragic moment, introduces the falling movement of the fourth part (*Umfehr,* translated as a "return"), in which Scarlett attempts to reconstruct her life and to preserve both Tara and Ashley's affection in Atlanta. The novel concludes with a catastrophe, in which Scarlett loses her love of Ashley in disillusionment, as well as the love of her own husband, who departs after Melanie's death.[25]

It is uncertain whether Howard—a professional dramatist educated at Berkeley and at Harvard—had recognized the novel's compatibility with this conventional tragic scheme and the unity of action which results from such comparison; his various treatments of its dramatization, between 1936 and 1937, into seven, ten, zero, eight, and eleven sequences, respectively, betray a different, episodic view of the narrative. While admitting to Selznick that "for screen purposes it is, I think, well to think of the book as Scarlett's story and of Scarlett herself as a character whose actions are consistently motivated by what she conceives to be the tragedy of an unrealized love," Howard began his fifty-page "Preliminary Notes on a Screen Treatment of *Gone with the Wind*" of December 14, 1936, with the pronouncement that "our chief difficulty will come from the lack of organization of the material of the second half of the novel—that is to say, the entire extent of the book after Scarlett's return to Tara from the siege of Atlanta."

The screenwriter also noted that "Part Five of the novel tells us how, as Rhett Butler's wife, Scarlett finally pays the piper for the very strength which has pulled her through. Unfortunately for our purposes, this accomplishment requires nearly two hundred pages of disjointed incident covering some five years." Perceiving that "there can be no doubt that the screen is at this point crying out for a swift final sequence" and that "there is at least two of everything in this book," Howard compressed over half of the novel's narrative into the final two of the seven sequences of his "Preliminary Notes." In contrast with the economy of this radical abridgment, his second sequence is devoted almost exclusively to the hospital bazaar and to Rhett's chivalrous return of the wedding ring that Melanie had donated selflessly to the Confederate cause.

Howard himself professed to having retained far too much story material "even in this considerably reduced treatment," yet, sensibly, did not question allotting adequate space early in the script for the exposition of the principal characters at Tara and at Twelve Oaks. "I should regret omitting the charming passage between Mammy and Scarlett," he declared, "as Scarlett dresses for the barbecue and Mammy forces her to eat so that she will not display an unladylike appetite." With respect to the important, recurring dream that haunts Scarlett through the latter half of the book, Howard confessed to Selznick without misgiving that he was "not fond of dream scenes on the screen" and had "not found any practicable way to include it" in his treatment.

In his letter to Howard of January 6, 1937, Selznick himself discouraged the screenwriter from attempting to preserve every element of the novel in the adaptation, yet stressed that any part chosen for inclusion must remain faithful to the original book. "I recognize, perhaps even more than you, the problem of length," the producer cautioned, disclosing that he was prepared for a treatment that might result in a film with a screening time of two and a half hours. "But even getting down to that length is going to be tough," he admitted. "We must prepare to make drastic cuts, and these cuts, I think, must include some of the characters because my feeling, based on experience adapting well-known and well-loved books, is that it is much better to chop out whole sequences than it is to make small deletions in individual scenes or sequences."

Contrary to the case of his earlier adaptation for MGM of *David Copperfield* (1935), which he cited, Selznick observed that both the recentness of the publication of Mitchell's novel and the existence of a contemporary audience "simply passionate about the details of the book"—which the novelist herself had recognized in her refusal to participate in the film enterprise—dictated "very strongly indeed" against alteration of the narrative. "These minor changes may give us slight improvements," Selznick conceded, "but there will be five or ten million readers on our heads for them; where, for the most part, they will recognize the obvious necessity of making drastic cuts."

With respect to Selznick's adaptations of two Dickens novels (*David Copperfield* and *A Tale of Two Cities*) for MGM in 1935, a remarkably high degree of fidelity to the original texts had been exhibited already, particularly when compared with other notable film adaptations of novels that had been released during this same period. Still, in terms of the books' sheer length, *Gone with the Wind* exceeded *David Copperfield,* the longer of the two Dickens novels, by twenty percent.[26] With respect to a motion picture's fidelity to an original literary source, in his 1949 doctoral dissertation for the University of Chicago Lester Asheim observed a seventeen- and an eighteen-percent deviation from the novels in the cases of Selznick's adaptations of, respectively, *David Copperfield* and *A Tale of Two Cities*; in comparison, *Wuthering Heights* (Goldwyn/United Artists, 1939) and *Les Misérables* (20th Century-Fox, 1935) deviated by thirty and forty-four percent, respectively.[27]

Selznick had not been opposed always to exploiting an adaptor's license by tampering more extensively with a literary source, as is indicated by his production of Tolstoy's *Anna Karenina* (1935) with Greta Garbo, to which Asheim assigned a deviational score of thirty-six percent.[28] However, it should be noted in contrast that Philip Dunne, who

prepared the filmscripts for 20th Century-Fox of, among other titles, *The Count of Monte Cristo* (1934), *The Last of the Mohicans* (1936), and *How Green Was My Valley* (1941), estimated—with some exaggeration—that, in adapting less canonized literary material for the screen, it was this studio's practice to "discard something like 90 percent of what the [original] author wrote."[29]

Ethan Mordden surmised in *The Hollywood Studios* that "Selznick plumed himself on fidelity to text, not because so many readers demanded that their favorite novel be so honored—what lobby could Dickens claim?—but because Selznick believed that The Novelist is Right."[30] On the contrary, the producer believed that a novel's success was determined by the response of its readership and not simply by the efforts of its author—a conviction which he expressed to Howard in his comments of January 6, 1937, which address the latter's "Preliminary Notes." Selznick cautioned:

> I have learned to avoid trying to improve on success. One never knows what chemicals have gone to make something that has appealed to millions of people, and how much the balance would be offset by making changes that we in our innocence, or even in our ability, consider wrong.
>
> I am embarrassed to say this to you who have been so outstandingly successful in your adaptations, but I find myself a producer charged with re-creating the best-beloved book of our time, and I don't think any of us have tackled anything that is really comparable in the love that people have for it.

Nevertheless, Selznick suggested without hesitation the elimination from the filmscript of the character of Will Benteen, who marries Suellen O'Hara in the latter half of the novel and manages Tara in Scarlett's absence, in spite of Benteen's articulation of a major theme of Mitchell's novel in his homily over Gerald O'Hara's grave. Asheim noted that the characters and scenes that were chosen for dramatization in film adaptations exhibited a direct relationship to the principal romance depicted in the particular stories.[31] The central heterosexual romance's relevance to deployment of secondary narrative action was recognized also by David Bordwell in *The Classical Hollywood Cinema.*[32]

In agreement with this prevalent Hollywood attitude, Selznick proclaimed that Will Benteen "plays no part of importance in the story of Scarlett or in the story of Scarlett and Rhett; and I think that in weighing what characters go and what characters stay, those who do not play a vital part in the lives of our two leads or in their story, are those which must go first." The producer was more generous in his concern over the fate of the ex-convict Archie, who serves in the novel to escort Scarlett and other ladies in their carriages in Atlanta under Melanie's sponsorship during the unsettling period of Reconstruction. This character's peculiar humor may have reminded him of the comical driver Barkis in *David Copperfield* who was included as a minor character in the 1935 film. "I, too, would like to keep Archie," Selznick admitted to Howard, "although I frankly doubt we are going to have the room." He added that "this is the sort of character that certainly we should fight to keep, but before we get through I am afraid that we are going to have to make many sacrifices of this kind." Accordingly, Archie does not appear in any of Howard's filmscripts.

In his comments to Howard of January 6, 1937, Selznick also expressed concern over the element of slavery in the story, although what worried him more than depicting enforced servitude was acknowledging characters' racism. "I personally feel quite strongly that we should cut out the [Ku Klux] Klan entirely," he wrote Howard, adding that "there is nothing in the story that necessarily needs the Klan." With respect to the vigilantism against the predominantly black inhabitants of Shantytown following the assault upon Scarlett by two of its vagrants, Selznick cautioned against identification with the KKK—contrary to what was written in the novel. "The revenge for the attempted attack can very easily be identified with what it is without their being members of the Klan," he rationalized. "A group of men can go out to 'get' the perpetrators of an attempted rape without having long white sheets over them and without having their membership in a society as a motive."

PROBLEMS WITH HOWARD'S INITIAL SCREENPLAY AND ITS FIRST REVISION

"It is obvious that some radical amputation of book material will be obligatory," Howard conceded to Selznick in his letter of February 12, 1937, which accompanied the draft of a 250-page filmscript. The screenwriter admitted indecision "on what to cut out or on how to cut it out." Because Howard felt that the "book itself is so unwieldy," revision was advised only of material already selected for inclusion in this first script. "What you are getting is *Gone with the Wind* reduced from a thousand to 250 pages," he explained and estimated that "weeding" of its abridged dialogue and of "dead wood" would eliminate another fifty pages; "then you and I use the axe and I sew up the wound," added Howard, who explained that his original draft of *Arrowsmith* was equal in length to the filmscript of *Gone with the Wind* initially submitted to Selznick and that much revision of the former work had followed in the company of the novelist.

The common misconception that Howard's initial filmscript was 400 pages in length and corresponded to a running time on the screen of six hours has plagued many of the publications documenting the production of this film. The earliest appearances of this claim are in Thomas's biography of Selznick ("Howard's labors brought forth a mountainous script that would have required five and a half hours to unreel on the screen"), in Lambert's *GWTW* ("[Howard's original filmscript] was over four hundred pages long, almost six hours' running time on the screen"), and in Flamini's *Scarlett, Rhett, and a Cast of Thousands* ("Howard produced a first draft from the 1037-page novel.

Despite massive cutting, it was a tome of 400 pages which would have run on the screen for over six hours."). This error continued to inform subsequently published works, such as the monograph by Bridges and Boodman, and Bartel's *The Complete "Gone with the Wind" Trivia Book*. Despite having access to the Selznick collection in his research for his book *Showman*, Thomson himself could not resist the influence of this legend, claiming that "by mid-February [1937] David had the script: 400 pages of it, enough for six and a half hours." He added, "Of course, that was too much, even making the book as two movies."[33]

This misconception is hardly trivial because the claim of a 400-page filmscript supports the erroneous thesis that both Howard and Selznick were overwhelmed by the magnitude of Mitchell's text and that they were unable to shorten the narrative in any organized fashion. In fact, the threat of excessive duration was posed less by the length of Howard's adaptation than it was by Cukor's predicted pacing of the acting. This film's editor, Hal Kern, estimated that the screen-play submitted to him by Selznick in 1938—which conformed to the version completed by Howard at the end of the previous year—would require about 26,000 feet of film or approximately four hours and twenty minutes (Kern's figure exceeds the length of the revised, released film by as much as forty minutes). "MGM's estimate was 29,000 feet [approximately half an hour longer than Kern's estimate and over an hour longer than the completed film], and David asked me why theirs was so different from ours," Kern reported. "I had to tell him that they were timing at what they knew to be Cukor's tempo, which was invariably slower than most."[34]

Howard's attitude in his undertaking of this picture's scenario was consistent with that expressed in his essay on screenwriting in *We Make the Movies*, an anthology of articles written by leading figures of the American film industry in 1937 concerning their own professional roles. "The screenwriter's task is really a job of adaptation hack writing, cut to the dimensions of the director's demands," and "the process by which the screen adaptor goes to work is in itself designed to cancel out inspiration," Howard himself lamented in its pages.[35] Nevertheless, unlike the more elite sources of many of his previous adaptations, Mitchell's novel tested this literate professional's tolerance. According to his "Preliminary Notes," what irritated Howard most about *Gone with the Wind* was a fault which he attributed to the novelist: "Scarlett bores me stiff after she marries Rhett," he remarked. "She turns into Fran Dodsworth, that is to say, a greedy woman whose only activity is being stupid about the sympathetic characters."

Howard's initial draft of 368 shots followed the story line of the principal characters with minor alteration. In general, the dialogue was not reproduced verbatim but was either paraphrased or invented to serve several original scenes. An example of a paraphrase is Ashley's remark to Scarlett in the library at Twelve Oaks, which in the filmscript reads, "Marriage isn't for people as different as you and I," and which reflects two statements made by him in the original scene in the novel—specifically, "Love isn't enough to make a successful marriage when two people are as different as we are"; and, "Can't I make you see that a marriage can't go on in any sort of peace unless the two people are alike?" An example of the invention of dialogue occurs in the scene that was fabricated involving the characters of Rhett Butler and Belle Watling, who were to be pictured together in public, seated in the prostitute's wagon and observing Scarlett's first arrival in Atlanta; asked by Belle whether he recognized the newcomer, Rhett was to reply simply that they had "never met officially," after which Belle was to rejoin, "Then I don't have to worry on her account."

Generally, most scenes were exploited neither for their spectacle nor for their dramatic potential. Instead, Howard abbreviated many of the conventions of the stage in the interest of condensing the novel's narrative to an acceptably short film length. "It does not matter how excellent a picture may be," he professed in *We Make the Movies*, "it is, in my opinion, too long if it runs beyond an hour and a half."[36] Thus, one of the results was that much of the novel's climactic episode of Scarlett's escape from an evacuated and burning Atlanta on the eve of its invasion was not chosen by Howard for dramatization.

Missing also from Howard's first filmscript is the scene of Ashley's returning to Melanie's arms after the war, before the eyes of Scarlett, who, in the novel, is restrained by Will Benteen from interrupting their embrace; this reunion was omitted entirely from the original screenplay, Howard electing instead to have Scarlett merely recount the news of Ashley's return during the writing of a letter to Aunt Pitty, in which the end of the war also is mentioned. Similarly, the scene in the novel in which Melanie unwittingly aids Scarlett's adulterous scheme by pleading with Ashley to accept the offer of partnership in Atlanta and not to move his family to New York was removed and replaced by Scarlett's informing Frank Kennedy that she has telegraphed the proposal to Ashley at Tara; "We'll make out, Ashley and I—you see if we don't!" she announces, indifferent to her husband's feelings.

While his low personal opinion of the novel inhibited exploitation of much dramatic material, Howard stooped to invent several scenes of vulgar melodrama. For example, Rhett proposes to Scarlett immediately after informing her of her second husband's death; thus, Howard robbed her of the delightfully selfish admission at a more appropriate moment later in the novel that she will agree to marry Butler in good part because of his money. In another scene, Rhett is allowed to overhear a tête-à-tête between Scarlett and Ashley, during which criticism of her husband's conduct is audible; afterward, the inveterate eavesdropper privately suffers an emotional breakdown, yet steels himself sufficiently during the following scene in which Scarlett refuses him conjugal rights. Although the miscarriage of the Butlers' second child is omitted, Rhett's sexual assault on Scarlett and her grateful summons to him from her pil-

low the following morning ("Rhett! Rhett, darling! Wake up, Rhett! It's your bride calling!" she cries in Howard's version) is followed by Butler's unrepentant confession of his having left their bed to enter that of Belle for more wanton purposes. This declaration precedes the accidental death of their daughter, "Bonnie," suggesting that the child's demise was justified eminently by her parents' conduct.

One of Howard's other inventions was that Scarlett does not sell her half of the milling business to Ashley, as she does in the novel, goaded by Rhett; instead, she offers it to Wilkes as a gift in observance of his birthday. After her departure from Ashley's office following her presentation of the gift and an embrace that is criminally interpreted by his spinster sister, India, Scarlett is shown cowering in her bed chamber, while India is seen condemning Butler's wife as an adulteress before others in Atlanta; both shots are prescribed for melodramatic alternation. It is worth noting also that with the omission by Howard of Johnnie Gallegher, the manager of Scarlett's second sawmill, Ashley's business acumen is never questioned, whereas in the novel he is portrayed as one who can barely break even, while his less scrupulous rival prospers.

Scarlett appears more susceptible to stereotypical feminine weakness in Howard's first screenplay, in which she faints upon learning from her father of her mother's death. Gerald himself does not appear to die from drinking and riding, as he does in the novel—possibly as a solution to the omission of Will Benteen from the script, so that Benteen's homily and his concomitant apology for O'Hara's irrational behavior were no longer necessary; instead, Howard allowed the paterfamilias simply to fade away from the script after suffering a brief delirium at the dinner table. Charles Hamilton also was granted a dignified demise. In the filmscript, a series of dissolves was designed to lead from the wedding ceremonies of Scarlett and Charles and Melanie and Ashley to tearful farewells at the train station and to Charles's expiring in Ashley's arms from a fatal battle wound; shots were to follow of Scarlett unhappily being fitted for a black widow's habit and finding herself to be the mother of an unwanted son. In the novel, Charles less heroically succumbs to pneumonia following a case of the measles contracted in a camp far from the enemy lines.

Scarlett's dramatic oath is made in the novel after she returns to Twelve Oaks and views the sad remains of its destruction by the Yankees; in the filmscript, however, it is delivered at Tara. Howard also chose to employ it as part of this character's reaction to her shooting a marauder and appropriating his wallet and horse. After defiantly proclaiming lines which ultimately are heard immediately before the film's intermission—and which to most viewers epitomize Scarlett's spirit ("As God is my witness, the Yankees aren't going to lick me! I'm going to live through this and when it's all over I'm never going to be hungry again! No, nor any of my folks! As God is my witness!")— and while dragging the corpse of the vanquished trespasser out the door, she adds with comic irony in Howard's first draft, "And he [*sic*] certainly has His own way of providing." Less dramatically, in the filmscript Rhett does not conclude his marriage with Scarlett with the remark, "My dear, I don't give a damn," as he does at the end of the novel; instead, undoubtedly in fear of the censorious Production Code Administration (PCA), Howard has him confessing, "I wish I cared. But I don't."

Kitsch and high camp were part and parcel of Howard's earliest conception of the filmscript. Given his association with the *New Republic* as a contributor, the screenwriter was aware of its criticism of Mitchell's novel (literary editor Malcolm Cowley complained in the September 15, 1936 issue that "*Gone with the Wind* is an encyclopedia of the plantation legend . . . false in part and silly in part and vicious in its general effect on southern life today"), and likely shared many of these negative opinions.[37] This bias may be apparent in his choice to employ the most hackneyed imagery in settings. Although Howard allowed that Tara should be constructed "only partly in the Neo-Grecque [i.e., neo-classical] style, for it has been added to haphazard," he recommended giving the mansion "all the charm required to satisfy the old plantation legend." More grandly, Twelve Oaks was to be "monumentally placed on a hill top," and Howard suggested that the structure should be "monumental according to the stateliest classic architectural manner," contrary to the more ordinary and historically acceptable form envisioned by Margaret Mitchell. An establishing shot of slavery at Tara was described as follows: "All the elements of homeward bound labor are united, singing, in the avenue of cedars which approaches the house"; and of the music itself to be selected for this scene, Howard recommended a bromide of "either some traditional negro melody or the Stephen Foster song, 'My Old Kentucky Home.'"

"My single object is to put the book roughly into picture form, sequence by sequence and scene by scene, including in it as many picture ideas as may occur to me, but making no particular effort towards a finished script," Howard admitted in *We Make the Movies*. "I proceed therefore on the theory that the sooner the first draft is on paper the sooner the real work will begin." He also advised that "it is not well to put too much of one's heart into this first draft."[38] Script pages were reduced to 197 numbered sheets in the revision of April 12, 1937, although these were supplemented by enough inserts on yellow-tinted paper to increase the total to 290 pages. While these optional scenes were not believed by Howard to be "absolutely essential to the screening of the picture," they were considered to be desirable if the film was to be presented in two parts—a possibility that Selznick had begun to consider.

Howard himself admitted that "the script as written treats the portion of the story which follows the return to Tara too briefly to carry conviction." At this time, the screenwriter invented a new context for Gerald O'Hara's death, placing his fatal fall from the saddle during the angry pursuit of Jonas Wilkerson and a tax collector who threaten to foreclose on Tara. Will Benteen was returned to the filmscript in the appended pages in order that an abridged version of the graveside homily—and the book's theme—might be presented.

"I feel that my sticking so closely to the Scarlett-Rhett story has robbed the book of a lot of historical size," Howard lamented specifically. Nevertheless, a most unusual invention that contributed to this revision was a montage of comical vignettes in which this couple's honeymoon travels were extended to include Rome, Venice, and Paris. Fabricated for these were such comments from Scarlett as—spoken in a carriage outside the Vatican—"I know I was brought up to be religious, Rhett, but I don't find churches as much fun as I used to." In a box at the Paris Opera, she exclaims, "Fiddle-dee-dee! If I don't like the music why shouldn't I talk? And if you really want me to love you you'll take me back to Atlanta and give me a chance to show all the old folks."

Howard wrote to Mitchell on June 5, 1937, "I had planned—during the period when I was fool enough to believe that my work on your book would have been finished when my contract said—to drop in on you with all that behind both of us." Apparently, the screenwriter had been satisfied with his part to this date. "As you know, none of those connected with the picture has yet got down to brass tacks," he continued, and informed her that he was returning to the studio that July for revisions in order to complete the script to Selznick's satisfaction, and also that he would be collaborating with both producer and director at this time.[39]

Friendly correspondence had developed between novelist and screenwriter, and both enjoyed swapping skeptical remarks on the subject of Selznick's desire to adapt the book as faithfully as possible. Without doubt, Howard was impressed favorably by Mitchell's having been awarded the Pulitzer Prize for fiction in May 1937, and Mitchell may have been surprised equally to see Howard's photograph on the cover of *Time* magazine the following month . . . . "He is one of the most effectively organized workmen now making a living in the entertainment business," the magazine reported, "[and] his incisive mind likes to condense rambling yarns like *Dodsworth* . . . and *Gone with the Wind*." His working schedule in Hollywood that spring (during the period of the filmscript's first revision) was described as "characteristically methodical" by the article, which, most flatteringly, concluded that, "if Nobel Prizeman Eugene O'Neill . . . is posterity's playwright, if Maxwell Anderson is a poet's playwright, Sidney Howard is a playwright's playwright [because] common sense and order govern his muse."[40]

"I know so little about the movies that I thought the script was already finished," the novelist confessed in a letter to the screen-writer on June 9, 1937. Mitchell was referring to the manuscript that had lain visibly on George Cukor's desk during his visit to Atlanta that April, and which she herself reputedly had avoided asking to examine. Nevertheless, she appeared to be hungry for news of the film project. "Picture scripts are written and later rewritten in collaboration with the director who has, after all, to make the picture," Howard responded on June 14. "The script of *Gone with the Wind* is written but not yet re-written."[41]

This advanced stage of "pre-production" to which Howard was referring began shortly afterward, when Cukor was enlisted for film script revision. (Cukor had visited Howard briefly at the writer's farm in the Berkshires but, according to biographer Patrick McGilligan, had neither read nor remembered to bring a copy of the novel for discussion.)[42] "Cukor, Howard, and I have been spending practically every day—starting sometime between nine and ten and running sometime between twelve-thirty and one-thirty—on the script of the picture," Selznick wrote on July 29, 1937. "This will persist for some weeks, as will the hours in the afternoon that Cukor spends with Howard on the details of the script." At the same time, Selznick began to consider creation of the role of "production designer" and assignment of William Cameron Menzies to this new position; as originally envisioned, Menzies' duties were to include his complete "storyboarding" of the screenplay and supervision of the film's art direction, special effects, and color cinematography.

CRITICISM FROM THE PRODUCTION CODE
ADMINISTRATION AND MORE REVISION

The significant changes in Howard's second filmscript revision, dated August 24, 1937, and composed of 460 shots on 239 numbered pages, involve action during the film's second half. The Butlers' honeymoon was returned to the States in this version, and scenes of the couple's nuptials in New Orleans, of their return to Atlanta and to the building of an ostentatious Victorian mansion, and of their failure to integrate themselves into traditional southern society (several members of which are represented reacting with "disdain" during the housewarming party) were to be presented in quick succession as a series of shots directed by Slavko Vorkapich (Hollywood's leading specialist of this form of montage sequence). Tastefully, Howard no longer hurried Rhett into proposing matrimony to Scarlett in the same scene in which he informs her of her second husband's sudden death. Sadly, Gerald O'Hara's burial does not include the graveside homily by Will Benteen because of the latter character's removal from the filmscript.

Instead of Benteen, it is Mammy who serves to restrain Scarlett from interfering with Melanie and Ashley's embraces during their reunion after the war, telling her, with an approximation of Benteen's words, "He's her husban', ain' he?" When Ashley visits privately with Scarlett afterward, he also delivers the tax bill due on Tara which was received from "our friend Wilkerson" and on which were to be written legibly "Third Notice" and "$300," for presentation in separate inserts or close shots. Scarlett brazenly returns to Tara to write the check for the tax payment in the presence of her sister, Suellen, to whom Frank Kennedy originally had been affianced, and afterward offers Ashley a partnership in the sawmill enterprise in Atlanta. Less complexly, Rhett was no longer involved in Scarlett's acquisition of the latter property and so was not betrayed by her offer of partnership to Wilkes, which was contrary to the conditions of Butler's instrumental loan to her for its purchase in the novel.

The description of Rhett's angry rape of his wife following India's accusation of Scarlett's infidelity with Ashley is unusually suggestive for motion pictures of this period and was written likely on Selznick's request; he may have hoped that his ultimately agreeing to omit these planted scenes from the shooting script might increase his bargaining power with the censors and allow the retention of less objectionable but more important adult material. (In contrast with the scene in the following passage, it should be remembered that more understatement was employed for this part of the film as it was shot and released, in which Rhett is shown to mount the grand staircase while lifting his struggling wife in his arms and promising, "This is one night you're not turning me out.") The screenplay includes the following directions:

> The night lamp is burning on the table as Rhett enters with Scarlett. He drops her on the bed. She shrinks from him in terror. He looks at her for a moment and then, dropping on his knees beside the bed, reaches towards her and drags her to him. She fights him off with what strength she has left but can put up no defense against his power. His lips meet hers and she lies in his arms helpless. Fade out.

A far more graphically rendered scene is that of Melanie in labor. "I think it's coming now," cries Scarlett amid many flies and much perspiration, and a series of shots which soon follows is described in the screenplay as: "Melanie's knees draw up in agony . . . Scarlett's face is distorted with horror . . . Prissy's hands place scissors in Scarlett's hands . . . [and] Melanie has fainted." In the novel, Mitchell herself summarized Scarlett's perception of the episode as a "nightmare of screaming pain and ignorant midwifery" which included Prissy's misplacing the scissors, spilling the basin of water on the bed, and dropping the newborn baby.

On January 12, 1938, Franclien Macconnell offered a number of suggestions to Selznick on Howard's revision of August 24, including the advice to emphasize the animosity of the sibling rivalry between Scarlett and Suellen in order to assuage audience outrage over the fact that the former steals the latter's beau in a marriage of convenience during the second half of the story. More importantly, she recommended not omitting reference to the dream that haunts Scarlett through the course of the second half of the novel, because it provides a rare instance of Rhett's exhibiting tenderness toward his wife, when he wakens and comforts her after one of its occurrences; furthermore, Macconnell added, "in the end Scarlett realizes the meaning of it"—that is, that "it is not Ashley, but Rhett and the safe haven of his arms that she has been seeking." On the lighter side, concerning the scene in the library at Twelve Oaks when Rhett exposes his supine eavesdropping after Scarlett has hurled and broken porcelain in angry reaction to Ashley's rejection of her declaration of love, Macconnell expressed regret over the "omission of Rhett's line, spoken from the depths of the sofa, 'This is too much.' . . ." (Rhett's response was rewritten much later.)

"Some spirit of madness moved Selznick to load the kit and kaboodle on a private car and bring them East to work with me here," Howard wrote Mitchell on October 7, 1937, while rehearsing his play, *The Ghost of Yankee Doodle Dandy*.[43] Selznick had invited Howard and Cukor to join him in a discussion with Joseph Breen, director of the PCA, concerning candidacy of scenes in the script for revision and censorship. Afterward, on October 14, Selznick received a seven-page letter from Breen listing objections to portions of the script of August 24, "all of which . . . may . . . easily be changed in order to bring the basic story into conformity with the Production Code." In particular, Breen demanded:

> There ought to be at no time *any suggestion of rape*—or the struggles suggestive of rape; Rhett should *not* be so definitively characterized as an immoral, or adulterous, man; the long scenes of childbirth should be toned down *considerably*; Scarlett should *not* offer her body to Rhett in the scene in prison; and the character of Belle should *not* definitively suggest a prostitute.
>
> [Breen's emphasis]

The association known as Motion Picture Producers and Distributors of America (of which SIP was a member) required that a film's release be prohibited without issuance of a certificate of approval signed by Breen and bearing the seal of his office (which was sponsored by the film industry itself as a form of self-regulation). For twenty years following inauguration of Breen's directorship in 1933, deference to the Production Code was enforced, although the judgments of its office might be influenced by arbitration. An appeal from Selznick to Will Hays, president of the PCA (aka the "Hay's office"), and payment of a $5,000 fine for violation of a Code provision were necessary in order to license the release of *Gone with the Wind* with the "damn" intact in Rhett's concluding utterance.

Concerning the filmscript of October 1937, Breen reminded Selznick of the "*very great importance*" of the deletion of "such action and dialogue which *throws emphasis upon the pain and suffering of childbirth*"; specifically, Breen demanded, "there should be no *moaning* or loud *crying*," and recommended that "these scenes of childbirth be cut to *an absolute minimum* in order merely to suggest Melanie's suffering." On Scarlett's proposition of prostitution to Rhett in order to raise the tax money due on Tara, Breen cautioned, "It might be that you could have her put forth the blunt suggestion to Rhett, 'Will you marry me?'"; he insisted that "*this is very important*." During the scene in which Rhett confronts Scarlett following her appearance at Melanie's party amid rumors of an adulterous affair with Ashley, "there should be no suggestion here that Rhett

is about to rape Scarlett." Apparently, Cukor had offered the censor assurances that the actor portraying Rhett would merely "take [the actress portraying Scarlett] in his arms, kiss her, and then gently start with her toward the bedroom." Nonetheless, the Code director reiterated, "It is our thought that you should *not* go so far as to throw her on the bed."

Breen also advised that neither Rhett, Ashley, nor Dr. Meade be presented as *offensively drunk* in the scenes in which they comically pretend to be inebriated in order to delude a Yankee captain into believing that rather than having participated, as Scarlett's avengers, in the raid on Shantytown following her assault by two of its vagrants, they were partying instead in Belle's house of prostitution. Furthermore, he suggested "the elimination of the word 'establishment' from Rhett's speech [i.e., 'Much as I regret to say it . . . we've all been together at an establishment conducted by a friend of mine and the captain's. A Mrs. Belle Watling . . .'], and the substitution, possibly, of 'refreshment parlor,' making the line read, 'We've all been together at a refreshment parlor.' In this same speech, we ask that you delete the expression, 'there were ladies . . .'" Breen also asked that the phrase "as God is my witness" be removed from Scarlett's oath and the filmscript—very likely because Howard's use of the marauder's violent death as background violated more than one of the Biblical Commandments.

Howard's final filmscript revision of 1937, dated November 27 and composed of 315 shots on 231 numbered pages, addressed many of these objections and reflects some of the suggested changes. Scarlett's defiant oath was eliminated altogether. Instead, after she has killed the Yankee scavenger and acquired his wallet and horse as spoils of war, "the triumph dies out of Scarlett's face as she backs through the door, the body dragging after her"; before a fade out, she simply remarks, "I reckon I must have changed since I came home." Another effect of Breen's objections was the alteration of the brief scene of Charles Hamilton's honeymoon with Scarlett (credited to William Cameron Menzies in the previous filmscript), in which the groom approaches the matrimonial bed in his dressing gown as Scarlett shakes in fear and protest under the sheets. In the November revision, Scarlett stares in "almost comic bewilderment" at Charles, who smiles "pathetically" at her and at his marching orders, which were to be arranged visibly on the bedside table for the camera's view and audience's amusement.

Reference to the Vorkapich montage of Scarlett's elopement with Rhett disappeared in this fourth filmscript and instead her in-laws in Atlanta were to be informed of the marriage by telegram, after which Mammy exclaims that "Miss Scarlett ain' nuthin' but a mule in horse harness. . . ." Decently, Ashley no longer complains to Scarlett privately of Rhett's behavior in the Butlers' new home. When Rhett visits the prostitute Belle Watling—who is described radiantly in the November revision as the "eternal Magdalene with a heart of gold"—he is reminded properly by her that there is still Bonnie's future of which to think; the insertion of Belle's observation that "the child's worth more than the mother" was calculated to appeal to the Catholic "Legion of Decency," which influenced the formation and enforcement of the Production Code. Afterward, Rhett is motivated to lecture Scarlett on their need to cultivate greater respectability for the children's sake. Not surprisingly, the passionate scene preceding the off-screen rape of Scarlett by Rhett was removed from the filmscript.

All shots of childbirth were deleted also. Still, inspired by a scene in the novel, the filmscript has Dr. Meade advising Scarlett to give Rhett another baby quickly in order to check her husband's dissipation following Bonnie's death; Howard also enlists Melanie to help coax Butler on this mission and to announce that she herself is pregnant with another child. An additional scene was invented in which Scarlett, wearing a nightdress, waits for Rhett to pass her open bedroom door on his drunken path to his private quarters; although she confesses her procreative intention upon his appearance, he remains too demoralized by Bonnie's death to comply and retreats to his bed, while Scarlett sobs alone in hers.

Influenced by Macconnell's comments on the previous script, in the November revision Howard introduced Scarlett's dream within the context of this character's conversation with Rhett when she awakens to his comforting arms after having suffered from the dream during their honeymoon. Selznick also asked Macconnell for comments on this revision. Her response addressed two important issues, one concerning the question of who was to manage Tara after Gerald O'Hara's death—in Scarlett and Ashley's absence and in lieu of Will Benteen, who had been removed from the script—and the other concerning proper identification of Jonas Wilkerson when this character arrives to announce his plan of acquiring Tara when taxes are not paid by the O'Haras.

With respect to the latter scene, Macconnell believed that Wilkerson should be identified as the vengeful former overseer of Tara, which he is in the novel, and not simply as an anonymous Yankee carpetbagger, as he appears in the earlier filmscripts. "Since his connection with Emmie Slattery [the daughter of the O'Haras' 'poor white trash' neighbors who had been responsible for spreading an infection to Scarlett's ministering mother with fatal results] has already been established in the script, there would be no harm in introducing the woman herself at that point, for her flashy smartness would offer a significant contrast to Scarlett's shabby, poverty-stricken attire," Macconnell suggested, and she advised that this comparison might illustrate "by implication" changes wrought by the Union's program of Reconstruction. "Gerald could enter [the] scene just in time to hear Wilkerson's threats and Scarlett's final outburst," she explained. "The intimation that he might lose Tara penetrates his bewildered brain and the scene logically paves the way for his death, as in the script."

Howard had written to Mitchell the day before completing the November 27 revision that Selznick, upon departing

New York, had asked that the screenwriter return to California early the following year for further work on the filmscript. Sardonically, Howard confessed to the novelist that he was looking forward to this trip, "not only because I should hate like the devil to turn the job over to some other writer but because I am interested to see how much money a picture producer is willing to spend to pay men for not being allowed to earn their pay." Howard continually objected to Selznick's editorial role. Frustration also grew from the producer's insistence that fidelity to the novel be observed ("It's not a movie script," Howard complained elsewhere, "it's a transcription from the book"), although the author of the phrase "dramatizing by equivalent" refused to desist from invention in each of his submitted drafts.[44]

"Sidney and I have a terrific job on our hands," Selznick admitted to Cukor on February 25, 1938. "I am weighing every word and every line most carefully, and Sidney's ideas are, as usual, excellent." Nevertheless, the producer remained adamant on the necessity of the screenplay's faithfulness to the original narrative, and wrote:

> I am also double-checking against the book once more and substituting valuable lines wherever I can for ordinary lines in the script. We are also double-checking against our story department's notes on things that they missed from the book [i.e., Macconnell's comments]; on [Wilbur] Kurtz' notes [as the production's historical advisor, and one whom Mitchell had recommended]; on production notes; on Hal Kern's cutting suggestions [as film editor]; on research notes from a society that complains about inaccuracies; and on Hay's office notes.

It may be of questionable value to ask whether Selznick's attention to these details was obsessional or commendable for one in the position of an independent Hollywood motion-picture producer at this time, yet certainly it may be said that his insistence upon fidelity was extraordinary. "The ideal script, as far as I am concerned would be one that did not contain a single word of original dialogue, and that was 100 percent Margaret Mitchell, however much we juxtaposed it," he informed Macconnell on December 5, 1938, only five days before the fire sequence was filmed on the studio's lot. Because of Howard's temporary refusal to continue on this project, Selznick had begun to work with other writers. Having completed the screenplay of *Made for Each Other* (1939), Jo Swerling accompanied the producer on a trip to Bermuda in order to assist with revising the screenplay of *Gone with the Wind*. Dissatisfied, Selznick sought Oliver H. P. Garrett upon returning to the States and facing the beginning of the film's production phase, although his collaboration with this screenwriter would prove to be disappointing also. F. Scott Fitzgerald himself was loaned to Selznick in early January of the following year for three weeks' work remaining on his contract as a screenwriter with MGM. Recognizing that the "author of *The Great Gatsby* and *Tender is the Night* was required to use only dialogue that came from Margaret Mitchell's novel," biographer Matthew Bruccoli observed correctly that the most frequent comments recorded in this screenwriter's copy of the filmscript are "cut" and "book restored."[45]

"As start day drew nearer, the quantity of writers multiplied, and it was all the newcomer could do to digest the masses of material accumulated in the previous two years," David Thomson observed in reference to the many files of revised filmscript pages by different screenwriters that are preserved in Selznick's collection. "The panic was building and with it the desperate confidence that [Selznick] could do more and more."[46] Undoubtedly, fidelity allowed for this self-assurance. "Naturally, and unfortunately, and with great beatings of breasts and letting of blood, we have had to make a great many cuts of scenes which we all love, but this is forced on us by the limitation of the length of any motion picture," Selznick conceded to Mitchell on January 24, 1939—two days before the filming of scenes with principal players commenced. "In what remains, however, we have been as faithful as possible; and even when we have had to make transpositions and alterations we have usually been able to find lines out of the book." On January 25 he advised the chairman of his board of directors, "Jack" Whitney:

> Don't get panicky at the seemingly small amount of final revised script. There are great big gobs that will be transferred from either the Howard script or the Howard-Garrett script, and it is so clearly in my mind that I can tell you the picture from beginning to end, almost shot for shot.

SCRIPT REVISION CONTINUES THROUGHOUT THE FILM PRODUCTION

Selznick knew that he could afford repeated investment in the script's revision because of the delay encountered in scheduling this film's production dates because of difficulties posed by casting. On October 1, 1938 he wrote Ed Sullivan, for publication in the latter's column in the *New York Daily News,*

> You have been in Hollywood enough to realize that players under contract to a studio cannot be secured by another studio just for the asking, even for such a project as *Gone with the Wind.* The public's choice clearly was Clark Gable for Rhett Butler. . . . But you must have a rough idea as to how willing MGM would be to give up Gable for a picture to be released by another company—and bear in mind that my company was under an exclusive contract with United Artists. Accordingly, the only way I could get him was to distribute the picture through MGM, and this meant I had to wait until my contract with United Artists had expired. . . . Therefore, *Gone with the Wind,* with Clark Gable as Rhett Butler, couldn't under any circumstances have been made one day sooner.

The result of his contract with United Artists was that Selznick undertook the making of nine other feature-length motion pictures during the production of this one epic film. Specifically, between the purchase of the screen rights to *Gone with the Wind* in 1936 and its release as a completed film in the final month of 1939, Selznick personally produced *The Garden of Allah* (1936), *A Star Is Born* (1937), *The Prisoner of Zenda* (1937), *Nothing Sacred* (1937), *The Adventures of Tom Sawyer* (1938), *The Young in Heart* (1938), *Made for Each Other* (1939), *Intermezzo* (1939), and *Rebecca* (begun in 1939 but released in 1940), all of which were distributed by United Artists according to the terms of a contract which also provided for the release of *Little Lord Fauntleroy* in April 1936. Selznick's inability to cast an actress in the role of Scarlett until he was permitted to film *Gone with the Wind* inspired an extraordinary talent search which effectively maintained heightened publicity for the motion picture during its lengthy period of preparation.

Selznick did not wait for a final shooting script of *Gone with the Wind* before preparing its budget. Various indices produced from the novel by the SIP story department served as "blueprints" for planning as much as did Howard's revisions of the continuity script. In *David O. Selznick's Hollywood,* Ronald Haver recounted that, late in 1936,

> Barbara Keon, Selznick's script secretary, Lydia Schiller, and several of the other women in the office began breaking the novel down, indexing every major event and action, cross-indexing this for time periods, seasonal changes, the historical background, and then making separate indexes for characterizations, dialogue topics, character relationships, clothing, descriptions of interior and exterior sets, so that even before there was an official script, there were ten detailed reference scripts that could be used as guides in the extensive pre-production work that was obviously going to be necessary.

From these breakdowns and from budgets prepared by Jack Cosgrove (for special effects), Raymond Klune (for production management), Walter Plunkett (for costumes), and Lyle Wheeler (for sets), the figure that emerged was two and a half million dollars—or, as Haver observed, the "entire year's production budget for Selznick International."[47]

This same figure was cited in negotiations with MGM, which, on August 24, 1938, presented Selznick with its promise of the loan of Clark Gable for use in *Gone with the Wind* and of its underwriting as much as half of the estimated budget in exchange for the film's worldwide distribution rights and half of its gross revenue. Several months earlier, MGM had offered to buy the production outright for $900,000 with the understanding that Selznick would be retained as producer. Selznick also considered co-producing the film with Warner Bros., which had offered the services of three of its leading stars—Errol Flynn (for $100,000 less than Gable's salary), Bette Davis, and Olivia de Havilland—and an investment up to $2.1 million, together with a lower distribution fee. Executive autonomy, financial reward, star appeal, and studio values were primary factors in Selznick's decision to co-produce with MGM. Still, the filmmaking ran over budget before completion, and in order for the production to maintain its independence from the distributor, a loan was necessary of one and a quarter million dollars, which required a personal guarantee of repayment by John Hay Whitney and which was arranged through Attilio Giannini (who was a member of the SIP board of directors and represented both United Artists and the Bank of America).

Although Mitchell's correspondence with Howard abated with the latter's absence from the film project, her friendship with Susan Myrick (whom she had recommended to Selznick as a technical advisor and dialogue coach) continued to provide the novelist with "inside" information. "Your letter had a laugh in every line," Mitchell wrote Myrick characteristically on February 10, 1939. "I must admit some of my laughter was on the wry side—especially when you described Twelve Oaks," the novelist explained, ignorant of Howard's complicity in its design. "I had feared, of course, that it would end up looking like Grand Central Station, and your description confirms my worst apprehensions."[48]

Stories of the difficulty experienced by Selznick in reducing Mitchell's narrative to a practicable shooting script remained a favorite topic of discussion for both correspondents. "Sue, it does sound incredible that the script is not finished," Mitchell gibed. "I have an idea (and correct me if I'm wrong) that they are using Sidney Howard's script for the first part of the movie—and it followed (so I am told by Mr. Howard) the book closely."[49] Because the novelist had refused to look at the screenplay, she was unaware of problems in earlier versions. "Well, dearie, you got another thought [coming]," wrote Myrick on February 14 in a similar manner of jest. Declaring that the "Howard script is beautiful" and was "just the book in spirit, every inch," Myrick related that

> David [Selznick], himself, thinks He is writing the script and tells poor Bobby Keon ["script girl"] and Stinko Garrett what to write. And they do the best they can with it, in their limited way . . . [The resulting] opus does follow the book in a fashion but it does such queer things.[50]

Oliver Garrett had developed a reputation as a collaborator and adaptor and was an old acquaintance of Selznick's, having participated as a member of the producer's wedding party in 1930. He had collaborated with Dudley Nichols on *The Hurricane* for producer Samuel Goldwyn and director John Ford in 1937 and had received co-credit with Joseph L. Mankiewicz as screenwriter of the Gable vehicle, *Manhattan Melodrama*, which Selznick produced for MGM in 1934. His approach to literary adaptation is characterized by his work with J. Grubb Alexander on *Moby Dick* (1930), with Benjamin Glazer on *A Farewell to Arms* (1932), and with Maurine Watkins on *The Story of Temple Drake* (1933; based upon William Faulkner's novel, *Sanctuary*)—films which demonstrate eccentric deference to cinematic norms and extensive alteration of literary sources. The original manuscripts of the two principal shooting scripts of *Gone with the Wind*, dated January 16,

1939, and February 27, 1939, credit both Sidney Howard and Oliver Garrett on the title pages.

Myrick also informed Mitchell on February 14 of the following scene:

> So George [Cukor] just told David he would not work any longer if the script was not better and he wanted the Howard script back. David told George he was a director, not an author, and he (David) was the producer and the judge of what is a good script (or words to that effect) and George said he was a director and a damn good one and he would not let his name go out over a lousy picture and if they didn't go back to the Howard script (he was willing to have them cut it down shorter) he, George, was through.[51]

Cukor's departure was announced to the press the same day. Haver acknowledged disputes over the film's script and "concept" as major reasons for this rift ("Selznick and Menzies had decided on a florid theatrical look and feel for the picture, while Cukor was minutely detailing his characters, an approach that Selznick felt did not catch 'the big feel, the scope and breadth of the production,'" he wrote) but also proposed Gable's displeasure with Cukor as a contributory factor.[52] In his biography of the director, Patrick McGilligan also posited Gable's homophobia as a primary reason (Cukor having been a homosexual who may have been privy to some bisexual activity in Gable's past).[53] "I'm going to beg you not to go into that bullshit about, 'What happened on *Gone with the Wind*?'" Cukor himself pleaded of an interviewer. "It's as though I asked you, 'What happened [in grade school] when your teacher sent you home? You peed your pants and you were sent home—now tell me the truth of it.'"[54]

Mitchell admitted amusement over the production's problems. "I hate to say 'I told you so' but there is no one but you to whom I can say it," she wrote Myrick on February 28, explaining:

> Before I signed the contract I told Katharine Brown and the other Selznickers assembled in the room they were making a great mistake, for the picture could not be made from that book. They all laughed. . . . They said it was a natural. . . . I said yes indeed and thank you, but I knew how that book was written. It had taken me ten years to weave it as tight as a silk pocket handkerchief. If one thread were broken or pulled, an ugly ravel would show clear through to the other side of the material. Yet they would have to cut for a script, and when they began cutting they would discover they had technical problems they had never dreamed about. . . . Now they have run into exactly the problem I foresaw. And may God have mercy on their souls.[55]

Selznick had written to Mitchell with another entreaty for assistance on January 24, shortly after principal filming had begun. "If you sympathize with our plight," he begged of her at the conclusion of his request, "I hope that if you still feel that you want to steer clear of the script you will at least understand and forgive my cry of distress." Mitchell again refused. "Have they got a script yet?" she queried Wilbur Kurtz on March 11. "As you can gather, I do get a great deal of fun out of this affair, and my greatest sense of enjoyment comes from a sense of thanksgiving that I have nothing to do with it and am not in Hollywood."[56]

In two of the books that Richard Harwell edited, the following seventeen writers and "tinkerers" (in alphabetical order) were credited with contributing to the assembly of the filmscript: John Balderston, F. Scott Fitzgerald, Michael Foster, Oliver Garrett, Ben Hecht, Sidney Howard, Barbara Keon, Wilbur Kurtz, Val Lewton, Charles MacArthur, John Lee Mahin, Edwin Justus Mayer, Winston Miller, Selznick himself, Donald Ogden Stewart, Jo Swerling, and John Van Druten.[57] Although it had become a common practice in Hollywood to exploit the talents of numerous individuals during the writing of a screenplay, the fact remains that this list of contributors is very lengthy—indeed, it is padded. Even without Bradbury Foote (a writer hired by MGM to prepare a script of *Gone with the Wind* with a "happy ending"), unassigned and uncreditable persons—namely, Keon, Kurtz, Lewton (Selznick's West Coast story editor), and MacArthur—account for almost a quarter of the names cited, and over half—namely, Balderston, Fitzgerald, Foote, Foster, Mahin, Mayer, Miller, Stewart, Swerling, and Van Druten—did not sustain more than tentative association with the preparation of the screenplay. Of the three screenwriters remaining (i.e., Garrett, Hecht, and Howard), Howard had unquestionably the longest tenure.

"In those days, the major studios operated on the principle that the more writers on a script, the better it was going to be. . . . It was not uncommon to have three, four, even six writers on a screenplay," observed I. A. L. Diamond, who began his career as a screenwriter in the 1940s and who later collaborated with Billy Wilder on several film productions, including *Some Like It Hot* (1959) and *The Apartment* (1960).[58] Donald Ogden Stewart, who contributed to the screenplays of *Dinner at Eight* and *The Prisoner of Zenda,* concurred that "producers had a theory that the more writers they had to work on scripts, the better the scripts would be."[59] An exceptional project for MGM, *The Wizard of Oz* (which completed its production ahead of *Gone with the Wind* in 1939 and was directed by Victor Fleming and at least three others) also reputedly employed the talents of ten to fourteen writers in the preparation of its script. (Fleming, who was Clark Gable's favorite director, was contracted for work on *Gone with the Wind* following Cukor's departure.)[60] John Lee Mahin, who worked on both pictures and has been described as Gable's favorite writer, claimed that screenwriters were treated as "factory boys" at MGM, which at one time maintained over one hundred writers under contract for purposes including collaboration and revision.[61]

Being ignorant of Hollywood's peccadillos, Mitchell confessed to Myrick on April 17, 1939 that the latter's letter of April 9, "which announced that Sidney Howard was back on the script, kept us [i.e., the novelist and her hus-

band, John Marsh] laughing all day" and that "every time we thought of the history of the script and the full circle which has been made we laughed again." She added, "I would not be at all surprised to learn that the script of the sixteen other writers had been junked and Mr. Howard's original script put into production."[62] (Mitchell's count derived from Myrick, who, in her letter of April 9, had confessed, "I haven't the faintest idea how many folks that makes in all who have done the script. I lost count after the first ten and all I know is Howard is somewhere around the sixteenth, though he may be the twentieth." Harwell later claimed that Myrick "counted better than she thought.")[63] Although neither provide a figure for the number of screenwriters employed on the project, accounts of the script situation two months earlier by John Lee Mahin and Ben Hecht when they worked separately and consecutively as writers on the film project follow this same story line. "I said, 'For God's sake, let's go back to Margaret Mitchell's book and Sidney Howard's wonderful script,'" Mahin professed. "Sidney did the first script and then they'd brought in some people and they fooled around with it."[64] In his autobiography, *A Child of the Century,* Hecht offered a similar opinion—namely, that Howard's work was superior to the revisions undertaken prior to his own engagement. The stage of filmscript revision that had been endured by Hecht himself, sequestered as he had been for a week in his own apartment with Selznick and Fleming, was recounted more with humor than with credibility. According to him, the trio worked eighteen-to-twenty-hour shifts each day and subsisted on a diet of bananas and salted peanuts. Hecht also admitted that he had not read the novel and was confused by Selznick's attempts to relate its story. "I argued that surely in two years of preparation someone must have wrangled a workable plot out of Miss Mitchell's Ouidalike flight into the Civil War," he wrote, in mocking reference to *Gone with the Wind* and Marie Louise de la Ramée, the prolific Victorian-era English romance novelist who used the nom de plume Ouida. "After an hour of searching," Hecht continued, "a lone copy of Howard's work was run down in an old safe."[65]

Harwell objected that Hecht's account of the film's screenwriting is "so full of demonstrable untruths and exaggerations (as is the rest of that autobiography) that it should be heavily discounted." Specifically, this scholar observed that Hecht wrote fallaciously "of the difficulty of finding a copy of Howard's script discarded three years before, of toasting the 'dead craftsman' (seven months before Howard's untimely death in August 1939), etc., etc."[66] Selznick and Fleming reputedly collapsed at the end of the week, concluding the collaboration. "The wear and tear on me was less," Hecht claimed, "for I had been able to lie on the couch and half doze while the two darted about acting . . . David specializing in the parts of Scarlet [*sic*] and her drunken father and Vic playing Rhett Butler."[67]

Although Selznick had desired no further involvement with Howard following the latter's refusal to return to the project as requested in October 1938, the screenwriter was again on the payroll for five hundred dollars a day the following April. Material from this period includes another original honeymoon scene of the Butlers in Europe—now in Vienna. The setting of Bonnie's nightmare also changed from Atlanta to London. Because father and daughter are presented alone and far from their home in the States, the object of Butler's reprimands is no longer Scarlett—who is chastised by him in the novel for her lack of compassion—but an anonymous English nurse. This unhappy excursion is the only scene in the film to be played before a European backdrop.

A more significant contribution to the screenplay during this same period was the revision of the final scene of the film, which previously had concluded simply with Scarlett, abandoned on the threshold. The new version reads thus:

> From the last shot of Scarlett,
> Dissolve to:
> Ext. Tara—Day
>
> Scarlett standing in front of Tara, where she stood with her father at the beginning of the picture, and with Rhett at the end of the honeymoon. She is looking out over the land, and there may be singing, the ghosts of the negro voices of the old days. Over the singing, she hears three voices clearly: her father's, Ashley's, and Rhett's.

GERALD'S VOICE

> Land's the only thing in the world that lasts.

ASHLEY'S VOICE

> Something you love even better than me . . . Tara.

RHETT'S VOICE

> You get your strength from the red earth of Tara.

She fills her lungs, and her head comes up, and she is able to face whatever the rest of her life may hold for her.

Selznick's influence may be perceived in the affirmative quality of this scene, which was developed further following Howard's final departure from the project. Consistent with the novel, the new ending transforms the story line from a tragedy, concluded by Scarlett's defense mechanism of "thinking about it tomorrow" because "tomorrow is another day," to a narrative with a sentimental plot, at the end of which one experiences awe or admiration for the protagonist rather than Aristotelian pity and fear. The effect is more an apotheosis than a catharsis. One is reminded also—even by the career of this fictional character—that Selznick's greatest gift, according to William Cameron Menzies, was an "ability to make people transcend themselves."[68]

The power of Selznick's influence also attracted criticism. In his biography of Mitchell, *Southern Daughter*, Darden Asbury Pyron argued that although Selznick sought fidelity to the novel and achieved it "to a remarkable degree," the adaptation is representative more of Hollywood than of

the story. "Vivien Leigh was just too beautiful, and she played the role with too much intelligence," Pyron complained. "If Scarlett is courageous and indomitable, she is also coarse, vulgar, violent, mean-spirited, vengeful, and uncultured." He also observed that, with exception of the black parts, the film eliminated most characters of lower-class origins. "The net effect of Selznick's omissions confirms the themes he chose to celebrate—nostalgia for the innocent, lost world of the plantation South."[69]

Selznick has been faulted, too, for his picture's stereotypical treatment of Afro-Americans and its inadequate exposition of racial issues. "The film's most controversial aspect remains its portrayal of race relations," concluded Catherine Clinton in her review of this film in *Past Imperfect: History According to the Movies*. "*Gone with the Wind* may be the first plantation film to feature Afro-American characters who *don't* spontaneously burst into song, but the picture still reflects historian U. B. Phillip's 'plantation school' view of the Afro-American experience which portrayed happy-go-lucky 'darkies' loyal to benevolent masters."[70] In *Toms, Coons, Mulattoes, Mammies, and Bucks: An Interpretive History of Blacks in American Film*, Donald Bogle offered a fair assessment of this film's position. "The problem with Civil War spectacles has never been that they presented Negroes as slaves—for how else could they be depicted?—but that the films have humiliated and debased them far beyond the calling of the script," he observed and noted that "the really beautiful aspect of [*Gone with the Wind*] was not what was omitted but what was ultimately accomplished by the black actors who transformed their slaves into complex human beings."[71]

A special concern of other commentators remains the issue of Selznick's extensive involvement in the film's production. Negative comparisons of Selznick's role have been made with parts played by other producers in script development. Donald Ogden Stewart described Selznick as a "terribly overbearing person" who always insisted that the producer was "*right,* and you weren't supposed to argue with him"; in contrast, Stewart remarked, "Irving Thalberg never did that. Irving would try to help you, encourage you: 'No, this isn't it, try it again.' But David was a much more overriding sort of personality."[72]

Contradicting this testimony regarding Thalberg, however, are numerous instances of his ability to "bear down" during his active involvement in the story conferences for *Grand Hotel* (1932), which were described by Thomas Schatz. Transcripts of sessions between the producer, associate Paul Bern, and writer-director Edmund Goulding during the preparation of what was described as "perhaps the consummate expression of the MGM style during Thalberg's regime" document that "at some point in virtually every conference Thalberg would launch into detailed analysis, often running on for minutes at a time, laying out the entire story line or untangling some particular script problem." Thalberg asserted once over Goulding's objections, "Over my dead body you'll cut that scene," and Schatz observed that the "discussions became more direct and practical, the negotiations less congenial, and the general atmosphere more intense" the closer these sessions approached the film's production date.[73]

In a monograph on Goldwyn, Richard Griffith related how Sidney Howard had categorized motion-picture producers into two kinds: "the kind who clears a space in which his writers and directors can do their work, and the kind who tries to write the story himself on both the script and the directorial level."[74] Very likely, for Griffith these two categories referred, respectively, to Goldwyn and to Selznick. "For myself," Howard himself wrote in the essay for *We Make the Movies,* "I prefer the type which undertakes to produce, more or less, the picture the director and screenwriter have given him." Of the other type of executive, "of which there are too many examples," the screenwriter described a "producer who is neither director nor writer and would like to be both." Howard concluded that "his determination to get his picture script written and rewritten until it coincides exactly with his own conception is more than likely to choke out the last germs of spontaneity and life," and noted that the inability of this type of producer to value another's view "frequently leads him to engage a whole series of writers, both in collaboration and in sequence."[75]

It is important to note that the above remarks were published in 1937 following the course of the "Goldwyn touch" on adapting *Dodsworth* and thus date from very early in the planning stages of *Gone with the Wind,* when Howard served as the sole adaptor of Mitchell's novel. Goldwyn's contributions to the screenwriting of *Dodsworth* are worth recounting in detail in view both of Howard's subsequent experience with Selznick and of the legend which developed that Howard's original treatment of Mitchell's novel was superior to much of the filmscript's later revision by others, among whom Selznick has been cast as the principal bungler by most commentators.

Acting for Lewis, Howard originally offered Goldwyn the option on *Dodsworth* for a mere $20,000, which the producer declined. Afterward, Howard purchased the rights himself, but adapted the work first as a play, which opened to rave notices at New York's Schubert Theater in 1934, whereupon Goldwyn purchased the rights from the playwright for $160,000. "This way I buy a successful play, something already in dramatic form," the producer purportedly told Howard. "With this, I have more assurance of success and it's worth the extra money I pay."[76] A variation of this claim is cited by A. Scott Berg in *Goldwyn: A Biography* in a manner more characteristic of Goldwyn's own *parole*: "This way, I buy a successful play. Before it was just a novel."[77]

More ironic still is the story that Goldwyn remained unsatisfied with the property, which he believed should focus not on Dodsworth's retirement and marital difficulties in Europe but on work in the automobile industry, and thus Edward Chodorov was paid $50,000 to write a different screenplay. Chodorov eventually submitted a script that was not very different from the original; "Mr. Goldwyn," he himself tried to explain, "this isn't a story about automobiles." Not satisfied, the producer hired five other writers, who labored over the project another two years. "The expenditure was enormous," Chodorov recalled. "There must have been eight different drafts before [Goldwyn] realized that I was right, that you couldn't tamper with Sidney's play construction."[78] The film follows the original version for the most part, and Howard is credited as the screenwriter.

In his biography of the producer, Lawrence J. Epstein argued:

> In being dissatisfied with the Chodorov draft, Goldwyn was merely exercising his artistic conscience. As Goldwyn saw it though, the two years and the substantial sums of money paid out to five different rewrite men had not been wasted. To be dissatisfied and not to try seemed worse to him than the two years of additional effort which, as their result, justified the original effort as being the best possible adaptation of the original Lewis work.[79]

Howard's negative opinion of this process is surmised easily, and one may suspect also that the screenwriter later believed that Selznick exhibited tendencies similar to those of Goldwyn. Nevertheless, in view of the uneven success of Howard's initial screenplays of *Gone with the Wind,* a more reasonable conclusion than his is that Selznick was justified in reserving the right to "exercise" his own "artistic conscience" by demanding further revisions.

In summary, commentary on script development for *Gone with the Wind* has been surveyed in this chapter and, by comparing the novel, the initial screenplay, and numerous revisions, the record of a significant part of this film's making has been emended. In the process, Selznick's influence on the adaptation process is revealed to have been a major constructive force, and a more accurate account has been offered of the complexity of the collaboration involved in screenwriting.

Contrary to opinions expressed by this film's only credited screenwriter, it is apparent after an examination of his successive drafts that the novel had not been adapted adequately by Sidney Howard in the filmscript's earliest versions. Selznick was aware of defects in these scripts but valued Howard's literary cachet; by commissioning him repeatedly for further revisions, the producer hoped that this screenwriter might be influenced to create what was expected. This endeavor was compromised fundamentally because Selznick espoused fidelity to the original novel, whereas Howard sought to invent "equivalent" narrative and dialogue, whether appropriate or not. Other writers were enlisted when Howard temporarily withdrew from the project.

Overall, Selznick's "manipulative style" as producer assured that the drama and spectacle of Mitchell's novel were realized as much as possible. Toward this end, Selznick saw that the undertaking of the picture's shot compositions and continuity design by William Cameron Menzies followed closely upon the script's development. Without a doubt, the magnitude of this film's success is as much a testament to the producer's role in its making as it is to the authority of those elements that contributed to the novel's acclaim.

Notes

1. Bordwell et al., *Classical Hollywood Cinema,* 94, 135-136.

2. Ibid.

3. Sklar, *Movie-made America,* 239-240.

4. Schatz, *Genius of System,* 178-179.

5. Harwell, *"Gone with the Wind" as Book and Film,* 49; Allen Hervey, *Anthony Adverse* (New York: Farrar and Rinehart, 1933).

6. Bob Thomas, *Selznick,* 286 (see n. 7: "After the immense success of *Gone with the Wind,* [Selznick] sent Margaret Mitchell $50,000, doubling her return from the movie rights"); Kahn, *Jock,* 122 ("[Whitney] and Selznick, on dissolving [SIP] in 1942, generously donated $50,000 to an Atlanta charity of Margaret Mitchell's choice, and while they were at it [gave] her an additional $50,000 for her own benefit—thus in effect doubling their initial purchase price for her book.").

7. Selznick to Howard, 6 January 1937. A brief summary of the racial controversy surrounding Griffith's picture is provided in the entry for *The Birth of a Nation* in Bawden, *Oxford Companion to Film,* 72: "Originally entitled *The Clansman,* the film followed its source novel [by Thomas Dixon, Jr.] in its bias towards the White Southern viewpoint (Griffith's father had been a veteran of the Confederate army). It was acclaimed for its outstanding merits—richly organized structure, dynamic editing, and dramatic use of space—but there was an outcry against its offensive portrayal of the negro. . . . The National Association for the Advancement of Colored People NAACP) launched an effective boycott and continued to picket cinemas where it was being shown until the Second World War." Picketing of this film's presentation is not uncommon even today. See also Staiger, *"The Birth of a Nation*: Reconsidering its Reception," 195-213.

8. Adams, "A Fine Novel," 1.

9. Flamini, *Scarlett, Rhett, and Cast,* 4.

10. Irene Selznick, *Private View,* 211-212.

11. Sennwald, "The Screen," 39.

12. Edwards, *Road to Tara,* 167; and Pyron, *Southern Daughter,* 307.

13. Harwell, *"Gone with the Wind" as Book and Film,* 38.

14. Balio, *Grand Design,* 1.

15. Mitchell, *Gone with the Wind,* 119-120.

16. Richard Corliss, *Talking Pictures,* 5.

17. *Time* (March 19, 1934), 36-37.

18. Howard, *Sinclair Lewis's "Dodsworth",* vii-viii, x, and xvii.

19. Howard, "Hollywood on the slide," 50; White, *Sidney Howard,* 33.

20. Mitchell, *"Gone with the Wind" Letters,* 72. In her letter, Mitchell also expressed an interest in Lamar Trotti (who was born and raised in Atlanta) as a candidate for screenwriter of *Gone with the Wind*; Trotti later wrote the story on which *Young Mr. Lincoln* (1939) was based and received an Academy Award as screenwriter of *Wilson* (1944).

21. Ibid., 79.

22. Ibid., 93.

23. Ibid., 96, 98, and 99.

24. Bob Thomas, *Selznick,* 139 and 146.

25. Freytag, *Technik des Dramas,* 102; Freytag, *Freytag's Technique of Drama,* 114-140. See also Carlson, *Theories of Theatre,* 258-259 ("Freytag's book . . . served well into the twentieth century as the standard manual for young playwrights"); and Bordwell et al., *Classical Hollywood Cinema,* 168.

26. Mitchell's *Gone with the Wind* (1936) runs 1,037 pages, while *David Copperfield* (New York: Heritage Press, 1935) is 821 pages long. (Originally serialized, the latter novel was published first in volume form in 1850 by Bradbury and Evans of London and ran 624 pages.)

27. Asheim, *From Book to Film* (see Tables 1 and 3, on pp. 74 and 114, respectively). With respect to methodology employed in this study, note p. 19: "The analysis procedure . . . consisted broadly of three steps: viewing the film; reading the book; comparing the book with the script. It was decided that the film would be seen prior to reading the book in order that no preconceptions be brought to the film which would hamper the complete objectivity of the analysis of manifest content"; and p. 39: "A problem presented by the comparative technique employed . . . is that of establishing a basis for comparison. In this study, the base is the novel; taking it as a norm we can chart the deviations from it made by the script to show the extent to which the several parts of the original are retained or altered by adaptation." Deviational scores were determined on the basis of changes of dialogue, characters, actions, scenes, setting, and sequences. Note also that such an analysis

of *Gone with the Wind*—in the forms of film, novel, and filmscript(s)—was not undertaken in Asheim's study.

28. Ibid.

29. "Philip Dunne: Fine Cabinetmaker," in McGilligan, *Backstory,* 157; interviewed by Tina Daniell.

30. Mordden, *Hollywood Studios,* 209.

31. Asheim, *From Book to Film,* 284 and 290.

32. Bordwell et al., *Classical Hollywood Cinema,* 16-17.

33. Bob Thomas, *Selznick,* 146; Lambert, GWTW, 42; Flamini, *Scarlett, Rhett, and Cast,* 199; Bridges and Boodman, *"Gone with the Wind": Definitive Illustrated History,* 25; Bartel, *Complete "Gone with the Wind" Trivia Book,* 50; Howard, *Gone with the Wind: Screenplay,* 7; and Thomson, *Showman,* 227.

34. Haver, *Selznick's Hollywood,* 246.

35. Naumberg, *We Make the Movies,* 32.

36. Ibid., 41.

37. Cowley, "Going with the Wind," 161-162.

38. Naumberg, *We Make the Movies,* 37.

39. Howard, GWTW: *Screenplay,* 15.

40. *Time* (June 7, 1937), cover and 32-33.

41. Mitchell, *Letters,* 150.

42. McGilligan, *Cukor,* 135.

43. Mitchell, *Letters,* 168.

44. Howard, GWTW: *Screenplay,* 17.

45. Bruccoli, *Some Sort of Epic Grandeur,* 450.

46. Thomson, *Showman,* 271.

47. Haver, *Selznick's Hollywood,* 241.

48. Mitchell, *Letters,* 249-250.

49. Ibid.

50. Howard, GWTW: *Screenplay,* 25 and 29.

51. Ibid., 24-25.

52. Haver, *Selznick's Hollywood,* 270.

53. McGilligan, *Cukor,* 148-153.

54. Interview by Stephen Farber for Oral History of the Motion Picture in America (transcript in University Research Library, University of California, Los Angeles), 15-16.

55. Howard, GWTW: *Screenplay,* 20.

56. Ibid., 29-30.

57. Ibid., 30; Harwell, *"Gone with the Wind" as Book and Film,* xx.

58. Froug, *Screenwriter Looks at Screenwriter,* 149.

59. "Donald Ogden Stewart: Politically Conscious," in McGilligan, *Backstory,* 341; interviewed by Allen Eyles and John Gillett.

60. Harmetz (*Making of "Wizard of Oz,"* 26) and Stempel (*Framework,* 72) both cite ten; Fricke et al. (*"Wizard of Oz": Pictorial History,* 44, 77, and 84) account for fourteen.

61. "John Lee Mahin: Team Player," in McGilligan, *Backstory,* 250 and 254; interviewed by Todd McCarthy and Joseph McBride.

62. Mitchell, *Letters,* 270.

63. Howard, GWTW: *Screenplay,* 30.

64. "John Lee Mahin: Team Player," in McGilligan, *Backstory,* 255.

65. Hecht, *Child of Century,* 489.

66. Howard, GWTW: *Screenplay,* 25 and 28.

67. Hecht, *Child of Century,* 489.

68. Behlmer, *Memo to Selznick,* xiv.

69. Pyron, *Southern Daughter,* 389-391.

70. Catherine Clinton, "Gone with the Wind," 132.

71. Bogle, *Toms, Coons, Mulattoes, Mammies, and Bucks,* 88.

72. "Donald Ogden Stewart: Politically Conscious," in McGilligan, *Backstory,* 341. Emphasis is Stewart's.

73. Schatz, *Genius of System,* 108, 110-111, and 115.

74. Griffith, *Samuel Goldwyn,* 6.

75. Naumberg, *We Make the Movies,* 44.

76. Easton, *Search for Sam Goldwyn,* 137; Arthur Marx, *Goldwyn,* 209-210.

77. Berg, *Goldwyn,* 277.

78. Arthur Marx, *Goldwyn,* 218-219.

79. Epstein, *Samuel Goldwyn,* 75.

Linda Troost and Sayre Greenfield (essay date 1998)

SOURCE: Troost, Linda and Sayre Greenfield. "Introduction: Watching Ourselves Watching." In *Jane Austen in Hollywood,* edited by Linda Troost and Sayre Greenfield, pp. 1-11. Lexington: University Press of Kentucky, 2001.

[*In the following essay, first published in 1998, Troost and Greenfield present an overview of several adaptations of Jane Austen's works for film and television.*]

The past few years have seen a proliferation of Jane Austen adaptations. Between 1970 and 1986, seven feature-length films or television miniseries, all British, were produced based on Austen novels; in the years 1995 and 1996, however, six additional adaptations appeared, half of them originating in Hollywood and the rest influenced by it.

The boom started in the United Kingdom in September 1995 with the "wet-T-shirt-Darcy" *Pride and Prejudice* miniseries written by Andrew Davies, and crossed the Atlantic in December with the opening of Emma Thompson's high-profile adaptation of *Sense and Sensibility*. The success of both these productions lifted the art-house film *Persuasion* (written by Nick Dear and released in late September but previously aired on British television in April 1995) out of potential obscurity and brought a new—and older—audience to Amy Heckerling's Hollywood film from earlier in the summer (July), an updating of *Emma* entitled *Clueless*. The next year, 1996, was the big one for fans of Austen in the United States. *Pride and Prejudice* came to the Arts and Entertainment Network (A&E) in January, and in the same month *Persuasion* and *Sense and Sensibility* enjoyed much wider U.S. distribution. It was also The Year of *Emma*.[1] In July 1996, Gwyneth Paltrow appeared as Austen's beautiful heroine for Hollywood's Miramax Films, written and directed by Douglas McGrath, and, in November, Britain's Meridian Broadcasting produced Andrew Davies's telefilm for ITV starring Kate Beckinsale (which came to A&E in February 1997). With such competition, the BBC, which had been developing its own miniseries of the novel, put its plans "on hold for the foreseeable future" (Sawyer).

As a result of the manifold productions, Jane Austen has become even more popular. Publishers have brought out tie-in editions of the novels, Emma Thompson and Nick Dear have published their screenplays, Sue Birtwistle and Susie Conklin have written two heavily illustrated books designed to accompany writer Davies's adaptations: *The Making of Pride and Prejudice* and *The Making of Jane Austen's Emma*.[2] Membership in the Jane Austen Society of North America (JASNA) jumped 50 percent over the course of 1996 alone (4,000 members as of September 1997), and Austen-L, an E-mail list based at McGill University in Canada, has more than 600 subscribers.

The interest in Austen and in adapting her novels has, of course, been operative all through this century. Andrew Wright describes attempts to set *Pride and Prejudice* to music, to rewrite the book for the stage, and so forth, and he lists more than sixty radio, television, film, and stage productions of Austen's various works between 1900 and 1975. If the recent phenomenon has seemed more intense, one must credit, first of all, the technology that allows such intensity. In the early 1970s, global culture was not so tightly meshed as it is now nor could the marketing practices be so efficient. For instance, the only possible place on U.S. television for such BBC versions of Austen as the 1971 *Sense and Sensibility* or the 1972 *Emma* was public television's *Masterpiece Theatre*. Neither series, indeed, crossed the Atlantic. In the 1990s, however, the TV adaptations can sell not only through PBS but also the

Arts and Entertainment Network (the telefilm of *Northanger Abbey* of 1986, a controversial production was the first to combine American and British resources—the BBC and A&E). Also, the current films have an established habit of video renting and buying on which to rely. For example, the BBC sold 200,000 video copies of the 1995 *Pride and Prejudice* within a year of the first airing (Nichols), 50,000 of them in the first week (Davies). The adaptations before 1986 did not have these cultural practices so well established. After all, prior to the 1980s, few homes had VCRs in them.[3]

Technological changes have also enhanced the opportunities for hyping the films. The television and Hollywood publicity machines have become very good both at appealing to a niche audience, in ways that Deborah Kaplan explores in her essay in this volume, and at expanding that niche. Specialized TV networks, instant books of the screenplays and of the filming process, videocassettes, CDs of the soundtracks, and official websites all collaborate to allow those enamored of Austen to indulge their taste further, and at the same time, these hot spots can spark and then expand even a mild interest. Idling through the World Wide Web, a viewer may decide to check if there is anything on Austen. Suddenly she discovers references to the Austen-L mailing list, she visits the Republic of Pemberley at www.pemberley.com, and the powers of reinforcement begin their work. The privacy of reading or of renting a video becomes easily supplemented and overwhelmed by this newfound ability to use and indulge Austenian knowledge in more public locations.

Naturally, such interest can be generated by the films only because Austen's novels maintain their attractions and because the producers and writers have targeted their audience well. What in Jane Austen's novels has made them so readily adaptable to film in the 1990s, and exactly what changes have they required to be successful in this period? Investigating the Austen film phenomenon of 1995-96 along these two lines, this collection of essays sheds light on the most culturally successful features of the novels, on the six film and television adaptations, and on us, the culture that watches these adaptations.

When agreements among our contributors emerge on these issues, they do not result from any particular effort that we, the editors, have made to "scold them into harmony" (Austen 169). Indeed, disagreements on the quality of the films and the emphases of Austen's novels do occur. How faithful films are to the books and the nature of the alterations may occasion some dispute, as when Lisa Hopkins argues that the Davies adaptation of *Pride and Prejudice* diminishes the splendors of Pemberley whereas Elisabeth Ellington proposes the reverse (this differing perception may result partly from British versus American perspectives). Likewise, Cheryl Nixon emphasizes the many changes this same television adaptation has made in the portrayal of Darcy, while Lisa Hopkins and Rebecca Dickson find this small-screen translation essentially faithful to the novel. Casey Diana bucks a tendency among some other contributors toward suspicion of the films by arguing for their pedagogical usefulness. Even perceptions of how the films were received can differ: Carol Dole notes the positive reviews of Dear's 1995 version of *Persuasion,* but Amanda Collins finds the production condemned relative to the praise heaped upon Thompson's *Sense and Sensibility.* We leave decisions on such disputes to the discretion of our readers, yet the attractions of the novels as raw material for the films and certain definable tendencies in the recent adaptations do emerge from this collection.

The qualities that make Austen's novels appealing material for the large and small screen include values that, if not immutable, have been continually appreciated over the last two hundred years. Austen's characters strike a perfect balance between recognizable types and individuals with complex motivations and idiosyncratic personalities. Readers and watchers identify with them and yet cannot fully predict their behaviors. Perhaps heroines such as Marianne Dashwood and Catherine Morland push the typical end of the scale while Emma Woodhouse and Anne Elliot push the idiosyncratic end, but such differences merely broaden the appeal of the Austen canon as a whole. The concerns at the center of Austen's plots—sex, romance, and money—are central concerns in our own era. The details of developing love and the constraints of limited finances provide difficulties that lend her storylines interest for the 1990s reader of sufficient maturity—and these elements of plot, like Austen's characters, can translate to film mostly intact.

Those concerns we share with Austen and her original audience, however, cannot alone account for the burst of interest at this time. Austen also assists in her own modern-day success by providing experiences we are not used to, allowing a reactionary escapism to a simpler time as it was lived by a comfortingly wealthy and leisurely class, as Casey Diana and Suzanne Ferriss note. In her essay, Ellington posits a nostalgia for an older English country-side that renders the Austen films visually attractive to us. One might note, too, the revival of interest in both Georgian architecture (see any recent housing development) and high-waisted dresses (visit any Saks Fifth Avenue),[4] additional features of this nostalgia. Indeed, reaction against the perceived crassness of modern life may have encouraged the Merchant-Ivory films and their successors over the past decade: the appeal of nineteenth-century upperclass society to viewers who want nuance, social sensitivity, and an education—particularly in British historical detail—to count for something.

One may conclude along with Amanda Collins that this desire for a genteel past is a retreat from reality since the most successful films generally leave out those sections of society that have other, grosser tastes and ignore sections of the world with less well-known cultural patterns than England's. We seek difference, but a familiar difference, and our schooling and reading have already made the Merchant-Ivory or Austenian worlds familiar, as Rachel Brownstein (quoting Monica Lauritzen) suggests. In these films, we can hide from the uncertainties of complex twentieth-century existence, where a war in Yugoslavia or a disease in Africa may affect an island in northern Europe or the larger island of North America. Carol Dole's essay complicates this position by intimating that the appeal of Austen in our time derives not simply from the longing for a more socially restricted, elegant life but from Austen's ambiguity toward that culture and partial criticism of it. While we may desire to escape to the world of this older, genteel class, we are simultaneously uneasy about such a wish: Austen gives us the historical fantasy yet provides harsh ridicule of those who are too snobbish in their class distinctions. Therefore, to love Austen is to adore Culture (in the old, high sense of the word) but to remain aware, as she is, of some of its attendant dangers.

Among the greatest attractions of Austen's culture, whether presented by book or film, may be its devotion to manners. In recent years, we have realized that post-1960s culture has lost some of its grace, hence the rise in popularity of Judith Martin (a.k.a. "Miss Manners") and summer camps for etiquette. Our fascination with Austen taps into this fascination with social polish. We may not want to live in this world, but it is fun to visit. An appreciation of manners requires a sophisticated knowledge of social customs, a sensitivity toward others, and the self-restraint for which Rebecca Dickson directly pleads in her essay. In an era of tell-all biographies and talk shows that exploit that all-too-easy impulse for self-exposure, it is difficult not to yearn for some greater degree of reticence in society.

For reticence, however, to communicate passions effectively, as Jane Austen's novels do to the right audience, that readership or viewership must possess social confidence and cultural sophistication. Other segments of the film and television audience—perhaps those who feel constrained into unpleasant social roles or numbed into powerlessness—appreciate depictions of the individual bursting through all social restraints and all concepts of historical accuracy. For them, the adventures of Hercules or Xena, Warrior Princess, can provide a more thorough escape. But the audience educated for Merchant-Ivory's 1986 adaptation of E. M. Forster's *A Room with a View,* Mike Newell's 1992 film of Elizabeth von Arnim's 1922 novel *Enchanted April,* or Thompson's adaptation of *Sense and Sensibility* sees less need for, or possibility of, escaping cultural restrictions. This audience can do without clashes between disparate sections of society or between different nations with mutually incomprehensible social codes and objectives. It wants a game of comprehensible dimension. Limit the field to a little bit of ivory, two inches wide, and the rules become manageable and reassuring. One can acknowledge some degree of corruption in society and feel one could, nevertheless, succeed in it; there is no need to destroy the powers of "civilized" darkness and march off into the virtuous desert like Conan the Barbarian.

For such specific powers of appeal, the 1990s audience may be more open than the audience of previous decades.

First, to state the obvious, the audience is largely female: at the Pittsburgh opening of Thompson's *Sense and Sensibility,* sold out an hour before its showing, the male half of this editorial team found himself in a distinct sexual minority, and at the 1997 meeting in San Francisco of the Jane Austen Society of North America, he noticed that generally only 20 percent of those attending sessions were male. Perhaps a plethora of television stations has made us all more assertive in having our particular tastes catered to, and a mainly female audience that prides itself on social sophistication may be less willing than it was in the 1970s to put up with films aimed at adolescent males. In addition, cultural winds may have blown a larger potential audience toward Austenian concerns. The election of Bill Clinton and Tony Blair to leadership in the United States and the United Kingdom respectively suggests that their political positions, combining fiscal responsibility with claims of social sensitivity, tap into a broad base—and those concerns seem remarkably central to Austen's novels.

Although the recent spate of Austen adaptations depends on novelistic features—such as plot, character, and the general social milieu—that translate readily to film, translations too faithful to the books cannot achieve broad enough appeal for the movie industry, even if we could agree what "faithfulness" to Austen might mean. In less than two hundred years, the cultural environment has altered enough to require considerable adaptation of the novels (how many of us these days understand the significance of owning a barouche as opposed to a curricle?). These changes from text to film offer us the chance for some sharp cultural self-definition. Certain alterations, of course, derive from the shift in form. Films will shorten the stories, and even a six-hour television miniseries must abbreviate long patches of dialogue or the readings of letters. More important, the translation to a visual medium encourages a far greater reliance on images: words cannot exist without a picture. One sees this already in the 1979 BBC miniseries of *Pride and Prejudice* written by Fay Weldon. The director, Cyril Coke, cannot merely have Elizabeth Bennet, after she has rejected Darcy, read his explanatory letter without finding some visual equivalent. Instead, we get long shots of Darcy's receding figure as we hear the letter being read. The 1996 McGrath adaptation of *Emma* must find some action to fill those spaces where Austen herself simply describes the heroine's feelings—and so scenes of Emma writing in a journal accompany her voice-over.

The unremitting images, however, provide far more than visual equivalents for Austen's text; the images inescapably change the emphasis. The matter of costumes, for instance, makes this shift clear. Austen, writing for contemporaries who do not need the word-painting, emphatically spares us details about clothing, but film must show its actors mostly clothed—and in historically correct costume—so it cannot avoid placing more value on a superficial concern such as fashion than Austen would. The oddness of the costume, its difference from our own style

of dress, cannot help but attract our attention, too. Often, however, directorial decisions invent images, as when director Simon Langton and writer Andrew Davies remove Darcy's clothes in the 1995 *Pride and Prejudice*.[5] This episode tells us more about our current decade's obsession with physical perfection and acceptance of gratuitous nudity than it does about Austen's Darcy, but the image carves a new facet into the text. Lisa Hopkins argues that such scenes empower women by making men the object of the gaze, and Cheryl Nixon points out that this titillating picture not only added symbolic depth for her students but also enlivened the character of Darcy. Amanda Collins goes further, arguing that most of the Austen movies (though not *Persuasion*), by their natural enough choice of beautiful lead actors, promote the equation of human physical beauty with worth, a Shaftesburian attitude Jane Austen seems directly critical of at times. For instance, the splendid appearance of Gwyneth Paltrow in *Emma* can, as Nora Nachumi indicates, undercut the satire directed against the character she plays. More generally, Deborah Kaplan worries that the emphasis on physical appearance simplifies the complexities of Austen's narration into that more associated with genre fiction. The human image is not the only change: scenery can intrude into the films as well, transforming Austenian satire on the Picturesque into an outright endorsement of the Picturesque. Moreover, this shift comes at the cost of social awareness, Ellington suggests. The simplest visual choices for a film can easily remold the values of the novels.

The delicate touch of Austen's satire may suffer much in the cinematic transformations of the novels. Nora Nachumi explores the difficulties of reproducing Austen's ironic narrator on-screen, concluding that the thoroughly modernized *Clueless* does a better job than some other films. Carol Dole notices the satire diverging to two extremes in the more faithful adaptations, with attacks on the class system becoming stronger (though perhaps less humorous) in *Persuasion* and the Davies version of *Emma* and attacks on class-consciousness growing merely superficial in the Americanized worlds of Thompson's *Sense and Sensibility* and McGrath's *Emma*. These films are not without satiric dimensions, but the directors and writers do not always seem to trust their audiences with subtlety—and perhaps with some wisdom: after all, in the movie theater or during a first showing on television, one cannot reread some previous sentence to double check for a suspected irony.

Not only the social commentary loses subtlety and balance; the passions in the stories also suffer coarsening in their compression. The emotions displayed by some characters receive considerable heightening and, as a number of contributors to this volume find, the films elevate and celebrate romance beyond any level the novels justify. Cheryl Nixon in particular emphasizes that Austen's men are modernized out of their repressions into displays of feeling. Austen generally celebrates male restraint, but film directors cannot tolerate such a value—or at least think the modern viewer cannot. And when the leading men of the films can be prodded into displaying affection toward children, so much the better, as Devoney Looser indicates, for their desirability.

If the idea and physique of the New Man of the 1990s reshapes Austen's on-screen heroes, her heroines require even greater adaptation by current films. The imprint of modern feminism on the films, however, is not any clearer than the status of feminist thought in Austen's original texts. Some of the movies at least superficially heighten the feminism to increase their appeal. Amanda Collins and Kristin Samuelian, for instance, note that Thompson's *Sense and Sensibility* creates female characters, particularly young Margaret, with whom a liberated audience can identify. Looser calls such shifts the "mainstreaming of feminism," showing heroines who can tackle physical activity, social conventions, and love all equally well. Suzanne Ferriss identifies versions of *Emma* that go in both directions, with the heavily adapted *Clueless* taking power away from the women it depicts, relative to Austen's heroines, and the two *Emmas* enhancing the depiction of women's power. On the other hand, Rebecca Dickson and Kristen Samuelian find the cinematic representations ultimately undercutting the subtle feminism Austen promoted in the novels. The late twentieth century still has not sorted out women's roles, and the on-screen depictions of Austen's characters echo the ambiguous position of women in the 1990s: feminist, traditionalist, or sometimes both, depending on whom one asks. Each screenwriter, director, and viewer sees the characters as reflecting his or her ideas of womanhood, and that may be the secret of Austen and the film adaptations: they play simultaneously to both camps and reach twice the audience. Both feminists and traditionalists can easily claim Jane Austen as their own.

Changes to Austen's texts made for the differing tastes and politics of the modern audience bring out the conflict not only between two discrete eras or philosophical stances but between two modes of reception: reading versus watching. Most of the essays in this collection will, naturally enough, favor the experience of reading (hence the decision to identify adaptations more often by screenwriter than director). To write on Austen is to be a reader, and to be a reader is to value the relative exclusivity and discipline of reading. Both fans of Jane Austen ("Janeites") and literary critics are primarily book people, and in times when we imagine that literacy is under assault, the degree of literacy required to read Austen or write criticism becomes all the more valuable by its relative scarcity. In *Pride and Prejudice,* Caroline Bingley understands that signs of reading are socially valuable, even if she does not understand how to enjoy reading itself:

> Miss Bingley's attention was quite as much engaged in watching Mr. Darcy's progress through *his* book, as in reading her own; and she was perpetually either making some inquiry, or looking at his page. She could not win him, however, to any conversation; he merely answered her question, and read on. At length, quite exhausted by the attempt to be amused with her own book, which she had only chosen because it was the

> second volume of his, she gave a great yawn and said, "How pleasant it is to spend an evening in this way! I declare after all there is no enjoyment like reading! How much sooner one tires of any thing than of a book!—When I have a house of my own, I shall be miserable if I have not an excellent library."
>
> [Austen 55]

Miss Bingley desires the appearance of high literacy, but she wants it on the cheap.

The problem that film adaptations of Austen's works present to a person already interested in her novels is essentially the fear of success. On the one hand, we may wish the films good commercial fortunes as a way of seconding our own appreciation, but on the other hand, this very confirmation of our taste renders our appreciation less exclusive, less a way of marking our superiority. We may both welcome and fear the invasion of the Caroline Bingleys onto our turf. In this sense, watching ourselves watching proves an exhilarating and disquieting experience, for we stand in a superior position and may well be suspicious of our own sense of superiority.

Insofar as the audience for the films consists largely of those who have already read the novels, we pay the admission, purchase or rent the videotape, or at least turn on the television to see to what extent these new versions of Austen measure up to our standards. For this audience, the films complicate the process of reading and do not replace it. The producers and distributors, however, seem to assume that seeing comes before reading, and so they picture an audience with less time, less knowledge, and less patience than the reader of Austen possesses. Of course, these hawkers of Austen may well be gathering new readers for her, too. Casey Diana's pedagogical experiment on her students portrays how the films may prepare an audience for reading, representing a shortcut to appreciation for those compelled to read one of her books or for those simply intrigued by the film into a subsequent perusal of the written texts.

However, for readers of Austen, a fear remains that these films (and the proliferating Internet websites devoted to them) may substitute for the novels. Instead of reading Austen, the Caroline Bingleys of the 1990s may just visit the Colin Firth websites and buy CDs of music from Austen's era, thinking that they are participating in High Culture. Undoubtedly the films and the spin-off products do substitute for the novels for some people, and they certainly provide a different (and complementary) experience from reading Austen's original works. The films are, by necessity, "E-Z" Austen, but we need not fear they will replace or degrade the novels. The film and television adaptations are attuned to one cultural moment as Austen's novels have proven themselves not to be. Every generation needs a film or video remake of *Pride and Prejudice* whereas Austen's novels have fit a succession of cultural moments for nearly two hundred years. That is the reason they form part of the literary canon. The films get remade because they do not inhabit a long sweep of time comfortably.

Our collection begins by looking at this sweep of time, with Brownstein's consideration of how successive remakes of *Pride and Prejudice* and *Sense and Sensibility* have brought different aspects of Austen's novels to the foreground, appealing to the varying cultural tempers of each era. A glance at the films that have seemed less successful than the recent ones in attracting an audience may also show how the immediacy of the film medium may inhibit longer-term appeal. The 1983 television adaptation of *Mansfield Park* and the 1987 of *Northanger Abbey* certainly received less critical comment in their day than the recent films have in theirs, and their ways of fleshing out the novels may be responsible: one seems too pedantic; the other, too flighty.

Watching a film almost inevitably presents the viewer with a denser texture than does reading. As we read, we fill in spaces that the text leaves blank, and we do not all fill them in the same ways. In recognizing this distinction, we see what Roman Ingarden identifies as "the opposition of the literary work of art itself to its various possible concretizations and, in particular, to its aesthetic concretizations" (241). With varying degrees of specificity, we imagine Edmund Bertram's appearance or Northanger Abbey's servants, each according to what suits our notions. The films leave vastly less interpretive room. Who has not been disappointed, sooner or later, in some Austen character's looks on-screen? The size of the ballrooms and the mansions, the patterns of the clothes and design of the country dances, the nature of expressions that pass across the faces—all these receive definition. Even the most accurate translation of an Austen novel to film may stand at a disadvantage to the book because of its detail in the face of our various understandings or misunderstandings. Much of the indeterminacy that powers our delight in arguments about Austen gets too settled by the films.

Yet even were we united in our tastes, the filmed versions would create aesthetic problems. On the one hand, we may not want to know as much as a film adaptation gives us. The *Mansfield Park* production, for instance, takes 35 minutes to get through the first 40 pages of the novel (until the arrival of the Crawfords), about 14 percent of the film to cover the first 8 percent of the book. This section of the series provides wonderfully detailed views of the texture of life at Mansfield Park, in the sort of production that Roger Sales in his book on representation in Regency England calls "heritage" television (17-25), but at the cost of our imaginations, whether accurate or not. Moreover, while we may know that Edmund Bertram is not particularly physically striking, do we really want his earnestly bad hairstyle thrust constantly into our vision? At least in the novel, even if we had imagined him to look this way, we are mostly allowed to forget that impression.

On the other hand, any film production of a well-loved novel runs the risk of not conforming to what we may have imagined. The distinctive BBC/A&E *Northanger Abbey* introduces scenes of Catherine's gothic imaginings at length, a persistently vocalized sound track, and a cart-wheeling servant lad in the garden at the Abbey. All in all, it gives us the delights of the unexpected, but it certainly leaves any devoted reader open to imagining other, perhaps more appropriate, ways of filling in the spaces in that text. The German Expressionist and Freudian elements interpolated into the film may startle not only the passionate Janeite but even the dispassionate scholar.[6]

The recent round of film and television productions, however, demonstrates by its collective success that writers, producers, set designers, costumers, composers, choreographers, food stylists, and actors can supplement the text with sights and sounds in a most appealing way. But the productions may suffer from being so fully attuned in their texture to our present tastes and imaginations that this texture will not always appeal so easily to future audiences. Once on film, those images are fixed in a way that Austen's writing (by virtue of its medium and her skill) avoids. These adaptations, then, have more to tell us about our own moment in time than about Austen's writing. In watching them, we watch ourselves.

Notes

1. The year 1996 also saw "Furst Impressions," a version of *Pride and Prejudice* aimed at children and starring Wishbone, a Jack Russell terrier. In the 1997-98 season, the thespian dog starred in a remake of *Northanger Abbey* entitled "Pup Fiction."

2. Roger Sales reports that, in Britain, *The Making of Pride and Prejudice* made the top of the nonfiction best-seller list in December 1996 (228).

3. The Austen film industry has been quick to catch on, however. The 1940 *Pride and Prejudice* appeared on video in 1985. Between 1985 and 1996, six of the seven British television adaptations produced between 1970 and 1986 were released on video. The productions from the early 1970s, none of which were shown in the United States, were obviously released to capitalize on current interest (only the 1971 BBC *Sense and Sensibility* has not made it to video, apparently because it was preempted by the 1985 production).

4. Fashion has been reluctant to revive the high-waisted dress, but Hilary Alexander credits its recent reappearance to the "sexy allure" of Gwyneth Paltrow in *Emma*. She also points to the Regency-inspired work of John Galliano for the summer 1996 *haute-couture* collection he designed for Givenchy. One should observe, however, that high-waisted minidresses were already appearing in the wardrobe of the very fashionable Cher "Emma" Horowitz (*Clueless*) the previous summer, no doubt as part of a 1960s revival rather than as an allusion to Austen.

5. Even though the BBC had just released a "heritage television" (Sales 237) production of *Pride and Prejudice* in 1989, rumors were circulating in the British press during October 1990 about a new ver-

sion that would feature nudity and "explicit sex" (Roth #589, 599, 640, 669, 733). Although the Davies version did contain some partial nudity, the explicit sex never quite materialized.

6. For an analysis of the psychoanalytic elements at work in this production, see Roberts.

Works Cited

Alexander, Hilary. "Emma's Exotic Empire." *The Electronic Telegraph* 13 Sept. 1996. Online at www.telegraph-.co.uk (10 Oct. 1997).

Austen, Jane. *Pride and Prejudice.* Ed. R. W. Chapman. Rev. Mary Lascelles. 3d ed. Vol. 2 of *The Novels of Jane Austen.* 6 vols. Oxford: Oxford UP, 1966.

Birtwistle, Sue, and Susie Conklin. *The Making of Jane Austen's Emma.* London: Penguin, 1996. Includes Andrew Davies's screenplay.

———. *The Making of Pride and Prejudice.* London: Penguin, 1995.

Davies, Caroline. "BBC Pride as 50,000 Buy Austen Video." *The Electronic Telegraph* 25 Oct. 1995. Online at www.telegraph.co.uk (10 Oct 1997).

Dear, Nick. *Persuasion.* Methuen Film Series. London: Methuen, 1996.

Ingarden, Roman. *The Cognition of the Literary Work of Art.* Trans. Ruth Ann Crowley and Kenneth R. Olson. Evanston: Northwestern UP, 1973.

Nichols, Peter M. "Literary Cycle: Bookshelf, Broadcast, Video Store." *New York Times* 7 Sept. 1997. Arts and Leisure section. Online edition.

Roberts, Marilyn. "Catherine Morland: Gothic Heroine after All?" *Topic: A Journal of the Liberal Arts* 48 (1997): 22-30.

Roth, Barry. *A Bibliography of Jane Austen Studies, 1984-94.* Athens: Ohio UP, 1996.

Sales, Roger. *Jane Austen and Representations of Regency England.* With "Afterword." New York: Routledge, 1996.

Sawyer, Evelyn. E-mail to Kali Pappas. 11 July 1997. Online at www.ocf.berkeley.edu/~kip/emma.news.html (10 Oct. 1997).

Thompson, Emma. *The Sense and Sensibility Screenplay and Diaries.* Rev. ed. New York: Newmarket, 1996.

Wright, Andrew. "Jane Austen Adapted." *Nineteenth-Century Fiction* [now titled *Nineteenth-Century Literature*] 30 (1975): 421-53. Contains an annotated list of pre-1975 adaptations.

Ken Gelder (essay date 1999)

SOURCE: Gelder, Ken. "Jane Campion and the Limits of Literary Cinema." In *Adaptations: From Text to Screen, Screen to Text,* edited by Deborah Cartmell and Imelda Whelehan, pp. 157-71. London: Routledge, 1999.

[*In the following essay, Gelder explores the relationship between literature and the cinema via an analysis of the movie* The Piano, *noting that even though the film was not an adaptation, it elicited critical analysis that designated it as "literary."*]

Jane Campion's film *The Piano* (1993) poses some interesting problems in terms of the relationship between literature and cinema. We can begin by noting that the film itself attracted the kind of sustained analytical criticism which worked to designate it as 'literary', even though it was not actually an adaptation. This meant that when the novel-of-the-film appeared a year later—co-written by Jane Campion and Kate Pullinger—it could only be identified as somehow *less* literary than the film: as if the film was more of a novel than the novel itself. The novel-of-the-film in fact answered some of the film's over-hanging enigmas and resolved some of its ambiguities. In other words, it clarified (even simplified) the film, and no doubt for these as well as other reasons it received almost no critical attention as a literary text. Certainly it is unusual to come across a case where a film is seen as more complex, nuanced and worthy of sustained 'literary' critique than the novel to which it is attached. In Campion's next project, a 1996 adaptation of Henry James's novel *The Portrait of a Lady* (1881), quite the opposite would seem to be true: that such a great novel would inevitably remain more complex and nuanced than the film. On the other hand, Campion's reputation by this time was secure enough for her scriptwriter, Laura Jones, to restructure this conventional view of novel-to-film adaptation by imagining Henry James to be 'turning [in his grave] with pleasure' at the film version (see Jones 1996: x). For Jones, novel-to-film adaptation involves an initial loss and a subsequent gain: 'you empty out in order to fill up' (Jones 1996: vi). Indeed, her screenplay even 'widens James's circle a little, stretches it a fraction' (Jones 1996: viii), returning us to the sense provided by *The Piano* that—those initial losses in an adaptation notwithstanding—a film can actually become something *more* than a novel. At the very least, then, a certain kind of productive entanglement occurs between the 'literary' and the 'cinematic'; let us also note that this entanglement works to limit possibilities, too, as the following discussions hope to show.

Literary Genealogies and Postcolonialism

Campion herself had given *The Piano* a precise kind of literary genealogy, speaking of her special debt to Emily Brontë's *Wuthering Heights* (1847). In an interview with Miro Bilbrough in the Australian journal *Cinema Papers,* she pays tribute to Brontë, as well as the American poet Emily Dickinson. For Campion, *Wuthering Heights* is 'a powerful poem about the romance of the soul' (Bilbrough 1993: 6) which provided an inspirational precursor for the not dissimilar narrative of *The Piano*: a thoroughly constraining arranged marriage (in the 1850s in this case) to a cold bourgeois property developer, and a tempestuous love affair with a man more in tune with nature and sexuality which, by contrast, is thoroughly liberating. More interestingly, the stark landscape of the moors in *Wuthering Heights* seemed to Campion to translate perfectly to the location of *The Piano*, the west coast of New Zealand's North Island, as if Brontë's novel and her film had somehow become synchronic:

> For me, and for many New Zealanders, the relationship with very wild beaches, especially the black sands and the west coast beaches around Auckland and New Plymouth, and the very private, secretive and extraordinary world of the bush, is a kind of colonial equivalent to Emily Brontë's moors.
>
> (Bilbrough 1993: 6)

Campion's remark in *Sight and Sound* that 'I feel a kinship between the kind of romance that Emily Brontë portrays in *Wuthering Heights* and this film' (Bruzzi 1993: 6), plays up this compatibility. In this sense, *The Piano* is quite a different project to Jean Rhys's *Wide Sargasso Sea* (1966), which had itself turned to Charlotte Brontë's *Jane Eyre* (1847) in order to emphasize not the synchronicity between texts and locations but, rather, their incommensurable differences. For Rhys, the Caribbean—being so *unlike* Brontë's England—worked to estrange *Jane Eyre* from itself, providing a postcolonial point of departure from that earlier novel. Campion, however, fuses her own project and *Wuthering Heights* together, to the extent—especially through the unrelenting rain-sodden images of the forests, and the beach in the opening sequence which is so turbulent as to make landfall a sheer impossibility—of making New Zealand strange instead. As a consequence, the postcolonial project of *The Piano* is much more internally compromised.

The grafting of a *Wuthering Heights*-based sensibility onto mid-nineteenth century New Zealand in fact ran the risk of obscuring issues specific to the latter's postcolonial development. The role of Maori, for example, who mostly shadow the film or appear fleetingly in ambiguous poses—like the 'effeminate' Maori reclining on a branch of a tree in one scene—has proved a source of contention among critics. Stella Bruzzi's homage to the film in *Sight and Sound* manages to ignore the role of Maori altogether, reading the film entirely through its *Wuthering Heights* framework—and both broadening and consolidating the film's European literary genealogy by comparing its heroine, Ada, with Flaubert's *Madame Bovary* (Bruzzi 1993: 8). For Bruzzi, the binary of austere patriarchal culture (repressive) and a feminine, sexual nature (liberatory) provides the key to *The Piano*; its modernity lies in Ada's ability to '*transcend* the limitations of such disempowered nineteenth-century heroines as Emily Brontë's Catherine' through 'self-knowledge' (Bruzzi 1993: 7; my italics). Bruzzi's article attracted a response in *Sight and Sound*'s letters pages from Richard Cummings, who sees Ada's romantic attachment to Baines in *The Piano* as a 'cop out' since, although the latter has Maori facial decorations, he nevertheless 'remains an Englishman' and manages to save Ada by getting her out of New Zealand and back to civilization (Cummings 1994: 72). 'In a post-colonial world', Cummings says, 'this is not only condescending, but so Eurocentric as to be totally anachronistic'

(Cummings 1994: 72). Bruzzi's counter-response perhaps only exacerbated the problem, seeing Cummings' account as 'reductive' and defending Campion's portrayal of Maori in the film *à la* Margaret Mead by claiming them as 'a positive force who remain unfettered by colonial notions of sin and guilt and do not censor sexuality or desire', adding that they 'in some way represent the unconscious of suppressed—and oppressed—characters such as Ada's husband Stewart' (Bruzzi 1994: 64).

This romantic view of indigenous people as the 'unfettered' unconscious of a repressed civilized world simply extends the binary which underwrites Bruzzi's article, of course—but it is also pertinent to the 'literary' appreciation of the film itself, which (in spite, or perhaps because, of the marginal presence of Maori) talked up the role of the 'unconscious' in *The Piano* and linked it to the feminine, the 'lyrical' and the poetic. In 1995 the film journal *Screen* published three articles which polarized *The Piano* by seeing its use of the repression (civilization, patriarchy) versus liberation (nature, sexuality, femininity, Maori) binary either positively as the key to the film's literariness, or negatively as something inhibiting and overly romantic, especially from a postcolonial perspective. One of the articles is by Stella Bruzzi, and extends the tribute she had paid to *The Piano* in *Sight and Sound,* seeing the film as an expression of Ada's capacity to 'unbalance' patriarchal restrictions (Bruzzi 1995: 266). A second article, by Sue Gillett, is a kind of lyrical panegyric to *The Piano* which tries to mimic the feminized (or feminist) 'unconscious' of the film through its very letter. But the third article, by Lynda Dyson, sees this turn to the 'unconscious'—and the association of the unconscious with Maori in the film—in negative terms only, as 'primitivist'. For Dyson, the grounding of the film in the kind of 'romantic vision' associated with Brontë's *Wuthering Heights* is precisely responsible for both the 'primitivist' representations of Maori and the obscuring of this feature in the film's critical reception. *The Piano*'s 'critical acclaim', she suggests,

> not only ignored the film's colonial setting but, by focusing on links between *The Piano* and the English literary canon, Campion and her work were appropriated as distinctly 'European'. While this appropriation can be understood within the context of the relationship between the metropolitan centre and the periphery—historically the 'privileging norms' of the European cultural canon have defined 'cultural value' in the colonial context—it also seemed to consolidate the 'whiteness' of the text.
>
> (Dyson 1995: 275)

For Dyson, then, the literariness of *The Piano*—owing so much to 'the European cultural canon'—inhibits its postcolonial potential. It prevents the film from functioning critically in relation to that canon, in the way that (for example) Rhys's *Wide Sargasso Sea* does in relation to *Jane Eyre*. By Campion's own account, as we've seen, the film transplants *Wuthering Heights* onto colonial New Zealand, as if the novel and the place are somehow made for each other.

WHERE IS NEW ZEALAND IN *THE PIANO*?

There never was a great nineteenth-century New Zealand novel: in this sense, the film of *The Piano* fills a literary gap. Yet the 'New Zealand' it evokes—derived from the atmospherics of Brontë's English novel, 'unconscious', feminine, lyrical, turbulent—may raise, rather than solve, problems of authenticity and appropriateness. In fact, the New Zealand identity of the film itself was contested, partly because Campion at the time of production had been living in Sydney, Australia, and partly because the film was financially backed by the French company CIBY 2000. The New Zealand film journal *Onfilm* noted these facts but claimed 'Kiwi sensation' Campion as a New Zealander all the same, albeit of a certain bohemian type (Pryor 1993: 25). Former Australian Prime Minister Paul Keating had claimed Campion's film for *his* country, however, praising *The Piano* as 'another triumph for the Australian film industry' (cited in Burchall 1993: 17). Some commentators had placed *The Piano* primarily in the context of earlier Australian—rather than New Zealand—films, taking it as broadly 'antipodean'. Although she emphasizes *The Piano*'s Anglo-European literary precursors, Stella Bruzzi nevertheless positions it cinematically alongside Gillian Armstrong's 'Australasian' film *My Brilliant Career* (1979) and Peter Weir's *Picnic at Hanging Rock* (1975), both 'high quality' Australian period costume dramas. But she also internationalizes *The Piano* by discussing it in relation to Caryl Churchill's *Cloud Nine* (1979) and, in fact, she invokes a range of contemporary British and American films and novels throughout her discussion by way of further comparison, including A. S. Byatt's *Possession* (1989). Other critics extend this international framework of influence—in particular, citing other examples of 'literary cinema', as well as novels themselves. For the *New Statesman & Society*'s film critic Jonathan Romney, *The Piano* 'bears obvious comparison' with John Fowles's *The French Lieutenant's Woman* (1981) through its depiction of 'Victorian mores from the standpoint of twentieth-century irony' (Romney 1993: 33). Jan Epstein compares Ada's muteness in *The Piano* with Oskar in *The Tin Drum* (1979), 'who at the age of three stopped growing by an act of will' (Epstein 1993: 20). Bruzzi also mentions Sally Potter's *Orlando* (1992) and Christine Edzard's *Little Dorritt* (1987).

Australian novelist Helen Garner had regarded the plot of *The Piano* as 'so original and seductive that I can hardly resist' (Garner 1993: 32), disavowing influences from elsewhere altogether. Other commentators have seen not just influence, however, but derivation. For Richard Cummings, *The Piano* 'has its roots in the original Rudolph Valentino version of *The Sheik*, in which another white woman awakens her eroticism with a pseudo-Third World character' (Cummings 1994: 72). The New Zealand location of Campion's film disappears entirely under the broad sweep of this comparison: from 'antipodean' to 'Third World'. The colonial romantic drama, of course, is a well-established cinematic genre and it would be quite possible to talk down *The Piano*'s uniqueness—and specificity—by situat-

ing it in this context. Think, for example, of Ken Annakin's film *Nor the Moon By Night* (1958), which has a woman go out to a similarly rain-soaked, muddy Kenya to marry a man who is cool towards her, only to be attracted to the man's brother—who, like Baines, is coded as close to nature and speaks the Zulu language fluently. But perhaps New Zealand returns to *The Piano* through another, more localized example of the colonial romance. Jane Mander's *The Story of a New Zealand River* (1920) has probably been the least acknowledged of all the sources for Campion's otherwise 'original' film. This colonial romance—a minor novel in early twentieth-century New Zealand literary history which, incidentally, has no Maori characters in it at all—concerns Alice and her daughter, who travel up river to the North Auckland frontier to meet Alice's husband-to-be, Roland, an enterprising but cold-hearted forester. Alice, however, finds herself attracted to David Bruce, an altogether more compassionate man. There certainly are clear comparisons to be drawn between this novel and *The Piano* in the exacting framework of colonial romantic drama. Alice even brings a piano with her—but this is the focus only of the earlier part of Mander's novel, and is never given the kind of symbolic resonance it has in Campion's film. Campion's treatment of Ada's piano in fact works to lift the film out of the generic constraints of the colonial romantic drama, making it seem 'original' once more—and allowing a suitably 'literary' mode of criticism to flourish in relation to it.

READING *THE PIANO* (THE FILM)

The combination of a symbolically enriched piano and a mute, impassioned heroine enabled commentators to talk up the 'literary' features of Campion's film. *The Piano*'s metaphors were seen as always open and ambiguous, and necessarily so. For Vikki Riley, Campion's film manufactures 'an entire system of signs and symbols, a Manichean universe which must be interpreted as a synergy of separate, albeit ambiguous motifs and gestures . . . Campion delights in matching and mismatching the symmetrical and asymmetrical implications of its design principles' (Riley 1995: 62). This may be why Riley sees Campion's feminism as 'out of sync with . . . feminist debate in the English speaking world' and yet at the same time 'so refreshingly accurate' (Riley 1995: 63): somehow asymmetrical and symmetrical at the same time. For cultural critics Ruth Barcan and Madeleine Fogarty, *The Piano* actively prevents viewers from arriving at 'any "one" interpretation . . . rendering a final interpretation unperformable' (Barcan and Fogarty 1995: 28). These two critics trace some of the differences of opinion found in commentaries on the film, and attempt to 'deconstruct' them—asserting, finally and liberally, that *The Piano* 'validates a position of ambivalence' (Barcan and Fogarty 1995: 27).

Openness (to different interpretations) and ambivalence (where even polarized interpretations are each true in their own right) give Campion's film its special 'literary' qualities: like a novel, *The Piano*'s meanings seem unable to be reduced or closed off. Philip Bell makes exactly this point:

'the film', he says, 'resists . . . reductionist analysis through the integration of its various modes of story-telling and its rich *mise-en-scène*' (Bell 1995: 59). Bell is particularly keen not to reduce the piano itself to a symbol of 'the female unconscious' (Bell 1995: 59). Nevertheless, he is also compelled to invoke the explanatory force of French psychoanalytical theory, thus running the risk of being reductive in spite of himself: 'Without reducing this complex figure [the piano] to one psychoanalytically specific term, it might be seen as signifying what Kristeva calls the "semiotic" realm . . . of pre-oedipal subjectivity' (Bell 1995: 59). Kristeva's 'semiotic' becomes the master key to the meaning of the piano in the film, and, as Bell sees it, Ada's task as she bargains over the keys is to retain as much of this feminized 'pre-oedipal subjectivity' as she can under the pressures of a 'patriarchal' symbolic order. For Bell, Ada and her muteness come to stand for the predicament of all women, particularly the female film-goer:

> the 1990s women watching *The Piano* are once again constituted as a *movie* audience, a reminder that the meanings conveyed by the moving images on the big silver screen are more like those set in motion by the ontological flows of music than by the digital or discrete signs of realistic literary (verbal) forms. Such an experience is not easy for the audience to talk about. They therefore 'love' the movie without analysis or critique.
>
> (Bell 1995: 58)

Here Bell uses the predicament of 'literary cinema' to polarize—rather than entangle—the two terms in this partnership. He sets up a binary which in fact recovers the 'cinematic' at the expense of the 'literary', triggering off a string of unimpeachable oppositions: film and novel; visual and verbal; lyrical and realistic; feminine and (by implication) masculine; mute and analytical; the unconscious and the symbolic order. These binaries segregate the 'literary' and the 'cinematic' in ways not dissimilar to some earlier film theorists, such as Rudolf Arnheim in *Film as Art* (1957) and Siegfried Kracauer in *Theory of Film* (1960). Bell's representation of women in this passage (as film-goers, but unable to conceptualize, replacing analysis with 'love') is obviously patronizing. But at the same time he suggests, through the example of *The Piano,* that film is nevertheless something *more* than the novel, something that can transcend the kind of analysis that depends on or is constrained by words alone (a position represented in the film itself by Ada's husband Stewart). Helen Garner agrees, seeing Campion's film as unleashing an 'unconscious' which, by its very nature, would seem to resist the closure of analytical literary criticism: 'to talk narrative would allow me a luxury that is denied to reviewers but which all Campion's work urges us towards—holding back as long as possible from analysis, letting the film's imagery work on us privately; as Jung would say, "letting the unconscious take precedence"' (Garner 1993: 32). In this sense, then, *The Piano* is something more than 'literary cinema' itself: it transcends even this particular genre.

The turn away from analysis is seen positively here, as if the film exceeds verbal critique to take its viewers into the realm of ecstasy. But a subsequent 'backlash' against Campion's film showed that analysis could be withdrawn for quite different reasons: because the film's symbols and metaphors weighed so heavy upon it as to render *The Piano* virtually unreadable (see, for example, Grimes and Barber 1994: 3; Martin 1994: 14). Film critic John Slavin gave perhaps the most considered account of the film in these terms. For Slavin, Campion's foregrounding of the 'subconscious' of her heroines means that she forgoes 'the requirements of coherent narrative in favour of a paradigm of isolated and exaggerated signifiers' (Slavin 1993: 28). Slavin's main objection is that the piano is simply unable to carry the kind of symbolic weight it seems burdened with. The implication that it represents Ada's 'voice' and 'independence', for example, does not properly explain why she so quickly acquiesces to Baines' 'improper suggestions', giving herself and her piano over to him (Slavin 1993: 30). Slavin, however, recognizes that he is showing a preference for what Bell had disparagingly called 'realistic literary . . . forms':

> It may be argued that in contrasting narrative and symbolic constructions in the film I'm judging it as though it is a literary text, that what I'm presenting is once again a case for the long playing debate of naturalistic depiction against the symbolic/geometric of which modernism has been such an energetic exemplar.
>
> It is certainly true that there is a prevailing philosophy in our film schools of 'Show, don't tell!', that is, of the striking visual moment as superior to the written or spoken word. . . .
>
> I have no argument with a cinema of signs. In such a cinema the symbolic brings order to the imaginary and in the process aestheticises it. Signs, however . . . emerge out of the organic/dramatic nature of the narrative text and that text is the negotiating agent between them and their socio-political context.
>
> (Slavin 1993: 30)

We have already seen critics valorizing the 'Show, don't tell!' approach in *The Piano*—which makes it seem more literary than literature in its privileging of the symbolic over the verbal. Slavin, however, requires a restrained, monogamous relationship between the two, where symbols bring 'order' to the 'imaginary' (in which case, the 'unconscious' is now much *less* 'unfettered') and are themselves entirely compatible with the verbal/narrative. In Campion's film, however, the 'striking image dominates the *mise en scène,* the dramatic development' (Slavin 1993: 30); it is excessive rather than restrained and compatible, promiscuous rather than monogamous. 'Her symbols', Slavin concludes, 'are hysterical high points of a subtext turned inside out' (Slavin 1993: 30).

READING *THE PIANO* (THE NOVEL)

Slavin's commentary sees *The Piano* negatively, as too symbolic, too metaphorical. It is a film that destabilizes, rather than transcends, the otherwise monogamous partnership between terms in the genre of 'literary cinema'. Other critics, however, such as Bell, Riley and Garner, see this same feature as a positive thing, a mark of *The Piano*'s distinctly 'cinematic' or hyper-literary character. No matter which critical view prevails, the subsequent novel-of-the-film could only be seen in the wake of all this as *lacking*. The novel of *The Piano* certainly seems to provide the kind of monogamous, settled relationship between word and image that Slavin yearns for. It has a primarily explanatory project, filling out the missing histories of various characters (Ada in particular) and accounting for how they came to be as they are. Its task is, in fact, to make the film more coherent. In this sense, the novel can be seen as restricting the film's imaginative scope. Interestingly, Campion's co-author Kate Pullinger laid part of the blame for this on Campion herself, who had written two initial chapters: 'She [Pullinger] was . . . restrained by Campion's first chapters, which covered Ada's motherlessness, her father's decaying estate, her life until the age of sixteen and her music teacher—and restrained again by her willingness to fax pages to Campion for amending, then picking up with the details as Campion saw them . . .' (Field 1994: 8). This sense that the novel is 'restrained' in relation to the film is consistent with those earlier readings which had seen the film as excessive, as open and ambiguous. 'Everything in the film is much more open to interpretation,' Pullinger says. 'For instance, a lot of people who have seen the film think that Ada was married before, because the evidence in the film which says she wasn't is so easy to miss' (Field 1994: 8). Her interviewer, Michelle Field, agrees, and as a consequence is also unable to see the novel's project in positive terms (Field 1994: 8).

These perspectives help to fix the novel-of the-film in a secondary, slighter role as something less than the film. The novel's project is first and foremost to explain rather than to allow the imagination a free, 'unfettered' rein: not 'Show, don't tell!' but 'Tell, don't show!' It thus completes a film which had valorized incompleteness, and in doing so it runs the risk of saying *too much*. In this sense, of course, the novel is not restrained at all; it, too, has its own mode of excess, performing the sort of explanations that some of the commentators cited above had wilfully foregone in relation to the film.

The novel-of-the-film certainly makes the symbolic role of the piano clearer—and in the process reveals a theme which it shares with the film, and which speaks directly to the characteristics of Campion's kind of 'literary cinema'. In her earlier life as a child (which the novel details) the piano comes to stand for Ada's mother, and her attachment to it is pre-Oedipal: 'as she played Ada conjured a soft, warm figure composed of music and polished wood and called it "Cecilia"' (Campion and Pullinger 1994: 35). Her music teacher, Delwar, seems to underwrite this attachment with his own playing, which transports Ada 'into another world where everything had the texture of silk and all was warmth and small rooms made cozy by hearthfires at night' (Campion and Pullinger 1994: 171). Their rela-

tionship is more erotic than disciplinary—so much so, that their sex flows naturally from a duet they play together. More importantly, the piano helps them fit 'naturally' together, sharing the same 'rhythm' (Campion and Pullinger 1994: 171), as if the pre-Oedipal attachment to the piano is not disturbed by Delwar, with Ada retaining the autonomy it had given to her. Playing the piano, then, is linked to pleasure, even ecstasy, and this in turn is linked to an image of the autonomous self and an 'unfettered' unconscious. The unconscious is privileged, in other words, while the disciplinary role—which requires restraint, learning, culture, work and *someone defined as other to you*—is given a greatly reduced significance.

In New Zealand, however, this relationship is traumatically unsettled. Ada's daughter, Flora, already sees the piano in a disciplinary way, refusing to practice (Campion and Pullinger 1994: 148); her betrayal of Ada may very well follow on from this refusal. When he purchases the piano, Baines asks Ada to teach him how to play, placing *her* in a disciplinary position and so compromising her autonomy. The piano recovers its unconscious, pre-Oedipal character, however, when their relationship becomes sexual: 'George Baines was not her husband; now he was no longer her pupil either' (Campion and Pullinger 1994: 146). Yet the unconscious/discipline binary does not fully separate itself out here. Rather, it becomes entangled. During the sex with Baines, Ada feels 'lost to the world' (Campion and Pullinger 1994: 151), still pleasured and playful and in the realm of the unconscious. Yet negotiating with Baines for the piano keys (she only ever partially recovers her piano) and learning more about sex from him at the same time, Ada is also aware that her body is 'no longer her own' (Campion and Pullinger 1994: 150). The novel both knows this and occasionally forgets it: sometimes the piano-as-Baines *is* associated only with pleasure, play and the 'unfettered' unconscious. By contrast, Stewart, Ada's husband, is associated with the denial or suppression of pleasure: with organization, work and production, with discipline and its virtues. (Like Ada, the Maori in the novel and the film are seen as 'naturally' unproductive.) When he punishes Ada and Flora by locking them inside his house, the novel tells us: 'Stewart had decided to teach Ada a lesson' (Campion and Pullinger 1994: 161). Lessons/work are seen here as restricting, restraining; pleasure is seen in contrast to this, as excessive and unrestrained and therefore always potentially compromised. Ada is a character, then, who tries to recover as much pleasure as she can. But the novel, like the film, stops short of presenting her as utterly unrealistic by putting her in a relationship which requires her to negotiate for her pleasure, to see pleasure-as-excess (improvisation, autonomy) always in a dialectical relationship with work-as-restraint (learning lessons under the guidance of others: negotiating and bargaining, rather than being autonomous and 'unfettered').

So the novel presents us with a sense of the unconscious/pleasure not as 'unfettered' at all, but as always potentially compromised, always coming up against its own limits.

The piano might well signify this anyway: the heaviness of the instrument keeps it on the beach for a time, and people literally have to work together to get it up the cliff and into the house. This is one of the few 'material' moments in the film, when the work of others is shown as the means to a pleasurable end for the piano's owner, when the 'unfettered' imagination is seen to depend upon organized labour. The piano thus has both a symbolic force and a material presence: it produces pleasure for Ada, but it is also—albeit reluctantly in this context—there to be worked upon, negotiated over, transacted, compromised, the subject of deals and directions with and by other people, autonomous and yet commercial.

Its role, in fact, speaks directly to the location of the film itself in what Pierre Bourdieu has called 'the field of cultural production'—which may well explain why the film takes the piano for its title (Bourdieu 1993). *The Piano* was the first of Campion's feature films to achieve substantial commercial support, thanks to the work of her producer, Jan Chapman—a 'tough negotiator' who managed to secure an 'extraordinary deal from CIBY 2000' (Connolly 1993: 7). But *The Piano* is also an 'arthouse' piece of literary cinema which would otherwise wish to distance itself from the compromises built into commercial deal-making. Campion has accounted for her own filmmaking history in this way: 'My first idea of cinema wasn't commercial cinema, it was personal-expression cinema. I still like to think that the two aren't mutually exclusive—and I hope that *The Piano* proves that' (Connolly 1993: 7). These comments polarize the commercial and the arthouse/personal at the same time as trying to reconcile them: as if they, too, can live monogamously with one another. In the interview in *Onfilm,* Campion represents CIBY 2000 as a commercial venture which has, in spite of itself, come to recognize and privilege the value of arthouse cinema:

> I think the curious thing about CIBY 2000 is that it's really a vision of one man, Frances Bouygues. . . . His years on earth were numbered and he wanted to leave a sort of tribute . . . he chose to do that through alternative cinema, art cinema. What I love about it is he actually loves art. You've got so much money, what are you going to do with it? I think in the end the thing that meant something was to have his heart moved, his soul, his spirit.
>
> (Pryor 1993: 25)

This sentimental account of the other party in Jan Chapman's 'extraordinary deal' puts a corporate backer in a role which is even more idealized than Ada's in Campion's film: as someone who actually *does* recover the kind of 'unfettered' pleasure or ecstasy associated with playing (or in his case, paying for) the piano. Indeed, in the context of women making deals with men, CIBY 2000's French representative is comparable not so much with Baines in *The Piano* as with Delwar (who is only in the novel-of-the-film); he certainly does not resemble Stewart, apparently having no repressive or constraining function at all as far as film production is concerned. Campion and her financial backers, in other words, fit together in terms

of their position in the cultural field as smoothly as Ada and Delwar as they play their duet together. But we should remember that this duet was a pre-Oedipal moment in the novel-of-the-film which later events undermine. Campion's happy synthesis of commercial transactions and the 'spiritual' world of art is not unlike her earlier blending of the atmospherics of *Wuthering Heights* and New Zealand: two incommensurable places are yoked together. But it relies on a disavowal of commercial pressures. In another interview, Campion proclaims: 'I'm not really trying to sell myself. . . . I don't need to sell myself, I've got work' (Schembri 1993: 13). The interviewer wonders if those pressures help to make her film more 'conventional' than it might have been:

> Under fire, she slips into arrogance. So suggesting that Campion opted for a more conventional shooting style in *The Piano* compared with her previous films, for instance, draws a duly liberal, if slightly uncomfortable, response. 'I don't agree with you at all about that. I don't think this is conventional at all.'
>
> (Schembri 1993: 13)

This disavowal of one of the consequences of commercial negotiation in film production—selling one's self, 'selling out'—helps Campion retain an image of *The Piano* as an autonomous and 'unfettered' form of 'personal expression'. Such an image no doubt assists in the identification of the film as 'literary cinema', even though it was never actually adapted from a novel, and it also allows *The Piano* to be received through a mode of literary criticism which valorizes these qualities. This is in spite of the fact that the ethics of 'selling out' or compromising one's self is the central theme of Campion's film, a point which the Australian critic Kerryn Goldsworthy registers with something close to horror:

> But what seems to me to be the inescapable moral of this movie is that a gifted woman must pay with her gift for true love. And the idea of the spectacularly gifted Jane Campion's beautiful and inspired film conveying this message makes my hair stand on end.
>
> (Goldsworthy 1993: 47)

We have seen a set of critical responses to *The Piano* that, in their privileging of the unconscious, of metaphor, of the imagination, displace the role of commercial transactions in the film—or, as in the last example, mention it only in order apparently to wish it wasn't there. For so many commentators, *The Piano* comes to stand for 'literary cinema' in its purest form: so pure, in fact, that the cinema is the only place for it. Any other place, including the place of commentary and criticism, seriously 'reduces' *The Piano*'s force. So the production of the novel-of-the-film becomes a kind of abject event—in which case, it may not be surprising to hear Kate Pullinger rebelliously admit 'that while I was writing it, I had this other version in my head which I called *The Anti-Piano*' (Field 1994: 8). Here the novel and the novel-of-the-film are coded as opposites: one is appropriate to the field of literature, while the other is inappropriate. This is because, in this case at least, the movement from film to novel is seen as regressive, as a debasement—not entirely unlike the movement from film to video. Indeed, for Philip Bell *The Piano* is precisely a film made to 'be seen at the theatre, not on the video', as if its cinematic location simply cannot be transgressed. This, he says, is because the film 'needs a space of black, or silence, as a zone to ward off the world which clatters and hums outside . . .' (Bell 1995: 60). In this account, *The Piano* must remain cinematic so that its autonomy is never compromised; it must remain sealed off in some kind of pre-Oedipal dark space, utterly separate from those other forms (the novel-of-the-film, the video of the film, the outside world 'which clatters and hums', analytical commentary) which seem to refuse to allow it to be what it is.

The Making of a Literary Adaptation

In Jane Campion's 1996 adaptation of Henry James's *The Portrait of a Lady,* autonomy—as something both desirable and impossible—turns out to be a central theme. Isabel is a heroine who wishes for independence and yet finds her independence increasingly compromised as she goes along. This theme may carry over into the adaptation itself, which begins by announcing its own independence from James's novel through an apparently unrelated prologue which presents a number of young Australian women talking about 'the kiss'. For Lee Marshall, the prologue immediately secures the film's autonomy from its literary source: 'this is a film which renders the debate about faithfulness to the source text irrelevant. . . . This is clear from the title sequence, which features a group of Aussie girls discussing love' (Marshall 1997: 9). Lizzie Franke, in her article on the film in *Sight and Sound,* initially sees Campion's prologue in the same way: 'The opening few minutes of Jane Campion's *The Portrait of a Lady* are sublimely designed to disorientate any viewer corseted into certain expectations of the literary-adaptation piece' (Franke 1996: 6). Identifying with the Australian girls, however, Franke goes on to recall her own teenage years and, as a consequence, recovers the literary tradition the film seemed at first to have disavowed: 'For those were the years when we started cramming our heads with ideas and aspirations, reading Austen, George Eliot, the Brontës, James and others' (Franke 1996: 6). An otherwise 'disorienting' scene that was initially viewed as independent of James's novel thus comes to evoke a field of great literary precursors (including James himself), in relation to which Campion's literary adaptation is then more properly and respectfully located. With *The Piano*, the issue was one of cinematic uniqueness, as if this work of 'literary cinema' is—in spite of its own literary genealogies—nothing other than cinematic. But even the scene that is most 'irrelevant' to James's novel in Campion's *The Portrait of a Lady* reminds Franke that this work of 'literary cinema' remains literary first and foremost.

How independent—how autonomous—can a work of 'literary cinema' hope to be? Of course, if the literary source remains unread, then from a film-goer's point of view the cinematic adaptation is all there is. Campion herself has noted that only '[o]ne in 10,000 people reads the novel, and of those who read it, many don't bother finishing it' (Campion 1997: 72). From this directorial perspective, the novel is 'finished' by the film itself, as if the adaptation somehow completes or even replaces James's own work—giving us quite the opposite relationship to the one we had seen with the film and novel of *The Piano*. Philip Horne, on the other hand, tries to recover the authority of Campion's literary source by seeing her adaptation as much *less* independent from Henry James, the Australian prologue notwithstanding. In particular, he notes that the dialogue in the film is often lifted wholesale from James's original novel (Horne 1997: 20). For Horne, Henry James sets up the terms of judgement for an adaptation of his own novel: Campion's film could not be any less autonomous from its source than this! Brian McFarlane also restricts the scope of the adaptation, regarding the prologue in Campion's film as 'downright silly', complaining about 'some artfully or pointlessly angled shots' and arguing overall that the 'film is at its least impressive when it seems most earnestly straining to be "cinematic"' (McFarlane 1997: 37). This last remark re-opens the binary implicit in the otherwise monogamous partnership of 'literary cinema', disparaging the latter term and in the process curtailing an adaptation's ability to secure at least some kind of independence from its source. In *Novel to Film* (1996), McFarlane discusses the film adaptations of five classic novels, including Peter Bogdanovich's 1974 adaptation of Henry James's novella *Daisy Miller* (1878). His emphasis is on an adaptation's faithfulness to the narrational mode of the literary source, the criteria for which in this case are again laid out by Henry James himself: 'By this, I mean the Jamesian device, variously described by the author and his critics as the use of a "centre of consciousness"' (McFarlane 1996: 139). At the same time, McFarlane recognizes that in cinema a character's inner turmoil 'is also . . . shown rather than told'. We return here to the question of a proper relationship between literature and cinema—proper enough to keep the 'literary cinema' partnership faithful and monogamous. For McFarlane, the slide toward a 'cinematic' independence from the source novel is the thing that most unsettles the properness of this partnership: 'The problem', he concludes, 'lies in deciding what exactly is being shown' (McFarlane 1996: 139). This is, indeed, the problem: an undecidability inhabiting the relationship between literature and cinema which enables the latter to be faithful and independent, monogamous and promiscuous, restricted or compromised by the source novel, and yet 'separate' or autonomous from it, all at the same time.

As I have noted, the theme of autonomy—as desirable and yet impossible—is central to Campion's adaptation of *The Portrait of a Lady*. The heroine, Isabel, wants to be able to 'do what she likes', to travel broadly and take 'chances', and she is encouraged along these lines by the small fortune provided by her generous benefactor, Ralph Touchett. We might observe in passing just how Touchett's relationship to Isabel recalls Frances Bouygues' relationship to Campion—as a benign corporate backer 'who wanted to leave a sort of tribute' which works inevitably to produce Campion, as Ralph does with Isabel, as a transnational. A new introduction by Regina Barreca to the 1997 Penguin film tie-in edition of James's novel talks up Isabel's autonomy in order to characterize her as a new heroine for the 1990s: 'At the end of the novel', Barreca says, over-enthusiastically, 'Isabel Archer is free' (James 1997: xv). Scholarly articles on Henry James and his heroine, perhaps not surprisingly, offer a more restrained view: Debra MacComb sees Isabel Archer as someone who negotiates her space within the framework of a partnership (MacComb 1996), while Jessica Berman takes the Jamesian woman as someone who, like America itself at the time, needed to 'temper its tendency to individuality' in relation to others (Berman 1996: 73). Campion's film certainly remains faithful to this particular theme, showing Isabel to be continually compromised by her various relationships with men, Gilbert Osmond in particular. Yet faithfulness itself is rendered unstable in the film, with Isabel imagining the possibility of being promiscuous (as in the dream-sequence where she is fondled by all her admirers) even as she acknowledges the restrictions that marriage to Osmond imposes upon her.

A certain kind of female masochism works itself out through this tension, as Mark Nicholls has noted in an article entitled 'She Who Gets Slapped'—where he also seems to suggest that Campion relishes the fact that Isabel's yearnings for independence remain unsatisfied (Nicholls 1997: 43-7). But another approach to this theme may be taken by turning back to available distinctions in the field of cultural production. Campion's film is also all about 'taste': it sets up a binary between tastes which are open, and tastes which are closed or restricted. The aesthete Gilbert Osmond cultivates the latter, as Ralph tells Isabel: 'I should have said that the man for you would have had a more active, larger, freer sort of nature. . . . I can't get over the sense that Osmond is somehow—well, small . . . I think he's narrow. . . . He's the incarnation of taste' (Jones 1996: 63). Isabel, however, thinks that Osmond's tastes are 'large' and 'exquisite' (Jones 1996: 64). The film shows her to be quite deluded about Osmond's highly refined tastes, while at the same time it suggests that Isabel is drawn to them precisely because they *are* so 'narrow' (which is where her 'masochism' really lies). The film thus sets up a predicament for its heroine that shows her openness and independence to be compromised by tastes that, although 'exquisite' and attractive to her, nevertheless work to restrict her freedom and compel her faithfulness. In other words, the film speaks about its *own* predicament as a literary adaptation. This is recognized in the partnership built into the generic term 'literary cinema', which articulates the sense that one is drawn to a form of cultural production that is itself restricted in terms of circulation ('One in 10,000 people . . .') but which requires one to cultivate a certain faithfulness or respect towards it—and yet, because cinema exerts its own influences and can have a much broader circulation than the literary source anyway, a certain kind of openness or unfaithfulness (or even a kind of promiscuity) is achieved at the

same time. Literary cinema may thus very well be in Isabel's words both 'exquisite' and 'large', as if there is no contradiction between these two features. It is a cross-over form of cultural production in this respect, negotiating a space for itself between the restricted circulation of the literary source and something altogether much broader or 'mainstream'. We can return to Pierre Bourdieu here, noting—as Bridget Fowler does in her book *Pierre Bourdieu and Cultural Theory* (1997)—his unimpeachable opposition between aesthetic taste on the one hand, and popular taste (the 'popular aesthetic') on the other (Fowler 1997: 160). Elsewhere, Simon During has talked about what he calls the 'global popular', mostly referring to the movie blockbuster form which is 'distributed and apparently enjoyed everywhere' (During 1997: 808). We have seen that *The Piano* was also a transnational film, and so is *The Portrait of a Lady,* yet their global popularity is tempered by their generic identification as 'literary cinema' and their association with 'narrow' or 'exquisite'—or literary—tastes. Perhaps we can mutate During's term accordingly, by seeing literary cinema as an example of what might in this case be called the 'restricted (global) popular'.

Nicholas Zurbrugg (essay date 1999)

SOURCE: Zurbrugg, Nicholas. "Will Hollywood Never Learn?: David Cronenberg's *Naked Lunch.*" In *Adaptations: From Text to Screen, Screen to Text*, edited by Deborah Cartmell and Imelda Whelehan, pp. 98-112. London: Routledge, 1999.

[*In the following essay, Zurbrugg presents a critical analysis of David Cronenberg's adaptation of* Naked Lunch *by William Burroughs, theorizing that the film was a successful rendition of the text because of the collaborative nature of Burroughs and Cronenberg's relationship.*]

> My nephew . . . was not an author. . . . Very few of those employed in writing motion picture dialogue are. The executives of the studios just haul in anyone they meet and make them sign contracts. Most of the mysterious disappearances you read about are due to this cause. Only the other day they found a plumber who had been missing for years. All the time he had been writing dialogue for the Mishkin Brothers. Once having reached Los Angeles, nobody is safe.
>
> (Wodehouse [1935] 1954: 236-7)

> If you go to Hollywood. . . . And if you really believe in the art of the film . . . you ought to forget about any other kind of writing. A preoccupation with words for their own sake is fatal to good film making. It's not what films are for. . . . The best scenes I ever wrote were practically monosyllabic. And the best short scene I ever wrote . . . was one in which the girl said 'uh huh' three times with three different intonations, and that's all there was to it.
>
> (Chandler, in Gardiner and Walker 1984: 138)

> For God's sake Bill, play ball with this conspiracy.
>
> (*Naked Lunch*, 1993)

Like P. G. Wodehouse and Raymond Chandler, William Burroughs has long anticipated the worst from mainstream cinematic adaptations. Writing to the painter Brion Gysin in a letter of 24 May 1977, for example, he memorably complains: 'What can happen to your script is not to be believed. It's like you came back from Istanbul and there was a Dali bent watch right in the middle of your picture. You write a part for James Coburn and you wind up with Liberace' (Morgan 1988: 541).

One way or another, Burroughs suggests, Hollywood invariably imposes the kind of pseudo-surreal effects that the French cultural theorist Paul Virilio equates with 'the poverty of the trivial dream, which is so curiously lacking in variety and imagination that the representation of our desires becomes a load of drivel, with endless repetitions of a few limited themes'. For Virilio, the same can be said for both 'digital imagery' in particular, 'which merely imitates the special effects and tricks of old 3D cinema' (Virilio [1993] 1995: 71), and for the accelerated pace of media culture in general, which in his terms ruins 'the pause of luminous contemplation' and exhausts 'the fragile sphere of our dreams' (Virilio [1993] 1995: 70-1).

As his notes on the American multimedia performance artist Robert Wilson's 'visionary' capacity to present 'beautiful life-saving dream images' indicate, Burroughs regards dreams as both a poetic necessity, circumventing 'the crippling conventions of dramatic presentation' and 'soap opera plots', and quite literally as 'a *biological necessity*' (Burroughs 1991: 17). In this respect, Burroughs—like Virilio and Wilson—is best understood as an ecologist of the dream, striving to remedy what Walter Benjamin calls 'the shock effect of the film' by identifying multimediated forms of 'heightened presence of mind' and re-establishing 'time for contemplation and evaluation' (Benjamin [1936] 1970: 240).

Likewise, as the subtitle of *Nova Express*—demanding 'WILL HOLLYWOOD NEVER LEARN?' (Burroughs 1966: 70)—suggests, Burroughs seems to have little sympathy for the mass-cultural banality of what he thinks of as the American 'non-dream'. So far as Burroughs is concerned:

> America is not so much a nightmare as a *non-dream*. The American non-dream is precisely a move to wipe the dream out of existence. The dream is a spontaneous happening and therefore dangerous to a control system set up by the non-dreamers.
>
> (Burroughs [1969] 1974: 102)

Paradoxically perhaps, some quarter century after the French edition of *The Job* first published this warning, the independent Canadian film-maker David Cronenberg met Burroughs for the first time in New York and initiated a project to film Burroughs' supposedly 'unfilmable' anti-novel, *The Naked Lunch* (1959), for mass-market distribution, and against all odds, to endorse Burroughs' prodigal career with the seal of Hollywood approval.

Cronenberg carefully defines his plans for *Naked Lunch* (1993) as the attempt to create 'a combination of Burroughsian material but put into a structure that's not very Burroughsian'. Such an adaptation, Cronenberg contends, 'still deserves to be called *Naked Lunch*' by virtue of "accurately reflecting some of the tone of Burroughs, what his life stands for, and what his work has been"' (Emery and Silverberg in Silverberg 1992: 65). For his part, Burroughs affirmed that Cronenberg's script offered 'a good example of the cinematic license the film-maker takes . . . to realize his vision on film' (Burroughs 1992b: 14-5).

Significantly though, far from considering Cronenberg's film to have anything of the interactive quality of his early 1960s cut-up experiments in the Beat Hotel with Brion Gysin, Harold Norse and Ian Somerville, when they 'held constant meetings and conferences with exchange of ideas and comparison of cut-up writing, painting and tape-recorder experiments' (Burroughs 1983: Introduction), Burroughs clearly regarded Cronenberg's film as 'a profoundly personal interpretation' rather than any kind of collaboration, stipulating that he 'had no writing input into the script whatsoever, and only courtesy rights to request any changes, which I didn't' (Burroughs 1992b: 15).

Cronenberg, by contrast, relates how he felt 'forced to . . . fuse my own sensibility with Burroughs and create a third thing that neither he nor I would have done on his own' (Cronenberg 1997: 162); at once confirming Burroughs' dictum that: 'No two minds ever come together without, thereby, creating . . . a third mind' (Burroughs 1979: 25), and partially fulfilling Burroughs' dream of 'taking over a young body' in 'an experiment of transference which would be of benefit to both of us, perhaps of incalculable benefit, but in all fairness not without danger' (Burroughs 1974: 28-9).

What are the advantages and disadvantages of a cinematic adaptation that foregrounds 'the tone' of a writer, what their life 'stands for' and what their 'work has been'? And what are the most obvious benefits or dangers of placing literary 'material' within a structure that's 'not very' typical of its author? In Burroughs' case, such questions are best considered in terms of the significant differences in 'tone' between Cronenberg's highly personal but in many ways predominantly mainstream cinematic adaptation of *Naked Lunch,* the more dynamic collaborative register of earlier adaptations of Burroughs' writings such as Antony Balch's underground classics *Towers Open Fire* (1963) and *The Cut-Ups* (1967), and such subsequent increasingly 'overground' ventures as Howard Brookner's *Burroughs: The Movie* (1983), Gus Van Sant's *Drugstore Cowboy* (1989), and Robert Wilson, Tom Waits and Burroughs' collaborative opera, *The Black Rider* (1990).

But what does it mean to 'adapt' a novel for the screen? And what, after all, is a novel? Such questions seem best approached by comparing Burroughs' and Cronenberg's writings and observations about text/screen adaptation. Burroughs dismisses soap opera as being 'not—sort of—

even *below* lowbrow' (Burroughs 1990: 47), and speculates that 'if you have a film that has, oh say, ten good minutes in it' that's 'a pretty good film', '[a] *very* good film, actually. You can't expect much more' (Burroughs 1990: 45). He generally concedes, however, that most novels lend themselves to certain 'old, old' formulas.

> Take any novel that you like, and think about making a film out of that novel. Or say in one sentence what this book is about. 'What is *Lord Jim* about?' . . . Two sentences, 'Honour lost. Honour regained.'
>
> (Burroughs 1990: 43)

But as he equally readily emphasizes, 'some novels won't break down like that', and even if they do, 'just because you can get a novel into one sentence doesn't mean you can make a film out of it'.

> You can get *The Great Gatsby* into a couple of sentences, but you can't make a film out of it. What is this about? 'Poor boy loses girl. Poor boy tries to get girl back, which results in tragedy.' 'Poor boy loses girl to rich man, and tries to get her back. Does get her back for a brief interlude, and then there is a tragic dénouement, because he's trying something that isn't going to work—he's trying to put back the clock.' But this isn't film material.
>
> (Burroughs 1990: 43)

And why isn't this 'film material'? Because—for Burroughs at least—the impact of *The Great Gatsby* arises not so much from its plot as from what Barthes defines as the 'grain' of the text, or what Chandler equates with a 'particular preoccupation with words for their own sake' (in Gardiner and Walker 1984: 138). 'It's all in the prose, in Fitzgerald's prose. That's where Gatsby exists', Burroughs concludes, and nothing but nothing, can translate this into film:

> Well, you remember the end of *The Great Gatsby,* that's one of the famous scenes in English prose, like the end of 'The Dead' by James Joyce, the famous 'snow falling faintly—like the descent of their last end, upon all the living and the dead'. There's no way that you can put that effectively into film. I mean, you can show snow, but what does that mean? It doesn't mean anything. And the same way with the end of *The Great Gatsby*. And all they could do was a voice-over.
>
> (Burroughs 1990: 43)

While Burroughs insists that film cannot do language's job more effectively, he acknowledges that words are equally powerless to emulate such cinematic effects as the *trompe-l'oeil* montages in Antony Balch's film *Bill and Tony* (1972). Here—in a 'little experiment' in 'face-projection', 'intended to be projected onto the faces of its cast'—Balch and Burroughs 'are seen first independently, then side-by-side, introducing themselves (as each other) and then speaking short texts', before dubbing each other's voices in the otherwise identical 'second half' (Balch 1972: 12). Even a summary of *Bill and Tony* becomes daunting, and

as Burroughs concludes: 'there's no way you could put that on the printed page' (Burroughs 1990: 43).

Contending that '[w]hen someone says, "Well, the film didn't do justice to the book", or vice versa, they're talking about things which aren't the same medium', generally observing that whenever 'Hollywood gets hold of something that's a classic . . . the results are usually terrible' and speculating that 'films made from quite mediocre books' usually 'make the best films', Burroughs concludes that '[t]he film must stand up as a separate piece of work, quite apart from the book' (Burroughs 1990: 43-5), resting his case upon the precedent of *Chandler* v. *Hollywood*.

> Raymond Chandler was once asked, 'How do you feel about what Hollywood has done to your novels?' He reportedly answered, 'My novels? Why, Hollywood hasn't done anything to them. They're still right there, on the shelf.'
>
> (Burroughs 1992a: xv)

But as Chandler indicates, Hollywood certainly does do things to novels, not least by contorting verbal complexity into what Beckett dismisses as the 'sweet reasonableness of plane psychology à la Balzac' (Beckett 1934: 976). Or as Homer Mandrill puts it in Burroughs' *Exterminator!*, Hollywood poetics (like redneck politics) compulsively turns the clock back 'to 1899 when a silver dollar bought a steak dinner and good piece of ass' (Burroughs 1974: 106), and—one might add—when a silver dollar also bought a good, no-nonsense read, rather than what P. G. Wodehouse memorably calls 'those psychological modern novels where the hero's soul gets all tied up in knots as early as page 21 and never straightens itself out again' (Wodehouse [1935] 1954: 246).

As the author of convoluted anti-narrative which 'actually caused at least one unprepared square to vomit on the carpet' (Nuttall [1968] 1970: 108), Burroughs very reasonably warns that '[i]t is probably an understatement to say that the novel does not obviously lend itself to adaptation for the screen' (Burroughs 1992a: xiii). In turn, as the ill-fated adapter of a 'mother of epics' into which he felt he could at best 'dip', rather than read 'from start to finish', Cronenberg determined 'to be absolutely ruthless when it came to using Burroughs' material' (Silverberg 1992: 161-2):

> I started to think about what I didn't want to do with *Naked Lunch*. I didn't want it to be a movie about drugs . . . I wanted it to be about writing . . . I wanted the movie to have characters . . . I wanted a woman to have an important character . . . I wanted it to have narrative cohesiveness.
>
> (Cronenberg, in Silverberg 1992: 164-5)

At the same time, Cronenberg's 'wants' list admits a number of symbolic exceptions. Following his early sense 'that drugs were for jazz musicians' (Silverberg 1992: 164), Cronenberg sets the scene for *Naked Lunch* with 'meandering alto sax notes from Ornette Coleman, gracing the highly stylized graphic design of the opening credits' (Conomos 1992: 16). Thereafter Cronenberg evokes addiction increasingly indirectly in terms of alien invasion imagery, as 'a metaphor for control'. 'I understood the metaphorical side. That's what I responded to' (Silverberg 1992: 164).

But Burroughs' vision is as much about low-life as hi-sci-fi life, and one neglects Burroughs' more or less direct evocations of the 'junk-sick dawn' at one's peril. As the virtuosity of *Naked Lunch*'s early pages suggests, Burroughs is at once the Balzac, the Baudelaire and the Ballard of New York's underworld, confidently charting its sordid, spectral or stomach-turning detail in narrative hovering between dispassionate restraint and paranoid anxiety, and generally anticipating the alacrity with which his later 'routines' evince 'simultaneous insight and hallucination', as 'three-dimensional fact merges into dream, and dreams erupt into the real world' (Burroughs 1993: 243, 300).

While Cronenberg's evocation of addiction in terms of the mechanized, fluid-emitting Mugwump offering 'the teat on its head to addicts eager to partake of its irresistible substance' (Duncan, in Silverberg 1992: 94-6) certainly suggests the presence of alien creatures in the real world, the prospect of his plastic monsters in a vaulted, Hammer style 'Mugwump dispensary' (Duncan, in Silverberg 1992: 96) smacks of the world of Dr Who rather than of Dr Benway. Cronenberg accurately observes that there is 'a lot of hi-sci-fi and horror imagery in Burroughs', particularly the 'Mugwumps, and all kinds of creatures' (Cronenberg, in Silverberg 1992: 166). But as a glance at *Naked Lunch* indicates, most of Burroughs' creatures are not so much exotic 'hi-sci-fi' mutants as vagrant 'terrestrial dogs' (Burroughs 1966: 18). Alienated both at home and abroad, these are quintessentially flesh-and-blood aliens, whether clinically described in terms of the kind of 'real scene' in which 'you pinch up some leg flesh and make a quick stab hole with a pin', before fitting the dropper 'over, not in the hole and feed the solution slow and careful so it doesn't squirt out the sides', or whether self-consciously caricatured in such 'pin and dropper' routines as:

> She seized a safety-pin caked with blood and rust, gouged a great hole in her leg which seemed to hang open like an obscene, festering mouth waiting for unspeakable congress with the dropper which she now plunged out of sight into the gaping wound.
>
> (Burroughs [1959] 1982: 20)

Occasionally, to be sure, Burroughs' world rocks to the 'Monster Mash', as mutants like Bradley the Buyer spread terror 'throughout the industry':

> Junkies and agents disappear. Like a vampire bat he gives off a narcotic effluvium, a dank green mist that anesthetizes his victims and renders them helpless in his enveloping presence. . . . Finally he is caught in the act of digesting the Narcotics Commissioner and destroyed with a flame thrower—the court of inquiry ruling that such means were justified in that the Buyer

had lost his citizenship and was, in consequence, a creature without species and a menace to the narcotics industry on all levels.

> (Burroughs [1959] 1982: 27)

But usually Burroughs depicts business as usual. Blandly concluding: 'Isn't life peculiar?' (Burroughs [1959] 1982: 15), he catalogues an underworld populated by such everyday grotesques as Willy the Disk, 'blind from shooting in the eyeball' (Burroughs [1959] 1982: 17); by the unwashed, such as 'Old Bart . . . dunking pound cake with his dirty fingers, shiny over the dirt'; by the frailty of 'spectral janitors, grey as ashes, phantom porters sweeping out dusty old halls with a slow old man's hand, coughing and spitting in the junk-sick dawn'; or by shameless 'old junkies'—'Really disgust you to see it' (Burroughs [1959] 1982: 15).

Ironically, while Cronenberg spares his viewers graphic representation of the 'unspeakable congress' between 'dropper' and 'wound' (Cronenberg, in Silverberg 1992: 20), his most powerful symbols of addiction evince an almost Burroughsian propulsion towards 'only the most extreme material' (Burroughs 1993: 262). Indeed, as Emery and Silverberg report, initial responses to the film's evocations of 'unspeakable congress' between the latex organs of 'fifty Mugwumps suspended horizontally and attended to by a hundred "slaves"' (Silverberg 1992: 71), occasionally proved equally disturbing to both Cronenberg and cast:

> Of the hundred extras . . . three defected. One of the defectors, a lawyer, said, 'I just can't have my clients see me sucking on a Mugwump teat,' and fled. One visitor who thoroughly enjoyed his encounter with a Mugwump, however, was Burroughs. 'I was impressed with the Mugwump,' he says. 'He's very engaging, rather simpatico.' . . . . This rather worried Cronenberg, who had designed the Mugwumps . . . to resemble old, elongated junkies that represent the evil spirit pervading the film.
>
> (Silverberg 1992: 71-2)

Both enjoying the Mugwump's immediate 'simpatico' presence, and condoning the 'masterstoke' of Cronenberg's 'substitution of . . . Mugwump jissom—for the rather more mundane heroin and marijuana depicted in the novel', Burroughs generously concludes: 'One of the novel's central ideas is that addiction can be metaphorical, and what could underscore this better than the film's avoidance of actual narcotics?' (Burroughs 1992a: xiv).

Naked Lunch is self-evidently anything but a purely metaphorical novel without reference to the 'actual'. As Burroughs himself emphasizes, it abounds in 'endless parenthesis' (Burroughs 1989: 128), multiplying realistic and metaphoric perspectives across his 'banquet of thirty, forty components' (Mailer 1965: 42), and hinges upon a sense of obligation towards all facts at all levels, whether metaphoric or literal, indirect or direct. Writing to Jack Kerouac on 18 September 1950, for example, Burroughs insists that '[f]acts exist on infinite levels' and that 'one level does not preclude another' (Burroughs 1993: 71), and in a letter to Kerouac of 12 February 1955 he still more explicitly determines to refine an 'absolute, direct transmission of *fact* on all levels' (Burroughs 1993: 265).

In turn, *Naked Lunch* unequivocally asserts that there is 'only one thing a writer can write about: *what is in front of his senses at the moment of writing*', and that its title 'means exactly what the words say . . . a frozen moment when everyone sees what is on the end of every fork' (Burroughs [1959] 1982: 218, 1). If Allen Ginsberg's sensitivity to the literal quality of Burroughs' 'actual visions' leads his poem 'On Burroughs' Work' (1954) to caricature them as being free from 'symbolic dressing' (Burroughs 1993: 40), Cronenberg's admiration for the general—rather than the local—satirical register of *Naked Lunch* leads him to overemphasize its symbolic content by treating much of the novel's most disturbing verbal content 'in a metaphorical way' (Cronenberg, in Silverberg 1992: 64).

At the same time, Cronenberg frequently modifies the particularity of the novel's detail in terms of his general insights into what Burroughs' life as a whole 'stands for' and 'what his work has been' (Cronenberg, in Silverberg 1992: 65). Acknowledging, for example, that his treatment of *Naked Lunch* is 'not as aggressive and predatory in its homosexuality' as Burroughs' novel, Cronenberg hints that his film may be closer to reality than the novel itself, insofar as it reflects Burroughs' more tentative evocations of his sexuality in 'letters, prefaces and other things': 'I was trying to see beyond, to the reality of the situation, which is much more ambivalent and ambiguous in terms of sexuality' (Silverberg 1992: 163). At such points Cronenberg's film becomes 'as much an adaptation of Ted Morgan's biography of Burroughs, *Literary Outlaw* . . . as it was *Naked Lunch*' (Rodley, in Silverberg 1992: 171).

But, as Burroughs remarks in *Interzone,* he is far more interested in Paul Klee's notion of art with 'a life of its own', placing the artist in 'real danger' (Burroughs 1989: 128), than in literary self-portraiture. While Cronenberg certainly evokes this kind of danger thematically, his general approach is often that of a biographical *roman-à-clef,* rather than that of a more dangerously corrosive *roman-à-Klee.* Gaining much of its iconic force from the deadpan detachment of Peter Weller, who as 'Lee' seems a deadringer both for a younger Burroughs and a younger Joseph Beuys, Cronenberg's *Naked Lunch* invites the viewer to play 'Spot the Bowles', to 'Spot the Ginsbergian "Martin"' and to 'Spot the Kerouacian "Hank"'. Declining to play, Burroughs bluntly observes: 'I don't recognize anyone I ever knew in those characters' (Burroughs 1992b: 15).

Far from arising from the concrete details of veiled autobiography, *Naked Lunch*'s impact surely derives primarily from its evocations of what Burroughs calls the 'poltergeist knockings and mutterings of America's putrefying unconscious' and the 'incredibly obscene, thinly disguised references and situations that slip by in Grade B Movies'

(Burroughs 1993: 259). Reluctant to offer a literal translation of Burroughs' cathartic 'shitting out my educated Middlewest background' (Burroughs, in Morgan 1988: 264) for fear of being 'banned in every country in the world', Cronenberg takes *Naked Lunch* to Disneyland, mechanizing and masking its menace with all the inventions of 'a heavy-duty effects movie' (Cronenberg, in Silverberg 1992: 161, 166).

Dispensing with Burroughs' most offensive characters and delegating their dialogue to 'effects that also talk a lot', *Naked Lunch* enlivens its decimated cast with the 'Bugwriter'—a robotic 'talking sphincter' (Duncan, in Silverberg 1992: 99, 101) with all the charm of what Burroughs calls 'a Dali bent watch' (Morgan 1988: 541). As Lyden Barber observes (1992: 34), the more one sees of this pulsating incarnation of Dr Benway's routine about 'the man who taught his asshole to talk' (Burroughs [1959] 1982: 133-5), the more tiresome it becomes, and the more grateful one feels for Burroughs' inspired role as Benway in the brief adaptation of the operating scene from *Naked Lunch* (Burroughs [1959] 1982: 66-7) in Howard Brookner's *Burroughs: The Movie* (1983).

Put another way, Burroughs' most forceful accounts of his literary crises derive not so much from the iconic quality of obscene descriptive detail, as from the ironic discursive energy with which Burroughs introduces such detail. Nowhere is this more apparent than in a letter to Kerouac (7 December 1954) outlining the difficulties of writing in 'a popular vein' (Burroughs 1993: 242), recording the involuntary genesis of *Naked Lunch*'s 'interzone' section, and generally generating the vitriolic humour so frequently missing from Cronenberg's adaptation of his novel.

> I sat down seriously to write a best-seller Book of the Month Club job on Tangier. So here is what comes out first sentence: 'The only native in Interzone who is neither queer nor available is Andrew Keif's chauffeur . . . Aracknid is the worst driver in the Zone. On one occasion he ran down a pregnant woman in from the mountains with a load of charcoal on her back, and she miscarried a bloody, dead baby on the street, and Keif got out and sat on the curb stirring the blood with a stick while the police questioned Aracknid and finally arrested the woman.' I can just see that serialized in . . . *Good Housekeeping.*
>
> (Burroughs 1993: 241-2)

Amusingly confirming that nothing about 'Burroughs in Tangier' was ever *Good Housekeeping* material, Paul Bowles' reminiscences suggest the ways in which Burroughs' distinctive performative energies subsequently offered remarkably good film-making materials to such early collaborative adaptations of his work as Balch's *Towers Open Fire* (1963). Doubtless the same cinematic energy might also have invigorated Cronenberg's adaptation of *Naked Lunch* had the disparity between fact and fiction not led to his exclusion from the film for fear that his presence 'might jar the viewer out of the story' (Burroughs 1992b: 15).

The litter on his desk and under it, on the floor, was chaotic, but it consisted only of pages of *Naked Lunch,* at which he was constantly working. When he read aloud from it, at random (any sheet of paper he happened to grab would do) he laughed a good deal, as well he might, since it is very funny, but from reading he would suddenly (paper still in hand) go into bitter conversational attack upon whatever aspect of life had prompted the passage he had just read.

(Bowles 1959: 43)

Following Bowles' lead, and remarking how 'Burroughs' humour is peculiarly American, at once broad and sly', Mary McCarthy persuasively argues that while there are 'many points of comparison between Burroughs and Swift', what saves *Naked Lunch* 'is not a literary ancestor but humor'. More specifically, McCarthy explains:

It is the humor of a comedian, a vaudeville performer playing in 'one,' in front of the asbestos curtain of some Keith Circuit or Pantages house long converted to movies. . . . Some of the jokes are verbal ('Stop me if you've heard this atomic secret' or Dr Benway's 'A simopath . . . is a citizen convinced he is an ape or other simian. It is a disorder peculiar to the army and discharge cures it'). Some are 'black' parody (Dr Benway, in his last appearance, dreamily, his voice fading out: 'Cancer, my first love'). . . . The effect of pandemonium, all hell breaking loose, is one of Burroughs' favorites and an equivalent of the old vaudeville finale, with the acrobats, the jugglers, the magician, the hoofers . . . all pushing into the act.

(McCarthy [1963] 1991: 4-5)

Sadly, Cronenberg virtually pushes such humour out of 'the act' in order to save his film from degenerating into what he calls 'a very nasty kind of soft, satirical social satire of the *Britannia Hospital* variety, with no emotional content and without the beauty, grace and potency of Burroughs' literary style' (Silverberg 1992: 161). But Burroughs' style is quintessentially a 'nasty' mixture of beauty, grace and the worst extremes of *Britannia Hospital* and *Carry On* humour, and any attempt to rarify it falls on its face. Lee's deadpan rendition of 'Bobo's death', for example—a funeral soliloquy stifling the bedpan hilarity of Benway's account of the quite literally 'sticky end' of Professor Fingerbottom, whose 'falling piles blew out the Duc de Ventre's Hispano Suiza and wrapped around the rear wheel'—prompts alarm rather than amusement, and the suggestion, 'You sound as if you could use a drink' (Burroughs [1959] 1982: 165). While Burroughs resists simplistic categorization as 'a stand-up comedian' (Bockris 1981: 27), his writing is certainly that of a 'sit-down' comedian, and Cronenberg's fork-waving and lunch-contemplating 'Lee' pales before Harry Dean Stanton's far more convincing Burroughsian presence as the sardonic Bud in Michael Nesmith's quirkily urban magic-realist *Repo Man* (1984).

In this respect, Cronenberg's greatest successes are surely his humourless evocations of the long-gone scenes that Burroughs distils from 'many sources: conversations heard and overheard, movies and radio broadcasts' (Burroughs 1986: 19). From the opening shot of Lee's silhouetted fedora, we enter what Burroughs persuasively calls a 'masterful thriller' (Silverberg 1992: 14) made up of third-hand images borrowed by Cronenberg from Burroughs, and borrowed by Burroughs from 'Grade B movies' (Burroughs 1993: 259). Yet as John Conomos observes (1992: 16), against all odds such refined cinematic simulation is 'extraordinarily atmospheric'. Typifying Cronenberg's tendency to borrow images and phrases from both *Naked Lunch* and other Burroughsian novels, Lee's visit to the 'bug drug' building builds on the opening section of *Exterminator!*; an episode written in surprisingly cinematic prose, rich in anecdotal bit-parts and still richer in such evocative sound-bites as Lee's catch-phrase—'Exterminator! You need the service?'—and the 'older' Cohen brother's rant—'You vant I should spit right in your face!? You vant!? You vant? You vant!?' (Burroughs 1974: 4, 3). Clearly sharing Burroughs' acute 'ear for dialogue' (Burroughs 1986: 185), even if unwilling or unable to find a way of integrating Burroughsian utterance into his film, Cronenberg beefs things up with a bonus one-liner from the Chinese druggist whose abrupt four-worder brings *Naked Lunch*'s last six lines (quoted here in full) to their fragmentary conclusion.

"They are rebuilding the City."
Lee nodded absently. . . . "Yes . . . Always . . ."
Either way is a bad move to The East Wing. . . .
If I knew I'd be glad to tell you. . . .
"No good . . . no bueno . . . hustling himself. . . ."
"No glot . . . C'lom Fliday"

(Burroughs [1959] 1982: 232)

Is this appropriate mainstream movie dialogue? One thinks not. And yet as Paul Bowles remarks, Burroughs' improvisations offered a remarkably theatrical spectacle: 'Surely . . . worth hearing, and worth watching', as he 'stumbled from one side of the room to the other, shouting in his cowboy voice' (Bowles 1959: 43). In turn, subsequent expatriate celebration of Burroughs' voice on the Paris-based English Bookshop's LP, *Call Me Burroughs* (1965), prompted the American poet Emmett Williams to write:

The first time I heard Burroughs' voice . . . I thought: Mark Twain must have talked like this . . . and I'm sure he likes apple pie. Later when I first heard these excerpts from *The Naked Lunch* . . . Twain . . . and apple pie were still in evidence, plus a large dose of Texas Charley the medicineshow man selling tonic to a lot of rubes. . . . His voice is terrifyingly convincing.

(Williams 1965: n.p.)

It is precisely this terrifyingly convincing voice that the British film-maker Antony Balch uses to capture the viewer's attention in the opening scene of Burroughs' first major cinematic adaptation and collaboration, *Towers Open Fire*. Described as 'an 11-minute collage of all the themes and situations in the book, accompanied by a Burroughs soundtrack narration' (Balch 1972: 10), *Towers Open Fire* rushes in where Cronenberg fears to tread (and where

Cronenberg can no longer tread), documenting Burroughs shooting up, partially documenting Balch masturbating to Burroughs' incantation 'silver arrow through the night', and offering little other characterization or narrative continuity than fleeting images of Burroughs and Gysin inside or outside the Paris Beat Hotel.

Towers Open Fire opens with a static close-up of Burroughs staring blankly at the camera for fifty seconds or so, before finally blinking and almost smiling, as a burst of trance music signals a cut to the next scene in which he acts as chairman of 'The Board'. Nothing happens, one might say. Or at least, nothing happens but Burroughs' impassive reading and audition of the horrendous 'old white schmaltz' droned out by 'the District Supervisor' in *The Soft Machine*. Here, for a highly unnerving minute, the viewer quite literally has 'no place to go' other than this forced encounter with disquieting dramatization of what the next sentence in *The Soft Machine* calls: 'Most distasteful thing I ever stood still for'.

> Now kid what are you doing over there with the niggers and the apes? Why don't you straighten out and act like a white man? After all they're only human cattle—You know that yourself—Hate to see a bright young man fuck up and get off on the wrong track— Sure it happens to all of us one time or another—Why the man who went on to invent Shitola was sitting right where you're sitting now twenty-five years ago and I was saying the same things to him—Well he straightened out the way you're going to straighten out. . . . You can't deny your blood kid—You're white white white—And you can't walk out on Trak—There's just no place to go.
>
> (Burroughs [1961] 1968: 140-1)

As becomes evident, Burroughs in the 1960s was altogether different to the Burroughs of the 1990s who claimed to be 'relieved' that Cronenberg did not ask him to 'write or co-write' the screenplay for *Naked Lunch*; who expressed surprise that writers still 'think they can *write* a film script, not realizing that film scripts are not meant to be read, but acted and photographed' (Burroughs, in Silverberg 1992: 14); and who generally argued that 'the rule of film is that movies move, with minimal talk' (Silverberg 1992: 13). Here, in black and white, Burroughs demonstrates the considerable impact of maximal 'talk' set against almost wholly motionless imagery, writing for— and reading and acting in—a cinematic adaptation built both around and upon the auratic energy of his cinematic presence.

Four years later, Balch's film *The Cut-Ups* (1967) explored still more radical text-screen collaboration and adaptation. On the one hand, as Gysin explains, Balch randomly spliced documentary footage of his collaborators:

> Antony was applying . . . the 'cut-up' technique where he simply took all the footage he had and handed it over to an editor, just telling her to set up four reels,

and put so many feet on each one in order—one, two, three, four, and start again, the same number.

> (Gysin 1997: 177)

On the other hand, Gysin and Burroughs produced an independent made-to-measure soundtrack, patiently intoning such mind-numbing greetings as 'Yes—hello', before juggling with the question, 'Does this image seem to be persisting?' and other phrases 'taken directly from the Scientology classes that [Burroughs] was going to at the time' (Gysin 1997: 180). As Gysin relates, predictably neither *Towers Open Fire* nor *The Cut-Ups* enjoyed commercial success when first screened at the Academy Cinema, Oxford Street, which 'finally asked if we could please take them off the screen because they'd had such a high incidence of people forgetting very strange things in the theatre'. Surprisingly, though, even greater hostility awaited them in New York, where even the artistic underground recoiled from Burroughs' 'very heavy aura' as a writer who 'had shot his wife' and 'published the most shocking book of its time' (Gysin 1997: 182).

Neither literary adaptation nor literary adoption seemed on Burroughs' cards in the late 1960s and early 1970s, and only in 1974 did his 'aura' grow lighter, following the success of his first New York readings. Recalling that 'Burroughs had gotten very paranoid in London', Andreas Brown describes how '[y]ou could see his face change as he realized that people wanted to hear him' (Bockris 1981: 77-8). In New York, as in Tangier and Paris, Burroughs once again wowed his contemporaries with his prowess as a performer and raconteur of semi-autobiographical texts, and in his film *Burroughs: The Movie* (1983), Howard Brookner gave Burroughs *carte blanche* to adapt or perform his writings and generally reminisce about the past. Here we see a besuited Burroughs reading on stage at a desk; a begarbed Burroughs in operating theatre greens, acting out one of the Dr Benway routines from *Naked Lunch*; and an avuncular Burroughs, nostalgically guiding Grauerholz around his old St Louis haunts. Without doubt, Burroughs was back in town.

In May 1983, Burroughs' induction into the American Academy and Institute of Arts and Letters marked his formal literary rehabilitation, and in October 1983, the first major public screening of *Burroughs: The Movie* at the New York Film Festival offered him the approval of independent cinema culture. Five years later, Hollywood itself confirmed that Burroughs was no longer *persona non grata,* as fact, fiction and Burroughs' conflicting personae as literary outlaw and grand old man of American letters coalesced in his role as Tom the Priest—based on The Priest in *Exterminator!* (Burroughs 1974: 156)—in Gus Van Sant's film *Drugstore Cowboy* (1989). Here, as in *Burroughs: The Movie*, Burroughs exemplifies the streetwise old-timer, this time guiding Bob (played by Matt Dillon) around town. And here, once again, Burroughs worked on his script, suggesting to Van Sant that his character—the 'middle-aged' junkie Bob Murphy—should become 'an old junkie', and describing 'how he would have behaved in Murphy's circumstances'. When Van Sant's 'rewrite didn't really capture it', Grauerholz 'rewrote four scenes for William . . . and then William put his own unique polish on it, his own imprimatur' (Grauerholz, in Miles 1992: 14).

The following year, Burroughs entered his final collaboration with the post-modern multimedia avant-garde, writing the libretto for Robert Wilson's opera *The Black Rider* (1990). Hailing Burroughs as a fellow visionary willing 'to destroy the codes in order to make a new language', Wilson welcomed the opportunity to set Burroughs' 'dreamy, cloud-like texts' against his own antinaturalistic practice of telling stories 'visually, in scenery and in gestures' (Wilson 1992: 50-1). Wilson set Burroughs' words within multimedia narratives evincing 'an ongoing thing . . . a continuum . . . something that never, never finishes', unlike commercially viable cinematic 'one-liners' in which 'you get information in three seconds, and then that's it' (Wilson 1992: 52). This time, collaborative multimedia adaptation and integration of Burroughs' writings struck gold, and (as Burroughs reports) when *The Black Rider* opened at Hamburg's Thalia Theatre in March 1990, 'There were fifteen curtain calls, which is almost unheard of' (Burroughs 1994: 70).

Revered as a living legend on almost all fronts, Burroughs now presented the ideal subject-matter for Hollywood legend. And so it came to pass, in Cronenberg's strangely puritanical homage to the undeniable 'beauty, grace and potency' of much of 'Burroughs' literary style' (Cronenberg, in Silverberg 1992: 161): a film made too late to integrate the dynamic authorial performances in *Towers Open Fire* and *The Cut-Ups,* made too cautiously to countenance the burlesque Burroughsian 'routines' authorially hammed to perfection in *Burroughs: The Movie,* made too conventionally to opt for the 'dreamy, cloud-like' logic welcomed by Wilson in *The Black Rider,* and made too wisely to replicate the authorial self-caricature in *Drugstore Cowboy.*

Cronenberg's adaptation of *Naked Lunch* surely works best when its camera-work lugubriously glides through beautifully observed sets with exemplary deceleration, partially compensating for its sins of omission with remarkable atmospheric intensity and spectacular 'adult' special effects, generating what Burroughs calls a 'miasma of paranoia' (Burroughs 1992b: 15) entirely commensurate with the 'dead-end despair' (Burroughs 1993: 255) permeating the bleaker sections of his 'very funny book' (Burroughs 1990: 38).

As Cronenberg indicates, writing as demanding as Burroughs' fiction almost inevitably places the cinematic adapter in a no-win situation, in which they can at best 'dip' into their subject, 'a little bit here, a little bit there' (Cronenberg, in Silverberg 1992: 161). Given such circumstances, Balch, Brookner, Van Sant and Wilson suggest, the most winning way to work with living experimental authors may well be the 'double-dipping' strategy of integrating the interactive 'special effects' offered by *collaborative* intertextual adaptation.

SOCIO-HISTORICAL AND CULTURAL IMPACT

Thomas H. Pauly (essay date 1982)

SOURCE: Pauly, Thomas H. "*Gone with the Wind* and *The Grapes of Wrath* as Hollywood Histories of the Depression." In *Movies as Artifacts: Cultural Criticism of Popular Film,* edited by Michael T. Marsden, John G. Nachbar, and Samm L. Grogg, Jr., pp. 164-76. Chicago: Nelson-Hall, 1982.

[*In the following essay, Pauly discusses the screen adaptations of* Gone with the Wind *and* The Grapes of Wrath, *noting that despite vast differences in the way critics viewed these films, they both addressed issues of survival during times of financial and social upheaval albeit from very different viewpoints.*]

Popular culture of the later Depression years was dominated by *Gone with the Wind* and *The Grapes of Wrath.* As novels, these two creations topped the best seller lists during 1936, 1937, and 1939. Interest in both works was then renewed in early 1940—perhaps even reached its greatest peak—when both opened as movies within weeks of one another (*Gone with the Wind* on December 15, 1939, and *Grapes of Wrath* on January 24, 1940). Though both were tremendous box office successes, their critics responded to each quite differently. While the reviews of *Gone with the Wind* strove to top one another with accounts of all the gossip, glitter, and money involved in the making of *Gone with the Wind,* those discussing *The Grapes of Wrath* stressed the outstanding quality of the film itself. "No artificial make-up, no false sentiment, no glamor stars mar the authentic documentary form of this provocative film," asserted Philip Hartung in his review of *The Grapes of Wrath* for *Commonweal.*[1] Similarly, Otis Ferguson was confident enough of the dissatisfaction *Gone with the Wind* would bring that he postponed going,[2] but he opened his review entitled "Show for the People," "The word that comes in most handily for *The Grapes of Wrath* is magnificent . . . this is the best that has no very near comparison to date."[3] Despite the overwhelming critical preference for Ford's movie, however, it won only one Oscar (Best Director) in the 1940 balloting, whereas Selznick's extravaganza swept all the major awards in 1939 except one (Best Actor). Clearly, the latter film was the people's choice. At issue here was an intense, unacknowledged debate over what the age preferred in its movies. In an era fraught with intense sociological upheaval, *Gone with the Wind* seemed consciously intended to project its audience into a realm of sentiment and nostalgia beyond the confines of actual experience. As Lincoln Kirstein complained in the opening paragraph of his scathing review for *Films*:

> . . . history has rarely been told with even an approximation of truth in Hollywood, because the few men in control there have no interest in the real forces behind historical movements and the new forces that every new epoch sets into motion. *Gone with the Wind* deserves our attention because it is an over-inflated example of the usual, the false movie approach to history.[4]

Implicit in these remarks is a charge often leveled against the movies produced during this era. Critics and historians of the cinema repeatedly call attention to Hollywood's striking reluctance to address itself to the problems of the Depression. Nothing, they point out, could have been further from the bread lines and the deprivation photographed by Dorothea Lange than the social comedies of Lubitsch, the slapstick of the Marx Brothers, and the polished dance routines of Fred Astaire and Ginger Rogers. Nonetheless, as Andrew Bergman has asserted and then persuasively demonstrated in his book on films of the Depression, *We're in the Money,* "People do not escape into something they cannot relate to. The movies were meaningful because they depicted things lost or things desired. What is 'fantastic' in fantasy is an extension of something real."[5] In other words, the "dreams" the audience is said to have demanded, those for which they spent the little extra money they had, were not mere illusions or abstractions but exciting, imaginative articulations of their greatest hopes and fears, their deepest doubts and beliefs. On this score, *Gone with the Wind* possesses a significant measure of both historical validity and importance. The fact that it was far and away the most successful film of the decade probably had less to do with the glittering surface that so annoyed the critics than the common ground it shared with *The Grapes of Wrath.* Though it was less daring and less accomplished than Ford's work as an artistic creation, *Gone with the Wind* was similarly preoccupied with the problem of survival in the face of financial deprivation and social upheaval. Both movies also demonstrate a nostalgic longing for the agrarian way of life which is ruthlessly being replaced by the fearful new economic forces of capitalism and industrialization. By way of extension, both reflect an intense concern for the devastating consequences of these conditions upon self-reliant individualism and family unity, two of America's most cherished beliefs. In each case, however, serious concern for these implications is dissipated into indulgent sentimentalism so that the audience's anxieties are alleviated rather than aggravated.

Even if the script had been available, *The Grapes of Wrath* dealt with issues that were too familiar and too painful to have been made during the early thirties. Yet, in deciding to produce a movie of this controversial novel at the time he did, Darryl Zanuck was sufficiently concerned about the specter of the Depression that he decided to mute and even eliminate some of the more charged aspects of Steinbeck's social criticism.[6] As Mel Gussow has explained, "For Zanuck, *The Grapes of Wrath* and *How Green Was My Valley* were not really social documents but family pictures of a very special kind; movies about families in stress."[7] Thus, the movie's emphasis falls upon the sentimental aspect of the conditions confronting the Joads. At the outset, this takes the character of the loss of a home, which deprives the family of its essential connection with the land. Tom's initial return assumes the character of a search for a place of refuge from the suffering and hostility he has been forced to endure in prison and on his truck ride. That everything has changed is made clear by his encounter with Casy; but the full impact of this upheaval is registered only when he beholds the vacant, crumbling house in which he was raised and hears Muley's distracted tale of how his reverence for the land has been desecrated. "My pa was born here," he insists; "We was *all* born on it, and some of us got killed on it, and some died on it. And that's what makes it ourn. . . ."[8] Equally striking in this regard is the later scene where Grampa asserts, "I ain't a-goin' to California! This here's my country. I b'long *here.* It ain't no good—but it's mine,'"[9] and then underlines his points by distractedly gripping his native soil.

In dramatizing the intense suffering these people experience, these lines serve the more important function of locating its source. The former agrarian way of life predicated upon man's intimate attachment to the land has given way to an economy of industrialization with its efficiency, practicality, and inhumanity. For Tom and his fellow farmers, there is no possibility of retaliation. The fury that drives Muley to take up a gun produces only frustration and helpless dejection because there is no enemy to shoot. The man on the caterpillar turns out to be his neighbor who is trapped by the same problem of survival. The machines that level their homes, like the foreclosures which are delivered in dark, sinister automobiles, cannot be associated with particular individuals; they are the weapons of a system devoid of both personality and humanity.

THE MAN:

> Now don't go blaming me. It ain't *my* fault.

SON:

> Whose fault is it? . . .

THE MAN:

> It ain't nobody. It's a company. He ain't anything but the manager. . . .

MULEY (BEWILDERED):

> Then who *do* we shoot?

THE MAN:

> . . . Brother, I don't know.[10]

Deprived of the only home he has known, Tom Joad joins his family in their quest for a new one. However great may be their need for food and money, keeping the family together, Ma Joad makes clear, is the most pressing concern. She sees that nourishment involves the spirit as well and in the face of the increasingly depersonalized world confronting her, the shared concerns of the family offer the only remaining source of humanity. These become the basic issues by which the audience measures the significance of the ensuing trip to California. As Ford dramatizes them, the policemen who harass the Joads, the strawbosses who dictate to them, the thugs who break up the dances and union gatherings are, like the handbills that bring them to California, products of a sinister conspiracy beyond human control. They combine with the inhospitable landscape encountered to create an environment in which the family is unable to survive. Grampa and Gramma die before the destination is reached; Connie cannot stand up to the punishment inflicted upon him and flees; Casy is killed by the growers' hired guns; having avenged Casy's death, Tom is forced to flee for his life.[11]

The Grapes of Wrath, however, is more than a mere drama of defeat. The futility of individualism and the breakdown of the family furnish, in the end, a distinct source of optimism. Having witnessed the miserable living conditions in which the Joads have futilely struggled to endure—the filthy tent in the clapboard road camp, the concentration of starving people in Hooverville, the gloomy squalor of the cabin at the Keene ranch—the audience is now introduced to a utopia of cooperative socialism which has been as scrupulously sanitized of communism as it is of filth. In contrast to the derogatory view expressed earlier in the movie, working with the government is shown to offer a more valid prospect of salvation than fighting against the prevailing conditions; at the Wheat Patch camp, the spirit of Tom's involvement with Casy is realized without the self-defeating violence and killing. Here, as George Bluestone notes, the Joads find "a kind of miniature planned economy, efficiently run, boasting modern sanitation, self-government, cooperative living, and moderate prices."[12] Here, people work together with the same automatic efficacy as the flush toilets. Cleanliness nourishes kindness, the caretaker explains with the serene wisdom of his kindly confident manner (does he remind you of FDR?).

Even the language has been changed to accord with this new society; one finds here not a shelter, a house, or a home, but a "sanitary unit." Though this community has been conceived to accord with the depersonalized society outside its gates, it has also incorporated a basic respect for human dignity. It is a world characterized by its Saturday dance with its democratic acceptance, its well-controlled exclusion of the forces of anarchy, its ritualistic incorporation of the outdated family into a healthy new society—a new society which would actually be realized only two years later in the "comfortable" concentration camps for Japanese-Americans during World War II. Above all, the Wheat Patch camp episode affords a bridge to the "new" ending Zanuck was moved to write for his movie.[13] As Tom and the Joad truck return to the outside world and strike out in different directions, they have no idea where they are going, but they all have renewed hope that they can find salvation just by being with "the people."

> Rich fellas come up an' they die, an' their kids ain't no good, an' they die out. But we keep a'coming. We're the people that live. Can't nobody wipe us out. Can't nobody lick us. We'll go on forever, Pa. We're the people.[14]

Such conviction, Zanuck concluded, was not to be thwarted by the "No Help Wanted" originally indicated in Nunnally Johnson's screenplay,[15] so he gave them an open road—which, appropriately enough, leads off to nowhere.

The Grapes of Wrath is a fine movie, but it is considerably flawed. Furthermore, for all its "documentary" technique, it is badly distorted history. Its depiction of the plight of the migrant worker contributes considerably less to our understanding of the conditions of the Depression than its suspicion of big business, its manifest agrarianism, and, above all, its sentimental concern for the breakdown of the family. Given the striking commercial success of the movie, one cannot help wondering what it was the public went to see—an artistic masterpiece, a direct confrontation with the reality of the Depression, or its handling of the above concerns. Of the three, the last was perhaps the most important, for this was the one striking point of resemblance between it and the biggest box office movie of the decade. *Gone with the Wind* succeeded as well as it did in large part because it so effectively sublimated the audience's own response to the Depression. For them, the panoramic shot of the Confederate wounded littering the center of Atlanta was not a matter of fact but of feeling. All concern for the scene's historical authenticity simply vanished in the face of its dramatization of the sense of helplessness and devastation they themselves had experienced.

Amidst these circumstances, Scarlett's subsequent return to Tara bears a striking resemblance to Tom's homecoming, in her quest for refuge from the adversities she has endured. Yet her expectation is shattered by the same scene of desolation that Tom discovered. For her, also, there is the same decaying ruin in place of the secure home she formerly knew. Tom's encounter with Muley seems almost a rerun of Scarlett's even more painful confrontation with her father, whose demented condition strikingly illustrates the magnitude of change resulting from the war's upheaval. As in *The Grapes of Wrath*, this breakdown in the integrity of the family is associated with the destruction of an agrarian way of life, which strikes at the very core of Scarlett's emotional being. The burned soil of Tara that Scarlett grips in the concluding scene of Part I is fraught with the same significance which attended Grampa's similar gesture in *The Grapes of Wrath*.

Scarlett's response, however, marks an important point of difference. Unlike Tom Joad, who took to the road and sought to survive by working with his family, Scarlett resolves to be master of her destiny. Her moving declaration, "As God is my witness . . . I'll never be hungry again," pits her will against the prevailing conditions. Her determination is such that she not only antagonizes the remnants of her family but she also exploits them; having slapped Suellen, she proceeds to steal her prospective husband, Frank Kennedy. Nonetheless, her actions are prompted by some of the same motives that carried the Joads to California.

In the characterization of Scarlett is to be found most of the complexity that *Gone with the Wind* possesses. As the reviewer of the *New York Times* observed, "Miss Leigh's Scarlett is the pivot of the picture."[16] Were she merely a bitch or strong-willed feminist, the appeal of this movie would have been considerably diminished. In order to appreciate the intense response she elicited from the audience, one has to understand the particular way in which Scarlett's return to Tara and her subsequent commitment to rebuilding it qualifies her initial assertion of independence and results in a tragic misunderstanding that brings her downfall. In the opening scenes of the movie, Scarlett wins the audience's sympathy for her determined spirit of rebellion. It is she who provides critical perspective on the glittering world of plantation society. Tara and Twelve Oaks, with their surrounding profusion of flowers and lush background sweep of countryside, are as magnificently attired as the people who congregate there and therefore are perfect settings for the featured scenes of dressing and undressing, posturing and strutting. The main function of women in this world is providing ornamental beauty. The illusion of grace and elegance they sustain is predicated upon a harsh standard of propriety, a painfully tight corset. Parties become major moments in their lives in helping them to achieve their ordained goal of marriage, but their area of decision is limited to the choice of a dress or hat. Since the threat of a rival is the only war they can be expected to understand, they are all herded off to bedrooms to freshen their appearances and restore their frail energies while the men debate the future of the South. Given the stifling confinement of this role, Scarlett balks. Like the other women, she entertains a vision of marriage and consciously attends to her appearance, but, unlike them, she is determined to act on her wishes. Thus, while her rivals retire according to the convention of the submissive female, she slips downstairs to confront Ashley in the belief that he will not be able to resist her assault.

The war, which pre-empts Scarlett's fight for Ashley, dramatically affirms these and all the other deficiencies of this society, but as a "lost cause," it also forces Scarlett to determine her highest priorities. At first, she displays only a selfish interest; its tragedy is for her a source of gain in relieving her of an unwanted husband. However, the flames of Atlanta which occasion a nightmare of emotion as they destroy the Old South, illuminate a new romantic potential in Scarlett's deepening relationship with Rhett. During their flight, their affair of convenience, predicated upon the same spirited, but pragmatic, individualism which alienates them both from plantation society, achieves a new

level of interdependency in the intense feelings they exchange and share. Having been stripped of her gentility, her vanity, and finally her self-confidence, Scarlett is reduced to her greatest moment of need. At this point, Rhett's selfishness, which reveals itself to have been basically an emotional shield, also gives way. For the first time, both reach out for something greater than themselves. The result, however, is not a common understanding. Rhett proposes a marriage and a new future, only to discover that Scarlett prefers to retreat to the past. Survival, she has come to believe, lies in the red earth of Tara. Rejected, Rhett goes off to fight for the cause. Thus, the situation which brought Rhett and Scarlett together propels them along separate paths in search of ideals which ironically the war is at that moment destroying. Though they survive to marry one another, the decisions forced by the war constitute an insurmountable breach which the conclusion of the movie simply reaffirms, as Rhett goes off to Charleston in search of "the calm dignity life can have when it's lived by gentle folks, the genial grace of days that are gone," while Scarlett heeds her father's words calling her back to Tara.

In his concerted effort to reproduce the novel as thoroughly as possible, Selznick felt that the increased emphasis he accorded to Tara was one of the few points of departure. "I felt," he explained in one of his memos, "that the one thing that was really open to us was to stress the Tara thought more than Miss Mitchell did."[17] For him, Scarlett's character was grounded in Tara, in agrarianism and the family, just as the identity of the Joads was. Yet, in according it much the same meaning, he dramatized its tragic consequence quite differently. Scarlett's vow never to be hungry again as she grips the burned soil of Tara at the end of Part I moves the audience with its stirring determination, but this vow is severely qualified by the scene's logic. Quite simply, Tara, or "terra," cannot provide the nourishment she requires.[18] The turnip she ravenously devours and then vomits is strikingly emblematic of Tara's true value. In the first place, the fact that the earth is red is an obvious signal that the soil sustains crops with great difficulty. Without the slaves and strong-willed owners, Tara is not even capable of generating enough capital to pay its taxes. The main reason for Scarlett's determination to return to Tara, however, transcends all these considerations. Tara is home—its essence is to be found more in the echoing sound of her father's voice and the heart-tugging strains of Max Steiner's music.[19] For her, Tara is the sphere of her father's influence, a refuge where matters were firmly under control and she was treated with tolerance and indulgence.[20] Yet this is equally foolish, for she discovers that her father has been broken by the war and now relies on her for the consolation she has expected him to provide. Nowhere are the disadvantages of Tara revealed more dramatically than in the buckboard visit of Jonas Wilkerson whose association with the new economic forces supplanting agrarianism recalls the nameless men of *The Grapes of Wrath* in their sinister cars.

Since money has become the only source of power, Scarlett must seek beyond Tara for survival. Scarlett appears to marry Frank Kennedy to pay the taxes on Tara, but she obviously sees that he is associated with the prospering forces of industrialization. Consequently, in becoming his wife, she really becomes a businesswoman. These conflicting allegiances to Tara and to her lumber mill place Scarlett in the paradoxical position of shunning the role of wife and mother in order to uphold her passionate commitment to family and the home. Her identification with business and its ruthless practices now loses her the audience's sympathy, yet, because she never understands the character and consequences of what she is doing, she proves more tragic than villainous. Her determined quest for the greatest margin of profit is not to be understood as her predominant aim. Much more essential is her desire that Tara be rebuilt. To do so is not only to eliminate the desperate state of poverty to which she had been reduced, but also to restore the spiritual strength of her family home. Only the audience, however, comprehends the hidden cost. Frank becomes her lackey and her marriage no more than a working partnership. She herself becomes a social pariah. Most important, Scarlett begins to die from emotional starvation, as her business absorbs her energies without providing any of the attention and compassion she has always craved. The sorrow she drowns with liquor following Kennedy's death is neither anguish nor a pained sense of confinement—it is a strange lack of feeling.

Once again, Rhett comes to offer her salvation. Despite his manifest contempt for propriety, Rhett's invasion of her privacy and his cynical proposal of marriage are joyfully welcomed, because they offer Scarlett an opportunity to escape her business and enjoy her own home. Unfortunately, the seeds of her undoing have already been sown. The self-reliant determination of her struggles has rendered her temperamentally incapable of filling the role of the devoted wife she would like to be. Rhett's gifts—the house and even Bonnie—all simply deprive her of the thing she needs most—a challenge. For this, she returns to Ashley, whose embodiment of the devoted husband she must destroy in order to win. Her visit with the dying Melanie causes her finally to realize this, as well as the fact that Rhett is a much worthier ideal. Sensing her folly, she rushes home to find that he has indeed become unreachable. As a mother without a child, a wife without a husband, Scarlett is left by Selznick at the end of the picture turning to a home she can inhabit only in her dreams. The famous concluding line of the novel, "tomorrow is another day," is almost drowned out in the movie by the emotionally charged flashback scene of Tara with Gerald O'Hara's words echoing in the background.[21] Thus, Scarlett stands at the end a strong-willed individualist in possession of all the wealth the audience could imagine, yet no better off than they because of her inability to realize her impossible dream of a happy home and a loving family.

At the height of the Depression, thirteen million workers were unemployed. People who had enjoyed marked prosperity during the twenties suddenly found themselves struggling just to stay alive. Equally troubling was their inability to comprehend the reasons for this devastating reversal. As Leo Gurko has observed, "The decade of the thirties was uniquely one in which time outran consciousness . . . the misery of the country was equalled only by its bewilderment."[22] The absence of checks and balances in the market place, which was supposed to provide the ordinary citizen with opportunity, seemed only to be making the rich richer and the poor poorer. Everywhere, big business seemed to be prospering. The general lack of knowledge about those who ran it or how it operated simply added to the pervasive belief that these companies were somehow profiting at the expense of the suffering individual. Similarly frustrating was the helplessness and loss of dignity caused by unemployment. No longer was the working man able to fill his expected role as head of the household. Either he could not support his family or he was forced to strike out on his own in order to do so. Consequently, his traditional source of consolation now only contributed to his distress. In the cities, where these problems were most acute, the idea of "getting back to the land" seemed to offer a ready-made solution. As Broadus Mitchell explains:

> In the cities, unemployment emphasized crowding, squalor, and cold; the bread lines were visual reproaches. In the country, on the other hand, was ample room. Further, in the cities, workers won bread by an indirect process which for some reason had broken down. But life in the rural setting was held to be synonymous with raising family food. The thing was simple, direct, individually and socially wholesome.[23]

This solution, of course, turned out to be most impractical. Yet it reveals the direction in which the people's anxieties were working. Coming at the end of the Depression as they did, *Gone with the Wind* and *The Grapes of Wrath* appealed to viewers who had lived through this ordeal. Both succeeded in large measure because they so effectively tapped the emotional wellsprings of this urban audience which was their chief patron. Repeatedly, the viewer found himself confronting these same troubling issues; but they were presented in such a way that he was reassured that everything would work out just as he hoped it would. At the same time, neither could have been as compelling had this sentimentality not been treated with a subtlety and understanding notably lacking in similar films like *Our Daily Bread.*

Notes

1. Philip T. Hartung, "Trampling Out the Vintage," *Commonweal 31* (February 9, 1940), p. 348.

2. Otis Ferguson, "Out to Lunch," *The Film Criticism of Otis Ferguson,* ed. Robert Wilson (Philadelphia: Temple University Press, 1971), pp. 280-81.

3. Otis Ferguson, "Show for the People," *Film Criticism,* p. 282.

4. Lincoln Kirstein, "History in American Films *(Gone with the Wind)*" in *American Film Criticism from the Beginnings to Citizen Kane,* ed. Stanley Kauffmann (New York: Liveright, 1972), p. 372.

5. Andrew Bergman, *We're in the Money: Depression America and Its Films* (New York: New York University Press, 1971), p. xii.

6. For a discussion of these deletions, see George Bluestone, *Novels Into Film* (Berkeley: University of California Press, 1971), pp. 156-161. Warren French discusses other important differences between the novel and the film in *Filmguide to The Grapes of Wrath* (Bloomington: University of Indiana Press, 1973), pp. 22-27.

7. Mel Gussow, *Don't Say Yes Until I Finish Talking: A Biography of Darryl F. Zanuck* (Garden City, N.Y.: Doubleday, 1971), p. 95.

8. Nunnally Johnson, *The Grapes of Wrath*, in *Twenty Best Film Plays*, ed. John Gassner and Dudley Nichols (New York: Crown Publishers, 1943), p. 338. There may be minor variations between these quotes and the actual movie since this filmscript is not the final version.

9. *Twenty Best Film Plays*, p. 345.

10. *Twenty Best Film Plays*, p. 338.

11. The movie, for some reason, doesn't include Noah's desertion, though the scene was apparently filmed.

12. *Novels Into Film*, p. 165.

13. Mel Gussow reports that Zanuck wrote Ma's speech which concludes the film, p. 92.

14. *Twenty Best Film Plays*, p. 377.

15. *Twenty Best Film Plays*, p. 377.

16. Frank Nugent, *"Gone with the Wind," The New York Times Film Reviews: A One Volume Selection* (New York: Arno Press, 1971), p. 185.

17. David O. Selznick, *Memo From David O. Selznick*, ed. Rudy Belmer (New York: Viking Press, 1972), p. 212.

18. Despite this meaning which emerges from the dramatized pronunciation of Tara, the plantation was most probably named after the famous hill in County of Meath which for centuries was the seat of the ancient kings of Gerald O'Hara's native Ireland.

19. The Tara theme song, which echoes through the movie, subsequently became a popular song entitled, appropriately enough, "My Own True Love."

20. To some extent, Scarlett's failure to find a satisfying husband can be traced to the fact that none was able to measure up to the image she had of her father when she was a young girl.

21. For its demonstration of the quintessential spirit of the Hollywood ending, the recent four-hour ABC-TV special on "The Movies" concluded with this scene.

22. Leo Gurko, *The Angry Decade* (New York: Dodd Mead & Co., 1947), p. 13.

23. Broadus Mitchell, *Depression Decade: From New Era Through New Deal 1929—1941* (New York: Rinehart & Co., 1947), p. 107.

Michael Selig (essay date 1992)

SOURCE: Selig, Michael. "From Play to Film: *Strange Snow, Jacknife,* and Masculine Identity in the Hollywood Vietnam Film." *Literature/Film Quarterly* 20, no. 3 (1992): 173-80.

[*In the following essay, Selig examines Hollywood adaptations of texts that dealt with the Vietnam war, characterizing them as unique opportunities that allow scholars to study the process of adaptation within the context of Hollywood's ideological stance towards the U.S. involvement in that conflict.*]

HISTORY AS MELODRAMA

For nearly ten years Hollywood ignored the story possibilities of the Vietnam "war." This was so much unlike Hollywood's production practices in other postwar eras that, in fact, the *absence* of films generated some critical discussion. Generally, it was assumed that Hollywood's reluctance to tackle the subject was a result of the industry's resistance to filming any controversial topic. However, one might more precisely note how the history of U.S. intervention in Vietnam is a difficult subject to adapt to Hollywood's narrative forms. Until recently, the industry had considerable trouble fashioning this history to fit the pattern of the conventional and the pleasurable. Quite simply, we "lost the war," and as a result the triumphant ending of the conventional Hollywood film, and especially the war film, is no longer credible.

Jacknife is only one of the many recent Vietnam films from Hollywood.[1] In many ways, it is typical of Hollywood films about veterans, treating war and its aftermath as domestic melodrama (e.g., *The Best Years of Our Lives, Pride Of The Marines, The Men,* and *Coming Home*). The film's central character, Megs aka Jacknife (Robert DeNiro), reenters the life of his "war buddy" David (Ed Harris), who is living with his sister Martha (Kathy Baker) in the house they grew up in. David's and Martha's father is dead, and their mother has moved to Florida. Megs returns in order to resolve an incident during the war which left both himself and David injured, and their mutual friend, Bobby, dead. As the film progresses, David and Megs make conflicting demands on Martha—sweetheart for Megs, mother for David—demands which, at least for David, threaten his home and his desperate sense of self. Martha in turn consistently criticizes David for his drinking and Megs for his crude manners. Megs awkwardly romances Martha, and his psychological healing is characterized by his attempts to restrain his violent temper and be tender toward her. Eventually, Megs and Martha "make love" in a scene which intends to convince us that Megs has in fact successfully healed himself. Ultimately, though, the veterans' bonding and the resolution of their war-time trauma mark the film's triumphant conclusion.

Jacknife is certainly subject to most of the criticisms that have plagued each new release of a film about Vietnam. Most obviously, it reiterates the proposition that the U.S. GI was a victim—here in a liberal, humanist guise like that of *Coming Home* or *Born On The Fourth Of July*, rather than in the reactionary one of Rambo. In either case, the Vietnamese are virtually nonexistent, and with their effacement the historical and political background of U.S. intervention in Vietnam is also effaced. Like all of Hollywood's Vietnam films, though, the authority and authenticity of *Jacknife*'s narrative, its "seriousness," is not premised on politics but on a specifically Hollywood-style melodramatics. Robert Lang's comments on melodrama are particularly helpful in focusing on this distinction: "the essential struggle is for individual identity within a familial context" (1).

Even though *Jacknife* is not much different from other Hollywood films about Vietnam in this regard, as an adaptation of a stage play, *Strange Snow,* the film offers us something unique: the opportunity to explore how the process of adaptation works within the context of Hollywood's consistent ideological stance toward U.S. intervention in Vietnam. By comparing the play with the film, the pressure to conform both history and the original material to Hollywood convention becomes more apparent. *Jacknife*'s restructuring of the play *Strange Snow* into a domestic melodrama permits the kind of contrived resolution typical of Hollywood's films about Vietnam, and a sense of victory where historically there was none.

Popular political discourse in the U.S. commonly draws on metaphors of the individual and the familial; it dates at least as far back as the Civil War and Reconstruction, as George Forgie has demonstrated in his book *Patricide in the House Divided*.[2] That the popular discourse about U.S. military involvement in Vietnam is limited to a focus on the individual instead of the social, the familial instead of the historical, is in evidence in the characterization of this history as a "trauma"—in other words, as a psychological issue rather than a political one. Gaylyn Studlar and David Desser note this when they discuss the manner in which Hollywood is "rewriting" the "war" in Vietnam as:

> a "trauma," a shock to the cultural system. Commonly used phrases such as "healing the wounds of Vietnam" are quite revelatory of this idea. . . . In reality, the attempt to cope with the national trauma of Vietnam confronts less a physical than a psychic trauma.
>
> (9)

In this sense, Hollywood's Vietnam films are something like a "talking cure," implementing a metaphorical psychoanalytic discourse to resolve the open-ended and unsatisfactory conclusion (for U.S. interests) to the historical Vietnam. This "talking cure" is in fact nurtured by what has come to be called the "cinematic apparatus," that is by

the conventional Hollywood mechanisms for placing the spectator in the position of a desiring subject.

As a result, U.S. intervention in Vietnam is never confronted on the grounds in which it challenges political identity—as, for example, an ideological commitment to freedom and democracy. Instead, Hollywood representations of Vietnam are consistently limited to questions which focus on the threat Vietnam poses to personal identity, and as Susan Jeffords has argued, the threat to a specifically masculine identity:

> . . . it becomes clear that the representation of the soldier and combat in contemporary American culture is more than simply a resurgence of militarism or nationalistic fever, but is instead a forum for the reaffirmation and reconstitution of the masculine. . . .
>
> (62)

Accepting Jeffords's argument, the question then becomes how the Hollywood Vietnam film specifically works to help contrive this "reaffirmation and reconstitution of the masculine." In her essay, "Desire in Narrative," Teresa de Lauretis argues that "All narrative . . . is overlaid with what has been called an Oedipal logic" (125). Raymond Bellour has recognized this as particularly apparent in Hollywood cinema: "The American film['s] massive attempt at socio-historical representation is basically shaped by . . . a classical Oedipal scenario . . . [one which] means accepting the place of the subject in the . . . family" (Bergstrom 93).[3] If Hollywood films consistently manifest both an Oedipal melodramatic narrative and a visual style organized around a masculine subject position, then we can begin to see how specific Hollywood Vietnam films engage this mechanism in order to attempt to resolve this "trauma" we consistently call "Vietnam."[4]

CONTRADICTION IN THE HOLLYWOOD VIETNAM FILM

Like most adaptations of stage plays, the transformation of *Strange Snow* into *Jacknife* required the addition of several scenes, not just to provide for a variety of settings and a more "filmic" display of action, but also to extend the fairly brief two acts into a feature-length story. Significantly, the film's extension of the play's more muted Oedipal tendencies into full-blown melodrama involves not only changes in the representation of the relationships between the principal characters. An adaptation from stage play to Hollywood film also requires the implementation of different spectatorial positions, ones which tend to constitute an identification between the viewer and a desiring male subject. As a result, the adaptation of play to film in this case engenders several contradictions which are typical of the Hollywood Vietnam film text.

One contradiction centers on the film's reification of the "authentic" view of Vietnam as that of the foot soldiers. The consistent affirmation of the infantry veteran's perspective as the only truthful perspective on Vietnam tends to paralyze the nonveteran's voice, to silence those who weren't "there."[5] This conflicts with the more general and economically necessary inclusion of a mass audience for these films, which depends on the pleasurable identification between heroic protagonist and spectator. In other words, the Vietnam film is faced with contriving an identification between the veteran-subject and the viewer, who is not likely to be a Viet vet, while at the same time reifying the exclusion of the nonveteran's perspective on the "war." The terms of this contradiction between exclusion and inclusion are typically constructed along the lines of gender. The excluded term is represented as female—not necessarily women characters, although this is common, but also feminized male characters (e.g., the long-haired protester or the feminized Vietnamese).[6] This leads to a further contradiction, as the Oedipalized construction of a male subject and a masculine identity both needs "woman" as the opposite figure against which man is defined and over which he triumphs, but which also must ultimately exclude or domesticate that figure. What Teresa de Lauretis notes about narrative in general, then, is also true of the Hollywood Vietnam narrative: "In this mythical-textual mechanics, the hero must be male . . . because, whatever its personification, the obstacle is . . . female" (118-19).

Finally, as an adaptation of a stage play, *Jacknife* tends toward the verbal rather than the visual. Whereas many other Vietnam films attempt to enact a "talking cure" with images of action, employing a conventionally active and pleasurable masculinization of the subject (e.g., in the character of Rambo or in *Platoon*), *Jacknife*'s construction of male subjectivity is dependent on contriving a literal "talking cure"—Megs can't stop talking about Vietnam, and David will be forced to in order to be "cured." The characteristic voice-over narration of many Vietnam films (e.g., *The Iron Triangle, Platoon, Apocalypse Now*), as well as the aggressive and overwhelming "dialogue" of Robin Williams in *Good Morning Vietnam*, is similarly focused on talking about Vietnam in order to subject to language the threat Vietnam poses to the self—much as the Vietnam films attempt to subject the threat of the Asian Other to the cinematic Symbolic. The force of the "theatrical" versus the "filmic" in *Jacknife* is most evident in the *film's* addition of seemingly uncinematic group therapy sessions, which is where the film ultimately leaves the recovering David.

From Play to Film

The change in title from play to film, *Strange Snow* to *Jacknife* (the nickname of the film's central character), is indicative of the film's greater focus on masculine identity. The sequence which accompanies the opening credits affirms this. Whereas the play opens with Megs's early morning assault on David's and Martha's home, the film's credit sequence offers the viewer Megs's preparation—from the alarm clock which brings him to consciousness (along with us as spectators) to the sequence's conclusion, a shot of David's and Martha's home from Megs's point of view. Unlike the play, where of necessity the viewer

maintains a distanced perspective, the film immediately provides for the viewer's identification with a desiring male subject.

In the opening scenes, the alteration of the play to provide for an identification with Megs is evident even in seemingly minor moments. In both play and film, for example, Megs wakes Martha and David and then exits in order to retrieve some "breakfast beer" from his car. During his absence, David tells Martha, "He's not my friend. He's just somebody I know." In the play, several more lines are exchanged between Martha and David before Megs reenters. In the film, however, Megs is seen overhearing the first part of this conversation, again placing the viewer in a position to share his perspective as he reenters the scene.

Megs's point of view, however, does not completely dominate the film. The character's lack of a stable identity, here played out as emotional instability, tends to keep the viewer at some distance. In the first half of the film especially, Martha's curiosity about Megs and his "endearing," even if eccentric, behavior matches that of the viewer, offering a surrogate point of view that challenges any exclusive identification with Megs.[7] The film also establishes a greater depth to the character of Martha than the play does. Although still very much the stereotype of a virginal school teacher, the intensity Kathy Baker brings to the portrayal of the character's sexual innocence implies both unsatisfied desire and some past trauma.

In fact, all three characters exhibit a history and desires which at least initially are translated into varying degrees of identification with each character's point of view.[8] This is evident in the film's addition of several sequences which involve only one of the three. In one scene, for example, Martha spies a young couple in the hall after school. The point of view shots which structure this sequence establish her as the subject of a desire which up to this point in the film are as fundamental as Megs's or David's to the progress of the narrative. Similarly, David's desire for a stable household and the restitution of parental authority is acted out in a scene where he visits Bobby's parents and virtually begs them to let him do chores around their house.

This instability in the characters' identities is not only manifested in the film's visualization of varying points of view; it also becomes the focal point around which the film extends the play's action. Narratively, this instability is linked to a sense of a traumatic history, both the fictional history of each character and the history of U.S. intervention in Vietnam. The latter, of course, grants the film its dramatic consequence. More significantly, though, by tying the restitution of a stable masculine identity to the history of the Vietnam war and its aftermath, an emotional resolution can be acted out for this unresolved history.

The stabilizing of each character's identity, and thus the spectator's position in relation to them, is dependent on working out the characters' histories through the resolution of Oedipal conflicts which structure the narrative of both the film and the play. The play, however, does not focus so specifically on the characters' acting out of desire, nor on the restitution of masculine identity to resolve the history of U.S. involvement in Vietnam.

In the film, though, the relationships reconstruct the triad of father, mother/lover, and son. Megs's entry into the lives of David and his sister disrupts the equilibrium of their household. Megs is not the first or only Father the narrative introduces, either. Bobby, the friend who died in Vietnam, took care of Megs and David while over there, and significantly he gave them their nicknames, exercising the power of the Symbolic. David's actual father is also dead, though not forgotten. He is introduced through David's desire to have "decked him" on his return from Vietnam, to have repayed him for the jingoistic slant he had given to enlistment. This revenge against the Father is frustratingly incomplete, though, as his father died before his return from Nam. This Oedipal frustration is symbolically overdetermined by the injury to David's leg, indicating the threat of castration and loss of identity that makes Vietnam so horrific. Like *Coming Home* and *Born On The Fourth Of July,* the injury and the loss of identity are tied together in a clichéd lamenting for the lost glory days of high school athletic prowess.[9] In the film, an additional brief scene of Megs and David playing basketball concludes with David hurting his leg and angrily lashing out at Megs. More significantly, as the film reaches its climactic confrontation between David and Megs over their injuries in Vietnam, David enters the local high school and destroys the trophy cabinet, including the photographs that continue to glorify his "heroic" achievements on the football field.

Paralleling this unstated historical conflict between Megs and David, and central to the working out of desire in the film, is Megs's romantic interest in David's sister, which results in a conflict over the allegiance of the sole significant woman in the film. In the play, David's resistance to this budding romance centers on differences in social class. Although David drives a truck, his pre-Vietnam ambitions to be a professional are consonant with his suburban Connecticut background and with his sister's middle-class sensibilities. Megs, however, is decidedly working class, and both the play and the film quite unimaginatively represent this through crude manners and a greater sense of sexual freedom.

In contrast, the film makes no significant distinction between David's and Megs's careers, and it also doesn't identify the difference in sensibilities between Martha and Megs with class differences. David's resistance is premised specifically on the threat Megs poses to his relationship with Martha, that is on the Oedipal conflicts it engenders. Several scenes are added to the play which make this clear. Twice, David sees Megs out with Martha, and he angrily exits without their knowledge. Following the second scene, he confronts Martha and demands that she no longer see Megs, in a moment partially derived from the play.

But the film extends this scene into a temporary reconciliation, where in Martha's bedroom she forces him to accept that she cannot be the woman he "wants her" to be. David exits, acting the hurt child.

For Martha, her resistance to Megs's romantic interest is represented in overtly masculine terms as her frigidity (compare Fonda's character in *Coming Home*). As mentioned earlier, though, the film's representation of her sexuality also inaugurates a sense of female history and consciousness that seems to challenge the predominance of a masculine point of view. Nevertheless, in contrast to the play, the film provides for considerably more focus on Vietnam and the predominance of the male characters' subjectivities. This is accomplished in part through several flashbacks of Vietnam and the moment of David's injury and Bobby's death, flashbacks presented from Megs's and David's points of view. In contrast, Martha's "trauma" is revealed in the clichéd and far less spectacular terms of a dialogue between her and Megs about her unsatisfying first sexual experience. In other words, the historical "trauma" is far more dramatically and distinctively represented in the case of the men.

Even more significantly, in the film the point at which Martha and Megs make love takes place about two-thirds of the way into the story, providing a pivotal moment in the film's progress toward a resolution. In the play, this scene comes at the end and is in fact never enacted. In the scene in the film, Martha's resistance to Megs's sexual advances is reversed without any apparent motivation, and on the very same night that she had violently rejected him. Much like *Coming Home,* the woman's subjectivity is established in opposition to masculine dominance, effaced by premising that subjectivity on her sexuality and then using it as the ground on which masculine identity is acted out. As in *Coming Home,* following the male subject's sexual satisfaction (and the apparent satisfaction of the woman), he is empowered, initiated into the role of the Father while she is virtually forgotten. Discussing the construction of the masculine bond in other popular texts about U.S. involvement in Vietnam, Susan Jeffords comments that the masculine "become[s] reinforced by its passage through women, by its appropriation and rejection of women's bodies" (39).

In the Hollywood Vietnam film, this empowerment is typically enacted through the spectator's identification with the heroic subject's access to the Symbolic, through his power to name Vietnam and thus contain its threat to the masculine self. In the play, *Strange Snow,* there is no parallel, as the characters are left without a resolution to their Vietnam-era trauma. In contrast, by giving voice to the past, the film concludes with the authentication of male subjective experience, an authentication based on the restitution of masculine identity and the contradictory exclusion and domestication of the female. Just as the anti-war film presents a foxhole bonding of male enemies (as in *The Iron Triangle*) the "coming home" Vietnam films present the camaraderie of psychologically distressed veterans, and the exclusion of the female, as the key to a resolution of their problems, and the narrative. As Susan Jeffords notes, ". . . the masculine bond depends on . . . an affirmation of difference—men are not women. The motif of this struture is thus one of exclusion, and its primary shape is a hierarchy defined by participation in/exclusion from the experience of war" (59-60). In *Coming Home,* Luke convinces Bob Hyde that he's "not the enemy," and immediately following he asserts the authenticity of his experience by addressing high school students, telling them, "I've been there." Sally Hyde is relinquished to her psychotic husband. In *Born On The Fourth Of July,* Ron Kovics reconstitutes his postwar identity by voicing opposition to U.S. involvement in Vietnam as a member of Vietnam Veterans Against the War, and the film's resolution comes with his address to the Democratic National Convention. The threat to male identity posed by his mother and the Mexican prostitutes is left far behind.

In *Jacknife,* the authenticity of personal experience is also premised on the camaraderie of the veterans and the exclusion of the female. In the film's penultimate scene, Megs tells David that he should no longer depend emotionally on Martha, because "She doesn't know. She wasn't there." This exclusion is visualized in a shot-reverse shot pattern with her standing alone in opposition to the "war buddies," whose point of view shots dominate this scene. In the film's final moments, David is seen giving voice to his experience in group therapy, which he had earlier rejected, while Megs prepares to leave town. However, Megs returns to Martha to complete the restitution of his identity, which was premised primarily on his sexual conquest. The film's commitment to both her exclusion from the experience of Vietnam *and* her domestication is necessitated by her maternal threat to David's self-realization, and by the film's structuring of Megs's masculine identity in opposition to her feminine one. While we see Megs return to Martha, David's narration voices the role the figure of "woman" plays in the film: "Bobby said we'd all find girls. And then finally things would make sense."

Conclusion

The adaptation of play to film involves both the transformation of the story and, of necessity, its visualization. Both the play and the film attempt to subject the history of U.S. involvement in Vietnam to the personal and the emotional, effacing a genuinely historical perspective. The humanistic sensibilities of the play are contradicted mostly by its ethnocentrism—by the total absence of a Vietnamese perspective—while the film is further limited by its patriarchal precedents, that is by the mobilization of Hollywood's conventionally pleasurable Oedipal textual mechanics. As a result, the film's narrative progresses toward a restitution of masculine subjectivity—toward an authentic and authoritative masculine perspective—providing the closure and the sense of victory missing from both the play and the historical Vietnam. Yet, the historically real victory belonged to the Vietnamese, and the attempt by *Jacknife,* like all the Hollywood Vietnam films, to refash-

ion the dominance of a Western male subjectivity engenders a series of contradictions which challenge the film's effectiveness as a "talking cure." As each new Vietnam film is released, and as each becomes a focus for ever more "talk" about Vietnam, it creates the desire for the production of yet another Vietnam film, one which will finally put the "trauma" to rest. Whereas Hollywood initially ignored the potential stories about U.S. involvement in Vietnam, lately it has discovered a way to produce a seemingly never-ending cycle of films which incite a desire that can't be satisfied.

Notes

1. *Jacknife* was a fairly successful film, though not probably up to expectations considering some fairly significant pre-release publicity centering on its stars, especially Robert DeNiro. The film is listed in *Variety*'s top 50 the first week of its release in March 1989, having been released in only two theaters. The film continues to appear in the top 50 for another 90 days, though never higher than number 19. After release on video, it appears on the top 50 list in *Variety* for nine weeks, the highest ranking sixteenth with a majority of weeks in the middle of the charts. The film has had a fairly long run on pay cable television, still showing at the time of this writing.

2. In early film melodrama, the significance of family to political ideology in a war and postwar situation is especially evident in *The Birth of a Nation.*

3. The significance of the Oedipal to Hollywood film melodrama is also considered by Lang: "Melodrama [is] Hollywood's fairly consistent way of treating desire and subject identity. . . . Hollywood's way of organizing experience parallels the way of psychoanalysis . . . that way is to tell stories, in images, and the masterplot . . . is Freud's myth of Oedipus" (12-13). Kaja Silverman similarly situates the centrality of masculine identity in Hollywood's representation of a postwar era. In an extended discussion of *The Best Years of Our Lives,* she notes the confrontation with a "loss of belief in the family . . . and the adequacy of the male subject" (118).

4. This is not necessarily to assert any essentialist or scientific truth to psychoanalytic discourse (or that discourse's ability to explicate the pleasure of a film text). Rather, it's a recognition of the power of psychoanalytic categories and tools of criticism to explicate ways we organize our collective as well as our personal history, to see with these categories the historical operations of ideology.

5. For a discussion of the "paralysis of response" on the reader's or viewer's part, see Jeffords 30-42.

6. See Jeffords, White, and Selig on the "feminization" of the Other, as well as other (that is, alternative) perspectives on the conflict in Vietnam.

7. Even as the "excluded" perspective of the nonveteran is engaged, it's focused on developing an under-

standing of the veteran as a subject, even if it's a subject of peculiar consciousness at this point. One might compare the film *Heroes,* or the spectator's positioning in relationship to the Green Berets character during the wedding in *The Deer Hunter.*

8. This discussion of the transformation of the play to a film text is intended to outline the possible positions offered to the spectator and not to take up the issue of how those positions are variously occupied by different spectators and/or groups of spectators.

9. This desire for the restitution of the lost glory days of athletic prowess characterizes a number of films about returning veterans from previous wars as well. For examples, see *The Best Years of Our Lives, Pride of the Marines,* and *The Men.*

Works Cited

Bergstrom, Janet. "Alternation, Segmentation, Hypnosis: Interview with Raymond Bellour." *Camera Obscura* 3-4 (1979): 71-104.

de Lauretis, Teresa. *Alice Doesn't: Feminism, Semiotics, Cinema.* Bloomington: Indiana UP, 1984.

Forgie, George. *Patricide in the House Divided: A Psychological Interpretation of Lincoln and His Age.* New York: W. W. Norton, 1979.

Jeffords, Susan. *The Remasculinization of America: Gender and the Vietnam War.* Bloomington: Indiana UP, 1989.

Lang, Robert. *American Film Melodrama: Griffith, Vidor, Minnelli.* Princeton: Princeton UP, 1989.

Selig, Michael. "Boys Will Be Men: Oedipal Drama in *Coming Home." From Hanoi to Hollywood: The Vietnam War in American Film.* Eds. Linda Dittmar and Gene Michaud. New Brunswick, NJ: Rutgers UP, 1990. 189-202.

Silverman, Kaja. "Historical Trauma and Male Subjectivity." *Psychoanalysis and Cinema.* Ed. E. Ann Kaplan. New York: Routledge and AFI, 1990.

Studlar, Gaylyn, and David Desser. "Never Having to Say You're Sorry: *Rambo's* Rewriting of the Vietnam War." *Film Quarterly* 42.1 (Fall 1988): 9-16.

White, Susan. "Male Bonding, Hollywood Orientalism, and the Repression of the Feminine in Kubrick's *Full Metal Jacket." Arizona Quarterly* 44.3 (Autumn 1988): 120-44.

Thomas Hemmeter (essay date 1994)

SOURCE: Hemmeter, Thomas. "Adaptation, History, and Textual Suppression: Literary Sources of Hitchcock's *Sabotage.*" In *Literature and Film in the Historical Dimension: Selected Papers from the Fifteenth Annual Florida State University Conference on Literature and Film,* edited by John D. Simons, pp. 149-61. Gainesville: University Press of Florida, 1994.

[*In the following essay, Hemmeter reviews the textual antecedents of Alfred Hitchcock's film* Sabotage, *proposing that the director used both the novel and play versions of* The Secret Agent *by Joseph Conrad.*]

In reacting against ahistorical textual readings of films, the field of cinema studies embraces the historical analysis of films both as products of historical forces and as producers of historical perspectives. Such studies generally examine the production practices of studios, the social conditions of audiences, and the economic and ideological pressures on filmmakers and the film industry. While this historical criticism does valuable service by filling in the historical context, sometimes the textual history of the film is neglected. Filmed adaptations of literary sources are particularly fertile sites of textual history since the films express both historical evaluations of their own periods and historical re-evaluations of the earlier period producing the literary source. A third historical period is implicated as well—that of the film criticism analyzing filmed adaptations. Dudley Andrew reminds us that in their own making of history, critical analyses are not above history—there is a historical dimension to their discourse.[1] In examining all three historical dimensions of Alfred Hitchcock's *Sabotage,* adapted from a Joseph Conrad work, it is clear that the critical discourse has worked to repress certain aspects of the film's textual history.

In 1907 Joseph Conrad published a novel entitled *The Secret Agent.* In 1936 Alfred Hitchcock directed and released a film entitled *Sabotage.* (He could not title his film *The Secret Agent* because he had used that title for his film adaptation of Somerset Maugham's *Ashenden* released the same year.) From 1965 to 1990 the critical conclusion has been that the Conrad novel is the single literary source of the Hitchcock film. Why Hitchcock chose to adapt such a dense, gloomy novel dominated by a sardonic narrator when he had success with more popular literary sources published between 1915 and 1935 remains a minor puzzle to most Hitchcock scholars. Tom Ryall notes that the novel preceded the popular cycle of spy thrillers which began around 1914 with World War I and continued into the 1930s.[2] Why would Hitchcock seek out a difficult text by an unpopular, if highly respected, writer concerned with pre-war social and political malaise?

One obvious answer to this question is found when noting historical parallels between the Edwardian decade building to World War I and the 1930s decade building up to World War II. Another possible answer to this question is that Hitchcock may not have gone back only to the 1907 novel; he may have also used as a source the play *The Secret Agent,* which Conrad adapted from his own novel. This intervening text complicates the easy equation of Edwardian and 1930s England. The absence of this dramatic adaptation of Conrad's novel in the discussion of Hitchcock's adaptation choices in *Sabotage* is a significant gap in the critical discourse (including Hitchcock's own) on the novel. I will argue that this discourse gap is also a historical gap, and that a textual history of the adaptation process evident in *Sabotage* reveals filmmaker and critics to be engaged in a type of history making which Pierre Sorlin, analyzing historical films, calls an effort to define their own vision of the past.[3] In the case of *Sabotage* a crucial aspect of this critical history making is the suppression of the intervening dramatic text of *The Secret Agent* in the discussion of the film's literary sources. A study of filmed adaptations reminds us that history is an act of forgetting as well as remembering.

Conrad adapted the play *The Secret Agent* from his novel in the years 1919-22, and it enjoyed a short run on the London stage in November, 1922.[4] The historical facts regarding Conrad's play strongly suggest that Hitchcock saw the work on stage. Hitchcock is known to have been a habitué of the London theater and to have been in London when Conrad's play was staged.[5] The only critic to cite Conrad's drama *The Secret Agent* as the literary source of *Sabotage,* Donald Spoto also notes Hitchcock's habit of inveterate theater-going.[6] One suspects the common critical preference for the Conrad novel as the literary source to have something to do with a preference for a more respectable precursor text: the novel enjoyed at least limited critical success (*TL* 878), while the play had a mercifully short run and was not critically admired.

An examination of the text of the play reveals details which give it claim, along with the novel, as one precursor text of *Sabotage.* The overall contours of the novel's plot remain in Conrad's play: the domestic tranquility of Verloc, an inactive double agent, his wife Winnie, and her retarded brother Stevie is disturbed by the demand from Verloc's superior that he sabotage the Greenwich Observatory with a bomb; the bomb's premature explosion prompts the police, Verloc's anarchist colleagues, and the reader to investigate what happened, leading first to the false conclusion that Verloc blew himself up and then to the realization that Stevie lost his life when Verloc sent him with the bomb; and when Winni Verloc discovers finally that her brother has died, she kills Verloc and finally herself after she is betrayed by another anarchist. (The play has her go mad rather than commit suicide.) The chief difference between novel and play is the latter's focus on the Verlocs, eliminating the saturnine narrator and much of the material on anarchists and double agents. The generic requirements of drama require a more condensed narrative, leading Conrad to announce that, in adapting his novel for the stage, he decided to focus on Winnie instead of Verloc, the secret agent (*TL* 838).

The film reproduces this focus on Winnie as the central member of a love triangle, like the play producing a discourse which places personal relations in the foreground at the expense of the novel's broad political and social issues. The film removes what little remained in the play about political matters, moves the Verlocs from a pornog-

raphy shop to a movie theater, and blends the police investigator and the anarchist lover of Winnie into one character. The film's major alteration is in plot: Where both novel and play have the bomb explode about one-third of the way through and lead us through investigations in which we are partially in the dark, the film delays the bombing until two-thirds of the way through and focuses on the aftermath—Winnie's reactions and those of her policeman-lover. The film also does not have Winnie commit suicide or go mad; instead, it has her joining a gay crowd of Londoners with her unwelcome lover.

Though the two precursor texts seem to offer the same basic narrative to adapt, there are some telling details in Conrad's play which mark it as a source. The stage directions specifically describe Stevie as dressed in an apron to do domestic chores,[7] a detail that does not appear in the novel but does appear in the film. The explosion in the movie theater at the end of *Sabotage* is another variation from the novel which the play anticipates in a line from an anarchist who dismisses just such a plan as ineffectual, "Blow up churches, theaters full of people—that's no good" (*DT* 35). And we can easily imagine a line from the play like "the police can do nothing" (*DT* 57), ringing in Hitchcock's head. Many other references or verbal images which echo in Hitchcock's film—the repeated use of the carving knife Winnie uses to kill Verloc or the reference to Stevie's death as accidental, "as if he had been run over by a bus" (in the film he dies in a bus)—appear in both novel and play, but stand out more forcefully in the latter since they are not embedded in the novel's dense text.

The argument here is not for a greater fidelity of film to play than to novel. Indeed, Conrad's novel includes details which might be argued to be inspiring certain film events. For example, during a famous scene in *Sabotage* Verloc, instructed to bomb Picadilly Circus, visualizes the destruction when the fish tank he has been staring at in an aquarium dissolves into an image of collapsing structures. The novel's narrative describes a character's imagination of a bomb's destructive power as "the overlighted place changed into a dreadful black hole belching horrible fumes choked with ghastly rubbish of smashed brickwork and mutilated corpses".[8] No lines from the play convey the imaginative fears of characters so visually.

Though one may find many parallels between film and novel, the ignored play stands as another source precisely because it expresses a historical pattern of textual suppression. In adapting his novel for the stage, Conrad suppressed most of his novel's overt political material; in adapting novel/play for the screen, Hitchcock suppressed most of the overt references to sex and buried the political material even more deeply than the play had done. Anarchists, foreign agents, and revolutionaries become shadowy figures, clearly elements of a MacGuffin, the plot pretext which creates external conflicts about which the characters are concerned but the viewer is not. This process of narrative suppression (MacGuffinizing), begun by Conrad's play which greatly reduces the role played by political agents in the novel, is continued in the film.

The film also expresses material that both Conrad's novel and play suppressed: the actual killing of the boy. The novel has the bombing simply happen in a narrative ellipsis, which has the effect of hiding the killing itself. In the play, Act 2 and part of Act 3 are concerned with people all talking about the bombing, but the real concern is not the event but the consequences for Winnie and for others in British society. Hitchcock's film reverses the emphasis: suppressing the broad social effects, *Sabotage* shows the gradual movement towards the boy's death itself. The effects of his death are narrow, focused on Winnie and her lover. Like all adaptations, which both preserve and cancel out the original text, *Sabotage* both conceals and reveals material from its predecessor text. The suppression of the dramatic text—by Conrad, by Hitchcock, and by critics discussing *Sabotage*—extends this textual process.

The critical history of the film text reveals a similar pattern of expression and suppression. The credits cite Conrad's novel as the literary source, and the two book-length works on Hitchcock's British films both assume that Hitchcock adapted his film from Conrad's novel (*AH* 126-127).[9] Even articles focused specifically on the nature of Hitchcock's adaptation in *Sabotage* assume that Conrad's novel provided the director with his source material.[10] Never mentioned (except in the critical biography by Spoto) is the fact that there are two Conrad works entitled *The Secret Agent*. The 1922 play, a source closer in time, is also more closely related in spareness of structure and in medium to the 1936 film than is the novel. Yet the critical heritage assumes that Hitchcock, who by 1936 had adapted ten plays into films and who suffered some studio pressure to use popular plays as source material (*AH* 179, *passim*), adapted *Sabotage* from the single novelistic source.

Without the intervening dramatic text to complicate historical assumptions, critics of *Sabotage* are free to dehistoricize the film into a typical studio adaptation with no firm relation to any historical period. On the one hand, its relationship to Edwardian England is denied; Hitchcock's film is "more reflective of [his] own time and place than of Conrad's".[11] On the other hand, its relationship to the social realities of England in the 1930s is denied; it is one of a vogue of spy thrillers and melodramas which hint "unwittingly" of events abroad.[12] Part of this critical project to dehistoricize *Sabotage* has to do with that common habit in adaptation criticism, privileging the literary source text and marginalizing the derived film text, which Eric Rentschler notes has the effect of overlooking vast intertextual space between film and source.[13]

A facet of this critical practice is the assumption of a unitary, coherent predecessor text, in this case Conrad's novel. A corollary assumption is that there is a direct historical link between the novel's fictional events and those of the Edwardian period. With a single preceding text as an anchor, the twenty-nine years between the novel and the film become unified—an uncluttered linear skin stretched over the intertextual space between film and novel. This historical simplification allows easy ideological parallels; e.g., as Conrad's novel is concerned with international and social problems leading to World War I, Hitchcock's film is concerned with problems leading to World War II. The 1930s assumes a profile similar to that of the Edwardian period, and the historical conclusion is that Britain repeated its mistakes or answered its challenges in two traumatic international stuggles. When Conrad's 1922 play enters the picture, however, the easy parallel disappears and the entire forty years from 1900 to 1939 become a complex historical fabric, not two parallel threads in England's political struggle against international chaos and violence.

To shift the discussion from broad historical and political grounds to means of production, it might be argued that the intervening dramatic text has been ignored because of conditions in the British film industry of the 1930s. Tom Ryall's study, *Alfred Hitchcock and the British Cinema*, goes a long way toward answering what Eric Rentschler argues is a central question of any adaptation study: Why does the artist adapt certain material at certain times (*GF* 4)? Although Ryall's study examines economic, studio, and artistic influences on Hitchcock's work (*AH* 85-184), with *Sabotage* he focuses on genre and adaptation. Ryall concludes that Hitchcock, working to produce entertainment films, was bound to a great degree by the conventions of popular art, particularly the thriller genre, whose vogue in the 1930s led the director to choose a number of similar literary properties for adaptation. He places *Sabotage* in what he calls Hitchcock's "thriller sestet": *The Man Who Knew Too Much* (1934), *The 39 Steps* (1935), *The Secret Agent* (1936), *Young and Innocent* (1937), and *The Lady Vanishes* (1938). What binds these six films together is a uniformity of literary source: unlike earlier films derived from middlebrow literary and dramatic adaptations, these six films drew on such traditions of popular culture as the crime and spy novel (*AH* 179).

But there is an interesting gap in Ryall's account, a gap which suggests that historical studies of films should not be limited to accounts of studio production constraints and of ideological apparatus imposed by economic and sociological conditions of a historical period. Although he draws a clear distinction between *Sabotage* and *The 39 Steps*—the latter has a dark tone derived from Conrad's novel while the former is light in tone because it adapts a popular novel—a unifying impulse leads Ryall to erase his own distinction and lump Conrad's novel in with other popular novels. Ryall's privileging of popular sources as one reason for Hitchcock's superior 1930s films requires the marginalization of middlebrow literary sources, as he mentions in particular dramatic adaptations (*AH* 128, 131-32). It makes sense, then, that as he suppresses the historical and textual differences of Conrad's novel from the other five suspense novels which Hitchcock adapted—the novel *The Secret Agent* was earlier in time and hardly popular— Ryall also suppresses the dramatic text of *The Secret Agent*. The play constitutes a middlebrow dramatic adaptation, though unsuccessful, and Ryall describes such adaptations as studio-enforced mechanisms to which Hitchcock had to flee when personal projects failed in the 1925-1933 years (*AH* 173). The 1922 text of *The Secret Agent* had to be suppressed.

TRUFFAUT:

> Making a child die in a picture is a rather ticklish matter; it comes close to an abuse of cinematic power.

HITCHCOCK:

> I agree with that; it was a grave error on my part.[14]

In discussing with Francois Truffaut his decisions to have a young boy blown up by a bomb in his 1936 film *Sabotage,* Hitchcock typically backs away from a violation of audience expectations, apologizing for alienating his viewers' sympathies. This is a common Hitchcock maneuver, as we find him, for example, apologizing for his film experiments in *Rope* (*HI* 130-31). Of course, Hitchcock loved technical experiment and indulged this interest in many films besides *Rope,* just as he indulged the habit of killing off attractive characters in films besides *Sabotage* (e.g., *Psycho, Vertigo, Frenzy*). Indeed, Hitchcock often complains about studio decisions demanding that a killing be suppressed or that a handsome leading man be declared innocent, as in the changed endings of *The Lodger* and *Suspicion.* Despite his disclaimer, in killing the innocent boy in *Sabotage,* Hitchcock succeeded in expressing what he wanted. His later confession of regret may be seen as an attempt at suppression.

Naturally Hitchcock does not correct Truffaut's assumption that *Sabotage* is based on Conrad's novel (*HI* 75), as indeed it was in part. The critical suppression of the less respectable literary source, a failed play, itself an adaptation, is met by Hitchcock's own suppression. One motive has to do with the ambivalence (or downright hostility) of British studio executives in the 1920s and 1930s toward art films, which may have lent some respectability to a film but were at odds with commercial success (*AH* 89). One distributor in particular, C. M. Woolf, came into conflict with Hitchcock more than once because he "nurtured a suspicion of Hitchcock's artistic qualities" (*AH* 164). Hitchcock would be safer claiming a novel distant in time—its unpopularity forgotten, its author famous enough to lend some prestige to the film—than to claim a pretentious play which was known to have not drawn an audience.

Another motive for Hitchcock's suppression is his own ambivalence toward drama. Though he thought that dramatists are more skilled than novelists in adapting their material for the screen (*HI* 50), in a sense the closeness of film to drama presented him problems in adapting plays. Hitchcock needed to narrate dramatic materials in cinematic form and felt embarrassed over his version of *Juno and the Paycock* because it resisted cinematic transformation (*HI* 48; *LT* 104-105). Indeed, Hitchcock claimed he felt he had stolen something when he was praised for *Juno,* leading him to declare his intention to avoid literary

masterpieces; his preferred method was to read a story once, forget the material and start to create cinema (*HI* 48-49). Suppression of the original text—he was unable to remember the story material drawn from sources on which his films are based—was clearly a working method for Hitchcock. It is an easy extension of this working method to see Hitchcock repressing a play like *The Secret Agent* whose discourse, closer to that of film, would resist his imaginative translation.

As in his statement on killing the child in *Sabotage,* Hitchcock's words are not entirely to be trusted. Suppression is so contrived a part of his working methods and his publicity that he also may have suppressed certain debts to Conrad's play. Though known to have worked extensively on scripts for most of his films, Hitchcock never has claimed screenwriting credit. The suppression of the play *The Secret Agent,* beyond the obvious publicity and business value of putting forward the more prestigious novel as the putative source text, expresses Hitchcock's mode of adaptation. To adapt is to conceal certain sources by overtly revealing an obvious source.

The act of Hitchcock and the critics to privilege the novel as the single source text of *Sabotage* is a historical act of suppressing other predecessor texts. In discussing the discourse of adaptation in the context of the theory of intertextuality, Christopher Orr challenges the notion of a singular literary source as a determining pretext for a filmed adaptation. A literary source is one of a series of pre-texts showing the same narrative conventions as the film adaptation. "The act of adapting a text from another medium is, in effect, the privileging or underlining of certain quotations within the film's intertextual space".[15] Orr would have us look at cultural codes and ideological practices in the adapted film's production as well as comparative discursive practices to guard against reductive discussions of fidelity of film to literary source. What is fascinating in the case of *Sabotage* is that studies like Ryall's of *Sabotage*'s conditions of production lead to conclusions similar to those of critics applying the discourse of fidelity of film to novel. Neither approach uncovers the historical document of the intervening third text, the play *The Secret Agent,* which challenges the singular notion of a literary source more definitively.

In *The Film in History,* Pierre Sorlin notes that "history is a society's memory of its past" and that each society creates its own version of the past according to its social organization (*FH* 16-17). Important in this historical memory, of course, is forgetting; in the process of selecting certain events, encounters, and documents to remember, others are selected to be forgotten. In discussing the literary source of *Sabotage,* film critics of the 1960s, 1970s, and 1980s have decided not to recall the intervening dramatic text of *The Secret Agent* and instead to remember the Conrad novel, joining Hitchcock in creating an oversimplified version of *Sabotage*'s textual history. Dudley Andrew says that history is not a sequence of events but "the revaluation by which events are singled out and understood in successive eras" (*CF* 127). The suppression of Conrad's play as a source of *Sabotage* extends Andrew's notion. As an adapted text, *Sabotage* has been revalued by successive generations who have chosen to foreground one facet of its textual past, its debt to the Conrad novel, and efface another facet, its debt to the failed Conrad play. The full complexity of the film's intertextuality has not been singled out for historical memory. Adaptations present history as an act of forgetting as well as remembering.

Notes

1. Dudley Andrew, *Concepts in Film Theory,* Oxford: Oxford University Press, 1984. Hereafter cited in the text as *CF.*

2. Tom Ryall, *Alfred Hitchcock & the British Cinema,* Urbana: University of Illinois Press, 1986. Hereafter cited in the text as *AH.*

3. Pierre Sorlin, *The Film in History: Restaging the Past,* Totowa, New Jersey: Barnes & Noble, 1980. Hereafter cited in the text as *FH.*

4. Frederick R. Karl, *Joseph Conrad: The Three Lives,* New York: Farrar, Straus and Giroux, 1979. Hereafter cited in the text as *TL;* Jocelyn Baines, *Joseph Conrad: A Critical Biography,* New York: McGraw-Hill, 1960.

5. John Russell Taylor, Hitch: *The Life and Times of Alfred Hitchcock,* New York: Pantheon, 1978. Hereafter cited in the text as *LT.*

6. Donald Spoto, *The Dark Side of Genius: The Life of Alfred Hitchcock,* Boston: Little, Brown, 1983.

7. Joseph Conrad, *The Secret Agent: A Drama in Three Acts,* London: T. Werner Laurie, 1923. Hereafter cited in the text as *DT.*

8. Joseph Conrad, *The Secret Agent,* 1953 Anchor edition. New York: Doubleday, 1907.

9. Maurice Yacowar, *Hitchcock's British Films,* Hamden, Connecticut: Archon Books, 1977.

10. Michael Andregg, "Conrad and Hitchcock: *The Secret Agent* Inspires *Sabotage,*" *Literature/Film Quarterly* III, no. 3 (Summer 1975): 215-225; Goodwin, James. "Conrad and Hitchcock: Secret Sharers." In *The English Novel and the Movies,* edited by Michael Klein & Gillian Parker, 218-227. New York: Ungar, 1981.

11. Steve Vineberg, "Two Routes into Conrad: On Filming *Under Western Eyes* and *Outcasts of the Islands,*" *Literature/Film Quarterly* XV, no. 1 (January 1987): 22-27.

12. Tony Aldgate, "Ideological Consensus in British Feature Films, 1935-1947." In *Feature Films as History,* edited by K. R. M. Short 94-112. Knoxville: University of Tennessee, 1981.

The view that Hitchcock's 1930s films do not reflect socio-political reality is widely held, supported by film historian like Roy Armes. Critics like Furhammar and Isaksson (139), attempting to counter that view, nevertheless feel constrained to put films like *Sabotage* in the suspense genre, a category whose structural demands weaken the film's political impact. Sam Simone, who devotes a book to establishing Hitchcock's overt political intentions in the 1940s films, agrees that his 1930s films were not as ideologically open because of governmental and studio censorship as well as the suspense structures (22). Hitchcock tried to warn the United States against Nazi sabotage in the 1940s films, but *Sabotage* is not a prior effort to rouse the English to the Nazi threat because it is seen as a part of a generic pattern of thriller adaptations and thus politically irrelevant. See: Roy Armes, *A Critical History of British Cinema,* London: Tantivy Press, 1977; Leif Fruhammar, and Folke Isaksson. *Politics and Film,* Translated by Kersti French. New York: Praeger, 1971; Sam P. Simone, *Hitchcock as Activist: Politics and the War Films,* Ann Arbor: UMI Research Press, 1985.

13. Eric Rentschler, "Introduction: Theoretical and Historical Considerations," In *German Film and Literature,* ed., Eric Rentschler (New York: Methuen, 1986) 1-8. Hereafter cited in the text as *GF.*

14. Francois Truffaut, *Hitchcock,* New York: Simon & Schuster, 1967. Hereafter cited in the text as *HI.*

15. Christopher Orr, "The Discourse on Adaptation," *Wide Angle* VI, no. 2 (1984), 72-76.

Leonard J. Leff (essay date December 1996)

SOURCE: Leff, Leonard J. "Hollywood and the Holocaust: Remembering *The Pawnbroker.*" *American Jewish History* 84, no. 4. (December 1996): 353-76.

[*In the following essay, Leff outlines the adaptive and production history of Edward Lewis Wallant's* The Pawnbroker, *calling it the foundation for such films as* Schindler's List *and various other pictures dealing with the Holocaust.*]

"Hollywood is just interested in making money. . . . No, to Hollywood, culture is just a dirty word. Callow, that's the word for American culture. They have so much to learn from the Europeans."[1]

—Selig (the brother-in-law) in Edward Lewis Wallant's *The Pawnbroker*

In a 1961 novel by Edward Lewis Wallant, Sol Nazerman runs a pawnshop near the Harlem River in New York. A former inmate of the Nazi concentration camps, he has social contacts—a woman with whom he has sex, an assistant who helps him in the store, a sister and her family who share a comfortable suburban home in Mount Vernon with him. But he shuts out the world to grieve for himself and the wife and children he lost in the Holocaust. Grim and ethnic, peppered with phrases like *oy vay* and *gay shluphin*, the novel was unusual screen fare in the year that Elizabeth Taylor won an Oscar for *Butterfield 8*.

Gerald Mast notes in *A Short History of the Movies* that the American cinema of the 1960s "became more a directors' cinema."[2] As an account of *The Pawnbroker* shows, though, the roots of the so-called Hollywood Renaissance were not only exceptionally tender—especially for downbeat pictures—but nurtured as much by studios or producers as directors or auteurs. Adapted for the screen and released by Allied Artists, *The Pawnbroker* (1965) was a story of repression and survival. And so, behind the scenes, was the story of the independent producers who, in association with actors, artists, and technicians, created the first stubbornly "Jewish" film about the Holocaust.

Movie company story editors of the early 1960s read virtually everything, even fiction, that concerned the Holocaust. *The Pawnbroker*, though, was not only about the annihilation of the Jews and its consequences—that was rare enough in 1961—but had the rawness of a bleeding wound. The gloomy novel opens as the "subtly deformed" (31) Sol Nazerman tramps to work. The snow he crunches could have produced a pleasant sound, but "the sight of the great, bulky figure, with its puffy face, its heedless dark eyes distorted behind the thick lenses of strangely old-fashioned glasses, dispelled any thought of pleasure" (5). For the anomic, the proper pronoun is indeed *its*, not *his*.

The story arc of *The Pawnbroker* rises, regressively, retrospectively, toward the death anniversary of Sol's wife and children. Instead of action, though, the novel works via memory and things, like glasses. Again and again the stolid pawnbroker dons or removes the "round, archaic" (197) glasses he had found during his internment. These "weird glasses" (168) lead his nephew to wonder whether Uncle Sol can "penetrate and understand" the "murkinesses" of the universe (75), and they so embarrass his niece that she wants to buy him "a decent pair . . . tortoise shell, those heavy, movie-producer kind" (29). The "unique spectacles" (71) "cut into the flesh of his nose" (191), but Sol goes on wiping (95) and cleaning (134) and rubbing them (85). They are his shield against past "spectacles" like the Holocaust and his weapon against present "spectacles" like Mount Vernon (and Harlem) culture, in one scene "picking up flashes of sunlight and flinging them at [another character] like tiny darts" (109).

Sol does not lack a sense of irony. When the Jewish cop on the beat tries to bully him into giving away a Hamilton Beach mixer, he merely shrugs. "Here he was in the classic role of the interrogated again, and Leventhal was playing the part of the oppressor. It was getting confusing; soon you wouldn't know the Jews from their oppressors, the black from the white" (44-45). He cannot be ironic about what haunts him, though, especially when it occurs with the force of a cinematic cut. "Suddenly [Nazerman] had the sensation of being clubbed. An image was stamped *behind* his eyes like a bolt of pain" (6). The horrendous scenes that follow, italicized in the text, do not conform to the usual survivor's dreams "of improbable paradises, of equally mythical and improbable enemies; cosmic enemies, perverse and subtle, who pervade everything like the air."[3] Instead, Sol's daydreams (or flashbacks) have the grit of documentary footage, as when he recalls the "*mountain of emaciated bodies, hands, and legs tossed in nightmare abandon, as though each victim had died in the midst of a frantic dance, the hollow eyes and gaping mouths expressing what could have been a demented and perverse ecstasy*" (146). Sol has seen too much. "*They could see the whole thing from where they stood in the camp square*" (76) on the night the dogs had hunted down Rubin. Now Sol makes love to Tessie, Rubin's widow, another aggrieved survivor, and struggles not to see the ghosts that surround them. "Yes," he tells her, "I have escaped. I am safe within myself. I have made an order for myself, and no one can disturb it" (91). On the final pages of the novel, though, when his assistant dies, Sol can no longer control his "glass-covered eyes" (6). The stoic weeps, and then, gradually, he "wiped his eyes clear again. . . . wetness dried on his cheeks and a great calm came over him" (205). He prays for the dead, his assistant and the others. More importantly, he forgives himself.

Like many in Hollywood, Paramount readers thought *The Pawnbroker* "tremendous" but found "no way to whip up any enthusiasm here, especially the moment 'small picture' was mentioned."[4] Metro-Goldwyn-Mayer had another idea. Bill Zimmerman (of the story department) and Red Silverstein (of foreign distribution) read the book and thought an adaptation at least possible, less as an MGM production than an MGM release. Though the novel was far darker and (apropos the Holocaust) more personal than *Exodus* (1960) or the forthcoming *Judgment at Nuremberg* (1961), it ended affirmatively and, if quickly produced, could perhaps ride the minor wave of box office interest in "Jewish" cinema. MGM's Joseph Vogel had once hoped to make "a succession of deals with Hollywood's independent producers to put M-G-M on a competitive par with its more alert rivals."[5] *The Pawnbroker* (likely to appeal to a maverick filmmaker) could test that plan.

Shortly after publication of *The Pawnbroker*, Zimmerman and Silverstein sent the novel to a confrere on the East Coast, the home of many of Hollywood's independent producers. Roger Lewis had worked in advertising at Warner Bros., 20th Century-Fox, and finally, throughout the 1950s, United Artists. He had served briefly as UA's director of promotion and exploitation, then resigned to write for television (he won an Emmy for an episode of "The Defenders") and look for "serious" work in motion pictures. *The Pawnbroker*, he later said, was so serious that it "scared hell out of me." He nonetheless took on the property when Zimmerman and Silverstein hinted that Rod Steiger, a "bankable" actor, was interested in the lead role.

In fact, Zimmerman and Silverstein had never spoken to Steiger. Zimmerman knew that Steiger was in New York in a play and thought that Lewis could persuade him to shoot a picture during the day. Lewis was annoyed—and, worse, soon learned that Joe Vogel, like Rod Steiger, had never heard of Wallant's novel. Silverstein hastened to explain that he and Zimmerman wanted Steiger engaged before they approached Vogel about the production: unless a star was attached, a movie about the Holocaust would languish in the front office.[6]

By early 1962 Steiger had read the novel and talked salary ($75,000 and ten percent of the net), but he wanted to see a screenplay before he committed.[7] MGM seemed more encouraging—only because it wanted to exploit the Eady Pool, a British law that afforded the American film industry a generous rebate of distribution costs for pictures shot in England. Since the smaller the budget the greater the protection against loss, MGM tentatively proposed a *Pawnbroker* shot in London for $400,000. Lewis was skeptical. The setting of the narrative thundered the new world, *New York,* and though $400,000 would buy more abroad than at home, it was still a paltry amount.[8]

As MGM tarried, Lewis formed a partnership with Philip Langner (whose father ran the Theatre Guild) for production of *The Pawnbroker* as "A Theatre Guild Film."[9] Langner put up $7,200 in exchange for one-third of the picture. "Without [Langner] the project would never have happened," Lewis told one interviewer, "so he's entitled to what he got. But I had to give away a hell of a lot for his $7,200."[10] Lewis and Langner optioned the novel for $1,000 and drafted a crude prospectus for private investors. *The Pawnbroker,* Lewis wrote, is "a vehicle that will garner attention and awards all out of proportion to the cost."[11] The announcement won notice. For instance, Groucho Marx (among others) wanted to play Sol—an odd but not inconceivable choice since Bert Lahr had starred in *Waiting for Godot* in 1956 and (as Bottom) in *A Midsummer Night's Dream* in 1960.[12] When no money appeared to be forthcoming, however, Lewis called on United Artists.

UA was the logical home for *The Pawnbroker*: the company not only had a long association with independents (Otto Preminger chief among them) but experience with the Eady Pool, which was then financing the first of the James Bond pictures and Tony Richardson's adaptation of *Tom Jones.*[13] David Picker loved Wallant's novel yet referred Lewis to Arnold Picker, head of UA's executive committee and "a hard ass."[14] About "Jewish" pictures, Picker told Lewis, the figures spoke for themselves. UA had bought *Exodus* in manuscript for $250,000 plus five percent of the profits. As early as 1958, over one year before publication, UA told Preminger (the director) that the studio would promote *Exodus* not as "a book about ancient Israel, but rather one of events that took place in *contemporary* history" (emphasis added). The campaign, in other words, would "keep foremost the idea that this is not a book specifically for Jewish interest, but rather that its contents are exciting universally." *Exodus* stayed on the

best seller list for 79 weeks and sold three million copies in paperback. The global box office was just under $20 million. *Judgment at Nuremberg,* on the other hand, produced one year later and encumbered in part by the salaries of its cast and the length of its narrative, had shown the concentration camps in documentary footage and was on its way to losing $1.5 million at the box office.[15]

Exodus and *Judgment at Nuremberg* (originally a television production) were pre-sold. Since *The Pawnbroker* was not, UA conditioned its support on Lewis' paring the budget to $350,000 and eliminating the Holocaust theme. "'People don't wanna see pictures about concentration camps,'" Picker told Lewis. Lewis argued. "'Well,'" Picker said, "'there're other injustices.'"[16] (In Hollywood each minority group had its season: when he adapted *The Brick Foxhole* for the screen, as *Crossfire* [1947], Dore Schary was forced to change the victim of Richard Brooks's novel from homosexual to Jew.) Lewis was disheartened. He was also $30,000 in debt.[17] Then Rod Steiger orally agreed to play Sol. MGM offered Lewis $2,000 to go to London to scout locations and a writer. At last *The Pawnbroker* was moving.

In London Canadian writer Ted Allan, who would later collaborate with Jan Kadar on *Lies My Father Told Me* (1975) and John Cassavetes on *Love Streams* (1984), agreed to adapt Wallant's novel for $6,000 (salary deferred) plus four percent of the net. To assure his fragile hold on MGM—and future access to UA—Lewis told Allan that the screenplay should deliver the "data" about the concentration camp "in [Nazerman's] words, rather than show it in literal scenes." He also wanted to alter the novel's presentation of two female characters. Tessie was another hostage of the Holocaust and too "depressive." Shimon Wincelberg (a Jewish friend) had told Langner that Tessie was "repulsive" and that "Wallant (though presumably a Jew) knows very little about lower-class Jews (or concentration camps, or nazis [sic]) and was able only to characterize them in crude stereotypes."[18] Wincelberg may well have been thinking of the appearance of Sol's lover at the beginning of chapter four:

> Tessie Rubin opened the door to Sol and gave him access to a different kind of smell from that of the hallway of the apartment house. The hallway, with its tile floors and broken windows, smelled of garbage and soot; Tessie's apartment gave forth the more personal odors of bad cooking and dust. . . . She had a large, curved nose, and her face was very thin; there were hollows in her temples, and her eyes, stranded in the leanness of all the features, were exceptionally large and dismal. She threw her arms outward, splayed her legs in exhaustion: their thinness was grotesque, because her torso was heavy and short, with huge breasts.
>
> (46-47)

The slovenly Tessie nurses both her father and her self-pity. Her dying father whines at her and bickers with Sol, whom she uses as willingly as do his sister Bertha, Bertha's husband, and their children. At dinner with the relatives he dislikes, Sol watches his brother-in-law and niece smile at each other "in a glow of intellectual rapport. You wouldn't even guess they were Jews, Bertha thought proudly" (27). No one reading the novel would guess otherwise. Wallant treats the needy customers of the pawnshop with a compassion he denies the other Jews of the story. From Tessie and Bertha to the venal cop Leventhal and the parasitical survivor Goberman (who collects for the Jewish Appeal), *The Pawnbroker* eerily echoes the Jews of the Nazi propaganda posters and the Cruikshank pen-and-inks for *Oliver Twist*. Roger Lewis was no doubt thinking of them when he asked the screenwriter to reconsider the "crude stereotypes."

The other female character of concern was the social worker, Marilyn Birchfield, who reaches out to the pawnbroker. Following a botched robbery of the shop, Sol's assistant takes a bullet intended for his boss. "For an instant [Sol] saw the immaculate face of Marilyn Birchfield and he said as in a dream, 'No, no, I am too dirty; you must go away from me.' And then she was gone, banished by his voice, and for a moment he thought he recognized the delicate shape of regret, until that, too, disappeared" (201). Though Sol later calls on Morton (his nephew) for support, Lewis thought that focusing on the social worker rather than the young man would lend the movie audience "a sense of hope and fulfillment that they, and the theme, deserve."[19]

Marilyn Birchfield "reads" gentile with her American smile and her social philosophy of good deeds, and though Sol's returning to Morton rather than her would loosen the thread of anti-Semitism that runs through the novel, it would also help reassure Hollywood investors accustomed to a fadeout on the heterosexual couple. Granted, Lewis wanted a screenplay reasonably true to Wallant's novel. He also intended to show MGM that the picture would be commercial, however, and to that end he wanted to cast a Caucasian as the woman who played the girlfriend of the Latino assistant. As he told Allan, "It's a chance, as in the book, to give us a good sex bit."[20]

Ted Allan finished the first draft in spring 1962, when the studios were retrenching and averse to Holocaust pictures, no matter how circumspect the "data." The screenplay was funereal and the ending dour; unlike Sol in the novel, Sol in the script reaches out to no one—neither his nephew nor Marilyn Birchfield. The screenplay was also chock-full of Jewish characters and Jewish "bits." MGM's Bill Zimmerman read Allan's work and found the "business of Sol's Jewishness" disagreeable. "Granted that he is a Jew and one of millions persecuted or murdered by the Nazis, our audience need not be reminded of it to the extent that this script does it. For example, the Hebrew memorial candle on Page 34 (which, aside from this issue, is meaningless for the bulk of our audience); the use of the word 'kike' on Page 25; the 'Jewish Holiday' reference on Page 124." Also, the script "badly" needs comedy relief, "easily available" fortunately in a scene featuring Jesus (the shop assistant) and his "cronies and their easy girls in a jukebox

bar, etc." Finally, the picture needs an "obligatory" scene of Sol and Marilyn at the close. The couple do not need "a sunset background, but at least they should figuratively touch hands in some manner."[21]

Again *The Pawnbroker* stalled. MGM was "too financially destitute at the moment," Philip Langner told one associate, too consumed by its runaway production of *Mutiny on the Bounty* (1962) to bankroll *The Pawnbroker*. Confiding in *Variety* reporter Thomas Pryor in a personal letter whose typos and syntax mirror his indignation, Lewis said that he was "holding a nice fat bag which included a gaurantee [sic] to Steiger they [MGM] now found some legal techincaility [sic] for saying they were not bound by, and, of course, my own obligation for the the the [sic] advance [on a screenplay]."[22] Though committed to the project, Ted Allan must also have been frustrated: he had not yet been paid and probably wondered whether he ever would be.

Steiger generally liked the screenplay, and by June 1962 Lewis was at work in London on a revised second draft that would hold Steiger yet lure backers (the producer hoped). Steiger was also in London, and nearby. "He would come in and he would have little notes and things about scenes that he had decided on or thought about the night before and he would act them out and he would weep, and I would weep almost," Lewis recalled. "And I would weep, not like Rod, who was moved by his own ideas and his own acting, but because it was so bad."[23] Looked at another way, the weeping marked the strong commitment of the actor. And, clearly, he was the production's linchpin.

The second draft of *The Pawnbroker* (according to the title page, "by Ted Allan and Rod Steiger") set the structure and retained the dark cast of Wallant's novel and Allan's first draft. Countering the opinion of the studios, Steiger thought that Nazerman's Jewishness and the accent on the camps were essential. Accordingly, the ending was bleak, with the pawnbroker slumped over the figure of Joseph, formerly Jesus. "Sol cries, his pain now finding full expression at the death of his 'son', at JOSEPH's sacrifice, and we know there is hope again for him—and for us." Though he had wanted a more explicit scene, with Marilyn, Lewis was not averse to shopping around the revised screenplay. In order to reproduce it, however, he had to ask his partner for money. "I don't have it," he told Langner, and "I will be digging into my slender resources before I leave here since the corp. account is practically nil." The screenplay was slender, not full length, the result of pruning Lewis had done "in anticipation of the director's involvement." At eighty-four pages it was too short. Rereading it months later, Allan himself conceded that "it needs a lot of work. It lacks passion and originality."[24]

The screenplay alone hardly accounted for lack of interest in *The Pawnbroker*. One problem was budget. Lewis could pay no more than $10,000 for a director, and he had been cautioned against many who worked for less, as Hollis Alpert noted when he wrote Lewis "to warn you against

John Cassevetes [*sic*]." Another factor was the London production base. "It was ridiculous," Sidney Lumet told one reporter, referring to Soho standing in for Spanish Harlem. "I had read the book before, loved Wallant's work, and was furious at the kind of treatment it had been given, so turned it down."[25]

Others responded negatively. Stanley Kubrick found Steiger not "all that exciting" and turned down the project. Karyl Reisz (whose parents had been interned and executed in Poland) told Lewis that for "deep, personal" reasons he "could not objectively associate himself with any subject which has a background of concentration camps." Mirroring the corporate culture of the studios, others saw *The Pawnbroker* as a professional cul-de-sac. Stage director Franco Zeffirelli was ardent for film credentials, but *The Pawnbroker* was "not the kind of subject [he] would wish to direct, certainly not as his first Anglo-American venture." More candid, producer Michael Balcon refused because of the "subject matter" and the fear (more than justified) that the major circuits would have "certain reservations" about the picture.[26] Lewis, who was speaking to agents rather than to directors or producers themselves, suspected that the go-betweens had not "made clear the fact that we are handling [the camps] symbolically, not realistically, in the script."[27] So unique—and so taboo—was the "realistic" content of *The Pawnbroker* in early 1962 that it discouraged both investors and artists.

In August 1962 Ely Landau stepped forward. An accomplished television producer, Landau was making his first picture, *Long Day's Journey into Night,* whose cast and theatrical origins would guarantee it wide press coverage and thus a fair chance at profit. He offered to pay off Lewis and Langner's past expenses on *The Pawnbroker* in return for eighty percent of the producers' share of the picture. Expecting far more than two-thirds of twenty percent of the picture (Langner would have taken one-third of that twenty percent), Lewis naturally made a counteroffer. Landau was "a mercurial guy who changes his mind ten times a day," Lewis told Ted Allan, "and, faced with our determination to draw the line and mean it, which [Landau] apprently [*sic*] didn't think was going to happen, he's already begun to back flip."[28] Lewis had no other prospects, though, and, faced with an able negotiator, sold Landau eighty percent of *The Pawnbroker.*

By early 1963, at his base camp in the Time-Life Building, Landau had read, without pleasure, yet another revision of Allan's screenplay, and by early spring he had asked Morton Fine and David Friedkin (who won sole screen credit) to rework it. Their 178-page first draft (dated 14 May 1963) was very descriptive, occasionally almost florid, and though they renamed the Jewish cop *Morrow,* their Sol was more Jewish than Allan's, especially in his morbid, dry humor.

Keenly attentive to point of view, as Resnais had been in *Hiroshima Mon Amour* (1960), Fine and Friedkin portrayed the scenes of Sol in the New York suburbs as though

they were "all happening on this side of a swoon . . . no distortion, absolute realism . . . a constant flux of voices and figures which ebb in, then out of focus. And overlapping of dialogues [*sic*], so that oftentime a speech which starts to have moment becomes lost as something new starts. And during the INTERCUTTING, the rising emetic effect on Sol is patent." Lewis' desire for closure has Sol reach out, finally, for Morton. "I need you," he says into a pay phone after the shooting. "Come to me." Per Lewis' desire for a "good sex bit," the screenplay called for intercourse between Jesus and his girlfriend as well as Sol and Tessie—but no nudity, in those scenes or others.[29]

In their second draft dated 21 August 1963 and thirty-five pages shorter than their first, Fine and Friedkin revised, among others, the scene that would give *The Pawnbroker* its place in the annals of American film censorship. At the pawnshop Jesus' girlfriend unzips her dress a little.

As she does the CAMERA MOVES IN to hold [her and Sol] in a TIGHT TWO SHOT.

MABEL

Look . . .

Sol doesn't move. And now with a languid gesture, looking down at her own breasts, she reaches for Sol, her fingers in back of his neck: gentle gesture for him to look . . . to come closer . . . gently . . . soothingly urging him.

MABEL

Just look, that's all.

As Sol looks, the voice of a concentration camp guard orders him to look at the Nazi soldier who sexually menaces Sol's wife, Ruth. The third draft, four pages shorter and finished seven days later, suggests that the producers were apprehensive about the nudity, for Fine and Friedkin designated "a TIGHT TWO SHOT *from over her shoulders*" (emphasis added). The decision on what to show would finally be answered on the set and, later, in the editing room. Already, though, before Landau had hired the director and editor who would win accolades for the film, *The Pawnbroker* was courting controversy, for, nudity aside, an honest presentation of the Holocaust would itself go well beyond the boundaries of "good taste" in American cinema of the early 1960s.[30]

"The successful adaptation," John Ellis writes in *Screen,* "is one that is able to replace the memory of the novel with the process of a filmic or televisual representation."[31] On those terms Fine and Friedkin's sixth draft (the shooting script) assured the film's success. Abandoning the pitch black tone of the novel, it nonetheless hews closely to the outlines of the story, especially the characterization of Sol, and yet is potentially strong enough to stand apart from the novel that had seeded it.

The shooting script is not conventionally faithful to the novel. It rearranges or omits scenes. It lightens the characterization of Tessie. It dampens hope at the end of the story. Subtly, it changes even Sol. During the Holocaust he had lost all that he loved, he confesses to Marilyn Birchfield late in the film. There was nothing he could do, and now, as the death anniversary approaches, he feels frightened. The emotion puzzles him. As he says, "It's been a long time since I felt . . . fear." Judith Doneson calls the pawnbroker "a weak, almost feminine, figure," and a link between "fear" and a humbled masculinity does not seem so remote, not according to the theory that the Holocaust "feminized [all] European Jewish men, who were castigated as incapable of protecting their families and were therefore led sheepishly to the slaughter."[32]

Seeing *The Pawnbroker* through the lens of gender rather than Jewish history could universalize the Holocaust, rendering it if not (as Doneson says) a metaphor for all human suffering,[33] then a statement on masculinity and its discontents. More so than the novel, though, the screenplay and film treat the feminization without losing the specificity of the Holocaust. Sol is surrounded with weak men. His brother-in-law (not a Holocaust survivor) literally lies prostrate at the beginning of the film, content to be led by his wife and supported by Sol, the "man of the house." One pawnshop customer stutters (he's a pederast in the novel), another lisps. The gangster Rodriguez and the hood Robinson condescendingly call Sol *uncle*, grudgingly recognizing his masculinity, but to their consternation he does not flinch at gunpoint. They may also envy the pawnbroker: though neither "weak" nor "feminine," Rodriguez and Robinson are both gay and thus more "other" than Jews are.

Sol best shows his manhood through his paternal interest in Jesus, the one character in the film whose self-doubts change the direction of the story. In their kitchen, in an odd scene, Jesus' mother supervises her son's bath as he teaches her to say "I am a good boy" in English.[34] When he goes to a nightclub—where an artiste ends her dance act by tearing off her wig and showing she's a man—he tells Mabel that the pawnbroker's "been working my back off all afternoon." When he tells her they should "just go up and sit and talk awhile," she pins his lethargy on his weak sex drive and says heatedly, "I don't like you working too hard 'cuz I don't like you using all your energy." Later he will show her what he can do, he snaps back, but when they have sex, she mounts him. (In the crosscut scene, Sol mounts Tessie.) The barb about "using all your energy" burrows under Jesus's skin: as he knows, day in and day out, a man must *prove* his manhood. Accordingly, when the hoods taunt him about working in the pawnshop ("a chicken business") and about his on-again off-again plan to rob it, he finally cooperates with them not only to steal the money but to show that he's man enough to do so.

Sol may well feel anxious about his manhood: when forced to "look . . . look" (at Ruth and the German officer) he is unable to "act like a man." A minor but telling change from novel to screenplay lets us infer that his "fear" has cultural as well as gendered roots.

Wallant's Sol is Polish. As Dorothy Bilik says in her monograph on Holocaust fiction, the pawnbroker was one of the "secularly educated, assimilated European Jews." And as Annette Insdorf reports in her book on Holocaust film, "Polish-Jewish civilization was highly developed between the wars and included experimental education (a Montessori school in Vilna), progressive politics (the *Bund*, a Jewish Socialist party), and ripe artistic movements (Yiddish writers' groups like *Di Khalyastre*)."[35]

The cinema's pawnbroker is German. As Rod Steiger's unaccented English (purged of "Jewish" syntax and Yiddish expressions) hints, the German Jews were not only the most assimilated of Europe but tended to consider themselves superior to others. They were free, they thought, of the Orthodoxy that characterized many Polish Jews and felt they were Germans before they were Jews. The death camps were in Poland, where the peasantry was notorious for its anti-Semitism, so when the German Jews were isolated from other German citizens they were puzzled, not least because they were so close to the social history that had produced the Nazis. If an awareness of the *shoah* dawned later—and more profoundly—on German Jews than on Poles, then the cinema's Nazerman may have found it harder than his counterpart in the novel to understand and accept what had happened to him as a man, a German, and a Jew. As such, the screen version of *The Pawnbroker* adds nuance to the character's fear.

The Pawnbroker was rehearsed and shot in New York in fall 1963, under the direction of Sidney Lumet and on a budget beyond the $350,000 once proposed. The principal set (only a few were constructed) was the pawnshop, created by Richard Sylbert and lit, coldly, carefully, by Boris Kaufman. It was (as Lumet wrote later) "a series of cages: wire mesh, bars, locks, alarms, anything that would reinforce a sense of entrapment,"[36] and Lumet used each barrier evocatively. Assistant director Dan Eriksen found many of the actual locations: the bleached landscape of Sol's Levittown home; the peculiar second-story church where Jesus's mother worships; the city park where Sol meets Marilyn for lunch (originally to have been the end of a dock, a movie cliche); Marilyn's Lincoln Towers apartment, whose balcony overlooks smokestacks near the center of the frame and a railroad yard of clattering and clanging trains; and the exterior of the pawnshop on 116th and Park Avenues, next door to the Radiante Bar that offers little light and less hope as Sol passes by at the end of the picture.

Along with the locales, the black-and-white cinematography hardens the grittiness of the production. In the 1950s even "small pictures" (like *Tea and Sympathy*) or serious dramas (like *Vertigo*) had been shot in color to compete with television. Once color reached television in the 1960s, though, Hollywood returned to monochrome, and Boris Kaufman was one of its masters; he had worked on American documentaries before he turned to features, and pictures like *12 Angry Men* and *On the Waterfront* foreshadowed the "realism" of *The Pawnbroker*.

Lumet had good camera sense. He had collaborated with Kaufman on *12 Angry Men* and *Long Day's Journey into Night* and worked fast, usually with two or three takes per shot. He was generous with actors, and the performers responded well, especially Jaime Sanchez (Jesus Ortiz), Eusebia Cosme (Mrs. Ortiz), and Brock Peters, who plays the gay racketeer (Rodriguez) living in a white house with a live-in white lover. Thelma Oliver, portraying Mabel as vulnerable yet brash, had not known that she would bare her breasts; she cried when told, and since (as Eriksen recalls) no "protection footage" was shot, she knew that the nude scene would probably appear in the final cut.[37] Lumet shot the sequence on a cleared stage, and, characteristically, the production quickly moved on.

Rod Steiger was immersed in the role of Sol Nazerman. He had shaved his head (his own idea, he told reporter Arnold Abrams) and hidden "his strong upper lip" behind a gray mustache. "There may be more money to be made in a musical comedy," he told the press, "but at least I feel I've done something worthwhile when I complete a film like this."[38] Lumet and Steiger were especially attentive to Sol's glasses. He has two pairs, one modern with black rims (the "movie-producer kind") and the other round with wire rims, like those Wallant describes. He keeps the latter at the pawnshop and uses the others elsewhere, until the scene with Mabel. Then, during the last third of the picture, he wears only the older pair, the spectacles that augur the looming and long-suppressed confrontation with the memory of the Holocaust.

Steiger and Lumet worked well together, especially in the last scene. The old-fashioned glasses press against Sol's forehead as he kneels over the dead Jesus, as he shapes a cry that never comes. That mute scream anchors the picture in "Jewishness." According to Annette Insdorf it represents not only "the helpless reaction to continued anti-Semitism, as illustrated by the client who calls [Nazerman] a 'money-grubbing kike'" but also "the emblem of the Holocaust survivor, the witness of a horror so devastating that it cannot be told."[39]

By Christmas 1963 *The Pawnbroker* was in the hands of the editor, Ralph Rosenblum, whose account of the picture in two chapters of *When the Shooting Stops* constitutes the only other production history of the film. Rosenblum and Lumet edited *The Pawnbroker* in January and February 1964. They cut out scenes of the cop and the parasite Goberman and, appeasing the brother-in-law in the Wallant novel (who says that Hollywood has "so much to learn from the Europeans"), added the Holocaust flashcuts which Rosenblum has discussed at length.

According to a February 1964 advertisement in *Variety*, the Landau Company was "dedicated to the production of quality motion pictures for that world-wide audience seeking meaningful and provocative screen entertainment."[40] The *meaningful* would not be the *provocative* shot of Mabel's breasts (assuming it passed the censors) but the integrity of *The Pawnbroker*'s representation of a cataclysmic moment in human history.

Throughout early spring 1964 Landau and Lewis looked on as Lumet and Rosenblum tuned *The Pawnbroker,* and by summer the filmmakers were ready to show the $930,000 production to potential distributors. The latter may have been wary of the content of the film, especially the nudity, which could attract audiences but also litigation. Hoping to establish the bona fides of the picture and soften the censors' anticipated resistance to it, Landau arranged to open *The Pawnbroker* abroad. Lewis later recalled that he had long wanted to screen *The Pawnbroker* at the Berlin Film Festival, and as the award-winning *Bicycle Thief* (1950) had shown, an international reputation could not only trump the Production Code Administration (PCA) office but help a "serious" film set box office records. In early summer 1964 a motion picture trade association panel sponsored by the United States Information Agency chose *The Pawnbroker* as the American entry for Berlin, where it could score an artistic—and political—coup. On 2 July, when the Festival screened the picture, Landau and Steiger were there (and lauded), apparently on the production's budget. Lewis and Langner were also present, on Langner's money, and feeling forgotten.[41]

Lewis was the one constant in *The Pawnbroker,* from the option on the novel through (and beyond) the international premiere of the picture, a point overlooked when Rosenblum says that Landau "found [Wallant's] book, optioned it, and hired two men to write the script before the director ever came on the scene. None of this can be fairly omitted from the story of the film's success."[42] In fall 1964 Lewis could only watch as the months passed and the Berlin publicity evaporated. Lewis begged Landau for prints to show around Los Angeles, and Landau, through an intermediary, responded "that, at the moment, there are only two PAWNBROKER prints in the United States that have the final version. Both of these prints are being used for screenings here. At such time as we make others, I will notify you and will be happy to send one to you." Landau was probably showing *The Pawnbroker* to likely distributors, and probably garnering more compliments than offers. The nudity was one bottleneck, the Holocaust theme another. "I don't think that Hollywood should deal with anything but entertainment," Paramount head Adolph Zukor had told the press in 1939. "The newsreels take care of current events. To make films of political significance is a mistake."[43] As late as 1962 Paramount had turned down *The Pawnbroker* because it was a low-budget production; another factor was no doubt the "depressive" content.

Finally, one copy of *The Pawnbroker* reached Hollywood. Contravening the protocol for feature films, Landau had not sent the shooting script to the Production Code office for vetting,[44] so agency director Geoff Shurlock may have felt sandbagged. Shurlock quickly screened the picture, though, and on New Year's Eve 1964 told Landau that the bare breasts and one of the sex scenes of Jesus and Mabel were "unacceptably sex suggestive and lustful."[45] The phrase was boilerplate left over from the tenure of former PCA director Joe Breen and calculated to force the producers into concessions. Another month passed. On 29 January Landau pleaded the moral gravity of the picture but was told that the Production Code would continue to hold the line on nudity and that Landau's only recourse would be a formal appeal.

Another month passed. Landau had arranged for Allied Artists to release *The Pawnbroker,* which, technically, the company could not do without the Production Code seal. Bosley Crowther, whose *New York Times* censure of the PCA's treatment of *Bicycle Thief* helped gain wide release of the picture, reported on 9 March 1965 that the New York censors had licensed *The Pawnbroker* sans cuts and that the Motion Picture Association appeals board (the parent of the PCA) would soon hear the issue.[46]

On 29 March 1965 representatives of Allied Artists told the appeals board that *The Pawnbroker* "will play specialized theatres for the most part, catering to adult audiences."[47] Allied Artists could have released the picture via a subsidiary and thus saved the cost and suspense of a confrontation with the Motion Picture Association. Since 1958, however, Allied Artists (a publicly traded company) had been frequently in the red; the price of its stock was hovering in the low single digits, and its next earnings report would show a $1.5 million loss. Allied Artists needed more than an "art house" hit. A Production Code seal—and controversy—could only help sell an otherwise difficult picture.

Landau assured the appeals board that the nudity was necessary to *The Pawnbroker* and that, more important, he would not exploit it in the advertising. The debate that followed was vigorous. Joe Mankiewicz, the independent producer whose *Suddenly Last Summer* had been a Production Code cause célèbre, defended Landau and *The Pawnbroker* while Spyros Skouras, the former exhibitor whose *Cleopatra* had taken down Twentieth Century-Fox and his presidency of the studio, led the opposition. Another major player, not even present, was Ephraim London, whom Landau had talked with, probably openly, about his plans to sue the Association in the wake of an unfavorable decision. London, having argued the *Miracle* case before the Supreme Court and thus curbed the authority of state and municipal censors, would gladly have taken on the Motion Picture Association, and Landau wanted to do so—despite the thought that other independent producers would have been too soft to join in as plaintiffs.[48] Based on a 6-3 vote, though, the Association granted *The Pawnbroker* an "exception" conditional on "reduction in the length of the scenes which the Production Code Administration found unapprovable."[49] Paramount head Barney Balaban warned that "any self-serving statement that the picture is unique and the so-called 'exception' applies only to this particular film is meaningless. The decision is obviously a precedent for the next and the next and we will learn where it ends only after it is too late." Balaban (the son of Russian Jewish immigrants) was probably swayed by other factors. In 1948 he had told Harry Warner that the return of Loeb and Leopold in *Rope* would have an

"adverse influence on [the] standing of our Jewish people in the nation." "Hollywood was itself a means of avoiding Judaism," Neal Gabler says, yet Balaban had toured the concentration camps; too shaken to tell even his family what he had seen, he may have been as averse to Jewish survivors as Jewish killers. Such points of view were not uncommon, as a prominent Los Angeles rabbi showed after release of *The Pawnbroker.* "All [the Jews] talk about is the Holocaust and all the sufferings," Edgar Magnin told Gabler. "The goddamn fools don't realize that the more you tell gentiles that nobody likes us, the more they say there must be reason for it."[50]

Whatever else, Balaban was right about precedents. The "reductions" of nudity were minimal, and the press cheered the producers' victory. "If the Motion Picture Code has been broken, it is time that it was re-written," James F. O'Neill wrote in the Washington *Daily News* in late spring 1965. "When you consider what the dirty-movie houses get away with, and what the legitimate stage is offering in the way of artistic achievement, and some of the trash which Hollywood uses to lure the morons, *The Pawnbroker* evolves as a most tasteful, dynamic and dramatic motion picture."[51] The unspoken achievement was of course the presentation of the Holocaust: *The Pawnbroker* was an acid test of Rabbi Magnin's point of view, and the fray over the nude scenes would be long forgotten before another "Jewish" film superseded the harshness of the concentration camp scenes in the Lewis and Landau production.

The Catholic Legion of Decency tabbed *The Pawnbroker* "C" (for "Condemned"), assured, as one official wrote, "that a condemnation is necessary in order to put a very definite halt to the effort by producers to introduce nudity into American films." Years before, when, according to one bishop, "Jewish control of the industry [was] alienating many of our people," the Catholics might also have been swayed by other factors. The times had changed, though, and *The Pawnbroker* would become the first "C" picture to play St. Paul, Minnesota, a strongly Catholic city; according to *Variety,* "this may mark a letting down of the bars here for such films."[52]

Having cleared the censors, the producers now had the harder task of selling a Holocaust picture (the nudity notwithstanding) to an audience of Jew and gentile alike. Landau opened *The Pawnbroker* in Los Angeles at the Pantages Theater, "either suicide or prescient genius," noted the reviewer for the *Hollywood Reporter.* The theater generally screened standard American fare, such as the Sinatra "rat pack" farce *Ocean's Eleven,* which Lewis recalled (in an oral history) was playing in reissue the night *The Pawnbroker* previewed there. The Pantages was RKO's "'key West Coast theatre,'" and the fact that it played *The Pawnbroker* let other exhibitors know that Allied Artists and RKO saw the production as a "big" picture.[53]

Major bookings and critical acceptance of *The Pawnbroker* followed, and so did Academy Award nominations.

Rod Steiger lost the Oscar to Lee Marvin (for *Cat Ballou*), and, worse for investors, Landau and *The Pawnbroker* lost to Fox and *The Sound of Music*. The outcome was no surprise to Quincy Jones, who scored the picture. "Hollywood has a funny sort of prejudice toward films that come out of the East and since *The Pawnbroker* was really an East coast production, the industry resisted everything about it."[54]

Playing only key cities, *The Pawnbroker* grossed almost $3 million. Then, for the smaller houses, American-International took over domestic distribution. A-I cut the nudity, won an innocuous "A 3" from the Catholic rating board and thus, according to *Variety,* opened up the picture to five- to ten-thousand more bookings. A-I reported that *The Pawnbroker* was only two feet shorter: the shot of the bare breasts had been removed "by using a lab blowup that cuts the girl's body off at shoulder level."[55] (The video bears the A-I logo but is the original Allied Artists release.) Soon Landau rued his pledge about advertising, for *The Pawnbroker* took in $1.5 million in Italy alone, thanks to what the producer called the "sex pitch" that had "proved to be a mainstay" in Italian posters for the film.[56] Domestically, the Motion Picture Association suppressed one "prominently displayed" part of the movie poster "showing the negro prostitute on top of the man."[57]

A beachhead for nudity in motion pictures, *The Pawnbroker* has—unjustifiably—been seen less often as an important picture about Jews, Jewish survivors, and the Holocaust. In the late 1950s *Me and the Colonel* (1958) and *The Diary of Anne Frank* (1959) had touched on the war but tiptoed around the Holocaust. Business was business, even on Broadway. When he directed *Anne Frank* in New York, Garson Kanin had had the playwrights delete Anne's allusion to the constancy of Jewish persecution, "an embarrassing piece of special pleading," he said. "The fact that in this play the symbols of persecution and oppression are Jews is incidental, and Anne, in stating the argument so, reduces her magnificent stature."[58] Jews endorsed the strategy: when *Anne Frank* went to Hollywood, the Jewish Film Advisory Committee applauded the authors of the screenplay for expanding the "universal" meaning of the play.[59]

As Sidney Lumet understood and as Judith Doneson says, "Jewish particularism was not popular in the fifties." At the end of that decade Lumet had read Herman Wouk's *Marjorie Morningstar* and, eager to direct it, flown west to confer with Jack Warner, who had once said that had he known about the Jewish connection to *Rope* he "would not have made any deal to release the picture." Scanning early sketches for the major set of *Marjorie Morningstar,* Lumet was astonished that the resort looked more like Brentwood than the Catskills. Production designer Dick Sylbert was mute, so Warner explained. "'You see, Sidney,' he said, 'we don't want a picture with a narrow appeal. We want something more universal.' I said, 'That means we don't cast any Jews, right?' I was on the three o'clock plane home."[60]

Those associated with *The Pawnbroker* had had doubts about the "particularism" of the story. "In keeping with the screenplay and the original novel," noted Rosenblum, writing more than ten years after release of the picture, the flashbacks portray none of the gross Nazi atrocities. "There were no ovens or executions or horrid human experiments. The story revealed the destruction of an identity," a "human" rather than "Jewish" identity. *Pace* Rosenblum, the flashbacks are not about suffering but Jewish suffering, and they anchor the film in the memory and "particularism" of the Holocaust. *The Pawnbroker* is significant because Sol Nazerman, Jew, is the central character. Absent his Jewishness or his life in the Nazi camps there is (as Patricia Erens says) no story.[61]

What then accounted for the relatively brisk box office of *The Pawnbroker*? "Thelma Oliver reveals a forceful personality (and a lovely body, too) as the Negro prostie," *Variety* told industry readers. Though the controversy over the nudity of *The Pawnbroker* surely attracted audiences, current events also produced box office interest in the Holocaust and thus the picture. Raul Hilberg's *The Destruction of the European Jews* had been published in 1961, and Hannah Arendt's account of the Eichmann trial (which lasted from April to December 1961) had appeared in *The New Yorker* in 1962-63 and then, hardbound, in *Eichmann in Jerusalem* in 1963. Both books enjoyed chiefly an intellectual readership; as Irving Howe said, as maddening as were Arendt's views, they "enabled us to finally speak about the unspeakable."[62] The trial itself and the hanging in May 1962 had been one of the major stories of 1961 and 1962 in the American press. "We want the nations of the world to know," Israeli prime minister David Ben-Gurion had said of the accusations and the proceedings, and reporters had spread the word.[63]

McCarthyism was over and the flight to the suburbs and the attendant struggle for assimilation *fait accompli*. In Hollywood and beyond, though, as Stephen Whitfield notes, some Jews "began to realize that the Jewish legacy was perhaps worth nurturing, if the alterative was the blurring of the differences between Jews and their neighbors, if the social contract contained a clause envisioning the end of the Jewish people." More generally, as Lester Friedman notes, there was a burgeoning awareness of ethnicity. Jews and others were now proud to identify themselves as members of a minority group,[64] and *The Pawnbroker* may have garnered a Jewish audience interested in a taste of Jewish history, one that had been less whitewashed than *Gentleman's Agreement* and *Crossfire,* one that addressed the screen taboo of the twentieth century, the Holocaust.

Both the "general American" and the "minority" audience of the 1960s were curious about others' heritage and history. And like a Western told by a Native American, a Jewish picture about the Holocaust was a novelty. On television in 1959, then on film in 1961, *Judgment at Nuremberg* had been the stalking horse for *The Pawnbroker,* less because, as Annette Insdorf notes, *Judgment* "fit the bristling new material of the Holocaust into an old narrative form, thus allowing the viewer to leave the theater feeling complacent instead of concerned or disturbed,"[65] than because it raised questions that *The Pawnbroker* could answer. Who were the (anonymous) Jews of *Judgment at Nuremberg*? Telling the story of six rather than six million and how they suffered, died, and were mourned, *The Pawnbroker* personalizes the past.

Finally, no less than Sidney Lumet, Boris Kaufman, Ralph Rosenblum, or others, Rod Steiger was crucial to the popular success of *The Pawnbroker*. Having won an Oscar for *On the Waterfront* (1954) and been nominated for *The Pawnbroker* before it entered general release, he had enough celebrity to sell tickets to the picture yet not so much celebrity that it absorbed the character he played. Justice prevails in *Judgment at Nuremberg* not only because the occasion demands it but because Spencer Tracy sits on the bench. More character actor than star, Steiger has no congenial screen persona that allows us to "excuse" or feel "complacent" about the pawnbroker. He brings Sol Nazerman (not Rod Steiger) dynamically to life, as a Jew, an abrasive, often unpleasant Jew, angry about the Holocaust; in short, he adds to the credibility and "particularity" of the character and assures the story the "small-picture" status that, paradoxically, makes it so powerful.

Ilan Avisar, author of *Screening the Holocaust: Cinema's Images of the Unimaginable*, finds *The Pawnbroker* offensive. Jesus' death, for instance, Christianizes Sol, who, when he presses his hand down on a receipt spike after the assistant dies, adopts the stigma of the cross. In a more persuasive reading, though, Annette Insdorf sees the spearing as the legacy of a Nazi rather than Christian concept. Sol "wounds himself, rendering flesh a mere object" and thus "makes concrete one of the film's central themes: survivor guilt."[66]

Avisar says that *The Pawnbroker* debases its Jewishness by drawing a "bogus analogy between the horrors of the Holocaust and living conditions in Spanish Harlem."[67] Lumet had drawn that analogy—but not without an awareness of its flaws, flaws that were, not coincidentally, present in the novel. The latter, for instance, opens on Sol at the pawnshop, where he has his first flashback. The film, on the other hand, opens on Germany before the war, then cuts to the suburbs, blunting rather than reinforcing a connection between the Holocaust and Harlem. And long before the Berlin screening of *The Pawnbroker*, Lumet had continually tinkered with shots of the three Nazis who arrest Sol's family—shortening the shots, then lengthening them, then shortening them again so that the comparison of the three Nazis and the three pawnshop robbers would be hinted at rather than hammered.[68]

Finally, Lumet and his collaborators erected a wall of more than italics (Wallant's device) to separate the concentration camp scenes from those in New York. Quincy Jones scored the present-day scenes with jazz and the backstory scenes with classical music. Boris Kaufman shot the latter to look hallucinatory—less dark, less "aural,"

less percussive, less densely composed than the New York scenes. And because the past unfolds in fractional seconds rather than whole seconds, it stands in keen and exceptionally filmic contrast to the present, a contrast sharpened by the fact that the concentration camp scenes (unlike those in the novel) are so elliptical that we cannot "read" them.

Roger Lewis once described himself as "often a little too conciliatory [*sic*]."[69] And so perhaps was *The Pawnbroker*, if not too conciliatory then (for some critics) too universal. The picture testifies nonetheless to the spirit of independent production and, more so, the horror of the event that the story both dramatizes and memorializes. As early as spring 1962, less than three weeks before Eichmann's execution, Lewis, a Jew and a former vice president for advertising, said that he wanted to do not *a* picture but *this* picture, *The Pawnbroker*, "because of the years I spent peddling millions of miles of horseshit on film and hating about 99% of it . . . and then having all the smart guys tell that this one wasn't commercial, would never go, etc."[70]

This picture, *The Pawnbroker*, was the work of *collaborateur*s rather than *auteur*s, which may account for its strengths and no doubt its weaknesses. Whatever its inherent successes or miscalculations, it was the foundation for the widely seen American miniseries about the *shoah* and, later, for the most honored and widely seen of all such theatrical films, *Schindler's List*. As Jesus tells Sol, "You my teacher." For the Holocaust pictures that followed, *The Pawnbroker* served the same function.

Notes

1. Edward Lewis Wallant, *The Pawnbroker* (New York, 1962), 28. Subsequent references to the novel will be from this edition, with page numbers indicated parenthetically within the text of the essay.

2. Gerald Mast, *A Short History of the Movies*, 4th ed. (New York, 1986), 430-31.

3. Primo Levi, quoted in Lawrence L. Langer, *The Holocaust and the Literary Imagination* (New Haven, Conn., 1975), 51.

4. Martin Rackin, Letter to Roger Lewis, 25 January 1962, Box 1, "Correspondence" Folder, Roger Lewis Collection, Western Heritage Center, Univ. of Wyoming, Laramie (henceforth RLC).

5. "Gun Fight at the M-G-M Corral," *Time*, 5 August 1957, 69.

6. Roger Lewis, "Oral History," Audiotape, n.d., #3216, RLC.

7. Lewis, Letter to Daniel Petrie, 30 January 1962, Box 1, "Correspondence" Folder, RLC.

8. Lewis, "Oral History."

9. Ted Allan, "Foreword," Allan and Rod Steiger, *The Pawnbroker: A Screenplay*, Ts., n.d., Box 2, RLC.

10. Fred Baker and Ross Firestone, eds., *Movie People: At Work in the Business of Film* (New York, 1973), 17.

11. Allan, "Foreword."

12. Philip Langner, Letter to Lewis, 29 March 1962, Box 1, "Correspondence" Folder, RLC.

13. Tino Balio, *United Artists: The Company That Changed the Film Industry* (Madison, Wisc., 1987), 237.

14. Lewis, "Oral History."

15. Balio, 213, 201, 133, 145.

16. Lewis, "Oral History."

17. Baker and Firestone, 22.

18. Shimon Wincelberg, Letter to Langner, 26 July 1962, Box 1, "Correspondence" Folder, RLC.

19. Lewis, Letter to Allan, 19 February 1962, Box 1, "Correspondence" Folder, RLC.

20. Lewis, "Notes on [Allan] Screenplay for 'Pawnbroker,'" Ts., n.d, Box 1, "Miscellaneous" folder, RLC.

21. WSZ [William S. Zimmerman], Comments on shooting script, Ts., 28 May 1962, Box 1, "Correspondence" folder, RLC.

22. Langner, Letter to Robin Fox, 7 June 1962, and Lewis, Letter to Thomas Pryor, 15 June 1964, both Box 1, "Correspondence" Folder, RLC.

23. Lewis, "Oral History."

24. Lewis, Letter to Langner; Lewis, Letter to Richard Gregson, 18 July 1962; Allan, Letter to Lewis, 2 August 1962; all Box 1, "Correspondence" Folder, RLC.

25. Hollis Alpert, Letter to Lewis, n.d., Box 1, "Correspondence" Folder, RLC; Sidney Lumet, "Keep them on the hook," *Films and Filming*, October 1964, 19.

26. John Boulting, Letter to Stanley Kubrick, 1 June 1962; Dan Cunningham, Letter to Lewis, 14 May 1962; Dennis van Thal, Letter to Lewis, 18 May 1962; Michael Balcon, Letter to Lewis, 26 July 1962, all Box 1, "Correspondence" Folder, RLC.

27. Lewis, Letter to Larry Backman, 22 May 1962, Box 1, "Correspondence" Folder, RLC.

28. Lewis, Letter to Allan, 30 November 1962, Box 1, "Correspondence" Folder, RLC.

29. Morton Fine and David Friedkin, "First Draft Script," *The Pawnbroker*, 14 May 1963, Box 2, RLC.

30. Fine and Friedkin, "Revised Draft," *The Pawnbroker*, 21 August 1963, Box 2, RLC.

31. John Ellis, "The Literary Adaptation," *Screen*, May-June 1982, 3.

32. Fine and Friedkin, "Revised Draft," *The Pawnbroker*, 28 August 1963, Box 2, RLC; Judith Doneson, *The Holocaust in American Film* (Philadelphia, 1987),

112; Michael Kimmel, *Manhood in America: A Cultural History* (New York, 1996), 278.

33. Doneson, 11.

34. Unless otherwise indicated, dialogue from *The Pawnbroker* has been transcribed from the soundtrack of the film.

35. Dorothy Seidman Bilik, *Immigrant-Survivors: Post-Holocaust Consciousness in Recent Jewish American Fiction* (Middletown, Conn., 1981), 80; Annette Insdorf, *Indelible Shadows: Film and the Holocaust*, 2nd ed. (New York, 1989), xvi.

36. Sidney Lumet, *Making Movies* (New York, 1995), 102.

37. Dan Eriksen, telephone interview with the author, 13 June 1996.

38. Steiger, quoted in Arnold Abrams, "Film Crew Gives Status to Back Yard on LI," 9 October 1963, 3, clipping, "Publicity" Folder, Box 2, RLC.

39. Insdorf, 33.

40. Landau Company, Advertisement, *Variety*, 12 February 1964, 19.

41. Harold Myers, "'Pawnbroker' Scores in Berlin Fest; Ovation for Steiger," *Variety*, 3 July 1964, 1; Lewis, "Oral History."

42. Ralph Rosenblum and Robert Karen, *When the Shooting Stops . . . the Cutting Begins: A Film Editor's Story* (New York, 1979), 165.

43. Alfred Markim, Letter to Lewis, 22 October 1964, Box 1, "Correspondence" Folder, RLC; Zukor, quoted in Neal Gabler, *An Empire of Their Own: How the Jews Invented Hollywood* (New York, 1988), 340.

44. Ely Landau, telephone interview with the author, 19 May 1980.

45. Geoffrey Shurlock, Letter to Markim, Landau Productions, 31 December 1964, Motion Picture Association of America, New York (henceforth MPAA).

46. Bosley Crowther, "New Decision Due on Movie Nudity," *The New York Times*, 9 March 1965, 30.

47. "Code Seal For 'Pawnbroker' Is Indicated," *Motion Picture Daily*, 24 March 1965, clipping, *Pawnbroker* file, MPAA.

48. Landau, telephone interview.

49. Appeals Board, Motion Picture Association of America, MPAA, "Minutes," 23 March 1965.

50. Barney Balaban, Letter to Ralph Hetzel, Acting President, Motion Picture Association of America, 29 March 1965, MPAA; Gabler, 300; Magnin, quoted in Gabler, 348-49.

51. James F. O'Neill, Washington *Daily News,* clipping, Pawnbroker file, MPAA.

52. "Draft," *The Pawnbroker* file, Legion of Decency Archive, Department of Communication, United States Catholic Conference, New York; Frank Walsh, *Sin and Censorship: The Catholic Church and the Motion Picture Industry* (New Haven, Conn., 1996), 85; *Variety Daily,* 1 June 1966, clipping, RLC.

53. Review of *The Pawnbroker, Hollywood Reporter,* 16 April 1965, clipping, RLC; Lewis, "Oral History."

54. Baker and Firestone, 189-90.

55. *Variety Daily,* 3 August 1966, clipping, RLC.

56. "'Pawnbroker' Tops Italo B. O. Chase," *Variety Daily,* 14 March 1967, clipping, *Pawnbroker* file, MPAA.

57. Michael Linden, Letter to Jack Goldstein, Allied Artists, 5 November 1965, MPAA.

58. Kanin, quoted in Lawrence Graver, *An Obsession with Anne Frank: Meyer Levin and the Diary* (Berkeley, 1995), 89.

59. Doneson, 72.

60. Doneson, 72; Jack L. Warner, Letter to Barney Balaban, 5 March 1948, *Rope* file, Warner Bros. Collection, Univ. of Southern California, Los Angeles; Lumet, *Making,* 54.

61. Rosenblum, 149; Patricia Erens, *The Jew in American Cinema* (Bloomington, Ind., 1984), 285.

62. "Myro," review of *The Pawnbroker, Variety,* 6 July 1964, clipping, *Pawnbroker* file, MPAA; Howe, quoted in Howard Morley Sachar, *A History of the Jews in America* (New York, 1992), 841.

63. Ben-Gurion, quoted in Jack Wertheimer, *A People Divided: Judaism in Contemporary America* (New York, 1993), 29.

64. Stephen J. Whitfield, "Our American Jewish Heritage: The Hollywood Version," *American Jewish History* 75 (1986): 334; Lester D. Friedman, *Hollywood's Image of the Jew* (New York, 1982), 171.

65. Insdorf, 7.

66. Ilan Avisar, *Screening the Holocaust: Cinema's Images of the Unimaginable* (Bloomington, Ind., 1988), 125; Insdorf, 33.

67. Avisar, 124.

68. Lewis, "Notes re Screening Revised Rough Cut 'The Pawnbroker,'" Ts., 14 February 1964, Box 1, "Miscellaneous" folder, 4, RLC.

69. Lewis, Letter to Allan, 19 February 1962, Box 1, "Correspondence" Folder, RLC.

70. Lewis, Letter to Allan, 9 April 1962, Box 1, "Correspondence" Folder, RLC.

Catherine Jurca (essay date summer 1998)

SOURCE: Jurca, Catherine. "Hollywood, the Dream House Factory." *Cinema Journal* 37, no. 4 (summer 1998): 19-36.

[*In the following essay, Jurca proposes that* Mr. Blandings Builds His Dream House *can be interpreted as an effort to clearly express national allegiance by the American film industry.*]

COMMUNISTS, HOUSING, AND HOLLYWOOD

In the September 1948 issue of *Harper's,* real estate developer William Levitt issued his famous postwar pronouncement on the relationship between homeownership and national allegiance: "No man who owns his own house and lot can be a communist. . . . He has too much to do."[1] Levitt had a vital personal interest in his prescription for national stability through the pressures of domestic responsibility. He was angling to sell houses, thousands of them, and the feasibility of his capitalist venture depended on substantial government cooperation with materials and financing. Levitt delivered his assessment of the homeowner's loyalty with the force of a punchline, but the sentiment behind his remark also carried serious weight for a country concerned about the presence of Communists, the absence of adequate housing, and the possible connections between these issues.

The return of veterans, a marriage boom, and the construction hiatus during most of the Depression and war years combined to cause an unprecedented housing shortage in the aftermath of World War II. Declaring it the worst deficiency "since 1607 when John Smith wondered where he would spend his first night in Virginia," the editors of *Fortune* devoted the April 1946 issue to the housing crisis; when the situation had scarcely improved by the next year, they followed up with an article called "The Industry That Capitalism Forgot."[2] They estimated that three million new homes were needed to alleviate the problem and focused on the efforts of Wilson Wyatt, Truman's newly appointed housing expediter, to stimulate the construction of single-family dwellings. *Fortune* reported that Americans, particularly veterans and the poor and lower middle class, "are strikingly in favor of positive government action to end the severe shortage."[3] In a national survey conducted by the magazine, nearly half of those polled "went so far as to advocate government construction of homes on a large scale, a much more drastic attack on the shortage than anything Mr. Wyatt has proposed."[4] While this response hardly signaled an upheaval of popular opinion in favor of socialized housing, *Fortune* played up the public's extreme dissatisfaction with the situation and the measures the government had taken to resolve it. If houses were credited with helpfully coercing homeowner loyalties (one of the undercurrents as well of Herbert Hoover's "Own Your Own Home" campaign in the twenties), there was always the danger that an inadequate supply of houses might begin to look like an inadequate supply of good Americans.[5]

It was in this special housing issue that *Fortune* editor Eric Hodgins first published his short story "Mr. Blandings Builds His Castle," which recounts the exaggerated financial, legal, and emotional obstacles that a New York City couple confront when they try to solve their own housing crisis by building a house on the suburban frontier of Connecticut. By the end of the year Hodgins' story had become a best-selling novel, under the more American and democratic title *Mr. Blandings Builds His Dream House,* the name also given to the 1948 film version, a co-venture between RKO and David O. Selznick's Vanguard Films that starred Cary Grant and Myrna Loy as the beleaguered advertising copywriter and his wife.

The screen rendition of Jim and Muriel Blandings' bumbling transformation from "modern cliff-dwellers" to satisfied homeowners coincided with Hollywood's own problems with the Communist menace, as well as an economic crisis precipitated by increased production costs, cuts in foreign revenues, a declining domestic market, and the antitrust lawsuit and threat of divestiture. Even for an industry that seemed to operate in a perpetual state of crisis, the confluence of economic catastrophe and political uncertainty after the war generated unusual concern and widespread media attention. The popular press generally shared *Time*'s assessment: "Seldom has Hollywood been so worried about its future."[6] Already fearful for their profits, studio executives "were scared stiff by what they thought was the average movie-goer's indignation over Communism."[7] Although public sentiment was vehemently anti-Communist, evidence suggests that rampant public outrage at its influence in the movie industry did not materialize in the immediate wake of the investigations of the House Un-American Activities Committee in 1947, the resultant contempt of Congress charges against the Hollywood Ten, and the studio executives' univocal denunciation of Communism and institution of the blacklist in November of that year. On November 2, the *New York Times* reported that a survey by its correspondents revealed outright disapproval of HUAC's methods in Dallas, Chicago, Omaha, Denver, Los Angeles, and San Francisco and indifference to the hearings in Boston and New Orleans; at the behest of the producers, George Gallup conducted an Audience Research Poll from which he concluded that "the public has little awareness of possible Communist influences, if any, in pictures being produced today" and that the hearings "will have little immediate effect on the boxoffice."[8] Citing the same poll, *Newsweek* attributed the decision to purge Communists from their ranks, in the absence of strong public feeling in the matter, to the studios' "desperately needing," in a moment of financial weakness, to generate some "good publicity."[9]

Economics rather than ideology dictated Hollywood's response to the Communist hearings, but the solution to the economic problem of bad publicity was to assuage public doubts about the industry's ideological commitments in the press but also within the medium of film. After all, the alleged results of Communist infiltration were the creation of such openly pro-Soviet movies as *Mission to Moscow*

(1943) and the insertion of subtle "un-American" propaganda into more average fare, for example, the unsympathetic banker in *The Best Years of Our Lives* (1946).[10] Hollywood films were presumed to take advantage of the power to disseminate unsettling political ideas, despite the tight control that the mostly conservative executives exercised over film content and their single-minded drive for profits. Government censure threatened government censorship, and the press drew analogies between the adoption of the Production Code in 1930, the formation of the Production Code Administration (PCA) in 1934, and the moguls' timely repudiation of the Ten.[11] In order to prove its Americanism, industry commentators anticipated that Hollywood would shy away from "any plots . . . that cut deep into contemporary life" for fear of having its product branded "subversive"; increasingly conscious of "bad relations with the public," it would risk no more "films containing any 'social significance' lest they be considered 'red.'"[12] The studios' reactionary response would mean an end to social problem films such as RKO's own controversial *Crossfire* (whose director and producer were fired and blacklisted following the investigations) and a renewed emphasis on "unadulterated escapism."[13]

Mr. Blandings looks like precisely the kind of harmless fluff that the press predicted the film industry would churn out following the hearings. Contemporary reviewers agreed that this movie about "average people who live in average homes and are troubled by average worries" was as "light, and frequently slight" as even the most mindless audience, or the most mindless congressmen, could dare hope.[14] And yet with the production and release of this film, Hollywood intervened in an urgent domestic issue, and reviewers were not loathe to make the connection between social context and film. According to *New York Times* film critic Bosley Crowther,

> If the much-talked-about housing problem could be as happily resolved for all as it is for those fortunate people who watch "Mr. Blandings Builds His Dream House" on the Astor's screen, then one of our major dilemmas in the domestic area would be a national boon. For the business, as here represented, of a man putting a roof over his family's head is so harmlessly entertaining and so conducive to a feeling of good-will that, made the experience of a nation, it could change the destiny of the world.[15]

The review proceeds as though the experience of watching characters find housing in *Mr. Blandings* helps to alleviate a shortage of actual houses, as though representing house building were tantamount to doing it. In 1950, Gilbert Seldes reflected in *The Great Audience* that Hollywood's parodic treatment of the housing crisis constituted "propaganda by inaction," in which the film industry had "take[n] the side of those who conspired to prevent action" by refusing to do anything but distract people with "light entertainment"; for Crowther, however, it is precisely "harmless" entertainment that actively changes the world, insofar as it makes us forget about our social problems.[16]

My point is not that Crowther misreads the film but that he falls for it completely. With Hollywood under particular pressure to make "good films about a good world," as Dore Schary, its executive producer, blandly remarked upon joining MGM later in 1948, the payoff of a trivial domestic plot that affirms house building and homeownership was more substantial than the rhetoric of harmless escapism or, for that matter, the rhetoric of conspiracy would suggest.[17] *Mr. Blandings* does not express a commitment to movies without commitments; rather, its ability to generate "a feeling of good-will" and the national and international implications of that feeling suggest that it may be best understood as an adept exercise in public relations at a volatile time in studio history.

As a co-production between RKO and David O. Selznick, who put together the original package and whose releasing organization (SRO) was granted U.S. and Canadian distribution rights and responsibility for all advertising and publicity, *Mr. Blandings* complicates the notion of single studio authorship.[18] As Douglas Gomery has argued, the vertically integrated studios thrived on corporate cooperation not competition; thus for Gomery, the studio as auteur argument is flawed because it overly concerns itself with differences among films at the level of production and ignores the fundamental economic collaboration in distribution and exhibition that made the system work.[19] In my reading of *Mr. Blandings,* I want to suggest a kind of compromise scenario, what might be called a studios-as-auteur theory, that does not lose sight of the distribution and exhibition context and treats the final product as the unique expression of a singular, and singularly besieged, industry, not of a particular studio. All Hollywood was under attack in the late 1940s, and a clever and natural way to counteract industrywide charges of Communist influence, which at its most basic level was just another word for "un-American," was to take advantage of film's persuasive powers to dramatize the industry's allegiance to American values and institutions within film itself.[20]

Film critics past and present have observed that in the forties, Hollywood films were widely recognized as crucial ideological tools in the campaign to convert the rest of the world to capitalism and democracy; as the place where "millions around the world obtain most of their ideas about the United States," they possessed a "unique ability to sell American goods and American ideas in every land."[21] But commentators have virtually ignored the vital role that Hollywood films could play in inculcating those same virtues at home. The film industry made its product available for nationalist propaganda in times of domestic crisis such as war. *Mr. Blandings* suggests the ways in which the medium of Hollywood could also be adapted to address a crisis of its own. Through its strategic conflation of writing advertisements, building homes, and making movies, *Mr. Blandings* is able to advertise itself and the project of filmmaking in general as scrupulously loyal to American institutions such as the home and family and also as central to their production. And like many good advertisements, *Mr. Blandings* does its work by appearing to sell nothing at all. A "good film," it quietly constructs the "good world" to which it also refers. At a time of much-

publicized doubt about Hollywood's allegiances, what this film cunningly sells above all is an image of itself as antecedent to both American dream houses and the Americans who inhabit them.

ADVERTISING AND THE AMERICAN DREAM

The problem of the apartment in *Mr. Blandings* is the problem of the city writ small. The film begins with a series of satiric indictments of New York City, narrated in a voice-over by Dore Schary, that focus on the overcrowding and discomfort of metropolitan life. The critique is integrated into the narrative when the scene shifts to the Blandings' flat, illustrating through extended comic business the predicament of squeezing a family of four into an apartment that is spacious not only by New York standards but spectacular given the lingering housing shortage: one reviewer referred to the Blandings as "those people lucky enough to have even an apartment [they] don't like."[22] While decent housing was still difficult to come by, the exaggerated, even fictitious deficiencies of the apartment affirm the contemporary political imperative of relocating the family to a proper home environment, which is to say, a private house outside the city.[23] Jim and Muriel each sing "Home on the Range" as they take turns in the shower, but neither one immediately intuits the message behind the music, however much the audience understands what it is they really want. Long before they decide to build, Muriel has designs on their apartment; when she shows Jim a sketch of some of the structural and decoration changes to the living room she is considering, he refuses to put any money into a place they don't even own. He deflates her sentimental use of the word "home" to get her way, saying that "home" doesn't make it "a national shrine." Jim doesn't yet recognize that homes are indeed national shrines, while Muriel fails to perceive that apartments don't count. The film teaches that there's no point being sentimental about a place that you rent; only a house that you own can be a shrine.

The strange precociousness of the Blandings' daughters gives concrete form to the perils that city life poses to the family as well as to the American social system. The first advertisement in the film appears at the breakfast table, when Betsy reads with tragic intonation a classified ad about which she has written a school theme: "Forced to sell, farm dwelling, original beams, barn, apple orchard, trout stream, seclusion, will sacrifice." Her subsequent plea on behalf of the farmer and against "middle-class people like us" is restrained and mechanical; Betsy parrots the lessons on social responsibility she has learned from the teacher at her expensive progressive school, a woman who, incidentally, lambastes advertising for its parasitism. Both girls are strangely affectless throughout the film; as disinterested witnesses of and commentators on the chaos that ensues, Betsy and Joan come across as more adult than the parents. The unnatural worldliness of apartment children, who were allegedly exposed to the pernicious, nondomestic influences that their peers, raised in private houses, were spared, was a complaint dating back to the emergence of apartment hotels in New York City in the late nineteenth century and echoed nationally in the twentieth.[24] Although much is made of the daughters' approaching womanhood and the need for each to have her own bathroom, which is underscored when Jim walks in on Joan early in the film, the daughters' precociousness is not sexual but political. Budding radicals who discuss pressing social problems over breakfast, these cantankerous young ladies need to learn that decrepit farmhouses are social opportunities for the middle class and not evidence of America's social decay.

Jim fails to respond to his daughter's testimony about what she calls "the disintegration of our present society" with either the desire to buy the property or proper sympathy for the farmer's plight, and she denounces his inability to see "the whole sordid picture." Jim can't see the picture because he is incapable of responding to the rhetoric of economic coercion and sacrifice. The classified ad indicates merely that "a fellow wants to sell his house so he puts an ad in the paper." Unable to interpret the farmer's ad as evidence of his victimization or even as a canny attempt to exploit the sympathies of city folk, Jim can't understand why Betsy mourns a man's free choice to alienate his property.

Nevertheless, it is an advertisement that advises Jim about the proper emotional and financial connection to the place he lives. His fifteen-thousand-dollar-a-year job as an advertising copywriter provides the economic foundation for the house, but advertising also, importantly, enables sentimental recognition of the home. Having fended off appeals from his wife and children, Jim instantly succumbs to a magazine real estate ad that features a picture of an old farmhouse with the caption "Come to peaceful Connecticut: Trade city soot for sylvan charm." It is not only effective, it's irresistible; as the voice-over assures us, "the ad was enough to convince Jim." The broken-down farmhouse that this advertisement inspires the Blandings to purchase is indistinguishable from the one described in the classified ad his daughter read, down to the orchards and trout stream, and the colonial decorating scheme they choose for the interior matches the living room sketch that Muriel originally had produced for their apartment. Jim's susceptibility to the ad is demonstrated by his instantaneous, instinctive response to it; he automatically converts the caption into his personal advertising copy: "Would you spend $7,000 to tear out someone else's walls, when for a few thousand more you could find a nice old place in Connecticut, fix it up, and have the kind of dream house you've always wanted?" He is addressing his secretary here, but the point is not that he is trying to sell her, nor that the slick professional advertisement sells him, but rather that it induces him to sell himself. And the ad works on Jim by playing upon his sentimental impulses as well as his fiscal pragmatism. His unwillingness to spend seven thousand dollars to rehabilitate an apartment some other man owns motivates his desire to spend more money on a "dream house." The advertisement enables him to forge the necessary connections between house and home, finan-

cial ownership and emotional investment, that had eluded him during the film's opening scenes.

But Jim loses his initial insight into the mutuality of feeling and finance that is embedded in the very term *home-owner* when he is forced to adopt a position that opposes the sentimental value of the home to its economic value. *Mr. Blandings* prepares us for this opposition before Jim has a chance to articulate it: it cuts from an exterior shot of Jim and Muriel walking into the dilapidated farmhouse they have fallen in love with to a shot of the pair sitting in the office of their lawyer and best friend, Bill Coles. By substituting a lawyer's office for the missing interior of the farmhouse, the camera exposes the financial unsoundness of the Blandings' purchase before the lawyer has the chance. The Blandings think they are entering their dream house, but they are about to learn that they are really entering into a terrible investment.

In his lawyer's office, Jim tries to defend his gross miscalculations about the financial value of the old house by comparing it to a "fine painting": both are "beautiful," and their beauty exempts them from economic considerations—"you can't measure the things you love in dollars and cents." Although the home has its sentimental genesis in an advertisement, he turns to painting in an effort to detach the home from commercial interests. This artistic analogy consistently frames the Blandings' understanding of their house and accounts for their failure to understand its economic value until the end of the film. A structural engineer tries to persuade the Blandings that they must tear down the old farmhouse and start fresh. In order to demonstrate the house's lean, he has the couple peer at the house through an old window frame. While the view through the frame reveals the building's structural and thus financial unsoundness, the frame itself turns the house into an object of aesthetic contemplation. The house becomes a painting, something beautiful not practical, and they reject the recommendation.

After failing to find an engineer who shares their view of the house, the Blandings finally do consult an architect, whose modest house plans they so revise and complicate that the anticipated cost of the project soars from $10,000 to $21,000. At this point the Blandings decide to abandon their dream and sign a twenty-year lease on their apartment, but on their way out of the architect's office, Muriel notices a painting of their proposed house, with the words "The Residence of Mr. and Mrs. Jim Blandings" printed underneath. The painting convinces the Blandings to proceed with construction, that no price is too great to procure an object that cannot be evaluated in economic terms. As Jim insisted earlier, "You don't ask how much was the paint, how much was the canvas," and even if you accidentally discover that paint and canvas come to $21,000, the information is not particularly relevant to your emotional investment in the home.

The instantaneous appeal of the painting seems to align it with the original advertisement for Connecticut real estate, but the former denies the sentimental possibilities of ownership that the latter underscores. Paintings appeal to viewers by persuading them that the object of representation—the home—exists in the realm of the aesthetic and sentimental rather than the economic. The film ultimately privileges the advertisement over the painting, however, because its lesson is not only that you can measure the things you love in economic terms, but that the economic is, in fact, the primary measure: dollar-and-cents value is precisely why you love them. The parallel anxieties of mounting bills as construction proceeds and Jim's fast-approaching slogan deadline for the WHAM ham account provide the dramatic tension—what passes for a plot. Obsessed with the details and difficulties of building, Jim has "lost the touch" and faces the prospect of losing his job and thus his dream house before it is even completed. The actual cost of the house wildly exceeds their initial budget; he registers the impending economic catastrophe by equating the construction of the house with the destruction of his home. In other words, he substitutes domestic problems for financial problems. Money and matrimony are intertwined most dramatically when he confuses an excess of bills and his best friend, Bill, with whom he imagines Muriel is having an affair. At the climax of Jim's economic and emotional crisis he confesses to his wife that he "hate[s]" the house, at which point Mr. Tasander, the local worker who drilled his well, comes over to see him about "a little matter of $12.36." This is the final straw; Jim has a fit, empties his pockets, and invites Mr. Tasander to help himself to anything in the house. It turns out that Mr. Tasander has come to return $12.36 that he mistakenly overcharged the Blandings. The economic moment, when the homeowner realizes that it is impossible to overspend on a house that he owns, collapses with the sentimental moment, his realization that he "love[s] this house." The cynical lawyer's subsequent endorsement of their home-building project, his final pronouncement that "maybe there are some things you buy with your heart, and not your head," misses the point of Jim's revelation. It is the unexpected dividend that convinces Jim of the home's sentimental value.

Economic investment and return are incorporated into the sentimental view of the home at just the moment when Jim's failure to produce an acceptable slogan for WHAM jeopardizes their future in the expensive new dream house. Only an advertisement can save the Blandings' home, and it comes at least nominally from within the home, when their black maid, Gussie, blurts out the slogan that becomes the center of a national ad campaign: "If you ain't eatin' WHAM, you ain't eatin' ham." Indeed, Gussie's main function in the film is to spout potential jingles to sell the ham she loves. She actually fights to keep it on the Blandings' breakfast table after Jim complains that he doesn't want to eat what he is responsible for cramming down one hundred million throats. She pleads with him: "The children like WHAM . . . Mrs. Blandings likes it too. And I consider it very tasty." He then parodies the virtues of the ham, its "succulent goodness [and] sugar-smoked tenderness," but Gussie understands his mockery

as promotion. She responds honestly to his satire: "You don't have to sell me; I like it." This remark, taken together with the final slogan that is inspired by pure affection for the product, not only marks Gussie the consumer as the natural advertiser in the movie but also naturalizes advertising itself. For his cynical affirmation she substitutes a sincere endorsement. Advertising not only evokes sentiment but is generated out of sentiment: loving something is identical to advertising it.

In its commitment to the notion of the consumer as a natural advertiser, *Mr. Blandings* embraces an exaggerated version of the "advertising state of mind that today meets and cooperates with advertising effort," as described in 1946 by a founding partner of the Caulkins and Holden agency, one of the first generation of "respectable" advertising professionals.[25] According to Caulkins, the modern advertiser worked *with* consumers not *on* them; their roles were complementary rather than antagonistic. Like last year's model, however, this sunny view of advertising was virtually obsolete by the time he had issued it. By the mid- and late forties, the profession increasingly articulated a more subtly coercive agenda that favored manipulative depth psychology in market research. Although the influential and persistent view of the advertiser as "hidden persuader" was largely a development of the 1950s, its direct antecedents were in the immediate postwar period, when advertisers sought to facilitate the reconversion of the American economy by "reduc[ing] the friction in distribution."[26] One might imagine that the pent-up desires of millions of Americans for the goods and services that had been difficult or impossible to obtain in the long years of the war would have been enough of a distributive lubricant, but advertisers in this period experimented with techniques for penetrating consumers' "unconscious minds" in order to ascertain "why they really want or don't want certain things" and how best they might be made to want them.[27]

In *Mr. Blandings,* the only unconscious is Jim's, and it is featured so that it may be repudiated as a source of advertising genius. The significance of the advertiser's unconscious was articulated by James Webb Young, an executive at J. Walter Thompson and an important figure in the history of advertising. In a lecture delivered to the Business School at the University of Chicago, Young claimed that the way to form ideas was to let the unconscious (sleeping) mind do the work of synthesizing bits of information that had been gathered and contemplated in advance; once the idea was released, the conscious mind then polished and perfected it.[28] While trying to produce the WHAM slogan, Jim falls asleep and awakes to some fresh ideas and fresh perspectives on old ones, only to have them rejected by his secretary. He gives up and goes home, where Gussie miraculously utters the slogan that becomes the center of a new campaign and saves his job. In *Mr. Blandings,* the solution is to let the consumer speak rather than the unconscious, any unconscious. Through Gussie's sincere endorsement of WHAM, advertising is manifested as the consumer's spontaneous and honest expression of love for a product; the film reverts to a nostalgic view of advertisers as deft channelers of the consumer's conscious desires and not crude manipulators of her psyche. Organic rather than parasitic, advertising is trustworthy because it gives consumers what they really want—advertisers and consumers speak with the same voice.

Thus the production of advertisements occurs in the home, where consumption takes place. Advertising is reinforced as both the economic and sentimental foundation of the home in the film's final moments, when the camera cuts from an over-the-shoulder shot of a magazine ad featuring Gussie in a white chef's hat and apron, uttering her successful slogan and holding out a platter of ham, to a shot of Jim, the picture of affluence, picking up and reading a novel about his adventures in home building. The camera then pulls back to reveal the completed house and the happy extended family in the foreground, with Gussie at the upper border of the frame. The visual marginalization of Gussie corresponds to the verbal shift from "*I consider it very tasty*" and the potential slogan, "You don't have to sell *me; I* like it," to the actual slogan: "If *you* ain't eatin' WHAM, *you* ain't eatin' ham." Gussie may be represented as an enthusiastic consumer, but as a black woman and servant, in a long tradition of "mammy" commercial icons and trademarks, she is also quite clearly an advertisement waiting to happen. She is insignificant to the film's narrative development, but in her cultural availability as the spokeswoman for the commodity, she is crucial to its narrative resolution.

The final advertisement translates her personal fondness for WHAM exclusively into an eagerness to serve it to the white family, but what's at stake here is much bigger than ham. The ending of *Mr. Blandings* articulates a nationalist agenda like the one Lauren Berlant attributes to *Imitation of Life* (1934).[29] Through her timely ad, for which she receives a ten-dollar-a-week raise, Gussie (played by Louise Beavers; who also starred as Delilah Johnson in the original *Imitation*) stabilizes the nation's fundamental domestic units, the white family and its free-standing private house. She appears as a virtual slave in the service of these institutions—how else could the Blandings get her to leave New York City for *their* dream house off in the Connecticut countryside?[30] Black women in this film are devoted consumers of hams so that white families may be devoted consumers of homes.

Advertisements generate homes, but they also generate Americans; home building is a process of American formation. Dore Schary's authoritative opening voice-over identifies Jim as a "typical New Yorker," which is also a code for the typical American: "In any discussion of contemporary American life we must inevitably start with Manhattan, New York City, USA." Despite, or perhaps because of, Jim's representativeness, however, he knows virtually nothing about American history, and his ignorance forms a comic leitmotif of the film. The construction of the Colonial-style house doubles as an education in American culture and history through which he may lay claim to his rights as an American citizen.

According to the Yankee realtor who sells them the farmhouse, General Gates watered his horses there during the Revolutionary War; whoever buys that house, he says, "is buying a piece of American history" in addition to plenty of closet space. Jim has never heard of General Gates and doesn't know the Revolutionary from the Civil War, but much of the appeal of the house lies in the possibility of owning a national landmark. A few moments later, when he fantasizes about the perfect dream house, he imagines an English country estate, complete with a mastiff and fox-hunting music playing in the background. The transition from the fantasy of the English estate to the reality of the New England Colonial coincides with the process of his Americanization. As his difficulties mount, Jim frequently invokes his identity as an "American" to assert vague "rights as a citizen," only to have them repeatedly denied and qualified by his attorney. It turns out that the only specific right that Jim is genuinely committed to is his right as an American to own his own home. By the end of the film, Jim enjoys this fundamental right and makes a pretty speech defending it, in which he speaks on behalf of "kids who are just starting out," those who don't make $15,000 a year writing advertising copy. Advertising copywriters in major Manhattan firms made a good deal more than this; Jim's salary was originally supposed to be $25,000 but was adjusted because the filmmakers considered the figure absurdly high to make him a plausible national average, however inadequate the final sum was to the task.[31] By cutting his salary and cutting the scene in which a couple of these "kids" (Mr. Tasander's son and daughter-in-law) admire and desire the finished house and hope some day to have "a little place of their own, with the Government's help," Jim Blandings is allowed to stand in and speak for a population that is erased from the film.[32] To be American is not simply to dream about a home of your own but to have it, without the assistance of the government. It is to embrace advertising as the foundation of dream houses.

SELZNICK'S DREAM HOUSE

Not surprisingly, part of the meaning of this film that advertises the virtues of advertising—and is also, as we shall see, designed as an advertisement *for* film—resides in its promotion. One of the people in charge of its advertising and exploitation was Paul MacNamara, vice-president of public relations for the Selznick organization and former promotion manager for the Hearst magazine group.[33] Just before going to work for Selznick in 1945, MacNamara had achieved instant fame for a national publicity stunt: in honor of Independence Day, he had persuaded every magazine in the United States to put the American flag on its July 1944 cover. He described this feat in a book on Selznick and Hollywood. "It was intended as a patriotic gesture on the part of the magazine business, to get people thinking about the print media in a favorable way."[34] A classic public relations move, the point was not to sell directly a particular product or service or even to champion a company but to extol the virtues of an industry. By pushing its patriotism, that is, by making nationalist sentiment seem a constitutive feature of the periodical press, Mac-Namara created a salutary image of an entire medium.

For *Mr. Blandings,* which he considered "a promotion man's dream," MacNamara attempted a similar and no less spectacular national publicity maneuver.[35] Indeed, part of the ingenuity of the exploitation campaign lay in its manifest excesses and transparency, which made the promotional work within the film appear comparatively discreet. Cashing in on the housing shortage and an anticipated building boom, the Selznick Releasing Organization arranged for corporate tie-ins with a number of companies that sold home furnishings and building materials—Aetna Steel, Bigelow-Sanford Carpet, Paragon Art and Linen, Sherwin Williams Paints, to name a few—that were to amount to some $3.5 million in free print advertising for the film.[36] The most important and profitable tie-in was with General Electric. Ads in newspapers, popular periodicals, and building and architecture trade magazines, as well as promotional materials that GE sent to its retailers across the country, boasted: "Mr. Blandings' Dream House has come true! And it's an all General Electric Dream!"[37] Marking its transition to postwar manufacturing, GE assembly lines were producing a new, all-electric kitchen which they rushed from the East Coast to Hollywood so that it could appear in the film. According to the General Electric/*Mr. Blandings* promotional kit, the media blitz was designed to make "every resident . . . automatically think of General Electric whenever he thinks of fine homes," in other words, to weave together the "General Electric Dream" and the American Dream.[38]

MacNamara's magic promotional touch made itself felt in what Selznick called "one of the most sensational stunts in a long time," the construction of over seventy "Blandings Dream Houses" in cities across the country that were raffled off and some of the proceeds given to various nonprofit organizations as part of the "charitable tie-up."[39] The Dream Houses were built with labor, materials, furnishings, and, of course, GE appliances and fixtures (down to the light bulbs), donated by companies likewise eager to stimulate America's homeownership habit. Not content simply to depict the virtues of ownership on the screen, SRO credited *Mr. Blandings* with actively helping to resolve the housing shortage. Although the press releases from Selznick's office didn't claim that the film was in itself a positive step toward ending the housing crisis, as Crowther's review had done, they asserted the beneficial effects of the Dream House campaign on homeownership: "The number of home owners in 1948 . . . will be increased by at least 73."[40] They likewise reported optimistically on the "alarming mass movement of America's population from rural to urban centers": the Dream Houses "will effect a migration of at least 73 American families back to the country," by which they meant "the suburbs of major American cities."[41] Cary Grant made a special appearance at the construction site of the Los Angeles Dream House, where he confused movie and real-world experiences of the housing crisis: "In my role of Jim Blandings in the film which sponsors the construction program I

came to know the trials and troubles of an average American family building a home today and I hope this project throughout the nation may in some way help alleviate the dire lack of housing."[42] Seventy-three houses, seventy-three homeowners—certainly a modest assault on the shortage, but to the extent that it actually provided Americans with their houses, it reflected the intensity of the film's and the filmmakers' commitment to the American home.

The idea of turning film into a sponsor of American houses also finds its way into the text of *Mr. Blandings.* As a promulgator of homeownership, domesticity, and American citizenship, it strives to sell itself as the ideal salesman of these national virtues. A figure for the kind of advertisement that the film valorizes, which expresses rather than fabricates consumer desire, helping people to name and thus to have what it is they really want—a ham, a home—*Mr. Blandings* proposes itself as the originator of homeownership and American citizens. The film is framed by opening and closing shots of two different American "dream" houses: the Southern Colonial that iconographically denotes a David O. Selznick project, and the completed New England Colonial home that the film has labored to produce. The prominent juxtaposition of these structures suggests a causal relation between the house of Selznick—a former RKO-Pathé production facility before it became the headquarters of Selznick International—and the Blandings' all-American home. The relation between them is reinforced through the allegorization of filmmaking as house construction. The opening credits are superimposed on architectural blue-prints and replace the usual details of house plans. An unnaturally long close-up of the architect's business sign, whose office happens to be located in a cozy house, reveals it to be virtually identical to the well-known sign used at the beginning of the film to announce a Selznick release. Even the carpenters who build the Blandings' house on-screen are the actual set builders for RKO pressed into service—real movie carpenters playing real housing carpenters. Through studios that look like houses, business interiors masked as homes, and Hollywood moguls who pass themselves off as architects, film domesticates itself.

A film about a social problem that's not a problem at all, or nothing, at least, that Hollywood can't solve, *Mr. Blandings* affirms its makers' allegiance at a time of national uncertainty about the loyalties of the American movie industry. When Emmett Lavery, the president of the Screen Writers Guild, testified before HUAC in 1947, he reported that Communist influence in Hollywood was negligible, because "nothing sends people out of theaters faster than a play or movie that is anti-anything." Hollywood's duties ran in the other direction: "We should make the people aware of the very active love they have for the institutions of this country."[43] Selznick himself condemned anyone who "hides behind constitutional privileges" for "placing his dollars above his loyalties to the industry, and far more importantly, to the nation."[44] After industry executives voted unanimously to support a blacklist and fire the Ten,

Eric Johnston, president of the Motion Picture Association of America, issued a policy statement that defended the firings based on the "disservice" the "actions" of the Ten did "their employers," which "has impaired their usefulness to the industry."[45] Unlike Selznick, Schary, a New Deal liberal, had much sympathy for the "unfriendly" witnesses and spoke eloquently in defense of their civil liberties when he testified before the committee on October 29, 1947, but similar concerns for the industry, if not fears for the nation, led him to cave in to pressure from his peers.[46] It is precisely *Mr. Blandings*'s loyalty to the nation and its institutions that attests to its loyalty to the industry. It served Hollywood by serving itself up as a testimony to these commitments. While alleged Communists such as John Howard Lawson asserted the privilege of free speech before HUAC by proclaiming, "I know my rights as an American citizen," *Mr. Blandings* instead champions the right to Americanize oneself by investing in a home.[47] Its rhetoric of rights based on the nationalizing force of private property made it a suitable advertisement for moviegoing in general. Its release in southern California was planned "in conjunction with a simultaneous tremendous advertising campaign urging the public to go to the movies. Not just to a theatre playing [*Mr. Blandings*] but to any movie."[48] Its success would be a triumph not only for Selznick and RKO but for the industry as a whole.

Despite excellent reviews, however, *Mr. Blandings*'s performance at the box office proved disappointing. With waves of releases scheduled in American cities from spring until fall (the building season) of 1948, frantic memos from Selznick to his publicity and advertising departments argued for a title change to "The Love Nest" or "The Wolf and Mrs. Blandings" in order to broaden its appeal and urged them to shift their advertising away from house building to the nonexistent love triangle (which Schary thought misleading). Selznick conducted his "own little Gallup Poll among people who have not seen the picture" and was horrified to discover their response: "Who wants to see a picture about house building?"[49] Although the makers of *Mr. Blandings* thought they were exploiting a pressing contemporary problem, the idea that houses were built one at a time, with infinite pain, already bordered on nostalgia. The audiences who didn't want to see the film were, in fact, never going to be building their own houses. Its release coincided with the expansion, and shortly the explosion, of the kind of mass-produced, on-site residential construction that made extensive postwar suburbanization possible. Selznick may have inspired Levitt (the *Harper's* article cited at the beginning of this essay describes Levitt's real estate office as "a smallish building, Selznick-colonial in style"), but Levitt certainly outdid him as a builder. The rise of Levittowns corresponded with the studios' imminent, if impermanent, collapse; the factory production of houses helped to precipitate the demise of the factory system in Hollywood. Perhaps another way to explain *Mr. Blandings*'s poor box office is to say that a growing number of people were beginning to find that they preferred living in decentralized dream houses to watching movies about them. Homeowners were too busy to be

Communists, and they were spending less of their leisure time in movie theaters. Levitt personally encouraged changing patterns of leisure: houses on the Long Island development came with a television set and washing machine (Bendix, not GE).[50] By the midfifties, after Howard Hughes had run RKO into the ground, a more ominous picture of the relationship between film and homeownership emerged, when the moribund studio sold its Encino location ranch, where the Blandings' dream had been filmed, as suburban development in the San Fernando Valley boomed.[51] At last Hollywood was really supplying Americans with their homes.

Notes

1. Eric Larabee, "The Six Thousand Houses That Levitt Built," *Harper's* 197 (September 1948): 84.

2. "*Fortune* Survey," *Fortune* 33 (April 1946): 266; "The Industry that Capitalism Forgot," *Fortune* 36 (August 1947): 61-67, 167-170.

3. "*Fortune* Survey," 266.

4. "The Promise of the Shortage," *Fortune* 33 (April 1946): 101.

5. Even in the late nineteenth century, homeownership was advocated as a means of social control among the poor and foreign-born. Josiah Strong anticipated Levitt's remark, albeit without the latter's good humor: "Let a man become the owner of a home, and he is much less susceptible to socialistic propagandism" (in *Our Country: Its Possible Future and Its Present Crisis* [1886; reprint Cambridge, Mass.: Harvard University Press, 1963], 176). The pamphlet *Good Homes Make Contented Workers* (Philadelphia: Industrial Society Associates, 1919) made the case more plainly: "A wide diffusion of home ownership has long been recognizable as fostering a stable and conservative habit. . . . The man owns his home, but in a sense his home owns him" (unpaginated).

6. "Paradise Lost?" *Time*, January 19, 1948, 87.

7. "Pink Slips," *Time*, December 8, 1947, 29.

8. Larry Ceplair and Steven Englund, *The Inquisition in Hollywood: Politics in the Film Community, 1930-1960* (Garden City, N.Y.: Anchor Press, 1980), 353.

9. "Hollywood's Super-Purge," *Newsweek*, December 8, 1947, 24, 25. Thus the famous meeting of the moguls at the Waldorf Hotel on November 24, 1947, which produced the proclamation banishing Communists from motion pictures, also resulted in a decision to establish a public relations committee to offset the negative publicity that Hollywood was receiving from the conservative press and special-interest groups.

10. For contemporaneous accounts of problematic Hollywood films, see William Walton, "Kangaroo Court under Klieg Light," *New Republic*, November 3, 1947, 8-9, and Samuel Shaffer, "Red Scenario,"

Newsweek, August 25, 1947, 22. For a discussion of pro-Soviet Hollywood movies made during World War II, see Clayton R. Koppes and Gregory D. Black, *Hollywood Goes to War: How Politics, Profits and Propaganda Shaped World War II Movies* (1987; reprint Berkeley, Calif.: University of California Press, 1990), 185-221, and Thomas Doherty, *Projections of War: Hollywood, American Culture, and World War II* (New York: Columbia University Press, 1993), 144-145, 267-268.

11. See Raymond Moley, "Movie Troubles—Past and Present," *Newsweek,* December 8, 1947, 92, and Walton, "Kangaroo Court." Although officially the code was designed to control the moral content of films, Gregory Black has shown that throughout the thirties it was frequently used to weaken social problem films and to prevent sensitive political films from being made. See his *Hollywood Censored: Morality Codes, Catholics, and the Movies* (Cambridge: Cambridge University Press, 1994), 246-291.

12. "Paradise Lost?" 88; Gladwin Hill, "'Safe and Sane' Films New Hollywood Rule," *New York Times,* November 30, 1947, VI, 6.

13. "Hollywood: An Industry Gets Over the Jitters," *Newsweek,* May 10, 1948, 60.

14. Rose Pelswick, review, *New York Journal-American,* March 26, 1948, 11; review, *Saturday Review of Literature,* May 8, 1948, 22.

15. Bosley Crowther, review, *New York Times,* March 26, 1948, 26.

16. Gilbert Seldes, *The Great Audience* (New York: Viking, 1950), 97, 99, 98.

17. Cited in Thomas Schatz, *The Genius of the System: Hollywood Filmmaking in the Studio Era* (New York: Pantheon, 1988), 446.

18. In January 1947, Dore Schary moved from executive producer at Vanguard Films, which Selznick created as a B-movie money-maker to finance his prestige films, to studio production head at RKO. Schary was still under contract to Selznick, and as part of the deal six of Schary's Vanguard projects went to RKO and Selznick got part of the profits, including 60 percent of the equitable interest of *Mr. Blandings.* Although Selznick was an independent producer and ran a distribution company, he was, in the words of Schatz. "a virtual studio unto himself" (*The Genius,* 9), relying upon the production facilities and talents of the major studios as well as their theater chains, in which he needed to place his own films and those he marketed on behalf of others.

19. "Historians' interest in competition for maximum box-office revenues (i.e. the difference between films) has only served to ignore the total and necessary corporate cooperation which existed on the levels of distribution and exhibition" (Douglas Gomery, *The Hollywood Studio System* [New York: St. Martin's Press, 1986], 193).

20. Writers who were critical of the hysteria over Communism noted that the word was bandied about with very little understanding of what it actually denoted; "Communism" was invoked whenever anyone wanted to suggest something "synonymous" with "un-American" (J. L. Benvenisti, "As Americans See Communism," *Commonweal,* November 14, 1947, 110). Similarly, Hollywood's involvement in antitrust legislation damaged its credibility as a democratic and fundamentally American industry. See, for example, Donald M. Nelson, "The Independent Producer," *Annals of the American Academy of Political and Social Science* 254 (November 1947): 49-57.

21. Herman A. Lowe, "Washington Discovers Hollywood," *American Mercury* 60 (April 1945): 407-408. See also Garth Jowett, *Film: The Democratic Art* (Boston: Little, Brown, 1976), 384-386.

22. Review, *Newsweek,* April 5, 1948, 85.

23. *Cities Are Abnormal,* ed. Elmer T. Peterson (Norman: University of Oklahoma Press, 1946) indicates the range of postwar anti-urbanism. Cities had replaced neighborhoods and communities with mere crowds; ecologically irresponsible, they posed threats to the public's physical, moral, and psychological health. In a nuclear age, the concentrated populations of cities came to be seen as helpless targets of nuclear attack. In the political climate of the time, cities also came to be understood in terms of their un-Americanism, as the historical gathering place of foreign immigrants and the locus of social and political unrest. For Louis Bromfield, cities were un-American because it was the fact, rather than the possibility, of homeownership that made the United States democratic. American cities were a threat to national security because they offered virtually no opportunities for average Americans to stabilize their politics by stabilizing their economic relation to the place they lived. Americans could either have a nation of Jeffersonian homeowners or a nation of Marxist rabble. See his "To Clear the Dross," 183-198.

24. "The children of hotel residents become precocious, wayward and self-assertive, and learn from strangers many things the knowledge of which should be kept from them as long as possible" (Everett N. Blanke, "The Cliff-Dwellers of New York," *Cosmopolitan* 15 [July 1893]: 356). The theme of the premature grown-up is amplified in a chapter devoted to children in Norman S. Hayner's sociological study *Hotel Life* (Chapel Hill: University of North Carolina Press, 1936), 119-131.

25. Earnest Elmo Caulkins, *"And Hearing Not—": Annals of an Adman* (New York: Scribner's, 1946), 227. American advertising's focal shift from the product to the consumer in the twenties and thirties is described in Roland Marchand, *Advertising and the*

American Dream: Making Way for Modernity, 1920-1940 (Berkeley: University of California Press, 1985).

26. Robert F. Elder, "Why Market Research Should Be Major Management Function," *Printer's Ink,* May 31, 1946, 52. Vance Packard exposed the advertiser's bold manipulation of the consumer psyche in *The Hidden Persuaders* (New York: David McKay, 1957).

27. Ernest Dichter, "Have You Tried Psychological Research?" *Printer's Ink,* January 3, 1947, 29; "What Is Depth Interviewing?" *Printer's Ink,* February 15, 1946, 36. Behavioral psychologist John B. Watson, formerly of Johns Hopkins University, probed the consumer's mind for the J. Walter Thompson Agency in the twenties, but it was only after World War II that advertising agencies were uniformly touted as sophisticated psychological laboratories.

28. James Webb Young, *A Technique for Producing Ideas* (1940; reprint Chicago: NTC Business Books, 1994). I am grateful to J. D. Connor for bringing Young's work to my attention.

29. See Lauren Berlant, "National Brands/National Body," in *Comparative National Identities: Race, Sex, and Nationality in the Modern Text,* ed. Hortense Spillers (New York: Routledge, 1991), 110-140. Berlant reads *Imitation* in light of the history of Aunt Jemima and argues that in both cases, investment in the embodiment of the black female is linked to the consolidation of white personal, corporate, and national identities. In the thirties and forties, Louise Beavers made a successful career out of playing the film version of Aunt Jemima; according to Donald Bogle, she was the first actress to become a "distinctive mammy figure" (*Toms, Coons, Mulattos, Mammies, and Bucks: An Interpretive History of Blacks in American Films* [New York: Viking, 1973], 62). For comprehensive studies of African Americans in advertising, see Marilyn Kern-Foxworth, *Aunt Jemima, Uncle Ben, and Rastus: Blacks in Advertising, Yesterday, Today, and Tomorrow* (Westport, Conn.: Greenwood Press, 1995), and Jan Nederveen Pieterse, *White on Black: Images of Africa and Blacks in Western Popular Culture* (New Haven: Yale University Press, 1992).

30. A reviewer remarked the absurdity of transplanting Gussie along with the family: "How in the world the Blandings ever persuaded their cook to move from midtown Manhattan to Connecticut is something that no home owners with a couple of children around the premises, will ever be able to understand" (Leo Mishkin, review, *Morning Telegraph,* March 26, 1948). Clipping in the David O. Selznick Collection at the Harry Ransom Humanities Research Center at the University of Texas at Austin (hereafter the Selznick Collection), box 3654, folder 1.

31. For an account of the film's production, see Eric Hodgins, "Mr. Blandings Goes to Hollywood," *Life,* April 12, 1948, 110-118. A 1948 congressional subcommittee report on income distribution announced that only 2.9 percent or 1 in 34 American families made more than $10,000 per year. Cited in Frederick Allen, *The Big Change: America Transforms Itself, 1900-1950* (New York: Harper, 1952), 210.

32. Text is from the script dated July 25, 1947, Selznick Collection, box 1064, folder 12.

33. Technically, *advertising* referred to paid promotions in media such as newspapers and magazines, while *exploitation* suggested all other kinds of promotions, including the unpaid publicity that studios worked so hard to generate for their films. According to Jane Gaines, exploitation meant merchant cooperation and tie-ins almost exclusively by the late 1930s. See "From Elephants to Lux Soap: The Programming and 'Flow' of Early Motion Picture Exploitation," *Velvet Light Trap* 25-26 (Spring 1990): 29-43.

34. Paul MacNamara, *Those Were the Days, My Friend: My Life in Hollywood with David O. Selznick and Others* (Metuchen, N.J.: Scarecrow, 1993), 17.

35. Ibid., 85.

36. Company names and estimates are from the "National and Local Advertising and Promotion Schedule," Selznick Collection, box 3824, folder 6. Since the 1920s, studios had used the tie-in for free set decoration, film advertising, and star publicity. Charles Eckert discussed the Warner-GE Better Times Special, a star-filled train that traveled from Hollywood to Roosevelt's inauguration in 1933 by way of New York City for the opening of *42nd Street* and marketed various General Electric appliances in large cities along the way. See "The Carole Lombard in Macy's Window," *Quarterly Review of Film Studies* 3 (1978): 1-21. Eckert was ultimately less interested in the impact of these publicity practices on the look of particular scenes or on the kinds of films made than in Hollywood's impact on the shape and character of consumerism. In his account, Hollywood begins to look like the original "hidden persuader."

37. General Electric promotional kit, Selznick Collection, box 3829, folder 1.

38. Ibid. The kitchen appeared in a short scene that was cut during final editing. According to MacNamara, a GE employee saw *Mr. Blandings* at a sneak preview, noted the absence of the kitchen scene, and reported back to his bosses in New York, who were furious. Rather than risk a lawsuit, RKO and Selznick agreed that the kitchen scene had to go back in. It is omitted from the version available on video, as well as from both copies of *Mr. Blandings* at the Library of Congress. I have not been able to verify the accuracy of MacNamara's account.

39. Memo from Selznick to MacNamara and Bob Gillham (May 28, 1948), Selznick Collection, box 1498, folder 14.

40. Press release, undated, Selznick Collection, box 3829, folder 2.

41. Press release, undated, Selznick Collection, box 3829, folder 2.

42. Press release (May 23, 1948), Selznick Collection, box 3810, folder 19.

43. Cited in Sidney Olson, "The Movie Hearings," *Life,* November 24, 1947, 146.

44. Telegram from Selznick to Bartley Crum (October 20, 1947), Selznick Collection, box 2356, folder 1.

45. "Film Industry's Policy Defined," *Variety,* November 26, 1947, 3.

46. Schary discusses his position, expresses regret over the handling of the situation, and defends his compliance with the blacklist in *Heyday: An Autobiography* (Boston: Little, Brown, 1979).

47. Cited in "Lawson and Thomas Clash at Hearing," *Variety,* October 29, 1947, 20.

48. Press release (September 27, 1948), Selznick Collection, box 3829, folder 2.

49. Memo from Selznick to MacNamara and Gillham (April 21, 1948), Selznick Collection, box 1498, folder 14. An anonymous reader for *Cinema Journal* rightly wondered whether the film's relatively poor showing at the box office might have had more to do with other factors such as Cary Grant's transition from romantic lead to jealous husband and father. This account is certainly plausible, but we will probably never know exactly why *Mr. Blandings* did not do well; what is most interesting to me is that Selznick discounted other possibilities in favor of its subject matter.

50. Jowett dates the significant commercial expansion of television and its arrival as "a true mass medium in the United States" (*Film,* 347) from 1948, which saw the number of stations increase from seventeen to forty-one, the sale of sets climb 500 percent over the previous year, and the first attempt at network service, which attracted important national advertisers.

51. Betty Lasky describes the gutting of RKO under Hughes and the sale of Hunter Ranch in *RKO: The Biggest Little Major of Them All* (1984; reprint Santa Monica, Calif.: Roundtable, 1989), 194-228.

Pauline Turner Strong (essay date 1998)

SOURCE: Strong, Pauline Turner. "Playing Indian in the Nineties: *Pocahontas* and *The Indian in the Cupboard*." In *Hollywood's Indian: The Portrayal of the Native American in Film,* edited by Peter C. Rollins and John E. O'Connor, pp. 188-205. Lexington: University Press of Kentucky, 1998.

[*In the following essay, Strong analyzes Hollywood's approach to Native American characters and culture using* Pocahontas *and* The Indian in the Cupboard *as representative examples.*]

Hollywood has long taken a leading role in shaping the American tradition of "playing Indian." This chapter considers how this tradition is mobilized in two family films released in 1995: Disney's heavily marketed *Pocahontas* and the Columbia/Paramount adaptation of Lynne Reid Banks's popular children's novel *The Indian in the Cupboard.* Borrowing a concept from Donna Haraway, I would place my "situated knowledge" of these films and their associated playthings at the intersection of, first, my scholarly interest in the production and significance of imagined Indians in Anglo-American culture; second, my memories of "playing Indian" at school, at summer camp, and in Camp Fire Girls during my childhood; and, finally, my experiences rearing two daughters (ages seven and ten when the films were released). In other words, this is what Kathleen Stewart would call a "contaminated" critique, one that is complexly influenced by my participation in the cultural phenomena that it analyzes. I write as a pianist who has played "Colors Of The Wind" (the theme song from *Pocahontas*) so often for my daughters' school choir that it runs unbidden through my mind; as a parent who has spent much of a weekend "playing Indian" on CD-ROM, helping seven-year-old Tina "earn symbols" for a computer-generated wampum belt so that we could be inducted as "Friends of the Iroquois"; and, above all, as a cultural critic whose views are influenced both by the insights of my daughters and by my hopes for their generation.

As I sit at my computer composing this essay, a three-inch plastic Indian stands beside the monitor. He wears a scalp lock, yellow leggings and breechcloth, a yellow knife sheath, and a yellow pouch. Next to him is the case for our videocassette of *The Indian in the Cupboard,* with the cover reversed, as directed, so that the case simulates a weathered wooden cabinet. Beside the cabinet is a plastic skeleton key, almost as large as the miniature Indian, that can be used to open the cabinet. Although it is possible to purchase the Indian figurine and the key independently, as well as figurines of other characters in the film, ours were packaged with the video, just as a locket was packaged with *The Little Princess.*

Equipped with the miniature Indian, the cabinet, and the key, I can, if I wish, imitate Omri, the nine-year-old American boy whose coming-of-age story is told in the film. Omri, like his English namesake in the novel, is given an Indian figurine that comes to life when locked inside a magical cabinet. My figurine does not come to life, but it nevertheless mocks me as it stands by my computer, underscoring my embeddedness in several traditions—European and Anglo-American, popular and scholarly—that have locked miniature Indians in cabinets, be they late-Renaissance wonder cabinets, children's toy collections, tourists' and collectors' displays, or museum dioramas.

If I wish to simulate Omri's mastery over life I must turn to the CD-ROM version of *The Indian in the Cupboard,* where with my cursor I can animate an Indian figurine—one that, like the miniatures that open the film, appears to be "antique," made of painted porcelain or wood rather than plastic. The figurine reminds me of a miniature cigar-store Indian or a ship's figurehead, as do the seven other Indian figurines on Omri's toy shelf. When I move the cursor in order to place the figurine in the cabinet and turn the key, it "comes to life" and begins to talk to me. Like Omri's miniature friend in the film, this animated Indian is named Little Bear. He identifies himself as an Onondaga of the Wolf clan and introduces me to his Ungachis, his "friends" on the toy shelf. He gives me the name of Henuyeha, or "player."[1] I accompany Little Bear to a promontory overlooking his palisaded village, where his people live in three longhouses.

Descending to the village I meet the Ungachis, whom I will later bring to life as my guides. I recall the many American Indians who have made their living as guides for hunters or anthropologists, as well as the YMCA organization Indian Guides, to which my brother and father once belonged (an organization parodied to good effect in the Disney film *Man of the House*). Foremost among my Onondaga "friends" is a clan mother, Gentle Breeze, who will introduce me to Onondaga words, stories, and symbols referring to the ancestors of the clans—Turtle, Bear, Wolf, Snipe, Beaver, Hawk, Deer, and Eel—as well as to the underwater Panther, the Keeper of the Winds and his Spirit Animals, the Peacemaker, and the Tree of Peace. Another Ungachi, a "chief" named He Knows the Sky, will point out and tell me stories about Grandmother Moon, the Path of the Dead, the Bear, the Seven Children, and Star Girl. ("What I like about the Onondaga," says ten-year-old Katie upon hearing the story of how Star Girl guided the starving people home, "is that it's not only boys and men who do important things.")

An Ungachi named Shares the Songs will teach me to play water drums, a flute, and a variety of rattles, challenging me to remember ever more complex rhythms. Swift Hunter will teach me to recognize and follow animal tracks, while Keeper of the Words will show me how to make a headdress in the style of each of the Six Nations of the League of the Onondaga. Two children will teach me their games: from Blooming Flower I will learn how to decorate carved templates with beads; from Runs with the Wind, how to play a challenging memory game with seeds of corn, squash, and several varieties of beans.

Succeeding in these various activities requires patience, attentiveness, and a well-developed memory. Each time I succeed I am rewarded with a symbol for my "wampum belt" and the kind of effusive praise Anglo-American children expect. Upon its completion a ceremony is held to present me with the wampum belt and to name me an Ungachi, a "Friend of the Iroquois." I am feasted with a meal of corn, pumpkin, potatoes, squash, deer, roasted turkey, and cornbread. This concludes the ceremony, which I have experienced as a disconcerting example of what Michael Taussing calls "mimetic excess." The resonances are many and diverse: Camp Fire Girl "council fires" at which, proudly wearing my deerskin "ceremonial gown" and the

beads I had "earned," I paid homage to Wohelo ("Work, Health, Love"); campfires under the stars at Camp Wilaha and Camp Kotami; classroom lessons and plays about the first Thanksgiving; the councils of "The Grand Order of the Iroquois," a fraternal organization founded by anthropologist Louis Henry Morgan (Bieder); the assimilationist group of reformers known as the "Friends of the Indian" (Prucha); and Vine Deloria's caustic dismissal of "anthropologists and other friends" in *Custer Died for Your Sins*.

Despite my initial discomfort with the power of bringing miniature Onondagas to life—and especially with the power to turn them back into mute "plastic"—I find myself intrigued and charmed by this simulated world. So is Tina, whose favorite game is one in which we bring an English trader to life and barter with him for trade goods. In the process we learn a fair amount about Iroquois hunting, farming, manufactures, and desires for trade goods. (The other Anglo-American figurine—and the only character drawn from the film besides Little Bear—is the cowardly cowboy Boone, with whom we experience the terrors of Omri's room from the perspective of a person three inches in height.) By the time Tina and I are presented with our wampum belts, we have been introduced to many aspects of Onondaga life in the early eighteenth century: the forest, the river, and the clearing; the architecture and layout of the village; corn, beans, and squash, the Three Sisters; the powers of various animals; the Onondaga names and legends of the moon, Milky Way, and several constellations; the manufacture of goods and the practice of reciprocity; the importance of clans and clan matrons. We have heard many Onondaga words and learned to recognize a few. With the exception of the trader and his goods, however, we have encountered no evidence of Iroquois relations with European colonists or with other indigenous peoples.

Little Bear's world is one of order, beauty, and tranquility, free of disruptions from warfare, disease, displacement, or Christian evangelism. It serves simultaneously to arouse powerful feelings of nostalgia and nostalgic feelings of power. This is a world under control; a world in which people treat each other with respect; a world pervaded by the soothing, rhythmic music of flutes, rattles, and vocables. It is a world in which human relationships tend to be free of conflict, a world in which—as both the textual and celluloid Omri teaches his friend Patrick—"you can't use people" (Banks, *Indian* 129). That we enter this world through the conceit of controlling the lives of miniature Indians and "mastering" the knowledge they have to teach us; that in this world the stereotypical Iroquois warrior is replaced by people living outside of history; that we feel we can be "Friends of the Iroquois" without confronting the political and economic claims that very friendship would make upon us, whether in 1720—the era in which the CD-ROM is set—or today: such ironies pervade *The Indian in the Cupboard* in all its incarnations.

Destabilizing stereotypes is tricky, as others easily rush in to fill a void. In L. R. Banks's original series of four novels, the figure of Little Bear explicitly replaces the stereotypical Plains Indian with a more localized and complexly rendered representation. When Little Bear comes to life, he does not live up to Omri's expectations of an Indian: he lives in a longhouse rather than a tipi, walks rather than rides a horse, and is unaware of the custom of becoming "blood brothers." In other ways, however, Little Bear more than meets stereotypical expectations: he is a fierce "Iroquois brave" who has taken some thirty scalps; he is volatile, demanding, and interested in "firewater"; he becomes "restive" while watching a Western on television; his English is broken and, early on, mixed with grunts and snarls; he initially thinks of Omri as the "Great White Spirit," only to be disillusioned when the boy fails to live up to his expectations of a deity (20-23, 148). Even so, the most racist typifications are voiced not by the narrator but by "Boohoo" Boone—who, when brought to life, denigrates "Injuns" and "redskins" as "ornery," "savage," and "dirty," only to be convinced otherwise by Omri and Little Bear (99-101). These passages and cover illustrations reminiscent of nineteenth-century dime novels have attracted some criticism (Slapin and Seale 121-22), but the moral of the tale is clear: although Omri at first cherishes his power over Little Bear, calling him "my Indian," he comes to respect Little Bear as an autonomous human being with his own life, times, country, language, and desires (Banks, *Indian* 70, 82).

Lynne Reid Banks is an Englishwoman who spent the war years in Saskatchewan, and the friendship between Omri and Little Bear plays on the alliance between the English and Iroquois during the French and Indian War (1754-63). The historical context of the books, however, is almost completely absent in both the film and the CD-ROM, which transpose Omri from England to New York City. In contrast to the CD-ROM, the film takes place completely in Omri's world, except for a brief visionlike sequence in Little Bear's world. For this reason the film has far less Onondaga content than the CD-ROM, though what there is has been carefully rendered, following the advice of Onondaga consultants Jeanne Shenandoah[2] and Oren Lyons (Yankowitz 31). Nevertheless, the film is just as nostalgic as the CD-ROM. When Little Bear, preparing to return to his own time, asks whether the Onondaga are always a great people, Omri sadly answers in the affirmative, then reluctantly reveals that "it isn't always so good" for them. This is indisputable, but the scene misses a valuable opportunity to show something of the resiliency and the contemporary life of Iroquois people. Portrayed in the past or in miniature, and without visible descendants, Little Bear is out of place, out of time, and an object of intense longing (as Susan Stewart has suggested for miniatures more generally). The film does nothing to help viewers imagine Little Bear's descendants as persons who share a world with Omri even as they share a tradition with Little Bear.

Nevertheless, the film is more successful than the book or CD-ROM in presenting Little Bear as far more than a typification. As played by the Cherokee rap artist Litefoot (Yankowitz), Little Bear dominates the film, even at three inches tall. This Little Bear is not to be patronized. He earns Omri's respect and teaches him to appreciate the awesome responsibility that comes with power over other human beings. Given their relationship, it is particularly jarring to have power over Little Bear, voiced by Litefoot, when playing Omri's role on the CD-ROM. The CD-ROM encourages the Henuyeha, in the spirit of playful learning, to mimic just what Omri learned *not* to do—albeit in the spirit of understanding Little Bear's world. It is doubly disconcerting to possess a plastic figurine of Little Bear. Omri's rejection of objectifying human beings was, predictably, lost on the marketing department—and doubtless on many of its young targets, who may well have added Little Bear to their collection of *Pocahontas*-related figurines from Burger King.

Although the marketing of *The Indian in the Cupboard* and its translation onto CD-ROM undercuts the narrative's critique of objectifying and manipulating human beings, the tensions and contradictions among the message, the medium, and the marketing of Disney's *Pocahontas* are far more blatant. On one level *Pocahontas* can be dismissed as a commercial product through which Disney's powerful marketing machine has revived and exploited the public's perennial fascination with playing Indian— "bringing an American legend to life" in order to hawk beads, baubles, and trinkets to would-be Indian princesses and to those who would seek to please them.[3] On another level, however, Disney's interpretation of the Pocahontas legend—which, following Sommer, we might call the United States' "foundational romance"—makes a serious statement about ethnocentrism, androcentrism, commodification, and exploitation as barriers to the dream of interethnic harmony that Smith and Pocahontas represent. Disney's *Pocahontas* purports to offer a far broader and more devastating cultural critique than *The Indian in the Cupboard*: a critique of the commodity form itself, albeit a consummately commodified critique.

To consider *Pocahontas* in terms of how it meets the challenges posed by its own message takes us beyond the usual attempts to measure the film solely against an uncertain and elusive historical reality. Pocahontas may be the first "real-life figure" to be featured in a Disney film, but the pre-Disney Pocahontas was already a highly mythologized heroine known only through colonial and nationalist representations—from the beginning, a product of Anglo-American desire. Disney has drawn on various versions of what Rayna Green calls "the Pocahontas perplex," giving new life and ubiquitous circulation to those versions deemed resonant with contemporary preoccupations. That is to say, the animated Pocahontas is located within the colonial and neocolonial tradition of noble savagism that Berkhofer analyzes in *The White Man's Indian*: the natural virtues she embodies and self-sacrifice she offers are those found in Montaigne and Rousseau, Thoreau and Cooper, Helen Hunt Jackson and *Dances with Wolves*. This is not to imply, to be sure, that Pocahontas is entirely a product of Western colonialism, but that we "know" her only within that arena—which, after all, is tantamount to not knowing her very well at all.

Outside of promotional material, the film's message is articulated most fully in "Colors Of The Wind," the Academy Award-winning song advertised as summing up "the entire spirit and essence of the film." Responding to Smith's recitation of all that the English can teach the "savages," Pocahontas chides him for thinking "the only people who are people" are those who "look and think" like him. Adapting a famous saying of Will Rogers, she urges Smith to "walk the footsteps of a stranger," promising that he will learn things he "never knew" he "never knew."[4] This Pocahontas is, above all, a teacher. Not, as one might expect, a teacher of the Powhatan language, culture, and standards of diplomacy, for the time-consuming process of learning to translate across cultural and linguistic borders is finessed through her mystical ability, as another song puts it, to "Listen With Your Heart." Rather, Pocahontas, a veritable child of nature, is a teacher of tolerance and respect for all life.

This unfortunate impoverishment of Pocahontas's teachings produces a truly awkward moment in the film, when Pocahontas magically switches from English to her native language on first encountering Smith. ("She was just speaking English a moment ago!" observed my daughters when they first saw this scene.) Although a few Algonquian words are sprinkled through the film, and Smith learns how to say "hello" and "goodbye," Disney's *Pocahontas* gives no sense of the intelligence, dedication, patience, and humility needed to "learn things you never knew you never knew." In being figured within the series of recent Disney heroines that includes Ariel, Beauty, and Jasmine (of *The Little Mermaid, Beauty and the Beast,* and *Aladdin,* respectively), this most famous of North American cultural mediators is removed from the series that also includes Malinche, Sacajawea, and Sarah Winnemucca. The ability to "listen with your heart" conquers all cultural distance for Pocahontas and John Smith.

This is not to say that it is entirely implausible that Pocahontas teaches Smith tolerance and respect for all life. One of the subtly effective moments in the film is the animated sequence corresponding to the passage in "Colors Of The Wind" about walking in the footsteps of a stranger. The footsteps shown are the tracks of a Bear Person, a concept as unfamiliar to most film viewers as it is to John Smith. "Colors Of The Wind" challenges not only ethnocentrism but also androcentrism, and the bear scene goes beyond Disney's ordinary anthropomorphizing to open a window onto an animistic view of the world. More often, however, Pocahontas's relationship to animals (for example, to Meeko the raccoon and Flit the hummingbird) is trivialized,[5] appearing not unlike Cinderella's relationship with her friends, the mice and birds, in the classic Disney film.

In another verse of "Colors Of The Wind" Pocahontas contrasts Smith's utilitarian and possessive thinking with her own intimate knowledge of nature. She scolds Smith for seeing the earth as "just a dead thing you can claim," for she knows that each rock, tree, and creature "has a life, has a spirit, has a name." Then, in the most sensual sequence of the film—or indeed of any previous Disney animation—Pocahontas entices Smith to run through the forest's hidden trails, to taste the earth's sun-ripened berries, to roll in the grasses of the meadow, enjoying all these riches "for once" without wondering "what they're worth." The seductive and precocious Pocahontas, who stalks Smith like a wildcat and then rolls with him in the grass, is a "free spirit" who embodies the joys of belonging to an enchanted and uncommodified world. This is not the first time the young Pocahontas has been sexualized—precedents include Smith's own writings as well as John Barth's *The Sot-Weed Factor*—but it is a startling departure for a Disney children's film. Pocahontas's overt sexuality no doubt has multiple motivations, but at one level it marks her as an intrinsic part of the natural world (as a "tribal Eve," according to Supervising Animator Glen Keane) (Hochswender 156).

It is the clear contrast between utilitarian possessiveness and sensual spirituality in scenes and lyrics like these that Russell Means pointed to in calling *Pocahontas* "the single finest work ever done on American Indians by Hollywood" by virtue of being "willing to tell the truth." But the film's critique of capitalist appropriation is enunciated by the same Pocahontas whose licensed image saturates the marketplace—along with that of her father, Powhatan, who, even more ironically, is modeled after and voiced by the same Russell Means who has demonstrated against the use of Indian images as mascots for sports teams. One can only wonder: what is the exotic, sensual, copyrighted Pocahontas if not the mascot for a feminine, earthy, New Age spirituality?

An eager and willing student of Pocahontas, John Smith learns to see maize as the true "riches" of Powhatan's land and presents the gold-hungry Governor Ratcliffe with a golden ear of corn. The play on "golden" makes for an effective scene, but totally excluded from the film is that other sacred American plant, tobacco, which became the salvation of the Virginia economy thanks to John Rolfe, the husband of a mature, Christian, and anglicized Pocahontas never seen in the film. Is this story—told in Barbour's biography and elsewhere—reserved for *Pocahontas II*? Probably not, for the historical Pocahontas's capture by the English as a hostage, transformation into Lady Rebecca Rolfe, and fatal illness during a trip to London does not resonate as well with an Anglo-American audience's expectations as the legend of Smith's capture and salvation by an innocent, loving, and self-sacrificing child of nature.[6]

Resonating with expectations, of course, is what creating a "timeless, universal, and uniquely satisfying motion picture experience" is all about. In imagining Pocahontas the filmmakers relied to some extent on consultation with Native people and scholars, but more on what resonated with their own experiences, desires, and sense of "authenticity" (so central to the Anglo-American tradition of "playing Indian," as Jay Mechling has pointed out). Lyricist Stephen Schwartz said of the composition of "Colors Of The Wind" that "we were able to find the parts of ourselves that beat in synchronicity with Pocahontas," while animator Keane declared, "I'm cast as Pocahontas in the film" (Hochswender 156). I suppose this is something like listening with one's heart, but there is a significant tension between such identification and "walk[ing] the footsteps of a stranger." This is not the Pocahontas we never knew we never knew, but the Pocahontas we knew all along, the Pocahontas whose story is "universal"—that is, familiar, rather than strange and shocking and particular. This is a Pocahontas whose tale, like that of Simba in *The Lion King* or Omri in *The Indian in the Cupboard,* fits into the mold of the Western coming-of-age story: Pocahontas, yearning to see (as the song goes) "Just Around The Riverbend," grows from youthful irresponsibility to mature self-knowledge through courage and love. It is a Pocahontas who speaks what is known in anthologies (for example, Suzuki and Knudtson) as "the wisdom of the elders," and communes with a Grandmother Willow who appears to be a kindly descendant of the animated trees in *Babes in Toyland.* It is a Pocahontas who, despite a tattoo and over-the-shoulder dress loosely consistent with John White's watercolors of sixteenth-century coastal Algonquians (Hulton, Josephy 183-93), has a Barbie-doll figure, an Asian model's glamour (Hochswender), and an instant attraction to a distinctly Nordic John Smith. In short, Disney has created a New Age Pocahontas embodying Americans' millennial dreams for wholeness and harmony while banishing our nightmares of savagery without and emptiness within.

Just as the dream of tolerance and respect for all life is voiced in song, so too is the nightmare of savagery and emptiness. While the dream is figured as feminine and Indian in the lyrical "Colors Of The Wind," the nightmare is presented as masculine and—at least initially—English in the driving and brutal "Savages." Mobilizing stereotypes akin to Boohoo Boone's, but considerably more vicious, this song describes Pocahontas's people as worse than vermin, as "filthy little heathens" whose "skin's a hellish red," as a cursed and disgusting race, as evil, "barely human," and "only good when dead."

"Savages" presents, at its dehumanizing extreme, the ideology of ignoble savagism—less typical, as Bernard Sheehan has shown, of the earliest years of the Jamestown colony than of the years after 1622, when Powhatan's kinsman Opechancanough launched a war of resistance against the English. In the context of the film, however, appearing as the English prepare to attack the Powhatan people, it is extremely effective, serving ironically to underscore the savagery of the English colonists rather than that of the "heathen." Earlier, in the opening to "Colors Of The Wind," Pocahontas had gently challenged the ideology of ignoble savagism by asking Smith why, if it was she who was the "ignorant savage," there was so very much he did not know. Characterized as wise and gentle, if mischievous and spirited, Pocahontas is clearly not an ignorant savage. With this already established, the colonists' rhetoric of savagery turns back upon them—at least until Powhatan, advised by a diviner, leads his people in a

similar chorus, calling the "paleface" a soulless, bloodless demon distinguished only by his greed. It is the English who are "different from us," who are untrustworthy killers, who are "savages."

Powhatan's portion of "Savages" purports to offer a portrait of the English colonists from the point of view of the colonized. Given what has gone on thus far in the film, and what we know of subsequent history, the accusation rings true. But this passage, too, ultimately rebounds against those who utter it. John Smith is captured and laid out, the executioner's tomahawk is raised, Smith is about to be mercilessly executed . . . and Pocahontas throws her body upon his, successfully pleading with her father for his life. The savagery of fear and intolerance is vanquished through the power of "listen[ing] with your heart."

So the story goes, in Smith's telling, at least. It may be, as Gleach suggests, that this was all an elaborate adoption ceremony in which Smith became a vassal of Powhatan, who ruled over an expanding group of villages. It may be, as I have proposed (in "Captivity in White and Red"), that Pocahontas was playing a traditional female role in choosing between life and death for a sacrificial victim. It may be that the incident is best understood as part of Smith's imaginative and self-serving fabrication of himself—what Greenblatt calls "Renaissance self-fashioning." I would not fault Disney for repeating the rescue as it is commonly known in a film advertised as "an American legend," but the litany "Savages! Savages!" is quite another matter. Its ideological work, in the end, is to level the English and the Powhatan people to the same state of ethnocentric brutishness, portraying ignoble savagism as natural and universal rather than as having particular cultural and historical roots. When these lyrics are disseminated outside the context of the film, in songbooks and on the soundtrack, they may have a particularly harmful impact upon a young and impressionable audience. We don't play the soundtrack in our house, but friends with younger children tell me that, to their horror, they have caught their children singing "Savages, Savages" among themselves, having internalized a racist epithet that remains potent and degrading.[7]

The filmmakers are quite aware that they are in risky territory here and characterize the episode as dealing with "one of the most adult themes ever in a Disney film." The theme is "the ugliness and stupidity that results when people give in to racism and intolerance," and it is refreshing to have it aired, particularly by a studio with a history, even recently, of racist animation. But a more responsible treatment of the theme would be considerably more nuanced, distinguishing between English colonialism and Powhatan resistance, and between the English ideology of savagism and coastal Algonquian attitudes toward their own enemies—whom, as Helen Rountree shows, they generally aimed to politically subordinate and socially incorporate, rather than exterminate and dispossess. This could be done by telling more of Pocahontas's and Powhatan's subsequent dealings with Smith, whom they treated, respectively, as "brother" and *weroance* (a ruler subordinate to Powhatan, the *manamatowick* or supreme ruler).

That *Pocahontas* raises a number of difficult and timely issues is a tribute to its ambition and seriousness of purpose. Indeed, the film begs to be taken as a plea for tolerant, respectful, and harmonious living in a world torn by prejudice, exploitation, ethnic strife, and environmental degradation. So, too, does *The Indian in the Cupboard*, albeit in a more limited fashion. That both films and their associated products and promotions are rife with tensions and ironies exemplifies the limitations of serious cultural critique in an artistic environment devoted to the marketing of dreams. That our children are bombarded with plastic consumables and impoverished caricatures while being admonished to treat other cultures, other creatures, and the land with respect should prompt us to find ways to teach them—and learn from them—the difference between producing and consuming objectified difference, on the one hand, and sustaining respectful relationships across difference, on the other.

In a society founded on objectification, differentiation, and commodification the lesson is a hard one, and one that has characteristically been expressed in an oppositional "Indian" voice. If *Pocahontas* and *The Indian in the Cupboard* can be viewed only with ambivalence because of their own participation in processes of objectification and commodification, the forms of "playing Indian" to which each gives rise may offer genuine possibilities for unlearning these processes and imagining new ones, that is, for learning things we never knew we never knew.[8]

"I love that part of the song," Katie has told me, and Tina and I agree. We often find ourselves singing Pocahontas's lines, and sometimes we stop to wonder at the paradoxical form of learning they suggest. As a first step on a transformative journey, we locked the plastic Indian in his videocase cupboard once and for all and stepped outside to find Star Girl in the night sky.

Notes

This essay, dedicated to Jane Cauvel upon her retirement from The Colorado College, is adapted from "Animated Indians: Critique and Contradiction in Commodified Children's Culture," *Cultural Anthropology* 11, 3 (August 1996): 405-24. It is published here with the permission of the American Anthropological Association. While certain new material is included, the original version contains more extensive references and acknowledgments, as well as lyrics and illustrations that were deleted from this version because of copyright restrictions.

1. Onondaga words are treated more or less as proper names on the CD-ROM, and I have anglicized them in this essay. Consulting the sparse published documentation on the Onondaga language, I am delighted to find that Little Bear's term for "player," Henuyeha, is a nominalization of the form used for playing the indigenous game of lacrosse (Hewitt 625). The term for "friend" that I anglicize as Ungachi is transcribed as *onguiatsi, mon ami* in Shea's French-Onondaga dictionary.

2. Jeanne Shenandoah was also a consultant for the CD-ROM, as were Rick Hill and Huron Miller.

3. This and subsequent unattributed quotations are taken from Disney press releases.

4. Paraphrasing the lyrics to "Colors Of The Wind" (because of copyright restrictions) does an injustice to Stephen Schwartz's fine poetry, which may be found in song books and on the notes to the soundtrack.

5. The trivialization of Pocahontas's relationship to animals was brought to my attention by a chastening response to the review of *Pocahontas* I posted on H-Net on June 30, 1995. On the electronic list devoted to "teaching social studies in secondary schools," Paul Dennis Gower Sr. replied, "PUHLEASE!!!!!! It is, after all, a cartoon. It has a talking raccoon, for crying out loud."

6. The rest of Pocahontas's story would make for an intriguing drama indeed if treated something like Disney's underpublicized *Squanto: A Warrior's Tale*, which does not hesitate to portray the brutality of Squanto's English kidnappers as well as a likely course of events leading to Squanto's allegiance to the English settlers at Plymouth. *Pocahontas: Her True Story*, a televised biography from the Arts & Entertainment network, provides a useful counterpoint to the Disney film but does not do justice to Pocahontas's tale or to the historical context of visual imagery (which is treated transparently as illustrative material, unlike the more historicized treatments of Josephy and Strong's "Search for Otherness").

7. This was a key objection of an open letter regarding *Pocahontas* posted by more than a hundred members of the NatChat listserv on July 18, 1995.

8. This outcome—utopian, perhaps, but consistent with Omri's own course of development—requires that commodified images be taken as "teachable moments" pointing toward more complex, less objectified, understandings.

Works Cited

Banks, Lynne Reid. *The Indian and the Cupboard*. New York: Doubleday, 1981.

———. *The Mystery of the Cupboard*. New York: William Morrow, 1993.

———. *The Return of the Indian*. New York: Doubleday, 1986.

———. *The Secret of the Indian*. New York: Doubleday, 1989.

Barbour, Philip. *Pocahontas and Her World*. Boston: Houghton Mifflin, 1969.

Barth, John. *The Sot-Weed Factor*. Toronto: Bantam Books, 1980.

Berkhofer, Robert F. *The White Man's Indian: Images of the American Indian from Columbus to the Present.* New York: Random House, 1977.

Bieder, Robert E. "The Grand Order of the Iroquois: Influences on Lewis Henry Morgan's Ethnology." *Ethnohistory* 27 (1980):349-61.

Deloria, Vine. *Custer Died for Your Sins: An Indian Manifesto.* New York: Macmillan, 1969.

Gleach, Frederick W. "Interpreting the Saga of Pocahontas and Captain John Smith." In *Reading Beyond Words: Contexts for Native History,* 21-42. Ed. Jennifer S. H. Brown and Elizabeth Vibert, eds. Peterborough, Ontario: Broadview Press, 1996.

Green, Rayna. "The Pocahontas Perplex: The Image of Indian Women in American Culture." *Massachusetts Review* 16, 4 (1975): 698-714.

Greenblatt, Stephen. *Renaissance Self-Fashioning: From More to Shakespeare.* Chicago: University of Chicago Press, 1980.

Haraway, Donna J. *Simians, Cyborgs, and Women: The Reinvention of Nature.* New York: Routledge, 1991.

Hewitt, J. N. B. "Iroquoian Cosmology, Second Part." *43rd Annual Report of the Bureau of American Ethnology, 1925-26.* Washington, D.C.: U.S. Government Printing Office, 1928.

Hochswender, Woody. "Pocahontas: A Babe in the Woods." *Harper's Bazaar* (June 1995): 154-57.

Hulton, Paul. *America 1585: The Complete Drawings of John White.* Chapel Hill: University of North Carolina Press and British Museum Press, 1984.

Jennings, Francis. *The Invasion of America: Colonialism and the Cant of Conquest.* New York: W. W. Norton, 1975.

Josephy, Alvin M., Jr. *Five Hundred Nations: An Illustrated History of North American Indians.* New York: Alfred A. Knopf, 1994.

Mechling, Jay. "'Playing Indian' and the Search for Authenticity in Modern White America." *Prospects* 5 (1980): 17-33.

Prucha, Francis Paul. *Americanizing the American Indians: Writings by the "Friends of the Indian," 1880-1900.* Cambridge: Harvard University Press, 1973.

Rountree, Helen. *The Powhatan Indians of Virginia: Their Traditional Culture.* Norman: University of Oklahoma Press, 1989.

Sharpes, Donald K. "Princess Pocahontas, Rebecca Rolfe (1595-1617)." *American Indian Culture and Research Journal* 19, 4 (1995): 231-39.

Shea, John Gilmary. *A French-Onondaga Dictionary, from a Manuscript of the Seventeenth Century.* 1860. New York: AMS Press, 1970.

Sheehan, Bernard W. *Savagism and Civility: Indians and Englishmen in Colonial Virginia.* Cambridge: Cambridge University Press, 1980.

Slapin, Beverly, and Doris Seale. *Through Indian Eyes: The Native Experience in Books for Children.* Philadelphia: New Society Publishers, 1992.

Smith, John. "A True Relation of Such Occurrences and Accidents of Noate as Hath Hapned in Virginia." In *The Complete Works of Captain John Smith (1580-1631),* 1:3-117. Philip L. Barbour, ed. Chapel Hill: University of North Carolina Press, 1986.

———. "The Generall Historie of Virginia, New England, and the Summer Isles." In *The Complete Works of Captain John Smith (1580-1631),* 2. Philip L. Barbour, ed. Chapel Hill: University of North Carolina Press, 1986.

Sommer, Doris. *Foundational Fictions: The National Romances of Latin America.* Berkeley and Los Angeles: University of California Press, 1991.

Stewart, Kathleen. "On the Politics of Cultural Theory: A Case for 'Contaminated' Cultural Critique." *Social Research* 58, 2 (1991): 395-412.

Stewart, Susan. *On Longing: Narratives of the Miniature, the Gigantic, the Souvenir, the Collection.* Durham, N.C.: Duke University Press, 1993.

Strong, Pauline Turner. "Captivity in White and Red." In *Crossing Cultures: Essays in the Displacement of Western Civilization,* 33-104. Daniel Segal, ed. Tucson: University of Arizona Press, 1992.

———. "The Search for Otherness." In *Invisible America: Unearthing Our Hidden History,* 24-25. Mark P. Leone and Neil Asher Silberman, eds. New York: Henry Holt, 1995.

Suzuki, David, and Peter Knudtsen. *Wisdom of the Elders: Sacred Native Stories of Nature.* New York: Bantam, 1992.

Taussig, Michael. *Mimesis and Alterity: A Particular History of the Senses.* New York: Routledge, 1993.

Yankowitz, Joan. *Behind the Scenes of "The Indian in the Cupboard."* New York: Scholastic, 1995.

THEATER AND HOLLYWOOD

Lynda E. Boose and Richard Burt (essay date 1997)

SOURCE: Boose, Lynda E. and Richard Burt. "Totally Clueless?: Shakespeare goes Hollywood in the 1990s." In *Shakespeare, the Movie: Popularizing the Plays on Film, TV, and Video,* edited by Lynda E. Boose and Richard Burt, pp. 8-22. London: Routledge, 1997.

[*In the following essay, Boose and Burt discuss Hollywood's influence in the popularization of Shakespearean drama in the late 1990s, noting the changes wrought by filmmakers in an attempt to appeal to contemporary audiences.*]

A short sequence in the 1995 summer film comedy *Clueless* (dir. Amy Heckerling) offers what might be considered a mini-allegory of Shakespeare's circulation within the popular culture of the 1990s. Based on Jane Austen's *Emma,* the film narrates the coming of age of "Cher," a Beverly Hills high school ingenue and media-savvy teen queen who reformulates the pleasures of discourse into side-by-side telephone conversations conducted on mobile telephones. In the manipulation of cultural capital as a means for asserting status, Cher (Alicia Silverstone) clinches her superiority inside of a contest that defines itself through Shakespeare. When her stepbrother's excessively Harvard girlfriend misattributes "to thine own self be true" to Hamlet and Cher corrects her, the girlfriend then rejects Cher's substitution of "that Polonius guy" and slams home her apparent victory with the smugly dismissive line, "I think I remember *Hamlet* accurately." But Cher beats her, point, set, and match, with the rejoinder that while she, by comparison, may not know her *Hamlet,* she most certainly does know her Mel Gibson!

We begin with *Clueless* because it complicates present moves in cultural studies about Shakespeare. With its Los Angeles location and youth market for Shakespeare, *Clueless* offers an opportunity for certain kinds of questions. For openers, just who is its Shakespeare joke on—the girlfriend, Cher, or just whom? Just what is the high-status cultural currency here, and how does "Shakespeare" function as a sign? Does the fact that Cher knows *Hamlet* not via the presupposed Shakespearean original but only via Mel Gibson's role in Zeffirelli's movie signify her cultural illiteracy—or her literacy? Or does this exchange perhaps point us away from any presumptive original, be it Jane Austen's or Shakespeare's, and direct us instead toward a focus on just its mediating package, what might be called the Hollywoodization of Shakespeare in the 1990s? In a postmodern way that effectively mocks all the presumed distinctions between high and low culture, *Clueless* does not merely relocate high culture to a low site (Los Angeles): after all, this is Beverly Hills, not the Valley, and no one is more vigilant than Cher and her friends about maintaining standards and eschewing tastelessness. Instead, *Clueless* elaborates on films like *L. A. Story* (dir. Steve Martin, 1991) in which Steve Martin begins by reciting a speech in praise of L.A. that parodies John of Gaunt's deathbed speech to Richard II, substituting "this Los Angeles" for the concluding words, "this England"; and on Jean-Luc Godard's *Lear* (1987), in which William Shakespeare Junior the Fifth goes to Hollywood to produce his ancestor's plays, which end up being edited by Woody Allen. Like these two films, *Clueless*'s repeated reference to technologies such as movies, televisions, mobile phones, head sets, car radios, CDs, computerized wardrobes, intercoms, and other devices that record, transmit, amplify, and likewise reshape meaning formulate the mediating power of Los Angeles as the contemporary site where high/low distinctions are engaged in endlessly resignifying themselves.

Cher's recording of *Hamlet* could be located in a wider range of 1990s *Hamlet*(s). The *Hamlet* created by the 1990s wasn't big just among the literati—he was so big that he was making guest appearances in all sorts of unexpected places, with different implications of its gendered reception. In 1991, Oliver Stone cast the Kennedy assassination through the lens of *Hamlet* in *JFK.* In 1994, Danny DeVito and the US Army found *Hamlet* to be the perfect force for transforming wimps and misfit soldiers into the STRAK army company that concludes *Renaissance Man* (dir. Penny Marshall) reaffirming the male bond in "Sound Off" lyrics that inventively substitute "Hamlet's mother, she's the Queen" for the usual female object of cadenced derision. Similarly, Disney's 1994 *The Lion King* (dir. Roger Allers and Ron Minkoff), reworked *Hamlet* for a younger generation. In 1995, Kenneth Branagh released his *A Midwinter's Tale,* a film about a provincial English production of *Hamlet,* and then in 1996 and 1997 his own full-length and abridged versions of *Hamlet.*

Ultimately, however, it was Arnold Schwarzenegger's 1992 film, *The Last Action Hero* (dir. John McTiernan), that most clearly allegorized the transformation of Hamlet from melancholy man into an image that could be valued by the young male consumers to whom the newly technologized violence of the 1990s was being played. In a displacement explicitly fictionalized as the direct product of a young male viewer's contemporary fantasies of masculinity, on screen the image of Olivier hesitating to kill the praying Claudius literally dissolves into a Schwarzenegger Hamlet who is actively engaged in "taking out the trash" of the something-rotten Denmark into which he is thrust. And in a clever bit of metatheatricality, the substitution of Schwarzenegger, America's highest paid actor of the early 1990s, is situated as the ultimate insurance that movie houses will stay open and movies will keep on playing. Kids like the film's ardent young filmviewer will keep right on getting sucked into the action-packed worlds of heroically imagined male violence that is both promulgated by American film and simultaneously guarantees the industry its seemingly unassailable hegemony. Though ironic, it is nonetheless true that the *Hamlet*(s) of the 1990s construct a world even more obsessively masculine than did the *Hamlet*(s) that preexisted any articulated feminist critique of popular culture. Mel Gibson as Hamlet means *Hamlet* as *Lethal Weapon Four.* But Mel also means Hamlet as Hollywood Hunk, an object of desire who, like Glenn Close's Gertrude, projects an image implicitly accessible to female and male viewers alike.[1] Zeffirelli's film may well be *Lethal Weapon Four*; but Hamlet-as-Mel suggests Shakespeare's prince as a 1990s model of unrestrictedly appropriatable desire, and it was through an appropriation of Mel-as-Hamlet that Cher triumphs over her truly clueless adversary, eventually winning a college guy (read: Harvard Law) boyfriend at the film's close.

Rather than assessing the various new *Hamlet*-sites in terms of possibilities for contradictory readings or as evidence anew of an American cultural imperialism, we are more interested in the critical developments that such a proliferation may signal. In the wake of the present displacements of book and literary culture by film and video culture and the age of mechanical reproduction by the age of electronic reproduction, the traditional literary field itself has already, to some extent, been displaced as an object of inquiry by cultural studies. And the Shakespeare moment in *Clueless* perhaps interests us for the very way it enacts this displacement, invoking the high status literary text only to dismiss it in favor of the actor's performance. For Shakespeare studies, what the transition from a literary to an electronic culture logically presages is exactly what, in fact, seems to be happening: an increased interest in the strategies of performance accompanied by a decreased focus on the poetic and rhetorical, the arena where New Criticism once so powerfully staked its claim.[2] If Michael Berube (1995) is right in assessing that the move to cultural studies primarily involves taking a less serious relation to criticism and its subjects, then Shakespeare (and Renaissance) Studies appears to be following suit, its dialogue lightening up a bit. New ways of reading the transvestism of the Renaissance stage, for example, are being discovered by contextualizing the cross-dressed Shakespeare heroine alongside pop culture figures like Michael Jackson and Madonna (see Garber 1992, 1995) and films like *The Crying Game* (dir. Jordan, 1992; see Crewe 1995).

It could be said that this shift to a cultural studies approach opens new possibilities for a kind of Shakespeare criticism with wider appeal to a non-academic public (which presumes, of course, that the Shakespearean academic necessarily wants such a popular audience.) It must also be said, however, that the shift raises a number of new questions, many of which relate to the new influence that Hollywood, Los Angeles, and American capitalism are already exerting on the popularization of Shakespeare. The media in 1990s America—film, video, television, and advertising—seemed suddenly prepared to embrace the Bard with all the enthusiasm (and potentially crushing effect) that such whole-hearted American embraces have come to harbinger for much of the world. Thus the question of potential diminishment that has always been raised about putting Shakespeare on film reappears, reinvigorated by the very technologies that make Shakespeare more accessible. We have yet to imagine how Shakespeare will be staged on the Internet, but for many of those who, unlike Cher, do know their Shakespeare, the transfer from "live" theater to the absent presence of the technologically produced filmic (or digitized) image invites a distinct ambivalence much like that which betrays the voice of *New York Times* writer Frank Rich, here writing in 1996 about Fredericke Warde, the star of the recently rediscovered silent 1912 *Richard III*. Noting that Warde blamed what he perceived as a "fall off" of Shakespeare theatrical productions on schools and literary societies for turning acting texts into objects of intellectual veneration, Rich, for whom the discovery of this venerable old Shakespeare film seems to have acted as catalyst for his own lament for a lost golden age, characterizes Warde as a thoroughly clueless innocent, someone who "didn't have a clue that movies were

harbingers of a complete cultural transformation that would gradually lead to the desensitized pop media environment of today."[3]

In the larger sense, however, Shakespeare's disappearance, his status as ghostwriter, precedes the 1990s. In some ways, the present historical moment only clarifies the way Shakespeare has always already disappeared when transferred onto film. Taken on their own terms, films like Greenaway's *Prospero's Books,* Derek Jarman's *Tempest,* and Godard's *Lear* involve not merely the deconstruction of Shakespeare as author but his radical displacement by the film director; and the interest in any of these films could legitimately be said to lie less in its relation to Shakespeare's play than in its relation to the director's own previous *oeuvre.* Even films which adapt the Shakespeare script as faithfully as does Branagh's *Much Ado About Nothing* speak within a metacinematic discourse of self-reference in which, through film quotation, they situate themselves in reference as much to other films as to a Shakespeare tradition.[4]

Yet judging from the commentary and the advertising matrix surrounding the release of the most recent Shakespeare adaptations, the fact that Shakespeare is the author seems to be becoming not only increasingly beside the point but even a marketing liability—an inference that *Los Angeles Times* movie critic David Gritten quite clearly picks up from the voices of both the director and producer of Ian McKellen's 1995 *Richard III*:

> Here on the set of *Richard III,* a film adaptation of one of the world's best known plays starring a bunch of distinguished classical actors, it comes as a surprise that everyone is trying to play down the S-word. The S-word? That stands for "Shakespeare." He's the guy who wrote *Richard III* some four hundred years ago, in case you weren't quite sure. In truth, the people behind this *Richard III* . . . are hoping to attract those very people who aren't quite sure of the film's provenance. "I'm encouraging everyone working on this film not to think of it as Shakespeare," says director Richard Loncraine. "It's a terrific story, and who wrote it is irrelevant. "We're trying to make the most accessible Shakespeare film ever made," says producer Lisa Katselas Pare.
>
> (Gritten 1995: 39, 41)

The similar trend that Don Hedrick points out in an essay in this collection—that any mention of Shakespeare is exactly what was under avoidance in the marketing of Branagh's *Henry V*—is a truism equally applicable to Zeffirelli's *Hamlet.* Likewise, Gus Van Sant (1993: xxxviii) notes about the making of *My Own Private Idaho* that while the foreign producers wanted to put in as much Shakespeare as possible the American producers wanted to cut out as much as possible.[5] Yet just when we might assume that the Bard's name was truly a marketing liability or that veneration of Shakespeare had come to be regarded in popular contexts as uncool,[6] the notably cool film director Baz Luhrmann put out a new *Romeo and Juliet* that is unquestionably situated in the pop culture, made-for-teens film market and is called *William Shakespeare's Romeo and Juliet.*[7]

The popularization of Shakespeare on film, video, and television—which began inside the stalwartly liberal tradition of noblesse oblige attempting to bring culture to the masses—now finds itself, in America at least, in a strictly market-responsive milieu in which literary knowledge is in general a decidedly low capital, frequently mockable commodity, caught within the peculiarly American ambivalence about intellectualism, and therefore to be eschewed at all costs. When Gus Van Sant imports the various Hal and Falstaff scenes from the *Henry IV* and *Henry V* plays and sticks them into *My Own Private Idaho*'s world of contemporary Portland gay hustlers and street dwellers, neither the film nor the characters speaking the lines register any acknowledgment that they are drawing upon Shakespeare. If this film is a Shakespeare spin-off, no one has to admit knowing it. But as a market screening device, the omission must have worked, since only those people who had read the Henriad or read commentary on the film in specifically "intellectual" magazine and review venues seemed conscious of any Shakespeare connection. The same might be said of *L. A. Story*. While many members of the audience may have picked up the allusions to *Hamlet* and other Shakespeare plays, only a Shakespearean would have read the movie as a rewriting of the play. Likewise, the connection between *Clueless* and Jane Austen's *Emma* got intentionally excluded from the film's promotional packet and was left to become known via strategically leaked news items designed to be circulated by word of mouth to intrigue the elite without turning off the intended teen market.

But while pride in anti-intellectualism has long roots as an American tradition and is a force which the 1980s and 1990s have seen assume a renewed political ascendancy, quite the opposite has historically been true of British cultural life, where Shakespeare and the English literary tradition have long been a rallying point of national superiority. The quotation of Shakespeare lines seems, in fact, to be used in Britain as a special, high-status kind of sublanguage, a signalling code of sorts that regularly shows up in the language of even British detective novels. It is thus frankly impossible to imagine the making of a British film like *Clueless* in which success would be correlated with a pride in *not* knowing one's Shakespeare. Nonetheless, the apparent dominance of Hollywood capitalism so thoroughly determines the market that Britain's famous Shakespearean actors now find even themselves playing roles within plays which require that they "not think of [the play] as Shakespeare."

But Hollywood's relationship to Shakespeare is marked by more than just the avoidance of the S-word. When Gus Van Sant turned to the Shakespeare narrative that he then consciously veiled in *My Own Private Idaho,* he even approached it through a layered mediation, essentially rewriting not Shakespeare's second tetralogy but Orson Welles's version of the second tetralogy, *Chimes at Midnight.* Van Sant's film thus participates in a peculiarly American norm by which Hollywood, up until Branagh's box office successes of the early 1990s, chose to maintain a significant distance from the direct—or "straight Shakespeare"—adaptational model that made both Olivier and Welles famously associated with all that was once included in the meaning of "a Shakespeare film." And while American television has shown some "straight" American versions of Shakespeare that do not modernize the verbal idiom or rewrite the story (most notably, televised versions of filmed theatrical productions, such as the American Conservatory Theater's famous 1971 *The Taming of the Shrew*), apparently the last instance in which a definably Hollywood film seriously tried to produce Shakespeare straight was Stuart Burge's 1970 *Julius Caesar*—itself an attempt to remake Joseph Mankiewicz's far more successful 1953 *Julius Caesar.* And although Japanese, German, Russian, Swedish (and etc.) straight Shakespeare films apparently feel perfectly comfortable doing Shakespeare with casts made up from their own national back lots, when Hollywood has made that same commitment, the casting list betrays a special American insecurity in its inevitable compulsion to import a large number of Royal Shakespeare Company actors to surround the American star.

Perhaps because Shakespeare is such a signifier for British cultural superiority, America's relationship to the Bard has frequently been marked by all the signs of a colonized consciousness. All in all, the preferred American approach to Shakespeare has been decidedly oblique; up until the sudden, Branagh-inspired boom in straight Shakespeare of the mid-nineties, Hollywood has distinctly felt more comfortable reworking Shakespeare into new, specifically American narratives such as Woody Allen's *A Midsummer Night's Sex Comedy* (1982) or Paul Mazursky's *Tempest* (1982), for example. America's best made for film Shakespeare productions may, in fact, be the musicals *Kiss Me, Kate* (dir. George Sidney, 1953) and *West Side Story* (dirs. Robert Wise and Jerome Robbins, 1961), where the Bard is recreated within a particular theatrical idiom that is thoroughly home-grown.

Even on the English side of the Atlantic, where Shakespeare has been apotheosized into the primary signifier for patriotism, nationhood, and national culture, the end of a tradition of turning Shakespeare plays into big fuss, high culture, capital-letter films has already been allegorized in the film *The Playboys* (dir. Gillies MacKinnon, 1992). An Irish acting troupe touring Ireland in the 1940s witnesses its Americanized production, part *Othello*, part adaptation of *Gone With the Wind,* be displaced and their troupe broken up by the arrival of the real thing, the Hollywood movie and a newly opened movie house in the town they have just played. To be sure, the late 1980s saw the English tradition of Shakespeare film refurbished by Kenneth Branagh into an enterprise comparable in energy to that of the 1940s when Sir Laurence Olivier was making *Richard III, Henry V, Hamlet,* and, in 1955, starring in Stuart Burges's *Othello.* But what Branagh has done is infuse the filming of Shakespeare with a marketeer's sense of popular culture. In his productions, high and low culture meet in moments where Shakespeare's scripts get subtly reframed inside of references to Hollywood pop culture: Branagh's adaptation actually rewrites *Henry V* as Clint Eastwood's "dirty Harry,"[8] and his *Much Ado about Nothing* opens with a witty visual evocation of *The Magnificent Seven.*

The sudden contemporary renaissance in filmed Shakespeare is British-led, but by 1995 even British casting practices had changed to reflect the exigencies of market capitalism. Following in the direction that Zeffirelli had been the first to seize upon, the new British productions were now promoting their global commerciality through a mixture of what has been derisively referred to as a cast made up of "British actors" and "American stars."[9] Branagh's 1989 *Henry V* had been filmed with a British cast. But by the time of *Much Ado About Nothing,* the British principals were surrounded by American pop film stars that made brothers out of America's most popular black actor (Denzel Washington) and America's most popular teen heart-throb (Keanu Reeves). There were, admittedly, some problems with casting Americans: in Branagh's *Much Ado,* Don John's line about Hero, "She's a very forward March chick," was cut for fear that Keanu Reeves would appear to be reverting to American slang rather than reciting Shakespeare.[10] And as Alan Bennett, who, when making a film of his play *The Madness of George III,* had to retitle it as *The Madness of King George* because American backers feared their audiences would think they had missed the first two parts, ruefully comments: "apparently . . . there were many moviegoers who came away from Branagh's film of *Henry V* wishing they had seen its four predecessors" (1995: xix). Yet the trend of using American stars continues, sometimes with particularly fortuitous implications that suggested new levels of narrative. In a production released in 1995, the presence of American actors Annette Bening and Robert Downey, Jr in Richard Loncraine's World War II-era rewrite of *Richard III* provided a fitting way for the film to mark Edward IV's queen, Elizabeth, and her brother, Lord Rivers, as distinctive outsiders to the royal family, and, through dress and hair-style, encourage visual allusions that suggested Bening-cum-Elizabeth, outsider wife to Edward IV, as that famous American divorcee and outsider wife to another King Edward, Wallis Simpson. By 1995 Branagh, too, had gone American: Hollywood's Lawrence Fishburne played the Noble Moor to Branagh's Iago; and in 1996 Branagh's *Hamlet* included such box office draws as Billy Crystal (first gravedigger), Robin Williams (Osric), Charlton Heston (the Player King), and Jack Lemmon (Marcellus). Yielding to the implicit logic of such casting, Baz Luhrmann simply invited the stars of his *Romeo and Juliet* "to speak the famous lines in their own American accent."[11]

In what seems relatively new to British filmed Shakespeare (albeit certainly not to staged productions), the plays were also being cut loose from the tradition of the pseudo-"Elizabethan" setting and relocated in the viewer's own milieu: a 1991 British film of *As You Like It* featured Rosalind in levis, and 1995 saw Britain rehistoricizing its own history by taking *Richard III* into the modernized territory that 1980s stage productions of the histories (especially the English Shakespeare Company's "Wars of the Roses" extravaganza) had shown to be highly viable. Thus, shortly after Great Britain solemnly celebrated the fifty-year anniversary of the end of World War II, *Richard III* replayed that history by reinscribing it into the cycle of dark days that had eventually led to the Tudor triumph, British mythology now promising an Elizabeth (II) for an Elizabeth (I). By the end of 1995, it was increasingly clear that the trademarks of pop culture were determining the productions of not only such well-known popularizers as Zeffirelli, but had caught up with the Shakespeare industry at large and were putting it into the fast lane. According to the *L. A. Weekly*'s review of the 1995 *Othello*:

> Writer-director Oliver Parker has opted for a spin on *Othello* that would make Shakespeare himself dizzy. With more pop than poetry, more snap than savvy, this variation of the tragedy finds the ever-appealing Lawrence Fishburne center court. . . . The production may be trashy and too fast by half—it makes Mel Gibson's galloping *Hamlet* seem sleepy—but the tenderness in Fishburne's eyes is startling. . . . While there's nothing wrong in mucking around with the classics when it comes to adaptations, the selectiveness of Parker's approach puzzles. Why, for instance, is there something so creepy and so very O. J. in the initial love scene between Othello and Desdemona . . . ?
>
> (Dargie 1995: 67)

Similarly, Margo Jefferson noted that Shakespeare's "metaphors and cadence . . . passions, convictions, and conflicts must meet up with ours in a world of rock, rap, gospel, and schlock pop, all just a radio station away from Prokofiev and Mozart. Shakespeare must adjust to city street and suburban mall English" (1996: C11). All in all, the message from the mid-nineties would seem to be that Shakespeare was busting out all over: Branagh having shown Hollywood that there was a market, production money seemed suddenly to be flowing; Branagh released his complete, uncut *Hamlet* (1996); Trevor Nunn—having demonstrated his entitlement on stage by directing big bucks productions of *Les Miserables* and *Cats*—directed a new *Twelfth Night* that debuted at Telluride (1996); another *Romeo and Juliet* in addition to Baz Lurhmann's 1996 production was on its way out; the Loncraine/McKellen *Richard III* (1994) had broken new ground in terms of reframing Shakespeare inside of pop-culture strategies; and, using an inventive new format for producing a Shakespeare film, Al Pacino had allegorized his own experience of playing *Richard III* in a documentary called *Looking for Richard* (1996).

Just how Hollywood's new interventions in a territory hitherto tacitly conceded to the Brits must look to the newly colonized former colonizer forms the potential subtext for Ian McKellen's remark about the difficulty he had in finding producers in Hollywood to fund the kind of *Richard III* film he wanted to make: "Of course, if Ken or Mel, or best of all Arnie or Sly were cast as Richard, it would have been easier" (McKellen 1996: 25-6). Baz Luhrmann (an Australian) put "William Shakespeare" in the title of his *William Shakespeare's Romeo and Juliet*, almost as if to insist on its authenticity. And as if to emphasize some kind of essential difference between the English kind of Shakespeare and the kind implicitly associated with American models, the Telluride announcement for Trevor Nunn's *Twelfth Night* (1995) asserts, with a barely concealed sneer: "the film succeeds in part due to Nunn's decision to ignore the box office lure of Hollywood stars, and to cast all the parts with outstanding British actors who can actually speak Shakespeare's lines with proper cadence and clarity."[12] Perhaps because he rightly sensed that strategies such as the above would fail, Kenneth Branagh made a more canny compromise, casting American stars not as leads but in multiple cameo parts for his 1996 *Hamlet*.[13] In these terms, the film promo that was most risky of all is that for Adrian Noble's *A Midsummer Night's Dream* (1996), the cast was made up not of Hollywood stars but a core of the same actors who played in the (1995) Royal Shakespeare Production. Perhaps for this reason the film's US release was delayed.

However much a British director might wish to preserve a British Shakespeare, American production money is the hidden engine that drives Britain's Shakespeare films. The disappointing overall outcome of the 1980s televised BBC Shakespeare series was due, at least in part, to Time-Life Corporation's determination to produce televised "classics" that would exhibit a uniform fidelity to imagined assumptions about Shakespeare's text and times.[14] Doing "culture" for an educational enterprise apparently provoked one extreme of the American colonial response. But Hollywood hegemony over the global market combined with the new, bottom-line-only mentality of the 1990s may now threaten Shakespeare from quite another direction. In light of Hollywood's 1995 decision to revise the heavy puritanism and somber morality of *The Scarlet Letter* (dir. Roland Joffe, 1995) into a film that would be more fun for an audience and would get rid of that "downer" of a Hawthorne ending, can a film of Nathum Tate's *King Lear*, in which Demi/Cordelia lives and marries Bruce/Edgar be far behind?

Of all the films of the 1990s, some of the most innovative come from an avant-garde tradition whose energies are infused both by popular culture and an international mode of film production. Through avant-garde filmmaker Peter Greenaway's very attempt to unpack the place that intellectual and aesthetic elitism has played in Western culture, *Prospero's Books* (1990), forms in many ways an important investigation of the idea of "the popular." A meditation on *The Tempest*, the film reproduces Shakespeare's play as caviar to the general and grants few if any concessions to the popular; Greenaway's revision of *The Tempest* relocates Prospero in the image of the elite filmmaker bidding farewell to a tradition that he himself, as technological magus, participates in destroying. In a science fiction bound together by a technologically produced iconography of western culture stretching from the pages of Renaissance humanism to computer-generated models of virtual reality, the revels seen as ending in this latest rendition of Shakespeare's final play are played out as a kind of intellectualized, nostalgic farewell to even the existence of a culture that might be called learned or elite. The book disintegrates, and before us we see a virtual meltdown of all that symbolizes the learned tradition, even the word itself. Yet in a kind of acknowledgment—indeed, almost an allegory—of the end of the twentieth century's new culture and its new possessors, it is Caliban, its implied inheritor, who reaches into the flood and saves the First Folio from the literary armageddon on screen before us. Meanwhile, at the margin, orchestrating the deluge, stands the figure of the maker—the Gielgud who is Prospero who is Shakespeare who is Peter Greenaway—mournfully bidding culture—at least as he and we have hitherto imagined it—into oblivion. Elite reproductions, whether avant-garde or devoted to the "classics," as well as popular productions, then, meet in the disappearing of Shakespeare.

Dealing with specifically filmic reproductions or appropriations of Shakespeare means that "the popular" must be thought through not only the media and institutions in which Shakespeare is now reproduced—mass culture, Hollywood, celebrity, tabloid—but above all, youth culture. For as Shakespeare becomes part of pop culture and Shakespearean criticism (especially film criticism) follows suit, both move into an arena increasingly driven by a specifically youth culture, and Hollywood has clearly picked up on that fact. The animated versions already released for more than a dozen of the plays and scheduled for additional releases are only the most literal version of this development. Clearly playing to the potent consumerism of what is recognized as a notoriously visual subculture, all four of the so-called "big" tragedies have recently been reproduced in sophisticated comic-book form, appropriate for college students; major Shakespeare critics are turning their talents to readings of MTV videos; and teen idols like Keanu Reeves are being lifted out of movies like *Bill and Ted's Excellent Adventure* (dir. Stephen Herek, 1989) to play Van Sant's modern-day Prince Hal in America's contemporary Shakespearorama.[15] But the production that went the furthest in enunciating itself as a teen film was the 1996 production of *William Shakespeare's Romeo and Juliet*, orchestrated by a director whose claim to fame rested in his previous direction of *Strictly Ballroom* (1992) and starring Leonardo DiCaprio as Romeo (star of the sitcom "Growing Pains," co-star of *What's Eating Gilbert Grape* [dir. Lasse Hallstroem, 1994] and star of *Basketball Diaries* [dir. Scott Kalvert, 1995]) plus Clare Danes (star of MTV's "My So-Called Life") as Juliet. Two journalists (Maslin 1996: C12; Corliss 1996: 89-90) compared the film to an MTV rock video; MTV News did a segment on it; MTV itself aired a half-hour special on the film three times the week before its United States release; and, also the week before release, the film sponsored the TV show

"My So-Called Life," ads blaring forth clips from the soundtrack CD with music by bands such as Garbage, Radiohead, Everclear, and Butthole Surfers. As has become standard for all films, even a website was announced.[16] Perhaps the ultimate statement of just how thoroughly *William Shakespeare's Romeo and Juliet* had constructed itself as a youth culture film lay in the way it was market-tested. At the screened tests done at U.C. Berkeley the summer before its opening, studio moguls handed out market surveys that specifically asked that those who filled them out be only those viewers who were thirty-nine or younger.[17] The marketing campaign proved successful: *Romeo and Juliet* came in first at the box office the week of its release in the United States.[18]

Yet the strategies of casting teen idols and the co-construction of youth culture as popular culture were themselves part of the box office stroke mastered some time ago by Zeffirelli in both *Romeo and Juliet* and *The Taming of the Shrew*. Indeed, as Robert Hapgood aptly suggests in an essay that is part of this collection, if Zeffirelli's *Hamlet* was less of a success than were his earlier Shakespeare films, it was because his *Hamlet* was far less oriented to a young audience. In all American-made film versions of *Romeo and Juliet,* the culture has inscribed itself into forms of racial tension replayed within an ethnically marked youth culture, as in *West Side Story, Valley Girl* (dir. Martha Coolidge 1988), *Love Is All There Is* (dir. Joseph Bologna and Renée Taylor 1996) and the Luhrmann production, which was set in a Cuban-American community, Verona Beach. The trend toward making films directed almost exclusively at youth culture is a global one, and the 1987 Finnish-made film, *Hamlet Goes Business* (dir. Aki Kaurismaki), confirms its relevance through the film's staging of Ophelia's suicide: after gazing at a photo of Hamlet, Ophelia drowns herself in a bathtub while listening to a teen pop lyric in which the boyfriend wishes only to make up with his girlfriend so that all his dreams will be fulfilled. Yet while the inventiveness of some of these popularizations should rightly be applauded, at some point the devolution of Shakespeare to pop culture/youth culture (for which we may also read masculine culture) must give some critics, particularly feminists, pause: if we may read the increasing portrayal of regressively stupid white males (*Forrest Gump* [dir. Robert Zemekis, 1994] and *Dumb and Dumber* [dir. Peter Farallay, 1994]) as a kind of Hollywood pandering to the anti-intellectual machismo of its adolescent buyer, just what kind of an American *Hamlet* is destined to succeed Mel Gibson's action hero is indeed a topic to puzzle the will.

Given that popularization is linked to youth culture, the crucial question for cultural critics rests, finally, with the pedagogical implications of Shakespeare's popularization on film, TV, and video. Popularization has meant the proliferation of representations, on the one hand, and thus an enlargement of what can be legitimately studied as part of the Shakespeare canon. But it has also meant the disappearance of (what was always the illusion of) a single, unified Shakespeare whose works could be covered. Stu-dents in today's average, college-level Shakespeare course are now more often shown select scenes from two or more versions of a given play than they are a single production in its entirety (productions like the 1980s BBC Shakespeare renditions, initially aired on a PBS series, that were ultimately designed and marketed specifically for classroom purpose). CD-ROM editions of the plays necessarily further this fragmentation.[19] With film and/or digital image as the version through which Shakespeare is primarily known, Shakespeare's accessibility is guaranteed, but along with this move to film comes a perhaps inevitable new sense of Shakespeare's reproduction, one which offers certain challenges to cultural criticism of Shakespeare as it is now practiced.

Consider, once again, the scene of Shakespeare pedagogy as narrated in *The Last Action Hero*. In this film, the kid who plays hookey in order to see action films starring Schwarzenegger grudgingly returns to class in time to hear his teacher regaling the students with the pleasures of *Hamlet*. The scene offers a bit of caviar to the theater-going elite in the private knowledge that the teacher is being played by Joan Plowright, Olivier's wife of many years and herself a renowned Shakespearean actress. The in-joke is included, but it is at the same time made purely extraneous to the pleasures of *The Last Action Hero,* where pleasure is distinctly located in the smash-bang thrills of pop culture. As the truant takes his seat and the teacher informs the students that they may recognize the actor, Sir Laurence Olivier, from his work in a television commercial or from playing Zeus in *Clash of the Titans* (dir. Desmond Davis, 1981), the relevance of Shakespeare seems most vividly represented by the comically outmoded 16mm projector through which the old Olivier film is being shown. The old-fashioned, dated feel of Olivier's film may be accounted for, at least in part, by the way the scene in *The Last Action Hero* marks a new relation between the plays and their audience, one in which the aura that pervaded the filmed Shakespeare "classics" is gone, and, with it, the sense of embodied intimacy between the audience and Shakespeare himself. The displacement of Olivier by Arnold Schwarzenegger marks the disappearance of an older sense of the actor as someone who actually knew Shakespeare, who communed with him, understood his mind, and perhaps at times even thought that he himself was Shakespeare.

Nonetheless, this film marks neither the unequivocal triumph of a new American cultural imperialism nor the displacement of a Shakespeare understood to be English by one who has become brashly American. As much as the film would seem to dismiss Shakespeare, it may also be understood as playing out one more version of the way that America, through the aesthetic medium that is as peculiarly American as the stage is English, tries to come to terms with its own, unregenerate fascination with the Bard of Avon. As apparently irrelevant as *The Last Action Hero* would seem to make Shakespeare, in this and all such recent filmic moments in which the Bard is suddenly invoked, William Shakespeare is still somehow a necessary signifier. He is that which must be posited and the debt that must be acknowledged before—and in order for—popular culture to declare itself so unindebted to the S-guy that it may get on with the production of itself and its own narratives.

Notes

1. The issue of just whose sexual fantasies Gibson's image plays to is itself an example of the contradictory impulses that the culture's new sophistication about media now allows. On the one hand, in vehement defense of the hunky hero's body as an object for female fantasies only, Mel's spokesMEN have gone so far as literally to deny the right of any fanzines (the new, technologized fan magazine produced by fans and circulated on Internet) to produce gay narratives about Gibson—the narratives that are, of course, encouraged by the distinctly homoerotic overtones of the male partnered relationship in the *Lethal Weapon* film series—overtones that have indeed become progressively more blatant as the rejection of them has become simultaneously more vocal. For more on Mel, see Hodgdon (1994). If there is any gender equality to be offered at all, it is probably to be found only in the newly explicit bisexuality of pop culture's film star images that sexualize us all into universal consumers. In particular, see Marjorie Garber's chapter on "Bi-sexuality and Celebrities" (1995).

2. It appears that Shakespeare's legitimacy, at least in the United States, depends on his status as screen writer rather than playwright. In a program on Shakespeare in the weekly television series *Biography This Week,* with interviews of British scholars like Andrew Gurr and Stanley Wells, the narrator concluded by remarking that "Shakespeare is now Hollywood's hottest screenplay writer" (broadcast November 9, 1996, on A& E). And Al Pacino's *Looking for Richard,* which includes footage of Pacino at the reconstructed Globe and interviews of Branagh and Gielgud, nevertheless focuses on the American film stars acting in the play.

3. See Rich (1996): Rich goes on to say, "But if audiences inevitably giggle a bit at the 1912 *Richard III,* they should also look at it as a window on an even more distant past when Americans didn't have to be spoon fed a great dramatist but were united in their passion for one who gave them characters who mirrored their own complex humanity, not to mention sublime poetry, along with the requisite dose of sex and violence. Exciting as this extraordinary find is [i.e., the movies], we will see in its frames the ghosts of something far larger that we have lost."

We would add as well that the use of American film stars in Shakespeare film productions is nothing new. Witness the Max Reinhardt *A Midsummer Night's Dream* with James Cagney and Mickey Rooney or the Joseph Mankiewicz *Julius Caesar* with Marlon Brando; and of course, there is a long tradition of Shakespeare burlesques in America and elsewhere. See Levine (1988). What has changed, in our view, is the reception of American stars in Shakespeare, both among the viewing public and academia. Moreover, the present moment of Shakespeare reproduction includes new spin-off products from films in addition to videos, many of which are regularly cross-referenced: CD-ROMs; laserdiscs; soundtrack CDs; MTV specials; Internet websites.

4. The opening sequence with its quotation from *The Magnificent Seven* of the four riders galloping abreast, for example.

5. Hollywood's skepticism about Shakespeare is of course nothing new. Shortly before his death in 1984, Richard Burton commented "Generally if you mention the word Shakespeare in Hollywood, everybody leaves the room, because they think he's box office poison" (Levine 1988: 53). As we make clear, the Brits' responses to this skepticism differ in the 1990s.

6. That it is uncool is clearly the message in John Power's (1996) review of Al Pacino's *Looking for Richard*: "Through it all, the movie spotlights Pacino's dewy eyed reverence for Shakespeare, which is touching in its unadorned dweebiness. . . . Most stars would sooner die than look this uncool."

7. Several months prior to opening, the Luhrmann film had apparently been market tested on the summer Shakespeare classes at U.C. Berkeley. According to one of the teachers, the questionnaire the viewers were asked to respond to actually included a query that asked "whether the Shakespeare language in the film had bothered you or not." Our thanks to Grace Ioppulo for telling us about the market survey.

8. See Don Hedrick's essay in this collection.

9. Consider that as recently as the mid-1980s the notion of casting Hollywood rather than British actors in Shakespeare film was still a joke. In *Dead Poets Society,* a teacher played by Robin Williams mimics Marlon Brando playing Antony in *Julius Caesar* (which Brando had done) and John Wayne as Macbeth (a conjunction apparently only imagined, to our knowledge).

10. Our thanks to Lance Duerfahrd for bringing this change to our attention.

11. See "Production Notes," http://web.idirect.com/-claire/rjintor.html, 2.

12. John Storey, Telluride publicist.

13. The Nunn strategy distancing his film from American efforts went wholly lost on the American journalists/publicists. The *New York Times* ran a full-page ad with a blurb from a critic comparing it favorably to "To Wong Foo" and "The Birdcage," a comparison that was, in fact, echoed by *Time* Magazine's David Ansen (Ansen 1996) and in the film's own website.

14. Even the BBC felt the pressure of contemporary popular English culture. Roger Daltrey, lead singer of The Who, played Dromio in *The Comedy of Errors,* and John Cleese of *Monty Python* played Petruchio in *The Taming of the Shrew.*

15. The choice for defining pop film's Shakespearean daughter is another face familiar from L.A. teen films, Molly Ringwald, who played both Miranda in Mazursky's *Tempest* and Cordelia in Godard's *Lear.*

16. An ad for a website appears on the video of the Parker *Othello,* and a website address appeared at the end of movie theater trailers of Branagh's *Hamlet.*

17. According to one teacher, the questionnaire included a query that asked "whether the Shakespeare language in the film bothered you or not." For other adolescent responses, see Smith 1996. Of course, age may take its revenge on youth through the use of Shakespeare. Consider the rehabilitation and recovery of George III and with him the institution of the monarchy through the use of *King Lear* and *Henry IV, Part 2* in the 1994 film of *The Madness of King George* (dir. Nicholas Hytner).

18. E! Television, November 4, 1996.

19. From MLA and Shakespeare Association conventions of the past few years, many academics are familiar with the brilliant scholarly tool into which Pete Donaldson has turned the multi-media, multi-production model. See also Al Braunmuller's excellent CE-edition of *Macbeth.* Further electronic Shakespeare can be found in the CD-ROMs released by Fox International of *William Shakespeare's Romeo and Juliet* and Castle Rock Entertainment of Oliver Parker's *Othello.* In 1997, Stephen Greenblatt's Norton edition of Shakespeare was published both as a book alone and as a book with a CD-ROM (one CD-ROM for students and another for professors).

References

Ansen, David (1996) "It's the 90s, So the Bard Is Back," *Time,* November 4, vol. 128, no. 19, 73-4.

Bennett, Alan (1995) *The Madness of King George,* New York: Random House.

Berube, Michael (1995) *Public Access,* New York and London: Routledge.

Burr, Ty (1996) "The Bardcage," *Entertainment,* November 15, 353: 49.

Corliss, Richard (1996) "Suddenly Shakespeare," *Time,* November 4, vol. 148, no. 21, 88-90.

Crewe, Jonathan (1995) "In the Field of Dreams: Transvestism in *Twelfth Night* and *The Crying Game,*" *Representations,* 50: 101-23.

Dargie, John (1996) "*Othello,*" *L.A. Weekly,* December 27.

Garber, Marjorie (1992) *Vested Interests: Cross-Dressing and Cultural Anxiety,* New York and London: Routledge.

———. (1995) "Some Like It Haute," *World Art,* 1, 30-3.

Gritten, D. (1995) "Shakespeare Is One Happening Dude," *Los Angeles Times,* December 27: 39, 41.

Hodgdon, Barbara (1994) "The Critic, the Poor Player, Prince Hamlet, and the Lady in the Dark," in *Shakespeare Reread: the Text and New Contexts,* ed. Russ McDonald, London and Ithaca: Connell University Press.

Jefferson, Margot (1996) "Welcoming Shakespeare into the Caliban Family," *New York Times,* November 12: C11, C16.

Levine, Lawrence (1988) "Shakespeare in America," in *Highbrow/Lowbrow: The Emergence of Cultural Hierarchy in America,* Cambridge, MA: Harvard University Press.

Maslin, Janet (1996) "Soft, What Light? It's Flash, Romeo," *New York Times,* November 1: C1, C12.

McKellen, Ian (1996) *William Shakespeare's Richard III,* Woodstock, New York: the Overlook Press, 25-6.

Powers, John (1996) "People Are Talking About Movies," *Vogue,* vol. 186, no. 10, October, 210.

Rich, Frank (1996) "A Banished Kingdom," *New York Times,* September 21, 19.

Smith, Lynn (1996) "Language Barrier Can't Keep Apart Lovers of 'Romeo and Juliet,'" *Los Angeles Times,* November 7, F15.

Van Sant, Gus (1993) *Even Cowgirls Get the Blues and My Own Private Idaho,* New York: Faber & Faber.

Christopher C. Hudgins (essay date 1997)

SOURCE: Hudgins, Christopher C. "*The Last Tycoon*: Elia Kazan's and Harold Pinter's Unsentimental Hollywood Romance." In *Hollywood on Stage: Playwrights Evaluate the Culture Industry,* edited by Kimball King, pp. 158-83. New York: Garland Publishing Inc., 1997.

[*In the following essay, Hudgins presents an analysis of Pinter's script for* The Last Tycoon, *characterizing it as an effective study of the Hollywood film industry as revealed through the life of its main character.*]

Early in the first chapter of *The Last Tycoon,* F. Scott Fitzgerald writes these lines for his narrator, Cecilia: "You can take Hollywood for granted like I did, or you can dismiss it with the contempt which we reserve for what we don't understand. It can be understood, too, but only dimly and in flashes. Not half a dozen men have ever been able to keep the whole equation of pictures in their heads. And perhaps the closest a woman can come . . . is to try to understand one of those men" (Fitzgerald 3).[1]

Despite its casual if historically accurate sexism, the proposition seems reasonable: get to know an industry by fathoming the depths of one of its most knowledgeable captains. But this aesthetic plan, which remains at the core of Harold Pinter's adaptation, disturbed many reviewers of Elia Kazan's 1977 film. Some thought the film ineffectual in its portrayal of Hollywood and moving in its portrayal of Monroe Stahr and his failed love, while others argued that exactly the reverse was the case. Not surprisingly, the minority of reviewers who were clever or subtle enough to praise the film found its double focus on the Hollywood industry and on the personal life of Monroe Stahr to be unified, of a piece, suggesting that both elements were effectively developed and at least clearly related.[2]

In arguing that the film is actually a beautifully unified work of art, I will primarily rely on the published version of Pinter's screenplay and on my transcription of the film, though several other scripts provide interesting insights. The Harold Pinter Archive at the British Library includes four different drafts of the screenplay, while the American Film Institute's Mayer Collection holds two copies of the script, one bearing revisions labeled 10/30/75, evidently notations made during production.[3]

The Harold Pinter Archive also includes an undated five-page letter to producer Sam Spiegel in which Pinter summarizes his "random thoughts" after re-reading the novel "in complete ignorance of what you have in mind for the movie" (Box 32). In section one he comments that the staying power of the novel is due to Fitzgerald's romanticism: "He saw life and lived it with a disregard of sordid reality or banal explanations. Everything he created was touched by this same penchant for life as a fleeting, mysterious, occasionally lyric experience. The past, what it was like and how it touched the present, is the keystone of his work." In section seven, Pinter notes that "All there was to the sentimental side of the man's nature was a longing for the past, an unexplained attachment to his dead wife, who remains nebulous, a common first draft failing." And he suggests that the script should not go beyond the six chapters which Edmund Wilson includes in his edition: "since the novel is unfinished," he writes, "one owes it to Fitzgerald to try to stay within the limits he indicated, which I believe to be a romantic love story about a complex and meaningful man" (section 4).[4]

Pinter clearly admires Irving Thalberg, Fitzgerald's model for Stahr, calling him a "pope of pop art," "probably the most dedicated of the movie makers. . . . He was more than a showman. He knew the influence films had upon the public, and for that reason felt a responsibility toward his work that is virtually non-existent today" (section 4). But he also recognizes his flaws, writing in a note file dated 1 January 1994 (Box 32), apparently to himself, "The whole thing to do with dream and reality. For Stahr, making films is reality—or are films themselves reality? All aspects of reality outside of film activity don't seem to mean very much to Stahr. Since his dead wife was an important ingredient to this activity, to what extent is she real?" (7).

Centering on how unrealistic Stahr is in his perceptions of women, how romantic, Pinter goes on to suggest that in his marriage Stahr has not known a real woman, only a film star: "The assumption that they were happily married must therefore be a false assumption" (7). He adds, "Kathleen is real, but because real, elusive. (Reality being elusive whether it's actual or fabricated!). But the fabricated reality of films is a much easier one to master and control. Actual facts are clearly far more slippery. Kathleen is both concrete and slippery," and she "has him in thrall." In sum, Pinter remarks "Stahr is a man of aspiration and dream but of appreciable limitation. Reality impinges upon him in the shape of Kathleen. Reality obtrudes into the world of Hollywood, or begins to. The Hollywood world has enormous influence upon the world, while remaining in many respects isolated from it" (9).

In these notes, Pinter centers on two elements that unify the personal and the social/industry aspects of the script he later completed. As we've seen, he labels Stahr a dreamer in both arenas, though such dreaming *can* have positive as well as negative connotations; he also suggests that Stahr wants to "master and control" his reality, implying that such a wish for dominance extends both to the industry and to Kathleen. Mastering and controlling this industry through imaginative talent is at least partially admirable, but attempting to extend such mastery into the private world is fraught with peril, ethically and pragmatically in this instance. It doesn't work with Kathleen, on one level because Stahr is jousting with a phantom, his illusion of what the woman is; on a second level, his attempt to "keep" Kathleen, not to lose her, doesn't work because of Stahr's own failure of will, because of his inability, outside the world of industry, to make hard, brave decisions.

Understanding Stahr in love, and in work, is difficult because the character's complexity is so subtly evoked through unmediated action in the film. In the Edmund Wilson edition, the last Fitzgerald note is "ACTION IS CHARACTER" (163), which eerily echoes Pinter's own comments and practice. Since his first film, *The Servant* (Losey, 1963), Pinter has typically eliminated most first-person narration, a practice he continues even in his most recent script for *Lolita* (unpublished, unproduced, 1995). He said about *Accident* (Losey, 1967) that he'd hoped to provide "Just a level, intense look at people, at things. As though if you look at them hard enough they will give up their secrets. Not that they will, for however much you see and guess at there is always something more" (Esslin 228). In another interview, Pinter says "Let the action speak for itself"; one needs to avoid "sentimentality"—instead, simply "look at it as hard as possible" (Ciment 21).

Avoiding sentimentality, looking hard, recognizing that there is always more than what appears in characters' actions, these are difficult tasks for the artist, presenting difficult interpretive problems for an audience. Still, in films based on Pinter's scripts, subtle indicators of a range of valid interpretive responses usually comment on such actions. In *The Last Tycoon,* some of these clearly are Kazan's, but in many instances such indexes of interpretive response—montage, broader structural or echoing techniques, images that garner meaning through repetition—are in the script. Kazan, as a matter of fact, says that he was "reverential" toward Pinter's script, not toward Fitzgerald's unfinished novel (Silver and Corliss 43).

With more leisure for considered response than the reviewers, a good many critics still fail to read these indexes of intended response (Hans Robert Jauss's term) very well with regard to the film's depiction of Hollywood and the power struggle going on there in the thirties.[5] *The Last Tycoon*'s portrayal of Hollywood is actually fully but subtly developed. With occasional comic or even satiric tone, Kazan and Pinter succinctly evoke both the glories and the absurdities of the industry, the potential aesthetic triumphs and the difficulties one must overcome to achieve those triumphs given the system and the very human nature of those who inhabit it.

The opening scenes of *The Last Tycoon* begin to evoke the nature of the industry and its art, as well as Stahr's masterful, powerful role within it; they also serve as a structural subtext for the love plot to come. First showing us a variety of the industry's product and then the process behind the creation of that product, the film describes Stahr's relationship with every aspect of that process. We see him interacting with an almost Dickensian variety of writers, actors, and directors, and we also see his work within the overarching structure of the Board of Directors and the omni-present but never visible money men in New York. By measuring Monroe Stahr (Robert De Niro) against Pat Brady (Robert Mitchum playing a character based on Louis B. Mayer), these early scenes establish Stahr's aesthetic and managerial superiority and also prepare us to recognize Brady's resentment of his success and his passionate wish to destroy Stahr as soon as any opportunity presents itself. In short, the film depicts an industry in transition, at the beginning of the takeover of the money men, who continue, by and large, to triumph over those like Stahr who attempt to blend a commercial product with heart-felt aesthetic concerns.

The two screenings that open the film center our attention on female betrayal and on the mystery of women for men. A tenor emoting on the soundtrack, we first see in close up, black and white, a woman's face in front of a man's face, their embrace and her seemingly sincere kiss as she excuses herself. As the staff exchange obvious signals, a car pulls up, machine gun fire rings out, the man falls, and we cut to a shot of a mirror reflecting the woman's touching up her lipstick, apparently unconcerned. The camera cuts back to the man's head on the floor, a round, overturned table rolling back and forth in front of his face. In voiceover, we hear a man's voice saying "The end is too gory. Cut one roll of the table," and then we cut to the screening room, shot in color, as Monroe Stahr adds that the signal is too obvious, killing the surprise, that it should be cut (1/1 and 2).[6]

A beach scene from *Dark Moonlight* follows, again in black and white, with no soundtrack this time, a man in a

tuxedo pouring champagne, alone on the beach, as a woman walks away from him toward the sea. In voice over, Stahr says "No, no, don't go to him at all. Stay on her. You don't need him. Stay on her all the way down to the edge of the sea. She's the one we're interested in" (194/3). This scene again demonstrates Stahr's sharp aesthetic judgment and the deference with which the others treat him. Like the gangster sequence, it also evokes the mystery of the feminine for the male. The shot suggests that the woman is leaving this paragon of male sophistication, and we wonder why, perhaps puzzling at the subtle connection of the two scenes showing women in very different circumstances leaving men behind. Clear echoes of this scene's beach imagery structurally link it to both of Kathleen's scenes with Stahr at his Malibu house.

One of the early scripts in the Pinter Archive includes a third screening scene showing the hero getting his girl at the last minute even though she is on the brink of marrying another man (Box 30). Cutting from bride and father waiting in a church vestibule, the camera shows us a rumpled man asleep in the alley. Lifting his hat, he says "Come on," and runs with his lady past limousines to drive off in a scruffy two-seater, her veils flying, romantically blissful. Had this scene made the final cut, it would have also ironically commented on Stahr's romanticism and its sources.

The cuts between the black and white "product" and the color scenes in the screening room shot, in combination with the voiceover, emphasize for us the difference between the illusion of film and the reality of the process of making it. That's doubly ironic, of course, given the film within the film structure. The voiceovers subtly suggest that reality and illusion can indeed overlap, the one influencing the other. Stahr's line about being interested in the woman, not the man, captures his own version of reality, which colors the way he wants his pictures, while also pointing toward his fascination, indeed obsession, with a certain type of woman, or at least his vision of what women should be.

This motif of betrayal and feminine mystery and ambiguity from the male "eye" continues as the film cuts away from the next color scenes with the old studio guide (John Carradine) to another black and white sequence, a scene with Didi (Jeanne Moreau) in a negligee making polite conversation on the phone with her absent husband about their child and how much she misses him as Rodriguez (Tony Curtis), bare chested, comes into the shot. When she hangs up, Didi rejects Rodriguez's advances, and he asks if she wants him to go. She at first tells him yes, but as he embraces her from behind, she turns, sensuously returning his embrace, her nails palpitating the flesh of his back, changing her "yes" to "no." In this instance, we are surprised, almost shocked, when we cut to a color shot of the crew who have been shooting this sequence.

Expecting another cut to the screening room, we are even more emphatically made aware of the process of manufacturing a movie, startled at the sudden shift from this slightly different illusion to the "reality" of the frame film. The scene also prepares us to recognize the similarities in Stahr's relationship with Kathleen, who has betrayed her fiancé with him and who gives him a series of ambiguous responses about how she regards their relationship, about what she really wants. The most specific echoing is the image of the embrace, which parallels in a variety of ways Stahr's forceful, commanding caressing of Kathleen's body in their second scene at the beach house. And finally, the scene continues to characterize Stahr, for he is in the background, here, seemingly omni-present throughout the studio, observing his director, Ridingwood (Dana Andrews), failing his task and his star (195-7/8-13).

The sequence in the Board of Directors dining room includes two other revealing commentaries on Stahr's relationship to his product. As we absorb the vision of Hollywood apart, distanced from the culture of the thirties, the luxury of the table, the fastidious dress of diners, Popolos (Tige Andrews) suggests to Stahr that they make *Manon* with a happy ending. Stahr replies, "It's been making money without a happy ending for a century and a half" (212/42). The line captures his balance, his recognition of the conditions of his industry; a profit is usually required, but he uses that logic here to justify an aesthetic end. And the idea for a *Manon* film carries subtextual implications for the "real" love story that's just beginning to develop. Of the two operas based on the Abbé Prevost novel, *Manon Lescaut,* Puccini's is the more relevant. Noted for his realism, Puccini's central interest in most of his mature work is the psychology of his heroines, who are madly in love, guilty about it and destroyed in the end. In *Manon,* though, a young man from a good family destroys his life for a courtesan. If the audience catches it, the allusion is ominous for Stahr's infatuation with Kathleen, who does have something of the courtesan about her, as we'll see.

During this same scene, Brady asks about the South American picture, which Stahr says is a go. Brady here takes the risk of criticizing the budget, but Stahr counters with his comment that "It's a quality picture," adding "It's time we made a picture that isn't meant to make money. Pat Brady's always saying at Academy dinners that we have a certain duty to the public. Okay. It's a good thing for the company to slip in a picture that'll lose money. Write it off as good will" (213-214/42). Again, the balance of Stahr's perspective, almost neoclassical, is the point; he advocates aesthetic responsibility, but he's also cognizant of a long-term financial advantage, the good will that such a picture can produce to the company's profit. As Stahr leaves the dining room before most of the board, moderate, not a glutton, without taking a drink, Brady's response is "Boy . . . ," ironically labeling his immaturity relative to the much younger Stahr.

Another of these subtly revealing and unifying screening sequences, relatively late in the film, is perhaps the most significant in both its characterization of Stahr and in its subtextually labeling how we may understand the film as a whole. A rough cut of the nightclub scene that concludes the Didi/Rodriguez movie, the sequence follows Stahr's reading the letter from Kathleen telling him that she is to be married and the scene where Cecilia is so distraught with Stahr's ignoring her once more. Black and white, it opens as Didi and Rodriguez act out their characters' nostalgically repeating the opening gambits for their affair; but we discover that she has decided to leave him and return to her husband. As Rodriguez, the bar owner, plays the piano, Didi, now revealed as his singer, breathes these lyrics: "You have the choice / Brown sugar or white / You have the choice . . . / Love's dear delay / Love's dread delight." *She* breaks off and walks away, saying "I owe it to him. I must go to him." And then sings once more, "You had the choice today / But you would never say / No, you would never say" (105). Rodriguez tells her that he'll never forget her; Didi at first agrees, but when the heart-broken bar-keep bitterly tells her to remember him to her husband, who will never know her as he has, she lashes out, telling Rodriguez that she's lied, that she'll forget him by tonight. In the film, she goes around the corner, leans against a wall, and sobs; as melodramatic music mounts, Rodriguez looks up from his piano, apparently having heard her. We cut to Stahr, in color, watching.

As Brady and one of his yes men mouth platitudes about French girls having depth, Stahr criticizes a line of dialogue from the scene and demands that it be re-shot, despite the $50,000 cost to do so. Though he's complimented the make-up and hair people, Stahr is clearly in an extremely bad state of mind; as he leaves Brady is impotently disgruntled. This screening room sequence continues to characterize Stahr as concerned about aesthetic quality, but here there is no justification or rationalization about the bottom line, and his judgement is called into question for the first time. The line he objects to is "Nor I you," Didi's response to Rodriguez that she won't forget him. Though the line is believable given her French-accented, non-native English, Stahr, like Rodriguez, has just had his hopes dashed by Kathleen's letter. He allows his personal despair to interfere with his professional judgement, and lashes out at Boxley (Donald Pleasence), the British writer who has written the scene, and at his Board, with none of his usual self-confident good humor.

Brady files Stahr's behavior as one more affront in the mounting number that accrue to provoke his final attack. The scene subtextually labels Stahr's situation since like these two fictional characters, he has tried to replay his earlier relationship with his dead wife with Kathleen. Didi's song also labels his later failure at relationship, foreshadowing the scene to follow, his second visit to the Malibu house with Kathleen. As we'll see, Stahr *will* have "had the choice" of trying to convince her to marry him, but he will put it off, frightened, the song suggests, by "Love's dread delight." The line subtly implies the ambivalence Stahr feels at the idea of loving someone who is not the perfect woman of his fictive imaginings, someone who does not adore his world of film and the power he wields.

This scene also labels Kathleen's previous behavior and that to come. Like Didi, and like Christine Linde in *A Doll's House,* Kathleen at first feels obligated to break off the relationship as forcefully as possible in a perhaps misguided attempt to be kind to the person rejected for reasons of duty. Didi says she owes a return to her husband; Kathleen says much the same thing about her fiancé. But Stahr concentrates on Didi's tearful remorse around that corner, emblematically centering on this aspect of the fiction's suggestion, hoping that Kathleen's letter revealing her *intentions* to marry may be similarly ambivalent and revocable. Unfortunately, even tragically, he has not paid attention to the need for forceful choice, the need to *say* what he seeks in his personal life with the same immediacy and decision he typically manages in his professional life.

The unifying connection, here, between the social, Hollywood plot and the personal, love plot is clear. Before this first major lapse on Stahr's part, roughly three-fourths of the way through the script, the film fully captures the nature of the industry in Stahr's relationship with his writers, with his actors, with his directors and with his staff. That relationship is typically portrayed as efficient and beneficent, both productive and caring whenever possible. As a whole, the portrait continues to emphasize the contrast and confusion between illusion and reality. Stahr's relationship with the Board, and with New York, of course, changes radically, mirroring both what happened historically to the industry and the source in Stahr's personal heartbreak for his own loss of professional control.

The scene with an old studio guide conducting a group of college girls through the studio follows the introductory screening room sequence. Here we see a miniature of the industry's relation to its public, its patrons' willing suspension of disbelief and their adulation of ever-so-distant, romantic stars. As the slightly comic but sympathetic old man takes off his hat, he guides the college girls into Minna Davis's dressing room. He claims contact with the mighty in telling them that he himself made the call to Mr. Stahr to announce his wife's final illness.[7] Photographs of Davis over his shoulder prepare us for the cut to a large painting, framed with elaborate lights, as if capturing her in a make-up mirror, an angelic image. That prepares us to recognize Kathleen's striking resemblance to this idealized portrait—not too difficult, since it's a painting of Ingrid Boulting with shorter blonde hair.[8] Manipulated by the industry-sponsored tour, the college girls' adulation of both Minna Davis and Stahr provides one of many comments on how Hollywood figures replace royalty in the American consciousness given its need for emblems of a life beyond the petty reality of day-to-day existence.

Once more foregrounding the illusion/reality motif, on a huge soundstage, the guide describes how Hollywood creates an earthquake scene. You rock the camera, he says, his old, thin body swaying back and forth, and then, repeating the gesture, more impressively describes rocking the room and throwing in a lot of dust. A girl suggests the addition of flying bricks, to which he jovially agrees. After the Didi and Rodriguez shoot, a sequence of cuts between Brady's office and Stahr's office leads up to the "real" earthquake at night. We see Brady's secretary feeling ill, in retrospect queasy from the pre-tremor, and then we see a chandelier swaying in Brady's office, a crack appearing in the ceiling of Stahr's office, panic in Brady's office. In one of my favorite touches, probably Kazan's, Brady abandons his daughter, seeking shelter himself under the frame of his office door, almost instinctively cunning, self-serving, and emotionally distant from even Cecilia (Theresa Russell). Cuts back and forth to the exterior, to the failed power plant, lights flashing on and off, and so on, establish the devastation outside the office.

The filmmakers walk a fine line here. They make this earthquake much less "corny" than any film utilizing the techniques the guide describes, but they also use those slightly melodramatic power station shots, sirens in the background, the frantic concern for Stahr's safety, and so on to emphasize the trauma of the event. Emblematically, the scenes which follow mark the major ground shift in Stahr's life, but within the context, still, of the illusory. For as Stahr hastens out into the back lots, taking control, aware of every nuance of his studio's property, we focus on a water tower's leaking a waterfall, then on the resulting flood. We see a minuscule village and palm trees swept away, meshing the illusion of the studio's stock in trade with the "reality" of this event. And finally, Stahr sees two women clinging to one another, riding the head of "Siva" down the flood.

Stahr's first response in the film is to remark, "Christ, we need that head next week" (25, 26). The script's identification of the head with "Siva," though, is typical of Pinter's use of images as subtextual labels. As Michael Millgate points out in his insightful essay on the novel, this scene is crucial in its making clear the relevance of Hollywood for Fitzgerald's vision of experience. Even with the ordinary and fake materials of the illusion factory in the foreground, the scene is "very nearly a miracle." In the novel, Fitzgerald writes that the head of the goddess "meandered earnestly on its way, stopping sometimes to waddle and bump in the shallows with the other debris of the tide." A worker tells Stahr, "We ought to let 'em drift out to the waste pipe, . . . but DeMille needs that head next week" (25). And then a vision of Stahr's dead wife climbs down from the floating head of the goddess. Millgate observes that this scene captures "The essential quality of experience for [Fitzgerald,] . . . the continual queerness and the occasional miracle of it, no less [a miracle] . . . for occurring always amidst commonplaces, vulgarity, and a good deal of evil" (297). He concludes that this "controlled and particularized realization of the miracle—the often absurd miracle—at the heart of ordinary experience" is the "essential achievement of Fitzgerald's mature fiction" (298).

Pinter's script captures that "queerness of experience" with arresting, evocative forcefulness. Stahr, already established as a man at the peak of his powers, a legend, but alone, isolated, suddenly has a woman float into his life, radically altering his fate, moving the ground he stands on, for all the world like that knock on the door one sunny morning in Pinter's adaptation of *The Trial*. In this film, we see a gorgeous closeup of Kathleen atop that goddess head, full blown, and cut back and forth between her and Stahr's absorbed stare. When we cut to the aftermath, Stahr dismissing his servant in his mansion, he takes a pill for his heart and begins to read those scripts. But he has entered a bedroom glaringly white to discover his dead wife, alluring, removing her cape, saying "I've come back." Boulting plays Minna Davis in this scene with the same hair we've seen in her earlier dressing room portrait. We cut to the "real" masculine bedroom, Stahr interrupting his lonely work, as he does recurringly from this point, calling on his staff to find the girl's phone number. The scene suggests both the unfruitful nostalgia that initially provokes Stahr's obsession and the illusory nature of his vision of this woman.

The use of Siva, often spelled "Shiva," underlines what a two edged sword such miracles of queerness can be. Most simply, Shiva is the Destroyer, but gradually "it came to be felt that Shiva destroyed in order to make room for new creation. . . . By a further development . . . Shiva stands for life itself, tremendous vitality," and becomes associated with "the illusion-creating power that has produced the beautiful and terrible phenomenal world" (Noss 280-5). Even if we do not bring to the film such detailed metaphoric association, the image of the goddess, and of Kathleen's descent into the floodwaters, suggests that Stahr has a chance for a new, more vital life, but that he also may be destroyed.[9]

Several evocative scenes with his writers flesh out the portrait of Stahr as the titan of his industry. For example, when young Wylie White (Peter Strauss) chases Stahr down in the streets outside the writers' quarters, we see the bustle of cowboys, horses, Indians who greet Stahr, and a wagon of chorus girls passing by that distract Wylie. The scene comically blends the illusory with the "real" as the two discuss Wylie's latest script, a crane in the background lifting the head of the goddess across the sky. Wylie has discovered this sunny morning that two other writers, his friends, have been assigned to the same script he's been working on and is politely complaining to Stahr about it. Stahr's response, first is that he's sorry: "What can we do? That's the system" (215/44).

When Wylie points out that Stahr has invented the system, the producer, not unkindly, responds that the problem is "You've distorted the girl. By distorting the girl you've distorted the story." In the midst of several other rapid-fire business conversations, he adds that he's not interested in Wylie's fantasies. As he signs some papers a secretary has driven up to him on Wylie's back, asserting their relative positions, he tells the young writer: "You've given her a secret life. She doesn't have a secret life. You've made her a melancholic. She is not a melancholic." What's impor-

tant is the way Stahr sees the girl, who "stands for health, vitality, love. You've made her a whore" (216/45). Wylie asks: "So how do you want the girl?"; Stahr replies, "Perfect." "Gee," says Wylie, echoing Brady's immature "Boy," at the Board's luncheon. Once more, Stahr's aesthetic concerns are responsibly linked to the bottom line, his assigning multiple writers to the same task in the interest of efficiency.

In the novel, the implications of this linkage of aestheticism with business emerge more explicitly in a conversation Stahr has with Boxley. There, Fitzgerald has the older writer complaining that the industry's system of mass production is all wrong. Stahr replies: "That's the condition. . . . There's always some lousy condition." He uses an example of making a picture about Rubens: "Our condition is that we have to take people's own favorite folklore and dress it up and give it back to them. Anything beyond that is sugar" (105), and he encourages Boxley to "give us some sugar."

At his best, Stahr struggles within the limitations of the financial conditions of the system to give the public something more than just mass production entertainment, and goes out of his way to try to help his writers do just that. In his scene with Wylie, Stahr teaches the youngster what he wants aesthetically. The problem is that Stahr wants that product to be based on *his* imagination, his wish to see the girl as the exemplum of healthy love. At times, Stahr's imagination is aesthetically shallow, completely the opposite of his insistence on making *Manon* with its unhappy ending. That Stahr wants the girl perfect also comments on his problems with perceiving Kathleen. Despite the fact that Stahr cannot see beyond his "scripting," we can see that there is much of the melancholic about Kathleen, a little of the whore, and certainly a "secret life," at first beyond his ken.

The film's Boxley scene accomplishes a similar dual purpose. The meeting with the three writers in Stahr's office follows Stahr's lonely trip up the stairs to his bedroom after his first failed meeting with Kathleen. In response to Boxley's complaint that he cannot work with the "hacks" Stahr has saddled him with, Stahr acts out a scenario to demonstrate how to capture the interest of an audience without the kind of stilted "talk" Boxley himself has written. The producer's story of a woman's coming into a room, emptying her purse, repacking it but leaving a nickel on the table, allows De Niro to work brilliant business to Pleasence's rapt attention: he mimics the woman's beginning to burn a pair of black gloves just as her phone rings; as suspense creates a captivating illusion without even the trappings of a shoot or set, Stahr speaks into the phone, in slight falsetto, "I've never owned a pair of black gloves in my life," hangs up, and goes back to burning those gloves in the fireplace. Suddenly, he says, we notice another man in the room, watching the girl. He stops, Boxley wants to know what happens next, and Stahr replies "I don't know. I was just making pictures" (229/65).

The scene is the most effective in the film at suggesting the brilliant talent behind Stahr's extremely early success.

He has the audience in his office (and us) on the edge of their seats with the mystery of the scene, with its suspense. We want to know who the girl is, why she's burning those gloves, what horrible crime she's covering up, and who that mysterious man is. Along with Boxley, we want to know "What was the nickel for?" Stahr has one of the other writers reply that "The nickel was for the movies." When Boxley laughingly asks "What do you pay me for? I don't understand the damn stuff" (229/65), Stahr replies, "Yes you do. Or you wouldn't have asked about the nickel."

Again, Stahr is trying to help his staff to do good work. Though perhaps paternalistic, he's still trying to get the best he can from a "distinguished English writer" who has more to offer than he's been able to tap as yet. The scene also provides an echoing label for our better understanding of the film's conclusion, where Stahr repeats these lines as we watch Kathleen burning his letter in its distinctive blue envelope rather than the black gloves. Echoing this scene, Stahr's once more saying that he doesn't know what happens, that he was just making pictures, suggests that he has desperately wanted to believe that he could control his life, script it as he wished with the characters playing the roles he dictates, as creatures of vitality and health and virtue, should he desire it. Kazan comments that "I was just making pictures" at the film's conclusion is "full of self-scorn. . . . I think that's the best line in the picture. . . . It says, in effect, 'That's what I've done all my life, and I've got such a habit of looking at things as though they were pictures, and in my own life it's become that'" (Silver and Corliss 43).

The producer's similarly encouraging scene with the admittedly difficult Didi on the set, warmly reassuring her about both her aging appearance and her talent (218-20/46), is prepared for by the hilarious scene in his busy office with Rodriguez, who's come to Stahr for advice about his impotence (!) once neither doctors nor cat houses have been able to help (207-9/39-40). The film adds several wonderfully comic bits to the script to emphasize that Stahr's kindness has somehow managed to alleviate the problem. Though we don't hear the specific advice, when Stahr and Rodriguez emerge into his outer office, Stahr cuts off Rodriguez's thanks with "Just play the part the way I said." We see Rodriguez, all grins, running gleefully across the lawn, vaulting into his convertible BMW roadster, and peeling away, tires squalling. Later we see him and his remarkably plain wife at the writer's ball, both positively aglow.

This scene once more comments on the illusion/reality theme as Rodriguez wonders how he can appear in a love scene when he can't make it with his own wife, whom he adores. Stahr's response, on one level a cover story for the office to hide the subject of their real discussion, also implies that Rodriguez should play real life just as he would a part. Though the scene reinforces Stahr's beneficent kindness, it also suggests that at least a part of the reason for that kindness for his actors is to improve his product.

The cumulative picture of Hollywood that emerges is that actors can indeed be prima donnas who must have their nurse maids to perform well. Cumulatively, too, the scene adds another element to the film's death and aging subtext, a typical Pinter motif. The dead if beloved actress Minna Davis, the fading Didi, the impotent Rodriguez in despair at his loss of vitality, the comic/absurd death of the editor in the screening room, and, above all, Stahr's emblematic heart disease and implied early death at the film's conclusion, all subtly imply that the choice of action "today" that Didi's song refers to is of great importance.

Stahr is too complex a hero always to be kind, even self-interestedly so. A streak of cruelty emerges both in his treatment of Didi's director, Red Ridingwood (Dana Andrews), and in his treatment of the Board. The film succinctly summarizes thirties Hollywood's directing system as Stahr dismisses Red from the picture. Like the writers, most directors were interchangeable, piece workers as far as the studios were concerned. Kazan economically suggests just what a slouch Ridingwood is, though, as he shows us the director lounging about, not communicating with the actors until an assistant lets him know that Stahr is on the set, more concerned with getting through the shooting schedule than with the quality of what he captures on film (8, 51-2). Stahr pulls him off the set, and, as the director gripes about his difficult leading lady, tells him that he just can't handle her, that another director is already on the set. Retrieving Ridingwood's coat from a waiting car, he reiterates, "You haven't touched what she's able to do." We see the pleasing results of Stahr's decision later in the rough cut screening, a remarkable contrast to Didi's attitudinizing in her first scene with Rodriguez.

The Last Tycoon's portrait of the Board and its relationship to the money people in New York amounts to a detailed examination of the central condition that constrains Stahr, within which he maneuvers brilliantly until his crisis, his earthquake. The first scene in Pat Brady's office, which follows the screening room sequences, begins with a voiceover as Stahr wearily lies down on his couch in his own modern office. Brady says "I love him," referring to Stahr. We cut to Brady pouring a drink, the first thing we see him do, in front of a tiger skin rug. After a shot of clearly expensive carved wooden lions on a shelf, Brady in his next breath complains to New York lawyer Fleishacker (Ray Milland) that New York has forgotten him, primarily because he has so loyally and generously supported Stahr. Fleishacker tries to reassure him, but Brady tells him he wants to see the recognition, pounding his desk, "I want to see it on this table. I want to feel it" (198-9/15). His own huge portrait glowering over the office and its wild animal decor suggests the savage egotism that drives Brady, despite that pose of loyal support.

The imagery repeated in the "leather" room that Stahr later ridicules at Brady's home during his meeting with Brimmer (Jack Nicholson), the animal skins are also in the foreground as Cecilia later discovers the nude secretary in her father's office closet (250-52/102). Brady's frequent drinking and the fact that his office contains no books, unlike Stahr's bookshelf-lined, tasteful, less grandiose quarters, furthers our unsympathetic response, as does that selfish disregard for his daughter during the earthquake sequence. Just before Cecilia's discovery of her father's peccadillo, he utters the real feeling subtextually and imagistically implied in his first scene: "It's Stahr! That goddamn little Vine Street Jesus! He's in my hair night and day. . . . He sits like a goddamn priest or rabbi and says what he'll do and what he won't do. I'm half crazy" (251/102).

The opening scene with Brady also begins to capture his basic dislike for the medium, his hatred of both writers and actors; Fleishacker, representing "New York's" sensibilities, echoes him. As Brady sees his daughter pull up outside with Wylie, he says "Did you see that bastard touch my daughter?" and replies to the lawyer's question that "He's a goddamned writer"(199/15). The lawyer responds: "I was looking in at the writers' building this morning. I watched them for fifteen minutes and there were two of them didn't write a line." When Cecilia comes in and gives her father a warm hug, before he's introduced Fleishacker asks if she's an actress, perhaps a label for Brady's typical behavior with starlets. Brady proudly comments: "She's too intelligent to be an actress. She'll be graduating next June from Bennington with honors" (200/17). The line suggests both Brady's real opinion of the people who work for him and implicitly that of the Board and of New York, again in marked contrast to Stahr's attitudes.

As we've seen, the Board luncheon scene accentuates the group's concern for the bottom line, exclusively. Fleishacker and Brady exchange meaningful glances in this scene and several others, suggesting their collusion. Brady is purposeful in his bringing up the budget for the South American picture, of course, to foreground it for New York's representative, but at this point Stahr's success has made him too powerful to be vulnerable. Stahr appeals to the Marcus (Morgan Farley), clearly held in some awe by the rest, who backs him up as the one responsible for the company's huge profits, as the person to whom the company owes it all. That irritates both Brady and Fleishacker, but they can do nothing at this point. Emblematically, Morse is a very old man who now leaves the table, carried in the arms of his muscular servant, the victim of an unnamed disease. The scene implies that Stahr may soon be in trouble, his support on thin ice, the old ways fading.

The Last Tycoon's sympathy is clearly with its namesake and against the Board and its alliance, through Brady, with the New York money men, for the sequences involving the Board include the broadest comedy in the film. Other than Marcus, undercut in different ways, the Board members are painted, perhaps even caricatured, as shallow, uncultured, uninteresting and uneducated. That's particularly evident in Popolos (Tige Andrews), the Greek who constantly wails on about both the glories of the American system and his opinion that all communists are "fairies,"

and in the pathetic yes-man Eastwick and his reiterated "There are other aspects, of course."[10] The film's conclusion, as the Board fires Stahr, makes clear that this pathetic group readily follows Brady's lead, who in turn has sucked up to New York and its fear of the consequences of Stahr's mishandling the writer's representative, Brimmer, the communist, a threat to Popolos' vision of the American way of life, the bottom line.

This evocative portrait of the conflict within the industry during a time of transition and change for the United States in general is very specifically related to Stahr's failure in his personal life, as we've suggested. After his sighting of Kathleen, Stahr constantly interrupts his business day for her, providing ammunition for Brady's and Fleishacker's hostile off-screen reports to New York. He takes a call at the Board luncheon about the girl's phone number, he calls Edna, whom he mistakes for Kathleen, from the set of Didi's film, and he refuses to talk to Brady about an "urgent call" from New York as he rushes off to meet her, Brady ominously watching from his window. Given Brady's informing Stahr that he's with Fleishacker and its timing, that call Stahr brazenly, heatedly refuses with "Not now!" (222/54) is almost certainly about the South American quality picture.

After meeting Kathleen, Stahr basically ignores his company table at the Writer's Ball when he discovers her there, another of those queer coincidences, and leaves in ardent pursuit. With mounting disregard for his best professional interests, he ignores an impressive list of callers at his home after his first idyllic night with Kathleen, including one from his chief supporter, Marcus. Soon after his discovery of Kathleen's letter announcing her impending marriage, we see his demanding a reshoot of the conclusion of Didi's movie despite the $50,000 price tag. After Kathleen's phone call and the second scene at the Malibu house with her, Stahr keeps an office full of people waiting as he writes draft after draft of a letter to her. And in marked contrast to his previously caring behavior, he is cold and ineffective at Didi's preview celebration, insisting on leaving early with Cecilia for the Malibu house, the site of his brief happiness. Finally, ecstatic over Kathleen's apparent agreement to go away with him for the weekend, he tells his secretary to cancel all of his appointments, including the one with Brimmer scheduled at Brady's home. At that very moment, he gets Kathleen's telegram; his smile at the cartoons he's been screening turns into a blank stare as he says, immobile, muttering, "Keep going." (263/127).

That final poleax is the blow that drives him to drink for the first time and to drunkenly attack Brimmer, who decks him, Brady again ominously watching through a window. Clearly caused by heartbreak, the scene provides Brady with enough to fire Stahr the next morning, the Board slavishly following New York's orders: "They've instructed me" Brady pontificates, "to tell you that they no longer hold you competent to negotiate with the writers. . . . They don't consider that trying to beat up the writer's representative is in the best interests of the company" (273/142). Though only as New York's puppet, Brady has won, and he's vengeful about it in a way he would never have dared before, advising Stahr that New York "said be sure to go see a doctor about your eye," blackened by Brimmer's punch.

Stahr has abandoned his balanced ability to cope with all comers, then, because he has lost Kathleen, but his professional fall carries with it a few positive implications for his potential personal growth. At first, Stahr has had no life beyond the movies, dwelling obsessively on his dead wife, whose picture is everywhere, over his shoulder at the office, in his bedroom, his study. Joss Marsh links that nostalgia to one of Fitzgerald's central problems, "modern man's removal from his direct experience into a half world of dangerous dreams," which can fracture relationships (102). But Stahr begins to struggle to learn to live in the present, outside the studio; after the first Malibu scene, we no longer hear much about Kathleen's resemblance to his dead wife. Stahr also makes an effort to get beyond his wish to dominate in his personal life as much as he does in his professional life, but that's finally ineffective because he cannot accept women as complex, independent equals. He wants them "perfect," like the screen's romantic icons. The film illustrates Victor Cahn's argument that in Pinter's version of competition between men and women, mystery about women troubles men "far more than it does his female characters" (7).

Monroe Stahr fails at love, loses his chance for two interrelated reasons. In the first place, his will, his courage to be, is not strong enough to force him into action when he is not assured of his own control; Kathleen's mystery, her secret life, perhaps her own ambivalence, places her beyond his limited experience and, like Prufrock, he simply can't risk, despite his desperate wish to do so. He cannot understand someone who is not of the film world, as he is, someone who wants a life different than his own, a "quiet life," as Kathleen reiterates. Secondly, Monroe Stahr is addicted to power, again because of his work; he attempts to dominate and control Kathleen at a number of points, sometimes successfully, but his final effort backfires, and he loses everything he cares about as direct result, personally and professionally. And then he dies.

There are three central scenes in this progression. After pejoratively establishing Stahr's initial fascination with Kathleen because of her resemblance to Minna Davis, the film shows her yielding to Stahr's very forceful pursuit after the Writer's Ball and agreeing to have lunch with him someplace where he is not known. Following a joyful idyll at a beach cafe, they end up at Stahr's unfinished house in Malibu, a typical Pinter image, going back that evening when Kathleen suggests a return, apparently overcome by passion. Millgate writes that the "most beautiful image of the book's sustained awareness of the ordinary queerness of experience is the scene of the consummation of Stahr's and Kathleen's love, which he finds a parallel for the opening image of the novel's earthquake sequence: everything

in the novel "is afloat and moving, in an earnest and bumbling way that is at the same time a rapid drift toward the waste pipe. Nothing stands still and no one can afford to wait for things to be just right" (299).

In *The Last Tycoon,* too often at first Stahr typically waits; Kathleen acts. He does not try to approach Kathleen when she kicks off her shoes and lies on the grass; she's the one who kisses him first in the parking lot and suggests that they go back to the beach house. With delightfully romantic music in the background, we cut to the pair at night, Stahr bringing her a candle; back turned, she begins to take off her dress, covering herself with a blanket and coming toward him. He reaches behind him, weak-kneed, clutching a post. Dropping her dress, she embraces him, and then begins to undress him. They pull back and smile, the gentle music ends, we hear the surf, and cut to a shot of an electric heater; then we cut to their naked bodies, Stahr kneeling beside her head and kissing her. She looks up at him as he nestles a pillow under her head, and covers her with a blanket. By now, the moment is wondrous, natural, comfortable, full of hope for their future.

At this point, Kathleen wonders "when it's settled," adding that "there's a moment when you needn't, and then there's another moment when you know nothing in the world could keep it from happening" (241/85). That implies a good bit of very real experience, but it is also her credo, this yielding to powerful emotion, one which Stahr has not been able to live by. She goes on to say she knows why Stahr had liked her "at first," and asks about Minna Davis. He tells her that he doesn't remember "what we were like. She . . . became very professional. She was very successful. She answered all her fan letters. Everyone loved her. (Pause). I was closest to her when she was dying" (241-2/85). Stahr's lines suggest the kind of distance in his marriage which Pinter describes in those early notes. There's both an envy and a resentment in his description of Minna Davis' professional success. The lines about their closeness during her illness also suggest a recognition that she was actually someone different then, someone other than the professional persona she previously depended on.

As if in response to Stahr's admission, Kathleen gets up and playfully dons an apron, asking if the maid lives in or just comes for breakfast, adding that there would be lots of work to do looking after Mr. Stahr. At one level, this is a request for clarification, an opportunity for Stahr to respond, an offer to "live in" rather than being a passing fancy. But he cannot take advantage of the implied opportunity, instead questioning her about her plans for the future—"Are you going to stay in California?" The question is incongruous, jarring, a non-sequitur. And she does not reply. He pursues it: "What's the mystery?" and she refuses to tell him. Still, Monroe Stahr has made some progress. When Kathleen tells him he looks tired, he insists that he's not and "shows her" by beginning to make love to her again. Retrospectively, this scene is an emphatic contrast to his scene with Cecilia when she has offered herself to him in his office and he's told her that he's too tired to "undertake anything." And now, when Kathleen remarks that she looks like Minna Davis in her cheekbones, he says "No, it's here," as he begins to cover her body. The implied suggestion is that he is no longer so obsessed with the resemblance to Minna.

The next morning, though, he continues to pry into Kathleen's mystery, and she tells him the story of her marriage to a deposed king who had become a drunkard and tried to force her to sleep with his friends. She tells Stahr she should have left her king "long before." That deepens her mystery—why has she left him? when? what gave her the courage? is it true? But the scene concludes as he says "I don't want to lose you," and Kathleen replies, "I want a quiet life," certainly an implied rejection, now, of what he is (244/87). At the parking lot, their leave-taking is cold and anti-climactic until she suddenly goes to him, but Stahr cannot take advantage of this moment either, and their cars go off in separate directions, for the audience a gentle, sad foreshadowing.

When Stahr gets home, though, he's infatuated, ignoring those callers, taking a pill. When the Butler brings him the letter that Kathleen has claimed to have lost in the car, he doesn't read it at first, smelling its perfume as he puts it aside for a stack of scripts. The strange gesture emblematically suggests his cowardice, that his business life, steeped in illusion, carries elements with it of both obsession and escape from any full experience of reality. When he finally reads the letter, he starts up the stairs, switching off the lights himself, as we hear Kathleen, in voiceover, informing him that she is soon to be married and won't see him after today. She adds that she intends his interest to fade now, all at once. As the door of his bedroom shuts behind him, the emotional tone is bewilderingly sad.

But after we watch the screening of the rough cut of Didi's movie with its emphasis on choice and on a leave-taking that she does not really want, we see Stahr pick up the phone in his office to answer a call from Kathleen and cut to the Malibu house. Her call poses several interpretive possibilities. It may suggest that Kathleen's mood when she has composed the letter was much different than it was after their night of love at the beach, but it certainly emphasizes that she was lying when she said that she'd lost that letter in the car, that at least for the moment she chose to leave the letter with him despite that night at the beach. It also emphasizes that she cannot stick with the decision the letter communicates, that she must see him again, even though that means she will betray her fiancé, like Didi, a second time. That should set off bells of opportunity in Stahr's head.

But at the Malibu house in the late afternoon, Stahr just probes the mystery of the husband-to-be and then tries to dominate her. Kathleen replies to his questioning, haltingly, that the man is an American who took her away, presumably from her husband, and brought her here to live in his house. "He's an engineer," she adds. "He'll be back

. . . next week." Indicated by Pinter's ellipsis, her brief pause both calls into question her truthfulness about that schedule and suggests its importance by centering our attention on it. When she adds that they are getting married, seemingly a redundancy, Stahr asks if she's in love with him. There is at least some courage there. And she replies: "Oh yes. It's all arranged. He saved my life. *Pause.* I just wanted to see you once more. *Pause.* It's all arranged" (256/112).

Pinter's dialogue here is typically subtle and evocative. Kathleen's repeated response to Stahr's question about love, "It's all arranged," coupled with "He saved my life," and her very pithy "Oh, yes," implies that she may not be in love with this man, that she is marrying him out of a sense of obligation. Retrospectively, Didi's returning to her husband because she "owes it to him" reinforces such a reading. Stahr's response, though, to this possibility is not to offer her his life, or to object to her going ahead with the plan. Instead, he attempts to control her, in marked contrast to that gentle lovemaking. He commands her to stop walking, to come back and to open her cape and to close her eyes. Though she hesitates at the cape command, she obeys. He traces first her face, then her throat, then her breasts, and finally her belly. As he does so, she opens her eyes, moves closer to him, and kisses him. He finally takes her in his arms. The scene clearly echoes that first shot of Rodriguez embracing Didi after her call to her husband, when she has first asked him to leave and then asked him to stay. Stahr has taken advantage of the moment, here, but only in a limited, nearly hostile way. On one level, he means to underline their passion for each other as a reason for her not to marry; on another, though, he simply takes advantage of her own passionate nature, insistent on control, inarticulate about that *choice* offered him by her phone call and her ambivalence.

With the implication hanging in the air that they have made love once more, we cut to Stahr's car, driving rapidly along the road at night, clearly some hours after the scene at Malibu. Kathleen comments on how quickly night falls here, with no twilight, echoing *Godot* and emblematically labeling her own mood. Then, apparently a non-sequitur, she says "I suppose some parts of America are gentle" (257/113). The suggestion is that this experience, unlike the first, has not been. But Stahr simply replies, "Sure," and then changes the subject, asking if she's leaving California.

The line echoes both his earlier question to Kathleen and his repeated question to Cecilia about when she's going back to college, and similarly suggests his nervousness, his not knowing what to say, his ineptitude around "real" women. But Kathleen's response is "We might . . . I might . . . I don't know." The pauses and the progression again suggest that she may not be certain that she will marry at all, even now. In the film, at this point he suddenly stops the car. He says "Listen—" but doesn't complete the sentence. Kathleen says "What?" There's a pause, and Stahr says "Nothing." Kathleen turns to him, from across the seat. During a much longer pause, she looks at him as he stares straight ahead. And then he decorously drops her off a block from the engineer's house.

Kathleen's urging Stahr on, asking him what he means to say, subtly suggests that she would *like* him to say something. The novel's narrative is more specific: "They looked at each other and her eyes asked, "Shall I marry The American?" He did not answer" (114). Still, this Pinter scene, like the Fitzgerald, suggests the low point of Stahr's courage; in the face of any uncertainty, he is paralyzed, he cannot act. But the next day, as preface for the third central scene in this progression, we see him writing draft after draft on that blue stationery, ignoring all business in his mobbed office. His courage has returned to at least some degree. We never see the contents of that letter, but Stahr gets a call at his home in response. In a quiet voice, Kathleen tells him that she has gotten his letter. He says he must see her, asking her to come away for the weekend. She replies at first that "It's very difficult." Then she says she can't. At his repeated urging, she says "I'll tell you tomorrow." But he refuses to take that for an answer, commanding her again, "No. You must say yes now" (262/122). The camera cuts to Kathleen, in her kitchen nook, saying yes into a phone (262/123).

That phone in Kathleen's kitchen "catches" her in yet another lie, for she's told him at their leave-taking after the first Malibu scenes that she doesn't have one (244/89), perhaps to protect against the possibility of a call when her fiancé might be there. Stahr's behavior here echoes his attempts at domination during the second Malibu interlude, and he's ecstatic that it has apparently worked once more. We're not so convinced as he that his romantic script will evolve the way he's written it for himself, confident with little basis in reality. Her telegram about her marriage that next noon confirms our suspicions, but Kathleen's mystery remains intact, for perhaps, as in the novel, her fiancé simply comes home earlier than expected. On the other hand, she may have told a lie to be rid of Stahr, to pursue her obligation to the American, like Didi. Neither we nor Stahr will know, but the central implication remains the same—Stahr has lost his chance by not acting courageously when he had his opportunity, by "not saying" as Didi's song has it. This time the queer events that so often shape our reality have been profoundly negative.

The novel is much more specific about the implications of the slightly different scene it paints when Stahr asks her for that weekend: "It is your chance Stahr. Better take it now. This is your girl. She can save you, she can worry you back to life. She will take looking after and you will grow strong to do it. But take her now—tell her and take her away. Neither of you knows it, but far away over the night The American has changed his plans. . . . In the morning he will be here" (115).

The coda with Stahr's drunken and fruitless brawl with Brimmer follows rapidly, leading to his dismissal. We see Kathleen act out Stahr's second rendition of the tale of the mysterious girl with the purse, in the final moments burning Stahr's blue envelope instead of the gloves and embracing a man with light brown hair in a brown tweed jacket and brown shoes (158), decidedly not the elegant Stahr. Stahr stares into the camera and says, once more, "I don't want to lose you," and we see him walk into the darkness of that soundstage, a man at the end of a short life, bereft of all he has treasured.

The film version of Fitzgerald's unfinished novel appears fruitfully ambiguous in its conclusion on a number of levels, but the emotional mood of this ending, in general terms, is of tragic loss, both for the potential aesthetic promise of Hollywood and for the possibility of life-mending love that Stahr throws away through a want of courage. Less ambiguously, I'd suggest, Kazan and Pinter do provide an interpretive gloss by explicitly comparing Stahr to a very particular kind of Prufrock. At the second screening session, the one after Stahr has seen Kathleen on the head of the goddess, as he's seeking her phone number, the screen shows us a woman in high dudgeon asking a man in stentorian tones, "How dare you ask me that question." During the first Malibu sequence, Stahr places a pillow under Kathleen's head. She has previously remarked that the incomplete swimming pool at the Malibu house will require a "constant supply of nereids, to plunge and gambol" (238/79) as she ridicules Stahr about being here, alone with his movie projector. Through repetition and echo, Pinter calls our attention to the line three times.[11]

Briefly to refresh the reader's memory of Eliot, late in the poem his persona asks if it would have been "worth it, after all, / . . . among some talk of you and me, / . . . To have squeezed the universe into a ball / To roll it toward some overwhelming question, / . . . If one, settling a pillow by her head, / Should say: "That is not what I meant at all." Prufrock decides that no indeed, he does not have the courage to ask this lady with the pillow by her head that overwhelming question, and as a consequence he lingers in the chambers of the sea "By sea-girls wreathed with seaweed red and brown / Till human voices wake us, and we drown."

Like Prufrock, successful or no, Monroe Stahr has measured out a part of his life with coffee spoons, afraid of the mystery of women, of not knowing the answer to that question, afraid of intimacy and love beyond his romantic illusions. Those nereids will not sing for him, certainly, since he has been so afraid to dare that question. But even if we notice such a pattern of enriching allusion, or are convinced by my noticing it, *The Last Tycoon* is more complicated than most *carpe diem* poems, for it links the romanticism of an industry often reflective of our need to escape reality to the personal downfall of one of its titans. The industry that has absorbed Monroe Stahr's life finally destroys it.

In his recently published book, David Mamet writes: "Perhaps there was a Golden Age of Drama in the movies, perhaps not. And perhaps I delude myself to think that the business was once overseen by filmmakers rather than exploiters. The difference, to me, between those two categories is this: Each wants to make money, but the filmmaker intends to do so by making a film" (120-121). In *The Last Tycoon,* filmmakers Elia Kazan and Harold Pinter capture a wonderfully precise and evocative portrait of Hollywood during its time of crisis, at the beginning of the end of the Golden Age, by focusing narrowly, looking hard, at one of its most talented and creative captains and his personal strengths and weaknesses. It is both ironic and encouraging that in the difficult film climate of twenty years ago the two could make such a rich narrative film adaptation. They have managed to work honorably and well within those conditions that Stahr tells Boxley are always there in one way or another.

Notes

1. I have used Edmund Wilson's 1941 edition of *The Last Tycoon* since that is clearly the version Harold Pinter worked from. I will mine Matthew J. Bruccoli's 1993 edition, *The Love of the Last Tycoon: A Western,* whenever appropriate.

2. See, for example, Crist, Kael and Farber.

3. Thanks to the wonderful staff in the Manuscript Room at the British Library and to the very helpful librarians at the American Film Institute. For a more complete analysis of the film materials in The Harold Pinter Archive at the British Library, please see the descriptive essay by Steven H. Gale and myself in *The Harold Pinter Review: Annual Essays 1995.* The Foundation at the University of Nevada, Las Vegas, provided funds for these research trips, for which I am very grateful.

4. Both Spiegel and Kazan later echo Pinter's ideas about not going beyond chapter 6. See Farber, 15, and Phillips 158-59. The Fitzgerald notes in the Wilson edition include plot lines expanding on the writer's union situation and detailing the increasingly melodramatic battle for control of the studio between Stahr and Pat Brady, a figure largely based on Louis B. Mayer. Both men take out murder contracts on the other; though Stahr decides on a transcontinental plane to abort his plan, ironically he dies when the plane crashes before he can cancel the hit. Though speculation, many critics agree with Ernest Hemingway in his letter to Maxwell Perkins: "Scott would never have finished it with that gigantic, preposterous outline" (Phillips 156).

5. See, for example, Repf.

6. Pagination throughout refers to Pinter's published script. The first numeral is the page number, the second Pinter's scene number. Where the dialogue in the film differs from the original, I will list only the scene number, quoting from my transcription.

7. Spiegel says that the inspiration for the guide sequence sprang from his taking Pinter on a Hollywood tour during a three-week visit. They met a guide with the studio for forty years, who told of Garbo often seeing him and complimenting him on his work, which made him cry (Alpert 11).

8. Boulting's casting and performance has evoked a good bit of negative criticism. Producer Spiegel says that Pinter's initial response to her tests was that he needed to find an actress, that Boulting couldn't get into repertory in London. Pleased with Boulting's work, in the interview Spiegel bets that Pinter is now eating his words (Alpert 14). In a 6 June 1996 letter to me, Pinter writes: "I thought the finished film did have a number of virtues but was destroyed at its very centre by the casting of the girl, who simply couldn't act."

9. In an unpublished 1984 interview, I asked Pinter about several such arresting images or scenes in his filmscripts, centering briefly on the one in *The Pumpkin Eater* where a mad Jamaican minister comes to Jo's distinctly upper class door. Pinter replied that our experience was indeed often that way, that "a mad Jamaican may appear at our door at any moment." That captures something of the same spirit of the "miracle of the queerness of experience" that Millgate finds in Fitzgerald, which I think runs throughout Pinter's canon.

10. "Eastwick" does not appear as a "named" character in the published script, surfacing in handwritten revisions in one of the two scripts at the American Film Institute.

11. None of these images occur in the novel. Stahr's action with the pillow appears in Pinter's published script as do the repeated references to the nereids. The screening clip with "How dare you ask me that question" does not appear in the published script nor in the scripts at the British Museum but is included in the handwritten revisions in the American Film Institute script.

Works Cited

Alpert, Hollis. *"The Last Tycoon." American Film.* March 1971, 8-14.

Cahn, Victor L. *Gender and Power in the Plays of Harold Pinter.* New York: St. Martins, 1993.

Ciment, Michael. "Visually Speaking: 'Reunion': Harold Pinter" (an interview). *Film Comment* 25 (1989), 20-22.

Crist, Judith. "Tycoon." *Saturday Review.* 11 Dec. 1976.

Esslin, Martin. *Pinter: The Playwright.* London: Methuen, 1984.

Farber, Stephen. "Hollywood Takes on 'The Last Tycoon.'" *New York Times.* 21 March 1976, 2:15.

Fitzgerald, F. Scott. *The Last Tycoon.* Ed. Edmund Wilson. New York: Charles Scribner, 1941.

The Love of the Last Tycoon: A Western. Ed. Matthew J. Bruccoli. New York: Cambridge, 1993.

Gale, Steven H., and Christopher C. Hudgins. "The Harold Pinter Archive in the British Library." *The Pinter Review: Annual Essays 1995.* Ed. Francis Gillen and Steven H. Gale. Tampa: Univ of Tampa, 1996.

Kael, Pauline. "Tycoon." *The New Yorker.* 29 Nov 1976.

Kazan, Elia. *The Last Tycoon.* Paramount. Screenplay, Harold Pinter. Sam Spiegel, Producer. Robert De Niro, Tony Curtis, Robert Mitchum, Jeanne Moreau, Jack Nicholson, Donald Pleasence, Ingrid Boulting.

Mamet, David. "The Screenplay." *Make Believe Town.* New York: Little, Brown, 1996, 117-125.

Marsh, Joss Lutz. "Fitzgerald, *Gatsby,* and *The Last Tycoon*: the 'American Dream' and the Hollywood Dream Factory—Part II." *Literature Film Quarterly* 20 (1992), 102-108.

Millgate, Michael. "Scott Fitzgerald as Social Novelist: Statement and Technique in *The Last Tycoon.*" *F. Scott Fitzgerald: Critical Assessments, Vol. III.* Ed. Henry Claridge. Near Robertsbridge, East Sussex: Helm, 1991. 283-9.

Noss, John B. *Man's Religions.* New York: Macmillan, 1967.

Phillips, Gene D., S.J. *Fiction, Film and F. Scott Fitzgerald.* Chicago: Loyola, 1986.

Pinter, Harold. *The Last Tycoon.* Typescript. The Mayer Collection. The American Film Institute.

——. "*The Last Tycoon.*" The Pinter Archive at the British Library. Typescripts, correspondence, notes. Boxes 30-32.

——. *The Last Tycoon. The French Lieutenant's Woman and Other Screen Plays.* London: Faber, 1982. 191-277.

——. Letter to the author. 6 June 1996.

——. *Lolita.* An unpublished screenplay. Author's collection.

Repf, Joanna E. "*The Last Tycoon* or 'A Nickel for the Movies.'" *Literature/Film Quarterly* 16 (1988), 78-81.

Silver, Charles, and Mary Corliss. "Hollywood Underwater: Elia Kazan on *The Last Tycoon.*" *Film Comment.* Jan.-Feb. 1977, 40-46.

R. Barton Palmer (essay date 1997)

SOURCE: Palmer, R. Barton. "Hollywood in Crisis: Tennessee Williams and the Evolution of the Adult Film." In *The Cambridge Companion to Tennessee Williams,* edited by Matthew C. Roudané, pp. 204-31. Cambridge: Cambridge University Press, 1997.

[*In the following essay, Palmer traces the impact and influence of Williams's writing on the development of American theater and film.*]

WILLIAMS ON FILM: SOME PRELIMINARY
THOUGHTS

In the English-speaking world, the two principal performance arts, theatre and film, have developed together in the twentieth century. An important common element of the British and American commercial theatres is that each has enjoyed a cooperative and mutually beneficial relationship with the respective national cinema since the beginning of the sound film era. In the case of Great Britain, this relationship was eased for several decades by the proximity of the commercial film studios, most of which were once located in the Greater London area, to the West End theatrical district; such proximity made it possible, in many cases almost inevitable, for creative personnel in the theatre to work part-time on film projects, and vice-versa. The move of the American film business to California from its New York base at the beginning of the studio period (c. 1912-20) posed difficulties for actors, writers, directors, and production artists wishing to work in both fields, and yet many have done so. Indeed, in the nineties, this trend shows no sign of abating, even with the dispersal of film production into a number of regional centers outside California.

Throughout the studio period (c. 1920-70), Hollywood benefited not only from the labors of those who had been trained on and worked mainly for the commercial American theatre. American filmmakers also looked to Broadway as they looked to the bestseller list: for source materials, for "properties" whose appeal to American consumers had already been well demonstrated. A play fresh from a successful Broadway run is also "pre-sold" in the sense that many filmgoers are acquainted with it even if they haven't attended a performance, and thus, so the industry reasoning runs, may be the more easily persuaded to see a film version. The result is predictable: many successful American commercial theatre productions are very attractive to filmmakers and regularly provide the source for successful film releases.

Thus we should expect that the widespread success achieved by and critical acclaim bestowed upon Tennessee Williams during his postwar Broadway career would have made his plays and other works desirable properties for cinematic adaptation. In fact, all of Williams's stage successes have been turned into films that, on the whole, have been received well by audiences and critics alike. However, the story of the transference of Williams's plays is by no means a simple one. The film business and the commercial theatre are institutions with quite different histories, requirements, traditions, and positions within the culture industry. Thus each had quite distinct reasons for valuing Williams as a writer and vastly divergent modes of shaping for presentation the dramatic texts he wrote. The result is that the Tennessee Williams who is central to the history of the American commercial theatre is substantially different from the Tennessee Williams who played a significant role in the development of the postwar American cinema. To judge the impact of his work on American culture, a consideration in some depth of both histories or versions of the author is necessary.

The purpose of this essay is to offer a critical history of the early and most important stage of the relationship between Tennessee Williams and the Hollywood cinema. That relationship, extending for more than two decades, is complex and multileveled, much more so than in the case of other American playwrights whose popularity resulted in movie versions of their works. With Eugene O'Neill, Arthur Miller, or William Inge, or, indeed, every other American playwright, of sole importance are the films in question, the screen versions themselves, which may be plumbed for their aesthetic, sociological, and institutional values or which may be examined to determine the whys and wherefores of the adaptation process.

With Williams, in contrast, such a concentration on the films would disregard a connection between the author and Hollywood that is arguably much more important. For unlike other noted playwrights, Williams's work strongly influenced the development of the film industry itself. Indeed, it is hard to imagine the course of fifties and early sixties cinematic history without his plays as source material; and if we could imagine such a history, it would be quite different from the one that actually played out on the screen. To my knowledge, no other author through his works alone has had this kind of influence on the history of a national cinema.

From this point of view, seven of the fifteen films based on Williams's work are of major importance: *The Glass Menagerie* (1950), *A Streetcar Named Desire* (1951), *The Rose Tattoo* (1955), *Baby Doll* (1956), *The Fugitive Kind* (1960), *Cat on a Hot Tin Roof* (1958), and *Sweet Bird of Youth* (1962). Though they have been analyzed by a number of scholars, all of the film versions of Williams's plays merit further, in-depth treatment, at least in terms of discussing the adaptation process, which raises interesting cultural and aesthetic questions that would in every instance repay further examination. Regrettably, space limitations make that impossible here. Focusing on Williams's impact on the cinema means that this chapter often departs from purely textual analysis. In fact, it has proved necessary to offer here a somewhat detailed account of developments within the film industry. These may not seem at first closely connected to the issues raised by adaptation, which is often approached formally through an assessment of the changes that have been made in transferring a source text from one medium to another. However, adaptation in the case of Williams must be understood in a larger sense, as designating how one medium comes to relate to another in a process that is centered upon but certainly not confined to the generation of texts. The discussion that follows of Williams's relationship to Hollywood will, I hope, make this point clear.

A NEW TYPE OF HOLLYWOOD FILM

Tennessee Williams rose to prominence during the immediate postwar era that witnessed a revitalization, perhaps even a rebirth of the American commercial theatre. Along with other new voices and innovators, most prominently Arthur Miller and William Inge, Williams succeeded in transforming the customary themes and form of the serious Broadway drama that had held sway during the early forties. These plays often featured high-minded or politically engaged comment on the American scene expressed by somewhat predictable patterns of exposition and resolution. Audiences were afforded intellectual stimulation and "dramatic" satisfactions of a traditional kind, with clear-cut divisions between rising action, climax, and falling action. A useful example is Lillian Hellman's critically acclaimed and commercially successful *Watch on the Rhine,* where the morality play opposition of democratic patriot to opportunistic fascist fellow traveler is resolved after much suspense by the former's cold-blooded elimination of the latter. The protagonist, appropriately named Freidank ("freethinker"), agonizes over the need for such killing, thereby exemplifying both a social democratic hatred of war and a desire for peace based on international comradeship. With its timely themes and intense drawing-room dramatics, the play was quickly and easily transformed by Hollywood into a successful star vehicle for Bette Davis (1943, directed by Broadway old hand Herman Shumlin).

For Williams, breaking with this Broadway tradition meant abandoning a moralistic or political analysis of American society for an exploration of the psychosexual inner lives of the emotionally traumatized and socially marginalized, those either dispossessed of happiness or indisposed to grasp it. His main characters became tortured loners who had been bypassed by the great American dream of public acclaim and bourgeois material success, often because of some sexual crime or indiscretion that alienated them from more respectable others. The drama that entangled them was always personal, seldom political, a function of complexly intimate relations with family or with fellow travelers met by chance on the road of self-confrontation.

Williams realized the usually tragic and often violent lives of such characters through a poetically rich blend of realist and expressionist techniques. The power and emotional intensity of his dramas revealed well-made theme plays to be by comparison mistakenly committed to the portrayal of irrelevant public selves. Not surprisingly, Williams's plays required new forms of stagecraft because missing fourth-wall sets often did not suit his more fluid conceptions of time and space; his characters, in turn, could only be fully realized by a different kind of naturalistic acting capable of representing conflicted, multilayered selves: the so-called "Method" that had recently come into vogue with the founding of the Actors Studio.

Williams, perhaps most notably with his early smash-hit productions such as *A Streetcar Named Desire* and *Sweet Bird of Youth,* appealed to a sophisticated and well-educated audience of playgoers much affected by the growing fashion for psychotherapy and the widespread endorsement of Freudian theory as an explanation of the human condition. They applauded Williams for putting sex on the theatrical agenda and sympathized with the guilt-ridden vulnerability of his protagonists. Responding to a contradictory historical moment that featured an intensifying Cold War but the proclamation of the "end of ideology," these playgoers did not resent the nearly complete absence of social and political themes in Williams's work, or the pessimistic bleakness of his vision. Because Williams was committed to thematizing sex and psychological discontent in new, more central ways, his plays seemed startlingly realistic, appeared despite their poetry and intellectual schemata to move beyond the restricting decorum of the previous theatrical age and make direct contact with life as it was really lived, warts and all.

Disdainful of an American cinema devoted to happy endings and flat characters, Broadway audiences were eager for an art that provided difficult satisfactions rather than the deceptive pleasures of wish fulfillment. In short, the vein of taste mined by Williams, Miller, Inge, and others was resolutely high cultural, accommodating of tragic themes and modernist techniques, scornful of traditional pieties, including what had hitherto been a more or less tacit ban on those "adult" subjects such as homosexuality, drug addiction, sexual predation, and prostitution so central to Williams's conception of dramatically arresting character. Catering to a minority, elite culture, the Broadway stage in the immediate postwar era could (and did) readily adapt to the new vision offered by Williams and others.

In contrast, the Hollywood film industry by the late forties had established itself solidly in another, rather distant area of cultural production: providing for general audiences clean, wholesome entertainment conforming to a detailed series of protocols—the Production Code. Based on Victorian notions of uplift, the Code proclaimed, in part, that "Art can be morally evil in its effects. This is the case clearly enough with unclean art, indecent books, suggestive drama. The effect on the lives of men and women is obvious."[1] Hollywood thus was committed to banishing from significant representation or often even mere mention the themes Williams found so compelling and unavoidable. This was by no means a situation unique to Williams. Literary modernism in general, with its distaste for didacticism and commitment to the truth, however unpleasant, of human behavior, could not easily be accommodated to the demands of a medium that endorsed older, opposed theories of art and cultural production.

In 1947, when Williams was making a name for himself with the popular and critically acclaimed New York production of *A Streetcar Named Desire,* Hollywood films were still closely vetted by the Production Code Administration, a censorship office that had been founded by the film producers themselves in 1934 in response to intense Catholic lobbying efforts for "cleaner" films and over which a prominent Catholic layman, Joseph Breen, still magisterially presided. The Code, and the censors who put it into force, demanded not only that various aspects of

human existence be avoided by Hollywood films, but that these vehicles of mass entertainment should also be structured by the central principle of nineteenth-century melodrama: evil was to be punished and good rewarded, while any sympathy for wrongdoing should be eliminated by compensating moral value (such as the unlikely reform in the last five minutes of hitherto enthusiastic sinners).

During the forties, the Hollywood studios were in general careful not to offend the more traditionally minded within their audience and eagerly promoted an idealized vision of American values and society. This was especially apparent for the duration of the war when Hollywood, in exchange for being allowed to continue to produce and exhibit films, energetically supported the aims of the government, making many morale-boosting and enlistment-encouraging films that emphasized traditional American optimism and solidly bourgeois values. The marketing strategy of appealing to a general, undifferentiated audience while not offending the morally conservative among them proved immensely successful. By war's end box-office receipts hit an all-time high; weekly attendance almost equaled the nation's population, which was at that time almost 120 million, a truly staggering figure that indicates how central moviegoing had become for many, who must have attended religiously numerous times a week.

Though film producers were always eager for material of demonstrated popularity—stories, novels or plays—they could transform into films, such an industry would seem to have little use for most of Williams's plays, which might be unprofitably restricted in their appeal because they were too arty. Furthermore, what Williams wrote was almost certainly too adult to make into movies that would meet with the ready approval of the Production Code Administration. The one obvious exception was *The Glass Menagerie,* made into a film version that was released in 1950 and directed by Irving Rapper. Williams's first stage success featured no violence and only, by way of sexual content, the Oedipal themes conventional in *Bildungsroman* narrative, at that time a Hollywood staple. *The Glass Menagerie* dramatizes the treacherous and sometimes uncrossable passage into adult life as well as the discontents of romance for women who must await the call of sexual desire. Amanda Wingfield is eager for her shy daughter Laura to be swept away by a "gentleman caller" even as, paradoxically, this overbearing mother makes it difficult for Laura's brother Tom to grow into healthy independence and sexual maturity (the conventional sexual politics of the film version are discussed in more detail below). Yet even this play, to Williams's chagrin, offended Joseph Breen in part when a scenario was submitted to him; the zealous censor thought that the relationship between Tom and Laura bordered on an incestuous attachment. Breen demanded excision of some of the dialogue in the emotional *scène à deux* where brother and sister acknowledge their mutual affection prior to Tom's departure for the Merchant Marine.

After 1946, Hollywood's most profitable year, however, the fortunes of the studios shifted radically. And in a short time what Williams had to offer in his groundbreaking later plays seemed not only acceptable, but desirable. In fact, the somewhat surprising result is that Williams soon became the most adapted of America's dramatists, with his plays and even a novella, *The Roman Spring of Mrs. Stone* (1961), providing the source for some of Hollywood's most critically acclaimed, most popular, most financially successful films during the fifties and early sixties. Against all odds, Williams's texts became key sources in the development of an "adult" form of cinematic entertainment, one radically different from the standard studio fare of the Hollywood boom during the middle forties.

At the end of the 1940s, the American film industry experienced a number of difficulties that led to a rapid and long-term decline in attendance and profits. An essential element of Hollywood financial success had been vertical integration, with production, distribution, and first-run theatrical exhibition existing under one corporate umbrella. Such economic muscle allowed the major studios to corner screen time and hence rental returns through blind bidding (the securing of exhibition contracts before a trade show of the film) and block booking (the offering of desired films for exhibition only in a block of less desirable ones). In a 1948 case involving Paramount, the US Supreme Court ruled that these trade practices and vertical integration itself were illegal. The major studios were all subsequently forced to sign consent decrees that led to their divestiture of theatrical holdings. Without a secure market for their product, the studios could no longer function as "factories" turning out hundreds of films annually by assembly-line methods. A gradual switch was made to one-off production that emphasized blockbuster or "special" projects, with each film the result of ad hoc financial and contractual arrangements. At the same time, payrolls were trimmed and the vast studio infrastructures dismantled.

Deprived of its formula for economic success, Hollywood lost its traditional main market as well: middle-class urbanites who lived close to downtown and neighborhood theatres. Lured by suddenly cheap housing, this class of Americans moved en masse to newly built suburbs, then far from movie theatres and frequently off public transportation routes. A substitute for cinema-going that was home-centered soon appeared in the form of television, which expanded rapidly in the course of the fifties until, by the end of the decade, most families in the country owned a set and tuned in many hours a week. With the establishment of a consumer economy devoted to the production of "durables" and the emergence of entertainment alternatives, Hollywood's traditional customers increasingly chose to spend their discretionary income on washing machines, vacation travel, and do-it-yourselfing. By the beginning of the fifties, weekly attendance was down to about sixty percent of immediate postwar levels, while production costs soared in an otherwise booming economy. Thousands of movie theatres around the country closed their doors forever as it appeared that Americans after forty years had finally wearied of their fascination with the motion pictures.

Producers attempted to reverse their declining fortunes with two principal strategies, one of which was particularly important in bringing the works of Tennessee Williams to the screen. First, the competition from television encouraged a differentiation of product as filmmakers attempted to outclass the fuzzy, black and white images and tinny audio then available on the tube by impressing viewers with wide-screen Technicolor epics in stereophonic sound. With its limited budgets, television programming could offer little in the way of stars or spectacle; blockbuster films of the period, by contrast, normally featured "all-star casts," exotic location shooting, and bravura action set-pieces in an attempt to woo back paying customers. This strategy was at least a partial success as the studios managed to stay in business.

Television, however, was also limited in a second way that Hollywood hoped to exploit: by the new medium's status as a governmentally regulated industry subject to Federal Communication Commission (FCC) guidelines, including production protocols similar to, but sometimes even more stringent than Hollywood's own, which were, of course, industry generated. If television had taken over to some degree Hollywood's former function as the provider of audiovisual entertainment for a mass public of all ages and tastes, then the film industry could colonize a new area of production, one whose popularity with a segment of the filmgoing public had been established by the exhibition successes of art films, especially Italian neorealist productions like *Bicycle Thief* (Vittorio de Sica, American release 1949). Though film exhibition in general suffered greatly from the late forties through the fifties, theatres that specialized in screening art films, mostly from Europe, became much more numerous and profitable at this time, indicating that there was a loyal audience of educated adults who would pay to see a "film" even if they despised Hollywood "movies" as the mindless products of a hopelessly compromised culture industry.

Because European films were not produced with input from the Production Code Administration (PCA), they often transgressed the official standards the industry had established, especially with regard to sexual representation. In fact, the term "art film" by decade's end had become, if only in part, a euphemism for soft core pornography. Normally all films, including imports, needed a certificate of approval from the PCA in order to secure exhibition contracts. *Bicycle Thief*'s importers were refused such a certificate by Joseph Breen, who objected to two scenes: one in which a young boy pauses by the side of a wall, apparently to relieve himself; and another in which a thief is pursued into a bordello whose inhabitants, though fully clothed and otherwise decent, are obviously engaged in the world's oldest profession. Despite the film's renown as an internationally acclaimed artistic triumph and protests from the American liberal establishment, Breen stuck by his decision.

Surprisingly, *Bicycle Thief* enjoyed an immensely successful run in the teeth of Hollywood's official condemnation,

eventually and improbably winning the Oscar for best foreign film in a turnabout that chagrined and embarrassed
Breen. Even the Catholic Church refused to go along with
the PCA and did not put the film on its forbidden list. The
lesson for film producers was obvious. There was a market
for films that were "artistic" and violated or at least tested
hitherto generally accepted limitations on the representation of sexual themes; the PCA had lost clout in its defense of what now began to seem unnecessarily old-
fashioned or prudish standards, and exhibitors could do
well even with controversial films that lacked PCA approval, but only if these could be justified artistically.

A STREETCAR NAMED DESIRE: THE FIRST ADULT FILM

Conditions within the industry, in other words, were right
for the production of American films on the European
model, films that would be both intellectually satisfying
and titillating. This was a trend to which Williams's
groundbreaking plays could make an important contribution, provided that they were adapted in the proper fashion. At first, however, Hollywood only showed interest in
Tennessee Williams's more conventional work. The studios' initial experience with the young author was with a
play not much different from the accustomed Broadway
serious drama of the period. *The Glass Menagerie* bears
the marks of strong influence from the Lillian Hellman
family problem play (*The Little Foxes* [1939] or, perhaps
even a closer analogue, *The Children's Hour* [1934]). Interestingly enough, it had first been written as a screenplay
for Metro-Goldwyn-Mayer (MGM) during Williams's un-
eventful employment there (it was rejected as unsuitable).
After the play's outstanding Broadway success, however,
the Hollywood studios (including a chagrined MGM)
fought a bidding war for the rights to film it, with Warner
Brothers proving eventually victorious.

The Glass Menagerie was adapted to fit a time-honored
and commercially successful formula, with Williams's poignant and ambiguous memory play transformed into a
straightforward melodrama that attested to the persever-
ance and final triumph of its sympathetically evoked female leads. Though radically different from Williams's
conception of the endearing but pathetic Laura, Jane Wyman here reprised her critically acclaimed role as a handicapped but resilient young woman. In Williams's story,
she is a cripple rather than the deaf mute whose portrayal
won her the Oscar in *Johnny Belinda* (Jean Negulesco,
1948). Like most women's pictures of the period, Rapper's version of *The Glass Menagerie* ends happily, with
family members reconciled and Laura eagerly awaiting the
imminent arrival of a flesh and blood gentleman caller to
rescue her from the discontents of maturation.

The tragic tone imparted by the playwright to Laura's isolation, Amanda's delusions of grandeur, and Tom's self-
serving reconstructions of the familial past needed to be
altered substantially in the transference to the screen if a
conventional woman's picture were to be the result. And

Williams was appalled at what was done to his play. Rapper's film was, in the playwright's opinion, "the most awful travesty of the play I've ever seen . . . horribly
mangled by the people who did the film script."[2]

Nonetheless, the core elements of *The Glass Menagerie*,
once provided with a more upbeat interpretation and resolution, were eminently suitable source material for a standard Hollywood film. Not only does the play, with its social realist perspective, make an important connection
between psychological and economic hardships, a common element in many of the gritty film dramas of the period; it also, except for flashback narration by a character,
then an almost standard technique in Hollywood films,
avoids modernist dramatic devices and moves steadily,
Ibsen-like, from exposition, through complication, to an
emotion-revealing conclusion. Hollywood films depended
above all else upon an unambiguous and dynamic narrative to hold audience interest. And Williams provides the
basis for a strong one in this play even though, characteristically, this element of dramatic construction did not particularly fascinate him and he sometimes experienced difficulties with devising a second act that would resolve the
issues raised in the first.

Though the playwright was hardly pleased, the film version of *The Glass Menagerie* was moderately successful
and bears close comparison with Rapper's greatest triumph in the woman's picture genre: *Now, Voyager* (1942),
a much-praised Bette Davis vehicle. That film also explores the depth of female discontents with a gender system that accommodates women, if at all, as passive objects of desire whose appearance and manner mean
everything. *Now, Voyager*'s at-first hysterical main character, Charlotte Vale, successfully struggles to achieve a pro-
visional independence and adulthood, though she is denied
the satisfactions of married life. Like the film version of
The Glass Menagerie, Now, Voyager offers an obviously
contrived happy ending, a wish fulfillment that entertainingly transcends the tragic conclusion of such exploration,
which is the developmental dead-end of lonely, barren
spinsterhood. Though oppressed by mothers who refuse to
stop infantilizing them, both Charlotte and Laura prove in
the end able to embrace maturity—the message of uplift
most common in the many woman's pictures of the period
that deal with young adulthood.

In contrast, Williams's second stage success, *A Streetcar
Named Desire,* though it likewise offers two sympathetic
women characters, could not have been transformed even
by the knowledgeable and experienced Irving Rapper into
anything resembling a woman's picture. With its revelation and dramatization of sexual misconduct, its delineation of a horrifying descent into madness, its portrayal of
women driven and even controlled by desire, the play, in
fact, offered themes that could not be accommodated to
any standard Hollywood schema. Though Williams had
garnered the acclaim of the critics and a Pulitzer Prize for
A Streetcar Named Desire, which continued to pack in
standing-room-only crowds, filmmakers were for two years

uninterested in pursuing the possibility of a screen adaptation—with one exception, William Wyler, one of Hollywood's most commercially successful and esteemed directors.

Correctly reading the changes in popular taste and impatient with the restrictions posed upon American filmmaking while imports demonstrated that the cinema was capable of producing sophisticated art, Wyler thought *Streetcar* would be a commercial success as a vehicle for Bette Davis, an actress he had worked with on prestigious adaptations of Lillian Hellman and Somerset Maugham. He recognized that, alone of noted American writers, Tennessee Williams had authored a text that could be the source of a film both artistic and sensational, the potent marketing combination of many European art films. Davis had played strong-minded, sexually aggressive Southern women twice in her career for Wyler, first in the Warners antebellum epic *Jezebel* (1939) and later in his acclaimed version of *The Little Foxes* (1941). By the late forties, Davis had developed a screen persona nicely balanced between sympathetic roles and more villainous portrayals, an ambiguity Wyler took advantage of when he directed Davis in *The Letter* (1940), where she is successfully cast as Somerset Maugham's most notorious heroine, a seemingly ordinary and respectable woman capable of the most outrageous sexual deception and violent crime, a character similar in important ways to Blanche DuBois.

Davis would likely have made a powerful Blanche, but Wyler was so discouraged by Breen's initial pronouncements on the project that he abandoned it, turning instead to Sidney Kingsley's Broadway hit *Detective Story* (1950) for his next film. This play dealt with, in part, an abortion doctor rather than a rapist, and Wyler more easily negotiated approval from Breen, despite the fact that many alterations were required from the PCA before a certificate was forthcoming.

Though it likewise raised strenuous objections from the censor, *Detective Story* was a very different kind of property from *Streetcar*. Kingsley's drama treats sexual subject matter that was from a PCA perspective objectionable, but it is hardly an erotic text, with its dramatic center the psychological breakdown a New York detective experiences as he tries to go about the performance of his duties. Williams's play, in contrast, not only treated sexual themes prominent on the Code's forbidden list—the homosexuality of Blanche's late husband, her evidently aggressive sexual appetite, and Stanley's violent rape of his wife's sister. It also exuded animalistic sexuality, with Stanley's attack the culmination of profound feelings of attraction/repulsion between the two main characters.

If, as Williams has emphasized, the rape in part represents the destruction of an old-fashioned gentility by the harsher, material forces of modern life, it also fittingly resolves Blanche's suspension between manipulative illusion and self-awareness. Taken by the brutish Stanley, Blanche becomes the seducer seduced and must face up to her own compulsive, predatory sexual urges. Her madness results not only from the undeniable horror of violation, but from the recognition that she has played a role in its advent. The complexity of Williams's conception is that Stanley and Blanche are compounded equally of sympathetic and unsympathetic elements. And the dramatic power of their explosive confrontation derives from the ways in which this evolving relationship is highly sexualized, with Stella's passion for Stanley and Mitch's carefully orchestrated desire for Blanche functioning as illuminating counterpoint.

In short, *Streetcar* not only takes sex as a theme; the play represents the power and destructiveness of desire, constructing itself as an erotic object that seduces the playgoer into an eagerness for the fateful, final encounter. Despite its hard-boiled look at sex, *Streetcar*, however, is never merely crude or suggestive like much popular American fiction, especially the works of Mickey Spillane, James M. Cain, and Erskine Caldwell, all of whom were notorious at the time for treating similar themes and enjoyed a wide readership. Williams's artfully ambiguous characterizations of Stanley and Blanche, and the poignant poetry of the play's dialogue, make *Streetcar* a powerfully moving if bleak examination of the human condition. Or, as director Elia Kazan, who was quite conversant with bottom-line Hollywood thinking, told film producer Jack Warner, "1/ It is about the three Fs; 2/ It has class."[3]

Remarkably, Williams's play was transferred to the screen with even fewer alterations than the playwright had suffered through while watching a Hollywood version of *The Glass Menagerie* emerge. The successful Broadway run, helped by the blatantly steamy title, had given the play a notoriety that, with its implied promise of commercial success, appealed to talent agent Charles Feldman, who bought the screen rights with the hope of breaking into the film business as a producer. If the pessimism of Williams's vision in *The Glass Menagerie* had been judged—and probably correctly—as box-office poison by Warner Brothers, the playwright's unremitting portrayal of sexual compulsion and violence in *A Streetcar Named Desire* was seen by Feldman as the quality most potentially attractive to filmgoers, despite the tragic consequences for Blanche of enduring the journey of desire to its bitter end.

Such suffering for a less-than-virtuous female main character did not violate then-acceptable notions of a poetically just ending. In fact, a popular film series at the time, what is now known as *film noir* or "dark cinema," often featured sexually aggressive or transgressive *femmes fatales* who met with violent retribution at the hands of the men they victimized. Functioning as a cultural other to the woman's picture, *noir* films thematized a self-righteous and often unambiguous misogyny, with fatally attractive women winding up dead, imprisoned, or otherwise punished. *Streetcar*'s downbeat conclusion, in other words, would be acceptable to filmgoers used to similar portrayals of feminine misadventure. Williams's change of subject matter from his first to second play meant that as far as film adaptation was concerned his dramatic conception would be less altered.

The irony involved, of course, is that *The Glass Menagerie* was in most ways closer to the kind of films Hollywood had become accustomed to making. But by a happy coincidence of authorial vision and cultural trends, Williams had subsequently begun to write just what some within the film business correctly thought would be hugely successful. *A Streetcar Named Desire* was just similar enough to the *film noir* to be easily marketable. And yet its startling differences from the standard Hollywood movie in the representation of sexual themes eminently suited Williams's play to be the source of the first Hollywood production in a new genre: the adult art film.

Afraid, perhaps, of controversy, the major studios all passed on *Streetcar*. But with the newly emerging possibilities of independent production, a screen version could be conceived and planned outside the mainstream of the business. Williams himself took a very active part in the project, an unusual step for an author at the time. However, he was very eager that his hit play be filmed and with Feldman's help approached Elia Kazan, who had directed the stage production, in hopes of convincing him to oversee the film version as well.

Kazan's career at the time usefully exemplifies how it was possible to work successfully both in Hollywood and on Broadway. In 1950, he was Broadway's hottest director, having brought to the stage what are arguably the three most important serious plays of the immediate postwar era: Arthur Miller's *All My Sons* (1947) and *Death of a Salesman* (1949) and Williams's *Streetcar* (1947). Kazan, however, had also achieved critical and commercial success with quite different film projects, all more or less standard genre pieces with strong melodramatic elements: the most important of these being *A Tree Grows in Brooklyn* (1945), *Gentleman's Agreement* (1947), and *Pinky* (1949), the last of which was coincidentally the highest-grossing film of that year.

Kazan was at first reluctant to do the project, not foreseeing, perhaps, that he could preside over the making of a very different kind of film, one that would not be forced to conform to Hollywood's Victorian aesthetic. Kazan's eventual agreement to what Williams and Feldman proposed altered the director's Hollywood career. The film version of *Streetcar* he directed would inaugurate a commercial American art cinema to which Kazan himself, immediately thereafter abandoning more conventional melodrama, would go on to make a number of notable contributions: *Viva Zapata!* (1952), *On the Waterfront* (1954), *East of Eden* (1955), and *A Face in the Crowd* (1957).

Williams thought, and rightly so, that Kazan's participation was essential to the preservation of his vision, for the director had been in large measure responsible for the effective shaping and nuancing of the complex dramatic elements in *Streetcar*. Feldman, however, knew that Kazan

was perhaps even more vital to the making of financial and technical arrangements. Kazan was not only a directorial genius, but a shrewd businessman eager for the commercial success his films had achieved. By now, he knew how to oversee a well-run production and keep financial backers happy. Persuaded by his friendship for Williams and the $175,000 fee he was offered (a huge amount at the time), Kazan undertook the job. Feldman was then quite quickly able to secure the agreement of Warner Brothers to finance a substantial part of the production costs. The studio would also loan its facilities and technicians in return for distribution rights and a profit share.

In the emerging world of fifties film production, such arrangements would soon be standard, profitable ones for independent producers like Feldman who were willing to take risks on unusual, perhaps marginal projects in the hope of turning a substantial profit. The importance of these contextual factors for the particular film version of Williams's play that eventually emerged can hardly be overemphasized. The conditions within the American film industry that resulted in large part from the studios' financial difficulties made it possible for Williams's play to be purchased and conceived as an independent commercial project, with hopes of its being adapted in a more or less "faithful" fashion. Kazan's version of *Streetcar* would have been unthinkable during the heights of studio success just a few years previously when steady profits were being made from a very different kind of product.

But more than financial arrangements were necessary if this project were to be successfully realized. The next and perhaps most difficult hurdle for Feldman, Williams, and Kazan to clear was the PCA, then weakened somewhat by the defiantly successful release of *Bicycle Thief* but still a potent force in Hollywood. The arrangement with Warner Brothers specified that the film version of *Streetcar* would have to be awarded a PCA certificate; there was to be no possibility of an uncertificated release if Williams and Feldman were to live up to their contract. Initial negotiations with the PCA resulted in objections to three aspects of Williams's play, the first two of which were settled rather easily by compromise. Blanche's husband would no longer be identified as a homosexual, but simply as a weak (read impotent) man, a change Kazan was actually in favor of since he disliked the suggestion of "perversion." Blanche's sexual hunger for young men, her "nymphomania" (in fifties terms), would have to be downplayed to make it less obvious to younger viewers but still clear enough to more experienced adults. Kazan was quite well experienced with the rhetoric Hollywood directors, writers, and actors had developed in order to represent, but only by nuance and suggestion, the facts of sexual desire and activity. He would have no problem in making sure that Blanche's disreputable sexual history was something only the more sophisticated could infer and did not think that these changes of emphasis would mar Williams's vision.

Breen also wanted the rape scene excised or somehow relieved of its terrifying significance, and this was a change neither Kazan nor Williams could agree to. Here Breen was adamant that even a nuanced treatment was objectionable, but, Williams and Kazan countered, the rape was the plot's central event, the necessary culmination of the highly charged, contradictory relationship between Stanley and Blanche that holds the spectator's interest from the outset. Were it removed in some fashion or another resolution substituted, the story, and the characters whose development it traced, would no longer make any coherent sense.

Though the Code was unambiguous on this point and Breen was personally unsympathetic to the artistic problems involved, the PCA found itself in a difficult position as it attempted to respond to a rapid evolution in popular taste and yet maintain its role as guarantor of a moralistic rationale for Hollywood films. After the *Bicycle Thief* embarrassment, Breen could ill afford another public incident that suggested his office was narrow-minded in its opposition to modern art. Williams's play, after all, had won the Pulitzer Prize. And yet any obvious endorsement of the screenplay proposed by Kazan and Williams would set a dangerous precedent for future decisions. Sensing Breen's dilemma, Kazan decided to avoid overt disagreement. The rejected script would stand. When shooting it, Kazan simply did not respond to Breen's objections that the rape scene be removed, staging and filming the sequence of events subtly if unmistakably. After viewing the completed film, Breen demanded some minor changes in the ending of the story, with the result that Stella appears to be resolved never again to trust her brutal husband, an interesting example of compensating moral value. But the core of Williams's drama remained on screen for filmgoers to enjoy and ponder, the Code that hitherto had prevented such screen treatment of sexuality having been breached. Kazan's version of Williams's play thereby inaugurated a new kind of Hollywood film, one whose increasing frankness and explicitness would demand by 1967 the abandonment of the Code altogether and the development of a ratings system to take its place.

The film's outstanding success with audiences was aided considerably by a casting thoroughly suited to the particular requirements of the commercial film industry. Though Jessica Tandy had created an excellent Blanche for the initial New York stage production that otherwise served as the basis of Kazan's film, Warners demanded an established film star in the featured female lead, standard industry practice at a time when marketing was based on an individual film's generic affiliations and star players. The choice of Vivien Leigh, who had appeared as Blanche in the London production, was fortuitous. More so than Broadway plays, Hollywood films depended on what we might term the "production history" of stars as well as their public images to create complex and appealing resonances of meaning.

Who better to portray the dark underside of Southern belledom than the actress famous for the screen incarnation of fiction's most famous Southern belle in *Gone with the Wind* (1939), one of the industry's most celebrated films? Who better to imitate the descent into madness of a genteel woman struggling with her sexual hunger than the successful actress whose fragile mental state and growing marital unhappiness, soon to result in adulterous misadventure, were then sensational public knowledge? It is no accident that Vivien Leigh was picked to portray an aging and mentally unstable actress who forms a liaison with a handsome young gigolo in a later Williams adaptation: *The Roman Spring of Mrs. Stone* (José Quintero, 1961); that film benefits from the same aspects of Leigh's star persona. Most important, perhaps, the casting of Vivien Leigh as Blanche effectively linked the spectator's knowledge about the sexual transgressions of film stars (i.e., Hollywood as the locus of an energizing sexual naughtiness) to the similar thematics of Williams's drama. No such effect could have been achieved with the less-than-notorious Jessica Tandy. Leigh, of course, was easily outclassed as an actress by Marlon Brando's powerful Method performance, but the way she is overwhelmed on screen by his personal magnetism and expressive abilities perfectly suits the themes and plot of Williams's play.

More important, of course, for the play's representation of sex, its arousal of desire was the casting of Marlon Brando as Stanley. It is certainly no exaggeration to say that Brando's sizzling incarnation of Stanley had much to do with the Broadway success of Williams's play. The American commercial theatre had seldom seen an actor of such raw physical magnetism. Because film, being based on photography, possesses better resources for eroticizing and idealizing the human body than live theatre, Kazan was able to make Brando's Stanley, with his complex mix of sympathetic vulnerability and terrifying aggressivity, even a more central, affecting part of the film, of which Brando became the undisputed star.

Just as Williams's play deeply affected the kind of film Hollywood thereafter would make, so Brando's performance—the first time American filmgoers had been treated to a full-blown Method characterization—transformed the traditional screen image of appealing maleness. Yet this development would have been impossible without Williams's play. A year earlier, Brando's first screen part, as a paraplegic veteran in *The Men* (Fred Zinnemann, 1950), had permitted him only to create a rather one-dimensional portrait of sympathetic Americanness—exactly the kind of role most available for handsome, young male leads at the time, and to which he would likely have been largely condemned had it not been for a film version of *Streetcar.* Even though his performance as Stanley pushed his career in a somewhat different direction, Brando was still unable to escape such parts entirely, as his conventional portrayals in such films as *Teahouse of the August Moon* (Daniel Mann, 1956) and *Guys and Dolls* (Joseph L. Mankiewicz, 1955) bear witness.

Of this there is no doubt. Williams's creation of Stanley Kowalski, as well as similar male leads such as Chance Wayne in *Sweet Bird of Youth* and Brick Pollitt in *Cat on a Hot Tin Roof,* contributed centrally to a radical transformation of what Americans had previously valued as ideal, male qualities. This transformed image of masculinity, though enhanced by the essentially theatrical techniques of Method performance, achieved cultural importance because of its dominant screen—not stage—presence in the fifties, a trend inaugurated and made possible by Kazan's *Streetcar.* The most important aspect of Williams's vision is that his male characters are less the bearers of sexual desire—the traditional male role in American theatre and film—and more its object, thereby assuming what is conventionally a female position. Such feminization is homo-erotic to some degree, but it creates an appeal from which female viewers are by no means immune, especially because the plays themselves offer strong women characters, perhaps most prominently Maggie in *Cat on a Hot Tin Roof,* who play the traditional male role of desiring subject.

Through weightlifting, then an activity quite socially marginal, Brando obsessively shaped his body into an erotic object, set off in *Streetcar* by the famous white T-shirt that quite self-consciously revealed rippling biceps and powerful forearms that are often emphasized by Kazan's staging. The T-shirt is only in part a signifier of Stanley's social class. It is much more the emblem of unrestrained and unabashed sensuality, an index of the character's perpetual state of mental undress, a flimsy, easily discarded concession to civilized values. Brando should be applauded for making his Stanley so attractively brutish, the appealing id whose emergence to dominance Blanche struggles against so fruitlessly.

Williams, however, must be given credit for creating a role that would bear successfully this kind of interpretation. In any event, Kazan's *Streetcar* was a success, at least in part, because it put into play and made irresistibly appealing a different approach to the male body that, while explicable perhaps because of Williams's homosexuality, fitted into, even as it decisively shaped, a larger cultural trend that was, initially at least, largely played out on the movie screen by a group of new male stars. During the fifties and early sixties, Marlon Brando, Montgomery Clift, Paul Newman, Robert Redford, and Laurence Harvey all appeared in Williams films that effectively showcased their strong heterosexual appeal; James Dean, in all probability, was prevented only by his premature death from doing so. Once again, what Williams had to offer resonated with, but also helped transform a fundamental aspect of how the cinema had traditionally attracted viewers—by directing an erotic gaze at the idealized female body. Significantly, Vivien Leigh's body is never eroticized or glamorized in the film. Her Blanche becomes instead the bearer of a desire that, while directed at young men, finds with poetic justice its true object in the dangerous appeal of Stanley.

The Tennessee Williams Film: A Subgenre

A Streetcar Named Desire did extremely well at the box office and was one of the most critically acclaimed films of 1951, an otherwise fairly grim year for Hollywood. The movie received ten Academy Award nominations—in all the major categories—and three awards, for female lead Vivien Leigh and supporting players Kim Hunter and Karl Malden. The lesson of this success was not lost on Hollywood, whose filmmakers eagerly awaited the production of more Williams properties to transform into moneymaking films. After *Streetcar* had achieved, in both its forms, an international renown for the playwright, Williams did not disappoint his enthusiastic publics. He began the most prolific period of his career, penning in quick succession a number of plays, all of which with one exception (*Camino Real* [1953]) became Broadway hits. Film producers competed eagerly for production rights to these properties, hoping to emulate Kazan's triumph; in the process they made the young playwright Hollywood's hottest author. Tennessee Williams seemed destined to achieve the same kind of success on the screen as he had enjoyed on the stage.

What had made Williams appealing to a general film, as opposed to a more elite theatrical audience, however, was quite different. Broadway spectators, though certainly riveted by Williams's handling of sexual themes, could appreciate his complex articulation of tone, which often ranged from the tragic to the almost farcical; though finding themselves engaged by Williams's psychological realism, which created powerful sympathy for his suffering protagonists, they could value the less emotional and more intellectual qualities that become more prominent in the plays after *Streetcar*: the self-conscious deployment of schematized ideas, mythological cadres, and expressionistic sets, among other somewhat anti-realist elements.

To judge from contemporary accounts, *Streetcar*'s screen triumph resulted primarily from its careful articulation of sexual, anti-romantic tension between the two leads, a tension energized and made appealing by the artful eroticization of Marlon Brando's body; moreover, in this play Williams does not stray far from the social realist aesthetic then the conventional basis for most Hollywood representation. Or, to put it another way, *Streetcar,* like *The Glass Menagerie,* is more an Aristotelian than a Brechtian play; its primary appeal is emotional, not intellectual, though it is certainly true that the playwright is here interested, as elsewhere, in the binary opposition of essential human qualities, roughly identifiable as "gentility" and "sensuality." Williams wrote two other plays that more or less conformed to the pattern established by *Streetcar: Cat on a Hot Tin Roof* and *Sweet Bird of Youth.* The film versions of both proved very popular with audiences even if critics often complained that, inevitably altered in accordance with Hollywood protocols, they were less than artistically triumphant. Together with *Streetcar,* they constitute the most significant subgenre of the Hollywood adult film during the fifties and early sixties.

What of the rest of Williams's dramatic work? Predictably, film viewers were to demonstrate a deep interest only in some of what Williams had to communicate as an artist, were enthusiastic about only those plays belonging to a certain, somewhat narrow type. Not surprisingly, the playwright was urged to return to this thematic and dramatic pattern by both his own creative tendencies and the acclaim of the filmgoing public. However, all of Williams's fifties plays (*Camino Real* again excepted), because of the playwright's fame and demonstrated commercial appeal, were adapted for the screen soon after their stage success.

The Rose Tattoo (Daniel Mann, 1956), though certainly not an artistic or commercial failure, exemplifies some of the problems involved in adapting for the movies a Williams' play that is quite different from *Streetcar* despite some obvious, even fundamental similarities. *The Rose Tattoo*, like *Streetcar*, traces the developing relationship between a woman who has experienced sexual obsession and a man she does not love and yet finds compellingly attractive even though she thinks him coarse and brutish. Again, as in *Streetcar*, the principal dramatic tension derives from the way in which the woman is forced to face the truth of her own lustful feelings, abandoning illusions about more refined versions of mutual attraction; here too the plot turns on a sexual encounter as she surrenders, after much resistance and equivocation, to the man's clumsy seduction. Even the settings of the two plays are much the same. For the raw ungentility of impoverished New Orleans, *The Rose Tattoo* offers an expressively similar substitute: a poor fishing village on the Gulf coast where a drama about elemental passions can likewise appropriately be set.

And yet *The Rose Tattoo* differs from *Streetcar* in two ways that made it difficult to adapt with the same kind of success for the screen. First, Williams's tone is here complexly seriocomic. The play offers a carnivalesque meditation on the intimate connection between the loftier and baser human elements, suggesting how the conflict between lust and propriety that destroys Blanche can be embraced and thereby transcended. Serafina Delle Rose, who feels an unquenchable desire for her husband Rosario, discovers after his death that he was unfaithful to her. His mistress, whom Serafina meets, even had a rose tattoo to match Rosario's. Serafina (whose name refers to the highest class of angels) then destroys the urn containing Rosario's ashes and succumbs to the inept seduction of Alvaro Mangiacavallo, a half-wit who ironically possesses a body almost identical to that of Rosario.

But Serafina's acceptance of an oafish lover (his name means "eat a horse") is by no means tragic. Instead, it signifies her psychologically healthy abandonment of demands upon passion that a frail human nature cannot support. Love can neither be eternal nor faithful in its object, Williams suggests. The flesh and blood rose tattooed on Rosario's chest, with its duplicate on his mistress, does not properly signify Serafina's angelic vision of love, which, of course, is always, already compounded with lust. By destroying the shrine she has made of Rosario's ashes, that is, the eternal, transmuted form of his body, Serafina is enabled to accept a mockingly ironic reincarnation in the person of Alvaro, a sexual object that must, and yet cannot be taken seriously. The angelic is brought to earth, but the descent is gently comic, in no way a tragic fall.

Thus, and here is the second and perhaps more important point, *The Rose Tattoo* decisively alters the sexual dynamics of *Streetcar*. The play debunks any serious approach to passion by refusing to allow Serafina to take her lover's betrayal as anything but a revelation of her own narrow-minded idealism. Serafina must surrender to the banality of lust, as represented by the irresistible physicality of Alvaro, even acknowledge that her daughter has the right to desire her sailor boyfriend. And so *The Rose Tattoo* is less an erotic object than a humorous, if intellectually schematic, meditation on the discontents and joys of eroticism itself. In the expressionist manner, the characters are more flat than round, more the representatives of human tendencies and qualities than psychologically complex individuals whose fate is meant to engage the spectator emotionally. The play disavows the tragic implications of passion so tellingly displayed in *Streetcar*. Thus the film version, even though it deploys the attractive bodies of Anna Magnani and Burt Lancaster in the featured roles, cannot transform them into a compellingly glamorous spectacle. Famous for her steamy roles in Italian neorealist films, Magnani, though often clad only in her underwear, cuts more a comic than erotic figure as Serafina. As a result of the notorious beach scene in *From Here to Eternity* (Fred Zinnemann, 1953), where, clad only in bathing trunks, he makes passionate love to Deborah Kerr in the surf, Lancaster became a male lead often called upon to seduce the leading lady with powerful tenderness. Yet the role of Alvaro Mangiacavallo demanded he make more use of his not inconsiderable gifts for energetic farce.

In general, Mann's film simplifies the intellectual scheme of Williams's play by melodramatizing all the dramatic encounters in the Hollywood fashion; thus the film lacks the sharply distanced comic energies of the stage version. At the same time, limited by Williams's dramatic and thematic conceptions, Mann fails to deliver the explosive eroticism of *Streetcar* despite exceptional casting obviously calculated to achieve such an effect. The screen version of *The Rose Tattoo* was a disappointment to playwright and filmgoers alike. Related difficulties insured a disappointing reception for both *Baby Doll* (Elia Kazan, 1956) and *The Fugitive Kind* (Sidney Lumet, 1960), the first of which recycles *Streetcar*'s director and the second its male lead in an attempt to duplicate the earlier film's success.

The marketing campaign for *Baby Doll* aroused a storm of largely irrelevant controversy by playing on Williams's then well-established reputation as an author of smutty stories. The film's poster featured Carroll Baker posed seductively in a crib, a gambit that along with its double entendre title falsely implied that the story was somehow concerned with the sexual predation of, if not little girls, then innocent gamines. The Catholic Legion of Decency condemned the film (probably without a viewing), while Bishop Fulton J. Sheen of New York called from the pulpit for its suppression. Reverend James Pike, a prominent Protestant clergyman, disputed Sheen's contention, if not his judgment of the film, declaring that adult viewers should be able to exercise freedom of choice and, if morally upright, would not be harmed by filmgoing of any kind. Williams's *Baby Doll* thus earned the dubious distinction of being the only film to spark a full-fledged and much-reported ecclesiastical debate, one that brought into focus the conflict between an older and an emerging view of how the film industry should function in American society.

Catholic protests and an attendant boycott probably did much to suppress business at the box office, but the film itself, quite different from its advertised image, undoubtedly contributed heavily to what must be counted a commercial failure. Based on two one-act plays that had not been produced on Broadway (27 *Wagons Full of Cotton* and *The Unsatisfactory Supper*) and which were stitched together mostly by Kazan, who was the creative motor behind the project, *Baby Doll* is a riotously funny black comedy treating the "love" triangle that develops between Archie Lee Meighan (Karl Malden) and his business rival Vaccaro (Eli Wallach) for the affection of Archie Lee's wife (Baker), who has refused to consummate their business-deal marriage until her twentieth birthday, on the eve of which the play's action begins. Because Vaccaro's real interest in Baby Doll is to persuade her to sign a statement attesting that Archie Lee burned down Vaccaro's cotton gin, the film does not develop its romantic triangle in an erotic fashion. In fact, the most intimate moment the two characters share is when Baby Doll spies upon Vaccaro napping in her crib. Though the performers, especially Baker, are often pictured in various states of undress (by this time a hallmark of Williams's movies), the film offers little more than innuendo and seductive teasing.

Significantly, *Baby Doll* was certificated without much dispute by Joseph Breen's successor at the PCA, Geoff Shurlock. Kazan undoubtedly constructed the most satisfactory version of this material by Williams, whose own attempt to recycle it as *Tiger Tail* proved a stage failure in the late seventies. Like Blanche DuBois, Archie Lee, Vaccaro, Baby Doll, and her Aunt Rose Comfort are all shakily rooted characters who fear dispossession even as they attempt to construct financial and emotional security for themselves. Their comic failures to do so are lightheartedly staged by Kazan, who is aided by the vibrant Method performances of Malden and Wallach. Though an undoubted artistic success, *Baby Doll* obviously did not give the filmgoing public the Williams they wanted to see and which the advertising campaign had promised them they in fact would.

In contrast, *The Fugitive Kind* (Sidney Lumet, 1960) offered film audiences what they wanted to see: a very sexy, yet sensitive Marlon Brando, who becomes the object of three women's desires. But Lumet and Williams hardly

give their viewers the dramatic form they would have preferred or even one, for the most part, they would have been able to appreciate. Williams's story, with its complex reworking of classical myth, depended upon a scheme of reference unknown to most filmgoers; without it, both the relations of the characters and the direction of the plot become hard to follow if not positively opaque. Like *Baby Doll*, the film is important for students and admirers of Williams because it presents most satisfactorily material that was of great interest to him. This modern update of Orpheus's tragic end was first staged as *Battle of Angels* in 1940, in a production whose overall problems insured a quick, and for Williams heartbreaking, cancellation. For most of two decades, he rewrote, and a second stage version, entitled *Orpheus Descending*, was produced on Broadway in 1957, where it enjoyed limited success. For the film version, Williams collaborated closely with screenwriter Meade Roberts and thereby exercised a great deal of control over the screenplay's ultimate form.

In the film, Lumet and Williams opt for greater realism, an artistic decision that accords with the fundamental Hollywood aesthetic. Hence the film omits the play's two old women who function as a kind of Greek chorus, commenting on the action; likewise, the setting is opened out from the store run by Lady (Eurydice) to different, authentic exteriors. While the mode of presentation and the cadre of the play are in this way made more naturalistic, little change is made in the characters' motivations. Their actions, removed from their mythic setting and now more resolutely a part of the everyday world, thus seem irrational, confusing, unengaging. The relationship between Val (Orpheus) and Lady, played effectively by Anna Magnani, fails to generate much in the way of passion or pathos because the significance of their bond, that is, its incomplete triumph over death, has been eliminated. Though the film artfully emphasizes the sensual, androgynous appeal of Brando's body in a series of initial scenes added to the playscript, the overall result is a somewhat confusing melange of representational modes, as Williams's material is only inadequately accommodated to the requirements of screen realism. A similar problem besets Peter Glenville's film version of *Summer and Smoke* (1961), a play with a strongly expressionistic cadre and characters who quite schematically represent a binary opposition of ideas. Though played effectively by the charismatic Laurence Harvey and beautiful Geraldine Page, the romantic pair in *Summer and Smoke* are prevented by the thesis of Williams's play—the conflict between body and soul—from generating the passionate sympathy that Stanley and Blanche had aroused.

On the screen, that aspect of Williams's thematics is only recaptured effectively in *Cat on a Hot Tin Roof* (1958) and *Sweet Bird of Youth* (1962). Both plays were directed on Broadway by Elia Kazan with the film versions overseen by Richard Brooks, who made a reputation in the fifties and sixties with well-executed adaptations of literary properties, most prominently the two Williams plays, but also works by Dostoevsky, Conrad, Sinclair Lewis, and Truman Capote. In their focus on male crisis, both films owe something to Brooks's fascination with issues of ethics and character; like the title figure in his *Lord Jim* (1964), Brooks's Brick Pollitt and Chance Wayne, played similarly by a quite kinetic and ultra-masculine Paul Newman, win through to redemption after painful self-examination and consciously chosen suffering. In each case, Williams's ambiguities and tragic realities are eliminated in favor of a life-affirming coupling, a change certainly instituted by Brooks, who, when he took on the two projects, was a commercially successful director interested in making literary films with a wide appeal. Happy endings were still an important part of the Hollywood formula, even in the late fifties and early sixties, and Brooks was well aware of this.

Like the stage versions they are adapted from, these two films, however, bear the marks of a greater influence from Elia Kazan. Specifically, they reflect strongly the interpretation of Williams that emerged from the director's close collaboration with the playwright on the Broadway version of *Streetcar*. It would certainly be incorrect to say that in these three stage and one film versions Kazan reduces the complexity of Williams's themes to something like a formula. And yet, like *Streetcar*, the films of *Cat on a Hot Tin Roof* and *Sweet Bird of Youth* emphasize sexual tensions, now viewed in a traditionally romantic way, while downplaying the questions of moral responsibility and self-understanding that are also important elements of Williams's dramatic conception in each case.

The two later films are also similar to *Streetcar* in offering a thoroughgoing eroticization of the male body, an eroticization that is now claimed very forcefully for heterosexuality despite the feminized nature of the two male main characters. David Thomson has observed of Kazan's stage and screen work that "he invariably needed some kind of sexual investment in a show—imaginative and actual."[4] And Kazan had no interest in the homosexual undertones of Williams's plays (witness his ready agreement to Breen's demand that Blanche's husband not be characterized as a closet gay). Except for the notorious film *Splendor in the Grass* (1961), Kazan's obsession with the erotic is nowhere more clearly evident than in *Cat on a Hot Tin Roof* and *Sweet Bird of Youth,* the screen versions of which are perhaps even more dominated by their identification of personality and sexual choice than the stage productions. Clearly, Brooks was eager to out-Kazan Kazan and succeeded in so doing. If Kazan did not turn Williams's multileveled explorations of the human dilemma into a rather narrow formula for screen success, Brooks did.

When first produced in 1955, Kazan's *Cat on a Hot Tin Roof* was a hit with audiences and critics alike, garnering Williams his second Pulitzer. It is perhaps surprising that a film version took three years to produce, but the storm of controversy that raged over *Baby Doll,* as well as that film's disappointing performance at the box office, undoubtedly played a role in the delay, as did the fact that this Williams play was even more concerned with sex, es-

pecially the impotence and possible homosexual inclinations of its protagonist, than *Streetcar*. In any event, by 1958 the Production Code had been weakened by further assault from filmmakers catering to increased audience demand for adult dramas. In particular, Otto Preminger's film version of F. Hugh Herbert's popular Broadway sexual farce, *The Moon is Blue* (1953) had been released without a PCA certificate and had profited from the notoriety; a full-scale Legion of Decency protest about the story's casual treatment of sexual liaisons failed to keep it from being one of the year's top-grossing films. Though "sexual perversions" were still officially banned from screen treatment, homosexuality could now be raised as an issue because the PCA could no longer enforce the letter of the Code; the screen version of William's play, in fact, would hardly be the first film to do so. In concession to public taste, however, the issue still needed delicate, indirect handling.

Williams's play, fittingly enough, leaves the issue of Brick's sexuality unresolved. Does he refuse to sleep with Maggie because Skipper's confession of love has made him face his own homosexual desires? Or is he disgusted by the "mendacity" of those around him, the deception and lying of which Maggie too is self-confessedly guilty, having betrayed her husband with his best friend? Brooks's film, in all likelihood, would not have become the biggest grosser of 1958 and one of the most financially successful films ever produced and released by MGM if the director and screenwriter James Poe had not opted clearly for the second of these explanations for Brick's declining moral and psychological state. Ben Gazzara and Barbara Bel Geddes, who had starred on Broadway, were replaced by the much more charismatic and attractive Paul Newman and Elizabeth Taylor in what proved a successful attempt to transform Williams's tragic vision of characters disgusted by mendacity who must, if they are to survive, invent a more powerful lie (i.e., Maggie's false proclamation of pregnancy). By adding a long scene between Brick and Big Daddy in which the father offers marital counsel and a vision of responsible family life that the son eventually accepts, Brooks is able to motivate Brick's eventual decision to go along with Maggie's lie in a spirit of reconciliation. Melodramatized in a typical Hollywood fashion, and accommodated to filmgoers' expectations for engaging romance, *Cat on a Hot Tin Roof* became a standard, early 1960s adult film, with its initial implications of sexual irregularity and disfunction dispelled by a plot that restored a solidly bourgeois normality to the Pollitt household. This combination had proven box-office dynamite the year before in another provocative, but ultimately conservative film: *Peyton Place* (Mark Robson, 1957).

Sweet Bird of Youth received a similar treatment from Brooks. The play version dramatizes the progressive narrowing of Chance's possibilities. Despite frantic efforts to attain a chance at celebrity through manipulation and even blackmail, he finally has no choice but to accept a horrifying death in life, a castration that is his poetically just reward for the betrayal of Heavenly and his own youth. In contrast, the film's Chance never is forced to abandon his drive toward self-fulfillment; he simply must recognize that he is more interested in having Heavenly than pursuing the fading dream of a film career with the help of the Princess. He must suffer, of course, for the error in judgment that harmed Heavenly, who must endure an abortion and damage to her reputation. Chance's girl in the film version, however, is spared the more horrible fate Williams originally imagined: a hysterectomy made necessary by the venereal disease Chance infects her with.

Williams's play uses its first-act setting in a rented hotel room to express Chance's entrapment with an equally desperate fellow traveler, the fading movie star whose life, fatally dependent like his own on transient physical beauty, is ironically enough the best he can hope for. In contrast, Brooks opens his film with a bravura sequence that establishes Chance as the very height of early sixties cool, expressed by his reflector sunglasses and arrogant, in-charge demeanor; here is a character who knows what he wants and has every intention of being successful in obtaining it. For Williams's hero, castration is the ultimate sign of his feminization, the reduction of his drive for success to a harlotry that delivers him into the power of those who would punish him for it. Brooks's Chance, because he has never completely surrendered himself to the career he so desperately wants, needs a less drastic lesson in the meaning of life. With his nose broken by Heavenly's brother, he can no longer hope to become a screen idol, for his youthful good looks were his sole acting asset. And yet he had previously rejected the Princess's offer to help him break into the business in order to make a last appeal for Heavenly, a move he knows will likely bring down the violent wrath of her family. So the disfigurement he subsequently suffers simply seals the bargain he had already agreed to. Bleeding but not dismembered, he is driven away by Heavenly in her Cadillac convertible at film's end in a scene that rhymes with the opening sequence picturing him at the wheel of the Princess's car. If Chance is now less confident, less able to direct his life, he has exchanged such freedom for the obvious benefits of a beautiful, rich woman's love, a finale that Brooks does not present with even a hint of irony. The film's Chance becomes the stock "Mr. Right" of pulp romance, a desirable catch whose selfishness must be transformed into what he himself knows is a better trait: the desire to give all in order to deserve and obtain the love of the woman who wants him.

WILLIAMS AND HOLLYWOOD: SOME CONCLUSIONS

Though audiences loved the film, critics were nearly unanimous in their disapproval, and yet Williams himself, perhaps disingenuously, said that Brooks's recasting of his tragic drama "was probably better than the play."[5] The playwright's remark, I think, is suggestive for a judgment of Hollywood's version of Williams. Undeniably, the films based on the plays, with the exception of *A Streetcar Named Desire* and *Baby Doll,* are inferior artistically to the successful stage productions that inspired them. Cer-

tainly, the adaptation process, fueled by the commercial success of the filmed *Streetcar,* was most successful when it confined the rich and varied *œuvre* of the playwright to certain narrow themes and representational modes that were in accord with film industry practice and the demonstrable desire of its consumers. Overall, Williams's plays are melodramatized in the process, that is, provided with characters able to achieve, after a purgatorial journey of self-discovery, a happy ending for themselves. And yet such melodramatization in some cases simply alters the tonality of the dramatic perspective Williams originally adopted, substituting more optimistic resolutions. Films such as *Sweet Bird of Youth* show how Williams's tragic figures might have escaped the horrible fates to which their own actions work to condemn them. If we are to believe the playwright, these alternative visions did not strike him, at least in every instance, as either disagreeable or dissatisfying.

This is fitting for two reasons. First, unlike many authors, notably fellow playwright Arthur Miller, Williams was eager from the beginning of his career that his stage successes be transformed into artistically significant films; in the case of *Streetcar,* for example, he worked diligently with Charles Feldman to make sure that his play had the same strong impact on filmgoers as it had on theatre audiences. In this regard, his early collaboration with Elia Kazan, who was also vitally interested in both mediums, is of great importance. Second, though this was not his aim, Williams provided Hollywood with source material that transformed the industry. *Streetcar* broke the hitherto impenetrable barrier established by the Production Code to the making of adult entertainment; this startlingly innovative production was the first in a distinguished series of American art films in the fifties and sixties, a genre to which Williams was to contribute several times more during the period. Perhaps even more important, the male roles in Williams's plays, reaching a wider audience through various film versions, popularized a different kind of masculinity, offering images of desirable, vulnerable, and yet aggressive maleness that profoundly affected American ideas about gender. Such roles, in particular, made Marlon Brando and Paul Newman the period's most acclaimed stars. Both went on to build an enduring popularity on parts often written in deliberate imitation of Williams's characters; compare, among a host of examples, the tortured, alienated loners played by Newman in *The Hustler* (Robert Rossen, 1961) and Brando in *Reflections in a Golden Eye* (John Huston, 1967), films whose way was paved most obviously by *Streetcar* and *Cat*. If the American cinema of the late fifties, sixties, and early seventies is densely populated by attractive yet emotionally sensitive men who lack decisiveness and are prone to failure, then Tennessee Williams must be credited for inaugurating what is, in part, a revolution in taste, but also, and more important, a transformation of the national character. And this would never have happened without the wholesale transference of his artistic vision from the stage to the commercial screen.

Notes

1. Quoted in Leonard J. Leff and Jerold L. Simmons, *The Dame in the Kimono* (New York: Doubleday, 1990), 288. My account of Hollywood censorship is much indebted to the detailed history of the subject offered in Leff and Simmons.

2. Quoted in Maurice Yacowar, *Tennessee Williams & Film* (New York: Frederick Ungar, 1977), 14.

3. Quoted in Leff and Simmons, *Dame*, 174.

4. *A Biographical Dictionary of Film* (New York: Knopf, 1994), 388.

5. Quoted in Yacowar, *Tennessee Williams*, 98.

Varun Begley (essay date May 1998)

SOURCE: Begley, Varun. "On Adaptation: David Mamet and Hollywood." *Essays in Theatre* 16, no. 2 (May 1998): 165-76.

[*In the following essay, Begley explores David Mamet's relationship to the theater and film industry, using one of the author's many adapted works as an example.*]

"If it's not quite 'Art' and it's not quite 'Entertainment,'" says Hollywood producer Bobby Gould at the opening of David Mamet's *Speed-the-Plow*, "it's here on my desk" (3). For more than twenty years, audiences have been similarly situated with respect to Mamet's work. The Mamet persona of the 1980s—evoked in plays, film scripts, films, *GQ* commentaries, essay collections, Madonna premieres, and innumerable critical articles and reviews—was cloaked in an aura of late-modern literary and mass-media stardom. The mishmash of adjectives required to delineate this peculiar celebrity suggests a complex set of mediations surrounding present notions of the literary, the artistic, and authorship itself, especially in relation to the vertiginous modes of contemporary media culture. In the case of Mamet, these mediations have directly challenged critical methodology. Critics have often been forced to disentangle the "serious" or literary aspects of the author from the trappings of popular culture and his own unusual notoriety.

At the same time, it is an uncomfortable proposition to write in one breath about Mamet's plays, the films he has written and directed, and the films he has merely written, as though all spoke to a hypostatized David Mamet who transcends context. The methodological fiction which enables inter-media studies entitled "David Mamet" has something in common with the aggrandizing marketing strategy which advertises the Sidney Lumet film *The Verdict* as "written by David Mamet," or, indeed, Edward Zwick's 1986 romantic comedy *About Last Night . . .* as "based on a play by David Mamet." Put in a more positive form, it seems that one of Mamet's most significant works has been the ongoing production of a particularly disparate

literary and filmic career. To assume a univocal identity, merely for the sake of simplicity, is to ignore the questions of medium, mediation, and authority which the phenomenon of David Mamet has thrown into relief.

As an alternative to a monumentalized Mamet, I propose to focus on the instabilities of authorship and imprimatur manifested in two encounters with Hollywood. I am also concerned with the rhetorical and ideological consequences of authorial positioning in relations between theatre and film, with a view toward the larger problem of cultural adaptation. The discussion takes the form of a triangulation between three distinct cultural texts, which, considered together, bear on questions of authority and adaptation in relation to literary and filmic modes of production. The first presentation is the extreme case of Mamet's *Sexual Perversity in Chicago* and its filmic realization, *About Last Night . . .*, which may in the simplest terms be grasped as the elaborate 80s mythification of a particularly sparse and bitter 70s dramatic text. The second presentation is Mamet's *Speed-the-Plow*, which acts to concretize and personify the implied yet absent Hollywood functionaries who adapted and authored *About Last Night. . . .*

This interpretive scenario is intended as a corrective to the mythic and narrative categories by which we usually understand this kind of cultural relation. The habitual attitudes of elitism and populism alike point to a solitary, heroic Mamet in conflict with the mass culture machine. Dogmatic biases toward mainstream film are certainly germane in relation to Mamet. Hierarchical conceptions of authorship persist, perhaps most revealingly in relation to films which he scripted but did not direct. Steven Gale, for example, remarks that *The Verdict* (1982) "is generally considered the writer's best screenplay," and proceeds to describe what he takes to be Mamet's use of "uninflected" Eisensteinian shots in the first nine minutes of the film (161, 164).

Beyond whatever disservice this argument may render to the film's director, Sidney Lumet, there is a substantial tension in the idea of the screenwriter as author of the *mise en scène* in this case, particularly since Gale alludes to Mamet's admission of being "'completely ignorant' about the 'visual' area of directing films" (164) prior to *House of Games* (1987). Or, to take another example, in his article "The Recent Mamet Films," Dennis Carroll claims that in relation to *We're No Angels*, "one has to make allowances for the considerable divergence between Mamet's wryly comic published screenplay . . . and the labored film realization by Neil Jordan" (185). Without clarifying what "wryly comic" or "labored" might mean, Carroll proceeds to discuss the film and its characters, as played by Robert De Niro, Sean Penn, Demi Moore, and Hoyt Axton, before concluding that this "work" belongs "squarely within the corpus of Mamet's thematic and moral concerns as delineated in his major plays" (188).

This last view is characteristic of identity-thinking in relation to authorship, presuming some unmediated relationship between "David Mamet" and whatever works bear his stamp, however imbricated they may be within disparate spheres of cultural production. To search for and reproduce an imagined literary Mamet independent or in spite of context is tacitly to reinstate the venerable hierarchy of art and popular culture, and to ignore one of the most singular features of Mamet's career and one of the most obsessive of his fixations. The arguments concerning Mamet and film are not merely incidental to the more "serious" study of his major plays, but instead constitute a useful limit in thinking through the dialectic of authorship in contemporary culture.

At first glance, however, a comparison between Mamet's *Sexual Perversity in Chicago* (1975) and its Hollywood incarnation *About Last Night . . .* (1986) seems a futile exercise. On the surface the two works, produced more than a decade apart, exhibit little more than passing similarity. The film, a loose adaptation of Mamet's circular, fragmentary, acerbic play on 1970s urban sexual morality, smooths the rough edges into a linear 1980s narrative of capitalist redemption, in which a disaffected young Chicagoan finds affluence and romance through suffering, repentance, and entrepreneurial hard work. Indeed the transfiguration of Mamet's play is so drastic as to call into question the notion of adaptation itself. Is adaptation an imitation, a retelling, or a re-production of some originary text? Isn't all cultural and aesthetic production a re-presentation of some presumed, ineluctable category of human life—psychology, myth, history? Is not representation itself a name for the fundamental epistemological dilemmas of language and vision, the ceaseless mediation of the real world to consciousness?

The problem of the play and the film can thus be quickly reduced to a Platonic truism: all art is adaptation, in which case the comparison of *Sexual Perversity* and *About Last Night . . .* is either willful and arbitrary or driven by some quasi-biographical motive to trace the fate of Mamet's work. Yet even in these terms *About Last Night . . .* is not *Homicide* or *House of Games* (both written and directed by Mamet), but instead an adulterated, unabashed, unregenerate star-vehicle for Rob Lowe, Demi Moore, and James Belushi, co-written by Denise DeClue and *Saturday Night Live* veteran Tim Kazurinsky. Thus to the film theorist or philosophically inclined aesthetician, *About Last Night . . .* is a qualitatively distinct and formally independent entity, exemplary only in the thoroughgoing mediocrity of its 1980s romance. To the literary biographer of David Mamet, the film can appear as little more than a scandalous footnote, a further testament to the clichéd thematics of unprincipled greed and expediency which mark popular perceptions of mainstream Hollywood.

In this way, the philosophical and literary objections to *About Last Night . . .* as an authentic instance of Mamet-adaptation conspire to neatly re-enact the familiar biases alluded to above. According to another view, however, the very "looseness" of the adaptation—in comparison to more faithful film versions of Mamet plays, such as *Glengarry*

Glen Ross—broadens the axes of structural and ideological difference to the point that the relation between filmic and theatrical modes of production can be more closely observed.

The dialectic of identity and difference with respect to adaptation is teasingly invoked from the outset of the film. *About Last Night . . .* opens with a verbatim enactment of *Sexual Perversity*'s opening exchange—in which Bernie relates an alleged sexual episode to Danny—yet we are immediately plunged into a radically different urban space. Intercut with the credits, we overhear snatches of dialogue, in a bar, on the street, in a train, until, on the scene's closing line ["D:You think she was a pro? / B:A pro, Dan . . . / D:Yes. / B: . . . is how you think about yourself. You see my point?" (17)], the camera pulls back to reveal a lush green softball field, dotted by healthy young urbanites in various stages of afternoon inebriation, flanked by the majestic skyscrapers of Chicago's downtown loop. This sequence is shot like an ad for the Chicago tourist board; the benign admixture of nature and civilization seems a vindication of enlightened urban planning. The tableau recalls a harmonious separation between the worlds of commerce and leisure; indeed the softball game acts as a kind of ideological posterboard for the luxuriant yuppie Saturday after a long week's work.

The film thus begins to flesh out the bare semiotic bones of a play which uses metonymic shorthand—a few barstools, a desk, a bed—to denote the range of public and private space, so that the stage itself acts as a metaphor for a fragmented, denatured, urban world. Virtually every scene in the film, however, lingers lovingly on the urban landscape—Wrigley Field, the Chicago Art Institute, restaurants, bars, parks, the lakeshore. These images all conspire toward the illusion of filled, integrated, vital space. The play is much more explicitly concerned with the pathology of urban life, the violent pulse of its libidinal energy, the phantasmagoric mythologies of sexual and social identity which structure the experience of its alienated citizens. The film, by contrast, is more quiescent in its representation of a fully reified, monumental environment which, whatever the individual psychological travails of the population, is still fundamentally conceived as a place of benevolent opportunity.

Clearly, in the representation of the social world the play and film begin to specify very different ideological programs. Before taking this analysis further, however, it is helpful to elaborate the narrative differences between the two texts. Composed predominantly of short scenes, *Sexual Perversity in Chicago* concerns two men, Bernie and Dan, and two women, Deborah and Joan—two dubious friendships which suffer when Deborah and Dan conduct a brief, doomed affair. In circular fashion, the play begins and ends with extended dialogues in which Bernie and Dan engage in adolescent sexual banter, typified by Bernie's drunken observation—"Tits and Ass. Tits and Ass. Tits and Ass. Tits and Ass. Blah de Bloo. Blah de Bloo. Blah de Bloo. Blah de Bloo" (58).

The construction of masculinity in the play hinges on the desperate, incantatory use of sexual terminology and aggressive (though implausible) anecdote to compensate for the utter dysfunction of the urban sexual world and the collapsing myth of masculine identity. This is a language with only the barest of contents, which, in its expression, registers only terror or rage. In the midst of a violent argument, Deborah tells Dan, "You're trying to understand women and I'm confusing you with information. 'Cunt' won't do it. 'Fuck' won't do it. No more magic. What are you feeling. Tell me what you're feeling. Jerk" (58).

There is the sense here of a profound, dehumanizing logic at work in urban sexual relations; in this respect, *Sexual Perversity* mirrors the male business world of *Glengarry Glen Ross,* in which inadequate salesmen are derided as "cunts" and the implicitly erotic motifs of "closing" and narrative seduction constitute the mythology of making a deal. Both plays are part of a critique of a cultural ethos in which business is sexual and sex is commercial. With its ominous subtext of rape and molestation, *Sexual Perversity* underscores the sociopathology of desire in a culture dominated by the acquisitive, exploitative logic of American business (Bigsby 51). The play is a portrait of commodified human relations, of characters conditioned to confront each other as objects, for whom the language of consumer society holds no promise of human relationship.

About Last Night . . . re-visions Mamet's dystopian 70s drama through the lens of the Reagan years. The film borrows snatches of dialogue from the play in a grand and unexpected sublimation of the entire ethos of sexual and economic malaise, in which the pathology of Dan and Deborah's relationship is miraculously reconfigured as the failure of Dan, now squarely identified as the protagonist, to effect a separation between friendship, relationship, and career. Deborah is now the living, breathing embodiment of a particular 1980s notion of progressive femininity: an intensely sexy and sexual career woman (graphic designer), who grapples with issues of closeness and caring, and struggles in vain to socialize Danny into the world of adult coupledom. The play's ambiguous reference to Deborah's lesbian experiences is restated as a mild, endearing pillow-talk joke. Indeed sex itself is scarcely the problem in *About Last Night . . .* (this is, after all, Rob Lowe and Demi Moore); the camera lingers lovingly on the apparent ecstasy and improbable physical beauty of its two stars. Deborah is even able to remark, as the couple breaks up, that "good sex" was all they had (while in the play both accuse each other of being a "lousy fuck").

In the film Bernie is played by the amiable though slightly obnoxious Jim Belushi, who reinvents the character as a humorous sidekick, a bad influence who nonetheless evolves a more supportive and less adolescent practice of friendship by the end. The reference to his childhood molestation is omitted, as is his venomous encounter with Joan—"You don't want to get come on to, go enroll in a convent. You think I don't have better thing to do? I don't

have better ways to spend my off hours than to listen to some nowhere cunt try out cute bits on me? . . . I mean, what the fuck do you think society is, just a bunch of rules strung together for your personal pleasure." (20,21) The position tacitly advanced by the play—that the mythic rules of society are in fact a kind of structural annihilation of pleasure—is here assimilated to 1980s self-help philosophy. Life is difficult and challenging, yet it is not only possible to adapt to one's proper roles, but infinitely desirable as well.

As a demonstration of this creed, Danny is given a career as an unhappy restaurant supply salesman with a corrupt and philandering boss. Against this rather ludicrous character is set the apron-clad, honest small businessman, a sympathic and sentimental figure who Danny must "cut off" if he is to keep his job. Predictably, this wrenching ethical dilemma causes an argument with Deborah, setting in motion the causal sequence which will eventually lead to the end of the relationship. Only by quitting his job and opening a small diner of his own is Danny able to find personal fulfillment, and, in a colossal revision of the play, win Deborah back at the end.

Sexual Perversity's circularity is given a thoroughgoing linear coating of classical Hollywood veneer. Unease about the commercialization of sexual culture in the play is fully exteriorized and symbolically negated by the emergence of an entire commercial culture and ethic which must be separated, balanced, and harmonized with the spheres of sex and friendship if any image of happiness is to be projected or sustained. Danny's journey is thus within the constellation of yuppie mythology, which afforded the illusion of metaphysical depth in the upwardly-mobile schema of career, family, friendship, and self-image: a paradigm which spawned a philosophy of "coping" and the inevitable commodification of various aspects of the yuppie lifestyle (health food, fitness, pop psychology, Landcruisers, etc.).

Yet despite its complicity in validating this specific 80s ideological program, *About Last Night . . .* remains naively, almost obsessively fixated on the utopian possibility of integrated experience and personal fulfillment, which, interestingly, does not conclude with Danny ascending the corporate ladder, but instead with the curious return of an anachronistic, old-world social space of small business and old-fashioned chaste courtship. On the one hand, this unexpected resolution may justifiably be read as the specious conflation of hyper-aggressive modern cultural, economic, and urban logic with the sentimentalized serenity of old-world values—an ideological construction mediated by the figure of Ronald Reagan himself, who seemed to embody both extremes. On the other hand, *About Last Night . . .* speaks to the problem of imagining a better life within the reified mythic and conceptual categories available to modern consciousness, a double-bind which imprints on contemporary culture the often incongruous iconography of ideology and utopia, progressivity and nostalgia, naivete and despair (Jameson 147-48).

Here a word should be said about the structural and perceptual differences between theatrical and filmic modes of representation in this case. One need not invoke an excess of psychoanalytic film jargon to detect *About Last Night* . . .'s obsessive relation to the iconic faces and bodies of its stars. The camera constantly seeks privileged perspectives in order to highlight nuances of character and emotion, and, presumably, to engage the fetishistic economy surrounding Rob Lowe and Demi Moore—a lovemaking scene shot from outside the bedroom window, for example, with the intervening windowframe and billowing curtains providing a discreet source of added titillation. Consequently, the film organizes and eroticizes its spaces along standard Hollywood lines of empathy, identification, and second-order voyeuristic fascination.

In addition, many such sequences are complicated by a kind of picture-postcard aesthetic, which demands that the image be completely harmonious, balanced, and framed. For example, when Danny and Deborah exchange intimacies on the Chicago lakefront, a full snapshot view of the downtown Loop occupies the background, with the Sears tower and Hancock building looming as vaguely phallic intimations. These particularly filmic proclivities find apotheosis in what we might think of as music-video montage, in which stultifying pop songs with titles like "So Far, So Good" are played over two- or three-minute episodic sequences consisting of, say, Rob Lowe and Demi Moore painting their apartment in studiously casual ripped shirts, making love (see above), and collecting the Sunday paper from the front stoop in their underwear, and all of this begins to signify something like "the deepening of the relationship." There are at least three such sequences in the film—Falling in Love, The Relationship Deepens, and Danny Takes Initiative and Opens His Own Restaurant— and each, while surrogating for dialogue, constitutes a well-nigh indissoluble narrative/semiotic unit in its own right.

It is difficult to know how to react to this last phenomenon, since at one level the music-montage does allow the audience a very quiescent, some might say narcotic, libidinal interlude, insofar as one "gets" the narrative point in the first few seconds and then has the opportunity to project, identify, or just unequivocally look without the usual attendant compulsions of narrative progress. At the same time, however, this affect closely resembles a kind of cognitive deadness. Its very success as diegetic filler is predicated on the criterion of instant recognizability, and in this respect the music-montage speaks directly to the most abject habits of consumerism, and relies almost exclusively on conventionalized and superficial means of representing experience.

Whatever the ideological valence of the music-montage, it exemplifies a distinctively filmic sensibility at work in *About Last Night* . . ., the main imperative of which is to flesh out, complete, and enclose what I described earlier as the bare bones of the play. By contrast, the determinations of the play are essentially theatrical. *Sexual Perversity* depends on the epistemological constraints of theatremaking—the constancy of the stage, the temporal and logical gaps between scenes, the material absence of the city which is its central concern—in order to convey a fragmented, denatured, and ultimately circular style of life. Independent of narrative divergences, this adaptation gestures toward the symbolic negation of theatrical representation. The film radically transfigures not only the literal content, but also the structural and ideological bases of the play, in accordance with the formal and ideological dictates of the film medium. Considered in this way, *About Last Night* . . . is paradoxically the most authentic of Mamet adaptations, if the criterion for authenticity is not fidelity or adherence, but instead the transformation of the original into a new and singularly filmic entity.

Against this reading, however, the rhetoric of *About Last Night* . . . is most quickly and intuitively restaged at the level of cultural commonplace: the mythologized relation of American theater to film, typically conceptualized or encoded as an encounter between dominant and marginal cultural forms, in which the aspiring actor or playwright enters into a Faustian bargain with the corporate Hollywood machine. Thus the myth of the serious writer (Odets, Faulkner, Fitzgerald) drunkenly co-authoring a B-grade suspenser or saccharine romance figures as the tragic confrontation between art and commerce and the dissolution of more traditional modes of authorship in the face of the new technocracy. The playwright, organizer of language and emblem of the protected aesthetic world of the theater, is pitted against his Hollywood counterpart, the venal producer, emblem of the commodification of culture and pitiless manipulator of capital.

Against this conceptual backdrop, Mamet's *Speed-the-Plow* assumes a complicated place. The 1988 opening of this play about Hollywood occasioned a media frenzy worthy of a Hollywood premiere. Coverage of the event was fueled by the casting of Madonna, the showbiz sexiness of its subject-matter, Mamet's peculiar insider/outsider relationship to Hollywood, and a muted populist identification with the tough-talking, straight-shooting Chicago writer who would provide some final word on the barbarities of L.A. (Brewer 49, 57). Ironically, the late-modern spectacle of *Speed-the-Plow* is perhaps most easily grasped as the hard-nosed, uncompromising Chicagoan who once wrote "Film is a collaborative business: bend over" (*Some Freaks* 11), attacking the windmill of Hollywood by putting its administrators onstage.

But this is only the skin of the onion. In an altogether different way than the many reflexive, critical films about Hollywood—beginning with Preston Sturges's *Sullivan's Travels* (1941)—*Speed-the-Plow* contributes to the critique of Hollywood by virtue of its very theatricality, which structurally negates or at least displaces the filmic mode of production which is the implied content or raw material of the play. This is a fancy way of saying that *Speed-the-Plow* derives much of its force from being a play about film, and this stark fact seems at once the most obvious and least understood aspect of its significance and appeal.

The content of the play, however, renders its relation to Hollywood ambiguous. On center stage is the author's mythic counterpart, film producer Bobby Gould; yet the play is emphatically un-filmic in its structure, offering only three characters and three fairly traditional scenes which alternate between Gould's office and home. Newly installed in a position of some authority, Gould must decide whether to "green-light" a vapidly commercial buddy-picture, or instead a literary tract entitled *The Bridge,* an almost equally laughable apocalyptic parable about "the historical effects of radiation" and "The End of the World" (42).

The play initially fashions the decision as one between the bottom-line pragmatics of entertainment and the presumably ennobling ethical dimensions of art, although the presentation of the two alternatives, particularly the ponderous and unconvincing fragments of *The Bridge,* eventually make this seem a false choice. Further, *Speed-the-Plow* humanizes the options through the characters who serve as supplicants to Gould and proponents of the two texts: Charlie Fox, the caustic junior producer with whom Gould shares fragmentary locker-room banter and easygoing misogyny, and Karen, the enigmatic saint-cum-whore office temp who sleeps with Gould at the end of scene 2, after first showering him with distended messianic monologues.

From the outline it is clear that *Speed-the-Plow* is oriented by severe dualities. Centered on Gould are two scripts, two competing characters, two ostensible ethical systems, and two implied models of language-use. Similarly, Fox is both jocular comrade and brutal competitor, and Karen is either a beatific voice of sainted reason or an ambitious whore. Finally, there are the two paradigms of film production. The first proposes a mechanical assemblage of narrative and marketing hooks in the commercial Hollywood style, and the second advocates faithful adherence to the originary and notably turgid literary pretensions of an anonymous author whom Fox deems "An Eastern Sissy Writer" (23). The first project is described as follows:

Fox:

Ah. Now that's the *great* part, I'm telling you, when I saw this script . . .

Gould:

. . . I don't know how it got past us . . .

Fox:

When they get out of *prison,* the Head Convict's Sister . . .

Gould:

. . . a buddy film, a prison film, Douggie Brown, blah, blah, some girl . . .

Fox:

Action, a social . . .

Gould:

Action, blood, a social theme . . .

Fox

(*simultaneously with "theme"*): That's what I'm *saying,* an offbeat . . .

Gould:

Good. Good. Good. Alright. . . .

(13)

And this, in part, is how Karen characterizes *The Bridge* to Gould:

He says: years later: it did not occur to him 'til then that this was happiness. That the thing which he lacked, he says, was *courage.* What does the Tramp say? "All fears are one fear. Just the fear of death. And we accept it, then we are at peace." And so, you see, and so all of the *events* . . . the *stone,* the *instrument,* the *child* which he met, *led* him there. . . . in his . . . yes, you see—I know that you see—and that's, that's to me, that's the perfection of the story, when I *read* it . . . I almost, I wanted to sit, I saw, I almost couldn't come to you, the *weight* of it . . . (*Pause.*) You know what I mean.

(47-48)

Even the briefest glance at Karen's speech will take in the many abstract nouns—happiness, courage, fear, death, etc.—which presumably take on a more concrete social or ethical significance in the full context of the radiation-odyssey. Conversely, the less-than-subtle array of symbols—stone, instrument, child, etc.—we would expect to conform to abstract concepts beyond the world of the story. Karen's somewhat desperate use of italicized emphasis struggles to accord an overblown "weight" to this hackneyed and risible allegory, to close the circle, as if by metaphoric fiat the author (or Karen) could conjure the literary world of *The Bridge* in complete parallel relation to our own.

This is a model of authorship which presupposes a singular and relatively omnipotent authorial voice, a unified and self-contained aesthetic world, and close connections between the literary work and the society in which we live. Mamet's method of parody, by contrast, is a metonymical shorthand, such that if "rock = death" and "child = happiness" in the ostensible universe of *The Bridge,* these two prepubescent metaphors indicate to us, by sheer reduction and distillation, the majesterial arrogance of the would-be prophetic narrative.

Ironically, the exchange between Gould and Fox is closely aligned with Mamet's metonymic technique. The various hooks—Douggie Brown, prison film, buddy film, some girl, etc.—assert no larger metaphoric significance, but instead merely stand as narrative markers of entertainment-value potential. The criterion here is recognition and familiarity, and in this respect Mamet's reductive parody of

The Bridge is consonant with Fox and Gould's construction of the Douggie Brown vehicle. Further complicating matters is the fact that the buddy-film narrative is presented dialogically, the offspring of a minute's banter between two film professionals for whom the rudiments of the story are largely habitual and unconscious, erected on the thin premise of a second-rate anonymous script which Fox "found . . . in the file" (8). The originary buddy-film idea, as one more severed, authorless, optioned "property" within the ominous corporate file, is something approaching a paradigm of late-modern commercial film production.

The parody of Hollywood, however, is not facile or one-sided in this case, particularly in relation to the vacuously literary alternative. Mamet deepens the issue by presenting a false option, and this gesture implicates the audience, Mamet, and the entire play, and in turn sounds a more dialectical note of falsity in the broader marketplace of culture. As noted earlier, Gould and Fox paradoxically exemplify a brutalizing creative honesty in the context of mass culture, and their method is to some degree at one with that of Mamet himself, to the extent that the latter has condensed and arranged his material according to expedient and familiar parodic hooks—the corruption of Hollywood, the literary pretensions of the East, etc.

Further, the audience paradoxically owes Gould some measure of allegiance. His job is to mediate the exigencies of text, finance, and production; to arrange the star, genre, and clichés; and to authorize a chain of signification over which, ultimately, he has no control. "Green-lighting" is a mechanical, commercial metaphor for his authorial contribution, and as such it roughly parallels that elemental decision on the part of the consumer regarding whether to go and see the movie, once it is made. Gould is middleman in a chain of authorship beginning anonymously "in the file," and ending with the unseen, godlike Head of the Studio. His position is therefore dislocated from the hypothetical originary creative act and the ultimate horizon of corporate capital, which remains similarly uncertain. Gould is a kind of *ur*-consumer. Ultimately, he compels partial identification, to the extent that his profession is a reciprocal search for "Those Things Which the Public Will Come In To See" (54).

The ambiguity of the connection to Hollywood makes it tempting to bracket the problem and assimilate *Speed-the-Plow* to the canon of Mamet's drama. Clearly, Mamet has often dramatized unusual and closely-observed commercial relationships and behaviors severed from traditional familial and communal ties, thereby estranging conventional expectations of dramatic raw material. In this respect there is a continuity between *Speed-the-Plow* and Mamet's other work. Yet as a theatrical referent, the Hollywood studio is different from, say, a real estate office or pawn shop (cf. *Glengarry Glen Ross* and *American Buffalo*), in that it is in part a sideways allusion to a distinct cultural medium, an instance of culture speaking to itself. Nor is this a neutral form of address. One must at least provisionally acknowledge the de facto hegemony of film in relation to other narrative media—economically, and in a certain way, structurally as well. In theory, any novel, play, or historical event is susceptible to film adaptation, and in principle this process may not be reversed. The parasitical nature of mainstream film has historically been a source of despair for experimental or modernist filmmakers, and has frequently led to calls for a new cinema which will realize the radical and epistemologically distinct potentialities of the film medium. The French New Wave, for example, was partly a reaction against the post-war "tradition of quality" in French cinema, which consisted predominantly of versions of nineteenth-century literary classics (Cook 538-88). Various camps within literary modernism evinced a similar distaste for commercial film as the authorless and faceless instrument of manufactured need, devoid of creative expression—a dubious regression of culture, answerable only to the exigencies of the commodity.

Thus attacks on mainstream film have tended to center on the barbarity of mechanized corporate authorship and its lack of an authentic and singular aesthetic vision, while defenses of commercial filmmakers, such as Hitchcock, have traditionally emphasized the transcendence of directorial style along the lines of literary originality. Biases against commercial film in general, and film adaptation in particular, therefore imply an attitude toward literary authorship, whether it is viewed as a lost or debased originality, or resurrected as authorial/directorial style.

Similarly, the literary media of theatre and fiction necessarily assume a position in relation to Hollywood, if by no other means than continuing to exist apart. Mamet has said that a frequent comment made to writers by "Hollywood people . . . , if they don't understand something or it's not bad enough for them, is, 'It's very theatrical. It's too theatrical.' That is used as a curse word. Also as an irrefutable statement. What are you going to say? 'It's not theatrical'?" (qtd. in Savran 142)

In this way *Speed-the-Plow* is not merely a parody of Hollywood but rather an analogue or photo-negative of the kind of film adaptation exemplified by *About Last Night. . . .* To the extent that film adaptation annihilates the literariness or theatricality of a particular work, according to its own spectacularizing logic of production, so too does *Speed-the-Plow* theatricalize what is most resolutely prosaic and un-filmic about Hollywood. Distinct from other recent plays which touch on Hollywood (such as David Rabe's *Hurlyburly* or Sam Shepard's *True West*), *Speed-the-Plow* is reflective of a remorseless structural purity in its staging of film production, a notably reductive and elemental aesthetic which ironically resembles that of the Douggie Brown film. The play has a taut and formalistic seamlessness which militates against metaphoric meanings or social referents. There is a sense of the action being completely and fully enclosed, internally bounded by the many abstract dualisms, the stark sexual triangle, and the buddy-film banter with which it opens and closes. *Speed-*

the-Plow encapsulates and delimits Hollywood, mirroring *About Last Night . . .*, which enacts a similar containment on *Sexual Perversity*. This is something more subtle and complex than simple parody, to the extent that it refashions the mythic animus between author and producer, and refuses the consolations of the literary and the filmic, art and entertainment, as secure and independent cultural domains.

Taken together, the three texts of the triangle—and the relationship of Mamet and Hollywood they suggest—point to the reified quality of thought as it pertains to both extremes. Hypostatizing Mamet entails significant ideological and hierarchical assumptions about literary authorship, which are silently buttressed by similarly monolithic conceptions of Hollywood. Further, these conventional categories disguise an element of complicity. Hollywood adaptations may serve as expedient markers of inferiority in validating a deeper appreciation of the original—"the novel was more profound," "it worked better on stage," "they changed the author's intention," etc. But the latent populism of mainstream adaptation can also serve as consolation. Commercial adaptations of difficult originals sublimate the unsettling modernist fantasy of an originary authorial voice and autonomous aesthetic world, removed from the brutal marketplace of existence. The filmic adaptation implicitly neutralizes the radical potential of autonomous art—as something distinct from consumer culture—by hearkening wistfully back to a superseded and fantastical era in which originals were still necessary. In this peculiar union of nostalgia and contempt the adaptation may redeem the egalitarian consumerist utopia of the present, and with it the subcutaneous pangs of a guilty life.

Thus a mainstream adaptation like *About Last Night . . .* engages populist fantasy through the symbolic annihilation of the original's bitter and subversive theatrical aura, together with its disquieting elitist overtones. At this level the film producer, as guardian of entertainment values, is a figure of comparative capitalist honesty, in contrast to the aestheticizing pretensions of the unhappy litterateur. Conversely, a scathing performance like *Speed-the-Plow* holds a dramatic mirror to the culture industry—adapts the adapters, as it were—enabling a highbrow identification with the author's literary superiority while gratifying prurient interest in the fetishized space behind the scenes.

The degree to which author, producer, and consumer have become relative rather than absolute subject-positions is perhaps an index of late modernity. To take another prominent example, Michael Crichton's voracious appetite for the technical minutiae surrounding dinosaurs and DNA cloning, sexual harassment, airline disasters, and emergency room medicine has led him to author bestselling novels, and to script, produce, or direct everything from *Coma* to *The Lost World* and *E.R.* Independent of the question of relative value, Mamet's career is anterior to Crichton's—aesthetically, if not chronologically—to the extent that Mamet's work is grounded in the traditions of modern

drama and the paradigm of the playwright as author of a singular and autonomous aesthetic world. The late- or post-modern aspects of Mamet's career derive their significance in relation to Mamet's foothold in the more orthodox forms of cultural modernity. The question of Mamet and Hollywood serves historically as a boundary or limiting instance in conceptualizing the present politics of authorship and adaptation.

Clearly, it is often more comfortable to think identity than to think difference. In a certain way, Mamet's own self-presentation—his essays on women, poker, Hollywood, and the company of men, for example—has oriented perceptions of the author toward an identity with the content and milieu of his works. The actor Joe Mantegna, who has appeared in many Mamet plays and films, remarked "David writes what he loves: men playing poker, living in this world of danger and guns, smoking, and rough talk. He loves it. He's not a voyeur; he's a participant" (Kane, "Interview" 266). Mamet appears to be first and foremost a player, engaged in the same machinations in life and production as his characters are in representation. Ironically, the mythology of the Mamet persona conspires both toward the tough-talking machismo of the iconoclastic author/hero, and toward an affinity for the invisible capitalist depredations of his ostensible "other," the Hollywood producer.

In this way Mamet contributes to a more genuinely dialectical view of authorship, by partaking fully in the bravado of originality while undercutting the recourse to monological origin. To the extent that authorship is a foundational category in thinking about culture, the dialectical author signals the relative instability of received cultural oppositions—art and entertainment, literature and media culture, theatre and film. In addition, author, producer, and consumer are increasingly mere potentialities in the dialectics of culture, empty markers of hypothetical performances. This is the *mise en scène* of the commodity, and it begs renewed attention to both the political rhetoric of culture—how a representation is made, by whom, for whom, and to what end; and the lateral rhetoric of culture—how a particular text or performance is speaking within the marketplace.

Mamet's various roles have enacted a certain authority, a "vision" for which he is justly credited. At the same time, his work has unabashedly implicated itself in the vicissitudes of the mass media and commercial culture. It is certainly now fashionable to look skeptically on the myth of origins; postmodernist chic has made much of originals, copies, and simulacra in relation to the image and technology; we mistrust the omniscient author and celebrate His demise. There is an element of truth in such hip consumerist relativity which can act as a corrective to the fossilized literariness of much high-minded critique. The Mamet persona has been performed across a wide band of culture, and even without the solace of transcendent authority there is a lesson in his willingness to play the game.

Works Cited

Bigsby, C. W. E. *David Mamet.* London: Methuen, 1985.

Brewer, Gay. *David Mamet and Film.* Jefferson, NC: Mc-Farland, 1993.

Carroll, Dennis. "The Recent Mamet Films: 'Business' Versus Communion." Kane, *David Mamet* 175-90.

Cook, David. *A History of Narrative Film.* New York: Norton, 1981.

Gale, Steven. "David Mamet's The Verdict: The Opening Cons." Kane, *David Mamet* 161-74.

Jameson, Fredric. "Reification and Utopia in Mass Culture." *Social Text*: 1 (1979): 130-48.

Kane, Leslie, ed. *David Mamet: A Casebook.* New York: Garland, 1992.

———. "Interview with Joe Mantegna" Kane, *David Mamet* 249-70.

Lumet, Sidney, dir. *The Verdict.* Screenplay by David Mamet. Based on the novel by Barry Reed. With Paul Newman, James Mason, Charlotte Rampling, Jack Warden, Milo O'Shea, and Lindsay Crouse. TCF/Zanuck-Brown, 1982.

Mamet, David, dir. *House of Games.* Written by David Mamet. With Lindsay Crouse, Joe Mantegna, Mike Nussbaum, and Lilia Skala. Orion, 1987.

———. *Sexual Perversity in Chicago and The Duck Variations.* New York: Grove, 1978.

———. *Some Freaks.* New York: Vintage, 1989.

———. *Speed-the-Plow.* New York: Grove, 1988.

Savran, David. *In Their Own Words: Contemporary American Playwrights.* New York: Theatre Communications Group, 1988.

Zwick, Edward, dir. *About Last Night . . .* Screenplay by Tim Kazurinsky and Denise DeClue. Based loosely on the play *Sexual Perversity in Chicago* by David Mamet. With Rob Lowe, Demi Moore, James Belushi, and Elizabeth Perkins. Tri-Star, 1986.

Joseph H. O'Mealy (essay date 1999)

SOURCE: O'Mealy, Joseph H. "Royal Family Values: The Americanization of Alan Bennett's *The Madness of George III.*" *Literature/Film Quarterly* 27, no. 2 (1999): 90-96.

[*In the following essay, O'Mealy presents an analysis of the screen adaptation of* The Madness of George III *as an example of Hollywood's tendency to downplay and simplify the political and constitutional issues explored in the original play.*]

When the film version of Alan Bennett's *The Madness of George III* appeared as *The Madness of King George,* the story circulated that the American backers had insisted on the title change because they feared the sequel-saturated Americans, not having seen the previous two Georges, would be confused.[1] This joke sounded plausible enough. After all, everyone knows that Hollywood producers have never gone broke underestimating the intelligence of the American people. Like the poodle in the microwave, however, the story is probably apocryphal—though with typical slyness, the author himself claims it was true. "This was a marketing decision," Bennett writes in the preface to the published version of the screenplay, "a survey having apparently shown that there were many moviegoers who came away from Kenneth Branagh's film of Henry V wishing they had seen its four predecessors."[2]

That alterations must be made between stageplays and screen adaptations is no news. The transformation of *The Madness of George III* into *The Madness of King George,* however, seems less conditioned by the technical differences between the two media, than, as the title change suggests, by the playwright's and the director's calculated adjustments to the cultural expectations and tastes of two different audiences.

Bennett wrote his stageplay for the narrow constituency of the Royal National Theatre, those better than average educated and monied Londoners and Anglophile tourists for whom theatre-going is a habit. He and Nicholas Hytner, who directed the stage production and the film version, knew that the film needed to reach a world-wide audience, of which the Americans represent the most lucrative part. The screenplay Bennett adapted from his own drama and the directing choices Hytner made in the film reflect this awareness. In an ironic reversal of the words Bennett puts in the mouth of William Pitt, by being "projected on a larger screen," the film version of George III's bout with madness in the late 1780s downplays the "groundwork of politics" as it embraces the "domestic melodramas" of generational conflict and marital disruption, those dynamics of the dysfunctional family American audiences know so well from daytime confessional television. By downplaying and simplifying the political and constitutional issues featured in the drama and foregrounding the family in crisis, Bennett also finds himself working in another very American mode, that of classic American family dramas like *Death of a Salesman* and *Long Day's Journey Into Night.* Either way, high or low, Bennett and Hytner have revised the play with an eye on the American audience.

The structure of the play rests upon the strict dichotomies of space and ideology Bennett identifies as "Windsor," the King's stronghold, and "Westminster," the Parliamentary redoubt. Except for the odd scene set at royalist Kew and the Prince of Wales's Carlton House, the play moves back and forth between these simple oppositions. Act One is almost symmetrical, with eight scenes set at Windsor alternating with six scenes at Westminster and two at Carlton House. Though a little more diffusely arranged, ultimately Act Two's tally is neat: five scenes on royalist grounds versus five scenes set among the Whig opposition, capped of course by the play's grand finale at St. Paul's Cathedral. The audience at the National would presumably recognize the implications of such a structure, in addition to being more familiar with the positions represented by Pitt and Fox. Such careful crosscutting establishes both the centrality and fevered antagonisms of the political struggle at the time. More than a figurehead, George III is in many respects the embodiment of the state. His own conflicted health of mind and body becomes emblematic of the nation's. Whichever political faction can lay claim to speak for or through the reigning monarch becomes therefore, through a syllogistic relationship, the state.

The movie audience is presumed to be less historically astute, so Hytner "opens up" the film enough to lose that oscillation between Windsor and Westminster, with all its attendant implications. A farmyard, a cricket game, a Lincolnshire field break up the intense volleying back and forth between the Pitt and Fox factions for control of the King's person. In fact, the production crew seems so indifferent to the historical acumen of the moviegoer that the film's opening scene contains a close-up of a door at Westminster—actually Eton College—with the clearly visible grafitto "1862" carved into the wood. After all, if the audience doesn't know who George III is, is it likely they'll know the difference between 1862 and 1788?

Changes in the cast of characters between play and film also offer revealing glimpses into Bennett and Hytner's strategies for their new audience. A fair number of figures disappear, and while minor comic butts like Sir Boothby Skrymshir and his dim nephew Ramsden, who pop up here and there seeking patronage from both the Tory and Whig factions, aren't much of a loss, when Edmund Burke disappears and Richard Brinsley Sheridan is reduced to a spear carrier at Carlton House, it becomes clear that the play's political content, complete with its complex relationship to the late Georgian literary sphere, is being diluted. Gone are allusions to Goethe and Gibbon, as well as the witty exchange prompted by Burke's asking Sheridan if he could ever abandon politics:

SHERIDAN:

> As distinct from the theatre, you mean? I don't know. There's the drama, of course. The temperament. And the acting, I suppose.

BURKE:

> What would you miss about politics?

SHERIDAN:

> I'm talking about politics.[3]

The other major casualty in the move from play to film is Dr. Ida Macalpine, a twentieth-century physician, who turns up at the end of the play to propose the porphyria theory of the King's illness. Never happy with this intrusion—"this didn't entirely work"—Bennett recalls that "when the play was revived the following season, the scene was omitted" (*King George* xx). When writing the film version Bennett turned to generic American movies of "thirty years ago" to solve this expository problem. In his favorite scenario, as two of the King's pages empty chamber pots in the river, one would wistfully predict that some day the world would know his master was not mad but suffering from porphyria. He would raise the chamber pot in the air, and the faces of other supposed royal sufferers from porphyria—Mary, Queen of Scots, Queen Anne, and James I—would beam down from the heavens (*King George* xx), accompanied no doubt by a chorus of stringed instruments and an angelic choir.

Bennett knows his Hollywood clichés, but also knows that film can offer less camp ways of providing this information to the viewers. In the introduction to the play version, written two years before he undertook the screen adaptation, he notes quite ruefully that "in a film one could deal with this explanation in the final credits" (*George III* xx), and dispense with the doctor ex machina of Ida Macalpine. Which, in the end, is precisely what he did.

In fact, Bennett's play already contains many film-like touches, especially in the transitions between scenes. For examples, he will elide the action, creating by a change in lighting a dissolve of sorts, from Pitt speaking to the King to Pitt addressing the House of Commons. Or Bennett will cut from the King being strapped into his restraining chair to the Prince of Wales being cinched into his girdle. With his film version, however, Bennett adds to these grammatical conventions the vocabulary of film conventions, generic conventions designed to appeal to an audience raised on the American film noir and western.

Take for instance Lady Pembroke. The stage directions describe her as an "impressive sight," a handsome woman of "around fifty" (*George III* 10). Once the King's dementia loosens his inhibitions, he finds her irresistible, and often tries to wrestle her to the floor; the film keeps that comic frustration, but creates a very different Lady Pembroke. As played by Amanda Donohoe she looks a couple of decades short of fifty, a ripe and luscious Mistress of the Robes to the Queen, who, as embodied by Helen Mirren, is not exactly the German dumpling Bennett placed on stage either.[4]

Even more to the point, the screenplay turns Lady Pembroke into a conventional femme fatale. Early on she flirts with Greville, the King's new equerry and the film's Everyman figure, through whose eyes the audience is meant to apprehend this alien culture of royalty. Later, she coolly seduces him in order to give the Queen access to the King after he has been removed from Windsor and incarcerated at Kew.[5] On the basis of this one encounter the susceptible Greville falls in love with Lady Pembroke, but, at the end of the film, when he attempts to renew their intimacies, she curtly brushes him off with a simple statement of fact: "it was what was required, Mr. Greville, that was all" (*King George* 71). Greville's disillusioning initiation into the mores of the aristocracy is of course the stuff of any education novel, but his sexual conning by a woman with an ulterior motive would also be very familiar to any fan of film noir.

The film's most shameless invocation of an American film convention comes at the climactic moment in the plot, when the Regency Bill is about to be put to a final vote in Parliament. If a vote is taken, the Prince of Wales is sure to be declared Regent, and George III will be put away forever. In the play, news that the King has recovered his wits is enough to squelch the Prince of Wale's accession. The film restages the classic cavalry rescue scene. Pitt cannot turn the tide with a few words in the House; the King himself must appear at Westminster—racing from Kew in a carriage trying to beat the clock, with the usual suspenseful intercutting between preparations for the vote and the progress of the King, slowed down by flocks of bleating sheep (the MPs?) blocking the roadway.

Needless to say, the King does arrive in time, the MPs flood out of their chamber, Parliament hails George III as their monarch, the Prince of Wales faints at being foiled, and a thoroughly entertaining and thoroughly familiar episode from the Saturday serials comes to a close. This sequence seems to have originated in the brain of the director, but Bennett writes amusingly about how the lengthy process of revision and the exigencies of collaboration wore down his resistance: "Had Nicholas Hytner at the outset suggested bringing the King from Kew to Westminster to confront the MPs, I would have been outraged at this adjustment to what had actually happened. By the time I was plodding through the third draft I would have taken the King to Blackpool if I thought it would have helped" (*King George* xxi).

The largest single change from play to film is, however, the introduction of Maria Fitzherbert, the secret wife of the Prince of Wales. Bennett says he added her because "the plot needed thickening"—which is true—and because he "wanted Mrs. Fitzherbert to have her own story and not just be sitting around as the companion to the Prince" (*King George* xv). Though the evidence of her own story is debatable, Mrs. Fitzherbert indisputably does place the Prince of Wales in a family context. In the play Prinny surrounds himself with a male coterie, chief among them his younger brother Frederick, the Duke of York, and comes across as a fat foppish dilettante whose major concerns in life are furniture design and the agonies of tight corsetting. Maria humanizes the film's Prince, who, as played by Rupert Everett, is neither convincingly fat nor especially foppish—though clearly foolish. Her sweet concern for the King's health stands in sharp contrast to the maneuverings of every one else in the Prince's camp, and even checks the Prince's own baser tendencies to place his own advancement over his father's recovery. When Maria urges the Prince to remember the family ties instead of impatiently desiring power, ("This is your father, sir. Be kind"), Fox notes that "she has more sense than he has" (*King George* 60). Nor is this Prince totally unfeeling. When the Prince peruses the Regency Bill for the mention

of a provision for Maria, who as a Catholic is legally prohibited from marrying the heir to the British throne, and finds none, he assures her, "It will happen, Maria, I promise you" (60), suggesting a devotion, however temporary, that dispels some of the self-absorption which defined his character in the play.

Most of Bennett's treatment of the family relations in the film is not as radical as his introduction of Maria Fitzherbert. The changes between stage and screen are few but telling. Most apparent is the recession of the political allusions and ambience which necessarily grants additional prominence to George III's family dilemma. The play's strongly defined political context keeps the family narrative, which Bennett pays a great deal of attention to, from dominating. The film loosens this political underpinning, and the family melodrama takes most of the attention by default. The film's rapid pacing and abbreviated scenes also sharpen the domestic dialogue. The Prince of Wales's remark when his mother slaps him after his father has tried to choke him—"Assaulted by both one's parents in the same evening! What is family life coming to?"—appears in both play and film. On the stage it is embedded in a long scene, while in the film it serves as the punchline for a thirty-second scene. As a result, the film audience is far more likely to remember its ironic comment on domestic tranquility.

Bennett chooses to foreground pathos more often than comedy in his depiction of the King's domestic relations. This serves to paint the King's tragedy as a personal one, the plight of a good family man—George did after all father fifteen children with the same woman and had no apparent mistresses—whose mental collapse is exacerbated by his anxiety about his loved ones. In one instance, Bennett uses a documented example of the King's dementia, his conviction that London was being flooded, to augment the audience's appreciation of George as a good father to his large brood. In actuality, George was desperate to rescue from the rising waters a manuscript he had been working on (Macalpine/Hunter 41). On stage, however, when he begins to rave, he insists that the children be carried to higher ground, and in the film this expression of fatherly concern becomes a full scene, with George hustling the youngest children out of bed in various degrees of distress and hysteria, and carrying them up to a rooftop.

This family-centric emphasis colors even the use Bennett makes of Shakespeare in both play and film. A reading of the Act IV reunion of Lear and Cordelia is the catalyst for, or at least an indicator of, the restoration of George III's wits. Anthony Lane has praised this scene for its bold proposition that "art—neither quackery nor dreadful discipline but the consolations of poetry—will finally draw the fever from the lunatic" (88)—a subtle and powerful reading, but not one likely to occur to most viewers of the film, who are more liable to agree with the interpretation of Shakespeare's play that Bennett has Thurlow deliver: "Tragic story. Of course, if that fool of a messenger had just got that little bit more of a move on, Cordelia wouldn't have been hanged, Lear wouldn't have died, and it would have ended happily . . . which I think would have made a much better ending. Because as it is, it's so damned tragic" (*King George* 67). By having Thurlow reduce the tragedy to a family quarrel reconciled, and regret that the father and daughter can't live happily ever after, Bennett is of course having his fun with this middlebrow view, which in the eighteenth century also found expression in Nahum Tate's happy ending version of Lear. And though twentieth-century American audiences may have only an intermittent acquaintance with Shakespeare and a minimal understanding of the principles of tragedy, most will applaud this affecting parallel between the restoration of Lear to his daughter and the imminent restoration of George to his wife and children—a reunion the film underlines with a scene of the two youngest children, Amelia and Adolphus, rushing to greet Papa on his return to Windsor. Almost as neatly as Nahum Tate, then, Bennett has domesticated and sentimentalized Lear.

The best example in the film of a greater foregrounding of the family comes in the very last scene, at St. Paul's Cathedral. On stage, only the King and Queen mount the staircase in their state robes to commence the Thanksgiving ceremony. The film offers the whole family, thus not only celebrating the restoration of the King and the rescue of the nation from its crisis, but gathering together royal parents and all the children, even the Prince of Wales and Duke of York, in a display of public solidarity. Bennett transfers stage dialogue from an earlier interview between the two oldest princes and their parents to the movie's final public and domestic scene.

KING:

> We must try to be more a family. There are model farms now, model villages, even model factories. Well, we must be a model family for the nation to look to.

When the Prince of Wales replies that he wants something to do, however, Bennett supplies the King with some new advice:.

KING:

> Smile at the people. Wave to them. Let them see we are happy! That is why we are here.
>
> (*King George* 74).

The sight of the royal family on the steps of St. Paul's, waving to the cheering crowds—the parents sincerely, the children in varying degrees of sullen obedience—neatly fulfills the Queen's request at the beginning of the movie that her eldest son make a greater effort at public relations. "George, smile, you lazy hound. It's what you're paid for. Smile and wave. Come on, everybody, smile and wave" (*King George* 11). Despite the personal cost, the royals thus grant the nation the image of a happy family. In this way, Bennett slips in a slyly contemporary view of the figurehead role of the British royal family. Most Americans can remember Charles and Diana on those very steps of

St. Paul's, and know how that rosy venture in public relations finally ended. Nor would they have much trouble catching the contemporary allusion in the play's wittiest line—"to be heir to the throne is not a position; it is a predicament" (*George III* 63)—though in the film Bennett helps them out by substituting "Prince of Wales" for "heir to the throne," just in case they don't know the two are synonymous.

Not surprisingly, American tastes and values exert their most powerful influence upon Bennett's recasting of George III's mental relationship to the recently "lost" American colonies, and upon the question of the efficacy of the several therapeutic treatments, especially Dr. Willis's "restraining" method, designed to cure the King's supposed madness.

In the play George refers to America with longing and regret. His mania may be due in part to this pining, for as Anthony Lane notes, "when a man loses his colonies . . . his wits will not be far behind (87). A similar melancholic tone is present in the film, though not uniformly. George's elegiac speech on the "forests, as old as the world itself, meadows, plains, immense solitudes," is carried over to the film, but without the second half which broadens the perspective: "Soon we shall lose India, the Indies, Ireland even . . ." (*George III* 25). The film insists on an American focus, and through the addition of at least three new scenes, crafts a new narrative trajectory for George to follow vis-à-vis the United States.

He starts out reluctant to accept the loss. When addressing Parliament he drops the word "former" from a reference to his North American possessions, and has to be corrected by a cough from the Lord Chancellor (*King George* 9). Some time later, when Pitt gently reminds him that the United States "are a fact, sir," he becomes "furious, and thrusts his face into Pitt's and seems about to explode," suggesting another link between the loss and incipient irrationality (author's direction, *King George* 15). A few scenes later he thrashes at thistle with a twig, shouting to himself, "This is the way we deal with America, sir. I'll teach you, sirs. Take that, Mr. Colonist," clearing progressing even further toward a breakdown (*King George* 20).

Since most Americans with any knowledge of George III probably think of him as the tyrant that patriots like Washington fought to defeat, the danger of course lies in the possibility that George will lose the American viewers' sympathy over these political matters. George's loss of the colonies must be therefore characterized as a personal loss, one that any anxious parent might agonize over, but which a healthy person will learn to deal with. Bennett and Hytner wisely have cut the scene in the play where Willis attempts to force the King to name the thirteen American colonies as part of his therapy (*George III* 74-75). George refuses, and his resistance can only be read, in the play, as a refusal to be reconciled, a refusal that the film wants to avoid. So after the King has recovered and he and Pitt are once again in the Library, Bennett has written a new scene that clarifies the therapeutic nature of the King's ordeal. George III can now talk about America with resignation—he can finally let go.

KING:

. . . But what of the colonies, Mr. Pitt?

PITT:

America is now a nation, sir.

KING:

Well, we must get used to it. I have known stranger things. I once saw a sheep with five legs.

(King George 70).

Bennett's little deflationary joke at the end softens the capitulation, but surely the American viewers won't mind, priding themselves on being good sports and also knowing that, although the English can't help acting a little superior, in their heart of hearts, they secretly wish to be like their American cousins.

Bennett's attitude toward the therapist himself, Dr. Willis, also seems to have undergone a trans-Atlantic sea change from stage to film. The one virtue of having Dr. Macalpine barge into the story and announce to the stage audience that none of the medical treatments—not just Sir Lucas Pepys's coprophilia, but also Willis's bondage and discipline—actually worked is that the King's ordeal takes on a horrific irony. And, as Ben Brantley notes, irony "is Mr. Bennett's element" (13). Porphyria's cyclic nature would have led to remission regardless of treatment, a point the stage version underlines when the King rebuts Pitt's opinion that Willis's regime had "done you some service, sir." "No," George replies, "It is Time that has done me the service" (*George III* 88).

The film reverses those sentiments. After the King suggests that Willis must have done him some good, Pitt answers, "I think it is time has done you the service, sir" (*King George* 70). Now George the patient seems to believe in his doctor. Anthony Lane's suspicion that the film "chooses to fudge" the question of whether Willis's treatments actually helped is correct (87). The question is why?

Again the American audience intervenes. Bennett's diary entry for November 17, 1980, offers a revealing assessment of the American capacity for earnest self-improvement. Taken to an Alcoholics Anonymous meeting in New York's Greenwich Village by a friend promising a "theatrical event," Bennett feels very much out of place. And not because he's not an alcoholic. Dreading the moment when he must stand up and tell his story, Bennett imagines saying, "My name is Alan and I'm English and I don't do this sort of thing." Luckily some woman monopolizes the meeting with her own story, and Bennett escapes, his privacy intact. He concludes his account, however, with a back-handed compliment: "Still, as so often with Americans, one comes away thinking that they do this kind of thing so much better than we do, and that, wanting irony, they show each other more concern" (*Writing Home* 109-110).

It is this perceived American lack of a sense of irony that almost requires Bennett to recast the impact of Dr. Willis on the madness of King George. If all the indignities that Willis serves up are as pointless as the obviously crackpot theories of the other doctors, the American audience might become dispirited. The graphic display of the King's blistering with heated cups, and the sight of a once proud and generally benevolent man strapped by force into a chair, gagged with a filthy rag, and broken by repeated insults are bad enough. It would be intolerable to think that all this has gone for naught and that passive acceptance would have led to the same result. The irony might be almost as sadistic as the treatment. As Bennett's earlier observations on the AA meeting suggest, Americans tend to put greater faith than the English in therapeutic ventures. Taking arms against a sea of troubles is not a strategy to be debated in the home of the self-help movement. Action is a moral imperative, success goes to the enterprising, and Willis's scheme is nothing if not bold. No stiff upper lip for the Americans, thank you.

As a result, the film audience is left with the distinct possibility that Willis might have made a difference. Though he looks like a cross between "a male nanny and rather sinister social worker," as played by Ian Holm, Willis inspires a great deal more confidence than those doctors, "looking like grotesques in a Hogarth print," who normally attend the King (Baruma 16). On stage, Willis hears that he is not welcome at the St. Paul's service, and is dismissed without hesitation: "Be off, sir. Back to your sheep and your pigs. The King is himself again" (*George III* 93). The theatre audience already knows, thanks to Dr. Macalpine, that the King will have other attacks in 1802 and 1810, and that the doctors would "have done better to leave him alone" (*George III* 93). The irony in the King's dismissal of Willis is thus double-edged: he will be back and once again do more harm than good. In the film this irony is diminished. One of the last shots in the film is of Willis mixing in with the crowd at St. Paul's, no longer at the King's side, but nearby, ever ready, just in case. The following statement does appear on screen just before the credits: "The colour of the King's urine suggests he was suffering from porphyria, a physical illness that affects the nervous system. The disease is periodic, unpredictable— and hereditary." But only a careful cinematic reader will catch the ironic implications. Moviegoers will probably have already kicked over their popcorn boxes in their rush for the exit.

For these viewers, Mr. and Mrs. King, as the royal couple playfully call themselves in private, have apparently ridden out another storm in their unapologetically bourgeois marriage. Clouds may one day gather again on the horizon, but then what family doesn't have its troubles?

Notes

1. Anthony Lane, "Power Mad," *The New Yorker,* January 6, 1995, 86. Even though *The Madness of King*

George was an Anglo-American co-production (Channel Four Films and The Samuel Goldwyn Company), the American audience's needs carried a great deal of weight. The policy at Channel Four Films has been to make their films "accessible to as wide an audience as possible." Recently, the thick Scottish accents in Trainspotting were re-dubbed by Channel Four "so that Americans would understand what they were saying" (*New York Times,* August 6, 1996, B4).

2. Alan Bennett, *The Madness of King George,* London: Faber and Faber, 1995, pp. xiii-xiv. Note: all future references to the screenplay will be indicated by *King George* in the text.

3. Alan Bennett, *The Madness of George III,* London: Faber and Faber, 1992, p. 6. Note: all future references to the stageplay will be indicated by *George III* in the text.

4. As also witnessed by the casting of the lean, handsome Rupert Everett as the puffy toad Prince, the universal law that movie stars must be more glamorous than stage actors is not challenged by this film.

5. This episode is completely invented by Bennett. In actuality the Queen was given apartments at Kew (see Ida Macalpine and Richard Hunter, *George III and the Mad-Business,* London: Allen Lane, 1969, p. 31).

Works Cited

Bennett, Alan. *The Madness of George III*. London: Faber and Faber, 1992.

Bennett, Alan. *The Madness of King George*. London: Faber and Faber, 1995.

Bennett, Alan. *Writing Home*. London: Faber and Faber, 1994.

Brantley, Ben. "Swimming in Irony." *The New York Times Book Review,* October 1, 1995: 13-14.

Buruma, Ian. "The Great Art of Embarrassment." *The New York Review of Books,* February 16, 1995: 15-18.

Lane, Anthony. "Power Mad." *The New Yorker,* January 6, 1995: 86-88.

Macalpine, Ida and Richard Hunter. *George III and the Mad-Business.* London: Allen Lane, The Penguin Press, 1969.

FURTHER READING

Criticism

Haskell, Molly. "Is it Time to Trust Hollywood?" *The New York Times* (January 28, 1990): 1, 36-37.

Discussion of the relationship between works of literature and their adapted versions on-screen, noting the importance of judging films as independent works of art.

Kovacs, Lee. *The Haunted Screen: Ghosts in Literature and Film.* Jefferson: McFarland and Company, Inc. 1999, 181 p.

Collection of essays on ghost stories and their film adaptations from the 1930s to the 1990s.

Leff, Leonard J. "A Thunderous Reception: Broadway, Hollywood, and *A Farewell to Arms.*" *Hemingway Review* 15, no. 2 (1996): 33-51.

Traces the adaptive history of Hemingway's *A Farewell to Arms,* both on stage and film.

Masavisut Nitaya, George Simson, and Larry E. Smith, eds. *Gender and Culture in Literature and Film East and West: Issues of Perception and Interpretation.* Honolulu: College of Languages and Literature, University of Hawaii, 1994, 296 p.

Essays focusing on gender and cultural differences as highlighted in various works of Western and Eastern literature and film.

Margolies, Alan. "'Kissing, Shooting, and Sacrificing': F. Scott Fitzgerald and the Hollywood Market." In *The Short Stories of F. Scott Fitzgerald: New Approaches to Criticism,* edited by Jackson R. Bryer, pp. 65-73. Madison: The University of Wisconsin Press, 1982.

Explores Fitzgerald's relationship with Hollywood screenwriting in the context of his short stories.

Sconce, Jeffrey. "Narrative Authority and Social Narrativity: The Cinematic Reconstitution of Bronte's *Jane Eyre.*" *Wide Angle* 10, no. 1 (1988): 46-61.

An analysis of a 1940s adaptation of *Jane Eyre,* focusing on the ways in which screenwriters adapted the novel to suit contemporary audiences.

Simons, John D., ed. *Literature and Film in the Historical Dimension: Selected Papers from the Fifteenth Annual Florida State University Conference on Literature and Film.* Gainesville: University Press of Florida, 1990, 183 p.

Selected essays from a conference focusing on the exploration of the relationship between aspects of history, literature, and film.

Wood, Gary. "Stephen King and Hollywood." *Cinefantastique* 21, no. 4 (February 1991): 24-51.

An overview of various film adaptations of Stephen King's works.

Jews in Literature

INTRODUCTION

Jews have been a presence in continental literature since the Middle Ages and in American literature since the nineteenth century. Scholars note that Christian writers have been fairly consistent in representing Jews in terms of the ethnic stereotype, but that trend has been shifting in the second half of the twentieth century toward a more complex and realistic characterization. In literature as well as in western culture, Jews have been traditionally portrayed as foreign, mysterious aliens associated with money (especially money-lending) and power in society. Shylock, one of the central characters of William Shakespeare's drama *The Merchant of Venice* (1600), perhaps best exemplifies this kind of characterization.

Modern critics have actively investigated the attitude of many major writers toward Jews as evidenced in their personal writings as well as in their works. For example, Maud Ellmann has explored the image of Jews projected in the works of T. S. Eliot and Ezra Pound, finding implied anti-Semitism in the case of Eliot, and very overt anti-Semitism in Pound's poetry and radio speeches delivered during World War II. Leopold Bloom, the hero of James Joyce's *Ulysses* (1922), has been the subject of numerous studies, notably by Harry Girling. Ronald Granofsky has connected elements of anti-Semitism in the writings of D. H. Lawrence with his ideas regarding race and masculinity. Pointing out both conscious and subconscious strains of anti-Semitism in the writings of Virginia Woolf and Stevie Smith, Phyllis Lassner has discussed the two writers' responses to the coming of World War II. In a similar vein, Susan Rubin Suleiman has examined Jean-Paul Sartre's *Refléxions sur la question juive* (1946), discovering buried anti-Semitic elements in this essay criticizing the treatment of Jews in France.

In the latter part of the twentieth century, the image of Jews in literature has been transformed by the Holocaust, a watershed event for Jews and many gentiles who have struggled to find a way to express their thoughts and feelings about the horrific events of World War II. When critics discuss Jews in literature in this century, they usually refer both to Jewish characters in literature and to Jewish authors. In the case of either group, the Holocaust has proven a defining moment in history. After the events of World War II, gentile writers have written more sympathetically about Jews in European and American society. Some critics have noted that Jews have become a symbol of persecution, endurance, and moral courage in late-twentieth-century literature. Many Jewish writers, on the other hand, have undergone a painful personal journey to re-examine their identity and heritage. They have also written about the paradoxical process of trying to find a language and a literary framework for writing about events that seem to be, by their very nature, unimaginable and unutterable. Scholars have praised such writers as Elie Wiesel, Nelly Sachs, Ernst Weichart, and Hermann Kasack for their courage in articulating the Holocaust experience. Much critical attention has been focused on the portrayal of the Holocaust in literature—whether personal accounts by survivors, in documentary and historical writings, or in prose fiction and poetry. Such scholars as Lawrence L. Langer, Sidra DeKoven Ezrahi, Edward R. Isser, and Michael André Bernstein have explored various aspects of the literature of the Holocaust, from implications for Jewish writers' religious faith to the enacting of Holocaust experiences on stage.

REPRESENTATIVE WORKS

Yehuda Amichai
Lo me-'akshav, Lo mikan [*Not of This Time, Not of This Place*] (novel) 1963

Aharon Appelfield
Badenheim (novel) 1939

Saul Bellow
Dangling Man (novel) 1944
Mr. Sammler's Planet (novel) 1969

Wolfgang Borchert
Draussen vorder Tür [*The Man Outside*] (novel) 1947

Theodore Dreiser
The Titan (novel) 1914
The Hand of the Potter (novel) 1918

T. S. Eliot
The Wasteland (poetry) 1922
After Strange Gods (essays) 1934
Notes toward a Definition of Culture (criticism) 1949

Peter Finkelgruen
Haus Deutschland: oder Die Geschichte eines ungesühnten Mordes (novel) 1992

E. M. Forster
The Longest Journey (novel) 1907

John Galsworthy
Loyalties (novel) 1922

Graham Greene
A Gun for Sale (novel) 1936
Brighton Rock (novel) 1938

Lillian Hellman
Watch on the Rhine (drama) 1941

Ernest Hemingway
The Sun also Rises (novel) 1926

John Hersey
The Wall (novel) 1950

Laura Z. Hobson
Gentleman's Agreement (drama) 1946

William Hoffman
The Trumpet Unblown (novel) 1955

James Joyce
Ulysses (novel) 1922

Hermann Kasack
Die Stadt hinter dem Strom [*The City beyond the Ruins*]
    (novel) 1947

D. H. Lawrence
Aaron's Rod (novel) 1922
England, My England (novel) 1922
The Captain's Doll (novella) 1923

Sinclair Lewis
Arrowsmith (novel) 1925

Arthur Miller
Focus (drama) 1945
Incident at Vichy (drama) 1964

Clifford Odets
Till the Day I Die (drama) 1935

Ezra Pound
The Cantos (poetry) 1948
Radio Speeches (speeches) 1978

Nelly Sachs
The Chimneys (poetry) 1967

Jean-Paul Sartre
Refléxions sur la question juive (essay) 1946

Bernard Shaw
Man and Superman (drama) 1905

Robert Sherwood
There Shall Be No Night (novel) 1940

Isaac Bashevis Singer
The Séance and Other Stories (short stories) 1968
Enemies, A Love Story (novel) 1972

Stevie Smith
Novel on Yellow Paper (novel) 1936
Over the Frontier (novel) 1938

C. P. Snow
The Conscience of the Rich (novel) 1958
Corridors of Power (novel) 1964

Ernst Weichert
Der Totenwold [*The Forest of the Dead*] (novel) 1947

Peter Weiss
Die Ermittlung [*The Investigation*] (novel) 1965

Patrick White
Riders in the Chariot (novel) 1961

Elie Wiesel
La Nuit [*Night*] (autobiography) 1958
Les Chants des Morts [*Legends of Our Time*] (novel) 1964

Virginia Woolf
Three Guineas (novella) 1938
Between the Acts (novel) 1941

Richard Wright
Native Son (novel) 1940

OVERVIEWS AND GENERAL STUDIES

Esther L. Panitz (essay date 1981)

SOURCE: Panitz, Esther. "Alienation and the Cult of the Individual." In *The Alien in Their Midst: Images of Jews in English Literature*, pp. 162-70. Rutherford, NJ: Associated University Presses, Inc., 1981.

[*In the following excerpt, Panitz presents a summary of the changing image of the Jew in English literature from the time of Geoffrey Chaucer to the twentieth century, and concludes that stereotypical thinking about Jews still remains.*]

The certitude that had been part of Browning's life reinforced his cheerful eagerness. Yet in the midst of all that pleasant ambience, the earlier frustrations and conflicts of the Victorian Age grew into the nativisms and doubts of the twentieth century. Scientific skepticism and an emphasis on empiricism helped erode individual morality, which had been based on accepted social values. In the political arena, imperialism, which had once engendered a sense of pride in England's customs and institutions, came to be regarded as a system of induced slavery. Economically, living standards improved for British workers because of the increased power of the Labor Movement. However, unionization alone was not the key to a happier, more meaningful existence for everyone. To compound the difficulty, a belief in the classless society as the ideal state did little to secure man's goals or purposes in life. Similarly, substituting the group for the individual did not solve private moral dilemmas. Socialism may well have been the herald of the new age, and scientific determinism was quite prepared to plot human behavior both for the present and for the future. Unfortunately, such attempts at interpreting the modern condition did little to reassert man's significance in the world or to clarify his goals. The result in Britain was literature that reflected man's alienation from himself, from others, and from the many ideals that he had once held.

In keeping with this new sense of individualism, George Bernard Shaw revolted against sterile plodding nineteenth-century melodrama. He declared that he would let his characters "rip," that the flow of ideas and action in which they engaged would form a natural, if sometimes illogical order of events. Such a policy produced slightly mad sets of human beings who peopled his plays. In *Man and Superman* it was the Jewish brigand, Mendoza, transformed as devil in a dream sequence, against whom the hero, Jack Tanner, argued his case. He protested that truth, beauty, and justice, which properly belong in hell, made that place all the more boring. Shaw had grafted his own reversal of values onto the medieval tradition of the Jew as devil. He was still the fiend, though only in a dream, and he bore a stereotypical Jewish surname, "Mendoza." Were all the virtues to be consigned to Hades, the Jew would become their proper guardian.

In this journey on the road to rebellion, Shaw also modified the usual association of Jews with wealth. In *Major Barbara* the Jew, Lazarus, was the silent partner in Andrew Undershaft's million-dollar munitions plant. But while Undershaft and Lazarus were prepared, like Barabas of old, to make war for the sake of profits, the rationale for their course of action had changed. Undershaft was convinced that poverty is worse than death. Therefore he and Lazarus had to foster wars everywhere to insure a continuous demand for their military hardware. Only in this way could they have guaranteed their factory workers the benefits of full employment. Even Major Barbara, Undershaft's evangelist daughter, knuckled under to the lure of her father's and Lazarus's millions: like the miser's gold of long ago, such wealth would breed, growing in direct proportion to increases in casualties and deaths on the battlefield. And by the time the play had run its course, Barbara would have no scruples about using ill-gotten gains for religious and charitable purposes.

Shaw's satire cut deep. Its very outrageousness proclaimed its Swiftean quality. But there were differences. Unlike Swift's, Shaw's irony did not dwell on the issue of Jews as a "stiff-neck'd people," a loathsome collectivity bound together to work its evil upon unsuspecting Anglicans. In fact, Shaw once admitted the superior wisdom of doing business with Jews and thought it advantageous, from a profit motive, to prefer their company to Christians.[1] The association of Jews with money-getting did not lead him to condemn them as a group. But by the time Shaw had completed destroying *all* the idols of his fellow human beings, he had come round to *Heartbreak House.* There all the values of Western civilization broke down; there men, ambiguous and contradictory, were separated from one another, and there, happiness, to be achieved by reaching the seventh degree of concentration into nothingness, was to be found in imbibing rum. In Shaw's literary world, then, the Jew was merely another characterization to be used for iconoclastic purposes. But even for Shaw, the literary image of the Jew still grew from the traditional Christian way in which he had earlier been perceived. Either he was the devil, or was associated, in however novel a fashion, with the accumulation of wealth.

Unlike Shaw, James Joyce did see his Jewish protagonist in ethnic terms. What was new, however, was that now the Jew's ethnicity and alienation were taken for granted by the author. He did not pass judgment on these aspects; he merely recorded the reactions they evoked in the Jew and in those about him. This he achieved by emphasizing the Israelite and Irish strains in the characters he shaped.[2]

James Joyce's *Ulysses,* one of the great masterpieces of twentieth-century literature, is a symbolic, naturalistic, poetic novel of man's eternal quest for identity. Here Joyce blended actual events and interior monologues in the lives of Leopold Bloom, an unprepossessing middle-class Jewish advertising salesman from Dublin, of his sexually adept singer-wife, Molly, and of Stephen Dedalus, a young Catholic teacher, to show how each of these people, within the same twenty-four-hour period of June 16, 1904, tried to learn to know himself.

For each, the acts engaged in on their journeys, both actual and metaphorical, were disarmingly simple, but like all simplicities they had profound implications whose depths derived both from the inner significance Joyce attached to them and from the parallels drawn to the wandering of the Homeric Ulysses. Thus, in the first third of the book, Stephen, like Telemachus of old, began by seeking his father, and finally, toward the end of the volume, met up with Bloom, a modern Ulysses, wise, yet foolish and devious; mediocre, yet perceptive and sensitive. In the search Telemachus-Stephen not only engaged in all those activities common to the human species, breathing, sleeping, eating, hearing, seeing, talking, eliminating, but he also fantasized, rebuked himself for his treatment of his dying mother, taught school, wrote incomplete verse, and mistrusted his friends, who, in their arrogant, patronizing ways also represented Penelope's suitors, who had finally to be defeated.

In the second third of the book, Bloom too began the day's activities inauspiciously. He fed the cat, brought his wife, Molly, breakfast in bed, read a note from his daughter, and delivered a message to his wife from her lover and concert manager, Blazes Boylan. He also went to the baths to prepare for his attendance at Paddy Dignam's funeral; he stopped at the newspaper office to sign a contract for placing an ad; he spoke with Mrs. Breen on O'Connell Bridge and wandered into different pubs where he thought of his wife's past and current lovers. He also waited at a maternity hospital for the birth his neighbor's, Mrs. Purefoy's, child. Finally, he rescued Stephen from a brothel after a street brawl with the police. But the significances of these routine activities were to be found in the preoccupation of his mind with images of his dead son, Rudy, and with his failure as a husband to Molly. He was tempted to reform her, physically and spiritually, much as Ulysses also sought to return to Penelope. All of Bloom's hells did not exactly parallel Ulysses', but that did not matter. Like Ulysses, Bloom too was an exile in an alien land, in the midst of those who refused to understand him.

For this reason, Joyce made his Everyman a converted Jew and fashioned Bloom precisely not as a Jew who would be distinguished by his own formal credal adherences, but rather as one who was not part of the ethnic majority and therefore remained alienated. Certainly, none of Bloom's formal acts ever proclaimed his original Jewishness. Throughout the work, his one distinguishing characteristic, his attachment to an orange grove in Palestine, spoke volumes for his nationalistic yearnings, but it did little to enlarge upon any specific non-Christian orientation to life that he may have had. On the contrary, he had eaten pork, and found some solace in hearing the mass, though in his mind he tended to deride the physical implications of Communion. Yet Christians in other literature were also prone to similar musings. Had not Browning's Renaissance bishop who ordered his tomb at St. Praxed's said as much, that lying there for centuries he would hear "the mutter of the mass" and "see God drunk and eaten all day long?" It was not Bloom's acceptance or rejection of any one or more Christian practices that set him apart from the lower middle classes among whom he lived. It was merely that all the others felt him to be different.

Throughout the book these differences arose in such a way as to emphasize the distinctiveness of race. This was a universal condition that Joyce caught and whose various facets he detailed in a multitude of situations. Thus Bloom was prepared to tell a sick joke at his own expense at Paddy Dignam's funeral, but was not allowed to conclude

it. Stephen's headmaster, Mr. Deasy, had indulged in silly rantings over Jewish control of the world. At the newspaper office, Bloom encountered some intellectual anti-Semites who associated Shakespeare's (spurious) Jewish origin with greed and uxoriousness. In the final meeting between Stephen and Bloom, the old blood-libel story, now seen as a variant of the Hugh of Lincoln legend, was sung. It was almost as though *The Prioresses Tale* had come full circle.

However, unlike his predecessors, similarly masters in the art of fiction, Joyce did not stoop to the caricaturized convention of the Jew, whose alleged evil was always to be associated with the immoral uses of wealth and vulgar taste. Joyce was not a Dickens, nor a Thackeray, nor a Trollope. But, first among the great novelists of the new age, he saw the Jew merely from the angle of an ethnic uniqueness, as one who was distinct from the rest of that society in whose midst he dwelled. With the possible exception of George Eliot, no British author had previously manifested such intuition or insight into the specifics of the Jewish psyche. Critics have seen resemblances between Joyce himself and Bloom, and it is true that Joyce laughed at himself. But that is inconsequential. What is important was that Joyce did not pass judgment on those differences which defined the Jew in popular terms. Instead, he merely recorded the emotional reactions of Bloom and his acquaintances to each other.

Bloom's alienation was revealed in that scene at Barney Kiernan's Pub in Little Britain Street, where an unnamed citizen mocked the excesses to which Irish patriotism was prone. Like the one-eyed cannibalistic cyclops of old who threatened Ulysses, here the anonymous citizen, molded to gigantic proportions and accompanied by a ferocious dog, cursed Bloom in the elaborate mode of a Celtic epic. But he cursed him for the sheer pleasure of it, even when Bloom tried to reason with him or weigh all the issues of any problem. To the citizen's description of the rule of fearful autocracy in the British Navy, Bloom responded with

> "Isn't discipline the same anywhere? I mean wouldn't it be the same here if you pit force against force?"

But the citizen's reaction was violent.

> "Didn't I tell you? As true as I'm drinking this porter, if he was at his last gasp, he'd try to downface you that living was dying."[3]

After the citizen, with the help of his confrères, had completed his catalogue of Irish martyrdoms at the hands of the English, the French, the Spaniards, and the Germans who had usurped the English throne, everyone "had a laugh at Bloom," for he did not fit his own description of a national as one who belongs to a nation "of the same people living in the same place."[4] While the others guffawed, the citizen spat at Bloom. Yet Bloom was not to be outdone. He identified himself as belonging to a race that was "Robbed . . . Plundered. Insulted. Persecuted." In his willful obtuseness, the citizen asked Bloom if he were talking about the new Jerusalem. Once Bloom answered, using the word, *love,* the citizen, deliberately misinterpreting Bloom's equation of love with life, called the Jew "a new apostle to the gentiles."[5]

This was a harsher treatment of Bloom than had occurred during the earlier episodes, at Paddy Dignam's funeral, or at the newspaper office where the editor swore at Bloom but did not threaten him. But the citizen's new and further level of degradation evoked a response from Bloom that appeared pathetic, courageous, and somewhat ludicrous all at the same time. Like Ulysses of old, Bloom, having shown his historic affiliation with his race, went on to shout

> ". . . three cheers for Israel,"

as his friend Martin Cunningham tried to get him away from the citizen's shouted obscenities, or the crude advice of the shady narrator who ranted with

> "Arrah, sit down on the Parliamentary side of your arse for Christ's sake and don't be making a public exhibition of yourself,"

along with other choice expressions contributed by

> all the ragamuffins and sluts of the nation round the door.

Finally, Bloom managed to retort,

> "Mendelssohn was a jew and Karl Marx and Mercandante and Spinoza. And the Saviour was a jew, his father was a jew. Your God."

To the rather bitterly humorous interpolation by the "good Christian, Martin"

> ". . . he had no father,"

Bloom modified the answer by saying,

> ". . . well, his uncle was a jew . . . your God was a jew, Christ was a jew like me."

These words put the citizen into such an apoplectic state that he swore,

> "by Jesus, says he, I'll brain that bloody jew man for using the holy name. By Jesus, I'll crucify him, so I will. Give us that biscuit box there.[6]

The hilarity that such lines called forth was matched only by Joyce's parody of newspaper articles, which, describing the tin box's clattering after Bloom in his wagon, ultimately elevated that clatter to the level of an earthquake, an earthquake to which church and state responded, to their glory.

The catastrophe was terrific and instantaneous in its effect . . . there is no record extant of a similar seismic disturbance in our island since the earthquake of 1534, the year of rebellion of Silken Thomas. . . . all the lordly residences in the vicinity of the Palace of Justice were demolished and that noble edifice itself, in which at the time of the catastrophe, important legal debates were in progress, literally a mass of ruins beneath which it is to be feared all the occupants had to be buried alive.

Because the earthquake was accompanied by a cyclone, the headgear and the silk umbrella with its initialed gold head that bore the arms and house number of the Recorder of Ireland were discovered in other "remote parts" of the island. Expressions of sympathy poured in from all over the world.

> Messages of condolences are being hourly received from all parts of the different continents and the sovereign pontiff has been graciously pleased to decree that a special *missa de profunctis* shall be celebrated simultaneously by the ordinances of each and every church of all the episcopal dioceses subject to the authority of the Holy See in suffrage of the souls of those faithful departed who have been so unexpectedly called from our midst. The work of salvage, removal of debris, human remains, etc. has been entrusted to Messrs. Michael Meade and Son, 159 Great Brunswick Street, and Messrs. J. C. Martin, 77, 78, 79 and 80 North Wall, assisted by the men and officers of the Duke of Cornwall's Eighth Infantry under the general supervision of H. H. H. Rear Admiral, the Right Honorable Hercules Hannibal Habeas Corpus Anderson, K.E., K.P., P.C., C.K.B., M.P., D.S.C., S.O.D., MF. H., MR. I.A., BL., MUS. DOC., P.L.G., FT. C.D., F.R.U.I., F.R.C.P.I., and F.R.C.S.I.

Joyce then pricked the rhetoric of his own style by reminding the reader that the fight between the citizen and Bloom began over some misplaced horse bets. The last paragraph of the chapter reverts to a mock-heroic biblical tone and Bloom's escape from Kiernan's tavern is compared to Elijah's ascent to heaven, where the customers beheld Him, even him, Ben Bloom, Elijah amid clouds of angels ascended to the glory of the brightness at an angle of 45 degrees over Donohoe's in Little Green Street like a shot off a shovel.[7]

If aspects of nationalism and faith set Bloom apart from others in Kiernan's Pub, then at the maternity hospital where he stopped to inquire after a neighbor, Mrs. Purefoy, he alone revealed a whole range of emotions alien to Stephen, to his friends, and to some of the medical students. Bloom was compassionate and humane, while the rest jested at fertility, childbirth, and the life giving process,[8] much as Ulysses' crew ate the divine oxen of the sun's pasture, for which their ship was destroyed by a thunderbolt and they were all killed.

In their biting jests at any affirmation of life, Stephen and his colleagues parodied all styles of language, from the biblical, to the hortatory Anglo-Saxon mode, to the medieval scholastic forms of writing and on to an imitation of the turgid prose of the seventeenth century metaphysicians. Through it all, the young men seemed to be saying that in the end all life winds down to a nothingness.

> . . . the aged sisters draw us unto life: we wait, fatten, sport, clip, clasp, sunder, dwindle, dig over us dead they bend . . . and as no man knows the ubicity of his tumulus nor to what processes we shall thereby be ushered nor whether to a Tophet or to Edenville in like ways all hidden when we would backward see from what regions of remoteness the whatness of our wholeness hath fetched his whenceness.[9]

Joyce pitted Bloom against any such ascription of emptiness of meaning to life.[10] Bloom alone rejoiced that after a hard labor, Mrs. Purefoy gave birth to a boy. While the young men scored him in elegant eighteenth century clarity of language for his compassion, they also adverted to his alienism and commercial propensities, and added ugly innuendos concerning his own private sexual behavior.

> But with what pleasure let it be asked of the noble lord, his patron, has this alien, whom the concession of a gracious prince has admitted to civil rights constituted the lord paramount of our internal polity? Where is now that gratitude which loyalty would have counselled? During the recent war, whenever the enemy had a temporary advantage with his granados did this traitor to his kind not seize the moment to discharge his peace against the empire of which he is a tenant at will rather than tremble for the security of his 4%? Or is it that being a deluder of others, he has at last become his own and his only enjoyer? Far be it from candor to violate the bed chamber of a respectable lady, the daughter of a gallant major [Molly Bloom], or to cast the more distant reflection upon her virtue, but if he challenges attention there . . . then be it said so. . . . But this new exponent of morals and healer of ills is at his best an exotic tree, which when rooted in its native orient grove and flourished and was abundant in balm, but transplanted to a clime more temperate, its roots have lost their quondam vigor while the stuff that comes away from it is stagnant, acid and inoperative.[11]

In a later episode, corresponding to the Homeric incident where Circe converted Ulysses' crew to swine, Bloom too, now completely dominated by his inner fantasies, viewed himself as a transvestite, eager to be debased, in a masochistic way, by the woman he had known, or was about to know, in a brothel. For having given a pig's trotter to a passing dog, he was arrested as a nuisance, and then was subjected to a Kafkaesque nightmare trial, in which his bankrupt attorney, J. J. O'Molloy, indulging in those stupidities of legal jargon which shape a form of black humor, pleaded Bloom's innocence of any sexual misconduct. He ascribed Bloom's guiltlessness either to his strange origin or to his insanity. Here, in a parody of a dramatic scene, O'Molloy spoke up in "pained protest":

> This is no place for indecent levity at the expense of an erring mortal disguised in liquor. We are not in a beer-garden, nor at an Oxford Rag nor is this a travesty of

justice. My client is an infant, a poor foreign immigrant who started scratch as a stowaway and is now trying to turn an honest penny. The trumped up misdemeanor which is due to a momentary aberration of heredity brought on by hallucination, such familiarities as the alleged guilty occurrences being . . . permitted in my client's native place, the land of the Pharaoh. *Prima facie,* I put it to you that there were no attempt at carnally knowing. Intimacy did not occur and the offense complained of Driscoll [Bloom's former maid servant] that her virtue was solicited, was not repeated. I would deal in especial with atavism. There have been cases of somnambulism in my client's family, of the accused, if the accused could speak, he could a tale unfold of one of the strangest that have ever been narrated between the covers of a book. He himself my Lord is a physical wreck from cholera's weak chest. His submission is that he is of Mongolian extraction and irresponsible for his action. Not all there in fact . . .

> By Hades, I will not have any client of mine gagged and badgered in this fashion by a pack of curs and laughing hyenas. The mosaic code has superceded to the law of the jungle. . . . when in doubt persecute Bloom.[12]

After the nightmare of the trial receded from Bloom's mind and the awaited execution was averted, he imagined himself the leader of the Irish people. Acting magnanimously on their behalf, he offered them a magical incantation of Hebrew letters of the alphabet, words meaning "phylacteries," "the sons of the covenent," "unleavened bread," "Germanic Jewry," and the term "insanity." Finally transformed into a Messiah, or Godhead, he was then pilloried in imitation of the Crucifixion.[13]

The net effect of such images, including the one where Bloom, transformed into a woman, gave birth to eight metallic children, all of whom became controllers of vast amounts of public wealth, strengthened the conventional caricature of the Jew as given to alien ways, immorality, arrogance, and lust for power. But in this instance, Joyce ascribed the fantasies to the victim himself; the Jew had come to believe what others were saying about him. Such negative connotations thereby lent themselves all the more easily to facile use by the Jew's detractors and calumniators, while they yet, by the very insanity of their argument, gave credence to those who would laugh such inanities to scorn. Joyce, by delineating the true inner reactions of Stephen, his friends, and the Irish populace to Bloom's very existence, and by portraying Bloom's own confused longing for love, security, and identity in what was a sterile Dublin wasteland, had made it possible to see Bloom, despite his alienation, as a veritable Ulysses, an Everyman who would endure.

In the light of Bloom's responses to those about him—he would affirm life while others mocked it; he would offer love while that unknown citizen in Kiernan's Pub counseled hate—there would be ample reason to agree with one critic that Bloom possessed Ulysses' classic temper, his heroic spirit.[14] In this sense, not only would Bloom persist, but he would also be aware of moral certainties in himself and others. Yet, after Bloom had rescued Stephen from the brothel, paid his bill there, comforted him after a cuff on the head by an exasperated soldier, talked with him in a cabman's shelter, and then finally engaged him in a long series of topics confined to the didactic logic and style of a catechism, there was communication, but little conscious understanding between the two men.

> What reduced to their simplest reciprocal form were Bloom's thoughts about Stephen's thoughts about Bloom and Bloom's thoughts about Stephen's thoughts about Bloom's thoughts about Stephen?
>
> He thought that he thought that he was a Jew, where as he knew that he knew that he knew that he was not.[15]

Put colloquially, when it came down to the nitty-gritty, Bloom thought that Stephen thought that he (Bloom) was a Jew, while Stephen knew that he (Bloom) knew that he (Stephen) was not. Were this to be taken as literally as it sounds, the great gulf of separation between Stephen and Bloom had not been bridged.

Yet certain most-respected students of Joyce's *Ulysses* have insisted that Stephen, in his unconscious quest for love, charity, and compassion, found those qualities in Bloom (hadn't Bloom counseled love and pity for Mrs. Purefoy, and even for the "ragamuffins" in the pub?), and that Bloom, seeing in Stephen a new crystallization of his long-dead son, Rudy, was reintegrated once more, now to assert his rightful role as a husband to his unfaithful wife, Molly. It has also been suggested that Stephen, the young, rejected, and rejecting intellectual, sought not only his father, but also a justification for a creative reawakening of his literary talents, and that his temporary meeting with Bloom granted him that moment of clarification, a Joycean epiphany, which enabled him later to write his masterpiece, *Ulysses*.[16]

For those who would insist upon a spiritual basis for this novel, Stephen-Joyce-Telemachus would then be returning to his spiritual father, Ulysses-Bloom-God, and in the Christian sense, Christ, in whom all would merge and be one. To carry this analogy further, Stephen and Bloom, talking together in the cabman's shelter, participated in the rite of atonement (at-one-ment), partook of communion with Stephen drinking cocoa, the drink of the gods, while Bloom, in his kitchen, was both God and celebrant. Since by such consumption Stephen became one with God, he would be reinvested with creative-artistic powers. Stephen, then, to fulfill his mission, would have to leave the Father-God, in order to go off and forge the artistic reshaping of his race, its "uncreated conscience in the smithy of his soul."[17] Such a rendering would omit the Christian sacrifice of the Son; unless, of course, Stephen, as one with Bloom-God, fashioned-created with his word.

Like other modern writers, Joyce was fascinated more by the psychology than the structure of myths. Homeric par-

allels were able to provide suitable frames for Joyce's *Ulysses*, but while the Homeric Ulysses was of epic proportions, Bloom was not. It has been argued that it would be immaterial to wonder whether after the Stephen-Bloom meeting, Bloom's self-assertion, equated with Molly's giving him breakfast in bed, would be realized, or whether Molly in her long unfinished, two-thousand-word reverie would really revise her relationship with her husband. Most critics, with one exception,[18] have refused to consider the consequences of such uncertainties.[19] For them, the Stephen-Bloom meeting, temporary though it was, was sufficient to resolve the difficulties. Yet were Bloom of truly heroic proportions and Stephen a youth destined to grow to magnificence, the intent of Joyce's work would be diminished. Both Stephen and Bloom would have lost their human qualities, and the alienation in which Joyce fashioned them would lose its meaning. Was not Joyce essentially implying that Stephen and Bloom had come together once, only to drift apart again? But the "epiphany" of each, even so, would remain with them.

Ulysses, a novel that vibrates with the reality of human interactions, relationships that constitute the fabric of modern society, reveals both Stephen and Bloom as archetypes of twentieth-century man, lost, alienated, with few relevant values to replace the old certainties of home, nation, and faith. Perhaps Matthew Arnold, writing long before *Ulysses* appeared in print, expressed the true understanding of the Ulysses-Bloom, Telemechus-Stephen and Penelope-Molly story.

> Ah, love, let us be true
> to one another! for the world, which seems
> to lie before us like a land of dreams,
> so various, so beautiful, so new
> hath really neither joy, nor love, nor life
> nor certitude, nor peace, nor help for pain
> and we are here as on a darkling plain,
> swept with confused alarms of struggle and flight
> where ignorant armies clash by night.[20]

In *Ulysses,* James Joyce built a whole edifice on the tenuousness of human relationships made more fragile by the doubt cast forth in *Dover Beach.* It would also appear that Graham Greene reacted to the emptiness inherent in Arnold's warning by peopling his novelist's world with alienated characters. But whereas Joyce relied on interior thought and half-formulated, often paradoxical emotions to stress the uncertainty and aimlessness of his characters, Greene utilized authorial comments, involved plot sequences, and contrived coincidences to fashion people who, at the very end, were frequently brought to the brink of salvation through the proddings of the Catholic Church. Though a much younger man than Joyce, Greene was a master craftsman of that realistic type of writing which antedated Joyce. Greene produced novels, short stories, and dramas designed both to entertain and to instruct. Practically all of these works, whether shaped for didactic purposes or constructed as popular literary amusements, found their justification in Greene's Catholicism, which served either as an embellishment, or as itself constituting the religious allegory by which the tale could be resolved.

Such religious teachings frequently involved the Judas theme of betrayal, a motif whose application Greene intensified through an adept use of irony, particularly in *This Gun for Hire,* an "entertainment," as he called it, and in its sequel, *Brighton Rock.* James Raven, the betrayed hero of *This Gun for Hire,* was not a Christlike prototype, but a murderer and denizen of the underworld, whose passing Greene likened to that of the Christian Savior. In *Brighton Rock,* Pinkie Brown, the seventeen-year-old boy leader of a razor-wielding gang involved in the racetrack-protection racket, was evil incarnate. Yet, in forcing his young bride into a sham suicide pact so as to accomplish her murder, he forgot that it was her death, not his own, that he had intended:

> and looking out as if it was he who'd got to take some sort of farewell of the bike and the bungalow and the rainy street, he thought of the words in the Mass:
>
> He was in the world and the world was made by Him and the world knew Him not.[21]

In both novels, the actual agents who betrayed the murderous nonheroes to the police were women, regarded either as representatives of humanity or as forces for natural justice. But, beyond the women, the very springs of evil themselves against whom Greene's rootless young men were pitted, were Jews.

This Gun for Hire is a swift, suspenseful thriller in which James Raven, a member of a gang involved, like Pinkie's, in the racetrack-protection frauds, was hired by one Cholmondeley (alias Davis, alias Davenant, and at odds with a seamy, mysterious, theatrical producer called Cohen), an agent of a wealthy Jewish steel mogul, Sir Marcus, to murder the humanitarian minister of a small European nation. Raven accomplishes his assignment, and the remainder of the novel consists of a double pursuit in which the police chase Raven, and Raven himself seeks Cholmondeley, his initial betrayer who had paid for the assassination in marked, stolen notes. But the heroine, Anne Crowdor, fearful that the murder will lead to war, finally betrays Raven to her fiancé, Mather, the detective in charge of the case.

The ostensible purpose of the murder had indeed been political. Since the martyred minister had been an ardent advocate for peace, his death at English hands might have led to a confrontation between England and the unnamed European country whose representative he was, a state of affairs from which Sir Marcus, the wily Jewish director of Midland Steel, alone would benefit. Much like Andrew Undershaft of Undershaft and Lazarus in Shaw's play *Major Barbara,* Sir Marcus would secure enormous profits from any future battle. But whereas Shaw laughed up his sleeve when his Andrew Undershaft convinced his daughter that war was a desirable end because it insured wealth and prestige for the leaders while spurring employment for the population as a whole, Greene allows his Sir Marcus no humor whatsoever. For that alien, detestable creature, squatting over his millions much as T. S. Eliot's Jew squatted on his window-sill in contempt, was incapable, like Dickens's millionaire Mr. Merdle, of consuming any substantial food (for how could a devil eat as humans ate?). Greene's heroine, Anne Crowdor, recognized the malevolence of Sir Marcus and his tool, Cholmondeley, so that her first impulse was to agree with Raven in seeking the death of these malefactors. But simple justice demanded an awareness of Raven's own murderous deed. In the end Anne rationalizes her own betrayal of Raven to the authorities by convincing herself that his killing the minister would have made armed conflict inevitable.

Her disclosure of Raven's guilt compounds the irony of the final act before the police closed in on him. Moments before his imminent demise, he managed effectively to kill the villains of the piece and thereby evoke sympathy for himself, a sympathy heightened by reiterated descriptions of his appalling early childhood and adolescence. Greene, in fact, reached the very height of pity for the physically repulsive Raven, with his harelip and miserable eyes. Readers are informed that had Raven himself, as part of a poor, despised class, realized that the minister was a pacifist, he would not have agreed to the dastardly act. Further, Greene compares Raven with a scapegoat, one forced to suffer the evils of others. Had he not indeed, from one standpoint, suffered for the evils of Sir Marcus and Cholmondeley, even though he himself had originally been a willing partner in the enterprise?

By supplying these reasons for Raven's basically purposeless killing—a killing whose only real motive was the two-hundred pounds promised the penniless Raven—Greene cleverly mythologized his nonhero into a symbol of a universal sufferer. In his flight from justice, Raven reflected that "foxes have their holes, but the son of man. . . ."[22] Raven's search for Cholmondeley and his attempts to elude the police occurred during the Christmas season in the Midlands industrial town of Nottwich. In his reaction to the reproductions of the Nativity scene in a storefront, Raven saw his own fate as Christ's, at the hands of a society that manipulated a legend out of an actual historic occurrence.

> They twisted everything, even the story in there, it was historical, it had happened, but they twisted it to their own purpose. They made him a god because they could feel fine about it all, they didn't have to consider themselves responsible for the raw deal they'd given him. He'd consented, hadn't he? That was the argument, because he could have called down "a legion of angels," if he'd wanted to escape hanging there. On your life he could, he thought, with better lack of faith, just as easily as his own father, taking the drop at Wandsworth [about to be hanged in prison], could have saved himself when the trap opened. He stood there with his face against the glass, waiting for somebody to deny that

reasoning, staring at the swaddled child with a horrified tenderness—"the little bastard"—because he [Raven] was educated and he knew what the child was in for, the damned Jews and the double-crossing Judas, with no one ever to draw a knife in his side when the soldiers came for him.[23]

Christlike, then; and by the time Raven had Mather within sight of his automatic, he was unable to shoot. He

> couldn't work up any sourness, any bitterness at his betrayal . . . but he had been marked from his birth for this end, to be betrayed in turn by everyone until every avenue into life had been safely closed. . . . as he fixed his arm at the long reluctant last and Saunders [Mather's assistant] shot him in the back through the opening door, death came to him in the form of unbearable pain. It was if he had to deliver this pain as a woman delivers a child and he sobbed and moaned in the effort. At last it came out of him and he followed his only child into a vast desolation.[24]

For all the sympathy Greene garnered about him, James Raven plainly was not a Christian in the deepest meaning of the term. Only Pinkie Brown of *Brighton Rock* surpassed him in evil.

Pinkie was hard and his name seemed ineradicable, like the rock-candy manufactured in the seaside resort of Brighton, whose letters remained clearly imprinted even at the end of the sweet stick. *Brighton Rock* then became the story of Pinkie's criminal career. He was only a seventeen-year-old boy, yet he had inherited the leadership of a gang of crooks when its chief mobster, a criminal named Kite, was betrayed by a cheap journalist, Fred Hale, to a notorious Jewish gangster. This racketeer, Colleoni, was in league with the police. At Colleoni's request, James Raven, the Raven of *This Gun for Hire*, had first disposed of Kite before he proceeded to tackle that innocent, pacifist foreign minister.

Pinkie, as the new leader of Kite's mob, had to assert his independence and avenge his predecessor's murder. This he attempted to do by having his razor-wielding hooligans "carve up" Fred Hale. Though Hale died of natural causes just before he was to have been slashed, the intent of Pinkie and his cohorts had clearly been murder. Their motive might have remained hidden had it not been for Ida Arnold, a sleazy, voluptuous blonde of easy virtue, who had earlier taken a liking to Hale and suspected that he had been done away with. Ida, as the representative of decent society and eager to see justice done in its natural way, equated the whole matter with "an eye for an eye, a tooth for a tooth." She manages effectively, through a whole series of strange coincidences, to force Pinkie to his own death, when he, in turn, is almost about to succeed in persuading his young bride, Rose, into preceding him in "a sham suicide pact." To hide the fact that Hale had really been murdered, Pinkie had been forced to marry Rose. He wished now to dispose of her through her own self-destruction, for he regarded his wife as a threat to his vir-

ginity. He identified such chasteness with the purity of his religion and with his role as leader. But Ida Arnold, the stickler for what was right, had destroyed all that with her constant prying. In fact, Greene applied the measure of everyday morality to Ida's quest for truth so doggedly that her pursuit of righteousness became tedious. At last it grew horrible even for Rose, who was a symbol of Catholic goodness, and whose own search for theological certainty was fulfilled by an old priest who comforted her after Pinkie's death. After her confession that she had prepared to take her own life, he reassured her that it was better to live in sin an entire lifetime than to believe that any soul might suffer damnation in the afterlife.

On another occasion Greene had wondered why there had been such a to-do about *Brighton Rock,* for all he had written was the story of one man's journey to hell,[25] but its implications reach far beyond Pinkie's descent into the netherworld. On his way he gathers sympathy from author and reader and Rose, who though her intended suicide would have placed her in "mortal sin", did not want Pinkie to face the darkness by himself.[26] The priest's blessing could also extend posthumously to Pinkie; did not divine mercy include the damned? Only the Jewish gangster is so evil in mind and spirit, that having no compassion he cannot even reach into Pinkie's hell. And while Colleoni has that satisfying glow about him like one who controls "Parliament . . . cash registers . . . policemen and prostitutes,"[27] it is Ida, stalking justice, who manages to separate Rose from Pinkie, when all along as good and evil "they should have remained together."[28]

Why Pinkie merited God's forgiveness but Colleoni and Ida did not is beyond explanation. Equally mystifying is the fact that the priest's word would provide scant consolation for Rose. Returning to her room, she would find that record Pinkie had once made for her at a cheap shop in Brighton, a record which she had hidden in a cupboard and to which she would now listen. She would shortly discover "the horror of it all" in the words of her dead husband: "God damn you, you little bitch, why can't you go back home for ever and let me be?"[29] What is clear however is that Greene's villainous protagonists are miraculously transformed by death, while the evil forces that sometimes join them or are at odds with them, the Jews and their followers, Colleoni of *Brighton Rock* and Sir Marcus of *This Gun for Hire* are never redeemed.

It would be simple enough to explain Greene's predilection for stereotyped Jewish villains—in *Orient Express,* it had been two merchant Jews, in *This Gun for Hire* and *Brighton Rock,* an armanents king and mobster—who served as modern day evidences of old anti-Semitic biases. Far more troublesome, however, would be the observation that Jews, or their unwitting representatives, had a part in doing Greene's evil geniuses to death. There has been a considerable amount of literary concern over Greene's fascination with his own morally and or physically repulsive fictive creations. Explanations with regard to his Manichaean or Jansenist tendencies have not been found want-ing.[30] Yet the key question with regard to Greene's be-trayed evildoers has not been asked. Were the Jews, or sometimes unwilling partners like Anne Crowder of *This Gun for Hire* or Ida Arnold of *Brighton Rock*, themselves the means by which divine justice was brought to bear, or were they still the emissaries of the devil?

Such queries would not be applicable to Evelyn Waugh's characterizations of Jews in his novels. These portrayals were merely extensions of stereotypes by earlier writers. This is all the more amazing in that Waugh's surrealist stories were mainly repetitions of one Shavian theme, the downfall of Western civilization with its humanistic val-ues. In his madcap universe, his protagonists bordered on the comic, the satiric, and the insane. Yet his Jews were still cast in the old mold. In *Decline and Fall* Dr. Augus-tus Fagan, the headmaster of Llanabba Castle, a public school in Wales, was a swindler. The scheming Jesuit priest of *Vile Bodies,* Father Rothschild S.J., was a fraudulent Jew, privy to the confidences of a Prime Minister. In *Hel-ena* the Wandering Jew was prepared to sell religion as a useful commodity, and in *Men at Arms* even the Jewish refugees in Yugoslavia in World War II were cheats and hypocrites, involved in questionable trade arrangements, who did the Partisans out of what was rightfully theirs.

W. Somerset Maugham was also content to evoke the old ghosts of anti-Semitism. His Jews, or those approximating them, remained pushy and always on the edge of society, where they never quite made it. Elliott Templeton, of *The Razor's Edge,* despised a brash young Jew for engaging in questionable deals in art and antiques, the very sort of chi-canery that was Templeton's own stock-in-trade. And al-most to a man, the fellow passengers aboard ship in the story, "Mr. Know-All," of *Cosmopolitans,* disliked Max Kalada, who, Jewish or not, was plainly depicted as the stereotype of the Jewish fixer.

Anti-Semitism in John Galsworthy's play *Loyalties* is based on totally different premises than those of the works of Maugham and Waugh. Written in 1922, not long after the period when Joyce was experimenting with his rootless individuals but before Greene had commenced his fascina-tion with seedy, isolated people on the fringes of society, *Loyalties* was a drama that dealt neither with murderous heroes, nor with ambivalent, quixotic, erratic personalities. Instead, its protagonists were typical representatives of Britain's upper and middle classes who put a premium on place and position in society.

The theme of this play was simple enough: except for rare occasions, most people placed group, class, religious, and ethnic loyalties to one another above moral considerations. To protect the reputation of any member of a specific clique was paramount. Under such circumstances silence and falsehood were to be fostered as part of a discreet, if somewhat subverted sense of honor.

In this story, a status-seeking young Jew, Ferdinand De Levis, who won almost one thousand pounds at the races

by entering a filly for whose keep he had paid, then had those monies stolen from him by the animal's original owner. That was Ronald Dancy, a typical upper-class of-ficer, who, together with his friends, frequented assorted racing and social clubs. Dancy and his peers lived by the gentleman's code of English society, which demanded loy-alty at the price of honesty. The drama itself involved opening trial negotiations instituted by De Levis, where circumstantial evidence had already emphasized the likeli-hood of Dancy's guilt. That guilt was later corroborated through the intervention of two representatives of the middle classes, one of whom was an Italian, a rather re-cent immigrant to England.

As an officer in Britain's colonial forces and a military ad-venturer, Dancy strongly believed in the superiority of the English mind and temperament. This would partially ex-plain why he saw nothing wrong in using the stolen money to pay off a "debt of honor" to the daughter of that Italian immigrant. This payment then released Dancy from any claims of affection she might have had upon him and al-lowed him to marry a woman of his own class. To Dancy such a transaction appeared as legitimate as robbing the Jew in the first place, the more so since the racing animal originally belonged to him. By the time the drama reached its denouement, De Levis, unlike Shylock, did not demand his pound of flesh. He only wanted justice done, and was prepared to donate his recovered purloined funds to char-ity. For his part, Dancy, still convinced of the morality of the gentleman's code of behavior, refused to accept his so-licitor's suggestion or that of one of his John Bullish friends that he either go off to fight in Morocco, or through diplomatic contacts seek a position at the Spanish War Of-fice. Instead, as his wife tried to postpone the moment of her husband's arrest, Dancy, in the bedroom, fired a bullet through his heart.

Throughout his ordeal, Dancy's friends remained loyal to him, even though they were aware of his guilt. Their com-mon bond of anti-Semitism provided the justification for their action. To begin with, Charles Winsor, the owner of the country house where the theft occurred, and his wife, Lady Adela, implied that De Levis's wealth was ill-gotten and that he was thoroughly disliked both for his flashy ways and for having entered into a wager over some par-lor trick with Dancy. Winsor and Lady Adela saw nothing wrong in Dancy's accepting the silly bet, but were still an-noyed at De Levis's stupidities, such as his hankering after social status. After De Levis had openly accused Dancy of the theft, Dancy's colleagues banded together to blackball De Levis's admission to the latest in a series of social clubs. The only basis for his acceptance would have been a common decision on the part of all concerned to keep the matter of the robbery quiet. But since De Levis was both practical and astute enough to realize that he was tol-erated only for his wealth, once that was gone the only re-course he had left was to recoup his losses. In acting on this premise, De Levis had broken the gentleman's code of behavior. He bruited the notion of the theft about the club-rooms; he refused to duel with Dancy so as to settle the matter at swords' point, and remained impervious to Dancy's request. Dancy wanted De Levis to apologize to him in writing for having had the effrontery to impute thievery to a gentleman and an officer. De Levis's adamant opposition only intensified the animosity that Dancy's peers felt toward him, while they found excuses for Dancy's behavior in the notion that he craved excitement and wondered whether two jury men, who appeared to be Jews, would not be prejudiced against Dancy. A potent dislike of Jews had prompted a prosperous middle-class merchant, Mr. Gilman, to offer evidence on Dancy's behalf, evidence that ironically enough became Dancy's undoing. When Gilman turned to a law clerk, assisting Dancy's solicitor, and said

> "I don't like—Ebrews. They work harder, they're more sober, they're honest and they're everywhere. I've nothing against them, but they get on so,"[31]

he was voicing a common British complaint.

Like Shaw, Galsworthy had also abjured the well-made play of French extraction. He earnestly believed that a successful play depended upon the presentation of fully integrated, wholly realized characters, whose thoughts, motives, and actions would then determine the natural unfolding of the narrative. But *Loyalties* did not measure up to such a standard. Its attempt to weigh the consequences of anti-Semitism in a starkly personal, highly dramatic way among believable human beings led instead to the emphasis on plot over personality. The figures who then emerged, Dancy as a typical British colonial, the British upper society women who viewed a trial as a much needed thrill in their otherwise boring lives, the liquor-drinking, bridge-playing club members, the immigrant with his artificial Italian accent, and even De Levis himself—all proved to be uninspiring creations who mouthed hackneyed statements. To Dancy's ugly but familiar epithet of "damn Jew" hurled at him, De Levis responded almost in kind. Using words that Disraeli in another context had once made famous, De Levis said:

> "My race was old when you were all savages. I am proud to be a Jew."[32]

There was only one insightful moment in the play that relieved the commonplace quality of such lines. That was when Jacob Twisden, the solicitor, convinced at last of Dancy's guilt, refused to defend him any further. Though Twisden chose this course against the inclination of his heart and will, it was an option that proved that on rare occasions and under extreme duress, the law will win out over group loyalties. It would appear that the only one in this play who cherished such a victory was the dramatist himself, who in real life had had some legal training.

At one moment during the chase in *This Gun for Hire*, James Raven overheard two women discussing the merits of *Loyalties*. They commented on its profundity and noted how humane the author was and that he was also a promi-

nent antivivisectionist. Greene's irony here could not have been more trenchant, for Greene himself was writing of rootless outcasts, while Galsworthy dealt with people whose very close ties to each other reinforced their prejudices.

Though he was a later contemporary of Shaw and Joyce, and much of his work preceded Greene's literary output, Galsworthy did not properly belong to that generation of writers concerned with the isolated individual. Shaw's Jewdevil, Mendoza, and Jack Tanner in the dream-sequence in *Man and Superman* may have spoken at cross-purposes; Leopold Bloom and Stephen Dedalus, when they finally met, may have answered each other in catechismal form, but they did not communicate. Anne Crowdor listened to James Raven while other thoughts were crowding her mind, and Pinkie Brown was prepared to subvert all of Rose's ideas because he bore no emotional relationship to her, but Dancy and De Levis found a means for communication in the shared antipathy they felt to one another.

An attempt has elsewhere been made to show that C. P. Snow, in his novel sequences called the *Strangers and Brothers* series, was also interested in the essential isolation of the individual in society, hence his all-inclusive title for most of his fiction. While men ought in reality to have been brothers, they were in essence only strangers to one another.[33] But such an interpretation would put an undue strain upon the whole thrust of Snow's work. Snow was always more concerned with personal and group interactions in their relationships to the use and abuse of power than he was with the unique individualities of the characters he created.

Though his novels were not autobiographical, Snow used his own *persona* or mask in the guise of one Lewis Eliot, who, like himself, was at home both in the world of the humanities and in science. In the *Strangers and Brothers* sequence, Snow managed effectively to fashion Eliot as his narrator. At the same time, through clever reminiscing and effective cross-referencing to new sets of circumstances in a variety of his novels, Snow also allowed Eliot to grow to maturity. Eliot's own dynamism then permitted him to move in various circles of society with comparative ease. A barrister by profession, he was also an academician at an anonymous Cambridge college. He had close ties with eminent scientists, classicists, historians, administrators, statesmen, and politicians in government. Each one of the novels in this series then deals with a multitude of moral problems refracted against Eliot. Inevitably, those problems arose when power was to be altered in some fashion in some school, group, family, corporate entity, or governmental institution. Frequently, these institutions were intended as microcosms of larger ruling units. The changes in power structure that went on in the cloistered college of a university bore implications for the administration of a country. The adoption, for example, of a radical nuclear policy by England in the fifties not only played havoc with the fates of individual politicians enmeshed in the intrigue for power, but would ultimately alter England's capacity for self-government. Though Eliot's sympathies in any one of these given situations were never hidden, his passion for dispassionate observation resulted in a style of writing by Snow that was both analytic and introspective, one that flowed from the traditions set in motion by Jane Austen, George Eliot, and Anthony Trollope.

Unlike the other novels in the *Strangers and Brothers* series, C. P. Snow's *The Conscience of the Rich* did not involve itself with either the machinations of a group of masters at a college or the maneuverings of civil service officials in a defense ministry. Instead, it centered on the interrelationships of an enormously wealthy Anglo-Jewish merchant-banking family in their town house in Bryanston Square, London. Here Lewis Eliot was concerned not only with the destructive effects of power exercised by March *père*, Leonard, or Mr. L. as he was called, on March *fils*, Charles, but also with the wrenchings and distortions of Charles's inner personality which arose from quite another cause. For C. P. Snow's theme in *The Conscience of the Rich* was that while Charles's inherited wealth had originally limited his choice of vocation and therefore denied him freedom, his Jewishness compounded his sense of shame at being an alien, albeit a successful one, in a society that would never accept him wholly. Therefore his was a "sick conscience."

Briefly, while the plot of the novel read like a good scenario, it also served as a frame for Charles's psychological complexities and pinpoints his father's authoritarian eccentricities. At the very outset of the novel, Charles, a classmate of Eliot's, refused, after he had handled himself well in his first case in court, to continue with his chosen profession. He would not remain a lawyer because he feared that this was the course that all bright, rich young Jews of his class and community were destined to take. Instead, he chose medicine and married the daughter of a doctor; his wife was Jewish and a contributor to a Communist journal. He incurred the wrath of his father and the opposition of his assorted relatives for his break with tradition. Charles's fight for independence appeared to be more damaging to his father's ego than was his sister Katherine's marriage to Francis Getliffe, a young Cambridge physicist who was a Christian. Eliot observed that by marrying a Jewess "in the orthodox manner," Charles rationalized his defection from the legal profession and compensated for his sister's alliance with a Gentile. But Eliot was not certain that Charles's marriage would free him from self-doubts. The remainder of the novel's plot then fulfilled Eliot's pessimistic appraisal. A rejected lover of Charles's radical wife managed to create a government crisis by implicating Charles's uncle, Sir Philip, a Cabinet minister, in unethical behavior, while Charles's wife, to uphold her Marxist beliefs, refused to release certain materials that would have lifted the shadow of suspicion from the March establishment. At the very end, Charles's father cut him off completely from his inheritance.

The patent objective of this novel was to show the decline in power of a wealthy Jewish banking house, modeled closely on that of the Rothschilds. But some of the attitudes it presented vis-à-vis twentieth-century British Jews might have been as commonly prevalent as those held by Mr. Gilman in *Loyalties,* who had come forward to bolster Dancy's reputation. Though the Marches were all sober, clever people "who had got on so," Katherine March had balked at going to socials composed exclusively of Jewish young people, while Charles himself was ashamed of his heritage. Snow would have his readers believe that Leonard March was more distressed at his son's marrying a girl of his own faith, but of leftist leanings, than at his daughter Katherine's becoming the wife of a Gentile academician. The connection between Jews and wealth had by now acquired a new aspect.

To this composite portrait of the wealthy Jewish merchant and the rebellious son, Snow had on another occasion added a scientific genius who was a Jew by accident of birth. David Rubin in *Corridors of Power* was really no different from his Christian counterpart, Francis Getliffe, in *The Conscience of the Rich.* Yet of David Rubin, Snow has written

> He was the most polite of men. He had been born in Brooklyn, his parents still spoke English as a foreign language. But he had his own kind of assurance, it did not surprise him to be told that he was the favorite for that year's Nobel physics prize.[34]

Could the ascription of assurance to David Rubin in spite of his alien origin have been anything but another example of stereotypical thinking? Again, when Eliot introduced Francis Getliffe's daughter, Penelope, who was in love with a wealthy young scion of impeccable Anglo-Saxon lineage, the reader was told:

> She was nineteen . . . Junoesque and in a rosy, flowering fashion, beautiful . . . Where that particular style of beauty came from, no one could explain; if I had not known, it would not have occurred to me that her mother was Jewish.[35]

Despite his analytical tendencies, the author could not help but think of Jews in preconceived and standardized terms.

Once such type casting led him to affirm that Jews were superior intellectually to non-Jews. This observation was not in keeping with the impartial tone Snow usually consigned to Lewis Eliot in the *Strangers and Brothers* series.[36]

One of the constant factors in an analysis of anti-Semitic attitudes would be attributing superior intelligence to Jews, an intelligence frequently associated with a certain unscrupulousness of character. If on the other hand Gentiles somehow were lacking in certain Christian mental endowments, they more than compensated for it by virtuous traits of temperament and personality. In several essays and articles, George Orwell, an earlier contemporary of Snow's, showed his awareness of such judgments; he regarded them as part of that larger irrationality which he equated with anti-Semitism in Britain during the two or more decades before the Second World War. But he was, at best, only able to describe its manifestations. Jews, he presumed, competed with native Britons for employment and housing; during the war years they profited from goods and services that arose in connection with the black market; had Hitler not persecuted them, they would have applauded his policies and economics; as German refugees they frequently denigrated British taste, customs, and manners. And on one occasion Orwell himself apparently believed that, at the height of the Blitz, Jews availed themselves in larger numbers than any other group of the shelters in the London Tube. On the other hand, the author refused to accept the canard that Jews were responsible for the deaths of one hundred citizens; when a bomb bursting nearby caused them to flee to the entrance of an underground station, the victims died in the crush. Still, the basic question as to why the Jews should have served as the scapegoat during the trying days of World War II eluded Orwell. While he would have urged the application of scientific methods to determine the root causes of anti-Semitism, he realized that this was not feasible. Many Britishers who might have had innate feelings of anti-Semitism would never own up to them at a time when Jews were being destroyed by Hitler. For this reason Orwell imagined that the English sense of decency would have revolted at more overt manifestations of anti-Semitism. This also made for an effective censorship of more forthright expressions of prejudice in a majority of the newspapers. What passed for anti-Semitic statements were then to be found in the everyday conversations and remarks of ordinary citizens, in the writings of the pro-Fascist groups, of the intelligentsia, and of the pacifists.[37]

If we judge his essays, Orwell's own view of anti-Semitism was that of the rational, liberal intellectual, opposed to tyranny at all costs. He regarded anti-Semitism as a popular neurosis incapable of eradication, an element that had always existed in Britain and that spread ultimately from the lower to the middle classes. However, such factors as the traditional British respect for law and the rights of the individual, the relative security of the country in the decades preceding the Second World War, and the very civilized tone of British society inhibited any truly radical growth of anti-Semitism.[38]

Orwell was noted more for his influence as an essayist and journalist than for his effects on others as a writer of fiction. His treatment of the imagined Jew in that well-known negative utopia 1984, written shortly before his death, however, would give the lie to his reasoned thinking elsewhere, that the gentleness of the British way of life would militate against an extreme outburst of hatred against the Jew. In the nightmare world of 1984, society was divided into three superstates, each one always in conflict with the other two on the periphery of empire. Here, the Jew had

already acquired the dubious distinction of being public enemy number one, in the superstate that mattered in the novel, Oceania. It was highly probable that in 1984, the Jew himself, Emanuel Goldstein, as the arch villain of the piece, did not even exist as a character; rather, he was the corporate imaginative creation of the leaders of the state. As an oligarchy that formed the Inner Party, these leaders had to fashion an object upon whom all human energies, formerly directed into avenues of sex, ambition, and power, could now be unleashed. That object then became the Jew, and man's normal drives, originally committed to love, to the need for interpersonal relationships, and to a sense of achievement for work well done, were now all transformed to hate. The weekly two-minute hate sessions aimed at televised pictures of Emanuel Goldstein, the obscure intellectual traitor directing a conspiracy, served the vital function of energy release for all of Oceania's population—for the leaders of the Inner Party and the Outer Party, and for the Proles, or proletariat, whose only purpose was to breed others like themselves to form the mass population of the state.

Essentially, 1984 is a journalistic novel that depicted a future science-fiction horror world, where war was peace, ignorance was strength, freedom was slavery, and every word in the language was to have only one meaning. Its rather thin plot was the story of the successful obliteration of Winston Smith's human qualities by a member of the Inner Party, O'Brien, who may or may not have been the idol, Big Brother, that the population at large was forced to worship. Winston Smith was destroyed as a human being because he himself dared to seek historical truth. Yet the key issue in 1984 was neither Smith's search for common reality, nor the fact that he and his girl friend, when confronted with the more immediate dangers of torture, betray each other to the authorities, but that Orwell recognized the relationship between alienation and power only too well. For Orwell viewed power as truly successful only when all human ties, bonds, relationships, and emotions were destroyed. Basically, Julia and Winston Smith betrayed each other because the naked power of government to which they had always been subjected had first destroyed the sense of fellowship between any two people. Here was power used in a totally different fashion from the way it was in the worlds of Snow's novels. There, the overriding considerations were always the means by which the individual and the group in any given situation manipulated each other in the interests of power. But in 1984, Orwell clearly established the belief that at some time in the future in Western society, power would simply be worshiped for its own sake. In one of those excruciatingly painful series of interrogations, O'Brien admitted that his own demise, or that of any other leader, was of no moment, for power, always to be adored for its own sake, would insure the eternal existence of Oceania. But such power became effective only after the very quality of warm emotional relationships among thinking people had been eradicated by members of the Inner Party. In other words, total alienation of individuals from each other, was the single element that allowed them to be ruled by others, that permitted naked power to hold sway.

And of course the third element, besides alienation and power, had to be the Jew, to serve as the object on whom all of man's energies, released and transformed into hate, could wreak their vengeance. Under the circumstances it would appear rather simplistic to be overly concerned as to whether or not Emanuel Goldstein represented Leon Trotsky in a novel considered by some to have been a vicious parody of Stalin's Russia. For Orwell's Goldstein fulfilled a far greater role than that ever allotted to Trotsky. After all, Trotsky was assassinated, but Orwell's villain had to be maintained forever, and hence could not be allowed to appear ludicrous as his medieval Jewish forebear of a devil did. Goldstein, in fact, had to remain eternally sinister, otherwise what would become of a negative Utopia if its inhabitants could not continually refresh their own sense of virtue by coming into contact with the wellsprings of palpable evil? This, then, was the image of the Jew to which utter alienation and the worship of power had led.

From Chaucer's day until the present, Christian writers have seen the Jew as an alien in the midst of English society. They have justified this view by insisting that the Jew had always related in some evil fashion to money and to the desire for power over others. Through the centuries, relationships between Jews and Christians in England changed because of different historical developments, but the image of the Jew found in Christian literature still found its rationale in his supposedly alien qualities. Every literary era from the days of the Norman invasion to the twentieth century has borne witness to this thesis. It is the one constant factor in the Christian composite portrait of the Jew in English literature.

By recounting a version of the blood-libel legend, Chaucer's *Prioress* neatly summed up the attitudes of the Medieval Church toward the Jews. Even after they had been expelled from England in 1290, Jews were still regarded as devils, usurers, Christ-killers, swindlers, liars, thieves, and cheats, outside the closed, hierarchical scheme of God's ordered universe. They were also endowed in legend with being the artificers of blood-curdling deeds.

Such themes repeated themselves with regularity in the medieval Mystery plays, which vilified Jewish characters or turned them into grotesques for the amusement of the audience. The same pejorative attitudes toward Jews as were exemplified in these works were also to be found in *The Prioresses Tale,* based on a story of one of the miracles attributed to the Virgin Mary. Whether Chaucer himself believed what he allowed his gentle Prioress to say has been questioned, but evidence has been gathered here to show that Chaucer was very much a man of his age. For him and for other medieval writers, Jews were still the "demonic aliens."

The coming of the Renaissance, with its emphasis on man's capacity to bend the resources of the universe to his will, contributed a slightly different perspective to the image of the Jew in English literature. He was still of the devil's party, and still possessed all those loathsome qualities common to moneylenders. But by now he had allegedly acquired an uncanny ability to add power to his wealth, and to use it for international purposes. The Elizabethan villain of a stage Jew was thus able to evoke bitter envy and grudging admiration from his Christian audience. This was best exemplified by Barabas in Marlowe's *Jew of Malta,* and to a lesser degree by Shylock, in *The Merchant of Venice,* whose financial successes were a constant reproach to Antonio.

Shakespeare's genius at characterization momentarily lifted Shylock above that fiendish caricature in which Barabas and other Jewish moneylenders had customarily been grounded. On occasion, Shylock's genuine human emotions seem to have added a sense of tragic grandeur to his character, a grandeur over which some later critics and actors waxed sentimental. But despite his artistic enlargement, Shylock remained an illusory character. He was not an authentic Jew, nor was Portia a real woman. The client whose case she so brilliantly argued was an unheard-of entity—a merchant who lent money gratis and refused to take interest. The play itself was likewise a fantasy, and its Jewish miser, for all of his excursions into the realm of human feeling, was as strange and alien as his medieval ancestor, the Jew devil of the Mystery plays.

Despite historic differences between the Medieval and Renaissance periods, it would appear that writers perceived Jews in pretty much the same way throughout those years. Artistically, of course, the generalized view of the evil Jews' plotting in *The Prioresses Tale* was quite different from the specific skulduggery of Marlowe's Barabas, or from Shylock's more sophisticated villainy. But essentially, for Marlowe and Shakespeare, the Jew was still very much what medieval Christian society had conjured him up to be in Chaucer's day. The medieval heritage of *The Merchant of Venice* had consigned Shylock to the money-grubbing realities of the Rialto. Only the new people, Antonio, Portia, Bassanio, and their friends were fit inhabitants of the idealized Belmont.

Puritan comprehension of the uses of wealth molded Jewish usurers to different proportions from those of their medieval predecessors. The horror of Christian associations with such moneylenders, international or otherwise, diminished when Cromwell, relying on Calvin's view that lending at moderate rates of interest was acceptable church doctrine, paved the way for the Jews to return to England. At the same time, reinvigorated millenial hopes prompted Christian writers to refurbish those medieval alternatives of death or conversion as the ultimate affirmation of the reigning faith. Without invoking the usual dire penalties, poets and essayists from John Donne to Abraham Cowley urged the Jews to accept Christianity. Formally, the emphases were upon Christianity's Hebraic roots and on the need for Jews to acquire spiritual grace. Yet neither Milton's appeals to right reason, nor the deistic thinking of the Cambridge Platonists proved essential for the Jews to take up quarters in England once again. More to the point was the conviction of Oliver Cromwell and his associates that legitimizing Jewish residence in England would prove beneficial to the trade of the realm. Finally, in a spirit of omission rather than commission, Cromwell recognized Jews as being present in his country. Thereupon, criticism of Jewish usurers grew muted in official governmental circles, while it expanded among disaffected aristocrats and middle-class merchants.

Because the Restoration and the eighteenth century were periods of wit and reason, the villainy of the Jewish usurers was rescaled for comic purposes. No longer were they incarnate villains who poisoned wells, or crucified children as a willful travesty of Christ's passion. Instead, the tradition of aristocratic satire in prose and verse, in the writings of Dryden and Pope and Swift, made effective use of the ludicrous aspects of Jewish villains. In the situation comedies and picaresque novels of the times, they also emerged as mindless misers. They had grown ridiculous, shaped by wealth into buffoons and lotharios trying to scale the social ladder. In their absurd attire and speaking some outlandish dialect, they appeared as alienated as their medieval forebears. This was now the composite picture of the average Jewish miser as he appeared in the works of middle-class poets, novelists, and dramatists, who rang all the changes upon his proverbial financial assets. For Daniel Defoe, Tobias Smollett, Henry Fielding, Samuel Richardson, and many others, the Jew had to use his wealth to maintain stumpets and frustrate the financial schemes of honest Christians. What intellectuals had complained of in this rational age—that the Jews were a necessary evil in a perfectly balanced world—popular writers were proving in their stories and dramas. And over all that dislike for the Jews there hovered an intense resentment concerning any wealth they may have accumulated. In time, the effects of such assets upon these fictional and dramatic creatures allowed them to evolve into fops and dandies. This new tradition of the effete Jewish character then found its full justification in later descriptions of aristocratic Jews, or Christian aristocrats with Jewish tendencies, securing niches in a society that rejected them.

On the other hand, occasional sentimental portraits of kindly misers were the result either of changes in the political temper of the times, or of humanitarian impulses that accompanied a rise in sentimentalism. Tobias Smollett's incredibly beneficent miser in *The Adventures of Ferdinand, Count Fathom,* may have been intended as the literary equivalent of a political change of heart, when a short-lived Naturalization Bill benefiting the Jews passed Parliament. But when the law was shortly repealed because of popular opposition to it, literary characterizations of good Jews also faded from the scene. The exception was Richard Cumberland's play, *The Jew,* depicting a miser who starved himself to aid impecunious Christians. This served as a dull offering upon the altar of English tolerance. Its sentimentalism was due in part to the incipient romanticism of the times. Sir Walter Scott's shaping of Rebecca in *Ivanhoe* was also based on those altered perceptions concerning emotion and characterization in literature. Scott's views of Rebecca may indeed have been influenced by those intricate displays of feeling with which Samuel Richardson had earlier endowed his virtuous heroine Clarissa Harlowe.

In a different context, romanticism gave new impetus to that old legend of the Wandering Jew, who, having rejected Christ, was doomed to roam the earth endlessly. His conversion and, by implication, the conversion of his race, which the medievalists had demanded upon pain of death, and for which seventeenth-century metaphysicians pleaded, now was redirected in verse by the Romantics. Wordsworth, Coleridge, Byron, and Shelley were both attracted and repelled by his strange qualities. Sometimes the Wandering Jew was also seen as a reflection of the poets' own inner selves.

In the wake of the vast industrial and technological changes that occurred during the Victorian period, the old bugaboo of the cash-nexus, that unfortunately wealth was the only element that determined human relationships, occupied the minds of some of the greatest of writers. Almost to a man they attributed this negative obsession with wealth to Jews, and thereby helped perpetuate the vision of the Jew as an alien. This was particularly true of Dickens, Thackeray, and Trollope. Dickens's early thief, Fagin, was the prototype for all his later villains, both Jew and Gentile, who by their meretricious hankering for wealth were bent on destroying society. Thackeray, in *Vanity Fair,* had Christians pursuing wealth with as much avidity as the nouveaux riches of *Our Mutual Friend.* Trollope's venal clergyman, Mr. Emilius, of *The Eustace Diamonds,* and Augustus Melmotte, the crooked millionaire of *The Way We Live Now,* who may have had Jewish blood in their veins, based their very existence on money.

Dickens, Thackeray, and Trollope also fixed their comic genius upon that arch aristocrat of Jewish origin, Benjamin Disraeli. In his own novels he too bewailed the nefarious uses to which wealth was put by unscrupulous individuals. But lurking behind that occult fascination with riches, which absorbed so many of Diaraeli's windy protagonists, was the author's own conviction that the Sidonias of the Jewish race, and their aides-de-camp, the Adam Bessos and Henry Baronis of this world, engaged in international finance for beneficent ends. To Disraeli's detractors, however, such ubiquitous money merchants were dubious characters at best, who by their financial speculations advanced the cause of the Jewish race, but yet deceived the world. The heady rhetoric of the Prime Minister's novels, dealing with the alleged superiority of the "Arabian Race," of whom the Jews were presumably the first offspring, lent credence to Disraeli's critics. However, the Prime Minister was firmly convinced that England would be rejuvenated by the message of the eternal traditions coming form the East—from Sinai and Calvary. Implicit in his view of a reawakened England was the social and political emancipation of the Jewish community.

A more immediate result of Disraeli's aspirations was Dickens's caricature of him as James Harthouse, the dandified seducer of *Hard Times.* Disraeli's fictional creations were also the butts of Thackeray's humor—the American consul at Jerusalem, in *Notes of a Journey from Cornhill to Grand Cairo,* who reached the Holy City to await the millennium; the sultry heroine, Miriam, in *Codlingsby,* who parodied Eva of *Tancred*; and Codlingsby himself, whose diction echoed the asinine sentiments of many of Disraeli's heroes. Not to be outdone, Trollope based his characterization of Ethelbert Stanhope, the ne'er-do-well of *Barchester Towers,* on Lady Bertie, another character in *Tancred,* and modelled the "Jew-priest" of *The Eustace Diamonds* on Disraeli himself.

Such negative views of aristocrats with "Jewish" ambitions eager to transform English society, or of Jews as the proprietors of misbegotten wealth, helped perpetuate an alienated image of the Jew in literature. His distinctiveness was further intensified by the prevailing passion for racial classification. The two parameters of Darwinian philosophy were applied to distinctive groups everywhere. Were they fit to survive and had their evolution into their present state shown them to have been in lock-step agreement with progress? Even authors who might have been interested in the religious, ethnic, and cultural values of the Jewish group contributed to this overriding concern with race. George Eliot was later claimed as the prophet of a restored Zion because of her novel *Daniel Deronda,* yet she did not eschew racist qualities in her descriptions of her Jewish characters. Toward the end of the century, such perceptions about Jews sometimes degenerated into obscene physical descriptions. This is what George Du Maurier's *Trilby* was all about.

Alone of the Victorians, Robert Browning seemed free from anti-Semitic prejudice. This may have been owing to his vast erudition, to his profound insight into human personality, and perhaps to the fact he lived in Italy for many years. But his sensible comprehension of Jews and Jewish culture was not truly representative of the historical period in which he lived, and his search for a rational balance in life was not to endure. Instead, the religious, economic, and political contests which tore Victorian society apart led to the alienation of modern man. Other psychological and sociological factors reinforced this sense of individual isolation so prevalent in modern times.

In their treatment of the Jews, writers now reacted against that period by dealing with them as rootless individuals in a stream-of-consciousness technique, or by resorting to older styles of writing where many of the accepted notions as to how Jews think and believe were merely variations on earlier literary treatments. Always the rebel, Shaw delighted in reversing the theme of the Jew's association with money and with the devil. In Shaw's topsy-turvy world, millionaire bankers benefited others through man-made wars, and the devil, as Jew, guarded dull virtues in hell. Joyce's Jew, Bloom, was no longer the devil in hell, but isolated in the world. Like man himself, Joyce contended, the Jew was dispossessed. Bloom suffered both from an inability to communicate with others and from a loss of his own identity. That his condition did not change at the end of the novel was part of Joyce's commentary on modern man.

Like Joyce, Greene also dealt with individuals cut off from each other. Yet his stories were traditionally structured, and his Jews were cast in the same old mold of money-mad, vile evildoers. What was new about these antagonists was they they served to undermine Christian rogues and scoundrels, who in death assumed Christlike qualities.

There was little that was new about Evelyn Waugh's Jewish characterizations. They merely carried on the usual linking of Jews with wealth and power. This was all the more surprising in that Waugh's novels themselves were satiric, rebellious, and outrageous.

The same could not be said of Maugham's well-structured stories, where his Jews were merely extensions of older stereotypes. But Maugham's contemporary, John Galsworthy, in his play, *Loyalties,* was concerned with his hero's Jewish origins and his battle for social status in a Christian society. Delving more deeply than Galsworthy into the web of alien backgrounds, C. P. Snow pitted the alleged fascination with riches and power on the part of Jews against their religious and ethnic obligations. In *The Conscience of the Rich* and *Corridors of Power,* wealth won out. For George Orwell, the seeming villainy of the Jew served as part of a larger caricature—of a world gone mad with power. The only positive development at this time was that Galsworthy, Joyce, and Orwell had come to acknowledge the irrational nature of anti-Semitic prejudice.

Essentially then, while there were some changes in Christian attitudes to Jews in English literature as civilization itself progressed from medieval to modern times, stereotypical thinking concerning Jews still repeated itself with alarming regularity. If Marlowe's Barabas cleverly manipulated international relations by his wealth and brilliance, men in Orwell's day saw the intelligence of Jews bound up with unscrupulousness of character. If Chaucer's medieval Jewry used the blood of Christian children for religious purposes, in the secular world of the nineteenth and twentieth centuries it was calmly accepted that, out of personal greed and lust for power, the Lazaruses and Sir Marcuses encouraged the possible deaths of thousands in spurious wars. And just as the ancestors of medieval Jewry were considered representatives of the devil, so in some terrible future yet unborn, their descendants would all coalesce into some universal satanic figure to be called Emanuel Goldstein or by some other comparable nomenclature. Plus ça change . . .

Notes

1. George Bernard Shaw, *Everybody's Political What's What* (New York: Doubleday, 1944), p. 287; see also Lawrence Langner, *G. B. S. and the Lunatic* (New York: Atheneum, 1963), p. 162-73, for the belief that as a nonogenarian, Shaw justified Hitler's estimate of the Jews; Eric Bentley, "The Making of a Dramatist, 1892-1903," in *George Bernard Shaw: Twentieth Century Views* (Englewood Cliffs, N.J.: Prentice-Hall, 1965), p. 58, elaborates upon Shaw's view of the nature of dramatic art.

2. S. L. Goldberg, *The Classical Temper* (London: Chatto & Windus, 1969), p. 285 n. 17.

3. James Joyce, *Ulysses* (New York: Random House, 1932), p. 324.

4. Ibid., p. 325.

5. Ibid., p. 327

6. Ibid., p. 336.

7. Ibid., p. 338-39.

8. Ibid., p. 385.

9. Ibid., pp. 387-88.

10. Ibid., pp. 400-401.

11. Ibid., pp. 402-3.

12. Ibid., pp. 454-55.

13. Ibid., pp. 477, 485-88.

14. Goldberg, *Classical Temper,* pp. 185-87, 274-75.

15. Joyce, *Ulysses,* p. 666.

16. Cf. Edmund Wilson, *Axel's Castle* (New York: Scribner's, 1959), p. 202; Goldberg, *Classical Temper,* pp. 91-93.

17. James Joyce, *Portrait of the Artist As a Young Man* (New York: Viking Press, 1965), p. 263; William York Tindall, *A Reader's Guide to James Joyce* (London: James Hudson (paperback), 1971), pp. 222-23.

18. Arnold Kettle, *An Introduction to the English Novel* (London: Hutchinson Co. (paperback), 1972), 2: 132.

19. Goldberg, *Classical Temper,* pp. 290-91, nn. 28, 29.

20. Matthew Arnold, "Dover Beach," in *English Poets, Romantic, Victorian and Later,* ed. James Stephens, Edwin L. Beck, and Royall H. Snow (New York: American Book Co., 1934), p. 563.

21. Graham Greene, *Brighton Rock,* Compass ed. (New York: Viking, 1956), p. 348.

22. Graham Greene, *This Gun for Hire* in *Three* (New York: Viking, 1952), p. 145.

23. Ibid., p. 76.

24. Ibid., pp. 146-47.

25. A. A. DeVitis, *Graham Greene,* Twayne English Authors Series 3 (New York: Twayne, 1963), p. 152.

26. Greene, *Brighton Rock,* p. 332.

27. Ibid., p. 89.

28. Ibid., p. 180.

29. Ibid., p. 257.

30. DeVitis, *Graham Greene,* pp. 147-50.

31. John Galsworthy, *Loyalties, Laurel British Drama: The Nineteenth Century,* ed. R. W. Corrigan (New York: Dell Publishing Co. [paperback], 1969), p. 191.

32. Ibid., p. 174.

33. Jerome Thale, *C. P. Snow, Writers and Critics,* (Edinburgh & London: Oliver Boyd [paperback], 1964), pp. 30, 53-54, 57.

34. C. P. Snow, *Corridors of Power* (New York: Bantam, 1965), pp. 9-10.

35. Ibid., p. 125.

36. "Why Are Jews Successful?" *Christianity Today,* 13:15, April 25, 1969, p. 31.

37. George Orwell, *As I Please,* 1943-45 in *Collected Essays, Journalism and Letters of George Orwell* (= *Collected Essays*), ed. Sonia Orwell and Ian Angus (London: Penguin, 1968), 3:332, 333, 424.

38. George Orwell, *My Country Right or Left,* in *Collected Essays* ed. Orwell and Angus, 2:229, 213, 332-33, 427-28; 3:103, 112-14, 378-88, 412, 416, 419-20, 424, 426, 430; idem, *In Front of Your Nose,* 4:227, 357.

Stephen R. Haynes (essay date 1995)

SOURCE: Haynes, Stephen R. "Introduction." In *Jews and the Christian Imagination: Reluctant Witnesses,* pp. 1-11. Hampshire, England: Macmillan Press Ltd., 1995.

[*In the following excerpt, Haynes examines the conception of Jews in the imagination of Christian writers, focusing on what he suggests are largely unconscious attitudes toward them.*]

[*The Jews*] *are our supporters in their books, our enemies in their hearts, our witnesses in their scrolls.*

Augustine, *On Faith in Things Unseen*

The history of the nation of Israel is indeed unlike that of any other nation throughout human history. No other nation has been so blessed by God and yet so hated by

Satan. The factors of satanic persecution, divine judg-
ment for sin, and divine blessing honoring the promises
to Abraham are all evident throughout Jewish history.

John Ankerberg and John Weldon, *One World: Biblical*
Prophecy and the New World Order

Why this extraordinarily neurotic way of reacting to
anything to do with Israel—and to quite a lot of things
to do with Jews elsewhere?

Norman Solomon, "The Context of the
Jewish-Christian Dialogue"

"Jews are news." This phrase is sometimes offered as a fa-
cetious explanation for the international attention directed
at events in and around the State of Israel. It is a half-
joking justification for the incommensurate scrutiny Israel
seems to receive in the news media. But though the words
"Jews are news" have a modern ring, Jews actually have
held a position of unique prominence in the collective
imagination of the Christian West for centuries. In fact,
even a cursory survey of texts that have influenced Western culture reveals that Jewish existence, Jewish exile and
dispersion and Jewish stereotypes bear great symbolic
weight in our collective traditions.

An illustration of the important but ambivalent position reserved for Jews in the Western mind is found in Dante's
Divine Comedy. In Canto IV of *Inferno,* Dante's pilgrimage through the underworld takes him to limbo, where
those who lived virtuous lives in the era before Christ
spend eternity. These souls are cut off from the divine
presence, but they are spared the suffering with which the
other denizens of hell are afflicted. Significantly, the favored souls of limbo are of two distinct classes: There are
the virtuous pagans, a group that includes classical masters
like Virgil (Dante's guide through hell); and the so-called
saints of the Old Testament. This latter group of non-
Christians enjoy particular privilege. For as Dante learns
from Virgil, the Hebrew saints were granted paradise at
the time of Christ's harrowing of hell. Virgil names Adam,
Abel, Noah, Moses, Abraham, David, Jacob and Rachel
among the former inhabitants of limbo who have achieved
blessedness, despite lacking baptism.

"I would have thee know," Virgil informs the poet, "that
before these no human souls were saved." Descending
with Dante through the circles of hell, the reader realizes
that these pre-Christian saints have fared much better than
the baptized heretics and apostates who populate the lower
levels of hell, and whose screams are an audible reminder
of Christian truth. But if "Hebrews" such as Moses are objects of special blessing in Dante's *Inferno,* "Jews" like
Judas are less fortunate. In the final canto, Dante and Virgil arrive at the ninth circle of hell. Here, in the dark
realm inhabited by Satan himself, Dante is introduced to
the most infamous of Jews:

> 'That soul up there which has the greatest punishment,'
> said the Master, 'is Judas Iscariot, who has his head in-
> side [one of Satan's mouths] and plies his head
> without.'[1]

In Dante's memorable depiction, Judas the arch-traitor becomes literally and figuratively the devil's own.

Obviously, *Inferno* is about much more than treacherous
Jews and worthy Hebrews. Speaking quantitatively, Ro-
mans are more prominent in *The Divine Comedy* than are
Jews. Furthermore, scholars have noted that in relation to
other texts from the Middle Ages Dante's masterpiece is
conspicuous for its dearth of anti-Jewish polemic.[2] Nevertheless, all Jews—whether saints or sinners—are depicted
by Dante as being quite different than the rest of us. As
the only souls qualified to attain paradise without conscious faith in Christ, the patriarchs and matriarchs of the
"Old Testament" are *sui generis*; while Jesus' unfaithful
disciple personifies the unique perfidy of deicide. Thus,
despite the absence of explicit anti-Judaism, the overall
impression left by Dante's portrayal of Jews is of a people
comprised exclusively of saints and traitors. Of course, every character in the *Divine Comedy* has been eternally assigned to salvation or damnation. But even in the company
of souls whose destiny has been determined, Jews are special cases. To put this in spatial terms, there are no Jews in
Dante's purgatory.

A thesis of this book is that Jews must always be special
cases in products of the Christian imagination, because of
the uniquely ambivalent place which the Jewish people inhabit there. Thus, what is really noteworthy about Dante's
depiction of Jews is not the comparative sparsity of anti-
Jewish polemic in the *Divine Comedy,* but the fact that
neither Dante's honored Hebrews nor his despised Jews
can be confused with what we might call average human
beings. They are men and women of exemplary faith upon
whom the divine favor eternally rests; or they are betray-
ers of friends, murderers of the innocent, killers of God. In
Dante's calculus of transgression and punishment, God's
chosen people are either supernaturally virtuous or utterly
debased. Whatever else is said about the depiction of Jews
in this masterpiece of Christian literature, it is clear that
representatives of the Jewish people remain qualitatively
"other."

Lest we be tempted, however, to consider such dichotomous renderings of Jews as "Catholic" or "medieval," it is
useful to observe that an equally polarized apprehension of
the Jewish people is manifest in the documents of a rationalized and iconoclastic Reformation culture. A few hundred years after Dante, in texts that are confessional rather
than imaginative, blessed "Hebrews" and cursed "Jews"
are relegated to the same disparate positions of honor and
condemnation. The "Scots Confession" of 1560, for instance, offers a typological interpretation of the biblical
patriarchs according to which all the faithful of the "Old
Testament," including Adam, Noah and David, "did see
the joyful day of Christ Jesus and did rejoice." The glory
which adheres to the people and institutions of the Hebrew
Bible is extoled as belonging to the "true Kirk," an entity
preserved by God through all ages. The "Heidelberg Catechism" of 1563 again honors the Hebrew ancestors of
Christ, whose gospel was "revealed in the beginning in the

Garden of Eden, afterward proclaimed through the holy patriarchs and prophets and foreshadowed through the sacrifices and other rites of the Old Covenant, and finally fulfilled through [God's] own well-beloved Son." Yet in a nearly contemporaneous Reformed document, the "Second Helvetic Confession" of 1566, the appellation "Jew" is utilized exclusively in references to doctrinal error. The author(s) of this creed, determined to vilify what they perceived as the theological folly of Roman Catholicism, found it appropriate (and no doubt effective) to associate Catholics with those arch-heretics the Jews. Here, as in many Protestant creeds of the Reformation era, millenarianism is condemned as a "Jewish dream."

A century later, the authors of the "Westminster Confession" (1647) treat the relationship of Christian and pre-Christian humanity by introducing the distinction between a "covenant of works" and a "covenant of grace," a sophisticated Reformed version of the standard dichotomy between Christian freedom and "Jewish" legalism. With this bifurcated covenant, the Westminster divines imply that the church has superseded the synagogue, which depends on a covenant that is "incapable of life." Still, in order that the heroes of the "Old Testament" may be located on the salvific side of this divide, the two covenants do not strictly correspond to the eras before and after the advent of Christ. In fact, "under the law [the covenant of grace] was administered by promises, prophecies, sacrifices, circumcision, the paschal lamb and other types and ordinances delivered to the people of the Jews, all foresignifying Christ to come." In general, Protestant confessions in the Reformed tradition assign high status to the Hebrew patriarchs and matriarchs, since they "did see the day of Christ Jesus and did rejoice." At the same time, they reiterate the classic anti-Jewish distinction between works and grace and dismiss some of their opponents' views as "Jewish" errors and fantasies.

I have chosen Dante and the Reformed confessions as textual windows on the Christian imagination because both are regarded as representing relatively positive apprehensions of the Jewish people. The author of a recent book on the character of Judas and the growth of anti-Semitism in Europe has singled out the author of the *Divine Comedy* for making a "conscious effort to avoid connecting the perfidy of Judas with the dishonour of the Jewish people as a whole."[3] And theology in the tradition of Calvin is frequently recognized for its philosemitic attributes, including a high level of respect for the "Old Testament" and for biblical Hebrews and their descendants. I refer to these texts, then, as a way of suggesting that even in Christian documents where anti-Jewishness is relatively inconspicuous one is likely to encounter deeply ambivalent and dichotomous portrayals of Jews.

Other examples of the virtual inability of Christians to conceive of Jews as typical human beings are found throughout the history of preaching. In fact, one particularly intriguing aspect of Christian homiletical discourse is the perennial failure of preachers to distinguish between biblical and contemporary Jews; between, that is, the heroes and antiheroes of the Bible and the persons who reside across town or down the street. Like the association of "Jewish perfidy" with the treachery of Judas, the linking of biblical Hebrews and every subsequent generation of Jews is still quite common, and sermons are a medium in which it has thrived. Historian Frank Felsenstein cites a sermon delivered in London in 1648 as a prime example of the Christian tendency to paint all Jews with broad and ancient stereotypes. Felsenstein notes carefully how the anonymous preacher inexplicably switches from past to present tense in the process of describing Jewish perversity. In an almost imperceptible transition, he proclaims that the Jews who killed Christ *are* hypocrites, a generation of vipers, etc.[4]

Felsenstein makes much of this abrupt shift, and it provides an illuminating glimpse of the Christian mind at work. But this tactic is more of a commonplace in Christian preaching than Felsenstein seems to be aware. Not long ago I was in attendance when a respected Protestant clergyman preached on the New Testament story of Jesus and Zaccheus. Toward the end of his sermon, the preacher made the impassioned observation that "the Jews did not understand what Jesus was doing [in associating with Zaccheus], and they still don't understand!" As one who had over time become sensitized to negative Christian portrayals of Jews, this sudden but significant shift in attention struck me as unwarranted and pernicious. Within one sentence, the minister had jumped several thousand years and as many miles. The same "they" which in the biblical text refers to Jesus' contemporaries in first-century Palestine was being employed to denote living Jews of the congregants' acquaintance. I am certain that anyone caring to know would find that such back and forth movements between real Jews and the "Jews" of sacred text is typical in Christian discourse of all kinds.

Further examples could be compounded, but I hope the point is clear: Persons raised in the Christian tradition have great difficulty viewing Jews as human beings like themselves. Walker Percy's claims to the contrary notwithstanding,[5] when Christians are confronted by the word-sign "Jew," they are more likely to conjure theological types and antitypes, not to mention cultural and literary stereotypes, than to think of real individuals with the same hopes, failures and foibles as non-Jews. Some have misunderstood this mythologizing tendency and claimed that for Christians the only good Jew is a dead Jew, or a [converted] Christian. But the Christian attitude toward the Jew has never consisted in a simple desire to bring an end to the Jewish people through persecution or conversion. Rather, the crux of the Christian outlook is that every Jew, whether they are cast in an angelic or demonic role, is part of a chosen race that in some mysterious way represents God.

Ultimately, it was this assumption which allowed Jews to persist in a relatively secure state within pre-modern Christendom. But it also determined that Jewish actions and beliefs would become objects of unnatural scrutiny and bizarre fantasy. Furthermore, most Christians through the ages have believed that they understood the Jews' history and destiny with greater probity than Jews themselves. For in the Christian imagination the existence and survival of the Jew have been invested with religious significance, even—and especially—when Jews refuse to recognize this significance. This book will argue that, whatever else may be said about the status of Jews in Christian and post-Christian Western societies, Jews continue to function in the Christian mind as fundamental symbols in the divine alphabet.

This is an exploration of the way representative Christian authors imagine Jews to be. Many recent works have addressed the history of Jewish-Christian relations, some tracking a local ebb and flow and some the broader tidal movements in that history. This work is neither an exhaustive historical survey nor a detailed description of conditions in a single region or historical epoch, but a wide-ranging analysis of a complex of ideas that is located across the chronological and ideological spectra of Christian thought. I realize that ideas, however compelling, cannot be divorced from the real and ongoing history which Christians and Jews share. Nevertheless, it is not my primary aim to evaluate the historical effects of mythical thinking; rather, I wish to document the variegated expressions of a deep and deeply ambivalent mythical construct.

Over the last thirty years, a variety of Christian and Jewish scholars have written convincingly of the role of Christian belief in preparing the European mind for the advent of racial anti-Semitism and the Holocaust. I offer this study of the witness-people myth as a complement to rather than a repudiation of their work. I am keenly aware, in fact, that if the religious dynamics of anti-Judaism and anti-Semitism had not been investigated so thoroughly by those whose work I cite, I would not be free to take a novel approach to this subject matter. Using a history of ideas methodology, I hope to demonstrate that animosity toward Jews, while fundamental to Christian theology and infecting the New Testament itself, does not represent the bedrock of the Christian imagination as it applies to the Jewish people. In the depths of the Christian mind is a mythical complex more ambivalent and more subtle in its pernicious influence than pure Jew-hatred.

I will use "witness-people myth" as a handy term for labeling a complex of beliefs and assumptions that has informed the Christian mind across the centuries. Where it is present in more subtle ways I will use the phrase "witness-people thinking." When it appears as a self-conscious articulation of Augustine's systematized version of the witness-people myth, I shall use the terms "witness-people doctrine," "witness-people theory," and "witness-people theology." But readers should bear in mind that at no time has any developed witness-people doctrine been articulated self-consciously by an official church body. Even in Augustine's case, elements of his witness-people doctrine are found scattered throughout his writings. In fact, the

power of the witness-people myth is testified to by its longevity despite never being an element of church dogma or an unwritten test of faith.

I believe that the textual evidence cited in these chapters amounts to an implicit demonstration of my thesis that the witness-people myth is a deep structure in the Christian imagination. Perhaps Chapter 6 contains the strongest argument in this direction: If the witness-people myth is not deeply ingrained in the theological imaginations of Christians, then why is its presence routinely ignored by otherwise incisive Christian scholars who are seeking to reconstruct the church's theology of Israel? As I try to show in my analysis of Christian Holocaust theology,[6] scholars who are genuinely concerned with the effects of Christian ideology *vis-à-vis* Jews remain quite unaware of the myth's presence in their own discourse. In fact, it is precisely in their attempts to comprehend and repudiate historic Christian anti-Judaism that the Holocaust theologians inadvertently reaffirm the most fundamental Christian ideology about Jews—the conviction that the existence, fate, and redemption of the Jews are signs for God's church. Today, as in centuries past, well-meaning Christians have reverted to basic forms of cognition about Jewish existence and Jewish travail. Can Christians be liberated, then, from the hold of the witness-people myth? This question I will take up in the book's final chapter.

My overall aim is to comprehend in the most profound way possible my own religious tradition's ambivalence toward Jews—to comprehend both the "good" and the "bad" in the Jewish myth which is operative throughout Christian history, and to analyze the manifestations of the myth I have discovered in modern and contemporary Christian discourse. This ambitious aim has required me to formulate a wager. I am wagering that by assuming a broad perspective I will discover something deeper than persistent Jew-hatred, something in which all Christian notions about Jews, both "negative" and "positive," are rooted.[7]

I am very conscious of the fact that the term myth is employed in many ways by contemporary thinkers. For my purposes, the phrase "witness-people myth" refers to a complex of ideas and symbols that, often precritically and unconsciously, informs ideas about Jews among persons who share a cultural heritage or world view. I infer the existence of "the Christian mind" and "the Christian imagination" as sources and habitations for this myth. In this I have been influenced by two aspects of the structuralist conception of myth popularized by cultural anthropologists: that the nature of the mind reveals itself in the structure of myths as much as in the structure of language, and that the structure of myth is both formative and reflective of the human mind. To use Claude Lévi-Strauss's words, I want to understand "how myths think in men [*sic*], unbeknown to them."[8]

I believe that crucial for understanding the witness-people myth is the recognition that it is characterized by an inner tension produced by the coexistence of dual components that Lévi-Strauss calls "bundles." The bundles which distinguish the witness-people myth pertain to the reprobation and preservation/salvation of the Jewish people, and give rise to what I will refer to as the negative and positive dimensions of witness-people thinking. The ambivalence created by competing bundles is expressed in several pairs of notions which inform Christian discourse:

reprobation ("negative")	preservation ("positive")
the Jews:	but:
are killers of Christ	remain the people of God
are superseded	are not "cast off"
are dispersed	carry "books" that testify to Christ
are witnesses to judgment	disseminate the knowledge of God
must be preached to in love	will convert before the end of time
have lost their land	will be restored to their land.⁹

As will be demonstrated in the chapters that follow, these and similar ideas are found together in texts from every era of church history. Where Jews are concerned, we find simultaneous teachings of judgment and eventual redemption; policies of isolation/exclusion carried out amid protection from physical attack; affirmations of God-willed suffering along with warnings about Christian participation in Jewish persecution; and emphasis on the interplay of dispersion and preservation. Tension created by the often paradoxical convictions associated with the witness-people myth is finally resolved in the confidence that Jews are God's people and will return to God's favor.

As I am employing it, then, "myth" refers to a specific set of beliefs, assumptions and convictions about Jews that have been expressed consistently by Christians over centuries. But since I am concerned with charting the ways that mythical notions are transmitted in Christian texts, I have found it useful to combine this structuralist understanding of the term with a "semiotic" approach. As Roland Barthes elaborates it,[10] the semiotic or semiological understanding of myth begins in the observation that myth is a type of speech, a system of communication, a message. Myth functions as a semiotic system in that, like language, it is structured in terms of the relationship between a signifier, a signified and a third term—"the associative total of the first two terms"[11]—which is called the sign. According to Barthes, myth is a second-order semiotic system constructed on a previously existing linguistic semiotic chain. . . .

Barthes' diagram of interlocking semiotic chains suggests how myth gets hold of language in order to build its own system. Myth transforms a previously established *sign* into an empty *signifier* that has been "drained." Thus the *sign* in a language system becomes a signifier in a myth system, a system with its own signified. In the myth I am analyzing in this book, the *sign* of a language system (actually the identity of the *signifier* "Jew" with a group of

people believed to share common characteristics, history and origins) is taken over to form the empty signifier that is the basis of the myth. In the metalanguage of myth, this *sign* which identifies "Jews" with real Jews and "Jewish history" with an accepted version of their story becomes the signifier for a new signified (God, or God's designs). The association of "Jews"/real Jews with God becomes the sign (Barthes also calls it the signification) by which the myth is recognized. While this mythical Sign takes many forms—including associations of Jewish exile and divine punishment, Jewish preservation and divine providence, Jewish restoration and divine guidance, Jewish conversion and divine love—in each case the correlation of the Jew with God is central.

In claiming that the witness-people myth is both an ambivalent collection of assertions about Jews and a system of linguistic signs which Christian communities construct unconsciously, I intend no contradiction. The structuralist perspective on the witness-people myth elucidates how Christian notions about Jews are organized in the depths of the Christian imagination, while the semiotic perspective helps to explain how the imagination utilizes language to project these ideas upon real Jews. Each offers useful insight into the mysterious operation of the witness-people myth.[12]

Notes

1. *Inferno,* 34: 61-3, from *The Divine Comedy of Dante Alighieri,* Vol. 1, tr. John D. Sinclair (New York: Oxford University Press, 1939), 423.

2. Jews are conspicuously absent from Dante's hell. Although Caiaphas makes a brief appearance in canto XXIII, Dante's description of usurers in canto XVII is without explicit references to Jews. This is especially surprising given that "[b]y the twelfth century the terms 'Jew' and 'usurer' were synonymous. . . ." [Jeffrey Richards, *Sex, Dissidence and Damnation: Minority Groups in the Middle Ages* (London: Routledge, 1991), 113.]

3. Hyam Maccoby, *Judas Iscariot and the Myth of Jewish Evil* (New York: The Free Press, 1992), 117.

4. "Jews and Devils: Anti-Semitic Stereotypes of Late Medieval and Renaissance England," *Journal of Literature and Theology* 4:1 (March, 1990), 15-28; 25.

5. See Chapter 5

6. I am concerned that my treatment of Christian Holocaust Theology may lead some readers mistakenly to infer hostility on my part toward radical attempts to reformulate Christian thought in the post-Holocaust environment. I want to say explicitly, therefore, that my critique reflects not disapproval of the task Holocaust Theologians have undertaken, but my opinion that too many Christian responses to anti-Judaism have sought to redress this problem by carelessly reiterating mythical forms.

7. My concern with the phenomenon of ambivalence has forced me to keep the relatively positive aspects

of Christian mythical thinking constantly in view. If this is interpreted by some readers as a subtle apologetic for this type of thinking, I can only respond that this is not my intent.

8. From *Le Cru et le cuit,* cited in Terrence Hawkes, *Structuralism and Semiotics* (London: Routledge, 1977), 41. My discussion of Lévi-Strauss and Barthes is indebted to Hawkes' excellent introduction to their work.

9. The Restorationist teaching was not a consistent part of witness-people thinking until the seventeenth century. While Augustine did not believe the Jews would return to their land, many fathers of the church did not rule out such a return. On Restorationist and anti-Restorationist thinking in the first few centuries of church history, especially as it relates to Julian the Apostate's unsuccessful attempt to rebuild the Jerusalem Temple in 363 CE., see Edward H. flannery, "Theological Aspects of the State of Israel," in John Oesterreicher, ed., *The Bridge,* Vol. 3 (New York: Pantheon, 1958), 301-24; 306ff.

10. See "Myth Today" in Roland Barthes' *Mythologies,* tr. Annette Lavers (New York: Hill & Wang, 1972).

11. Ibid., 113.

12. See Ibid., 115.

Linda Nochlin (essay date 1995)

SOURCE: Nochlin, Linda. "Starting with the Self: Jewish Identity and Its Representation." In *The Jew in the Text: Modernity and the Construction of Identity,* edited by Linda Nochlin and Tamar Garb, pp. 7-19. London: Thames and Hudson, 1995.

[*In the following essay, Nochlin explores the representation of Jews in the visual arts and the underlying assumptions, cultural and literary, that they reflect. She concludes, however, that there are no sweeping generalizations that can be made about how Jews are depicted in art.*]

"Why do they hate us so much?" This is not merely an anguished cry torn from the heart—although, of course, it is that, too—but rather a perfectly rational question to ask in the face of the plethora of hostile, denigrating, and debasing representations of Jews—the Jew, Jewishness—collected and analyzed in the texts of this volume. That these representations are often contradictory—Jews are too smart and innately incapable of genius; Jewish women are natural wantons and asexual or frigid; Jews underhandedly control the international banking community and yet pollute the great cities with their fetid, crime-ridden slums; Jews are over-intellectual but over-emotional, hyper-rational but superstitious—does nothing to mitigate the force of their collective assault. On the contrary, it would seem to imply that we are and have been so hated that *only* mutually exclusive categories would seem large

enough to encompass the totality of our iniquity. A language of excess seems the natural vehicle for such vileness.

Sometimes, reading these texts and the myriad others detailing the dark face of anti-Semitic representation, I have actually felt compelled to run to the mirror. To what extent do I conform to the Jewish stereotypes reiterated time after time in these pages and detailed in Sander Gilman's book *The Jew's Body*?[1] While it is true that my ears do not stick out, my nose is far from hooked, and my lips are thin rather than thick and coarse, I do have flat feet and rounded shoulders (I remember gratefully that my husband, equally Jewish, had such high arches that as a child, he had to wear orthopedic shoes and do detestable exercises to correct them, and that he had shoulders so broad that he had trouble finding suits to fit; but, I remembered, his nose *was* slightly aquiline). While I had always associated my red hair and freckles with the Gentile world—Irish, perhaps, or Scottish—I learned that these were particularly ascribed to the diabolic or demonic aspects of Jewishness: Gauguin, for example, depicts the Dutch Jewish artist Meyer de Haan with red hair, red beard, and a cloven hoof in place of a hand, and the image is not merely his invention. At times, I would find myself surreptitiously looking at people on the street in my neighborhood on the Upper West Side of Manhatten or at a concert or movie or, more to the point, emerging from the local synagogue. Some of them, indeed—the older ones mostly—bore the stigmata of stereotypical Jewishness: the frog-like mouths, the large, uncomely noses, the squinty eyes, and the weak, hunched-over physiognomies of the classical anti-Semitic caricature. How delighted I was to see that the young people, on the contrary, even the ones walking to the Orthodox synagogue around the corner, were often tall, broad-shouldered, and fit beneath their prayer-shawls and yarmulkes, the young women fashionably if conservatively dressed: no hint of caricature here!

The terrible thing about the voluminous literature representing the Jew as excessive is the way it sticks in the mind, seeps into the unconscious, embeds itself in the deepest levels of my being even if I detest its assertions and, on the rational level, I realize its total irrationality. But I am irrational, too, or not merely rational. I am ashamed of myself for subscribing to these hateful, phantasmagoric pseudo-identities for even an instant; but something deep inside me cannot be gainsaid. Centuries of negative stereotyping cannot be erased so easily—not even in the minds of those who would discredit the anti-Semites and defend the Jews. Figures as intelligent and anti-anti-Semitic as Sartre may unconsciously subscribe to stereotypical notions of "the Jew," as Susan Suleiman points out in her perceptive essay in this volume. The minds of Jews who are not particularly "self-hating" themselves may share some of the anti-Semites' attitudes about Jewish "Others"—German Jews about Ashkenazis, for instance, or Jews with rural origins about their urban co-religionists. The almost universal opprobrium felt by Christian Europe for Jews and Jewishness, epitomized in the stereotypical construction of "The Jew," seeps into the most hidden layers of even the most enlightened and self-confident psyche, where it lies dormant until stimulated, roused to consciousness by an experience like working on this book.

If, as William James said, "The deepest principle in human nature is the craving to be appreciated,"[2] then the historical representation of the Jew as irredeemably detestable, corrupt, and physically and morally loathsome is destructive of this "deepest principle," for it denies all appreciation to any member of this alienated group simply by virtue of being born to it. Why do they hate *me* so much, when they, the anti-Semitic perpetrators of the articles, stories, and images discussed by our authors, don't even know me? I am unappreciated, made abject *a priori* simply because I am one of them. And the consequences of this belief have been more terrible than mere lack of appreciation. They have been extermination.

Hovering, unspoken for the most part, above the discourse about Jewish identity and representation after the middle of the twentieth century is the shadow of the Holocaust. It is hard to consider a character like Fagin objectively, to think of Lautrec's illustrations to *Au Pieds du Sinaï* within a limited historical context, because the thought of the terrible consequences, the ultimate corollary, of the "representation of the Jew as excess," inevitably intervenes; it may be brushed aside or taken into consideration—but cannot be dismissed.

For me, who had always taken for granted that I was Jewish, who had grown up in an almost completely Jewish community in Brooklyn, New York, during the thirties and forties, but had never particularly considered the content of that Jewish identity until I undertook the editing of this book, visiting Prague this summer was a revelation. I made the obligatory pilgrimage to the cramped "Jewish Quarter," now a tourist Mecca for Jews from all over the world, mainly, I suspect, from the United States. Cravenly avoiding the exhibition of children's art from Theresienstadt, I threaded my way through the old Jewish Cemetery, the oldest in Europe I understand, with its rows and layers of crooked and tilted grave stones (like the rounded shoulders of Jewish stereotype) and entered the so-called Pinkas School or Synagogue, founded in the sixteenth century. There was a sign asking for silence. Inside the building, a small group of dedicated young people were painstakingly recopying the names of the 77,000 or so Jewish victims of the Holocaust from the region who had been murdered by the Nazis, names that had been inscribed on the walls right after the war and then effaced in a so-called cleaning process by the Soviet invaders.[3] Reading the long lists of names, row after row of them, transcribed in colored pigment on the whitewashed walls of the synagogue, humble forerunners of the more monumental inscription on the bronze surface of the Vietnam Memorial in Washington, D.C., I was struck by the familiarity of the names I was reading: Ableman, Bruckenfeld, Anbinder, Cohen—this could have been the Brooklyn telephone directory of my youth. People with the same names as these were the ones

I was telephoning, playing with, visiting, or complaining to about rationing at the very time the bearers of these Jewish names in Prague, the members of *these* families, were being brutally taken from their homes, piled into box cars, and killed in the gas chambers. It was not that I didn't know such things before, but the walls of the Pinkas Synagogue suddenly made them concrete, gave specificity and recognizable identities to the anonymous "victims" in a way that made their fate all the more terrible in that the lists were so "ordinary," so much part of my childhood experience, and yet, at the same time, so horrifically different. More powerfully than any representation, the names, in their naked indexicality, an indexicality which here denied the very possibility of communication through an icon of the Holocaust, bore concrete witness to Jewish identity and its destruction. Consciously or not, the Hebrew interdiction against the graven image was in effect, and powerfully effective. Here, on the walls of the Pinkas Synagogue, the Jew and the text coincide absolutely and literally.

There too, in Prague, I read briefly the history of the Jews in the city: an ancient history, dating back to the Middle Ages, a familiar narrative of brief periods of acceptance—extremely circumscribed—followed by exiles or even pogroms, a rebuilding of the community, success, and security, followed by recurrent difficulty and renewed oppression and exile. There was almost no place in Europe where Jews could live with equanimity, in peace and security long enough to establish deep roots; no place where they could own land over a period of time; no place where they could have equal access to all the trades and professions, until well after the French Revolution. In Christian Europe, they were the irrevocable other, endowed with all the negative characteristics the Christian majority most hated and despised—in themselves primarily. Paranoid fantasies could always be fueled by selective fact-finding, heightened by vicious and exaggerated representation.

"Why do and did they hate us?" can be answered on the simplest level by replying "Because we were the ones singled out to be objects of hatred." Jews have always been the hated other since the beginning of the Christian era. Not only were they the Christ Killers, but they stubbornly refused to see the light of Christian salvation and stuck to the old dispensation. It is the shapes this hatred assumes, the substance of the paranoid fantasies, the social role played by the "phantasmagoric" Jew of racial abjection that varies, that is at once interesting and abhorrent.

The modern construction of the Jew and the establishing of a coherent Jewish identity may be said to have begun with the construction of modernity itself, in the nineteenth century. This construction is almost synchronous with, though hardly identical to, the growth of mass communication and the possibility of popular representation on a large scale. This fabric of Jewish identity is interwoven with the complex formation of anti-Semitism as an ideological position. Indeed, one might say that Jewish identity and the Jew of anti-Semitism are brought into being by the same representational trajectory. What we are interested in here is not some "real," essential Jewishness lurking beneath a surface of lies and clichés, a reduced essence beyond the excessiveness of the stereotypical Jewish persona of art, literature, and propaganda, but rather that excessiveness itself; the almost hysterical repetitiveness of myths and exaggerations, black or white, and the ambivalent fluctuations between these two poles, revealed in a subtle analysis like the one to which Bryan Cheyette's submits colonialist Jewish representation, which constitutes the repertory of represented Jewishness in modern times.

It may be the ultimate irony in the history of Jewish identity and the representation of the Jew that successful assimilation, in France and Germany during the "benign" nineteenth century, should be so intimately, indeed necessarily, connected with the formation of modern anti-Semitic stereotypes. "Anti-Semitism turned racist only on the fateful day, when, as a consequence of Emancipation, you could no longer pick Jews out of a crowd at first glance," declares Alain Finkielkraut in his provocative study of modern anti-Semitism and its variants, *The Imaginary Jew.*[4] Continues Finkielkraut: "Since the Jews—those revolting mimics—were no longer distinguishable by any particular trait, they were graced with a distinct mentality. Science was charged with succeeding where the gaze had failed, asked to make sure that the adversary remained foreign, to stigmatize the nation of Israel by enclosing it within a Jewish reality. . . . Racial hatred and its blind rage were essentially the Jews' punishment for no longer placing their difference on display."[5]

Jewish Identity and the Ambiguities of Visual Representation

If the terrible consequences of a politics of Jewish identity in the mid-twentieth century are brutally legible in the names of murdered victims inscribed on the wall of the Pinkas Synagogue, the relationship between Jewish identity and visual representation in the modern period as a whole is far more ambiguous. Although the coarse anti-Semitic caricatures discussed by Michèle Cone in her essay on anti-Semitism and art criticism under Vichy seem unequivocal in their visual venom, in other cases the representational spectrum and its variables present themselves with far greater complexity. Much depends on the position of the artist—Jewish or non-Jewish, more or less sympathetic to Jews, "neutral" or hostile—as well as the position of the viewer in relation to represented Jewishness. In the latter case, we might turn to the interesting example provided by Kathleen Adler in her essay on Sargent's portraits of the Wertheimer family: these portraits might well be taken for overt or covert anti-Semitic caricatures by viewers with varied attitudes towards "the Jews" themselves. Nevertheless, both the artist and his Jewish sitters saw them as extremely sympathetic, vital images of the wealthy art dealer and his family. For them, the portrait of Asher Wertheimer "served both as a likeness which satisfied the family and as an image which proclaimed the sitter's identity as a Jew—a Jew of a particular class, distinguished by his wealth."[6]

Contrast and Compare: Two Representations of Jews

How then is "Jewishness" constituted as a visual trope in the modern period? Can the artist establish a Jewish typology which is generally readable as Jewish without resorting to caricature or "negative" (I use the term provisionally and warily) imagery? How can we—and who are "we" *vis-à-vis* Jewish identity anyway?—distinguish between an image of Jews which is anti-Semitic and one which is "positive" (again, I use the other term of the dichotomy with extreme reluctance)? A detailed comparison of two nineteenth-century representations of very similar Jewish subjects reveals the complexity involved in attempting to separate "good" and "bad" images of Jews. The comparison will put up the work of the German artist Ludwig Knaus (1829-1910) against that of the French Jew Alphonse Lévy (1843-1918). Both Knaus's *Solomonic Wisdom* of 1878 and Lévy's *The Hebrew Lesson: The Portion,* one of the artist's most celebrated lithographs, first published in the periodical *La Plume* in 1895,[7] represent an older Jewish man transmitting the traditional wisdom of his people to a younger disciple.

Solomonic Wisdom is one of a group of genre paintings Knaus devoted to marginal groups, Gypsies as well as Jews. Although at first sight the image is a benign one, the ironic title directs the viewer to more or less subtle clues undermining the apparent coziness of the scene. The benign old man, taking his ease with his pipe, is not really benign; his dignity is farcical. This is a Jewish old-clothes dealer (a fairly common trade for Jews, deprived as they were of access to more dignified professions), teaching an unsavory young disciple, whose animalistic features and "typical" red hair betray his racial origins, the tricks of the trade, the sharp practices characteristic of the race.[8]

The old man's unchristian pride in profiting off the misery of others (Gentiles), the young man's unseemly avidity in absorbing the sordid lesson, are underlined by the abjectness of the setting—a squalid basement full of rags. The Jews, of course, are depicted as unaware of this squalor since it is their natural environment. Yet if the image is an anti-Semitic one, it is, at least for the modern viewer, a relatively subtle one, its ironic vision of Jewish domesticity directed to our attention as much by the title as by outright exaggeration of physiognomy, gesture, or setting. To a viewer of Knaus's day, however, like the art historian and critic Ludwig Pfau, this was an easily readable satire of Jewish sharp practices.[9] Looking back at the painting ten years later, in 1888, Pfau describes it as follows: "A gray-haired old-clothes dealer gives his redheaded offspring theoretical advice about how to get rich. The harmony between these two noble souls, for whom haggling has all the fascination of an art form, the cozy air of superiority of the smoking old man, who feels himself as completely at home in his over-crowded den as Mephistopheles in the witches' kitchen, and the knowing grin of the youth, whose eyes glisten like those of a cat when he hears a mouse rustling, are products of an extraordinary art of expression."[10] Once more, irony puts these Jewish figures in their place and bears witness to the skill of the artist who can convey the underlying racial character of the group with such authenticity.

But what are "we" (and by this I mean the modern, visually sophisticated spectator, Jewish or non-Jewish, interested in reading the inscription of value in visual imagery) to make of Alphonse Lévy's construction of Jewishness in *The Hebrew Lesson*? Clearly this is meant to be, and to some extent works as, a "positive" image. The old Hebrew teacher, a rabbi, teaches a young pupil to read the time-honored language of his people, thereby contributing to the continuation of Jewish identity in diaspora. Given the age of the pupil, it is possible, and probable, that this is a bar mitzvah portion: the boy is imbibing not merely an identifying language, but also the traditional wisdom that will enable him to take his place as an adult member of the Jewish community—to become a Jewish man, in short. The instruction represented, rather than being a training in stealth and abjection, a "negative" image, such as that depicted by the German Knaus, is the transmission of traditional religious wisdom (the very opposite, in its purity and unworldliness, from the ironically designated "Wisdom" of Knaus's denomination), "positive" in the best sense of the word.

But when we consider the representation as a representation, and not merely its iconography, the case is much less clear. Indeed, it constitutes a case of that representational ambiguity to which I have referred. What we have here is a gap-toothed, large-nosed old man, positioned close to the surface of the print in a pose of authority vaguely reminiscent of that established by Titian in his papal portraits, and his less than attractive, or even intelligent, young pupil with cap pulled low over his eyes as he struggles over the text, presented in close-up within a dark interior unmistakably shown as Jewish by the Hebrew inscription and seven-branched lamp hanging from the ceiling. It would seem to be no accident that the Lévy image at one time was included in what one authority on the artist, Elie Szapiro, has termed a "véritable anthologie antisémite," Furst's *Die Juden in der Karikatur* of 1923, and yet at another time served as the cover illustration for a special number of *La Vie illustrée* consecrated to the "Jewish world" on the occasion of the 1902 Zionist Congress in Basel.[11]

It seems to me that *The Hebrew Lesson* must be further contextualized, within both the frame of Lévy's production and that provided by his own statement of his intentions in a representation such as this. Alphonse Lévy made his reputation, and it was a considerable one in France in the latter part of the nineteenth century, as a purveyor of Jewish customs and folklore. He exhibited regularly in the Salon, but was best known for his lithographs and illustrations of Jewish family life and religious practice in Alsace, scenes already old-fashioned and replete with nostalgia when he depicted them.[12] Lévy was a draftsman of considerable skill, whose efforts were consecrated by an exhibition on the premises of *La Plume* in 1897. He was capable of work of considerable dignity and formal inventiveness, like the forceful poster of a man in a prayer shawl advertising the exhibition of his work, or the humorous but still effective *Preparations for Passover,* depicting an Alsatian-Jewish housewife putting herbs in the holiday soup as she looks out at the spectator challengingly from the bailiwick of her resplendent kitchen; still other works, less formally distinguished but not without pictorial interest, represent *Saturday Prayer; The Meeting with the Rabbi,* an outdoor scene indicating the Alsatian architecture in the background; *The Kapora Ceremony,* representing the swinging of a chicken over the heads of some startled children on the Eve of Yom Kippur; *The Matzo Balls,* also titled *The Good Jewish Housewife,* showing a buxom matron rubbing her hands with satisfaction, or flour, as she pauses to look up at the spectator in the midst of Passover food preparation; and a whole series of representations of the Jews of Algiers to whom Lévy turned for subject matter later in his life.[13] Lévy made his intention to celebrate rather than satirize Jewish family customs and religious practices explicit in a letter he published in *La Plume* in August, 1895. His inspiration, Lévy declares, was "the beauty, the charms of the religious group to which I belonged. It is in taking notice of all its picturesque qualities that I decided to depict it with my feeble talents."

But Lévy buys his benign image of Judaism at a price: the price of difference. By distinguishing between his "good" Jews—"I chose my models among the humble folk, the naively pious villagers for whom the tricks of our over-civilized society were still a mystery"—and the corrupt nogoodniks of the modern city, he makes it clear that he has no truck with the ambitious assimilationists of Paris. "Raised in a simple, humble milieu," the artist declares, "I was able to observe in my childhood the scenes that I try to represent . . . mores and character-types of a race still unspoiled by contact with the great centers. My models have not yet crossed the borders of the villages in Alsace or Lorraine; they are the ancestors of those whom Drumont attacks so vehemently today." And he continues with his apologia for his (rural) Jewish subjects: "The race is valiant, strong in its family virtues, its sobriety, its tenacity . . . and all these virtues are annihilated, are transformed by the emigration to the great cities."[14]

No more than Lautrec, in his poster for the outspokenly anti-Semitic novel of Victor Joze, would Lévy, apparently, look to the urban Jewish financier or businessman for sympathetic models.[15] Like the Mennonites, or Pennsylvania Dutch in the United States, or the country folk represented in the peasant novels of George Sand earlier in the century, called up to support the enterprise of Lévy's literary confrère Daniel Stauben in his *Scenes of Jewish Life in Alsace* in the 1850's, these quaint, marginal, nostalgically isolated Jews of the countryside seem to have been constructed almost explicitly to countervene the hostile representation of the Jews by the French anti-Semites of the period. Above all, Lévy's Jews are harmless and open about their identity—and they belong to the past. They would never try to "mingle," he implies, or to "get above themselves."

One might say that Lévy's representation of his Jewish subjects is in fact a sub-category of a broader representational formation: that reassuring nineteenth-century trope of difference which reconstructs the rural as the timeless, the pious, and the quaintly picturesque in the wake of the various Revolutions—1789, 1830, and 1848—in which portions of the peasantry had played an active and threatening role. Just as the picturesque and timeless peasant was called into representational play in an endless stream of banal Salon paintings during the period, so the "good rural Jew" with his or her charming, timeless customs, superstitions, and folkloristic idiosyncrasies, is summoned up to meet the perceived threat of the assimilated, smart, successful urban Jew, represented so unflatteringly by Lautrec in his Joze posters, or, on a more sinister level, by anti-Semitic caricaturists. One might even think of Chagall's earlier work, combining astutely measured dosages of fantasy, *shtetl* memories, and Cubist formal structure, as providing a Modernist version of this strategy of difference within Jewish representation.

I do not mean to imply that the only good Jew in modern representation is the rural Jew: far from it. The writer Israel Zangwill's popular *Children of the Ghetto,* as well as the important novel of Henry Roth, *Call It Sleep,* focus with enormous sympathy, and a sense of the human complexity, on the plight of the newly transplanted urban Jews of the late nineteenth and early twentieth century. Indeed, in the construction of Modernity, the shift from restrictive rural societies, no matter how picturesque, to open, urban ones, no matter how risky, can be viewed more fruitfully as a liberation rather than a corruption, for Jews as well as Gentiles, as Marshall Berman has pointed out in his classic examination of Modernism and Modernity *All that Is Solid Melts into Air*[16] and as he implies in his analysis of the apocalyptic final scenes of *Call It Sleep* in this volume.

THE NATURE OF THE CRITERIA

But, to return to our analysis of the specific work of Lévy with which we started, *The Hebrew Lesson: The Portion,* and the representational ambiguities that it offers to the interpreter: it seems to me that before we can deal properly with the idea of "ambiguous" semiology in Jewish representation, we must examine carefully what we have in mind when we talk about a "positive" or a "negative" image of a Jew. We need, that is, to consider the nature of the criteria themselves, and who has established them, rather than taking for granted that such and such a lithograph is a "good" one or another a "bad" one: we must also take account of the fact that the same image can be put to different uses.

While it is true that the Jew-as-Vampire caricatures discussed by Michèle Cone can only be read as unequivo-

cally negative, since the Jew in question is constructed as the signifier of an allegory of greed, and can be read in no other way, in the case of Lévy's *The Hebrew Lesson,* we must examine the all too easily taken for granted bias in criteria of Jewish negativity itself. Why, for example, does an image which represents a Jew as an old man with a single tooth and a big nose necessarily constitute a "negative" representation or, to put it more forcefully, an "anti-Semitic" one? Doesn't this notion of negativity itself derive from a certain deeply implanted, universalist notion of the "normal" (or more strongly, of the "beautiful"), deriving ultimately from Greek classicism, which condemns all other types to the realm of "otherness" or "deviance?" Similar deviations have been read into the thick lips and dark skin of the Black or even, in the eyes of Winckelmann and his more extreme, gynophobic followers, into the curving breasts and bulging hips of women which "deviate" from the masculine ideal type.

Here, it seems to me, we are forced to take into account the role played by both intentionality and contextuality in the construction of Jewish representation. To what else can we resort when the criteria of judgment are themselves ambiguous or even suspect? It seems to me that in such cases, the intention of the artist, suspect though it has been held in sophisticated critical discourse, as well as the context within which the work was created, must then be called into play. In a work like Lévy's *The Hebrew Lesson,* intentionality must be summoned to assist in the reading of the image. First of all, one needs to know that this is a Jew, a scene of Jewish life, and a scene of Jewish life created by a Jewish artist, for it to assume a sinister or contrarily, a benign, implication. Once one knows that the Jewish artist, Lévy, intended it as one of a series of representations of the practices of the rapidly vanishing Jewish communities of rural Alsace in the nineteenth century, communities which to a large extent ceased to exist after the German occupation of 1871, and which he clearly regarded with the same nostalgia that American Jews lavished on life in the *shtetl,* and that he devoted a great deal of time, warmth, and energy to his creation of *Scènes familiales juives,* we inevitably look at the work somewhat otherwise than if it had been intended as an anti-Semitic caricature. And this is true even when we discover that Lévy, in this series of lithographs, often seems to find caricature "irresistible," while at other times his "tenderness" towards his subjects seems evident.

And much also depends on the eye of the beholder. To the Jewish viewer, especially the religious Jew, or the Jew nostalgic about the vanished life of the rural Jewish communities of Europe, this may seem merely an accurate and basically sympathetic record of how poor (toothless, big-nosed) rabbis and their youthful students looked and behaved in the past. The passing down of Jewish wisdom from one generation to another seems an honorable and praiseworthy practice, certainly one that is completely harmless to non-Jews. To the non-Jew, and above all, to the anti-Semitic observer, who sees otherness as a threat and an insult, such an image might seem to bear witness to Jewish "conspiracy"; how "they" plot to maintain their special difference and apartness, or, more paranoid still, how "they"—ugly, hook-nosed, deformed, clannish—conspire to undermine Gentile hegemony with their secret language and nefarious rituals.

In conclusion, one might say that, as opposed to the implacable simplicity of the names inscribed on the wall of the Pinkas Synagogue, or the grotesqueries of out-and-out anti-Semitic caricature, when it comes to representing Jews, there are no simple formulae to be adopted, no good versus bad representations, and, more germane to the point of this collection, no one-dimensional modes of interpretation that may satisfactorily explicate or exhaust the meanings of representations of Jews and Jewishness—any more than there is a single, simple essential Jewish identity which exists waiting to be discovered. Admittedly, it is more difficult to find work in the visual arts which deliberately problematizes the issue of Jewish identity (rather than merely rendering it problematic by unconscious ambiguities of expression), than in the realm of literature. I am thinking, of course, of the examples of such deliberate refusal of narrative simplicity offered by Joyce and Proust, discussed by Connor and Kristeva respectively here. Nevertheless, certain examples of such problematization, often inscribed by foregrounding the formal structure or visual language of the work in question, immediately come to mind: Claude Lanzmann's film *Shoah,* for example, which refuses the easy pathos of realism; some of the Holocaust memorials described by James Young in his *The Texture of Memory: Holocaust Memorials and Meaning,* like the range of broken shards at Treblinka or the Memorial Tent at Yad Vashem ("stone heaviness on the outside, dark absence inside"); or the ambiguously resonant work of the artist Kitaj, one of whose works is reproduced on our cover—all refuse an easy representation of Jewish identity or experience. It is to be hoped that the essays in this volume, like this adventurous work in art and literature, rather than attempting to provide interpretative solutions or reductions of meaning, to foreclose the possibilities of significance, will, on the contrary, problematize the vexed issue of representing Jews or Jewishness by pointing out the multiplicity of possible meanings and the variety of interpretative strategies at the disposal of both authors and audience.

Notes

1. Sander L. Gilman, *The Jew's Body.* New York and London: Routledge, 1991.

2. Cited in Doris Grumbach, *Coming into the End Zone: A Memoir.* New York: W. W. Norton, 1991, p. 41.

3. The Pinkas Synagogue stands over the 11th-century foundations of what was possibly the first synagogue in Prague. The present building was begun in 1479. It was enlarged in 1535 and received its present facade in 1625. 77,297 Czech Jews were killed by the Nazis, and their names were inscribed beneath the vaults of the synagogue after the war. The synagogue was reopened in 1991, after being closed for over 20

years of so-called restoration, during which the Communist authorities permitted the written memorial to sink into invisibility. This information comes from the invaluable and accurate guide to Prague by Sadakat Kadri: *Prague.* London: Cadogan Books, 1993, p. 166.

4. Trans. K. O'Neill and D. Suchoff. Lincoln: University of Nebraska Press, 1994 (originally published as *Le Juif Imaginaire,* 1980), p. 83.

5. Alain Finkielkraut, *The Imaginary Jew,* p. 83.

6. Kathleen Adler, *see below,* p. 90.

7. *The Hebrew Lesson* was one of Lévy's most frequently shown works. Not only was it published in the prestigious *La Plume,* it was represented in the artist's one-person show of 1897 on the premises of the journal. See *Atelier d'Alphonse Lévy à Alger* (sale cat.), Paris: Hôtel Drouot, 1993, no. 112.

8. See *Ludwig Knaus, 1829-1910* (exh. cat.), Museum Wiesbaden, 1979, no. 96, p. 96, for extensive information about this painting and Knaus's attitudes toward his Jewish subjects.

9. It is perhaps not without relevance to the attitudes embodied in this painting to discover that 1878, the year it was created, was also when the Christian Socialist Party was founded in Berlin, the first political party grounded on anti-Semitic doctrine. See *Knaus,* p. 97.

10. Cited in *Knaus,* p. 169. The same boy appears again, as a single full-length figure, in *The First Profit,* another work from 1878 with a Jewish subject, an oil painting now in the Hermitage in St. Petersburg (*Knaus,* no. 97, pp. 169-70.) A pendant to *Solomonic Wisdom,* the young Jewish boy represented here has a certain youthful charm but also a feral look that bodes ill for the future. His racial "otherness" and associated moral insufficiency are conveyed by subtle hints rather than outright caricature: the slanted green "cats" eyes, the prominent spaces between the teeth, the big ears; above all, the complacent leer with which the youth shares his triumph with the spectator as he puts his first-earned coin into his purse.

11. See Elie Szapiro, "Réflexion sur les représentations et l'image du Juif en France au temps de "l'Affair Dreyfus," *Actes de la Journée d'Etudes autour de l'Affaire Dreyfus,* December 12, 1991, Paris: Ecole des Hautes Etudes du Judaisme, 1992, p. 45, and *Atelier d'Alphonse Lévy,* no. 112. However, as Szapiro himself points out, despite the fact that the issue is not in itself anti-Semitic, "son titre extérieur est la première impression qu'il donne le sont franchement." Nevertheless, as this author continues, "il offre pourtant huit autres reproductions d'oeuvr d'Alphonse Lévy, reproductions qui montrent, au contraire, avec quelle tendresse évidente, même si elle reste souvent teintée d'ironie, ce peintre savait représenter les aspects très différents du judaisme français de son temps." *Actes,* pp. 45-6.

12. For the best account of Lévy's career, see Elie Szapiro, "Alphonse Lévy et l'image du Juif en France au temps de l'affaire Dreyfus (1895-1902)," *Archives Juives: Revue d'histoire des Juifs de France* (Dossier: Les Juifs et l'Affaire Dreyfus), no. 27/1, vol. a, 1994, pp. 72-8.

13. Original, large-scale lithographs of these works, including a color version of the poster, and many more are available in two albums in the Salle d'Estampes, Bibliothèque Nationale, Paris: *Oeuvre d'Alphonse Lévy, Peintre, graveur et lithographe français, 1843-1918* (AA.4. Supplt. relié) and *Oeuvre d'Alphonse Lévy* (Dc. 356/in-fol. Form 3)/Mobile. Another volume of the artist's work, Alphonse Lévy, *Scènes familiales juives,* preface by Bernard Lazare, Paris: F. Juven, 1902 (In-dol., 10 p.m.h.) is missing from the collection. Several of the prints were exhibited at the Galerie Saphir Rive Droite, Paris, Summer, 1994. The *Scènes familiales juives,* in various avatars, keep popping up as illustrations, most recently for an English translation of Daniel Stauben's *Scenes of Jewish Life in Alsace,* a work originally published in serial form in the *Revue des deux mondes,* 1857 and 1859, and, translated by Rose Choren, by Methuen in London in 1979. The American edition contains numerous pale and worn-out versions of Lévy's richly modulated lithographs: see Daniel Stauben, *Scenes of Jewish Life in Alsace,* illustrations by Alphonse Lévy, ed. and trans. Rose Choron, Malibu, Joseph Simon: Pangloss Press, 1991.

14. Cited in Elie Szapiro, *Actes,* pp. 72-3.

15. See Gale Murray, *below,* p. 58. Of course John Singer Sargent, as Kathleen Adler points out, could create a positive, if ambiguous, image of wealthy, sophisticated urban Jews in his portraits of the Wertheimer family, *below,* pp. 83-96.

16. Marshall Berman, *All that Is Solid Melts into Air: The Experience of Modernity.* New York: Simon and Schuster, 1982.

Harley Erdman (essay date 1997)

SOURCE: Erdman, Harley. "Introduction." In *Staging the Jew: The Performance of an American Ethnicity 1860-1920,* pp. 1-13. New Brunswick, NJ: Rutgers University Press, 1997.

[*In the following excerpt, Erdman explores the influence of Jewish stage stereotypes on artists and audiences in the period between 1860 and 1920, showing how various artists both fulfilled and reshaped expectations of their performances.*]

The actor David Warfield used to tell a story about his professional debut as part of a second-rate West Coast company in the late 1880s. The play was Tom Taylor's Victorian melodrama *The Ticket-of-Leave Man,* a quarter-of-a-century-old English play that by then was an American stock repertory staple. The role was Melter "Aby" Moss, Jewish henchman and counterfeiter. When Warfield recounted the story to a journalist in 1926, after a long career that saw him celebrated first as the foremost Jewish "delineator" of the day and later as "the greatest living actor in English," he recalled the trepidation that accompanied the breakthrough of being cast in such a crucial role:

> I had no idea of the character of Morse [sic] but as he was a Jew, I supposed of course he must have an exaggerated nose. Now, I had no experience in mechanically simulating noses—no idea of the stuff of which such things were made. I should of course have used the regular make-up putty, but instead I obtained some of the stuff a glazier uses. With this I proceeded to build a pendant addition to my nose.
>
> I congratulated myself on the job. But . . . right after my entrance in the act my nose began to elongate, until it was like the trunk of a baby elephant—lengthy beyond my wildest dreams of what a Jew's nose should be. When I realized what was taking place, I became demoralized. Instead of calmly manipulating the thing into shape, as an accustomed actor would have done, I became panic-stricken. I roughly pushed my nose back and off, which gave it a bulbous, pear-shaped appearance. Thus it remained a few moments, then began to elongate again.
>
> By this time the audience had caught on. It snickered. My panic increased. When I again grabbed the thing, which had now assumed the proportions of a banana, my fingers left deep ridges in it. Under pressure it began to flatten and spread. It changed its grotesque shape with every squeeze I gave it. It was at a serious moment in the play—a sensationally dramatic moment, that was supposed to create the tensest suspense. But the audience saw nothing but my ever-changing nose. Instead of howling with rage as becomes a well-trained audience at the melodrama, it guffawed. I was hustled off the stage abruptly, ignominiously.
>
> I shall never forget the agony of humiliation I felt. The memory of that agony is with me still.[1]

This striking tale invites multiple readings, the obviously Freudian aside. First, there is Warfield, a Jewish actor, having to augment his appearance since his own markings of Jewish ethnicity apparently do not qualify as authentic enough to satisfy his audience's expectations. The chosen site of this augmentation? None other than that time-honored manifestation of Jewish difference, that badge of Semitic authenticity: the nose. Yet, in the process of performing this difference, which presumably the actor lacks but the character possesses, the inexperienced Warfield fails miserably, unable to embody somebody else's conception of himself.

That conception, and who authored it, becomes yet more complicated when one considers that Warfield, the son of immigrant parents, is performing for an American audience a part written by an Englishman for an English public, embodying traditional stock elements of English anti-Semitism as reflected in literary and dramatic images from Shylock to Fagin. However, Moss, unlike his Venetian-cum-Elizabethan forerunner who went cloaked in the gabardine of the Hebrews, does not have his Jewishness clearly inscribed in Taylor's written text. Nowhere in *The Ticket-of-Leave Man* does Moss call himself a Jew, nor does any other character refer to him as such, yet it remains understood throughout the script, by clues such as the character's name ("Moss" which suggests "Moses") and profession (counterfeiter, the traditional profession of the Victorian stage Jew) that Moss is nothing but a Jew and must be played as such in performance. The character's ethnicity, then, must express itself outwardly through other signs. It must be manifested through grotesque gestures, intonations, and appendages that can only be inscribed through performance. Hence the requisite putty nose.

And who exactly is this David Warfield? As his fame grew during the first decade of the twentieth century, the actor tended to elide issues of origin, to distance himself from the Jewish peddlers he made a fortune playing, to point out that "they" were not him. Magazine articles took pains to make visual points about Warfield the man—his sandy hair, blue eyes, modest nose—suggesting that he was not to be equated with the characters that he portrayed. When Warfield died in 1951, he was interred with Roman Catholic rites. In fact, a 1960s dissertation dealing with vaudeville comedy took for granted the irony that Warfield himself was not of Jewish heritage. The irony, however, points back the other way, since, as far as I have been able to ascertain, Warfield was born David Wohlfelt, the child of Orthodox Russian-Jewish immigrants.[2]

And to what extent do we accept the history of this performance as real? Warfield told many things to many journalists over the years, often contradicting himself from interview to interview. This story seems, like much melodrama itself, almost too perfectly constructed to be true. Consider the rising action of the dramatic elements: the neophyte's indecision, his nervous preparation, his initial entrance, the first sign of the *schnoz*'s melt, the mangling that takes the putty from bad to worse, the audience's mounting laughter, the exit in humiliation. If there is a grain of truth in the tale, it is difficult to sift it out from the storyteller's embellishment, aided as it is by the passing of more than thirty-five years of countless retellings. What's more, the tale carries its own curious footnote, a slip made by either Warfield or the journalist recording him, in that it misreports the name of the stage character in question. Moss is a name that may be Jewish. Morse, on the other hand, rarely is.

Where does authenticity reside in this story? To what extent is this fragment of history objectively real or merely a part of Warfield's public performance of himself? Is Wohlfelt the Jewish man more authentic a subject than Warfield the talented performer who played Jews but died Catholic? And is the performance itself to be seen as au-

thentically English or authentically American, given the disjuncture between the origins of the text and the participants in this particular performance? How does a historian answer these questions to make sense of this story?

The authenticity of ethnic identity is ultimately not the issue, neither in this story nor in the pages to follow. The real Warfield/Wohlfelt is not going to stand up and I am not going to try to make him. Rather, this story provides me with a vortex where the issues I am concerned with converge and collide. My subject, after all, is how Jews and gentiles performed Jewish characters on American stages in the last decades of the nineteenth century and the first decades of the twentieth. I am not concerned with the material circumstances of Jewish-American social history per se, but rather the fluctuating expectations gentiles have had of Jews and Jews have had of themselves, as represented by the performances of the commercial stage.

Most of these theatrical characterizations are not flattering. Many are specifically anti-Semitic. Perhaps as a result, Jewish representation from this long era, falling roughly between the Civil War and World War I, remains a topic many today would prefer to ignore, erase, or simply forget. "The memory of that agony," to cite Warfield, remains painful. However, I believe these performances merit historical excavation and critical examination. As Sander Gilman and Stephen Katz have argued, by accepting the central value system of a given culture, Jews prove the charges of the mainstream against them since they ultimately cannot stand apart from the performances expected of them. Therefore, "to understand Jewish identity in the Diaspora one must also understand the creation, generation and perpetuation of negative images of the Jew."[3] These negative images, in the tradition of Melter Moss, are the focus of Part One of this book.

However, my story cannot be told merely through a cataloging of Jewish stage characters who reflect gentile expectations of Jewish behavior. Men (and, to a far lesser extent, women) of Jewish heritage gradually became active agents in shaping these performances during this same era. As actors, directors, producers, playwrights, and patrons, they came to exercise influence and wield power in the popular performing arts. In this case, Warfield's example is once again instructive, for the actor went on to make his first fortune playing stage Jews who were not craven villains, but rather, endearing smalltime businessmen who transformed many of the ignominies associated with stage Jews into kinder qualities calculated to win an audience's sympathies. The point then, is not how Warfield failed at playing the Jewish villain but how he succeeded in reordering the elements of the popular image of the Jew, and in so doing, helped to renegotiate the terms by which Jewish males were to perform themselves as Jewish-American men.

Warfield, of course, did not manage this negotiation alone. As I show here, he was one figure in a complex network of performers, playwrights, producers, and theatergoers, both Jewish and gentile, who achieved positions of influence in the theater and transformed the nature of Jewish stage characters during this era. This transformation, like assimilation itself, came with compromise. The new performances had their own liabilities, which invoked new agonies and led to new ironies, even while they perpetuated many elements of the older negative images. These complex encounters are the focus of Part Two of this book.

By tracing the relationship between Jewish stage types and the artists fashioning and audiences receiving them from 1860 to 1920, I show how, in coming to power, Jews resisted, assimilated, or reordered images that a dominant culture constructed for them, and then emerged embodying new performances of themselves in ways that continue to impact Jewish-American culture today.

The tradition of Jewish characters in Western drama and literature before the twentieth century has been the subject of a number of important studies that have laid a solid foundation for my work here. The key seminal study, M. J. Landa's *The Jew in Drama* (1926), starts with the Hebrew origins of drama, then traces the genealogy of stage types in England from the Middle Ages into the twentieth century.[4] Edward Coleman's bibliography *The Jew in English Drama* (1943) remains the most comprehensive on the topic. Edgar Rosenberg's thoughtful and persuasive *From Shylock to Svengali* (1960) argues that "the image of the Jew in English literature has been a depressingly uniform and static phenomenon" in tracing the polarities of the Shylock and Shiva (evil and saintly) types.[5]

These studies have defined their fields through the boundaries of literature, whether dramatic or otherwise, and thus construct their histories through the examination of established and widely circulated texts. Recently, the fields of cultural and performance studies have pushed the limits of what constitutes legitimate subjects for historical inquiry. Louise Mayor's *Ambivalent Image* (1988), while not a work theoretically in line with cultural studies, defines its field more broadly to deal with the representation of the Jew in such diverse areas as drama, fiction, religious writing, and journalism.[6] More recently, Shearer West's "The Construction of Racial Type" (1993) and Frank Felsenstein's *Anti-Semitic Stereotypes* (1995) have provided excellent models for the incorporation of alternate discourses (from cartoons to popular sociology) into the history of England's representations of the Jews by constructing networks of associations between theater and other forms of representation. In a similar way, John Gross's creatively wrought *Shylock* (1993) is a history of responses to and receptions of Shylock, both on and off the stage.

Some of this scholarship has been enriched by the perspective that Jews themselves have had a hand in constructing these traditions. This framework is already evident in Edward Calisch's *The Jew in English Literature as Author and as Subject* (1909) and implicit in the way Louis Harap structures his useful *The Image of the Jew in American Literature* (1974). Above all, much of Sander

Gilman's outstanding work has both influenced and reflected these recent trends in scholarship by examining the interrelationship of diverse discourses to create a sort of cultural history of how Jewishness has been constructed.

My particular approach to this material is shaped by critical theory of the past fifteen years, which has posited an anti-essentialist, anti-foundational notion of human identity. William Boelhower's *Through a Glass Darkly* (1984) views ethnicity as a "kinesis" which takes place in cultural encounters, a process of perceiving and being perceived that resides outside the context of the subject. For Boelhower, ethnicity is processual, an act of interpretation, a way of defining oneself in relation and opposition to others. Judith Butler's razor-sharp *Gender Trouble* (1990) posits gender as a process, arguing that reified categories such as "woman" and "man" represent terms in process, ever becoming and constructing themselves. Thus, "various acts of gender create the idea of gender, and without these acts, there would be no gender at all." Since gender attributes "are not expressive but performative," this flux becomes apparent in the ways in which people perform themselves—performances that, even for a given individual, vary depending upon time, place, and situation.[7] In different ways then, both Boelhower and Butler articulate the instability of identity and posit a subjectivity grounded in action rather than essence.

I should make clear that none of this anti-essentialism makes ethnicity unreal. Ethnicity, as shaped by history, as lived in the moment, is all too real most of the time. The power of culture, as expressed in both the beauty of difference and the injustice of oppression, asserts itself continually. In fact, anti-essentialism ultimately foregrounds the importance of ethnicity since it posits difference as the ongoing creation of complex dynamics which can never be reduced to a gene visible under a microscope; it is a process for which we all bear an active responsibility for perpetuating, in both its positive and negative aspects, as we perform as both actors and audience members in daily encounters. Anti-essentialism also opens the way for the critical cultural historian since it foregrounds history as a way of understanding culture today, under the assumption that performances shape as well as reflect material reality.

This type of history points me to the boundary between ethnicities, to those "borders [that] bleed as much as they contain," to cite the anthropologist Dwight Conquergood.[8] David Warfield walked in that borderland when he performed himself as Wohlfelt or Warfield, Jew or gentile, Victorian villain or lovable peddler. For me, that borderland is usefully represented by the theater, a site where playwrights, directors, performers, and audiences constantly impact each other, with no subject ever emerging from any given performance the same as he or she went into it. Performance then, is both my subject of study and operative metaphor.

If ethnicity is something that bleeds over boundaries, then much more so is that ethnicity known as Jewishness, the ambiguities and uncertainties of which have frequently characterized a culture through two thousand years of Diaspora. As many commentators have pointed out, "Jew" has rarely meant the same thing to two people. At times, the term has signified the member of a race; at times, it has designated the practitioner of a religion. At times, it has denoted the member of a nation; at others, it has indicated the member of a culture. In European tradition, Jews were vilified and segregated as the unapproachable Other, quintessential foreigners lurking both within and without. In modern America, on the other hand, Jews have largely been subsumed into the category of white, of European, on the privileged side of the gulf that separates "us" from "them." At times, Judaism has been constructed in arch opposition to Christianity; at other times, it has been accepted into a conceit known as the "Judeo-Christian" tradition. Revolutionaries have seen Jews as too capitalist, while capitalists have seen Jews as too revolutionary. Some have seen Jews as the purest of pure races, others as the most mongrel of all mongrels. For some, Jews have been too brash and noisy; for others, they have been too sly and secretive. For some, Jews have been acquisitive misers; for others, they have been gaudy spendthrifts. Albert Sonnenfeld has noted that "for each ideology . . . the Jew is the necessary adversary."[9]

These ambiguities affect not only the way others define Jews but also the way Jews have defined themselves. Is a Jew somebody born of a Jewish mother, as the state of Israel's policy of return suggests? Is a practicing convert who abides by the tenets of religious law less Jewish than the daughter of Jewish parents who has stopped identifying herself as Jewish? Or is anybody who chooses to identify his or herself as a Jew, a Jew? Moreover, how does the term "Jewish-American" fit into this equation? Does it refer to someone American by nationality and Jewish by religion? American by citizenship and Jewish by nationality? The ambiguities multiply.

My purpose is to explore rather than to answer these questions, assuming that, while a term like "Jewish-American" can never be absolutely defined, it does comprise a variety of ways of living that can be practiced, an array of roles that can be performed. Examining how Jews have historically been performed in America is a way of exploring the modalities of being Jewish-American without reducing the term to a limiting definition.

Critics and historians have attempted such a genealogical overview of Jewish representations in American performance before, but to date the focus of scholarship has been on images prevalent after 1910. Figures like Fanny Brice, Al Jolson, Sophie Tucker, and the Marx Brothers, whose work has been immortalized through the media of mass production, hover very much present in the memory, giving the impression that these individuals, along with figures like Irving Berlin and George Gershwin, were the fountainheads of Jewish-American mainstream cultural representation. However, these "early" artists seem like pioneers only in relation to where we situate ourselves, here at the end of the twentieth century, from which perspective vaudeville, silent movies, and early Broadway have become synonyms for the "good old days." In fact, these major figures represent the third and fourth generations of Jews active in American theater and show business. Their work, both in what it rejects and in what it assimilates, builds directly on earlier traditions, performed by Jews and gentiles alike, stretching back into the middle years of the nineteenth century. These neglected earlier traditions then, are what concern me here.[10]

In my research, I have discovered a blossoming of Jewish-American stage representation in the second half of the nineteenth century, particularly after 1860. I therefore take this year as a rough starting date for my work. After 1860, stage Jews of one type or another began to turn up on American stages, becoming widespread in the years right after the turn of the century. Increasingly after 1920, however, performing Jewishness in mass culture increasingly required varieties of masking. In deference to *Awake and Singing,* Ellen Schiff's recent fine anthology of "classic" American Jewish plays, which starts in 1920, I stake out this earlier era as one characterized by heightened Jewish visibility in popular culture, even if in literary quality the performances may qualify resoundingly as "pre-classic."

The broad boundaries of my research then, are 1860 and 1920, though most of the performances I document and analyze fall between 1875 and 1915. In setting these boundaries, I have largely excluded certain artists like Eddie Cantor, Al Jolson, and Sophie Tucker, who have been well examined elsewhere and whose work extends into the next era.

This same period roughly parallels the successive waves of Jewish immigration to the United States: the initial, modest wave of mostly German Jewish immigrants who arrived mostly between the 1830s and 1870s, and the much larger wave of Eastern European immigrants, mostly from Russia, who came by the millions between 1881 and 1917, before more restrictive immigration laws sharply curtailed their numbers.[11] It seems clear that the preponderance of Jewish stage representations between 1860 and 1920 reflects the growing visibility of the Jewish in America, not to mention their growing presence in the theater world itself.

Given this outline, however, I want to refrain from invoking the theater as faithful mirror of society. If it seems to function at times like a mirror, it does so more like one at a funhouse, for Jewish stage representations of the time embodied curious amalgams of characteristics associated with both German and Eastern European cultures, with certain features and trends emerging in ways which did not directly coincide with immigration patterns. In some cases, as I show, society ended mirroring theater, rather than the reverse.

I am attracted to the theater not only because it both shapes and reflects cultural forces, but also because it conveniently offers me a concrete, defined site—a literal stage peopled with physical bodies—for analysis. I find it a fascinating laboratory of meanings and possibilities. In the period I am examining, however, the stage in America had a particular resonance which it no longer possesses today. As a phenomenon which catered to mass audiences from all walks of life, theater between the Civil War and World War I was peculiarly vital and self-sustaining; religious opposition to playgoing was largely a remnant of the past, and movies had not yet emerged as the nation's dominant mode of entertainment. Though from the purely aesthetic perspective one can bemoan its seemingly paltry artistic achievements, there is no question that the stage of this era, from saloon-style variety to grand opera, provided the main form of entertainment and recreation for an entire society. The performances I consider, then, are not coterie events but events that speak significantly and broadly to the types of socio-cultural issues with which I am most concerned.

In looking at theater, I cross a few boundaries, considering other forms which, while not to be conflated with the stage, bear enough connections to it to make their inclusion relevant. In a few instances, I consider early film which, while it was evolving its own codes and traditions, was a medium with many ties to the theatrical tradition. I also briefly consider the lyrics of Tin Pan Alley, whose work was directly connected to the stage, since songs were often published and marketed in conjunction with their interpolation into musical comedies, revues, and operettas.

I had originally envisioned a book with two easily distinguished, clearly divided sections. The first section was to consider how gentiles portrayed Jews for gentile audiences during this period. The second was to consider how Jews performed themselves for gentile audiences. Alas, in the course of my research, my borders began to bleed, my categories to come apart. True, the first section was simple enough to establish, if fuzzy around the edges; there clearly were "Jewish" performances in which Jews had little or no agency, whether as performers or audiences. These were the images and representations of a dominant culture considering a largely unknown Other. In the second category, however, I stumbled, precisely because perplexing figures like David Warfield seemed to fall betwixt and between classification. In this field where writers, directors, producers, comedians, and theatergoers all had hands in authorship, it became impossible to discern who exactly was performing what for whom. Polarities between Jew and gentile fell apart. So while for my first section I was able to fix certain forms where Jews were largely excluded, in my second section I was able to locate only transitional sites, a variety of performances and encounters in a borderland where Warfield, in his resplendent ambiguity, is a representative figure.

Some may wonder why I neglect to deal with the rich phenomenon of the American Yiddish-language theater, except in passing. After all, the era I am examining here corresponds closely to the peak years of New York City's Yiddish theater, which in both range and quality of productions, surely constitutes one of the outstanding ethnic moments in American cultural history. It would seem that the Yiddish stage bears a strong connection to the English-language performances analyzed here—a connection emphasized by the fact that figures like Jacob Adler performed the same role for both Yiddish- and English-language audiences, while others like Paul Muni actually crossed over from being Yiddish- to English-language stars. A number of significant directors and scenic artists also worked in both theaters, while many other notable Jewish-American performers were exposed to the Yiddish theater in their childhoods. Moreover, the audiences for these two theaters were never entirely mutually exclusive.

Ultimately, I believe that the arguments for excluding close examination of Yiddish theater are more persuasive than those for including it. First, from the purely logistical point of view, attempting to deal with the immense variety of stage types in the Yiddish theater looms as an enormous task that merits a book in itself, especially given that the Yiddish theater itself encompassed many of the same class, epochal, and generic distinctions as did the English-language theater.[12] More importantly, however, despite the network of informal connections tying the Yiddish-and English-language theaters in America, the strong case can be made for a disjuncture between these stages. In other words, twentieth-century Jewish performances in English represent a continuity with the nineteenth-century American theater not evident with the Yiddish stage of folk operettas, sentimental melodramas, and quasi-socialist problem plays. The break in language, in my view, reflects a break in tradition. What is most significant about Yiddish performances styles may be how relatively little of their *yiddishkeit* ever found its way into American theater. The Jewish producers of Broadway and early Hollywood, many of whom came from assimilated families that had immigrated before 1881, were all too ready to shunt aside the cultural politics of the Yiddish world.

Though my focus here is ethnicity, the issue of gender asserts itself throughout my analysis. While I had originally hoped to foreground gender issues in a way that offered a balanced treatment of Jewish female and male stage types during this period, such a balancing act proved difficult. The fact is, most of the performers portraying Jews during this time period were men, and the vast majority of the characters they played were male. Though the relative invisibility of the "Jewess" is discussed in these pages, such a discussion does not remedy the male-heavy historical imbalance, which remains reflected in these pages. In the course of my analysis, however, I try to make clear that I am often referring to males, not some hypothetical universal subject.

In earlier versions of this work, I had foregrounded class divisions among audiences, taking my cue from Lawrence Levine's notions of the "highbrow" and "lowbrow" forms which emerged during the nineteenth century. I had theorized, for example, clear distinctions between ways of staging Jews for working class and bourgeois audiences in the Victorian era. As I became more familiar with the material, though, I found it increasingly difficult to reduce the complexity of the late nineteenth-century performance scene, at least as it was reflected in these performances. The result is that, while I have tried to acknowledge class distinctions when relevant, they no longer serve as a point of orientation for my work. Suffice to say that Jewish presence in the theater was closely associated with those mass cultural forms possessing broad audience appeal that emerged near the turn of the century. I use the term "popular" to refer to these commercialized forms, which included vaudeville, Broadway musicals and comedies, the songwriting industry, and early film.

I should explain my use of other terms. By "Victorian," I am referring to a period of time roughly from the 1840s to the 1890s, which parallels the emergence of certain attitudes, classes, and cultural formations which are generally understood.[13] "American" is more problematic, the politics of its hemispheric implications aside.[14] In focusing on performances which took place in the United States, I have ended up including a wide variety of plays and events, not all of which were American in the strictest sense. In the international world of show business, where plays and players frequently crossed the seas in search of new audiences, facile national distinctions tend to break down.[15] *The Ticket-of-Leave Man,* for example, is a play from England, yet for decades it held the American stage as a stock-company standard, where it both influenced and was influenced by American audiences. Sarah Bernhardt and Henry Irving are two other continental figures who, due to the length and breadth of their repeated tours, became influential players on the American cultural scene. If one extends the importance of a given performance beyond the sanctified realm of author and performer to that of the audience, then national distinctions begin to break down. I have taken the liberty, then, of including as American here any show that could be said to have had a significant impact on audiences in the United States through repeated touring or performance.[16]

In appropriating the term American for my uses, I also acknowledge being New York-centric in my focus, a perspective justified by the fact that New York was the undisputed center of the national theater industry during this period in a way that it was not before and has not been since. In keeping with this perspective, all years given for plays are for their New York premieres, when known.

"Anti-Semitic" is another term which needs explanation. Historically, use of the term dates to 1879, when it was coined to describe a newfound racial antipathy toward the Jews, in contrast to earlier European prejudices, based more upon religious difference.[17] In common usage today, the word has two distinct though by no means mutually exclusive meanings. First, it is often used to describe certain acts or attitudes of a specifically vicious or hateful nature—the use of derogatory racial slurs, the painting of swastikas, the perpetuation of hate crimes. However, many

Jews also frequently invoke the term to describe institutionalized sets of attitudes and practices, which while perhaps not consciously malevolent, reflect deeply ingrained and no less invidious prejudicial perspectives. In these pages, I choose to use the term anti-Semitic only when referring to the former specific actions and attitudes; otherwise, almost every performance I discuss here would arguably qualify as anti-Semitic and the term itself would lose its meaning. Even in this narrower context though, the word's usage here ultimately remains subjective for it corresponds to my own notion of what is specifically hateful.

Finally, throughout this study, in referring to Jewish stage characters, I try to use ethnically inflected words that might previously have been used to refer to the specific stage types, not to mention to Jewish-American women and men in general. Therefore female characters here are frequently "Jewesses" while villains are sometimes "sheenies." It goes without saying that my purpose is not to offend but to construct a context through which we can more clearly understand these performances, sometimes in all their ugliness.

It should also be noted that, in language, what is politically acceptable comes and goes, influenced by and influencing the aspirations and anxieties of a given moment. At earlier times in American history, "Hebrew" and "Israelite" were seen as more polite ways of designating a person of Jewish faith than the somewhat crass and blunt "Jew." In contrast, the shortened form "Hebe" could once be used without giving offense. Today, the word most American Jews prefer to use to describe themselves and have others describe them is "Jewish," a term which comfortably suggests cultural and religious affiliations while eliding the stickier question of race and biology. In other words, it implies an ethnicity not innate and essential, but rather, an adjectival condition which modifies some more fundamental identity which remains elusive.

I do not divorce myself from this view. I accept the term's implications and use it as a way of reflecting my own understanding of what it means to be a Jew. This work ultimately reflects, I hope, the aspirations and anxieties of the moment, as we look to the next millennium to see what performing Jewishness in America can mean.

Notes

1. "Thirty-five Years of Stage Fright," *Pictorial Review,* February 1926, in the Warfield file of the Billy Rose Collection of the New York Public Library. The paragraphing here is my own. William C. Young, in *Famous Actors and Actresses,* specifies the time and place as Napa, California, 1888. On the subject of Warfield's reputation as a great actor, see *Outlook,* 26 October 1912. As late as the film *Gold-diggers of 1933,* a character could admiringly mention Warfield in the same breath as the heralded George Arliss—another actor who became famous playing a Jew. See my discussion of *Disraeli* in Chapter Six.

2. On Warfield's not being Jewish, see Paul Antonie Distler, "Rise and Fall of the Racial Comics," 171.

Sources give a variety of spellings for Warfield's family name, including "Wollfeld," but "Wohlfelt" is the one I have come across most often and the one I use here. Immigrant families themselves sometimes spelled their English names inconsistently or gradually changed the spelling over time.

3. Sander Gilman and Stephen T. Katz, *Antisemitism,* 18.

4. Landa laments that at the beginning of the twentieth century the Jew remained an "enslaved buffoon" but also suggests that the future might bring more positive portrayals of the Jew. See 308-310. Ellen Schiff's *From Stereotype to Metaphor* (1982) suggests that the modernist revolution indeed brought about such a liberation, making it possible for the Jewish character to "play any role intended for a human being," 247.

5. Edgar Rosenberg, *From Shylock to Svengali,* 297.

6. While Mayor descends at times into a mere catalogue-like listing, in its ambitious scope it remains an impressive piece of scholarship that has been of great use to me.

7. Judith Butler, *Gender Trouble,* 140-141.

8. Dwight Conquergood, "Rethinking Ethnography," 184.

9. Albert Sonnenfeld, "The Poetics of Anti-Semitism," 84. Sonnenfeld also articulates how Jews have been perceived in relationship to economic and political practices. On the position of Jews in America, see Albert S. Lindemann, *The Jew Accused,* 209. On the many meanings of Jew, see Geroge M. Kren, "The Jews: The Image as Reality," 285-287.

10. Distler's unpublished dissertation, "Rise and Fall of the Racial Comics," is the one pioneering survey, but it does not pretend to go into detailed analysis and confines its scope to a specific era of variety theater.

11. In making this generalization, I do not want to reduce the complexity of pre-Holocaust Jewish immigration to the United States to two simple waves. There were, for example, Sephardic Jews living along the eastern seaboard as early as the seventeenth century; there were many Eastern European Jews who arrived before 1881; there were some German Jews who arrived after 1881; there were Central European Jews arriving throughout this era who do not fit so neatly into one category or another. Hasia R. Diner has particularly emphasized the diversity of the mid-nineteenth century arrivals throughout *Time for Gathering.*

12. As is clear from Nahma Sandrow's *Vagabond Stars,* there was no single "Yiddish theater" in America; it was a highly diverse network of institutions spanning a broad range of styles, appealing to a wide variety of audiences. When extended to the international level, the whole question of Yiddish theater becomes even more complex.

13. Historians often refer to a large portion of this era as the "Gilded Age," but I prefer the term Victorian because it better reflects the time frame and conjures up the cultural milieu with which I am concerned than do other terms. If it reflects an Anglo-centrism, then it accurately reflects the stage world I am looking at, which was directly impacted by many English and Irish artists, as I make clear in Chapter One. The emergence of Jews in the theater, which I trace in Part Two, can thereby be seen as representing a departure from this Victorian era.

14. Some would argue that to use the term American to refer to the United States (as I do here) unfairly appropriates an entire hemisphere (the Americas) for a single and rather atypical country within that region. At the moment, however, I cannot find another adjective which so usefully serves my purposes and so I continue to use it, though I welcome others using it for their purposes as well. From having lived in Mexico, I know that, while I was a "norteamericano" to some of my Mexican friends, I remained an "americano" to the vast majority.

15. Heinz Kosok deals with this issue in greater depth in "Dion Boucicault's 'American' Plays."

16. In determining what is significant, I have exercised subjective judgment, influenced by the size of audience, length of run, and relevance to the issues I am discussing. In particular, I have excluded works by established British playwrights like Jones, Maugham, Pinero, and Shaw which, despite their importance in the history of dramatic literature, received mostly brief productions in the United States. On the other hand, Herbert Beerbohm Tree's production of *Trilby* cannot be ignored. Israel Zangwill's *The Melting-pot* receives extended treatment; though Zangwill was English, the play was not only set in the United States, but had its first production there and significantly shaped the public conversation on immigration.

17. For more detailed examinations of the rise of modern anti-Semitism, see Judith Marion Halberstom, "Parasites and Perverts," 101; Lindemann, *The Jew Accused,* 16; Kren, "The Jews: The Image as Reality," throughout.

Robert Schechter (essay date summer 1999)

SOURCE: Schechter, Robert. "Rationalizing the Enlightenment: Postmodernism and Theories of Anti-Semitism." *Historical Reflections* 25, no. 2 (summer 1999): 279-306.

[*In the following essay, Schechter examines the roots of anti-Semitic thought, beginning with François-Marie Voltaire in the Enlightenment and continuing into the nineteenth and twentieth centuries.*]

The Jews of France did not wait for postmodernism before criticizing the Enlightenment. In response to an anti-Jewish libelist who in 1786 accused the Jews of being "superstitious," Isaiah Berr Bing of Metz defended himself and his coreligionists in a published letter:

> I do not know what you call superstitious; is it to show the most inviolable attachment to a religion in which you do not dare ignore the mark of divinity? Is it to observe very scrupulously all that it prescribes? If it is in that that we appear superstitious to you, I shall willingly admit that we are, that I hope quite sincerely that we shall always be; in spite of the progress of fashionable philosophy, in spite of its aversion for the ceremonial, and for everything that it cannot, as it were, touch with its finger.[1]

Yet it would be mistaken to characterize Bing as somehow against the Enlightenment. Indeed, in his pamphlet he drew liberally from the *philosophes,* postulated the natural equality of men and urged religious toleration. His philippic against the tendency of "fashionable philosophy" to encourage what Max Horkheimer and Theodor Adorno would later call the "disenchantment of the world" was a rhetorical ploy designed to make his opponents appear overly abstract and cerebral. This was a prudent strategy, since Bing knew that his audience valued the piety and sincerity of the naïve believer over the intellectual dexterity of the hair-splitting rationalist. (If this statement seems doubtful, I hope to convince the reader of its veracity by the end of this essay.) Moreover, he knew that Christians tended to attribute precisely the traits he ascribed to his adversaries—a mentality of calculation and excess of reason over feeling—to the Jews themselves. Thus his apparent defiance of a dominant trend was really the expression of a widely-held set of values.

Yet historians and other retrospective observers have tended to reify the rhetorical figure of "fashionable philosophy"—conjured up as a serviceable straw man by any number of defensive eighteenth-century polemicists, not only maligned Jews—into a historical fact. They have posited an airy, abstract Enlightenment on the basis of accusations made in the heat of contestation, then ventured to determine the effect of this object on the people allegedly subjected to it. Not surprisingly, this version of the Enlightenment has come up wanting, first by conservatives advocating greater respect for "traditional" institutions and religious orthodoxy, and in the twentieth century by postmodernists who have determined that totalizing abstractions such as those attributed to the Enlightenment skew the perception of chaotic reality and violate the "right to be different."

Not surprisingly, evaluations of the "Jewish question" during and following the eighteenth century have similarly been affected by the construction of the Enlightenment as abstract and rationalistic. Thus Arthur Hertzberg argues in *The French Enlightenment and the Jews* that the poison of modern anti-Semitism is a legacy of the Enlightenment. Similarly, though more radically and with greater philo-sophical sophistication, Horkheimer and Adorno in their *Dialectic of Enlightenment* found anti-Semitism to be paradigmatic of the Enlightenment's allegedly destructive and violent tendencies. These two books afford an opportunity to re-evaluate the relationship between the Enlightenment and the Jewish question, which in turn will permit a re-examination of the values of the Enlightenment.

Arthur Hertzberg's *French Enlightenment and the Jews* takes as its point of departure the chilling paradox that "[t]he era of Western history that began with the French Revolution ended in Auschwitz."[2] The author's explanation of this terrible reversal was not simply that Europeans had failed to live up to the liberal Enlightenment principles of the Revolution, or that the dark forces of reaction had won them over, but that the Enlightenment itself was in some significant measure inimical to Judaism and the Jews. Thus, "Modern, secular anti-Semitism was fashioned not as a reaction to the Enlightenment and the Revolution, but within the Enlightenment and Revolution themselves."[3] Hertzberg's critique does not extend to the Enlightenment as a whole. Montesquieu is exempt because his "relativism" favored the acceptance of difference among peoples, and Hertzberg claims that "pro-Jewish" commentators in the late eighteenth-century debates on the Jews' legal status "invariably quoted from Montesquieu."[4]

The primary culprit in Hertzberg's scheme is Voltaire, against whom the "friends of the Jews . . . did battle."[5] Hertzberg maintains that Voltaire, though often remembered as an apostle of tolerance, made an exception of the Jews, whom he denounced as "ignorant," "barbarian," "superstitious," "fanatical" and asocial, insults he supposedly derived from classical authors, especially Cicero. Moreover, he argues that Voltaire, unlike "pro-Jewish" commentators, did not expect the vices typically attributed to the Jews to disappear upon an improvement in their legal condition; rather he "ruled the Jew to be outside society and to be hopelessly alien even to the future age of enlightened men."[6] And though Voltaire's alleged bias against Jews was the source of controversy in his own day and the subject of historiographical debate since the nineteenth century, Hertzberg has raised the stakes by claiming that Voltaire established a model of modern anti-Semitism on which future anti-Semites would draw when seeking an "enlightened" justification for their prejudices.[7]

Whatever merit there is to Hertzberg's claims about the road from Voltaire to Auschwitz could only be established by a study of postrevolutionary anti-Semitism, though even that project would be of doubtful value, since it would have to reify anti-Jewish statements made in various contexts into a "unit-idea" in the fashion of Arthur Lovejoy's *Great Chain of Being.*[8] Hertzberg's failure even to attempt to show a connection between the anti-Jewish statements of eighteenth-century authors and those of later writers, however, constitutes a serious shortcoming, since it is this very thesis which distinguishes *The French Enlightenment and the Jews* from previous books that have posited an "enlightened" form of anti-Semitism, especially in the writings of Voltaire.[9] More seriously still, I would submit, and will try to demonstrate later in this essay, that Hertzberg is mistaken even in his claims about the relationship between Voltaire's statements about the Jews and those of other eighteenth-century authors.

Yet before critiquing the specifics of Hertzberg's argument, it is instructive to compare his discussion to that of a more famous treatment of the relationship between the Enlightenment and the Holocaust: namely *Dialectic of Enlightenment* (1944), by the German-Jewish philosophers Max Horkheimer and Theodor Adorno. To be sure, *Dialectic of Enlightenment* was written as a work of social theory and cultural criticism rather than historiography, and its treatment of "Enlightenment" extends far beyond the historical period traditionally known as the Age of the Enlightenment. For Horkheimer and Adorno, Enlightenment is a mode of thinking characterized by "instrumental reason" rather than an historical epoch per se. It is evident wherever a capitalist mode of production is in place. Enlightenment is already present in embryonic form in Homeric times, as the ingenious "proprietor" Odysseus reveals through his mastery of nature (i.e., his ability to restrain himself in the face of the sirens' temptation) and his deception of anyone still in the thrall of a pre-representational, mythic attitude toward language (i.e., his ability to trick the blind cyclops Polyphemus by calling himself "No one.")[10] It remains in residual form as late as the era of fascism and monopoly capitalism, in other words the authors' own day, when its worst feature, domination, is all that survives, and a farcical version of liberal individualism barely conceals the eclipse of human agency, choice and responsibility.[11] Yet the Enlightenment as an era or a historically bounded movement, which the authors tend to designate with a definite article—*die Aufklärung* as opposed to *Aufklärung*—gets considerable attention in the *Dialectic,* and indeed is the period in which Enlightenment as a mode of thinking, as the "disenchantment of the world," appears in its most unalloyed form.[12]

Moreover, Horkheimer and Adorno, like Hertzberg nearly a quarter century later, took as their central problem the paradox that the Enlightenment *itself* contained a virulence capable of producing the horrors of National Socialism. The authors of the *Dialectic of Enlightenment* did not reduce the phenomenon of National Socialism to the Holocaust, and considered fascism more broadly as a force affecting all of society; yet they unequivocally regarded anti-Semitism as central to the paranoiac ideology of the Nazis, the Jews as their primary victims, and the gas chamber as the symbol of their descent into barbarism. Although Horkheimer and Adorno devoted a chapter to the subject of anti-Semitism, which they subtitled "The Limits of Enlightenment," they hinted at the problem in their earlier chapter, "The Concept of Enlightenment." There they argued that with the "disenchantment of the world" and the "extirpation of animism," the Enlightenment came to reduce all particularities to instances of universal concepts. For the scientist this meant that every object had to fit into universal schemas of species and genera. For the moralist

it meant that nothing was valuable—neither actions nor individuals—except insofar as it was valuable for something else, preferably a universal principle such as happiness or utility. Thus, "[f]or the Enlightenment, whatever does not conform to the rule of computation and utility is suspect." The increase in the activity of commodity exchange, whose dominant principle was fungibility, fed the habit of regularization, until "equivalence itself [had] become a fetish." As a result the Enlightenment "excise[d] the incommensurable. Not only [were] qualities dissolved in thought, but men [were] brought to actual conformity." Social distinctions were deemed absurd, but "under the leveling domination of abstraction" individuals formed what Hegel had called a "herd."[13]

With hindsight one can derive the implications of the Enlightenment mode of thought for the Jews. The Jews might be tolerated insofar as their presence is deemed useful—and indeed, as Hertzberg points out, the French monarchy tolerated the Jews precisely on the basis of utilitarian reasoning.[14] Yet they might be expelled, or worse, should their usefulness disappear. Their difference, their incommensurability, was a problem, and the undifferentiated herd viewed them as intolerable. Yet the question remains as to why the Jews should have received so much attention—as opposed to some other "other" such as Basques or Bretons. At one point Horkheimer and Adorno suggested that the "herd's" preoccupation with the Jews was accidental, and accordingly speculated, "The fact that anti-Semitism tends to occur only as part of an interchangeable program is sure hope that it will die out one day."[15] But the bulk of their analysis in the chapter, "Elements of Anti-Semitism," suggests the opposite: namely the historically necessary development of anti-Semitism.

From Roman times, according to this analysis, the Jews were forced into commerce, an activity which became "not their vocation but their fate," and consequently provoked the hostility of their impoverished customers.[16] Yet coexisting with this orthodox Marxian explanation—which made the Jews harbingers of modernity—was the more peculiar claim that, on the contrary, the Jews reminded moderns of the terrifying natural world from which Enlightenment had striven to liberate humanity. This "greater affinity to nature" was visible in "certain gestures and behavior patterns"—specifically flattery and entreaty—that society in the "bourgeois mode of production" wished to have "consigned to oblivion."[17]

There are important differences between Hertzberg's analysis of "enlightened anti-Semitism" and that of Horkheimer and Adorno. Specifically, as Gary Kates has noted, Hertzberg's argument contains a distinctly Zionist subtext.[18] By contrast, Horkheimer and Adorno maintained what Martin Jay has called an "indifference to Zionism as a solution to the plight of the Jews."[19] Moreover, in Hertzberg's account *laissez-faire* economists receive praise for viewing Jewish merchants as a counterforce to the restrictive trading practices of the guild system;[20] and "secular anti-Semitism" is identified exclusively with "the left," both before the Revolution, when Voltaire is improbably associated with that wing, and in the nineteenth century, when the main culprits are utopian socialists and Marx.[21] Horkheimer and Adorno, meanwhile, typically showed their Marxist colors by explaining ideas in terms of a materialist base and associating the worst type of thinking with capitalist mentalities.

Considering the differences between *The French Enlightenment and the Jews* and *Dialectic of Enlightenment*, one might question the wisdom of examining them together in an essay intended to contribute to a discussion on postmodernism. After all, postmodernism is usually associated with the left, and though Horkheimer and Adorno certainly fulfill that apparent prerequisite, Hertzberg's conservatism would seem to disqualify him, as would his Zionism, since the latter is intimately connected to the quintessentially modern project of nationalism. Moreover, Hertzberg's positivist method, which consists of finding quotations, lining them up as "pro-Jewish" or "anti-Semitic," judging their authors accordingly and looking for the influence of ideas on thinkers, is hardly compatible with the postmodern suspicion of binary opposites, its skepticism regarding influences and coherent doctrines, and its emphasis on the relationship between language and cultural practices.

Yet if Hertzberg is not a self-conscious practitioner of postmodern scholarship, his principal theme—the destructive nature of hostility to difference—is quite compatible with the most characteristic goals of postmodernism. Jean-François Lyotard defines "postmodern knowledge" as "refin[ing] our sensitivity to differences and reinforc[ing] our ability to tolerate the incommensurable."[22] Similarly, Zygmunt Bauman argues that postmodern ethics require a respect of others "precisely in their otherness." He writes:

> One needs to honour the otherness in the other, the strangeness in the stranger, remembering—with Edmond Jabès—that 'the unique is universal,' that it is being different that makes us resemble each other and that I cannot respect my own difference but by respecting the difference of the other.[23]

In this context, Hertzberg's story of a people condemned for their supposed inability to conform to new universal standards of rationality and accepted only insofar as they rejected what made them different (i.e., their identity) can be seen as an object lesson in the abusive effects of Enlightenment universalism. Though the question of assimilation was relevant to Jews from the late eighteenth century—when enlightened Europeans first invited them to take part in their society on their terms—it acquired a new significance in the context of postmodern concerns. Just as liberal calls for the assimilation of immigrants and absorption of regional identities into a modernizing state were being challenged by those who invoked, in post-1968 fashion, the *droit à la différence*, Hertzberg's book, itself published in 1968, seems to have confirmed an increasing distaste for the ethos of assimilation.[24] And just as postmodern feminists proclaim the need to recognize women as fundamentally different from men rather than conflating the terms "equal" and "identical,"[25] Hertzberg notes the damage done to Jews by those who wished to deny their specificity.

In addition to addressing postmodern concerns more generally, Hertzberg's argument resembles that of Horkheimer and Adorno in some important specifics. Both Hertzberg and the authors of *Dialectic of Enlightenment* share the belief that it was the extreme rationalism of the Enlightenment that anti-Semites could use as a weapon against the Jews. In some cases this rationalism appears simply as the horror of and desire to eliminate difference. Thus Hertzberg sees the Jews as a problem to many *philosophes* and revolutionaries who mistrusted their alleged "particularism"; and Horkheimer and Adorno saw the Jews as an affront to anyone who employed abstract *Verstand*—the Enlightenment's favored mode of intellection—when attempting to make sense of reality. In other cases the menacing rationalism is depicted in the more mundane terms of "enlightened" thinkers denouncing the Jews as primitive. Thus Hertzberg refers to Voltaire's disparaging comments about the Jews' alleged "barbarism" and "superstition," while Horkheimer and Adorno hypothesized an urbane aversion to the "mimetic" gestures of insufficiently civilized Jews still in the thrall of "nature."

To what extent does this picture of the Jews in conflict with rationality correspond with eighteenth-century French texts on the "Jewish question"? There is a good deal of evidence for the first claim—that the Jews posed a problem to "enlightened" thinkers simply because they were different, particular, or "other." Yet it must be remembered that this discomfort is precisely what made the elimination of discriminatory laws possible. For Pierre-Louis Lacretelle, the barrister who in 1775 defended two Jewish merchants excluded from setting up a store in Thionville despite a 1767 royal decree permitting nonguild members to establish retail shops, the issue was not whether a specific law had been violated. Rather, "The real question of this case" was "to determine whether Jews are men."[26] Of course, the problem was purely rhetorical, since Lacretelle had no doubt that Jews were "men." But since he implicitly believed in the natural equality of all human beings and assumed his audience shared this belief,[27] his point was precisely that their exclusion from equal participation in society absurdly implied that they were outside the human race. Similarly, the Comte de Mirabeau claimed that reducing Jews to the label "Jew" suggested they were nonhuman, and in arguing for equal property rights wrote, "The Jew is still more a man than he is a Jew . . . how could he not wish for a status in which he could become a landowner?"[28] Abbé Grégoire proved that the "regeneration" of the Jews was possible by noting, "[F]or a long time now it has been repeated that they are men like us, [that] they are [men] before they are Jews"[29]; and a member of the Paris Commune countered opponents to the proposed revolutionary decree on Jewish equality by writing, "To say that the Jews are incapable of satisfying the duties of society is to sustain that the Jew is more Jew than he is man."[30] Examples such as these could be multiplied, but the point is clear: the denial of Jewish specificity was a crucial strategy in the struggle for civic and political equality.

Nevertheless, the denial of difference cut both ways, and if it facilitated legal equality it simultaneously did violence to any components of Jewish identity deemed "particularistic." In an oft-quoted statement, the Comte de Clermont-Tonnerre urged his fellow deputies in the Constituent Assembly, "One must refuse the Jews everything as a nation and give them everything as individuals . . . they must form neither a political corporation nor an order in the state; they must be individual citizens."[31] Insofar as this exhortation pays homage to the individual, it appears to conform to a respect for difference. Yet it contained the hint of a threat, which Clermont-Tonnerre made explicit when he claimed that any Jews who did not wish to be citizens under the conditions laid out above should be "banished." He said, "It is repugnant that there should be a society of noncitizens in the state and a nation within the nation."[32] This was perhaps a rhetorical concession to opponents of his proposed legislation, since he went on to assure the Assembly that Jews did indeed wish to be citizens. Yet the statement reflected a real tension in the contract between the representatives of the revolutionary state and the Jews, according to which legal equality entailed a change in habits and beliefs that deviated from some (admittedly fictional) norm, as well as the elimination of allegedly "antisocial" practices such as endogamy and dietary restrictions. In a word—assimilation. Clermont-Tonnerre himself did not believe that this assimilation had to go beyond submission to French law and the relinquishing of corporate privileges of self-governance, and asked rhetorically, "Is there a law obliging me to marry your daughter? Is there a law obliging me to eat hare, and to eat it with you?"[33] In this respect he deviated from Hertzberg's picture of revolutionaries who made "demands . . . on the inner spirit and religion of the Jews."[34] Yet other proponents of Jewish "regeneration," most famously Grégoire, proclaimed the need for the Jews to abandon the Talmud—which supposedly produced superstitious beliefs and an aversion to sociability—and for the state to oversee religious instruction to prevent rabbis from teaching such nonsense.[35] He proposed the forced re-education of Jews, their removal from miasmic ghettos to rural surroundings, where they would learn the morally salutary as well as physically healthful vocation of agriculture.[36]

Grégoire toned down his coercive program of 1787 when the Revolution broke out and he stood a realistic chance of enacting "regenerating" legislation. In his *Motion en faveur de Juifs,* published between mid-October and late December 1789, he simply called for the formal abolition of the legal difference between Jews and Christians. Perhaps he reasoned that any restrictive proposals would play into the hands of those deputies opposed to all reform in the Jews' legal status. He may also have been responding to the anti-Semitic violence that had gripped Alsace in the summer and fall of 1789. Yet he did not retract his earlier *Essai,* and even proudly referred readers to it.[37] Whether or not he changed his mind about the *Essai* or some components of it, however, is less important than the fact that it reflected the widely-held belief that Jews would be better citizens to the extent they became more like their non-Jewish compatriots.

Even the Revolution's complete dismantling of Jewish communal autonomy, therefore, did not protect Jews from the accusation they were a "nation within the nation." The persistence of this epithet is not surprising when one considers that it indicated less an institutional structure than an attitude of exclusiveness and even hostility which Christians repeatedly attributed to the Jews. This is what the Alsatian anti-Semite François Hell meant when in 1779 he denounced the Jews as "a nation in the nation" and a "powerful little state in a large state."[38] And Napoleon evidently had something similar in mind when in 1806 he responded to accusations of persistent Jewish usury in Alsace by declaring the Jews a "nation within a nation."[39] He could not have been referring to communal structures since these had been abolished with the Revolution, and indeed Napoleon himself quickly responded to the perceived problem by establishing a neocorporate system of consistories—without the legal autonomy of the *ci-devant* communities, to be sure—by which Jewish "notables" could enforce civic virtue.[40]

If the hostility to difference was pervasive both in undisguised libels and proposals for the legal and moral "regeneration" of the Jews, as Hertzberg suggests, it was not limited to the "Jewish question." Indeed, the very relevance of this discourse lies in its ability to reveal a larger animosity to difference which was, as Horkheimer and Adorno claimed, characteristic of the Enlightenment. Thus the tendency to regard Jews as actually or potentially a "nation within the nation" is symptomatic of a political philosophy that insists on the indivisibility of the body politic. It bears a striking resemblance to Sieyès's denunciation of the nobility as *imperium in imperio,* which itself evokes Rousseau's claim that sovereignty must remain undivided.[41] Moreover, these taboos against particularism—with their ethical overtones aligning civic virtue with conformity and civic vice with nonconformity—constitute the moral-political version of a taboo against alterity in general. With respect to the latter prohibition, Horkheimer and Adorno claimed that "the Enlightenment recognizes as being and occurrence only what can be apprehended in unity . . ." And further, "To the Enlightenment, that which does not reduce to numbers, and ultimately to the one, becomes illusion."[42] In this respect, Jacobinism can be seen as merely the moralization of an epistemological principle. With it unity has been transformed from a condition of intelligibility to a moral imperative.

If the Enlightenment was inimical to the Jews insofar as they constituted an incommensurable "other," however, the second set of claims by Hertzberg and the authors of *Dialectic of Enlightenment*—namely that "enlightened" observers found the Jews insufficiently civilized, lacking in rationality, or overly proximate to nature—is less supportable.

For Hertzberg, Voltaire was the greatest and most influential of the "enlightened anti-Semites," and since this claim plays such a central role in the "enlightened anti-Semitism" thesis more generally, it is worth examining in some detail. As evidence of Voltaire's anti-Semitism, Hertzberg relies almost exclusively on biblical criticism and commentary on classical history, in which the *ancient* Hebrews are allegedly denounced as barbaric and superstitious. Thus the Jews of Abraham's time (!) are called "a small, new, ignorant, crude people."[43] Hertzberg alludes to "Voltaire's arguments against the Bible" as if Biblical criticism were identical with anti-Semitism. He goes to great lengths to find in Bayle and the English Deists "the crucial sources" of this critique without considering that indignant remarks about Saul's treachery against David or David's murder of Naboth do not constitute anti-Semitism; indeed the behavior of both kings is denounced in the Old Testament itself.[44] Elsewhere, the perfectly accurate claim that the Bible depicts God commanding the Israelites to kill idolaters is a "slur."[45] More evidence of Voltaire's anti-Semitism is found in his distaste for the Hebrew language, which evidently showed that the ancient Israelites "had no idea of that which we call taste, delicacy, or proportion."[46] His belief that the Jews borrowed Bible stories from Greek myths is yet another tell-tale sign of his anti-Semitism, as is his praise of Grotius for "his opinion that Alexander and Aristotle were superior to the Jews" of the fourth century B.C.[47]

As to Voltaire's animosity toward contemporary Jews, Hertzberg provides a single letter, buried in the immense corpus of his correspondence, in which he wrote that the *converted* Jews in the English colonies were "the greatest scoundrels who have ever sullied the face of the globe."[48] In the face of this lack of evidence, Hertzberg uses comments by *other philosophes* to indict Voltaire. Anti-Jewish remarks by Diderot and Holbach are unearthed, though these too were primarily directed against the ancient Jews.[49] Even so, Voltaire is judged guilty by association with a "*coterie*" of *philosophes,* which he simultaneously is presumed to have led.

Hertzberg might have made a more convincing case had he refrained from prosecuting Voltaire as a kind of anti-Jewish ringleader and simply argued that a tendency to criticize the Jewish religion as irrational was present in a number of Enlightenment thinkers. Yet even this claim would be meaningless outside the polemical context of these "anti-Semitic" statements. As Peter Gay has convincingly argued, Voltaire's criticism of Judaism and the biblical Jews served the strategic purpose of defaming the Church, his real enemy, and that he "struck at the Jews to strike at the Christians."[50] One finds support for this position in the *Dictionnaire philosophique,* in which Voltaire depicted the "fanaticism," "ignorance," and "barbarity" of the ancient Jews, but then revealed his contemporary anti-clerical agenda when he claimed that Christians "have imitated" the "cruelest and most intolerant people of all antiquity" in "their absurd furors."[51] Elsewhere, in a passage cited by Hertzberg, Voltaire insisted that the Christians were merely "uncircumcised Jews," the heirs to a religion they held in contempt. He wrote that the Jews of Roman times "kept all their customs, which are exactly the opposite of all proper social customs; they were therefore rightly treated as a people opposed to all others, whom they served, out of greed and hatred, out of fanaticism; they made usury into a sacred duty." Yet he went on to write a crucial addendum, "And these are our fathers."[52] This subtle mixture of humanism and calumny was meant to deflate a pretentious church by reminding it of its familial origins among a people it otherwise reviled and persecuted.

That Voltaire's strategy was not unique among the *philosophes* is evident from an examination of the writings of the baron d'Holbach, who similarly defamed the genealogy of "*l'infâme*" by associating it with its most celebrated adversary. Indeed, even the title of his principal work on Judaism, *L'Esprit du Judaïsme, ou examen raisonné de la loi de Moyse, et de son influence sur la religion chrétienne,* reveals his goal of determining the influence of the Judaism on Christianity. In this work Holbach summarized the history of the ancient Jews as the deeds of "a throng of people whom [a] healthy [sense of] morality would have us regard as monsters sullied by the most revolting cruelties and the most horrifying crimes."[53] The villain of the story is Moses, a cynical tyrant who has invented a religion for the sole purpose of enriching himself and his successors. Moses takes advantage of the credulity of the Jews, "this vulgar people, still incapable of reasoning."[54] He convinces them, through magic tricks that he learned in Egypt, of his special relationship to God. He invents the fable of Abraham and Isaac, since the barbarians he is trying to convince can only conceive of a God who demands blood sacrifices.[55] Moses and his successors the priests whip the common people into a "perpetual fanaticism" that enables them to conquer the territory of their neighbors.[56] Once established, the priests steal from the people on the pretext of requiring sacrifices for the expiation of their sins. They ally themselves with the monarchs, then attempt to usurp their authority, the result being a long and bloody series of civil wars that ends only with the destruction of Jerusalem and the dispersion of the Jews.

Throughout his narrative, Holbach makes it clear that his real enemy is the contemporary church. He treats the Jews as a dead people whose only significance lies in the lessons their history can teach contemporary Europeans.[57] Thus the priests of ancient Israel stand for the modern Catholic clergy, and the High Priest of the Temple represents the Pope. Demands for agricultural sacrifices are likened to modern tithes and indulgences.[58] The fanaticism and barbarity of the ancient Jews is seen again in the Christian people, and the conception of a bloodthirsty God that produced the barbaric story of Abraham and Isaac also explains the Christian belief in a "cannibal God" who could only redeem his sinful creatures by spilling the blood of his son.[59] Holbach sees the dangerous alliance between priests and kings reproduced in his own day, as well as the dangers of their quarrels.[60] He sees almost no meaningful difference between Judaism and Christianity. The latter is only "a reformed Judaism," and its believers are, in language identical to that of Voltaire, merely "uncircumcised Jews."[61] The principal defect of ancient Judaism, the "spirit of priesthood," is the defining character of Christianity.[62] The only difference is that Christianity has done more damage. Whereas the "prophets of Judea" only caused harm to "a little corner of Asia," "the Christian Priests have covered immense empires with corpses and blood."[63]

Thus Voltaire participated in a larger campaign of anti-clericalism in which "anti-Semitic" statements served the purpose of condemning the Church. None of this is meant to exculpate Voltaire, a project which would be as pointless as condemning him. For what it is worth, it is likely that Voltaire, like nearly all his contemporaries, "enlightened" or not, harbored prejudices against the Jews of his day. It may also be true that Voltaire "regarded the Jewish character as a continuity from ancient times to the present," a claim Hertzberg borrows from Hannah Emmrich's 1930 study, *Das Judentum bei Voltaire.*[64] That he considered Jews incapable of regeneration and "hopelessly alien even to the future age of enlightened men" is thoroughly unsubstantiated.[65]

More important than Voltaire's personal feelings, as Hertzberg acknowledges, is the reception of his statements by contemporaries and posterity. As noted above, Hertzberg does not even attempt to prove his assertion that Voltaire is "the major link in Western intellectual history between the anti-Semitism of classic paganism and the modern age," so there is little need to refute this claim.[66] As to the eighteenth-century reception of his statements, there is some support for the belief that contemporaries regarded Voltaire as hostile to Jews past and present. Thus Isaac de Pinto, taking offense to remarks in the *Dictionnaire philosophique,* defended the religion of his ancestors in a spirited rejoinder.[67] The Jansenist Abbé Guénée posed as a group of insulted Jews and undertook to disabuse Voltaire of his apparent misconceptions about the Jews and Judaism, clearly doing so because of outrage at what he rightly took as an attack on his own religion.[68]

Yet if Jews and defenders of the Bible took offense at Voltaire's statements about them, this does not mean that anti-Semites in eighteenth-century France drew much inspiration from him. The most infamous of these Jew-baiters was François Hell, an Alsatian bailiff who in the late 1770s organized the production of forged receipts to release Christians from loans owed to Jewish lenders; he then attempted to justify his action in a pamphlet entitled *Observations d'un Alsacien sur l'affaire présente des Juifs d'Alsace.* Yet Hell made no mention of Voltaire in his 86-page diatribe. Untroubled by this inconvenient omission, Hertzberg writes, "Though Hell never quoted Voltaire directly, it is clear from his book that he had read with great care the anti-Jewish pronouncements of the sage of Ferney."[69] In fact, this is not at all clear; and even if Hell had read Voltaire's writings on the Jews his own opinions were in direct opposition to them. While Voltaire saw the perse-

cution of the Jews as evidence of a deplorable popular fanaticism, Hell saw it as the "just wrath of Heaven."[70] Whereas Voltaire denounced the belief that Jews crucified Christian children at Passover and poisoned wells from which Christians drank as outrageous libels, Hell repeated these very accusations and used them to justify anti-Semitic violence.[71] In style as well as the content of his writing Hell was the very opposite of Voltaire. Voltaire ironically mocked what he disliked; Hell was a student of *sensibilité,* relying on tear-jerking tropes and narratives of domestic tragedy—complete with weeping wives and children—brought on by Jewish usury. His defiant abhorrence of irony was reminiscent of Rousseau, Voltaire's rival in content and style, and he had a Rousseauian persecution complex as well. Both are evident in his prediction that his opponents, the "sectarian[s] of tolerance whose eye sees fanatics everywhere" (hardly the words of a disciple of Voltaire) and "the *bel esprit* who runs after brilliance"— would "pronounce an edict of proscription against me." Yet he defiantly wrote, *"Et qu'importe?* I will immediately call my heart, which will absolve me." Further along these lines, he confessed (i.e., boasted) that he was "a bit agitated by an excess of patriotism," but added, "my sentiments are pure." His only desire was to "unmask crime," that is the crime of Jewish usury that forced him to take the technically illegal but morally justifiable action of forging receipts.[72] The implications of Hell's style and the content of his claims will be considered later, but for now it is sufficient to note that Voltaire, far from being an influence or inspiration upon Hell, was on the contrary inimical to the anti-Semitic message he was trying to send.

By contrast, in 1786 the anti-Semitic libelist Latour-Foissac did refer to Voltaire when accusing the Jews of "ignorance," "superstition" "fanaticism" and "barbarism." Yet the bulk of his pamphlet, like that of Hell, was a sentimental tableau in which gullible yet virtuous Christians are duped by clever, evil Jews.[73] It thus clashed with the elitist contempt for the unlettered *canaille* suggested by the reference to Voltaire. Yet, aside from Latour-Foissac's reference to Voltaire, Hertzberg shows nothing else to suggest that he had any impact on any anti-Semitic authors or statements in eighteenth-century France.

This does not mean that rationalist language was never used in the discourse on the Jews and Judaism. Grégoire, for example, lamented what he saw as the Jews' "acquired ignorance, which has depraved their intellectual faculties." He did not consider the Jews incapable of genius, and like contemporaries interested in improving their condition cited the German-Jewish philosopher Moses Mendelssohn as proof that they harbored the potential for intellectual greatness if given the proper conditions. Mendelssohn, moreover, was a sign that the Jews were "at least at the dawn of reason." Grégoire nevertheless claimed that "since the historian Josephus it took seventeen centuries to produce a Mendelssohn." In the intervening time the Jews had allegedly only borrowed ideas from their neighbors, "and what ideas!" Alchemy and cabbala were what the Jews in Grégoire's view had found most appealing. Most irrational, according to the author, was the Jews' attachment to the Talmud, "this sewer in which the deliriums of the human mind are accumulated."[74] Similarly, Mirabeau envisaged intellectual improvement as crucial to the program of "regeneration," and in a eulogy for Mendelssohn he opposed the philosopher to his ignorant coreligionists, especially the rabbis who "could not see without indignation that humanity and truth seemed dearer to Mendelssohn than the dark dreams of the Talmudists."[75]

Yet if commentators occasionally criticized the Jews for being insufficiently rational, persistently primitive or troublingly close to nature, the shortcomings much more often attributed to them were quite the opposite. Indeed, *pace* Hertzberg and the authors of the *Dialectic of Enlightenment,* they were denounced as *all too rational,* as overly cunning and calculating and in possession of the unnatural ability to conceal their thoughts and emotions. By contrast, their "victims," i.e., their debtors, were idealized as naïve innocents incapable of calculation, transparent in their emotional expression, but all the more virtuous for their natural simplicity. The binary opposition between the natural Christian and calculating Jew is unmistakable in the anti-Semitic pamphlets of the 1770s and 1780s. Specifically, Hell takes on the role of the simple citizen defending his compatriots from the depredations of clever Jews. As mentioned earlier, he "call[s] [his] heart" to prove his sincerity, which is apparently a rhetorical substitute for reason. This kind of cardiac language saturates his pamphlet, which he hopes will "reheat the hearts" of his compatriots, and if his "ideas [do] not appear . . . subtly fashioned enough or encased in a sufficiently elegant style," they have been "dictated by a patriotic heart."[76]

The dichotomy between "citizen" and "Jew" is clearest in Hell's representation of the paradigmatic fraudulent loan. The victim of usury is "the youth, in whom *reason is still weak* or bewildered by *the ardor of budding passions.*" He "cannot foresee," that is, cannot calculate, "the finesse of the fraud and the consequences of the commitment" to the loan.[77] In what amounts to a monetary seduction, the Jewish usurer repeatedly "offers his purse" to the "young man," who is naturally "susceptible to debauchery" (*enclin à la débauche*).[78] Each time the victim "avidly bites" at the contents of the purse, and his "passions, nourished by this food, grow." (*Les passions nourries par cet aliment croissent.*) "The prodigal son . . . returns," and "each time well-received, he receives" more money. But each time he must offer to pay a higher rate of interest. "The passions" of the young man "are kindled, the taste of dissipation is excited and quickly consumes" him. Yet the Jew, in contrast to the picture presented by Horkheimer and Adorno of a person in the thrall of natural or "mimetic" gestures, controls himself. He "seizes the moment at which [the young man] returns, "feigns an obdurate expression," (*fait mine d'être dur*) "refuses for a moment, but after prevailing upon the young man to sign IOUs the sum total of which is quadruple that of the loan, he gives in" and lends. Hell writes:

> It is thus that this young man of good family, corrupted by the fire of debauchery, drinking from the perfidious

cup of usury, swallows in one gulp the patrimony that he does not yet have and the dowry of the woman to whom he is not yet engaged.[79]

For Hell, then, it is the "young man of good family" who is close to nature, as his uncontrollable "passions" and his penchant for corporeal satisfaction—expressed in the digestive language of biting, swallowing and tasting—makes clear. It is the calculating Jew who controls his gestures and profits from the Christian's appetites. Yet Hell asks the reader to be sympathetic to the debauched young man, whose excesses should be forgiven—as the biblical metaphor of the prodigal son suggests—and whose errors are sentimentalized through their connection to domestic tragedy.

A strikingly similar rhetorical strategy is evident in Latour-Foissac's *Cri du citoyen.* Here the author recalls his experiences as a young officer away from home for the first time. Writing in the third person, he describes the naïve citizen, "[j]ust out of the hands of an instructor, under whom his petulant concern for liberty sighed." At this time "[his] open, honest and loyal heart is still in the heedlessness of a profound calm. . . ." Like the victim of usury in Hell's account, he is incapable of foreseeing the traps set by the calculating Jew. As soon as he arrives in the garrison town of Metz, he and his colleagues "become the object of the Synagogue's scrutiny." The Jewish moneylenders have already determined that this is one of the "opportune moments that can make seductive and pleasant the ruinous offers they make," presumably since the men are away from the supervision of their families and tempted to various forms of debauchery. In a revealing phrase the author claims that it is at precisely such "moments when *weakened reason becomes powerless,* that the Jews appear and deal their money." The officer tries to resist the temptation, but dissimulation triumphs over naïveté, and inevitably "the transaction will be completed, to the certain ruin of the unfortunate borrower."[80]

In addition to unequivocal anti-Semites such as Hell and Latour-Foissac, those who agitated for the legal improvement in the Jews' condition similarly considered them, in their unregenerated state, to be overly calculating and thus the opposite of natural, hence virtuous, citizens. Grégoire, although capable of denouncing the irrationality of the Talmud and rabbinical teaching, much more frequently accused the Jews of harboring a cold, commercial mentality and lacking the attachment to nature that would presumably increase their level of morality. He called rabbis "casuists," suggesting a hair-splitting rationality on their part, and claimed that "a multitude" of them "authorize . . . bad faith, equivocation, mental restrictions, hypocrisy." "Is it true," he asked, reserving judgment on the answer, "that, according to the Talmud, a Jew must . . . wish [a Christian] a *bon voyage* while adding, under his breath, 'like that of Pharaoh in the sea . . . ?'"[81] Thus he attributed a kind of duplicitous irony to Jews that would be seen as "aristocratic" during the Revolution. That irony, absent from the unambiguous, straightforward citizen, was a sign of the corruption of civilization, not a proximity to primitive "nature." Indeed, in his claim that Jews were not to blame for their decadent morality, Grégoire opposed them to the "peaceable Tahitians" presumed to be superior in morality not only to Jews, but to Europeans in general. He proposed a thought experiment: "bring [the Tahitians] on the scene . . . forbid them all means of subsistence except a retail commerce whose gains are precarious and small, sometimes nonexistent when agility and activity do not suffice to support imperious and ever reappearing needs," and "soon they will call to their aid cunning and trickery."[82] "Cunning and trickery," then, were absent from the moral economy of the noble savage; they were conditions that only obtained in a civilized, capitalist economy.

On those few occasions when Grégoire praised the Jews of his day, moreover, he did not praise their rationality, but their "natural" virtues. He noted that certain vices of civilization, such as drinking, libertinage, pornography and adultery, were not common among Jews. They were frugal, charitable to their poor and respectful of their elders, and Grégoire noted with Rousseauian approval that Jewish mothers breast-fed their children.[83] In other words, he praised their simple, natural affections, and hoped that someday these would not be limited to their domestic relations, but would extend toward their relations with Christians. Thus it was possible for him to predict that with regeneration they "would acquire sociability, sentiments, virtues, without losing the antique simplicity of their morals."[84] For that transformation to take place, the Jews would have to abandon the decadent occupation of commerce and return to the pastoral existence that Grégoire believed they had led in Biblical times. At that time, Grégoire prophesied:

> The rustic tasks will then call the Hebrew to our fields, once watered by the blood of his forefathers, and which at that time will be watered by his sweat; he will leave his manor to breathe the pure air of the hills: soon stimulated by interest, his once-soft arms will be strengthened by exercise, and this physical improvement will bring moral improvement too, for the first of arts is also the first in virtue.[85]

Grégoire also considered traditional crafts as regenerative work, but his main requirements were that the work be simple, traditional and, in keeping with physiocratic doctrine, productive.

Mirabeau similarly conceived of Jewish vice and the possibilities of regeneration in terms of an opposition between decadent commerce and virtuous work, especially agriculture. He had apparently inherited anti-commercial ideas from his father, one of the founders of physiocracy, and disparaged trade not only as economically sterile, but morally degrading as well. He idealized the farmer, writing, "The simple morals of the countryside, the regular diligence that [the farmers'] work requires, preserve his innocence and hospitable morality."[86] The merchant, by contrast, had "different habits, different principles, a completely different spirit." In a kind of psychopathology of commerce he wrote:

> Continually occupied with making a profit, avoiding losses, fighting foreign interests, consulting, provoking, tampering with his fortune, [the merchant] is incessantly agitated by restless activity. . . . The habit of seeing everything from the point of view of gain must naturally tighten his feelings; temptations are too frequent; overpricing is too hard to distinguish from taking prudent advantage of circumstances. The merchant, even an honest one, might eventually deceive himself and take the one for the other. He always stands to lose or gain in his relations with other men; insensibly he accustoms himself to regarding them as adversaries or rivals; his soul contracts, his sensitivity is deadened, sordid interest or ostentatious luxury too often take its place.[87]

If the ordinary merchant was subjected to such assaults on his morality, Mirabeau argued, then *a fortiori* the Jew, who saw nothing but contempt from his Christian neighbors, would be even less inclined to act honestly. It was not about the Jew's rationality that Mirabeau expressed concern, but his "sensitivity," which would be "deadened" by the effects of incessant calculation. His intellect operated effectively, even too effectively; it was his "feelings" that were "tighten[ed]" and his "soul" which was "contract[ed]."

. . . . .

The texts on the Jewish question in eighteenth-century France call for a re-evaluation of the relationship between the Enlightenment and the Jews. If Enlightenment rationality made it difficult to accept the Jews as an incommensurable other, rationality as a value in and of itself was rarely invoked in evaluations of the Jews and their level of morality. On the contrary, the Jews tended to receive praise insofar as they appeared "natural" and "sensitive" and criticism insofar as observers judged them to be calculating and clever. In the latter case they were typically opposed to an ideal Christian "citizen," either a peasant or a soldier, who embodied the qualities necessary for civic virtue: visible, affective (yet unaffected) intensity and proximity to nature.

It would be difficult to overstate the significance of this re-evaluation of "enlightened anti-Semitism," as it sheds light on the much larger question of just what the values of the Enlightenment were. Indeed, if Hertzberg and the authors of *Dialectic of Enlightenment* were mistaken about the relationship between the Enlightenment and the Jews, it is because they were mistaken about the respective value the Enlightenment placed on reason and "nature," rationality and sensitivity, or (to borrow a dichotomy from Jane Austen) Sense and Sensibility.

This is a very large claim, one that the eighteenth-century French literature on the Jewish question alone cannot prove. Yet other tendencies in eighteenth-century thought tend to corroborate the hypothesis that the Enlightenment placed a greater value on the senses and the emotions than is typically assumed. The most obvious piece of evidence in this respect is the corpus of sentimental literature that flourished in eighteenth-century Europe. Tear-jerking authors, from Richardson to Rousseau to Goethe, aimed not at the head but the heart, as did genre painters such as Greuze, upon whom Diderot famously lavished praise.[88] The valorization of sensation was not limited to art and novels. It was crucial to the century's most favored epistemology, known significantly as sensationalism. From Locke to Condillac to Hume, theorists of knowledge rejected the rationalism of Descartes in favor of a system in which feeling preceded both knowing and thinking. Even Kant's greatest work was, revealingly, *A Critique of Pure Reason,* a book that rejected the "dogmatic" belief that the Understanding alone could know the thing-in-itself.

In the philosophical subfield of ethics, sensation was again indispensable. Not only was *"un coeur sensible . . .* the precondition for morality."[89] In Hume's philosophy ethics derived from sensation, and in the *Preliminary Discourse* to the *Encyclopédie* d'Alembert argued that it was the prior sensation of injustice, either direct or indirect, that made knowledge of right and wrong possible.[90] To be sure, Kant had hoped to derive an ethics from rationality alone, i.e., from *a priori* principles without the aid of experience, and Horkheimer and Adorno made much of his failure to do so. They argued devastatingly that the autonomous individual postulated in the categorical imperative could just as easily (and justifiably) behave like a character invented by the Marquis de Sade as a restrained moralist such as Kant himself.[91] The failure itself is nevertheless indicative—as is Kant's desperate recourse to "practical reason"—of the Enlightenment's prior success (with Kant's help) at lowering philosophical expectations about the power of unaided reason. Sade's pornographic burlesque of philosophy, moreover, is itself evidence that the mind was not the summa for Enlightenment thinkers.

Horkheimer and Adorno used Sade as evidence that the Enlightenment had rationalized (in both senses of the word) vice and crime, but did not appreciate the implications of just what kind of vice and crime was being rationalized. The single-minded determination with which Sade's characters attempt to reduce sexual activity to a dispassionate, mechanical activity reveals the dangerous power the author attributed to the senses, which needed to be dominated if they were not to dominate their subjects. In a less overtly sexual way, the moral and political philosophers of the eighteenth century problematized the human will as a set of drives that conflicted with those of fellow human beings in civil society. Thus Kant, in his categorical imperative, wished to rationalize the will by requiring it to be fairly and feasibly universalized, and Rousseau, in his *Social Contract,* sought to domesticate it by making it conform to the consent of public-spirited citizens. In both cases the will was potentially dangerous— though elsewhere in Rousseau's writings strong desires are themselves evidence of virtue. But by recognizing that danger Kant and Rousseau, like Sade, showed their belief in the power of a force, the senses, which could with only great difficulty be governed by reason.

Even the Rousseauian-Jacobin fear of "particularism," which translated into a contempt for dissenting individuals and Jewish or noble "nations within the nation," can be seen as a kind of irrationalist organicism. Although Horkheimer and Adorno attributed the Enlightenment disdain for the incommensurable to its fetishistic need to "reduce to numbers, and ultimately to the one,"[92] when seen in the context of nascent nationalism this tendency appears to confirm Durkheim's claim that Rousseau (as well as Montesquieu) viewed society as an organism, as having a living identity irreducible to the sum of its parts.[93] Thus Rousseau, Sieyès and the republican nationalists of the revolutionary era were closer to animism than they were to the preferred rationalist physics of mechanism.

Of course, it would be wrong to deny that rationalism and the ethos of rationality played significant roles in the Enlightenment. Certainly *philosophes* were capable of singing reason's praises, and the desire of thinkers to understand both the natural and human world in terms of predictable laws is undeniable—though again it should be emphasized that these laws, according to empirical epistemology and the scientific method, could not be derived without the data of experience, and ultimately of the senses. But even this modified rationalism competed with a valorization of the senses as vehicles of knowledge, both physical and moral, and indeed as guarantors of ethically correct behavior. The tension between reason and sensation, the mind and the body, the head and the heart provided the stuff of philosophical speculation as well as imaginative literature throughout the century, as is evident in Hume, Rousseau, Kant and Sade. It is perhaps here, at the intersection of thinking and feeling, rather than the crossroads of myth and disenchantment, that one should locate the Dialectic of Enlightenment.

Yet what explains the error made by Hertzberg and the authors of *Dialectic of Enlightenment*? To be fair, it is an old mistake which does not belong to them alone. For more than two centuries critics have conjured up a largely fictitious image of a cold, dispassionate, bloodless Enlightenment. This essay began with a description of how Isaiah Berr Bing exaggerated the rationalist, materialist tendencies of "fashionable philosophy" for polemical purposes. Those who opposed the French Revolution—which had sought its justifying heritage in the philosophy of the eighteenth century—would have other reasons for presenting the Enlightenment as the apotheosis of rationalism.

For example, Edmund Burke was an heir to Enlightenment empiricism, which he consecrated in his paeans to human experience. His reluctance to alter established institutions, though later consecrated "conservative," does not mean that he was anti-Enlightenment, since the Enlightenment thinkers were themselves, as empiricists, respectful of human experience and reluctant to change institutions on the basis of abstract models. Thus Burke's defiant acclaim for the "prejudices" of peoples was not so different from Montesquieu's reverence for the "genius of the nation" and his caution with respect to altering institutions.[94] Yet the Revolution's appropriation of the *philosophes* made it desirable for Burke, as an opponent of the revolutionary program, to distance himself from the Enlightenment Pantheon. Thus he criticized the revolutionaries as abstract system builders and "metaphysicians," though it should not be forgotten that this was precisely the language that Voltaire had used to deride his adversaries.[95]

Similarly, Hegel viewed the Enlightenment through the prism of the Revolution, which for him took the form of Napoleon and the battle of Jena. He too critiqued the Enlightenment as an abstract, "gaseous" movement that fetishized the universal and ignored the particular.[96] This analysis, on which Horkheimer and Adorno would later rely and which conforms to Lyotard's and Bauman's conceptions of postmodernism as discussed earlier, bears more than a little resemblance to that of Burke, especially insofar as it justified Hegel's reputedly conservative call for the preservation of established institutions, however irrational.

Thus an overly rationalized, insufficiently sensitized Enlightenment was fabricated by Enlightenment thinkers themselves, for polemical and political reasons, then bequeathed to historians and philosophers as an object for evaluation. Some would reject it, others would embrace it, merely placing a positive spin on its fabled rationalism.[97] But in the process of judging the Enlightenment they would forget the extent to which it valued sensation, emotions and displayed an arational or even irrational reverence for nature, both in its order and its chaos.

Notes

1. *Lettre du Sr.I[saïah] B[err] B[ing], Juif de Metz, à l'auteur anonyme d'un écrit intitulé: Le Cri du citoyen contre les Juifs* (Metz, 1787), pp. 29-30; repr. in *Révolution française et l'émancipation des Juifs* (Paris: EdHis, 1968), vol. 8. Cf. Ronald Schechter, "Translating the 'Marseillaise': Biblical Republicanism and the Emancipation of Jews in Revolutionary France," *Past and Present* 143 (May 1994): 131.

2. Arthur Hertzberg, *The French Enlightenment and the Jews* (New York, 1968), p. 5.

3. Hertzberg, *French Enlightenment*, p. 7.

4. Ibid., p. 10.

5. Ibid.

6. Ibid.

7. On Voltaire's relationship to the Jews and Judaism see Heinrich Graetz, "Voltaire und die Juden," *Monatsschrift für die Geschichte und Wissenschaft des Judentums* XVI (1867): 321-30; Herbert Solow, "Voltaire and Some Jews," *Menorah Journal* XIII (1927): 186-97; Hanna Emmrich, *Das Judentum bei Voltaire* (Breslau, 1930); Pierre Aubery, "Voltaire et les Juifs," *Studies on Voltaire and the Eighteenth Century* XXIV (1963): 67-79; and Peter Gay, *The*

Party of Humanity: Essays in the French Enlightenment (New York, 1964), pp. 97-108.

8. Arthur O. Lovejoy, *The Great Chain of Being* (Cambridge, MA, 1936 and 1964), pp. 3-23. For a powerful critique of Lovejoy's approach see Quentin Skinner, "Meaning and Understanding in the History of Ideas," *History and Theory* 8 (1969): 3-53.

9. See note 8 above.

10. Max Horkheimer and Theodor W. Adorno, *Dialectic of Enlightenment,* trans. John Cumming (New York, 1972), pp. 43-80.

11. Horkheimer and Adorno, *Dialectic,* passim.

12. Ibid., p. 3.

13. Ibid., pp. 6, 12-13, 17.

14. Hertzberg, *French Enlightenment,* pp. 12-28, 64-71 passim.

15. Horkheimer and Adorno, *Dialectic,* p. 207. Elsewhere they wrote that "victims [of persecution] are interchangeable according to circumstances—gypsies, Jews, Protestants, Catholics, and so on. . . ." *Dialectic,* p. 171.

16. Ibid., pp. 174-5.

17. Ibid., pp. 112, 181-2.

18. Gary Kates, "Jews into Frenchmen: Nationality and Representation in Revolutionary France" in Ferenc Fehér, ed., *The French Revolution and the Birth of Modernity* (Berkeley, 1990), pp. 103-16. Hertzberg reveals his sympathies when he writes that the Zionist founders Leo Pinsker and Theodor Herzl "both independently *recognized that* modern anti-Semitism was . . . a new, secular, and continuing phenomenon." By implication, only a coherent and self-conscious Jewish nation, or nation-state, could protect the Jews from the hatred of non-Jews. Hertzberg, *French Enlightenment,* p. 5. Emphasis added.

19. Martin Jay, *The Dialectical Imagination: A History of the Frankfurt School and the Institute of Social Research, 1923-1950* (Boston and Toronto, 1973), p. 32.

20. Hertzberg, *French Enlightenment,* pp. 12-28, 64-71 passim.

21. Ibid., pp. 10-11, 357.

22. Jean-François Lyotard, "Excerpts from *The Postmodern Condition: A Report on Knowledge*" in Joseph Natoli and Linda Hutcheon, eds., *A Postmodern Reader* (Albany, 1993), p. 73.

23. Zygmunt Bauman, "Postmodernity, or Living with Ambivalence" in Natoli and Hutcheon, *Postmodern Reader,* p. 14.

24. On the assertion of the "right to be different" among Jews and regional minorities in post-1968 France,

see Judith Friedlander, *Vilna on the Seine: Jewish Intellectuals in France since 1968* (New Haven, 1990), p. 38-64.

25. On the division of feminists between advocates of "sameness" and "difference" see Carol Lee Bacchi, *Same Difference: Feminism and Sexual Difference* (Sydney, 1990).

26. "LVIIIe cause. Question d'état sur les Juifs de Metz," *Causes célèbres, curieuses et intéressantes, de toutes les cours souveraines du royaume, avec les jugemens qui les ont décidées,* vol. 23 (Paris, 1776), p. 65. Published separately as *Plaidoyer pour Moyse May, Godechaux et Abraham Lévy, Juifs de Metz. Contre l'hôtel-de-ville de Thionville et le Corps des Marchands de cette ville* (Bruxelles, 1775). On Lacretelle see David A. Bell, *Lawyers and Citizens: The Making of a Political Elite in Old Regime France* (New York, 1994), pp. 164-67, 175-80.

27. The "audience" did not merely include the court, but the reading public for whom legal briefs such as Lacretelle's were extraordinarily popular. On this phenomenon see Sarah Maza, *Private Lives and Public Affairs: The Causes Célèbres of Prerevolutionary France* (Berkeley, 1993).

28. Honoré Gabriel de Riquetti, Comte de Mirabeau, *Sur Moses Mendelssohn, sur la réforme politique des Juifs: et en particulier sur la révolution tentée en leur faveur en 1753 dans la grande Bretagne* (London, 1787), p. 66, repr. in *Révolution française et l'émancipation des Juifs* (Paris, 1968), vol. 1.

29. Abbé Henri Grégoire, *Essai sur la régénération physique, morale et politique des Juifs* (Paris, 1789), p. 118, repr. in *Révolution française et l'émancipation des Juifs* (Paris, 1968), vol. 3.

30. [Jean Debourge], *Lettre au comité de constitution sur l'affaire des Juifs; par M. de Bourge, représentant de la commune de Paris* (Paris, 1790), p. 31.

31. *Opinion de M. le comte de Clermont-Tonnerre, député de Paris. Le 23 décembre 1789* (Paris, 1789), p. 13. Cf. *Archives parlementaires,* vol. 10, pp. 754-56.

32. *Opinion de M. le comte,* p. 13.

33. *Opinion de M. le comte,* p. 12.

34. Hertzberg, *French Enlightenment,* p. 364.

35. Grégoire, *Essai,* p. 87.

36. Ibid., p. 124.

37. *Motion en faveur des Juifs, par M. Grégoire, curé d'Embermenil, député de Nancy; précédée d'une notice historique, sur les persécutions qu'ils viennent d'essuyer en divers lieux, notamment en Alsace, et sur l'admission de leurs députés à la barre de l'Assemblée nationale* (Paris, 1789), repr. in *Révolu-*

tion française et l'émancipation des Juifs (Paris, 1968), vol. 7.

38. François Hell, *Observations d'un Alsacien sur l'affaire présente des Juifs d'Alsace* (Frankfurt, 1779), p. 66.

39. Simon Schwarzfuchs, *Napoleon, the Jews, and the Sanhedrin* (London, 1979), p. 49.

40. On the Jewish consistories in France see Phyllis Cohen Albert, *The Modernization of French Jewry: Consistory and Community in the Nineteenth Century* (Hanover, N.H., 1977).

41. Abbé Emmanuel Joseph Sieyès, *Qu'est-ce que le tiers-état?* (1789; reprint Paris: Société de l'Histoire de la Révolution Française, 1888), p. 31. Cf. Jean-Jacques Rousseau, *On the Social Contract,* book II, ch. 2.

42. Horkheimer and Adorno, *Dialectic,* p. 7

43. Hertzberg, *French Enlightenment,* p. 303.

44. Ibid., p. 39, 39n.

45. Ibid., p. 304.

46. Ibid., p. 301.

47. Ibid., p. 303.

48. Ibid., p. 284.

49. Ibid., pp. 281-82, 308-12.

50. Peter Gay, *The Party of Humanity: Essays in the French Enlightenment* (New York, 1964), p. 103.

51. Voltaire, *Dictionnaire philosophique* (1764; reprint Paris, 1954), p. 402.

52. Hertzberg, *French Enlightenment,* pp. 302-3.

53. Paul Henri Thiry, baron d'Holbach, *L'Esprit du Judaïsme, ou examen raisonné de la loi de Moyse, et de son influence sur la religion chrétienne* (London [i.e. Amsterdam], 1770), pp. viii, ix.

54. Ibid., p. xiv.

55. Ibid., pp. 7-8.

56. Ibid., p. xv.

57. Though he mentions the modern Jews and even professes sympathy for their suffering, Holbach revealingly entitles his penultimate chapter, "The conduct and fate of the Jews from their captivity to their total destruction." This conceit is necessary for him to predict that Christianity will ultimately be destroyed as well.

58. Holbach, *L'Esprit du Judaïsme,* pp. 49-65.

59. Ibid, pp. xxi-xxii, 7-8, 176.

60. Ibid., pp. xv, 96.

61. Ibid., pp. i, 182.

62. Ibid., p. 56.

63. Ibid., p. 97.

64. Hertzberg, *French Enlightenment*, p. 300. Cf. Hannah Emmrich, *Das Judentum bei Voltaire* (Breslau, 1930).

65. Hertzberg, *French Enlightenment*, p. 10.

66. Ibid.

67. [Isaac de Pinto], *Apologie pour la nation juive, où réflexions critiques sur le premier chapitre du VIIe tome des oeuvres de M. de Voltaire au sujet des Juifs. Par l'auteur de "l'Essai sur le luxe"* (Amsterdam, 1762).

68. Abbé Antoine Guenée, *Lettres de quelques Juifs portugais et allemands à M. de Voltaire: avec des réflexions critiques, & c: et un petit commentaire extrait d'un plus grand* (Paris, 1769).

69. Hertzberg, *French Enlightenment*, p. 288.

70. Hell, *Observations*, p. 11.

71. Ibid., pp. 11-18. For Voltaire's denunciation of medieval anti-Jewish fanaticism and false beliefs regarding alleged ritual crimes, see *Essai sur l'histoire générale* (Geneva, 1756), 343; and "Le philosophe ignorant" in J. Van Den Heuvel, Ed., *Mélanges* (Paris, 1961), p. 929.

72. Hell, *Observations*, pp. 3-4. On Rousseau's preoccupation with "unmasking," see Jean Starobinski, *J.-J. Rousseau: la transparence et l'obstacle* (Paris, 1971), esp. pp. 84-101.

73. [Philippe-François de Latour-Foissac], *Le Cri du citoyen contre les Juifs de Metz. Par un capitaine d'infanterie* (Lausanne [Metz], 1786).

74. Grégoire, *Essai*, pp. 87, 116, 161-3.

75. Mirabeau, *Sur Moses Mendelssohn*, p. 28.

76. Hell, *Observations*, pp. 3-4.

77. Ibid., p. 40.

78. Whether "susceptible to debauchery" means desiring the sex money will presumably buy or defenseless in the face of the Jew's monetary debauchery of the young man is (perhaps deliberately) ambiguous.

79. Hell, *Observations*, pp. 40-1.

80. Latour-Foissac, *Cri du citoyen*, pp. 5-24. Emphasis added.

81. Grégoire, *Essai*, pp. 87-8.

82. Ibid., p. 67.

83. Ibid., pp. 65-7, 80-1.

84. Ibid., p. 139.

85. Ibid., p. 124. Cf. Schechter, "Translating the 'Marseillaise,'" p. 121.

86. Mirabeau, *Sur Moses Mendelssohn*, p. 86.

87. Ibid., p. 87.

88. Simon Schama, *Citizens: A Chronicle of the French Revolution* (New York, 1989), pp. 145-62; and Anita Brookner, *Greuze: The Rise and Fall of an Eighteenth-Century Phenomenon* (Greenwich, CT, 1972).

89. Schama, *Citizens*, p. 149.

90. David Hume, *An Enquiry Concerning the Principles of Morals* (London, 1751), esp. section 1; and Jean Le Rond d'Alembert, *Preliminary Discourse to the Encyclopedia of Diderot*, trans. and intro. Richard N. Schwab (Chicago, 1995), pp. 12-13.

91. Horkheimer and Adorno, *Dialectic*, pp. 81-119.

92. Ibid., p. 7.

93. Emile Durkheim, *Montesquieu and Rousseau: Forerunners of Sociology*, trans. Ralph Manheim, foreword Henri Peyre (Ann Arbor, 1960).

94. Burke, *Reflections on the Revolution in France* (London, 1790). Cf. Montesquieu, *De l'esprit des loix*, esp. pt. 6, bk. 31, ch. 4.

95. Burke, *Reflections*, passim. I have found 25 variations on the term "metaphysics" and 15 on "abstract," all of them pejorative, in the *Reflections*.

96. Hegel, *Phenomenology*, §488-595. On the "gaseous" nature of Enlightenment religion see §586. Similarly, Burke referred to the "spirit of liberty" as a "wild gas." *Reflections*, ed. Conor Cruise O'Brien (Harmondsworth, 1969), p. 90.

97. Most recently, Jürgen Habermas has praised the Enlightenment as a period during which rational individuals could discuss issues dispassionately in the "political public sphere," and lamented the replacement of this golden age by a late-capitalist culture of public opinion management. *The Structural Transformation of the Public Sphere: An Inquiry into a Category of Bourgeois Society*, trans. Thomas Burger and Frederick Lawrence (Cambridge, MA, 1991).

REPRESENTING THE JEW IN LITERATURE

Harold Fisch (essay date 1971)

SOURCE: Fisch, Harold. "The Twentieth Century." In *The Dual Image: The Figure of the Jew in English and American Literature*, pp. 80-97. New York: Ktav Publishing House, Inc., 1971.

[*In the following excerpt, Fisch explores the treatment of Jewish characters in various twentieth-century literary works and suggests that in these works the Jew emerges as "a symbol of the moral victory of the human spirit."*]

LIBERALS AND REACTIONARIES

When we turn to the twentieth century we note that in spite of the generally soberer presentation of Jews the mythological outline remains. In E. M. Forster's early novel, *The Longest Journey* (1907), the Jewish Hegelian philosopher from Cambridge, Stewart Ansell performs a task in relation to the hero Rickie similar to that of Deronda in relation to Gwendolen in George Eliot's novel. He is the cultural and moral catalyst. He exposes the emptiness and triviality of the English upper class, its petty hypocrisies, and serves as a kind of lay-confessor to Rickie who is seeking moral integrity but constantly lapsing into self-deception and weakness. It is Ansell who screws him to the sticking point and forces him, simply through the effect of character and example, to be true to himself. In the great central scene where the accounts are cleared (there is always such a scene in a Forster novel) Ansell occupies the front of the stage: "He seemed transfigured into a Hebrew prophet passionate for satire and truth."

One of Ansell's functions is to be the representative of the honest middle classes—his father is a provincial draper—bringing honesty and realism into the world of the decayed gentry. He also strives to make them appreciate Stephen, the illegitimate half-brother of Rickie who seems to represent the life of the earth, of the proletariat. Ansell's function in the social structure is thus that of a symbolic reconciler of opposites. His message is the same as that of Margaret Schlegel in *Howard's End* later on (1910)—"only connect!" It is given to the Jew to achieve both the necessary detachment and the necessary moral vision for this purpose.

The place of the Jew in the newly evolving social pattern is a natural preoccupation of twentieth century writers, conscious as they are of the disruption of the nineteenth century class system. This applies also to Glasworthy's thoughtful and balanced study of the Jew in an alien society. His *Loyalties* (1922) is a piece of social analysis in dramatic form rather than a profound work of art, but its human insight and subtlety of characterisation are nonetheless impressive. In his study of the *nouveau riche* Jew, Ferdinand de Levis, trying to establish himself among the English upper-class, he shows how, in spite of the gentlemanly tolerance of the English, the Jew in a moment of crisis is neither a fellow nor an equal, but an outsider whose presence is a source of wrath and embarrassment, and whose cause by being just does cease to be obnoxious.

The crisis occurs when Ferdinand discovers that a large sum of money belonging to him has been stolen at a house-party. His suspicions rightly settle upon a fellow guest, Captain Ronald Dancy, whose known impecuniosity and recklessness and certain other circumstances make it appear probable that he was the thief. The other decent-minded English folk, however (including General Canynge and Charles Winsor), are seen to band themselves together to protect Dancy not because they believe him innocent

but because he is an officer and a gentleman. For them, Ferdinand's appeal to the law is simply bad form. Other characters however, such as Adela Winsor, are capable of weighing the case up impartially and getting beyond immediate class-loyalties. Eventually the truth comes to light, when two of the stolen bank notes turn up in the office of Dancy's solicitor, Jacob Twisden, and are traced back to Dancy himself who had used them to pay a "debt of honour." Twisden himself shows by his conduct that there is a sanction beyond *esprit de corps,* namely, integrity and justice. The presence of the Jew in gentile society, however unlovable he personally may be (and de Levis *is* unlovable), is indeed always a test of the quality of its justice.

De Levis is not a very comprehensive study in Jewish social psychology; he has no religious consciousness, either positive or negative. But in the play it is rather the social psychology of the English in their reaction to the Jew which is under scrutiny. De Levis illustrates well the dramatic situation of the Jew who is never quite accepted as a full member of the group and who reacts to the subtle discrimination by acute nervousness, suspicion, vindictiveness, and envy. His position has thus something in common with that of Shylock, and indeed many a passage in the play shows the influence of Shakespeare's study of the Jew in a hostile environment. But de Levis's final reaction when the climax is reached is quite different, and in a way more convincing, than Shylock's (convincing, that is, as realistic Jewish psychology). He turns up at the solicitor's office to make it clear that he has no interest in pressing the case to a conclusion now that he has been proved morally right:

> Don't mistake me. I didn't come because I feel Christian; I am a Jew. I will take no money—not even that which was stolen. Give it to a charity. I'm proved right. And now I'm done with the damned thing.

De Levis has the vices of an industrious go-getter for whom material calculations matter more than they should; but he is, unlike Shylock, neither mean nor avaricious, and indeed he has that oriental love of colour and display, and those bursts of magnanimity and ostentation so lacking in Shylock but so characteristic of even very ordinary Jews. Glasworthy of course had the advantage (that Shakespeare lacked) of seeing Jews close up, and he used his opportunities to good purpose. Whilst not producing a work of classic depth or spiritual insight, he nevertheless produced a very interesting, and also very true, social document. The middle-class objection to Jews voiced by one of the characters, illustrates Galsworthy's power of irony and the keenness of his observation:

> They work harder; they're more sober; they're honest; and they're everywhere. I've nothing against them, but the fact is—they get *on* so.

This scientific and judicial study of the Jewish problem as a social issue, shows us that the attempt is to be made to humanise the figure of the Jew in literature and to try to strip it of mythical features. And that is the dominant trend in the twentieth century. The Jew tends to be demythologized, to become neutral, to resemble any other middle class citizen. In the century of the common man the Jew has become the quintessential symbol of that common man!

This is evidently the tendency in the portrayal of Leopold Bloom in James Joyce's *Ulysses* (1922), probably the most important twentieth century work of fiction in which the Jew occupies the centre of interest. But Bloom is no longer "the Jew" of Dickens or of George Eliot; he is—at least on the surface—undistinguished and unheroic. He is simply unaccommodated man himself—Everyman in short—going about, through the space of one day and one night, his simple and everyday avocations.

The figure of Bloom had originally been suggested to Joyce by the story of a Dublin Jew named Hunter who was rumoured to be a cuckold. Additional features of Bloom's situation and character were provided by a friend and benefactor of Joyce, Ettore Schmitz (Svevo), an assimilated Jewish manufacturer of Trieste with some literary talent. Bloom does not have much association with Jews and Judaism, but there are authentic touches. Hebrew phrases go round in his head. There is a recurrent reference to an illustrated prospectus issued by an association of Palestine orange-growers (*Agudath Netaim*) which Bloom has been carrying round in his pocket throughout the day in his life which the novel records. Joyce also found in Bloom a reflection of his own problems. Having left his hometown of Dublin in 1904 after an unsettled youth and a Catholic upbringing, Joyce evidently found in the Jews an analogy to himself and his own situation. He too was an exile and a wanderer. But so was mankind as a whole. In this respect it may be said that we are all Jews!

Ulysses is the first major novel in which the Jew functions as a symbol of a universal condition. And that universal condition can be summed up in the word *alienation*. Victim, impotent lover, cuckold, dreamer, and frustrated wanderer, Bloom represents some of the permanent features of the twentieth century view of man: he resembles the antiheroes of Kafka, Faulkner, and Bellow. In short he has become a *persona* of Everyman. We sense something abnormal in the man who claims to have a fixed and assured relation to his environment. Alienation has become the normal condition of mankind, and it is the great distinction of Joyce to have seen this so early on and to have given this phenomenon a classic literary expression in the figure of Bloom-Everyman.

Bloom is also a clown, and as such he arouses in the reader the traditional comic reaction associated with the Jew figure in earlier literature. And it is not only the Jew who is a clown. Twentieth century man has frequently seen himself in the image of a clown—helpless, absurd, and vainly trying to make sense of a hostile, or at least uncongenial, environment. In this respect Bloom is the precursor of Charlie Chaplin, Willy Loman, and of Vladimir and Estragon

in Beckett's theatre of the absurd. At the end of the 'Cyclops' episode in *Ulysses*, Bloom is seen being pursued out of Barney Kiernan's public house by the mordantly anti-semitic Citizen and his dog. Bloom escapes in a jarvey chased by the dog, whilst the Citizen hurls a biscuit-tin at his head which barely misses him. The scene is one of uproarious farce, pure clowning:

> Did I kill him, says he, or what?
> And he shouting to the bloody dog:
> —After him Garry! After him, boy!
> And the last we saw was the bloody car rounding the corner
> and old sheepface on it gesticulating and the bloody mongrel
> after it with his lugs back for all he was bloody well worth
> to tear him limb from limb.

It is of course not true to say that *Ulysses* lacks the elements of the mythological. The whole scene of Bloom's exit from the pub is, as is well known, a parodic rendering of Ulysses' escape from the cave of the Cyclops in Homer's *Odyssey*. In Joyce's handling it becomes the escape of a very non-heroic Ulysses from a Dublin tavern with a roaring Citizen in pursuit temporarily 'blinded' (like the Cyclops) because the sun is in his eyes. There is also mythological enlargement of another kind. With one of those Joycean lurches of tone which we encounter throughout the novel, Bloom becomes transformed momentarily into Elijah ascending to heaven in his chariot:

> When, lo, there came about them all a great brightness and they beheld the chariot wherein he stood ascend to heaven. And they beheld Him in the chariot, clothed upon in the glory of the brightness, having raiment as the sun, fair as the moon and terrible that for awe they durst not look upon him. And there came a voice out of heaven, calling: *Elijah! Elijah!* And he answered with a main cry: *Abba! Adonai!* And they beheld Him even Him, ben Bloom Elijah, amid clouds of angels ascend to the glory of the brightness at an angle of forty-five degrees over Donohue's in Little Green Street like a shot off a shovel.

Here notwithstanding the final note of bathos there is no doubt that the Jew Bloom has acquired a prophetic grandeur; the wonder of the past is upon him, "the glory of the brightness" looking absurdly out of place over Donohue's in Little Green Street.

Here once again is that conjunction of everyday beggary and sabbath magnificence with which Zangwill had endowned his characters, and ben Bloom Elijah as a comic rendering of the dual image is not entirely unlike that great king of schnorrers, Manasseh Bueno Barzilai Azavedo da Costa.

But Joyce's intuition of the dual image is subtler than this. And here we find a further myth-pattern. Throughout the length of the novel, Bloom is seeking his spiritual "son" Stephen Dedalus, whilst Stephen is seeking his spiritual "father" Bloom. Their union towards the end is all too short-lived, but it is in a way the climax of the story. Bloom finds in the young poet and intellectual a substitute for his own lost infant Rudy, whilst Stephen finds in the kind and unassertive middle-aged Jew a father-figure more congenial to him than his own natural father, the boorish Irishman Simon Dedalus. Bloom and Stephen thus fall into the classic pattern of unheroic father and attractive offspring that we find in *The Merchant of Venice, Ivanhoe,* and *Daniel Deronda* (Lapidoth and Mirah). Bloom is not black, not disreputable, but he has a tinge of grey: he is the *homme moyen sensuel;* whilst Stephen represents hope, beauty, and vision. Bloom's own line has come to an end; he has a daughter, but his son is dead, his wife unfaithful, and he himself impotent. But in the young Irishman with the Hellenic name who affirms the spirit of man in literature Bloom finds his true heir. It is a re-enactment of the Pauline fable of the olive-tree, with Stephen as the branch of the wild olive restored to the native root of the good olive tree. In the Homeric *schema* it is the reunion of Ulysses with his long-estranged son Telemechus—the homecoming of the wanderer, the intimation of a messianic fulfilment.

The Jewish mythic stereotypes which we have noted in earlier examples from lesser writers are thus still active, guiding both author and reader in their reaction to the rituals being enacted in the fable. For all the twentieth century desire to get behind the myth and depict the Jew on the basis of social realism, myth tends to return either unconsciously or in the form of burlesque. In George Bernard Shaw's play, *Man and Superman* the Jew-Devil figure of medieval legend returns in the burlesque form of Mendoza the Jewish bandit. Mendoza who meets the hero Tanner in the Sierra Nevada reappears later in his dream as the Devil, whilst Tanner himself is re-incarnated as Don Juan. The two proceed to an interesting discussion of love, metaphysics, and the future of the human race. But the real Devil-Jew still functions in the collective unconscious (as twentieth century anti-semitic propaganda has shown). In an actively religious sensibility such as that of Graham Greene he comes back to the surface.

Greene's *Brighton Rock* (1938) is a novel conducted at the level of theological symbolism or allegory. Pinkie is the villain, but he lives within the world of spiritual realities (*i.e.,* Catholic spirituality). He knows Heaven and Hell, Sin and Grace. On the other hand, the Jew, Colleoni, knows only the *World.* His self-possession is the sign of his utterly negative and corrupt function.

> His old Semitic face showed few emotions but a mild amusement, a mild friendliness; but suddenly sitting there in the rich Victorian room, with the gold lighter in his pocket and the cigar case on his lap, he looked as a man might look who owned the whole world, the whole visible world that is, the cash registers and policemen and prostitutes, Parliament and the laws which say "this is Right and this is Wrong".

Pinkie is damned: but Colleoni is not damned in the same way, for he is "the Prince of this World," *i.e.,* he is, in strictly theological terms, the Devil himself. Here is the old medieval conjunction of Jew and Devil. Colleoni subtly leads Pinkie on to his damnation and final catastrophe. He knows all that goes on in Pinkie's surroundings. His agents and his power are all pervasive. He does not personally commit acts of violence, but all the forces of evil are at his command.

Colleoni is not a Jew just by chance; he is rather *the* Jew. As he passes Pinkie in his car, he appears to symbolise the eternal Jew, "not Colleoni at all . . . but any rich middle-aged Jew returning to the Cosmopolitan after a concert in the Pavilion". But if the Jew is the Devil, he is also (to complete the triangle) Judas. The attack on Spicer by "the Jews" (*i.e.,* Colleoni's gang) is a symbolic re-enactment of the crucifixion and betrayal of Jesus. Spicer's cry to Pinkie carries that particular theological reference when he exclaims in his anguish, "Pinkie. For Christ's sake."

A Gun for Sale (1936) presents the same Jew-Devil archetype in the person of Sir Marcus, ruler of the brothels and the steel industry. Through murder and conspiracy he manipulates the fate of nations and threatens the world with War. This will not only give a boost to the armaments industry (over which he presides) but will further his diabolical plans for the human race generally. In a transparently allegorical central scene, the heroine, Anne, and the main protagonist, Raven spend Christmas eve in a dark and freezing hut like the holy family, there being "no place for them at the inn." Like Christ, Raven will be killed through the forces of law and order, with the Jew in the background playing a sinister and dominant role. The fact that Raven is also a murderer gives an extra paradoxical twist but does not destroy the theological *schema.* On the contrary it serves to emphasize the fact that he bears upon himself the guilt of the human race, the burden of original sin which will be discharged at the moment of his passion. He gives up the ghost amid unbearable pain, and the world is saved, for the time being, from War.

This novel, like all Graham Greene's writings, combines the maximum of realism (sordid realism we should add) with the maximum of fantasy. In a way this gives a curious strength and tensile quality to his vision of everyday life whether in Brighton or Nottwich or the underside of London. But, nevertheless, realism is constantly subverted or side-tracked, and one finds oneself suddenly in a looking-glass world of medieval monsters and monks' tales. The authors of the medieval Mysteries dealt with the same range of myth and symbolism that Greene treats of, but they did not claim as he does to hold the mirror up to contemporary life. It is this double effort which gives to Graham Greene's work its tension and depth; but it also gives it a certain brittleness. It has a quality of prodigious anachronism. The portraits of Sir Marcus and Colleoni, with their medieval gargoyle features, are examples of such anachronism.

The fabulous Jew of Greene's imagination has counterparts in occasional parentheses in the work of T. S. Eliot—

also, it should be noted, a poet strongly influenced by the Catholic tradition:

> My house is a decayed house,
> And the jew squats on the window sill, the owner,
> Spawned in some estaminet of Antwerp.

The word "spawned" serves to emphasise his subhuman nature. Elsewhere, however, Eliot is capable of voicing the medieval veneration of the *pre-Christian Jew* (*i.e.,* the prophets and heroes of the Old Testament):

> In the days of Nehemiah the Prophet . . .
> In Shushan the palace, in the month Nisan,
> He served the wine to the king Ataterxes,
> And he grieved for the broken city, Jerusalem;
> And the King gave him leave to depart
> That he might rebuild the city. . . .
> So they built as men must build
> With the sword in one hand and the trowel in the other

(Chorus from The Rock, 1934)

Here again determining the dividing line between the "good" Jew of Biblical times, and the "bad" Jew of to-day is the compulsive mechanism of the dual image.

THE AMERICAN SCENE (THE NON-JEWISH WRITERS)

In spite of the well-established myth of America as the melting-pot where races and nations would fuse together, and the stereotyped images of prejudice dividing one national group from another would consequently disappear, the image of the Jew projected both in the work of Jews and non-Jews on the North American continent during the first half of the twentieth century does not differ significantly from that which we have found in England.

Thomas Wolfe for a while enjoyed the favours of a Jewish mistress who established him in the world of wealthy and cultivated men of letters, yet in his writings he vacillates between a fascination for the intensity and vigour of Jewish life, and an almost obsessive disgust for the persons of the New York Jews such as Mr. Rosen ("Death and Proud Brother") with his unctuousness, his wealth, and his pearly teeth:

> He would wear striped trousers and he would walk up and down upon rich carpets, he would be splendid and full of power like a well-fed bull.

The medieval conjunction of Jew and Devil, still active in the imagination of Graham Greene, has little theological edge for the American writer sadly lacking as he is in a sense of the middle ages, but something very like that archetype is still discernible in F. Scott Fitzgerald's *The Great Gatsby* (1925) in the portrait of Meyer Wolfsheim "the man who fixed the World's Series back in 1919." The reference is to the baseball championships of that year, but the wording suggests manipulation on a universal scale. This figure of ominous and diabolical power is a "small flat-nosed Jew"; he has "bulbous fingers" and a sentimental tendency to weep for friends who have met a violent death.

Evil Jews are also to be found in the novels of Theodore Dreiser. During the period of the rise of Nazism Dreiser compromised himself as a spokesman of American anti-semitism. He complained that the Jews were an obnoxious racial entity.

> They do not blend as do other elements in this country, but retain, as they retain in all countries, their race solidarity and even their religion.

These words were written in 1935. Dreiser persisted almost until his death in 1945 in opposing to the standard liberal American attitude to Jews his own special right-wing prejudices—prejudices which have never really disappeared from the American consciousness although they may have been driven into that outer darkness where the Ku Klux Klan and the Birch Society still hold sway. And yet even Dreiser in *The Hand of the Potter* (1918) balances his evil characters with a fine old Jewish *pater familias* who is as noble as his son is evil—a reversal of the usual stereotyped juxtaposition of black father and white offspring. Dreiser's Jewish fathers are not all noble and patriarchal. In *The Titan* (1914) one of the hero Cowperwood's mistresses is the daughter of a certain Isadore Platow, a wealthy furrier of Chicago:

> He was a large, meaty, oily type of man—a kind of ambling, gelatinous formula of the male, with the usual sound commercial instincts of the Jew, but with an errant philosophy which led him to believe first one thing and then another so long as neither interfered definitely with his business.

Dreiser is pulling the stops a little too obviously. Such a description could almost have been written by a computer if it had been programmed with details of the standard Jewish "black" portraiture of the eighteenth and nineteenth centuries.

A somewhat more unusual anti-Semitic portrait which could certainly not have been manufactured by a computer is to be found in Ernest Hemingway's celebrated novel, *The Sun Also Rises* (1926). Robert Cohn is a Jew who in order to normalize his relationship with a hostile and cynical gentile world turns himself into a boxing champion. But in spite of his physical expertise and his success with the fascinating Lady Brett Ashley, he remains the outsider. He has successfully adapted himself to the *mores* of the tough set around him with their interest in the bull-fight (a typical Hemingway occupation), but the cloven hoof shows through in Cohn's unwillingness to get drunk like Jake, Bill, Mike, and other sound human specimens. The unhealthy sobriety of the Jew is as distasteful as his self-indulgence. Strangely enough, both are imputed to the Jew in the examples we are discussing, but then logical consistency is not a feature of myth. Hemingway is said to have drawn his character from the life, and if so it is easy to imagine that the real Robert Cohn was probably no more obnoxious than de Levis in Galsworthy's play. However, Hemingway has chosen to take the angle of vision of the hard bohemian characters who have trodden their moral sympathies underfoot. There is a Nietzschean transvaluation of values here, a refusal to admit the tenderer emotions, to temper toughness of mind, male aggressiveness, with any of the traditional Judeo-Christian virtues. Thus he kills those women characters who are too weak to share in the new dispensation (e.g., Catherine in *A Farewell to Arms*), he shuts out the undrinking Jew, and finally destroys himself as well. It is a plan ultimately destructive of human values.

The alien Jewish male is more often than not an unattractive figure in earlier American fiction, but Leslie Fiedler has reminded us of the ubiquity of the desirable Jewish female, the archetypal "Jew's Daughter". She appears in Hawthorne (*The Marble Faun*), in Melville (*Clarel*), and in a host of minor novelists. She may also be identified as Marjorie Morningstar, the good Jewess, beside the bad Jew, Noel Airman, in Herman Wouk's celebrated bestseller of 1955. There is a more serious portrait of the good Jew in Sinclair Lewis's *Arrowsmith* (1925). He is Professor Max Gottlieb, the true medical scientist, devoted, self-sacrificing, and holding aloft his ideals in a world of corruption and second-rate talent. The Jew as moral mentor appears in Richard Wright's classic negro novel *Native Son* (1940). Max is the Jewish lawyer who speaks to the heart of Bigger Thomas, the Negro convicted for murder and rape. The Jew being also an outsider and a victim may sympathize with the Negro and undersand his bitter and savage frustrations. Thus it is Max, the Communist Jew, who discovers and saves the human image in the soul of the Negro. The novel reads a little sentimentally thirty years later when we are no longer so sure of finding a solution for all the world's racial problems in a socialist paradise. Moreover, we are no longer sure that for all their community of social experience the Negro and Jew are destined to walk hand in hand into a future of freedom and bliss. A latter-day Negro poet, LeRoi Jones gives us an image of the Jew the precise opposite of that projected in Wright's novel. He sees them as

> Selling fried potatoes
> and people, the little arty bastards
> talking arithmetic they sucked from the
> arab's head.

And he muses on—

> how we beat you
> and killed you
> and tied you up
> and marked this specimen
> "Dangerous Germ
> Culture." And put you back
> In a cold box.

Lurking behind the new sinister image of the Jew in Negro literature is the memory of the long hot summers of the sixties when Negro violence in a dozen cities made Jewish store-owners its chief victim, when the Negro proletariat saw in the successful Jewish bourgeoisie the symbol of all that it hated in America. Here in Richard Wright and in LeRoi Jones is an indication of the still potent contradictions set up by the archetypal dual image of the Jew.

DEMYTHOLOGIZING THE JEW

Is there any possibility of demythologizing the Jewish image? The fact is, as we have seen, that the Jew impinges on the non-Jew (and on himself) in a traumatic fashion. "The word *Jew*" Karl Shapiro has said, "retains its eternal shock." How is one to render this except by imputing either extraordinary virtue or extraordinary vice to the person who causes the shock? And that, of course is the way of mythology. The twentieth century has made a major effort to avoid this seeming necessity and to down-tone the Jew, to neutralize him. We saw this process at work in the portrayal of Leopold Bloom in James Joyce's great novel, but we saw also that mythology returns in the mock-epic style and through the structure of relationships between the characters. Joyce's novel ultimately testifies to the permanence of the extraordinary in the portrayal of the Jew.

More decidedly neutral portraits of Jews appear in the novels of G. B. Stern, such as *Tents of Israel* (1924), and *The Young Matriarch* (1942). Except for their cosmopolitanism and the intensity of their family relationships and loyalties, they are like any other group of middle class folk. Plays on Old Testament subjects by Christopher Fry, Laurence Housman, and James Bridie also tend to treat the material in normal, tragic (or even sometimes, comic) terms. In much present-day American literature too the Jew becomes a neutral figure; he does not drag in the Jewish problem wherever he goes. This is true of the work of Pearl Buck, Damon Runyan and many others. But it may be suggested that the effort to neutralize the Jew has not really succeeded. A note of unreality creeps into the portraiture. The reader cannot convince himself that wings and/or cloven hoof are not somewhere hidden under the seemingly ordinary outer dress. Character-drawing is too disarming, too emphatically casual. No-one who is really like everyone else has to go out of his way to say so again and again.

This is ultimately the criticism that should be made against so distinguished a novel, for instance, as C. P. Snow's *The Conscience of the Rich* (1958). Snow has chosen to analyze the impact of the social and political changes of the '30's on a rich upper-class family of bankers, the Marches. The Marches are English Jews, but they have the instincts of the landed gentry. Jewish shading is provided by the rather strong sense of family loyalty, a feeling for the family's past generations, and a somewhat ritualized pattern of behaviour when they are together. But they are certainly not Jewish in any fundamental way.

> The Marches were secure, they were part of the country, *they lived almost exactly the lives of other wealthy men.*

(my italics)

The crisis comes when the son Charles decides to forego the family fortune and the responsibilities that go with it, marry a communist, and go in for a medical career. Charles though earnest, is not a moral visionary or an interpreter and critic of society like Stewart Ansell in E. M. Forster's novel. In Snow's novel, the detached spectator is a non-Jew, Lewis Eliot. It is he who observes the doings of the Marches and their upper class world from the position of middle class independence, whilst the Jew has become part of the fixed order of English life with little to distinguish him from his social background.

We have been suggesting that to neutralize the portrait of the Jew in this way, to make him ordinary and everyday, is to lean over backwards. The note of unreality creeps in through the very lack of polarization. To this it might be objected that there are, as a matter of fact, ordinary Jews who live lives scarcely distinguishable from those of non-Jews belonging to the same social class, and that C. P. Snow was almost undoubtedly painting the Marches from the life. He had observed just such a Jewish family. One cannot deny that Snow's novel and similar writings by G. B. Stern and others have *descriptive* truth and that the characterization often carries conviction. What is wrong is the plot, or more precisely, the *history* of the characters—the things that happen to them. The fact is that Jewish history is not neutral history. As George Eliot had sensed, the things that happen to Jews are not things that happen to ordinary people. Galsworthy also understood this. De Levis in *Loyalties* is an unextraordinary person, but his dramatic situation has the specificity of Jewish existence. This is what is lacking in *The Conscience of the Rich*. There is an existential gap. Jews living in the twentieth century cannot be isolated from Jewish history without some prejudice to the realism of the portraiture. Jewish history may not be enjoyable for those living it, but friend and foe will surely agree that it is nothing if not remarkable.

It may be suggested that the only satisfactory way of de-mythologizing the Jew is to take the emphasis off the Jew as a person and to place it on Jewish history. It is first and foremost Jewish history which makes the Jew strange and remarkable, not the supposed extremes of his personality. This is the implication of a work by an American non-Jewish writer which should be mentioned. It is John Hersey's *The Wall* (1950), the story of the Warsaw Ghetto revolt and the Jewish martyrdom at the hands of the Nazis—a theme central to modern Jewish history and of immense importance for the literary portrayal of the Jew from now onwards. *The Wall* presents its Jewish characters in the Ghetto as—in the first instance—perfectly ordinary everyday characters; some of them are noble, some ignoble; but most of them have ordinary human failings and weaknesses. This we may say, so far, is the neutral or journalistic portrayal of the Jew—and Hersey is first of all a journalist. But we become quickly aware that the extraordinary *history* in which these people are involved—and indeed have always been involved—creates of them in the end fabulous personalities. The elements of heroism,

nobility, and an inner sense of superiority in the face of evil, seem to be bestowed upon the Jew by the very nature of his situation. It is this which Hersey recognizes as the final meaning of the Ghetto tragedy. Jewish history is not neutral history; it is the history of trial and sacrifice. The Jew becomes inevitably a symbol of the moral victory of the human spirit, not because as an individual he is necessarily better than anyone else, but evidently because he is called upon to be a witness to the work of God in the world. The "Suffering Servant" acquires a dignity not on account of his character but on account of his situation. It is an existential not a moral distinction which primarily marks the Jew out from his fellows. And in this Hersey has come near to a valid rendering of the Jewish image for the twentieth century reader.

In a poetically conceived novel from the Antipodes, *Riders in the Chariot* (1961), Patrick White records the spiritual impact of the Holocaust on one Himmelfarb, a German Jewish professor who has survived Auschwitz to settle down as a labourer in a small Australian township. As well as being a "suffering servant," he is also a visionary, a mystic. But his vision of the "Chariot," though serving to define his specific Jewish existence, also links him mysteriously with other suffering characters—an eccentric maiden lady who finds the Chariot in trees and animals, and a half-educated Negro artist who has achieved it in paint.

The Jewish fate is what makes the Jew different, but it can be shared by others whose lives have been touched by the same magic spell of triumph and tragedy.

Harry Girling (essay date 1990)

SOURCE: Girling, Harry. "The Jew in James Joyce's *Ulysses*." In *Jewish Presences in English Literature*, edited by Derek Cohen and Deborah Heller, pp. 96-112. Montreal, Canada: McGill-Queen's University Press, 1990.

[*In the following essay, Girling presents a detailed examination of the character of Leopold Bloom in James Joyce's novel* Ulysses, *focusing on Joyce's conception of Bloom's typical and atypical Jewish traits.*]

Unlike the Jews discussed in the previous chapters, the Jew in James Joyce's *Ulysses*, Leopold Bloom, is usually thought of as an Everyman figure. Not that he is going about looking for his soul, like the central character of the medieval play of *Everyman*. Rather he is like the man in the street, but larger and plumper than life; he is nothing and everything at the same time. He is a fairly faithful husband with a constant hankering towards an adulterous intrigue; he earns enough to get by, though he has to resort to various stratagems to stay afloat; he has quite good taste in music, but his chief interest in art is in trying to find out whether marble goddesses have a nether orifice; he has lots of acquaintances and no particular chums; he is fairly greedy and a bit fastidious; inclined to avoid trouble except when he is suddenly a hero; a father pining for a dead son who miraculously is endowed with a spiritual heir; a restless traveller who comes home as if he will never leave it again.

So the only remarkable thing about Leopold Bloom is that he is a Jew. Come to that, he is not much of a Jew at all, with neither a sense of Jewish lineage nor a Jewish upbringing. His father, not he, swallowed the bait of the Society for the Conversion of the Jews, gave up his religion and changed his name from Virag to Bloom. But Leopold knows himself to be, and is known as, a Jew in a nation—the Irish—and a society—Dublin—where Jews are few and are even said to be non-existent. His name is Jewish, his appearance is Jewish, and he himself, if the ragbag of his mind contained the material to say so, would not shrink from the final banality of claiming that he has a Jewish soul. Bloom is probably circumcised, for he was born when his father was still Jewish, though Joyce does not say so, not even when Bloom is admiring his own penis in the bathtub, "the limp father of thousands, a languid floating flower" (71).[1] The chief model for Leopold Bloom was a writer Joyce befriended in Trieste, Ettore Schmitz, an Italian Jew who published the delightful *Confessions of Zeno* under the pen name of Italo Svevo in 1923. Zeno is not a Jew; the chief quality he shares with Bloom is a charming incapacity for taking himself seriously.

We may wonder why James Joyce chose to make his man in the middle, the average sensual man, a Jew. There is no obvious answer. The reader may decide that Leopold Bloom epitomises, merely by his survival, the shifts and compromises that have controlled the lives of all the people in the twentieth century who have been so fortunate as to survive war and catastrophe—an emergence millions of Jews were cruelly deprived of. Bloom's journey through Dublin on a single day represents in some fashion the itinerary of a twentieth-century survival. Such a view does not take in anything resembling the holocaust, but who in the first quarter of the twentieth century would have dared to contemplate, in his most terrified imaginings, the horrors that the second quarter was to bring forth?

James Joyce's *Ulysses* was published by Shakespeare and Company in Paris on Joyce's fortieth birthday, 2 February 1922. Parts of the book, which he had been writing since 1914, had been published in periodicals from 1918 onwards. The publication history is a fascinating story of struggle against censorship and suppression, a struggle which ended in America after the epoch-making judgment given in the New York District Court by Justice Woolsey in October 1933 and the subsequent publication of the novel by Random House. The corresponding publication in Great Britain by John Lane did not take place until 1936.

These bare written-out dates—1914, 1918, 1922, 1933, 1936—cannot be thought of as mere figures. As we look back to 1933 and 1936 from the last decades of the twentieth century, we are aware of the gathering shadows that were soon to close upon Europe and the world, the darkness and tragedy of the Nazi attempt at world domination, and all the agony of the "final solution." The years 1914-18 bring to mind another kind of mass slaughter, another European tragedy, as devastating though not as evil as the Nazi destruction. Amid all these annals of doom it is difficult to come back to the date in the middle, the year 1922, and to find there some lights of hope shining, of which *Ulysses* was one.

We cannot expect to find euphoria in the years immediately after the ending of the European war in November 1918. The frantic rejoicing of Armistice Night in London marked the end of a universal disaster, but hard after came both every kind of local disaster and the influenza epidemic that claimed more victims than the war had done. Yet many people wanted to believe that the "war to end wars" would serve as a permanent warning to competing nations and that the Treaty of Versailles would establish permanent peace. In spite of all discouragements, until 1939 some idealists continued to hope that the nations could avoid war, believing in the League of Nations with a fervour that the United Nations Organization, with its cynical great-power share-out, never inspired.

One of the reasons for hope in the years after 1918 was that four great empires, the Russian, the Austrian, the Prussian, and the Ottoman, had all crumbled, dismantling some ancient fortresses of reaction and repression. Tsarist Russia had been the European example of institutionalized persecution of Jews. Anti-Semitism was everywhere, of course, but governmental authorization for it was more flagrant in Russia than elsewhere. It was Russia that made the world familiar with the word and the event *pogrom,* and not without reason were brutal police everywhere called "Cossacks." But can one say that the Tsarist anti-Semitism was worse than the Stalinist? One way in which it was better was that Jews were allowed to emigrate from the land of oppression, to flood across the Atlantic and also to other free countries round the world, there to establish the first durable form of the new Zion, part of which was the Lower East Side, New York.

The break-up of the old continental empires (which allowed the British, French, and American empires to acquire some new overseas colonies) liberated some national minorities that had aspired for centuries to become nations. The years after 1918 also saw several new states looking round them in new-found pride: Balkan states, Baltic states, Czecho-Slovakia, Poland, Hungary. They did not all become democratic havens of tolerance, but those that did lit up in a glory that was to prove desperately short-lived. Many lost their independence in 1939 or before, some betrayed by enemies, some by false friends such as those whose abandonment of Czecho-Slovakia made the war inevitable.

Two of the small states that achieved or advanced towards freedom after 1918 were Israel and Ireland. Israel had not moved very far towards statehood in 1922, but the essential step had been taken: after the Balfour Declaration of 1917 promising a Jewish national home, the military defeat of Turkey enabled the League of Nations in 1922 to grant a mandate to Great Britain to bring it about. Many years of difficulty and struggle were to follow before the state of Israel was proclaimed on 15 May 1948, but the mandate of 1922 can be regarded as the first hint of Zion—as Leopold Bloom calls it, "the golden city which is to be, the new Bloomusalem" (395). Also in 1922, more than two centuries of wrongs and self-sacrificing resistance came to an end in Ireland when the Irish Free State was established by the ratification of a treaty with Great Britain on 8 January. The failed rebellion during Easter 1916 had made another fifteen martyrs for old Ireland, fifteen martyrs for the Crown, as the ballad of Kevin Barry would put it; but this time all the hanged men

> Are changed, changed utterly:
> A terrible beauty is born.

Although the poet, W. B. Yeats, did not mean it thus, the "terrible beauty" was Irish freedom, born in 1922 after the years of oppression. Ireland had suffered, from 1919 to 1921, the post-war years of terrorism and counter-terrorism when the Black and Tans, British mercenaries, fought the Irish Republican Army. After the treaty, Ireland did not spend long on the arts of peace. The civil war between the Free State Army and the Irish Republican Army began in June 1922 (just after Joyce's fortieth birthday and the publication of *Ulysses*). Irishman shot Irishman until 1926, when the last guerilla fighters surrendered. "Irelan' sober is Irelan' free" says Jack Boyle, drunker than ever, at the end of Sean O'Casey's *Juno and the Paycock*. There is not much possibility of Ireland becoming habitually sober (who would wish it?); more than sixty years later there still seems little possibility of Ireland becoming free of the shadow of a gunman. For the last twenty years the civil war has moved to Ulster, and Irishmen shoot Irishmen not because they are "die-hards" or "staters" but because they are Catholics or Protestants. And who can say when the shooting will end in the golden city of Zion?

> —But it's no use, says [Bloom]. Force, hatred, history, all that. That's not life for men and women, insult and hatred. And everybody knows that it's the very opposite of that that is really life.
>
> —What? says Alf.
>
> (273)

What? indeed. There is an answer, in one word, but it will be better to make further acquaintance with Leopold Bloom and with James Joyce before coming back to it.

The present task is to rediscover, looking back across all the horrors of the twentieth century, the "radical innocence" (Yeats's phrase) of the moment in 1922 when *Ulysses* was published, to discern in the novel the intertwined cord of Jewish freedom and Irish freedom, with the promise that any interest in Joyce's masterpiece is "self-

delighting, self-appeasing, self-affrighting" (still Yeats) even if the focus is no more than the emerging portrait of a Jew. After all, those tourists (not few) whose only interest in foreign places is in seeking out the old synagogues—in Florence, Athens, Bombay - usually find some incidental entertainment in the streets they pass through on their way to the Jewish shrines.

Joyce made a brief statement about the purpose of his book when he sent an elaborate scheme of the episodes and their very rich system of symbolic equivalences to his friend Carlo Linati in 1920. "It is the epic of two races (Israel—Ireland) and at the same time the cycle of the human body as well as a little story of a day (life) . . . It is also a kind of encyclopedia."[2]

Of all the ways in which *Ulysses* could be described, an "epic of two races (Israel—Ireland)" is not the most obvious. These threads are easily traced, but they are only strands in a total whose complexity, variety, subtlety, and fascination are beyond description. Though Joyce himself rejoiced in the layers of symbolism, the intricate correspondences, the constant cross-referencing, the wealth of historical detail, his intimate knowledge of Dublin streets and places, and above all the basic structuring of episodes from Homer's *Odyssey*—any admirer can spin out other comparisons and footnotes that are relevant and valuable—an interested reader can dispense with the whole apparatus of explanation and follow the story page by page. Some pages are transparently clear, some so obscure that no clues can help, some so perverse that they look like an elaborate leg-pull, and some so winning that the reader wants them to go on forever.

The preliminary indications given here do not amount to the elementary guidelines that are supposed to be necessary for a reading of *Ulysses*. No guidance of any kind is required. It is not even obligatory to read through from the beginning—the book may just as well be started anywhere in the middle. The few descriptive lines extracted below are meant to provide some continuity to the narrative, with the implicit assumption that Leopold Bloom, a genial soul, will introduce the reader to the glories of *Ulysses* and to the genius of James Joyce.

The three principal strands in the novel are the episodes from Homer's *Odyssey*, the succession of events in a single day in Dublin, and the coming together of the two principal characters, Leopold Bloom and Stephen Dedalus. Each of these strands runs through the whole narrative, and each forms an independent pattern by which the whole novel could be followed.

Ulysses was a leader in the Greek army which besieged Troy for ten years. As if this absence from home were not enough, after the fall of Troy, Ulysses was unable to return to his kingdom of Ithaca for another ten years, having been delayed by various adventures such as a near escape from the man-eating giant Cyclops and a one-year sojourn on the island of Aeaea, governed by Circe, a sorceress who turned his companions into swine. When Ulysses at last arrived in Ithaca, he found his wife Penelope importuned by a swarm of suitors, whom he drove off with the help of his son, Telemachus. The Penelope of Joyce's story, Bloom's wife Molly, has the last say in the book, a rambling monologue of several thousand words, explaining in remarkable detail how she did not reject the sexual advances of any suitor who came along, yet still kept her loyalty to her Poldy.

All the events in *Ulysses* took place on "16 June 1904" (In recent years this 16th day of June has been celebrated in Dublin and round the world—*urbi et orbi*—as Bloomsday.) The day begins with breakfast, fried bacon for Stephen Dedalus and a fried kidney for Leopold Bloom, and ends in a shared drink of Epp's cocoa in Bloom's house in Eccles Street during the early hours of the morning. Various historical events that took place on 16 June 1904 crop up in the book, such as the sinking of a ferry in New York harbour and the Gold Cup horse race at Ascot in England, but none of the events mentioned have anything to do with the nations of Ireland and Israel, which, it seems, allowed the first Bloomsday to pass without any world-stirring happening. The day marked Joyce's first meeting with his wife, but neither Sinn Fein nor the Zionist movement took any notice.

The most direct comparison of Ireland and Israel in *Ulysses* occurs in a piece of quoted oratory recited among a crowd of gossipers in a newspaper office. To a slightly sceptical eye, the oratory does not seem particularly convincing, but the piece gains an adventitious importance because it was one of four paragraphs selected by Joyce for a gramophone recording in his own voice. He must have thought it an adequate sample of his masterwork. The context is a discussion about the revival of the Irish language, one of the channels for the expression of Irish nationalism in the early years of the twentieth century, when Irish Home Rule seemed to be a lost cause, when the violence of the Fenians had burnt itself out and the violence of Sinn Fein had hardly started, and the Abbey Theatre had not yet raised the mythical banner of Kathleen ni Houlihan. It was a time for windy oratory, a time when battle lines were being drawn in nothing more permanent than the spilt beer on any pub counter.

The comparable debate in the Zionist movement at the beginning of the century concerned the use of Hebrew as the language of Jewish national revival. There was a good deal of rabbinic opposition to the use of the language of prayer as the language of political agitation. Yiddish, the language of the revolutionary socialist Bund, was recommended as more suitable. Of course, Hebrew was chosen as the language of the Zionist movement, of the kibbutzim, and of the state of Israel, and today's flourishing literature, culture, and political system demonstrate the appropriateness of the choice. The state of Eire, on the other hand, has never managed to install Irish as more than a second language, and, in spite of every encouragement, threat, and bribe, Irish is still no more than a marginal addition to the governmental system. But who was to know that Irishmen would refuse to speak Irish, who among those theorists arguing in a newspaper office in 1904 that they ought to? Or, for that matter, who could guess it in 1922 when *Ulysses* appeared? "Sufficient for the day is the newspaper thereof" (114).

The orator purports to represent a not very likely meeting between an Egyptian high priest and a youthful Moses, when the high priest, speaking like an imperialist cabinet minister, scolds the Jews for their obstinate fatuity in belonging to an inferior race.

> Why will you jews not accept our culture, our religion and our language? You are a tribe of nomad herdsmen: we are a mighty people. You have no cities nor no wealth: our cities are hives of humanity and our galleys, trireme and quadrireme, laden with all manner merchandise furrow the waters of the known globe. You have but emerged from primitive conditions: we have a literature, a priesthood, an agelong history and a polity . . . Israel is weak and few are her children: Egypt is an host and terrible are her arms . . .
>
> —But, ladies and gentlemen, had the youthful Moses listened to and accepted that view of life, had he bowed his head and bowed his will and bowed his spirit before that arrogant admonition he would never have brought the chosen people out of their house of bondage, nor followed the pillar of the cloud by day. He would never have spoken with the Eternal amid lightnings on Sinai's mountaintop or ever have come down with the light of inspiration shining in his countenance and bearing in his arms the tables of the law, graven in the language of the outlaw.
>
> (117)

Elsewhere the pleasure of reading any page of this novel is made richer by reference to places and people appearing on several other pages. Here the contextless quotation from the orator is exposed as self-contradicting, self-ridiculing, and hence its absurdity can stand by itself. Are we to think of an Irish Moses coming down from Sinai with the tables of the law graven by God in Irish, only to find that not a soul among the chosen people can read them? It would make matters worse if Moses himself could not read the Hebrew commandments on the tablets and had to apply to the erudite high priest (conveniently on hand in the desert) for a translation. The first person we meet in Joyce's Dublin who is able to speak Irish is a crassly insensitive Englishman who drives Stephen out of his lodging. As for Bloom, he remembers so little of the Pesach service that his father used to read when he was a small boy that he has Moses leading the people out of Israel "out of the land of Egypt and into the house of bondage *alleluia*" (101). Israel had seen so much more of the house of bondage than of promised land that (in the year 1904 at least) it offered no good omen for Ireland. Stephen, who is one of the auditors of the citation of the windy orator, responds by suggesting that they should all go for a drink next door, and offers a story of two old women who climb Dublin's Mount Sinai—Nelson's column—and spit down secular plumstones from the top.

Stephen serves as the registrant of spoken comments about Jews, since they are rarely made directly to Bloom. The first note of anti-Semitism comes from the Britisher Haines, who is sharing a lodging with Stephen and another friend, Buck Mulligan. Haines gives voice to the common slur when he accuses "German jews" of wanting to take over his country (18). In the first decade of the twentieth century, a few Jewish capitalists were blamed for the manifold sins of British imperialist exploitation. This view is extended by Mr Deasy, the owner of a private school Stephen is temporarily teaching in. Deasy, who speaks for the Protestant [elite] in Ireland, regards his deeply rooted prejudices as equivalent to historical analysis. No doubt he would produce another collection of slanders against the Catholic Irish if the opportunity arose. "England is in the hands of the jews. In all the highest places: her finance, her press . . . Old England is dying . . . They sinned against the light . . . And that is why they are wanderers on the earth to this day" (28). Stephen's reply is not spoken; it appears as an interior monologue and is the first example of the innovative literary method that makes this novel so remarkable. Words sounded inside the head are as much part of the ongoing situation in which they appear as would be spoken dialogue or explicit action. Stephen's memory supplies him with a view of Jewish merchants in Paris; he does not contradict Deasy's slander but picks up his false interpretation of appearances and transforms it into a lament for the impermanence of Jewish endeavours.

> On the steps of the Paris Stock Exchange the gold-skinned men quoting prices on their gemmed fingers. Gabble of geese. They swarmed loud, uncouth, about the temple, their heads thickplotting under maladroit silk hats. Not theirs: these clothes, this speech, these gestures. Their full slow eyes belied the words, the gestures eager and unoffending, but knew the rancours massed about them and knew their zeal was vain. Vain patience to heap and hoard. Time surely would scatter all. A hoard heaped by the roadside: plundered and passing on. Their eyes knew the years of wandering and, patient, knew the dishonours of their flesh.
>
> (28)

The reinterpretation indicates that the very stereotype that served as the hook on which prejudices were hung can be regarded, in its exotic guise, as an occasion for participation by a sympathetic observer in the sufferings of defenseless victims. Stephen goes on to produce a sentence that might be engraved as a comprehensive comment on the sorrows of the twentieth century. "History, Stephen said, is a nightmare from which I am trying to awake" (28).

Stephen's thought could well be of the long history of cruelty and suffering in Ireland. Its lapidary force speaks for all the people who look backwards only with horror and who have little hope in looking forward. But Stephen would rather not discuss Ireland. Much later in the day, drunk and battered and bored to distraction by Bloom's long-winded discourse about work for all and a tidysized income for all the Irish, Stephen in desperation interrupts, "We can't change the country. Let us change the subject" (527).

Change: "Mr Leopold Bloom ate with relish the inner organs of beasts and fowls. He liked thick giblet soup, nutty gizzards, a stuffed roast heart, liverslices fried with crustcrumbs, fried hencods' roes. Most of all he liked grilled mutton kidneys which gave to his palate a fine tang of faintly scented urine" (45).

How does a kidney manage to be attractive and repulsive at the same time? It looks interesting, it tastes nice, it slips down easily. But on second thought, it has too functional an appearance, its texture is suspiciously smooth, it lacks fibre, and the after-taste might make anyone wonder. Some people never start to like kidneys, others give them up, and those who declare themselves to be kidney-eaters do so rather defiantly. There is something about undisguised flesh-eating, something about eating a working organ, as if the sheep would like to have it back, and something, alas, to do with the production of urine, don't ask too closely. Why isn't a mutton kidney called by a different name from our own kidneys? Why doesn't it have a euphemism like "sweetbreads"? What if we decide that Leopold Bloom, here met for the first time, is somehow like a kidney? If he is, that is how James Joyce made him for his readers, his consumers. But to say a Jew is like a kidney would be an absurdity, obviously anything can be compared with anything and what sense would such a comparison make? Anyhow no Jew could be compared with the pork kidneys that Bloom enjoys for his breakfast on this memorable day.

The attempt here is to see what kind of Jew James Joyce made in Leopold Bloom.

We find out more about the mind of Bloom than of anyone else in literature, including Hamlet. Perhaps Marcel Proust says more about what goes on in his mind, but Proust is so resolutely intellectual and artistic that no thoughts that do not come up to an A level, or at least B+, are ever admitted. Whereas the thoughts of Bloom hardly ever rise above a C level, and some are frankly D or E, though never a failing F. Bloom's thoughts are never shocking or disgusting, but most of them are so ordinary, so shallow in their humdrum continuity, that the only thing that seems to be as exterior and as unremarkable as they are is the earth itself, and all the miscellaneous objects that clutter its surface. Yes, we all know that there are large forces working beneath the surface and over it—gravity here, cosmic rays out there, television in the sky, potatoes in the ground, somewhere an earthquake cooking up, and plenty of weather. But, when we look around, we see nothing of these forces, nor do we observe the beautiful landscapes that painters discover; we see trees and dogs, people and motorcars, some ordinary-looking buildings and some scraps of paper blown by the wind. Our minds are likewise stuffed with thoughts so shallow and with trivialities so boring that even a psychoanalyst would refuse to listen to them. So is Bloom's mind. But when Joyce renders the shifting spectacle of Bloom's commonplace thinking, the result is fascinating, dramatic, poignant, and above all else illuminating—a new world that reveals the whole panorama of twentieth-century living and all the potentialities of twentieth-century fiction. A reader feels like some watcher of the skies when a flying saucer skims into his ken.

Bloom's unfocused wisps of thought, which attach themselves to the sight of two horses at nosebag time, give a brief and complete sample of the impressions, judgments, and memories that pass across the surface of his mind in a second or two, more quickly than the spelt-out words. He switches from recollection to describing visual impressions because a poster advertising *Hamlet* has reminded him of Ophelia's suicide, then recalls his own father's suicide, then the day when he had to recover his father's body. But look at the horses:

> He came nearer and heard a crunching of gilded oats, the gently champing teeth. Their full buck eyes regarded him as he went by, amid the sweet oaten reek of horsepiss. Their Eldorado. Poor jugginses! Damn all they know or care about anything with their long noses stuck in nosebags. Too full for words. Still they get their feed all right and their doss. Gelded too: a stump of black guttapercha wagging limp between their haunches. Might be happy all the same that way. Good poor brutes they look. Still their neigh can be very irritating.
>
> (63)

Bloom's thoughts are always transitory. A moment before thinking about his father, he had been trying to get a glimpse of a lady's legs as she climbed into a jaunting car, and had wondered why the King always dresses like a soldier for his portraits, never as a fireman or a policeman. Yet when he pauses by the pair of nags he grasps a sequence of essentials that, in Stephen Dedalus's phrase in *A Portrait of the Artist as a Young Man,* comes to "the whatness of all horse." This is because Bloom, without realizing it, is momentarily a poor brute of a horse himself. He too is a poor juggins (a simp, an easy mark), satisfied by a nosebag, bearing a rather limp stump between his legs too, with a line in repetitive talk that gets on everyone's nerves. So he catches a reflection of himself in a mirror that his thoughts have fashioned from the two horses in the street. Joyce discovered that the language of a drifting slack consciousness makes a more vividly true self-portrait the further the stream of trivialities moves beyond deliberate control.

What happens when Bloom sees himself not as a horse but as another long-nose, a Jew? Will there be a "whatness of all Jew"? As the day goes on, Bloom becomes more like Ulysses returning to Ithaca, less like a kidney-eater on the lookout for erotic adventure. His Jewishness belongs, not quite typically, to the beginning of his day. The implied recognition of Bloom and Stephen as father and son, Ulysses and Telemachus, take the form of a shared drink of

cocoa and parallel arcs of urination side by side in the garden. The exchange of their Jewish-Irish identities consists of some doubtful comparisons of the Hebrew and ancient Irish alphabets, and Stephen's chanting of the folk-ballad about "the jew's daughter" who, with her little penknife, cuts off the head of a little schoolboy. Neither in fake philology nor in legends of ritual murder—age-old incitements to massacres of Jews—is there much possibility of mutual understanding. Better they not try to talk.

> Both then were silent?
>
> Silent, each contemplating the other in both mirrors of the reciprocal flesh of theirhisnothis fellowfaces.
>
> (577)

The most satisfying experience to accost Bloom during his epic day is a vision of a Zionist settlement. It originates from a picture he notices when buying his breakfast kidney. Having put the kettle on to boil, he goes to the pork butcher, Dlugacz, and, while waiting to be served, admires the vigorous hips of the servant-girl from next door who is standing in front of him at the counter. Idly picking up a piece of the cut paper that the butcher uses for wrapping, he finds a picture of cows in a "model farm at Kinnereth on the lakeshore of Tiberias" (48), and the name Moses Montefiore catches his eye. He recognizes the name but his mind wanders to mornings in the cattle market, a breeder slapping a "ripe-meated hindquarter," and by easy transition his gaze rests on the hindquarters in the skirt in front of him, inviting a lecherous mind to a slap; perhaps he will follow her into the street if the butcher hurries up. So much for Kinnereth. Instead, Dlugacz meets Bloom's eye—in spite of his pork butchering he is also Jewish—and flashes the possibility of mutual recognition, Jew meeting Jew. "A speck of eager fire from foxeyes thanked him. He withdrew his gaze after an instant. No: better not: another time" (49).

Outside in the street, the girl has gone, and Bloom's attention returns to the Zionist advertisement. The address is in Berlin—Bleibtreustrasse—Remain True Street. Can Bloom remain true to a tradition he has never known, to a community he has never entered? He can at least be true to himself, if he could find out what being a Jew means. For the moment he dreams of growing oranges in Ottoman Palestine.

> Orangegroves and immense melonfields north of Jaffa. You pay eighty marks and they plant a dunam of land for you with olives, oranges, almonds or citrons . . . Your name entered for life as owner in the book of the union . . .
>
> Nothing doing. Still an idea behind it.
>
> He looked at the cattle, blurred in silver heat. Silver-powdered olive trees. Quiet long days: pruning, ripening.
>
> (49)

The vision does not last, a cloud covers the sun, and a desolate scene takes the place of the orange groves.

No, not like that. A barren land, bare waste. Volcanic lake, the dead sea: no fish, weedless, sunk deep in the earth . . . A dead sea in a dead land, grey and old. Old now. It bore the oldest, the first race. A bent hag crossed from Cassidy's clutching a naggin bottle by the neck. The oldest people. Wandered far away over all the earth, captivity to captivity, multiplying, dying, being born everywhere. It lay there now. It could bear no more. Dead: an old woman's: the grey sunken cunt of the world.

Desolation.

Grey horror seared his flesh.

(50)

Unlike Bloom in 1904 and Joyce in 1922, we can see that Bloom (and Joyce) chose the wrong symbol for their overwhelming sense of desolation about the future of the Jewish people, picturing the land of the first Zionist pioneers as a "dead land, grey and old." Yet, if we change the place to mid-Europe in the 1940s, the same desolation comes over us. We know too well where the "barren land, bare waste" was situated. No one could have anticipated in advance the places and the terrifying circumstances of the extermination camps. But Joyce by sympathetic imagination has made himself aware of Jewish tragedies stretching forwards as well as backwards in time; these are the grey horrors that sear Bloom's flesh. Joyce could not know about the multiplying orange groves and the dunam of land awaiting Leopold Bloom in the state of Israel.

Bloom after all is chiefly a survivor: he lives through cuckoldom and whoredom and boredom as well as anti-Semitic scorn and opprobrium. Yet on the right occasion (not frequently) he shows that he can be a fighter and stand up to persecution, wringing reluctant admiration from his detractors. As one of them says with a sneer, "Old lardyface standing up to the business end of a gun" (273).

The most notable occasion of this is called "Cyclops," from the episode in the Homeric story. Ulysses and his companions are captured by the one-eyed giant Cyclops, but they escape after Ulysses thrusts a stake into the one eye. The blinded giant hurls a rock at the retreating ship large enough to sink it, but it misses, and Ulysses survives once again. The monster in Dublin is an old and gnarled Irish patriot nicknamed "the Citizen" who sits in the corner of Barney Kiernam's pub fighting for Ireland with his ugly mouth, seconded by his repulsive dog Garryowen, and exacting his toll of pints from all comers. The episode is narrated by a despicable voice from the Dublin gutter, a collector of bad debts on behalf of a merchant called Moses Herzog. "'Circumcised?' says Joe. Ay, says I. A bit off the top" (240). Bloom is seen through the eyes of this boozer and sponger when he ventures into Kiernan's on a charitable errand, looking for a friend who will help to clear the insurance money for the widow of an acquaintance who has just died. Bloom takes no drink and does his best to agree with everyone in the idle talk that eddies round the subjects of hangmen, sport, recent trials, flog-

ging in the navy, and the wrongs of Ireland. But he gets into trouble when he stretches the notion of "persecution" beyond indignation against the injustices perpetrated by the Sassenach, the British hyenas.

—Persecution, says [Bloom], all the history of the world is full of it. Perpetuating national hatred among nations . . .

—What is your nation if I may ask? says the citizen.

—Ireland, says Bloom. I was born here. Ireland.

The citizen said nothing only cleared the spit out of his gullet and, gob, he spat a Red bank oyster out of him right in the corner . . .

—And I belong to a race too, says Bloom, that is hated and persecuted. Also now. This very moment. This very instant.

Gob, he near burnt his fingers with the butt of his old cigar.

—Robbed, says he. Plundered. Insulted. Persecuted. Taking what belongs to us by right. At this very moment, says he, putting up his fist, sold by auction off in Morocco like slaves or cattle.

—Are you talking about the new Jerusalem? says the citizen.

—I'm talking about injustice, says Bloom . . .

—But it's no use, says he. Force, hatred, history, all that. That's not life for men and women, insult and hatred. And everybody knows that it's the very opposite of that that is really life.

—What? says Alf.

—Love, says Bloom. I mean the opposite of hatred. I must go now . . .

—That chap? says the citizen. Beggar my neighbour is his motto. Love, moya! He's a nice pattern of a Romeo and Juliet.

(271-3)

The word "love" is not in itself conclusive or resounding, and in its various forms, "lerv," "loov," and "luv," the sound has been even more debased by popular songs since Joyce's day. But "love" is a word that can mean a great deal, as the poets and philosophers have shown us. Bloom does not make it mean very much—he is no poet or philosopher—he is just the kind of average man who makes everything he says or thinks irretrievably ordinary, boring, banal. Yet in an unexpected way he is making an assertion about the banality of goodness that stands in opposition to what Hannah Arendt, in a striking phrase about Eichmann, called "the banality of evil." What is Bloom referring to, as far as his own experience of "love" demonstrates it? Just a bit of kindness, consideration, thoughtfulness, a share of his wife's bed-warmed flesh, a few lascivious thoughts, some memories of his father and of his dead son, an odd reminiscence of "silly Milly" his daughter (as she calls herself to him); the act of picking up someone knocked down by a bully. (It is said the idea for *Ulysses* started when Joyce was picked up, after a scuffle, by a Mr Hunter, who people said was a Jew.) How can this banality of love stand against the whole banality of evil, against the operating machinery of a modern state, against railways merely being efficient, against small officials just doing their jobs, against whole populations who, in indifference or fear, look the other way, against the everyday habit of listening to a Mozart quartet while terrible crimes are going on a few yards away? Hope, Bloom seems to say, is in letting love be as humdrum, unexciting, and uninspiring as common courtesy—and as unremarkable as casual masturbation. But never unheroic. Not something to die for but something to survive for.

The next time Bloom pokes his head into Kiernan's pub he is attacked, though not for his words about love. Nonsensically he is accused of betting on a hot tip and making a packet from a bookmaker without standing drinks all round, as custom demands. A collection of absurd misunderstandings has added up to the situation when he is condemned for a fault and doesn't even know what he is accused of.

> Mean bloody scut. Stand us a drink itself. Devil a sweet fear! There's a jew for you! All for number one. Cute as a shithouse rat. Hundred to five . . .
>
> —Don't tell anyone, says the citizen, letting a bawl out of him. It's a secret.
>
> And the bloody dog woke up and let a growl.

(Here some of the pub loafers hold down the citizen while others get Bloom out into a jaunting car—a stand-in for Ulysses's ship. He shouts back defiantly while the citizen is "on his high horse about the jews.")

> —Mendelssohn was a jew and Karl Marx and Mercadente and Spinoza. And the Saviour was a jew and his father was a jew. Your God.
>
> —He had no father, says Martin . . .
>
> —Well, his uncle was a jew, says he. Your God was a jew. Christ was a jew like me.
>
> Gob, the citizen made a plunge back into the shop.
>
> —By Jesus, says he, I'll brain that bloody jewman for using the holy name. By Jesus, I'll crucify him so I will. Give us that biscuitbox here.

(279-80)

This Cyclops, like his Homeric counterpart, hurled after Ulysses—Bloom—a Jacobs' biscuitbox which missed its target, so that the hero escaped. But Leopold Bloom fled from the pub in a fast car, rather in the way that Elijah ascended to heaven in a fiery chariot. "And there came a voice out of heaven, calling: *Elijah! Elijah!* And He answered with a main cry: *Abba! Adonai!* And they beheld Him even Him, ben Bloom Elijah, amid clouds of angels ascend to the glory of the brightness at an angle of forty-five degrees over Donohoe's in Little Green Street like a shot off a shovel" (283).

Leopold deserves his apotheosis, though his escape is by no means the end of his story. But his ascent completes his specifically Jewish incarnation: he becomes less Jew and more Greek, less Bloom and more Ulysses, a traveller like Sinbad the Sailor and Tinbad the Tailor and Jinbad the Jailer (607) and all the other alliterators.

And Leopold the Jew? The most that James Joyce seems willing to say is that Leopold survives as part of the history that makes the nightmare from which the twentieth century is trying to awake. That awakening Joyce wrote out cryptically in *Finnegans Wake*. But both Ireland and Israel did awake, however difficult and fraught with problems their awakening has been. Perhaps one day Israel and Ireland will become boring enough, banal enough, to awake into a new day of love and peace—the day when the guns will stop. Then they will persuade all the world to celebrate Bloomsday.

Notes

1. All references to *Ulysses* are to the Penguin edition of the corrected text, ed. Hans Walter Gabler with Wolfhard Steppe and Claus Melchior (Harmondsworth, Middlesex, England: Penguin Books Ltd, 1986).

2. Richard Ellmann, *Ulysses on the Liffey* (NY: Oxford University Press 1972), 186.

Susan Rubin Suleiman (essay date 1995)

SOURCE: Suleiman, Susan Rubin. "The Jew in Sartre's *Réflexions sur la question juive*: An Exercise in Historical Reading." In *The Jew in the Text: Modernity and the Construction of Identity,* edited by Linda Nochlin and Tamar Garb, pp. 201-18. London: Thames and Hudson, 1995.

[*In the following essay, Suleiman discusses Jean-Paul Sartre's* Réflexions sur la question juive *in the context of French attitudes toward Jews in the 1940s. Suleiman points out anti-Semitic elements in Sartre's language even as he is criticizing anti-Semitism.*]

> . . . that book is a declaration of war against anti-Semites.
>
> Jean-Paul Sartre[1]

> Sartre is transformed in the third part of his essay into the antisemite against whom he rails in the first part.
>
> Elaine Marks[2]

In a sense, this essay will be nothing more than my attempt to fill in the gap between those two statements, both of which I consider true. Can a "declaration of war against anti-Semites" become itself, at least in part, anti-Semitic? The idea, although paradoxical, is not totally surprising: in the heat of battle, much can easily stick to your skin, without your always knowing whether it is your muck or your enemy's.

Sartre was not an anti-Semite, nor did he harbor any love for anti-Semites. His book *Réflexions sur la question juive* (*Anti-Semite and Jew*) was perceived, at the time of its publication in 1946, exactly as he described it more than thirty years later: a declaration of war against anti-Semites. Because of that book, followed by his unwavering support for the state of Israel, Sartre remained a hero to French Jews until his death and beyond.[3] Some of the first Jewish readers of *Réflexions* found their lives transformed by the experience; among them was twenty-year-old Claude Lanzmann, a young assimilated Jew lucky enough to have survived the war in Paris with all his family. "I remember, I walked the streets differently [after reading Sartre's book], I could breathe again, because the simple fact that the war was over had not changed the way one felt inside," Lanzmann told two interviewers in 1987. Even after the Holocaust, he explained, anti-Semitism persisted in France, and so did the shame and fear experienced by many Jews. But Sartre's book "gave us a feeling of recognition." Against a certain hateful French tradition—one for which "the anti-Semitism of the Nazis was not a foreign tongue," Lanzmann grimly notes—Sartre embodied "another way of being French." It was thanks to Sartre's book, Lanzmann concludes, that he was "once again able to walk with head held high." And the ultimate word of praise: "We could compare Sartre's *Reflections on the Jewish Question* to Zola's 'J'Accuse.'"[4]

I too am a Jewish reader with a long-standing admiration for Sartre. Although I was too young to read *Réflexions sur la question juive* when it first appeared, I read it around fifteen years later, when I was in graduate school; the first chapter, "Portrait of the Anti-Semite," became, for a while, my bible. Sartre not only explained the phenomenology of racism but also gave a striking description of how some human beings, possessed by a "nostalgia for impermeability," are "drawn to the permanence of stone" (20-21). Besides its poetic resonance, Sartre's imagery helped me to understand the thornier analyses of his *L'Etre et le néant* (*Being and Nothingness*): the anti-Semite's desire for stone-like permanence was none other than a refusal of the human condition of "l'être pour soi," a state of chronic incompletion and approximation. Furthermore, the "Portrait of the Anti-Semite" complemented and formed a philosophical commentary on one of Sartre's most brilliant works, the novella *L'Enfance d'un chef* (published in 1939), whose antihero-protagonist is a fictional embodiment of the "portrait."[5]

For all these reasons, I considered *Réflexions sur la question juive* a crucially important book. Imagine my surprise when, upon rereading it after many years, I found myself growing more and more angry and offended. My new responses were provoked not by the first chapter, which I still consider magnificent, but by the third, where Sartre discusses "the Jew." The peculiar effects produced by his argumentation and rhetoric in that chapter warrant detailed analysis, for they amount to nothing less than an "anti-Semite effect" (like Roland Barthes's "reality effect," a

textual phenomenon). If even a staunchly anti-anti-Semitic work can produce such an effect, that fact is worth pondering.

To return to my two epigraphs, the gap I am seeking to fill is neither psychological nor conceptual; as I have suggested, conceptually the two statements are not contradictory. The gap that interests me is empirical, a gap in reading: by what process can one move from reading this well-known work primarily as an act against anti-Semitism, to reading it *also* as an example of anti-Semitism *malgré soi*? And what are the consequences of such a move, for an understanding both of Sartre and of French anti-Semites and Jews? I call these questions empirical rather than hermeneutic (though, of course, they concern interpretation), because they involve specific instances and experiences of reading in specific historical contexts. They are all the more interesting in that they concern "the Jewish question," a notoriously ambiguous concept with a complicated history.

"LA QUESTION JUIVE"

From the start, the "Jewish question" was indissociable from reflections on identity and difference. Tracing the history of the term as it emerged in the 1840's, chiefly in Germany, Jacob Toury notes that its meaning was different from earlier "questions" regarding the Jews: "the emerging 'Jewish question' was not the question of individual rights and of equality between private citizens, but rather the question of the corporate status of Jewry as a whole."[6] The "Jewish question" (*die Jüdische Frage,* then *Judenfrage*) in this modern sense could only emerge when a significant number of Jews had entered civil society as fully fledged citizens, after the French Revolution. As long as the Jews of Europe were isolated in ghettos and physically marked off as Other, there was no question about their separate status; that question arose when they were no longer in the ghetto, indeed when they could be perceived as occupying an inordinately large space in mainstream public life. It was the problematic relation between the Jews' "corporate status"—or, as more virulent and "scientific" versions would later formulate it, their "racial identity" as Jews—and their status as citizens of nation-states that "the Jewish question" posed. But in fact, not much real questioning went on in most versions of "the Jewish question," because (as Toury puts it) "the 'Jewish question' as a slogan did not take roots until it had established itself as an anti-Jewish battle-cry" (p. 92). In other words, those who wrote on the question from the start already knew the answer: the Jews were not only unassimilable, a separate "corporation"; they also constituted a threat, as a group, to the well-being of the nation.

Complications occurred when Jewish writers also began writing about the *Judenfrage,* in order to refute the terms in which it was raised by anti-Semites. Most Jews who wrote about the "Jewish question" in Germany in the mid-nineteenth century "utterly denied the existence . . . of a 'Jewish nation' and of a 'Jewish national character'"

(Toury, p. 101). For them, Judaism was a religion, not a "corporation": there was no such thing as "the Jewish question," unless it meant simply the right of all citizens to freedom of religion. Still later, however, the question of a Jewish national identity was raised in a positive way by Jewish theorists of Zionism. Theodor Herzl's book on the necessity of a Jewish state, *Judenstaat* (1896), bore the subtitle: *Versuch einer modernen Lösung der Judenfrage* ("Attempt at a Modern Solution of the Jewish Question").

To "reflect on the Jewish question," and even more so to reflect on "Reflections on the Jewish question," is necessarily to grapple with political concepts of identity and difference. Put that way, the question of how one reads Sartre's nearly fifty-year-old book takes on a decidedly contemporary ring.

A first ambiguity: why did Sartre choose the title he did, for a book published less than two years after the end of a war whose most notorious slogan was "the final solution"? Solution to what? To the "Jewish question." Clearly, he was being provocative—but provocation is a double-edged sword. For his "war against anti-Semites," Sartre chose a title that evoked tens and hundreds of anti-Semitic pamphlets and articles and special issues of newspapers published in France from the 1880's through the Second World War. From Edouard Drumont to Robert Brasillach, virulent French anti-Semites were concerned about "the Jewish question." In April 1938, Brasillach devoted a whole issue of his weekly newspaper *Je suis partout* (subtitled *Le grand hebdomadaire de la vie mondiale,* "the great weekly of world life") to "La Question Juive." The main message of this special issue, as spelled out by Brasillach and his colleague Lucien Rebatet, was that Jews should be stripped of French nationality: "It is impossible, as many liberals believe, to belong to two nations, the Jewish and the French," wrote Brasillach. "We demand that Jews be returned to their condition as Jews," wrote Rebatet—which meant, for him, "stripping Jews of French citizenship, and of all the rights that go with it."[7]

True, some Jewish publications during those years also used the phrase "question juive"—but after the rise of Nazism, such use was defensive: it was a matter of countering the Nazi or Nazi-inspired use of the term. Thus in 1934, a collective volume titled *La Question Juive* began by citing the persecutions of "Mr. Hitler"; the volume's aim, stated in the introduction, was to "show impartially and clearly the activity undertaken by Israelites [a euphemism preferred by assimilated, upper-middle-class French Jews, instead of "Juifs"] in every domain to make their homeland, France, more prosperous, happier, greater! . . . the Israelites have well served the French family of which they are an integral part, so that they could not be separated from it without doing it grave harm." One "patron" of the volume noted, in a letter reprinted at the end, that in his opinion there should be no "Jewish question" at all. But given what was happening in Germany, he added, it would be both foolish and cowardly to pretend it didn't exist.[8]

By the time of the war, the "Jewish question" had acquired unmistakably anti-Semitic overtones, in France as in Germany. Furthermore, Sartre's title must surely have evoked, for his French readers of 1946, one of the more ignominious institutions of the Vichy regime: the Commissariat Général aux Questions Juives, founded in March 1941, which continued to function until April 1944, shortly before the fall of the regime. The Commissariat was headed during its most active period (May 1942 to February 1944) by Louis Darquier de Pellepoix, who had been a founder of the Comité anti-juif de France (French Anti-Jewish Committee) before the war. During a public speech for the Comité, in May 1937 at the Salle Wagram, Darquier made his memorable statement: "It is extremely urgent to resolve the Jewish question, whether the Jews be expelled or whether they be massacred."[9]

In 1941, before he became Commissaire, Darquier founded a private institute with the support of the Germans, the Institut d'Etude des Questions Juives (Institute for the Study of Jewish Questions, IEQJ), one of whose first activities was the organization of the exhibition "Le Juif et la France." This exhibition, held at the Palais Berlitz on the Boulevard des Italiens from September 1941 to January 1942, brought in, at a conservative estimate, 200,000 paying customers.[10] The catalogue essay (by one J. Marquès Rivière) stated in its opening sentences: "Whether we like it or not, it's a problem. A sore point since forever . . . *the Jewish question dominates the world.*"[11] The proclaimed aim of the exhibition was to instruct and enlighten: the visitor was to learn, by means of "statistics, tables, quotations, documents . . . everything he needs to know in order to defend himself personally and to defend the community of which he is a part against Jewish control."[12] The theme of race dominated both the exhibition and the lectures that accompanied it. More generally, race dominated the preoccupations of the IEQJ, whose secretary-general stated in a public speech in September 1941 that Judaism was not a matter of religion: "for us the Jew is a race and it is on that ground alone that we want to stand."[13] What this meant concretely, in 1941, was that the French Jews who had converted, either in 1940 or before, out of religious conviction or in order to escape persecution, could not count on being "exempted."

Although the IEQJ did not have government status, its position on the "Jewish race" was hardly different from the official Vichy position, as spelled out in the "Jewish laws" of October 1940 and March 1941; the 1941 law defined as Jewish "anyone, regardless of religion, who had at least three grandparents of the Jewish race"—but if the person was married to a Jew, then two grandparents sufficed. As for what constituted "grandparents of the Jewish race," they were grandparents who "belonged to the Jewish religion."[14] Evidently, the "Jewish race" was not easy to define, even for convinced racists. As Michel Leiris pointed out a few years after the war, "the Jews are sufficiently undefinable from an anthropological point of view . . . so that even the Nazis had to fall back on the criterion of religion as a means of discrimination."[15] This difficulty notwithstanding, the IEQJ renamed itself in 1943 as "Institut d'Etude des Questions Juives et Ethno-Raciales" (Institute for the Study of Jewish and Ethno-Racial Questions) under the directorship of an expert in the field of "ethno-racism," Dr. Georges Montandon. Shortly before that, Darquier succeeded in getting the minister of National Education to create a chair at the Sorbonne in the "history of contemporary Judaism," to which a certain Henri Labroue was named in November 1942. He did not have any students, but continued to profess; so much for Jewish Studies under Vichy.[16]

What does all this have to do with Sartre's *Réflexions sur la question juive,* a book whose justly famous opening chapter is the devastating portrait of the anti-Semite? Clearly, Sartre had no connection to Darquier or to his Commissariat or his ethno-racial institutes, other than the connection of an outraged critic. His "Portrait de l'antisémite" (first published separately in *Les Temps Modernes* in November 1945) can be read as a cruelly accurate depiction and analysis of the anti-Semitic personality embodied in Darquier and others of his ilk. But all the more so, the question persists: why did Sartre choose a title as provocatively loaded with anti-Semitic overtones (in 1946) as "la question juive"? One possible answer is that for him the question did not carry anti-Semitic overtones; just as *die Judenfrage* had been adopted by Jewish writers in Germany in the nineteenth century, so "la question juive" had been discussed by Jews and philo-Semites in France. The only trouble with this answer is that it does not adequately take account of the influence of the war and the years immediately preceding it, when "the Jewish question" was a monopoly of the racist Right. I have a strong suspicion that in the immediate postwar years, the words "question juive" (like *Judenfrage* and "the Jewish question") had become so closely associated with Nazism and with the "final solution" that no Jewish or pro-Jewish writer would use them except in quotation marks. Indeed, even today, many people cringe before a non-quotational use of that phrase. It is not an accident, I think, that the title of Sartre's book in English was not "Reflections on the Jewish Question," but *Anti-Semite and Jew.* The idea is the same, but the words are less tainted.

It is possible, of course, that Sartre wanted to provoke by using a loaded term. Interestingly, his explicit provocation with this phrase is directed not at the anti-Semite but at what he calls "the democrat"—the liberal, humanist universalist who claims that since all human beings are equal, "There is no Jew, there is no Jewish question" ("Il n'y a pas de Juif, il n'y a pas de 'question juive'," 67). Sartre attacks this figure in the short second chapter of the book, using an argument that will appear familiar to contemporary theorists of identity politics. Despite his goodwill, says Sartre, the democrat ends up paradoxically close to the anti-Semite, for he too wants to destroy the Jew. Whereas the anti-Semite wants to destroy the Jew as a man, leaving only his Jewishness, the democrat wants to destroy the Jew as a Jew, leaving only his humanity (68). By insisting, against the democrat, that there *is* a "Jewish

question" (the sentence I quoted above is the only occurrence of that phrase in the book—in quotation marks, attributed to the democrat), Sartre thus prepares the way for his own solution to the question. His solution, laid out in the book's fourth and final chapter, is that Jews must take responsibility for ("assume," in the French sense) their Jewishness instead of trying to deny it or hide it. The "authentic" Jew will claim his rights as a citizen *and* as a Jew. Just as a woman who votes, in societies where she has the vote, is fully equal to a male voter without having to "undergo a sex change when she enters the voting booth," so a Jew has full rights as a citizen without having to strip himself of his Jewishness (177). Only the "inauthentic" Jew tries to hide his Jewishness, or as Sartre puts it, "flees from it." The authentic Jew, by assuming his Jewishness, will achieve what his inauthentic counterpart never succeeded in doing: over the course of time, and with the goodwill of Gentiles who are determined to combat anti-Semitism, he will become assimilated into French society (181-2).

In other words, the authentic Jew will finally cease being a Jew. For as Sartre had stated earlier, "the Jew is a man whom other men call Jew" (83); but once the Jew, having chosen authenticity, becomes fully accepted by others, he will no longer be called Jew. It follows inevitably, although Sartre doesn't actually say it, that the Jew will cease to exist. The insensitivity of this argument—since it ends up denying Jewish existence in a more absolute fashion than any "democrat" ever dreamed of—as well as its ignorance of Jewish history and traditions (since it claims they don't exist) has been pointed out by some Jewish critics from the moment Sartre's *Réflexions sur la question juive* was published.[17] Generally, their criticisms have been circumspect, given Sartre's immense intellectual prestige both at the time of publication and later—and given the undeniable courage and brilliance with which he declared his opposition to anti-Semitism, at a time when already anti-Semitism was making a quiet comeback in France.[18] Also praiseworthy was his sincere assertion, at the end of the book, that anti-Semitism was, finally, not the Jews' problem: it was the French who had to change their attitudes, admit their fault, and mend their ways.

Jewish readers recognized his goodwill and were, on the whole, grateful. Still, in one way or another, many Jewish critics writing in French, then and now, have criticized him for not acknowledging the positive existence of Jews; even Albert Memmi, who considered himself a disciple of Sartre and dedicated his 1962 book *Portrait d'un juif* to him, points a strong criticism when he writes, negating Sartre's own words without naming him: "the Jew is not only one whom others consider a Jew. If he were only that, he would, as a Jew, be nothing but pure negativity. . . . The Jew is also a history and traditions, institutions and customs; he has an abundance of properly positive traits."[19]

Sartre has been rightly criticized for defining the Jew only as an absence, a negative quantity. What very few critics appear to have noticed—and this is especially true of those writing in French—is that Sartre does in fact attribute "positive" traits to the Jew, not in the sense of desirable or positively valued, but in that of a positive quantity opposed to zero. All of Chapter Three, the longest chapter in the book, is devoted to a description of what Sartre calls the "inauthentic" Jew, who is most certainly endowed with presence. It is in this description—which, he emphatically declares, is not a "portrait" (157)—that Sartre himself undergoes the metamorphosis Elaine Marks noticed: he becomes, in the space of his writing, an anti-Semite.

"LA RACE JUIVE"

I repeat, "in the space of his writing." What happens in this third chapter is a textual and discursive event: the production of an "anti-Semite effect." How does this happen? Or put another way, how did I became aware of it? Suddenly, in the middle of a page: "I will not deny that there is a Jewish race" ("Je ne nierai pas qu'il y ait une race juive," 73); and at the same time gradually, through the accumulation of details, as the text repeatedly corrects itself, explains itself, finds exceptions to itself, and squeezes itself into a corner. Only a close reading—and furthermore, only an intertextual close reading that situates this text in relation to the anti-Semitic discourses of the Vichy era and of the 1930's—can fully demonstrate my meaning here. While the whole chapter calls for such a reading, in the interest of concision I will follow a single major track, that of race.

Sartre broaches the matter of race very soon after the beginning of the chapter, in a passage that must be quoted in full:

> Je ne nierai pas qu'il y ait une race juive. Mais il faut d'abord nous comprendre. Si l'on entend par race ce complexe indéfinissable où l'on fait entrer pêle-mêle des caractères somatiques et des traits intellectuels et moraux, je n'y crois pas plus qu'aux tables tournantes. Ce que j'appellerai, faute de mieux, caractères ethniques, ce sont certaines conformations physiques héritées qu'on rencontre plus fréquemment chez les Juifs que chez les non-Juifs. Encore convient-il de se montrer prudent: il faudrait plutôt dire *des* races juives. On sait que tous les Sémites ne sont pas Juifs, ce qui complique le problème; on sait aussi que certains Juifs blonds de Russie sont plus éloignés encore d'un Juif crépu d'Algérie que d'un Aryen de Prusse Orientale. En vérité, chaque pays a ses Juifs et la représentation que nous pouvons nous faire de l'Israélite ne correspond guère à celle que s'en font nos voisins. Quand je vivais à Berlin, dans les commencements du régime nazi, j'avais deux amis français dont l'un était Juif et l'autre non. Le Juif présentait un "type sémite accentué"; il avait un nez courbé, les oreilles décollées, les lèvres épaisses. Un Français l'eût reconnu sans hésiter pour israélite. Mais comme il était blond, sec et flegmatique, les Allemands n'y voyaient que du feu; il se divertissait parfois à sortir avec des S.S. qui ne se doutaient pas de sa race et l'un d'eux lui dit un jour: "Je suis capable de reconnaître un Juif à cent mètres." . . . Quoi qu'il en soit et même en admettant que tous

> les Juifs ont certains traits physiques en commun, on ne saurait en conclure, sinon par la plus vague des analogies, qu'ils doivent présenter aussi les mêmes traits de caractère

(73-5).

(I shall not deny that there is a Jewish race. But we must be clear at the start. If by race is understood that indefinable complex into which are tossed pell-mell both somatic characteristics and intellectual and moral traits, I believe in it no more than I do in ouija boards. What, for lack of a better term, I shall call ethnic characteristics, are certain inherited physical configurations that one encounters more frequently among Jews than among non-Jews. But one is well advised to be prudent: we ought to say Jewish *races*. It is known that not all Semites are Jews, which complicates the problem. We also know that certain blond Jews of Russia are still further removed from a woolly-headed Jew of Algeria than from an Aryan of East Prussia. In truth, each country has its Jews and our picture of an Israelite hardly corresponds at all to our neighbors' picture. When I lived in Berlin at the beginning of the Nazi regime, I had two French friends one of whom was a Jew and one of whom was not. The Jew was of a "marked Semitic type": he had a hooked nose, protruding ears, thick lips. A Frenchman would have recognized him as a Jew without hesitation. But since he was blond, lean, and phlegmatic, the Germans were completely taken in. He occasionally amused himself by going out with S.S. men, who did not suspect his race. One of them said to him one day: "I can tell a Jew a hundred yards off." . . . Whatever the case may be, even admitting that all Jews have certain physical traits in common, one could not conclude from that, except by the vaguest of analogies, that they must also show the same traits of character.)[20]

Following Sartre's tortuous, not to say burlesque, path here, we come up with the following remarkable series of thoughts: he does not deny that there is a Jewish race—a rather uncomfortable affirmation, using a double negative and a verb (*nier*) that requires the subjunctive (*qu'il y* ait), which introduces a shadow of a doubt. But let's be clear, he continues: by race, he does not mean a combination of "somatic" (sounds more scientific than "bodily") traits and character traits. No, by ethnic characteristics (ethnic, racial, the terms are apparently equivalent in his mind) he means "certain inherited physical configurations" that are found more frequently among Jews than non-Jews. Note the careful phrasing, avoiding excessive generalization in this delicate area of ethnic science: those physical configurations are not "always" found in Jews, just "more frequently." Indeed, one must be prudent (*encore convient-il d'être prudent*—a properly ponderous turn of phrase) for "it is known" (*on sait*—an impersonal piece of knowledge, a certainty) that not all Semites are Jews, which complicates the problem (this is becoming very serious science). In truth (*in truth*), every country has its own Jews, and our (*our*—that is, French) representation of "the Israelite" (it is more polite to call them Israelites) is not at all like that of our neighbors. The proof of this important piece of truth is that during the year Sartre spent in Germany, the Germans never realized that one of his friends, *whom a*

Frenchman would immediately have recognized as jewish (israelite with a small i) *because of his hooked nose, protruding ears and thick lips,* went totally unrecognized by the Germans! Would you believe it, those stupid S.S. men never suspected his race! One of them even told him, one day, "I could detect a Jew from a hundred meters away." . . . But whatever the case may be, and even admitting that all Jews have certain physical traits in common (here, no subjunctive is used: *même en admettant que tous les Juifs* ont *quelques traits en commun*), nothing would allow one to conclude, except by the vaguest analogy, that they must also present the same character traits. He has thus circled back to the original position: Jewish race equals physical traits but not character traits. In the process, a subjunctive of possible doubt has been replaced by the indicative, albeit in a concessional phrase ("even admitting that").

But the concessive phrasing appears to be an affectation, for the anecdote that precedes it has already made clear that Sartre and the S.S. man he ridicules are equally certain of their ability to recognize "their own Jews," if not each other's Jews. Was Sartre aware of the perfect symmetry between himself proclaiming that "any Frenchman would have recognized him as Jewish" and the S.S. man who claimed he "could tell one from a hundred meters away"? Another noteworthy thing about the anecdote (is it an *histoire juive,* a Jewish joke?) is that Sartre appears to have a certain trouble deciding whether his friend is a Jew or an Israelite, with or without a capital "i." This trouble occurs often in the book, and in several cases a sudden "Israelite" appears after a series of "Jews," all referring to the same person. Until recently in France, "Israelite" was the polite way of referring to French Jews (especially as opposed to Eastern European Jews), and upper-middle-class Jews preferred that nomination. Since Sartre's point in this book was precisely that Jews should not be ashamed of their Jewishness, it would have been logical for him to use only "Juif" (today, most French Jews prefer that term). Curiously, it is his occasional use of the euphemism that strikes one as jarring, indicating unease. In this instance, after some wavering he finally chooses "israelite" and follows it with a mention of his friend's "race" (without quotation marks).

Now at the Commissariat Général aux Questions Juives, they also had some uncertainty on the point of Israelite versus Jew. So much so that in September 1942, Darquier sent out a circular to his staff: Jews were not to be called Israelites, because that would designate them as a religion, not a race. But since they were a race, they had to be referred to as *Juifs.* The word *israélite* was to be used exclusively as an adjective referring to religion, as in *la confession israélite* or *le culte israélite.*[21] Sartre, less consistent, uses "israelite" but associates it with "race."

Why bring Darquier and his racist nonsense back into this discussion? Because I cannot help hearing an echo in Sartre's discourse, almost as if he were in dialogue with Darquier—or with the "expert" Dr. Montandon, director of the Institute for the Study of Jewish and Ethno-Racial Questions. Shortly after taking up his post in 1943, Montandon defined the first aim of the Institute as "the study of questions relating to peoples and races and, particularly in the spiritual, social, political and economic realms, the investigation of the field of activity of persons belonging to the people of Jewish race in France and in the world."[22] Sartre, on the contrary, insists that the "physical traits" of the "Jewish race" are not linked to character traits; therefore, we can conclude that he was repudiating Montandon's kind of "ethno-racial" science. Yet, his very use of the term "Jewish race" in a pseudo-scientific sense and his association of it with physical characteristics that "can be recognized by any Frenchman"—characteristics, furthermore, that correspond almost exactly to Montandon's enumeration of the traits of the "Jewish racial type"—hooked nose, protruding ears, thick lips—strike me as troubling.[23] It is as if he were saying to Montandon: "All right, I accept your notions about their physical characteristics; but you're quite wrong if you think I'll go any further. Character traits? Ah ça alors, non!"

The problem is, he has gone too far already. Edith Thomas, a left-wing writer who was roughly the same age as Sartre, noted in her diary in June 1942: "The wearing of the Jewish star has the virtue of proving to us that there is no such thing as the Jewish race; only one Jew in ten has the classical type that people attribute to them and that is also found, even much more so, among Spaniards and Arabs. . . . The Jews are therefore not *a* race."[24] Sartre, by admitting that all Jews "have some physical traits in common," has ventured down a slippery slope. And this is only the beginning: he will slip much further. I am convinced, incidentally, that he was unaware of where his words were leading him. But that is no reason to stop tracking them—on the contrary, it is the most interesting reason for doing so. I offer, briefly, a few more items from his "race track."

After the above passage, the word race is discussed explicitly one more time, in a complicated maneuver that shows Sartre again engaging with the anti-Semite's discourse, again apparently repudiating it but also echoing it in a troubling way:

> Cette communauté juive qui n'est basée ni sur la nation, ni sur la terre, ni sur la religion, du moins dans la France contemporaine, ni sur les intérêts matériels, mais sur une identité de situation, pourrait être un lien véritablement *spirituel* d'affection, de culture et d'entraide. Mais ses ennemis aussitôt diront qu'elle est ethnique et lui-même [le Juif], fort embarrassé, pour la désigner, usera peut-être du mot de race. Du coup, il donne raison à l'antisémite: "Vous voyez bien qu'il y a une race juive, ils le reconnaissent eux-mêmes et d'ailleurs s'assemblent partout." Et, en effet, si les Juifs veulent puiser dans cette communauté une fierté légitime, comme ils ne peuvent s'enorgueillir, ni d'une oeuvre collective spécifiquement juive, ni d'une civilisation proprement israélite, ni d'un mysticisme commun, il faudra bien pour finir qu'ils exaltent des qualités raciales. Ainsi l'antisémite gagne à tous les coups (103).

(This Jewish community which is based not on nation, land, religion—at least not in contemporary France—or material interests, but only on an identity of situation, might indeed be a true *spiritual* bond of affection, of culture, and of mutual aid. But its enemies will immediately say that it is ethnic, and he [the Jew] himself, at a loss how to designate it, will perhaps use the word *race*. With that, he justifies the anti-Semite: "You see, there is such a thing as a Jewish race, they themselves recognize it, and besides, they stick together everywhere." And, in fact, if the Jews want to draw a legitimate pride from this community, they must indeed end up by exalting racial qualities, since they cannot take pride in any collective work that is specifically Jewish, or in a civilization properly Israelite, or in a common mysticism. Thus the anti-Semite wins on all counts.)[25]

Besides the appalling ignorance Sartre displays here about Jewish history and about specifically Jewish contributions to culture (it appears that he has never heard of the Hebrew Bible or the Kabbalah, for starters), the most remarkable thing about this passage is its suggestion that the Jews' own racism is what provokes the blame of the anti-Semite, whose words Sartre proceeds to quote: "You see, there is such a thing as the Jewish race, they themselves recognize it, they set themselves apart." Then, to top things off, Sartre *seconds* the anti-Semite: since the Jews have nothing to be proud of, "they must indeed end up by exalting racial qualities. . . . Thus the anti-Semite wins on all counts." But the anti-Semite "wins" here only because Sartre agrees with him—agrees with him about the Jews' lack of history and cultural achievement, and agrees with him that the Jews themselves are racists. It is worth recalling that the theme of "Jewish racism"—with its corollaries, Jewish arrogance and Jewish power—was a commonplace of anti-Semitic propaganda in the 1930's. Thus, the front page of *La France enchaînée,* "Organe du Rassemblement Antijuif de France" (headed by Darquier), carried this banner headline in its issue of April 19, 1938: "L'Union Sacree S'Impose contre le Racisme Juif!" ("A Holy Alliance Must Oppose Jewish Racism!").[26] Anti-Semites from Brasillach to Rebatet harped on the "clannishness" of Jews, their refusal to mix with others. Sartre *repeats* the anti-Semitic slogan about "Jewish racism" even as he apparently deplores it.

Note that in this passage, Sartre appears to take his distance from the idea of a "Jewish race," since he has the anti-Semite say: "You see, there is such a thing as a Jewish race," as if addressing someone who contested that notion. Yet—and this is my next item on the list—after this passage I count six explicit uses of the word "race" by Sartre himself, in his own name and without quotation marks, referring to the Jews.[27] This is not counting several other instances where he discusses "Jewish racial traits" without actually using the word "race." For example, in the following extraordinary passage, where he not only offers us his final definition of "ethnic traits," but tells us another anecdote that functions as a fully fledged *histoire juive*:

Quand les Juifs sont entre eux, en effet, chacun d'eux n'est, pour les autres et, par suite, pour lui-même, rien de plus qu'un homme. Ce qui le prouverait, si c'est nécessaire, c'est que, très souvent, les membres d'une même famille ne perçoivent pas les caractères ethniques de leurs parents (par caractères ethniques nous entendons ici les données biologiques héréditaires que nous avons acceptées comme incontestables). Je connaissais une dame juive, dont le fils, vers 1934, était contraint par sa situation de faire certains voyages d'affaires en Allemagne nazie. Ce fils présentait les caractères typiques de l'Israélite français: nez recourbé, écartement des oreilles, etc., mais comme on s'inquiétait de son sort, pendant une de ses absences, sa mère répondit: "Oh! je suis bien tranquille, il n'a absolument pas l'air juif."

(123-4).

(When Jews are among themselves, in effect, each one is, for the others and consequently for himself, nothing more than a man. What would prove this, if it were necessary, is that very often members of the same family do not perceive the ethnic characteristics of their relatives (by ethnic characteristics, I mean here the hereditary biological givens which we have accepted as incontestable). I knew a Jewish lady whose son had to make some business trips into Nazi Germany around 1934. This son had the typical characteristics of the French Israelite—hooked nose, protruding ears, etc.—but when we expressed anxiety about what might happen to him during one of his absences, his mother replied: "Oh, I am not worried; he absolutely does not look Jewish.")[28]

I want to laugh at the joke, but in another way I want to cry. Note how Sartre has slipped, here, from the earlier concessive construction ("even admitting that all Jews have certain physical traits in common") to pseudo-scientific affirmation, and from statistical probability ("certain physical configurations that one encounters more frequently among Jews") to ethnic essence: "the hereditary biological givens that we have accepted as incontestable." *Who* has accepted these "givens" as incontestable? The fact is, by 1946 very few anthropologists believed in the possibility of defining an ethnic group, or even a race (for the two are not, despite what Sartre seemed to believe, synonymous) in terms of "hereditary biological givens." And absolutely no reputable anthropologist, or any other scientist, believed in the existence of a "Jewish race." That idea had been dismissed, by Ernest Renan and others, as early as the 1890's. By the 1940's, only Nazi theorists of "racial hygiene" and "ethno-racial experts" like Dr. Montandon believed that nonsense.[29] Which leaves one wondering, truly wondering, who Sartre's "we" were. . . .

Perhaps we find an answer twenty pages later: "It is known [*On sait*] in effect that the only ethnic characteristics of the Jew are physical. The anti-Semite has seized upon this fact and transformed it into a myth: he claims to detect his enemy by a mere glance."[30] Sartre, too, can detect a "French Israelite" at a glance. Incidentally, his use of the presuppositional *on sait* and *nous savons* ("we know") in these pages deserves a whole separate analysis, as does his use of pronouns in general. Barbara Johnson has noted that an author "can proclaim 'I am this'; but when the image is repeated as 'you are that,' it changes completely. The content of the image may be the same, but its interpersonal use is different."[31] In the discursive system of *Réflexions sur la question juive*, Sartre never even says "You are that" to the Jew. Instead, he addresses an impersonal *on* or a *nous* and says "*He* is that," pointing to the Jew. Independently of the content of his statements (which, as it happens, is already deplorable), his systematic opposition of *on* and *nous* ("we French") to *il* (the Jew) reproduces on the linguistic level the opposition between Frenchmen and Jews that was (and is) a hallmark of racist anti-Semitic ideology.

The last, and perhaps most disturbing, item on Sartre's "race-track": despite his earlier insistence that Jewish "ethnic traits" were only physical, not moral or psychological or other, Sartre spends a large part of this chapter outlining the psychological, intellectual, moral, and economic characteristics of the "inauthentic" Jew, who turns out to be none other than "the Jew" *tout court*. Once again, Sartre *thinks* he is defending the Jew against the anti-Semite's myth, but actually reinforces the myth. The Jew whose portrait he draws is hyper-self-conscious and introspective, has perverse sexual tastes, is tactless and anxious, loves money, and has an inordinate taste for abstraction and rationalism. Bergson's concept of intuition, according to Sartre, cannot "rightfully" (*à bon droit*) be called irrationalist, the way Kierkegaard's or Novalis's thought can; it is, rather, simply rationalism by another name—a "*debaptized* rationalism" (*un rationalisme débaptisé*)![32] Is there any clearer way of saying that Bergson's is a "Jewish philosophy"?

Almost invariably, Sartre begins with an *on dit* ("it is said") that sums up a stereotyped trait—and then, instead of contesting "what is said," he proceeds to *explain* it as the result of a choice by the "inauthentic" Jew. Thus, in the matter of money: "The Jew loves money, it is said. . . . In truth, if the Jew loves money, it is not because he has a peculiar taste for copper or gold coins or for bills."[33] No, it's because money is more "abstract" than land or real estate. Conclusion, after three pages of further explanations: "One sees all the background factors involved in the Jew's taste for money" (*On voit tous les arrière-plans que comporte le goût du Juif pour l'argent*), where it is no longer an unidentified, presumably anti-Semitic *on* who says that the Jew loves money, but Sartre himself.[34]

An even quicker switch occurs in the discussion of Jewish anxiety: "We shall content ourselves in conclusion with indicating in broad strokes what is called [*ce qu'on appelle*] Jewish anxiety. For Jews are often anxious. An Israelite is never sure of his position or of his possessions."[35] We are not dealing with a noble, metaphysical angst in the case of the Jew—it is simple material anxiety for possessions and home that Jews are gripped by, as Sartre "explains" them.[36]

Such are "les traits principaux de la sensibilité juive" (157, "the principal traits of Jewish sensibility"). It would seem that Montandon was right after all: "la race juive" is not only a set of physical traits, but a whole complex of character traits as well.

Some years ago, I saw a Charles Addams cartoon in *The New Yorker*: it showed a man in a barber's chair, looking in the mirror held up behind him by the barber. Actually, there was a whole series of mirrors one behind the other, with the man's bland face reflected in them—in all except one, where his face appeared transformed into that of a werewolf. I thought of that cartoon as I reread Sartre's book. In the beginning and the end, the mirror reflects Sartre the sincere enemy of anti-Semitism and generous defender of the Jews. Somewhere around the middle, the werewolf appears.

CONCLUSION, OR, A QUESTION OF READING

Given Sartre's genuine desire to combat anti-Semitism and defend the Jews (recall the ringing sentences of his final paragraph, so often quoted: "Not one Frenchman will be free so long as the Jews do not enjoy the fulness of their rights. Not one Frenchman will be secure so long as a single Jew—in France or *in the world at large*—can fear for his life"[37]), how can we explain the truly unfortunate "anti-Semite effect" produced by his text? And why did none of his French readers, at the time the book came out, notice this effect (or, if they noticed it, why didn't they say so)? Why, for that matter, did so few American readers notice it?

To the first question, there is an almost ridiculously simple, yet compelling answer; and there is a slightly more complicated one as well. The simple answer is that Sartre sounded like an anti-Semite when speaking about the Jews, because all he knew about them he learned from anti-Semites—in other words, he didn't do his homework. Consider the following exchange in his last interview with Benny Lévy, and notice Lévy's growing amazement. He begins by asking Sartre whether he has changed his mind about the Jews not having any history, and Sartre says yes, but he still doesn't know much about Jews and his not knowing Hebrew is a big obstacle; he certainly knew even less when he wrote *Réflexions sur la question juive*, he adds.

B.L:

But when you wrote your book surely you had put together some documentation?

J.-P.S:

No.

B.L:

What do you mean, no?

J.-P.S:

None. I wrote without any documentation, without reading one Jewish book.

B.L:

> But how did you do it?

J.-P.S:

> I wrote what I thought.

B.L:

> But taking off from what?

J.-P.S:

> Taking off from nothing, taking off from anti-Semitism, which I wanted to combat.[38]

"Taking off from anti-Semitism," is it surprising that Sartre's portrait of the Jew sounds anti-Semitic? It is the opposite that would be surprising.

The more complicated answer is that, like most Frenchmen during the war, Sartre was bombarded by anti-Semitic discourses in the press, on the radio, in newsreels, posters, not to mention ordinary conversations—before the war as well—with people like his stepfather or Simone de Beauvoir's parents, whose anti-Semitic views were quite strong; and that he "soaked it up" without even being aware of it. This is what Christian Delacampagne has called Sartre's being "a man of his time": "These fragments of antisemitism cannot appear as such to Jean-Paul Sartre himself because, in his youth, they constituted a normal opinion in his milieu, an opinion so normal that it was never questioned, and because it is very difficult to rid oneself of such opinions."[39] When you think about it, both answers make Sartre look bad. I don't know what to do about that.

Perhaps the more interesting question is the second one, about what readers have or have not noticed in Sartre's text. Given the conscious good intentions of Sartre's book, which appeared when he was at the height of his prestige as the leader of the new existentialist philosophy in France, it is understandable why none of his contemporary French readers noticed, or allowed themselves to notice, the text's disturbing underside. All the more so since, by the time the book appeared, the unambiguous first chapter, "Portrait de l'antisémite," had already been published in *Les Temps Modernes* and been greeted as a courageous gesture against a reviving anti-Semitism. (By late 1945 and 1946, anti-Semitism in France was visible again despite the postwar purges.) Still, one wonders: didn't Sartre's contemporary French readers, or at the very least his contemporary Jewish readers, catch any echoes of the Institute for the Study of Jewish and Ethno-Racial Questions? *Le Monde juif,* the monthly journal of the then recently founded Centre de la Documentation Juive Contemporaine, printed documents about Darquier's Commissariat Général aux Questions Juives in practically every issue throughout 1946. Yet, when Sartre's book came out, they published the most hyperbolically positive review of any I have read from that time, praising Sartre's courage, his greatness as a writer, and so on.[40]

It was not that Sartre's Jewish readers had forgotten the wartime propaganda about "la race juive" and "la question juive" when they read his book; on the contrary, they remembered them all to well, but Sartre's whole persona was too prestigious, and too strongly identified in their mind with a pro-Jewish stance, for them to hear the anti-Semitic echoes in his discourse. In other words, they were too close to the historical and intertextual context to "make the mistake" (that is what they would have called it, and undoubtedly that is what it would have been) of putting Sartre anywhere near the anti-Semites. I surmise that they noticed the problem with the "portrait of the Jew," were momentarily troubled, then turned their eyes to the more comfortingly negative portrait of the anti-Semite, and even of the "democrat" who would deny Jewish specificity.

This explanation, although plausible, does not help us much to understand why later admiring readers, even professional reader-scholars and critics, have refused to take a long, hard look at Sartre's representation of the Jew. I recently read a 200-page British thesis devoted to *Réflexions sur la question juive,* which does not once appear troubled: according to the author, Sartre "selects certain common anti-Semitic myths" only in order to demystify them.[41] It is very hard to rid oneself of idolatry, and for many of us Sartre was (continues to be) an idol. When I delivered a first version of this essay at a conference of twentieth-century French specialists at Dartmouth College (March 1994), and a month later in a public lecture at Yale University's French department, I was accused by a few indignant colleagues and graduate students, including some old friends, of having totally misunderstood Sartre's text—and furthermore, of having accused Sartre of "being an anti-Semite." (Others, it is true, congratulated me for having described their own reading experience).

As for the American reception of *Anti-Semite and Jew* at the time of its publication, the prestige and celebrity factor played a big role as well, for Sartre was as famous in the United States by 1948 (when the translation appeared) as he was in France. But that did not prevent some American Jewish critics from picking up the anti-Semitic echoes in his text. Thus Gustav Ichheiser in 1949 noted: "He overtly denounces anti-Semitism but unconsciously is not without sympathy with those values and sentiments which are at the bottom of what he denounces."[42] Harold Rosenberg, in a much longer article that same year, praised Sartre for his courageous action in a historical "moment of intense confusion" after the downfall of Nazism; but he went on to criticize Sartre sharply and extensively: "on the basis of his authentic-inauthentic conception, Sartre has consciously permitted himself to accept the anti-Semite's stereotype of the Jew."[43] Did Rosenberg know about the Commissariat Général aux Questions Juives and the Institut d'Etude des Questions Juives et Ethno-Raciales? Probably not. But he didn't have to, because their stereotypes and theories of the Jew were the same as those of Nazi or Nazi-inspired anti-Semites everywhere. Paradoxically, it was Rosenberg's distance from the specific French context that allowed him to see the similarities between Sartre's "portrait of the Jew" and the standard discourse of virulent anti-Semitism.

The same, I would say, was true of Elaine Marks, writing much later (in 1972). Her remark about Sartre being transformed into the anti-Semite he was attacking was based on her intuitive recognition of the anti-Semitic echoes in his text. What I have tried to do here is to study in detail how the "anti-Semite effect" was produced on the level of Sartre's language and rhetoric, and also to document the intertextual context from which his own discourse unfortunately "took off."

Notes

1. Interview with Benny Lévy, "The Last Words of Jean-Paul Sartre," trans. Rachel Phillips Belash, *Dissent* (Fall 1980), p. 418. Sartre died in April 1980; the interview appeared in French in *Le Nouvel Observateur,* March 10, 17, and 24; reprinted in J.-P. Sartre and Benny Lévy, *L'Espoir maintenant.* Lagrasse: Verdier, 1990.

   I wish to thank the following for their help: Sharon Bhagwan for her superb research assistance; Michel Contat, Dorothy Kaufmann, and Stanley Sultan for their careful reading of the manuscript and their critical suggestions; Denis Hollier and Sandy Petrey for disagreeing with me, forcing me to make my own position clearer.

2. Elaine Marks, "The Limits of Ideology and Sensibility: J.-P. Sartre's *Réflexions sur la question juive* and E. M. Cioran's *Un Peuple de solitaires,*" *The French Review* 45, no. 4 (March 1972), p. 784.

3. See, e.g., Salomon Malka, "Une couronne pour Sartre," *L'Arche: Le mensuel du judaisme français* (May 1981), who eulogizes Sartre one year after his death, mentioning *Réflexions sur la question juive* as one indication of Sartre's lifelong "fidelity to Judaism and Israel" (p. 61). I discuss the critical reception of *Réflexions* at the end of this essay. Jean-Paul Sartre, *Réflexions sur la question juive.* Paris: Gallimard, "Folio essais," 1954, p. 54; originally published (by P. Morihien), 1946. Page references, to the 1954 French edition, will be given in parentheses in the text. Unless otherwise stated, all translations from French and German are my own.

4. Interview with Gertrud Koch and Martin Löw-Beer, "Sartre's 'J'accuse.' Ein Gespräch mit Claude Lanzmann," *Babylon: Beiträge zur jüdischen Gegenwart,* 2/1987, pp. 75, 76, 77.

5. I have analyzed *L'Enfance d'un chef* in detail in my *Authoritarian Fictions: The Ideological Novel as a Literary Genre.* Princeton University Press, new edition with new preface, 1993, pp. 244-56.

6. Jacob Toury, "'The Jewish Question': A Semantic Approach," in *Yearbook of the Leo Baeck Institute,*

vol. 11. London: Horovitz Publishing, 1966, p. 95. Subsequent page references are given in parentheses in the text.

7. Brasillach's article, "La Question Juive," appeared on the front page of *Je suis partout,* 15 April 1938; Rebatet's "Esquisse de quelques conclusions," p. 9. A note on p. 1 states that the articles in this special issue—which also contains a large number of anti-Semitic cartoons—were written and asembled by Rebatet.

8. *La Question Juive vue par vingt-six éminentes personalités,* ed. W. Simon. Paris: E. I. F., 1934, introduction by W. Simon pp. 11-12; the "patron" is Louis Schmoll, a lawyer letter p. 108.

9. "Il faut de toute urgence résoudre la question juive, que les Juifs soient expulsés ou qu'ils soient massacrés." Cited in Jean Laloum, *La France antisémite de Darquier de Pellepoix.* Paris: Editions Syros, 1979, p. 17. Laloum gives a detailed history of the Commissariat Général aux Questions Juives, on which my own account is largely based. See also Michael Marrus and Robert Paxton, *Vichy France and the Jews.* New York: Basic Books, 1982.

10. For a detailed study which cites that figure as the low figure, see André Kaspi, "'Le Juif et la France,' une exposition à Paris en 1941," *Le Monde Juif* 79 (1975), pp. 8-20. The exhibit ran from September 5, 1941 to January 15, 1942.

11. "Qu'on le veuille ou non, c'est un problème. Agitée depuis toujours . . . *la question juive domine le monde,*" *Le Juif et la France,* exh. cat., Palais Berlitz, Paris, 1941, p. 7; emphasis in text. Besides the essay, the catalogue contains photographs of installations and a map of the two floors of the exhibition, as well as a preface by the secretary-general of the IEQJ, P. Sézille. As befits the exhibition's didactic mission, the catalogue essay is divided into sections on "Jews in the Middle Ages," "Jews and Revolutions," "Jewish Customs and Mores," "The Secret Power of the Jews," "The Jews Masters of Peoples," and so on.

12. "Les chiffres, les statistiques, les tableaux, les citations, les documents de toute nature que nous avons réunis pour l'édification du public . . . lui apprendront sans effort tout l'essentiel de ce qu'il doit savoir, et pour se défendre personnellement, et pour défendre la collectivité dont il est solidaire, contre l'emprise judaique," ibid., preface (2 pp., unnumbered), by P. Sézille.

13. "Pour nous le Juif est une race et c'est sur ce terrain seul que nous voulons rester." Cited in Kaspi, "'Le Juif et la France,'" p. 13.

14. The texts of the various laws of 1940 and 1941 which defined persons of the "Jewish race" are quoted in Laloum, *La France antisémite,* pp. 90-92.

15. Michel Leiris, "Race et Civilisation" (1951) in *Cinq études d'ethnologie.* Paris: Gonthier, 1969, p. 22.

16. See Laloum, *La France anti-sémite,* p. 73 and pp. 67-8; Marrus and Paxton, *Vichy France and the Jews,* p. 298. Dr. Montandon was the author of several works of "ethno-racial science," including the notorious little pamphlet *Comment reconnaître et expliquer le Juif?.* Paris: Nouvelles éditions françaises, 1940, in which he enumerates the physical and moral characteristics of the "Jewish race." Montandon's clinical work as an "ethno-racial expert" (consisting in measurements to determine whether a given person was "of the Jewish race" or not) is described by Marrus and Paxton, in tragicomico-grotesque terms, pp. 300-01.

17. See, e.g., the long article signed Rabi, "Sartre, portrait d'un philosémite," *Esprit* (October 1947), pp. 532-46. Rabi notes that Sartre reduces Jews to objects, whereas they want to be subjects: "We know that we have a common history . . . ," p. 539; Arnold Mandel, "Retour aux 'Réflexions,'" *L'Arche* 61 (February 1962), p. 48: "In Sartre's postulate there is a categorical negation of Jewish being as belonging to a culture and inheriting a history; Albert Memmi, *Portrait d'un Juif.* Paris: Gallimard, 1962, offers an indirect criticism of Sartre, as I discuss below.

18. Tony Judt, *Past Imperfect: French Intellectuals, 1944-1956.* Berkeley: University of California Press, 1992, pp. 184-6, has faulted Sartre for not condemning Communist anti-Semitism in the Soviet Union and Czechoslovakia in the early 1950's, at the time of the Slansky trial. Sartre's silence, as Judt rightly points out, was due to his anti-anti-Communism at the height of the Cold War. This moral lapse inspired by "global politics" does not diminish the importance of Sartre's denunciation of anti-Semitism at home right after the war.

19. Memmi, *Portrait d'un Juif,* p. 81: "le Juif n'est pas uniquement celui que l'on considère comme Juif. S'il n'était que cela, il ne serait, en tant que Juif, que pure négativité. . . . Le Juif est aussi histoire et traditions, institutions et coutumes, il déborde de traits proprement positifs."

20. Sartre, *Anti-Semite and Jew,* trans. George J. Becker. New York: Grove Press, 1960, pp. 61-2. I have modified the translation somewhat for the sake of precision. Most notably, I have removed the quotation marks around "Aryan." Evidently, the translator felt bothered by Sartre's uncritical use of that disreputable word—he puts it into quotation marks almost each time it occurs. Werner Cohn, "The 'Aryans' of Jean-Paul Sartre: Totalitarian Categories in Western Writing," *Encounter* (December 1981), pp. 87-8, has shown that Sartre referred to "Aryans" quite frequently in this book (17 times), mostly without quotation marks; but Cohn cites evidence to show that even some Jewish writers in the 1940's, in Germany and the United States, used the term uncritically—a fascinating case of being contaminated by the words of the enemy.

21. Cited in Laloum, *La France antisémite,* pp. 76-7.

22. Cited in Laloum, ibid., p. 74, "l'étude des questions se rapportant aux peuples et aux races et, en particulier, dans les domaines spirituel, social, politique et économique, l'investigation du champ d'activitée des personnes appartenant au peuple de race juive en France et dans le monde."

23. Montandon's *Comment reconnaître et expliquer le Juif?* is divided into 2 parts: "Caractères physiques du Juif" and "Portrait moral du Juif." Under physical characteristics (p. 23), Montandon mentions "a strongly convex nose," "fleshy lips," and "eyes not deeply set into their orbits" as primary traits; secondary traits are "curly hair" (indicating "negroid ancestry") and "large, protruding ears."

24. Edith Thomas, *Pages de journal, 1939-1944,* ed. Dorothy Kaufmann. Paris: Viviane Hamy, 1995, pp. 181-2: "Le port de l'étoile juive a ceci d'excellent c'est qu'il nous prouve que la race juive n'existe pas; un sur dix juifs seulement a le type classique qu'on a l'habitude de leur attribuer et qui se retrouve aussi bien et même beaucoup mieux chez les espagnols, les arabes. . . . Les juifs ne sont donc pas *une* race." Entry dated June 24, 1942. Thomas would fit Sartre's definition of the "democrat," since she also states, 18 days before (June 6, 1942), p. 180, that "there is no such thing as the Jewish question" (*il n'y a pas de question juive*). According to her, "the Jewish problem is an imposture." "Democrat" or not, Thomas's views here strike me as less problematic than Sartre's. Thomas, incidentally, was actively involved in the Resistance; Sartre was not.

25. *Anti-Semite and Jew,* p. 84; translation slightly modified.

26. Reproduced in Laloum, *La France antisémite,* following p. 88.

27. In some recent discussions with French friends, I have been repeatedly reminded that the word "race" in French is often used in a general way, with no racist overtones, to mean nation or community linked by a common heritage. Nevertheless, Sartre's use of "Jewish race" is astonishing given the shameful history of that term in the 1940's; besides, as was clear in the first passage quoted, he uses the word "race" in connection with Jews not in its loose sense but in a pseudo-scientific sense.

28. *Anti-Semite and Jew,* pp. 101-02, translation modified. Inexplicably, the English version *omits* the first sentence of this passage (which occurs in the middle of a page). Did the translator consider it too compromising?

29. For a detailed study, see Robert N. Proctor, *Racial Hygiene: Medicine under the Nazis.* Cambridge, MA: Harvard University Press, 1988. Although the concept of "race" is still a subject of debate, it is clear that by the 1940's—partly in response to Nazi theo-

ries—the supposedly biological "givens" of race were largely discredited. Ashley Montagu's study, *Man's Most Dangerous Myth: The Fallacy of Race,* first came out in 1942. New York: Columbia University Press; later editions 1945, 1952, 1961. For a contemporary synthesis, see (among many) Anthony Appiah, "The Uncompleted Argument: Du Bois and the Illusion of Race," in *"Race," Writing, and Difference,* ed. Henry Louis Gates, Jr. University of Chicago Press, 1986, pp. 21-37. As for the "Jewish race," a good brief account of early uses of this term in France is in Michael Marrus, *The Politics of Assimilation: The French Jewish Community at the Time of the Dreyfus Affair.* Oxford: Clarendon Press, 1971, ch. 2. Marrus notes that although at that time French Jews themselves often used the term, they "did not mean by 'race' the same thing as Drumont . . . they meant a sense of community with other Jews" (p. 27). Marrus points out that the enormously influential Ernest Renan *revised* his idea about a "Jewish race" in response to Drumont's anti-Semitic racism: by the early 1890's, he strongly opposed the idea that there was a "distinctly Jewish racial type" (pp. 21-2).

30. *Anti-Semite and Jew,* p. 118, translation modified. "On sait en effet que les seuls caractères ethniques du Juif sont physiques. L'antisémite s'est emparé de ce fait et l'a transformé en mythe: il prétend déceler son ennemi sur un simple coup d'oeil," *Réflexions,* p. 144.

31. Barbara Johnson, "Thresholds of Difference: Structures of Address in Zora Neale Hurston," in Gates, *"Race," Writing, and Difference,* pp. 322-3.

32. *Réflexions,* p. 141. Becker's translation does away with Sartre's Christian image: "a rationalism that has undergone a change of name," p. 16.

33. *Anti-Semite and Jew,* p. 126, translation modified. "Le Juif aime l'argent, dit-on. . . . A vrai dire, si le Juif aime l'argent, ce n'est pas par un goût singulier pour la monnaie de cuivre ou d'or ou pour les billets," *Réflexions,* p. 153.

34. *Anti-Semite and Jew,* p. 128, translation modified; *Réflexions,* p. 156. Again, Becker softens the Eng. version by inserting a crucial adjective, not in Sartre's text: "Thus we see all the background for the Jew's *alleged* taste for money."

35. *Anti-Semite and Jew,* p. 132, translation modified. "Nous nous contenterons, pour finir, d'indiquer à grands traits ce qu'on appelle l'inquiétude juive. Car les Juifs sont souvent inquiets. Un Israélite n'est jamais sûr de sa place ou de ses possessions," *Réflexions,* p. 161.

36. Again, the demon of intertextuality confronts me: Montandon entitled his book "How to recognize and explain the Jew?" (*Comment reconnaître et expliquer le Juif?*). Sartre, *Anti-Semite and Jew,* p. 124, translation modified, writes, in the midst of a whole series of "explanations": "It seems to me that one might explain in the same way the famous Israelite 'lack of tact.' Of course, there is a considerable amount of malice in this accusation." "Il me paraît que l'on pourrait expliquer de la même façon le fameux 'manque de tact' israélite. Bien entendu, il y a dans cette accusation une part considérable de malveillance," *Réflexions,* p. 151. If the accusation is malicious, why "explain" the trait it points to? Sartre's own uneasiness, or perhaps his own split personality with regard to the Jew in this text, is particularly apparent here. Could it also be that—being himself an ultra-rationalist, introspective, anxious man with "perverse" sexual tastes, uncomfortable with his body—he identifies with the "inauthentic" Jew?

37. *Anti-Semite and Jew,* p. 153. "Pas un Français ne sera libre tant que les Juifs ne jouiront pas de la plénitude de leurs droits. Pas un Français ne sera en sécurité tant qu'un Juif, en France et *dans le monde entier,* pourra craindre pour sa vie," *Réflexions,* p. 185, emphasis in text. Suddenly, I notice even here: is Sartre *opposing* Frenchmen to Jews? Or are French Jews included among the "Frenchmen who will not be free," etc? Oh dear. Maybe it is impossible to speak about Jews, or any other ethnic group, from outside the group without running into such problems.

38. "The Last Words of Jean-Paul Sartre," pp. 418-19. Fourteen years earlier, Sartre had already stated in an interview that he had some regrets over his approach in the *Réflexions*: "I should have treated the problem from a double point of view, historical and economic. I limited myself to a phenomenological descriptoin"; quoted in Michel Contat and Michel Rybalka, *Les Ecrits de Sartre.* Paris: Gallimard, 1970, p. 140.

39. Christian Delacampagne, *L'invention du racisme: Antiquité et Moyen-Age.* Paris: Fayard, 1983, p. 27. I discovered Delacampagne's discussion of *Réflexions* only after writing the first draft of this essay (thanks to the author himself). In the few pages he devotes to Sartre's book, Delacampagne cites many of the same phrases and passages I found most disturbing; he concludes that the anti-Semitic echoes are typical of "the most traditional anti-Semitism, that of the French Right before the war" (p. 27). Delacampagne informs me, however, that he no longer believes in his demonstration. I do!

40. Review by Jean-Albert Hesse, *Le Monde juif* (May-June 1947), p. 33.

41. Anthony Blend, "Sartre and the Jewish Question," M. Phil. thesis, University of Southampton, 1988, p. 138 (at the library of the Centre de la Documentation Juive Contemporaine, Paris).

42. Gustav Ichheiser, book review, "*Anti-Semite and Jew* by Jean-Paul Sartre, trans. by George J. Becker," *American Journal of Sociology* 55, no. 1 (July 1949), p. 111.

43. Harold Rosenberg, "Does the Jew Exist? Sartre's Morality Play About Anti-Semitism," *Commentary*, 7, no. 1 (January 1949), p. 15.

Maud Ellmann (essay date 1996)

SOURCE: Ellmann, Maud. "The Imaginary Jew: T. S. Eliot and Ezra Pound." In *Between "Race" and Culture*, edited by Bryan Cheyette, pp. 84-101. Stanford, CA: Stanford University Press, 1996.

[*In the following essay, Ellmann identifies elements of their stance toward Jews in the works of T. S. Eliot and Ezra Pound, concluding that the two poets "projected their own darkness" upon them.*]

> These tears are shaken from the wrath-bearing tree.
>
> —T. S. Eliot, "Gerontion"

T. S. Eliot and Ezra Pound, like Coleridge and Wordsworth, tend to be coupled in literary history and hence to be regarded as accomplices. There are many similarities between them: both rejected the "huge looseness" of the United States, together with its liberal individualism, and fled to Europe in pursuit of pastures old. Both adopted a radical conservatism which, in Pound's case, led to fascism; yet both wrote poetry whose experimentalism poses a puzzling contrast to their political authoritarianism. The most damning resemblance, however, is the antisemitism revealed by both in varying intensities. While Eliot denied the presence of antisemitism in his poetry and attempted to conceal its symptoms in his prose, Pound's prejudices grew increasingly fanatic, culminating in his fascist broadcasts for Rome Radio during World War II.[1] Although he was arrested for treason and incarcerated in a mental hospital, Pound did not repent his ways until 1967, when he reportedly expressed regret for what he lamely termed the "suburban prejudice" of antisemitism.[2] His last years, however, were spent in utter silence, which suggests a more profound and harrowing remorse, of the kind expressed in his last fragments of *The Cantos*: "Let the Gods forgive what I / have made."[3]

Compared to Pound's obsessive vitriol, Eliot's scattered and equivocal discourtesies against the Jews scarcely merit the charge of antisemitism. However, George Steiner has pointed out that "Eliot's uglier touches tend to occur at the heart of very good poetry (which is *not* the case of Pound)."[4] Pound, when seized with hatred, degenerates into obscenity; yet the "uglier touches" in *The Cantos* rarely violate the incandescent lyric passages. *The Cantos* would have benefited from the "caesarian Operation" Pound performed upon *The Waste Land*—removing, among other infelicities, its impalatable passages of antisemitism—but Eliot's early poems would never have survived such cuts.[5] For their aesthetic power depends upon the wrath that bore such figures as the syphilitic Jew, "Spawned in some estaminet of Antwerp," who "squats on

the windowsill" in "Gerontion" (1917); or "Rachel *née* Rabinovich," who "Tears at the grapes with murderous paws" in "Sweeney among the Nightingales" (1920); or the ghastly image in "Burbank with a Baedecker; Bleistein with a Cigar" (1920), in which "the rats" are yoked together with "the Jew" as fellow vermin of the underworld:

> The rats are underneath the piles.
> The Jew is underneath the lot.[6]

This image, which resembles Pound's scatalogical Hell Cantos, also resembles Nazi propaganda films, where juxtaposition is similarly used to insinuate a kinship between rats and Jews. Yet animal imagery is such a commonplace in Jew-baiting and other forms of racist rhetoric that it is strange that Eliot succumbed to the cliché, even if he approved the sentiment. So strange is it that Christopher Ricks has convinced himself that Eliot, at moments like these, is satirizing the *vox populis,* rather than expressing his own views. According to Ricks, even a poem as offensive on first reading as "Burbank with a Beidecker; Bleistein with a Cigar" dissolves into a "multiplicity of partial dramatisations," in which the poet cannot be conclusively identified with any of the poem's points of view.[7]

Another notorious passage occurs in "A Cooking Egg," where Eliot writes:

> The red-eyed scavengers are creeping
> From Kentish Town and Golder's Green.
>
> (*Collected Poems*, p. 45)

These lines probably refer to a popular mythology that Jews were particularly susceptible to eye disease.[8] In the hearings of the 1903 Royal Commission on Alien Immigration, Dr. F. A. C. Tyrell contended that trachoma, a disease of the eyes, was "very largely a disease of race. . . . The Jewish people are peculiarly prone to trachoma." From this standpoint, he was anxious about admitting them into British society. However, other doctors disagreed, arguing that the disease was prevalent in overcrowded districts, "whether occupied by aliens or Christians," being particularly "common among the poor Irish."[9] Either way, eye disease was perceived as an effect of overcrowding and therefore as a malady of urban life. In this respect the English myth of Jewish eye disease resembles the German myth of Jewish flatfootedness, an ailment likewise attributed to "citification." Since the nineteenth century, as Sander Gilman has observed, Jews had been regarded as the embodiments of urban civilization, and their supposed flatfootedness imputed to their sinister work as merchants. At the same time, the malformed foot—like the evil eye to which the image of the "red-eyed scavengers" alludes—also harks back to medieval representations of the devil.[10]

These passages, and others like them in the work of Eliot and Pound, cast doubt on the redemptive power traditionally ascribed to art: its capacity to cure life's ills, absolve its sins, correct its errors, or sublimate its passions.[11] At their worst moments, Eliot and Pound confront us with an art mired in paranoia and delusion, infernal and beyond re-prieve. But it is important to remember that Eliot repeat-edly denied his antisemitism, regarding the accusation as "a terrible slander on a man."[12] Some of his denials took the form of doctoring his prose: the different editions of *Notes Towards the Definition of Culture,* for example, re-veal an attempt to clarify, if not to withdraw, his previous reservations about Jews. The first edition of 1948 con-tained the following statement:

> In certain historical conditions, a fierce exclusiveness may be a necessary condition for the preservation of a culture: the Old Testament bears witness to this.

A footnote continued:

> Since the diaspora, and the scattering of Jews amongst peoples holding the Christian Faith, it may have been unfortunate both for these peoples and for the Jews themselves, that the culture-contact between them has had to be within those neutral zones of culture in which religion could be ignored: and the effect may have been to strengthen the illusion that there can be culture with-out religion.[13]

In the 1962 edition, however, Eliot revised the first part of this footnote to read as follows:

> It seems to me highly desirable that there should be close culture-contact between devout and practising Christians and devout and practising Jews. Much culture-contact in the past has been within those neutral zones of culture in which religion can be ignored, and between Jews and Gentiles both more or less emanci-pated from their religious traditions.
>
> (p. 70)[14]

The first footnote holds the Jewish diaspora responsible for both the Jews' and the Christians' lapse from ortho-doxy, whereas the second exonerates the Jews for this di-lution of tradition. In the revised edition, we are told that only "emancipated" Jews or Christians need be kept apart; "devout" practitioners of either faith may be trusted to withstand the adulterating influence of "culture-contact" with the other. Unpleasant as it is, the second footnote cannot be accused of antisemitism, but merely of a general distrust of laxity.

Even with its original footnote, *Notes Towards the Defini-tion of Culture* caused Eliot less trouble than the previous work, *After Strange Gods* (1934), which he withdrew from print after its first edition. Later he explained to Pound: "'After Strange Gods' is not a good book. Intemperate and unjust, and expresses emotional state of its author rather than critical judgment. . . . I let 'After Strange Gods' go out of print."[15] It was in this work that Eliot made his no-torious pronouncement that "any large number of free-thinking Jews" is "undesirable" in Christian society.[16] By quoting this passage out of context, however, critics have tended to overlook the ambiguities in which it is embed-ded, especially its intertextual preliminaries. Eliot begins by defining his concept of *tradition*:

> Tradition is not solely, or even primarily, the mainte-nance of certain dogmatic beliefs; these beliefs have come to take their living form in the course of the for-mation of a tradition. What I mean by tradition in-volves all those habitual actions, habits, and customs, from the most significant religious rite to our conven-tional way of greeting a stranger, which represent the blood kinship of "the same people living in the same place."[17]

Curiously, Eliot's quotation, "the same people living in the same place," derives from the Cyclops episode of James Joyce's *Ulysses,* in which Leopold Bloom, the Jewish hero, is attempting to define the word *nation* to a bunch of drunken Irish antisemites:

> Bloom was talking and talking with John Wyse and he quite excited with his dunducketymudcoloured mug on him and his old plumeyes rolling about.
>
> —Persecution, says he, all the history of the world is full of it. Perpetuating national hatred among nations.
>
> —But do you know what a nation means? says John Wyse.
>
> —Yes, says Bloom.
>
> —What is it? says John Wyse.
>
> —A nation? says Bloom. A nation is the same people living in the same place.
>
> —By God, then, says Ned, laughing, if that's so I'm a nation for I'm living in the same place for the past five years.
>
> So of course everyone had the laugh at Bloom and says he, trying to muck out of it:
>
> —Or also living in different places.
>
> —That covers my case, says Joe.
>
> —What is your nation if I may ask? says the citizen.
>
> —Ireland, says Bloom. I was born here. Ireland.[18]

In this hilarious exchange, Joyce seems to be anticipating Hannah Arendt's argument that antisemitism is the conse-quence of modern nationalism.[19] If the nation is defined by sameness, as Bloom ventures (or by "blood kinship," as Eliot amplifies), the Jews are bound to be perceived as for-eign bodies at the heart of consanguinity. Bloom, however, claims his Irishness on grounds of birthplace—"I was born here. Ireland"—while he later claims his Jewishness on grounds of "race": "And I belong to a race too, says Bloom, that is hated and persecuted" (*Ulysses,* p. 273). In *After Strange Gods,* Eliot advocates cultural homogeneity, enshrined in his concept of tradition, which is defined as the tendency to sameness in communities; yet he under-cuts this argument by quoting Bloom—the most free-thinking of Jews—in words that Joyce has already con-signed to the ridiculous: "the same people living in the same place."

In 1940 Eliot had an exchange of letters with J. V. Healy, who complained of Pound's antisemitism and also alluded to Eliot's tendencies in this direction. Eliot replied sharply, "As for Mr. Pound, I have already made it clear that I do not associate myself with any of his opinions about Jews. I am no longer in a position to communicate with him."[20] Previously, Eliot had challenged Healy to provide evidence for his allegation; Healy had replied by pointing out the passage on free-thinking Jews from *After Strange Gods*:[21]

> The population should be homogeneous; where two or more cultures exist in the same place they are likely either to be fiercely self-conscious or both to become adulterate. What is still more important is unity of religious background; and reasons of race and religion combine to make any large number of free-thinking Jews undesirable. There must be a proper balance between urban and rural, industrial and agricultural development. And a spirit of excessive tolerance is to be deprecated.
>
> (p. 19)

Eliot defended this passage by insisting that he was objecting to "free-thinking," rather than to Jews per se: "It should be obvious that I think a large number of free-thinkers of any race to be undesirable, and the free-thinking Jews are only a special case." Healy replied: "Assuming that you meant what you now claim to mean, it still strikes me as unfortunate that you should pick on Jews (free-thinkers or not) at a time they were being hounded and tortured."[22] At this point Eliot took umbrage and the correspondence ended acrimoniously. Nonetheless, Eliot probably regretted his remark about free-thinking Jews, since his friend John Hayward, in his edition of Eliot's *Selected Prose* (1953), cut short the excerpt from *After Strange Gods* to end two sentences before the offending passage.[23] To describe this editing as white-washing would be extreme, but the passage looks a good deal less "intemperate and unjust" (in Eliot's words) thanks to its abbreviation.

In 1957, Eliot was again accused of "unambiguous signs of antisemitism," this time by an anonymous reviewer in the *Times Literary Supplement,* who evaded Eliot's subsequent demands for chapter and verse.[24] Christopher Logue replied instead, citing as evidence the passages from Eliot's early poetry discussed above; an editorial from *The Criterion* where Eliot commended the policy statement of *The British Lion,* a fascist publication; and of course, the notorious passage from *After Strange Gods.*[25] In his reply, Eliot demonstrated that Logue, through selective quotation, had misrepresented his editorial in *The Criterion*; but he offered no defenses of his other works, only pointing out that Logue had missed two further passages regularly arrayed against him, including the 1948 footnote in *Notes Towards the Definition of Culture*. It seems that Eliot had finally wearied of self-exculpation.

"Between the conception / And the creation . . . / Falls the Shadow."[26] The contrast between Eliot's intentions toward the Jews and the aspersions that he cast upon them makes one wonder what shadow fell between conception and creation, what unconscious forces tempted him into a prejudice he earnestly disowned. William Empson offers the brilliant suggestion that the "Jew" in Eliot's writing is a stand-in for his Unitarian father:

> Eliot wanted to grouse about his father, and lambasted some imaginary Jews instead. . . . Unitarians describe themselves as Christians but deny that Jesus was God, whereas Eliot was beginning to feel a strong drag towards a return to the worship of the tortured victim. . . . Now if you are hating a purse-proud business man who denies that Jesus is God, into what stereotype does he best fit? He is a Jew, of course.[27]

The value of Empson's reading is its specificity: rather than accusing, he attempts to penetrate the singularity of Eliot's ambivalence. Without this attention to textual and biographical detail, the critic, in exposing antisemitism, always runs the risk of witch-hunting, of re-enacting the paranoia of the antisemite toward the Jew. What was it that troubled Eliot so much about the Jews that he compromised his reputation as a moralist to snub them? Part of the answer may be found in his correspondence with Healy, where Eliot (confirming Empson's suspicions) insists that the Jewish religion, "shorn of its traditional practices, observances and Messianism . . . tends to become a mild and colourless form of Unitarianism." To justify his misgivings about "free-thinking Jews," he argues that the "Jew who is separated from his religious faith is much more deracinated thereby than the descendant of Christians, and it is this deracination that I think dangerous and tending to irresponsibility."[28] Taking Eliot at his word, the remainder of this essay argues that the fear of "deracination" or displacement is the wellspring of much of the antisemitism to be found in Eliot as well as Pound. For both writers, Jewishness comes to stand for the deracinating, mongrelizing, disembodying effects of writing; and the imaginary Jew becomes the mirror image of the poet himself, his diabolical *semblable*.[29]

. . . . .

In his essay "The Music of Poetry" (1942), Eliot compares the relations between words in language to the relations between classes in society:

> Ugly words are . . . words not fitted for the company in which they find themselves; there are words which are ugly because of rawness or because of antiquation; there are words which are ugly because of foreignness or ill-breeding (e.g. *television*): but I do not believe that any word well-established in its own language is either beautiful or ugly. . . . Not all words are equally rich and well-connected: it is part of the business of the poet to dispose the richer among the poorer, at the right points.[30]

This image presents poetic and political ideals as interchangeable: just as a government enforces rank and precedence, so the poet must regulate the pecking order of his words. Immigration should also be controlled, for verbal foreigners, like verbal upstarts, disturb the rooted traditions of the tongue. The poet's task, Eliot claims, is to use "the right word *in the right place,* the rightness depending upon both the explicit intention and an indefinite radiation of sound and sense."³¹ What goes for language goes for people, too, who are best advised to stay where they were born. In *Notes Towards the Definition of Culture,* Eliot argues that "it would appear to be for the best that the great majority of human beings should go on living *in the place* in which they were born" (p. 52, my emphasis). Though he permits some cultural diversity in so-called "satellite" communities, he insists that these subserve a central "orthodoxy," whose role is to maintain the purity of Christian doctrine. Any restlessness within these satellites endangers their integrity, unbalancing the delicate economy of difference. As Terry Eagleton remarks, "When the human beings begin to move, Eliot's structures begin to crumble."³²

For Eliot believes the boundaries of *meaning* to depend upon the boundaries of the speech community. In the epigraph to *Notes Towards the Definition of Culture,* he cites the definition of definition from the *Oxford English Dictionary*: "Definition: I. The setting of bounds; limitation (rare). . . ." To define, then, is to confine, to delimit, to put things in their places and to keep them there. *Dis*placement, on the contrary, erodes the bounds of definition, creating social and semantic turmoil. The fear of such displacement, whether of deracinated peoples or uprooted words, resurfaces throughout Eliot's literary and cultural criticism. In his famous discussion of "dissociation of sensibility," for instance, he accuses Milton of allowing sound to take the place of sense, thus forsaking meaning for mellifluence. According to Eliot, "Language in a healthy state presents the object, is so close to the object that the two are identified." In Milton, however, the pleasure "arises from the *noise*": from a language that refuses to subordinate itself to objects, delighting in the "mazes" of its own sonority. By dissolving meaning into music, Milton bequeathed a fallen language to generations of poets in his wake. Eliot argues that Swinburne's writing, centuries later, exhibits the same deviance: "It is the word which gives [Swinburne] the thrill, not the object."³³

Once word and object are dissociated, the author's personality assumes the limelight, with catastrophic consequences for his poetry. In an essay of 1919, Eliot objects to poems that "make you conscious of having been written by somebody"—and it is the *writtenness,* as much as the *somebody,* that irks him.³⁴ He implies that the author's personality breaks forth when word and object break asunder, when language refuses to defer to what it means. Ideally, words should efface themselves before their referents, as should the somebody who wrote them down. Eliot's famous theory of "impersonality" was devised, at least in part, to counteract displacement, specifically the displacement of the meaning by the word, but also the displacement of the old by the new, the tradition by the individual, the poem by the poet. He introduced the theory in his famous essay "Tradition and the Individual Talent" (1919), where he condemns the Romantic cult of originality, arguing that the values of tradition have been overshadowed by the greed for novelty. He argues that the writer who seeks novelty "*in the wrong place*" merely "discovers the perverse" (*Selected Essays,* p. 21). Instead, the modern writer should cultivate impersonality, sacrificing individual for universal values: only by undergoing this "extinction" in his art can he hope to gain distinction in eternity, purified of self-indulgent idiosyncracies.

In the early 1930s, Eliot renews this crusade, inveighing against "the whole movement of several centuries towards the aggrandisement and exploitation of personality." In its "proper place," he argues, personality may not be damnable; but now that the eternal values of the Church have surrendered to the vagaries of liberal individualism, the author's personality has grown increasingly obstreperous: "It seems to me that the eminent novelists who are nearly contemporary to us, have been more concerned than their predecessors—consciously or not—to impose upon their readers their own *personal view of life*" (*After Strange Gods,* p. 53). Their personalities are therefore *out of place,* having exceeded their permitted bounds; and this displacement is responsible not only for the cult of personality but for every other form of modern "heresy." In *After Strange Gods,* Eliot draws a distinction between "blasphemy," which he admires, and "heresy," which he deplores, arguing that "no one can possibly blaspheme . . . unless he profoundly believes in that which he profanes" (p. 52). This implies that blasphemy is a backhanded form of faith; like the psychoanalytic patient, who denies desires so that they may surface into consciousness ("No, I *don't* want to kill my father!"), the blasphemer, by denying religion, affirms that it is worth the trouble of repudiating. Eliot may have borrowed this idea of blasphemy from *A Rebours* (1884), where Huysmans argues: "Since sacrilege depends on the existence of a religion, it cannot be deliberately and effectively committed except by a believer, for a man would derive no satisfaction whatever from profaning a faith that was unimportant or unknown to him."³⁵ Heresy, on the contrary, seeks faith *in the wrong place,* fetishizing substitutes and simulacra, and thus creates "strange gods"—like Yeats's ghosts, or Pound's Confucius, or Lawrence's dark deities of Mexico—which threaten to dislodge the long-established icons of the West (p. 41).

According to Eliot, Matthew Arnold instigated modern heresy by substituting literature for faith: "Literature, or Culture tended with Arnold to *usurp the place of* religion" (*Selected Essays,* p. 424, my emphasis). As a result of this displacement, religious writings are now appreciated solely for "literary merit," and religious rituals for entertainment value, having been deprived of "the beliefs with which their history has been involved."³⁶ Arnold, Eliot claims, "discovered a new formula: poetry is not religion, but it is a capital substitute for religion—not invalid port, which may lend itself to hypocrisy, but coffee without caffeine, or tea without tannin" (*Use of Poetry,* p. 26). In Arnold's philosophy, poetry supplants belief in the same way that the sound of Milton's verse supplants its sense. In either case, the fetishism of the signifier, of the written or acoustic substance of the word, takes the place of eternal truths, substituting form for content, sound for meaning, rite for faith.

For Eliot, the only way that poets can resist the spread of "heresy" is to return to speech: "every evolution in poetry is apt to be, and often to announce itself to be a return to common speech" (*On Poetry*, p. 31). Speech, because it necessarily involves "one person talking to another," presupposes a community of speakers, and thus confirms the "vital connection between the individual and the race" (*On Poetry*, p. 31; *After Strange Gods*, p. 48). Writing, as opposed to speech, is a solitary, even narcissistic, activity: we write, as we read, alone in silence. Eliot bemoans the fact that "most poetry is written to be read in solitude" (*On Poetry*, p. 17). Disparaging "such individual benefit from poetry," he pleads for "something that it does collectively for us, as a society." An oral literature, such as the poetic drama he struggled to revive, might reunite what he describes as "that mysterious social personality which we call our 'culture'" (pp. 18, 23). If the writer spoke directly to his audience, he would be obliged to honor their collective values instead of flattering his reader's private predilections and his own. Writing, on the contrary, entails the dangerous privacy in which the cult of personality expands, while the author, as a social servant, disappears from view.

It is these anxieties about displacement that give rise to Eliot's imaginary figure of the Jew. At one level the free-thinking Jew stands for the heresy of liberal individualism, epitomized by Unitarianism, that Eliot deplores. Having been raised as a Unitarian himself, his wish to segregate the Jews conceals another wish to cordon off his own free-thinking past. The Jews, for Eliot, represent the adulteration of traditions severed from their living speech and native soil. Yet Eliot himself is doubly displaced, being exiled from a land of exiles, and thus suspiciously resembles those deracinated Jews who endanger his ideal of rootedness. His struggle to transplant himself to England, by dispossessing his American past ("History is now and England"[37]), requires him to disavow his own affinity with the wandering Jew.

At a deeper level, though, Eliot's distrust of Jews corresponds to his distrust of writing. Sooner or later, written words are destined to desert the place of their origination; like Jews, they refuse to remain in the place where they were born. The wandering of words, like the wandering of peoples, erodes the boundaries of the speech community; and Eliot's attempts to control the movements of nomadic Jews correspond to his desire to delimit the dissemination of the written word. Constantly disowning or revising his past writings—especially his remarks about the Jews—Eliot had reason to resent the errancy of written words, their independence from the will of their creator. At the same time, though, his poetry exploits this very errancy, uprooting words from other authors, texts, and nations: "great poets steal." *The Waste Land,* for example, performs a textual diaspora in which the writings of the past deracinate themselves and recombine with words of other ages, languages, and authors, in a limitless process of miscegenation. Thus Eliot, by banishing free-thinking Jews from his utopia, was attempting to banish from himself the forces of displacement exemplified in both his life and his art.

. . . . .

Most of Eliot's expressions of antisemitism occur in his early writings of the 1920s, at a time when such remarks were fashionable. As Leonard Woolf, himself a Jew, observed, "I think T. S. Eliot was antisemitic in the sort of vague way which is not uncommon. He would have denied it quite genuinely."[38] In the 1930s, however, Eliot as editor of *The Criterion* warned Pound that he would terminate their correspondence unless the latter desisted in his Jew-baiting. It seems that Eliot was forced to act upon this threat, judging by his letter to Healy of 1940: "I am no longer in a position to communicate with [Pound]." In the 1930s, therefore, Eliot decisively repudiated antisemitism, though he may have persisted in it without knowing it; but this is an altogether different prejudice from Pound's maniacal crusade against the Jews.

Robert Casillo has distinguished four stages in Pound's career of antisemitism: the first, when he absorbed in childhood the fashionable prejudices of suburban Philadelphia; the second, when he returned to America in 1910-11 and grew alarmed, like Henry James, by the multitudes of recent Jewish immigrants: "There is no swarming like that of Israel once Israel has got a start."[39] The third stage occurred in the late 1920s through the 1930s, when Pound, obsessed with economics, seized upon the quaint idea of "usury" as the key to the decline of the West. During this stage Pound also borrowed from Tadeusz Zielinski the idea that Christianity originated in the Dionysian mysteries ("Christ follows Dionysus / Phallic and ambrosial") but was later corrupted by the Judaic tradition, which produced the flesh-hating austerities of Protestantism.[40] Only in the 1930s, though, did Pound reach the fourth stage of blaming the Jews for all the sins of usury. In his fascist broadcasts for Rome Radio, his antisemitism, like the Nazis', took a racial rather than religious form, in which he vilified the Jews as excrement, disease, and vermin.[41] It is tempting to dismiss these broadcasts as the ravings of a lunatic, except that the views expressed in them were held so widely at the time that madness had become the norm, and reason the anomaly. The fact that the neo-fascist party in Italy, which made important gains in the 1994 elections, decorated its headquarters with the sayings of Ezra Pound shows that we cannot afford either to forget or to extenuate his diatribes against the Jews.

To vilify him in return, however, is to collude in his pursuit of scape-goats and to overlook the complex sources of his antisemitism. Pound's prejudice, like Eliot's, makes sense only in the context of a whole entanglement of phobias, in which the dread of Jews features as a symptom rather than a cause. The next section of this essay investigates the ingenuity of Pound's delusion, the rigor of its blindness to itself, by unraveling the meanings impacted in his personal mythology of usury. Usury means excessive interest rates, but Pound capitalizes on the word itself until it encompasses all forms of exorbitance—especially writing, which he comes to regard as a usurious excess or excrement of speech. In Pound's work, antithesis begets antithesis: usury is opposed to economic health in the same way that writing is opposed to speech, or space to time, or excrement to semen. To track down this contagion of antitheses, it is useful to begin with his analysis of music in *Antheil and the Treatise on Harmony* (1927). Pound opens this work with the complaint that "the element most grossly omitted from treatises on harmony up to the present is the element of Time."[42] He believes that the essence of music is measure, which originates in "the age-lasting rhythms of the craft, cloth-clapping, weaving, spinning, milking, reaping" (p. 88). These crafts obey the living rhythms of nature rather than the deathly ticking of the metronome.

> The early students of harmony were so accustomed to think of music as something with a strong lateral or horizontal motion that they never imagined any one, Any One could be stupid enough to think of it as static; it never entered their heads that people would make music like steam ascending from a morass.
>
> (p. 11)

This "steam," Pound thinks, disfigures rhythm. Wagner, for example, "produced a sort of pea soup, and . . . Debussy distilled it into a heavy mist, which the post-Debussians have desiccated into a heavy dust cloud" (p. 40). It is chords, according to Pound, which are responsible for turning music into swamp gas; being "spatial," chords coagulate the moving energies of rhythm. For this reason Pound compares the analysis of chords to studying "the circulation of the blood from corpses exclusively" (p. 23). Like Henri Bergson, who believed that the fundamental error of western thought was to misconceive of time in terms of space, so Pound believes that everything went wrong in music when space usurped the precedence of time.

"Clogs are spatial," Pound announces to Louis Zukofsky in a letter of 1936, dated "anno XIV" in deference to the fascist calendar. Here Pound is referring to the "clog" of usury; but it is through such metaphors that his early, aesthetic antipathy to space insinuates itself into his later economic theory. "Monetary reform occurs in Time," he writes: the same element of time that inheres in music. When this "Yellyment of Time" prevails in the economy, money moves with unimpeded rhythm. "Whereas clogs (as the German railway signs tells [*sic*] us, are Spatial. raumlich)."[43] Space produces clogs and constipation on the one hand, incontinence and foetor on the other, resulting in a kind of sphincteral collapse of the economy.

Usury, Pound argues, arose in the same era in which space crept into music and corrupted it: by "1200 / or after 1221," at the latest, "it All went to rot."[44] Usury spatializes money in the same way that writing spatializes speech, through an operation Pound describes as "satanic transubstantiation":

Only spoken poetry and unwritten music are composed without any material basis, nor do they become "materialised."

The usurers, in their obscene and pitch-dark century, created this satanic transubstantiation, their Black Mass of money, and in so doing deceived Brooks Adams himself, who was fighting for the peasant and humanity against the monopolists.

". . . Money alone is capable of being transmuted immediately into any form of activity."—This is the idiom of the black myth![45]

Since spoken poetry and unwritten music exist only in time, they cannot be "materialised," and hence cannot be bought or sold. The same "majestic rhythm" that articulates their movement should ideally regulate the flow of cash.[46] Pound believes that money should be treated as a "ticket," because tickets are "timed," and the "timing of budgets" is crucial to economic rhythm.[47] Instead, money has degenerated into a fetish, which hoards the very energies it should unleash. The usurers, in their "obscene and pitch-dark century," spatialized money, which henceforth petrifies and putrifies.

Just as money hoards the powers of production, so writing hoards the energies of speech and music. Once committed to the page, poetry and music undergo "satanic transubstantiation," for they stagnate in space when they should flow in time. According to this logic, writing, insofar as it is spatial, represents the "usury" of speech: for writing clogs the moving energies of speech in the same way that usury obstructs the rhythms of exchange. In Pound's mythology, usury not only blocks financial circulation but also infiltrates the body, deranging its interior economy. In the Hell Cantos, where Pound invents his own inferno for the usurers, the human body is turned inside-out and back-to-front:

> Standing bare-bum.
> Faces smeared on their rumps,
>   wide eye on flat buttock,
> Bush hanging for beard.
>   Addressing crowds through their arse-holes,
> Addressing the multitudes in the Ooze. . . .
>
> (XIV 61)

In this Bosch-like vision, the anus takes the place of mouth and genitals at once and, in defiance of Pound's principle of "clear demarcation," substitutes its "Ooze" for speech and sperm. For usury has seized "Control of the outlets" (CIV 738): be they the outlets of the market, the organs of the news, or even the orifices of the human body. In 1921, Pound proposed the extraordinary theory that the world began with a cosmic ejaculation, whose spermatic force still circulates through art and nature, dispensing incarnation as it moves. The brain itself, he postulated, is a clot of genital fluid, restless to enflesh a second cosmos.[48] The Hell Cantos, however, show how usury derides this spermatic thrust ("phallic and ambrosial") and substitutes the anus's perverse fecundity: "a continual bum-belch / distributing its productions" (XV 65).

This bum-belch is a non-origin, which parodies the very notion of a source. To purify the currencies of words or flesh or finance, Pound believes that it is necessary to return to sources, be they the classics, time, the mint, the phallus, or the sun. But usury is money "created out of nothing," as Pound quotes wrathfully from Paterson, the founder of the Bank of England.[49] It corresponds to the attempt in discourse "to lift zero by its own bootstraps."[50] Having no origin, it also has no destination, and thus defies the very principle of teleology. Wherever usury's influence has spread, foul aftergrowths engorge their origins. Thus Pound, following Dante, condemns usurers and sodomites to the same circle of his inferno, because both seek wealth or pleasure "without regard to production" (XLV 230n), and thus without regard to ends. "By great wisdom sodomy and usury were seen coupled together," Pound writes, for both are enemies of generation.[51] *The Cantos* constantly lament the "*coitu inluminatio*" which has been supplanted by these usurious excesses (e.g., LXXIV 435). In a healthy economy, "any note will by paid"; "the deposits," Pound repeats, "will be satisfied" (LXXXVI 564; XXXVIII 190). But neither sodomy nor the "buggaring bank" is ever satisfied or cashed into production (LXXVII 468). Instead, both fester in the sty of the between. Teeming in darkness, they create an excremental universe, exuberant as the spermatic one they imitate.

It is this *betweenness* that worries Pound more than any of the other crimes of usury, because it undermines the temporal order. "Entering all things," usury *defers*. It comes *between* the stonecutter and the stone, "*between* the young bride and her bride-groom":[52]

> between the usurer and any man who
>   wants to go a good job
>   (perenne)
> without regard to production—
>
>   a charge
> for the use of money or credit.
>
>   (LXXXVII 569)

This passage suggests that any form of interest interrupts production, breeding difference and delay where coitus and generation should occur. Elsewhere, however, Pound insists that even interest had an origin in nature before it was corrupted into usury; for nothing can come of nothing, no matter what the wretched Paterson might say. "The idea of Interest existed before the invention of metal coin," he argues. "And there is MUCH more justification for collecting interest on a loan of seed, on a loan of she-goats and buck-goats, than on a loan of non-breeding, non-breedable metal."[53] He insists that money should "represent something . . . such, namely As rams and ewes."[54] But usury inflates the sign out of all proportion to the signified, so that money stands for nothing but its own unnatural fecundity. "Money is now the NOTHING you get for SOMETHING before you can get ANYTHING," wrote Frederick Soddy, an economist whom Pound admired despite his name.[55]

"Money is an articulation," Pound wrote in 1951. "Prosody is an articulation of the sound of a poem. Money an arti / say National money is articulation of total purchasing power of the nation."[56] It is by means of money that nations articulate their power; by means of prosody that poems budget their expenditure of sound. So close is this analogy between the flow of money and the flow of words that Pound believes the purification of one economy will magically decontaminate the other. Economic "mess" is both the cause and consequence of "muddling and muddying terminology" (*Guide to Kulchur*, p. 31):

> Messes of cliche supplied by Iouce and the restuvum to maintain the iggurance spewed out by the Oozevelt Anschauung.
>
> And the Ooze was possible because writers did not keep the language clean.[57]

This rant, though it appears in a letter of 1954, shows Pound to be arrested in the widespread antisemitism of the 1930s, when the New Deal was frequently maligned as the "Jew Deal" (Pound also calls it the "spew deal"). During this period, the American upper classes, fanatically opposed to Roosevelt, accused the president of being mad, unprincipled, dishonest, alcoholic, syphilitic, Communist—and sometimes, Jewish; many referred to him derisively as "Rosenvelt," although his ancestry, in fact, was Dutch.[58] In the letter quoted above, Pound blames the Ooze of Roosevelt (and the Ooze of usury) on writers who failed to purify the dialect of the tribe. But elsewhere he blames the fall of language on the rise of usury. In *Guide to Kulchur*, he argues that the "infamy which controls English and U.S. finance has made printing a midden, a filth, a mere smear" (p. 184). "Gold bugs against Any order," the usurocracy inscribes the currencies of money and language alike with its excremental signature, its "smear" (LXXXVII 572).

It is through this smear that usury disseminates itself through history, manifesting itself wherever monuments and records are destroyed. If the world was created by an ejaculation, hell's bum-belch is busy decreating it by blotting out its history. "My generation was brought up ham ignorant of economics," Pound frets in a radio broadcast. "History was taught with Omissions of the most vital facts. Every page our generation read was overshadowed by usury" (*Radio Speeches*, p. 339). It is by "destroying the symbols," he declares, that Usura spreads her empire of forgetfulness, and she even keeps herself under erasure. An "octopus," she disappears behind her ink, behind the filth to which she has reduced the printed word (see XXIX 145). The Jews, Pound thinks, are doubly implicated in the crime of usury, for they not only practice it but they refuse to represent or even name their God. Their taboo against the graven image colludes with that compulsion to undefine, erase, unname, unrepresent that Pound identifies with usury. Indeed, the term *semitic* in Pound's writing actually comes to *mean* erasure, particularly the erasure of history: "Time blacked out with the rubber" (VII 25). However, he does not restrict this accusation to the Jews, but extends it to the Protestants whom he regards as their descendants. Protestantism, for Pound, is nothing more than "jewdianity

. . . renewed jewdianity, reJewed whichianity"; it conspires with Judaism "semitically to obliterate values, to efface grades and graduations."[59] When Canto C declares that usury is "beyond race and against race" (798), this is because the semitic is ultimately doomed to obliterate *itself* by destroying boundaries and embastardizing breeds.

Of all usury's assaults on definition, the last and consummate is its erasure of the proper name. In Canto XCVI, Pound despairs of finding anyone "whom the Ooze cannot blacken," because "the stench of the profit motive has covered their names" (XCVI 662). No name is proof against this Ooze, this smear, this "semitic" process of obliteration. What is more, the law of libel forces Pound himself to collude in the erasure of the name, for many of the Semites he would like to damn sneak through *The Cantos* under pseudonyms. "That ass Nataanovitch," for instance:

> Or some better known -ovitch
> whose name we must respect because of the
> law of libel
>
> (XXXV 172)

Pound attacks the law of libel in his *Guide to Kulchur*: "The purpose of law is to eliminate crime not to incubate it and cause it to pullulate" (p. 186). This law flouts Pound's first principle of language and economics: "to call things by their right names—in the market" (XXXIV 168; cf. *Selected Prose,* p. 333). Whereas "clear definition" purges the economy, withdrawing names from circulation only helps to breed the crimes they signify. Like usury, they pullulate in darkness.

Unnamed and unnaming, smearing names with their semitic Ooze, the Jews defy the very principle of definition. Yet Pound, in spite of his crusade for clarity, inculpates himself in this semitic process of erasure. In his typescripts, he uses the £-sign to delete his errors, thus transforming his own name into a wandering obliteration. His first name, too, becomes a synonym for erasure. When he first read *Ulysses,* he disapproved of Bloom's cloacal pleasures, writing coyly to Joyce: "I don't arsk you to erase. . . ."[60] It is of course the arse that Pound would like to ask Joyce to erase; but Joyce noticed that "arse," "erase," and Ezra are virtually anagrams for one another. In *Finnegans Wake,* Ezra is spelt with an "s" ("Esra"), thus exposing its proximity to "arse," "erase," and even "usura."[61] These puns suggest that Pound (£) himself is the usurious currency; while Ezra (Esra) is the other face of the same coin, the hinter-face that belches into hell ("Faces smeared on their rumps / Addressing the multitudes in the Ooze"). As regards his identification with the Jews, Pound himself is disarmingly candid: in *Guide to Kulchur,* he acknowledges his own "nomadic" temperament and adds that "it is not for me to rebuke brother Semite for a similar disposition."[62] It seems that there is more than a fraternal bond between the poet and the race—"beyond race and against race"—that he abominates: for the semitic principle is enshrined in his own name: Ezra the prophet, Ezra the wanderer, Ezra the pound. And if, as *The Cantos* say,

"there is / no end to the journey" (LXX 477), how could Ez defeat Ooze, or Esra erase Usura?

. . . . .

John Berryman, in an essay called "The Imaginary Jew" (1945), describes an occasion of his youth when he was accused of being Jewish by a drunken Irishman in Central Park. "You talk like a Jew," the drunk insisted.

> "What does that mean?" Some part of me wanted to laugh. "How does a Jew talk?"
>
> "They talk like you, buddy."
>
> "That's a fine argument! But if I'm not a Jew, my talk only—"
>
> "You probably are a Jew. You look like a Jew."
>
> "I *look* like a Jew? Listen," I swung around with despair to a man standing next to me, "do I look like a Jew? It doesn't matter whether I do or not—a Jew is as good as anybody and better than this son of a bitch—" I was not exactly excited, I was trying to adapt my language as my need for the crowd, and my sudden respect for its judgment, possessed me. . . .
>
> "You look like a Jew. You talk like a Jew. You *are* a Jew," I heard the Irishman say. . . .
>
> "I'm *not* a Jew," I told him. "I might be, but I'm not. You have no bloody reason to think so, and you can't make a Jew by simply repeating like an idiot that I am."
>
> "Don't deny it, son," said [a] red-faced man, "stand up to him. . . ."
>
> "Jesus, the Jew is excited," said the Irishman.

The argument continues, violent and ridiculous, long into the hot summer night. In the days afterwards, however, Berryman comes to the conclusion that his persecutors were right: he *is* a Jew.

> The imaginary Jew I was was as real as the imaginary Jew hunted down, on other nights and days, in a real Jew. Every murderer strikes the mirror, the lash of the torturer falls on the mirror and cuts the real image, and the real and the imaginary blood flow down together.[63]

This essay, too, has traced the imaginary Jew back to the mirror in which Eliot and Pound gazed unknowingly into their own souls. Both reviled in the Jew what they feared and cherished in themselves: their exile from their homeland and their diaspora among the texts that bear their names. Pound projected onto the imaginary Jew the anal fantasies and phobias enciphered in his name—a persecutor he could never overcome. His anti-semitism, like Eliot's, is founded on identification, and his writings represent a lifelong struggle to exorcise his unknown self.

Freud argues that the psychic mechanism of identification originates in fantasies of cannibalism, whose aim is to possess the object unconditionally. For this reason, identification is "ambivalent from the very first," since eating can preserve the object only at the cost of its destruction:

"The object that we long for and prize is assimilated by eating and is in that way annihilated as such." However, in the case of mourning, the object, once incorporated, preys upon the ego in return, until the latter is "totally impoverished."[64] The work of mourning thus consists of the struggle to devour, but also to disgorge, the things we love.

This theory casts some light on Pound, who is consumed with what he hates, forever struggling to eliminate his own obsession in the form of scatological abracadabras. Both Pound and Eliot reveal the dangers of identification, of this consuming love in which the object has to be destroyed. These dangers also lurk in any politics based upon identification, whether of the right or of the left. To identify oneself as male or female, white or black, gentile or Jew is always to produce a hated double: it is to repeat the error of Eliot and Pound, who projected their own darkness upon the Jews. To avoid this error, we must look beyond the pieties of identity politics to rediscover the radical singularity of human experience. The mirror of identification must be broken if the real and the imaginary bloodshed is to cease.

Notes

1. Eliot reportedly denies the presence of antisemitism in any of his poetry in an unpublished letter to Edward Field, 17 March 1947, in the T. S. Eliot Collection of the University of Texas at Austin (G462). I have not seen this letter.

2. Michael Reck, "A Conversation between Ezra Pound and Allen Ginsberg," *Evergreen Review* 55 (June 1968), pp. 27ff.

3. Canto CXX, *The Cantos* (New York: New Directions, 1970), p. 803. Further references to *The Cantos* will be designated by the Canto number (in Roman numerals) and the page number (in Arabic numerals).

4. George Steiner, letter to *The Listener,* 29 April 1971; cited in Christoper Ricks, *T. S. Eliot and Prejudice* (London: Faber, 1988), p. 28.

5. Letter from Pound to Eliot [24 December 1921], in *The Letters of T. S. Eliot,* ed. Valerie Eliot (London: Faber, 1988), vol. 1, p. 498.

6. "Whatever you do . . . avoid piles," Eliot cautioned a friend after an operation to remove his own in 1951: see Peter Ackroyd, *T. S. Eliot* (Harmondsworth: Penguin, 1984), p. 303. See also T. S. Eliot, *Collected Poems and Plays* (London: Faber, 1969), pp. 37, 56, 41.

7. Ricks, p. 38.

8. I am grateful to John Simons for this suggestion. Another example of Jewish eye disease may be found in the abominable unpublished "Dirge" in T. S. Eliot, *The Waste Land: A Facsimile and Transcript,* ed. Valerie Eliot (London: Faber, 1971), p. [121]:

Full fathom five your Bleistein lies

Under the flatfish and the squids.

Graves' Disease in a dead jew's eyes!

When the crabs have eat the lids.

The whole passage in the manuscript was marked "?? doubtful" by Pound.

9. Cited in Colin Holmes, *Anti-Semitism in British Society, 1879-1939* (London: Edward Arnold, 1979), p. 37.

10. Sander Gilman, *The Jew's Body* (London: Routledge, 1991), ch. 2, esp. pp. 38-49.

11. For a powerful attack on this tradition, see Leo Bersani, *The Culture of Redemption* (Cambridge, Mass.: Harvard University Press, 1990).

12. Quoted by Ricks, p. 61.

13. T. S. Eliot, *Notes Towards the Definition of Culture* (London: Faber, 1948), p. 71.

14. I am grateful to Ronald Schuchard for drawing my attention to this alteration.

15. Letter from Eliot to Pound, 28 December 1959, in Pound Archive, Beinecke; quoted in Maud Ellmann, *The Poetics of Impersonality: T. S. Eliot and Ezra Pound* (Cambridge, Mass.: Harvard University Press, 1987), p. 35.

16. T. S. Eliot, *After Strange Gods* (London: Faber, 1934), p. 19.

17. Ibid., p. 18.

18. James Joyce, *Ulysses* (London: Bodley Head, 1986), pp. 271-72.

19. Hannah Arendt, *The Origins of Totalitarianism* (1951; rpt. New York: Harcourt Brace Jovanovich, 1973), Part I: "Antisemitism."

20. Letter to J. V. Healy, 19 June 1940, T. S. Eliot Collection, University of Texas at Austin (G334); discussed by Ricks, p. 54.

21. T. S. Eliot, Letter to J. V. Healy, 10 May 1940, in T. S. Eliot Collection (G333).

22. Ibid.; cited by Ricks, p. 44.

23. T. S. Eliot, *Selected Prose,* ed. John Hayward (Harmondsworth: Penguin, 1953), pp. 20-21; the four sentences that follow Hayward's excerpt are the most notorious. I am grateful to John Simons for drawing my attention to this ellipsis.

24. "Classical Inhumanism," rev. of Geoffrey Wagner, *Wyndham Lewis, Times Literary Supplement,* 2 August 1957, p. 466.

25. *Times Literary Supplement,* 6 September 1957, p. 533. The editorial cited by Logue is in *Criterion* 7 (1928?), p. 98: "The accusations made by *The Brit-*

ish Lion against British Communists may all be true, and *the aims set forth in the statement of policy are wholly admirable.* The *Lion* wishes to support 'His Majesty the King, his heirs and successors, the present Constitution, the British Empire and the Christian Religion'. These are cardinal points. We would only suggest that the British Lion might very well uphold these things without dressing itself up in an Italian collar." Christopher Logue quotes only the passage italicized above. Eliot's views are more clearly expressed in another editorial in *Criterion* 8 (1928), p. 288, where he declares his preference for Charles Maurras and *Action Française* over fascism: "I am all the more suspicious of fascism as a panacea because I fail so far to find in it any important element, beyond this comfortable feeling that we shall be benevolently ordered about, which was not already in existence. Most of the concepts which might have attracted me in fascism I seem already to have found, in a more digestible form, in the work of Charles Maurras. I say a more digestible form, because I think they have a closer applicability to England than those of fascism." He concludes with the statement: "Both Russian communism and Italian fascism seem to me to have died as political ideas, in becoming political facts" (p. 290). In general terms, Eliot seems to feel that fascism, whatever its success in Italy, cannot be imported into Britain because of its incompatibility with monarchism.

26. Eliot, "The Hollow Men," V (1925), *Collected Poems,* p. 85.

27. William Empson, *Using Biography* (1984); cited by Ricks, p. 47.

28. Letter to Healy, 10 May 1940, T. S. Eliot Collection, University of Texas at Austin; cited by Ricks, p. 44.

29. Extended versions of these arguments may be found in my book, *The Poetics of Impersonality,* pp. 23-61; 149-99; and in my essay "Ezra Pound: The Erasure of History," in Derek Attridge, Geoff Bennington, and Robert Young, eds., *Post-Structuralism and the Question of History* (Cambridge: Cambridge University Press, 1987), pp. 224-62.

30. T. S. Eliot, *On Poetry and Poets* (London: Faber, 1957), pp. 32-33.

31. T. S. Eliot, "The Varieties of Metaphysical Poetry," The Turnbull Lectures, ms., T. S. Eliot Collection, Houghton Library (bMS Am 1261), III; cited in Ellmann, *The Poetics of Impersonality,* p. 54.

32. Terry Eagleton, "Eliot and a Common Culture," in Graham Martin, ed., *Eliot in Perspective: A Symposium* (London: Macmillan, 1970), p. 281.

33. T. S. Eliot, "The Metaphysical Poets" (1921), in *Selected Essays* (London: Faber, 1951), p. 288; "Swinburne as Poet" (1920), *Selected Essays,* p. 327; "Milton I" (1936), in Frank Kermode, ed., *Selected Prose* (London: Faber, 1975), p. 262; "Swinburne as Poet," *Selected Essays,* p. 327.

34. "The Method of Mr Pound," *Athenaeum,* no. 4669 (1919), p. 1065.

35. J.-K. Huysmans, *Against Nature [A Rebours],* trans. Robert Baldick (Harmondsworth: Penguin, 1959), p. 162.

36. T. S. Eliot, *The Use of Poetry and the Use of Criticism* (1933; rpt. London: Faber, 1971), p. 135.

37. T. S. Eliot, *Little Gidding* (1942), V, *Collected Poems,* p. 197.

38. Quoted by Peter Ackroyd, *T. S. Eliot* (Harmondsworth: Penguin, 1984), p. 304.

39. Henry James, *The American Scene* (Bloomington: Indiana University Press, 1968), p. 131.

40. Ezra Pound, "Hugh Selwyn Mauberley (Life and Contacts)," lines 37-38, in *Collected Shorter Poems* (London: Faber, 1968), p. 206. See, for instance, Tadeusz Zielinski, *Our Debt to Antiquity,* trans. Strong and Stewart (London: Routledge, 1909), p. 123.

41. See Robert Casillo, *The Genealogy of Demons: Anti-Semitism, Fascism, and the Myths of Ezra Pound* (Evanston, Ill.: Northwestern University Press, 1988), pp. 4-8.

42. Ezra Pound, *Antheil and the Treatise on Harmony* (1927; rpt. New York: Da Capo Press, 1968), p. 9.

43. Letter to Louis Zukofosky, TS (March? 1936), Pound Archive, Beinecke Library, Yale University.

44. Letter to Boris de Rachewiltz, TS (31 May? 1954), ibid.; cited in Ellmann, "Ezra Pound: The Erasure of History," p. 250.

45. Ezra Pound, *Selected Prose: 1909-1965,* ed. William Cookson (London: Faber, 1973), p. 21.

46. Ezra Pound, *Gold and Work,* Money Pamphlets by £, no. 2 (London: Peter Russell, 1951), p. 12; rpt. in *Selected Prose,* p. 346.

47. Ezra Pound, *Impact: Essays on Ignorance and the Decline of American Civilization,* ed. Noel Stock (Chicago: Henry Regnery, 1960), pp. 91-92. See also XCIX 706: "You forget the timing of budgets/That is to say you probably don't even know that/Officials exist in time."

48. Ezra Pound, Postscript to Rémy de Gourmont, *The Natural Philosophy of Love* (London: Casanova Society, 1926), pp. 179, 169, 174; rpt. in Pound, *Pavannes and Divagations* (Norfolk: New Directions, 1958), pp. 203-14.

49. XLV 233; LXXIV 468; see also *Selected Prose,* pp. 290, 308, 338; and Christopher Hollis, *The Two Nations* (London: Routledge, 1935), ch. 3.

50. Ezra Pound, *Guide to Kulchur* (1938; London: Peter Owen, 1952), p. 78.

51. *Impact,* p. 233; *Selected Prose,* p. 265.

52. XLV 230; Addendum for C 798.

53. *Ezra Pound Speaking: Radio Speeches of World War II,* ed. Leonard J. Doob (Westport, Conn.: Greenwood, 1978), pp. 176-77; see also *Selected Prose,* p. 318.

54. *Radio Speeches,* p. 176; cf. *Selected Prose,* p. 347.

55. Frederick Soddy, "The Role of Money" (1934), in Montgomery Butchart, ed., *Money* (London: Stanley Nott, 1945), p. 268.

56. Letter to Agresti, TS (5 July 1951), Pound Archive, Beinecke Library, Yale University.

57. Letter to Sister Bernetta Quinn, TS (1954), ibid.

58. Myron I. Scholnick, *The New Deal and Anti-Semitism in America* (New York: Garland, 1990), pp. 62-68.

59. Letter to Boris de Rachewiltz (1 August 1954), Berg Collection, New York Public Library; Pound, *Guide to Kulchur,* p. 185.

60. *Pound/Joyce: The Letters of Ezra Pound to James Joyce, with Pound's Essays on Joyce,* ed. Forrest Read (London: Faber, 1966), p. 157.

61. James Joyce, *Finnegans Wake* (1939; rpt. New York: Viking, 1967), p. 116.

62. *Guide to Kulchur,* p. 243; see also my "Floating the Pound: The Circulation of the Subject of *The Cantos,*" *Oxford Literary Review* 3 (1979), p. 26; and Daniel Pearlman, "Ezra Pound: America's Wandering Jew," *Paideuma* 9 (1980), pp. 461-81.

63. John Berryman, "The Imaginary Jew," *The Freedom of the Poet* (New York: Farrar, Straus and Giroux, 1976), pp. 364-66.

64. "Group Psychology" (1921), in the Standard Edition of *The Complete Psychological Works of Sigmund Freud,* trans. James Strachey (London: Hogarth, 1953-74), vol. 18, p. 105; "Mourning and Melancholia" (1917), vol. 14, p. 253.

Phyllis Lassner (essay date 1996)

SOURCE: Lassner, Phyllis. "'The Milk of Our Mothers' Kindness Has Ceased to Flow'": Virginia Woolf, Stevie Smith, and the Representation of the Jew." In *Between "Race" and Culture,* edited by Bryan Cheyette, pp. 129-44. Stanford, CA: Stanford University Press, 1996.

[In the following essay, Lassner points out ambivalent images of Jews in several works by Virginia Woolf and Stevie Smith, respectively, noting that the coming of World War II was a milestone event in both writers' thinking about Jews.]

Among the constantly shifting boundaries of canon formation, perhaps no other text so represents the intersection of gender, modernism, and anti-militarism as Virginia Woolf's *Three Guineas.* In its experiments with genre and form, it constructs a history and theory of fascism through a feminist pacifist polemic. Invoking the figure of Antigone as muse of women's war resistance, *Three Guineas* argues that the history of continuous conflict is evident in the ethos of the patriarchal family and state. Written at the moment World War II is about to begin, even its timing has revolutionary appeal. *Three Guineas* impugns myths of a united nation's victory over the external enemy by exposing as an internal danger England's failure to integrate women into its political economy. Woolf's method interrogates the very logic of a nation's polity as she calls for internal insurrection rather than debates on geopolitical solutions. In a shifting voice that reflects its decentering text, the narrator entreats, parodies, rages, and finally even challenges the oratory of her esteemed contemporary, Churchill. But instead of calling for self-sacrifice in a nation proud of its isolation, Woolf calls for a Society of Outsiders who disclaim the very idea of nationhood.

Three Guineas' self-reflexive, self-questioning form serves as a model by which to question Woolf's ideological assumptions as well as other texts by British women writing about World War II. Nowhere is this more paradigmatic than in her taxonomy of outsider/insurrectionists. "Fighting together" against the "monster Tyrant, Dictator" who "is making distinctions not merely between the sexes, but between the races" are women and Jews (pp. 102-3). In the late 1930s, this linkage is not gratuitous. Woolf's linkage of women and Jews as victims of fascist oppression forms a text that demands explication if we are to understand the consequences of her approach to the formation of fascism. As Jane Marcus has written, "*Three Guineas* was Virginia Woolf's attempt to articulate a unified intellectual position that would connect" the separate battles against the oppressive discourses and structures of "capitalism, imperialism, anti-feminism, and patriarchal culture," the sum of which Woolf constructs as the origins of fascism.[1] In turn, Woolf's text can be read as a critical method by which to examine the representation of Jews in novels of the 1930s and 1940s by British women writers. Adopting her own method of seeking correspondences, I will compare Woolf with the representation of the Jew, women, and fascism in texts also of the 1930s by Stevie Smith. Of different minds about the origins of fascism and the destiny of the Jew, they also inscribe different consequences for their rhetorical strategies.

Marcus explains the self-questioning method of *Three Guineas* as "a nonaggressive feminist/pacifist polemic of 'correspondence' . . . suggesting agreement and [a] harmonious . . . community formed by letter-writing . . . answerable to each other as well as to her" (p. 147). Taking Woolf at her word, one must assume that harmony is achieved only if she too is answerable, not only to her correspondents but to the precepts of her "anti-authoritative," non-aggressive intentions (p. 147). That Woolf took this warrant seriously is evidenced by her responses to those who wrote to her about *Three Guineas*.[2] As Brenda Silver shows, many readers were persuaded by Woolf's rhetoric and her extensive notes and quotations, and indeed, were inspired by Woolf's faith in the written word at a time when the Nazis were twisting words into lessons of hate.[3] Others criticized her denial that women can be militaristic or wish to be politically active. Lady Rhondda writes that she cannot join Woolf's Outsiders' Society if she is to activate her own antiwar views as editor of *Time and Tide* (Silver, p. 263). Complicating the issue of whether and how to take moral responsibility for war is such a desire to be involved; this could be at the personal level of "looking after people rather than [being] . . . looked after" or, as the pacifist Naomi Mitichison considered, one might engage in "revolutionary actions arising from 'intolerable situations' that one shares with one's 'fellow-beings'" (Silver, pp. 263, 264). Such an intolerable situation could be envisaged in the Nazi drive to power and Europe's defensive rearmament, events that made it impossible for other correspondents to "stand aside indifferently . . . when bombs are killing their families and destroying their homes" (Silver, p. 267).

Woolf responded to both compliments and criticisms in letters, in her reading notebooks and diaries, in her essay "Thoughts on Peace in an Air Raid," written to an American audience in 1940, and by implication, in her last, posthumously published novel, *Between the Acts*. Because *Three Guineas* is her response not only to the immediate events leading up to World War II but to what she saw as continuous male aggression, we can see all of her writing in the thirties as a plea to "attack Hitler in England" by responding to his "savage howl" with a call for "the emancipation of man."[4] "Thoughts on Peace in an Air Raid" asks women to reject the "desire to dominate and enslave" that produces "subconscious Hitlerism," just as the "talk of white feathers," she reminds Shena Simon on January 22, 1940, sharpened "the spur of the fighting cock" in World War I.[5] Woolf's images in these writings coincide with her method of dramatizing ideas in *Three Guineas* and thus invite us to see correspondences between its arguments and those figured in her other writing that confronts "the whole iniquity of dictatorship, whether in Oxford or Cambridge, in Whitehall or in Germany, in Italy or in Spain."[6] The symbolic weight of images that achieved political force in *A Room of One's Own* and would shape her fiction emerged in *Three Guineas* as a political rhetoric counterattacking not only the institutional fascism of the patriarchal family but the oratorical power of Mussolini and Hitler.

Part of Woolf's imagistic method is to counter the names of villains with those of victims. Naming Jews as victims of fascism establishes her knowledge not only of Jewish persecution in Nazi Germany but, since she is also critiquing Britain's home-grown fascism, of British antisemitism. In fact, Marcus tells us that Woolf "called herself a Jew," and Woolf herself records in her diaries and letters that she and her Jewish husband planned to commit suicide if the Nazis invaded, because they would both be arrested. How-

ever the Woolfs may have disagreed about the inherent roots of fascism, they certainly concurred about its consequences.[7]

In 1932 Woolf sketched a portrait of "The Great Jeweller," included in her list of "Caricatures," and later developed it into a short story, "The Duchess and the Jeweller." This is not a work that has received any critical attention, although Woolf herself felt "a moment of the old rapture" when copying the story (*Diary,* vol. 5, p. 107). Her "rapture" is clear testament to Woolf's creative drive, for she had to revise the story twice before it was published in *Harper's Bazaar* (London, April 1938; New York, May 1938). The revisions, however, were not her idea but were demanded by her New York agent "on grounds that it was 'a psychological study of a Jew' and thus, because of widespread racial prejudice in America, unacceptable to his (unnamed client)" (*Diary,* vol. 5, p. 107).

The jeweller in question, Oliver Bacon, has worked himself up from "sell[ing] stolen dogs on Sunday" in the alleyways of Whitechapel to become owner of a Mayfair shop famous from Germany to America (p. 249). Being "the richest jeweller in England," however, only marks him as socially vulnerable, for the presence of his most prestigious client, the Duchess of Lambourne, in "the dark little shop in the street off Bond Street" only calls attention to his inability to escape "the dark alley" he left behind (pp. 249, 250). Having decided, against his practical judgment, to save the Duchess from her gambling debts and buy her suspect pearls, he is defeated by her promise of a weekend at her country estate. He has been seduced by the vision of her daughter Diana into buying what turn out in the end to be fake pearls. In fact, the successful jeweller is cut down by the very symbols he attaches to the Duchess's prestige: "the swords and spears of Agincourt" which still aggressively defend Britain's imperial sovereignty (p. 253). In a web of ironies, the world of the Duchess, which is the guarantor of Oliver Bacon's success, remains intact because of his presence as hidden protector. Whenever he buys the Duchess's jewels, he underwrites the power that keeps her estate safe from the likes of him. At the end, the Duchess's duplicity joins forces with Bacon's self-delusion, and he is refigured once again as "a little boy in the alley" (p. 253).

The repetitions which produce the tale's comic ironies take on a different pallor if we examine the published text against the earlier drafts. To be sure, earlier markers of the jeweller's Jewish identity are removed. His original name, Theorodoric, then changed to Isidore Oliver, is, in the published version, ambiguous. Mispronunciations such as "pet" for "bet" are deleted as are references to "crowds of Jewesses."[8] Such changes, however, do not expunge the published story of earlier resonances, for as Susan Dick reports, "In revising the story for publication, VW removed all *direct* references to the fact that the jeweller is a Jew, along with *some* of the details associated with stereotypes of the Jew."[9] Those details and references that remain shape a different kind of irony when read in relation to those Woolf deleted. For example, the published portrait focuses on features that have stereotyped Jews throughout western literature, but in terms that call attention to that stereotype while denying its presence.[10] The narrator introduces us to Oliver Bacon by his "nose, which was long and flexible, like an elephant's trunk" and which

> seemed to say by its curious quiver at the nostrils (but it seemed as if the whole nose quivered, not only the nostrils) that he was not satisfied yet; still smelt something under the ground a little further off. Imagine a giant hog in a pasture rich with truffles; after unearthing this truffle and that, still it smells a bigger, a blacker truffle under the ground further off. So Oliver snuffed always in the rich earth of Mayfair another truffle, a blacker, a bigger further off.
>
> (p. 249)

The very length and twists of this passage resemble the nose it describes, and thus represent Oliver Bacon as the feature most bound to concern Woolf's New York publisher. In addition to their suggestiveness, the sheer number of words Woolf must use to recast the Jewish nose implicates her synecdoche in a suspicious gesture that both elides his Jewish identity and disparages it. While Bacon is a name for both Jews and non-Jews, and thus seemingly innocuous, its link to the hog's character—gluttonous and unclean—leads us on a regrettable course, especially as the place where Oliver learns his craft, the alleyways of East End Whitechapel, is known by Londoners to be a native habitat of the Jew. This is also true of the location of his first shop, Hatton Garden, which Joseph Bannister's 1907 work *England under the Jews* calls a "London nosery."[11] To depict Oliver Bacon as having "dabbled his fingers in ropes of tripe" would seem to reinforce his surname as a sign of non-Jewish character, but since the Jewish identity is present for her English readers, albeit obscured from Americans, the image indicts the Jew nonetheless as desecrating his own tradition, particularly as the ropes of tripe suggest the ropes of pearls which the venal nature of "the hog" cannot resist. As it highlights itself, the repeated and extended imagery that shapes the jeweller's nose and character invokes the revision process, which only highlights the absent antecedents that had been found offensive.

Woolf's two-faced imagery of the jeweller is ironized even more acutely by that which shapes his career. The "wily astute little boy . . . sells stolen dogs on Sunday," an apprenticeship which Woolf creates as a parable of the jeweller's rise to the purlieus of Mayfair by landing him in a shop, not on Bond Street, but "off" (pp. 249, 250). Travestying the Christian sabbath condemns Oliver Bacon to a limbo he is made to deserve. That this is the pale of Jewish jewellers is shown by Margery Allingham's story of the thirties, "The Hat Trick," in which a socialite reports buying a curio "from old Wolfgarten in one of those cute little streets off Bond Street [who] gave me his solemn word by everything he feels to be holy that it's quite u-nique."[12] Based on this Jewish geography, it is no wonder that the Duchess brings her fake pearls to Bacon's es-

tablishment and not one appointed to do business with the king; she simply knows where to bring a shady deal. Oliver is neither a fence, like Fagin or Mr. Benjamin in Trollope's *The Eustace Diamonds,* or even a Mr. Carat in Maria Edgeworth's "The Good Aunt," who buys the aunt's jewels when she needs money but is exposed as a criminal. But as Anne A. Naman points out, these are models for "associating the figure of the Jewish jeweller with criminal deviations from that profession," which thus plays to the audience's acceptance of Jewish characteristics adding up to sleazy characters (p. 119).

These models become even more arresting when we see how much Oliver Bacon and the Duchess share with Trollope's Mr. Benjamin and Lizzie Eustace. Like the Victorian pair, who take advantage of each other's vulnerability and desire, the Duchess and the jeweller "were friends, yet enemies . . . ; each cheated the other, each needed the other, each feared the other, each felt this and knew this every time they touched hands" (p. 251). Although Woolf pities the jeweller for being taken in by his desire for the golden Diana and her world, and satirizes the Duchess as bloated with "prestige, arrogance, and pomp," clearly "the daughter of a hundred Earls" (p. 251) is less at risk at any time than is any Jew in 1938. Woolf accedes to the demand that she not "offend" readers by encoding her "psychological portrait of the Jew" in a dangerous game, one which pits the "wily" Jew against readers who, if they play by Woolf's rules, might share her triumphant last word.[13] For other readers, and this would include other correspondents to *Three Guineas,* such a rhetorical strategy questions Woolf's solidarity with those who are "shut out . . . because you are Jews" and therefore questions her call to fight "the tyranny of the Fascist state" and reject one's own "desire to dominate and enslave."[14]

I single out 1938 because it was the year of publication of "The Duchess and the Jeweller" and *Three Guineas* and coincides with Woolf's diary entries: "Jews persecuted, only just over the Channel" and "The Jews obsess [Leonard's mother]" (*Diary,* vol. 5, pp. 189, 191). Mrs. Woolf was not alone in her obsession, for her son too was "obsessed with" newspaper reports and photographs of "wholesale torture" and saw this persecution as part of a program of "liquidation of tens of thousands of persons, classified . . . for destruction."[15] Given the depth of his concern—although Virginia refers only to that of her mother-in-law—it is not farfetched to see Leonard figured in *Three Guineas* as one of the "outsiders" she would save.[16] He could also be one of the pamphlet's correspondents; his political activism aligns him with the man to whom *Three Guineas* responds and with those who wrote to her later.[17] As we have seen, although a number of these responses survive, Virginia's diary refers only vaguely to Leonard's doubts about *Three Guineas* (vol. 5, pp. 118, 126, 127, 133, 141).[18] We do not have his specific questions, but we can reasonably assume that although the Woolfs had agreed on international peace plans after World War I, by the 1930s, when Leonard was deeply anxious about the threat to Jews of a unique German fascism, his historically specific and pragmatic approach to geopolitics would be incompatible with Virginia's transhistorical, pancultural call to emancipate men's political consciousness.[19]

Such disagreement could have influenced Leonard's dislike of Virginia's 1936 novel, *The Years,* a reaction which made her feel not only "pessimistic, but . . . [that] these are disgusting, racking . . . days" (*Diary,* vol. 5, p. 22). Freema Gottleib speculates that their differences could easily have centered on a passage which "savour[s] of the genteel antisemitism which afflicted Chamberlain's England in the years immediately preceding the Second World War" ("Leonard Woolf," p. 28). The passage begins with North reading a poem to Sara, which is interrupted by the sound of the Jew, Abrahamson, taking a bath. As ritualistic as the bath itself, North and Sara keep repeating the words "The Jew," and with no intervening thought, express their joint disgust at the "line of grease" and hair they picture the Jew leaving.[20] Their direct discourse affirms the view that Woolf represents her character's prejudices rather than her own, and that juxtaposing Sara as a "shabby scapegoat" to the "scapegoats" of *Three Guineas* not only presages the Holocaust, but "transform[s] their diaspora into a conspiracy for 'Justice and Liberty'" (Marcus, *VW,* p. 42).

Two lines of the poem North is reading (Marvell's "The Garden") are printed in the novel and serve as both context and gloss on the passage in question: "Society is all but rude—/ To this delicious solitude. . . ." (*Years,* p. 365). If what North and Sara say about the Jew implicates them in the "rude" society of their "polluted" diaspora (p. 366), what of the narrator/author who has safely absented herself from the characters' direct discourse? North helps us to locate the narrative voice. He reflects that Sara's words refer to her poverty, but her "excitement . . . had created yet another person; another semblance, which one must solidify into one whole" (p. 368). Typical of Woolf's dialectic form, uniting disparate entities into a symbolic bond, the vision here joins the hunchback Sara and the Jew, just as *Three Guineas* joins women and Jews into a Society of Outsiders. Unfortunately, the critical distance which is at stake here collapses with this union, for the very history invoked by the novel's references to dates, the suffragist movement, and the two world wars, distinguishes between the plights of women and Jews as definitively as the novel relates their fates. As Zwerdling argues, because Woolf was so distraught over the coming war and the fragmentation of personal and political relations, she could no longer construct a vision of providential union. Instead, she engages in "antiromantic deflation, the deliberate juxtaposition of beautiful and sordid" in order to represent the "sinister implications . . . of a return from civilization to barbarism" (pp. 315, 306).

The last section of *The Years,* "Present Day," invokes a significant intersection on that "return"—the time when Woolf was writing *The Years* and when North and Sara share their revulsion at the Jew. This is a time, as we now know, when Woolf was aware that ambivalence toward

Jews endangered them as never before, and yet she risks a moral ambiguity that is never clarified. Why, one must ask, are there no images other than that of the Jew to represent the "sordid"? Abiding by Woolf's own vision, the question remains: Where does she position herself as "outsider" when, on the one hand, there is no positive identification with that other outsider, the Jew, and no narrative distance from the "sinister implications" of his portrait?

That Virginia Woolf was capable of "genteel antisemitism" has been well documented. Looking back at her feelings about marrying Leonard, she wrote to Ethel Smyth: "How I hated marrying a Jew . . . how I hated their nasal voices & their oriental jewellry and their noses and their wattles" (Aug. 20, 1930).[21] She added, however, "What a snob I was: for they have immense vitality and I think I like that quality best of all." Allowing for Woolf's personal ambivalence, the question remains one of literary representation and its impact on readers, especially those concerned with her moral and political vision. How do we explain her failure to unify the one vision she never abandoned—that between her art and politics—in short, her failure to integrate her avowed sympathy for the plight of oppressed Jews with her representation of them? The answer lies, I believe, in Woolf's constructions of history, which, while uniquely her own, invest as well in tenets of a modernist aesthetic. If *The Years* is filled with historic moments and mimesis, it is also, as Jane Marcus shows, infused with "mythical motif," allusive of Sophocles' *Antigone,* Wagner's *Ring of the Nibelung,* and Jane Harrison's studies of matriarchal myth (*Languages,* pp. 36-37). Working "as Gotterdammerung," the novel interprets history as apocalypse, and becomes a chronicle of purgation and regeneration (p. 57).

Nowhere is the effect of this mythic history more apparent than in the scene in question where the graphic particulars of plumbing mock a mythic figure—the Jew—Abrahamson, the father and son of Jewish history and myth. In the "sordid" history of how two characters in England between the wars perceive the Jew, the modernist moment fails to distinguish between "genteel anti-semitism," Nazi racial policy, the plight of an impoverished and handicapped woman, and that of a Jew in 1936. The combination of mythic drama and political novel allows elements of each to bleed into the other so that the pungent critique of patriarchal fascism elides the difference between the disenfranchisement of the daughters of educated men and the Jew endangered by a historic moment. This is a moment that may be continuous with earlier persecutions, but within the scope of Woolf's voracious newspaper reading and historical imagination could be recognized as unique.[22]

Woolf's last novel, *Between the Acts,* written when war had already broken out, combines a sense of history as both continuous and riddled with crisis, the effect of which is a confrontation and denial of history.[23] As enacted by the pageant, the characters' dialogue and reflections, and the imagery, history in this novel points to 1939 as a juncture in the continuum of English time from its primordial roots through cultural efflorescence and barbaric regressions. That 1939 marks a downward trend is evinced by a moment of startling violence, when Giles Oliver stomps to death a snake in the throes of strangling on a toad it cannot swallow. All too similar to a stormtrooper, Giles epitomizes the masculine aggression that Woolf felt was responsible for the return to war. Zwerdling argues convincingly that "Giles's behavior is . . . very close to the Fascist threat he fears . . . a good indigenous example of the ethos Woolf had seen in the first days of Italian Fascism" (p. 308). But Giles is unexceptional in the history of England, for the seemingly idyllic village that spawned him suffers from disharmony and xenophobia, as attested to by Miss La Trobe and the Manresas. If Miss La Trobe suffers the indifference of her audience, and Mrs. Manresa is derided as vulgar energy, it is the absent Ralph Manresa who is made to suffer from the text's own ironies. Represented as the construction of village gossip, Ralph is only known as "a Jew, got up to look the very spit and image of the landed gentry, supplied from directing City companies—that was certain—tons of money" (*Between the Acts*, p. 40).

The alien Jew in this novel is the creation of a home-grown fascism which in its anonymous indirect voice is distinct from that of the author and narrator. The quintessential outsider, he is represented only by his garish car and wife, figured, therefore, as an absence, not only from the ancestral country home and the pageant, but from the saga of English history. The Jew's absence and the images which paradoxically mark his presence dramatize the novel's theory of that history as disjunctive; indeed, it is consistent with mocking the Olivers for being two-hundred-year-old newcomers to Pointz Hall, or oppressive, as in Isa Oliver's constrained life. Unlike the Olivers, however, who are pictured at the end of the novel as integrated into the ebb and flow of their national and personal histories, the Jew's position in the novel remains disjunctive and oppressive. Even more extreme than his position in English history, Woolf's novel acknowledges the Jew's rescue as necessary but can't tolerate his difference. The villagers express sympathy: "And what about the Jews? The refugees . . . People like ourselves, beginning life again" (p. 121). Woolf herself showed such sympathy when she sold her *Three Guineas* manuscript to help refugees, but she cannot tolerate the Jew's presence in her fiction of English history.

At the very moment when history was taking a radical turn, Woolf's representation of the Jew is justified by her views of historical process. The title, *Between the Acts*, evokes the two world wars, suggesting that history is both successive and regressive, and that intervals dramatize the conflicts in personal and social relations that make war continuous. Historical time marks continuous sequences of conflict that repeat themselves, because the belief in change is more expedient than recognizing the return of repressed violence. As Rachel Bowlby shows, *Between the Acts* undoes "any stable conception of time on which to peg a conception of history or historical change" because

it challenges "the distinction between serial time and repetitive time."[24] Because serial time is a masculine construct that denies the repetition of man-made violence, it takes the woman writer, as Judith Johnston asserts, to end such repetition, to create the possibility for historical change "even with only the end of an old inky pen" (p. 274).

As Woolf's historical critiques show, change from violence to peace is possible only if authoritarian impulses are recognized as destructive. Reading Freud in 1939 confirmed her belief in "subconscious Hitlerism" but also prompted her revisionary idea that "though many instincts are held more or less in common by both sexes, to fight has always been the man's habit, not the woman's" (*Three Guineas*, p. 6). Woolf committed her writing to the political act of exposing the more insidious aggression sanctioned by social structures. But as Freud also argued, unresolved ambivalence only activates aggression, and this is a dynamic embedded in images of those oppressed people Woolf would save from such hostility. Woolf's construction of gender and unconscious aggression are connected by one of *Three Guineas'* correspondents, Vita Sackville-West: "Is it not true that many women are extremely bellicose and urge their men to fight? . . . I am entirely in agreement with you that they ought not to be like that, but the fact remains that they frequently are."[25]

Woolf's failure to recognize her ambivalence toward her fellow outsiders is made possible by her visionary historical "farsightedness that thought in centuries rather than in decades" (Johnston, p. 260) and across culture and nations.[26] Just as she sees World War II growing out of the chaos of World War I and their "similarities" greater than their differences (Zwerdling, p. 288), so she identifies fascism in English patriarchy as indistinct from German and Italian. That Woolf viewed the Second World War as both coterminous with the last and yet apocalyptic in its own right destroyed her belief in a struggle for change. With boundaries between past and present and war and peace dissolving, there can be no action, including writing, that will turn civilization away from its death instinct. Her conclusion agreed with Freud, as she recorded in her diary on December 9, 1939: "If we're all instinct, the unconscious, whats all this about civilisation, the whole man, freedom & c?" (vol. 5, p. 250).[27] This transhistorical, pancultural view collapses distinct events into an epic battle with the barbarians within and at the gates, and disrupts belief in "individuality and the words and names used to protect this identity."[28]

Woolf's historic vision is challenged by her own creative process. In the second draft of "The Duchess and the Jeweller," the jeweller's name, Isidore Oliver, marks him as Jewish. Like his compatriot, Ralph Manresa, he disappears but is then resurrected as other outsiders: he becomes Oliver Bacon, oppressed by a narrator in league with social prejudice, and supported only when he becomes a gentile woman—Isa Oliver—whose oppression can now be blamed on patriarchal fascism. If Woolf does not distinguish between English patriarchy and the fascism of Hitler and Mussolini, neither does she distinguish her own rhetoric of sympathy for the Jews from her stereotypical portraits and omissions. Woolf's recognition of the political consequences of unconscious aggression is the reality test by which we can view her ambivalent images of Jews and their disturbing presence in her construction of a mythic history and pessimism about change.

In the same years Woolf was writing *Three Guineas,* other British women writers were self-consciously confronting British antisemitism as a phenomenon deeply entrenched in British culture but distinguished from other political injustices for its particular dangers in the 1930s. One writer who serves as a respondent to Woolf is the poet Stevie Smith, who wrote *Novel on Yellow Paper* in 1936 and *Over the Frontier* in 1938. Smith's experimental forms and narrative voice construct an inquiry into war and oppression that questions the political implications of Woolf's vision of history. Smith's narrator confronts both herself and her readers with an ambivalence toward Jews that impugns the viability of a "Society of Outsiders" at a time when a form of fascism had emerged under a particular "tyrant/dictator" whose racial politics were unique in their enforcement. Read together, Woolf's polemics and images of Jews and Smith's novels provide a critique of women's construction of their own roles in a total war on the outsider.

In two volumes of unmediated, monologic discourse, Smith's female hero, Pompey Casmilus, conducts an inquiry into the role of individual and collective consciousness in the history of war and aggression. With great glee, she indicts Britain's imperial past, as the perpetrator of violence in both its acts and rhetoric, but confronts personal political consciousness as having a formative role in the collective.[29] Historical event is represented in personal reflection which, because it is driven by unresolved ambivalence, emerges as hostile speech that colludes with a masculinist war machine. In 1938, the year *Over the Frontier* is published, the aggressive impulses that were seething in the first volume materialize in a midnight ride over the frontier of reality and fantasy, enacting a "racial hatred that is running in me in a sudden swift current, in a swift tide of hatred" (p. 159). But Pompey does not ride alone, for although her lover, Major Tom Satterthwaite, is too sick to accompany her, she makes sure that we do, for in her direct discourse she not only shares her words with us, she implicates us in them. Unlike Woolf's construction of harmonious correspondents, Smith challenges her readers to react against her and thus discover their own politics.

Like Virginia Woolf, Smith preferred writing as her act of political protest, and also experimented with forms that would question intersections of realism and representation. Instead of reifying mythological structures to envision historical process, however, Smith deploys them to expose their dangers to political discourse. Thus even Pompey Casmilus's name ironizes her political consciousness. The men for whom she is named signify a historical continuum

of aggression that infuses her identity and consciousness by inscribing her into the myths that justify violence and war. The war god and the general whose patronymics she bears and whose violence she inherits are the icons of myths that give us power over the "dreams that come to us in the night that are full of cruelty" (p. 56). As Pompey's name and the novel imply, art and myth are implicated in both power and cruelty, because their persuasive force often serves ambiguous representations of power and cruelty. The only plot these novels can claim is the unraveling of Pompey's ambivalences as a critical exegesis of art's collusion with myths of power. Her zany, whirlwind associations, readings of history, painting, and myth, decenter the power of coherent explanation by revealing how it occludes distinctions between self-determination and the oppression of others. The result, she shows, is how easily art and myth are appropriated to justify violence and war. Pompey's "Januslike-double-faced" feelings toward "Jewfriends" represent that occlusion in order to show how oppression of the other inheres dangerously in self-determination (*Yellow Paper,* p. 13).

Over the Frontier begins with Pompey's ironic self-reflections on Georg Grosz's painting of a horse and rider, "Haute Ecole." She analyzes not only her reactions to the painting but her associations with its historical and political contexts. It thus becomes impossible for her to appreciate the "passion and integrity" of the "ferocious and captive animal" without considering the artist's and viewer's complicity in the enigmatic quality of "his degenerate rider" (pp. 16, 11, 15). As Pompey veers through Grosz's career and life, her reading of "Haute Ecole" is clarified by its relation to his "cynical and malicious" satires, his portfolio of "war suffering," her associations with "the tearing seering suffering of Germany after the war," Grosz's "escape to America," and her own escape into art from "the shame and dishonor the power of the cruelty" that stretches "to the very last outposts of the black heart of despair" (pp. 12, 14, 15, 16). The allusion to Conrad's *Heart of Darkness* invokes not a male bastion of brutality, but Pompey's questioning "of the heart feminine," which, because it is just as "numb and ripe for death," can mobilize the cruel messages of art and myth as her ride over the frontier testifies (pp. 17, 18).

Pompey's ride into war's theater of cruelty begins in *Novel on Yellow Paper,* when she confronts her "mixed feelings towards the Jews" (Spalding, p. 18). Indulging her self-pity at being "the only goy" at a party hosted by Jewish friends, she discovers a miracle cure by identifying with the aggression of her namesakes (*Yellow Paper,* p. 11). She can be "shot right up" by deciding that "a clever goy is cleverer than a clever Jew" (p. 11). This is the power that she would later realize is part of the "cruelty [that] is very much in the air now, it is very dangerous, it is a powerful drug that deadens as it stimulates" (*Frontier,* p. 56). In 1936 and 1938 Stevie Smith interrogates myths of Anglo-Saxon moral hegemony by implicating a woman's voice in the rhetoric of the enemy's racial politics. Oppressed as much by the self-containment of her Jewish friends as she is by identifying with their oppression, she assumes an ambiguous position of addressing and expressing the social and political constructions of antisemitism:

> Do all goys among Jews get that way? Yes, perhaps. And the feeling you must pipe down and apologize for being so superior and clever: I can't help it really my dear chap, you see I'm a goy. It just comes with the birth. It's a world of unequal chances, not the way B. Franklin saw things. But perhaps he was piping down in public, and apologizing he was a goy. And there were Jews then too. So he put equality on paper and hoped it would do, and hoped nobody would take it seriously. And nobody did.
>
> *(Yellow Paper, p. 11)*

Given Pompey's self-parodying voice, we could easily add: and neither does she, were it not for the fact that this passage represents the start of her journey to "the other side of the dividing line of pain in art" and between "the awful aloofness of the artist" and her cooptation into feeling morally superior (*Frontier*, pp. 67, 61). Never letting either us or herself off the hook, Pompey warns: "For you see I will not let you escape the issue, nor myself either" (p. 67).[30]

Pompey's journey takes her through a history of personal vulnerability that is transmuted into imperial aggression. The change occurs when she denies that her insecurity leads to defensiveness that in turn must find a scapegoat to feel safe. That Stevie Smith should choose the figure of the Jew and antisemitism as her test case in 1936 and 1938 testifies to her recognition of "the full danger in [Pompey's] pride at being a goy, for it is 'as if that thought alone might swell the mass of cruelty working up against them [the Jews]'" (Spalding, p. 120). So vulnerable herself, Pompey situates her ambivalence toward the Jew in social and historical contexts that expose the precariousness of both representing and identifying with the Jew. Unlike Woolf's Jewish jeweller, who despite revision is nonetheless indelibly branded with the dirt of his search for gold, Smith's Jewish entrepreneur is saved by Pompey's uncensored "play" with "Mr. Freud['s]" idea that "Gold is Dirt," allowing her to see that

> hostility burns from empire blue eyes to the dark eyes of Israel, lord of the hidden river. And in each separate mind the significance of gold is a separate thing . . . in the mind of Empire-Blue-eyes, the significance of gold is fury and pride and a great beacon of light and power. Blue-eyes looks like he would lay a trail of bullets around the Board Room table. . . . And in the eyes of Israel what is the significance of Gold? Unity, flexibility, secrecy, control. Israel has lapped round that course already so many times, so many, many times, and his eyelids are a little weary. O.K. Israel, keep it under your hat.
>
> *(Frontier, pp. 84-85)*

Pompey has no access to the power of "Board Room tables," but her position as narrator privileges the voice of the vulnerable woman as sharing and shaping the forces of oppression, which in turn shape the representation of the Jew. Her position as participant-observer in the history of British imperialism is thus one of both power and powerlessness, but never one of absence or passivity, a status that is particularly important because all other voices in the novels are filtered through Pompey's. It is by dint of her position as audience that we can assess Pompey's relation to her "Jew-friend," Igor Torfeldt, whose "so-racial bonework of the face, and the blond blond hair and blue-grey eyes" make Pompey think Jews "look so patient, so souffrant, so sicklied o'er, bleached, albinoed and depigmented, by What of the Sorrows of Werther by the Dark Tarn of Auber, With-Psyche-his-soul-and-nobody-to-hold-his-paddy-paw" (*Frontier*, p. 72). The Jew "bleached" of his otherness is no better off, however, than Pompey's other Jew-friend, "very essentially civilized, urbane and international . . . old Jew Aaronsen," who also performs for her, not only on the piano but on the international stock market (*Frontier*, p. 197). As consumer of the Jews' gifts, Pompey is no innocent bystander, but implicates herself in myths that construct the Jew's character as originating not only in that of "*Our Lord,*" but in that of crucifier, both victim and villain, always responsible for his own vilification (p. 73).

The myths that construct the Jew as timeless Other are historicized by Pompey's representation of Igor's audience. She mimics those onlookers who praise the blond Igor as the Aryan "saviour . . . among the best type of young Jew, the aristocracy of Israel" (p. 73). Her next move, however, reveals the danger embedded in this praise, for she connects this revision of the Other to her nation writ large—Britain, the colonizing empire, and Britain's historic similarity to Germany, the supremacist, colonizing enemy (p. 73). In the face of the coming war, Pompey reviews the propaganda and jingoism that have historically justified Britain's imperial infamies through its rhetoric of pragmatism and restraint.[31] But it takes her reading of a German military memoir to provide the perspective from which Pompey can be critical of her own complicity with her nation's rhetoric and its construction of the Other. Pompey's reading is infused with satiric glosses that debunk myths of "our so darling pet Lion of these British Isles" by mocking Germany's admiration for Britain's "ethical imperialism" (pp. 104, 101). The joke is on both nations, for Britain's succès d'estime is based on convincing itself and her admiring enemy of an untroubled correspondence between its rhetoric of "justice and freedom" and its colonizing much of "the earth under its sway" (p. 102). But just as Pompey must join the ranks of the genteel antisemites in order to authenticate her mockery of them, so she must become a warrior in order to gain the authority of her anti-imperialist gloss.

Pompey's journey into "a heart of darkness" takes her through England's ignoble past and Germany's threatening future to argue on the basis of their similarities that her vision of history will locate their differences in her responses to war and the Jews (p. 48). War breaks out for Pompey at British headquarters in a German schloss, where her holiday becomes a nightmare flight into espionage, death, and imprisonment. Embedding a British spy maneuver into the German landscape erases and yet imprints boundaries between offensive and defensive, allies and foes, male militarism and female pacifism. In uniform and on horseback, Pompey is transformed into Georg Grosz's military icon, and once she discovers her "secret heart of pride and ambition, of tears and anger," she assumes the character of crucifier, of Grosz's "degenerate rider" (pp. 221, 11). Calling herself "Pompey *der* Grosse," she defends herself by shooting the "rat face" monster who reflects the "cruelty" she has seen on faces in all the places she values as civilized, including her own (pp. 228-29, 252). Cruelty, she discovers, is a function of civilization itself, whether defined as the British lion or as one's friends, because by nature of its collective self-interest, civilization is exclusionary and constructs the outsider as antipathetic.

When Pompey is finally challenged by another voice, it is to clarify the origins and impact of her "sensitive conscience," whether it has been constructed by her own narrative or as the object of patriarchal military history (p. 158). Both her lover and her military commander ask her, "On whose side are you?" and then press her even further when she chooses her friends: "And the Jews?" (pp. 158-59). Still choosing friends, she sacrifices the antipathetic Other to the very history in which she colludes as writer and as actor. As a result, she confirms art's conspiracy with myths of power; and until she realizes that her uniform is no outer garment, but rather an expression of "the racial hatred that is running in me," she remains a prisoner of war (p. 159). The running narratives of Pompey's personal and political monologue reach their final destination at the intersection of her perspective and ours. She sees herself reflected in the German Prince Von's celebration of British imperial history, but we can see her two volumes as a process of self-questioning that is very different from the prince's mythic construction of her homeland.

Out of that interrogation emerges a vision of history that is concurrent with modernism and with fascism but that identifies the historic moment as riven with a unique fascistic danger.[32] Going over the frontier for Stevie Smith explodes boundaries between offensive and defensive cruelty and universalizes guilt for war's violence, but it also constructs differences that become Pompey's saving grace. Whatever surreality Pompey's fantasy of war assumes, through her meditations and reflections, war's events are transformed from mythic representation to an analysis of culture. This analysis takes English history out of Prince Von's hands and subjects it to a kind of scrutiny that celebrates a different kind of Englishness. As one myth after another is demolished by Pompey's fantasied experience, it is replaced by the developing sense that:

> In England there is no national ideology . . . to be carried through, to be expressed in a word and impressed

upon a people, as in Germany it is expressed and impressed, with what of an original pure intention we cannot know, with what of a calamity in event we know too well.

(pp. 258-59)

Smith's prophecy of that calamitous event, a second world war, disrupts pancultural views of fascism, distinguishes past from present, and her voice from that of Woolf's. She imagines historic process as a debate which is knowledge-bearing in its confrontation not only with herself and her correspondents but with the consequences of discovering differences between a self-questioning rhetoric and that which is already persuaded of its truth. Through her relentless questioning, Pompey Casmilus represents the possibility for historical change and for freeing the representation of the Jew from the historical dangers of ambivalence.

Notes

1. Jane Marcus, *Virginia Woolf and the Languages of Patriarchy* (Bloomington: Indiana University Press, 1987), pp. 55, 78.

2. For an account of the debate about *Three Guineas* that originally appeared in *Time and Tide* (25 June 1938), pp. 887-88, see Jane Marcus, "'No More Horses': Virginia Woolf on Art and Propaganda," *Women's Studies* 4 (1977): 203-14.

3. Brenda R. Silver, "*Three Guineas* Before and After: Further Answers to Correspondents," in Jane Marcus, ed., *Virginia Woolf: A Feminist Slant* (Lincoln: University of Nebraska Press, 1983), p. 269.

4. *The Diary of Virginia Woolf,* ed. Anne Olivier Bell (New York: Harcourt Brace, 1984), vol. 5 (1936-1941), pp. 142, 169; *The Letters of Virginia Woolf,* ed. Nigel Nicolson and Joanne Trautmann (New York: Harcourt Brace, 1975), vol. 6, p. 379.

5. "Thoughts on Peace in an Air Raid," in *Collected Essays* (New York: Harcourt Brace, 1967), p. 174; *Letters,* vol. 6, p. 379.

6. *Three Guineas*, p. 103. Catherine F. Smith observes that in *Three Guineas* "ideas are imaged and dramatised" as a "visionary method" of "making society equitable and just" through the mind and writing of the woman narrator ("*Three Guineas*: Virginia Woolf's Prophecy," in Jane Marcus, ed., *Virginia Woolf and Bloomsbury* [Houndmills: Macmillan, 1987], p. 226). Beverly Ann Schlack sees precursors of Woolf's "explicitly bitter anger of *Three Guineas* towards 'manhood and patriotism, politics, and war' throughout her career" ("Fathers in General," in Jane Marcus, ed., *Virginia Woolf: A Feminist Slant*, p. 70.

7. *Virginia Woolf and the Languages of Patriarchy,* p. 120. For an analysis of the Woolfs' political dis-

agreements, see Laura M. Gottlieb, "The War Between the Woolfs," in Marcus, *Virginia Woolf and Bloomsbury,* who opts for Virginia's approach.

8. See "The Duchess and the Jeweller," unsigned and undated typescripts, at the Berg Collection of the New York Public Library, quoted with their permission and that of Quentin Bell.

9. Editorial note, *The Complete Shorter Fiction of Virginia Woolf,* 2nd. ed., ed. Susan Dick (New York: Harcourt Brace, 1989), p. 309; my emphasis.

10. For analyses of these literary stereotypes, see Harold Fisch, *The Dual Image: A Study of the Jew in English and American Literature* (London: World Jewish Library, 1971); Esther Panitz, *The Alien in Their Midst: Images of Jews in English Literature* (East Brunswick, N.J.: Assoc. University Press, 1981); Anne A. Naman, *The Jew in the Victorian Novel* (New York: AMS Press, 1980); Bryan Cheyette, "Jewish Stereotyping and English Literature," in Tony Kushner and Ken Lunn, eds., *Traditions of Intolerance* (Manchester: Manchester University Press, 1989).

11. Quoted by Sander Gilman in his discussion of the Jew's nose as "the iconic representation of the Jew's phallus" as a carrier of disease, *The Jew's Body* (New York: Routledge, 1991), p. 126.

12. Margery Allingham, "The Hat Trick," in *Mr. Campion and Others* (1939; Harmondsworth: Penguin, 1959), pp. 52-53.

13. I am grateful to Karen Alkalay-Gut for this insight. Naman argues that using Jewish or other typed traits to define Jewish character and focusing on the Jew's "moral traits and social roles rather than psychological complexities and environmental circumstances" suffuses his character with prejudice (p. 10).

14. *Three Guineas,* p. 103; "Thoughts on Peace," p. 174.

15. Phyllis Grosskurth, "Between Eros and Thanatos," review of vol. 6 of *Letters of Virginia Woolf, Times Literary Supplement,* Oct. 31, 1980, p. 1225; *The Journey Not the Arrival Matters* (London: Hogarth, 1970), p. 12. Leonard Woolf's youthful "bitterness and ambivalence" toward his Jewish identity developed into pride as he became concerned with anti-semitism, beginning with his novel *The Wise Virgins* and story "Three Jews" and concluding with his account of his visit to Israel in 1957 (*Sowing: An Autobiography of the Years 1880-1904* [New York: Harcourt Brace, 1969], p. 196). See Freema Gottlieb, "Leonard Woolf's Attitude to his Jewish Background and to Judaism," *Transactions of the Jewish Historical Society of England, 1973-75,* pp. 25-38, for an analysis of Leonard Woolf's ambivalence.

16. Critics have used the Woolfs' complex marriage to explain their intellectual and political differences. Both Grosskurth and Cynthia Ozick ("Mrs. Virginia Woolf," *Commentary* [August 1973]: 33-44) link their marital tensions both to Leonard's attitude toward Virginia's illness and to Virginia's ambivalence about Jews. Louise de Salvo notes Virginia's "repulsion" toward Leonard's family, but then, stringing together bits and pieces from Leonard's letters and from various intensely invested and therefore biased sources, states, as definitive and incontrovertible truth, that Leonard's "cruelty" and "betrayal" were to blame for the Woolfs' tensions. Virginia, by contrast, is beatified as his forgiving victim (*Conceived with Malice* [New York: Dutton, 1994], pp. 69, 59, 87). Though de Salvo allows for the marriage to develop productively, nowhere does she consider the historic and political implications of Virginia's "rabid anti-Semitism," p. 69.

17. Leonard felt that Germany's harsh punishment at the end of World War I led to an inevitable rise of militarism, but also felt that the Labour Party should "commit itself to a policy of resisting any further acts of aggression by Hitler" by ensuring Britain's military strength; see *Downhill All the Way* (London: Hogarth Press, 1970), p. 243.

18. Laura Gottlieb purports to compare the political writing of both Woolfs, but she analyzes only *The Intelligent Man's Way to Prevent War,* whose approach to ending war she finds "narrow" but to which she admits Leonard had only "limited involvement" (p. 247), and ignores his *Barbarians at the Gates.* Her argument that Leonard was jealous of Virginia's "intrusion into the field he had designated as his own" dismisses the validity of their different approaches as well as the possibility of taking his response to *Three Guineas* seriously (p. 242). Alex Zwerdling offers a careful analysis of the intellectual, political, and emotional bases of the Woolfs' different views about the coming war in *Virginia Woolf and the Real World* (Berkeley: University of California Press, 1986).

19. Wayne K. Chapman and Janet M. Manson show how the Woolfs collaborated and influenced each other's thinking about war and peace throughout the period of World War I and afterwards in their hopes for the League of Nations; see "Carte and Tierce: Leonard, Virginia Woolf, and War for Peace," in Mark Hussey, ed., *Virginia Woolf and War* (Syracuse: Syracuse University Press, 1991).

20. *The Years* (London: Hogarth Press, 1937), p. 366. Freema Gottlieb also shows that this representation coincides with a "Nazi typology," which justified closing swimming baths to Jews in 1933 because, as Sartre showed in his study of antisemitism, "the body of the Jew would render the bath wholly unclean" (p. 29).

21. In *The Elephant and My Jewish Problem* (New York: Harper & Row, 1988), Hugh Nissenson reports a conversation with Quentin Bell, who said that "when

she was young, Virginia had a Jewish problem. Leonard, too, if the truth be told. It's a common English ailment. It doesn't mean much" (p. 156).

22. Preparing for *Three Guineas,* Woolf carefully searched the daily newspapers for evidence of masculinity and militarism. See Zwerdling, p. 299, and Brenda Silver, *Virginia Woolf's Reading Notebooks* (Princeton: Princeton University Press, 1983). The hostility and aggression that Sara shares with North challenge Patricia Cramer's thesis that the novel expresses "feelings of peace and love that Woolf associated with maternal and woman-to-woman love" ("Loving in the War Years," *Virginia Woolf and War,* p. 206).

23. Leonard Woolf felt that though "the hero of this novel—is England and the pageant of English history . . . the war itself is not referred to except once obliquely"; quoted in Zwerdling, p. 353, from the Leonard Woolf Papers, I R, University of Sussex Library.

24. *Virginia Woolf: Feminist Destinations* (Oxford: Blackwell, 1988), pp. 149-50. Elizabeth Abel compares the novel to Freud's conception of a progressive patriarchal order that ignores the relationship between Hitler, antisemitism, and the powerful authority Freud himself invokes. Although she sees the novel's "present-time reality" recreating an oppressive patriarchal past, she never mentions the presence and absence of Jews, *Virginia Woolf and the Fictions of Psychoanalysis* (Chicago: University of Chicago Press, 1989), p. 116. Judith Johnston sees the novel challenging "the humanist myth of a continuous cultural lineage from Greek to . . . British empires" ("The Remediable Flaw," in *Virginia Woolf and Bloomsbury,* p. 260).

25. *Letters of Vita Sackville-West to Virginia Woolf* (New York: William Morrow, 1985), p. 415. Sackville-West offers a different view of responsibility for World War II in her dystopic novel, *Grand Canyon* (London: Michael Joseph, 1942), which was a plea for the United States to enter the war and save itself and the world from repeating a politics of appeasement. Woolf's use of combative language has been noted by Zwerdling, among others.

26. Pamela Caughie argues in *Virginia Woolf and Postmodernism* (Bloomington: Indiana University Press, 1991) that more important than resolving conflict is to recognize "how our descriptions create them" (p. 207), but Deborah Guth, "Fiction as Self-Evasion in *Mrs. Dalloway,*" *Modern Language Review* 84 (Jan. 1989), shows how Woolf's evasiveness prevents this. Brenda R. Silver shows how "the authority of anger" in *Three Guineas* is emotionally and ideologically directed ("*Three Guineas* Before and After"). I would insist that Woolf's representation of Jews is both evasive and directed; while her anger at patriarchal oppression is justified, the vituperative

tone embedded in her portraits of Jews is dangerous and questions her authority.

27. Louise de Salvo asserts that Woolf's final depression results from being unable to reconcile Freud's insistence on unconscious fantasy with her experiences and memory of childhood sexual abuse, *Virginia Woolf: The Impact of Childhood Sexual Abuse on Her Life and Work* (New York: Ballantyne, 1989). I maintain that her despair is overdetermined, that the war meshes with memories of abuse and loss, and that reading Freud was disturbing because it also made her recognize so much of her unresolved ambivalence. Andrea Freud Loewenstein's psychological model of ambivalence toward the Jew in modern British writers such as Graham Greene and Wyndham Lewis, *Loathsome Jews and Engulfing Women* (New York: New York University Press, 1993), is very useful in pointing to the convergence of political attitudes and rhetorical strategy.

28. Nora Eisenberg, "Virginia Woolf's Last Words on Words: *Between the Acts* and 'Anon,'" in Jane Marcus, ed., *New Feminist Essays on Virginia Woolf* (Lincoln: University of Nebraska Press, 1981), p. 257.

29. Joyce Carol Oates sees Pompey's voice as "quirky, rambling, ingenuous, stubborn, funny-peculiar." See "A Child with a Cold, Cold Eye," *New York Times Book Review,* Oct. 3, 1982, p. 11. David Garnett discusses her candor in *The New Statesman and Nation,* Sept. 5, 1936, p. 321.

30. Frances Spalding notes Smith's criticism of George Orwell, who, as Loewenstein shows in this volume, expressed ambivalence toward the Jews despite his avowed sympathy for them and his analysis of British antisemitism. See *Stevie Smith: A Biography* (New York: Norton, 1988). Sanford Sternlicht maintains that Smith is not interested in politics, but despite her own disclaimer, the discourse on antisemitism in *Over the Frontier* is thoroughly politicized. For Smith's political values in relation to Storm Jameson, see my essay, "A Cry for Life," in M. Paul Holsinger and Mary Anne Schofield, eds., *Visions of War* (Bowling Green: Popular Press, 1992).

31. Paul Rich sees "the British right in the inter-war years as dominated by a more traditional Victorian idea of status and gentility" ("Imperial Decline," in *Traditions of Intolerance,* p. 37).

32. Tony Kushner discusses the survival of British antisemitism during the war, despite the decline of Oswald Moseley's British Union of Fascists ("The Paradox of Prejudice," in *Traditions of Intolerance*). Hermione Lee notes Pompey's lack of "patience with pacifism in the face of the Nazis" in relation to her concern with the aggression of men and women; see "Stevie Smith," in Harold Bloom, ed., *British Modernist Fiction, 1920-1945* (New York: Chelsea House, 1986), p. 320.

Ronald Granofsky (essay date winter 1999)

SOURCE: Granofsky, Ronald. "'Jews of the Wrong Sort': D. H. Lawrence and Race." *Journal of Modern Literature* 23, no. 2 (winter 1999): 209-23.

[*In the following essay, Granofsky traces Lawrence's anti-Semitic attitudes to his ideas about race, culture, and masculinity.*]

In *The Captain's Doll,* a novella from the early 1920s, D. H. Lawrence takes his protagonist, Captain Alexander Hepburn, from post-war occupied Germany to Tyrolean Austria in amorous pursuit of the much younger Countess Johanna zu Rassentlow, familiarly known as Hannele, after the captain's wife has died under suspicious circumstances. The two travel together to a mountain glacier and stay at a hotel full of tourists, among whom are "many Jews of the wrong sort and the wrong shape." As is often the case in Lawrence's fiction, it is unclear here whether the comment is the narrator's free indirect rendering of the thoughts of the protagonist or the narrator's own description separate from Hepburn's perception. In any case, these Jews are people who, on the one hand, are condemned for pretending to be something they are not—"so that you might think they were Austrian aristocrats, if you weren't properly listening, or if you didn't look twice"—but, on the other hand, are appreciated somehow, for "they imparted a wholesome breath of sanity, disillusion, unsentimentality to the excited 'Bergheil' atmosphere."[1] In isolation, the remark might seem frivolous, even quite common by between-the-wars standards, but, together with many other racist statements in Lawrence's writings, the rather off-hand description raises questions about a major twentieth-century author who remains in some respects enigmatic. For one thing, it raises the question of what, for Lawrence, would be Jews of the right sort and shape.

The issue of Lawrence and race is entangled in his writing within a nexus of competing ideological and psychological formulations, and to untangle it is no easy task. In my view, race for Lawrence is one of many related categories that make up a worldview that is keyed upon gender concerns, specifically as those concerns arise out of an adult reaction against the early dependency of a highly sensitive male child upon his mother. Long ago, Christopher Caudwell cuttingly used Lawrence's own pseudo-scientific phraseology to express Lawrence's view of the human dilemma as "the yearning of the solar plexus for the umbilical connexion."[2] I believe that the vexed issue of Lawrence and race can be brought into sharper focus than has previously been the case if it is positioned within the context of his struggle, in the displaced form of his fiction, to free himself from the debilitating aspects of that umbilical connection. At the very time when Lawrence was frequently crossing national boundaries in his life, there is in his writing an ongoing exploration of the boundaries that serve to protect the vulnerable self's integrity, alongside a defensive aggression in the form of misogyny or racism when the boundaries of the self are threatened. Lawrence's negative attitude toward Jews is obdurate because he associates them with both a female threat to the self and with a more general tendency to breach category confines, a tendency whose dynamic recalls the more immediate female threat.

There are times, mostly fairly early on in his life, when Lawrence seems anxious to rise above the racism of his era. In a 1913 letter to Gordon Campbell, Lawrence writes that "[i]t is no use hating a people or a race or humanity in mass. Because each of us is in himself humanity."[3] He was even capable of imagining himself becoming racially other in the poem "Tropic" from *Birds, Beasts and Flowers* (1923): "Behold my hair twisting and going black. / Behold my eyes turn tawny yellow / Negroid; / See the milk of northern spume / Coagulating and going black in my veins."[4] Even here, however, an element of escape from maternal dependency can be read into the white milk turning black, an image, conceivably, of maternal lactation negated as much as of racial otherness. Similarly, Lawrence was capable of identifying with Jews, if in a decidedly negative manner: "[Gibbon] says the Jews are the great *haters* of the human race . . ." he writes in a letter of May, 1918, "I feel such profound hatred myself, of the human race, I almost know what it is to be a Jew."[5]

Usually, however, the Lawrence we see declaiming on race is a Lawrence who comes close to justifying Kingsley Widmer's hyperbolic label, "the modern rebellious Protestant psychopath as intellectual artist."[6] There is certainly enough material in Lawrence's writing to suggest strongly that he held views that we would today call racist and anti-Semitic. His letters are full of such convictions, while his fictional characters complain, for example, of "Chinese and Japs" who "teem by the billion like . . . vermin," or of "niggers" who wallow.[7] However, one of the seemingly most damning pieces of evidence of all may well be misleading. We have been conditioned by the history of this century to equate with racism Lawrence's concept of the superior wisdom of "blood consciousness," what he termed at one point his "great religion."[8] But we may question whether Lawrence's "blood consciousness" really is an ideology of race. Jascha Kessler, for one, certainly thinks that it is: "No wonder Lawrence's later books were popular in Nazi Germany," she writes in a 1964 article, "his blood theory led him directly into totalitarian ideology. For to Lawrence blood was not merely a trope, or a spiritual symbol: it was the quintessence of the racial."[9] Christopher Heywood, however, has suggested that Lawrence's blood consciousness owes a great deal to the neurological, non-racial writings of the Frenchman Bichat and the Englishman Hall.[10] In the letter in which Lawrence sets out his "great religion," the blood is opposed to the intellect. He repeats the opposition metaphorically in comparing the body to a candle flame and the intellect to the light from the candle shed on objects around it. His interest, he claims, is in the flame itself, not in the objects illuminated. The context of blood here, then, sounds very much like the Cartesian mind—body split, not like a racial concept at all. Nor is Lawrence's use of blood as a symbol in his own fiction—for example, in the chapters "Coal Dust" and

"Rabbit" in *Women in Love* (1920)—invariably racial. Blood has highly charged connotations, and for many of Lawrence's readers there is undoubtedly a connection between Lawrence's "blood knowledge" and his willingness in his leadership fiction to contemplate the spilling of blood, but we should be careful not to place such matters on racial hangers when Lawrence clearly had no intention of doing so. Lawrence's closet is filled enough with skeletons as it is.

As James F. Scott has suggested, most readers of D. H. Lawrence "are at least casually aware that [he] thought in racialistic and ethnocentric terms."[11] Nevertheless, most critics of Lawrence's work, it is fair to say, have gingerly stepped around the issue of his racial opinions as if it were something a dog had left in the way, or else they have quickly berated Lawrence and gone on to more interesting subjects. Jeffrey Meyers' biography of Lawrence is a good example. Meyers spends just under three pages and a footnote detailing Lawrence's Jewish friends and his anti-Semitism, concluding somewhat laconically that "Lawrence's tirades against Jews did not prevent him from having Jewish friends and publishers."[12] True enough, but that tells us little. Meyers makes no attempt to understand either the racism itself or the Janus-like letter writing that sees Lawrence rail against Jews when communicating with the anti-Semitic Robert Mountsier (who acted as his American agent for a time) while denouncing Montsier's prejudices to Jewish friends or acquaintances.[13] The few writers who do try to grapple with Lawrence's attitudes to race can be divided roughly into three camps. Representing one extreme is Bertrand Russell's well-known suggestion that one can draw a straight line from Lawrence to Auschwitz.[14] Emile Delavenay, under the immediate impact of the Second World War, strongly condemned Lawrence's use of the anti-Semitic and anti-humanistic ideas of such writers as Houston Chamberlain and his admirer Otto Weininger.[15] Similarly, Kessler directly associates Lawrence's blood knowledge with Nazism's racial theories and eugenic practices. For Kessler, blood racism is a new form of racism in world history, one that may be identified with the primitivism which Lawrence and other Modernists were so attracted to: Lawrence "is stonily serious about race; for without differentiation according to race, there is no differentiation of blood, and without blood differences no distinctions can be possible between the 'gods' of the blood, hence no innate superiority exists, no absolutes by which to gauge inferiority, no means for establishing servile races. . . ."[16]

A little further removed in time from the war than Delavenay and Kessler, there have been a variety of defences of, or explanations for, Lawrence's remarks on race. One interesting example is Barbara Mensch's book entitled (using Adorno's term) *D. H. Lawrence and the Authoritarian Personality,* in which Mensch argues that Lawrence was fascinated by "the authoritarian personality" but always countered such a character in his fiction with a liberal one.[17] For Mensch, Gerald Crich's death in *Women in Love,* in fact, shows "that Lawrence views authoritarianism as a fatal flaw."[18] Similarly, she argues, although *The Plumed Serpent*'s Cipriano is comparable to Adolf Eichmann, it is the much different Don Ramón whom the novelist endorses.[19] It is generally true that when a Lawrence character speaks of extermination it is of the human species, not of one particular race. It is perhaps worth mentioning, however, that, outside his fiction, Lawrence was capable—even before the First World War—of calling for the extermination of the English, although the rhetorical excess here suggests a venting of spleen rather than a serious desire. In a July, 1912 letter to Edward Garnett, he writes of the English, "Curse the blasted, jelly-boned swines, the slimy, the belly-wriggling invertebrates, the miserable sodding rotters. . . . God blast them, wish-wash. Exterminate them, slime" (*Letters I,* p. 422).[20] Daniel J. Schneider has criticized Delavenay's attack on Lawrence as a distortion of Lawrence's position, one that ignores the writer's often critical attitude to Chamberlain's ideas. Delavenay, Schneider suggests, was strongly influenced by the historical events that occurred in Europe after Lawrence's death in 1930 (an influence that Delavenay has acknowledged).[21] Indeed, a major hurdle to a clear understanding of the subject of Lawrence and race is the way in which European Fascism developed after his death. He could not possibly have imagined those developments, and we cannot forget them.

Finally, in something of a middle position between the accusers and defenders of Lawrence on race is the argument of Judith Ruderman. Agreeing that Lawrence was anti-Semitic, Ruderman insists, rightly I think, that this should form not our conclusion but more properly a starting point for a discussion of the writer's worldview. After detailing Lawrence's anti-Semitic remarks in fiction and non-fiction alike, Ruderman concludes that he was neither a rabid racist nor a blameless product of his time.[22] Her most suggestive remark on the subject is that "Lawrence's attitudes toward the Jews . . . express certain tensions found at the core of his work," tensions that might "reveal fruitful connections between misogyny and anti-Semitism,"[23] the same collocation, in fact, that Susan Griffin postulates in her study of pornography.[24]

I would also place the claims of Paulina S. Pollak in this middle camp. Although her 1986 article is wholly censorious of Lawrence's anti-Semitism, it makes an effort to understand the sources of the prejudice. Where a good deal of Ruderman's work on Lawrence, and, by extension, her essay on his anti-Semitism, place the emphasis on pre-oedipal problems between mother and child—a position with which I generally agree—Pollak argues for a straightforwardly oedipal reading of father-son antipathy. Pollak makes several interesting points in her attempt to demonstrate that Lawrence fits the "model of the personality prone to acts of anti-Semitic persecution";[25] however, there are problems with her argument. First, it is ahistorical: the individual predicted by the model tends to see hostility everywhere in the outer world, and Pollak assumes that such a description fits Lawrence. But Lawrence's anti-Semitic remarks date to prewar days, while his view of the entire world as hostile dates only from 1915, when such a conviction is perfectly understandable for a man who had a novel suppressed by court order and was being watched as a potential wartime threat because he had spoken out against the war and had a German wife. According to the model, the individual disposed toward anti-Semitism feels threatened because of his or her own inadequate feelings of self and by the fact that Jews, on the contrary, have "the courage to be different."[26] The idea of inadequate self-definition points us in the right direction, but the suggestion that Jewish apartness constitutes a threat does not make sense in Lawrence's case. Lawrence valued what he called "otherness" very highly. In the specific example of the "Jews of the wrong sort" in *The Captain's Doll,* the narrator is criticizing not the Austrian Jews' attempts to be different but their desire to assimilate. Pollak's argument, moreover, depends upon the Christian view of the Jews as representative of the father who kills the son, a situation that is inverted in the oedipal paradigm. These implications of alleged Jewish deicide do not apply to other ethnic or national groups derided by Lawrence, and, furthermore, there is the fact that, in life, it was his mother's death that Lawrence actually hastened and not his father's. Pollak is, of course, correct in her claim that "Lawrence's prejudice was buried at deep, emotional levels of his personality and served demanding psychic needs,"[27] but the sense of a vulnerable self in Lawrence derives from pre-oedipal patterns that are associated with the mother and, by extension, with women in general.

In my opinion, the extreme view of Lawrence as proto-Nazi—Kessler's position, in other words—is both right and wrong. It is right in the sense that Lawrence's post-war *Weltanschauung* is centered about the concept of differentiation (more precisely, hierarchy) but wrong in that race is not the key differentiating criterion for Lawrence even late in his career when, as in *The Plumed Serpent* (1926) most emphatically, it is said to be. In fact, race and other constructs, such as class, that are capable of hierarchical formulation are, in Lawrence, generally if covertly subsumed by the larger concerns of the gender struggle that is played out in his middle to late fiction as he continues to contend with the oldest hierarchy of all, that of mother and child. What is most crucial as a context for the condemnation of the Austrian Jews' efforts at assimilation in *The Captain's Doll* is thus the importance of maintaining rigidly demarcated boundaries of all sorts. In this sense, then, Lawrence's anti-Semitic attitude may be seen as a displacement of a fear of amorphous boundaries, ultimately those protecting his vulnerable sense of self. Women who try to suffocate men and Jews who try to hide their Jewishness have this in common for Lawrence: they do not respect the boundaries that make discrimination among individuals possible.

. . . . .

A remarkable short story from the volume *England, My England* (1922) may serve to illustrate the dynamic through which the mother-child paradigm becomes displaced, in this case, unto a married couple, in such a way that the displacement symbolically threatens the self-integrity of the male protagonist. In "The Blind Man," Maurice Pervin has returned from the battlefield of Flanders to his wife, Isabel, scarred and completely blind. They are able to achieve a generally satisfying relationship that is, however, marred by occasional bouts of depression on his side and a maddening feeling of weariness on hers. When Isabel's old friend Bertie Reid, a bachelor, comes to pay an extended visit, the unacknowledged problems come to a head. The two men dislike each other, and Maurice feels isolated to the point where he retreats to the stable and his animals for the feeling of warmth and security which he experiences there. Isabel sends Bertie out to check on Maurice, and the story ends in something of an epiphany. Maurice touches Bertie's face and head and asks Bertie to touch his scarred face in return. The result is a feeling of exhilaration for Maurice and one of collapse for Bertie.

"The Blind Man," like so many other stories of roughly the same time, obliquely but clearly expresses Lawrence's denial of his own illness and his belief in a vitalistic strength beyond any mere physical debility. However, the relationship of Maurice and Isabel has begun to founder on Maurice's dependency on her, an entirely reasonable one given the circumstances. One might posit an oedipal constellation at work when Maurice, upstairs changing, hears Isabel and Bertie talking and feels "a childish sense of desolation"; he "seemed shut out—like a child that is left out."[28] But there is more to it than that, for it is clearly a feeling of dependency rather than jealousy that distresses him: "[H]e had almost a childish nostalgia to be included in the life circle. And at the same time he was a man, dark and powerful and infuriated by his own weakness. By some fatal flaw, he could not be by himself, he had to depend on the support of another. And this very dependence enraged him" ("Blind," p. 66). The narrative strategy that Lawrence uses to solve the tense situation he has set up is ingenious both fictionally and psychologically. In effect, when Pervin lays his hands on Bertie Reid—whose own inadequacies have been described in terms of an "incurable weakness, which made him unable ever to enter into close contact of any sort" ("Blind," p. 68), especially with women—he is able to transfer, as it were, his own feeling of childish dependence unto the guest. As a result, it is Bertie's self-boundary that is destroyed: "He could not bear it that he had been touched by the blind man, his insane reserve broken in. He was like a mollusc whose shell is broken" ("Blind," p. 75). In a dynamic something like that of the original function of a scapegoat, Maurice Pervin seems to have overcome his own vulnerability by transferring it onto another person. While Lawrence clearly would like to think of himself as a Maurice Pervin, overcoming mere physical disabilities, he must fight against the barely acknowledged fears of a psychological collapse like that of a Bertie Reid (as the fact that Lawrence as a boy was known as "Bert" might suggest).

Just as the shell of the self must be hardened in order to maintain the sense of stand-alone selfhood, the separateness of recognizable others must also remain clearly demarcated or else anxiety about the viability of independence itself may be provoked. Herbert Howarth tries to excuse the "Jews of the wrong sort" remark by claiming in an endnote that they "form a positive of the story. The Jewish visitors refrain from exhilaration; they are in touch with the earthier Mother."[29] Scott commends Lawrence for never having "turned his anthropological speculation [on race] towards self-serving or exploitative purposes, as did so many political anthropologists of this period, for whom racial differences legitimated conquest."[30] Scott also qualifies Howarth's position somewhat, a stance he otherwise approves of: the Jews in *The Captain's Doll* are "representatives of an alien civilization older than Europe's, [who] possess a cultural wisdom which they cynically refuse to impart."[31] Both views, in my opinion, miss the centrality of Lawrence's critique of the effort of the Austrian Jews to assimilate, to break down the demarcating line excluding them from the heart of Austrian society. To paraphrase Ruderman, they dress Austrian but think Yiddish.[32] The same insistence on preserving differences is evident in a letter to Louis Golding, written around the time Lawrence was revising *The Captain's Doll*, discussing Golding's novel *Forward from Babylon* (1920): "I do wish it had been more Jewish. One can hardly see any difference between your vision and the English vision. I wish you had given one the passional truth of Reb Monash's Yidishkeit [*sic*]. . . . And a Jewish book should be written in terms of *difference* from the Gentile consciousness—not identity with it" (*Letters III*, p. 690).

Lawrence, then, wishes to insist on discriminating, separating out, one race from another. In the rejected epilogue to his commissioned history book, *Movements in European History* (1921), Lawrence uses what is perhaps his favorite metaphor, the growing tree, to describe his conception of the relationship among the races. He thereby suggests a fundamental unity and equality among races even as he is at pains to describe their separateness: "In its root and trunk, mankind is one. But then the differences begin. The great tree of man branches out into different races. . . . And each great branch has its own growing tip. . . . Every branch has its own direction and its own growing tip. One branch cannot take the place of any other branch. Each must go its own way, and bear its own flowers and fruits."[33] Such a formulation can apply to individuals as well, of course. Lawrence struggled throughout his life and writing career with boundary definitions in an effort to strengthen his own sense of selfhood, a sense badly damaged by mothering that tended to suffocate that sense and to violate boundaries, as the very title to his autobiographical *Sons and Lovers* (1913) serves to indicate. In *Fantasia of the Unconscious* (1922), Lawrence even seems to blame his mother indirectly for his consumption: "On the upper plane, the lungs and heart are controlled from the cardiac plane and the thoracic ganglion. Any excess in the sympathetic mode from the upper centres tends to burn the lungs with oxygen, weaken them with stress, and cause consumption. So it is just criminal to make a child too loving."[34] A similar fear of suffocation is evident in racist

remarks by Lawrence while in the then-Ceylon en route to Australia. There is something approaching hysteria here that suggests the need for hierarchy and separation in the service of racial discrimination: "Those natives are *back* of us—in the living sense *lower* than we are. But they're going to swarm over us and suffocate us. We are, have been for five centuries, the growing tip. Now we're going to fall. But you don't catch me going back on my whiteness and Englishness and myself" (*Letters IV*, p. 234). Boundary setting and violation are also important in *The Rainbow* (1915), particularly in the relationship of Anna and Will Brangwen, which is almost destroyed when Anna feels Will's dependence on her becoming a terrible burden, even a predatory threat, as we see in the chapter "Anna Victrix."[35] Anna "wanted to thrust him off, to set him apart" because she feels that she is being devoured (*Rainbow*, p. 173). In *Women in Love*, something of a reprise of this situation, but with much more deadly results, occurs in the relationship between Gerald and Gudrun as described in the chapter "Snowed Up": "As they grew more used to each other, he seemed to press upon her more and more. . . . [H]e dropped his respect for her whims and her privacies, he began to exert his own will, blindly, without submitting to hers."[36] Finally, we may view the poem "New Heaven and Earth" as the narration of a struggle to overcome extreme solipsism, a condition that is the inverse of engulfment but equally refuses both to recognize self-boundaries—"I shall never forget the maniacal horror of it all in the end / when everything was me . . ."—and to recreate a reassuring sense of boundary definition: "I put out my hand in the night, one night, and my hand / touched that which was verily not me, . . . I was greedy, I was mad for the unknown . . ." (*Poems*, pp. 257, 259).

Lawrence's anxiety about Jews violating boundaries leads to characterizations that, in some cases, go well beyond the one in *The Captain's Doll* in terms of fear and loathing. In *Women in Love*, one of Birkin's well-known philosophical principles is that there are two great drifts towards racial/cultural death in his era, tendencies in which dissolution is made inevitable by the break with the cultural balance between body and mind (*Women*, pp. 253-54). One is the "Arctic" way of the Northern peoples, a hyper-consciousness whose characteristics are personified most clearly in Hermoine Roddice and whose direction is exemplified by the icy death of Gerald Crich. The other is the "African" way of pure sensuality, the self-destructiveness of which is represented as early as *The Rainbow* by Anton Skrebensky, who, newly returned from Africa, invites his own vitalistic "annihilation" by Ursula Brangwen. In *Women in Love*, Birkin foresees Gerald's death in the snow as a fulfillment of the fate of "Arctic man" (*Women*, p. 254), which is predicated on the "white" races "having the arctic north behind them," while the African process is "controlled by the burning death-abstraction of the Sahara" (*Women*, p. 254). There is, however, an inconsistency in *Women in Love* between the ideology of these two processes of dissolution and Lawrence's portrayal of the cosmopolitan and avant-garde

Jewish artist Loerke (based loosely on the painter Mark Gertler) as a contemptible, even disgusting exemplar of dissolution. Loerke has taken the process of racial decay further along than anyone else in this novel and, arguably, anywhere else in Lawrence. Gudrun considers him "to be the very stuff of the underworld of life. There was no going beyond him" (*Women*, p. 427). Birkin calls him "'a little obscene monster of the darkness'" and suggests that he must be Jewish because, as a "rat" in "the river of corruption," he is far ahead in the process of dissolution (*Women*, p. 428).[37] Indeed, Lawrence wrote in October of 1916 to Mark Gertler about Gertler's painting "The Merry-Go-Round," a work he admired very much and had in mind for part of Loerke's Cologne piece, that "[i]t would take a Jew to paint this picture. . . . You are of an older race than I, and in these ultimate processes, you are beyond me, older than I am. . . . It will be left for the Jews to utter the final and great death-cry of this epoch: the Christians are not reduced sufficiently" (*Letters II*, pp. 660, 661).

It is Loerke's presumed Jewishness that would appear to be key to the negative, almost classically anti-Semitic portrayal, for, otherwise, it would seem, "he is a small, dark man of the type who, like Lewis in *St. Mawr* and Cipriano in *The Plumed Serpent*, conveys positive cultural values . . ." for Lawrence.[38] Although the portrayal of Loerke is an extreme example, the same anti-Semitic tendency is clearly present in other works: Alfred Kramer in *Mr. Noon* (1984) (based on Frieda's brother-in-law Edgar Jaffe) has "a drop too much of Jewish blood in his veins, and so we must not take him as typical of the sound and all-too-serious German professors for whom the word is God."[39] Nor should we forget the authoritarian leader Ben Cooley in *Kangaroo* (1923), a Jew who yearns for the love and support of Richard Somers but who is rejected and dies.

The narrative manoeuvre in *Kangaroo* is revealing in that it is wholly unconvincing, especially in terms of Lawrence's own formulation during this period of two antithetical urges in humanity, love and power: this polarity serves much more clearly than the earlier Arctic/African opposition to bring out the fear of engulfment that partly underpins Lawrence's anti-Semitism. In other words, the manoeuvre may lead to narrative confusion, but it clarifies the racism. The most lucid fictional enunciation of the contrast between love and power is put in the mouth of Rawdon Lilly in *Aaron's Rod* (1922). Lilly makes it clear that the love urge (whether directed at an individual, at humanity as a whole, or at God) leads to a loss of selfhood, whereas the power urge, he tells Aaron, is what protects the self: "'You've got an innermost, integral unique self, and since it's the only thing you have got or ever will have, don't go trying to lose it. . . . Your own single oneness is your destiny'" (*Aaron*, p. 295). In *Kangaroo* itself, a novel laced with anti-Semitic remarks, Ben Cooley initially represents the power urge, at least in his political platform and his tactics. But Lawrence simply does not know how to end the novel without the inconsistency of also associating Cooley with the love urge so that, in re-

jecting him, the Lawrence figure, Somers, will be rejecting love rather than power. Cooley's character was based on an Australian Jew, Major-General Sir Charles Rosenthal,[40] so Lawrence simply made him Jewish in this hastily written novel. But since Jews for Lawrence are associated with the threat of merger and of boundary violation, Cooley illogically becomes an exponent of the love urge.

In terms of Lawrence's non-fiction, we may look to his brilliant *Studies in Classic American Literature* (1924) for examples of the way love seems to threaten the self through merger with an other. In the essay on Poe, the fate of Roderick Usher is clarified through the perspective of love's dangers: "Love is the mysterious vital attraction which draws things together, closer, closer together." But there must be limits to the merging, for "[t]he central law of all organic life is that each organism is intrinsically isolate and single in itself."[41] Lawrence even issues a warning late in the essay: "Beware, oh woman, of the man who wants to *find out what you are*. And, oh men, beware a thousand times more of the woman who wants to *know* you or *get* you, what you are" (*Studies*, p. 76). And, of course, the symbolic incest in Poe's story represents the dangers of love-merger and boundary violation: "They would love, they would merge, they would be as one thing. So they dragged each other down into death" (*Studies*, p. 85). And "the result is the dissolution of both souls, each losing itself in transgressing its own bounds" (*Studies* p. 86). Similarly, when writing on Melville, Lawrence argues that "[e]very relationship should have its absolute limits, its absolute reserves, essential to the singleness of the soul in each person" (*Studies*, p. 152). As for Whitman, Lawrence's chapter on the poet, as one would expect, reads like one long tirade against love and merging: "This merging, *en masse*, One Identity, Myself monomania was a carry-over from the old Love idea. It was carrying the idea of Love to its logical physical conclusion" (*Studies* p. 182).

. . . . .

Insofar as Lawrence sees them as boundary interlopers, then, Jews represent or at the very least are a reminder of a dynamic that is far too dangerous to ignore. In addition, Lawrence seems to have accepted a classical tenet of anti-Semitism, that Jewish men have become feminized. Not only would such a belief add to their supposed tendency to traverse boundaries, gender boundaries in this case, but it would also align them directly with the very people whose presence is most dangerous to Lawrence's own sense of self-boundaries, women.[42] Returning to our touchstone on Lawrence and race, it is possible to argue that, judging by internal and external evidence, the Jews in *The Captain's Doll* are of the "wrong sort" not only because they want to assimilate but also because their race, even unassimilated, has become feminized. This qualification, of course, makes the racism no less objectionable, but it is an important nuance that we must take into account if we are to understand Lawrence's writing and, indeed, if we are to understand some of the psychological origins of racism itself. *The Captain's Doll* turns out to be subtextually about the power struggle inherent in any sexual relationship for Lawrence at this point in his career, where women represent the terrifying "devouring mother" within a relationship and where a man must do all he can to assert his maleness and priority. *The Captain's Doll*'s Mrs. Hepburn is considerably older than her husband, and she has brought her fortune to the marriage. The marriage for him, the narrator informs us, has been "a long slow weaning away" (*Fox*, p. 114), a phrase that echoes Lawrence's description of his own difficulties in gaining independence from his mother (*Letters I*, p. 527). As I have suggested elsewhere,[43] Hepburn's wife's fatal fall from her hotel window may be related symbolically to the comment in "Education of the People" (composed in 1920) that to save the sanity of our children we must pull down the mothers "from their exalted perches."[44] Now Hepburn will not be satisfied with Hannele until the terms of this new relationship are altered to reflect his belief in male priority. He has proved himself by attaining his own exalted perch on top of the glacier, thereby defeating the same "Arctic" world that, in *Women in Love,* proves fatal to Gerald Crich. Gerald dies not directly because of the interference of the racially-other Loerke but because of the woman to whom he had clung, at one point, as an infant clings to its mother: "Like a child at the breast, he cleaved intensely to her, and she could not put him away" (*Women*, p. 345). That Loerke and Gudrun form a tandem which excludes Gerald is suggestive of the conflation of women and Jews as threats and of misogyny and racism as the emotional reactions to those threats.

Similarly, in *The Lost Girl* (1920), Alvina Houghton is brought down by circumstances from her lofty position in the social edifice of her home town—a movement signalled by her descent into her father's coal mine—until her lover, the Italian Ciccio, her social inferior in English terms, feels able to assert his mastery. When Ciccio pays a call on the Houghtons, Alvina "stood on the doorstep above him" and looks down on him "from her height." Nevertheless, Ciccio beckons with his eyes, in which there is "a dark flicker of ascendancy," and Alvina steps "down to his level" to follow him.[45] When he kisses her, Alvina paradoxically comes alive even as she feels herself die; to complete the ascent-descent inversion, when Alvina runs indoors to her room, in the realization that she loves Ciccio, she "kneeled down on the floor, bowing down her head to her knees in a paroxysm on the floor" (*Lost*, p. 175). It is only in this way that the paradox inherent in the title of the novel—that to find herself Alvina must lose herself—may be actuated. In *The Fox,* one of two companion stories to *The Captain's Doll*, the male protagonist is again much younger than the female, a state of affairs that inevitably in Lawrence bears parent-child overtones. Henry Grenfel must vigorously combat those overtones in his relationship with Nellie March. And so he simply dismisses March's objection that she is old enough to be his mother, although, in fact, she is not; but even in his own mind, he must insist on his priority in a way that protests a little too much: "[h]e was older than she, really. He was master of her" (*Fox*, p. 23). In the final novella of the vol-

ume, *The Ladybird,* there is a curious inversion which is related, I believe, to Lawrence's childhood illnesses and dependence upon his mother. The severely wounded male protagonist, one of Lawrence's little dark men, who has been likened to "a child that is very ill and can't tell you what hurts it" (*Fox*, p. 163) and himself feels that he has lost his manhood as a result of his dependence, heals himself and "cures" the nervous unease of the Sleeping Beauty figure, Lady Daphne. No maternal care here.[46]

The fight in Lawrence for the priority of the son/husband over the mother/wife can be traced back at least to *Sons and Lovers* (1913), in which the issue is camouflaged by the much more obvious and dramatized struggle between Mrs. Morel and Miriam for the love of Paul. But clearly Mrs. Morel's death at the end of the novel liberates Paul, and Paul brings that death about (or at least hastens it, as Lawrence had done with his mother in life). He resorts to euthanasia, not murder. Nevertheless, the pattern is set whereby the death of the other (especially the motherly other) and/or what she represents is strongly connected to self-liberation. Paul Morel feeds his mother poisoned milk, thereby at once commenting upon the toxic nature of maternal nourishment (when administered, like Mrs. Morel's medicine, in too large doses) and avenging himself in a symbolically appropriate way. And we are back once again to the "milk of northern spume / Coagulating and going black in my veins" of "Tropic."

In *Aaron's Rod*, the inclusion of Jews among those who are immediately to be made slaves in the harebrained reactionary scheme of Argyle (a scheme that is endorsed in large part by Lilly) seems to be racially motivated and thereby to support Jascha Kessler's argument that Lawrence needs the idea of the differentiation of blood in order to provide for servile (and thus for superior) races. Argyle tells Levison, his interlocutor, that he would make slaves of "'[e]verybody, my dear chap: beginning with the idealists and the theorising Jews . . .'" (*Aaron*, p. 279). However, we must think back to the earlier scene at the Royal Oak pub and Lawrence's description of Aaron's apparently ongoing flirtatious relationship with the landlady, an obvious foreshadowing of his much more developed liaison with the Marchesa Del Torre. First, the landlady is called "a large, stout, high-coloured woman, with a fine profile, probably Jewish" (*Aaron*, p. 17). Her nose has "a subtle, beautiful Hebraic curve," and she herself is one "who loved intellectual discussion" (*Aaron*, p. 18). This is important in the light of Argyle's comments regarding "theorising Jews." Shortly afterwards, the narrator has apparently studied the woman's genealogy, for now she is simply "the Hebrew woman," and it is her lustfulness that is central rather than her intellectualism (*Aaron*, p. 23). There is an elision, then, between race consciousness and a threatening, because sexually demanding, femaleness. Theorizing Jews, people whom Argyle apparently feels a need to control, turn out, in the subtextual scheme of the novel as a whole, to be associated with lustful women who would enslave the male through the arts of seduction. Despite his best efforts, Aaron backslides in his flight from women when he has a brief and debilitating affair with the Marchesa. She, evidently, wants Aaron to play the mama in their relationship—a very interesting new wrinkle in Lawrence's fiction: "she seemed almost like a clinging child in his arms" (*Aaron*, p. 261). She wishes, he feels, "to curl herself on his naked breast" (*Aaron*, p. 272). Aaron's otherwise marked desire to be infantilized—his wish to be babied by Lilly, for example—is thwarted when the Marchesa treats him like the mother, herself the baby at the breast. I must stress that these connections are sub-textual and not readily apparent on a first reading. The fact that the landlady of the pub in *Aaron's Rod* is Jewish is a very minor detail in the novel, but why make her Jewish at all? Aaron is in flight from women, and, I am arguing, the fact of the landlady's ethnic identity may be under-stood within that context in this work, as, more generally, Lawrence's racism may be related to his attitude to women.

In his essay on Thomas Hardy, Lawrence goes off on one of his seemingly aimless tangents to discuss race. Once again, there is a strong connection here to gender, and, while the link is often covert in Lawrence, in this instance, the view of Jews as feminine is explicit, while Lawrence's wish to control their movements is easily discernible be-hind the projective manoeuvre of blaming women: "But in the terrible moment when they should break free again, the male in the Jew was too weak, the female overbore him. He remained in the grip of the female. . . . He had become the servant of his God, the female, passive. The female in him predominated, held him passive, set utter bounds to his movements, to his roving . . ." (*Phoenix*, p. 450). In another Lawrence essay, "The Two Principles," we see clearly how race and gender concerns become con-fused: ". . . some races, men and women alike, derive from the sun and have the fiery principle predominant in their constitution, whilst some, blonde, blue-eyed, north-ern, are evidently water-born. . . . Nevertheless, if we must imagine the most perfect clue to the eternal waters, we think of woman, and of man as the most perfect premise of fire" (*Phoenix II*, p. 234).

Delavenay suggestively claims that Lawrence was influ-enced by the Jewish anti-Semite Otto Weininger to see Ju-daism, in Weininger's words, as "'*saturated with feminin-ity*, with precisely those qualities the essence of which I have shown to be in strongest opposition to the male nature.'"[47] In short, races seem to be polarized for Lawrence by their degree of feminization. Races which he disapproves of—English and Jewish primarily—are either female in cultural predilection or produce men who are cowed to the point of impotence. Women become "cock-sure," men "hensure," in Lawrence's terms. Those of whom he approves—Italians for a time, American natives, Aztecs—put women in their place even if that place is one of human sacrifice, as in the notorious "The Woman Who Rode Away." Race becomes a displaced battleground for Lawrence's fight with women, a fight he would like to give the aura of political significance but which in reality stems from his childhood dependence upon his mother. In

that sense, the only race that finally matters to Lawrence is the "race" of men, that is, the male of the human species, as in *Sea and Sardinia* (1921): "One realizes, with horror, that the race of men is almost extinct in Europe. Only Christ-like heroes and woman-worshipping Don Juans, and rabid equality mongrels. The old, hardy indomitable male is gone."[48]

In a recent article, Howard J. Booth attempts to place Lawrence's attitudes to race within the context of psycho-analysis and of post-colonial theories about the construc-tion of subjectivity and colonized others in the imperial project. For Booth, Lawrence's writing generally repre-sents a refreshing openness to transformation by the en-counter with racial others, but the critic is puzzled by re-marks in the essay "On Being a Man," in which Lawrence is not so open in his description of an imaginary meeting of a racial other, in this case, an African-American in a train. Booth writes: "Though he criticises fixing the Afri-can—American with a single word, he then falls into a se-ries of stereotypes. It is solipsistic because the other is only important in so far as he offers an experience for the self. The hierarchies between white and black are not ques-tioned, they remain in place," and, indeed, the description in the essay ends "with Lawrence making an easy slide into issues of gender and heterosexual relations."[49] The question as to why "racist discourses infiltrate a passage where Lawrence is considering engagements with other-ness that change and transform the self positively"[50] might be answered by reference to the evidence that Lawrence prizes otherness not as a catalyst to self-transformation but as a reassurance that his self-boundaries are not threat-ened, the same sense he needs in his relations to women.

The eliding of race and gender terms of reference becomes a pattern in Lawrence's writing, but it is not always easy to discern because of the passionate, disconnected way of argumentation which he employs. There is a concealed concern in much of his fiction with a childlike dependence on a woman—often couched in terms far different from that concern. Lawrence will devote much of his creative life to imagining ways to protect his self-integrity from the threat of his own dependency on women, and in so doing he will strike out at other races, but particularly at Jews as a group, for their boundary crossings remind him uncon-sciously of his greatest fear. This is not to say that Lawrence's anti-Semitism is not racism but merely that, like all irrational beliefs, it has hidden causes that are worth exploring. In Lawrence's case, the hidden roots of anti-Semitism appear to lie in an equally irrational but more understandable (because traceable) misogyny. His work retains its fascination, among other things, as the creation of a tremendously conflicted man whose struggles can teach us something about race hatred.

Notes

1. D. H. Lawrence, *The Fox, The Captain's Doll, The Ladybird,* ed. Dieter Mehl (Cambridge University Press, 1992), p. 140. Henceforth referred to paren-thetically as *Fox*.

2. Christopher Caudwell, "D. H. Lawrence: A Study of the Bourgeois Artist," *D. H. Lawrence: Critical Assessments,* ed. David Ellis and Ornella De Zordo, vol. IV (Helm, 1992), p. 357.

3. George J. Zytaruk and James T. Boulton, eds., *The Letters of D. H. Lawrence,* vol. II (Cambridge University Press, 1981), p. 301. Henceforth referred to parenthetically as *Letters II.*

4. D. H. Lawrence, *The Complete Poems of D. H. Lawrence,* eds. Vivian de Sola Pinto and Warren Roberts (1964; Penguin, 1977), p. 301. Henceforth referred to parenthetically as *Poems.*

5. James T. Boulton and Andrew Robertson, eds., *The Letters of D. H. Lawrence,* vol. III (Cambridge University Press, 1984), pp. 242-43. Henceforth referred to parenthetically as *Letters III.* Compare such a statement with a letter of December 1919, in which Lawrence suggests that his travels have been so extensive that "I am turned into a wandering Jew" (*Letters III,* p. 435).

6. Kingsley Widmer, "Lawrence and the Nietzschean Matrix," *D. H. Lawrence and Tradition,* ed. Jeffrey Meyers (Athlone Press, 1985), p. 130. Widmer discusses Lawrence and Nietzsche and their "multiple racist bigotries" (Widmer, p. 130).

7. These sentiments are from *Aaron's Rod,* but they are typical of the fiction from *Women in Love* onward. See D. H. Lawrence, *Aaron's Rod,* ed. Mara Kalnins (Cambridge University Press, 1988), p. 97. Henceforth referred to parenthetically as *Aaron.*

8. James T. Boulton, ed., *The Letters of D. H. Lawrence,* vol. I (Cambridge University Press, 1979), p. 503. Henceforth referred to parenthetically as *Letters I.*

9. Jascha Kessler, "D. H. Lawrence's Primitivism," *Texas Studies in Literature and Language,* V (1964), p. 484.

10. Christopher Heywood, "'Blood-Consciousness' and the Pioneers of the Reflex and Ganglionic Systems," *D. H. Lawrence: New Studies,* ed. Christopher Heywood (St. Martin's Press: 1987), p. 104 *et passim.*

11. James F. Scott, "D. H. Lawrence's *Germania*: Ethnic Psychology and Cultural Crisis in the Shorter Fiction," *D. H. Lawrence Review,* X (1977), p. 142.

12. Jeffrey Meyers, *D. H. Lawrence: A Biography* (1990; Vintage-Random House, 1992), p. 133.

13. Mountsier seems to have had a way of bringing out the anti-Semite in Lawrence in their correspondence, especially when they are discussing such Jewish publishers as Thomas Seltzer and Benjamin Huebsch. A typical example occurs in a letter to Mountsier of March 1921: "I want you to act entirely on your own discretion: quite approve of your opening the Seltzer letter. I hate Jews and I want to learn to be more *wary* of them all" (*Letters III,* p. 678). To his Jewish friend S.S. Koteliansky, in November of the same year, he remarks that Mountsier "is one of those irritating people who have generalised detestations: his particular ones being Jews, Germans, and Bolshevists. So unoriginal." See Warren Roberts et al., eds., *The Letters of D. H. Lawrence,* vol. IV (Cambridge University Press, 1987), p. 113. Henceforth referred to parenthetically as *Letters IV.*

14. Emile Delavenay points out in an essay from 1987 that Russell's remark "was not intended to accuse Lawrence of complicity with the Nazis" but rather to condemn the "Germanic modes of thought" that were adopted by Lawrence and were responsible, ultimately, for Auschwitz. See "Further Thoughts on Lawrence and Chamberlain," *D. H. Lawrence Review,* XIX (1987), p. 174. However, Mark Kinkead-Weekes's biography of Lawrence's middle years places any scruples which Russell may have had when he made the remarks—and, indeed, his motives—entirely in doubt. See *D. H. Lawrence: Triumph to Exile 1912-1922* (Cambridge University Press, 1996), pp. 810-11 note 68.

15. Emile Delavenay, *D. H. Lawrence: The Man and his Work. The Formative Years: 1885-1919,* trans. Katharine M. Delavenay (Heinemann, 1972), pp. 298-99. In his Foreword to the English translation of his monumental work, a work begun in 1932 but completed in the late 1960s, Delavenay writes: "I have naturally been influenced by the experiences of the years after 1935. It is impossible for my generation to forget that some of the ideas which attracted Lawrence as early as 1915 were subsequently mobilized in the service of the worst crimes against mankind" (p. xvi).

16. Kessler, p. 484.

17. Barbara Mensch, *D. H. Lawrence and the Authoritarian Personality* (St. Martin's Press, 1991), p. 2.

18. Mensch, p. 72.

19. Mensch, pp. 243-45.

20. More ominous is Lawrence's opinion that it is acceptable to destroy defective specimens of humanity. In the late essay "Return to Bestwood" (written in 1926), for instance, he suggests that "[h]opeless life should be put to sleep, the idiots and the hopeless sick and the true criminal." See *Phoenix II: Uncollected, Unpublished, and Other Prose Works by D. H. Lawrence,* eds. Warren Roberts and Harry T. Moore (Viking, 1968), p. 265. Henceforth referred to parenthetically as *Phoenix II.*

21. See Daniel J. Schneider, "D. H. Lawrence and Houston Chamberlain: Once Again," *D. H. Lawrence Review,* XIX (1987), pp. 157-71. Delavenay responds to Schneider in the same issue of the journal in which Schneider's article appears. He also reiterates the importance of Lawrence's personal anti-Semitism, as well as his anti-democratic leanings. See "Further

Thoughts on Lawrence and Chamberlain," *D. H. Lawrence Review*, XIX (1987), pp. 173-80.

22. Judith Ruderman, "D. H. Lawrence and the 'Jewish Problem': Reflections on a Self-Confessed 'Hebrophobe,'" *D. H. Lawrence Review*, XXIII (1991), p. 107.

23. Ruderman, pp. 107, 108.

24. Susan Griffin, *Pornography and Silence: Culture's Revenge Against Nature* (Harper, 1981).

25. Paulina S. Pollak, "Anti-Semitism in the Works of D. H. Lawrence: Search for and Rejection of the Father," *Literature and Psychology*, XXXII (1986), p. 20.

26. Pollak, p. 20.

27. Pollak, p. 29 note 4.

28. D. H. Lawrence, *England, My England* (Penguin, 1974), p. 65. Henceforth referred to parenthetically as "Blind".

29. Herbert Howarth, "D. H. Lawrence from Island to Glacier," *University of Toronto Quarterly*, XXXVII (1967-68), p. 229 note 24.

30. Scott, p. 163.

31. Scott, p. 157.

32. Ruderman, p. 102.

33. D. H. Lawrence, *Movements in European History*, ed. Philip Crumpton (Cambridge University Press, 1989), p. 256.

34. D. H. Lawrence, *Fantasia of the Unconscious* and *Psychoanalysis and the Unconscious* (Penguin, 1971), p. 59.

35. As an example of this minutely explored aspect of the relationship between Anna and Will: "She found that, in all her outgoings and her incomings, he prevented her. Gradually she realized that she was being borne down by him, borne down by the clinging, heavy weight of him, that he was pulling her down as a leopard clings to a wild cow and exhausts her and pulls her down." See D. H. Lawrence, *The Rainbow*, ed. Mark Kinkead-Weekes (Cambridge University Press, 1989), p. 172. Henceforth referred to parenthetically as *Rainbow. The Rainbow* was written at a time when Lawrence could still identify to a certain extent with his female protagonists, and here Anna seems to be more Lawrentian than Will. Ursula Brangwen, the representative of the third generation in *The Rainbow*, experiences many of the events in Lawrence's own life. When she meets Rupert Birkin in *Women in Love*, however, she becomes more Frieda than Lawrence, while Birkin takes on the burden of Lawrence's views.

36. D. H. Lawrence, *Women in Love*, ed. David Farmer, Lindeth Vasey and John Worthen (Cambridge Uni-

versity Press, 1987), p. 441. Henceforth referred to parenthetically as *Women*.

37. Compare Lawrence's letter to J. M. Murry, in which he declares that Murry has betrayed not only Lawrence but everybody else as well. Nevertheless, "in Kot [S.S. Koteliansky] you met a more ancient Judas than yourself. There are degrees within degrees of initiation into the Judas trick. You're not half way on yet. Even Kot is miles ahead of you." See James T. Boulton and Lindeth Vasey, eds., *The Letters of D. H. Lawrence*, vol. V (Cambridge University Press, 1989) p. 205.

38. Margaret Storch, "'But Not the America of the Whites': Lawrence's Pursuit of the True Primitive," *D. H. Lawrence Review*, XXV (1993-1994), p. 49.

39. D. H. Lawrence, *Mr. Noon*, ed. Lindeth Vasey (Grafton-Collins, 1986), p. 128.

40. Robert Darroch, *D. H. Lawrence in Australia* (Macmillan, 1981), p. 61.

41. D. H. Lawrence, *Studies in Classic American Literature* (Penguin, 1971), p. 71. Henceforth referred to parenthetically as *Studies*.

42. Cornelia Nixon places Lawrence's misogyny in the context of other seemingly authoritarian thinkers of the time (Lewis and Yeats, for example), who tended to consider "democracy as feminine and authoritarianism as masculine." See *Lawrence's Leadership Politics and the Turn Against Women* (University of California Press, 1986), p. 6.

43. Ronald Granofsky, "Survival of the Fittest in Lawrence's *The Captain's Doll*," *D. H. Lawrence Review*, XXVII (1997-1998), p. 39.

44. D. H. Lawrence, "Education of the People," *Phoenix: The Posthumous Papers of D. H. Lawrence*, ed. Edward D. McDonald (1936; Heinemann, 1961), p. 621. Henceforth referred to parenthetically as *Phoenix*.

45. D. H. Lawrence, *The Lost Girl*, ed. John Worthen (Cambridge University Press, 1981), p. 174. Henceforth referred to parenthetically as *Lost*.

46. When Lady Daphne visits the recovering Count Dionys at the hospital for prisoners of war, he says to her: "'It troubles me . . . that I complain like a child, and ask for things. I feel I have lost my manhood for the time being'" (*Fox*, p. 171). Once he has recovered his health, however, his manhood returns, and, during a stay at the home of Daphne and her husband, the Count's lovemaking is curative for her. Daphne feels "as if she had slipped off all her cares. She did not care, she did not grieve, she did not fret anymore. All that had left her. She felt she could sleep, sleep, sleep—for ever" (*Fox*, p. 217). For an extended treatment of this issue in *The Ladybird*, see my "Illness and Wellness in D. H. Lawrence's *The Ladybird*," *Orbis Litterarum*, LI (1996), pp. 99-117.

47. Otto Weininger, *Sex and Character* (Heinemann, 1906), p. 306. Quoted in Emile Delavenay, "Lawrence, Otto Weininger and 'Rather Raw Philosophy,'" *D. H. Lawrence: New Studies,* ed. Christopher Heywood (St. Martin's Press, 1987), p. 140.

48. D. H. Lawrence, *Sea and Sardinia* (Penguin, 1971), pp. 68-69.

49. Howard J. Booth, "'Give me *differences*': Lawrence, Psychoanalysis, and Race," *D. H. Lawrence Review,* XXVII (1997-1998), p. 190.

50. Booth, pp. 190-91.

THE HOLOCAUST IN LITERATURE

Lawrence L. Langer (essay date 1975)

SOURCE: Langer, Lawrence L. "Acquainted with the Night." In *The Holocaust and the Literary Imagination,* pp. 31-73. New Haven, CT: Yale University Press, 1975.

[*In the following excerpt, Langer explores some ways in which various writers transformed their experience of the Holocaust into art.*]

> *Who will write us new laws of harmony?*
> *We have no further use for well-*
> *tempered clavichords. We ourselves*
> *are too much dissonance.*
>
> Wolfgang Borchert

> *In the beginning there was the Holocaust.*
> *We must therefore start all over again. . . .*
> *What it was we may never know; but*
> *we must proclaim, at least, that it was,*
> *that it is.*
>
> Elie Wiesel

The journey from documentation to art, from the gross horrors of the Holocaust to their imaginative realization in literature, is a devious and disconnected one, full of unexpected detours through terrain scarcely surveyed by earlier critical maps. Writers themselves have gone astray in this uncharted landscape, a circumstance best illustrated, perhaps, by Peter Weiss's *The Investigation,* an attempt to create with a minimum of alteration from the testimony of witnesses at the Auschwitz trial in Frankfurt between 1963 and 1965 a series of dramatic scenes which would convey the authentic reality of that experience by using only the language of history, the words of the men and women who themselves endured—as victims or tormentors—its fearful tenure in time.

The result on the stage is singularly undramatic, notwithstanding the loose verse form of the monologues and dialogues of the characters—the chilling evidence in its pages rarely rises above the cold, harsh surface of mere factual truth. By duplicating the details of history without embellishing them, while at the same time being highly selective in his use of them, Weiss eliminates any perspective which might offer his audience an entry into their implications; oddly, and certainly unintentionally, the result is not a new aesthetic distance, but an aesthetic *indifference,* a failure of the artist's imagination to seduce the spectator into a feeling of complicity with the material of his drama. *The Investigation* confirms more powerfully than any theoretical argument the need for a dimension in the literature of atrocity beyond the poetic distillation of court records, for something comparable to the wedding of history and innovation that made Weiss's own *Marat/Sade* (in its fullest stage version) such a brilliant success.[1]

Anyone present in the courtroom in Germany during the trial which furnished the substance of Weiss's Auschwitz play might have seen and heard impressive evidence of the human mind's inadequacy to absorb—to say nothing of perceiving the implications of—the naked facts of atrocity:

> The witness remembers one particular day in November, 1944: "Jewish children were brought to Auschwitz. A truck came and stopped for a moment in front of the Political Section. A little boy jumped off. He held an apple in his hand. Boger and Draser [SS men] were standing in the doorway. I was standing at the window. The child was standing next to the car with his apple and was enjoying himself. Suddenly Boger [one of the guards on trial] went over to the boy, grabbed his legs, and smashed his head against the wall. Then he calmly picked up the apple. And Draser told me to wipe 'that' off the wall. About an hour later I was called to Boger to interpret in an interrogation and I saw him eating the child's apple."

> Nobody can quite believe that he has heard right, but the witness reiterates the description of this insane act.

> "You saw it with your own eyes?"

> "I saw it with my own eyes."

> "You can swear to it in good conscience?"

> "Absolutely."[2]

Later the judge summons the witness back to the stand: "Is what you have told us the absolute truth?" Replies the witness: "I swear it is."[3]

Between the incomprehension of judge and jury and the certitude of the witness, the groping for a response and the incontrovertible facts of Auschwitz, lies that nocturnal realm which the writers I examine in this study inherited as their reality. Since such evidence clearly *dis*orients whatever human faculty might respond to it, piling atrocity on atrocity in the manner of *The Investigation* without providing an imaginative orientation for the development of this faculty could only paralyze it further. The writer bequeathed this evidence can deny it (surely the witness is lying); or he can ignore it (an aberration, totally uncharacteristic of modern reality); or he can accept its challenge, concede that the familiar structure of reality has crumbled, forge a path between incomprehension and response, and finally rebuild from the rubble of such testimony a grotesque literary edifice that will leave its inhabitants, like the judge and jury, incredulous and dismayed, but also, unlike the audience, better equipped to enter into the literal revelation through the avenue of accessibility laid out by the imagination of the artist.

"Normal men," insists David Rousset, whose *L'Univers Concentrationnaire* has given one name to the nocturnal realm just described, "do not know that everything is possible. Even if the evidence forces their intelligence to admit it, their muscles do not believe it. The concentrationees do know. . . . They are set apart from the rest of the world by an experience impossible to communicate." This recurrent notion, which we have encountered before and will meet again, expressed most often by writers who, like Rousset, nevertheless go on to "tell about" what they know only a few initiates will comprehend, illuminates the discontinuous and dislocated nature of their vision perhaps even more than the divided impulses driving them simultaneously to speech and silence, and culminates most fruitfully in the search for a metaphorical language to sustain the tensions that inspire it.

Thus, Rousset imagines this incommunicable experience as one ripe with decay that "shrivels away within itself" though it "still lives on in the world like a dead planet laden with corpses."[4] His grim simile aptly illustrates a vital paradox afflicting many writers themselves intimately involved with the Holocaust: for just as "surviving corpses" palpably contradicts our sense of a reasonable reality, so Rousset's language graphically summons up the very atmosphere of death-in-life that lay at the heart of his private experience. It conjures the writer to dredge from the mute abyss of anguish verbal tokens of that woe, even as it warns of the dangers that threaten to stifle the voice of the intruder who dares to wander through its depths.

One of the first to venture in this direction was Wolfgang Borchert, a young German who returned from the war maimed in spirit and ailing in body, conditions to which he shortly succumbed—in 1947 he was dead at the age of twenty-six. His most famous work, the play *Draussen vor der Tür (The Man Outside),* dramatizes the disillusionment of a soldier arriving in his homeland to find it drained of all meaning, hollow compensation for the years of senseless agony. But more important for our purposes are the stories and short prose pieces—half essay and half rhapsody—that Borchert left behind him. These illuminate the inner duality which the earliest writers in the tradition of atrocity seem to have experienced, the conviction that language was powerless to evoke their nightmare visions and the urgent need to find words to do so—a nightmare, as one commentator has suggested, which "imposes silence even while it demands speech."[5]

In a lyrical essay of late 1946 or early 1947, entitled "In May, In May Cried the Cuckoo" (intensifying the paradox, since May represents the crest of spring, the time of renewal, and also the month of the Third Reich's final collapse and war's end in Europe), Borchert struggles with the familiar question of "after such horrors, what language?" deeply tormented as he is by the writer's inability to draw on his customary treasury of words to express his vision of what men have committed and endured. Mourning the writer's isolation, he invokes the mocking cry of the cuckoo as a reminder of the abyss which history has sunk between the poet and his art:

> Cry, bird of loneliness, make fools of the poets, they lack your mad syllables, and their lonely distress becomes drivel, and only when they're dumb do they do their best, bird of loneliness, when mothercry hunts us through sleepless May nights, then we do our most heroic deed. The unspeakable loneliness, this icy male loneliness, we live then, we live without your mad sounds, brother bird, for the last, the ultimate cannot be put into words.[6]

Borchert makes the cuckoo a surrogate spokesman for "the true sounds of the world" which the helpless writer, overwhelmed by the enormity of the "truths," regards with frustration. In so doing, he himself becomes a spokesman for all those who looked out on their shattered world with dazed eyes and numbed memories and wondered how they would ever organize their sensations into meaningful verbal patterns.

The proposition that before 1939 imagination was always in advance of reality, but that after 1945 reality had outdistanced the imagination so that nothing the artist conjured up could equal in intensity or scope the improbabilities of *l'univers concentrationnaire*—this proposition, offered by several writers in the tradition of atrocity, is a crucial one, sustained by Borchert's own response to the postwar scene:

> For who among us, who then oh, who knows a rhyme for the rattle of lungs shot to pieces, a rhyme for the scream at the gallows, who knows the metre, the rhythm, for rape, who knows a metre for the bark of machine-guns, a sound for the new-smothered scream of a dead horse's eye, in which no further heaven is mirrored, not even the blazing of villages, what press has a sign for the rust-red of goods-trucks [i.e. *Güterwagen* = freight cars or box-cars, used for deporting Jews and other prisoners to concentration camps], this world-in-flames red, this dried-up blood-encrusted red on white human skin? Go home, poets, go into the forests, catch fish, chop wood and do your most heroic deed: Be silent! Let the cuckoo cry of your lonely hearts be silent, for there's no rhyme and no metre for it, and no drama, no ode and no psychological novel can encompass the cry of the cuckoo, and no dictionary and no press has syllables or signs for your wordless world-rage, for your exquisite pain, for the agony of your love. . . . Since for the grandiose roar of this world and for its hellish stillness the paltriest words are lacking. All we can do is: to add up, collect the sum, count it, note it down.[7]

But even while demanding silence, Borchert labors to discover a speech, a voice to express his "wordless world-rage" and "exquisite pain," to recapture the lost eloquence of the poet's tongue. Notwithstanding his demurral, his catalogue of the items of atrocity is more than a notation: the rust-red of box-cars and "dried-up blood-encrusted red on white human skin" are not statistics of death, adding up, collecting, and counting, but stark suggestive images of atrocity which draw on a landscape of extreme horror not wholly familiar to his readers, even though it is an inescapable part of the reality of their time. Untroubled by his apparent self-contradiction (which by now we can recognize as a symptom of the literature concerned with this problem), Borchert in the same passage proclaims: "We must make a note of our misery"—though he agrees that sparse illustration, never detailed explanation, is all one can hope for, with two hundred printed pages serving as a commentary on "the twenty thousand invisible pages, on the Sisyphus pages which make up our life, for which we know no words, no grammar and no punctuation. But on these twenty thousand invisible pages of our book stands the grotesque ode, the ridiculous epic, the most prosaic and bewitched of all novels: Our crazy spherical world, our quivering heart, our life! That is the book of our mad, bold, fearful loneliness on night-dead streets."[8]

Grotesque, ridiculous, crazy, mad—terms that do not describe an ordered world, or even a readily visible one. Perhaps the most convincing evidence that certain writers following World War II felt themselves confronted by a unique situation for which earlier literary traditions had not prepared them is the fundamental difference between Borchert's response and the reaction of writers to World War I. They shared with Borchert his shock and disillusionment, and were vividly aware of a rupture in historical tradition (and to some extent, in traditions of literary style), but neither Dos Passos nor Hemingway nor Erich Maria Remarque felt totally disabled by his experience—each turned willingly to a kind of literary realism that could satisfactorily echo "the true sounds of the world" of war and violence, as they had experienced it. Their sensibilities were jarred by the disjunctions between the rhetoric of peace and the brutal events of war, but this became the *basis* of their vision, not a barrier against it. Hemingway's aim was to describe "the way it was"; Borchert realized the futility of such an ambition, since the "ultimate" was indescribable.

Yet Borchert tried, and since his time a generation of writers has invented a new fictional grammar, or several, all designed to make each written page evoke ten unwritten ones. One of the peculiarities of the literature of atrocity is that (far more than Hemingway's literature of understatement) so much of it is a literature of innuendo, as if the author were conspiring with his readers to recapture an atmosphere of insane misery which they somehow shared, without wishing to name or describe it in detail. Borchert experimented with such a technique in a tale of 1946, called "Billbrook," about a Canadian airman walking at war's end through a dead and utterly demolished section of Hamburg. The landscape presents a desolation scarcely evokable; yet the precisely chosen images communicate horrors far in excess of their fragmentary nature. For example:

> He was standing at a big cross-roads. He looked back: No child? No dog? No car? He looked to the left: No child. No dog. No car. He looked to the right and in front: no child and no dog and no car. He looked along the four endless roadways: No house. No house? Not even a cottage. Not even a hut. Not even an isolated, still-standing trembling, tottering wall. Only the chimneys, like the fingers of corpses, stabbed the late afternoon sky. Like the bones of a giant skeleton. Like tombstones. The fingers of corpses, clutching at God, threatening heaven. The bare, bony, burnt, bent fingers of corpses. In whichever direction he looked, and he had the feeling that from the cross-roads he could see for miles in each direction: No living thing. Nothing. Nothing living.[9]

For the writer in quest of a new idiom, this scene provides a startling challenge; indeed, the specific physical image of the crossroads is invested with unusual metaphorical significance. The familiar sounds of civilization have abruptly disappeared—the cry or laugh of a child, a dog's bark, the whine of an auto engine—to be replaced by a stark visual silence that conveys its implications through a series of ominous and sinister similes of extermination. Borchert is "only" describing his native Hamburg, but the association of chimneys with corpses inescapably wakens memories of scenes which Borchert may never have witnessed but which were absorbed by his imagination and transformed into a kind of archetypal symbolic presentation of the inconceivable annihilation—the literal reduction to nothingness—that we identify with the Holocaust. It is a landscape without figures, an eerie, frozen *danse macabre* of inert forms sculptured against a background of silence—and through all this wanders the Canadian airman, from the town of Hopedale in Labrador, whose naïve and peaceful eyes survey this fantasy of death with fascinated incomprehension, as his comfortable assumptions succumb to the suasions of a reality too terrible to behold. The passage is saturated with negatives, in a desperate attempt to suggest presence by representing absence; the few chimneys projecting from the earth are metamorphosed into the pleading, accusing arms and fingers of corpses which suddenly clutter the barren landscape and assault the imagination with remembrances of things past that populate the desolate scene with the vividness of a waking dream. Yet Borchert has actually *mentioned* almost none of this.

Nothing is unaffected by this metamorphosis, including nature. For Hemingway nature usually provided solace and escape, at least temporary respite from disillusioning human reality. But (as in Nelly Sachs's poems) Borchert's story is encompassed by a landscape of horror, merges with it, and finally shares its grotesque atmosphere of gloom. The development comprises a remarkable demonstration of prose persuasion. The passage begins with a suggestion of the effect of this unholy pilgrimage on the airman himself: "He gazed stubbornly before him at the earth. But he could not recover his lost premature pride and his high-spirited mood. Lost, crumbled, dead." Then:

> Suddenly he saw that there was indeed something living in this dead houseless noiseless corpse-fingered city: grass. Green grass. Grass as in Hopedale. Normal grass. Millions of blades. Insignificant. Scanty. But green. And alive. Alive like the hair of the dead. Dreadfully alive. Grass, as everywhere in the world. Sometimes a little too gray, too dewy, too crumpled, dusty. But still green and alive. Everywhere living grass. He grinned. But the grin froze, because his brain thought of a word, a single word. The grin grew gray and dusty, like the grass in several places. But iced with too much hoar-frost. Graveyard grass, thought his brain. Grass? Good, grass, yes. But graveyard grass. Grass on graves. Grass of ruins. Gruesome ghastly gracious gray grass. Graveyard grass, unforgettable, full of the past, saturated with memory, eternal grass on graves. Unforgettable, shabby, mean: unforgettable gigantic grass carpet, over the graves of the world.[10]

Perhaps the ultimate cannot be put into words, but Borchert here has managed to envelop civilization in a shroud through which its spectral death-mask weirdly shines; his grim ironic hymn to the "greenness of the grass" is comparable to Melville's celebrated chapter on the "Whiteness of the Whale." As in Melville, the visible world of green gives way to the invisible spheres of gray, and by applying to inanimate matter epithets like "dreadfully," "gruesome," and "ghastly"—epithets that should properly be reserved for the *human* atrocities committed upon the grasses of the world during the period of his apprenticeship to life—Borchert (again like Nelly Sachs) forces all of reality into complicity with death, with the unforgettable agonies that haunt the memory of the past and permanently alter the physical, the spiritual, the psychological, and the emotional landscape of the present.

The gradual erosion of familiar reality, its displacement by a different, scarcely recognizable, threatening, amorphous externality providing no reassurance or support for the tottering spirit of the victim, is a theme which Borchert's successors would repeatedly exploit. To the protagonist of Borchert's tale, born in Hopedale, the grass at first offers a cause for relief, if not rejoicing: in the city of the dead, at least the green grass is alive. But in the passage quoted, a remarkable counterpoint is established between the expectations of Borchert's character and the direction in which the prose compels the reader. To the young airman, the grass seems "normal"; to the reader, it is transformed gradually into a sinister reminder that never again, or not for a long time, will he be able to contemplate grass without seeing it, as it were, under the influence of the graveyard, alive "like the hair of the dead." Perhaps the contrast is too stark, but the metamorphosis in attitude is underscored when we recall Walt Whitman's use of the identical image in *Leaves of Grass*. One is tempted to suggest, indeed, that Borchert offers a grim rejoinder to the innocent question of Whitman's child: "What is the grass?" The reality of Borchert's immediate past, pressing with obstinate

gloom on the imagination, casts ineradicable shadows on Whitman's cheerful alternatives ("I guess it must be the flag of my disposition, out of hopeful green stuff woven," or "I guess it is the handkerchief of the Lord"); Whitman's association of grass with death ("now it seems to me the beautiful uncut hair of graves") only confirms the distance we have traveled from transcendental conviction to the bizarre uncertainties of a post-atrocity era. Ironically, Whitman almost supplies writers like Borchert with an epigraph that describes the core of their vision—"And to die is different from what any one supposed"—"almost" because Whitman adds "and luckier,"[11] a supplement which must leave a bitter taste on the tongue of anyone who has sampled the ingredients with which writers like Borchert season their literary brews.

One of these writers was Ernst Wiechert, who never properly joined the fraternity himself but anticipated several of its problems and expressed them with extraordinary clarity and insight for his younger successors. A German novelist with an established reputation before the war broke out, Wiechert was arrested by the Gestapo in 1938 and eventually wound up in Buchenwald, where he spent five months before the efforts of his wife and friends (he was not Jewish), aided apparently by his fame as a writer, secured his release. During the war Wiechert wrote a brief account of his experiences in the concentration camp, which was published in 1947 as *The Forest of the Dead (Der Totenwald)*. The prologue to the work is gravely prophetic:

> This report is meant to be no more than a prelude to the great Symphony of Death which will some day be written by hands more competent than mine. I have but stood in the doorway and looked at the dark stage, and I have recorded not so much what my eyes have seen as what my soul has seen. The curtain had risen only part of the way, the lamps were dim yet, the great actors were still standing in the dark. But the spokes of the horrible wheel had already begun to turn, and blood and terror were dripping from it as it circled flashing in the dark.
>
> I was called upon, and now my voice must speak. Others will be called, and they will speak. But behind them all the Great Voice will be swelling from beyond, saying "Let there be night!"[12]

Actually, the book progresses slowly from what the "soul" has seen to what the "eyes" have seen, as Wiechert first assesses the influence his "new" life must irrevocably exert on his former one, then tries to realize visually, through the precision of language, the exact nature of this "new" vision of experience, and finally confesses—we almost anticipate it—his inability to record what words were never designed to describe, or eyes in fact to behold, or human creatures to suffer, thus reaffirming the barrier between art and reality which the unique nature of the Holocaust (with its attendant experiences) created whenever it touched the sensibilities of the writer.

In an effort to gain detachment and probably greater universality in *The Forest of the Dead*, Wiechert assumes the guise of an inmate named Johannes, but the autobiography is thinly veiled, and Johannes plays the role of a sensitive mind stunned by a reality it was unprepared to encounter:

> It is hard to describe the emotions which had stirred Johannes from the moment of arrival in the camp. It was not so much terror, or bewilderment, or a half-conscious numbness. It was more the sensation of an ever-growing coldness that spread gradually from deep within until it filled his entire being. It was as if the life he had lived up to now, and his whole world were freezing to numbness in this chill. As though he was gazing through a thick sheet of ice at very distant things. And in that distance moved the noiseless and unreal spirits of his past; the people he had loved, his books, his hopes and plans, all of them marked now, bearing the germ of death, and given to disintegration, without a purpose in a world in which these sons of pastors were now the ruling men ["sons of pastors" = SS guards]. He felt the cold break down his dream as frost breaks a flower stem. He felt a crack run through God's image, a crack that would not ever heal.[13]

Imagery of insulation abounds in the literature of atrocity—insulation separating two worlds, as here the comfortable past and inconceivable present of Johannes, or Borchert's once-vital grass "iced with too much hoarfrost"; and we recall Spender's writers hesitating to plunge into the modern centers of the "destructive element," gazing rather "at the furnace through a fire-proofed window in a thick wall." Fire and ice—Robert Frost was not the last to offer us these dismal alternatives, though his waspish humor traditionally excludes him from the ranks of those who have had genuine acquaintance with the night.

Most important in the Wiechert passage, however, is the effect of the present on the past: ice separates, it chills and freezes, but it does not preserve; it is here literally another destructive element, disintegrating the substances of memory ("people," "books," "hopes," "plans,")—customary companions to human solitude—and leaving a vacuum of values, a paralyzing, frozen, meaningless and inconsolable despair. And the last concession is the most difficult, but Wiechert submits to its promptings with a painful honesty: the crack in God's image sunders man from his spiritual heritage and destiny and returns us to Wiechert's own ominous echo of the Great Voice: "Let there be night!" A world darkened by the withdrawal of spiritual possibility is unusual, though not unique, in the history of literature; but the demonic powers that trod this God-abandoned landscape, and the acts carried out at their behest and under their supervision, tinted everything with an unfamiliar hue of death that even Dante's Inferno failed to reflect.

This is precisely what required the writer to devise a new palette of colors, and Wiechert added his voice—though in point of time his was one of the first—to the chorus of those who announced the futility of the endeavor, even while he experimented with shades and tones for sketching visions of the unspeakable. His evocation of prisoners huddled forlornly on the *Appelplatz*—the area where roll

call was held—is all the more remarkable when we consider that he is drawing on recollections of 1938, when Buchenwald was a comparatively "mild" prelude to the extermination camps that were to follow:

> When late in August, in the gray light of dawn, those thousands gathered for early roll call, bent down and freezing, in pouring rain, mud on the drill ground reaching above their ankles, many leaning on tall sticks to hold themselves upright, some in a serious condition clinging to the shoulders of their comrades, some on crude stretchers; when the wind drove puffs of fog about the columns, enveloping and then revealing them in the pale light; when at the foot of one of the trees or a light pole a man lay dying, half in the other world already, with his face open to the light of dawn, then all this was a picture of the damned arisen like a specter from Hades, or a vision out of Hell, beyond the brush of the greatest painter, beyond the needle of the greatest etcher, because no human phantasy or even the dreams of a genius can measure up to this reality, which has not had its like in centuries, perhaps never.[14]

The fog-shrouded atmosphere drives the spectator to rub his eyes to see whether or not he is dreaming, to deny what his vision confirms, to draw comparisons—as does Wiechert, instinctively searching for a literary vindication at the very moment of his consciousness that none could possibly exist—almost helplessly with the traditional Hell or Hades, which are clearly recognized as inadequate similes; and finally, as the fog rolls in and out of the scene, to retreat in awed silence. But Wiechert's prediction that no human fantasy and no dreams can "measure up to this reality" is premature, though he shrewdly defines the perspective which later writers will have to use in their approach to that reality: for "human phantasy" is precisely the combination of real and unreal that can evoke the moral and physical chiaroscuro Wiechert speaks of; and the atmosphere of dreams, already familiar to readers of Kafka, afforded an entry to the world of the Holocaust that was denied the advocates of literal realism.

To establish an order of reality in which the unimaginable becomes imaginatively acceptable exceeds the capacities of an art devoted entirely to verisimilitude; some quality of the fantastic, whether stylistic or descriptive, becomes an essential ingredient of *l'univers concentrationnaire*. Indeed, those who recorded details painstakingly in an attempt to omit none of the horror may have been unwittingly guilty of ignoring precisely the chief source of that horror—existence in a middle realm between life and death with its ambiguous and inconsistent appeals to survival and extinction, which continuously undermined the logic of experience without offering any satisfactory alternative. It is scarcely accidental that those who testify most intensely to the dilemma are writers who themselves were somehow intimately acquainted with the "reality" of the era, since they are the ones best equipped to understand the layers of apparent fantasy which obscured it. And perhaps the most singular appeal of their literary efforts is that the distortions wrought by their veils of fantasy only illuminate the terrors of the "reality" with an unholier glow.

Inevitably, writers concerned with the aesthetic interplay of fantasy and reality would turn to those phenomena of the half-conscious life where the two are tightly inter-twined—the world of dreams. More concretely, the influence of the reality of atrocity on the dreams of those who endured it—whether victims or spectators—forms a fascinating study in itself, and indeed at least one brief study of the subject has already appeared, which, though limited in scope *and* inference, offers some relevant background for the literature we are concerned with. Charlotte Beradt's *The Third Reich of Dreams* examines recurrent dreams of selected Germans between the years 1933 and 1945 (though the author herself fled Germany in 1939, returning after the war to complete her research). She is less interested in what the dreams reveal about the individual personalities of the dreamers than in what they disclose about the inner tension of a people collectively trapped (some willingly, others not) by an environment of "total authority" in which the "normal" development of character through the free expression of ideas and impulses is forbidden.

In other words, she explores the impact of a more broadly public and less explicitly brutal and repressive *univers concentrationnaire* on the psychic life, the realm of dreams, of the ordinary inhabitant of the Third Reich; and the results of her investigation are of special interest to us because they suggest and clarify some of the problems of characterization and style which novelists exploiting this material will have to confront: the creation of characters with divided and often uncomplementary sensibilities, or personalities so passive as to be virtually extinguished, or individuals with exaggerated impulses (like an extraordinary capacity for cruelty), which in a traditional setting would be acceptable only in surrealistic or ultramelodramatic literature. Thus, it is not surprising that in the dreams recorded the dreamers are usually involved in situations inconsistent with the expectations of logic or reason. According to Miss Beradt, a major value of these dreams is what they expose about the emotional states and motives of men when they become cogs in a giant machine; and though we dare not confuse the workings of that machine inside and outside the concentration camp, the dreams it inspired among nonvictims help to clarify the nature of the reality imposed on those who suffered a harsher fate. For example:

> When a person sits down to keep a diary, this is a deliberate act, and he remolds, clarifies, or obscures his reactions. But while seeming to record seismographically the slightest effects of political events on the psyche, these dreams—these diaries of the night—were conceived independently of their authors' conscious will. They were, so to speak, dictated to them by dictatorship. Dream imagery might thus help to describe the structure of a reality that was just on the verge of becoming a nightmare.[15]

The transfer and expansion of such visions into sustained works of the imagination has been the delicate and difficult task of the writers considered in this study, who almost uniformly acknowledged that the material of their art must somehow include a sense of a reality not merely on the verge of becoming a nightmare, but already become one.

The uncanny resemblance between the dreams recorded in Miss Beradt's book (and the very language she employs to describe them), and the substance of the literature of atrocity indicates an imaginative affinity that reaches far deeper than the accidental fulfillment of certain scattered dreams in real experience. It is by no means merely a matter of prophetic intuition, she suggests:

> These dreams are indeed reminiscent of mosaics—often surrealistic ones—whose single pieces had, as it were, been chipped from the reality that was the Third Reich. This justifies interpreting them as contributions to the psychology of totalitarianism, and permits one to apply them to the concrete situation they illuminate.
> . . .
>
> Set against a background of disintegrating values and an environment whose very fabric was becoming warped, these dreams are permeated by a reality whose quality is unreal [*irreale Realität*]—a combination of thought and conjecture in which rational details are brought into fantastic juxtapositions and thereby made more, rather than less, coherent; where ambiguities appear in a context that nonetheless remains explicable, and latent as well as unknown and menacing forces are all made a part of everyday life.[16]

Although "unreal reality" is intended as a description of dream-content, it serves equally well as an exact commentary on the paradoxical quality of the experience attested to by some of the witnesses mentioned in this chapter. Perhaps "irrealism" would be a more valid description of certain techniques that sought to enlarge on their testimony.

Dreams, of course, have long been literary devices for probing the unconscious motives and tensions of characters, but never before has their provenance been so clearly a moral and emotional reality shared by large masses of people. The private nightmares of Lady Macbeth or Dostoevsky's Svidrigaylov arise from situations afflicting only themselves or those closest to them: total strangers could not make much sense of Lady Macbeth's obsession with cleanliness or the rodents and spiders that haunt Svidrigaylov. The literature of atrocity, however, like the dream images in Miss Beradt's study, draws on a nonimaginative reality available to anyone familiar with even the barest details of the historical past it alludes to; accordingly (and unlike literary tragedy), it is compelled to employ the implications of fact to create its unique aesthetic appeal.

Thus, Miss Beradt is not far off when she observes "how closely the means employed in these dreams to describe life under the Third Reich coincide with the techniques contemporary German writers use to convey a dark past that eludes them when they approach it in a realistic fashion," or that the atmosphere of total if inexplicable oppression they exude resembles some episodes and parables from Kafka. In fact, she astutely continues, slipping un-consciously from dream analysis to literary criticism,

> the line between the comic and the tragic often be-comes blurred as their authors struggle to express the inexpressible. They describe phenomena typical of the period in the form of parables, parodies, and paradoxes. And situation is heaped on situation in a succession of snapshot images from which the echo of daily life re-verberates with frightening loudness or with equally frightening softness, emerging radically simplified but also radically exaggerated.[17]

The dreams thus become commentaries on a reality that insinuates itself into the sensibility of the dreamer (or the writer) and through some kind of ambiguous transforma-tion is altered into "a reality whose quality is unreal" but simultaneously more vivid and—perhaps most inexpli-cable of all—more tolerable and accessible to the imagina-tion. This atmosphere seems appropriate for such fiction because in these dreams (as in the experience of totalitar-ian reality that inspired them) the rigid framework of fa-miliar values has disintegrated, and a world appears where recognizable fears are masked by eccentric behavior—obliterating, as Miss Beradt points out, the boundaries be-tween tragedy and comedy and thus laying the foundations for the possibility of the absurd which, following a tribu-tary not far distant from the literature of atrocity, led to the drama of Beckett and Ionesco. Just as the moral enormi-ties committed (and suffered) during the Holocaust re-quired these authors to revise their conception of human character and of what represented "normal" behavior, so they had to alter their notion of literary setting, substitut-ing for the traditional environments of fiction a complex amalgamation of reality and unreality that gradually dis-placed previous norms and itself became the measure of what once was considered "normal."

Since the genesis of these authentic dreams may be traced to a reality akin to (but by no means identical with) the one that later stimulated the literature of atrocity, it is hardly surprising that some of them read like condensed anecdotes from their pages. To glance at only one or two by way of illustration: a twenty-two-year-old girl who felt her crooked nose identified her as a member of the "infe-rior" race dreamed in the early years of the Hitler era:

> "A peaceful family outing. Mother and I had brought along some cake and the folder containing our geneal-ogy. Suddenly a shout: they're coming. Everyone in the garden restaurant there on the Havel River knew who 'they' were and what our crime was. Run, run, run. I looked about for a hiding place high up. Perhaps up the trees? Atop a cupboard in the restaurant? All at once I found myself lying at the bottom of a pile of corpses with no idea how it got there—at least I had a good hiding place. Pure bliss under my pile of bodies, clutch-ing my papers in their folder."[18]

The omissions here are as significant as the included de-tails: the introduction of the threatening force without ex-planation (everyone "knew who 'they' were"); the abrupt

transition from familiar routine to macabre flight, without any attempt to establish a logical connection between the two; the reduction of tragedy by the absurd failure of the victim to respond to her dilemma with intense emotion (further compounded by the grotesquely comic sensation of "pure bliss" in the security of the death heap); and the remarkable anticipation of a later reality, which retrospec-tively, given our knowledge of the mass exterminations, controls the reader's response in a way that compels him to view what is "only" a dream through the shuddering (and partially distorting) lenses of historical fact. The mad-sane fictional universe of Jakov Lind is not far off.

One other example must suffice to illustrate the ingredients that constitute the unfamiliar yet never entirely unrecog-nizable reality of *l'univers concentrationnaire,* a hybrid of the nerve-wracking bewilderments of a Kafkan anti-hero and the spiritual futility of Dante's infernal sufferers:

> "While out for a walk we heard a rumor in the streets that people should keep away from their apartments be-cause something terrible was going to happen. We stood across the street and looked longingly up at our apart-ment where the blinds were drawn as if no one lived there.
>
> We went to my mother-in-law's apartment, the last place left to go—up the stairs, but we discovered strange people living there now—could it be the wrong building?
>
> We went up the stairs in the building next door, but it, too, was the wrong one—a hotel. We came out by an-other door and tried to find our way back, but now we couldn't even find the street any more.
>
> All at once we thought we'd found the house we so badly needed, but it was only the same hotel that had confused us once before. After we'd gone through this unnerving run-around for the third time, the woman who owned the hotel told us, 'It won't do you any good even if you do find that apartment. This is what is going to happen. . . .' And in the manner of Christ's curse on Ahasuerus [the legendary Wandering Jew], she pronounced:
>
> > 'There comes a law:
> > They shall dwell nowhere.
> > Their lot shall be
> > To wander ever through the streets.'
>
> Then she changed her tone and, as if she were reading out some proclamation, droned: 'In conjunction with said law, everything previously permitted is now for-bidden, to wit: entering shops and stores, employing craftsmen. . . .' Right in the middle of this horrifying scene something trivial occurred to me—now how was I to have my new suit made up?
>
> We left the hotel and went out *forever* into the dismal rain."[19]

The tension between the normal ("how was I to have my new suit made up?") and the abnormal (literally displaced persons, doomed to wander without cause forever in the rain) was a basic constituent of reality during the Holocaust. The departure from the "safe" and familiar apartment into an unspecified but threatening future (for which no one is prepared—the common response was to "walk around the corner," as it were, expecting to find the old apartment, the former security, with nothing changed) is an astonishing anticipation of the fate of millions (considering that the dream was recorded in 1935!). But the most revealing and useful detail, insofar as the later development of character and setting in fiction is concerned, is the preponderance of what we might call nostalgia over apprehension, the inability of the victims to confront the sudden events with concrete action, or even reflection, because nothing in their past was commensurate with the possibilities of physical and spiritual annihilation that lay before them. And since the dreamers themselves were relatively unselfconscious about the implications of their dreams (in this instance, the dreamer wasn't even Jewish, though her husband was), they are valuable to us chiefly as evidence of the influence the Third Reich had on the unconscious life of those affected by it, and as the raw material for a clearer understanding of the relationship between "irrealism" and "realism" as literary techniques for portraying the world of the Holocaust.

The raw material approaches the more finished forms of art—if not the final version—in dreams recounted by self-conscious authors who sought to articulate some of the tensions between the normal and abnormal alluded to earlier, and who therefore commented more elaborately on the implications of their dreams and the problems these implications posed to the literary imagination. One of these, a young Italian Jew named Primo Levi, spent a year at Buna-Monowitz, a munitions labor-camp associated with the main extermination camp at Auschwitz-Birkenau. Like so many others, Levi retrospectively acknowledged that the ordeal suffered by him and his fellow prisoners would never be erased from their consciousness, but would afflict their sensibilities permanently and transform their responses to life, awake and in dreams:

> So for us even the hour of liberty rang out grave and muffled, and filled our souls with joy and yet with a painful sense of pudency, so that we should have liked to wash our consciences and our memories clean from the foulness that lay upon them; and also with anguish, because we felt that this should never happen, that now nothing could ever happen good and pure enough to rub out our past, and that the scars of the outrage would remain within us for ever, and in the memories of those who saw it, and in the places where it occurred, and in the stories that we should tell of it.[20]

Levi goes on to describe the effects this "awful privilege" of his generation has had on the lives of himself and his contemporaries: like modern ancient mariners, they must plunge back into the "inexhaustible fount of evil" they have survived, but which has indelibly stained their future reality, and narrate to trapped but fascinated bridegrooms the "incurable nature of the offense" to humanity which they have endured and which "spreads like a contagion" across the landscape of contemporary history.

The permanently corrupting influence of such experiences inspired survivors, too, with recurrent collective dreams that later provided many writers with material for an imaginative universe existing between the bounds of fantasy and reality. Elsewhere Levi has commented on one peculiarity of the dream-phenomenon in *l'univers concentrationnaire*:

> My dream stands in front of me, still warm, and although awake I am still full of its anguish: and then I remember that it is not a haphazard dream, but that I have dreamed it not once but many times since I arrived here, with hardly any variations of environment or details. I am now quite awake and I remember that I have recounted it to Alberto [a fellow inmate] and that he confided to me, to my amazement, that it is also his dream and the dream of many others, perhaps of everyone. Why does it happen? Why is the pain of every day translated so constantly into our dreams, in the ever-repeated scene of the unlistened-to story?[21]

Levi's dream-state is a "ladder between the unconscious and the conscious," in which he tries to explain to friends and members of his family the essential truth of his camp experience—the railway cars, the train whistles, the hard wooden beds, the hunger, the lice, the beatings, the blood; but his listeners do not follow him, "they are completely indifferent: they speak confusedly of other things among themselves, as if I was not there." The gulf between the two worlds, not the poverty of language, is what imposes silence here, as if the speaker in the dream had not yet recognized the need for finding new ways of communicating his painful sense of a "different" reality to those still dwelling in the familiar and normal past. "This is the most immediate fruit of exile, of uprooting," Levi concludes: "The prevalence of the unreal over the real. Everyone dreamed past and future dreams, of slavery and redemption, of improbable paradises, of equally mythical and improbable enemies; cosmic enemies, perverse and subtle, who pervade everything like the air."[22]

As in the poems of Nelly Sachs and the passages by Wolfgang Borchert, the cosmic enemy becomes life itself, absorbed into the landscape and the atmosphere, pervading everything, an indefinable *threat*, always there to disturb one's waking hours and hover over one's dreams, announcing the impossibility of an episode at the very moment it occurs, deceptively reassuring at the instant of extremity, when the options of oblivion and eternity disrupt the "real" until the imagination can no longer acknowledge what it once considered "real." Many of these qualities are incorporated into a kind of archetypal dream of Levi's (as the dream was incorporated into his own future waking hours), adding an imperishable quality of apprehension to the consciousness of contemporary humanity, altering every prior conception of reality and chafing the imagination of those writers who have chosen to devote a part of their talent to the imaginative recreation of atrocity:

> It is a dream within a dream, varied in detail, one in substance. I am sitting at a table with my family, or with friends, or at work, or in the green countryside; in

short, in a peaceful relaxed environment, apparently without tension or affliction; yet I feel a deep and subtle anguish, the definite sensation of an impending threat. And in fact, as the dream proceeds, slowly or brutally, each time in a different way, everything collapses and disintegrates around me, the scenery, the walls, the people, while the anguish becomes more intense and more precise. Now everything has changed to chaos, I am alone in the center of a grey and turbid nothing, and now, I *know* what this thing means, and I also know that I have always known it; I am in the Lager [i.e. concentration camp] once more, and nothing is true outside the Lager. All the rest was a brief pause, a deception of the senses, a dream; my family, nature in flower, my home. Now this inner dream, this dream of peace, is over, and in the outer dream, which continues, gelid, a well-known voice resounds: a single word, not imperious, but brief and subdued. It is the dawn command of Auschwitz, a foreign word, feared and expected: get up, *"Wstawàch."*[23]

It is as if the *Angst* introduced to the modern era by Kierkegaard, Kafka, and their successors had finally acquired a local habitation and a name; certainly the "dawn command of Auschwitz" resembles the inaugural knell of Kafka's nightmare world, for "getting up" opens the odyssey into unreality of both Gregor Samsa and Joseph K. And in both instances, in Levi and Kafka, awakening signifies the termination of the "dream of peace" which for us represents conventional reality: the consolations of friends, family, nature, normalcy, a world whose irrevocable disappearance into an unrecapturable past is a premise of the art of atrocity. *Das wandlose Leben,* life without walls, in the graphic phrase of Charlotte Beradt—a life inflexibly shadowed by a particular kind of threat, permanently deprived of a particular kind of security, has begun. "Nothing is true outside the Lager" now represents reality; all the rest, says Levi, was the "real" dream. And it is not merely a clever but ephemeral slogan; even when it is not literally applied, as in the succeeding account of a dream-become-literature, it symbolizes a portion of the universe entrenched in the modern imagination.

Hermann Kasack's novel, *The City beyond the River* (*Die Stadt hinter dem Strom,* 1947), represents one of the earliest fictional attempts to create a literary mise-en-scène commensurate with this universe, though his account of its genesis is far more relevant to our purposes than the result, which is only moderately successful. According to Kasack, the germ of the novel was a vision he had in 1942, in which he saw "the expanses of a ghostly ruined city, that disappeared into infinity and in which people moved about like troops of imprisoned puppets." The vision, Kasack confesses (perhaps naïvely), may have been inspired by the war and the Nazi years, but he considers this (naïvely too) irrelevant. It is also connected, he says, to a dream of the previous year. In any event, Berlin (where he was living) was still intact, and he had not yet seen any place that had been touched by the war. His vision, he concludes, must have been an anticipation of reality; it inspired him to begin the novel, without knowing where it might lead.[24]

The novel, whose chief limitation is probably a *total* reliance on the descriptive techniques of realism to evoke an unrealistic atmosphere, takes a young man on a train journey across a river into a realm populated by strange figures, some known to him, who behave with a passivity he cannot comprehend, and who, we suspect sooner than he (and with an ease that minimizes the tension of the fiction), are actually dead. "At first," Kasack writes in his retrospective account, "I intended to get by with a few pages, in order to capture the vision of a life grown ghostlike. But the increasingly uncanny reality of the time repeatedly summoned up new images." Gradually, the content of his original vision became a reflection of the real world, one that "in its social, spiritual, and cultural structure appeared just as dubious and fragile, just as false and insecure," as the houses of German cities, which everywhere tottered on the brink of collapse. Then a strange thing happened, which temporarily convinced Kasack that he would be unable to finish his book: "Something occurred that completely paralyzed me, though I should have foreseen it:—reality had caught up with my vision. The reality which I had foreshadowed had become the arena of general existence—including the most bizarre details."[25]

When the landscape of life begins to resemble the landscape of art, and the work of the imagination becomes a retrospective prophecy, then the usual creative process is reversed, and the writer must reorient his own attitude toward experience. As Germany turned into the kingdom of the dead that he had supposedly anticipated in his novel, Kasack realized that "reality had not overtaken my vision, but had only confirmed it." This recognition—a slow process of nearly a year, according to Kasack—liberated him from his imaginative paralysis; after 1945—by then the war was over, and the full extent of the human desolation it had bred in Germany and beyond its borders was public knowledge—he completed his novel. Later, Kasack could describe its milieu in detail as an intermediate realm "where men exist only as images of life, without participating in it in the fullest sense, and where at the same time they are touched by death, without falling senseless into its lap." Human creatures whose mechanical gestures belie their reality, signs of civilization promising a vitality that dissolves as one approaches, the familiar giving way to the threatening, the individual consciousness sinking into anonymity—"when I searched for a fixed place," says Kasack, "where the images of our reality had settled, this middle-realm of the dead offered itself poetically as the clearest answer."

All this suggests that features of *l'univers concentrationnaire* reached beyond their barbed-wire boundaries to the imagination of writers, whose intimations of disaster floated in an atmosphere of apprehension until history gave substance to these "images of our reality" and persuaded a novelist like Kasack that, for his generation at least, death was less occult than life. He had begun his account of his novel's origin by admitting the possible influence of the Nazi regime on his vision; he ended on a far less ambiguous note: "Terror and the horrible should not be evaded. It is useless to cling to an idyllic attitude that the convulsions of the present are not prepared to acknowledge."[26]

The problem of writing about experience under circumstances in which death is more "real," a more accurate measure of existence—gruesome as that may sound—than life, was anticipated by Borchert in his landscape of a mutilated city whose corpselike rubble assumes a vitality of its own, and by Anthony Hecht in "More Light! More Light!" where the grave becomes the habitation of man and human creatures climb in and out of it in a grisly game of "house." It was foreseen in Ernst Wiechert's *Totenwald* (*Forest of the Dead*), where the germ of death infected his past life, freezing (and disintegrating) all values, cracking God's image, "as frost breaks a flower stem." Hermann Kasack preserved in detail—in fact, published during the war—the dream he alluded to earlier as preceding and helping to shape his subsequent vision of the "middle-realm" of death, and it provides an even sharper insight than Kasack's own commentary into the displacement of life by death as an imaginative framework for understanding the literature of atrocity. Not unexpectedly, Kasack calls his version *"Der Totentraum"*—the Dream of Death.

The account of the dream is so vivid, its treatment of the illogic of reality in a death-dominated atmosphere so artful, that one deplores all the more Kasack's inability to sustain this mood in his novel. In the dream, Kasack finds himself among the dead, having gained entry to their realm by committing a crime punishable by decapitation. He has been convicted and sentenced for slandering the gods of the state in public (this in the printed version; Kasack admits that in the actual dream, the "gods of the state" were the leaders of the Nazi party—reenforcing the curiously literal quality of the dream, in which apprehensions generated by reality are not very much distorted or disguised); the execution, similarly, was carried out before the eyes of all. But the abyss between life and death does not appear, the victim does not quickly lose consciousness, he feels no bodily pain but simply stands there with his blank neckstump: "a single sharp cut had separated [him] from life on earth, [leaving him] still in the midst of the enraged, heaving mob and at the same time in the place of death." In his dream, Kasack is surprised but not overwhelmed by the contradictions between his expectations and his experience: according to the laws of anatomy, the unity of head and body has been destroyed; but someone simply set his head on his neck "like a helmet,"[27] and he continues to function. The reader is gradually induced to accept the impossible as plausible by a matter-of-fact style that belies what it is describing (somewhat in the manner of Kafka). Like the dreamer, he clings to the memories of normality even as reality alters its usual visage: as the two worlds drift apart, the inhabitant of the realm of death makes vain efforts to communicate with the vanishing universe of "life," from which his "crime" has sundered him forever.

Thus, at first the dream-figure remains visible to those who had demanded his execution (as they remain visible to him), including his wife, his children, and his friends, and his instinct is to establish contact with the latter, to reassure them (and to assure himself) that the dead do not depart, but "observe everything on earth, as if they still belonged to the sphere of living creatures." The initial response of the "dead," then, is to refuse to accept the possibility that a permanent metamorphosis in their condition (and in the nature of reality) has occurred: "I told [them] of this strange intermediate state in which I found myself, but soon noticed that my voice made no more sound (because my organs had been severed); I noticed that no one heard me." Writing a message proves equally futile, as the letters dissolve before the eyes of the "living" before they can be deciphered: "everything seemed to have been written with water, nothing remained but some scarcely meaningful scratches of a broken pen, empty furrows on an empty sheet of paper." One is reminded of Joseph K.'s desperate attempt to prove that nothing has changed by pulling out his identity papers and thrusting them before the eyes of his mysterious accusers. In his dream, Kasack gradually acknowledges his changed environment, without abandoning hopes of reestablishing contact with normality, until he is literally split into a kind of Dostoevskeyan double, in the manner of Ivan Karamazov, uncertain which is his real "self," caught between two physical (and, symbolically, spiritual) realities:

> I continued to imagine myself visible on the surface of the earth, even though parts of me were drawn down to unfathomable depths and were condensed there into a phantom which I saw moving about like an external image of myself. I was already assigned to other prisoners of this hell, and noticed the shapes of guards approaching suddenly like cardboard figures, which reached gigantic proportions as I looked. The landscape of lava-like rocks in irregular layers stretched endlessly into the distance.[28]

Primo Levi's principle that "nothing is true outside the Lager" is transposed by Kasack into a dramatic illustration of his less specific conviction that terror and the horrible should not be evaded by the writer who has lived under their influence. At first the realities of death (the more "normal" condition, symbolically, one is tempted to say the "Lager-truth") appear in distorted form; the atmosphere of fear and desolation (the threatening shapes of the guards, for example) belongs to an alien environment. But anyone familiar with the uninitiated prisoner's initial response to his entry into a concentration camp will detect a remarkable imaginative sympathy between the actual accounts and Kasack's dream-vision, ostensibly not concerned with that experience at all—as if the threat of repression at home (Kasack's dream, after all, was unconsciously inspired by a desire to rebel against the sources of power in the state) possessed a secret kinship with the facts of oppression in the camps, the unreal reality of the authentic experience.

For example: Kasack's dream-figure receives advice and information which—given certain differences in emphasis to be expected of a dream—many an actual inmate might recognize:

From one of the dead who had already been in this circle of the underworld for some time I learned that some guards were friendlier, but most were increasingly fierce and malicious. He gave me many suggestions: for example, how I could avoid drinking at meals the hot brew that was like molten lead. By a clever turn of the hand I could unobtrusively pour out the contents of the bowl, without being noticed by the guards. But I was never able to ascertain this way of holding it.[29]

From the center of "the destructive element," events assume a strange logic—the question of self-protection and survival was always uppermost in the minds of the real prisoners—yet the will of the dreamer is still reluctant to assent to what experience proclaims (his inability to learn the "rules" of the death-realm); rather, he feels a compulsion to announce to those he left behind that the transition from life to death is continuous, not abrupt, that in death as in life there is "a way of torment leading to purification," and especially he feels a need to correct some of the misconceptions about death that he himself had expressed while still alive. Again one is reminded of the two worlds of Joseph K., the one in which he protests his innocence, and the one in which he seems unable to ignore the vague accusations which alter his life. The imagery of Kasack's dream supports such a schizophrenic reality: "I saw everything as one views a distant event through glass, approaching and drawing one towards it." First, verbal communication fails; then written messages; finally, visual contact grows dimmer, until what was once real becomes questionable, and all contact between the realms of life and death is broken off—the displacement is complete:

> But now I was compelled to notice that I myself, as earlier the handwriting and the paper, faded more and more from the eyes of my family, more and more withered away into invisibility, even though in death I remained physically embodied, so that I could hardly seem only a shadow to them.
>
> For a while I saw them anxiously running back and forth seeking me or some trace of me. But then they went about their usual business, without acknowledging my presence. And since they no longer thought of me, the bond that joined me to the life of the past gave way, and my dead visage lost sight of their forms. I still saw only the guards, who pressed toward me like a gray wall, and this time it was the wickeder ones who seized me. Then the earthly part of me was extinguished, and I knew nothing more of my death, because I had forgotten life.[30]

When life seems superceded by a condition of existence that the word or concept "death" insufficiently describes, a condition which perhaps we should call an eternal moment of apprehension fused with terror, then the artist has come close to defining the rational-irrational atmosphere that flourishes in most literature of atrocity, a broadly imaginative equivalent to Primo Levi's "dawn command of Auschwitz," which similarly banished his past life into the realm of unreality as "a brief pause, a deception of the senses, a dream"; in Kasack as in Levi, an immediate

threat, however incredible in its implications, variously embodied, dissipates the familiar world and compels the mind and the senses to accept its replacement, if only because the single alternative is to return to a void. To salvage some fragment of his past—a gesture, a memory, some token that an "awakening" must follow this interminable sleep—this is the aim of Kasack's dream-figure. His failure is also a failure of his "forgotten life" (of which he himself, of course, was once a part, and which in the dream he tries so desperately to contact); his reluctance to abandon the attempt reflects the difficulty with which the modern mind (and the creative imagination) accepts the fact that the events culminating in the Holocaust have altered that "forgotten life" beyond recognition; and the futility of his efforts, signified by the hiatus in his memory, suggests that anyone determined to communicate the profoundest implications of this rupture will have to find uniquely convincing ways of rejoining and revitalizing the two alien worlds.

But like the survivors in Nelly Sachs's "Chorus of the Rescued," "leave-taking" may be the only legacy to facilitate such a rehabilitation, a dubious eventuality indeed: perhaps all the artist can do is clarify the reality that lies behind such a rupture. No one will ever isolate the single most crucial crisis for the individual implicit in the Holocaust experience, but certainly included among a list of them must be a new association, or more precisely, a new and unprecedented alliance, with death. Ernst Wiechert's *Forest of the Dead,* Kasack's "Dream of Death," Borchert's spectral landscape of death in his native Hamburg, the young girl who dreamt of lying beneath a pile of corpses—these and countless other illustrations confirm the significance to the imagination of a realm whose features were subtly transforming the familiar contours of life and finally undermining their very stability. The traditional descents to the underworld recorded in the epic poets and Dante always culminated in a return to the living characterized by a spiritual strengthening, a celebration of the future, perhaps a temporary nostalgia (in some instances) for the departed, but never a permanent mood of despair. But the various landscapes of death we have encountered, physical or spiritual, are encompassed by gloom and shrouded with the melancholy fact that nothing—not love or understanding, not memory or hope—will ever again be the same.

An archetypal example of the fiction resulting from these circumstances, assimilating as it does many of the extraordinary responses to the reality of the Holocaust examined in this chapter, is Pierre Gascar's novella *The Season of the Dead,* a tale that begins with the idea of death—"Dead though they may be, the dead do not immediately become ageless"—and ends with the fact of death—"After a moment I wiped away my tears and went back to my dead." Death insinuates itself into the substance of the narrative until it no longer represents merely the termination of life, but the very marrow of existence, the secret at its heart. It is as if the narrator had reversed the direction of the pilgrim Dante's voyage and concluded the journey in the depths of the Inferno face-to-face with a secular incarnation of the negation of spirit, a truth far more mournfully essential than the radiant divine Rose of Paradise—that hunted man, haunted by fear, condemned to extermination, is reduced to nullity.

As a French soldier, not a Jew, who spent five years in German prisoner-of-war camps, Gascar must have been in a position, like his narrator, to observe the process whereby the mind moves imperceptibly toward the content of this vision, unaccustomed as it may be at first to the literally buried horror at the end of the ordeal. For the controlling metaphor of *The Season of the Dead*, the setting of the story, is a cemetery adjoining the French prisoner-of-war camp in the Ukraine, and the chief task of the narrator and his associates is to offer decent interment to those of his comrades who die, from whatever cause, during their imprisonment. A grave-digger (and prisoner) assigned to bury the "war dead," the narrator quickly realizes that this formula "had lost its heroic sense without becoming obsolete"[31]; and thus, in the beginning he unconsciously drifts into the role of reinterpreting, or rediscovering, the meaning of that traditional epithet, "war dead," to penetrate, as it were, the euphemism of death shorn of its heroic associations but as yet lacking a concrete image, an embodiment in the action of the narrative, to add moral and emotional flesh to this discovery.

Just as the men have entered their "second captivity" in this disciplinary prisoner-of-war camp (having previously attempted several abortive escapes), so the narrator slowly penetrates to a "second" sense of his own reality, and all men's, a sense in which death plays a new part, not only as a persistent threat, which is expected in wartime, but as a phenomenon that disfigures his attitude toward himself and the bond that links him to life. The feeling spreads to the other members of the cemetery detachment, who live, Gascar suggests, from "death to death," which distinguishes them from the other prisoners: "We belonged to another world, we were a team of ghosts returning every morning to a green peaceful place, we were workers in death's garden, characters in a long preparatory dream through which, from time to time, a man would suddenly break, leaping into his last sleep" (p. 185). Their routine, given the circumstances, may *seem* ordinary, but fortified by imagery like that in the passage above, which animates associations beneath the surface level of the narrative, it exercises a stealthy effect on our conception of their labor, and finally on the narrator's conception of it too.

The transition, as so often in the literature of atrocity, is made possible by the fate of the Jews, whose suffering, even in narratives like the present one (Kosinski's *The Painted Bird* and Semprun's *The Long Voyage* are other examples), where it does not constitute the central theme of the work, catalyzes the imagination as it expands to symbolic dimensions and ultimately magnetizes the narrator's attention with its fascinating and inscrutable appeal. For in their closely supervised confinement the only escape is for the eyes, and the only horizon, the endless

trains of Jewish deportees from the Ukrainian town adjoining the prison camp and the cemetery; until finally, in a silent communion with victims more irrevocably doomed than they, they read in the fate of the Jews a dramatic pantomime of their own destiny as men.

An unspoken bond unites the two groups, as if "some final inner process of preparation was taking place" (as indeed it was), though as yet their future is still a matter of anticipation, of intellectual formulation, rather than concrete and visceral fact. One morning, however, the prisoners make a discovery that approaches (though it does not yet quite reach) the intensity of an epiphany:

> we saw a man lying dead by the roadside on the way to the graveyard. There was no face; it was hidden in the grass. There was no distinguishing mark, save the armlet with the star of David. There was no blood. There is practically no blood in the whole of this tale of death.
>
> [pp. 189-90]

Death anonymous but embodied, a paradigmatic emblem of the mystery locked in the narrator's experience, with no assurance of a solution other than the visible testimony before his eyes—the challenge then as now is to transform the hidden features into a human identity and to distill some significance from this ominous death of the Jew. Groping for an attitude consonant with the grotesque truth implicit in the discovery of the corpse, the narrator concludes that "every death invents death anew," a harsh, unconsoling, even terrifying principle, since it stifles the prospect of life's renewal after the impulse to destroy has exhausted itself, as if death extended its stranglehold beyond the last act of the tragedy, preventing catharsis and poisoning the future—much in the spirit of the conclusion of *King Lear*.

As if to seal the finality of the rift between the idea of the tragedy of death as man's earthly lot and the grim principle enunciated by the narrator, the narrator together with his German guard visits the ancient Jewish cemetery of the Ukrainian district, where in a dramatic confrontation they explore familiar and unconventional attitudes toward the dead. The German, a pastor in peacetime who himself spent two years in a concentration camp for his "subversive" moral views, then was assigned to this comparatively safe post, traces the letters on the gravestones, reads out the Hebrew dates, and finds solace in the conviction, preached by his religion, that "death belongs to the past."

The narrator, on the other hand, intrigued by the strange breaking branch carved on most of the gravestones, converts its symbolism into the vexing inquiry: "when death has come, has one finished dying?" His subsequent reflection echoes the language and the very imagery of Nelly Sachs's poem: "Perhaps we are doomed to a perpetual leavetaking from that which was life and which lies in the depth of the night, as eternal as the patient stars"—a fearful constellation, illuminating each man's life with a kind of darkness visible, and casting a lurid glow on the ambiguous insight that every death invents death anew. If, as the narrator meditates aloud, "the moment of death is never over" (pp. 198-99) then life may be an immortality in reverse, a "demortality"—to coin a term in the absence of a vocabulary to describe his response—and the unidentified Jewish corpse, like his ancestors in the cemetery, are merely ultimate extensions of a condition that now must define the living as well as the dead.

Absorbed by these unorthodox but increasingly relevant premises, the mind finds it more and more difficult to accommodate itself to the old idea of a world where vitality and survival take priority as human values, and where the persistence of nature assures a hopefully recurring cycle of day following night and spring the winter:

> There was still the sky, the sky between the branches when you raised your head, an unyielding sky, still heavy with threats. Daylight is up there. I must be dreaming. It was as if when you pushed open the shutters after a night full of bad dreams the influx of light proved powerless to dispel the terrifying visions of the darkness from your eyes. And yet everything is there, quite real.
>
> [pp. 203-04]

Waking is dreaming, light is darkness, life is death: contradictions grow logical in this universe *if* we can adjust to the perspective of abnormality (from the point of view of our own safe normalcy) that Gascar's imaginative vision slowly unfolds before our eyes. Seeking to rescue experience from the shackles of a random chaos, the narrator reveals the possibility of a deeper secret meaning behind the facade of our comfortable reality:

> These things were on the scale of a cosmogony. Or worse: they took you into a universe which perhaps had always existed behind the solid rampart of the dead, and of which the metaphors of traditional rhetoric only gave you superficial glimpses: where . . . one could not keep body and soul together, where one really was bled white and died like a dog.
>
> [p. 214]

Thus, Gascar incorporates into his narrative the very dilemma which has inspired so much critical controversy—a *univers concentrationnaire* which refuses to be subjugated by the rules of traditional rhetoric, but which asserts the essential realities of its hell in spite of the dry husks of verbal formulae which contain or express them. The reader participates in the struggle, as the narrator concedes (like George Steiner) that monstrous orders disfigure a language, but insists that language did not present an insuperable barrier between the human imagination and the horror that beckoned beyond the solid ramparts of the dead. The vitality of that horror lurks in the imagery with which Gascar clothes his idea: "In those days the German language was like a landscape full of ravines, from the depths of which rose tragic echoes" (p. 215). One of these ravines is the treacherous transvaluation of values which experience daily confirms, for the French narrator quickly learns

that any expression of compassion for the Ukrainian Jews threatens his own safety: "fraternization had become conspiracy" (p. 216).

The German guard, on the other hand, the former pastor, authorized by the camp commandant to make some "human" approaches to the doomed Jews, desperately mouths the platitudes of his faith in a vain effort to salvage his own crumbling humanity in the presence of their fate: "This is the last form of priesthood open to me . . . the last power I've got. It's inadequate and clumsy, it needs to be exercised upon a living object, a single object" (p. 217). Unwilling to accept the axiom that the Jews are no longer living objects in any meaningful sense, the German utters the last gasp of a dying principle of love in the midst of an encroaching spiritual anarchy, and the narrator's response provides an apt climax to this little conversational parable on language and values, or more precisely perhaps, language and silence: "His lips went on moving. I said nothing. I would not have known what to say" (p. 217).

The failure of language and of the traditional values it expresses is one discovery impressed on the imagination of the narrator. But his education has far to go, for when he abandons the "way" of Ernst, the German pastor turned camp guard who preaches love even as he executes the heartless authority of his masters, the narrator has nothing but the graveyard to assure his identity, the "only innocent place" left, as he calls it, offering him a kind of immunity, though from what he does not specify—certainly, at least, from the delusions of language. Having spoken earlier of the German language as a landscape full of ravines, Gascar seems to transmute the metaphor into the subsequent activity of his narrator, a dramatic incarnation of the principle that the concreteness of the Holocaust repudiates the abstractness of the words used to describe it. For instinctively he is drawn away from life on the surface, to death in the depths, as he and his companions unite in a kind of "cult of the grave," whose weeds, in a phrase reminiscent of Borchert, "are the white hair of the dead" concealing some terrifying knowledge, some "haunting dream of underground" still to be disclosed to them (p. 218).

They decide to dig a trench from the nearby forest to the cemetery to drain off the rainwater that is scoring the graves, and in the process they are lured into physical labyrinths of extinction beyond the most extravagant excursions of the imagination, notwithstanding their prior experience with the anonymous corpse. For the ditchdiggers "accidentally" uncover, in a quest that merges the literal and the symbolic layers of the tale, a clandestine, subterranean charnel-house, a mass grave of half-decayed, hastily buried bodies—apparently Jews executed secretly before their arrival in the camp. They are naturally horrified by the spectacle, but the episode reaches far profounder dimensions, becoming a kind of parable of the Holocaust for all humanity, representing as it does the fundamental truth which the imagination must face with absolute immediacy, ungraced by any mitigating idea or deed—for Gascar, the grand metaphor of *l'univers concentrationnaire* is the kind of death suffered by the Jews, and here language plunges into the ravine as conviction wrestles with disbelief:

> This was death—these liquifying muscles, this half-eaten eye, those teeth like a dead sheep's; death, no longer decked with grasses, no longer ensconced in the coolness of a vault, no longer lying sepulchered in stone, but sprawling in a bog full of bones, wrapped in a drowned man's clothes, with its hair caught in the earth.

The narrator is forced by the discovery to distinguish between "the idealized dead," the inherited, civilized conception of what it means to die, and "the state of insane desolation to which we are reduced when life is done." The perception is equally essential for anyone seeking entry to the realms of the literature of atrocity, for it reverses the customary growth toward insight that fiction has trained the imagination to expect by transforming death into a vital image and reducing life to an aborted journey, "wreckage stranded in the cul-de-sac of an unfinished tunnel" (pp. 220-21).

For Gascar has created a pattern to complete the scheme of reality toward which the authors discussed earlier in this chapter were groping: the stench of the exhumed corpses gradually permeates the landscape (inner and outer) inhabited by the narrator and his friends; the grisly site of previous slaughter proclaims the appalling notice from underground that history has arrived at a unique stage in its cycle, foretold earlier in the title of the story—a season of the dead. No one can predict its duration, but its temporary triumph is undeniable; the pastor himself finally confesses to the narrator, "we ought to realize that there can't be any true life afterwards for us, who have endured these sights" (p. 227). But even such professions of disillusionment, like professions of faith, are suspect, because their rhetoric introduces an inescapable barrier between lips and imagination. True as the guard's statement may be, it cannot rival in potency of response the final insight of the prisoners themselves, caretakers in the cemetery of the world, who on "the fringe of the war, on the fringe of the massacres, on the fringe of Europe . . . seemed like hollow-eyed gardeners, sitters in the sun, fanatical weeders, busily working over the dead as over some piece of embroidery" (p. 233). In a world decimated of value, of the echoes of life, no other fruitful activity seems to remain; this is one of the most difficult lessons for the initiate into *l'univers concentrationnaire* to accept, since its consequences are so somber, the opportunities it offers for growth so limited—the mind instinctively recoils from the responsibilities it imposes.

Yet Gascar unerringly finds the dramatic equivalent for this melancholy conclusion in the last scene of *The Season of the Dead*, where against a background of rumbling convoys of mechanized death the narrator learns that the possibility of death as a personal tragedy has been eliminated from the universe, and that this in turn has altered the meaning of living, of survival itself. A spare grave is al-

ways kept empty, awaiting its corpse, and one morning his companion discovers that during the night it has been occupied by a living tenant, obviously a Jew from the town hiding from the Germans to escape deportation, who has another place of concealment during the day; and gradually, in a symbolic, silent communion with the grave through a series of laconic, surreptitious exchanges of notes—literally notes from underground this time—they identify him as one Lebovitch, whom the narrator had in fact met briefly in the nearby village earlier in the story. Thus, the unidentified corpse of a Jew who had inaugurated their initiation into the unreal reality of the underworld is ironically resurrected; and though he remains invisible to the end, he is given, in a grisly parody of human identity that is characteristic of the literature of atrocity, a local habitation and a name, which only make his doom seem more terrible than the fate of the faceless corpse, identified simply by his Star of David.

For Lebovitch—actually, in his brief notes he uses his initials, I. L., which the narrator is able to recognize—is the last hope of the principle of life in *l'univers concentrationnaire*, and though the prisoners grow obsessed with the challenge of keeping him alive, concealing provisions in the grave during the day that are gone the following morning, they are really paying homage, in a modern ritual of appeasement, to a power already dominating their souls: "our continual contact with death was beginning to open for us a sort of wicket gate into its domain" (p. 242). Before our eyes a replacement for Dante's Inferno is born, a creation of the Holocaust, shorn of allegorical trappings and theological dimensions, a literal hell that nevertheless treads on the boundaries of myth ("We continued to offer food to this Egyptian tomb," p. 244). In such an environment man is a victim even when he seems to control his actions; when a prisoner dies and Lebovitch's haven is occupied by an actual corpse, the narrator and his friend dig another spare grave alongside it, but with the uneasy feeling that they "were preparing to bury an unseen friend" (p. 245)—their affirmative efforts are governed by the force they think they are resisting. From his charnel-house Lebovitch offers his message to an unresponsive world, to a world which, given the opportunity, could respond only with silence: "They've killed them all . . . killed them all! What is loneliness?" (p. 245).

But Lebovitch is a man as well as a prophet, announcing the new apocalypse while simultaneously longing for his own survival, and his complementary question to his associates "beyond the tomb"—"Are there any exemptions?"—confirms the reluctance of the imagination to assent to a principle of existence that shatters the established limits of reality and utterly destroys the nostalgia of hope. Lebovitch's loneliness is undefinable, incommunicable—the traditional idea of society as the locale of man's destiny or as an impetus to the growth of moral values seems utterly ludicrous here—and as the narrator tries to comprehend how such a forlorn and abandoned victim could still think in terms of "exemptions," he furnishes a glimpse into the "locale" that would replace this shattered reality, now declared bankrupt by the Holocaust: "I was beginning to find out how rich and full was insanity's account compared with the meager bankbooks of reason" (p. 246). At this point, to approach life with the resources of reason and all the attitudes behind this noble concept is equivalent to embracing madness, given the nature of the narrator's milieu; but embracing madness is equally futile, and the only other option, honestly if sadly acknowledged by Gascar, is a lucid recognition of how events have disfigured human values and condemned men to inhabit a landscape permanently consecrated to death, a doom accurately prefigured in the harrowing image of Lebovitch the Jew and the paradox of his simultaneously occupied and empty grave.

All that remains is epiphany, but not one ripe with the promise of future life and spiritual redemption. In few other works of this sort does the profusion of imagery reach so insistently across the abyss of language to lure the imagination into the labyrinths of its unfamiliar world. If the experience of the narrator alienates him from himself, his own reservoir of usable values, what effect must it have on his audience? Hence Gascar chooses his metaphors and similes as weapons to assault the sensibilities and break down any remaining reluctance on the part of the reader to accept the "abnormal" world of his fiction as an accurate reflection of modern reality. As autumn darknes the Ukrainian countryside and slows down the cycle of nature, it is

> less like the morning after a bad dream or the lucid astonishment of life than the final draining away of all blood, the last stage of a slow hemorrhage behind which a few tears of lymph trickle, like mourners at life's funeral. Autumn brought a prospect of exhausted silence, of a world pruned of living sounds, of the reign of total death.
>
> [p. 247]

And we are invited, induced, persuaded to join the procession of mourners and share with the narrator his loss of the last two vestiges of hope that might preserve at least a faint gleam from the fading security of the past: the life of Lebovitch, and—it sounds almost weird in the context of the story—the love of a woman.

The first hope is of course vain: although the narrator confesses that the precarious existence of the Jew became for him "the last remaining symbol of a denial of death" (p. 247), he arrives one morning at the cemetery to find the planks of the spare grave thrown aside, and is greeted by a stark image that should waken memories of an earlier experience: "At the bottom of the grave there lay a black jacket without an armlet" (p. 248). Only this solitary and mute shred of evidence beckons the imagination toward the truth that "I. L." has vanished without a trace and "would never come back" (p. 248), a dismal symbolic affirmation of what the narrator had hoped desperately to deny, leaving only unanswered questions in the empty space of the grave—an epitaph of silence. And when soon afterwards the convoys cease to rumble across the plain, the epiphany expands into the remaining spiritual vacuum,

as I. L.'s private doom merges with the desolate fate of an entire race. Now, the narrator acknowledges, autumn has really arrived, the season of the dead is defined, and only the prospect of winter looms: spring, like love, has apparently perished with the victims of *l'univers concentrationnaire.*

Thus, when a love-theme is abruptly introduced near the end of the narrative, it is already anomalous, its resolution almost predictable: what have the emotions generated by this kind of feeling to do with a milieu like the one Gascar has portrayed? One evening the narrator notices a young Polish girl passing near the cemetery, and in a surge of the human in the very midst of its opposite, he clings to her image as a last refuge for his own withering "normal" affections. Her appeal—she is a stranger, and the narrator himself admits that he "knew nothing to suggest that she was worthy" (p. 240) of his devotion—remains a mystery; but in the rhythm of the story she introduces a faint echo of human promise against the reverberating crescendos of the negations of death. The girl, whose name is Maria and whose voice, we are told, could still express joy, temporarily disappears from the tale during the Lebovitch episode, but returns with autumn and bears with her in that austere landscape the possibility of romantic longing; and some deep independent impulse of the imagination, an unconscious "will-to-life" in the midst of all this terrible chaos of fear and suffering, seems to justify her presence at this crucial moment in the narrator's emotional existence.

Gascar has conjured up a dramatic confrontation between pre-Holocaust reality and *l'univers concentrationnaire,* but only to confirm what we have already suspected, what the narrator's experience has made inevitable: the irrevocable incompatibility of love and death. For as Maria visits the burial-ground and the narrator (with the sentimental guard's permission) rushes to the verge of the forest to embrace her in the sinister setting of a darkening sky and a rising wind, their fleeting union is only the prelude to a more enduring, eternal separation. The very language with which the narrator describes his bliss undermines its stability, as he equates the "ultimate salvation" of Maria's arms with an instant of "blindness" and "oblivion." In a world consecrated to death, the traditional rhetoric of love and religion (the implications of the name "Maria" are unavoidable) is confused with the vocabulary of nihilism, as words fail and only the image can express the tensions with which Gascar concludes *The Season of the Dead:*

> It was the only refuge within which to break the heavy, clipped wings that thought had set growing on one's temples, the only place where the mind, like a heavy-furred moth dazzled by the great light of death, could for an instant assuage its longing to return to the warm, original darkness of its chrysalis.
>
> [p. 249]

Alien to the narrator's universe, frightened by the urgency of his gestures, Maria kisses him and flees, but his instinctive effort to follow her is futile: "Within me and about me a great silence had fallen. After a moment I wiped away my tears and went back to my dead" (p. 249).

There is really no choice, as Gascar's grotesque metaphors assert; the tug of the chrysalis is inescapable, and clipped wings cannot, given what the narrator has endured, soar to a heaven of love. In an ironic reversal of the living epic hero's inability to embrace the spirit of his departed companion in the underworld, Gascar's unheroic narrator enters into his heritage of death-in-life while the still vital spirit of Maria fades into the hopeless distance. The immediacy of his proximity to death, to such death, imprisons his awareness and sensibility, destroying, for the present at any rate, the possibility of love. In the wake of the failure of its ultimate salvation floats the ultimate revelation that for him, as for I. L. and his fellow Jews, there is no exemption, and that he must now enact in his own destiny the answer to Lebovitch's horror-stricken question, "What is loneliness?" (p. 245).

Thus Gascar adds impressive imaginative testimony to Primo Levi's more restricted principle that, for him, "nothing was true outside the Lager," that all the rest was "a brief pause, a deception of the senses, a dream." The conception of two such worlds, disproportionate, estranged, coexistent but barred from communion by the unreconcilable quality of their assumptions, is an essential premise of the literature examined in the following pages. The gross distinctions between these worlds are by now clear, but subtle and elusive ones exist that are more difficult to explain. The role of death is a major source of confusion, and Gascar has done much to clarify it.

Some complementary and highly original insights are added in a unique and remarkable work, still untranslated, by Jean Améry, *Jenseits von Schuld und Sühne (Beyond Guilt and Atonement)*, in which the author tries to define the attitude of intellectuals like himself toward the wholly unanticipated ordeal of torture and humiliation which he endured in Auschwitz and other camps. For example, in a single lucid (and slightly sardonic) formulation, Améry illuminates (quite unintentionally, of course) the Maria episode in *The Season of the Dead*: "In the concentration camp there was no Tristan music to accompany death, only the bellowing of the SS and the Kapos [brutal inmates, often criminals, in charge of certain prison barracks]." But most significantly, Améry makes explicit a theme that Gascar and other authors considered in this study explore, without formulating it as precisely as Améry does.

Améry observes that one consequence of the camp experience was the "total collapse of the aesthetic idea of death." The intellectual, especially one of German training (Améry, an acrostic for Mayer, was himself Austrian), nourished by Schopenhauer, Wagner, Mann, and Rilke, was suddenly confronted with a reality that left him paralyzed and without resources, groping for a response: "There was no place in Auschwitz for death in its literary,

philosophical, or musical forms. No bridge led from death in Auschwitz to 'Death in Venice.'"[32] But traditionally, "death in its literary, philosophical, or musical forms" has provided the imagination of all men, not merely intellectuals, with metaphors for confronting and understanding our ultimate fate; art and metaphysics have collaborated in the past to derive eschatologies that make human destiny, even under the most adverse circumstances, endurable to the individual. In his striking antithesis between death in Auschwitz and "Death in Venice," Améry articulates what unwilling victims of *l'univers concentrationnaire* must have encountered with a mute dismay, and in the process discloses a major legacy of the camp experience, one that enriched the literary mind long before it reached the perceptions of the historian.

For after the empirical invalidation of the "aesthetic idea of death" which had fortified the prisoner against adversity in his "normal" life, he was left defenseless; and if in spite of this he tried to establish a spiritual or metaphysical attitude toward death, he stumbled once more, in Améry's words, "against the reality of the camp [*Lagerrealität*], which condemned the hopelessness of such an attempt." As a result—and here Améry contributes an invaluable distinction for anyone seeking to appreciate the literary imagination's use of *l'univers concentrationnaire*—the intellectual, like his nonintellectual comrade, concerned himself "not with death [*Tod*], but with the *process of dying* [*Sterben*]."[33]

Améry cites the example of an SS-man who slit open a prisoner's belly and filled it with sand, and suggests that, given such possibilities, an individual would scarcely occupy himself with *whether* one must die, or *that* he must, but *how* it would happen. Thus, a primary ingredient of the tragic vision is eliminated for the artist, who is faced with the challenge of infusing literature with a sense of "dying" commensurate with the *Lagerrealität* and creating an art beyond tragedy, where death in Auschwitz is translated into "Death in Auschwitz"—an art capable of incorporating implications about human experience unimaginable in the pre-Holocaust perfection of "Death in Venice." Where dying was omnipresent, Améry concludes, death withdrew.

Améry's analysis not only illuminates retrospectively the climax and other episodes in Gascar's *Season of the Dead*, but also sheds necessary light on the obsessive quality of the literature discussed in subsequent chapters. For a reader accustomed to the secure terrain of *Tod*, with its assumptions about cause and effect in human experience and the consolations of tragedy it makes available, inevitably feels an uncanny and often intolerable disquiet when cast adrift on the uncertain sea of *Sterben*, especially when we recollect that this "simple" dichotomy represents an estrangement vastly more far-ranging than the terms themselves imply. Perhaps the discomfort engendered by this situation accounts for some of the psychological and emotional rejection frequently provoked by the content of the literature of atrocity.

For as this literature usurps the bulwarks of our civilization—childhood, family, love, a sense of the human spirit, reason, an idea of the will as a faculty that shapes if it does not always control the future, and a durable faith in the uninterrupted processes of time and history—as this displacement occurs, the reader finds himself unconsciously maneuvered into an alien territory devoid of familiar landmarks; and if he persists, he becomes himself a temporary inhabitant of *l'univers concentrationnaire*, recreating, in collaboration with the artist, the features of a reality that history has declared extinct but which continues to haunt the memory and imagination with echoes of an unquenchable despair.

Notes

1. I base this judgment partly on my response to the New York City stage production of *The Investigation.* The Berlin production, which I have not seen, is said to have been far more imaginative.

2. Bernd Naumann, *Auschwitz,* trans. Jean Steinberg (London: Pall Mall Press, 1966), p. 133.

3. Ibid., p. 138.

4. David Rousset, *The Other Kingdom,* trans. Ramon Guthrie (New York: Reynal & Hitchcock, 1947), pp. 168-69.

5. "Jewish Values in the Post-Holocaust Future," *Judaism* 16 (Summer 1967): 267.

6. Wolfgang Borchert, "In May, in May cried the Cuckoo," in *The Man Outside,* trans. David Porter (London: Calder and Boyars, 1966), pp. 189-90.

7. Ibid., p. 190.

8. Ibid., pp. 190-91.

9. Borchert, "Billbrook," in *The Man Outside,* p. 58.

10. Ibid., pp. 59-60. (I have slightly modified the translation.)

11. Walt Whitman, "Song of Myself," in *Leaves of Grass and Selected Poems* (New York: Rinehart & Co., 1949), pp. 27-29.

12. Ernst Wiechert, *The Forest of the Dead,* trans. Ursula Stechow (New York: Greenberg Publishers, 1947), p. 1.

13. Ibid., p. 63.

14. Ibid., p. 70.

15. Charlotte Beradt, *The Third Reich of Dreams,* trans. Ariadne Gottwald (Chicago: Quadrangle Books, 1968), p. 9.

16. Ibid., pp. 16, 17.

17. Ibid., pp. 17-18.

18. Ibid., pp. 80-81.

19. Ibid., pp. 138-39.

20. Primo Levi, *The Reawakening,* trans. Stuart Woolf (Boston: Little, Brown, 1965), pp. 12-13.

21. Primo Levi, *Survival in Auschwitz,* trans. Stuart Woolf (New York: Collier Books, 1961), p. 54.

22. Levi, *The Reawakening,* pp. 107-08.

23. Ibid., pp. 221-22.

24. Hermann Kasack, "Die Stadt hinter dem Strom: Eine Selbstkritik," in *Mosaiksteine: Beiträge zu Literatur und Kunst* (Frankfurt am Main: Suhrkamp Verlag, 1956), pp. 350, 351. Translation mine.

25. Ibid., pp. 351, 352.

26. Ibid., pp. 352, 353, 354.

27. Kasack, "Der Totentraum," in *Mosaiksteine,* p. 355.

28. Ibid., pp. 356-57.

29. Ibid., p. 358.

30. Ibid.

31. Pierre Gascar, "The Season of the Dead," in *Beasts and Men and The Seed,* trans. Jean Stewart and Merloyd Lawrence (New York: Meridian Books, 1960), pp. 175-76.

32. Jean Améry, *Jenseits von Schuld und Sühne* (Munich: Szczesny Verlag, 1966), p. 33. Translation mine.

33. Ibid., p. 34.

Sidra DeKoven Ezrahi (essay date 1980)

SOURCE: Ezrahi, Sidra DeKoven. "The Holocaust as a Jewish Tragedy 2: The Covenental Context." In *By Words Alone: The Holocaust in Literature,* pp. 116-48. Chicago: The University of Chicago Press, 1980.

[*In the following excerpt, Ezrahi examines the way several Hebraic writers treat the Holocaust in their works, emphasizing the trauma and great personal and religious cost of turning such an experience into art.*]

ELIE WIESEL AND ISAAC BASHEVIS SINGER: FROM REALITY TO LEGEND

The major tensions which the Holocaust activated in Jewish beliefs and ethics as well as the engagement of traditional elements in the search for appropriate forms of expression are discernible in a body of European literature encompassing diverse languages and audiences. The novels of Elie Wiesel are perhaps the most widely read fictional representations of the clashes between inherited religious and moral values and the enormity and inscrutability of contemporary reality.

With the exception of his first book, *Night,* an autobiographical chronology of deportation and of existence and survival in the camps, and a few stories in *Legends of Our*

Time, Wiesel's narratives are located on the periphery of or retrospective to the concentrationary universe. *Dawn, The Accident,* and *The Town beyond the Wall* are set in the aftermath of the war, yet treat as morally compelling even in the post-Holocaust world those issues and relationships which arose in the concentrationary context: the roles and responsibilities of victim, victimizer, and spectator, the guilt and death-wish of the survivor. *A Beggar in Jerusalem* is located at the Wailing Wall just after the Six-Day War, yet is haunted by memories and spirits from the Holocaust. Even *The Oath,* the story of a pogrom which took place in the 1920s, can be read as a kind of microcosm of or a prelude to the Holocaust. *Gates of the Forest* explores three possibilities for Jewish survival during the Holocaust on the periphery of the ghettos and camps: alone in caves, with the partisans in the forests, and among the gentiles in disguise. In every one of these books, then, the narrative is haunted by echoes or premonitions of the cataclysm even though the center of dramatic action may be far removed from the actual scenes of massacre.

Wiesel is one of a number of Holocaust writers for whom survival seems to have dictated their choice of profession; when he was deported to Auschwitz from his Transylvanian hometown of Sighet, he was a fifteen-year-old heir to a world view in which, as he says, secular creations had no place:

> If someone had told me when I was a child that one day I would become a novelist, I would have turned away, convinced he was confusing me with someone else. . . . Novels I thought childish, reading them a waste of time. . . .
>
> As for France—whose language I chose for my tales—its name evoked visions of a mythical country, real only because mentioned in Rashi and other commentaries on the Bible and Talmud.[1]

This statement suggests a kind of pre-*Haskalah* ("Enlightenment") polarization of art and religion. It must, nevertheless, be remembered that it was in the innocence and single-minded piety of youth that Wiesel was suddenly severed from an insulated religious ambience and, overnight as it were ("night" lasted one year), thrust into a secular post-Holocaust universe. The contradictions between the attitudes and the literary conventions that were his heritage, and the medium of the modern French novel in which he chose to write are the main source of both the unique power and the weaknesses in his writing. The tension and its various resolutions can be demonstrated by identifying the elements of religious literature which have been introduced into the novel and the ways they have affected the nature and direction of the narrative. Wiesel has drawn primarily on the midrashic narratives which provide a prototype for the fusion of reality and legend.

The Canadian philosopher Emil Fackenheim has suggested a reading of Wiesel's fiction in terms which oversimplify the complexities of religious-oriented responses in the modern era; his definition of *midrash,* while partial, never-

theless illuminates some of the operations of that literary genre in the collective process whereby the past is rendered continually present. Auschwitz, by assimilation into latter-day *midrash,* becomes, potentially, a "root experience" which is incorporated into the dialectics of Jewish history.[2] While the lofty historical purposes which have been conferred by Fackenheim and others weigh perhaps too heavily on the work of Wiesel, I would isolate two elements which seem to characterize most of the classical midrashic narratives that undertake to interpret cataclysmic historical events and which inform the best of Wiesel's fiction: first, the quality of storytelling which is grounded in historical reality but which serves parabolical purposes ("when facts or texts become unacceptable, fiction or legend weaves the garland of nobler fancy," writes one midrashic commentator);[3] and, second, the mystery which lies at the heart of the Midrash and which is deliberately left unresolved. The principal mystery or contradiction which the *midrash* of catastrophe grapples with is the manifestation of divine providence in human affairs, and parallels have been drawn between the *midrashim* that were written at the time of the destruction of the Second Temple as both a witness and challenge to divine purposes, and the fragments of a violated theodicy that recur in Wiesel's narratives.[4] The antinomies and paradoxes which are countenanced within what remains a normative metaphysical framework constitute the essence of this literature and predominate in Wiesel's early novels particularly, where the bond between God and man, so often activated in classical *midrash,* is sorely tested. It is, therefore, a misdirected enterprise to read his novels either as theological tracts or as psychologically cogent character-studies (although at times, as we shall see presently, Wiesel himself seems to invite such readings and it is in such places that the creative tension between *midrash,* fiction, and philosophy dissolves).

The other literary component that Wiesel has adopted which originates in the pious literature is Hasidic legend—which in certain respects is a modern derivative of *midrash,* focusing more on human relations than on celestial drama. As experiments in the incorporation of legend into modern fiction, Wiesel's novels assimilate and adapt elements of structure as well as themes and perspectives from Hasidic lore. Yet, given what Buber calls the "formlessness" of most Hasidic tales, which are generally corrupted by oral transmission, Wiesel's narratives are more synthetic and contrived than their models, and his dramatic techniques are those of a modern novelist; nevertheless, some of the basic components of the legend—easily identified because they are so decidedly unmodern—are preserved: the relationship of master and disciple which reappears in many different guises in all of Wiesel's books; the master or mysterious stranger as wonder-worker; the repeated accounts of the attempts of holy men to hasten the advent of the messiah. The authority of the saint or master, who usually plays a central role in this fiction, is validated in most cases by the teller of the tale, who is clearly identified (frequently he is the narrator of the story); in that sense the latter becomes the master's disciple and scribe.

In most original Hasidic legends, the name of the rebbe as well as the name of the Hasid who transmitted the tale is mentioned; as one Lubavitcher Hasid explained, "the only way to know if a story is true is if it has testimony from witnesses—that is, true witnesses."[5]

It is this, the personal validation of events, which also accounts, in large measure, for the magnetism of Wiesel's presence in America as a "genuine" survivor, as one considered to be qualified to write about and interpret the Holocaust. Yet here, as in the case of the Hasidic rebbe, the question of credibility does not revolve around strict adherence to "reality." In addition to the numerous memoirists, other writers we have considered, such as Ilona Karmel, have presented a much more convincing realistic interpretation than Wiesel's of the possibilities of life under the sign of the Swastika. David Daiches offers Wiesel's novels as "important evidence, great documents" of World War II;[6] like traditional Hasidic legend, however, which is a record of specific events and often cites places and dates, this fiction is grounded in reality yet is sustained more by the spiritual authority of authentic testimony than by accurate documentary. Even in the autobiographical *Night* and the short sketches located in the camps in *Legends of Our Time,* there seems to be a saturation point beyond which the author refuses to dwell on sordid facts, on the struggle for "bread and soup." It seems as if the aesthetic forms and religious categories that are to constitute the shape and substance of Wiesel's fiction cannot be cultivated on a substructure of atrocity.[7] The novels that follow *Night* still contain aspects of Wiesel's own biography—of what actually happened, and of what might have happened: they are explorations of the various paths a fifteen-year-old religious Jew from Transylvania might have taken. But what emerges as significant is not these events *per se,* but their representational aspect in legends which transform private experience into public legacy.

Nevertheless, the balance between reality and legend is a very delicate one in this genre, and Wiesel's narratives are constantly in danger of being subverted by either too much or too little realism. On stylistic grounds, his occasional lapses into a kind of staccato, journalistic realism are startlingly intrusive; these are most evident in passages meant to provide a *mise-en-scène* in the postwar European metropolis such as one finds in *The Oath* or in *The Town beyond the Wall* ("That year Paris was in the throes of what seemed to be a philosophico-political struggle with its conscience. . . . Everybody talked existentialism, everybody discussed Communism . . ."),[8] or in passages meant to establish the simultaneity of past and present history by interspersing contemporary idiom with legendary memories of the past ("Occupy the cities," Israeli officer Gad tells his men in a scene from the Six-Day War in *A Beggar in Jerusalem.* "Surround all pockets of resistance and proceed with the attack. Leave the mopping up for later. Undertake no action which would risk breaking the initial thrust" [p. 170]. In this case the attempt to present a Hemingwayesque battle scene is disruptive to both the tenor and the pace of the narrative and subverts the very claim

to a realm of experience which transcends the one-dimensional, reality-oriented view of human history). Where Wiesel's stories are compelling, a generation or so after the war, it is in part because of the legendary quality which that period in history and that geographical location (the shtetl as well as the ghetto and the camp) already possess. Beyond that, Wiesel's almost unique position in the history of Holocaust literature in European languages lies in his attempt to convey in secular fiction the manner of thought and the literary modes practiced by believing Jews who perished; to apply, that is, to the most cataclysmic event of all, the internal methods by which the Jews of Eastern Europe traditionally grappled with and assimilated collective events and tragedies. Memory in this literature is collective, a partner in the unique interaction between past, present, and future which is the key to the Jewish perception of history. Wiesel acknowledges this when his narrator in *A Beggar in Jerusalem* rejects the imperalism of present reality by invoking the contemporaneity of Jewish history: the authentic legends, he says, are those told by people who are the "contemporaries of their ancestors," who are "unwilling to limit themselves to dates and locations. For them, chronological truth or nominal truth is only accidentally related to truth" (p. 45).

Yet, unlike myth, the midrashic manner commands a certain authenticity, and communal experience must be transmitted with a measure of realism as well as miracle. "God bent the heavens, moved the earth, and shook the bounds of the world, so that the depths trembled, and the heavens grew frightened," reports an ancient *midrash* on the revelation at Mt. Sinai; but, "although [such] phenomena were perceptible on Mt. Sinai in the morning, still God did not reveal Himself to the people until noon. For *owing to the brevity of the summer nights, and the pleasantness of the morning sleep in summer, the people were still asleep when God had descended upon Mt. Sinai . . ."* (emphasis mine).[9] It is the role of the witness or transmitter, then, to establish at least a degree of verisimilitude, and then to interpret and explore the event and to assign it a place in Jewish history. The quality of Hebraic legend, which is anchored in historical reality without purging it of the "contradictory multiplicity of events [and] psychological and factual cross-purposes," was identified by Erich Auerbach as characteristic even of early biblical narratives.[10]

Wiesel has defined his writing as an act of commemoration: "for me writing is a *matzeva,* an invisible tombstone, erected to the memory of the dead unburied" (*Legends of Our Time,* p. 25). It is also an act of resurrection—of return to that little town in the Carpathian Mountains just before the doors to the gas chambers were opened, at the moment when reprieve still seemed somehow possible. This is the moment captured graphically in the photographs that were taken in the camps, as Wiesel describes them in *One Generation After*:

> And from Treblinka—or is it Birkenau, Ponar, Majdanek?—this image which one day will burst inside me like a sharp call to madness: Jewish mothers, naked, leading their children, also naked, to the sacrifice.

. . . Look at the women, some still young and beautiful, their frightened children well-behaved. . . . And you, what are you doing? Go ahead, go on, snatch a flower, offer it to the mothers in exchange for their children—what are you waiting for? Hurry up, quickly, grab a child and run, run as fast as your legs will carry you, faster than the wind, run while there's still time, before you are blinded by smoke . . .

[p. 50]

Deceptively like the "still unravish'd bride of quietness" on Keats's Grecian urn—always about to be kissed—these innocent, naked Jewish mothers will always, inexorably, be leading their naked children to the sacrifice; but, frozen in that moment by the "artist" (in this case a German officer collecting "exotic souvenirs" for his photo album), they will never quite reach the "altar," and the writer is faced with the moral imperative to somehow still save them from the execution.

All of Wiesel's writing can be seen as an attempt to free these victims from their fate, to suspend history, if only for the moment. This is a theme which also appears elsewhere, especially in the poetic literature in which cameos of living memories stand out in temporary relief against the background of the inevitable. In numerous verses, Uri Zvi Greenberg graphically invokes the aborted lives of his family: "Here are mother and father / they have not yet been killed by their murderers."[11] Again, in a dream, he is transported to a snowy forest to cover the nakedness and feed the hunger of his young martyred nephew, "while he is still alive."[12] But since, unlike the urn or the photograph, the history-bound dream and the narrative are not arrested before the consummation of the death sentence, but must conclude by handing the victims back to the executioner, the story is repeated again and again. As Azriel, the only survivor of the town of Kolvillàg, tells his young interlocutor in Wiesel's *The Oath*, "all I can call my own is a forbidden city I must rebuild each day, only to watch it end in horror each night" (p. 9). Yet it is in the very repetition that the reality of character and situation is undermined. The same characters reappear with almost tedious predictability in Wiesel's fiction and eventually lose the husks of peculiarity; at this point, the commemorative impulse to embrace the entire spectrum of attitudes, modes of living, and personalities is transformed into a set of generalized codes which stand like a monument over a common grave, subsuming the richness and diversity of infinite particulars. And in the process, the imperative of history, to which the elegist must, after all, conform—that the testimony have its story, its *histoire*—is sometimes sacrificed to the legend. Just as we saw that, in a genre in which history is a springboard to eternity, an overdose of realism can dispel the aura and mystery of legend, so an attenuation of realism can betray the *ground* of legend; this is evident in the extreme in the confrontation of disembodied spirits in a passage entitled "Dialogues I" in *One Generation After*: "Tell me: do you know who you are?" one asks the other. "No. Do you?" "I don't." "Are you at least sure that you exist?" "I'm not. Are you?" "No. Neither am I" (pp. 31-32).

Often compressing reality until nothing remains but the shadows, Wiesel nevertheless persists in his efforts to establish the coordinates by which the individual can orient himself to the memories and the norms of a destroyed universe. Ironically, perhaps, Hebraic writing furnishes one of the few instances in the literature we are studying where a survivor of the Holocaust does not have to invent the cultural frames within which the events can be transmitted. In the contemporary rabbinic literature we find evidence of the process whereby the Nazi onslaught was met with the weapon that Jews have always used in self-defense, that of barricading themselves behind a wall of Torah and fighting the next round with God. The two-volume *Responsa from the Depths* is the record of the questions concerning ritual observance that were addressed to Rabbi Avraham Shapiro by inmates of the Kovno Ghetto, and his answers. As conditions in the ghetto worsened, the rabbi suspended more and more of the laws pertaining to ritual observances (though not the ethical imperatives) until very little remained of the commandments *but the framework of commandment itself.*[13] Similarly, in Wiesel's fiction the forms are preserved even if the content has been inverted. Wiesel retains the form of prayer in *Night*, though it comes out sounding like a curse; when the *Kapos* come into the barracks at Auschwitz to collect any new shoes that the inmates may have brought with them, Eliezer's own pair of new shoes are so coated with mud that they are not noticed: "I thanked God, in an improvised prayer, for having created mud in His infinite and wonderful universe."[14] And when Pinhas, the former director of a rabbinical school, who appears in Auschwitz in *Legends of Our Time*, fasts on Yom Kippur, or asks that the Kaddish be recited after his cremation, it is as an act of defiance: "here and now, the only way to accuse [God] is by praising him," he explains to his fellow inmates.[15] In the biblical tradition, euphemism is sometimes used to avoid explicit blasphemy: "bless God and die," Job's wife counsels her husband in a phrase generally translated as "*curse* God and die" (2:9). What is crucial is that the dialogue between man and God—even man's persistent invocation of a God who refuses to answer—is maintained. The evidence of either the indifference or the vengeance of God (it is hard to say which is worse) is in the fate that awaits Pinhas soon after his defiant act: "he left me a few weeks later," the narrator says, "victim of the first selection" (p. 61).

The inversion of the blessing and the dire fate of the blasphemer are also found in a Yiddish story by Isaac Bashevis Singer, "The Slaughterer." For over two decades Singer, who had emigrated from Poland to the United States in 1935, seemed to be deliberately avoiding the Holocaust in writing about the shtetl as if it still existed. In an interview with Irving Howe in 1966, he admitted that "at the heart of [his] attitude there is an illusion which is consciously sustained."[16] But some of the later stories in *The Seance* and the novel *Enemies, A Love Story* mark a clear turning toward a more direct confrontation with the effects of the Holocaust and an attempt to incorporate the challenges of the destruction into his own mythology and cosmology. In the powerful story "The Slaughterer," the growing abhorrence of the town *shohet* ("slaughterer"), Yoineh Meir, for the brutality of the ritual act of slaughter which he must perform leads him to challenge the divine authority that has sanctified it. The ancient ceremony of *shehitah* is suddenly transvalued into an act of savage murder. Yoineh Meir addresses God with the blasphemous "Thou art a slaughterer! . . . The whole world is a slaughter-house!"[17] This indictment of divine indifference to animal (and, by the extention that the post-Holocaust reader makes, to human) slaughter is reminiscent of Bialik's challenge of God after the Kishinev pogroms (the title of Bialik's poem is "On the Slaughter"). And, like the defiant Pinh]as in Wiesel's story but unlike the "pious blasphemers" of Singer's own earlier stories (such as Gimpel or Rabbi Bainish of Komarov, who are invariably saved from their impious words and deeds by a supernatural vision), Yoineh Meir is not rescued from his blasphemous declarations and desecrating acts; he is allowed to commit suicide—and his challenge, like that of Pinhas, remains, terrifyingly, without answer. If no more miracles are forthcoming, it is, ultimately, the "crust of bread" that emerges victorious—the crust of bread for which the hungry struggle, for which even "saints become criminal." "So that crust could change the natural order, could reverse the structure of creation!" concludes the narrator of Wiesel's *Town beyond the Wall* (p. 59).

It is, then, not only the death of the Jews but their degradation which must be redeemed after the Holocaust. Salvation in Wiesel as in Singer can no longer come through divine intervention. "Do you believe in God?" the narrator of *The Accident* asks the doctor who has just operated on him. "Yes, he answered. "But not in the operating room. There I only count on myself."[18] In the course of Wiesel's fiction, that "operating room"—the human arena—has become his central concern: as Robert Alter observed, "the theological center has shifted to the human spirit; it is pathetically finite man who is the source of miraculous aspiration, of regeneration, in a world where all life is inevitably transient."[19]

It is not a theodicy, then, which evolves out of a reading of this fiction, but an affirmation of the metaphysics of human potential and vision. For these writers the Holocaust seems to have left vast empty spaces that only human compassion can fill. The shift from the cosmic to the human plane appears also to have taken place abruptly, if belatedly, in Singer's writing, triggered not by the chronology of events but by a shift in the writer's perspective. Unlike the earlier fiction, most of the stories since *Short Friday* (*The Seance, Enemies, A Love Story, Friends of Kafka, Passions,* and so on) are located in the United States rather than in the shtetl, and most of the protagonists are survivors. Even in those later stories which are set in Europe, the concentration camp, while never dramatized directly, forms a kind of palimpsest with the shtetl which erases much of the former innocence and exuberance. The main focus in most of Singer's earlier fiction was on the battle between supernatural forces for hegemony over the soul of man, and Singer was frequently berated by the more sentimental guardians of Yiddish culture for overlooking the ethical dimension of Jewish community life. In this respect the stories in *The Seance* especially seem to represent a significant change in focus; there is greater concentration on the earthly plight of suffering humanity, on the problems of physical existence and coexistence. The drama in such stories as "The Seance" lies not in the battle between forces of good and evil in supernal regions, but in the psychological, moral struggle among men or between one man and his conscience. Human feelings have largely replaced cosmic forces as the prime movers in this drama. There is, particularly in the stories in *The Seance,* less of the purely erotic that dominated many of Singer's earlier stories, and more of simple affection and kinship. In "The Seance" and "The Letter Writer," the two stories in which these qualities are most manifest, something of the vitality that was part of the turbulent sexuality of the earlier work has been sacrificed. The characters are old and tired; they have seen much and suffered much, and their energies are exhausted. They are attracted to each other not out of strong passion but out of the very depth of their weakness.

And the ghosts and demons, it seems, have shared the fate of the community that believed in them. In the story "The Last Demon," from *Short Friday,* the narrator makes a rather astonishing confession that can perhaps be read as a sign of a change of direction in Singer's writing: "I, a demon, bear witness that there are no demons left. . . . I've seen it all, the destruction of Tishevitz, the destruction of Poland. There are no more Jews, no more demons. . . . There is no longer an Angel of Good nor an Angel of Evil. No more sins, no more temptations! . . . There is no further need for demons. We have also been annihilated. I am the last, a refugee."[20] Wallace Stevens, surveying another corner of the same destroyed universe, wrote, "How cold the vacancy / When the phantoms are gone and the shaken realist / First sees reality."[21]

The supernatural has not been entirely banished from Singer's cosmos, however, but has been transfigured. Unlike the grotesque and often malevolent role they played in the earlier tales, the ghosts in the later stories are universally benevolent. They may even be reincarnations of the dead martyrs, come to console the survivors:

> Yes, the dead were still with us. They came to advise their relatives on business, debts, the healing of the sick: they comforted the discouraged, made suggestions concerning trips, jobs, love, marriage. Some left bouquets of flowers on bedspreads, and apported articles from distant places. . . . If this were all true, Herman thought, then his relatives, too, were surely living. He sat praying for them to appear to him. The spirit cannot be burned, gassed, hanged, shot. Six million souls must exist somewhere.[22]

The "annihilation" of the demons, like the "demise" of Sholom Aleichem's fictional characters in Alterman's poem, suggests the link between the death of the Jews and the collapse of their cultural universe; in Singer's story the new phantoms represent both a different cultural framework (America) and different communal concerns: no longer the agents of temptation, sin, or redemption in a religious community, the spirits function more as social advisers or personal counselors in a vision permeated by both anguish and irony.

Writing from within Jewish literary and cultural traditions, Wiesel's, like Singer's, indictments of God or demotion of the supernatural places an even greater onus on man, on the surviving remnant of Israel. More than most writers, who peek but do not linger in the concentrationary universe, Wiesel has been unswerving in his attention to the dead and their legacy; led by repetition into frequent overstatement and redundance, he has nevertheless persisted in the attempt to transmute destruction and death into legend that can abide both within the canon of lamentational literature and within the province of the modern novel. Singer, on the other hand, who celebrated the teeming life of pre-Holocaust civilization, traces its shadows in a post-Holocaust diaspora. Both writers reveal the agonies inherent in the confrontation between a religious universe committed to continuity and salvation through and beyond the vicissitudes of human affairs, and the compelling reality of the discontinuities induced by catastrophe.

While Wiesel and Singer explore certain classical religious positions which were challenged by secular patterns of thought and finally violated if not altogether shattered by the Nazi cataclysm, they avoid positing any historiosophical overview which could provide an accounting for or a logically coherent response to the Holocaust. "Without God," Wiesel writes in an essay, "the attempted annihilation of European Jewry would be relevant only on the level of history . . . and would not require a total revision of seemingly axiomatic values and concepts. Remove its Jewish aspects, and Auschwitz appears devoid of mystery."[23] Yet he resists any suggestion that design or purpose can be extracted from the events, whether in traditional religious terms according to which individuals or communities are singled out for the glorification of God's name, or in terms of a process of Jewish history by which reconstruction follows destruction. He goes so far to avoid any intimation of a causal relationship between the devastation of Diaspora Jewry and the restoration of Zion as to alter the conclusion of a Talmudic *midrash.* In the original, Rachel intercedes on behalf of the bereaved remnant of Israel who survived the destruction of the Temple and were driven into exile, and she is assured by God that for her sake He will "lead the children of Israel back to their land"; in Wiesel's version of this *midrash,* a compassionate but impotent God can only descend from heaven, weeping, to join the Jews in their martyrdom.[24]

Other writers have drawn on the schema of return that is rooted in midrashic and biblical tradition (Jeremiah assured the survivors of his generation that God would "take you one of a city, and two of a family, and . . . bring you to Zion" [3:14]) as well as in contemporary political events. The most completely constructed philosophy of re-

turn predicated on the rebirth of the State of Israel and on legendary sources can be found in the poetry of U. Z. Greenberg: "By their merit [the martyrs'] we have the Land," he writes at the conclusion of his "Crown of Lamentation for the Whole House of Israel."[25] More fragmented responses can be seen in the writings of the younger Israeli writers we have mentioned, for whom Israel offers the pragmatic answer of self-defense and a capacity for revenge to the meek submissiveness of Europe's Jews. Hanoch Bartov's *The Brigade* reconstructs the brazen, self-confident attitude of a generation of Israeli soldiers who regarded the victims with disdain mingled with a determination to avenge their death. The soldiers in the "Jewish Brigade" tauntingly paint "Die Juden Kommen" on their armored cars and proceed through enemy territory, but their "attack" comes *after* the Allied victory and the most their avenging arm can achieve is the belated and rather absurd act of pelting a convoy of returning German soldiers with tin cans and stones. And when the Jewish soldiers finally encounter the refugees in the D.P. camps, all confidence in the simple equations of Jewish history vanishes before the otherworldly physiognomy that suffering has carved out of the faces of their kinsmen.

Yehuda Amichai's *Not of This Time, Not of This Place* is a more probing and sensitive exploration of the personal need for vindication which can yield no historic results. In his imagined return to a reconstructed Germany and his belated attempt to uncover and retaliate against the Nazis who were responsible for the deportation and death of his childhood friend, Joel assembles an "army" which includes an Indian tourist, an American film producer, and an Israeli figure skater. Action reduced to gesture and inflated rhetoric masking small deeds comprise the irony of diminished heroics of the would-be warrior and redeemer of his people: "I thought, I will blow a shofar to summon my army, as they used to do in the Bible," the narrator boasts. "But I said 'Let's order beer.'"[26] In the end it is Joel himself, Joshua manqué, who is conquered, petulantly confessing himself to be "like Jericho [with] a terrible army of conquerors [raging] on my ruins" (p.269). Amichai probes the deeper psychological needs for a redress of wounds carried since childhood, but here, as in Bartov's novel, nothing but the rubble of a former existence and the anonymous faces of a suspect generation of Germans, camouflaged by social decorum, confront the narrator's frenzied crusade. These novels reveal the frustration and futility of the attempts made by post-Holocaust Jews to leap over the unyielding gap of time and absorb the Holocaust into the unfolding drama of return and liberation.

In poetry Abba Kovner has delineated the internal struggle over alternative Jewish responses to an opportunity for resistance during the war itself. There have been many documentary and artistic accounts of the revolts in ghettos and camps, but only a few of them focus less on the historical events and more on the ethical and religious implications of conflicting forms of Jewish response to the threat of collective extinction. Kovner is able, both biographically and imaginatively, to link the call to arms with which the partisans confronted Jewish nonviolence during the Holocaust and the armed struggle for liberation which took place in Israel a few years later. The unfolding of the larger process of return, while not conceived as an imminent metahistorical or theological design as it is in Greenberg's poetry, does vindicate the blood of the martyrs who died with only the dream of Zion in their hearts no less than that of the soldiers who later fought and died under a national banner. Yet the poet's memory, like his poetry, is haunted by the thought of those whom the partisans left behind in the ghettos as they fled to the forests—often to suffer terrible retaliation at the hands of the Nazis for the escape of the few: Kovner's magnificent long poem "The Key Sank," which traces the prewar life and ghettoization of one small town in Poland and the escape into the forests of twelve youthful Resistance fighters, concludes with three short, staccato lines that compress so much of the anguish that the survivor carries with him into the future and that undermines any attempt at reading causality into events: "In the end / We are all vanquished. / The dead. And the living."[27]

MANÈS SPERBER: FROM KIDDUSH HA-SHEM TO KIDDUSH HA-HAYYIM

Like Kovner in his poems, Manès Sperber in one short novel explores the implications for Jewish tradition of the conflict between mutually exclusive forms of resistance to the Nazi threat. But unlike Kovner and other survivors possessed by one subject, Sperber, a Galician Jew who spent his young adulthood in Vienna as assistant to Alfred Adler and found asylum during the war years in France, places the Holocaust within the larger context of modern warfare and the struggle for human rights. His novel . . . *Than a Tear in the Sea* is part of a trilogy that portrays the lives and diverse activities of members of a Polish Resistance organization. Still, even within this wider purview, Sperber succeeds in insulating the events of the Holocaust and relating them primarily to the internal history and values of the Jewish people; in an essay introducing the novel, the author defines the particular historical challenge to which his narrative responds:

> Throughout the entire history of [the Jewish people], this Civitas Dei without a country . . . the survivors of each catastrophe discovered their invincibility anew. It was the invincibility of their faith; God was just, for he condemned their enemies to be transformed into murderers, while to the Jews he accorded the grace of being victims only, who thereby died sanctifying the Almighty. . . .
>
> Now, this had ceased to be true: the Hitlerite fury took the Jewish people by surprise: they were no longer inclined and in no way prepared to die for God. If, for the first time on Christian soil, Jews were going to be murdered *en masse* without any demands being made upon them in the name of Christ, European Jewry itself was *going to perish for nothing, in the name of nothing.*
>
> [p. viii]

The essence of this novel, then, is the challenge to the ultimate significance of martyrdom by such an unprec-

edented threat to the body as well as to the soul of the Jew—and the struggle for the proper Jewish response to an opportunity for resistance.

The setting of . . . *Than a Tear in the Sea* is the Jewish town of Wolyna and its environs. The town is defined by its own inhabitants through its history of suffering—of "wars, uprisings, pogroms, epidemics, great fires" (p. 7). So inured are they to disaster that when a stranger, Edi Rubin, who has escaped from the death camps, appears in their midst in order "to describe those camps in detail, to tell of the unimaginable organization for annihilation against which he must pronounce his warning" (p. 16), he is hardly listened to. Rubin does, however, succeed in convincing twenty-eight men from Wolyna, including Byrnie, the rabbi's son, to take to the woods to fight "so that, if it must be, they might at least die like men and not like sheep" (p. 17). Just as they reach underground headquarters, the roundup of the remaining Jews begins, and soon the town is empty and the mutilated corpse of the old rabbi lies in the village square. The twenty-eight Jews, together with some volunteers from the Armia Krajowa, the local unit of the Polish Resistance, succeed in ensnaring into a nearby ravine and slaughtering a number of Ukrainians in the service of the SS. But anti-Semitism erupts within the ranks of the Polish Underground itself, and most of the fugitive Jews are slaughtered. Byrnie remains alive long enough to confront Edi Rubin's cynicism and despair with his own faith, to invest in him the message of the Jewish people's death, and to pledge him to survival.

The novel opens in those halcyon days when an eternal rhythm of recurrence, and not the contingencies of the present, still regulates the lives of Wolyna's inhabitants. The narrative weaves an aura of legend reminiscent of a Chagall tapestry: the Jews of the town are carpet-makers and violinists, and include the usual quorum of Jewish types—a pious rabbi, his sensitive young son, a few panderers, good house-wives, innocent children. Character stereotyping, which we come to recognize as a hallmark of the commemorative enterprise that would sort out the general from the incidental, is particularly striking in Sperber's novel because the characters in his other fiction are much rounder and more individuated and, as André Malraux remarks in his introduction to the novel, when "a story in which psychological analysis plays a negligible role [is] written by a former assistant of Adler, [it] is a fact that gives pause for reflection." And, indeed, it is not psychology but something else which, as Malraux goes on to observe, governs a character like Byrnie, the rabbi's son: "Byrnie has all the ambiguous intensity of the great modern creations; but his language expresses what he has conquered, the presence within him of the eternal" (p. xix).

But whereas Malraux defines the "eternal" which abides in Byrnie as a "universal" quality, "the essential expression of the religious experience," and in this sense insists that "this is no more Jewish literature than Tagore is Vedantist literature" (p. xviii), I would argue that this is, on the contrary, precisely where Sperber exposes the particular agony that lies at the very core of Judaism after the Holocaust. Malraux opposes "history" to the "Eternal," recognizing, on the one hand, that "the townspeople of Wolyna take on the centuries of which Wolyna is composed," but contrasting this to what "Byrnie takes on [of] the Eternal." The "Eternal" as a "universal" force is thus understood to transcend both the parochial and the temporal. "Sperber," Malraux continues, "owes to Hegel his obsession with history as something intelligible; now, his entire narrative is a revolt against history" (p. xx). It is, however, not Hegel who has rendered history "intelligible" for Sperber (*The Phenomenology of Mind* figures in the novel as a lower form of perception of history, Hegel representing what Byrnie calls the "arrogance" of the human spirit who believes he is "his own creator" [p. 19]—but Judaism. And history, in Judaism, is coterminous with the Eternal. Byrnie's own perception of the Eternal (and of eternal values) is integral to his perception of Jewish history; although, in joining the partisans, he seems to have rejected his father's attitude toward martyrdom (the old rabbi dismissed Rubin's plea for armed resistance by adopting the traditional Jewish stance toward the persecutor as a "scourge" that God uses "to chastise us," and was concerned with ensuring that he and his people "die not as murderers but as martyrs" [p. 18]), Byrnie, no less than his father, sees divine providence in events—even in the imperative of action, of armed rebellion. A transcendent history may, then, subsume events, but it does not negate them. The "higher will" acts, mysteriously, *through* the Jewish community, even if that community is reduced to only twenty-eight men—or, eventually, to only one or two. It is, then, in a context in which the Holocaust is presented not only as the crucible of the individual or of the universal human spirit but as the agony of the soul of Israel that stereotyped characters appear in this literature—as representatives not of moral or religious positions such as those embodied by the dramatis personae of the Christian moralities, but of the clash of spiritual attitudes *in history,* under the aspect of eternity.

One of these attitudes legitimates the massacre of the Ukrainian collaborators by Byrnie's "partisans"; while armed resistance cannot begin to redress the evil done to the other Jews of the town, it does provide the men with a catharsis of sorts. Nevertheless, although Sperber seems to espouse a consistent historical overview, the time-hallowed values continue to clash with the imperatives of the hour within the soul of the protagonist who is still committed to the ancient tradition; it is Byrnie's resistance to setting up barricades on the Sabbath which finally leaves him and his men exposed to the guns of the Polish partisans.

A tentative faith in the transcendent spirit which orders the cosmos and leads Israel through the fires along inscrutable paths emerges from the clash of attitudes in . . . *Than a Tear in the Sea.* But in the entire trilogy of which this novel is a part, the faith that survives adversity is in the beneficence of the *human* spirit. Even Byrnie, who is most clearly invested with a kind of saintliness, is equally the personification of "human goodness"; a series of healing

miracles that he works as he lies dying are more the function of psychological perception than of divine powers. Even as he dedicates his life to God, he consecrates life itself; in casting his lot with the partisans rather than with the passive victims of Wolyna, he affirms the imperative of survival (*kiddush ha-hayyim*) which was articulated by Rabbi Nissenbaum, one of the spiritual leaders of Polish Jewry, as the equivalent of martyrdom (*kiddush ha-Shem*) in other times.[28] Yet even such survival cannot be anarchic, and when he feels that the very structure of the Law is being threatened by a pledge to survival at all costs, Byrnie barricades himself and his men behind the Torah. If they are destined not to survive, as he has anticipated, their deaths will at least have been carved out of the affirmation of life and the pride of self-defense as well as the glorification of God, like the deaths of the fighters in the Warsaw Ghetto. The spiritual magnetism of this young rabbi lends a kind of sanctity to his convictions and acts even over the ascetic saintliness of his elderly father, with which they seem to clash. And here Malraux seems justified in concluding that the "tragic conflict" in this parabolic novel, between martyrdom and armed resistance, "tends neither towards the victory of one or the other of the opposing values in it, nor to their reconciliation; it would seek to reveal the presence of a mystery rather than to achieve the solution of a puzzle" (p. xix). Yet behind this mystery lie the terrible, unremediable lacerations which the Holocaust inflicted in the body of normative Judaism.

ANDRÉ SCHWARZ-BART: THE LAST PASSION

Jewish suffering seems to have become a salient literary subject in post-Holocaust France with the award of the Prix Goncourt to three French-Jewish writers within seven years (1955-62) for novels in which the Holocaust figures as a theme. And, like the other two authors (Anna Langfus and Roger Ikor), André Schwarz-Bart reached Jewish circles mostly through the mediation of wider social acclaim. The scope of the public interest may be all the more remarkable as his novel, *The Last of the Just,* is, ostensibly at least, concerned with the internal processes of Jewish history. It is a quasi-factual account of the genealogy of the Levy family of Just Men whose tradition of self-sacrifice originates with the suicide of Yom Tov Levy and the other besieged Jews of York in 1185—whose ashes were "cast to the winds"[29]—and culminates in the martyrdom of Ernie Levy among the Jews in Auschwitz, where *his* ashes are cast to the winds.

In its focus on persecution as the organizing principle of communal memory, *The Last of the Just* is a fictional derivative of the medieval lamentation literature. And, just as the medieval authors of those elegies or elegiac chronicles were held accountable less for the facts than for the transmission of the events within a traditional normative framework, so in the case of Schwarz-Bart, accountability is measured less in terms of fidelity to history than in terms of the traditional codes by which experience is interpreted. Whereas questions of "validity" are hardly germane to an imaginative interpretation of history, the normative premises which such a writer invokes and the habit of a public literature through which, as Maurice Samuel put it, events "establish" [themselves] in the Jewish people," engage Schwarz-Bart in a special kind of dialogue and could account for the controversy which followed the publication of his book. The bond linking the generations of Levys is the spiritual genealogy of the *lamedvovnik,* the Just Man, who constitutes one of the thirty-six pillars of human goodness (*lamedvov* is the equivalent in Hebrew gematria of thirty-six) by which it is believed that the perpetuation of the world is ensured. In his fictional adaptation, Schwarz-Bart took liberties in molding the cultural meanings of the folk beliefs embodied in the legend. Propelled by the interest in the concept of the Just Men which Schwarz-Bart's book generated, Gershom Scholem wrote an essay explicating the origins and the substance of the legend, illuminating the discrepancies between the two versions but refraining from passing judgment: "As a novelist Schwarz-Bart is not bound by scholarly conventions and can give free reign to his speculative fantasy."[30] "Speculative fantasy" is of interest here as more than a deviation from scholarly conventions, however, as it is in the shifts and transformations of traditional sources that we can identify the orientations of each of these writers toward the Holocaust. Schwarz-Bart's major departure from the sources lies in his eschewal of the principle of the anonymity of the Just Man. By establishing the position as hereditary, he actually alters the concept of righteousness which was traditionally regarded as both self-effacing and socially unrewarded. No homage is paid to or canonization conferred upon the man whose saintliness is matched by his obscurity. Scholem elucidates the "anarchic morality" which underlies the *lamedvov* tradition: if there are no external markings of election, each man remains responsible as potentially just in the sight of God and should regard his neighbor as having the same potential and refrain from passing any moral judgment on him.[31] There are no designated saints whose function it is to relieve others of their troubles or their sins. The legend places emphasis on goodness which can never be hereditary but must involve the effort of a lifetime to acquire.

Schwarz-Bart's emendation of cultural and religious categories proves to be less an exploration of, or even a challenge to, traditional attitudes toward theodicy and Jewish destiny than an interpolation of extrinsic attitudes into the traditional forms. By changing the essence of the legend of the Just Man, Schwarz-Bart has delineated an altogether different way of being and of relating to the community from what has been indigenous to it. The Jews have had their revered leaders and even their "dynasties" of holy men, especially within the Hasidic community—but the idea of a kind of predestined assignation of individual martyrdom in the context of some sort of communal redemption is foreign to normative Judaism.

In spite of appearances, then, the organization of Jewish history around a succession of pogroms in this novel does not either serve or defy the specific purposes of the traditional poems and chronicles of lamentation—namely, commemoration of the martyrs and affirmation of faith in God at the moment of supreme sacrifice—but presents Jewish history as an adjunct to or a whipping boy for Christian history. It has already been observed, by Pierre Aubéry and other critics, that Schwarz-Bart's "vision of Jewish fate comes closer to the Christian punitive concept than the Jewish prophetic vision."[32] The roles of victim and victimizer appear as preordained and the Nazis, who in fact are portrayed in this novel more extensively and realistically than in most of the literature we are considering, become the latest in the inevitable procession of executioners. Their partners in this reiterated passion are the willing victims, the dynasty of Just Men. And the central character, the last of the Just Men, is the one who most clearly embodies this Christological role.

It should be stressed that it is not the subject but Schwarz-Bart's treatment of it that is striking within the Hebraic context. Jewish literature, as insulated as it may often appear to be, has reflected an ongoing dialogue with Christianity—in often subterranean but nonetheless persistent ways which focus variously on Jesus as an ancient model of Jewish martyrdom and on institutionalized Christianity in its historical relation to the Jews. Irving Howe points to the contemporary manifestations of this strange magnetism in the poetry of Yiddish writers such as H. Leivick and Itzik Manger.[33] Some of the most controversial expressions are to be found in the Yiddish writings of Sholem Asch—in his historical novels on the life of Jesus and in the Holocaust stories in his collection *Tales of My People,* in which the victims are portrayed as sacrificial lambs through a veil of gentle lyricism that belies the atrocities much as portraits of the crucifixion elevate physical pain into spiritual passion. Asch explicated his vision in an *Epistle to the Christians,* published in 1945: "Suddenly [at the moment of death in the camps] everything becomes understandable, realizable, clear, and beautiful. Suffering acquires a reason, an explanation—it is the highest price exacted for one's faith. . . . The prophet Elijah leads the way and makes a path for [the victims]. King David is among them as are the patriarchs and the prophets. And so is the Nazarene."[34] Other Hebraic writers reflect the dialectic between Judaism and Christianity through the more ambiguous role the Church has played in Jewish history and, most recently, in the context of the Holocaust. In Kovner's poem "My Little Sister," and in the Hebrew short story by Aharon Appelfeld "Kitty," the convent provides both a temporary refuge to the body and an ultimate lair for the soul of a young Jewish girl.

In Schwarz-Bart's novel, Christianity is represented both in the historical context of the interaction of the Church with the Jews and in the allegorical model presented by the figure of the suffering Christ. Ernie Levy appears as an archetype of the tormented Jew from earliest childhood when he is subjected to torture at the hands of his gentile playmates. As a youth he begins to court martyrdom by bravely facing a cordon of SA soldiers in the synagogue courtyard. "He is the lamb of suffering; he is our sacrificial dove," his grandfather declares (p. 175), and proceeds to initiate him into his otherworldly mission as a Just Man: "A day will come when all by yourself you will begin to glow . . ." (p. 179). From that point on, Ernie inflicts a succession of physical and spiritual stigmata upon his body and soul in anticipation of "offer[ing himself] heroically to the holocaust" (p. 185)—a process that culminates in the final martyrdom enacted when he abandons the asylum he has found in France and voluntarily forces his way into a transport bound from Drancy to Auschwitz.

The story of Ernie's last days, of his short love affair with Golda, consummated the day before her deportation and consecrated in the gas chamber, has the human warmth and gentle, legendary sentimentality of the most idyllic portrait of romance in the valley of the shadow of death. But Ernie's last role is not only that of the Romeo who has chosen to die with his Juliet, but of the martyr who has chosen to die with and for his people, to suffer little children to come unto him; he dies embracing the children whom he has accompanied from Drancy, crying tears of blood, the "blood of pity" (p. 406).

It is here, in the quality of mercy, that Ernie's passion acquires its ultimate significance. The final scene of the novel is one of the very few accounts in the literature of the last moments in the gas chambers—for, since there were no survivors, only an act of imagination can invoke that scene. Yet there is nothing grotesque or horrible about this passage, only an infinite sadness which pervades the conclusion of the novel, like the gas which permeates the cubicle of death. As Ernie encourages "his" children to "breathe deeply, my lambs, and quickly," to shorten the suffering and hasten the end, as the Jews recite together "the old love poem" which, "above the funeral pyres of history, the Jews . . . [had] traced in letters of blood on the earth's crust—'Shma Israel Adonai Elohenu Adonai Eh'oth [*sic*]'" (p. 407)—as one by one they die and Ernie and Golda embrace in one last loving gesture, it is not the horror of dying which emerges but a kind of hagiographic parable of mercy and comfort.

In the end, then, it is not simply the reenactment of the Jewish destiny of martyrdom which remains as Ernie's final legacy; although, as we have suggested, the inevitability of martyrdom is the organizing principle of the novel, what emerges is not an affirmation of metaphysical *purpose*. There are in fact occasional instances of religious doubt and even blasphemy in the novel; when Ernie is at his lowest, after receiving knowledge of his family's murder and before taking the decision to join the other imprisoned Jews, he rails against a Divinity that could have designed such a fate: "If it is the will of the eternal, our God, I damn his name and beg him to gather me up close enough to spit in his face" (p. 308). And the narrator, who introduced himself at the beginning of the novel as a "friend" of Ernie's, mourns Ernie's death in the words of a violated Kaddish which may be compared to the inverted prayers and ceremonies we have encountered in other fiction:

> And praised. Auschwitz. So be it. Maidanek. The Eternal. Treblinka. And praised. Buchenwald. So be it.

Mauthausen. The Eternal. Belzec. And praised. Sobibor. So be it . . .

[p. 408]

Yet, while these passages impugn divine beneficence, they do not rend the heavens asunder. There is a lack of real tension and hence of engagement between the fate of the victim and his inherited system of values. The compassion which Ernie embodies in his last moments becomes almost a messianic force which, in the lack of divine comfort, eases the dying multitudes into the next world. Although messianic expectations abound in lamentation literature, this is a vision of consummation which is rare, if not unique, and goes beyond even Asch's sentimental portraits of calvary in the concentration camps. As his life is snuffed out on a twentieth-century crucifix of gas, Ernie Levy becomes the Christ whom he has revered as the model of a Just Man—not the "blond Christ of the cathedrals," whose cross was "turn[ed] around" to make a sword to strike down all the generations of his descendants, but the Christ who, as Ernie tells Golda, was "a simple Jew . . . a kind of Hasid . . . a merciful man, and gentle" (pp. 351, 384). And in the last lines of the narrative the compassion of the last of the Just Men is generalized and canonized into a transcendental spirit:

> At times, it is true, one's heart could break in sorrow. But often too, preferably in the evening, I cannot help thinking that Ernie Levy, dead six million times, is still alive, somewhere, I don't know where. . . . Yesterday, as I stood in the street trembling in despair, rooted to the spot, a drop of pity fell from above upon my face; but there was no breeze in the air, no cloud in the sky . . . there was only a presence.

[p. 409]

This image resembles the metaphors of phantoms or clouds or other transmigrations of the souls of the martyred Jews which we frequently encounter in Hebraic literature. Yet the lyrical element of reconciliation wrought by pity and of transcendental harmony which concludes this tale of genocide is absent among the other writers, who reflect a tradition in which no human being is invested with the power to relieve the sins, or the sufferings, of another, a tradition in which the *Shekhinah* itself, an emanation of the Divine, is believed to have accompanied Israel into exile and to share in its suffering.[35] The same kind of reconciliation is effected in Schwarz-Bart's second novel, *A Woman Named Solitude*, the story of the massacre of the slaves of West Africa; the narrator of that novel instructs the reader that if he wishes to visit the site of the massacre, he will find mounds of bone and wall, testifying to a former human presence and randomly buried and dug up by the "innocent hoes of [today's] field workers." His concluding passage is an attempt to link this massacre with the Holocaust by the kinship of martyrdom and the author's sense of the written text as monument: "If [the reader] is in the mood to salute a memory, his imagination will people the environing space, and human figures will rise up around him, just as the phantoms that wander about the humiliated ruins of the Warsaw ghetto are said to rise up before the eyes of other travelers."[36]

The ghosts of these and other genocides still hover, then, over the ruins of their former homes—a presence that can be resurrected by the imagination which provides them with a foothold. The two novels are a double testament to the eternal recurrence of human suffering. The black woman Solitude, like Ernie Levy, is destined from birth for martyrdom by an inexorable historical process that ordains that certain groups be lambs and others butchers. And her passion, like that of Ernie Levy, is ultimately redeemed by the harmony and ascendancy of her being—and by the imagination of a compassionate artist who invokes the phantoms and transmutes a bloodbath into a gentle lyrical parable.

As Milton Hindus has written, Schwarz-Bart is "obviously universalistic in his aspirations . . . as an artist [and] . . . conceives of himself as a mediator between several cultures." His novels of suffering may then be read as attempts to travel the "road to the universal . . . through the particular"[37]—without, however, being necessarily constrained by the boundaries of the particular. In this sense, *The Last of the Just,* suffused as it is with a sense of Jewish destiny, with Jewish values and mores, remains, ultimately, outside the internal polemic in which the Jewish artist who is also the scribe struggles with ancient forms of collective perception and modern forms of collective death. Ernie Levy's messianic role is realized in his martyrdom; it is as if the world has been redeemed by the last of the Just, "dead six million times," and there is nothing beyond his death but a kind of *grace.* For most of the writers who are linked to the lamentation tradition, the struggle of man betrayed in Auschwitz by a helpless or indifferent God and a tarrying messiah only intensifies as it is multiplied by six million. And it is not human compassion which is primary in this struggle, but human *responsibility. The Last of the Just* is a call for sacrifice and mercy beside the more consistently Hebraic demand for human responsibility and divine justice. It is a message of comfort beside the demand for anguished engagement.

NELLY SACHS: FROM MOUNT MORIAH TO MAJDANEK

The perception of Jewish suffering as an invariable, eternal component in human history and the cosmic absorption of that suffering also appear as a recurrent theme in the poetry of Nelly Sachs.

Sachs's poems are free from the didacticism, apologetics, and sentimentalism which characterize the poetry of so many lesser Holocaust poets. Some of her most powerful poems are those which are universal lyrics of pain—especially the lullabies and laments to the slaughtered children ("O Night of the Weeping Children," "A Dead Child Speaks")—or those which reflect the poet's own personal angst as a survivor ("If I Only Knew," "We the Rescued"). Nevertheless, Sachs also invites a reading as a "public"

poet. Not only has she been accorded the status of the poet who "speaks for the fate of the Jews" by the Germans themselves (the quote is taken from the citation on the Frankfurt Peace Prize which she received in 1965)[38] and by many Jewish readers, but she has explicitly assumed that role; in a letter acknowledging her use of biblical and Hasidic sources in the mystery play *Eli,* she writes: "I just have the deep feeling that Jewish artists must begin to listen to the voice of their lineage, so that the old spring may awaken to new life. With that in mind I have attempted to write a mystery play of the sufferings of Israel."[39]

Biblical and Hasidic, even Cabbalistic, themes are woven into Sachs's poetry as into her play—but without the flesh of living transmission. They are *sources* rather than *traditions,* serving the search for an attitude toward death. As in the writing of Schwarz-Bart, it is death—the enormity, the mystery, the place of death—which is at the center of Sachs's poetry. Where other Hebraic writers do concentrate on dying, it is more for the legacy that the manner of dying leaves to the living than for the repulsive—or redemptive—power of death itself.

None of this figures into Sachs's postwar poetry, which is totally informed by the act of slaughter that brought the poet herself back to Judaism (an assimilated young woman living in Berlin and writing neoromantic poetry, she was forced to flee from Nazi Germany in 1940 and found a haven in Sweden). In the one instance where she reconstructs the Jewish town—the play *Eli* which, written in 1943, envisions the return of survivors to their hometown and their attempts to rebuild it—it is to fix the moment of death rather than to convey or recapture the spirit of life. As David Bronsen has said of the characters in the play—of the workers who dig up the rubble before laying new foundations—they are "archaeologists of the immediate past,"[40] discovering a ribbon or a skullcap or a shoe and trying to guess who its owner had been and to reconstruct the manner of his death. They are archaeologists, then, not of the kind who reassemble the shards of their own lost communal past and who try to leap back over death to recapture the pulse of a civilization, but of the kind who excavated Pompeii and were far more intrigued by the death-pose than by the life which was snuffed out by lava.

This point is, I believe, crucial to an understanding of Sachs's poetry, as the death of Israel becomes the essential fact on which attitudes toward mankind and toward the universe are based. The Bible appears here not as the epic of a living people, but as a kind of compendium of the signs of martyrdom which will furnish the references for future sacrifice. There is, in short, no *history* in Sachs's universe: there are archetypes of events and of relationships and functions, but there is no biography or history. It is not simply an absence of "reality," for, although the "facts" have been raised to the level of metaphor in her poetry, the agony and even the details of dying are conveyed here more powerfully than in many other, more graphic, descriptions of death in the camps. A close reading even suggests the specific correlatives of death by gas in the expressionistic lines of one poem, "Landscape of Screams," which appears in the volume of her selected poems, *O the Chimneys*:

> O, O hands with finger vines of fear,
> dug into wildly rearing manes of sacrificial blood—
>
> Screams, shut tight with the shredded mandibles of
>   fish,
> woe tendril of the smallest children
> And the gulping train of breath of the very old . . .
>
> [p. 127]

But this reality, the things and events of this world, takes on significance not in its peculiarity but in its symbolization of something beyond itself—of the eternal recurrence of the pattern, and even the manner, of death. The characters in *Eli* are nonspecific archetypes of social roles (Washerwoman, Baker Woman, Knife Grinder, Rabbi, and so on). Even those few who have names—such as Michael, the central character—are the embodiments of certain tasks (Michael represents, as Sachs herself explains in the postscript, one of the Thirty-six Just Men). And the ultimate division of roles is into those of murderer, victim, and survivor (weeper); the Knife Grinder, accused by the Old Woman that his grinding "carves up the world in pieces," answers that he grinds because "it's my trade," and the Old Woman acknowledges, "so it's his trade, / as it's mine to weep—/ and another's to die" (p. 335).

This is a recurrent image throughout the poetry as well as the play, the image of the "age-old game of hangman and victim, / Persecutor and persecuted, / Hunter and hunted—" (p. 340). Among the victims there are no persons but the totality of Israel as an abstract quantity of prospective martyrs: children, nursing mothers, old men, bakers, rabbis, and so on; they are not the archetypes that distill a living organism into its most representative members, such as we have encountered in other Hebraic writing. And among the hangmen, not only do the Nazis remain anonymous; they become at times no more than the dismembered instruments of a transcendent will. A recurrent synecdoche in the poetry is the "fingers of the killers"; in *Eli,* each finger represents a different form of death (one finger strangles, another administers injections, and so on), and in the poem "O the Chimneys," the "fingers" are the agents which build the chimneys that are to direct "Israel's body as smoke through the air" (p. 3). And even those devices of concentrationary death, the chimneys, are transfigured into latter-day conveyances for facilitating the flow of dust that is as ancient as the martyrdom of Jeremiah and Job:

> O the chimneys
> Freedomway for Jeremiah and Job's dust—
> Who devised you and laid stone upon stone
> The road for refugees of smoke?
>
> [p. 3]

The implication is that there can be more than one answer to the question, "who devised you?" The latest martyrdom

of Israel was, then, prefigured and preordained as long ago as in the time of Jeremiah and Job—and even before that, in the time of Abraham; one of the instruments of death has even been passed down from Mount Moriah to Majdanek:

> Above Moria, the falling off cliffs to God,
> there hovers the flag of the sacrificial knife
> Abraham's scream for the son of his heart,
> at the great ear of the Bible it lies preserved.
>
> . . . Job's scream to the four winds
> and the scream concealed in Mount Olive
> like a crystal-bound insect overwhelmed by impotence.
>
> O knife of evening red, flung into the throats
> where trees of sleep rear blood-licking from the
>   ground,
> where time is shed
> from the skeletons in Hiroshima and Maidanek . . .
>
> [pp. 127, 129]

The reference to Hiroshima suggests the unity of suffering; this is rare in the poetry of Sachs, which is explicitly concerned not with the universality of suffering but with the universal and eternal role of Jewish suffering; otherwise, this poem is fairly representative of the theme of recurrence that emerges in most of her Holocaust poems. Jewish history, or the continuum of Jewish existence, becomes a series of reenactments of the pageant of death which take place not in a civilization but in a barren landscape of screams. Death is consecrated by divine will—but not by the God of revelation and covenant, not by the God who is called into dialogue with man. The significance of this becomes sharper if we compare the above stanzas with similar passages that appear in the literature in which Mount Moriah is associated with Majdanek. In a Yiddish poem by H. Leivick, for example, unlike in Sachs's poem, the same imagery of continuity which affirms the cyclical nature of Jewish history also constructs an irony of juxtaposition or inversion that characterizes most of postwar lamentation literature. The speaker in Leivick's poem links the two places, the mountain on which Isaac was nearly sacrificed and the death camp in which thousands of Jews were actually slaughtered, in an effort to force God to honor His covenant with His people as they have honored theirs with Him.[41] A similar image appears in Aaron Zeitlin's Yiddish poem "Ani Ma'amin": "Who is so volcanic as my God? / If he is Sinai to me, / He is Maidanek as well." This poem, like Zeitlin's other poems, is a declaration of faith (one volume of his poetry is entitled *Poems of Hurbn and of Faith*), yet it is faith secured only after struggle and protest. And his God is a God who commands and who lives in history: "I believe / He suffers with me; / if I cry out against Him with me He cries . . ."[42] In Sachs's poems, God is unreachable and unaccountable, and the recurrence of martyrdom is accepted almost as a law of nature. Sachs herself, in a letter to Walter Berensohn in 1946, attaches a mission of enlightenment through suffering to the destiny of Israel: "When each of the peoples of the earth seeks for meaning, why should not Israel again offer mankind a draught from its own ancient source? I do not think it is enough to win fruit and home from our inherited earth when it is in our power together to fulfill the ancient call of our people—new and purified by suffering."[43]

There is, then, a "meaning" which Israel is meant to extract—and to share—out of its sufferings. But the ultimate resolution is not in the social message, or even in the messianic compassion which redeems the passion in a work like *The Last of the Just,* but in a kind of transcendental synthesis. Without attempting to present an exegesis of the metaphysics which informs Sachs's poetry, at the heart of which lies unfathomable mystery, I would only call attention to the manner in which Israel's latest martyrdom is absorbed into the larger, cosmic design; the speaker, like a seventeenth-century English metaphysical poet, reaches from the particular property which designated the victims—the numbers engraved on their arms in the camps—to a mystical, quasi-Cabbalistic, assimilation of numbers as components of an organic universe:

> When your forms turned to ashes
> into the oceans of night
> where eternity washes
> life and death into the tides—
>
> there rose the numbers—
> (once branded into your arms
> so none would escape the agony)
>
> there rose meteors of numbers
> beckoned into the spaces
> where light-years expand like arrows
> and the planets
> are born
> of the magic substances of pain—
>
> numbers—root and all
> plucked out of murderers' brains
> and part already
> of the heavenly cycle's
> path of blue veins.
>
> ["Numbers," p. 71]

The unity of the universe is so complete that no part of it can be violated without all the others being affected. The "Star" in *Eli* testifies to its role in accepting the "dust" of Israel as it traveled through the chimneys: "I was the chimney sweep—/ my light turned black—"; and the tree testifies: "I am only a tree. / I can no longer stand straight . . ." (p. 363). There is, then, terrible, cosmic sadness for the loss—"there, always, / where a place has been left / for heartbeats" ("Who knows where the stars stand," p. 103)—but the loss and the sadness are ultimately absorbed into the divine harmony:

> The child murdered in sleep
> Arises; bends down the tree of ages
> And pins the white breathing star
> That was once called Israel
> To its topmost bough.

> Spring upright again, says the child,
> To where tears mean eternity.
>
> ["The Voice of the Holy Land," p. 45]

Of her own verse, Sachs says that it is "always designed to raise the unutterable to a transcendental level, so as to make it bearable and in this night of nights to give a hint of the holy darkness in which quiver and arrow are hidden" (a reference to the prophet Isaiah, who says that "the Lord puts the arrow he had used back in its quiver so that it may remain in darkness").[44]

Just as Sach's universe is organic and totally interconnected, so all the poems written since 1946 are aspects of a unifying vision. At her death in 1970, this gentle poet left to her people a strange and beautiful volume of consolation which seeks refuge in a Divinity whose ways are inscrutable and in a community which fulfills its tragic mission in death.

PAUL CELAN: NO CONSOLATION

Paul Celan has been regarded by many as the most accomplished German lyric poet of recent decades. He and Sachs are among the few who did not exchange their language when they emigrated from Germany and whose writing remains, in part at least, rooted in German literary traditions. The German of Celan, it has been argued, was significantly influenced by the literary conventions of his adopted home, France; nevertheless, his language is such a unique construct of deeply rooted idiom and neologism that he can hardly be considered a "displaced" writer. As Alvin Rosenfeld writes: "When all else had been taken from Paul Celan, when his homeland had been occupied by the Nazis and his parents deported to one of the death camps, his language alone remained as a link to the past, and the poet lived in it as permanently and as securely as he ever did again in any physical landscape."[45] Celan was born in Czernowitz, capital of Bukovina (where most of the Jews spoke German), and barely escaped the death by gas that was the lot of his parents; he spent the war years in a work camp and then returned to Romania for a short time before his exile to Paris. His death in 1970 was, apparently, a suicide.

Celan's poetry, which explores vast territories of the human soul, is not concerned exclusively with the Holocaust, and it is not primarily as a poet of the Holocaust that he has been read; in fact, except for his widely acclaimed poem "Todesfuge," the depth of his involvement with the Jewish catastrophe and his extensive use of Jewish sources have often been overlooked. What is needed is a reading of Celan, as one would read other Hebraic writers, with an understanding of his origins so that one can appreciate his deviations. Celan himself described the landscape—internal as well as external—that was his heritage in an acceptance speech in 1958 when he was awarded the Bremen Literary Prize: "The landscape from which I come to you—by way of what detours! but are there even such things as detours?—this landscape may be unknown to most of you. It is the landscape that was the home for a not inconsiderable part of those Hasidic tales that Martin Buber recounted to us all in German."[46] Against this landscape, the question of continuity or discontinuity in the traditional perceptions of martyrdom is crucial to an understanding of the few poems which are clear responses to the Holocaust.

Celan is the artist who is most often invoked in the ongoing debate on the potential of aesthetic forms to capture the horrors of the concentrationary universe. The challenge, it will be recalled, was formulated by Adorno when he discussed the dangers inherent in any "artistic representation of the naked bodily pain of those who have been knocked down by rifle butts"; it contains the potential, he continued—"no matter how remote—to squeeze out pleasure." We saw that Borowski expressly banished "beauty" that would betray the sweat and blood of the victims, and that Hochhuth rejected for the stage, as providing too much distancing, the method used by Paul Celan in "Todesfuge," in which "the gassing of the Jews is entirely translated into metaphors."

Sachs and Celan are the most extreme examples of artists who have transmuted the ugly realities into works of aesthetic perfection without detracting from the horror. In Celan, in fact, the horror of physical defilement and psychological degradation is overshadowed by the spiritual emptiness and desolation experienced by the victim and the survivor in an abandoned universe. Here, ironically, Celan is more firmly rooted in traditional Jewish beliefs than Sachs, and therefore his despair is so much more endemic and shattering than her quiet acceptance. Using many of the same images and invoking many of the same associations as Sachs, he constructs a world as bleak and rudderless as hers is whole and mysterious. Sachs's repeated invocation of the dust of martyred Israel—the dust of ancient sacrifices and the ashes of contemporary incinerations—is echoed repeatedly in poems of Celan's, but whereas for Sachs the dust of today's sacrifice mingles with the sand of Sinai and the wisdom of Solomon and finds its resolution in the eternal process by which "the fingers" (of the murderers) which "emptied the deathly shoes of sand" will tommorow "be dust / In the shoes of those to come" ("But who emptied your shoes of sand," p. 9), Celan can offer no consolation in the cosmic design, or even in the artistic reconstruction of the event:

> There was earth in them, and
> they dug.
>
> They dug and dug, and thus
> Their day wore on, and their night. And they did not
>   praise God,
> who, they heard, willed all this,
> who, they heard, knew all this.
>
> They dug and heard no more;
> they did not grow wise, nor contrive any song,
> or any kind of language.
> They dug . . .[47]

The God whom they "did not praise" is the God of the covenant, the God who must be held accountable for the operations of history. In another poem, the victims' silence, their refusal to pray, is transformed into a prayer of defiance which is perhaps the most anguished of the blasphemies to be encountered in the literature:

> No one kneads us again of earth and clay,
> No one incants our dust.
> No one.
>
> Blessed art thou, No-one.
> For thy sake we will bloom.
> Towards
> thee.
>
> We were, we are, we shall remain
> a Nothing,
> blooming:
> the Nothing-, the
> No-one's Rose . . .
>
> ["Psalm," p. 183]

Jerry Glenn, in his analysis of this poem, notes that the "majority of interpreters . . . feel that the blasphemy is only apparent, and that Celan is here following the old Jewish law that the name of God must not be spoken, but rather a circumlocution must be found." By this interpretation, then, Celan is "actually affirming the God of Judaism."[48] This approach, it seems to me, represents a common attempt at plastering over the cracks that the Nazi earthquake caused in the foundations of Judaism which the artist, in his agony, reveals.

In Celan, as in several of the other writers we have considered, the ghosts of unfulfilled lives still haunt the natural world:

> Whichever stone you lift—
> you lay bare
> those who need the protection of stones:
> naked,
> they now renew the intervolving . . .
>
> ["Whichever Stone You Lift," p. 71]

In Sachs's universe, the stones are the petrified vessels of the generations of human history:

> We stones
> When someone lifts us
> He lifts the Foretime—
> When someone lifts us
> He lifts the Garden of Eden
>
> . . . For we are memorial stones
> Embracing all dying.
>
> We are a satchel full of lived life.
> Whoever lifts us lifts the hardened graves of earth.
>
> ["Chorus of the Stones," p. 35]

Sachs's poem concludes with the promise of dreams and angels that the stone which served as a pillow for the patriarch Jacob confers on Jacob's ancestors:

You heads of Jacob,
For you we hide the roots of dreams
And let the airy angels' ladders
Sprout like the tendrils of a bed of bindweed.

[p. 35]

But, for Celan, there is no blessing in the stones. His poem concludes with a curse:

Whichever word you speak—
you thank
perdition.

[p. 71]

Celan directly acknowledges the gap between his compatriot's quiet faith in an inscrutable Deity and his own angry prosecution of an accountable God, in a poem dedicated to Nelly Sachs:

. . . The talk was of your God, I spoke
against Him, I
let the heart that I had,
hope:
for His highest, His deathrattled, His
angry word . . .

["Zurich, Zum Storchen," p. 179]

Finally, whatever his brief against God, Celan casts his lot with the folk of Israel—especially in some of his earliest and some of his latest poems (in *Mohn und Gedächtnis* and in *Die Niemandsrose*). When he speaks of the victims he usually speaks in the first person plural, and his identification with the suffering lot of his people is nowhere more apparent than in his masterpiece, "Todesfuge": "Coal black milk of morning we drink it at evening / we drink it at noon and at daybreak we drink it at night."[49] In this poem, in which life and death in the camps are translated into surrealist metaphor without in any way betraying the situation, there is a clear juxtaposition of the people of Israel on the one hand, represented by the narrator and his fellow victims as well as by the vision of the biblical "Shulamith," and the Germans on the other, represented by "the man," clearly an SS officer, as well as by the vision of Goethe's "Marguerite." The clash here is not simply of two inexorable forces, but of two civilizations. And Celan's is not a legacy of consolation or resolution but of confrontation and defiance.

It can be said, then, that it is not a recounting of atrocities which produces the terror in the elegiac poetry and prose we have been reading, but the reflection of a world which has lost its center, a world abandoned by God and filled with the corpses of His worshipers. The echoes of phrases from lamentation literature appear all the more terrible here because the ultimate source of meaning and consolation which informed the interpretation of catastrophe throughout the generations has been withdrawn. In the Midrash, as in the Bible, all of nature, all of the cosmos, participates in the suffering of Israel. One *midrash* recounts that when the Temple was burning and the Jews were being slaughtered, Moses reprimanded the sun for shining on such devastation. The sun replied, in sorrow and shame, that it was forced by higher powers to shine[50] Compare this with the poems and stories of the *hurbn* in which the outside world—nature, the cosmos, Divinity—appears repeatedly either as a memory or a mockery. Although, as we have learned, a defiance which borders on apostasy accompanies the response to catastrophe in nearly every generation, never, I believe, in the lamentation literature does man's loneliness appear so vast and implacable or the desolation of his world so total. Tradition flounders here like a boat whose course was charted long ago but which has lost its compass and most of its crew.

And yet the classical themes continue to reverberate through Hebraic literature; to whom, to what force can the Jewish writer appeal other than to the God of his fathers, who still belongs to the folk of Israel, even in the hour of His eclipse and their death: "In whom can I believe, / If not in Him, my beloved God of cataclysm?" asks Aaron Zeitlin in his poem "Ani Ma'amin"; "I am a Jew, as He is God."[51] Even if the poet would construct his world anew, *ex nihilo,* his creation is the prisoner of memory, and for all the would-be autonomy of his imagination he resurrects the little town in Europe with its pious men and cradle-rocked children—and its watchful God. Jacob Glatstein writes:

. . . I'll be stubborn,
plant myself
in my own intimate night
which I've entirely invented
and admired from all sides.
I'll find my place in space
as big as a fly,
and compel to stand there
for all time
a cradle, a child,
into whom I'll sing the voice
of a father drowsing,
with a face in the voice,
with love in the voice,
with hazy eyes
that swim in the child's sleepy eyes
like warm moons.
And I'll build around this cradle a Jewish city
with a *shul,* with a God who never sleeps,
who watches over the poors shops,
over Jewish fear,
over the cemetery
that's lively all night
with worried corpses.
And I'll buckle myself up with my last days
and, for spite, count them in you, frozen past
who mocked me,
who invented my living, garrulous
Jewish world.
You silenced it
And in Maidanek woods
finished it off with a few shots.[52]

What emerges from a comparative study of these Hebraic writers is a pattern which at first appears surprising but which derives from the immeasurable trauma which the

Holocaust wrought not only in the flesh of Israel but in its spirit. For those writers who remain within the parameters of the tradition, the attempt to recreate the Holocaust in terms of its collective legacy is accompanied by the risk of exposing the ruptures, the discontinuities, and the cracks in the most fundamental codes of Jewish faith and conduct. On the other hand, those few writers, such as Schwarz-Bart and Sachs, who would "conquer" the Holocaust by seeking in the abyss the sparks of redemption or consolation have done so by going beyond the tradition, beyond the covenantal relationship between God and Israel, and beyond the internal literary and philosophical dialogue through which Israel has confronted catastrophe throughout the ages.

Notes

1. *One Generation After*, p. 78.

2. *God's Presence in History: Jewish Affirmations and Philosophical Reflections.*

3. Shalom Spiegel, introduction to Louis Ginzberg, *Legends of the Bible* (New York: Simon and Schuster, 1956), p. xxii.

4. Fackenheim, *God's Presence in History*, pp. 67-69, 77.

5. Quoted in Jerome R. Mintz, *Legends of the Hasidim: An Introduction to Hasidic Culture and Oral Tradition in the New World* (Chicago: University of Chicago Press, 1968), p. 250.

6. "After Such Knowledge . . . ," p. 108.

7. This is an inhibition which many of the *paytanim* who wrote poetic lamentations commemorating centuries of suffering did not share; see the *selihah* prayer by R. Shabbetai Cohen Ba'al ha-Shah in memory of the victims of Chmielnicki: "Their feet and hands they severed / and cut the corpse in half" (Bernfeld, *Sefer ha-Dema'ot*, vol. 3, p. 172). The elevation of reality to the level of legend or myth in the poetry of another Hebraic writer, Uri Zvi Greenberg, functions, as it does in Wiesel, as a prism through which otherwise intolerable reality can be filtered.

8. *The Town beyond the Wall*, p. 73.

9. Ginzberg, *Legends of the Bible*, p. 382.

10. *Mimesis*, p. 17.

11. "Ki ze Kevar Bekhi" [A time for tears], in *Rehovot ha-Nahar*, p. 80.

12. "Shir Min ha-Ya'ar: Haya Zoheket" [Song of the forest, an animal laughs], in ibid., p. 95.

13. Ephraim Oshry, *She'eilot u-Teshuvot mi-Ma'amakim* (New York, 1959).

14. *Night*, p. 47.

15. Wiesel, *Legends of Our Time*, p. 61.

16. "I. B. Singer," p. 60.

17. "The Slaughterer," in *The Seance*, p. 29.

18. Wiesel, *The Accident*, p. 72.

19. *After the Tradition*, p. 160.

20. "The Last Demon," in *Short Friday* (New York: Noonday Press, 1964), pp. 119, 129.

21. "Esthétique du Mal," in *The Collected Poems of Wallace Stevens* (New York: Knopf, 1954), p. 320.

22. "The Letter Writer," in *The Seance*, pp. 262-63.

23. *One Generation After*, p. 166.

24. *Ani Ma'amim*.

25. "Crown of Lamentation for the Whole House of Israel," in *Rehovot ha-Nahar*, p. 62.

26. *Not of This Time, Not of This Place*, p. 254.

27. "Ha-Mafte'ah Zalal," in *Mi-Kol ha-Ahavot*, p. 178. Translation mine.

28. Recorded by Nathan Eck in *Wandering on the Roads of Death* [Hebrew], quoted by Shaul Esh, "The Dignity of the Destroyed," *Judaism* 11, no. 2 (Spring 1962): 106-7.

29. *The Last of the Just*, p. 4.

30. "The Tradition of the Hidden Just Men," in *The Messianic Idea in Judaism* (New York: Schocken, 1971), p. 251.

31. Ibid., p. 256.

32. Paraphrased by Lothar Kahn, *Mirrors of the Jewish Mind: A Gallery of Portraits of European Jewish Writers of Our Time*, p. 215. See also Lisa Billig, "Voices out of the Holocaust," *Reconstructionist* 26, no. 15 (December 2, 1960): 24.

33. *World of Our Fathers*, pp. 450-51.

34. *One Destiny: An Epistle to the Christians*, trans. Milton Hindus (New York: Putnam, 1945), p. 26.

35. Megillah, 29a.

36. *A Woman Named Solitude*, trans. Ralph Manheim (New York: Bantam, 1973), p. 150. As moving as this passage is, it should be recalled that even the "ruins" of the Warsaw Ghetto were quickly obliterated and the city rebuilt.

37. "Across Different Cultures," *Midstream*, March 1973, p. 77.

38. Quoted in Marie Syrkin, "Nelly Sachs—Poet of the Holocaust," p. 15.

39. Letter dated January 27, 1946, which appeared in *Aufbau*, November 4, 1966, p. 22, quoted in David Bronsen, "The Dead among the Living: Nelly Sachs' 'Eli,'" p. 126.

40. Ibid., p. 121.

41. "Der Kheshbon Is Nokh Alts mit Dir, Bashefer" [The reckoning is only with You, Creator of the Universe], in *In Treblinka Bin Ikh Nit Geven,* p. 17.

42. "Ani Ma'amin," in Howe and Greenberg, eds., *A Treasury of Yiddish Poetry,* pp. 323-24.

43. *Aufbau,* October 28, 1966, quoted in Syrkin, "Nelly Sachs—Poet of the Holocaust," pp. 16-17.

44. Postscript to *Eli,* in *O the Chimneys,* pp. 387, 386.

45. "Paul Celan," p. 77.

46. Quoted in ibid., p. 76.

47. "There Was Earth in Them," in *Speech-Grille and Selected Poems,* p. 173.

48. *Paul Celan* (New York: Twayne, 1973), p. 121.

49. "Todesfuge," in Karl S. Weimar, "Paul Celan's 'Todesfuge': Translation and Interpretation," p. 85.

50. For a recounting of this *midrash,* see Louis Ginzberg, *Legends of the Jews,* vol. 4 (Philadelphia: Jewish Publication Society of America, 1946), pp. 303 ff.

51. Howe and Greenberg, eds., *A Treasury of Yiddish Poetry,* p. 322.

52. "I'll Find My Self-Belief," in Whitman, ed., *An Anthology of Modern Yiddish Poetry,* pp. 5-7.

Bibliography

Alter, Robert. *After the Tradition: Essays on Modern Jewish Writing.* New York: Dutton, 1971.

————. "A Poet of the Holocaust." *Commentary,* November 1973, pp. 57-63.

Fackenheim, Emil. *God's Presence in History: Jewish Affirmations and Philosophical Reflections.* New York: New York University Press, 1970.

Rosenfeld, Alvin. "Paul Celan." *Midstream,* November 1971, pp. 75-80.

Sidra DeKoven Ezrahi (essay date 1980)

SOURCE: Ezrahi, Sidra DeKoven. "History Imagined: The Holocaust in American Literature." In *By Words Alone: The Holocaust in Literature,* pp. 176-216. Chicago: The University of Chicago Press, 1980.

[*In the following excerpt, Ezrahi explores the responses of postwar American writers to the Holocaust, emphasizing a conflict many of them experienced between their creative imagination and obligation to historical truth.*]

> When six millions are slaughtered, in effect twice or thrice that number are [killed]. For the Jews [on all the other continents] die with them. All those that have not

yet [perished] are not dead simply because they do not know what has happened. . . . A cold shiver passes over me when I think of their remorse when they do get to know, after the War. . . . Oh, merciful and gracious God! If the circumstances had been reversed, we the Jews of the great European religious academies would have known what was taking place! We would have shrieked to the high heavens and shaken the whole world to its very foundations.

> Itzhak Katzenelson, *Vittel Diary*

The European writer—Jew or gentile, survivor or observer—could hardly escape the visions of a Holocaust which was enacted on his native soil. The Poles, as Rudnicki demonstrates, inhabit a land which was physically devastated by military attack and spiritually violated by the presence of the death camps. The Germans were at best observers—as, in fact, were most of the peoples of Europe, whose "undesired" neighbors were rounded up under their very eyes. François Mauriac recalls "the trainloads of Jewish children standing at Austerlitz station,"[1] a spectacle which was reenacted time and again for the non-Jew during the war years.

On the other side of the ocean, the American writer, unless he actually participated in the military liberation of the concentration camps, had no direct contact with the life and death struggles of the victims of Nazism. Nevertheless, an event of such enormity, which clearly carried far-reaching implications for the future of the Jewish people in particular and of mankind in general, could not be passed over in silence, even by Jewish writers in America who only a few years before were endorsing universalistic causes and may have been indifferent to or even contemptuous of their Jewish origins. Yet few if any of these writers possessed the resources from which an immediate response could be shaped. In retrospect, many years later, Saul Bellow articulated the challenge they had faced while at the same time acknowledging the empirical constraints inherent in their creative engagement with the subject:

> Just what the reduction of millions of human beings into heaps of bone and mounds of rag and hair or clouds of smoke betokened, there is no one who can plainly tell us, but it is at least plain that something was being done to put in question the meaning of survival, the meaning of pity, the meaning of justice and of the importance of being oneself, the individual's consciousness of his own existence. It would be odd, indeed, if these historical events had made no impression on American writers, even if they are not on the whole given to taking the historical or theoretical view. They characteristically depend on their own observations and appear at times obstinately empirical.[2]

When he referred to the "reduction of millions of human beings into heaps of bone . . . or clouds of smoke," Bellow could have been alluding to the atomic blasts as well as the Nazi Holocaust; Hiroshima weighs almost as heavily on the American conscience of the American-Jewish writer as Auschwitz preys on his Jewish sensibilities. And he is calling attention to a basic characteristic of the American temper, its fact-minded attachment to empirical criteria of validity. Finally, he is deploring the threat to the self, the loss of identity, which both the Nazi and the nuclear forms of mass extermination represented, perhaps even more than the threat to the entire corpus of Judaism which the destruction of European Jewry signified.

No single work expresses the historical insulation of the American-Jewish writer of the 1940s and his regard for the primacy of the self as effectively as Bellow's own first novel, *Dangling Man.* Published in 1944, before the war had ended, yet not before news of the destruction of European Jewry had received wide publicity, it concerns a young American (incidentally Jewish) who, in the end, resolves his own problems of alienation by enlisting in the army. Except for one dream-sequence filled with physical torture and murder which are associated with unspecified atrocities being committed in Europe, there is no sense of connectedness to the larger events in which he will, by his act of enlistment, be forced to take part. The novel concludes with a tenuous entry into history—but it is not until *Mr. Sammler's Planet,* published twenty-five years later, that there appears in Bellow's fiction a Jew who has lived through and absorbed the major cataclysms of Jewish history in the twentieth century. That quarter-century measures a gradual shift in the engagement as well as the familiarity of the American-Jewish writer with the fate of the Jews of Europe.

Even the writer whose sense of community was stronger in the forties than Bellow's could hardly have broken through the empirical barriers and assimilated into his writing the reports of horrors that were broadcast to him over the radio or glared at him from the newspapers; while they may have dwarfed and mocked his own "mercifully more humdrum" existence,[3] they could not, in their terrible strangeness, furnish new subjects for his art. As early as 1940, Shlomo Katz reported, with probing candor, a conversation which had taken place among a group of young Jewish writers. The writers remain anonymous in his essay, but the condition they describe may be considered as fairly representative. When the "news from Europe" started coming in, Katz reports, these writers, most of whom were American-born and had not written on Jewish subjects for some time—if ever—were nonetheless shaken: "The awareness of their Jewishness transformed the news from Europe into a personal injury and tended to replace other subjects in importance." One writer expressed the dilemma in which they all found themselves:

> How can I write of loneliness in New York, or poverty, or the despair felt by one of the economic outcasts, after I had just read some particularly gruesome piece of news from Germany or Poland? . . . True, one does not rule out the other, objectively. But keenly as I may feel the situation I wish to write about, I cannot help repeating to myself the particular piece of news I read about, and the loneliness of the great city as well as the tragedy of poverty recede in importance; for I visualize the victim in Poland or Germany and I know that he would be happy to exchange positions with the lonely

soul, and be thankful for it. I am then confronted with a new theme which in artistic intensity overshadows the one I originally conceived. You will admit that the prospect of one so crushed as to be humbly thankful for that against which we protest, and mind you, honestly and sincerely thankful, is certainly a more moving subject. My first hero who tears his hair in the loneliness of his room while listening to the monotonous ticking of the clock (but after a fair meal), and my heroine who is about to jump off the George Washington Bridge because she cannot practice her art as freely as she would like to while she remains on a W.P.A. project, become shadowy in outline. Again, I repeat, these subjects are still powerful and justify treatment, but I lose my approach; I fall out of the mood and can no longer do these subjects that justice which I feel is their due.

And yet, Katz explains, such a writer cannot incorporate into his art the themes which have come to haunt him, for "only the slimmest of cultural and psychic ties bind him to the Jews of Poland . . . Germany or Russia." Nearly every American-Jewish writer, son or grandson of immigrant parents, felt some personal bond, it is true, to an ancestral home or family in war-torn Europe. Yet the process of acculturation in America had been swift, and "between him and the European scene there lie years" of cultural estrangement.[4] The emotional bond, then, could prove not only insufficient as a creative resource for the writer, but positively detrimental to his art, and the paralysis of creativity which Katz diagnosed in 1940 was to worsen in the ensuing years.

On the most fundamental level, then, it is clear that the absence of direct experience or at least of a cultural ambience that could render the unlived experience familiar, as well as a paralyzing sense of the enormity of the unexplored event, impeded—and eventually shaped—the assimilation of the Holocaust into American, and particularly into American-Jewish, literature. Several stages can be identified in the slow process by which the remote event eventually entered the literature, a few of which correspond to specific historical developments and others to the gradual evolution of a literary milieu. The focus here is not, then, on a specific genre or genres of the literature of displaced and culturally unconnected persons, but on a phase in the literary history of a distinct community of writers. Like the Hebraic, the American literary response to the Holocaust can be examined within a specific and preexistent cultural context, although in the first case it is the proximity to and in the second the distance from the events that maintains the boundaries and the inner coherence of a distinct literary universe.

The war literature, which began to appear in America shortly after the demobilization, established the camps somewhere on the outer boundaries of human geography. During the next several years, which were marked by introspection and a sense of diffidence or vulnerability on the part of American Jews, the magnitude of the fascist threat was probed, but not the historical events of the Holocaust, by a number of serious as well as more popular novelists of the period; the novels by Saul Bellow, Arthur Miller, and Laura Z. Hobson which appeared in the mid-forties reflect a kind of transference of the patterns and fears of anti-Semitism into the American context. Some writers regarded themselves during this same period as spokesmen for the victims and combed the ruins of Europe for their testimonies. During the fifties, the growing documentation by survivors and historians lent greater visibility and familiarity to historical events, although a certain resistance to confronting the American "complicity of silence" or to dwelling on the particularity of Jewish suffering could also be detected during those years. The Eichmann trial proved to be a watershed in the American perception of the Holocaust, as it provided near-personal contact with survivors and an unprecedented immersion in the facts for those who followed it through the public media. The trial itself generated a number of poetic and fictional explorations into the concentrationary universe by writers such as Denise Levertov and Norma Rosen. And the heightened interest which the Eichmann trial precipitated may have been one of the factors behind the proliferation of translations into English of European literature of the Holocaust, which appeared in America in the 1960s. At the same time a number of survivor-writers, including Ilona Karmel, Zdena Berger, Elżbieta Ettinger, and Jerzy Kosinski published their novels in English, adding to an evolving literature that was to provide the outsider with a map of the landscape and possible avenues of approach to it. The realistic fiction written by American-Jewish writers in the sixties and seventies tries to make up for the lack of empirical resources by a thoroughly researched representation of events which were still unknown and by literary models which had not yet been established in the 1940s.

Yet the historical remove remains the basic existential premise on which any American writer confronts the Holocaust, and in the work of certain writers such as Irving Feldman and Arthur Cohen, it is this fact which constitutes the boundary and the resource as well as the ultimate challenge for the imagination. These writers represent two of the most radical attempts to possess the universe of camps and ghettos by a kind of literary fiat.

Parallel with the development of a realistic historical fiction on the one hand, which presupposes an acquired familiarity with the subject, and of a literature that engages history imaginatively on the other hand, have been attempts to distill the experience into its basic symbols and its moral or social legacies. A partial, though intriguing, early example of this is to be found in the parables of Isaac Rosenfeld, which explore the terror of the closed society. For a number of other writers, Jews and non-Jews, the Holocaust is a symbol of the ultimate in human suffering; in Arthur Koestler's words, Jewish suffering represents "man's condition carried to the extreme."[5] These writers range from the proletarian writers of the thirties and beyond, who incorporated the Holocaust into their litany of the class struggle against oppression, to Arthur Miller and Sylvia Plath, for whom personal agony finds its "objective correlative" in Auschwitz.

Where the imagination is not bound by imperatives of personal experience, the symbolic transmutations of historical events disengage more easily from the compulsion to "represent." As such, while nearly every European novel, poem, or play is a form of witness, for American literature the stark realities constitute a stimulus for a process essentially more introspective, self-referential, and autonomous with respect to the haunting memories and less charged with the moral responsibilities and dilemmas of survival and testimony.

THE HOLOCAUST AND THE LITERATURE OF WORLD WAR II

Even as the war literature began to appear, the fate of the Jews and the existence of the concentration camps remained as much on the periphery of consciousness as they had during the war itself.[6] In an occasional novel a soldier does stumble across a death camp or a D.P. camp or the ruins of a ghetto. Yet such a discovery is in most cases as abrupt and unintegrable as the discovery of a Martian spaceship would have been. It was an event which the Americans, British, and Russians experienced as liberators, and the condition of the prisoners they liberated was so unlike anything they had ever witnessed, even on the battlefield, that the event had to be isolated, circumscribed, in order to be communicated at all. In Stefan Heym's novel *The Crusaders,* the decision to liberate a camp near Neustadt is a "bootleg affair"[7] embarked on by one General Farrish; the camp itself is not even on the map—of either the Americans or the Germans. The description of the actual operation of the camp is stiff and reads rather like a textbook account of the system which the author must have come to understand only much later. But what this passage does dramatize with the force of authentic witness is the horror of the first sight of the camps for anybody outside the system. Perhaps the most telling sign of the fact that the very existence of the camps is extraneous to civilized concepts of social order is the wild, enraged reaction of the American soldiers who join the camp inmates in massacring the SS men who are found in the camp; as one of the Americans says, in reply to the officer who wants to capture these men alive so they can be brought to trial, we've "got to do this job before our civilized inhibitions catch up with us" (vol. 2, p. 704). Finally, as they evacuate the camp the dejected, disoriented soldiers look forward only to doing "some fighting, some clean fighting" (vol. 2, p. 706).[8]

Another American war novel, *The Trumpet Unblown,* by William Hoffman, illustrates even more forcefully the remoteness of the concentrationary universe from the experience or imagination of even the most war-weary soldier. In this novel, as in *The Crusaders,* American troops stationed in Germany on a mop-up operation discover traces of concentrationary existence. At one point they come across a barn piled high with charred corpses and force the German townspeople from nearby to dig some graves; in the course of this work, "they found a little life in some of the flesh. It was nothing much, just some stinking organisms, weighing a few pounds at the most, that had managed to live at least a week under ten feet of decomposing flesh. But there was life. The organisms responded to light and touch and sipped water. Sometimes lashless eyelids would flicker a few times before the organisms died."⁹ The anonymity and dehumanization to which the victims were subjected even before their deaths is never more apparent in the literature of the Holocaust than in this passage in which the word "man," "woman," or "child" is never used.

Frederick Hoffman, in analyzing this novel, draws no distinction in kind between the horrors of modern warfare and of the concentration camp. Shelby, a soldier who is one of the main protagonists in *The Trumpet Unblown,* is described as "as much a victim of the war as if he had spent the years in a concentration camp." Hoffman calls this book the *"terminus ad quem* of the literature of violence."¹⁰ But even though some of the imagery of decomposing bodies and severed limbs is common to both situations, there is an important distinction between the above passage and even the most lurid descriptions of combat in this novel and in most of the other novels which cover the same terrain; the distinction derives from the perception that the horrors of the concentration camp are the deliberate product of a social organization in which the victims and the victimizers are clearly and demonically defined and are not the blind casualties in a declared war between two parties who share the status of soldiers and enemies. Nor, for all the anonymity and routine of mechanized mass death in the concentration camps, were the victimizers insulated from the instant connection between their sadistic acts and the deadly results.

The soldiers who stumble upon the dying victims do not, of course, understand the operation of the system and its clear-cut distinctions; but they do perceive that there was a system behind this hideousness, whose sole purpose was the manufacture of pain and death. The existence of the camps as an incomprehensible social order located at the extreme borders of the imaginable is dramatized in the scene in *The Trumpet Unblown* in which a group of D.P.'s in striped pajamas, with "bald heads and lustreless eyes" (p. 200), comes out of the woods: "One of the D.P.s had somewhere gotten hold of an old trumpet. The other D.P.s collected around him and began to chant. It was not a song. It was a melodic wail. Then the trumpet came in. It was a straight, unwavering tone upheld by the voices. The music was barbaric and like no music ever written . . ." (p. 201). Even when the camps appear in the pages of a war novel, then, they are unassimilable, mysterious and, necessarily, tangential to the business at hand."¹¹

Among the American novelists and poets of the war, Randall Jarrell is one of the few who attempted to explore the concentration camp beyond the barbed wire delineation between the human beings on the outside and the skeletons on the inside. In his few Holocaust poems, as well as in his other war poems, Jarrell—the gentile from the American South—attempted to remake himself, according to M. L. Rosenthal, into "a sort of German-Austrian Jew-

ish refugee of the spirit."¹² But unlike Sylvia Plath, whom we will consider later and whom A. Alvarez described in nearly identical language when analyzing her homeopathic appropriation of Holocaust symbols (for Plath the adult is a survivor, "an imaginary Jew from the concentration camps of the mind"), Jarrell does not adopt these symbols as metaphors for his own personal suffering, but assumes the burden of the witness who inherits the dying victim's portion of pain. And yet, like Rudnicki and Gascar, he can not get beyond the death and the dying, for that is the sum total of the reality that greeted him and the other liberators of the camps. The closest he comes to a "life portrait" is in his imaginative evocation of the survivor in a "concentration camp burned by its guards, deserted by its prisoners, and not yet occupied by the Allies," in the poem "In the Camp There Was One Alive."¹³ Yet this survivor, abandoned in a "charred cave" in the burning camp, is himself only a heartbeat away from his own death, and his comforters are the already-dead who "come" to him in his last lonely moments. The poetic imagination still cannot take the solider-explorer beyond the terminus of the camp system.

Another of Jarrell's poems, "A Camp in the Prussian Forest," which is one of the most powerful of the Holocaust poems written in America, is concerned directly with death in the camp and with the ritual of burial and elegy that the observer would grant the corpses, both as a tribute to the victims and a defiance of the anarchy of death. Yet as in Gascar's story, the hideous facts of death resist the decorous finale that the poet would accord them, and the camp and its inmates remain inexorably outside the amenities that would civilize them. The speaker, who participates in the mass burial of "load on puffed load" of "corpses, stacked like sodden wood," saws a star from the pine tree which graces the grave (the tree, in a gentle pathetic fallacy, will "pine if it is able"), paints it, and plants it, along with a wreath of pine needles, in the soil that covers the bodies. But his gesture is mocked by the other form of death—the Zyklon B death and the crematory interment from which the dead emerge again as "smoke" to "foul" the memorial star and "chalk with ash" the needles of the pine wreath:

> The needles of the wreath are chalked with ash,
> A filmy trash
> Litters the black woods with the death
> Of men; and one last breadth
>
> Curls from the monstrous chimney . . .
>
>   ["A Camp in the Prussian Forest," pp. 167, 168]

Yet, the most forceful representation of the remoteness and mystery of the concentrationary universe lies not in the symbols but in the syntax of Jarrell's poem. The first line of the fifth verse begins innocently—almost jocularly—by invoking images of mass inebriation ("Here men were drunk"), but the reversal lies in the radical use of "drunk" not as an adjective but as a passive verb: "Here men were drunk *like water,* burnt *like wood*" (p. 167, emphases mine).¹⁴ By an act of grammatical transformation which excludes them from the rules of social discourse, the victims are reduced from agents to objects of normal human functions. This process continues in the next lines, in which the levels of communication are violated by an undifferentiated yoking of literal and metaphorical language:

> The fat of good
> And evil, the breast's star of hope
> Were rendered into soap.
>
> [p. 167]

Yet the speaker, nearly trapped in the uncharted regions of violated syntax and reified metaphor, is carried out of the concentration camp by the familiarity and continuity of a meter and rhyme scheme which threaten to break down in a few places but regain their regularity, and by the latent Christian imagery which is both mocked and affirmed in the final apostrophe:

> . . . and one last breath
>
> Curls from the monstrous chimney . . . I laugh aloud
> Again and again;
> The star laughs from its rotting shroud
> Of flesh. O star of men!
>
> [p. 168][15]

Because the perspective of the American soldier-poet or soldier-novelist must inevitably be from the outside, and must encompass a vast panorama of destruction with few if any *points d'appui* to facilitate identification with specific individuals, a whole range of empathetic emotions seems to be inaccessible to him. There is sympathy in Jarrell's poetry, but it is undifferentiated and must give way to horror and shock and to an ultimate despair at the inability to rescue character and personal destiny from the piles of ruined humanity. Those writers, survivors or expatriates from Eastern Europe, who were intimately acquainted with the way of life as well as the mutilated death mask of the victims, were able to reconstruct their world and to reassemble random bones into persons. But the first encounter of the outsider with concentrationary death defied all the literary conventions by which tragedy has been conveyed through character, martyrdom through spiritual authority, and agony through personality.

A small group of soldier-writers did, however, attempt to integrate the camps into a larger scheme of meaning which also had a personal, existential referent; they include Jewish novelists such as Irwin Shaw and Louis Falstein, in whose novels the discovery of the camps forms an important link in the protagonist's pursuit of his own identity, a process shared by some of the Jewish soldier-writers from Palestine for whom the European manoeuvres in which they participated served primarily as a catalyst for expeditions into their own souls.

Shaw's *The Young Lions* gained instant popularity and is in certain respects a good representative of the middlebrow war literature of the period and of the earliest perceptions of the Holocaust in the American imagination.

The private mission of the American Jew in Europe dovetails neatly in this novel with the ideological commitment that had incubated under the American left wing during the thirties. It is in this regard that such fiction differs markedly from other American novels of the Second World War; both Paul Fussell and Stanley Cooperman, in their studies of the literature of World War I in England and America respectively, demonstrate how the brutality of the Great War destroyed for the postwar writers both the sense of moral seriousness and the expectation of personal valor and glory that soldiers had carried with them into battle since time immemorial and that had shaped the aesthetic conventions of a long tradition of war literature. Although fascism was considered to be a valid and even compelling *causus belli,* war was no longer regarded by the combatants of the Second World War either as a pledge to social amelioration or as a "proving ground of combat"; "almost all of them agreed that Hitler and the Japanese had to be stopped, but they couldn't understand why somebody else than they, individually, shouldn't have done the stopping."[16] For the American-Jewish soldier-novelists, however, the war against Hitler was regarded as a mission in which they had a sanctified role to play, and something of the sense of personal valor and purpose was rescued by these writers from the lost chivalric tradition.

Aesthetically, however, these novels add little to the serious experiments which characterized much of the literature after World War II. Despite the epic sweep of events and plethora of characters, *The Young Lions* is so schematic that there is no room in all its six hundred and eighty-nine pages for coincidence. The two major themes, or convictions, which underlie the narrative may be summed up in what Frederick Hoffman calls the "'crusading spirit' (that is, that this is a 'must war' against a clearly seen, an obvious enemy)" and the "fear of an indwelling Nazism, a self-analytic devil search." Three wooden characters spar in this Manichean drama until both these convictions are vindicated: Noah Ackerman, the American Jew who "is going into the war to fight both the Nazi evil and its native American examples," Michael Whitacre, the American gentile who is Noah's disciple in moral education, and Christian Diestl, "the finest product of Nazi demonology."[17]

It is significant that the final scene, in which the extremes meet and are resolved, takes place in the woods adjacent to the concentration camp which has just been liberated and occupied by the American forces. The camp itself is not much more than a stage prop into which Christian Diestl wanders and from which, finding himself trapped by the masses of insurgent inmates who have been abandoned by the SS, he manages to escape in the striped prison clothes of a *katzetnik*. It is a stage prop for Noah Ackerman too who, having fought his private war in the army against American anti-Semitism, discovers the ultimate products of the same venom in the concentrationary universe—but at the same time discovers the potential for future regeneration in the person of his commanding officer, Captain Green, who has shown compassion as well as efficiency in his operation of the camp. "When the war is over," Noah shouts in the forest, only seconds before he is shot down by Diestl, "Green is going to run the world. . . . The human beings are going to run the world! . . . There's a lot of Captain Greens! . . . There're millions of them!"[18] Christian kills Ackerman as a German soldier killing an American soldier, while the Nazi in Diestl kills the Jew in Ackerman. Finally Diestl's nemesis materializes in the form of Whitacre, who has served his apprenticeship at Ackerman's side and must now try to live up to the legacy of the "human beings" with which Ackerman charged him.

Due reverence, mingled with a measure of disgust, is granted the camp inmates; the approach of the American soldiers to the camp is described in terms of an encounter with impenetrable horror that are characteristic of the war literature:

> The men in the trucks fell quiet as they drove up to the open gates. The smell, by itself, would have been enough to make them silent, but there was also the sight of the dead bodies sprawled at the gate and behind the wire, and the *slowly moving mass of scarecrows* in tattered striped suits who engulfed the trucks. . . .
>
> They did not make much noise. Many of them wept, many of them tried to smile, although the cavernous eyes did not alter very much, either in weeping or smiling. *It was as though these creatures were too far sunk in a tragedy which had moved off the plane of human reaction onto an animal level of despair—and the comparatively sophisticated grimaces of welcome, sorrow and happiness were, for the time being, beyond their primitive reach.*
>
> [p. 672, emphases mine]

Here, again, there can be no further penetration of the "mystery" of the death camp, of the system that prevailed there and that brought the victims to their present state, and no empathy for the separate individuals who now constitute a mass of skeletons differentiated only as the "dead," the "dying," the "critical," and the "out of danger" (p. 674). The scenario in the camp serves rather to establish Green's humanity—in his calm and just dispensing of rations and medical supplies and his dry-eyed but compassionate assent to one prisoner-rabbi's request to hold a mass Kaddish for all the dead. It is, ultimately, the American Green who comes to liberate the Jews in the camps— and it is the American in Noah Ackerman who liberates the Jew in him. Ackerman's earlier response to the crude anti-Semitic remarks directed against him by men in his own company is a microcosm of the American response to fascism; he becomes a powerful avenger, learning to fight even the most formidable bullies and brandishing a knife against any further threats. "As he walked toward the barracks, he realized suddenly that he had discovered the technique of survival" (p. 352). And even though he must ultimately die at the hands of Diestl, his death is avenged by his American buddy. Implicit in this is the lesson that the Jews of Eastern Europe were deprived of on any large scale: the lesson of the strength of arms that can secure justice.

This route is pursued even more doggedly in another minor novel of the period, Louis Falstein's *Face of a Hero.* A first-person narrative concerned primarily with the terrors and triumphs of airborne combat (the narrator, Ben Isaacs, like the author, was an aerial gunner in the Air Force), the novel incorporates a visit to an Italian D.P. camp for Jews who had escaped from camps and ghettos in Eastern Europe. The narrator's initial response, predictably, is one of strangeness, even alienation, of recognition that as an American he can never fathom the suffering of these people: "At that moment I was sorry I had come; I felt like an intruder from another world that did not know the smell of the crematoria and the yellow Star of David. And if they resented me I did not blame them. *They* were the survivors of the six million slaughtered Jews, not we American Jews."[19]

And yet if it is as an American that he has been spared the Holocaust that Hitler arranged for the Jews, it is also as an American that he has come to liberate the survivors. Again, like Noah Ackerman, it is the American soldier in Ben Isaacs who liberates the persecuted Jew in him; "were it not for the fact that I was a 'bombadier,'" he muses, the inmates "would have resented my intrusion." As it is, they practically worship him; they crowd around him, staring at him, touching him, asking him questions. An old woman begins to weep and scream: "A Jewish bombadier who has been bombing *him* [Hitler] has come to visit us! . . . There he is! May he live to one hundred and twenty, Riboinoy shel Oilom. Come, Jews, behold him!" (p. 190).

Like so many other Jewish soldiers who fought in the European theater, both Ben Isaacs and Noah Ackerman rediscover their Jewish origins by association—both voluntary and involuntary—with the victims of Nazism. Their Jewish consciousness is, then, activated and shaped in World War II by a reversion to European perspectives which the immigrant had abandoned when he reached American shores. The dying words of Ackerman's father, who at the beginning of the novel lies destitute in a damp hotel in Santa Monica, concern the brother whom he had left behind in Europe when he emigrated: Your uncle, Jacob Ackerman says to his son, "is not a stranger to you. He is a Jew and the world is hunting him, and you are a Jew and the world is hunting you" (p. 46). Months later, after the anti-Semitism at home and abroad has kindled in him a new sense of kinship with his people, Noah is identified in his own mind as "Ackerman, out of Odessa . . ." (p. 548).

Ben Isaacs is also made aware by Hitler that his destiny is inexorably linked to that of the Jews behind the barbed wire. Himself an emigré who had arrived in America at the age of fifteen, he returns to Europe "because Hitler made me conscious, again, that as a Jew I must assume the role of scapegoat" (p. 42). He is advised by his buddies to remove his dog tags before flying over Germany; as he does so he realizes that he "hadn't the slightest idea what they did to captured American soldiers of Jewish extraction" (p. 70)—but he is fearful that they accorded them the same treatment they accorded Jews of any other nationality.

Heroism, then, is the answer that Shaw and Falstein would give to the real or potential threat of fascism. Just as in other popular novels of the Holocaust, such as those of J.-F. Steiner and Leon Uris, and much of the Hebrew war literature, heroism is exalted above martyrdom, so in *Face of a Hero* and *The Young Lions* the hero, the Jew as American, finally supersedes and redeems the victim, the Jew as European.

Any American-Jewish writer who, after the war, would attempt to penetrate the concentrationary universe armed only by the imagination would risk being regarded—or regarding himself—as an "intruder." The soldier was in the unique position not only of liberating the few surviving victims but of avenging them and their dead. Nevertheless, most of the literature which reconstructs the engagement of the Jewish soldier with the Jewish victims is so schematic, ultimately serving primarily the patriotic and ideological purposes for which so much war literature is written, that it does not survive as art but as an attitude—as one of the first encounters, authenticated by direct experience, with the Holocaust in American literature.

AMERICAN PROJECTIONS OF THE HOLOCAUST

For many of the civilian American-Jewish authors writing in the years immediately following the war, the Holocaust prompted introverted responses similar to but even more insular than those we have just encountered in the war literature: in some cases it confirmed the faith in the strength of American ideals which, having proved triumphant in the war against evil in Europe, should ultimately prevail in the internal war against social injustice, while in other cases it served to highlight the anti-Semitism inherent in American society. What is common to this literature is a primary concern for the status of the Jews of America, for which the Holocaust serves as a point of reference, not as the focus of attention.

The belief in a dialectical process of moral ascent, which tried to embrace even the Holocaust as part of the great confrontation between the forces of good and evil, justice and injustice, socialism and fascism—the last flickering of the proletarian faith of the thirties—underwent a short revival in the postwar period. Clifford Odets's anti-Nazi play, *Till the Day I Die*, written in 1935, had focused on the clash between ideologies and glorified the sacrificial heroism of those dedicated to overthrowing the "animal kingdom" and establishing "a world of security for all mankind";[20] such a play could hardly be written in 1945. Alfred Kazin, in his autobiography *Starting Out in the Thirties*, writes of the optimism generated in his contemporaries by Odets and the ideals which his art embodied; he recalls that as he had watched Odets's plays he too had been convinced that

> history was going our way, and in our need was the very lifeblood of history. . . . It was as if the planet had locked in combat. . . . There seemed to be no di-

> vision between my effort at personal liberation and the apparent effort of humanity to deliver itself. Reading Silone and Malraux, discovering Beethoven string quartets and having love affairs were part of the great pattern in Spain, in Nazi concentration camps. . . . Wherever I went now, I felt the moral contagion of a single idea.

Ten years later, Kazin and his compatriots learned what pattern life had in fact taken in the concentration camps:

> One day in the spring of 1945, when the war against Hitler was almost won, I sat in a newsreel theatre in Picadilly looking at the first films of the newly-liberated Belsen. On the screen, sticks in black and white prison garb leaned on a wire, staring dreamily at the camera; other sticks shuffled about [while bulldozers worked]. . . . Then the sticks would come back on the screen, hanging on the wire, looking at us.[21]

It is difficult to hang the old ideologies on such sticks. Occasionally a writer like Albert Halper went so far as to attach the fate of the Jews to the sense of a general sellout of the old ideologies: "I do not pester my gentile friends about the plight of these five million expiring Jews, nor do I allow the cries of these Jews to interfere with my appetite," he said in a symposium, "American Literature and the Younger Generation of American Jews," sponsored by the *Contemporary Jewish Record* in 1944; "Hell, my gentile friends are as intelligent as I am. They know that the betrayal of the Jews is part of the whole stinking betrayal of the world. In time, a man learns to eat his dinner sitting on a garbage dump."[22] And yet, even if the conviction of a "single idea" of social justice had not proved as "contagious" as Kazin and others had envisioned, many writers clung to the promise of American democracy as the last haven for the Jew from international fascism. Even Budd Schulberg, who gained notoriety in Jewish circles in 1941 with his unsympathetic portrait of a ruthless, scheming Hollywood Jew (though, ironically, the novel, *What Makes Sammy Run?* which traces the unscrupulous rise of Sammy Glick in the movie industry, is also a testimony to the opportunities which America affords anyone ambitious enough to grab them), wrote a story as early as 1938 about a persecuted Polish Jew, Nathan, who meets an American Jew and is overwhelmed by the promise of security which he represents:

> There was something about Democracy, Nathan thought, as he listened to Mr. Brownstein. . . . The confidence: being able to lift up your head and look the moon in the face. Even when Mr. Brownstein bitterly denied there was Democracy in the States, where the Yids couldn't work for Universal Electric or get to be President, he leaned over the table and spoke at Nathan and waved his arms, and puffed his cigar . . . and grandly produced his business card like an American, a Walt Whitman Democrat, something whole, a man with a vote, a man to stare you down, no Polish Jew.[23]

Another writer who represents the same spectrum of cultural attitudes in popular literature is Ben Hecht, whose novel *A Jew in Love*, published in 1931, had exalted as primary the opportunity which America afforded the Jew of *disappearing as a Jew*. In a post-Holocaust story, "God Is Good to a Jew," the refugee from Hitler, far from seeking to emancipate himself from his racial origins, discovers, as he dies on a street in New York, that America is the one place where he is not persecuted as a Jew. Having barely escaped death in Poland, Aaron Sholomas dies finally not from being a Jew but from heart failure. Witnessing a neighborhood fire and assuming it to be a pogrom which will soon engulf him, he faints; as he gains consciousness he realizes that the crowd around him is a solicitous, not a murderous, group. "In these last moments of his life, the torn soul of Sholomas filled with love. . . . After many years and after a long journey [he thought], I have found that goodness does not vanish where the Jew stands. I have found a home." He dies at peace, dreaming of this miracle—"that a Jew would be lying dead among strangers and that the night would be filled with compassion."[24]

The distance between *A Jew in Love* and "God Is Good to a Jew" is the territory traveled by an American Jew who has confronted the Holocaust. As Stanley Yedwab said about a whole group of writers of whom Hecht was one, "fascism seemed to force the marginal Jew back to a Jewishness which he no longer possessed."[25] Hecht's "conversion" is stridently mapped out in two autobiographies published during and after the war. Even as he celebrated the opportunities America presented the Jew to live, or die, as a Jew, much as he had once celebrated the opportunity to assimilate, Hecht is filled with contempt for those Americans—Jews and non-Jews—who were prominent in politics and the arts and who did not speak out during the war. Although his credibility is not incontestable, and his abrupt about-face in Jewish sympathies may even be suspect, it is hard to disprove his contention that "the Americanized Jews who ran newspapers and movie studios, who wrote plays and novels, who were high in government and powerful in the financial, industrial and even social life of the nation were silent" while the atrocities were being committed.[26]

The silence of both the Jews and the gentiles during the Holocaust can be seen as a reflection—either in fear or in sympathy—of the specter of anti-Semitism which had haunted prewar America. World War II followed hard on two decades in which some of the most prominent writers in America had voiced opinions more modulated than but not altogether different in kind from those of the more vociferous anti-Semites in Europe. From Wolfe to Dreiser, from Eliot and Pound to Hemingway and Fitzgerald, in fiction, poetry, and polemical journalism,[27] the Jew in America was vilified, often along the very lines in which the traditionally anti-Semitic portraits of Jews had been drawn in European literature: the Jew as Shylock, the Jew as Machiavel, the Jew as polluter of Western culture. True, only Pound and a few others refused to recant once it became clear what the application of their prejudices in a fascist regime were leading toward. Wolfe wrote a denunciatory account of his trip to Nazi Germany, "I Have a

Thing to Tell You," and the novel *You Can't Go Home Again,* which included a sympathetic portrait of a Jewish refugee and eventuated in the banning of his books in Hitler's Germany; even Dreiser denied that he associated himself with the values of the Third Reich.[28] But their earlier attitudes, which reflected a certain climate of opinion in America, must have had no small influence on Jewish writers who, in spite of a large number of both realistic and ideological works reflecting American-Jewish life, had not yet acquired the cultural citizenship in American letters that they would eventually enjoy. One typical Jewish response to the religious tolerance embodied in the American ideal on the one hand and to the anti-Semitism manifested in American culture on the other is the self-deprecation or self-denial which can be found in the works of writers from divers periods, ranging from Mary Antin in the second decade of this century to Samuel Ornitz, Ben Hecht, and Budd Schulberg in the thirties and forties, Jerome Weidman in the fifties, and Philip Roth in the sixties. In the thirties and forties especially, the vigorous protestations of faith in America as the last stronghold of liberty and avenger of fascism can be seen, conversely, as a wishful evasion of the dangers inherent in the murky undercurrent of anti-Semitism that flowed through American society.

This undercurrent was brought to the surface in a new way in three novels of the immediate postwar period, Arthur Miller's *Focus* (1945), Laura Z. Hobson's *Gentleman's Agreement* (1946), and Saul Bellow's *The Victim* (1947). These novels, which are not commensurate in quality, illuminate at different levels the subtle and insidious manifestations of anti-Semitism in American society and expose the raw nerves of Holocaust-haunted American Jews. Hobson's novel is not much more than a screenplay strung together by a predictable narrative; Miller's is more substantive, though still a rather callow venture into fiction for the young playwright, while Bellow's novel is important both as an early indicator of thematic and structural directions in his own writing and as a serious attempt at an allegorical, rather than polemic, exploration of complex social and psychological issues.

Miller's *Focus* and Hobson's *Gentleman's Agreement* are both predicated on the rather improbable act of assumption of Jewish identity by an American gentile. In the case of Miller's protagonist, Lawrence Newman, it is an involuntary act—his purchase of eyeglasses results in such a change of physiognomy that he is suddenly taken for a Jew by all his associates and acquaintances. The initial response of Newman (a prototype of Miller's antihero, a man of average stature, whose conformity to prevailing social codes extends to membership in the anti-Semitic Christian Front) is bitter resentment at such mistaken identity, but eventually he comes to accept the burden of martyrdom that accompanies the physical transformation. In Hobson's *Gentleman's Agreement,* in which stick figures enact the pageant of pride and prejudice in inexorable ways which lead toward an agreeable end, the protagonist is a non-Jewish newspaperman, Philip Green, who decides to impersonate a Jew in order to represent from the "inside" the problem of anti-Semitism which he has been assigned to write about for *Smith's Weekly Magazine*. Both Miller and Hobson seem to assume that the "Jewish problem" would be more comprehensible to the American reader if perceived through the eyes of the gentile.

The assumption of Jewish identity on the part of Hobson's Green is, at least on the surface, far more credibly engineered than that of Miller's Newman. The occasion of mistaken identity—the acquisition of a pair of glasses—is improbable to the point of being ludicrous, unless one reads *Focus* as a satire on the myth of physically defined racial features. Ostensibly, the transformation occurs as suddenly and markedly as that experienced by Kafka's Gregor Samsa; Newman returns home with his glasses and stares at himself in the mirror:

> In the mirror in his bathroom, the bathroom he had used for nearly seven years, he was looking at what might very properly be called the face of a Jew. A Jew, in effect, had gotten into his bathroom. . . . Under such bulbous eyes . . . [his smile] was a grin, and his teeth which had always been so irregular now seemed to insult the smile and warped it into a cunning, insincere mockery of a smile, an expression whose attempt at simulating joy was belied, in his opinion, by the Semitic prominence of his nose, the bulging set of his eyes, the listening posture of his ears.[29]

This stereotype of racial characteristics, which corresponds to the standard anti-Semitic portrait of the Jew in American and European literature, is a boomerang of the typecasting which Newman himself had indulged in for years in his capacity as personnel manager for a large corporation which did not hire Jews. Just before his own credentials are called into question, he interviews a woman, a Miss Hart who, he is convinced, is a Jewess hiding behind a Christian name. Her appearance, in his eyes, is cheap, gaudy, and lustful; "he could not blot out the sheen of her dress and the dazzling pin she wore between her breasts. . . . She was overdressed, overpainted" (p. 35). Yet later, after he himself has been mistaken for a Jew, fired from the company for which he has worked for twenty-five years, and forced to look for a job, he encounters the same Miss Hart—*she* is on the hiring and firing end this time—and his realization that she is not Jewish changes his entire perception of her: "As a Jewess she had seemed dressed in cheap taste, too gaudily. But as a Gentile he found her merely colorful in the same dress, a woman who expressed her spirited nature in her clothes" (p. 83).

The arbitrariness of the criteria by which the destiny of a people is carved is nowhere more evident than in the ridiculous misperceptions from which most of the characters in this novel suffer. Even Newman's mother comments that he looks like a Jew with his new glasses, and the others, who notice the same change, waste no time in acting upon their perceptions: after losing his job, Newman is harassed by his neighbors and ostracized from those very ex-clusive circles from which he had once prided himself on excluding others. Soon, however, outward posture does acquire a corresponding inner dimension and Newman, like Hobson's Green, begins to "focus" on the world through Jewish eyes. At this point, for both men, mankind comes to be divided into Semites and anti-Semites (with a sprinkling of philo-Semites). In fact, since one's attitude toward the Jews becomes the only touchstone of character, most of the people in both novels emerge as one-dimensional characters, and the "Jewish problem" takes on the proportions of an epidemic. Newman's transformation coincides with the "intrusion" of a Jewish family into his neighborhood; as he sits in the subway he notices that a no-smoking sign has "Jew" written above the offensive smoker; the anti-Semitic graffiti scrawled on the pillars of the train station represent, to him, "a secret newspaper publishing what the people"—including himself, up to a point—"really thought" (p. 7). Phil Green suddenly discovers anti-Semites in taxicabs, hotels, offices—and even in his own family. The problem becomes so ubiquitous that an atmosphere of harassment is created which resembles, if only in its psychological effect, the early stages of the persecution of the Jews in Nazi Germany. True, each incident is fairly insignificant in itself. "No big things," Philip realizes after his first few days as a Jew; "no yellow armband, no marked park bench, no Gestapo. Just here a flick and there another. . . . Each to be rejected as unimportant."[30] Yet the Holocaust represents an intensification in degree, not in kind, for the oppressed American Jew. Newman, married now (to Miss Hart), goes to a movie theater which, it turns out, is featuring a film on the treatment of the Jews in Nazi Germany. The sympathies of the audience around him are not clearly with the victims. The parallel is obvious, and yet that scene constitutes the only instance in the novel where the Jews of Europe are specifically mentioned. Where they do appear, then, the victims of the Holocaust function more as a reference than as the center of the novel's concerns; one is, in fact, barely conscious in reading either of these novels that at the very hour that Philip Green is being turned away from a restricted resort and Lawrence Newman is being fired from his job, millions of Jews are being incinerated in Europe for the same "crime" of birth that Newman and Green are accused of. Ludwig Lewisohn wrote a scathing critique of Hobson's book soon after it appeared, in which he charged that "the six million martyrs, the monstrous theft of all Jewish property over half the world, the closed doors of America, these things, and I am speaking from *her* angle, seem not even to be within her grasp of knowledge."[31]

Yet Miller carries the problem one step further than Hobson. Lawrence, a little man trapped in the clichés of suburban living and of a small job in a large corporation, subscribes to all the prejudices that go with such status. As the enforced change produces certain internal adjustments, he abandons these stereotypes for a more ambiguous, autonomous mode of thought and behavior. And as his prejudices fall away, the novel itself develops from a satiric portrait of the mechanical thoughtlessness of the prejudiced man into a more psychologically complex character study. The transition is not altogether successful, and at times Miller's schematic inversions defeat what should be the organic nature of a growth in stature and in subtlety. But the shift is a significant one, and the concluding chapters are convincing enough to drive home the message that the protagonist must become his own adversary, the Christian Fronter must become a Jew, in order to become a man.

Saul Bellow's *The Victim* is a more consistent and penetrating psychological study than either *Focus* or *Gentleman's Agreement*. The victimization of the Jew in this novel takes place in the encounter between only two people, with few of the social supports which made anti-Semitism appear so rampant and so threatening in the novels of Miller and Hobson. Yet, on another level, *The Victim* is a probing allegory of the Holocaust as a process whereby prejudice and delusion take possession of the psyche. Using the Dostoyevskian technique of the "double," whereby the "other" appears as both victimizer and alter ego of the victim, with just a shadow of a doubt about the full reality of his being (like Yakov Golyadkin in *The Double,* Asa Leventhal awakens from sleep into the atmosphere of suspicion and harassment which materialize in the person of his tormentor), Bellow distills the concentrationary system into two of its most basic components: failure which seeks an external scapegoat and fear compounded by a sense of guilt.

Kirby Allbee, a onetime acquaintance of Asa Leventhal's, reenters Leventhal's life in a state of destitution, blaming him for having willfully caused his downfall. In the course of their succeeding encounters, it emerges that he holds Leventhal initially, and therefore ultimately, responsible for the chain of events which began with a few anti-Semitic remarks that Allbee had made at a party, after which Leventhal, determined, Allbee claims, to seek revenge, brought about the loss of Allbee's job, which in turn drove him to drink and to the loss of his wife.

While Leventhal, who is alone (his wife is visiting her mother) and, like Bellow's other solitary heroes, particularly vulnerable to such an attack, wrestles with whatever the germ of truth may be in this welter of accusations ("he liked to think 'human' meant accountable"),[32] all the while outwardly denying any responsibility, Allbee insists on identifying Leventhal's behavior with that of his "people" (p. 34)—insisting, that is, that in some deterministic sense, one's heritage is one's fate. The Holocaust is mentioned directly only in one scene when, to protect himself against the onslaught of incriminations against himself and his "people," Leventhal responds rather lamely, "I don't see how you can talk that way. . . . Millions of us have been killed. What about that?" (p. 133). But Bellow's novel delineates, on the individual level, the myth of the Jew which was propagated on the social level as the ideological justification for the extermination of a whole people. As the Nazis, needing a scapegoat to explain their destitute state after World War I, accused the Jews of stealing their jobs, ruining their economy, polluting their culture, defiling their family lives, and conspiring to usurp political power,

so Allbee accuses Leventhal of getting him fired, of bringing about his financial ruin, of precipitating his wife's death—and of belonging to a tribe that has violated the purity of American culture ("Last week I saw a book about Thoreau and Emerson by a man named Lipschitz," he sneers [p. 131]). Even the most natural acts take on sinister racial implications in the eyes of the anti-Semite. When Allbee finally meets Mary, Leventhal's wife, years after the series of encounters that eventuate in Allbee's eviction from Leventhal's apartment and from his life, he notices that she is pregnant, and smiling, he says to Leventhal, "Congratulations. I see you're following orders. 'Increase and multiply'" (p. 254). This last encounter is a meeting between the restored victimizer (Allbee in formal dress squiring around a has-been actress) and the restored victim (Leventhal, a prospective father, more secure in his job, protected from loneliness by his devoted wife, free from harassment) which nevertheless reinforces the old relationship. In a statement defining his sense of his own station in life, Allbee explains to Leventhal that he himself is "not the the type that runs things." He disappears as Leventhal, stunned, calls out to him, "Wait a minute, what's your idea of who runs things?" (p. 256). The implication is clear.

In all three of these novels, written just after the war, the Holocaust appears less as a historical event than as a demonic force inherent in Western society. The fear of a potential pogrom on American shores was, evidently, still greater than the empathy for the actual victims of events which had already taken place.

One writer who distilled the Holocaust into components even more basic and further removed from historical events than the substratum of anti-Semitism which Miller, Hobson, and Bellow had exposed was Isaac Rosenfeld. Remaining very much a loner in his literary experiments, yet pointing the way to a symbolic assimilation of the Holocaust as a common cultural heritage generalized beyond its particular historical coordinates, Rosenfeld produced a series of allegories in the postwar years which capture the essence of the concentrationary experience with a power and inexorability that even more accomplished artists have rarely achieved, either before or since. A confessed disciple of Kafka, Rosenfeld reconstructs the terror, if not the *mise-en-scène,* of recent history. "Terror" is in fact the key to an understanding of Rosenfeld's work, a key that he himself provided in two essays published in 1948 and 1949 in which he also revealed the extent to which the Holocaust haunted and informed his imagination. These essays are worth quoting at some length:

> We still don't understand what happened to the Jews of Europe, and perhaps we never will. There have been books, magazine and newspaper articles, eyewitness accounts, letters, diaries, documents certified by the highest authorities on the life in ghettos and concentration camps, slave factories and extermination centers under the Germans. By now we know all there is to know. But it hasn't helped; we still don't understand. . . . There is no response great enough to equal the facts that provoke it.

And even those people—the "innocent and the indignant, the relatives and coreligionists or friends of the victims"—who may be willing to admit and to try to understand the facts can never really give an accounting for their own "numbness" in the face of the screams that reached them from a distant continent: "When it comes to numbness we are no different from the murderers who went ahead and did their business and paid no attention to the screams," Rosenfeld continues, in one of the earliest and most relentless expressions of self-reproach by an American-Jewish writer.

Faced with such facts and such numbness, Rosenfeld concludes that "the concentration camp is the model educational system and the model form of government. War is the model enterprise." It is into such "models," he maintains, that we must fit all contemporary experience, as the humanistic cultural traditions have been violated and can no longer provide the structure and value system for human events: "There is no more good and evil—if there were, the screams would have been heard. There is only the terror."[33]

Yet even from such desperate pronouncements Rosenfeld emerges as a moralist. A few years earlier, at the height of the war, he had addressed himself to the "situation of the Jewish writer," and had concluded that, in spite of the fact that it is a burden on the artist, who "should first of all have the security of a dignified neutrality," to know that "he may at any time be called to account not for his art, nor even for his life, but for his Jewishness," nevertheless "out of their recent sufferings one may expect Jewish writers to make certain inevitable moral discoveries. These discoveries, enough to indict the world, *may also be crucial to its salvation*" (emphasis mine).[34]

It is, therefore, out of a moral commitment as deep as that of Kafka, as well as out of pessimism as great as that of his mentor, that Rosenfeld constructs his allegories of terror. Several of the stories which were published posthumously in *Alpha and Omega* (Rosenfeld died suddenly in 1956) are parables of the closed society, of which the concentration camp may be seen as the "model." "An Experiment with Tropical Fish" is a humourous fable of helpless beings trapped in a concentrationary system (the aquarium) in which the impulse to understand and influence one's environment is mocked by a total absence of autonomy. "The New Egypt" is an apocalyptic allegory of the totalitarian society in which even death, the surcease of suffering, is denied the enslaved citizens, who have been granted immortality to perform the Sisyphean task of constructing pyramids. The most sinister and uncompromising presentation of the "terror" is the portrait of the oppressor in "The Brigadier," which was part of a novel that was never published. Unsatisfied with the mere defeat of his enemy, the Brigadier-narrator strives to *possess* him by a total understanding of his character, as he is convinced that "victory will be impossible until we gain this knowledge" of the essential nature of the enemy. "What do we know?" he asks concerning his adversary (who bears close resemblance to the two biological groups singled out for extermination during World War II): "The enemy is darker than we, and shorter in stature. . . . His language . . . has nothing in common with our own . . . his religion is an obscenity . . ."[35] The Brigadier's tactics involve, in the first place, befriending his prisoners and winning their confidence and, when that yields little "knowledge," torturing and finally killing them: "I would feel an overwhelming hatred of the enemy, and become convinced that my hatred had brought me so much farther than love, to the very brink of knowledge" (p. 108). The perverse Nazi preoccupation with defining and labeling Jewish character and culture, exhibited in the careful preservation of a museum of Jewish artifacts in Prague, coupled with the assumption of the impenetrability and foreignness of the Jew, is generalized here into an epistemological drama of group sadism.

Rosenfeld's penetration into the psychology of hatred and the sociology of oppression was coupled with a kind of mystical faith in the redeeming power of "joy" as the obverse of terror, a version of Reichian principles which consists of "love and restoration" and the "creation of a new capacity . . . to experience our natural life to the full."[36] His Reichianism was never fully realized in his fiction, and in fact many of his stories appear to have remained in the experimental stage where the fusion between ideas and characters had not yet been perfected. Yet Rosenfeld pointed the way to a radically different absorption of the Holocaust into the imagination of the American writer, and if his writings never matured beyond a promising apprenticeship, he was engaged, like Kafka, in the major enterprise of what Theodore Solotaroff calls the sublimation of "his own and his people's needs and terrors in an absolute statement of the human crisis":

> The ghetto sensibility, which Rosenfeld himself loved, with all its hallucinations and hope and ironies both intact and transformed in Kafka's art, reached out in parables to comprehend and redeem the broken, fearful moral order of Europe.[37]

Kafka's pre-Holocaust statement that the suffering of the Jew is emblematic of the suffering of all mankind—"Man schlagt den Juden und erschlagt den Menschen"[38]—is echoed in Rosenfeld's post-Holocaust declaration: "As a Jew . . . I am all Europe."[39]

SALVAGING THE VOICES OF THE DEAD

Rosenfeld was to remain for many years largely without successors. While most writers, and their readers, had not yet emerged from the "numbness" that had prevailed during the war years, and a few others remained preoccupied with the possibility of a fascist threat to American Jews, a small group of writers and critics began to assume a kind of historical imperative by searching throughout Europe to piece together the story of what had happened—only to discover that the endless repetition of horror stories, which should lend them credibility and even familiarity in the eyes of the American visitor, served but to reconfirm how great the distance was that separated those who were there from those who had been spared.

Yet the refugees themselves seemed eager to tell their stories, which, they thought, must be of interest to American Jews. Rosenfeld observed that the journalistic reports were valuable because they merely "set down what [the writer] has seen and heard on a visit to [Europe's] surviving Jews. . . . [Such a book] has the courage . . . to stay near the thing itself and not to cast about for the usual reassurance."[40] For some writers the subject had to be left there, at the level of bare fact; for others these stories would eventually serve as resources for their own imaginative retellings. But for many years the ruthless realism of atrocity was largely avoided or at best transformed into the remote domain of nightmare or fable more reconcilable with the American faith in human goodness.

One writer who did not attempt any psychological or artistic incorporation of the European Jewish ordeal into the American experience but who was, unwittingly perhaps, to challenge the sanguine presuppositions underlying the American ideal was Meyer Levin. His concept of the role of the American writer was, quite simply, that of a midwife to the authentic recitations of the victims themselves. As a war correspondent, Levin had asked for "one special assignment—to uncover what had happened to the Jews"— and he had, by his own account, "sought out every survivor I could unearth, from the first who emerged from the subcellars of Paris, to the living cinders of the death-camp crematoria."[41] He faithfully collected information and recorded numerous testimonies, but he felt he would "never be able to write the story of the Jews of Europe,"[42] for in spite of the cultural familiarity and sympathy as well as the wealth of knowledge about the Holocaust reality that he had gained, he too, like the war poets and novelists, sensed the impenetrable mystery of the experience that he had not shared: "This tragic epic cannot be written by a stranger to the experience, for the survivors have an augmented view which we cannot attain; they lived so long so close with death that *on a moral plane they are like people who have acquired the hearing of a whole range of tones outside normal human hearing*" (*In Search*, p. 173, emphasis mine).

Yet when Levin, in his travels, came upon the work that he could finally regard as the "voice I had been waiting for, the voice from amongst themselves, the voice from the mass grave" (*The Obsession*, p. 35), it was in fact a story which *did* remain within the range of "normal human hearing." *Anne Frank: The Diary of a Young Girl*, which Levin discovered in its French edition, had not yet been accepted by any American publisher. Levin was instrumental in finding a publisher, but only after several editors had rejected the book because, as they wrote, "they were personally touched, but professionally they were convinced that the public shied away from such material" (*The Obsession*, p. 35). Later, when Levin discussed with various producers the concept of transposing the diary into a play, the reaction of Herman Shumlin was typical of the

sympathetic-but-realistic attitude that he was to encounter repeatedly; as Levin reports in *The Obsession*, Shumlin warned him that "it's impossible. You simply can't expect an audience to come to the theater to watch on the stage people they know to have ended up in the crematorium. It would be too painful. They won't come" (p. 36). And yet this diary, which of course did achieve, both in the original and in the theatrical and cinematic adaptations, popularity unmatched by any other documentary or artistic representation of the Holocaust, had the wide appeal it did not only because of the articulate, sensitive, and candid writing of a precocious thirteen-year-old girl but also, or perhaps especially, because of the sanguine tone which dominates the text, because of the absence of any direct account of the horrors and the loneliness that were the lot of most of the Jews who went into hiding during the war— and of the Franks and Van Daans themselves, after their arrest. Although Levin never acknowledges the fact, it is precisely because the book does *not* record that "whole range of tones outside normal human hearing" that it could be so well received by an audience who shared in what Bettelheim describes as the "general repression of the discovery" of the horrible facts of the concentrationary universe.[43]

Bettelheim claims that all the arrangements made by the Frank family in hiding ran counter to the requirements of self-preservation under such circumstances (he particularly cites their failure to prepare any escape routes to the free world or, while in hiding, to practice survival techniques in anticipation of possible arrest). Yet, while Bettelheim's simplistic assumption that if the Franks had "faced the facts," they would probably have survived, takes very little account of the utterly helpless and unprecedented situation in which the Jews found themselves (and this assumption, that adaptation to "extreme social circumstances"[44] would have been an almost certain guarantee of survival, is a dominant theme throughout *The Informed Heart*), his extension of this psychology of denial does facilitate our understanding of the reasons for the warm reception granted the diary and the play on which it was based: "[Anne Frank's] story found wide acclaim because . . . it denies implicitly that Auschwitz ever existed. If all men are good, there never was an Auschwitz."[45]

The circumstances attending the dramatic adaptation of the diary tend to confirm Bettelheim's observations. The need to affirm that "all men are good" and, by extension, that all men are brothers casts the manuscript that Anne Frank left behind her into the pale afterglow of the ideals of socialism and universalism that had informed so much of the American art of the thirties and that were suffering their own political martyrdom in the fifties. By circumventing the impenetrable "terror" that Rosenfeld had defined as the essence of the Holocaust, the drama of Anne Frank which opened on Broadway and played in theaters and moviehouses throughout the world succeeded also in avoiding the issue of Jewish identity which was at the core of the diary that Anne Frank had abandoned when she was arrested in her "secret annex." From a moving document of the plight of an assimilated Jewish family which nonetheless perceives its suffering and its destiny as part of the particularistic destiny of the Jewish people, the diary was transformed into a work of art which comprises both a litany of human suffering and a declaration of ultimate faith in universal goodness. The playwrights who converted the diary into a commercial drama availed themselves of a young girl's naive belief in the potential for human goodness to serve the defense of American liberal optimism against the evidence of pure evil. In the emphasis on Anne's faith there is an implicit denial of her fate—either as the innocent victim of demonic forces or as the Jewish victim of anti-Semitism. The adaptation of *The Diary of a Young Girl,* while it brought the Holocaust to the forefront of mass consciousness, did not really seek to dispel the curiously functional "amnesia" toward the events themselves, which was accompanied by a general unwillingness on the part of non-Jews in America to explore the "Jewish problem" and by a Jewish ambivalence toward accepting the role of messengers of the reality of evil in a society still largely animated by faith in the moral order.

Meyer Levin has recorded, fictionalized, litigated, and lamented this phenomenon for a quarter of a century. His discovery of the diary and his role in getting it published in America prompted him to bid for a chance at dramatizing it himself. The ensuing story of manipulation of the text by many hands not only is a thoroughly documented and tedious case history of the paranoia of Meyer Levin, but also highlights an important stage in the evolution of American attitudes toward the Holocaust.

A few parenthetical comments should be made at this point about the very act of converting the diary into a play, an act which cannot be judged independently of the mediocre talents of all those who engaged in the adaptation, but which also points to a certain inherent resistance of the original text to any modification. No matter how faithful the artistic adaptation might have been to the diary, it would necessarily have betrayed the very nature of the genre—for the numerous diaries which were written by the victims in hiding or in ghettos or camps, and posthumously published, constitute a peculiar genre with a beginning and a middle, but no end. The tragic impact of a diary like Anne's is a product of the interaction between the writer who, even in her last entries, affirms her belief that "it will all come right,"[46] and the post-Holocaust reader who, through the burden of hindsight, knows that it did not come right. The diary ends abruptly, randomly; the various versions of the play, answering to the exigencies of form, have their resolutions and their "moments of truth" that the imagination imposes on reality. Furthermore, the characters lose much of the mystery and complexity combined with the adolescent naiveté with which Anne perceives them when they are translated from the subjectivist perspective of a diary to the autonomy of stage personae. And all of the playwrights who tried their hands at the task failed particularly in the representation of the secret duality of Anne's character, for this "little bundle of contradictions" (p. 280), who could confide her true self

only to paper, must suddenly externalize and verbalize feelings which by their very admission violate that realm of privacy which is the diary itself.

But the central issue which Levin raises in documenting the history of his own and the Broadway versions of the play, an issue which reflects on the assessment of American willingness to relate to the particularity of Jewish suffering, remains an important measure of oth the popular and the more serious art of the fifties. What is deleted from the original text in the Broadway drama is the engagement with Jewish history (such as Anne's sister's pledge to become a nurse in Palestine) and the affirmation of Jewish destiny (exemplified in Anne's assertion of the uniqueness and purpose of Jewish martyrdom and her declaration of faith). That such omissions are the deliberate expression of an ideology which universalized the Jewish experience may be supported by a passage from Lillian Hellman's autobiography *Pentimento,* in which the writer who was the guiding spirit behind the Broadway play tells of having smuggled a large sum of money into Nazi Germany in 1937 for a friend who was engaged in buying the freedom of endangered persons; when Hellman asked her if the people for whom the money was intended were Jews, the friend answered, in a line which anticipates one of Anne's statements in the Broadway play, "About half. And political people. Socialists, Communists, plain old Catholic dissenters. *Jews aren't the only people who have suffered here*" (emphasis mine).[47]

On such grounds Meyer Levin tries to build a case for the existence of a kind of literary mafia of Communist sympathizers who engaged, during the McCarthy period, in a counteroffensive against ethnic perspectives and reflected a widespread liberal defensiveness against elevating Jewish particularism through the enormous emotional lever of the Holocaust. Through more balanced arguments, Edward Alexander has demonstrated how "resistant to [the] negative evidence" of recent events were the humanitarian, universalistic ideals which American Jews, no less than non-Jews, had rescued from the promise of the Enlightenment.[48] One can shore up this claim with a consideration of both the scarcity of literature in the fifties dealing with the Holocaust from a Jewish perspective and the reception given those works which did appear. A number of writers who participated in a symposium sponsored by *Congress Weekly* in 1951 told of the resistance with which their books, touching on the Holocaust or other manifestations of anti-Semitism, were greeted.[49] In fact the high degree of self-consciousness which dominates most of the symposia sponsored by Jewish literary journals in those years is in itself indicative of the conflict that Jews perceived between their identity as Americans and as Jewish writers, and the sense they still had of their own precarious status in the American literary community. This sense persisted well into the years that have been hailed as a period of "philo-Semitism" in America, which began as a belated penitential reaction to the Holocaust and peaked in the sixties.

The legacy of the thirties, then, which contained the slowly dying vestiges of gentile anti-Semitism as well as a persistent liberal resistance among Jews and non-Jews to differentiating the Jewish experience, was a recurrent issue which certain writers, such as Hobson, Miller, and Bellow, had begun to explore directly in their fiction, which others such as Rosenfeld reflected in their allegorization of the events, and which a few of the more polemically minded writers and journalists, such as Levin and Hecht, openly challenged in various literary and extraliterary forums. The publication of Hersey's *The Wall* in 1950 conferred the legitimization of gentile authorship and readership as well as a heroic perspective on what had been formerly perceived by Jews and non-Jews alike as a parochial and shameful subject. And if the drama *The Diary of Anne Frank*, which was first performed in 1955, did attempt to portray Jewish suffering, it was after purging it of its particularity. It would take another five to ten years before the cultural and spiritual requisites for a more specific and personal engagement with the events of 1933-45 would suffice to generate in American literature a more straightforward historical relationship on the one hand and a more profound assimilation of the implications of the Holocaust for non-survivors on the other.

The Man in the Glass Booth

The intensity and scope of the renewed engagement of American writers with the Holocaust were catalyzed by an event which took place sixteen years after the war. The Eichmann trial, coming as it did after a decade and a half of documentation and testimony on the part of scholars and survivors, forcing its entry into the homes of all Americans who committed the minimal act of turning on their television sets, ensued in a spate of literary activity unprecedented at any time since the war. Of course television was far more pervasive and influential in the sixties than it had ever been and, as evidenced by the impact that televised reports of the Vietnamese war were to have on the American people a few years later, could succeed in conveying remote events with unprecedented urgency and immediacy. Much of the literature written in the mid- and late sixties reflects the heightened historical consciousness which the trial precipitated. In some cases the creative mind, compelled to acknowledge the horrors that were now granted the status of higher reality by the legal process itself, responded by seeming to abdicate altogether the task of imposing form; Charles Reznikoff's series, *Holocaust,* which we have already considered, is a long documentary poem based on the records from the Eichmann and Nuremberg trials. Resembling Weiss's *Investigation* in its reproduction of excerpts of legal testimony from the trials of Nazi criminals, it shares with all the documentary art of the Holocaust the premise of minimal intervention in or manipulation of history on the part of the artist.

Other works of the period following the trial are more specifically concerned with the implications for Americans of the discoveries made during the proceedings. Two themes seem to dominate this body of literature: the first, influenced in no small measure by Hannah Arendt's interpretation of the trial, which was the filter through which most Americans were able to conceptualize what was otherwise a morass of indigestible, unintegrable facts,[50] concerns the "banality" and the "bureaucracy" of the Nazi evil. The second theme, which derives from the first, relates to the appropriation of the Holocaust not primarily as a historical event but as a complex of psychological possibilities. The thesis which Arendt and others espoused, which rendered the actions of the oppressor intelligible and even predictable under certain conditions, and which claimed "that this new type of criminal, who is in actual fact *hostis generis humani*, commits his crimes under circumstances that make it well-nigh impossible for him to know or to feel that he is doing wrong,"[51] denies, as it were, the historical circumscription of the Holocaust and engages the writer who did not experience the events in a process of self-scrutiny and speculation on the implications for the human species of the victimization and annihilation of the Jews. Again, as in the case of the immediate postwar literature which distilled the Holocaust into the ubiquity of the anti-Semitic menace, or the stories of Rosenfeld which reduced historic events to parables of the closed society, American writers seemed to avail themselves of the evidence produced at the Eichmann trial to try to possess not the events themselves but the moral options which prevailed in those times and which could be repeated under similar circumstances.

We have seen that a similar process took place at the same time in Israeli literature. The fact that the Eichmann trial proved to be such a watershed can, perhaps, be ascribed to a parallel development in the literary history of the two countries where large concentrations of Jews were removed from what had happened to the Jews of Europe. In a discussion among four Hebrew authors who had responded to the question of why contemporary Israeli writers had not previously given adequate literary expression to the Holocaust, Moshe Shamir is reported as having said:

> as for the catastrophe of European Jewry, it is not quite true to say that our literature has failed to reflect the tragedy, but we are troubled by the feeling that it has not yet found adequate expression. The difficulty is that "just as the catastrophe was something hellish and inconceivable, so we are waiting for a work that will express something of *our inability to grasp the catastrophe, the fact that we confront it with empty hands.*" . . . Until Hebrew authors feel the catastrophe as a personal tragedy, they will not be able to write about it. The trouble is that from the cold biological point of view, the Yiddish writers were "*inside* the burning house" while the Hebrew writers saw it from the outside. . . .
>
> There is . . . a recent event which has brought the subject home to the younger generation "as a personal, moral problem." That is the Eichmann Trial, not only in itself but against the background of the affluent society—Israeli version, in the Sixties of this century: the dramatic and shattering contrast between the world that the trial presented with such terrific force, and the life that surrounded the courthouse (emphases mine).[52]

Dalia Ravikovitz, a poet who represents the younger generation of Israeli writers, is quoted as saying that "especially after the Eichmann trial, . . . 'the Holocaust is like an exploding hand grenade; each of us has been struck by his private splinter, which he carries in his own body.'"[53]

Many American writers might have said what Shamir and Ravikovitz did about their former inability to personalize or internalize the Holocaust, and the thawing impact of the Eichmann trial which transformed the Holocaust into a "personal, moral problem." Denise Levertov wrote a trilogy of poems, "During the Eichmann Trial," which explores the challenge presented to Everyman by evil impulse, and Eichmann's failure to meet the challenge to look into the faces of his victims and pity them. The reflection in the glass booth, then, is our own reflection, and Eichmann becomes the example of a lesson not learned:

> He stands
>
> isolate in a bulletproof
> witness-stand of glass,
> a cage, where we may view
> ourselves, an apparition
>
> telling us something he does not know: we are members
>
> one of another.[54]

In the second poem in the trilogy, Levertov presents Eichmann as the agent of death in an inversion of the Edenic myth; a Jewish boy who is lured into Eichmann's orchard ("the Devil's garden") by the sight of one "yellow and ripe" peach is pounced on by "mister death . . . / who wanted that yellow peach / for himself." The anecdote is consistent with the previous portrait of Eichmann, the demon-as-technocrat, "mister death who signs papers / then eats" (p. 64). Levertov admits in a note that her poem, though based on an incident reported at the trial, is not an exact "report of what happened but of what I envisioned" (p. 65). The trial and the person of Eichmann become, then, triggers for the poetic imagination.

The literary fascination with this character as the embodiment of the human potential for blind obedience and criminal pitilessness[55] is significant in that it reflects an implicit acceptance of Eichmann's defense of himself as a mere cog in the machinery of Nazism and an implicit rejection of the prosecution's charge, echoed by Jacob Robinson, that "he was no average man and possessed no ordinary criminal skills."[56] The temptation of compliance with the dictates of the impersonal bureaucratic systems which control the lives of individuals in both totalitarian and democratic states is, perhaps, more familiar and more threatening to the American writer than the elusive ideology of evil on which the Third Reich was founded.[57]

One writer for whom the Eichmann trial provided a personal link not so much with the oppressors or the oppressive impulse as with the victims of Nazism is Norma Rosen. Her novel *Touching Evil* is a portrait of the intrusion of monstrous evil into the domestic realm, and of the incompatibility, to which Shamir alluded, between the concentrationary universe reconstructed at the trial and the "affluent society" beyond the courthouse doors. The narrative comprises a series of letters written by Jean Lamb to her absent lover, describing her own activities and those of her friend Hattie during the period that the Eichmann trial is being serialized on television. The premise by which historical experience is appropriated by these nonparticipants (and non-Jews) is one which honestly acknowledges the gap in experience and struggles with the need to repossess the events vicariously. Each of these two women has "extracted [her] private symbols of horror from the welter of horror symbols."[58] Jean, in her letters, reveals that the Holocaust has so invaded her personal life that her initial discovery of the concentration camps, just after the war, generated in her a pledge to withdraw from the pursuit of a normal life. Though she has retained the outward appearance of normalcy, she has remained unmarried and, of course, childless; the Holocaust has become her "personal catastrophe" (p. 78), and whenever she hears her name called—"Miss Lamb"—she feels, she says, "a tugging of the rope. 'Miss Lamb to the slaughter!' Not as victim, I never thought that, but as witness" (p. 97). The ultimate knowledge of the twentieth century is contained for her in the sum of the experience of the victim and the one who has touched evil through the imagination: "Between those who were there and those who dreamed they were there we've been through everything, haven't we? Between the survivors and the ones who didn't survive we know it all" (p. 57).

Jean's younger friend, Hattie, has learned of the Holocaust through the Eichmann trial, and Jean relives her initial reactions to the discovery of the concentrationary universe through her. Hattie, in an advanced state of pregnancy, is extraordinarily vulnerable to the onslaught of morbid facts that are reported at the trial and not only empathizes with all those pregnant women who, together with their fetuses or newborn infants, were tortured and killed by the Nazis, but in some mystical sense tries to internalize—and redeem—their plight. Her struggle culminates, after the birth of her own daughter, in a metempsychotic vision of the death and rebirth of children, which she relates to Jean as a possible scenario for a play:

> "the children talk about their happiness to be alive at first, and then each tells how he or she died. After each war, each atrocity, each death, the children fly down to their mothers' beds and disappear in them. Then the whole thing is repeated, and the children fly up again. New children. . . . New births. . . . New times. . . . New joys. . . . Centuries and centuries and centuries of joyful births and terrible deaths. . . . After a while we begin to see similarities . . . we see the same children over and over . . . those children haven't been lost. . . ."

[p. 237]

Hattie's own child, then, becomes the reincarnation of one of those infantile victims of the Holocaust, and the act of parturition is, for her, an act of resurrection.

The discovery of the Holocaust, imparted through the Eichmann trial, invades and transforms, in one way or another, the lives of all the characters in this novel who have followed the proceedings on television. The sign of contemporary civilization, which Jean compares to the monuments of other eras—to Stonehenge, the Parthenon, and the Great Pyramid at Giza—is the "piled up stick bodies at the bottom of a lime pit" (p. 73).

In an essay, Norma Rosen says her novel was conceived out of Bertolt Brecht's pronouncement that "he who can still smile has not yet heard the terrible news," and was shaped by the realization that the only role that she could adopt for herself as an American writer was the vicarious one of "witness—through the imagination," of "documenter of the responses of those who had (merely) 'heard the terrible news.'" The Holocaust, Rosen writes, is the "central occurrence of the twentieth century. It is the central human occurrence. It cannot therefore be more so for Jews and Jewish writers. But it ought, at least, to be that." It is, then, as a Jewish writer that she would convey in fiction not the "meaning of the Holocaust for Jewish history," but the "meaning to human life and aspiration of the knowledge that human beings—in great numbers—could do what had been done."[59] Again it is the Jewish experience yielding some lesson about the behavior and destiny of the species which is preeminent and, as in the novels of Hobson and Miller, the center of consciousness is a non-Jew. Finally, in an act reminiscent of the sacramental resolutions in Wallant's novels and consistent with a perspective that assimilates the Holocaust into prevailing religious or social codes in America, Jean, in her last letter to her lover, pledges herself to a search for "Jesús," a destitute Puerto Rican boy whom she has befriended and cared for and who has now disappeared.

As so often happens in these novels, the burden of the "terrible news" weighs too heavily on the frail shoulders of the well-meaning American protagonists, and their actions in a sane society can never be commensurate with their "knowledge" of the madness that prevailed under Nazism. The novel is, therefore, not altogether convincing on the psychological level; nevertheless, Rosen does achieve a partial balance between the narrative of commonplace events in the lives of a few people living in New York in 1961 and the subterranean forces of Holocaust evil and suffering which constantly threaten to subvert those events.

IMAGINATION IN PLACE OF HISTORY

Norma Rosen's assumption of the role of "witness-through-the-imagination" resembles in certain respects that of Irving Feldman in two Holocaust poems which appeared in his collection of poetry *The Pripet Marshes,* published in 1965. Directly acknowledging, as Rosen does, the gap between survivors and those who were not there, Feldman

attempts to make the experience his own in one poem, "The Pripet Marshes," through a leap of the historical imagination, and in another, "To the Six Million," through a mystical act of erotic possession.

In "The Pripet Marshes," Feldman transforms historical remove into historical prerogative. Unlike the survivor-writer, whose imagination is ultimately accountable to history—who, like Wiesel, for example, may suspend history momentarily in order to resurrect his friends and family but who must in the end surrender them to their historical deaths—the liberated fantasies of Irving Feldman allow him to manipulate history freely. The poem is a visionary transplantation of Feldman's own, American, family and friends into the ghetto in the Pripet Marshes (northwestern Ukraine) at the moment before the Germans are to arrive:

> Often I think of my Jewish friends and seize them
> as they are and transport them in my mind to the
> shtetlach and ghettos.[60]

As in Yeats's "Easter 1916," the speaker names the victims ("Maury is there, uncomfortable and pigeon-toed. . . . And Frank who is goodhearted. . . . And my mother. . . . And my brown-eyed son" [pp. 44, 45]), but unlike the elegist, he is spared the necessity of eulogizing them—for, after all, they are only the understudies for the real victims, whom the poet never knew. Only minutes before their martyrdom is to be enacted ("in the moment when the Germans are beginning to enter / the town"), the speaker snatches them back—for, freed from historical necessity, he has the divine power of the creator:

> But there isn't a second to lose, I snatch them all
> back,
> For, when I want to, I can be a God.
> No, the Germans won't have one of them!
> This is my people, they are mine.
>
>   [p. 146]

In the second poem, "To the Six Million," the autobiographical "exemption" which the speaker invoked in order to save lives in the first poem is transformed into a tragic mission. Through an act of the imagination no less radical than that exercised in "The Pripet Marshes," the poet takes upon himself the burden of the death of the six million—a burden imposed on him because he is a survivor ("survivor" here as one who was spared, was not touched by the events). Here, as in the first poem, the speaker does not eulogize the real victims, whom he never knew personally—and eulogy, it should be recalled, is one of the major tasks in nearly every work of art by a survivor of the Holocaust. He would appropriate the victims, then, not in their lives, but in their deaths. Again, like the soldier-writers who came upon the traces of death but could never reconstruct the lives of the victims, the American writer here relates only to the corpses and the desolation.

In the central part of the poem the speaker is alone in a ghost town, without either divine or human supports, and he asks himself, "survivor, who are you?" (p. 49). The terrible loneliness which underlies that question generates the search for historical coordinates by which the "I" can possess and merge with the dead victims. And here the historical exemption which the poet invoked to rescue Jews in "The Pripet Marshes" becomes an imperative to relive "the agony of the absence" (p. 51), for he who dies, dies only once, but he who remains must relive the death of the millions, over and over.

In the last section of the poem, the speaker persists in his attempt to possess the death of the six million, to merge with the collective destiny. In this section biblical images, mostly from Song of Songs, predominate, sanctifying, as it were, the erotic vision. Yet several of these images takes on an additional meaning, transforming the portrait of divinely sanctioned love into a vision of grotesque, concentrationary death. "And your necks that are towers, / Your temples that are as pieces / Of pomegranate within your locks" (p. 52), a direct quote from the Song of Solomon, can be construed not simply as the physiognomy of the beloved but also as the sight of multilated corpses: "necks as towers" can also be decapitated necks; "temples . . . as pieces of pomegranate" can also be bleeding skulls.

The speaker's search for a way into this death leads him through all the possible relationships to the dead ones; he appears alternately as mother, as child, as father, as brother, and as friend: "I must possess you, befriend you, / . . . and be your brother and your son" (p. 53). And, finally, the speaker appears as the bridegroom, and through a necrophilic act of love, succeeds in possessing—and reviving—the beloved dead, who is simultaneously widow and stillborn child:

> Sweetness, my soul's bride,
> Come to the feast I have made,
> My bone and my flesh of me,
> Broken and touched,
> Come in your widow's raiment of dust and ashes,
> Bereaved, newborn, gasping for
> The breath that was torn from you,
> That is returned to you.
>
> [pp. 53-54]

Despite the grotesqueness of the imagery, the concluding lines of the poem carry a serene resolution which the act of love and the liturgical tone of the poem have evoked: "My heart is full, only the speech / Of the ritual can express it" (p. 54).

Feldman's poems are among the most daring examples of the attempt of the creative writer to overcome what Shamir calls "the fact that we confront [the Holocaust] with empty hands," what the writers of A-bomb literature call, in relation to the events at Hiroshima and Nagasaki, "the differences between those who went through this historical experience and those who did not."[61] Both Feldman and Rosen, freed from historical imperative, perform an act of mystical transference in an effort to engage history. Another writer, Arthur A. Cohen, has appropriated the symbols of the Holocaust through a more radical fiat of the historical imagination. *In the Days of Simon Stern,*[62] which is a complex and diffuse but philosophically provocative novel by a contemporary American-Jewish thinker, is an apocalyptic legend of the founding of a secret "Society for the Rescue and Resurrection of Jews." The Society's compound, on the Lower East Side of New York, is inhabited by one thousand survivors of the Holocaust who have been gathered from the liberated camps in Europe. The story, narrated by blind Nathan Gaza (such symbols as Nathan's name, borrowed from the Sabbatean and other contexts, are overly transparent), focuses on the career of one Simon Stern, an American-born millionaire real-estate dealer who receives an annunciation of his mission as Messiah and tries to fulfill it by establishing the Society and reconstructing the broken lives of a collection of survivors. Based on the traditional belief that the Messiah will come in the wake of terrible cataclysm, the narrative is a concatenation of biblical and cabbalistic legends, theological discourses, and homilies loosely held together by an improbable narrative. The two themes which dominate the novel are the theme of rescue and rehabilitation, in America, of the survivors of the European Holocaust, and the related process by which Jewish history is reenacted—and thereby authenticated for the historically "deprived" American Jew—on American soil. Within the Society's compound a replica of the Temple of Solomon is constructed, and the narrative concludes with an emblematic holocaustic conflagration which destroys the Temple and the compound and scatters the inhabitants all over land. Cohen's novel is an ambitious, at times engaging, but seriously flawed attempt on the one hand to render the Holocaust theologically meaningful, and on the other hand to possess the Holocaust by means of a kind of shadow-play recapitulation of history.

In addition to the existential leaps of imagination by which writers such as Norma Rosen, Irving Feldman, and Arthur Cohen have attempted to appropriate the Holocaust in fiction and poetry, two distinct attitudes seem to characterize the Holocaust literature that has appeared in America in the years since the Eichmann trial. The first, which may be associated with the universalistic perspective of writers such as Rosenfeld and Levertov, attempts to extract the moral and emotional options from the extreme conditions of a holocaust and to explore their implications for post-Holocaust man. The second mode, which matured only with the accumulation of documentation that conferred a kind of familiarity on events totally outside the realm of the authors' experience, and which is formally derivative from the European literature, is a version of the historical novel.

There is a group of writers who can be said to have borrowed the loaded symbols and scenarios of the Holocaust in order either to achieve a kind of instantaneous emotional pitch or to demonstrate the misery of the human condition by reference to the most abject of its victims. Arthur Miller, who graduated from *Focus* to more explicit uses of the concentrationary experience, literally places the ruins of a death camp as a backdrop to the personal drama in *After the Fall*;[63] in the words of A. Alvarez, Miller "thumbed an emotional lift from Dachau"[64] in that play, invoking the horror of violent and anonymous death as a kind of atmospheric prop surrounding the death of Marilyn Monroe. Miller's *Incident at Vichy* is more specifically related to the Holocaust, but even here, in the interrogation room in Vichy, where a group of Jews and one German nobleman are gathered, the drama is enacted between abstract moral forces which assume, for the occasion, a variety of stereotyped identities. "Jew," says the psychiatrist Leduc, "is only the name we give to that stranger, that agony we cannot feel, that death we look at like a cold abstraction. Each man has his Jew; it is the other. And the Jews have their Jews . . ."[65] This play, according to Miller himself, is an "attempt to understand the fundamental . . . forces . . . operating in us today."[66]

A far more serious experiment with the emotional load of Holocaust symbols appears in some of the later poetry of the non-Jewish poet Sylvia Plath. The images of her skin as a Nazi lampshade, of ashes, a cake of soap, a gold filling to invoke visions of her own death ("Lady Lazarus"); the fantasy of her German-born father as a Nazi and herself as a Jewish victim, meant to represent the problematic father-daughter relationship ("Daddy"); the kitchen oven emblematic of the crematory ovens and the fat of the Sunday lamb recalling the fat of the Jews, while the speaker's "heart" is entered like a "holocaust" ("Mary's Song"),[67] are manifestations of the process by which Sylvia Plath came to regard herself as "an imaginary Jew from the concentration camps of the mind."[68] Irving Howe makes a strong moral and literary judgment about Plath's use of these images and raises some provocative questions relating to a major trend which we have identified in some of the Holocaust literature of the sixties in America:

> That dreadful events in the individual's psyche may approximate the sufferings of a people is indeed possible, but again it might be good to remember that Jews in the camps didn't merely "suffer": they were gassed and burned. Anyone—poet, novelist, commentator—who uses images of the camps in order to evoke personal traumas ought to have a very precise sense of the enormity of what he or she is suggesting. He or she ought to have enough moral awareness and literary control to ask whether the object and the image have any congruence. . . .
>
> Is it possible that the condition of the Jews in the camps can be duplicated? Yes. . . . But it is decidedly unlikely that it was duplicated in a middle-class family living in Wellesley, Massachusetts, even if it had a very bad daddy indeed. . . .
>
> To condone such a confusion is to delude ourselves as to the nature of our personal miseries and their relationship to—or relative magnitude when placed against—the most dreadful event in the history of mankind.[69]

Howe's critique of Plath touches on the question of the rightful and credible claims which can be made upon the memory and the images of the Holocaust. On the one hand, Plath's use of those symbols is a testimony to the widespread diffusion of the Holocaust images, their common currency, so to speak, in Western culture. On the other hand, it represents a kind of devaluation of the particularity as well as the monstrosity of the historical experience. Of course those who regard themselves as the guardians of the culture and destiny of a martyred people and who insist on considering the Holocaust as a nonanalogous horror, totally unrelated to any other acts of organized brutality or to any form of personal suffering, are in fact denying the process by which the events of the past become the shared heritage of humanity. Yet when James Baldwin compares black militant Angela Davis to the "Jewish housewife in the boxcar headed for Dachau,"[70] when the vocabulary of the events of 1933-45 is applied to any situation of intense emotional or social privation, the enormity and the moral inadmissibility of the concentrationary experience are diluted even as the widespread symbolic assimilation of the experience is achieved.

One group of American writers who cannot be accused of the "solipsistic fallacy" are the authors of the realistic fiction which proliferated in the sixties and seventies. Written for the most part by Jews, this fiction is one attempt to recoup the double loss experienced by American Jews: the loss of continuity with their communal origins as a result of the emigration from Europe, and the loss of the remaining bearers of the past as a result of the Holocaust. The latter loss renders the former irremediable and thus the search for avenues into the past becomes so difficult and, often, so guilt-ridden. Susan Fromberg Schaeffer's novel *Anya*[71] is a consummate example of the appropriation of the Holocaust and of the pre-Holocaust heritage through the vicarious acquisition of the details that constituted the events. The author's research into the period is so extensively displayed that it is almost as if she were making a bid for entry into unknown territory through an astounding command of maps and charts. It is a novel which could hardly have been written before scholarship and testimony had provided compensation for the existential distance and a novel like Ilona Karmel's *An Estate of Memory* had provided the literary model. *Anya* centers on one young woman's struggle to preserve her own and her daughter's lives, and traces her journey from the plenitude of life in a wealthy Polish-Jewish home through the scarcity of the ghetto, the eventual disappearance and death of the other members of her family, and her incarceration in the Kaiserwald camp, from which she ultimately escapes and is reunited with her daughter; Anya lives out the rest of her life as a "refugee" in New York. The authenticity achieved by a plethora of details is, nevertheless, undermined by occasional gaps in acquired knowledge—such as glimpses of Hasidic life which reveal a lack of familiarity with the subject—and the integrity of the narrative is violated by speculation on the "meaning" of survival in the last chapter. The novel is a good example of impressive erudition and a sensitive exploration of brutal experience, as well as of the lapses which are probably inevitable in the vicarious reconstruction of cataclysmic history.

In their reliance on meticulous reconstruction based on research, such novels exemplify a form of realism or naturalism which posits as morally acceptable the appropriation of the Holocaust through the autonomy and primacy of facts and the function of those facts in constraining imagination and personal fantasy. The tension between internal accountability to the imagination and external accountability to the victims expresses the heart of the dilemma of Holocaust literature in America. In the decades that have ensued since the liberation of the camps, American writers have engaged history vicariously through several avenues, the different stages and trends in literature revealing changing perspectives on the events and on their relevance to the American experience. The insular response of postwar Jewish writers to the events in Europe was the first indication of a tendency to extract a universal moral message out of the particularistic experience and to explore the relevance of such experience for post-Holocaust man. A parallel response which has become more prominent over the years derives from the impulse to possess the experience itself, either through a form of witness or historical reconstruction, or through a leap into fantasy charged with historical possibilities.

Notes

1. Introduction to Wiesel, *Night,* p. 7.

2. "Some Notes on Recent American Fiction," in *The American Novel Since World War II,* ed. Marcus Klein (Conn.: Fawcett, 1969), p. 160.

3. The phrase is from A. Alvarez, "The Literature of the Holocaust," p. 69.

4. Shlomo Katz, "What Should We Write?" p. 16.

5. *Thieves in the Night: Chronicle of an Experiment* (London: Macmillan, 1946), p. 351.

6. "L'univers concentrationnaire" remained peripheral during the war because the ghettos and camps did not fit into the strategic calculations of either side; on the rare occasions when camps such as Buchenwald were attacked by the Allied forces, it was the weapons-manufacturing plants which were adjacent and not the camps themselves that were the target of the bombing. The camp administrators did not in any way consider themselves subject to the regulations of international warfare and treatment of prisoners. Hitler's policy of genocide was carried out by special units set up for that purpose and was avoided by both the Axis and the Allied powers as an issue of belligerency. The extermination of the Jews of Europe seems almost coincidentally to have been carried out during the Second World War.

7. Stefan Heym, *The Crusaders,* vol. 2, p. 630.

8. In our discussion of the documentary reconstruction of Nazi trials, it will be recalled, we mentioned a related story by Borowski which dramatizes, from the perspective of the *katzetnik,* the incongruities between the pretenses of law to redress the crimes of Auschwitz and the lawless forces which had been unleashed. See above, chapter 2.

9. *The Trumpet Unblown,* p. 200.

10. *The Mortal No,* pp. 258, 257.

11. In the German war literature, on the other hand, the subject seems to be deliberately avoided. Theodore Frankel draws the portrait of the German soldier who fights heroically on the Russian and Polish fronts but never comes across or acknowledges the concentration camps which dot the countryside of Europe. Walter Dirks, who was an editor of the *Frankfurter Hefte,* is quoted in that essay as having forthrightly admitted: "My brother who died on the side of the road during the retreat from the Caucasus knew what was happening in Buchenwald and Dachau. . . . Of course, he was only a Landser [simple German G.I.], and possibly for that reason he had a better chance to learn what went on" ("The Unredeemed," p. 79). But, as Frankel points out, most of the fictional characters, also "Landsers," who appear in these novels never acknowledge knowing about and certainly never participate in, those atrocities. For that matter, hardly a Nazi appears in these novels. As I have already noted, the most detailed fictionalized account of the Holocaust circulating in Germany as late as 1954 was a translation of John Hersey's *The Wall.*

12. *Randall Jarrell* (Minneapolis: University of Minnesota Press, 1972), p. 6.

13. Introduction to "In the Camp There Was One Alive," in *The Complete Poems,* p. 405.

14. The same image, with somewhat altered meaning but the same effect, appears in another of Jarrell's Holocaust poems, "Protocals"; a child who died in Birkenau describes her death in the gas chamber where "the water drank me" (*The Complete Poems,* p. 193).

15. Jarrell's concern for the Jews of Eastern Europe does go beyond the confines of the camps; two poems on the plight of Jewish refugees, "To the New World (For an Emigrant of 1939)" and "Jews at Haifa," probe a more familiar human condition than that which was so inaccessible to the imagination of the liberator of the concentration camps.

16. Malcolm Cowley, *The Literary Situation,* quoted in Stanley Cooperman, *World War I and the American Novel* (Baltimore: Johns Hopkins Press, 1967), p. 221n.

17. Frederick Hoffman. *The Mortal No,* pp. 236-37.

18. *The Young Lions,* p. 680.

19. *Face of a Hero,* pp. 189-90.

20. "Till the Day I Die," p. 154.

21. *Starting out in the Thirties,* pp. 82-83, 166.

22. "Under Forty: A Symposium in American Literature and the Younger Generation of American Jews," *Contemporary Jewish Record,* February 1944, pp. 22-23.

23. "Passport to Nowhere," in Harold U. Ribalow, ed., *A Treasury of American Jewish Stories,* p. 570.

24. "God Is Good to a Jew," in ibid., pp. 419, 420.

25. "The Jews as Portrayed in American Jewish Novels of the 1930's," *American Jewish Archives* 10, no. 2 (October 1959): 152.

26. *A Child of the Century* (New York: Simon and Schuster, 1954), pp. 519-20.

27. See, for example, the polemic that was generated by the "Editorial Conference" in which the editors of the *American Spectator*—Theodore Dreiser, George Jean Nathan, Ernest Boyd, James Cabell, and Eugene O'Neill—participated in September 1933, and the responses to it from Michael Gold ("The Gun is Loaded, Dreiser," *New Masser,* May 7, 1935, p. 13), Hutchins Hapgood, and others.

28. "I have no hatred for the Jew and nothing to do with Hitler or fascism," Dreiser insisted when interviewed in the *New Masses* (April 30, 1935, p. 10).

29. *Focus,* pp. 24-25.

30. Laura Z. Hobson, *Gentleman's Agreement,* p. 97.

31. "Comment on Writing," *New Palestine* 37, no. 14 (April 14, 1947): 118.

32. *The Victim,* p. 139.

33. "Terror Beyond Evil," *New Leader,* February 1948, and "The Meaning of Terror," *Partisan Review,* January 1949, both reprinted in *An Age of Enormity: Life and Writing in the Forties and Fifties,* pp. 197, 198, 199, 206, 207.

34. "The Situation of the Jewish Writer," in *An Age of Enormity,* pp. 67, 69.

35. "The Brigadier," in *Alpha and Omega,* p. 104.

36. Rosenfeld, "The Meaning of Terror," in *An Age of Enormity,* p. 209.

37. Introduction to Rosenfeld, *An Age of Enormity,* p. 32.

38. Quoted in George Steiner, *Language and Silence,* p. 166.

39. "The Hand That Fed Me," in *Alpha and Omega,* p. 9.

40. "Terror beyond Evil," in *An Age of Enormity,* p. 198.

41. *The Obsession,* p. 28.

42. *In Search,* p. 173.

43. *The Informed Heart,* pp. 252-53.

44. Ibid., pp. 252-54.

45. Ibid., p. 254.

46. *Anne Frank: The Diary of a Young Girl,* trans. B. M. Mooyaart (Garden City: Doubleday, 1952), pp. 278-79.

47. *Pentimento: A Book of Portraits* (New York: New American Library, 1973), p. 113.

48. "The Holocaust in American-Jewish Fiction: A Slow Awakening," in *Judaism* 25, no. 2 (Spring 1976): 322. Alfred Kazin characterizes the same trends when he writes that in the postwar period "the left had nothing to say, did not even include the gas in its summary view of Hitlerism as the 'last decadent stage of capitalism'" (*New York Jew,* p. 195).

49. "Why I Wrote a Jewish Novel," symposium in *Congress Weekly,* November 26, 1951, reprinted in Ribalow, ed., *Mid-Century,* pp. 316-32.

50. As an example, Mary McCarthy, contributing to the polemic that developed over Arendt's book, wrote that for her, *Eichmann in Jerusalem* was "morally exhilarating," that the chaos and the suffering of those times were shaped in the book into "a plot and a lesson" ("The Hue and Cry," in *The Writing on the Wall and Other Literary Essays* [London: Weidenfeld and Nicolson, 1970], pp. 66, 67).

For another gauge of Arendt's widespread influence on American writers, see the numerous works which were dedicated to her, including Anthony Hecht's poem "More Light, More Light" (reprinted in *Norton Anthology of Modern Poetry,* ed. Richard Ellmann and Robert O'Clair [New York: Norton, 1973], p. 1026).

51. Arendt, *Eichmann in Jerusalem: A Report on the Banality of Evil,* p. 253. That this interpretation of the trial is not the only possible one, and that, therefore, those writers who reflect it are probably reflecting Arendt's hypothesis rather than their direct perception of what took place at the trial, may be deduced from Jacob Robinson's quite different analysis of the trial and the character of Eichmann in *And the Crooked Shall Be Made Straight* (Philadelphia: Jewish Publication Society of America, 1965).

52. Moshe Bar Nathan, "The Authors and the Party," *Jewish Frontier,* November 1963, pp. 4-7. This analysis of a discussion which originally appeared in Hebrew in *Ma'ariv* is quoted in Robinson, *And the Crooked Shall Be Made Straight,* p. 138.

53. Ibid., p. 139.

54. "During the Eichmann Trial," in *The Jacob's Ladder,* p. 63.

55. Michael Hamburger, who despite his German origins and prolonged periods of residence in the United States should probably be considered a British poet, wrote a poem which reflects the same attitudes toward Eichmann and toward the threat to humanity that the devil-as-technocrat represents:

Yet, Muse of the In-trays, Out-trays,
Shall he be left uncelebrated
For lack of resonant numbers calculated
To denote your hero, and our abstract age?
Rather in the appropriate vocabulary
Let a memorandum now be drawn up—
Carbon copies to all whom it may concern—
. . . Adolf Eichmann, civil servant (retired):
A mild man, meticulous in his ways,
As distinctly averse to violence
As to all other irregularities
. . . with a head for figures, a stable family life.
No abnormalities.
Never lost his temper on duty
Even with subordinates, even with elements earmarked
For liquidation.

Hamburger, like Levertov, calls upon mankind to find within itself the quality of "pity" which Eichmann lacked and which can save "man," "woman," and "child" from the cold, calculated hatred that kills remorselessly ("In a Cold Season," pp. 67-70). Along these lines, see also Muriel Spark, *The Mandelbaum Gate* (New York: Knopf, 1966), pp. 210—12.

56. *And the Crooked Shall Be Made Straight,* p. 58.

57. Even the occasional departure from the portrait of Eichmann as bureaucrat, as Everyman gone astray, such as Robert Shaw's novel and drama *The Man in the Glass Booth,* seems difficult to sustain. Shaw's exploration of the insane, criminal Nazi as "no average man" disintegrates under the revelation that the presumed Nazi is actually a Jew masquerading as Nazi masquerading as Jew. It is perhaps a confession of an evil so opaque that the outsider can only trace its shadows. The sharper features of Eichmann as "the enemy" are delineated by Italian-Jewish writer Primo Levi. His poetic address to Eichmann as "our precious / enemy, / You, forsaken creature, man ringed /with death," who came to disrupt the natural order of the universe is more consonant with the attitude of most survivors ("For Adolf Eichmann," trans. Ruth Feldman and Brian Swann, in the *Jewish Quarterly* 21, nos. 1 & 2 [1973]: 216).

58. *Touching Evil,* p. 55.

59. Norma Rosen, "The Holocaust and the American-Jewish Novelist," pp. 57-60.

60. "The Pripet Marshes," in *The Pripet Marshes and Other Poems,* p. 44.

61. The statement, made by a "nonhibakusha" writer named Kim Kokubo in a discussion with R. J. Lifton, reflects the opinions of many Japanese writers, both survivors and nonsurvivors (*Death in Life,* pp. 433 and 414 ff.).

62. *In the Days of Simon Stern* (New York: Random House, 1973).

63. *After the Fall* (London: Secker and Warburg, 1964).

64. "The Literature of the Holocaust," p. 67.

65. *Incident at Vichy,* p. 84.

66. Comment made in the course of a conversation with Norman Lloyd after the production of *Incident at Vichy* on "Hollywood Television Theatre" on NET, 1974.

67. The poems are from Plath's last collection, *Ariel.*

68. Alvarez, *The Savage God,* p. 19. See above, chapter 4.

69. Irving Howe, letter to the editor, *Commentary,* October 1974, p. 12.

70. Quoted by Shlomo Katz in "An Open Letter to James Baldwin," *Midstream,* April 1971, p. 3: see Baldwin's reply and Katz's rejoinder in the June/July issue of the journal, pp. 3-10.

71. *Anya* (New York: Macmillan, 1974).

Bibliography

Bellow, Saul. "Some Notes on Recent American Fiction." In Marcus Klein, ed., *The American Novel since World War II.* Greenwich, Conn.: Fawcett, 1969.

Bettelheim, Bruno. *The Informed Heart: Autonomy in a Mass Age.* Glencoe: Free Press, 1960.

Hoffman, Frederick. *The Mortal No: Death and the Modern Imagination.* Princeton: Princeton University Press, 1964.

Katz, Shlomo. "What Should We Write?" *Jewish Frontier* 7, no. 5 (May 1940): 15-17.

Levin, Meyer. *The Fanatic.* New York: Simon and Schuster, 1964.

———. *In Search.* New York: Horizon, 1950.

———. *The Obsession.* New York: Simon and Schuster, 1973.

Michael André Bernstein (essay date 1997)

SOURCE: Bernstein, Michael André. "Unrepresentable Identities: The Jew in Postwar European Literature." In *Thinking about the Holocaust after Half a Century,* edited by Alvin H. Rosenfeld, pp. 18-37. Bloomington: Indiana University Press, 1997.

[*In the following essay, Bernstein suggests that the Jew has not been treated in all his complexity in postwar European fiction, but rather as a representative of a "cemetery culture."*]

Ignorance about those who have disappeared undermines the reality of the world.

—Zbigniew Herbert, "Mr. Cogito on the Need for
Precision"

I

Initially, the tale may seem all too familiar. After so many
similar narratives, this story's trajectory from the gradual,
piecemeal reconstruction of a family's devastation at the
hands of the Nazis to bitter disappointment at the postwar
German legal system's callous refusal of justice, let alone
of repentance, for that murderous brutality moves us less
by its scrupulously assembled details than by our always
freshly triggered incomprehension at the sheer repetition
of such facts. This time, the first incarnation of the story is
as a combination memoir, detective story, legal brief, and
carefully restrained *cri de coeur* by journalist Peter Finkelgruen in his 1992 text, *Haus Deutschland: oder Die Geschichte eines ungesühnten Mordes*.[1] Finkelgruen is a German Jew, and although this fact is the foundation of his
story, it is *not* especially highlighted in the story's actual
telling. Briefly summarized, the book recounts how a
writer, returning "home" to Germany in the summer of
1988, accidentally comes across a small newspaper article
describing the imminent deportation "home" from Italy of
Anton Malloth, a former guard at the Theresienstadt concentration camp. The two notions of being-at-home become crucial, if antithetical, in the course of the book. For
Peter Finkelgruen this small shred of newsprint opens a
complex double movement, on the one hand into his family's past, and on the other into the tortuous legal bureaucracy of his country's present.

The Finkelgruens, we quickly notice, begin to seem as
emblematic of modern German Jewish family history as,
say, the Buddenbrooks do for an earlier and decidedly different social dispensation. Their fate is recorded as a kind
of *Entbildungsroman,* similar to that endured by millions
of others like—and, equally important, *unlike*—them, although each member of the family is always meticulously
individualized in spite of the leveling assaults directed at
them by a regime that insisted that all Jews were fundamentally identical in their difference from humanity. *Haus
Deutschland* covers three generations, beginning with Martin Finkelgruen, the successful businessman and decorated
World War I veteran who flees to Czechoslovakia after the
NSDAP assumed power. From Karlsbad, Martin Finkelgruen moved on to Prague, and from there, unable to keep
running faster than the advancing *Wehrmacht,* he was deported to Theresienstadt where, on 10 December 1942, he
was beaten to death by Malloth in the infamous *kleine
Festung*. His son Hans tried to reach the United States but
ended up in Shanghai, where he died in the Jewish ghetto
set up by the Japanese occupiers. Hans's and Esti's son,
Peter Finkelgruen, did survive, however, and although he
lived abroad for some time, he eventually returned to Cologne, where he became a successful writer.

Haus Deutschland is not just a family history, though as
such, it is an engrossing addition to the genre—almost as
compelling, if narrower in its historical compass and anecdotal richness, as works like the Austro-Jewish story, *Das
waren die Klaars*.[2] But Finkelgruen's account is also a legal murder-mystery, or rather, since there is no mystery
and no legal process, an indictment of a judicial refusal
that stands for all the greater refusals of a system and its
practitioners. Malloth had already been condemned to
death in absentia by a Czech court for war crimes, but the
German authorities ruled that there was "insufficient evidence" to substantiate the charges against him and de-
clined either to proceed further on their own or to extra-
dite him to the waiting Czech police.

With all the technical expertise of a professional reporter
and the growing intensity of a man who feels it is his own
intimate history that is at issue, Peter Finkelgruen proceeds to assemble ever more convincing proof of Malloth's crimes, including eyewitness evidence that the guard
had brutally murdered Martin Finkelgruen in front of numerous other prisoners. But in spite of the new evidence
so meticulously provided by Peter Finkelgruen, the state
prosecutor continues to resist trying Malloth, and at the
end, it is the murderer who goes free, now safely "at
home" in *Haus Deutschland* while an inconvenient reminder of the past like Peter Finkelgruen has been made
to realize he is clearly less than completely welcome there.

But my own story only begins here, just as Peter Finkelgruen's book itself soon takes on another form. Not long
after the publication of *Haus Deutschland,* the Düsseldorfer Schauspielhaus commissioned the Israeli dramatist Ye-
hoshua Sobol to write a play based on Finkelgruen's book.
That play, called *Schöner Toni* (Handsome Tony), after
one of Anton Malloth's nicknames, was translated from
Hebrew into German by Finkelgruen himself, with the assistance of Gertrud Seehaus, and had a successful premier
in Düsseldorf in June 1994.[3] Sobol follows the book quite
closely, but with instinctive dramatic intelligence he nar-
rows the focus to two settings: the Finkelgruens' temporary, and ultimately, vain Prague refuge, and the grandson's futile search for justice in present-day Germany. But
Sobol also highlights the non-Jewish women who accompanied the Finkelgruen men, especially Martin's Czech
lover, Anna, who survives Auschwitz, and Hans's wife,
Esti (Ernestine), who comes back from Shanghai completely broken by her ordeal. The play also contains some
comically grotesque dialogues of silence between the public prosecutor, eager to discover nothing, and a Malloth
obviously eager to oblige him. But what interests me more
is what the noted director, Bruno Klimek, added to the
text of the play to heighten the audience's sympathy for
the characters. When we first meet Anna, for example, she
is singing a Yiddish song, a detail for which there is no
warrant in either *Haus Deutschland* or the text of *Schöner
Toni*; and at a number of points the Finkelgruens are endowed with a kind of touching *Yiddishkeit* that is bound to
surprise anyone who is familiar either with the actual story,
or indeed with the class of German Jews that *Haus Deutschland* so ably portrays. In fact, all of the Finkelgruens,
three generations of them—Jews, Aryans, and what the

Nuremberg decrees so carefully demarcated as "Mischlinge erster Klasse"—are shown in Peter Finkelgruen's narrative to be thoroughly and completely German, identical in mannerisms, tastes, customs, and habits to the people from whom they were ferociously excised. Why, then, does Bruno Klimek, a genuinely gifted theater director and a man of impeccably antifascist and anti-anti-Semitic convictions, add such details, almost as if they were a matter of course, to his production?

I am not concerned here with suggesting that Bruno Klimek's addition of a visual and audible "Jewish" dimension to his characters, the surplus, in a sense, of an immediately decipherable network of codes designed to make it easier to identify the category of "being a Jew," stems from anything but the most unimpeachable of motives.[4] But I do think that what it highlights is just how troubling the issue of Jewish identity, and more specifically, the *representation* of European Jewish identity, has become in the aftermath of the Shoah. Nor is it only a matter of exotic stereotypes that all Jews are somehow supposed to embody, although elements of this belief can easily be shown to haunt philo-Semitic, as well as anti-Semitic, imaginings. Rather, it is as though in order for Jews to be represented at all by postwar European artists, they first need to be "made visible" by bringing out those features that endow them with a distinct, but supposedly communal, identity. For a dramatist, filmmaker, or novelist to show us a European Jew in the years before the Shoah, that Jew is almost always figured through a set of conventions as formulaic and unindividualized as the stock epithets used by oral poets as mnemonic devices to help listeners grasp instantly who is being talked about. Given the history of European Jewry, especially between 1932 and 1945, it is no doubt inevitable that the question of how—indeed, for most German and Austrian artists it should really be phrased as *a question of whether*—it is possible to represent Jews at all except by regarding them as "proto-victims of the Holocaust."

To put the matter as starkly and polemically as possible, I want to suggest that while it is possible for German and Austrian writers to sympathize, and even to sympathize deeply, with the catastrophic suffering inflicted on the Jews, it is much harder for them to imagine that many of those Jews could have been indistinguishable *in every way* from their neighbors, that they did not even possess any definably Jewish "family resemblance" that linked all those sentenced to extermination—except, of course, for the absolute universality of that sentence itself. To set into motion, and come very close to succeeding in, a plan to exterminate an entire race no doubt touches some absolute limit of representability in the sense of actually letting us feel with any inwardness, or even fully comprehend intellectually what took place.[5] But it can nonetheless be symbolically figured, difficult though the idea may be to admit, so long as any member of the group can be pictured as standing in for—which means in some immediately graspable way being identical to—everyone else for whom the same fate is intended. But if the victims are *not* distin-

guishable from the murderers until they have been made recognizable as victims by continuous ill-treatment, if their only allpervasive, shared characteristics are those imposed by their killers (on the model of the Nazi decree ordering all male Jews to add the name Israel and all females the name Sarah to their identification documents), then the original indistinguishability of killer from killed, the extermination, in this sense, of like by like, becomes a slaughter of identity rather than the attempted eradication of difference; as such it poses a much more intractable problem of both artistic and theoretical representation. If the murdered were as diverse as the murderers, then the metonymy on which a supposedly illustrative drama, film, or novel about the Shoah depends would be radically subverted; and while it remains possible to create a representation of an individual's entrapment within the Nazi killing machinery, it is not possible to make that person's catastrophe representative of the whole except in its ultimate terminus in death.[6]

But even if it could be argued that hunger, fear, exhaustion, terror, and hopelessness did indeed give the Jews imprisoned in the ghettos, and even more, those in the concentration camps, a set of common traits, this is manifestly not true of European Jewry before the Nazi victories. Elsewhere I have suggested a way of understanding how the annihilation of European Jewry in the Shoah has led writers, by what I call "backshadowing," to project a series of judgments, almost invariably negative ones, onto the daily lives of a large and heterogeneous population that is portrayed primarily—and uniformly—as "victims-in-waiting" of the coming genocide.[7] "Backshadowing" in this sense is a way to endow the past with the coherence of a linear unfolding: it works by a kind of retroactive foreshadowing in which the shared knowledge of the outcome of a series of events by narrator and listener is used to judge the participants in those events *as though they too should have known what was to come*. Thus, our knowledge of the Shoah is used to condemn the "blindness" and "self-deception" of Austro-German Jewry for their unwillingness to save themselves from a doom that was supposedly clear to see. I was struck by how often writers, especially Jewish writers—whether social historians, biographers, or novelists—in looking back from a postwar perspective on the life of Austro-German Jewry, found it hard to register, without the acquired certainty of backshadowing and the tone of patronizing incredulity to which it gives rise, that there is nothing self-evidently deluded in the fact that it was the *wrong* prediction, the fatally *incorrect* interpretation of public events that won the intellectual and emotional allegiance of the vast majority of European Jews. Or, to phrase the issue still more polemically: the wrong prediction did not have to be wrong; and its failure was, if anything, a good deal less likely than the (retrospectively) more accurate, pessimistic prognosis. My point here, though, is not to repeat arguments made in more detail elsewhere but to suggest that in the hands of postwar German and Austrian imaginative writers, dramatists, and filmmakers, backshadowing often works in a radically different way from the model I proposed in *Foregone Conclusions.*

In the hands of a philo-Semitic writer who wants to trouble the too easy sleep of his countrymen's conscience, a combination of compassion for the victims—rather than a judgment upon their supposed self-deception—fuses with an aesthetic need to make the victims both recognizable and representative in order to create a standardized and frequently sentimentalized figure whenever they depict European Jews in the years before the Nazi state. From the first moment we encounter such figures, no matter what activities they seem to be engaged in or the vicissitudes of their moment-by-moment existence, both their clear difference from the non-Jewish characters and their highlighted vulnerability mobilize our affective identification solely through their role as "soon-to-become victims" of a waiting terror. Whether it is the thoroughly assimilated Finkelgruens suddenly manifesting touching snatches of *Yiddishkeit,* or the very few Jews appearing in the supposedly even-handed Austrian bestselling novel, *Puntigam, oder, Die Kunst des Vergessens*—who are scarcely individualized at all and are only referred to in such general terms as "your famous grain Jews"—the Jew as an individual whose traits are not instantly universalizable hardly figures at all.[8] There is, in other words, a curious symmetry in the way backshadowing has structured the figuring of prewar European Jewry by postwar Jewish writers versus by Austro-German ones. In both cases, the Jewish community tends to be portrayed as a single, homogeneous entity. But where a writer like Aharon Appelfeld will satirize the self-delusion of Jews who act, think, talk, and live like other Austrians, thereby only blinding themselves to their preordained fate, postwar Austrian and German writers, if they are able to incorporate Jews into their fictions at all, will tend to standardize them in the exactly opposite direction. They tend to make each of them a visible, audible, and even gestural incarnation of a universal Jewishness whose inevitable destruction the audience ought to mourn and even feel a certain uncomfortable guilt about—much, perhaps, as American liberal audiences are expected to deplore the brutal but, it is also clearly implied, inescapable annihilation of the Native American tribes—who are invariably portrayed in *bien pensant* films and novels as the repositories of all the wished-for virtues lacking in the social fabric of present-day America. More often, however, it is the absence of Jews in Austro-German works that is most noticeable, for example, the painfully labored—becuase so overemphatic—avoidance of Jewish characters in Edgar Reitz's *Heimat* or, just as interesting, the astonishing decision in staging Erwin Sylvanus's 1957 play, *Dr. Korczak und die Kinder,* to represent the murder of Korczak and his orphans as a kind of Pirandellian *Sei personaggi in cerca d'autore* performed by a contemporary troupe of German actors without a single Jew in the company.[9] It is as though in order for the audience to "take in" even the barest facts of the Shoah, it is first necessary to make certain that they are not, as it were, doubly embarrassed by also having to confront a living Jew on the stage. The

Publikumsbeschimpfung is difficult enough for the audience to endure when it is addressed to them by a good German "dressed up" as a Jew; if it were articulated by a real Jew, enacting what was once done to his people by men and women intimately related to those purchasing tickets for that night's performance, then the collapsing of the distance between "spectacle" and history would become too troubling to put up with.

But I would also want to argue that when Jews do appear, the backshadowing of the genocide makes them in some fundamental way unrepresentable in their specificity and particularity. In a sense, the negative sublime of the Shoah itself, its ultimate unrepresentability, has been transferred wholesale to European Jewry almost independently of when or where they lived. For a contemporary German or Austrian writer to take on the voice of a Jew, to embody the consciousness of a Jew, even in a work set before the Nazi accession to power, means to have figured the Jew as he will be seen in the black light of genocide; but in so doing, the lure of sympathetic representation inevitably collapses into an erasure of the difference upon which real meaning depends. No wonder then that for most writers, it is easier simply to do without Jews altogether.[10]

In a way, of course, the Shoah gives only a guilt-induced "positive" turn to a centuries-long fundamental European difficulty in imagining Jews as particularized at all. At least since the eighteenth century, the Jew has been a phantasmic figure for the two most powerful political and theoretical movements of the Western imagination: the Enlightenment on the one hand, and its negative emanation, loosely definable as the anti-Enlightenment, on the other.

For the Enlightenment, with its cult of progress, faith in universals, and formally abstract notions of citizenship and community, Jewish particularism was inherently retrograde, tribal, and doomed to extinction by the rational process of human civilization itself. Jews could become full citizens precisely and only by ceasing in any significant sense to be or to think of themselves as Jews.[11] For anti-Enlightenment thinkers though, it was only the local, the communal, and the specific that gave one a real identity. The difficulty for Jews in this scheme of things, however, was that while they were undeniably "particular," they were also and always the incarnations of that most oxymoronic concept—a deracinated particularism. Jews were simply never "in the right place" or endowed with the "right roots" to be seen as individuals: they had local customs, but the wrong ones; their language as Jews (whether Yiddish or Hebrew) was not that of the province in which they lived; and their customs, though venerable enough, had no mystical connection to the soil or tribal practices of the region where they dwelt. For the Enlightenment, that is, Jews typified a distasteful particularism, no more representable than was Othello's handkerchief upon a neoclassic Parisian stage; to the anti-Enlightenment, Jews were the very *exemplum* of a sterile, vitiating universalism that lacked all of the vital, blood-and-soil nourished specificity that alone made a densely individualized representation imaginable.

II

I think there are as many ways of surviving survival as there have been to survive.

—Philip K., quoted in Lawrence Langer, *Holocaust Testimonies*

If there is one genre that by its very nature ought to resist these forms of radical reductionism, it is surely the survivor memoir. And indeed, it is striking how often such memoirs succeed in portraying the pre-Shoah life of the writer without relying upon the kind of historical backshadowing I have been tracing. It is their portrayal of the sheer variety of prewar European Jewish life, its irreducibility to any monological categories, whether of "self-deluding assimilationism" or "Yiddish communalism," that is ultimately almost as instructive in these memoirs as their testimony about the horrors of the ghettos and camps. Survivor memoirs show how deeply intertwined the problems of individuality and representation are, since every survivor's story is utterly unique and yet each also bears witness to a fate that, in one way or another, was endured by all those caught up in the Nazi death machinery. What these memoirs enact, in other words, is an exemplary lesson in how the identical end planned for all Jews by the Reich, and the similarity of suffering inflicted by the Nazis upon every Jew in their grasp, need not be projected backward to represent a standardized European Jewish life and consciousness *before* the Shoah.

But the very fact that we know the Shoah did take place, as well as our response to the individual experience of the survivor witness, has decisely changed the terms in which we theorize the limits of representation today. And in this domain, it is as senseless to seek any consensus among the survivor witnesses as it is to expect their picture of pre-Shoah European Jewry to share a set of common characteristics. Indeed, it is again the *differences* in the way survivors such as Primo Levi or Jean Améry understand their relationship to European culture that is so revelatory of the incoherence of the very category of "the survivor" as a group identity. For all the technical expertise and even occasional bravura of recent philosophical debates about representation and identity, I know of none that approach the depth and seriousness of that between Levi and Améry; and if I gesture only briefly toward a moment in their texts, it is because even in its most condensed formulation, the implications of their positions and the resonance they carry will be readily apparent.

Writing on the Shoah has repeatedly turned on the antithesis between identity as the set of individuating, singular traits that made up prewar Jewish existence, and identity as the obliteration of all difference, whether in the Reich's anti-Semitic legislation, in the camps themselves, or in the postwar representation of European Jewry. One side of the antithesis is unforgettably crystallized in Jean Améry's bitter formulation: "no bridge led from death in Auschwitz to *Death in Venice*."[12] The experience of torture and the death camp gave Hans Maier not merely a new name but a new identity, one that erased forever the consciousness that had constituted and understood itself through its relationship to culture. Representation itself had failed Améry. With nothing left to draw upon except his permanently reexperienced ordeal ("Anyone who has been tortured remains tortured"), Améry's post-Auschwitz identity remains—on principle—forever identical, not merely to what *he* became under torture, but to the new category of "the intellectual at Auschwitz."[13] Hence, of course, Améry's wounded reaction to Primo Levi, whom he called "The Forgiver"—not because Levi ever "forgave" the Nazis but because for Levi, personal identity remained profoundly linked to representation, not merely representation of one's biographical experiences, but the act of cultural imagining and representation itself. This, surely, is the central meaning of the muchanalyzed chapter "Il Canto d'Ulisse" in *Se questo è un uomo*.[14] Directly contrary to Améry's dictum, culture, in the specific form of Dante's lines about Ulysses in *Inferno* XXVI, *did* help Levi maintain a sense of identity, and even of continuity with his pre-camp self. Levi's recollection of Dante's great canto did not provide a bridge *to* Auschwitz; instead, it gave him a momentary bridge *back* to a way of thinking about himself that enabled him to answer in the affirmative to the question: "Is this a man?" On his first day in Auschwitz, Levi tried to grab an icicle to quench his unendurable thirst, "but at once a large, heavy guard . . . brutally snatched it away." When Levi asked, "Warum?," he received his first real lesson in the infernal logic of the camp: "Hier ist kein Warum." But in Dante's represented Inferno, rather than in the Nazis' actual one, explanation for each divine judgment is the principal thematic concern of the various *canti*. More pertinently still, the *form* of the poem, the strict *terza rima* that determines the shape and sound of every single line, is what helps Levi both to recall many of the crucial verses from the Ulysses canto as well as to realize which ones he has forgotten. In the rhyme scheme itself, in other words, there is a clear, formal *warum* for every lexical decision. It is this principle of form-giving imagination, of representation as a human activity, on which identity in the individualizing, anti-camp, and ultimately, contra-Améry sense, is shown to depend. Paradoxically, to maintain an individual identity is to be committed to representation; and the need to draw on cultural models to confirm one's humanity is ultimately a gift, not a lack or a weakness in either oneself or one's heritage.[15]

III

They will even take away our name: and if we want to keep it, we will have to find in ourselves the strength to do so . . . so that behind the name something of us, of us as we were, still remains.

—Primo Levi, *If This Is a Man*

There are many ways that a distrust of representation can work to nullify individual identity. In a curious sense, the insistence on the uncrossable abyss between Hans Maier's prewar Austrian culture and Jean Améry's forever frozen moment in the SS torture cellar at Breendonk is not unrelated to Bruno Klimek's addition of a sentimentalized *Yid-*

dishkeit to the characters in *Schöner Toni*. A radical severance from one's roots as an intellectual, assimilated *Austrian* Jew and a sentimentalizing of the German *Jew* as a type, are eerily consonant in their insistence on a single mode of existence, expressed through a fixed repertoire of tones that are supposedly common to all Jews whose lives were devastated by the Shoah. Klimek probably does not realize that he is removing any humanly specific identity by imposing traits on the Finkelgruens that make recognizable a *type,* not a person, nor that his reliance on the most readily available ethnic stereotypes only obscures the very identity to which he is trying to give form. But if Klimek falls *below* the challenge of representation, Améry, as his Nietzschean title makes clear, wants to find a new identity and discourse *outside* the canon of pre-Shoah figuration altogether.[16] It is as though the Nazis' creation of a system and a language beyond any humanity permanently obliges a Jew to bear witness in a mode beyond any form of cultural representation linked to a time before the Shoah. Lucidly, and with enormous, though ultimately, I think, self-damaging strictness, Améry denies any authenticity to the effort of sustaining, through individualized representation and cultural memory, a continuity of personal identity extending from a prewar self through the experience of the Shoah.

To the question of how a non-Jewish, Austrian or German writer today can represent Jews without either evading the issue of what was done to them or of letting that communal cataclysm obscure the individuality of the victims, I think Thomas Bernhard's 1988 play, *Heldenplatz,* provides one possible answer.[17] Set in a present-day Vienna that is saturated with the ugliest venom of its Nazi past, *Heldenplatz* is more than merely a brilliant dramatization of history as a "return of the repressed." Nor is it, as Viennese critics, both sympathetic and hostile, seem to have felt, only an indictment of Austria for its anti-Semitism, opportunism, and venality. The play is all these things; but for my purposes, it is also a work that shows it is possible to represent Jews as victims of Nazism without sentimentalizing or, for lack of a better term, "ghettoizing" their behavior and traits.[18] So deeply have the scars of Nazism marked the play's characters that the whole piece begins only after the suicide of its most important character, Professor Josef Schuster, who has killed himself out of fear and disgust at the lack of any real change in the mentality of his countrymen. Schuster, a refugee who returned from his Chair at Oxford to a position at the University of Vienna in a desperately miscarried attempt to rebuild something of his prewar life, has the futility of that hope brought home to him with a virulence that places Bernhard's perspective squarely on the side of the most pessimistic judgments in Jean Améry.[19] But even as the appalling memory of the *Anschluss* begins more and more to flood the consciousness of the surviving Schuster family members, and as the remembered cries of the delirious crowd hailing their *Führer* from the Heroes' Square of the book's title become increasingly audible to actors and audience alike, until the raucous noise fills the whole theater, the Schusters continue to be the idiosyncratic, difficult,

and in many ways personally unsympathetic people they have always been. They remain, that is to say, themselves—true to their own particular identities, though their identity as Jews has made any kind of existence in Austria utterly impossible.[20] The contemporary Viennese Nazi apologists and anti-Semites are incalculably worse, but the contempt Bernhard feels for them is secure enough of its grounds and precise enough in its focus that it need not insist upon the sanctity or uniformity of the victims. Nor is Bernhard concerned to "charm" his audience's sympathy by giving to the Jews he represents a set of endearingly ethnic—and hence, to a Viennese audience, reassuringly distancing—touches.

In Aharon Appelfeld's novel *Badenheim 1939,* one of the characters, uncomfortable with his Jewishness—as indeed are most of them—reacts to a question about his origins by insisting that he is "an Austrian citizen of Jewish origin."[21] In Appelfeld this is clearly an absurd reply, another sign of the suicidal self-delusions of a community whose toadying assimilationism and lack of authenticity, as much as the loathing of their enemies, made their annihilation a foregone conclusion. The phrase "an Austrian citizen of Jewish origin" is meant by Appelfeld to sound bathetic—an index of the depth of the speaker's willful obtuseness about the truth of his position. The words are risible because they have no meaning; and all of *Badenheim 1939* is intended to show that the words were *always* meaningless, and not only after the application to Austria of the Nuremberg Decrees, which formally stripped Austrian Jews of their civil rights and citizenship. If the words ever had any meaning, the implicit argument runs, the Shoah could never have happened. But if Appelfeld's vacationing Jews all resemble one another in their self-alienation and refusal to see what is happening everywhere around them, Thomas Bernhard's Schuster family, if it were so inclined, could accurately say of itself that by mannerism, education, and even, in a sense, by cultural arrogance, it is composed of "Austrian citizens of Jewish origin," without either an iota of self-hatred or the slightest delusion that the truth of the statement would save them from the malice of the country's anti-Semites. The Schusters—and their author—already know that the fury breaking out around them has nothing to do with their personal behavior or characteristics. Anti-Semitism, in this play, is a problem of the anti-Semite, not of the Jews, and once the implications of this perception *for artistic representation* are fully understood, the issue of identity can at last be extricated from both the condescending judgments and the clichéd sentimentalizations of backshadowing.

In a letter to Alexander Pushkin, Beztuzhev-Marlinsky wrote: "We have a criticism, but no literature."[22] So far, I admit that what I have offered here is little more than a theory in search of a literature-to-come.[23] And if much of twentieth-century Jewish history militates against the likelihood of that literature ever being written, it is also true that such an effort must be made if European Jewry is to be represented in all its vital complexity and not merely as an ineluctably foredoomed museum or, more often still, cemetery culture.

Notes

1. *Haus Deutschland: oder Die Geschichte eines ung-esühnten Mordes* (Berlin: Rowohlt Verlag, 1992).

2. George Clare, *Das waren die Klaars* (Berlin: Verlag Ullstein, 1980). Clare's own English version has a more melodramatic title, *Last Waltz in Vienna: The Destruction of a Family, 1842-1942* (London: Macmillan, 1981), but is otherwise identical to the German text.

3. I would like to thank the staff of the Düsseldorfer Schauspielhaus, and especially Barbara Reitz of the Dramaturgie-Sekretariat, for their unfailing and prompt help with all my inquiries. Her assistance included providing me with a copy of the theater's own working text of Sobol's play, which was invaluable for my research.

4. An analogous problem, for example, arises for American Jewish novelists when they wish to show that their characters, though fully integrated into society as a whole, are to be regarded as essentially and distinctively Jewish. A complex, but in principle, I think, definable set of conventions intended to accomplish precisely this kind of "rapid deciphering of ethnicity" can be found in the work of novelists such as Saul Bellow, Bernard Malamud, and Philip Roth. For a fine discussion of this question, see Benjamin Harshav, *Language in Time of Revolution* (Berkeley: University of California Press, 1993). But the resonance and implications of such conventions are profoundly different depending on whether they are employed on a German stage or in an American novel; and this fact alone has interesting implications for the ways in which history and immediate context decisively influence how formally similar codes actually function.

5. Of the enormous literature on this question, I have found these studies to be the most helpful: Berel Lang, ed., *Writing and the Holocaust* (New York: Holmes & Meier, 1988); James E. Young, *Writing and Rewriting the Holocaust: Narrative and the Consequences of Interpretation* (Bloomington: Indiana University Press, 1988); and Saul Friedlander, ed., *Probing the Limits of Representation: Nazism and the "Final Solution"* (Cambridge: Harvard University Press, 1992).

6. There is an exact analogy to the leveling of individual differences among the Jewish victims of the Shoah in the equally clichéd representation of the Nazi murderers as identical to one another. The "stage Nazi," that is, corresponds perfectly to the stereotypical Jew. But homogenizing the murderers turns history into a kind of puppet show devoid of individual decisions, choice, and, ultimately, moral responsibility. The readiness to participate in the genocide was always personal and could never be predicted, let alone, in any way "justified" on the basis of monolithic categories such as "German obedi-

ence," "national character," or any of the other readily available—and all too often invoked—typologies.

7. Michael André Bernstein, *Foregone Conclusions: Against Apocalyptic History* (Berkeley: University of California Press, 1994).

8. Gerald Szyszkowitz, *Puntigam, order, Die Kunst des Vergessens* (Vienna: Paul Zsolnay Verlag, 1988). An English translation by Adrian Del Caro, with a preface by Simon Wiesenthal, and an afterword by Jurgen Koppensteiner, is available as *Puntigam, or, The Art of Forgetting* (Riverside, Ca.: Ariadne Press, 1990). It is worth mentioning in this context that throughout *Puntigam,* there is a good deal of discussion of Nazi brutality, but almost exclusively as it was exercised upon local Austrian patriots, *not* on the Jews. We read, for example, that "one heard it whispered that in Mauthausen they had again hanged someone from *Sveti Jacob* [an anti-German irredentist movement] "but *nothing* about the Jews who were murdered at Mauthausen" (p. 187 of the English text).

9. Erwin Sylvanus, *Korczak und die Kinder* (Hamburg: Rowohlt Verlag, 1957). The play is available in an English translation by George E. Wellwarth in Michael Benedikt and George E. Wellwarth, eds., *Postwar German Theatre: An Anthology of Plays* (New York: E. P. Dutton, 1967). For a more detailed study of this issue, see Anat Feinberg, *Wiedergutmachung im Programm: Jüdisches Schicksal im deutschen Nachkriegsdrama* (Cologne: Prometh Verlag, 1988). I would like to thank Dr. Jeanette R. Malkin of The Hebrew University, Jerusalem, for recommending Anat Feinberg's book to me, as well as for suggesting the pertinence of the production of *Dr. Korczak und die Kinder* for my argument here.

10. For a lucid discussion of the way postwar German filmmakers have represented the Third Reich, see especially Anton Kaes, *From Hitler to Heimat: The Return of History as Film* (Cambridge: Harvard University Press, 1989).

11. On the theological roots of the conflict between a supposed Jewish "particularism" versus a Christian "universalism," see Daniel Boyarin, *A Radical Jew: Paul and the Politics of Identity* (Berkeley: University of California Press, 1994).

12. Jean Améry, *At the Mind's Limits: Contemplations by a Survivor on Auschwitz and Its Realities,* trans. Sidney Rosenfeld and Stella P. Rosenfeld (Bloomington; Indiana University Press, 1980) 16.

13. Améry's dictum, for all its dark brilliance, needs to be carefully questioned, not merely recited; it may perhaps open, rather than shut off, a whole series of questions on the relationship between pre-Nazi culture and the Holocaust. Améry seems to indict Mann's novella, and metonymically culture as a

whole, for the absence of such a bridge. But would not a culture that provided this "bridge" be much more alarming? What if, in other words, there were not a chasm, but rather, as has been argued by many people, a *continuity* between the Nazi atrocities and the highest forms of German creativity? In this context I am less concerned to explore that question than to ask in more general terms why we ought to require of any work of art that it serve as preparation for, or as a link to, the experience of torture and genocide? As I have argued elsewhere, to indict culture because of its helplessness either to prepare one for, or somehow actually to restrain, an event as lethal and cataclysmic as the Holocaust profoundly misunderstands the relationship between culture and lived experience: Very little about either cultural or individual human values can be learned from how they bear up in a situation *in extremis,* and the Shoah is not an appropriate, let alone a privileged, gauge for the authenticity or legitimacy of those values. See Michael André Bernstein, "Against Comfort," *Times Literary Supplement* 5 May 1995: 9-10.

14. Of the numerous critical pieces on the function of Dante in Levi's texts, the two I have found most useful are: Lynn M. Gunzberg, "Nuotando altrimenti che nel Serchio: Dante as vademecum for Primo Levi," in *Reason and Light: Essays on Primo Levi,* ed. Susan Tarrow (Western Societies Program, Occasional Paper No. 25, Center for International Studies, Cornell University, 1990), and Dalya M. Sachs, "The Language of Judgment: Primo Levi's *Se questo è un uomo,*" *Modern Language Notes* 110.4 (September 1995); 755-84.

15. For a different reading of the Levi-Améry connection, see Alvin H. Rosenfeld, "Primo Levi: The Survivor as Victim," in James S. Pacy and Alan P. Wertheimer, eds., *Perspectives on the Holocaust: Essays in Honor of Raul Hilberg* (Boulder, CO: Westview Press, 1995) 123-44. By looking at Levi both from the vantage point of the still-unresolved issue of whether or not his death was a suicide brought on by the memory of his time in Auschwitz, as well as from the undeniably darker and more pessimistic tones of his late texts such as *The Drowned and the Saved,* Rosenfeld questions the ultimate value of literary memory and representation as a means of self-preservation for Levi's consciousness.

16. The English translation of Améry's title, *Jenseits von Schuld und Sühne,* literally "Beyond guilt and repentance," as *At the Mind's Limits,* though it captures some of the sense of a boundary, completely loses the deliberate invocation of Nietzsche's *Jenseits von Gut und Böse* (Beyond good and evil).

17. My discussion of *Heldenplatz* here is obviously not intended to suggest that it is the only possible model, or that Bernhard is the only writer to have made an attempt to represent Jews without backshadowing or sentimentalization. My intent is not to provide an exhaustive inventory of texts and authors, but rather, to highlight a specific set of theoretical and practical dilemmas. And in this context, it is worth stressing that a list, no matter how complete, is not an argument, and an inventory, no matter how scrupulously assembled, is not an explanation, and all too often the compilation of discrete items of information is seen as a sufficient answer to problems of interpretation and understanding. See Thomas Bernhard, *Heldenplatz* (Frankfurt: Suhrkamp, 1988).

18. For a useful analysis of the play from a political and ideological perspective, see Eckhard Gropp, *Thomas Bernhards "Heldenplatz" als politisches Theater* (Bad Honnef: E. Keimer Verlag, 1994).

19. My linking of Bernhard's play with Améry's writings is far from arbitrary; not only are both writers centrally concerned with a crisis of representation and cultural memory/amnesia in postwar Austria, but it is also widely accepted that Bernhard's Professor Schuster was directly inspired by Améry himself.

20. For a fascinating instance of how determined many Austrian Jews were to preserve as much as possible of their pre-*Anschluss* cultural habits and attitudes, even in exile in Bolivia, see Leo Spitzer, "Andean Waltz," in Geoffrey Hartman, ed., *Holocaust Remembrance: The Shapes of Memory* (Cambridge: Basil Blackwell, 1994) 161-74.

21. Aharon Appelfeld, *Badenheim 1939,* trans. Dalya Bilu (Boston: David R. Godine, 1980) 21.

22. This is quoted in Michael Holquist, *Dostoevsky and the Novel* (Princeton: Princeton University Press, 1977) 12.

23. Recent American fiction offers an interesting parallel to some of the formal directions that the kind of representation I have been championing might explore. In 1982, Toni Morrison wrote a short story, "Recitatif," which narrates a lengthy relationship between two women, Twyla and Roberta. One of these women is black, the other white, and the whole story turns on racial questions; indeed, issues of race form the core of every incident in "Recitatif" and largely define the dialogues between the women. Yet, we are never told who is white, and who black, and the ambiguity is strictly maintained throughout the narrative. Morrison herself has said that she intended the uncertainty to be unresolvable and deliberately removed any authorial cues that might decisively settle the question. "Recitatif" appears in *Confirmation: An Anthology of African American Women,* ed. Amiri and Amina Baraka (New York: Quill, 1983) 243-61. For a searching analysis of Morrison's story, see Elizabeth Abel, "Black Writing, White Reading: Race and the Politics of Feminist Interpretation," *Critical Inquiry* 19 (Spring 1993): 470-98. Although I think "Recitatif" is only partially successful, it is a fascinating attempt; and it would be interesting to imagine a similar story, but with a German and a Jew as

its protagonists, endlessly discussing Christian-Jewish relations, the Shoah, postwar Jewish reactions to the reemergence of Germany as a world power, and so on, yet also leaving the reader unable to decide which speaker is which.

Edward R. Isser (essay date 1997)

SOURCE: Isser, Edward R. "The Antecedents of American Holocaust Drama." In *Stages of Annihilation: Theatrical Representations of the Holocaust*, pp. 32-43. Madison, WI: Associated University Presses, Inc., 1997.

[*In the following excerpt, Isser discusses American drama written about the Holocaust, noting that themes and imagery were often softened and diluted to make them more acceptable to theatergoers.*]

The Holocaust is an ineffable occurrence that defies the capabilities of the human imagination. Dramatic representations of the historical catastrophe must transform, or as Adorno has said, transfigure, the terror so that it can be endured by an audience. In the American theater this is accomplished usually by the imposition of melodramatic modes upon the historical model. Sententious messages, moral exemplars, uplifting endings, and heroic sacrifices are used to bring order out of the chaos; to make the unimaginable approachable and the unbearable manageable. Lawrence Langer refers to this as the Americanization of the Holocaust, and asserts that such representations "permit the imagination to cope with the idea of the Holocaust without forcing a confrontation with its grim details."[1]

The process of Americanization can be traced to the antifascist plays of the 1930s and early 1940s. These works, written by some of America's best known playwrights, bridged the cultural and spatial gap between American and European affairs. Most of these plays had nothing to do with Jews, but they nevertheless had a significant influence upon Holocaust dramaturgy. The antifascist plays offered effective strategies for overcoming audience apathy and revulsion in representing the Nazi movement.

Early antifascist dramas urged American involvement in European affairs at a time when public opinion was firmly opposed to intervention. Nazism was represented as an amorphous evil physically and spiritually encroaching upon the West. The authors strove to create empathy for the victims and to agitate public opinion against the movement. According to Susan and Bernard Duffy, the purpose of antifascist drama was "to chronicle Nazi atrocities in order to shock the audience, instill in them a sense of outrage, and move them into action."[2]

Examples of antifascist drama include Richard Maibaum's *Birthright* (1933), Leslie Reade's *The Shatter'd Lamp* (1934), Elmer Rice's *Judgment Day* (1934), *American Landscape* (1938), and *Flight to the West* (1940), Sinclair Lewis's *It Can't Happen Here* (1936), S. N. Behrman's

Rain from Heaven (1934), Clifford Odets's *Till the Day I Die* (1935), George S. Kaufman and Moss Hart's *The American Way* (1939), Clare Booth's *Margin for Error* (1939), Maxwell Anderson's *Candle in the Wind* (1941), Lillian Hellman's *Watch on the Rhine* (1941) and *The Searching Wind* (1944), the 1941 revision of Robert Sherwood's *There Shall Be No Night*, John Steinbeck's *The Moon is Down* (1942), and Edward Chodorov's *Decision* (1944). In addition, a number of works by European authors opposed to the Nazis were presented in New York at this time: Friedrich Wolf's *Professor Mamlock* (1937), Ernst Toller's *No More Peace* (1937), and Franz Werfel's *The Eternal Road* (1937).

Antifascist dramas use a number of theatrical and literary devices to bridge the physical and emotional gap between an American audience and events in Europe. Most popular are the conventions of reflected emotional involvement, the imminent threat scenario, redemptive heroic sacrifice, and the familial melodramatic structure. Reflected emotional involvement occurs in works such as *There Shall Be No Night*, *Watch on the Rhine*, *Flight to the West*, and *Candle in the Wind*. In these plays the protagonists, threatened by the Nazis, are romantically linked to American women. The women, without exception, are white, Protestant, and from proper homes in New England or Virginia. The women are presented as moral exemplars to the American people, and their willingness to sacrifice themselves for the men they love validates the righteousness of the antifascist cause. The imminent threat scenario occurs in *It Can't Happen Here*, *The American Landscape*, *The American Way*, and *Flight to the West*. In these plays Nazism is presented as a clear and present danger to the United States. No longer can the plight of Europe be ignored because the source of its misery, fascism, has arrived in America. The United States is threatened by Nazi takeovers and infiltration, but in each play an American comes forth willing to sacrifice himself to save the country from the Nazi threat.

Clifford Odets, Robert Sherwood, and Lillian Hellman wrote three distinctly different types of plays to express their outrage about the rise and spread of Nazism. Like all antifascist plays, their works strove to create empathy for the victims of fascism in order to counter the isolationism and apathy of the general public. Clifford Odets's *Till the Day I Die* (1935) tells the story of a young communist named Ernst Laustig who is tortured by the Gestapo, denounced by his comrades, and who commits suicide in order to offer a message of hope and strength to his yet unborn child. Robert Sherwood's *There Shall Be No Night* (1940) is about a Noble Prize winning Greek scientist named Karilo Vlachos who refuses to flee his homeland when the Italian and German Armies invade. The death of the avowed pacifist at the pass of Thermopile, and the stoicism of his faithful wife, are offered as moral imperatives to the American people. In Lillian Hellman's *Watch on the Rhine* (1941), the good German Kurt Mueller faces certain death when he decides he must return to Europe in order to aid his comrades. The play is set on the outskirts of

Washington, D.C., at the estate of a wealthy liberal matron named Fanny Farrelly. The plot includes numerous coincidences, Nazi spies, adultery, hints of incest, blackmail, murder, and finally a noble sacrifice and a family reconciliation.

The three dramatists, using diverse techniques, seek to demonstrate the imminent threat of Nazism to the world and to agitate their audiences to take action against it. The playwrights, however, approach the problem from contrasting perspectives. Odets presents Nazism as the enemy of all workers and suggests that it can only be defeated by an international "united front." Sherwood argues that Nazism is a fundamental threat to democracy and that America has a moral, Christian duty to preserve freedom on the planet. Hellman stresses a more secular position, but also concludes that Americans have a moral imperative to fight inequality and tyranny wherever it is found.

Hellman and Sherwood manipulate the emotions of their audiences by filtering the situation in Europe through American sensibilities. In *Watch on the Rhine*, the daughter of Fanny Farrelly returns after twenty years accompanied by her German husband. He is a brave "antifascist" who is the devoted father of their three children. The validity and goodness of his quest against the Nazis is reflected in the love and devotion of his American wife and his beautiful American children. The American audience that cannot identify itself with the character of Kurt Mueller can certainly feel empathy for his angelic Anglo-Saxon wife. A similar device is used by Sherwood in *There Shall Be No Night*. The Greek scientist Karilo Vlachos is married to a woman from a prominent New England family. The Vlachos household in Athens is decorated with American paintings and English is the language spoken. The Vlachos's son, Peter, proudly proclaims his American heritage and his desire to visit his mother's country. The sacrifice of the Greek scientist and his son for the cause of freedom are seen through the eyes of the American wife and mother. Sherwood also uses the character of a CBS radio reporter to provide even more of an American perspective.

Sherwood's use of the CBS radio reporter is a clever device that enables him to provide detailed information about the specific situation and to editorialize upon it simultaneously. This mode of narrative also allows the playwright to dispense with purely expositional dialogue. The representation of the radio broadcast in *There Shall Be No Night* is extremely effective and highly dramatic: The foreign correspondent breathlessly speaks into a microphone while his colleagues manipulate the equipment. Sherwood's insertion of edited historical documentation into the middle of his family melodrama adds to the perceived verisimilitude of the piece. By filtering that information through an American reporter, he further reinforces the connection between distant events and his intended audience. The reporter, Dave Corween, is clearly sympathetic to the Greek cause and colors his reporting accordingly.

Clifford Odets in *Till the Day I Die* must provide an American audience with a tremendous amount of background information in order to convey the political situation in Germany. He solves this problem, in part, by having his hero work on an illegal printing press. In the first scene, a character reads a flyer that the workers have produced. The delivery of information in this manner is more awkward and less dramatic than that provided by the radio reporter in *There Shall Be No Night*, but it is effective nevertheless.

Another device used by Odets, and later borrowed by Hellman, is the reading of the police dossier. Background on the behavior of a character and a chronological summary of historical and political events is provided quickly and dramatically. When the sadistic Nazi captain interrogates Ernst Tausig, he has the victim's file before him. In the third act of *Watch on the Rhine*, the dissolute Romanian aristocrat who works as a Nazi spy, utilizes a dossier to reveal the true identity of Kurt Mueller. The audience, in both instances, is kept on edge because they, like the protagonist, do not know the extent of information held inside the files. A final device of exposition used by Odets in *Till the Day I Die* is that of the formal report. A secret communist cell meets in the sixth scene of the play and the first order of business is the delivery of reports on insurgent actions. The second order of business is the reading of the roll of honor for those killed fighting the Nazis. Odets thus has another opportunity to add more background information and additional specific detail to the melodramatic framework of the piece. These strategies for delivering background information, historical context, and political explanation will be utilized by numerous later playwrights of Holocaust drama.

All three plays end with a redemptive act of tragic sacrifice that is meant to serve as a moral exemplar to the audience. In each case the goal of defeating the Nazis is represented as a messianic quest. Ernst Tausig's defiant suicide in *Till the Day I Die* is the heroic action of a man who has retained his humanity under barbaric circumstances. Karilo Vlachos in *There Shall Be No Night* tells his fellow soldiers before the fateful battle against the Nazis that their mission is noble and pious and will serve as a beacon for democracy. Kurt Mueller's farewell to his wife and children in *Watch on the Rhine* before he returns to Europe is a sentimental appeal against Nazism.

America's ambivalence toward Hitler, its phobic attitude toward communism, and latent antisemitism all contributed to the manufacturing of the mythic antifascist hero. This fictional construct was never a communist or a socialist. He was always a liberal democrat who embraced a value system identical to the American model. The phrase "anti-fascist," first used by Lillian Hellman in *Watch on the Rhine*, is a neutered descriptive term that is not threatening to American political or religious values.

One of the great heroes of antifascist drama is S. L. Jacobowsky. Jacobowsky, a refugee from Poland, is an eternal optimist who manages to outwit the Nazis at every turn. Although the character of Jacobowsky was created by Franz Werfel, the 1944 Broadway production was based upon a version written by S. N. Behrman. The controversial transformation of Werfel's play by Behrman demonstrated how the complexities and subtleties of the European wartime experience were simplified reductively for American consumption. Franz Werfel's original version of the play could be considered one of the earliest examples of Holocaust drama. S. N. Behrman's adaptation is probably the last great antifascist play. The difference between the two is the process of Americanization which transformed Werfel's dark tragicomedy into a sleek Broadway entertainment.

The creative genesis of *Jacobowsky and the Colonel* occurred in 1942 at a Hollywood dinner party thrown by Max Reinhardt in honor of Werfel. Werfel, who had recently escaped from France, entertained the guests by telling an amusing tale about a Polish Jew he had met during his travels. S. N. Behrman approached Werfel after the dinner and the two men discussed the dramatic possibilities of the story. Behrman claims that he suggested Werfel write a play along the lines of the anecdote but Werfel told him, "you must write it."[3]

Behrman began working on a dramatic adaptation and kept in contact with Werfel seeking advice and collaboration. Werfel, however, became dissatisfied in the direction that Behrman was taking the narrative and effectively fired him. Werfel, who had begun working on his own version of the play, believed that the piece needed to be Americanized, and sought out Clifford Odets to assist him. Odets agreed to collaborate and produced a script that was optioned by the Theatre Guild in New York. The Theatre Guild, and particularly its managing director Lawrence Langner, ultimately decided that Odets's version was "too ponderous and unplayable." They contacted S. N. Behrman and brought him back onto the project. Elia Kazan, who was directing the production, visited Werfel in California and sought his permission to use the Behrman version. According to Kazan the meeting did not go well:

> Why, he wanted to know, was his play being adapted? What was wrong with presenting a simple straightforward translation of his work? Who here was a better writer than himself? I said it was a matter of the American theatre audience. At this he began to yell at me. He said Americans had no dramatic literature worthy of the name . . . 'Savages!' he yelled. "You are savages here!" . . . This by-play went on throughout the interview, and I got nowhere.[4]

Lawrence Langner, however, worked out a deal with Werfel and the production went into rehearsal utilizing Behrman's text. Kazan directed the play as if it was a fairy tale: "The production must dance, its style must be light and charged with wit; every single person in the play must be a subtly comic figure."[5] The production opened in New Haven, Boston, and Philadelphia before its New York City premiere, and during the out-of-town period the script was rewritten and honed into a joyful comedic romp. Werfel, whose own version of the play in German was subtitled a "Comedy of a Tragedy," was angered that his work was being transformed into little more than a Boulevard drama.[6] After the play opened in Boston, Werfel demanded once more that Behrman be removed from the project. The Theatre Guild, however, refused Werfel's request and lawyers from both parties became involved. The final conclusion was that Behrman and Werfel shared joint authorship of the Broadway production, but Werfel received the lion's share of the royalties. Werfel quickly had his own version of the play translated into English and published. Behrman's recollection of the incident in 1972 is tinged with bitterness:

> Werfel and I were now enemies. I had given him a hit; the play was sold for a considerable sum to the movies; I never heard a word from him although he was not averse to collecting the major part of the royalties. The only one who later tried to shed light on it was a friend of Werfel's. He explained to me that German writers consider that no writing is any good unless it is symbolic and tragically serious. They love symbolic characters which represent profoundly somber abstractions. Werfel had by this time written his own version of the play and it was full of them. It became the libretto for a tragic German opera.[7]

The two versions of the play are radically different in style and emphasis despite their structural similarities. In both versions a refugee from Poland named Jacobowsky seeks to escape Paris before the invading German army arrives. Jacobowsky is able to secure a car, but is unable to drive. Meanwhile a Polish army officer, carrying important documents for his government-in-exile, also needs to leave Paris but has no means of transport. The colonel and Jacobowsky agree to travel together and the officer's adjunct drives the car. Instead of fleeing from the Germans, however, the colonel orders them to drive toward the front lines where his mistress is waiting. They pick up the girlfriend, Marianne, and wildly set off for the coast of France. Along the way Jacobowsky uses his cunning and good nature to secure food and supplies. At one point, after the car has been stopped by German soldiers, Jacobowsky extricates them from the situation and tricks the Nazis into giving them gasoline. The story ends happily when Jacobowsky and the colonel, their differences resolved, both escape to England.

In Behrman's drama the colonel is represented as a Don Quixote-like figure—a noble but slightly crazed romantic warrior. He is gruff, rude, domineering, and given to flights of fancy. The colonel's assistant, Szabuniewicz, is also broadly drawn in a manner much akin to Sancho Panza. Jacobowsky, portrayed as the only normal person in a world turned upside down, is forced to tolerate these two crazy men in order to escape.

Behrman's version of the story is ethnically and culturally neutered. The urgency for Jacobowsky's escape from the Nazis is never explicated. The only reason given is Jacobowsky's fear that he will be placed in a concentration camp. But he is never expressly referred to as a Jew and he does not call himself one. The only time Jews are mentioned is toward the end of the play. A Gestapo officer has been killed and all Jews and aliens are to be shot on sight. This information is used to heighten the dramatic tension and serves as a backdrop for a sentimental scene between Jacobowsky and Marianne.

Behrman's sententious message, delivered in one of the few political speeches of the play, is couched in the broadest and most general terms. Behrman's greeting card sentiment, that people everywhere should be concerned with injustice anywhere, is worded without ethnic reference:

> You remember when the Hitler pestilence first broke out in Germany all of us said, "What happens to Jacobowsky is none of our business." And when it spread from Vienna to Prague we said the same thing. "It's none of our business." But if instead we, and the British and the Americans and the Poles, had said: "It is our business—Jacobowsky is a man too. We can't allow human beings to be treated so"—in six weeks with six divisions we could have exterminated this pestilence in Germany.[8]

Jacobowsky is presented as a prototypical antifascist hero in Behrman's adaptation of Werfel's story. Jacobowsky becomes a metaphoric figure who stands for the downtrodden of Europe; he is the refugee Everyman of the Second World War. The extent of his Judaism, however, is limited to his name.

In Franz Werfel's version of the play the colonel is not the buffoonish clown that appears in Behrman's drama. Colonel Stjerbinsky is a mean spirited antisemite who actively loathes Jacobowsky. Jacobowsky, in turn, is a peevish character who is vain and a bit of a snob. The tension between the two opposites builds until it turns nasty and ugly. The cosmopolitan Jew and the fascistic army officer almost come to blows after a particularly brutal interchange:

COLONEL STJERBINSKY:

> Last night, when we were sleeping in the public dormitory in Dax, on those wretched mattresses, you and I next to each other-r-r—Stjerbinsky's luck—why did you star-r-re at me

JACOBOWSKY:

> I was wondering about your face and about your muttering.

COLONEL STJERBINSKY:

> My R-r-rosary. I was pr-r-raying. Under-r-r the blanket, because I was ashamed of you.

JACOBOWSKY:

> Do you always have such threatening eyes when you pray?

COLONEL STJERBINSKY:

> But you do not pr-r-ray, Jacobowsky. You wer-r-re str-r-rapping ar-r-round your-r-r stomach your-r-r money-belt . . . You wer-r-re afr-r-raid.

JACOBOWSKY:

> In this belt was my last bit of money and some dear souvenirs.

COLONEL STJERBINSKY:

> You wer-r-re afr-r-raid of me! Be Still! Mister-r-r S. L. Jacobowsky r-r-regards Colonel Tadeusz Boleslav of the noble family Pupicky-Stjerbinsky as a scoundr-r-rel, a pickpocket, a highwayman.[9]

The relationship between Jacobowsky and Stjerbinsky is on the brink of termination after this dialogue. The two men, however, cannot survive alone. The best qualities of each is lacking in the other. The bravado and strength of the colonel needs the cunning and sophistication of Jacobowsky to be effective. Jacobowsky, in turn, depends upon the colonel to provide physical safety and leadership. The two men symbolize the condition of gentiles and Jews in Europe and Werfel uses them to demonstrate the interdependency of the two groups.

The imminent demise of the relationship between Jacobowsky and Stjerbinsky creates a metaphysical crisis that demands supernatural intervention. At this crucial juncture, a strange apparition appears on the stage; it is the Wandering Jew and St. Francis of Assisi, riding a bicycle built for two. The Wandering Jew looks like a typical intellectual and speaks in a linguistic pattern that suggests a shtetl Jew. He explains why he looks so young to the incredulous colonel, "I do the best I can. When a person is two thousand years old, he should look about as I do" (75). St. Francis, appearing like a pale Minorite monk in sandals, speaks with a thick Italian accent and usually defers in conversation to the Wandering Jew.

The absurd and bizarre comedy of the scene—which foreshadows the grotesque post-war imagery of Ionesco, Genet, and Beckett—is overshadowed by the terror of the situation and the gravity of the mission shared by the Wandering Jew and St. Francis. The Wandering Jew, who has just spent two years in Dachau, explains the reason for their arrival:

> In the works of Eugène Sue and other authors you will read that I am the forerunner of the great wind. The wind is on the way. In Wiesbaden an armistice has been signed. The Germans will occupy the greater part of France and the entire coast. There's only a moment left. The advance troops are arriving in mayors' offices all over France. With extradition lists!

> (77)

After delivering the message, St. Francis and the Wandering Jew climb back on the bicycle and pedal off together. This unlikely pair, as disparate as the colonel and Jacobowsky, represent Werfel's mystic vision of a synthesis between Christianity and Judaism. The Wandering Jew tells Jacobowsky, "just let opposites get old enough and they'll meet, just like parallel lines in infinity" (76).

At the end of Werfel's play the colonel and Jacobowsky gain mutual respect and begin to take on the characteristics of each other. The final scene of the play takes place at the Mole de Nivelle in Saint Jean-de-Luz. The four travelers—Jacobowsky, Marianne, the colonel, and the adjunct—arrive at the pier where a boat is waiting to embark for England. A British officer greets the colonel and informs him that there is room on the boat for only two passengers. The colonel's adjunct, Szabuniewicz, apparently in little danger, departs the scene, but that still leaves three people for two spaces. Marianne is deeply upset at the thought of leaving Jacobowsky behind and refuses to get on the boat without him—"I saw a truck a while ago, on which they were carting away innocent people! I saw them drag all the Jews out of my little hotel and saw them tear the parents from their children! My ears are still ringing with their grief" (108). The British officer, however, will not allow Marianne to give up her place for Jacobowsky. "We are saving only English subjects and Allied officers, and no one else. If it is at all possible, we are willing to wink at various ladies attached to these gentlemen" (113). The colonel, behaving in a manner hitherto foreign to his personality, graciously praises Jacobowsky and attempts to cajole the Englishman into relenting. When the British officer refuses, the colonel selflessly announces that he will remain behind and share Jacobowsky's fate.

Jacobowsky rises to the occasion and makes a heroic and noble gesture to prevent the colonel from sacrificing himself. Jacobowsky produces two identical vials from his coat—one containing poison and the other water—and proclaims that he will throw one into the sea and drink the other. He tells his friends that his fate is now in the hands of Providence. If he drinks the poison then he will die immediately, thus freeing the colonel from his vow. If he drinks the water then it is a sign that he has divine guidance and therefore does not need the colonel's help. Jacobowsky believes that faith must be maintained regardless of the circumstances:

> Yes, Marianne, the Jacobowskys are to be exterminated, with the overt or secret approval of the world! But they will not be exterminated, although millions die. God is punishing us. He probably knows why. He punishes us by unworthy hands, who make us stronger while they weaken us. And then, filled with loathing, He exterminates them in turn. Do you know that the Wandering Jew and Saint Francis are on their way to America? But I . . . Between a life that is worse than death, and a death that is worse than this life, I shall escape through the little chink that God always leaves open for us (118).

The British officer, called the Dice Player, urges Jacobowsky to choose between the two vials. Jacobowsky throws one into the sea and drinks the other. He has chosen correctly and the officer, impressed by Jacobowsky's courage and determination, decides to bring him on board. "The arguments of your friends didn't convince me. You convinced me yourself! Your resoluteness and your will to live, you optimist! England can make use of you. The whole world needs you" (119).

The Colonel and Jacobowsky, now comrades in arms, walk onto the boat leaving Marianne behind. The Colonel pledges his eternal love to her and says he will return as a liberator of France. This Euripidean ending, complete with a pseudo deus ex machina, reveals the irony underlying the comedic structure of the piece. Werfel's play is indeed a tragedy of a comedy, and the playwright leaves little doubt that although Jacobowsky has gained salvation by fleeing Europe, millions of others have been left behind to die.

Jacobowsky and the Colonel is full of dark and forbidding images: the Wandering Jew who arrives from Dachau, the description of Jews being forcibly deported, and the desperation of a man driven to suicide. It is no wonder that the Theatre Guild in 1944 opted for S. N. Behrman's light-hearted script instead of Werfel's somber vision. Besides the obvious commercial appeal of Behrman's work, it was also politically expedient. It was of paramount importance that American involvement in the Second World War not be couched in terms of liberating European Jewry. Instead, the war had to be perceived by the public—if their support was to be maintained—as a war to preserve the American way of life.

A Werfel biographer, Lionel B. Steiman, concedes that "it may indeed be true that a straight translation of *Jacobowsky and the Colonel* would have been too alien to American taste and experience and that American audiences would have rejected it."[10] But he concludes that a major reason why such a translation would have failed was because the play discussed the fate of European Jews, which was a subject "no American audience in the year 1944 was yet prepared to hear."[11]

One of the most bitter and hotly contested subjects in Holocaust studies concerns who knew what and when. Apologists for Allied inaction have long argued that no one in the West really knew what was happening. Numerous books, however, such as Arthur Morse's *While Six Million Died* (1967), Henry Feingold's *The Politics of Rescue* (1970), and David S. Wyman's *The Abandonment of the Jews* (1984) assert that the Roosevelt and Churchill administrations were well aware of what was going on in Nazi-occupied Europe, but chose to ignore it. Haskel Lookstein in *Were We Our Brother's Keepers?* (1985) and Deborah Lipstadt in *Beyond Belief* (1986) argue that not only were politicians aware of the mass killings but so, too, was the general public and particularly the American Jewish community.

Behrman's decision to neuter the ethnic identity of Jacobowsky and his failure to refer to the suffering of European Jewry is problematic. Behrman, an assimilated Jew, chose to ignore the suffering of his co-religionists because, in part, it would have reduced the commercial viability of his play. Ironically, the Theatre Guild's production of *Jacobowsky* was still identified as a "racial comedy." Burns Mantle in his anthology *The Best Plays of 1943-44* suggests that the play's success was due largely to Jewish patronage: "There was a comedy-starved public of war victims of one class and another that was naturally sensitive to the appeal of racial comedy of the 'Jacobowsky' pattern. Something like 26 theatre parties, each of them taking over the capacity of the Martin Beck Theatre, had been organized before the comedy opened."[12]

The transformation of Werfel's play—the Americanization of the text by Behrman and Elia Kazan—and the dramaturgical strategies utilized by the authors of other antifascist dramas provided paradigmatic models for the later creation of American Holocaust drama. Plays such as Frances Goodrich and Albert Hackett's *The Diary of Anne Frank* (1955), Millard Lampell's *The Wall* (1960), Shimon Wincelberg's *Windows of Heaven* (1962), and Arthur Miller's *Incident at Vichy* catered to the taste of an American audience weaned on the upbeat endings, moral simplifications, heroic sacrifices, and exultant moments of antifascist drama. Works needed to be sanitized, accessible, and uplifting in order to be acceptable and profitable in the American market. As late as 1964, Leo Sullivan's review of the Arena Stage's production of Millard Lampell's revised version of *The Wall* revealed a continuing critical bias. Sullivan applauded the Arena's production because "its sense of comedy, coupled with the genuine suspense of plot, delivers 'The Wall' from being the depressing thing one might have expected."[13] For a Holocaust drama to be a commercial success in the 1950s and 1960s it had to be funny, suspenseful, and entertaining—in other words, it had to be like S. N. Behrman's version of *Jacobowsky and the Colonel*.

Notes

1. Lawrence Langer, "The Americanization of the Holocaust on Stage and Screen," *From Hester Street to Hollywood,* ed. Sarah Blacher Cohen (Bloomington: Indiana University Press, 1983), 214.

2. Susan Duffy and Bernard K. Duffy, "Anti-Nazi Drama in the United States 1934-1941," *Essays in Theater* 4, no. 1 (1985): 39.

3. S. N. Behrman, *People In A Diary* (Boston: Little, Brown & Co., 1972), 168.

4. Elia Kazan, *A Life* (New York: Alfred A. Knopf, 1988), 241.

5. Hermine Rich Isaacs, "First Rehearsals: Elia Kazan Directs a Modern Legend," *Theatre Arts* 28 (1944): 144.

6. Lionel B. Steiman, *Franz Werfel: The Faith of an Exile* (Ontario: Wilfred Laurier, 1985), 176.

7. Behrman, *People In A Diary,* 176.

8. S. N. Behrman, *Franz Werfel's Jacobowsky and the Colonel* (New York: Random House, 1944), 137.

9. Franz Werfel, *Jacobowsky And The Colonel: Comedy of a Tragedy,* trans. Gustave O. Arlt (New York: The Viking Press, 1944), 73-74.

10. Steiman, *Franz Werfel: The Faith of an Exile,* 176.

11. Ibid., 177.

12. Burns Mantle, ed. *The Best Plays of 1943-44* (New York: Dodd, Mead & Co., 1945), 236.

13. Leo Sullivan, "Reconstructed *Wall* Proves Good Drama," review of *The Wall,* by Millard Lampell, *Washington Post,* 31 January 1964, 9(B).

FURTHER READING

Criticism

Antler, Joyce. *Talking Back: Images of Jewish Women in American Popular Culture.* Hanover, NH: Brandeis University Press, 1998, 301 p.
 Collection of essays that explores the image of Jewish women in film, television, literature, and the culture at large.

Ben-Joseph, Eli. *Aesthetic Persuasion: Henry James, the Jews, and Race.* Lanham, Md.: University Press of America, Inc., 252 p.
 Explores Henry James's attitude toward Jews and the question of race in the contexts of his work, society, and history.

Clendinnen, Inga. *Reading the Holocaust.* Cambridge, England: Cambridge University Press, 1999, 227 p.
 Examines the experience of the Holocaust from both the victims' and the perpetrators' points of view using an historical and anthropological approach.

Cohen, Arthur A. *The American Imagination after the War: Notes on the Novel, Jews, and Hope.* Syracuse, NY: Syracuse University Press, 1981, 36 p.
 Discusses the works of Jewish writers in the post-World War II United States, focusing on their response to their jewishness and to the Holocaust experience.

Gross, John. Shylock: *Four Hundred Years in the Life of a Legend.* London: Chatto & Windus, 1992, 355 p.
 Explores the origin, development, continuing use, and ramifications of the Shylock figure in literature.

Harap, Louis. *Creative Awakening: The Jewish Presence in Twentieth-Century American Literature, 1900-1940s.* New York: Greenwood Press, 1987, 196 p.
 Comprehensive survey of Jewish writers and their works in America in the first half of the twentieth century.

Parry, Ann. "Idioms for the Unrepresentable: Post-War Fiction and the Shoah." *Journal of European Studies* 27, no. 4 (December 1997): 417-32.

Focuses on European writers' search for a language and a form in which to depict the Holocaust in their works.

Ricks, Christopher. *T. S. Eliot and Prejudice.* London: Faber and Faber, 1988, 290 p.

Detailed exploration of T. S. Eliot's portrayal of and attitude—conscious and unconscious—toward Jews as seen through his writings.

Roskies, David G. *Against the Apocalypse: Responses to Catastrophe in Modern Jewish Culture.* Cambridge, Mass.: Harvard University Press, 1984, 374 p.

Examines the response of Jewish writers to the Holocaust in the contexts of literature, history, society, and psychology.

How to Use This Index

The main references

Calvino, Italo
1923-1985 .... CLC 5, 8, 11, 22, 33, 39,
73; SSC 3

---

list all author entries in the following Gale Literary Criticism series:

BLC = *Black Literature Criticism*
CLC = *Contemporary Literary Criticism*
CLR = *Children's Literature Review*
CMLC = *Classical and Medieval Literature Criticism*
DA = *DISCovering Authors*
DAB = *DISCovering Authors: British*
DAC = *DISCovering Authors: Canadian*
DAM = *DISCovering Authors: Modules*
      DRAM: Dramatists Module; MST: Most-Studied Authors Module;
      MULT: Multicultural Authors Module; NOV: Novelists Module;
      POET: Poets Module; POP: Popular Fiction and Genre Authors Module
DC = *Drama Criticism*
HLC = *Hispanic Literature Criticism*
LC = *Literature Criticism from 1400 to 1800*
NCLC = *Nineteenth-Century Literature Criticism*
NNAL = *Native North American Literature*
PC = *Poetry Criticism*
SSC = *Short Story Criticism*
TCLC = *Twentieth-Century Literary Criticism*
WLC = *World Literature Criticism, 1500 to the Present*

The cross-references

See also CANR 23; CA 85-88;
obituary CA116

---

list all author entries in the following Gale biographical and literary sources:

AAYA = *Authors & Artists for Young Adults*
AITN = *Authors in the News*
BEST = *Bestsellers*
BW = *Black Writers*
CA = *Contemporary Authors*
CAAS = *Contemporary Authors Autobiography Series*
CABS = *Contemporary Authors Bibliographical Series*
CANR = *Contemporary Authors New Revision Series*
CAP = *Contemporary Authors Permanent Series*
CDALB = *Concise Dictionary of American Literary Biography*
CDBLB = *Concise Dictionary of British Literary Biography*
DLB = *Dictionary of Literary Biography*
DLBD = *Dictionary of Literary Biography Documentary Series*
DLBY = *Dictionary of Literary Biography Yearbook*
HW = *Hispanic Writers*
JRDA = *Junior DISCovering Authors*
MAICYA = *Major Authors and Illustrators for Children and Young Adults*
MTCW = *Major 20th-Century Writers*
SAAS = *Something about the Author Autobiography Series*
SATA = *Something about the Author*
YABC = *Yesterday's Authors of Books for Children*

Literary Criticism Series
Cumulative Author Index

Aiken, Conrad (Potter) 1889-1973 .... **CLC 1, 3, 5, 10, 52; DAM NOV, POET; PC 26; SSC 9**
See also AMW; CA 5-8R; 45-48; CANR 4, 60; CDALB 1929-1941; DLB 9, 45, 102; EXPS; HGG; MTCW 1, 2; RGAL; RGSF; SATA 3, 30; SSFS 8

Aiken, Joan (Delano) 1924- .... **CLC 35**
See also AAYA 1, 25; CA 9-12R, 182; CAAE 182; CANR 4, 23, 34, 64; CLR 1, 19; DLB 161; FANT; HGG; JRDA; MAICYA; MTCW 1; RHW; SAAS 1; SATA 2, 30, 73; SATA-Essay 109; WYA; YAW

Ainsworth, William Harrison 1805-1882 .... **NCLC 13**
See also DLB 21; HGG; RGEL; SATA 24; SUFW

Aitmatov, Chingiz (Torekulovich) 1928- .... **CLC 71**
See also CA 103; CANR 38; MTCW 1; RGSF; SATA 56

Akers, Floyd
See Baum, L(yman) Frank

Akhmadulina, Bella Akhatovna 1937- .... **CLC 53; DAM POET**
See also CA 65-68; CWP; CWW 2

Akhmatova, Anna 1888-1966 ..... **CLC 11, 25, 64, 126; DAM POET; PC 2**
See also CA 19-20; 25-28R; CANR 35; CAP 1; DA3; EW 10; MTCW 1, 2; RGWL

Aksakov, Sergei Timofeyvich 1791-1859 .... **NCLC 2**
See also DLB 198

Aksenov, Vassily
See Aksyonov, Vassily (Pavlovich)

Akst, Daniel 1956- .... **CLC 109**
See also CA 161

Aksyonov, Vassily (Pavlovich) 1932- .... **CLC 22, 37, 101**
See also CA 53-56; CANR 12, 48, 77; CWW 2

Akutagawa Ryunosuke 1892-1927 .... **TCLC 16; SSC 44**
See also CA 117; 154; DLB 180; MJW; RGSF; RGWL

Alain 1868-1951 .... **TCLC 41**
See also CA 163; GFL 1789 to the Present

Alain-Fournier .... **TCLC 6**
See also Fournier, Henri Alban
See also DLB 65; GFL 1789 to the Present; RGWL

Alarcon, Pedro Antonio de 1833-1891 .... **NCLC 1**

Alas (y Urena), Leopoldo (Enrique Garcia) 1852-1901 .... **TCLC 29**
See also CA 113; 131; HW 1; RGSF

Albee, Edward (Franklin III) 1928- . **CLC 1, 2, 3, 5, 9, 11, 13, 25, 53, 86, 113; DA; DAB; DAC; DAM DRAM, MST; DC 11; WLC**
See also AITN 1; AMW; CA 5-8R; CABS 3; CAD; CANR 8, 54, 74; CD; CDALB 1941-1968; DA3; DFS 2, 3, 8, 10, 13; DLB 7; INT CANR-8; LAIT 4; MTCW 1, 2; RGAL; TUS

Alberti, Rafael 1902-1999 .... **CLC 7**
See also CA 85-88; 185; CANR 81; DLB 108; HW 2; RGWL

Albert the Great 1193(?)-1280 ...... **CMLC 16**
See also DLB 115

Alcala-Galiano, Juan Valera y
See Valera y Alcala-Galiano, Juan

Alcayaga, Lucila Godoy
See Godoy Alcayaga, Lucila

Alcott, Amos Bronson 1799-1888 .... **NCLC 1**
See also DLB 1, 223

Alcott, Louisa May 1832-1888 . **NCLC 6, 58, 83; DA; DAB; DAC; DAM MST, NOV; SSC 27; WLC**
See also AAYA 20; AMWS 1; BPFB 1; BYA 2; CDALB 1865-1917; CLR 1, 38; DA3; DLB 1, 42, 79, 223, 239, 242; DLBD 14; FW; JRDA; LAIT 2; MAI-CYA; NFS 12; RGAL; SATA 100; WCH; WYA; YABC 1; YAW

Aldanov, M. A.
See Aldanov, Mark (Alexandrovich)

Aldanov, Mark (Alexandrovich) 1886(?)-1957 .... **TCLC 23**
See also CA 118; 181

Aldington, Richard 1892-1962 .... **CLC 49**
See also CA 85-88; CANR 45; DLB 20, 36, 100, 149; RGEL

Aldiss, Brian W(ilson) 1925- . **CLC 5, 14, 40; DAM NOV; SSC 36**
See also AAYA 42; CA 5-8R; CAAE 190; CAAS 2; CANR 5, 28, 64; CN; DLB 14; MTCW 1, 2; SATA 34; SFW

Alegria, Claribel 1924- .... **CLC 75; DAM MULT; HLCS 1; PC 26**
See also CA 131; CAAS 15; CANR 66, 94; CWW 2; DLB 145; HW 1; MTCW 1

Alegria, Fernando 1918- .... **CLC 57**
See also CA 9-12R; CANR 5, 32, 72; HW 1, 2

Aleichem, Sholom .... **TCLC 1, 35; SSC 33**
See also Rabinovitch, Sholem

Aleixandre, Vicente 1898-1984 ... **TCLC 113; HLCS 1**
See also CANR 81; DLB 108; HW 2; RGWL

Alencon, Marguerite d'
See de Navarre, Marguerite

Alepoudelis, Odysseus
See Elytis, Odysseus
See also CWW 2

Aleshkovsky, Joseph 1929-
See Aleshkovsky, Yuz
See also CA 121; 128

Aleshkovsky, Yuz .... **CLC 44**
See also Aleshkovsky, Joseph

Alexander, Lloyd (Chudley) 1924- ... **CLC 35**
See also AAYA 1, 27; BPFB 1; BYA 5, 6, 7, 9, 10, 11; CA 1-4R; CANR 1, 24, 38, 55; CLR 1, 5, 48; CWRI; DLB 52; FANT; JRDA; MAICYA; MAICYAS; MTCW 1; SAAS 19; SATA 3, 49, 81; SUFW; WYA; YAW

Alexander, Meena 1951- .... **CLC 121**
See also CA 115; CANR 38, 70; CP; CWP; FW

Alexander, Samuel 1859-1938 .... **TCLC 77**

Alexie, Sherman (Joseph, Jr.) 1966- .... **CLC 96, 154; DAM MULT**
See also AAYA 28; CA 138; CANR 95; DA3; DLB 175, 206; MTCW 1; NNAL

Alfau, Felipe 1902-1999 .... **CLC 66**
See also CA 137

Alfieri, Vittorio 1749-1803 .... **NCLC 101**
See also EW 4; RGWL

Alfred, Jean Gaston
See Ponge, Francis

Alger, Horatio, Jr. 1832-1899 .... **NCLC 8, 83**
See also DLB 42; LAIT 2; RGAL; SATA 16; TUS

Al-Ghazali, Muhammad ibn Muhammad 1058-1111 .... **CMLC 50**
See also DLB 115

Algren, Nelson 1909-1981 ..... **CLC 4, 10, 33; SSC 33**
See also AMWS 9; BPFB 1; CA 13-16R; 103; CANR 20, 61; CDALB 1941-1968; DLB 9; DLBY 81, 82, 00; MTCW 1, 2; RGAL; RGSF

Ali, Ahmed 1908-1998 .... **CLC 69**
See also CA 25-28R; CANR 15, 34

Alighieri, Dante
See Dante

Allan, John B.
See Westlake, Donald E(dwin)

Allan, Sidney
See Hartmann, Sadakichi

Allan, Sydney
See Hartmann, Sadakichi

Allard, Janet .... **CLC 59**

Allen, Edward 1948- .... **CLC 59**

Allen, Fred 1894-1956 .... **TCLC 87**

Allen, Paula Gunn 1939- .... **CLC 84; DAM MULT**
See also AMWS 4; CA 112; 143; CANR 63; CWP; DA3; DLB 175; FW; MTCW 1; NNAL; RGAL

Allen, Roland
See Ayckbourn, Alan

Allen, Sarah A.
See Hopkins, Pauline Elizabeth

Allen, Sidney H.
See Hartmann, Sadakichi

Allen, Woody 1935- .... **CLC 16, 52; DAM POP**
See also AAYA 10; CA 33-36R; CANR 27, 38, 63; DLB 44; MTCW 1

Allende, Isabel 1942- . **CLC 39, 57, 97; DAM MULT, NOV; HLC 1; WLCS**
See also AAYA 18; CA 125; 130; CANR 51, 74; CWW 2; DA3; DLB 145; DNFS; FW; HW 1, 2; INT CA-130; LAIT 5; LAWS 1; MTCW 1, 2; NCFS 1; NFS 6; RGSF; SSFS 11; WLIT 1

Alleyn, Ellen
See Rossetti, Christina (Georgina)

Alleyne, Carla D. .... **CLC 65**

Allingham, Margery (Louise) 1904-1966 .... **CLC 19**
See also CA 5-8R; 25-28R; CANR 4, 58; CMW; DLB 77; MSW; MTCW 1, 2

Allingham, William 1824-1889 ...... **NCLC 25**
See also DLB 35; RGEL

Allison, Dorothy E. 1949- .... **CLC 78, 153**
See also CA 140; CANR 66; CSW; DA3; FW; MTCW 1; NFS 11; RGAL

Alloula, Malek .... **CLC 65**

Allston, Washington 1779-1843 .... **NCLC 2**
See also DLB 1, 235

Almedingen, E. M. .... **CLC 12**
See also Almedingen, Martha Edith von
See also SATA 3

Almedingen, Martha Edith von 1898-1971
See Almedingen, E. M.
See also CA 1-4R; CANR 1

Almodovar, Pedro 1949(?)- .... **CLC 114; HLCS 1**
See also CA 133; CANR 72; HW 2

Almqvist, Carl Jonas Love 1793-1866 .... **NCLC 42**

Alonso, Damaso 1898-1990 .... **CLC 14**
See also CA 110; 131; 130; CANR 72; DLB 108; HW 1, 2

Alov
See Gogol, Nikolai (Vasilyevich)

Alta 1942- .... **CLC 19**
See also CA 57-60

Alter, Robert B(ernard) 1935- .... **CLC 34**
See also CA 49-52; CANR 1, 47, 100

Alther, Lisa 1944- .... **CLC 7, 41**
See also BPFB 1; CA 65-68; CAAS 30; CANR 12, 30, 51; CN; CSW; GLL 2; MTCW 1

Althusser, L.
See Althusser, Louis

Althusser, Louis 1918-1990 .... **CLC 106**
    See also CA 131; 132; CANR 102; DLB 242

Altman, Robert 1925- .... **CLC 16, 116**
    See also CA 73-76; CANR 43

Alurista
    See Urista, Alberto H.
    See also DLB 82; HLCS 1

Alvarez, A(lfred) 1929- .... **CLC 5, 13**
    See also CA 1-4R; CANR 3, 33, 63, 101; CN; CP; DLB 14, 40

Alvarez, Alejandro Rodriguez 1903-1965
    See Casona, Alejandro
    See also CA 131; 93-96; HW 1

Alvarez, Julia 1950- .... **CLC 93; HLCS 1**
    See also AAYA 25; AMWS 7; CA 147; CANR 69, 101; DA3; MTCW 1; NFS 5, 9; WLIT 1

Alvaro, Corrado 1896-1956 .... **TCLC 60**
    See also CA 163

Amado, Jorge 1912-2001 ... **CLC 13, 40, 106; DAM MULT, NOV; HLC 1**
    See also CA 77-80; CANR 35, 74; DLB 113; HW 2; LAW; LAWS 1; MTCW 1, 2; RGWL; WLIT 1

Ambler, Eric 1909-1998 .... **CLC 4, 6, 9**
    See also BRWS 4; CA 9-12R; 171; CANR 7, 38, 74; CMW; CN; DLB 77; MSW; MTCW 1, 2

Ambrose, Stephen E(dward)
    1936- .... **CLC 145**
    See also CA 1-4R; CANR 3, 43, 57, 83, 105; NCFS 2; SATA 40

Amichai, Yehuda 1924-2000 .. **CLC 9, 22, 57, 116; PC 38**
    See also CA 85-88; 189; CANR 46, 60, 99; CWW 2; MTCW 1

Amichai, Yehudah
    See Amichai, Yehuda

Amiel, Henri Frederic 1821-1881 .... **NCLC 4**
    See also DLB 217

Amis, Kingsley (William)
    1922-1995 ...... **CLC 1, 2, 3, 5, 8, 13, 40, 44, 129; DA; DAB; DAC; DAM MST, NOV**
    See also AITN 2; BPFB 1; BRWS 2; CA 9-12R; 150; CANR 8, 28, 54; CDBLB 1945-1960; CN; CP; DA3; DLB 15, 27, 100, 139; DLBY 96; HGG; INT CANR-8; MTCW 1, 2; RGEL; RGSF; SFW

Amis, Martin (Louis) 1949- .... **CLC 4, 9, 38, 62, 101**
    See also BEST 90:3; BRWS 4; CA 65-68; CANR 8, 27, 54, 73, 95; CN; DA3; DLB 14, 194; INT CANR-27; MTCW 1

Ammons, A(rchie) R(andolph)
    1926-2001 ...... **CLC 2, 3, 5, 8, 9, 25, 57, 108; DAM POET; PC 16**
    See also AITN 1; AMWS 7; CA 9-12R; 193; CANR 6, 36, 51, 73; CP; CSW; DLB 5, 165; MTCW 1, 2; RGAL

Amo, Tauraatua i
    See Adams, Henry (Brooks)

Amory, Thomas 1691(?)-1788 .... **LC 48**
    See also DLB 39

Anand, Mulk Raj 1905- .. **CLC 23, 93; DAM NOV**
    See also CA 65-68; CANR 32, 64; CN; MTCW 1, 2; RGSF

Anatol
    See Schnitzler, Arthur

Anaximander c. 611B.C.-c.
    546B.C. .... **CMLC 22**

Anaya, Rudolfo A(lfonso) 1937- ...... **CLC 23, 148; DAM MULT, NOV; HLC 1**
    See also AAYA 20; BYA 13; CA 45-48; CAAS 4; CANR 1, 32, 51; CN; DLB 82, 206; HW 1; LAIT 4; MTCW 1, 2; NFS 12; RGAL; RGSF; WLIT 1

Andersen, Hans Christian
    1805-1875 .... **NCLC 7, 79; DA; DAB; DAC; DAM MST, POP; SSC 6; WLC**
    See also CLR 6; DA3; EW 6; MAICYA; RGSF; RGWL; SATA 100; WCH; YABC 1

Anderson, C. Farley
    See Mencken, H(enry) L(ouis); Nathan, George Jean

Anderson, Jessica (Margaret) Queale
    1916- .... **CLC 37**
    See also CA 9-12R; CANR 4, 62; CN

Anderson, Jon (Victor) 1940- . **CLC 9; DAM POET**
    See also CA 25-28R; CANR 20

Anderson, Lindsay (Gordon)
    1923-1994 .... **CLC 20**
    See also CA 125; 128; 146; CANR 77

Anderson, Maxwell 1888-1959 .... **TCLC 2; DAM DRAM**
    See also CA 105; 152; DLB 7, 228; MTCW 2; RGAL

Anderson, Poul (William)
    1926-2001 .... **CLC 15**
    See also AAYA 5, 34; BPFB 1; BYA 6, 8, 9; CA 1-4R, 181; CAAE 181; CAAS 2; CANR 2, 15, 34, 64; CLR 58; DLB 8; FANT; INT CANR-15; MTCW 1, 2; SATA 90; SATA-Brief 39; SATA-Essay 106; SCFW 2; SFW; SUFW

Anderson, Robert (Woodruff)
    1917- .... **CLC 23; DAM DRAM**
    See also AITN 1; CA 21-24R; CANR 32; DLB 7; LAIT 5

Anderson, Roberta Joan
    See Mitchell, Joni

Anderson, Sherwood 1876-1941 ..... **TCLC 1, 10, 24; DA; DAB; DAC; DAM MST, NOV; SSC 1, 46; WLC**
    See also AAYA 30; AMW; BPFB 1; CA 104; 121; CANR 61; CDALB 1917-1929; DA3; DLB 4, 9, 86; DLBD 1; EXPS; GLL 2; MTCW 1, 2; NFS 4; RGAL; RGSF; SSFS 4, 10, 11

Andier, Pierre
    See Desnos, Robert

Andouard
    See Giraudoux, Jean(-Hippolyte)

Andrade, Carlos Drummond de ..... **CLC 18**
    See also Drummond de Andrade, Carlos
    See also RGWL

Andrade, Mario de .... **TCLC 43**
    See also de Andrade, Mario
    See also LAW; RGWL; WLIT 1

Andreae, Johann V(alentin)
    1586-1654 .... **LC 32**
    See also DLB 164

Andreas Capellanus fl. c. 1185- .... **CMLC 45**
    See also DLB 208

Andreas-Salome, Lou 1861-1937 ... **TCLC 56**
    See also CA 178; DLB 66

Andress, Lesley
    See Sanders, Lawrence

Andrewes, Lancelot 1555-1626 .... **LC 5**
    See also DLB 151, 172

Andrews, Cicily Fairfield
    See West, Rebecca

Andrews, Elton V.
    See Pohl, Frederik

Andreyev, Leonid (Nikolaevich)
    1871-1919 .... **TCLC 3**
    See also CA 104; 185

Andric, Ivo 1892-1975 .... **CLC 8; SSC 36**
    See also CA 81-84; 57-60; CANR 43, 60; DLB 147; EW 11; MTCW 1; RGSF; RGWL

Androvar
    See Prado (Calvo), Pedro

Angelique, Pierre
    See Bataille, Georges

Angell, Roger 1920- .... **CLC 26**
    See also CA 57-60; CANR 13, 44, 70; DLB 171, 185

Angelou, Maya 1928- ..... **CLC 12, 35, 64, 77, 155; BLC 1; DA; DAB; DAC; DAM MST, MULT, POET, POP; PC 32; WLCS**
    See also AAYA 7, 20; AMWS 4; BPFB 1; BW 2, 3; BYA 2; CA 65-68; CANR 19, 42, 65; CDALBS; CLR 53; CP; CPW; CSW; CWP; DA3; DLB 38; EXPN; EXPP; LAIT 4; MAICYAS; MAWW; MTCW 1, 2; NCFS 2; NFS 2; PFS 2, 3; RGAL; SATA 49; WYA; YAW

Angouleme, Marguerite d'
    See de Navarre, Marguerite

Anna Comnena 1083-1153 .... **CMLC 25**

Annensky, Innokenty (Fyodorovich)
    1856-1909 .... **TCLC 14**
    See also CA 110; 155

Annunzio, Gabriele d'
    See D'Annunzio, Gabriele

Anodos
    See Coleridge, Mary E(lizabeth)

Anon, Charles Robert
    See Pessoa, Fernando (Antonio Nogueira)

Anouilh, Jean (Marie Lucien Pierre)
    1910-1987 .... **CLC 1, 3, 8, 13, 40, 50; DAM DRAM; DC 8**
    See also CA 17-20R; 123; CANR 32; DFS 9, 10; EW 13; GFL 1789 to the Present; MTCW 1, 2; RGWL

Anthony, Florence
    See Ai

Anthony, John
    See Ciardi, John (Anthony)

Anthony, Peter
    See Shaffer, Anthony (Joshua); Shaffer, Peter (Levin)

Anthony, Piers 1934- .... **CLC 35; DAM POP**
    See also AAYA 11; BYA 7; CA 21-24R; CANR 28, 56, 73, 102; CPW; DLB 8; FANT; MAICYAS; MTCW 1, 2; SAAS 22; SATA 84; SFW; SUFW; YAW

Anthony, Susan B(rownell)
    1820-1906 .... **TCLC 84**
    See also FW

Antoine, Marc
    See Proust, (Valentin-Louis-George-Eugene-)Marcel

Antoninus, Brother
    See Everson, William (Oliver)

Antonioni, Michelangelo 1912- .... **CLC 20, 144**
    See also CA 73-76; CANR 45, 77

Antschel, Paul 1920-1970
    See Celan, Paul
    See also CA 85-88; CANR 33, 61; MTCW 1

Anwar, Chairil 1922-1949 .... **TCLC 22**
    See also CA 121

Anzaldua, Gloria (Evanjelina) 1942-
    See also CA 175; CSW; CWP; DLB 122; FW; HLCS 1; RGAL

Apess, William 1798-1839(?) .... **NCLC 73; DAM MULT**
    See also DLB 175, 243; NNAL

Apollinaire, Guillaume 1880-1918 .. **TCLC 3, 8, 51; DAM POET; PC 7**
    See also CA 152; EW 9; GFL 1789 to the Present; MTCW 1; RGWL; WP

Apollonius of Rhodes
    See Apollonius Rhodius
    See also AW 1; RGWL

Apollonius Rhodius c. 300B.C.-c.
　220B.C. .... **CMLC 28**
　See also Apollonius of Rhodes
　See also DLB 176

Appelfeld, Aharon 1932- ... **CLC 23, 47; SSC
　42**
　See also CA 112; 133; CANR 86; CWW 2;
　RGSF

Apple, Max (Isaac) 1941- .... **CLC 9, 33; SSC
　50**
　See also CA 81-84; CANR 19, 54; DLB
　130

Appleman, Philip (Dean) 1926- .... **CLC 51**
　See also CA 13-16R; CAAS 18; CANR 6,
　29, 56

Appleton, Lawrence
　See Lovecraft, H(oward) P(hillips)

Apteryx
　See Eliot, T(homas) S(tearns)

Apuleius, (Lucius Madaurensis)
　125(?)-175(?) .... **CMLC 1**
　See also AW 2; DLB 211; RGWL; SUFW

Aquin, Hubert 1929-1977 .... **CLC 15**
　See also CA 105; DLB 53

Aquinas, Thomas 1224(?)-1274 ..... **CMLC 33**
　See also DLB 115; EW 1

Aragon, Louis 1897-1982 .. **CLC 3, 22; DAM
　NOV, POET**
　See also CA 69-72; 108; CANR 28, 71;
　DLB 72; EW 11; GFL 1789 to the Present;
　GLL 2; MTCW 1, 2; RGWL

Arany, Janos 1817-1882 .... **NCLC 34**

Aranyos, Kakay 1847-1910
　See Mikszath, Kalman

Arbuthnot, John 1667-1735 .... **LC 1**
　See also DLB 101

Archer, Herbert Winslow
　See Mencken, H(enry) L(ouis)

Archer, Jeffrey (Howard) 1940- ...... **CLC 28;
　DAM POP**
　See also AAYA 16; BEST 89:3; BPFB 1;
　CA 77-80; CANR 22, 52, 95; CPW; DA3;
　INT CANR-22

Archer, Jules 1915- .... **CLC 12**
　See also CA 9-12R; CANR 6, 69; SAAS 5;
　SATA 4, 85

Archer, Lee
　See Ellison, Harlan (Jay)

Archilochus c. 7th cent. B.C.- .... **CMLC 44**
　See also DLB 176

Arden, John 1930- .... **CLC 6, 13, 15; DAM
　DRAM**
　See also BRWS 2; CA 13-16R; CAAS 4;
　CANR 31, 65, 67; CBD; CD; DFS 9;
　DLB 13, 245; MTCW 1

Arenas, Reinaldo 1943-1990 . **CLC 41; DAM
　MULT; HLC 1**
　See also CA 124; 128; 133; CANR 73, 106;
　DLB 145; GLL 2; HW 1; LAW; LAWS 1;
　MTCW 1; RGSF; WLIT 1

Arendt, Hannah 1906-1975 .... **CLC 66, 98**
　See also CA 17-20R; 61-64; CANR 26, 60;
　DLB 242; MTCW 1, 2

Aretino, Pietro 1492-1556 .... **LC 12**
　See also RGWL

Arghezi, Tudor .... **CLC 80**
　See also Theodorescu, Ion N.
　See also CA 167; DLB 220

Arguedas, Jose Maria 1911-1969 .... **CLC 10,
　18; HLCS 1**
　See also CA 89-92; CANR 73; DLB 113;
　HW 1; LAW; RGWL; WLIT 1

Argueta, Manlio 1936- .... **CLC 31**
　See also CA 131; CANR 73; CWW 2; DLB
　145; HW 1

Arias, Ron(ald Francis) 1941-
　See also CA 131; CANR 81; DAM MULT;
　DLB 82; HLC 1; HW 1, 2; MTCW 2

Ariosto, Ludovico 1474-1533 .... **LC 6**
　See also EW 2; RGWL

Aristides
　See Epstein, Joseph

Aristophanes 450B.C.-385B.C. .... **CMLC 4;
　DA; DAB; DAC; DAM DRAM, MST;
　DC 2; WLCS**
　See also AW 1; DA3; DFS 10; DLB 176;
　RGWL

Aristotle 384B.C.-322B.C. .... **CMLC 31; DA;
　DAB; DAC; DAM MST; WLCS**
　See also AW 1; DA3; DLB 176; RGEL

Arlt, Roberto (Godofredo Christophersen)
　1900-1942 .... **TCLC 29; DAM MULT;
　HLC 1**
　See also CA 123; 131; CANR 67; HW 1, 2;
　LAW

Armah, Ayi Kwei 1939- .... **CLC 5, 33, 136;
　BLC 1; DAM MULT, POET**
　See also AFW; BW 1; CA 61-64; CANR
　21, 64; CN; DLB 117; MTCW 1; WLIT 2

Armatrading, Joan 1950- .... **CLC 17**
　See also CA 114; 186

Arnette, Robert
　See Silverberg, Robert

**Arnim, Achim von (Ludwig Joachim von
　Arnim)** 1781-1831 ..... **NCLC 5; SSC 29**
　See also DLB 90

Arnim, Bettina von 1785-1859 .... **NCLC 38**
　See also DLB 90; RGWL

Arnold, Matthew 1822-1888 ..... **NCLC 6, 29,
　89; DA; DAB; DAC; DAM MST,
　POET; PC 5; WLC**
　See also BRW 5; CDBLB 1832-1890; DLB
　32, 57; EXPP; PAB; PFS 2; WP

Arnold, Thomas 1795-1842 .... **NCLC 18**
　See also DLB 55

Arnow, Harriette (Louisa) Simpson
　1908-1986 .... **CLC 2, 7, 18**
　See also BPFB 1; CA 9-12R; 118; CANR
　14; DLB 6; FW; MTCW 1, 2; RHW;
　SATA 42; SATA-Obit 47

Arouet, Francois-Marie
　See Voltaire

Arp, Hans
　See Arp, Jean

Arp, Jean 1887-1966 .... **CLC 5**
　See also CA 81-84; 25-28R; CANR 42, 77;
　EW 10; TCLC 115

Arrabal
　See Arrabal, Fernando

Arrabal, Fernando 1932- ... **CLC 2, 9, 18, 58**
　See also CA 9-12R; CANR 15

Arreola, Juan Jose 1918- .... **CLC 147; DAM
　MULT; HLC 1; SSC 38**
　See also CA 113; 131; CANR 81; DLB 113;
　DNFS; HW 1, 2; LAW; RGSF

Arrian c. 89(?)-c. 155(?) .... **CMLC 43**
　See also DLB 176

Arrick, Fran .... **CLC 30**
　See also Gaberman, Judie Angell
　See also BYA 6

Artaud, Antonin (Marie Joseph)
　1896-1948 . **TCLC 3, 36; DAM DRAM;
　DC 14**
　See also CA 104; 149; DA3; EW 11; GFL
　1789 to the Present; MTCW 1; RGWL

Arthur, Ruth M(abel) 1905-1979 ..... **CLC 12**
　See also CA 9-12R; 85-88; CANR 4; CWRI;
　SATA 7, 26

Artsybashev, Mikhail (Petrovich)
　1878-1927 .... **TCLC 31**
　See also CA 170

Arundel, Honor (Morfydd)
　1919-1973 .... **CLC 17**
　See also CA 21-22; 41-44R; CAP 2; CLR
　35; CWRI; SATA 4; SATA-Obit 24

Arzner, Dorothy 1900-1979 .... **CLC 98**

Asch, Sholem 1880-1957 .... **TCLC 3**
　See also CA 105; GLL 2

Ash, Shalom
　See Asch, Sholem

Ashbery, John (Lawrence) 1927- ... **CLC 2, 3,
　4, 6, 9, 13, 15, 25, 41, 77, 125; DAM
　POET; PC 26**
　See also Berry, Jonas
　See also AMWS 3; CA 5-8R; CANR 9, 37,
　66, 102; CP; DA3; DLB 5, 165; DLBY
　81; INT CANR-9; MTCW 1, 2; PAB; PFS
　11; RGAL; WP

Ashdown, Clifford
　See Freeman, R(ichard) Austin

Ashe, Gordon
　See Creasey, John

Ashton-Warner, Sylvia (Constance)
　1908-1984 .... **CLC 19**
　See also CA 69-72; 112; CANR 29; MTCW
　1, 2

Asimov, Isaac 1920-1992 ..... **CLC 1, 3, 9, 19,
　26, 76, 92; DAM POP**
　See also AAYA 13; BEST 90:2; BPFB 1;
　BYA 4, 6, 7, 9; CA 1-4R; 137; CANR 2,
　19, 36, 60; CLR 12; CMW; CPW; DA3;
　DLB 8; DLBY 92; INT CANR-19; JRDA;
　LAIT 5; MAICYA; MTCW 1, 2; RGAL;
　SATA 1, 26, 74; SCFW 2; SFW; YAW

Assis, Joaquim Maria Machado de
　See Machado de Assis, Joaquim Maria

Astell, Mary 1666-1731 .... **LC 68**
　See also DLB 252; FW

Astley, Thea (Beatrice May) 1925- .. **CLC 41**
　See also CA 65-68; CANR 11, 43, 78; CN

Astley, William 1855-1911
　See Warung, Price

Aston, James
　See White, T(erence) H(anbury)

Asturias, Miguel Angel 1899-1974 .... **CLC 3,
　8, 13; DAM MULT, NOV; HLC 1**
　See also CA 25-28; 49-52; CANR 32; CAP
　2; DA3; DLB 113; HW 1; LAW; MTCW
　1, 2; RGWL; WLIT 1

Atares, Carlos Saura
　See Saura (Atares), Carlos

Athanasius c. 295-c. 373 .... **CMLC 48**

Atheling, William
　See Pound, Ezra (Weston Loomis)

Atheling, William, Jr.
　See Blish, James (Benjamin)

Atherton, Gertrude (Franklin Horn)
　1857-1948 .... **TCLC 2**
　See also CA 104; 155; DLB 9, 78, 186;
　HGG; RGAL; SUFW; TCWW 2

Atherton, Lucius
　See Masters, Edgar Lee

Atkins, Jack
　See Harris, Mark

Atkinson, Kate .... **CLC 99**
　See also CA 166; CANR 101

Attaway, William (Alexander)
　1911-1986 .... **CLC 92; BLC 1; DAM
　MULT**
　See also BW 2, 3; CA 143; CANR 82; DLB
　76

Atticus
　See Fleming, Ian (Lancaster); Wilson,
　(Thomas) Woodrow

Atwood, Margaret (Eleanor) 1939- ... **CLC 2,
　3, 4, 8, 13, 15, 25, 44, 84, 135; DA;
　DAB; DAC; DAM MST, NOV, POET;
　PC 8; SSC 2, 46; WLC**
　See also AAYA 12; BEST 89:2; BPFB 1;
　CA 49-52; CANR 3, 24, 33, 59, 95; CN;
　CP; CPW; CWP; DA3; DLB 53, 251;
　EXPN; FW; INT CANR-24; LAIT 5;
　MTCW 1, 2; NFS 4, 12, 13; PFS 7;
　RGSF; SATA 50; SSFS 3, 13; YAW

Aubigny, Pierre d'
See Mencken, H(enry) L(ouis)

Aubin, Penelope 1685-1731(?) .... **LC 9**
See also DLB 39

Auchincloss, Louis (Stanton) 1917- .. **CLC 4, 6, 9, 18, 45; DAM NOV; SSC 22**
See also AMWS 4; CA 1-4R; CANR 6, 29, 55, 87; CN; DLB 2, 244; DLBY 80; INT CANR-29; MTCW 1; RGAL

Auden, W(ystan) H(ugh) 1907-1973 . **CLC 1, 2, 3, 4, 6, 9, 11, 14, 43, 123; DA; DAB; DAC; DAM DRAM, MST, POET; PC 1; WLC**
See also AAYA 18; AMWS 2; BRW 7; BRWR 1; CA 9-12R; 45-48; CANR 5, 61, 105; CDBLB 1914-1945; DA3; DLB 10, 20; EXPP; MTCW 1, 2; PAB; PFS 1, 3, 4, 10; WP

Audiberti, Jacques 1900-1965 .... **CLC 38; DAM DRAM**
See also CA 25-28R

Audubon, John James 1785-1851 . **NCLC 47**
See also ANW; DLB 248

Auel, Jean M(arie) 1936- .... **CLC 31, 107; DAM POP**
See also AAYA 7; BEST 90:4; BPFB 1; CA 103; CANR 21, 64; CPW; DA3; INT CANR-21; NFS 11; RHW; SATA 91

Auerbach, Erich 1892-1957 .... **TCLC 43**
See also CA 118; 155

Augier, Emile 1820-1889 .... **NCLC 31**
See also DLB 192; GFL 1789 to the Present

August, John
See De Voto, Bernard (Augustine)

Augustine, St. 354-430 .... **CMLC 6; DA; DAB; DAC; DAM MST; WLCS**
See also DA3; DLB 115; EW 1; RGWL

Aunt Belinda
See Braddon, Mary Elizabeth

Aurelius
See Bourne, Randolph S(illiman)

Aurelius, Marcus 121-180 .... **CMLC 45**
See also Marcus Aurelius
See also RGWL

Aurobindo, Sri
See Ghose, Aurabinda

Austen, Jane 1775-1817 ...... **NCLC 1, 13, 19, 33, 51, 81, 95; DA; DAB; DAC; DAM MST, NOV; WLC**
See also AAYA 19; BRW 4; BRWR 2; BYA 3; CDBLB 1789-1832; DA3; DLB 116; EXPN; LAIT 2; NFS 1; WLIT 3; WYAS 1

Auster, Paul 1947- .... **CLC 47, 131**
See also CA 69-72; CANR 23, 52, 75; CMW; CN; DA3; DLB 227; MTCW 1

Austin, Frank
See Faust, Frederick (Schiller)
See also TCWW 2

Austin, Mary (Hunter) 1868-1934 . **TCLC 25**
See also Stairs, Gordon
See also ANW; CA 109; 178; DLB 9, 78, 206, 221; FW; TCWW 2

Averroes 1126-1198 .... **CMLC 7**
See also DLB 115

Avicenna 980-1037 .... **CMLC 16**
See also DLB 115

Avison, Margaret 1918- .... **CLC 2, 4, 97; DAC; DAM POET**
See also CA 17-20R; CP; DLB 53; MTCW 1

Axton, David
See Koontz, Dean R(ay)

Ayckbourn, Alan 1939- ...... **CLC 5, 8, 18, 33, 74; DAB; DAM DRAM; DC 13**
See also BRWS 5; CA 21-24R; CANR 31, 59; CBD; CD; DFS 7; DLB 13, 245; MTCW 1, 2

Aydy, Catherine
See Tennant, Emma (Christina)

Ayme, Marcel (Andre) 1902-1967 ... **CLC 11; SSC 41**
See also CA 89-92; CANR 67; CLR 25; DLB 72; EW 12; GFL 1789 to the Present; RGSF; RGWL; SATA 91

Ayrton, Michael 1921-1975 .... **CLC 7**
See also CA 5-8R; 61-64; CANR 9, 21

Azorin .... **CLC 11**
See also Martinez Ruiz, Jose
See also EW 9

Azuela, Mariano 1873-1952 . **TCLC 3; DAM MULT; HLC 1**
See also CA 104; 131; CANR 81; HW 1, 2; LAW; MTCW 1, 2

Baastad, Babbis Friis
See Friis-Baastad, Babbis Ellinor

Bab
See Gilbert, W(illiam) S(chwenck)

Babbis, Eleanor
See Friis-Baastad, Babbis Ellinor

Babel, Isaac
See Babel, Isaak (Emmanuilovich)
See also EW 11; SSFS 10

Babel, Isaak (Emmanuilovich) 1894-1941(?) .... **TCLC 2, 13; SSC 16**
See also Babel, Isaac
See also CA 104; 155; MTCW 1; RGSF; RGWL

Babits, Mihaly 1883-1941 .... **TCLC 14**
See also CA 114; DLB 215

Babur 1483-1530 .... **LC 18**

Babylas 1898-1962
See Ghelderode, Michel de

Baca, Jimmy Santiago 1952-
See also CA 131; CANR 81, 90; CP; DAM MULT; DLB 122; HLC 1; HW 1, 2

Bacchelli, Riccardo 1891-1985 .... **CLC 19**
See also CA 29-32R; 117

Bach, Richard (David) 1936- .... **CLC 14; DAM NOV, POP**
See also AITN 1; BEST 89:2; BPFB 1; BYA 5; CA 9-12R; CANR 18, 93; CPW; FANT; MTCW 1; SATA 13

Bache, Benjamin Franklin 1769-1798 .... **LC 74**
See also DLB 43

Bachman, Richard
See King, Stephen (Edwin)

Bachmann, Ingeborg 1926-1973 .... **CLC 69**
See also CA 93-96; 45-48; CANR 69; DLB 85; RGWL

Bacon, Francis 1561-1626 .... **LC 18, 32**
See also BRW 1; CDBLB Before 1660; DLB 151, 236, 252; RGEL

Bacon, Roger 1214(?)-1294 .... **CMLC 14**
See also DLB 115

Bacovia, George 1881-1957 .... **TCLC 24**
See also Vasiliu, Gheorghe
See also DLB 220

Badanes, Jerome 1937- .... **CLC 59**

Bagehot, Walter 1826-1877 .... **NCLC 10**
See also DLB 55

Bagnold, Enid 1889-1981 ...... **CLC 25; DAM DRAM**
See also BYA 2; CA 5-8R; 103; CANR 5, 40; CBD; CWD; CWRI; DLB 13, 160, 191, 245; FW; MAICYA; RGEL; SATA 1, 25

Bagritsky, Eduard 1895-1934 .... **TCLC 60**

Bagrjana, Elisaveta
See Belcheva, Elisaveta

Bagryana, Elisaveta .... **CLC 10**
See also Belcheva, Elisaveta
See also CA 178; DLB 147

Bailey, Paul 1937- .... **CLC 45**
See also CA 21-24R; CANR 16, 62; CN; DLB 14; GLL 2

Baillie, Joanna 1762-1851 .... **NCLC 71**
See also DLB 93; RGEL

Bainbridge, Beryl (Margaret) 1934- . **CLC 4, 5, 8, 10, 14, 18, 22, 62, 130; DAM NOV**
See also BRWS 6; CA 21-24R; CANR 24, 55, 75, 88; CN; DLB 14, 231; MTCW 1, 2

Baker, Carlos (Heard) .... **TCLC 119**
See also CA 5-8R; 122; CANR 3, 63; DLB 103

Baker, Elliott 1922- .... **CLC 8**
See also CA 45-48; CANR 2, 63; CN

Baker, Jean H. .... **TCLC 3, 10**
See also Russell, George William

Baker, Nicholson 1957- .... **CLC 61; DAM POP**
See also CA 135; CANR 63; CN; CPW; DA3; DLB 227

Baker, Ray Stannard 1870-1946 .... **TCLC 47**
See also CA 118

Baker, Russell (Wayne) 1925- .... **CLC 31**
See also BEST 89:4; CA 57-60; CANR 11, 41, 59; MTCW 1, 2

Bakhtin, M.
See Bakhtin, Mikhail Mikhailovich

Bakhtin, M. M.
See Bakhtin, Mikhail Mikhailovich

Bakhtin, Mikhail
See Bakhtin, Mikhail Mikhailovich

Bakhtin, Mikhail Mikhailovich 1895-1975 .... **CLC 83**
See also CA 128; 113; DLB 242

Bakshi, Ralph 1938(?)- .... **CLC 26**
See also CA 112; 138; IDFW 3

Bakunin, Mikhail (Alexandrovich) 1814-1876 .... **NCLC 25, 58**

Baldwin, James (Arthur) 1924-1987 . **CLC 1, 2, 3, 4, 5, 8, 13, 15, 17, 42, 50, 67, 90, 127; BLC 1; DA; DAB; DAC; DAM MST, MULT, NOV, POP; DC 1; SSC 10, 33; WLC**
See also AAYA 4, 34; AFAW 1, 2; AMWS 1; BW 1; CA 1-4R; 124; CABS 1; CAD; CANR 3, 24; CDALB 1941-1968; CPW; DA3; DFS 11; DLB 2, 7, 33, 249; DLBY 87; EXPS; LAIT 5; MTCW 1, 2; NFS 4; RGAL; RGSF; SATA 9; SATA-Obit 54; SSFS 2

Bale, John 1495-1563 .... **LC 62**
See also DLB 132; RGEL

Ball, Hugo 1886-1927 .... **TCLC 104**

Ballard, J(ames) G(raham) 1930- . **CLC 3, 6, 14, 36, 137; DAM NOV, POP; SSC 1**
See also AAYA 3; BRWS 5; CA 5-8R; CANR 15, 39, 65; CN; DA3; DLB 14, 207; HGG; MTCW 1, 2; NFS 8; RGEL; RGSF; SATA 93; SFW

Balmont, Konstantin (Dmitriyevich) 1867-1943 .... **TCLC 11**
See also CA 109; 155

Baltausis, Vincas 1847-1910
See Mikszath, Kalman

Balzac, Honore de 1799-1850 ... **NCLC 5, 35, 53; DA; DAB; DAC; DAM MST, NOV; SSC 5; WLC**
See also DA3; DLB 119; EW 5; GFL 1789 to the Present; RGSF; RGWL; SSFS 10; SUFW

Bambara, Toni Cade 1939-1995 ...... **CLC 19, 88; BLC 1; DA; DAC; DAM MST, MULT; SSC 35; WLCS**
See also AAYA 5; AFAW 2; BW 2, 3; BYA 12, 14; CA 29-32R; 150; CANR 24, 49, 81; CDALBS; DA3; DLB 38, 218; EXPS; MTCW 1, 2; RGAL; RGSF; SATA 112; SSFS 4, 7, 12; TCLC 116

Bamdad, A.
See Shamlu, Ahmad

Banat, D. R.
See Bradbury, Ray (Douglas)

Bancroft, Laura
See Baum, L(yman) Frank

Banim, John 1798-1842 .... **NCLC 13**
See also DLB 116, 158, 159; RGEL

Banim, Michael 1796-1874 .... **NCLC 13**
See also DLB 158, 159

Banjo, The
See Paterson, A(ndrew) B(arton)

Banks, Iain
See Banks, Iain M(enzies)

Banks, Iain M(enzies) 1954- .... **CLC 34**
See also CA 123; 128; CANR 61, 106; DLB 194; HGG; INT 128; SFW

Banks, Lynne Reid .... **CLC 23**
See Reid Banks, Lynne
See also AAYA 6; BYA 7

Banks, Russell 1940- .... **CLC 37, 72; SSC 42**
See also AMWS 5; CA 65-68; CAAS 15; CANR 19, 52, 73; CN; DLB 130; NFS 13

Banville, John 1945- .... **CLC 46, 118**
See also CA 117; 128; CANR 104; CN; DLB 14; INT 128

Banville, Theodore (Faullain) de
1832-1891 .... **NCLC 9**
See also DLB 217; GFL 1789 to the Present

Baraka, Amiri 1934- . **CLC 1, 2, 3, 5, 10, 14, 33, 115; BLC 1; DA; DAC; DAM MST, MULT, POET, POP; DC 6; PC 4; WLCS**
See also Jones, LeRoi
See also AFAW 1, 2; AMWS 2; BW 2, 3; CA 21-24R; CABS 3; CAD; CANR 27, 38, 61; CD; CDALB 1941-1968; CP; CPW; DA3; DFS 3, 11; DLB 5, 7, 16, 38; DLBD 8; MTCW 1, 2; PFS 9; RGAL; WP

Baratynsky, Evgenii Abramovich
1800-1844 .... **NCLC 103**
See also DLB 205

Barbauld, Anna Laetitia
1743-1825 .... **NCLC 50**
See also DLB 107, 109, 142, 158; RGEL

Barbellion, W. N. P. .... **TCLC 24**
See also Cummings, Bruce F(rederick)

Barber, Benjamin R. 1939- .... **CLC 141**
See also CA 29-32R; CANR 12, 32, 64

Barbera, Jack (Vincent) 1945- .... **CLC 44**
See also CA 110; CANR 45

Barbey d'Aurevilly, Jules-Amedee
1808-1889 .... **NCLC 1; SSC 17**
See also DLB 119; GFL 1789 to the Present

Barbour, John c. 1316-1395 .... **CMLC 33**
See also DLB 146

Barbusse, Henri 1873-1935 .... **TCLC 5**
See also CA 105; 154; DLB 65; RGWL

Barclay, Bill
See Moorcock, Michael (John)

Barclay, William Ewert
See Moorcock, Michael (John)

Barea, Arturo 1897-1957 .... **TCLC 14**
See also CA 111

Barfoot, Joan 1946- .... **CLC 18**
See also CA 105

Barham, Richard Harris
1788-1845 .... **NCLC 77**
See also DLB 159

Baring, Maurice 1874-1945 .... **TCLC 8**
See also CA 105; 168; DLB 34; HGG

Baring-Gould, Sabine 1834-1924 ... **TCLC 88**
See also DLB 156, 190

Barker, Clive 1952- ...... **CLC 52; DAM POP**
See also AAYA 10; BEST 90:3; BPFB 1; CA 121; 129; CANR 71; CPW; DA3; HGG; INT 129; MTCW 1, 2

Barker, George Granville
1913-1991 .... **CLC 8, 48; DAM POET**
See also CA 9-12R; 135; CANR 7, 38; DLB 20; MTCW 1

Barker, Harley Granville
See Granville-Barker, Harley
See also DLB 10

Barker, Howard 1946- .... **CLC 37**
See also CA 102; CBD; CD; DLB 13, 233

Barker, Jane 1652-1732 .... **LC 42**
See also DLB 39, 131

Barker, Pat(ricia) 1943- ...... **CLC 32, 94, 146**
See also BRWS 4; CA 117; 122; CANR 50, 101; CN; INT 122

Barlach, Ernst (Heinrich)
1870-1938 .... **TCLC 84**
See also CA 178; DLB 56, 118

Barlow, Joel 1754-1812 .... **NCLC 23**
See also AMWS 2; DLB 37; RGAL

Barnard, Mary (Ethel) 1909- .... **CLC 48**
See also CA 21-22; CAP 2

Barnes, Djuna 1892-1982 .... **CLC 3, 4, 8, 11, 29, 127; SSC 3**
See also Steptoe, Lydia
See also AMWS 3; CA 9-12R; 107; CAD; CANR 16, 55; CWD; DLB 4, 9, 45; GLL 1; MTCW 1, 2; RGAL

Barnes, Julian (Patrick) 1946- .... **CLC 42, 141; DAB**
See also BRWS 4; CA 102; CANR 19, 54; CN; DLB 194; DLBY 93; MTCW 1

Barnes, Peter 1931- .... **CLC 5, 56**
See also CA 65-68; CAAS 12; CANR 33, 34, 64; CBD; CD; DFS 6; DLB 13, 233; MTCW 1

Barnes, William 1801-1886 .... **NCLC 75**
See also DLB 32

Baroja (y Nessi), Pio 1872-1956 ..... **TCLC 8; HLC 1**
See also CA 104; EW 9

Baron, David
See Pinter, Harold

Baron Corvo
See Rolfe, Frederick (William Serafino Austin Lewis Mary)

Barondess, Sue K(aufman)
1926-1977 .... **CLC 8**
See also Kaufman, Sue
See also CA 1-4R; 69-72; CANR 1

Baron de Teive
See Pessoa, Fernando (Antonio Nogueira)

Baroness Von S.
See Zangwill, Israel

Barres, (Auguste-)Maurice
1862-1923 .... **TCLC 47**
See also CA 164; DLB 123; GFL 1789 to the Present

Barreto, Afonso Henrique de Lima
See Lima Barreto, Afonso Henrique de

Barrett, Andrea 1954- .... **CLC 150**
See also CA 156; CANR 92

Barrett, Michele .... **CLC 65**

Barrett, (Roger) Syd 1946- .... **CLC 35**

Barrett, William (Christopher)
1913-1992 .... **CLC 27**
See also CA 13-16R; 139; CANR 11, 67; INT CANR-11

Barrie, J(ames) M(atthew)
1860-1937 .... **TCLC 2; DAB; DAM DRAM**
See also BRWS 3; BYA 4, 5; CA 104; 136; CANR 77; CDBLB 1890-1914; CLR 16; CWRI; DA3; DFS 7; DLB 10, 141, 156; FANT; MAICYA; MTCW 1; SATA 100; SUFW; WCH; WLIT 4; YABC 1

Barrington, Michael
See Moorcock, Michael (John)

Barrol, Grady
See Bograd, Larry

Barry, Mike
See Malzberg, Barry N(athaniel)

Barry, Philip 1896-1949 .... **TCLC** █
See also CA 109; DFS 9; DLB 7, 22█ RGAL

Bart, Andre Schwarz
See Schwarz-Bart, Andre

Barth, John (Simmons) 1930- ... **CLC 1, 2, █ 5, 7, 9, 10, 14, 27, 51, 89; DAM NOV; SSC 10**
See also AITN 1, 2; AMW; BPFB 1; C█ 1-4R; CABS 1; CANR 5, 23, 49, 64; CN█ DLB 2, 227; FANT; MTCW 1; RGAL█ RGSF; RHW; SSFS 6

Barthelme, Donald 1931-1989 ... **CLC 1, 2, █ 5, 6, 8, 13, 23, 46, 59, 115; DAM NOV█ SSC 2**
See also AMWS 4; BPFB 1; CA 21-24R█ 129; CANR 20, 58; DA3; DLB 2, 234█ DLBY 80, 89; FANT; MTCW 1, 2█ RGAL; RGSF; SATA 7; SATA-Obit 62█ SSFS 3

Barthelme, Frederick 1943- ...... **CLC 36, 11**
See also CA 114; 122; CANR 77; CN█ CSW; DLB 244; DLBY 85; INT CA-122

Barthes, Roland (Gerard)
1915-1980 .... **CLC 24, 8█**
See also CA 130; 97-100; CANR 66; EW 13; GFL 1789 to the Present; MTCW 1, █

Barzun, Jacques (Martin) 1907- ..... **CLC 51█ 145**
See also CA 61-64; CANR 22, 95

Bashevis, Isaac
See Singer, Isaac Bashevis

Bashkirtseff, Marie 1859-1884 .... **NCLC 2█**

Basho, Matsuo
See Matsuo Basho
See also RGWL; WP

Basil of Caesaria c. 330-379 .... **CMLC 3█**

Bass, Kingsley B., Jr.
See Bullins, Ed

Bass, Rick 1958- .... **CLC 79, 14█**
See also ANW; CA 126; CANR 53, 93█ CSW; DLB 212

Bassani, Giorgio 1916-2000 .... **CLC █**
See also CA 65-68; 190; CANR 33; CWW█ 2; DLB 128, 177; MTCW 1; RGWL

Bastian, Ann .... **CLC 7█**

Bastos, Augusto (Antonio) Roa
See Roa Bastos, Augusto (Antonio)

Bataille, Georges 1897-1962 .... **CLC 29**
See also CA 101; 89-92

Bates, H(erbert) E(rnest)
1905-1974 . **CLC 46; DAB; DAM POP█ SSC 10**
See also Gawsworth, John
See also CA 93-96; 45-48; CANR 34; DA3█ DLB 162, 191; EXPS; MTCW 1, 2█ RGSF; SSFS 7

Bauchart
See Camus, Albert

Baudelaire, Charles 1821-1867 . **NCLC 6, 29, 55; DA; DAB; DAC; DAM MST, POET; PC 1; SSC 18; WLC**
See also DA3; DLB 217; EW 7; GFL 1789 to the Present; RGWL

Baudouin, Marcel
See Peguy, Charles (Pierre)

Baudouin, Pierre
See Peguy, Charles (Pierre)

Baudrillard, Jean 1929- .... **CLC 60**

Baum, L(yman) Frank 1856-1919 ... **TCLC 7**
See also CA 108; 133; CLR 15; CWRI; DLB 22; FANT; JRDA; MAICYA; MTCW 1, 2; NFS 13; RGAL; SATA 18, 100; WCH

Baum, Louis F.
See Baum, L(yman) Frank

Baumbach, Jonathan 1933- .... **CLC 6, 23**
See also CA 13-16R; CAAS 5; CANR 12, 66; CN; DLBY 80; INT CANR-12; MTCW 1

Bausch, Richard (Carl) 1945- .... **CLC 51**
See also AMWS 7; CA 101; CAAS 14; CANR 43, 61, 87; CSW; DLB 130

Baxter, Charles (Morley) 1947- .... **CLC 45, 78; DAM POP**
See also CA 57-60; CANR 40, 64, 104; CPW; DLB 130; MTCW 2

Baxter, George Owen
See Faust, Frederick (Schiller)

Baxter, James K(eir) 1926-1972 .... **CLC 14**
See also CA 77-80

Baxter, John
See Hunt, E(verette) Howard, (Jr.)

Bayer, Sylvia
See Glassco, John

Baynton, Barbara 1857-1929 .... **TCLC 57**
See also DLB 230; RGSF

Beagle, Peter S(oyer) 1939- .... **CLC 7, 104**
See also BPFB 1; BYA 9, 10; CA 9-12R; CANR 4, 51, 73; DA3; DLBY 80; FANT; INT CANR-4; MTCW 1; SATA 60; SUFW; YAW

Bean, Normal
See Burroughs, Edgar Rice

Beard, Charles A(ustin) 1874-1948 .... **TCLC 15**
See also CA 115; 189; DLB 17; SATA 18

Beardsley, Aubrey 1872-1898 .... **NCLC 6**

Beattie, Ann 1947- ..... **CLC 8, 13, 18, 40, 63, 146; DAM NOV, POP; SSC 11**
See also AMWS 5; BEST 90:2; BPFB 1; CA 81-84; CANR 53, 73; CN; CPW; DA3; DLB 218; DLBY 82; MTCW 1, 2; RGAL; RGSF; SSFS 9

Beattie, James 1735-1803 .... **NCLC 25**
See also DLB 109

Beauchamp, Kathleen Mansfield 1888-1923
See Mansfield, Katherine
See also CA 104; 134; DA; DA3; DAC; DAM MST; MTCW 2

Beaumarchais, Pierre-Augustin Caron de 1732-1799 . **LC 61; DAM DRAM; DC 4**
See also EW 4; GFL Beginnings to 1789; RGWL

Beaumont, Francis 1584(?)-1616 .... **LC 33; DC 6**
See also BRW 2; CDBLB Before 1660; DLB 58

Beauvoir, Simone (Lucie Ernestine Marie Bertrand) de 1908-1986 .... **CLC 1, 2, 4, 8, 14, 31, 44, 50, 71, 124; DA; DAB; DAC; DAM MST, NOV; SSC 35; WLC**
See also BPFB 1; CA 9-12R; 118; CANR 28, 61; DA3; DLB 72; DLBY 86; EW 12; FW; GFL 1789 to the Present; MTCW 1, 2; RGSF; RGWL

Becker, Carl (Lotus) 1873-1945 ..... **TCLC 63**
See also CA 157; DLB 17

Becker, Jurek 1937-1997 .... **CLC 7, 19**
See also CA 85-88; 157; CANR 60; CWW 2; DLB 75

Becker, Walter 1950- .... **CLC 26**

Beckett, Samuel (Barclay) 1906-1989 .. **CLC 1, 2, 3, 4, 6, 9, 10, 11, 14, 18, 29, 57, 59, 83; DA; DAB; DAC; DAM DRAM, MST, NOV; SSC 16; WLC**
See also BRWR 1; BRWS 1; CA 5-8R; 130; CANR 33, 61; CBD; CDBLB 1945-1960; DA3; DFS 2, 7; DLB 13, 15, 233; DLBY 90; GFL 1789 to the Present; MTCW 1, 2; RGSF; RGWL; WLIT 4

Beckford, William 1760-1844 .... **NCLC 16**
See also BRW 3; DLB 39, 213; HGG; SUFW

Beckman, Gunnel 1910- .... **CLC 26**
See also CA 33-36R; CANR 15; CLR 25; MAICYA; SAAS 9; SATA 6

Becque, Henri 1837-1899 .... **NCLC 3**
See also DLB 192; GFL 1789 to the Present

Becquer, Gustavo Adolfo 1836-1870 .... **NCLC 106; DAM MULT; HLCS 1**

Beddoes, Thomas Lovell 1803-1849 .... **NCLC 3; DC 15**
See also DLB 96

Bede c. 673-735 .... **CMLC 20**
See also DLB 146

Bedford, Donald F.
See Fearing, Kenneth (Flexner)

Beecher, Catharine Esther 1800-1878 .... **NCLC 30**
See also DLB 1, 243

Beecher, John 1904-1980 .... **CLC 6**
See also AITN 1; CA 5-8R; 105; CANR 8

Beer, Johann 1655-1700 .... **LC 5**
See also DLB 168

Beer, Patricia 1924- .... **CLC 58**
See also CA 61-64; 183; CANR 13, 46; CP; CWP; DLB 40; FW

Beerbohm, Max
See Beerbohm, (Henry) Max(imilian)

Beerbohm, (Henry) Max(imilian) 1872-1956 .... **TCLC 1, 24**
See also BRWS 2; CA 104; 154; CANR 79; DLB 34, 100; FANT

Beer-Hofmann, Richard 1866-1945 .... **TCLC 60**
See also CA 160; DLB 81

Beg, Shemus
See Stephens, James

Begiebing, Robert J(ohn) 1946- .... **CLC 70**
See also CA 122; CANR 40, 88

Behan, Brendan 1923-1964 ...... **CLC 1, 8, 11, 15, 79; DAM DRAM**
See also BRWS 2; CA 73-76; CANR 33; CBD; CDBLB 1945-1960; DFS 7; DLB 13, 233; MTCW 1, 2

Behn, Aphra 1640(?)-1689 .... **LC 1, 30, 42; DA; DAB; DAC; DAM DRAM, MST, NOV, POET; DC 4; PC 13; WLC**
See also BRWS 3; DA3; DLB 39, 80, 131; FW; WLIT 3

Behrman, S(amuel) N(athaniel) 1893-1973 .... **CLC 40**
See also CA 13-16; 45-48; CAD; CAP 1; DLB 7, 44; IDFW 3; RGAL

Belasco, David 1853-1931 .... **TCLC 3**
See also CA 104; 168; DLB 7; RGAL

Belcheva, Elisaveta 1893-1991 .... **CLC 10**
See also Bagryana, Elisaveta

Beldone, Phil ''Cheech''
See Ellison, Harlan (Jay)

Beleno
See Azuela, Mariano

Belinski, Vissarion Grigoryevich 1811-1848 .... **NCLC 5**
See also DLB 198

Belitt, Ben 1911- .... **CLC 22**
See also CA 13-16R; CAAS 4; CANR 7, 77; CP; DLB 5

Bell, Gertrude (Margaret Lowthian) 1868-1926 .... **TCLC 67**
See also CA 167; DLB 174

Bell, J. Freeman
See Zangwill, Israel

Bell, James Madison 1826-1902 ... **TCLC 43; BLC 1; DAM MULT**
See also BW 1; CA 122; 124; DLB 50

Bell, Madison Smartt 1957- ...... **CLC 41, 102**
See also AMWS 10; BPFB 1; CA 111, 183; CAAE 183; CANR 28, 54, 73; CN; CSW; DLB 218; MTCW 1

Bell, Marvin (Hartley) 1937- ...... **CLC 8, 31; DAM POET**
See also CA 21-24R; CAAS 14; CANR 59, 102; CP; DLB 5; MTCW 1

Bell, W. L. D.
See Mencken, H(enry) L(ouis)

Bellamy, Atwood C.
See Mencken, H(enry) L(ouis)

Bellamy, Edward 1850-1898 ...... **NCLC 4, 86**
See also DLB 12; RGAL; SFW

Belli, Gioconda 1949-
See also CA 152; CWW 2; HLCS 1

Bellin, Edward J.
See Kuttner, Henry

Belloc, (Joseph) Hilaire (Pierre Sebastien Rene Swanton) 1870-1953 ...... **TCLC 7, 18; DAM POET; PC 24**
See also CA 106; 152; CWRI; DLB 19, 100, 141, 174; MTCW 1; SATA 112; WCH; YABC 1

Belloc, Joseph Peter Rene Hilaire
See Belloc, (Joseph) Hilaire (Pierre Sebastien Rene Swanton)

Belloc, Joseph Pierre Hilaire
See Belloc, (Joseph) Hilaire (Pierre Sebastien Rene Swanton)

Belloc, M. A.
See Lowndes, Marie Adelaide (Belloc)

Bellow, Saul 1915- . **CLC 1, 2, 3, 6, 8, 10, 13, 15, 25, 33, 34, 63, 79; DA; DAB; DAC; DAM MST, NOV, POP; SSC 14; WLC**
See also AITN 2; AMW; BEST 89:3; BPFB 1; CA 5-8R; CABS 1; CANR 29, 53, 95; CDALB 1941-1968; CN; DA3; DLB 2, 28; DLBD 3; DLBY 82; MTCW 1, 2; NFS 4; RGAL; RGSF; SSFS 12

Belser, Reimond Karel Maria de 1929-
See Ruyslinck, Ward
See also CA 152

Bely, Andrey .... **TCLC 7; PC 11**
See Bugayev, Boris Nikolayevich
See also EW 9; MTCW 1

Belyi, Andrei
See Bugayev, Boris Nikolayevich
See also RGWL

Benary, Margot
See Benary-Isbert, Margot

Benary-Isbert, Margot 1889-1979 .... **CLC 12**
See also CA 5-8R; 89-92; CANR 4, 72; CLR 12; MAICYA; SATA 2; SATA-Obit 21

Benavente (y Martinez), Jacinto 1866-1954 .... **TCLC 3; DAM DRAM, MULT; HLCS 1**
See also CA 106; 131; CANR 81; GLL 2; HW 1, 2; MTCW 1, 2

Benchley, Peter (Bradford) 1940- . **CLC 4, 8; DAM NOV, POP**
See also AAYA 14; AITN 2; BPFB 1; CA 17-20R; CANR 12, 35, 66; CPW; HGG; MTCW 1, 2; SATA 3, 89

Benchley, Robert (Charles) 1889-1945 .... **TCLC 1, 55**
See also CA 105; 153; DLB 11; RGAL

Benda, Julien 1867-1956 .... **TCLC 60**
See also CA 120; 154; GFL 1789 to the Present

Benedict, Ruth (Fulton) 1887-1948 .... **TCLC 60**
See also CA 158; DLB 246

Benedikt, Michael 1935- .... **CLC 4, 14**
See also CA 13-16R; CANR 7; CP; DLB 5

Benet, Juan 1927-1993 .... **CLC 28**
See also CA 143

Benet, Stephen Vincent 1898-1943 . **TCLC 7; DAM POET; SSC 10**
See also CA 104; 152; DA3; DLB 4, 48, 102, 249; DLBY 97; HGG; MTCW 1; RGAL; RGSF; SUFW; WP; YABC 1

Burke, Kenneth (Duva) 1897-1993 ... **CLC 2, 24**
See also AMW; CA 5-8R; 143; CANR 39, 74; DLB 45, 63; MTCW 1, 2; RGAL

Burke, Leda
See Garnett, David

Burke, Ralph
See Silverberg, Robert

Burke, Thomas 1886-1945 .... **TCLC 63**
See also CA 113; 155; CMW; DLB 197

Burney, Fanny 1752-1840 .... **NCLC 12, 54, 107**
See also BRWS 3; DLB 39; RGEL

Burney, Frances
See Burney, Fanny

Burns, Robert 1759-1796 . **LC 3, 29, 40; DA; DAB; DAC; DAM MST, POET; PC 6; WLC**
See also BRW 3; CDBLB 1789-1832; DA3; DLB 109; EXPP; PAB; RGEL; WP

Burns, Tex
See L'Amour, Louis (Dearborn)
See also TCWW 2

Burnshaw, Stanley 1906- .... **CLC 3, 13, 44**
See also CA 9-12R; CP; DLB 48; DLBY 97

Burr, Anne 1937- .... **CLC 6**
See also CA 25-28R

Burroughs, Edgar Rice 1875-1950 . **TCLC 2, 32; DAM NOV**
See also AAYA 11; BPFB 1; BYA 4, 9; CA 104; 132; DA3; DLB 8; FANT; MTCW 1, 2; RGAL; SATA 41; SCFW 2; SFW; YAW

Burroughs, William S(eward)
1914-1997 .. **CLC 1, 2, 5, 15, 22, 42, 75, 109; DA; DAB; DAC; DAM MST, NOV, POP; WLC**
See also Lee, William; Lee, Willy
See also AITN 2; AMWS 3; BPFB 1; CA 9-12R; 160; CANR 20, 52, 104; CN; CPW; DA3; DLB 2, 8, 16, 152, 237; DLBY 81, 97; HGG; MTCW 1, 2; RGAL; SFW

Burton, Sir Richard F(rancis)
1821-1890 .... **NCLC 42**
See also DLB 55, 166, 184

Burton, Robert 1577-1640 .... **LC 74**
See also DLB 151; RGEL

Busch, Frederick 1941- .... **CLC 7, 10, 18, 47**
See also CA 33-36R; CAAS 1; CANR 45, 73, 92; CN; DLB 6, 218

Bush, Ronald 1946- .... **CLC 34**
See also CA 136

Bustos, F(rancisco)
See Borges, Jorge Luis

Bustos Domecq, H(onorio)
See Bioy Casares, Adolfo; Borges, Jorge Luis

Butler, Octavia E(stelle) 1947- .... **CLC 38, 121; BLCS; DAM MULT, POP**
See also AAYA 18; AFAW 2; BPFB 1; BW 2, 3; CA 73-76; CANR 12, 24, 38, 73; CLR 65; CPW; DA3; DLB 33; MTCW 1, 2; NFS 8; SATA 84; SCFW 2; SFW; SSFS 6; YAW

Butler, Robert Olen, (Jr.) 1945- ...... **CLC 81; DAM POP**
See also BPFB 1; CA 112; CANR 66; CSW; DLB 173; INT CA-112; MTCW 1; SSFS 11

Butler, Samuel 1612-1680 .... **LC 16, 43**
See also DLB 101, 126; RGEL

Butler, Samuel 1835-1902 . **TCLC 1, 33; DA; DAB; DAC; DAM MST, NOV; WLC**
See also BRWS 2; CA 143; CDBLB 1890-1914; DA3; DLB 18, 57, 174; RGEL; SFW; TEA

Butler, Walter C.
See Faust, Frederick (Schiller)

Butor, Michel (Marie Francois)
1926- .... **CLC 1, 3, 8, 11, 15**
See also CA 9-12R; CANR 33, 66; DLB 83; EW 13; GFL 1789 to the Present; MTCW 1, 2

Butts, Mary 1890(?)-1937 .... **TCLC 77**
See also CA 148; DLB 240

Buxton, Ralph
See Silverstein, Alvin; Silverstein, Virginia B(arbara Opshelor)

Buzo, Alexander (John) 1944- .... **CLC 61**
See also CA 97-100; CANR 17, 39, 69; CD

Buzzati, Dino 1906-1972 .... **CLC 36**
See also CA 160; 33-36R; DLB 177; RGWL; SFW

Byars, Betsy (Cromer) 1928- .... **CLC 35**
See also AAYA 19; BYA 3; CA 33-36R, 183; CAAE 183; CANR 18, 36, 57, 102; CLR 1, 16, 72; DLB 52; INT CANR-18; JRDA; MAICYA; MAICYAS; MTCW 1; SAAS 1; SATA 4, 46, 80; SATA-Essay 108; WYA; YAW

Byatt, A(ntonia) S(usan Drabble)
1936- ...... **CLC 19, 65, 136; DAM NOV, POP**
See also BPFB 1; BRWS 4; CA 13-16R; CANR 13, 33, 50, 75, 96; DA3; DLB 14, 194; MTCW 1, 2; RGSF; RHW

Byrne, David 1952- .... **CLC 26**
See also CA 127

Byrne, John Keyes 1926-
See Leonard, Hugh
See also CA 102; CANR 78; INT CA-102

Byron, George Gordon (Noel)
1788-1824 ...... **NCLC 2, 12, 109; DA; DAB; DAC; DAM MST, POET; PC 16; WLC**
See also BRW 4; CDBLB 1789-1832; DA3; DLB 96, 110; EXPP; PAB; PFS 1, 14; RGEL; WLIT 3; WP

Byron, Robert 1905-1941 .... **TCLC 67**
See also CA 160; DLB 195

C. 3. 3.
See Wilde, Oscar (Fingal O'Flahertie Wills)

Caballero, Fernan 1796-1877 .... **NCLC 10**

Cabell, Branch
See Cabell, James Branch

Cabell, James Branch 1879-1958 .... **TCLC 6**
See also CA 105; 152; DLB 9, 78; FANT; MTCW 1; RGAL; SUFW

Cabeza de Vaca, Alvar Nunez
1490-1557(?) .... **LC 61**

Cable, George Washington
1844-1925 .... **TCLC 4; SSC 4**
See also CA 104; 155; DLB 12, 74; DLBD 13; RGAL

Cabral de Melo Neto, Joao
1920-1999 .... **CLC 76; DAM MULT**
See also CA 151; LAW; LAWS 1

Cabrera Infante, G(uillermo) 1929- . **CLC 5, 25, 45, 120; DAM MULT; HLC 1; SSC 39**
See also CA 85-88; CANR 29, 65; DA3; DLB 113; HW 1, 2; LAW; LAWS 1; MTCW 1, 2; RGSF; WLIT 1

Cade, Toni
See Bambara, Toni Cade

Cadmus and Harmonia
See Buchan, John

Caedmon fl. 658-680 .... **CMLC 7**
See also DLB 146

Caeiro, Alberto
See Pessoa, Fernando (Antonio Nogueira)

Caesar, Julius .... **CMLC 47**
See also Julius Caesar
See also AW 1; RGWL

Cage, John (Milton, Jr.) 1912-1992 . **CLC 41**
See also CA 13-16R; 169; CANR 9, 78; DLB 193; INT CANR-9

Cahan, Abraham 1860-1951 .... **TCLC 71**
See also CA 108; 154; DLB 9, 25, 28; RGAL

Cain, G.
See Cabrera Infante, G(uillermo)

Cain, Guillermo
See Cabrera Infante, G(uillermo)

Cain, James M(allahan) 1892-1977 .. **CLC 3, 11, 28**
See also AITN 1; BPFB 1; CA 17-20R; 73-76; CANR 8, 34, 61; CMW; DLB 226; MSW; MTCW 1; RGAL

Caine, Hall 1853-1931 .... **TCLC 97**
See also RHW

Caine, Mark
See Raphael, Frederic (Michael)

Calasso, Roberto 1941- .... **CLC 81**
See also CA 143; CANR 89

Calderon de la Barca, Pedro
1600-1681 .... **LC 23; DC 3; HLCS 1**
See also EW 2; RGWL

Caldwell, Erskine (Preston)
1903-1987 .. **CLC 1, 8, 14, 50, 60; DAM NOV; SSC 19**
See also AITN 1; AMW; BPFB 1; CA 1-4R; 121; CAAS 1; CANR 2, 33; DA3; DLB 9, 86; MTCW 1, 2; RGAL; RGSF; TCLC 117

Caldwell, (Janet Miriam) Taylor (Holland)
1900-1985 .. **CLC 2, 28, 39; DAM NOV, POP**
See also BPFB 1; CA 5-8R; 116; CANR 5; DA3; DLBD 17; RHW

Calhoun, John Caldwell
1782-1850 .... **NCLC 15**
See also DLB 3, 248

Calisher, Hortense 1911- ..... **CLC 2, 4, 8, 38, 134; DAM NOV; SSC 15**
See also CA 1-4R; CANR 1, 22, 67; CN; DA3; DLB 2, 218; INT CANR-22; MTCW 1, 2; RGAL; RGSF

Callaghan, Morley Edward
1903-1990 ...... **CLC 3, 14, 41, 65; DAC; DAM MST**
See also CA 9-12R; 132; CANR 33, 73; DLB 68; MTCW 1, 2; RGEL; RGSF

Callimachus c. 305B.C.-c.
240B.C. .... **CMLC 18**
See also AW 1; DLB 176; RGWL

Calvin, Jean
See Calvin, John
See also GFL Beginnings to 1789

Calvin, John 1509-1564 .... **LC 37**
See also Calvin, Jean

Calvino, Italo 1923-1985 .... **CLC 5, 8, 11, 22, 33, 39, 73; DAM NOV; SSC 3, 48**
See also CA 85-88; 116; CANR 23, 61; DLB 196; EW 13; MTCW 1, 2; RGSF; RGWL; SFW; SSFS 12

Cameron, Carey 1952- .... **CLC 59**
See also CA 135

Cameron, Peter 1959- .... **CLC 44**
See also CA 125; CANR 50; DLB 234; GLL 2

Camoens, Luis Vaz de 1524(?)-1580
See also EW 2; HLCS 1

Camoes, Luis de 1524(?)-1580 .... **LC 62; HLCS 1; PC 31**
See also RGWL

Campana, Dino 1885-1932 .... **TCLC 20**
See also CA 117; DLB 114

Campanella, Tommaso 1568-1639 .... **LC 32**
See also RGWL

Cassity, (Allen) Turner 1929- .... **CLC 6, 42**
See also CA 17-20R; CAAS 8; CANR 11;
CSW; DLB 105

Castaneda, Carlos (Cesar Aranha)
1931(?)-1998 .... **CLC 12, 119**
See also CA 25-28R; CANR 32, 66, 105;
HW 1; MTCW 1

Castedo, Elena 1937- .... **CLC 65**
See also CA 132

Castedo-Ellerman, Elena
See Castedo, Elena

Castellanos, Rosario 1925-1974 .... **CLC 66;**
DAM MULT; HLC 1; SSC 39
See also CA 131; 53-56; CANR 58; DLB
113; FW; HW 1; LAW; MTCW 1; RGSF;
RGWL

Castelvetro, Lodovico 1505-1571 .... **LC 12**

Castiglione, Baldassare 1478-1529 ...... **LC 12**
See also Castiglione, Baldesar
See also RGWL

Castiglione, Baldesar
See Castiglione, Baldassare
See also EW 2

Castillo, Ana (Hernandez Del)
1953- .... **CLC 151**
See also AAYA 42; CA 131; CANR 51, 86;
CWP; DLB 122, 227; DNFS; FW; HW 1

Castle, Robert
See Hamilton, Edmond

Castro (Ruz), Fidel 1926(?)-
See also CA 110; 129; CANR 81; DAM
MULT; HLC 1; HW 2

Castro, Guillen de 1569-1631 .... **LC 19**

Castro, Rosalia de 1837-1885 ... **NCLC 3, 78;**
DAM MULT

Cather, Willa (Sibert) 1873-1947 .... **TCLC 1,**
11, 31, 99; DA; DAB; DAC; DAM
MST, NOV; SSC 2, 50; WLC
See also AAYA 24; AMW; AMWR 1; BPFB
1; CA 104; 128; CDALB 1865-1917;
DA3; DLB 9, 54, 78, 256; DLBD 1;
EXPN; EXPS; LAIT 3; MAWW; MTCW
1, 2; NFS 2; RGAL; RGSF; RHW; SATA
30; SSFS 2, 7; TCWW 2

Catherine II
See Catherine the Great
See also DLB 150

Catherine the Great 1729-1796 .... **LC 69**
See also Catherine II

Cato, Marcus Porcius
234B.C.-149B.C. .... **CMLC 21**
See also Cato the Elder

Catton, (Charles) Bruce 1899-1978 . **CLC 35**
See also AITN 1; CA 5-8R; 81-84; CANR
7, 74; DLB 17; SATA 2; SATA-Obit 24

Catullus c. 84B.C.-54B.C. .... **CMLC 18**
See also AW 2; DLB 211; RGWL

Cauldwell, Frank
See King, Francis (Henry)

Caunitz, William J. 1933-1996 .... **CLC 34**
See also BEST 89:3; CA 125; 130; 152;
CANR 73; INT 130

Causley, Charles (Stanley) 1917- .... **CLC 7**
See also CA 9-12R; CANR 5, 35, 94; CLR
30; CWRI; DLB 27; MTCW 1; SATA 3,
66

Caute, (John) David 1936- .... **CLC 29; DAM**
NOV
See also CA 1-4R; CAAS 4; CANR 1, 33,
64; CBD; CD; CN; DLB 14, 231

Cavafy, C(onstantine) P(eter) ... **TCLC 2, 7;**
DAM POET; PC 36
See also Kavafis, Konstantinos Petrou
See also CA 148; DA3; EW 8; MTCW 1;
RGWL; WP

Cavallo, Evelyn
See Spark, Muriel (Sarah)

Cavanna, Betty .... **CLC 12**
See also Harrison, Elizabeth (Allen) Ca-
vanna
See also JRDA; MAICYA; SAAS 4; SATA
1, 30

Cavendish, Margaret Lucas
1623-1673 .... **LC 30**
See also DLB 131, 252; RGEL

Caxton, William 1421(?)-1491(?) .... **LC 17**
See also DLB 170

Cayer, D. M.
See Duffy, Maureen

Cayrol, Jean 1911- .... **CLC 11**
See also CA 89-92; DLB 83

Cela, Camilo Jose 1916-2002 .... **CLC 4, 13,**
59, 122; DAM MULT; HLC 1
See also BEST 90:2; CA 21-24R; CAAS
10; CANR 21, 32, 76; DLBY 89; EW 13;
HW 1; MTCW 1, 2; RGSF; RGWL

Celan, Paul ...... **CLC 10, 19, 53, 82; PC 10**
See also Antschel, Paul
See also DLB 69; RGWL

Celine, Louis-Ferdinand .. **CLC 1, 3, 4, 7, 9,**
15, 47, 124
See also Destouches, Louis-Ferdinand
See also DLB 72; EW 11; GFL 1789 to the
Present; RGWL

Cellini, Benvenuto 1500-1571 .... **LC 7**

Cendrars, Blaise .... **CLC 18, 106**
See also Sauser-Hall, Frederic
See also GFL 1789 to the Present; RGWL;
WP

Centlivre, Susanna 1669(?)-1723 .... **LC 65**
See also DLB 84; RGEL

Cernuda (y Bidon), Luis
1902-1963 .... **CLC 54; DAM POET**
See also CA 131; 89-92; DLB 134; GLL 1;
HW 1; RGWL

Cervantes, Lorna Dee 1954- .... **PC 35**
See also CA 131; CANR 80; CWP; DLB
82; EXPP; HLCS 1; HW 1

Cervantes (Saavedra), Miguel de
1547-1616 .. **LC 6, 23; DA; DAB; DAC;**
DAM MST, NOV; HLCS; SSC 12;
WLC
See also BYA 1, 14; EW 2; LAIT 1; NFS 8;
RGSF; RGWL

Cesaire, Aime (Fernand) 1913- . **CLC 19, 32,**
112; BLC 1; DAM MULT, POET; PC
25
See also BW 2, 3; CA 65-68; CANR 24,
43, 81; DA3; GFL 1789 to the Present;
MTCW 1, 2; WP

Chabon, Michael 1963- .... **CLC 55, 149**
See also CA 139; CANR 57, 96

Chabrol, Claude 1930- .... **CLC 16**
See also CA 110

Challans, Mary 1905-1983
See Renault, Mary
See also CA 81-84; 111; CANR 74; DA3;
MTCW 2; SATA 23; SATA-Obit 36

Challis, George
See Faust, Frederick (Schiller)
See also TCWW 2

Chambers, Aidan 1934- .... **CLC 35**
See also AAYA 27; CA 25-28R; CANR 12,
31, 58; JRDA; MAICYA; SAAS 12;
SATA 1, 69, 108; WYA; YAW

Chambers, James 1948-
See Cliff, Jimmy
See also CA 124

Chambers, Jessie
See Lawrence, D(avid) H(erbert Richards)
See also GLL 1

Chambers, Robert W(illiam)
1865-1933 .... **TCLC 41**
See also CA 165; DLB 202; HGG; SATA
107; SUFW

Chamisso, Adelbert von
1781-1838 .... **NCLC 82**
See also DLB 90; RGWL; SUFW

Chandler, Raymond (Thornton)
1888-1959 .... **TCLC 1, 7; SSC 23**
See also AAYA 25; AMWS 4; BPFB 1; CA
104; 129; CANR 60; CDALB 1929-1941;
CMW; DA3; DLB 226, 253; DLBD 6;
MSW; MTCW 1, 2; RGAL

Chang, Eileen 1921-1995 .... **SSC 28**
See also CA 166; CWW 2

Chang, Jung 1952- .... **CLC 71**
See also CA 142

Chang Ai-Ling
See Chang, Eileen

Channing, William Ellery
1780-1842 .... **NCLC 17**
See also DLB 1, 59, 235; RGAL

Chao, Patricia 1955- .... **CLC 119**
See also CA 163

Chaplin, Charles Spencer
1889-1977 .... **CLC 16**
See also Chaplin, Charlie
See also CA 81-84; 73-76

Chaplin, Charlie
See Chaplin, Charles Spencer
See also DLB 44

Chapman, George 1559(?)-1634 .... **LC 22;**
DAM DRAM
See also BRW 1; DLB 62, 121; RGEL

Chapman, Graham 1941-1989 .... **CLC 21**
See also Monty Python
See also CA 116; 129; CANR 35, 95

Chapman, John Jay 1862-1933 .... **TCLC 7**
See also CA 104; 191

Chapman, Lee
See Bradley, Marion Zimmer
See also GLL 1

Chapman, Walker
See Silverberg, Robert

Chappell, Fred (Davis) 1936- ..... **CLC 40, 78**
See also CA 5-8R; CAAS 4; CANR 8, 33,
67; CN; CP; CSW; DLB 6, 105; HGG

Char, Rene(-Emile) 1907-1988 .... **CLC 9, 11,**
14, 55; DAM POET
See also CA 13-16R; 124; CANR 32; GFL
1789 to the Present; MTCW 1, 2; RGWL

Charby, Jay
See Ellison, Harlan (Jay)

Chardin, Pierre Teilhard de
See Teilhard de Chardin, (Marie Joseph)
Pierre

Chariton fl. 1st cent. (?)- .... **CMLC 49**

Charlemagne 742-814 .... **CMLC 37**

Charles I 1600-1649 .... **LC 13**

Charriere, Isabelle de 1740-1805 .. **NCLC 66**

Chartier, Emile-Auguste
See Alain

Charyn, Jerome 1937- .... **CLC 5, 8, 18**
See also CA 5-8R; CAAS 1; CANR 7, 61,
101; CMW; CN; DLBY 83; MTCW 1

Chase, Adam
See Marlowe, Stephen

Chase, Mary (Coyle) 1907-1981 .... **DC 1**
See also CA 77-80; 105; CAD; CWD; DFS
11; DLB 228; SATA 17; SATA-Obit 29

Chase, Mary Ellen 1887-1973 .... **CLC 2**
See also CA 13-16; 41-44R; CAP 1; SATA
10

Chase, Nicholas
See Hyde, Anthony
See also CCA 1

Chateaubriand, Francois Rene de
1768-1848 .... **NCLC 3**
See also DLB 119; EW 5; GFL 1789 to the
Present; RGWL

Clarin
See Alas (y Urena), Leopoldo (Enrique Garcia)

Clark, Al C.
See Goines, Donald

Clark, (Robert) Brian 1932- .... **CLC 29**
See also CA 41-44R; CANR 67; CBD; CD

Clark, Curt
See Westlake, Donald E(dwin)

Clark, Eleanor 1913-1996 .... **CLC 5, 19**
See also CA 9-12R; 151; CANR 41; CN; DLB 6

Clark, J. P.
See Clark Bekedermo, J(ohnson) P(epper)
See also DLB 117

Clark, John Pepper
See Clark Bekedermo, J(ohnson) P(epper)
See also AFW; CD; CP; RGEL

Clark, M. R.
See Clark, Mavis Thorpe

Clark, Mavis Thorpe 1909- .... **CLC 12**
See also CA 57-60; CANR 8, 37; CLR 30; CWRI; MAICYA; SAAS 5; SATA 8, 74

Clark, Walter Van Tilburg
1909-1971 .... **CLC 28**
See also CA 9-12R; 33-36R; CANR 63; DLB 9, 206; LAIT 2; RGAL; SATA 8

Clark Bekedermo, J(ohnson) P(epper)
1935- .. **CLC 38; BLC 1; DAM DRAM, MULT; DC 5**
See also Clark, J. P.; Clark, John Pepper
See also BW 1; CA 65-68; CANR 16, 72; DFS 13; MTCW 1

Clarke, Arthur C(harles) 1917- .... **CLC 1, 4, 13, 18, 35, 136; DAM POP; SSC 3**
See also AAYA 4, 33; BPFB 1; BYA 13; CA 1-4R; CANR 2, 28, 55, 74; CN; CPW; DA3; JRDA; LAIT 5; MAICYA; MTCW 1, 2; SATA 13, 70, 115; SCFW; SFW; SSFS 4; YAW

Clarke, Austin 1896-1974 ... **CLC 6, 9; DAM POET**
See also CA 29-32; 49-52; CAP 2; DLB 10, 20; RGEL

Clarke, Austin C(hesterfield) 1934- .. **CLC 8, 53; BLC 1; DAC; DAM MULT; SSC 45**
See also BW 1; CA 25-28R; CAAS 16; CANR 14, 32, 68; CN; DLB 53, 125; DNFS; RGSF

Clarke, Gillian 1937- .... **CLC 61**
See also CA 106; CP; CWP; DLB 40

Clarke, Marcus (Andrew Hislop)
1846-1881 .... **NCLC 19**
See also DLB 230; RGEL; RGSF

Clarke, Shirley 1925-1997 .... **CLC 16**
See also CA 189

Clash, The
See Headon, (Nicky) Topper; Jones, Mick; Simonon, Paul; Strummer, Joe

Claudel, Paul (Louis Charles Marie)
1868-1955 .... **TCLC 2, 10**
See also CA 104; 165; DLB 192; EW 8; GFL 1789 to the Present; RGWL

Claudian 370(?)-404(?) .... **CMLC 46**
See also RGWL

Claudius, Matthias 1740-1815 .... **NCLC 75**
See also DLB 97

Clavell, James (duMaresq)
1925-1994 .. **CLC 6, 25, 87; DAM NOV, POP**
See also BPFB 1; CA 25-28R; 146; CANR 26, 48; CPW; DA3; MTCW 1, 2; NFS 10; RHW

Clayman, Gregory .... **CLC 65**

Cleaver, (Leroy) Eldridge
1935-1998 . **CLC 30, 119; BLC 1; DAM MULT**
See also BW 1, 3; CA 21-24R; 167; CANR 16, 75; DA3; MTCW 2; YAW

Cleese, John (Marwood) 1939- .... **CLC 21**
See also Monty Python
See also CA 112; 116; CANR 35; MTCW 1

Cleishbotham, Jebediah
See Scott, Sir Walter

Cleland, John 1710-1789 .... **LC 2, 48**
See also DLB 39; RGEL

Clemens, Samuel Langhorne 1835-1910
See Twain, Mark
See also CA 104; 135; CDALB 1865-1917; DA; DA3; DAB; DAC; DAM MST, NOV; DLB 12, 23, 64, 74, 186, 189; JRDA; MAICYA; SATA 100; YABC 2

Clement of Alexandria
150(?)-215(?) .... **CMLC 41**

Cleophil
See Congreve, William

Clerihew, E.
See Bentley, E(dmund) C(lerihew)

Clerk, N. W.
See Lewis, C(live) S(taples)

Cliff, Jimmy .... **CLC 21**
See also Chambers, James
See also CA 193

Cliff, Michelle 1946- .... **CLC 120; BLCS**
See also BW 2; CA 116; CANR 39, 72; DLB 157; FW; GLL 2

Clifton, (Thelma) Lucille 1936- .... **CLC 19, 66; BLC 1; DAM MULT, POET; PC 17**
See also AFAW 2; BW 2, 3; CA 49-52; CANR 2, 24, 42, 76, 97; CLR 5; CP; CSW; CWP; CWRI; DA3; DLB 5, 41; EXPP; MAICYA; MTCW 1, 2; PFS 1, 14; SATA 20, 69; WP

Clinton, Dirk
See Silverberg, Robert

Clough, Arthur Hugh 1819-1861 ... **NCLC 27**
See also BRW 5; DLB 32; RGEL

Clutha, Janet Paterson Frame 1924-
See Frame, Janet
See also CA 1-4R; CANR 2, 36, 76; MTCW 1, 2; SATA 119

Clyne, Terence
See Blatty, William Peter

Cobalt, Martin
See Mayne, William (James Carter)

Cobb, Irvin S(hrewsbury)
1876-1944 .... **TCLC 77**
See also CA 175; DLB 11, 25, 86

Cobbett, William 1763-1835 .... **NCLC 49**
See also DLB 43, 107, 158; RGEL

Coburn, D(onald) L(ee) 1938- .... **CLC 10**
See also CA 89-92

Cocteau, Jean (Maurice Eugene Clement)
1889-1963 .... **CLC 1, 8, 15, 16, 43; DA; DAB; DAC; DAM DRAM, MST, NOV; TCLC 119; WLC**
See also CA 25-28; CANR 40; CAP 2; DA3; DLB 65; EW 10; GFL 1789 to the Present; MTCW 1, 2; RGWL

Codrescu, Andrei 1946- .... **CLC 46, 121; DAM POET**
See also CA 33-36R; CAAS 19; CANR 13, 34, 53, 76; DA3; MTCW 2

Coe, Max
See Bourne, Randolph S(illiman)

Coe, Tucker
See Westlake, Donald E(dwin)

Coen, Ethan 1958- .... **CLC 108**
See also CA 126; CANR 85

Coen, Joel 1955- .... **CLC 108**
See also CA 126

The Coen Brothers
See Coen, Ethan; Coen, Joel

Coetzee, J(ohn) M(ichael) 1940- ...... **CLC 23, 33, 66, 117; DAM NOV**
See also AAYA 37; AFW; BRWS 6; CA 77-80; CANR 41, 54, 74; CN; DA3; DLB 225; MTCW 1, 2; WLIT 2

Coffey, Brian
See Koontz, Dean R(ay)

Coffin, Robert P(eter) Tristram
1892-1955 .... **TCLC 95**
See also CA 123; 169; DLB 45

Cohan, George M(ichael)
1878-1942 .... **TCLC 60**
See also CA 157; DLB 249; RGAL

Cohen, Arthur A(llen) 1928-1986 ...... **CLC 7, 31**
See also CA 1-4R; 120; CANR 1, 17, 42; DLB 28

Cohen, Leonard (Norman) 1934- ...... **CLC 3, 38; DAC; DAM MST**
See also CA 21-24R; CANR 14, 69; CN; CP; DLB 53; MTCW 1

Cohen, Matt(hew) 1942-1999 .... **CLC 19; DAC**
See also CA 61-64; 187; CAAS 18; CANR 40; CN; DLB 53

Cohen-Solal, Annie 19(?)- .... **CLC 50**

Colegate, Isabel 1931- .... **CLC 36**
See also CA 17-20R; CANR 8, 22, 74; CN; DLB 14, 231; INT CANR-22; MTCW 1

Coleman, Emmett
See Reed, Ishmael

Coleridge, Hartley 1796-1849 .... **NCLC 90**
See also DLB 96

Coleridge, M. E.
See Coleridge, Mary E(lizabeth)

Coleridge, Mary E(lizabeth)
1861-1907 .... **TCLC 73**
See also CA 116; 166; DLB 19, 98

Coleridge, Samuel Taylor
1772-1834 . **NCLC 9, 54, 99; DA; DAB; DAC; DAM MST, POET; PC 11, 39; WLC**
See also BRW 4; BRWR 2; BYA 4; CD-BLB 1789-1832; DA3; DLB 93, 107; EXPP; PAB; PFS 4, 5; RGEL; WLIT 3; WP

Coleridge, Sara 1802-1852 .... **NCLC 31**
See also DLB 199

Coles, Don 1928- .... **CLC 46**
See also CA 115; CANR 38; CP

Coles, Robert (Martin) 1929- .... **CLC 108**
See also CA 45-48; CANR 3, 32, 66, 70; INT CANR-32; SATA 23

Colette, (Sidonie-Gabrielle)
1873-1954 . **TCLC 1, 5, 16; DAM NOV; SSC 10**
See also Willy, Colette
See also CA 104; 131; DA3; DLB 65; EW 9; GFL 1789 to the Present; MTCW 1, 2; RGWL

Collett, (Jacobine) Camilla (Wergeland)
1813-1895 .... **NCLC 22**

Collier, Christopher 1930- .... **CLC 30**
See also AAYA 13; BYA 2; CA 33-36R; CANR 13, 33, 102; JRDA; MAICYA; SATA 16, 70; WYA; YAW 1

Collier, James Lincoln 1928- .... **CLC 30; DAM POP**
See also Williams, Charles
See also AAYA 13; BYA 2; CA 9-12R; CANR 4, 33, 60, 102; CLR 3; JRDA; MAICYA; SAAS 21; SATA 8, 70; WYA; YAW 1

Collier, Jeremy 1650-1726 .... **LC 6**

Collier, John 1901-1980 .... **SSC 19**
See also CA 65-68; 97-100; CANR 10; DLB 77, 255; FANT; SUFW

Cortes, Hernan 1485-1547 .... **LC 31**
Corvinus, Jakob
   See Raabe, Wilhelm (Karl)
Corvo, Baron
   See Rolfe, Frederick (William Serafino Austin Lewis Mary)
   See also GLL 1; RGEL
Corwin, Cecil
   See Kornbluth, C(yril) M.
Cosic, Dobrica 1921- .... **CLC 14**
   See also CA 122; 138; CWW 2; DLB 181
Costain, Thomas B(ertram)
   1885-1965 .... **CLC 30**
   See also BYA 3; CA 5-8R; 25-28R; DLB 9; RHW
Costantini, Humberto 1924(?)-1987 . **CLC 49**
   See also CA 131; 122; HW 1
Costello, Elvis 1955- .... **CLC 21**
Costenoble, Philostene 1898-1962
   See Ghelderode, Michel de
Costenoble, Philostene 1898-1962
   See Ghelderode, Michel de
Cotes, Cecil V.
   See Duncan, Sara Jeannette
Cotter, Joseph Seamon Sr.
   1861-1949 ...... **TCLC 28; BLC 1; DAM MULT**
   See also BW 1; CA 124; DLB 50
Couch, Arthur Thomas Quiller
   See Quiller-Couch, Sir Arthur (Thomas)
Coulton, James
   See Hansen, Joseph
Couperus, Louis (Marie Anne)
   1863-1923 .... **TCLC 15**
   See also CA 115; RGWL
Coupland, Douglas 1961- .... **CLC 85, 133; DAC; DAM POP**
   See also AAYA 34; CA 142; CANR 57, 90; CCA 1; CPW
Court, Wesli
   See Turco, Lewis (Putnam)
Courtenay, Bryce 1933- .... **CLC 59**
   See also CA 138; CPW
Courtney, Robert
   See Ellison, Harlan (Jay)
Cousteau, Jacques-Yves 1910-1997 .. **CLC 30**
   See also CA 65-68; 159; CANR 15, 67; MTCW 1; SATA 38, 98
Coventry, Francis 1725-1754 .... **LC 46**
Cowan, Peter (Walkinshaw) 1914- .... **SSC 28**
   See also CA 21-24R; CANR 9, 25, 50, 83; CN; RGSF
Coward, Noel (Peirce) 1899-1973 . **CLC 1, 9, 29, 51; DAM DRAM**
   See also AITN 1; BRWS 2; CA 17-18; 41-44R; CANR 35; CAP 2; CDBLB 1914-1945; DA3; DFS 3, 6; DLB 10, 245; IDFW 3, 4; MTCW 1, 2; RGEL
Cowley, Abraham 1618-1667 .... **LC 43**
   See also BRW 2; DLB 131, 151; PAB; RGEL
Cowley, Malcolm 1898-1989 .... **CLC 39**
   See also AMWS 2; CA 5-8R; 128; CANR 3, 55; DLB 4, 48; DLBY 81, 89; MTCW 1, 2
Cowper, William 1731-1800 ..... **NCLC 8, 94; DAM POET**
   See also BRW 3; DA3; DLB 104, 109; RGEL
Cox, William Trevor 1928-
   See Trevor, William
   See also CA 9-12R; CANR 4, 37, 55, 76, 102; DAM NOV; INT CANR-37; MTCW 1, 2
Coyne, P. J.
   See Masters, Hilary

Cozzens, James Gould 1903-1978 . **CLC 1, 4, 11, 92**
   See also AMW; BPFB 1; CA 9-12R; 81-84; CANR 19; CDALB 1941-1968; DLB 9; DLBD 2; DLBY 84, 97; MTCW 1, 2; RGAL
Crabbe, George 1754-1832 .... **NCLC 26**
   See also BRW 3; DLB 93; RGEL
Craddock, Charles Egbert
   See Murfree, Mary Noailles
Craig, A. A.
   See Anderson, Poul (William)
Craik, Mrs.
   See Craik, Dinah Maria (Mulock)
   See also RGEL
Craik, Dinah Maria (Mulock)
   1826-1887 .... **NCLC 38**
   See also Craik, Mrs.; Mulock, Dinah Maria
   See also DLB 35, 163; MAICYA; SATA 34
Cram, Ralph Adams 1863-1942 ..... **TCLC 45**
   See also CA 160
Crane, (Harold) Hart 1899-1932 .... **TCLC 2, 5, 80; DA; DAB; DAC; DAM MST, POET; PC 3; WLC**
   See also AMW; CA 104; 127; CDALB 1917-1929; DA3; DLB 4, 48; MTCW 1, 2; RGAL
Crane, R(onald) S(almon)
   1886-1967 .... **CLC 27**
   See also CA 85-88; DLB 63
Crane, Stephen (Townley)
   1871-1900 .... **TCLC 11, 17, 32; DA; DAB; DAC; DAM MST, NOV, POET; SSC 7; WLC**
   See also AAYA 21; AMW; BPFB 1; BYA 3; CA 109; 140; CANR 84; CDALB 1865-1917; DA3; DLB 12, 54, 78; EXPN; EXPS; LAIT 2; NFS 4; PFS 9; RGAL; RGSF; SSFS 4; WYA; YABC 2
Cranshaw, Stanley
   See Fisher, Dorothy (Frances) Canfield
Crase, Douglas 1944- .... **CLC 58**
   See also CA 106
Crashaw, Richard 1612(?)-1649 .... **LC 24**
   See also BRW 2; DLB 126; PAB; RGEL
Craven, Margaret 1901-1980 .... **CLC 17; DAC**
   See also BYA 2; CA 103; CCA 1; LAIT 5
Crawford, F(rancis) Marion
   1854-1909 .... **TCLC 10**
   See also CA 107; 168; DLB 71; HGG; RGAL; SUFW
Crawford, Isabella Valancy
   1850-1887 .... **NCLC 12**
   See also DLB 92; RGEL
Crayon, Geoffrey
   See Irving, Washington
Creasey, John 1908-1973 .... **CLC 11**
   See also Marric, J. J.
   See also CA 5-8R; 41-44R; CANR 8, 59; CMW; DLB 77; MTCW 1
Crebillon, Claude Prosper Jolyot de (fils)
   1707-1777 .... **LC 1, 28**
   See also GFL Beginnings to 1789
Credo
   See Creasey, John
Credo, Alvaro J. de
   See Prado (Calvo), Pedro
Creeley, Robert (White) 1926- .. **CLC 1, 2, 4, 8, 11, 15, 36, 78; DAM POET**
   See also AMWS 4; CA 1-4R; CAAS 10; CANR 23, 43, 89; CP; DA3; DLB 5, 16, 169; DLBD 17; MTCW 1, 2; RGAL; WP
Crevecoeur, Hector St. John de
   See Crevecoeur, Michel Guillaume Jean de
   See also ANW

Crevecoeur, Michel Guillaume Jean de
   1735-1813 .... **NCLC 105**
   See also Crevecoeur, Hector St. John de
   See also AMWS 1; DLB 37
Crevel, Rene 1900-1935 .... **TCLC 112**
   See also GLL 2
Crews, Harry (Eugene) 1935- ..... **CLC 6, 23, 49**
   See also AITN 1; BPFB 1; CA 25-28R; CANR 20, 57; CN; CSW; DA3; DLB 6, 143, 185; MTCW 1, 2; RGAL
Crichton, (John) Michael 1942- .... **CLC 2, 6, 54, 90; DAM NOV, POP**
   See also AAYA 10; AITN 2; BPFB 1; CA 25-28R; CANR 13, 40, 54, 76; CMW; CN; CPW; DA3; DLBY 81; INT CANR-13; JRDA; MTCW 1, 2; SATA 9, 88; SFW; YAW
Crispin, Edmund .... **CLC 22**
   See also Montgomery, (Robert) Bruce
   See also DLB 87; MSW
Cristofer, Michael 1945(?)- ... **CLC 28; DAM DRAM**
   See also CA 110; 152; CAD; CD; DLB 7
Croce, Benedetto 1866-1952 .... **TCLC 37**
   See also CA 120; 155; EW 8
Crockett, David 1786-1836 .... **NCLC 8**
   See also DLB 3, 11, 183, 248
Crockett, Davy
   See Crockett, David
Crofts, Freeman Wills 1879-1957 .. **TCLC 55**
   See also CA 115; 195; CMW; DLB 77; MSW
Croker, John Wilson 1780-1857 .... **NCLC 10**
   See also DLB 110
Crommelynck, Fernand 1885-1970 .. **CLC 75**
   See also CA 189; 89-92
Cromwell, Oliver 1599-1658 .... **LC 43**
Cronenberg, David 1943- .... **CLC 143**
   See also CA 138; CCA 1
Cronin, A(rchibald) J(oseph)
   1896-1981 .... **CLC 32**
   See also BPFB 1; CA 1-4R; 102; CANR 5; DLB 191; SATA 47; SATA-Obit 25
Cross, Amanda
   See Heilbrun, Carolyn G(old)
   See also BPFB 1; MSW
Crothers, Rachel 1878-1958 .... **TCLC 19**
   See also CA 113; 194; CAD; CWD; DLB 7; RGAL
Croves, Hal
   See Traven, B.
Crow Dog, Mary (Ellen) (?)- .... **CLC 93**
   See also Brave Bird, Mary
   See also CA 154
Crowfield, Christopher
   See Stowe, Harriet (Elizabeth) Beecher
Crowley, Aleister .... **TCLC 7**
   See also Crowley, Edward Alexander
   See also GLL 1
Crowley, Edward Alexander 1875-1947
   See Crowley, Aleister
   See also CA 104; HGG
Crowley, John 1942- .... **CLC 57**
   See also BPFB 1; CA 61-64; CANR 43, 98; DLBY 82; SATA 65; SFW
Crud
   See Crumb, R(obert)
Crumarums
   See Crumb, R(obert)
Crumb, R(obert) 1943- .... **CLC 17**
   See also CA 106
Crumbum
   See Crumb, R(obert)
Crumski
   See Crumb, R(obert)
Crum the Bum
   See Crumb, R(obert)

Davis, B. Lynch
See Bioy Casares, Adolfo; Borges, Jorge Luis

Davis, B. Lynch
See Bioy Casares, Adolfo

Davis, Gordon
See Hunt, E(verette) Howard, (Jr.)

Davis, H(arold) L(enoir) 1896-1960 . **CLC 49**
See also ANW; CA 178; 89-92; DLB 9, 206; SATA 114

Davis, Rebecca (Blaine) Harding
1831-1910 .... **TCLC 6; SSC 38**
See also CA 104; 179; DLB 74, 239; FW; RGAL

Davis, Richard Harding
1864-1916 .... **TCLC 24**
See also CA 114; 179; DLB 12, 23, 78, 79, 189; DLBD 13; RGAL

Davison, Frank Dalby 1893-1970 ..... **CLC 15**
See also CA 116

Davison, Lawrence H.
See Lawrence, D(avid) H(erbert Richards)

Davison, Peter (Hubert) 1928- .... **CLC 28**
See also CA 9-12R; CAAS 4; CANR 3, 43, 84; CP; DLB 5

Davys, Mary 1674-1732 .... **LC 1, 46**
See also DLB 39

Dawson, Fielding 1930- .... **CLC 6**
See also CA 85-88; DLB 130

Dawson, Peter
See Faust, Frederick (Schiller)
See also TCWW 2, 2

Day, Clarence (Shepard, Jr.)
1874-1935 .... **TCLC 25**
See also CA 108; DLB 11

Day, John 1574(?)-1640(?) .... **LC 70**
See also DLB 62, 170; RGEL

Day, Thomas 1748-1789 .... **LC 1**
See also DLB 39; YABC 1

Day Lewis, C(ecil) 1904-1972 . **CLC 1, 6, 10; DAM POET; PC 11**
See also Blake, Nicholas
See also BRWS 3; CA 13-16; 33-36R; CANR 34; CAP 1; CWRI; DLB 15, 20; MTCW 1, 2; RGEL

Dazai Osamu .... **TCLC 11; SSC 41**
See also Tsushima, Shuji
See also CA 164; DLB 182; MJW; RGSF; RGWL

de Andrade, Carlos Drummond
See Drummond de Andrade, Carlos

de Andrade, Mario 1892-1945
See Andrade, Mario de
See also CA 178; HW 2

Deane, Norman
See Creasey, John

Deane, Seamus (Francis) 1940- ...... **CLC 122**
See also CA 118; CANR 42

de Beauvoir, Simone (Lucie Ernestine Marie Bertrand)
See Beauvoir, Simone (Lucie Ernestine Marie Bertrand) de

de Beer, P.
See Bosman, Herman Charles

de Brissac, Malcolm
See Dickinson, Peter (Malcolm)

de Campos, Alvaro
See Pessoa, Fernando (Antonio Nogueira)

de Chardin, Pierre Teilhard
See Teilhard de Chardin, (Marie Joseph) Pierre

Dee, John 1527-1608 .... **LC 20**
See also DLB 136, 213

Deer, Sandra 1940- .... **CLC 45**
See also CA 186

De Ferrari, Gabriella 1941- .... **CLC 65**
See also CA 146

Defoe, Daniel 1660(?)-1731 .... **LC 1, 42; DA; DAB; DAC; DAM MST, NOV; WLC**
See also AAYA 27; BRW 3; BRWR 1; BYA 4; CDBLB 1660-1789; CLR 61; DA3; DLB 39, 95, 101; JRDA; LAIT 1; MAICYA; NFS 9, 13; RGEL; SATA 22; WCH; WLIT 3

de Gourmont, Remy(-Marie-Charles)
See Gourmont, Remy(-Marie-Charles) de

de Hartog, Jan 1914- .... **CLC 19**
See also CA 1-4R; CANR 1; DFS 12

de Hostos, E. M.
See Hostos (y Bonilla), Eugenio Maria de

de Hostos, Eugenio M.
See Hostos (y Bonilla), Eugenio Maria de

Deighton, Len .... **CLC 4, 7, 22, 46**
See also Deighton, Leonard Cyril
See also AAYA 6; BEST 89:2; BPFB 1; CD-BLB 1960 to Present; CMW; CN; CPW; DLB 87

Deighton, Leonard Cyril 1929-
See Deighton, Len
See also CA 9-12R; CANR 19, 33, 68; DA3; DAM NOV, POP; MTCW 1, 2

Dekker, Thomas 1572(?)-1632 . **LC 22; DAM DRAM; DC 12**
See also CDBLB Before 1660; DLB 62, 172; RGEL

Delafield, E. M. .... **TCLC 61**
See also Dashwood, Edmee Elizabeth Monica de la Pasture
See also DLB 34; RHW

de la Mare, Walter (John)
1873-1956 ..... **TCLC 4, 53; DAB; DAC; DAM MST, POET; SSC 14; WLC**
See also CA 163; CDBLB 1914-1945; CLR 23; CWRI; DA3; DLB 19, 153, 162, 255; EXPP; HGG; MAICYA; MTCW 1; RGEL; RGSF; SATA 16; SUFW; WCH

Delaney, Franey
See O'Hara, John (Henry)

Delaney, Shelagh 1939- .... **CLC 29; DAM DRAM**
See also CA 17-20R; CANR 30, 67; CBD; CD; CDBLB 1960 to Present; CWD; DFS 7; DLB 13; MTCW 1

Delany, Martin Robison
1812-1885 .... **NCLC 93**
See also DLB 50; RGAL

Delany, Mary (Granville Pendarves)
1700-1788 .... **LC 12**

Delany, Samuel R(ay), Jr. 1942- . **CLC 8, 14, 38, 141; BLC 1; DAM MULT**
See also AAYA 24; AFAW 2; BPFB 1; BW 2, 3; CA 81-84; CANR 27, 43; DLB 8, 33; MTCW 1, 2; RGAL; SCFW

De La Ramee, (Marie) Louise 1839-1908
See Ouida
See also SATA 20

de la Roche, Mazo 1879-1961 .... **CLC 14**
See also CA 85-88; CANR 30; DLB 68; RGEL; RHW; SATA 64

De La Salle, Innocent
See Hartmann, Sadakichi

Delbanco, Nicholas (Franklin)
1942- .... **CLC 6, 13**
See also CA 17-20R; CAAE 189; CAAS 2; CANR 29, 55; DLB 6, 234

del Castillo, Michel 1933- .... **CLC 38**
See also CA 109; CANR 77

Deledda, Grazia (Cosima)
1875(?)-1936 .... **TCLC 23**
See also CA 123; RGWL

Deleuze, Gilles 1925-1995 .... **TCLC 116**

Delgado, Abelardo (Lalo) B(arrientos) 1930-
See also CA 131; CAAS 15; CANR 90; DAM MST, MULT; DLB 82; HLC 1; HW 1, 2

Delibes, Miguel .... **CLC 8, 18**
See also Delibes Setien, Miguel

Delibes Setien, Miguel 1920-
See Delibes, Miguel
See also CA 45-48; CANR 1, 32; HW 1; MTCW 1

DeLillo, Don 1936- ..... **CLC 8, 10, 13, 27, 39, 54, 76, 143; DAM NOV, POP**
See also AMWS 6; BEST 89:1; BPFB 1; CA 81-84; CANR 21, 76, 92; CN; CPW; DA3; DLB 6, 173; MTCW 1, 2; RGAL

de Lisser, H. G.
See De Lisser, H(erbert) G(eorge)
See also DLB 117

De Lisser, H(erbert) G(eorge)
1878-1944 .... **TCLC 12**
See also de Lisser, H. G.
See also BW 2; CA 109; 152

Deloire, Pierre
See Peguy, Charles (Pierre)

Deloney, Thomas 1543(?)-1600 .... **LC 41**
See also DLB 167; RGEL

Deloria, Vine (Victor), Jr. 1933- ...... **CLC 21, 122; DAM MULT**
See also CA 53-56; CANR 5, 20, 48, 98; DLB 175; MTCW 1; NNAL; SATA 21

Del Vecchio, John M(ichael) 1947- .. **CLC 29**
See also CA 110; DLBD 9

de Man, Paul (Adolph Michel)
1919-1983 .... **CLC 55**
See also CA 128; 111; CANR 61; DLB 67; MTCW 1, 2

DeMarinis, Rick 1934- .... **CLC 54**
See also CA 57-60, 184; CAAE 184; CAAS 24; CANR 9, 25, 50; DLB 218

Dembry, R. Emmet
See Murfree, Mary Noailles

Demby, William 1922- .... **CLC 53; BLC 1; DAM MULT**
See also BW 1, 3; CA 81-84; CANR 81; DLB 33

de Menton, Francisco
See Chin, Frank (Chew, Jr.)

Demetrius of Phalerum c.
307B.C.- .... **CMLC 34**

Demijohn, Thom
See Disch, Thomas M(ichael)

Deming, Richard 1915-1983
See Queen, Ellery
See also CA 9-12R; CANR 3, 94; SATA 24

Democritus c. 460B.C.-c. 370B.C. . **CMLC 47**

de Montherlant, Henry (Milon)
See Montherlant, Henry (Milon) de

Demosthenes 384B.C.-322B.C. ...... **CMLC 13**
See also AW 1; DLB 176; RGWL

de Natale, Francine
See Malzberg, Barry N(athaniel)

de Navarre, Marguerite 1492-1549 ..... **LC 61**
See also Marguerite d'Angouleme; Marguerite de Navarre

Denby, Edwin (Orr) 1903-1983 .... **CLC 48**
See also CA 138; 110

Denham, John 1615-1669 .... **LC 73**
See also DLB 58, 126; RGEL

Denis, Julio
See Cortazar, Julio

Denmark, Harrison
See Zelazny, Roger (Joseph)

Dennis, John 1658-1734 .... **LC 11**
See also DLB 101; RGEL

Dennis, Nigel (Forbes) 1912-1989 ...... **CLC 8**
See also CA 25-28R; 129; DLB 13, 15, 233; MTCW 1

Dent, Lester 1904(?)-1959 .... **TCLC 72**
See also CA 112; 161; CMW; SFW

De Palma, Brian (Russell) 1940- ...... **CLC 20**
See also CA 109

Domecq, H(onorio) Bustos
    See Bioy Casares, Adolfo; Borges, Jorge
    Luis

Domini, Rey
    See Lorde, Audre (Geraldine)
    See also GLL 1

Dominique
    See Proust, (Valentin-Louis-George-Eugene-
)Marcel

Don, A
    See Stephen, Sir Leslie

Donaldson, Stephen R(eeder)
    1947- .... **CLC 46, 138; DAM POP**
    See also AAYA 36; BPFB 1; CA 89-92;
    CANR 13, 55, 99; CPW; FANT; INT
    CANR-13; SATA 121; SFW; SUFW

Donleavy, J(ames) P(atrick) 1926- .... **CLC 1,
    4, 6, 10, 45**
    See also AITN 2; BPFB 1; CA 9-12R;
    CANR 24, 49, 62, 80; CBD; CD; CN;
    DLB 6, 173; INT CANR-24; MTCW 1,
    2; RGAL

Donne, John 1572-1631 .... **LC 10, 24; DA;
    DAB; DAC; DAM MST, POET; PC 1;
    WLC**
    See also BRW 1; BRWR 2; CDBLB Before
    1660; DLB 121, 151; EXPP; PAB; PFS 2,
    11; RGEL; WLIT 3; WP

Donnell, David 1939(?)- .... **CLC 34**
    See also CA 197

Donoghue, P. S.
    See Hunt, E(verette) Howard, (Jr.)

Donoso (Yanez), Jose 1924-1996 ... **CLC 4, 8,
    11, 32, 99; DAM MULT; HLC 1; SSC
    34**
    See also CA 81-84; 155; CANR 32, 73;
    DLB 113; HW 1, 2; LAW; LAWS 1;
    MTCW 1, 2; RGSF; WLIT 1

Donovan, John 1928-1992 .... **CLC 35**
    See also AAYA 20; CA 97-100; 137; CLR
    3; MAICYA; SATA 72; SATA-Brief 29;
    YAW

Don Roberto
    See Cunninghame Graham, Robert
    (Gallnigad) Bontine

Doolittle, Hilda 1886-1961 . **CLC 3, 8, 14, 31,
    34, 73; DA; DAC; DAM MST, POET;
    PC 5; WLC**
    See also H. D.
    See also AMWS 1; CA 97-100; CANR 35;
    DLB 4, 45; FW; GLL 1; MAWW; MTCW
    1, 2; PFS 6; RGAL

Doppo, Kunikida .... **TCLC 99**
    See also Kunikida Doppo

Dorfman, Ariel 1942- ...... **CLC 48, 77; DAM
    MULT; HLC 1**
    See also CA 124; 130; CANR 67, 70; CWW
    2; DFS 4; HW 1, 2; INT CA-130; WLIT
    1

Dorn, Edward (Merton)
    1929-1999 .... **CLC 10, 18**
    See also CA 93-96; 187; CANR 42, 79; CP;
    DLB 5; INT 93-96; WP

Dor-Ner, Zvi .... **CLC 70**

Dorris, Michael (Anthony)
    1945-1997 .... **CLC 109; DAM MULT,
    NOV**
    See also AAYA 20; BEST 90:1; BYA 12;
    CA 102; 157; CANR 19, 46, 75; CLR 58;
    DA3; DLB 175; LAIT 5; MTCW 2; NFS
    3; NNAL; RGAL; SATA 75; SATA-Obit
    94; TCWW 2; YAW

Dorris, Michael A.
    See Dorris, Michael (Anthony)

Dorsan, Luc
    See Simenon, Georges (Jacques Christian)

Dorsange, Jean
    See Simenon, Georges (Jacques Christian)

Dos Passos, John (Roderigo)
    1896-1970 ... **CLC 1, 4, 8, 11, 15, 25, 34,
    82; DA; DAB; DAC; DAM MST, NOV;
    WLC**
    See also AMW; BPFB 1; CA 1-4R; 29-32R;
    CANR 3; CDALB 1929-1941; DA3; DLB
    4, 9; DLBD 1, 15; DLBY 96; MTCW 1,
    2; RGAL

Dossage, Jean
    See Simenon, Georges (Jacques Christian)

Dostoevsky, Fedor Mikhailovich
    1821-1881 . **NCLC 2, 7, 21, 33, 43; DA;
    DAB; DAC; DAM MST, NOV; SSC 2,
    33, 44; WLC**
    See also Dostoevsky, Fyodor
    See also AAYA 40; DA3; EW 7; EXPN;
    NFS 3, 8; RGSF; RGWL; SSFS 8

Dostoevsky, Fyodor
    See Dostoevsky, Fedor Mikhailovich
    See also DLB 238

Doughty, Charles M(ontagu)
    1843-1926 .... **TCLC 27**
    See also CA 115; 178; DLB 19, 57, 174

Douglas, Ellen .... **CLC 73**
    See also Haxton, Josephine Ayres; William-
    son, Ellen Douglas
    See also CN; CSW

Douglas, Gavin 1475(?)-1522 .... **LC 20**
    See also DLB 132; RGEL

Douglas, George
    See Brown, George Douglas
    See also RGEL

Douglas, Keith (Castellain)
    1920-1944 .... **TCLC 40**
    See also BRW 7; CA 160; DLB 27; PAB;
    RGEL

Douglas, Leonard
    See Bradbury, Ray (Douglas)

Douglas, Michael
    See Crichton, (John) Michael

Douglas, (George) Norman
    1868-1952 .... **TCLC 68**
    See also BRW 6; CA 119; 157; DLB 34,
    195; RGEL

Douglas, William
    See Brown, George Douglas

Douglass, Frederick 1817(?)-1895 .. **NCLC 7,
    55; BLC 1; DA; DAC; DAM MST,
    MULT; WLC**
    See also AFAW 1, 2; AMWS 3; CDALB
    1640-1865; DA3; DLB 1, 43, 50, 79, 243;
    FW; LAIT 2; NCFS 2; RGAL; SATA 29

Dourado, (Waldomiro Freitas) Autran
    1926- .... **CLC 23, 60**
    See also CA 25-28R; 179; CANR 34, 81;
    DLB 145; HW 2

Dourado, Waldomiro Autran
    See Dourado, (Waldomiro Freitas) Autran
    See also CA 179

Dove, Rita (Frances) 1952- .... **CLC 50, 81;
    BLCS; DAM MULT, POET; PC 6**
    See also AMWS 4; BW 2; CA 109; CAAS
    19; CANR 27, 42, 68, 76, 97; CDALBS;
    CP; CSW; CWP; DA3; DLB 120; EXPP;
    MTCW 1; PFS 1; RGAL

Doveglion
    See Villa, Jose Garcia

Dowell, Coleman 1925-1985 .... **CLC 60**
    See also CA 25-28R; 117; CANR 10; DLB
    130; GLL 2

Dowson, Ernest (Christopher)
    1867-1900 .... **TCLC 4**
    See also CA 105; 150; DLB 19, 135; RGEL

Doyle, A. Conan
    See Doyle, Sir Arthur Conan

Doyle, Sir Arthur Conan
    1859-1930 ... **TCLC 7; DA; DAB; DAC;
    DAM MST, NOV; SSC 12; WLC**
    See also Conan Doyle, Arthur
    See also AAYA 14; BRWS 2; CA 104; 122;
    CDBLB 1890-1914; CMW; DA3; DLB
    18, 70, 156, 178; EXPS; HGG; LAIT 2;
    MSW; MTCW 1, 2; RGEL; RGSF; RHW;
    SATA 24; SCFW 2; SFW; SSFS 2; WCH;
    WLIT 4; WYA; YAW

Doyle, Conan
    See Doyle, Sir Arthur Conan

Doyle, John
    See Graves, Robert (von Ranke)

Doyle, Roddy 1958(?)- .... **CLC 81**
    See also AAYA 14; BRWS 5; CA 143;
    CANR 73; CN; DA3; DLB 194

Doyle, Sir A. Conan
    See Doyle, Sir Arthur Conan

Dr. A
    See Asimov, Isaac; Silverstein, Alvin; Sil-
    verstein, Virginia B(arbara Opshelor)

Drabble, Margaret 1939- ...... **CLC 2, 3, 5, 8,
    10, 22, 53, 129; DAB; DAC; DAM
    MST, NOV, POP**
    See also BRWS 4; CA 13-16R; CANR 18,
    35, 63; CDBLB 1960 to Present; CN;
    CPW; DA3; DLB 14, 155, 231; FW;
    MTCW 1, 2; RGEL; SATA 48

Drapier, M. B.
    See Swift, Jonathan

Drayham, James
    See Mencken, H(enry) L(ouis)

Drayton, Michael 1563-1631 ..... **LC 8; DAM
    POET**
    See also DLB 121; RGEL

Dreadstone, Carl
    See Campbell, (John) Ramsey

Dreiser, Theodore (Herman Albert)
    1871-1945 .... **TCLC 10, 18, 35, 83; DA;
    DAC; DAM MST, NOV; SSC 30; WLC**
    See also AMW; CA 106; 132; CDALB
    1865-1917; DA3; DLB 9, 12, 102, 137;
    DLBD 1; LAIT 2; MTCW 1, 2; NFS 8;
    RGAL

Drexler, Rosalyn 1926- .... **CLC 2, 6**
    See also CA 81-84; CAD; CANR 68; CD;
    CWD

Dreyer, Carl Theodor 1889-1968 ...... **CLC 16**
    See also CA 116

Drieu la Rochelle, Pierre(-Eugene)
    1893-1945 .... **TCLC 21**
    See also CA 117; DLB 72; GFL 1789 to the
    Present

Drinkwater, John 1882-1937 .... **TCLC 57**
    See also CA 109; 149; DLB 10, 19, 149;
    RGEL

Drop Shot
    See Cable, George Washington

Droste-Hulshoff, Annette Freiin von
    1797-1848 .... **NCLC 3**
    See also DLB 133; RGSF; RGWL

Drummond, Walter
    See Silverberg, Robert

Drummond, William Henry
    1854-1907 .... **TCLC 25**
    See also CA 160; DLB 92

Drummond de Andrade, Carlos
    1902-1987 .... **CLC 18**
    See also Andrade, Carlos Drummond de
    See also CA 132; 123; LAW

Drury, Allen (Stuart) 1918-1998 .... **CLC 37**
    See also CA 57-60; 170; CANR 18, 52; CN;
    INT CANR-18

Dryden, John 1631-1700 .... **LC 3, 21; DA;
    DAB; DAC; DAM DRAM, MST,
    POET; DC 3; PC 25; WLC**
    See also BRW 2; CDBLB 1660-1789; DLB
    80, 101, 131; EXPP; IDTP; RGEL; TEA;
    WLIT 3

Duberman, Martin (Bauml) 1930- ..... **CLC 8**
See also CA 1-4R; CAD; CANR 2, 63; CD

Dubie, Norman (Evans) 1945- .... **CLC 36**
See also CA 69-72; CANR 12; CP; DLB 120; PFS 12

Du Bois, W(illiam) E(dward) B(urghardt) 1868-1963 ... **CLC 1, 2, 13, 64, 96; BLC 1; DA; DAC; DAM MST, MULT, NOV; WLC**
See also AAYA 40; AFAW 1, 2; AMWS 2; BW 1, 3; CA 85-88; CANR 34, 82; CDALB 1865-1917; DA3; DLB 47, 50, 91, 246; EXPP; LAIT 2; MTCW 1, 2; NCFS 1; PFS 13; RGAL; SATA 42

Dubus, Andre 1936-1999 ..... **CLC 13, 36, 97; SSC 15**
See also AMWS 7; CA 21-24R; 177; CANR 17; CN; CSW; DLB 130; INT CANR-17; RGAL; SSFS 10

Duca Minimo
See D'Annunzio, Gabriele

Ducharme, Rejean 1941- .... **CLC 74**
See also CA 165; DLB 60

Duchen, Claire .... **CLC 65**

Duclos, Charles Pinot- 1704-1772 .... **LC 1**
See also GFL Beginnings to 1789

Dudek, Louis 1918- .... **CLC 11, 19**
See also CA 45-48; CAAS 14; CANR 1; CP; DLB 88

Duerrenmatt, Friedrich 1921-1990 ... **CLC 1, 4, 8, 11, 15, 43, 102; DAM DRAM**
See also Durrenmatt, Friedrich
See also CA 17-20R; CANR 33; CMW; DLB 69, 124; MTCW 1, 2

Duffy, Bruce 1953(?)- .... **CLC 50**
See also CA 172

Duffy, Maureen 1933- .... **CLC 37**
See also CA 25-28R; CANR 33, 68; CBD; CN; CP; CWD; CWP; DLB 14; FW; MTCW 1

Du Fu
See Tu Fu
See also RGWL

Dugan, Alan 1923- .... **CLC 2, 6**
See also CA 81-84; CP; DLB 5; PFS 10

du Gard, Roger Martin
See Martin du Gard, Roger

Duhamel, Georges 1884-1966 .... **CLC 8**
See also CA 81-84; 25-28R; CANR 35; DLB 65; GFL 1789 to the Present; MTCW 1

Dujardin, Edouard (Emile Louis) 1861-1949 .... **TCLC 13**
See also CA 109; DLB 123

Dulles, John Foster 1888-1959 .... **TCLC 72**
See also CA 115; 149

Dumas, Alexandre (pere) 1802-1870 ...... **NCLC 11, 71; DA; DAB; DAC; DAM MST, NOV; WLC**
See also AAYA 22; BYA 3; DA3; DLB 119, 192; EW 6; GFL 1789 to the Present; LAIT 1, 2; RGWL; SATA 18; WCH

Dumas, Alexandre (fils) 1824-1895 .... **NCLC 9; DC 1**
See also DLB 192; GFL 1789 to the Present; RGWL

Dumas, Claudine
See Malzberg, Barry N(athaniel)

Dumas, Henry L. 1934-1968 .... **CLC 6, 62**
See also BW 1; CA 85-88; DLB 41; RGAL

du Maurier, Daphne 1907-1989 .. **CLC 6, 11, 59; DAB; DAC; DAM MST, POP; SSC 18**
See also AAYA 37; BPFB 1; BRWS 3; CA 5-8R; 128; CANR 6, 55; CMW; CPW; DA3; DLB 191; HGG; LAIT 3; MSW; MTCW 1, 2; NFS 12; RGEL; RGSF; RHW; SATA 27; SATA-Obit 60

Du Maurier, George 1834-1896 ..... **NCLC 86**
See also DLB 153, 178; RGEL

Dunbar, Paul Laurence 1872-1906 . **TCLC 2, 12; BLC 1; DA; DAC; DAM MST, MULT, POET; PC 5; SSC 8; WLC**
See also AFAW 1, 2; AMWS 2; BW 1, 3; CA 104; 124; CANR 79; CDALB 1865-1917; DA3; DLB 50, 54, 78; EXPP; RGAL; SATA 34

Dunbar, William 1460(?)-1520(?) .... **LC 20**
See also DLB 132, 146; RGEL

Duncan, Dora Angela
See Duncan, Isadora

Duncan, Isadora 1877(?)-1927 .... **TCLC 68**
See also CA 118; 149

Duncan, Lois 1934- .... **CLC 26**
See also AAYA 4, 34; BYA 6, 8; CA 1-4R; CANR 2, 23, 36; CLR 29; JRDA; MAICYA; MAICYAS; SAAS 2; SATA 1, 36, 75; WYA; YAW

Duncan, Robert (Edward) 1919-1988 .... **CLC 1, 2, 4, 7, 15, 41, 55; DAM POET; PC 2**
See also CA 9-12R; 124; CANR 28, 62; DLB 5, 16, 193; MTCW 1, 2; PFS 13; RGAL; WP

Duncan, Sara Jeannette 1861-1922 .... **TCLC 60**
See also CA 157; DLB 92

Dunlap, William 1766-1839 .... **NCLC 2**
See also DLB 30, 37, 59; RGAL

Dunn, Douglas (Eaglesham) 1942- .. **CLC 6, 40**
See also CA 45-48; CANR 2, 33; CP; DLB 40; MTCW 1

Dunn, Katherine (Karen) 1945- .... **CLC 71**
See also CA 33-36R; CANR 72; HGG; MTCW 1

Dunn, Stephen (Elliott) 1939- .... **CLC 36**
See also CA 33-36R; CANR 12, 48, 53, 105; CP; DLB 105

Dunne, Finley Peter 1867-1936 ...... **TCLC 28**
See also CA 108; 178; DLB 11, 23; RGAL

Dunne, John Gregory 1932- .... **CLC 28**
See also CA 25-28R; CANR 14, 50; CN; DLBY 80

Dunsany, Lord .... **TCLC 2, 59**
See also Dunsany, Edward John Moreton Drax Plunkett
See also DLB 77, 153, 156, 255; FANT; IDTP; RGEL; SFW; SUFW

Dunsany, Edward John Moreton Drax Plunkett 1878-1957
See Dunsany, Lord
See also CA 104; 148; DLB 10; MTCW 1

du Perry, Jean
See Simenon, Georges (Jacques Christian)

Durang, Christopher (Ferdinand) 1949- .... **CLC 27, 38**
See also CA 105; CAD; CANR 50, 76; CD; MTCW 1

Duras, Marguerite 1914-1996 . **CLC 3, 6, 11, 20, 34, 40, 68, 100; SSC 40**
See also BPFB 1; CA 25-28R; 151; CANR 50; CWW 2; DLB 83; GFL 1789 to the Present; IDFW 4; MTCW 1, 2; RGWL

Durban, (Rosa) Pam 1947- .... **CLC 39**
See also CA 123; CANR 98; CSW

Durcan, Paul 1944- .... **CLC 43, 70; DAM POET**
See also CA 134; CP

Durkheim, Emile 1858-1917 .... **TCLC 55**

Durrell, Lawrence (George) 1912-1990 .... **CLC 1, 4, 6, 8, 13, 27, 41; DAM NOV**
See also BPFB 1; BRWS 1; CA 9-12R; 132; CANR 40, 77; CDBLB 1945-1960; DLB 15, 27, 204; DLBY 90; MTCW 1, 2; RGEL; SFW

Durrenmatt, Friedrich
See Duerrenmatt, Friedrich
See also EW 13; RGWL

Dutt, Toru 1856-1877 .... **NCLC 29**
See also DLB 240

Dwight, Timothy 1752-1817 .... **NCLC 13**
See also DLB 37; RGAL

Dworkin, Andrea 1946- .... **CLC 43, 123**
See also CA 77-80; CAAS 21; CANR 16, 39, 76, 96; FW; GLL 1; INT CANR-16; MTCW 1, 2

Dwyer, Deanna
See Koontz, Dean R(ay)

Dwyer, K. R.
See Koontz, Dean R(ay)

Dwyer, Thomas A. 1923- .... **CLC 114**
See also CA 115

Dybek, Stuart 1942- .... **CLC 114**
See also CA 97-100; CANR 39; DLB 130

Dye, Richard
See De Voto, Bernard (Augustine)

Dyer, Geoff 1958- .... **CLC 149**
See also CA 125; CANR 88

Dylan, Bob 1941- .... **CLC 3, 4, 6, 12, 77; PC 37**
See also CA 41-44R; CP; DLB 16

Dyson, John 1943- .... **CLC 70**
See also CA 144

E. V. L.
See Lucas, E(dward) V(errall)

Eagleton, Terence (Francis) 1943- .. **CLC 63, 132**
See also CA 57-60; CANR 7, 23, 68; DLB 242; MTCW 1, 2

Eagleton, Terry
See Eagleton, Terence (Francis)

Early, Jack
See Scoppettone, Sandra
See also GLL 1

East, Michael
See West, Morris L(anglo)

Eastaway, Edward
See Thomas, (Philip) Edward

Eastlake, William (Derry) 1917-1997 .... **CLC 8**
See also CA 5-8R; 158; CAAS 1; CANR 5, 63; CN; DLB 6, 206; INT CANR-5; TCWW 2

Eastman, Charles A(lexander) 1858-1939 .... **TCLC 55; DAM MULT**
See also CA 179; CANR 91; DLB 175; NNAL; YABC 1

Eberhart, Richard (Ghormley) 1904- .. **CLC 3, 11, 19, 56; DAM POET**
See also AMW; CA 1-4R; CANR 2; CDALB 1941-1968; CP; DLB 48; MTCW 1; RGAL

Eberstadt, Fernanda 1960- .... **CLC 39**
See also CA 136; CANR 69

Echegaray (y Eizaguirre), Jose (Maria Waldo) 1832-1916 .... **TCLC 4; HLCS 1**
See also CA 104; CANR 32; HW 1; MTCW 1

Echeverria, (Jose) Esteban (Antonino) 1805-1851 .... **NCLC 18**
See also LAW

Echo
See Proust, (Valentin-Louis-George-Eugene-)Marcel

Eckert, Allan W. 1931- .... **CLC 17**
See also AAYA 18; BYA 2; CA 13-16R; CANR 14, 45; INT CANR-14; SAAS 21; SATA 29, 91; SATA-Brief 27

Eckhart, Meister 1260(?)-1327(?) ..... **CMLC 9**
See also DLB 115

Eckmar, F. R.
See de Hartog, Jan

Farmer, Philip Jose 1918- .... **CLC 1, 19**
See also AAYA 28; BPFB 1; CA 1-4R;
CANR 4, 35; DLB 8; MTCW 1; SATA
93; SCFW 2; SFW

Farquhar, George 1677-1707 ... **LC 21; DAM DRAM**
See also BRW 2; DLB 84; RGEL

Farrell, J(ames) G(ordon)
1935-1979 .... **CLC 6**
See also CA 73-76; 89-92; CANR 36; DLB
14; MTCW 1; RGEL; RHW; WLIT 4

Farrell, James T(homas) 1904-1979 . **CLC 1, 4, 8, 11, 66; SSC 28**
See also AMW; BPFB 1; CA 5-8R; 89-92;
CANR 9, 61; DLB 4, 9, 86; DLBD 2;
MTCW 1, 2; RGAL

Farrell, Warren (Thomas) 1943- ...... **CLC 70**
See also CA 146

Farren, Richard J.
See Betjeman, John

Farren, Richard M.
See Betjeman, John

Fassbinder, Rainer Werner
1946-1982 .... **CLC 20**
See also CA 93-96; 106; CANR 31

Fast, Howard (Melvin) 1914- .. **CLC 23, 131; DAM NOV**
See also AAYA 16; BPFB 1; CA 1-4R, 181;
CAAE 181; CAAS 18; CANR 1, 33, 54,
75, 98; CMW; CN; CPW; DLB 9; INT
CANR-33; MTCW 1; RHW; SATA 7;
SATA-Essay 107; TCWW 2; YAW

Faulcon, Robert
See Holdstock, Robert P.

Faulkner, William (Cuthbert)
1897-1962 .... **CLC 1, 3, 6, 8, 9, 11, 14, 18, 28, 52, 68; DA; DAB; DAC; DAM MST, NOV; SSC 1, 35, 42; WLC**
See also AAYA 7; AMW; AMWR 1; BPFB
1; BYA 5; CA 81-84; CANR 33; CDALB
1929-1941; DA3; DLB 9, 11, 44, 102;
DLBD 2; DLBY 86, 97; EXPN; EXPS;
LAIT 2; MTCW 1, 2; NFS 4, 8, 13;
RGAL; RGSF; SSFS 2, 5, 6, 12

Fauset, Jessie Redmon
1882(?)-1961 .... **CLC 19, 54; BLC 2; DAM MULT**
See also AFAW 2; BW 1; CA 109; CANR
83; DLB 51; FW; MAWW

Faust, Frederick (Schiller)
1892-1944(?) .... **TCLC 49; DAM POP**
See also Austin, Frank; Brand, Max; Challis, George; Dawson, Peter; Dexter, Martin; Evans, Evan; Frederick, John; Frost,
Frederick; Manning, David; Silver, Nicholas
See also CA 108; 152; DLB 256

Faust, Irvin 1924- .... **CLC 8**
See also CA 33-36R; CANR 28, 67; CN;
DLB 2, 28, 218; DLBY 80

Fawkes, Guy
See Benchley, Robert (Charles)

Fearing, Kenneth (Flexner)
1902-1961 .... **CLC 51**
See also CA 93-96; CANR 59; CMW; DLB
9; RGAL

Fecamps, Elise
See Creasey, John

Federman, Raymond 1928- .... **CLC 6, 47**
See also CA 17-20R; CAAS 8; CANR 10,
43, 83; CN; DLBY 80

Federspiel, J(uerg) F. 1931- .... **CLC 42**
See also CA 146

Feiffer, Jules (Ralph) 1929- ..... **CLC 2, 8, 64; DAM DRAM**
See also AAYA 3; CA 17-20R; CAD; CANR
30, 59; CD; DLB 7, 44; INT CANR-30;
MTCW 1; SATA 8, 61, 111

Feige, Hermann Albert Otto Maximilian
See Traven, B.

Feinberg, David B. 1956-1994 .... **CLC 59**
See also CA 135; 147

Feinstein, Elaine 1930- .... **CLC 36**
See also CA 69-72; CAAS 1; CANR 31,
68; CN; CP; CWP; DLB 14, 40; MTCW
1

Feke, Gilbert David .... **CLC 65**

Feldman, Irving (Mordecai) 1928- ..... **CLC 7**
See also CA 1-4R; CANR 1; CP; DLB 169

Felix-Tchicaya, Gerald
See Tchicaya, Gerald Felix

Fellini, Federico 1920-1993 .... **CLC 16, 85**
See also CA 65-68; 143; CANR 33

Felsen, Henry Gregor 1916-1995 ..... **CLC 17**
See also CA 1-4R; 180; CANR 1; SAAS 2;
SATA 1

Felski, Rita .... **CLC 65**

Fenno, Jack
See Calisher, Hortense

Fenollosa, Ernest (Francisco)
1853-1908 .... **TCLC 91**

Fenton, James Martin 1949- .... **CLC 32**
See also CA 102; CP; DLB 40; PFS 11

Ferber, Edna 1887-1968 .... **CLC 18, 93**
See also AITN 1; CA 5-8R; 25-28R; CANR
68, 105; DLB 9, 28, 86; MTCW 1, 2;
RGAL; RHW; SATA 7; TCWW 2

Ferdowsi, Abu'l Qasem 940-1020 . **CMLC 43**
See also RGWL

Ferguson, Helen
See Kavan, Anna

Ferguson, Niall 1964- .... **CLC 134**
See also CA 190

Ferguson, Samuel 1810-1886 .... **NCLC 33**
See also DLB 32; RGEL

Fergusson, Robert 1750-1774 .... **LC 29**
See also DLB 109; RGEL

Ferling, Lawrence
See Ferlinghetti, Lawrence (Monsanto)

Ferlinghetti, Lawrence (Monsanto)
1919(?)- ... **CLC 2, 6, 10, 27, 111; DAM POET; PC 1**
See also CA 5-8R; CANR 3, 41, 73;
CDALB 1941-1968; CP; DA3; DLB 5,
16; MTCW 1, 2; RGAL; WP

Fern, Fanny
See Parton, Sara Payson Willis

Fernandez, Vicente Garcia Huidobro
See Huidobro Fernandez, Vicente Garcia

Fernandez-Armesto, Felipe .... **CLC 70**

Fernandez de Lizardi, Jose Joaquin
See Lizardi, Jose Joaquin Fernandez de

Ferre, Rosario 1942- ...... **CLC 139; HLCS 1; SSC 36**
See also CA 131; CANR 55, 81; CWW 2;
DLB 145; HW 1, 2; LAWS 1; MTCW 1;
WLIT 1

Ferrer, Gabriel (Francisco Victor) Miro
See Miro (Ferrer), Gabriel (Francisco
Victor)

Ferrier, Susan (Edmonstone)
1782-1854 .... **NCLC 8**
See also DLB 116; RGEL

Ferrigno, Robert 1948(?)- .... **CLC 65**
See also CA 140

Ferron, Jacques 1921-1985 .... **CLC 94; DAC**
See also CA 117; 129; CCA 1; DLB 60

Feuchtwanger, Lion 1884-1958 .... **TCLC 3**
See also CA 104; 187; DLB 66

Feuillet, Octave 1821-1890 .... **NCLC 45**
See also DLB 192

Feydeau, Georges (Leon Jules Marie)
1862-1921 .... **TCLC 22; DAM DRAM**
See also CA 113; 152; CANR 84; DLB 192;
GFL 1789 to the Present; RGWL

Fichte, Johann Gottlieb
1762-1814 .... **NCLC 62**
See also DLB 90

Ficino, Marsilio 1433-1499 .... **LC 12**

Fiedeler, Hans
See Doeblin, Alfred

Fiedler, Leslie A(aron) 1917- .. **CLC 4, 13, 24**
See also CA 9-12R; CANR 7, 63; CN; DLB
28, 67; MTCW 1, 2; RGAL

Field, Andrew 1938- .... **CLC 44**
See also CA 97-100; CANR 25

Field, Eugene 1850-1895 .... **NCLC 3**
See also DLB 23, 42, 140; DLBD 13; MAI-
CYA; RGAL; SATA 16

Field, Gans T.
See Wellman, Manly Wade

Field, Michael 1915-1971 .... **TCLC 43**
See also CA 29-32R

Field, Peter
See Hobson, Laura Z(ametkin)
See also TCWW 2

Fielding, Helen 1959(?)- .... **CLC 146**
See also CA 172; DLB 231

Fielding, Henry 1707-1754 ..... **LC 1, 46; DA; DAB; DAC; DAM DRAM, MST, NOV; WLC**
See also BRW 3; BRWR 1; CDBLB 1660-
1789; DA3; DLB 39, 84, 101; RGEL;
WLIT 3

Fielding, Sarah 1710-1768 .... **LC 1, 44**
See also DLB 39; RGEL

Fields, W. C. 1880-1946 .... **TCLC 80**
See also DLB 44

Fierstein, Harvey (Forbes) 1954- .... **CLC 33; DAM DRAM, POP**
See also CA 123; 129; CAD; CD; CPW;
DA3; DFS 6; GLL

Figes, Eva 1932- .... **CLC 31**
See also CA 53-56; CANR 4, 44, 83; CN;
DLB 14; FW

Finch, Anne 1661-1720 .... **LC 3; PC 21**
See also DLB 95

Finch, Robert (Duer Claydon)
1900-1995 .... **CLC 18**
See also CA 57-60; CANR 9, 24, 49; CP;
DLB 88

Findley, Timothy 1930- . **CLC 27, 102; DAC; DAM MST**
See also CA 25-28R; CANR 12, 42, 69;
CCA 1; CN; DLB 53; FANT; RHW

Fink, William
See Mencken, H(enry) L(ouis)

Firbank, Louis 1942-
See Reed, Lou
See also CA 117

Firbank, (Arthur Annesley) Ronald
1886-1926 .... **TCLC 1**
See also BRWS 2; CA 104; 177; DLB 36;
RGEL

Fish, Stanley
See Fish, Stanley Eugene

Fish, Stanley E.
See Fish, Stanley Eugene

Fish, Stanley Eugene 1938- .... **CLC 142**
See also CA 112; 132; CANR 90; DLB 67

Fisher, Dorothy (Frances) Canfield
1879-1958 .... **TCLC 87**
See also CA 114; 136; CANR 80; CLR 71,;
CWRI; DLB 9, 102; MAICYA; YABC 1

Fisher, M(ary) F(rances) K(ennedy)
1908-1992 .... **CLC 76, 87**
See also CA 77-80; 138; CANR 44; MTCW
1

Fisher, Roy 1930- .... **CLC 25**
See also CA 81-84; CAAS 10; CANR 16;
CP; DLB 40

Fisher, Rudolph 1897-1934 .. **TCLC 11; BLC 2; DAM MULT; SSC 25**
See also BW 1, 3; CA 107; 124; CANR 80;
DLB 51, 102

Francis, Dick 1920- .... **CLC 2, 22, 42, 102; DAM POP**
See also AAYA 5, 21; BEST 89:3; BPFB 1; CA 5-8R; CANR 9, 42, 68, 100; CDBLB 1960 to Present; CMW; CN; DA3; DLB 87; INT CANR-9; MSW; MTCW 1, 2

Francis, Robert (Churchill)
1901-1987 .... **CLC 15; PC 34**
See also AMWS 9; CA 1-4R; 123; CANR 1; EXPP; PFS 12

Francis, Lord Jeffrey
See Jeffrey, Francis
See also DLB 107

Frank, Anne(lies Marie)
1929-1945 . **TCLC 17; DA; DAB; DAC; DAM MST; WLC**
See also AAYA 12; BYA 1; CA 113; 133; CANR 68; DA3; LAIT 4; MAICYAS; MTCW 1, 2; NCFS 2; SATA 87; SATA-Brief 42; WYA; YAW

Frank, Bruno 1887-1945 .... **TCLC 81**
See also CA 189; DLB 118

Frank, Elizabeth 1945- .... **CLC 39**
See also CA 121; 126; CANR 78; INT 126

Frankl, Viktor E(mil) 1905-1997 ...... **CLC 93**
See also CA 65-68; 161

Franklin, Benjamin
See Hasek, Jaroslav (Matej Frantisek)

Franklin, Benjamin 1706-1790 .. **LC 25; DA; DAB; DAC; DAM MST; WLCS**
See also AMW; CDALB 1640-1865; DA3; DLB 24, 43, 73, 183; LAIT 1; RGAL; TUS

Franklin, (Stella Maria Sarah) Miles (Lampe) 1879-1954 .... **TCLC 7**
See also CA 104; 164; DLB 230; FW; MTCW 2; RGEL; TWA

Fraser, George MacDonald 1925- ...... **CLC 7**
See also CA 45-48, 180; CAAE 180; CANR 2, 48, 74; MTCW 1; RHW

Fraser, Sylvia 1935- .... **CLC 64**
See also CA 45-48; CANR 1, 16, 60; CCA 1

Frayn, Michael 1933- .... **CLC 3, 7, 31, 47; DAM DRAM, NOV**
See also BRWS 7; CA 5-8R; CANR 30, 69; CBD; CD; CN; DLB 13, 14, 194, 245; FANT; MTCW 1, 2; SFW

Fraze, Candida (Merrill) 1945- .... **CLC 50**
See also CA 126

Frazer, Andrew
See Marlowe, Stephen

Frazer, J(ames) G(eorge)
1854-1941 .... **TCLC 32**
See also BRWS 3; CA 118

Frazer, Robert Caine
See Creasey, John

Frazer, Sir James George
See Frazer, J(ames) G(eorge)

Frazier, Charles 1950- .... **CLC 109**
See also AAYA 34; CA 161; CSW

Frazier, Ian 1951- .... **CLC 46**
See also CA 130; CANR 54, 93

Frederic, Harold 1856-1898 .... **NCLC 10**
See also AMW; DLB 12, 23; DLBD 13; RGAL

Frederick, John
See Faust, Frederick (Schiller)
See also TCWW 2

Frederick the Great 1712-1786 .... **LC 14**

Fredro, Aleksander 1793-1876 .... **NCLC 8**

Freeling, Nicolas 1927- .... **CLC 38**
See also CA 49-52; CAAS 12; CANR 1, 17, 50, 84; CMW; CN; DLB 87

Freeman, Douglas Southall
1886-1953 .... **TCLC 11**
See also CA 109; 195; DLB 17; DLBD 17

Freeman, Judith 1946- .... **CLC 55**
See also CA 148; DLB 256

Freeman, Mary E(leanor) Wilkins
1852-1930 .... **TCLC 9; SSC 1, 47**
See also CA 106; 177; DLB 12, 78, 221; EXPS; FW; HGG; MAWW; RGAL; RGSF; SSFS 4, 8; SUFW; TUS

Freeman, R(ichard) Austin
1862-1943 .... **TCLC 21**
See also CA 113; CANR 84; CMW; DLB 70

French, Albert 1943- .... **CLC 86**
See also BW 3; CA 167

French, Marilyn 1929- .... **CLC 10, 18, 60; DAM DRAM, NOV, POP**
See also BPFB 1; CA 69-72; CANR 3, 31; CN; CPW; FW; INT CANR-31; MTCW 1, 2

French, Paul
See Asimov, Isaac

Freneau, Philip Morin 1752-1832 ... **NCLC 1**
See also AMWS 2; DLB 37, 43; RGAL

Freud, Sigmund 1856-1939 .... **TCLC 52**
See also CA 115; 133; CANR 69; EW 8; MTCW 1, 2

Freytag, Gustav 1816-1895 .... **NCLC 109**
See also DLB 129

Friedan, Betty (Naomi) 1921- .... **CLC 74**
See also CA 65-68; CANR 18, 45, 74; DLB 246; FW; MTCW 1, 2

Friedlander, Saul 1932- .... **CLC 90**
See also CA 117; 130; CANR 72

Friedman, B(ernard) H(arper)
1926- .... **CLC 7**
See also CA 1-4R; CANR 3, 48

Friedman, Bruce Jay 1930- ...... **CLC 3, 5, 56**
See also CA 9-12R; CAD; CANR 25, 52, 101; CD; CN; DLB 2, 28, 244; INT CANR-25

Friel, Brian 1929- .... **CLC 5, 42, 59, 115; DC 8**
See also BRWS 5; CA 21-24R; CANR 33, 69; CBD; CD; DFS 11; DLB 13; MTCW 1; RGEL

Friis-Baastad, Babbis Ellinor
1921-1970 .... **CLC 12**
See also CA 17-20R; 134; SATA 7

Frisch, Max (Rudolf) 1911-1991 ... **CLC 3, 9, 14, 18, 32, 44; DAM DRAM, NOV**
See also CA 85-88; 134; CANR 32, 74; DLB 69, 124; EW 13; MTCW 1, 2; RGWL

Fromentin, Eugene (Samuel Auguste)
1820-1876 .... **NCLC 10**
See also DLB 123; GFL 1789 to the Present

Frost, Frederick
See Faust, Frederick (Schiller)
See also TCWW 2

Frost, Robert (Lee) 1874-1963 .. **CLC 1, 3, 4, 9, 10, 13, 15, 26, 34, 44; DA; DAB; DAC; DAM MST, POET; PC 1, 39; WLC**
See also AAYA 21; AMW; AMWR 1; CA 89-92; CANR 33; CDALB 1917-1929; CLR 67; DA3; DLB 54; DLBD 7; EXPP; MTCW 1, 2; PAB; PFS 1, 2, 3, 4, 5, 6, 7, 10, 13; RGAL; SATA 14; WP; WYA

Froude, James Anthony
1818-1894 .... **NCLC 43**
See also DLB 18, 57, 144

Froy, Herald
See Waterhouse, Keith (Spencer)

Fry, Christopher 1907- .... **CLC 2, 10, 14; DAM DRAM**
See also BRWS 3; CA 17-20R; CAAS 23; CANR 9, 30, 74; CBD; CD; CP; DLB 13; MTCW 1, 2; RGEL; SATA 66

Frye, (Herman) Northrop
1912-1991 .... **CLC 24, 70**
See also CA 5-8R; 133; CANR 8, 37; DLB 67, 68, 246; MTCW 1, 2; RGAL

Fuchs, Daniel 1909-1993 .... **CLC 8, 22**
See also CA 81-84; 142; CAAS 5; CANR 40; DLB 9, 26, 28; DLBY 93

Fuchs, Daniel 1934- .... **CLC 34**
See also CA 37-40R; CANR 14, 48

Fuentes, Carlos 1928- .. **CLC 3, 8, 10, 13, 22, 41, 60, 113; DA; DAB; DAC; DAM MST, MULT, NOV; HLC 1; SSC 24; WLC**
See also AAYA 4; AITN 2; BPFB 1; CA 69-72; CANR 10, 32, 68, 104; CWW 2; DA3; DLB 113; DNFS; HW 1, 2; LAIT 3; LAW; LAWS 1; MTCW 1, 2; NFS 8; RGSF; RGWL; WLIT 1

Fuentes, Gregorio Lopez y
See Lopez y Fuentes, Gregorio

Fuertes, Gloria 1918-1998 .... **PC 27**
See also CA 178; 180; DLB 108; HW 2; SATA 115

Fugard, (Harold) Athol 1932- . **CLC 5, 9, 14, 25, 40, 80; DAM DRAM; DC 3**
See also AAYA 17; AFW; CA 85-88; CANR 32, 54; CD; DFS 3, 6, 10; DLB 225; DNFS; MTCW 1; RGEL; WLIT 2

Fugard, Sheila 1932- .... **CLC 48**
See also CA 125

Fukuyama, Francis 1952- .... **CLC 131**
See also CA 140; CANR 72

Fuller, Charles (H., Jr.) 1939- .... **CLC 25; BLC 2; DAM DRAM, MULT; DC 1**
See also BW 2; CA 108; 112; CAD; CANR 87; CD; DFS 8; DLB 38; INT CA-112; MTCW 1

Fuller, Henry Blake 1857-1929 .... **TCLC 103**
See also CA 108; 177; DLB 12; RGAL

Fuller, John (Leopold) 1937- .... **CLC 62**
See also CA 21-24R; CANR 9, 44; CP; DLB 40

Fuller, Margaret
See Ossoli, Sarah Margaret (Fuller)
See also AMWS 2; DLB 183, 223, 239

Fuller, Roy (Broadbent) 1912-1991 ... **CLC 4, 28**
See also BRWS 7; CA 5-8R; 135; CAAS 10; CANR 53, 83; CWRI; DLB 15, 20; RGEL; SATA 87

Fuller, Sarah Margaret
See Ossoli, Sarah Margaret (Fuller)

Fuller, Sarah Margaret
See Ossoli, Sarah Margaret (Fuller)
See also DLB 1, 59, 73

Fulton, Alice 1952- .... **CLC 52**
See also CA 116; CANR 57, 88; CP; CWP; DLB 193

Furphy, Joseph 1843-1912 .... **TCLC 25**
See also CA 163; DLB 230; RGEL

Fuson, Robert H(enderson) 1927- .... **CLC 70**
See also CA 89-92; CANR 103

Fussell, Paul 1924- .... **CLC 74**
See also BEST 90:1; CA 17-20R; CANR 8, 21, 35, 69; INT CANR-21; MTCW 1, 2

Futabatei, Shimei 1864-1909 .... **TCLC 44**
See also CA 162; DLB 180; MJW

Futrelle, Jacques 1875-1912 .... **TCLC 19**
See also CA 113; 155; CMW

Gaboriau, Emile 1835-1873 .... **NCLC 14**
See also CMW; MSW

Gadda, Carlo Emilio 1893-1973 .... **CLC 11**
See also CA 89-92; DLB 177

Gaddis, William 1922-1998 ... **CLC 1, 3, 6, 8, 10, 19, 43, 86**
See also AMWS 4; BPFB 1; CA 17-20R; 172; CANR 21, 48; CN; DLB 2; MTCW 1, 2; RGAL

Gaelique, Moruen le
See Jacob, (Cyprien-)Max

Gage, Walter
See Inge, William (Motter)

Gelber, Jack 1932- .... **CLC 1, 6, 14, 79**
See also CA 1-4R; CAD; CANR 2; DLB 7, 228

Gellhorn, Martha (Ellis)
1908-1998 .... **CLC 14, 60**
See also CA 77-80; 164; CANR 44; CN; DLBY 82, 98

Genet, Jean 1910-1986 .. **CLC 1, 2, 5, 10, 14, 44, 46; DAM DRAM**
See also CA 13-16R; CANR 18; DA3; DFS 10; DLB 72; DLBY 86; EW 13; GFL 1789 to the Present; GLL 1; MTCW 1, 2; RGWL

Gent, Peter 1942- .... **CLC 29**
See also AITN 1; CA 89-92; DLBY 82

Gentile, Giovanni 1875-1944 .... **TCLC 96**
See also CA 119

Gentlewoman in New England, A
See Bradstreet, Anne

Gentlewoman in Those Parts, A
See Bradstreet, Anne

Geoffrey of Monmouth c.
1100-1155 .... **CMLC 44**
See also DLB 146

George, Jean
See George, Jean Craighead

George, Jean Craighead 1919- .... **CLC 35**
See also AAYA 8; BYA 2, 4; CA 5-8R; CANR 25; CLR 1; DLB 52; JRDA; MAICYA; SATA 2, 68, 124; WYA; YAW

George, Stefan (Anton) 1868-1933 . **TCLC 2, 14**
See also CA 104; 193; EW 8

Georges, Georges Martin
See Simenon, Georges (Jacques Christian)

Gerhardi, William Alexander
See Gerhardie, William Alexander

Gerhardie, William Alexander
1895-1977 .... **CLC 5**
See also CA 25-28R; 73-76; CANR 18; DLB 36; RGEL

Gersonides 1288-1344 .... **CMLC 49**
See also DLB 115

Gerstler, Amy 1956- .... **CLC 70**
See also CA 146; CANR 99

Gertler, T. .... **CLC 134**
See also CA 116; 121

Ghalib .... **NCLC 39, 78**
See also Ghalib, Asadullah Khan

Ghalib, Asadullah Khan 1797-1869
See Ghalib
See also DAM POET; RGWL

Ghelderode, Michel de 1898-1962 ..... **CLC 6, 11; DAM DRAM; DC 15**
See also CA 85-88; CANR 40, 77; EW 11

Ghiselin, Brewster 1903-2001 .... **CLC 23**
See also CA 13-16R; CAAS 10; CANR 13; CP

Ghose, Aurabinda 1872-1950 .... **TCLC 63**
See also CA 163

Ghose, Zulfikar 1935- .... **CLC 42**
See also CA 65-68; CANR 67; CN; CP

Ghosh, Amitav 1956- .... **CLC 44, 153**
See also CA 147; CANR 80; CN

Giacosa, Giuseppe 1847-1906 .... **TCLC 7**
See also CA 104

Gibb, Lee
See Waterhouse, Keith (Spencer)

Gibbon, Lewis Grassic .... **TCLC 4**
See also Mitchell, James Leslie
See also RGEL

Gibbons, Kaye 1960- .... **CLC 50, 88, 145; DAM POP**
See also AAYA 34; AMWS 10; CA 151; CANR 75; CSW; DA3; MTCW 1; NFS 3; RGAL; SATA 117

Gibran, Kahlil 1883-1931 .... **TCLC 1, 9; DAM POET, POP; PC 9**
See also CA 104; 150; DA3; MTCW 2

Gibran, Khalil
See Gibran, Kahlil

Gibson, William 1914- .. **CLC 23; DA; DAB; DAC; DAM DRAM, MST**
See also CA 9-12R; CAD 2; CANR 9, 42, 75; CD; DFS 2; DLB 7; LAIT 2; MTCW 2; SATA 66; YAW

Gibson, William (Ford) 1948- ... **CLC 39, 63; DAM POP**
See also AAYA 12; BPFB 2; CA 126; 133; CANR 52, 90, 106; CN; CPW; DA3; DLB 251; MTCW 2; SCFW 2; SFW

Gide, Andre (Paul Guillaume)
1869-1951 . **TCLC 5, 12, 36; DA; DAB; DAC; DAM MST, NOV; SSC 13; WLC**
See also CA 104; 124; DA3; DLB 65; EW 8; GFL 1789 to the Present; MTCW 1, 2; RGSF; RGWL

Gifford, Barry (Colby) 1946- .... **CLC 34**
See also CA 65-68; CANR 9, 30, 40, 90

Gilbert, Frank
See De Voto, Bernard (Augustine)

Gilbert, W(illiam) S(chwenck)
1836-1911 .... **TCLC 3; DAM DRAM, POET**
See also CA 104; 173; RGEL; SATA 36

Gilbreth, Frank B(unker), Jr.
1911-2001 .... **CLC 17**
See also CA 9-12R; SATA 2

Gilchrist, Ellen (Louise) 1935- .. **CLC 34, 48, 143; DAM POP; SSC 14**
See also BPFB 2; CA 113; 116; CANR 41, 61, 104; CN; CPW; CSW; DLB 130; EXPS; MTCW 1, 2; RGAL; RGSF; SSFS 9

Giles, Molly 1942- .... **CLC 39**
See also CA 126; CANR 98

Gill, Eric 1882-1940 .... **TCLC 85**

Gill, Patrick
See Creasey, John

Gillette, Douglas .... **CLC 70**

Gilliam, Terry (Vance) 1940- .... **CLC 21, 141**
See also Monty Python
See also AAYA 19; CA 108; 113; CANR 35; INT 113

Gillian, Jerry
See Gilliam, Terry (Vance)

Gilliatt, Penelope (Ann Douglass)
1932-1993 .... **CLC 2, 10, 13, 53**
See also AITN 2; CA 13-16R; 141; CANR 49; DLB 14

Gilman, Charlotte (Anna) Perkins (Stetson)
1860-1935 ..... **TCLC 9, 37, 117; SSC 13**
See also BYA 11; CA 106; 150; DLB 221; EXPS; FW; HGG; LAIT 2; MAWW; MTCW 1; RGAL; RGSF; SFW; SSFS 1

Gilmour, David 1949- .... **CLC 35**
See also CA 138; 147

Gilpin, William 1724-1804 .... **NCLC 30**

Gilray, J. D.
See Mencken, H(enry) L(ouis)

Gilroy, Frank D(aniel) 1925- .... **CLC 2**
See also CA 81-84; CAD; CANR 32, 64, 86; CD; DLB 7

Gilstrap, John 1957(?)- .... **CLC 99**
See also CA 160; CANR 101

Ginsberg, Allen 1926-1997 .... **CLC 1, 2, 3, 4, 6, 13, 36, 69, 109; DA; DAB; DAC; DAM MST, POET; PC 4; WLC**
See also AAYA 33; AITN 1; AMWS 2; CA 1-4R; 157; CANR 2, 41, 63, 95; CDALB 1941-1968; CP; DA3; DLB 5, 16, 169, 237; GLL 1; MTCW 1, 2; PAB; PFS 5; RGAL; WP

Ginzburg, Eugenia .... **CLC 59**

Ginzburg, Natalia 1916-1991 .... **CLC 5, 11, 54, 70**
See also CA 85-88; 135; CANR 33; DLB 177; EW 13; MTCW 1, 2; RGWL

Giono, Jean 1895-1970 .... **CLC 4, 11**
See also CA 45-48; 29-32R; CANR 2, 35; DLB 72; GFL 1789 to the Present; MTCW 1; RGWL

Giovanni, Nikki 1943- .... **CLC 2, 4, 19, 64, 117; BLC 2; DA; DAB; DAC; DAM MST, MULT, POET; PC 19; WLCS**
See also AAYA 22; AITN 1; BW 2, 3; CA 29-32R; CAAS 6; CANR 18, 41, 60, 91; CDALBS; CLR 6, 73; CP; CSW; CWP; CWRI; DA3; DLB 5, 41; EXPP; INT CANR-18; MAICYA; MTCW 1, 2; RGAL; SATA 24, 107; YAW

Giovene, Andrea 1904-1998 .... **CLC 7**
See also CA 85-88

Gippius, Zinaida (Nikolayevna) 1869-1945
See Hippius, Zinaida
See also CA 106

Giraudoux, Jean(-Hippolyte)
1882-1944 .... **TCLC 2, 7; DAM DRAM**
See also CA 104; 196; DLB 65; EW 9; GFL 1789 to the Present; RGWL

Gironella, Jose Maria 1917-1991 ..... **CLC 11**
See also CA 101; RGWL

Gissing, George (Robert)
1857-1903 .... **TCLC 3, 24, 47; SSC 37**
See also BRW 5; CA 105; 167; DLB 18, 135, 184; RGEL

Giurlani, Aldo
See Palazzeschi, Aldo

Gladkov, Fyodor (Vasilyevich)
1883-1958 .... **TCLC 27**
See also CA 170

Glanville, Brian (Lester) 1931- .... **CLC 6**
See also CA 5-8R; CAAS 9; CANR 3, 70; CN; DLB 15, 139; SATA 42

Glasgow, Ellen (Anderson Gholson)
1873-1945 .... **TCLC 2, 7; SSC 34**
See also AMW; CA 104; 164; DLB 9, 12; MAWW; MTCW 2; RGAL; RHW; SSFS 9

Glaspell, Susan 1882(?)-1948 . **TCLC 55; DC 10; SSC 41**
See also AMWS 3; CA 110; 154; DFS 8; DLB 7, 9, 78, 228; MAWW; RGAL; SSFS 3; TCWW 2; YABC 2

Glassco, John 1909-1981 .... **CLC 9**
See also CA 13-16R; 102; CANR 15; DLB 68

Glasscock, Amnesia
See Steinbeck, John (Ernst)

Glasser, Ronald J. 1940(?)- .... **CLC 37**

Glassman, Joyce
See Johnson, Joyce

Gleick, James (W.) 1954- .... **CLC 147**
See also CA 131; 137; CANR 97; INT CA-137

Glendinning, Victoria 1937- .... **CLC 50**
See also CA 120; 127; CANR 59, 89; DLB 155

Glissant, Edouard 1928- . **CLC 10, 68; DAM MULT**
See also CA 153; CWW 2

Gloag, Julian 1930- .... **CLC 40**
See also AITN 1; CA 65-68; CANR 10, 70; CN

Glowacki, Aleksander
See Prus, Boleslaw

Gluck, Louise (Elisabeth) 1943- .. **CLC 7, 22, 44, 81; DAM POET; PC 16**
See also AMWS 5; CA 33-36R; CANR 40, 69; CP; CWP; DA3; DLB 5; MTCW 2; PFS 5; RGAL

Glyn, Elinor 1864-1943 .... **TCLC 72**
See also DLB 153; RHW

Gobineau, Joseph-Arthur
1816-1882 .... **NCLC 17**
See also DLB 123; GFL 1789 to the Present

Godard, Jean-Luc 1930- .... CLC 20
See also CA 93-96
Godden, (Margaret) Rumer
1907-1998 .... CLC 53
See also AAYA 6; BPFB 2; BYA 2, 5; CA
5-8R; 172; CANR 4, 27, 36, 55, 80; CLR
20; CN; CWRI; DLB 161; MAICYA;
RHW; SAAS 12; SATA 3, 36; SATA-Obit
109
Godoy Alcayaga, Lucila
1899-1957 .... TCLC 2; DAM MULT;
HLC 2; PC 32
See also BW 2; CA 104; 131; CANR 81;
DNFS; HW 1; MTCW 1, 2
Godwin, Gail (Kathleen) 1937- ..... CLC 5, 8,
22, 31, 69, 125; DAM POP
See also BPFB 2; CA 29-32R; CANR 15,
43, 69; CN; CPW; CSW; DA3; DLB 6,
234; INT CANR-15; MTCW 1, 2
Godwin, William 1756-1836 .... NCLC 14
See also CDBLB 1789-1832; CMW; DLB
39, 104, 142, 158, 163; HGG; RGEL
Goebbels, Josef
See Goebbels, (Paul) Joseph
Goebbels, (Paul) Joseph
1897-1945 .... TCLC 68
See also CA 115; 148
Goebbels, Joseph Paul
See Goebbels, (Paul) Joseph
Goethe, Johann Wolfgang von
1749-1832 ...... NCLC 4, 22, 34, 90; DA;
DAB; DAC; DAM DRAM, MST,
POET; PC 5; SSC 38; WLC
See also DA3; DLB 94; EW 5; RGWL
Gogarty, Oliver St. John
1878-1957 .... TCLC 15
See also CA 109; 150; DLB 15, 19; RGEL
Gogol, Nikolai (Vasilyevich)
1809-1852 . NCLC 5, 15, 31; DA; DAB;
DAC; DAM DRAM, MST; DC 1; SSC
4, 29; WLC
See also DFS 12; DLB 198; EW 6; EXPS;
RGSF; RGWL; SSFS 7
Goines, Donald 1937(?)-1974 . CLC 80; BLC
2; DAM MULT, POP
See also AITN 1; BW 1, 3; CA 124; 114;
CANR 82; CMW; DA3; DLB 33
Gold, Herbert 1924- ... CLC 4, 7, 14, 42, 152
See also CA 9-12R; CANR 17, 45; CN;
DLB 2; DLBY 81
Goldbarth, Albert 1948- .... CLC 5, 38
See also CA 53-56; CANR 6, 40; CP; DLB
120
Goldberg, Anatol 1910-1982 .... CLC 34
See also CA 131; 117
Goldemberg, Isaac 1945- .... CLC 52
See also CA 69-72; CAAS 12; CANR 11,
32; HW 1; WLIT 1
Golding, William (Gerald)
1911-1993 ..... CLC 1, 2, 3, 8, 10, 17, 27,
58, 81; DA; DAB; DAC; DAM MST,
NOV; WLC
See also AAYA 5; BPFB 2; BRWR 1;
BRWS 1; BYA 2; CA 5-8R; 141; CANR
13, 33, 54; CDBLB 1945-1960; DA3;
DLB 15, 100, 255; EXPN; HGG; LAIT 4;
MTCW 1, 2; NFS 2; RGEL; RHW; SFW;
WLIT 4; YAW
Goldman, Emma 1869-1940 .... TCLC 13
See also CA 110; 150; DLB 221; FW;
RGAL
Goldman, Francisco 1954- .... CLC 76
See also CA 162
Goldman, William (W.) 1931- ...... CLC 1, 48
See also BPFB 2; CA 9-12R; CANR 29,
69, 106; CN; DLB 44; FANT; IDFW 3, 4
Goldmann, Lucien 1913-1970 .... CLC 24
See also CA 25-28; CAP 2

Goldoni, Carlo 1707-1793 .... LC 4; DAM
DRAM
See also EW 4; RGWL
Goldsberry, Steven 1949- .... CLC 34
See also CA 131
Goldsmith, Oliver 1730-1774 . LC 2, 48; DA;
DAB; DAC; DAM DRAM, MST, NOV,
POET; DC 8; WLC
See also BRW 3; CDBLB 1660-1789; DFS
1; DLB 39, 89, 104, 109, 142; IDTP;
RGEL; SATA 26; TEA; WLIT 3
Goldsmith, Peter
See Priestley, J(ohn) B(oynton)
Gombrowicz, Witold 1904-1969 .... CLC 4, 7,
11, 49; DAM DRAM
See also CA 19-20; 25-28R; CANR 105;
CAP 2; DLB 215; EW 12; RGWL
Gomez de la Serna, Ramon
1888-1963 .... CLC 9
See also CA 153; 116; CANR 79; HW 1, 2
Goncharov, Ivan Alexandrovich
1812-1891 .... NCLC 1, 63
See also DLB 238; EW 6; RGWL
Goncourt, Edmond (Louis Antoine Huot) de
1822-1896 .... NCLC 7
See also DLB 123; EW 7; GFL 1789 to the
Present; RGWL
Goncourt, Jules (Alfred Huot) de
1830-1870 .... NCLC 7
See also DLB 123; EW 7; GFL 1789 to the
Present; RGWL
Gongora (y Argote), Luis de
1561-1627 .... LC 72
See also RGWL
Gontier, Fernande 19(?)- .... CLC 50
Gonzalez Martinez, Enrique
1871-1952 .... TCLC 72
See also CA 166; CANR 81; HW 1, 2
Goodison, Lorna 1947- .... PC 36
See also CA 142; CANR 88; CP; CWP;
DLB 157
Goodman, Paul 1911-1972 ..... CLC 1, 2, 4, 7
See also CA 19-20; 37-40R; CAD; CANR
34; CAP 2; DLB 130, 246; MTCW 1;
RGAL
Gordimer, Nadine 1923- ...... CLC 3, 5, 7, 10,
18, 33, 51, 70, 123; DA; DAB; DAC;
DAM MST, NOV; SSC 17; WLCS
See also AAYA 39; AFW; BRWS 2; CA
5-8R; CANR 3, 28, 56, 88; CN; DA3;
DLB 225; EXPS; INT CANR-28; MTCW
1, 2; NFS 4; RGEL; RGSF; SSFS 2;
WLIT 2; YAW
Gordon, Adam Lindsay
1833-1870 .... NCLC 21
See also DLB 230
Gordon, Caroline 1895-1981 . CLC 6, 13, 29,
83; SSC 15
See also AMW; CA 11-12; 103; CANR 36;
CAP 1; DLB 4, 9, 102; DLBD 17; DLBY
81; MTCW 1, 2; RGAL; RGSF
Gordon, Charles William 1860-1937
See Connor, Ralph
See also CA 109
Gordon, Mary (Catherine) 1949- .... CLC 13,
22, 128
See also AMWS 4; BPFB 2; CA 102;
CANR 44, 92; CN; DLB 6; DLBY 81;
FW; INT CA-102; MTCW 1
Gordon, N. J.
See Bosman, Herman Charles
Gordon, Sol 1923- .... CLC 26
See also CA 53-56; CANR 4; SATA 11
Gordone, Charles 1925-1995 .... CLC 1, 4;
DAM DRAM; DC 8
See also BW 1, 3; CA 93-96; 180; 150;
CAAE 180; CAD; CANR 55; DLB 7; INT
93-96; MTCW 1

Gore, Catherine 1800-1861 .... NCLC 65
See also DLB 116; RGEL
Gorenko, Anna Andreevna
See Akhmatova, Anna
Gorky, Maxim .... TCLC 8; DAB; SSC 28;
WLC
See also Peshkov, Alexei Maximovich
See also DFS 9; EW 8; MTCW 2
Goryan, Sirak
See Saroyan, William
Gosse, Edmund (William)
1849-1928 .... TCLC 28
See also CA 117; DLB 57, 144, 184; RGEL
Gotlieb, Phyllis Fay (Bloom) 1926- .. CLC 18
See also CA 13-16R; CANR 7; DLB 88,
251; SFW
Gottesman, S. D.
See Kornbluth, C(yril) M.; Pohl, Frederik
Gottfried von Strassburg fl. c.
1170-1215 .... CMLC 10
See also DLB 138; EW 1; RGWL
Gould, Lois .... CLC 4, 10
See also CA 77-80; CANR 29; MTCW 1
Gourmont, Remy(-Marie-Charles) de
1858-1915 .... TCLC 17
See also CA 109; 150; GFL 1789 to the
Present; MTCW 2
Govier, Katherine 1948- .... CLC 51
See also CA 101; CANR 18, 40; CCA 1
Goyen, (Charles) William
1915-1983 .... CLC 5, 8, 14, 40
See also AITN 2; CA 5-8R; 110; CANR 6,
71; DLB 2, 218; DLBY 83; INT CANR-6
Goytisolo, Juan 1931- ... CLC 5, 10, 23, 133;
DAM MULT; HLC 1
See also CA 85-88; CANR 32, 61; CWW
2; GLL 2; HW 1, 2; MTCW 1, 2
Gozzano, Guido 1883-1916 .... PC 10
See also CA 154; DLB 114
Gozzi, (Conte) Carlo 1720-1806 .... NCLC 23
Grabbe, Christian Dietrich
1801-1836 .... NCLC 2
See also DLB 133; RGWL
Grace, Patricia Frances 1937- .... CLC 56
See also CA 176; CN; RGSF
Gracian y Morales, Baltasar
1601-1658 .... LC 15
Gracq, Julien .... CLC 11, 48
See also Poirier, Louis
See also CWW 2; DLB 83; GFL 1789 to
the Present
Grade, Chaim 1910-1982 .... CLC 10
See also CA 93-96; 107
Graduate of Oxford, A
See Ruskin, John
Grafton, Garth
See Duncan, Sara Jeannette
Graham, John
See Phillips, David Graham
Graham, Jorie 1951- .... CLC 48, 118
See also CA 111; CANR 63; CP; CWP;
DLB 120; PFS 10
Graham, R(obert) B(ontine) Cunninghame
See Cunninghame Graham, Robert
(Gallnigad) Bontine
See also DLB 98, 135, 174; RGEL; RGSF
Graham, Robert
See Haldeman, Joe (William)
Graham, Tom
See Lewis, (Harry) Sinclair
Graham, W(illiam) S(idney)
1918-1986 .... CLC 29
See also BRWS 7; CA 73-76; 118; DLB 20;
RGEL
Graham, Winston (Mawdsley)
1910- .... CLC 23
See also CA 49-52; CANR 2, 22, 45, 66;
CMW; CN; DLB 77; RHW

Grahame, Kenneth 1859-1932 ...... **TCLC 64; DAB**
See also BYA 5; CA 108; 136; CANR 80; CLR 5; CWRI; DA3; DLB 34, 141, 178; FANT; MAICYA; MTCW 2; RGEL; SATA 100; WCH; YABC 1

Granger, Darius John
See Marlowe, Stephen

Granin, Daniil .... **CLC 59**

Granovsky, Timofei Nikolaevich
1813-1855 .... **NCLC 75**
See also DLB 198

Grant, Skeeter
See Spiegelman, Art

Granville-Barker, Harley
1877-1946 .... **TCLC 2; DAM DRAM**
See also Barker, Harley Granville
See also CA 104; RGEL

Granzotto, Gianni
See Granzotto, Giovanni Battista

Granzotto, Giovanni Battista
1914-1985 .... **CLC 70**
See also CA 166

Grass, Guenter (Wilhelm) 1927- ... **CLC 1, 2, 4, 6, 11, 15, 22, 32, 49, 88; DA; DAB; DAC; DAM MST, NOV; WLC**
See also BPFB 2; CA 13-16R; CANR 20, 75, 93; DA3; DLB 75, 124; EW 13; MTCW 1, 2; RGWL

Gratton, Thomas
See Hulme, T(homas) E(rnest)

Grau, Shirley Ann 1929- .... **CLC 4, 9, 146; SSC 15**
See also CA 89-92; CANR 22, 69; CN; CSW; DLB 2, 218; INT CANR-22; MTCW 1

Gravel, Fern
See Hall, James Norman

Graver, Elizabeth 1964- .... **CLC 70**
See also CA 135; CANR 71

Graves, Richard Perceval
1895-1985 .... **CLC 44**
See also CA 65-68; CANR 9, 26, 51

Graves, Robert (von Ranke)
1895-1985 .. **CLC 1, 2, 6, 11, 39, 44, 45; DAB; DAC; DAM MST, POET; PC 6**
See also BPFB 2; BRW 7; BYA 4; CA 5-8R; 117; CANR 5, 36; CDBLB 1914-1945; DA3; DLB 20, 100, 191; DLBD 18; DLBY 85; MTCW 1, 2; NCFS 2; RGEL; RHW; SATA 45

Graves, Valerie
See Bradley, Marion Zimmer

Gray, Alasdair (James) 1934- .... **CLC 41**
See also CA 126; CANR 47, 69, 106; CN; DLB 194; HGG; INT CA-126; MTCW 1, 2; RGSF

Gray, Amlin 1946- .... **CLC 29**
See also CA 138

Gray, Francine du Plessix 1930- ..... **CLC 22, 153; DAM NOV**
See also BEST 90:3; CA 61-64; CAAS 2; CANR 11, 33, 75, 81; INT CANR-11; MTCW 1, 2

Gray, John (Henry) 1866-1934 ...... **TCLC 19**
See also CA 119; 162; RGEL

Gray, Simon (James Holliday)
1936- .... **CLC 9, 14, 36**
See also AITN 1; CA 21-24R; CAAS 3; CANR 32, 69; CD; DLB 13; MTCW 1; RGEL

Gray, Spalding 1941- ..... **CLC 49, 112; DAM POP; DC 7**
See also CA 128; CAD; CANR 74; CD; CPW; MTCW 2

Gray, Thomas 1716-1771 .... **LC 4, 40; DA; DAB; DAC; DAM MST; PC 2; WLC**
See also BRW 3; CDBLB 1660-1789; DA3; DLB 109; EXPP; PAB; PFS 9; RGEL; WP

Grayson, David
See Baker, Ray Stannard

Grayson, Richard (A.) 1951- .... **CLC 38**
See also CA 85-88; CANR 14, 31, 57; DLB 234

Greeley, Andrew M(oran) 1928- ..... **CLC 28; DAM POP**
See also BPFB 2; CA 5-8R; CAAS 7; CANR 7, 43, 69, 104; CMW; CPW; DA3; MTCW 1, 2

Green, Anna Katharine
1846-1935 .... **TCLC 63**
See also CA 112; 159; CMW; DLB 202, 221; MSW

Green, Brian
See Card, Orson Scott

Green, Hannah
See Greenberg, Joanne (Goldenberg)

Green, Hannah 1927(?)-1996 .... **CLC 3**
See also CA 73-76; CANR 59, 93; NFS 10

Green, Henry .... **CLC 2, 13, 97**
See also Yorke, Henry Vincent
See also BRWS 2; CA 175; DLB 15; RGEL

Green, Julian (Hartridge) 1900-1998
See Green, Julien
See also CA 21-24R; 169; CANR 33, 87; DLB 4, 72; MTCW 1

Green, Julien .... **CLC 3, 11, 77**
See also Green, Julian (Hartridge)
See also GFL 1789 to the Present; MTCW 2

Green, Paul (Eliot) 1894-1981 .... **CLC 25; DAM DRAM**
See also AITN 1; CA 5-8R; 103; CANR 3; DLB 7, 9, 249; RGAL

Greenberg, Ivan 1908-1973
See Rahv, Philip
See also CA 85-88

Greenberg, Joanne (Goldenberg)
1932- .... **CLC 7, 30**
See also AAYA 12; CA 5-8R; CANR 14, 32, 69; CN; SATA 25; YAW

Greenberg, Richard 1959(?)- .... **CLC 57**
See also CA 138; CAD; CD

Greenblatt, Stephen J(ay) 1943- ...... **CLC 70**
See also CA 49-52

Greene, Bette 1934- .... **CLC 30**
See also AAYA 7; BYA 3; CA 53-56; CANR 4; CLR 2; CWRI; JRDA; LAIT 4; MAICYA; NFS 10; SAAS 16; SATA 8, 102; WYA; YAW

Greene, Gael .... **CLC 8**
See also CA 13-16R; CANR 10

Greene, Graham (Henry)
1904-1991 .... **CLC 1, 3, 6, 9, 14, 18, 27, 37, 70, 72, 125; DA; DAB; DAC; DAM MST, NOV; SSC 29; WLC**
See also AITN 2; BPFB 2; BRWR 2; BRWS 1; BYA 3; CA 13-16R; 133; CANR 35, 61; CBD; CDBLB 1945-1960; CMW; DA3; DLB 13, 15, 77, 100, 162, 201, 204; DLBY 91; MSW; MTCW 1, 2; RGEL; SATA 20; WLIT 4

Greene, Robert 1558-1592 .... **LC 41**
See also DLB 62, 167; IDTP; RGEL; TEA

Greer, Germaine 1939- .... **CLC 131**
See also AITN 1; CA 81-84; CANR 33, 70; FW; MTCW 1, 2

Greer, Richard
See Silverberg, Robert

Gregor, Arthur 1923- .... **CLC 9**
See also CA 25-28R; CAAS 10; CANR 11; CP; SATA 36

Gregor, Lee
See Pohl, Frederik

Gregory, Lady Isabella Augusta (Persse)
1852-1932 .... **TCLC 1**
See also BRW 6; CA 104; 184; DLB 10; IDTP; RGEL

Gregory, J. Dennis
See Williams, John A(lfred)

Grekova, I. .... **CLC 59**

Grendon, Stephen
See Derleth, August (William)

Grenville, Kate 1950- .... **CLC 61**
See also CA 118; CANR 53, 93

Grenville, Pelham
See Wodehouse, P(elham) G(renville)

Greve, Felix Paul (Berthold Friedrich)
1879-1948
See Grove, Frederick Philip
See also CA 104; 141, 175; CANR 79; DAC; DAM MST

Grey, Zane 1872-1939 . **TCLC 6; DAM POP**
See also BPFB 2; CA 104; 132; DA3; DLB 9, 212; MTCW 1, 2; RGAL; TCWW 2

Grieg, (Johan) Nordahl (Brun)
1902-1943 .... **TCLC 10**
See also CA 107; 189

Grieve, C(hristopher) M(urray)
1892-1978 ..... **CLC 11, 19; DAM POET**
See also MacDiarmid, Hugh; Pteleon
See also CA 5-8R; 85-88; CANR 33; MTCW 1; RGEL

Griffin, Gerald 1803-1840 .... **NCLC 7**
See also DLB 159; RGEL

Griffin, John Howard 1920-1980 ..... **CLC 68**
See also AITN 1; CA 1-4R; 101; CANR 2

Griffin, Peter 1942- .... **CLC 39**
See also CA 136

Griffith, D(avid) Lewelyn) W(ark)
1875(?)-1948 .... **TCLC 68**
See also CA 119; 150; CANR 80

Griffith, Lawrence
See Griffith, D(avid) Lewelyn) W(ark)

Griffiths, Trevor 1935- .... **CLC 13, 52**
See also CA 97-100; CANR 45; CBD; CD; DLB 13, 245

Griggs, Sutton (Elbert)
1872-1930 .... **TCLC 77**
See also CA 123; 186; DLB 50

Grigson, Geoffrey (Edward Harvey)
1905-1985 .... **CLC 7, 39**
See also CA 25-28R; 118; CANR 20, 33; DLB 27; MTCW 1, 2

Grillparzer, Franz 1791-1872 . **NCLC 1, 102; DC 14; SSC 37**
See also DLB 133; EW 5; RGWL

Grimble, Reverend Charles James
See Eliot, T(homas) S(tearns)

Grimke, Charlotte L(ottie) Forten
1837(?)-1914
See Forten, Charlotte L.
See also BW 1; CA 117; 124; DAM MULT, POET

Grimm, Jacob Ludwig Karl
1785-1863 .... **NCLC 3, 77; SSC 36**
See also DLB 90; MAICYA; RGSF; RGWL; SATA 22; WCH

Grimm, Wilhelm Karl 1786-1859 .. **NCLC 3, 77; SSC 36**
See also DLB 90; MAICYA; RGSF; RGWL; SATA 22; WCH

Grimmelshausen, Hans Jakob Christoffel von
See Grimmelshausen, Johann Jakob Christoffel von
See also RGWL

Grimmelshausen, Johann Jakob Christoffel von 1621-1676 .... **LC 6**
See also Grimmelshausen, Hans Jakob Christoffel von
See also DLB 168

Grindel, Eugene 1895-1952
See Eluard, Paul
See also CA 104; 193

Grisham, John 1955- .... **CLC 84; DAM POP**
See also AAYA 14; BPFB 2; CA 138; CANR 47, 69; CMW; CN; CPW; CSW; DA3; MSW; MTCW 2

Grossman, David 1954- .... **CLC 67**
See also CA 138; CWW 2

Grossman, Vasily (Semenovich) 1905-1964 .... **CLC 41**
See also CA 124; 130; MTCW 1

Grove, Frederick Philip .... **TCLC 4**
See also Greve, Felix Paul (Berthold Friedrich)
See also DLB 92; RGEL

Grubb
See Crumb, R(obert)

Grumbach, Doris (Isaac) 1918- . **CLC 13, 22, 64**
See also CA 5-8R; CAAS 2; CANR 9, 42, 70; CN; INT CANR-9; MTCW 2

Grundtvig, Nicolai Frederik Severin 1783-1872 .... **NCLC 1**

Grunge
See Crumb, R(obert)

Grunwald, Lisa 1959- .... **CLC 44**
See also CA 120

Guare, John 1938- .... **CLC 8, 14, 29, 67; DAM DRAM**
See also CA 73-76; CAD; CANR 21, 69; CD; DFS 8, 13; DLB 7, 249; MTCW 1, 2; RGAL

Gubar, Susan (David) 1944- .... **CLC 145**
See also CA 108; CANR 45, 70; FW; MTCW 1; RGAL

Gudjonsson, Halldor Kiljan 1902-1998
See Laxness, Halldor
See also CA 103; 164; CWW 2

Guenter, Erich
See Eich, Guenter

Guest, Barbara 1920- .... **CLC 34**
See also CA 25-28R; CANR 11, 44, 84; CP; CWP; DLB 5, 193

Guest, Edgar A(lbert) 1881-1959 ... **TCLC 95**
See also CA 112; 168

Guest, Judith (Ann) 1936- .... **CLC 8, 30; DAM NOV, POP**
See also AAYA 7; CA 77-80; CANR 15, 75; DA3; EXPN; INT CANR-15; LAIT 5; MTCW 1, 2; NFS 1

Guevara, Che .... **CLC 87; HLC 1**
See also Guevara (Serna), Ernesto

Guevara (Serna), Ernesto 1928-1967 .... **CLC 87; DAM MULT; HLC 1**
See also Guevara, Che
See also CA 127; 111; CANR 56; HW 1

Guicciardini, Francesco 1483-1540 ..... **LC 49**

Guild, Nicholas M. 1944- .... **CLC 33**
See also CA 93-96

Guillemin, Jacques
See Sartre, Jean-Paul

Guillen, Jorge 1893-1984 .... **CLC 11; DAM MULT, POET; HLCS 1; PC 35**
See also CA 89-92; 112; DLB 108; HW 1; RGWL

Guillen, Nicolas (Cristobal) 1902-1989 ... **CLC 48, 79; BLC 2; DAM MST, MULT, POET; HLC 1; PC 23**
See also BW 2; CA 116; 125; 129; CANR 84; HW 1; LAW; RGWL; WP

Guillevic, (Eugene) 1907-1997 .... **CLC 33**
See also CA 93-96; CWW 2

Guillois
See Desnos, Robert

Guillois, Valentin
See Desnos, Robert

Guimaraes Rosa, Joao
See Rosa, Joao Guimaraes
See also LAW

Guimaraes Rosa, Joao 1908-1967
See also CA 175; HLCS 2; LAW; RGSF; RGWL

Guiney, Louise Imogen 1861-1920 .... **TCLC 41**
See also CA 160; DLB 54; RGAL

Guinizelli, Guido c. 1230-1276 ...... **CMLC 49**

Guiraldes, Ricardo (Guillermo) 1886-1927 .... **TCLC 39**
See also CA 131; HW 1; LAW; MTCW 1

Gumilev, Nikolai (Stepanovich) 1886-1921 .... **TCLC 60**
See also CA 165

Gunesekera, Romesh 1954- .... **CLC 91**
See also CA 159; CN

Gunn, Bill .... **CLC 5**
See also Gunn, William Harrison
See also DLB 38

Gunn, Thom(son William) 1929- .. **CLC 3, 6, 18, 32, 81; DAM POET; PC 26**
See also BRWS 4; CA 17-20R; CANR 9, 33; CDBLB 1960 to Present; CP; DLB 27; INT CANR-33; MTCW 1; PFS 9; RGEL

Gunn, William Harrison 1934(?)-1989
See Gunn, Bill
See also AITN 1; BW 1, 3; CA 13-16R; 128; CANR 12, 25, 76

Gunn Allen, Paula
See Allen, Paula Gunn

Gunnars, Kristjana 1948- .... **CLC 69**
See also CA 113; CCA 1; CP; CWP; DLB 60

Gurdjieff, G(eorgei) I(vanovich) 1877(?)-1949 .... **TCLC 71**
See also CA 157

Gurganus, Allan 1947- . **CLC 70; DAM POP**
See also BEST 90:1; CA 135; CN; CPW; CSW; GLL 1

Gurney, A(lbert) R(amsdell), Jr. 1930- ..... **CLC 32, 50, 54; DAM DRAM**
See also AMWS 5; CA 77-80; CAD; CANR 32, 64; CD

Gurney, Ivor (Bertie) 1890-1937 ... **TCLC 33**
See also BRW 6; CA 167; PAB; RGEL

Gurney, Peter
See Gurney, A(lbert) R(amsdell), Jr.

Guro, Elena 1877-1913 .... **TCLC 56**

Gustafson, James M(oody) 1925- ... **CLC 100**
See also CA 25-28R; CANR 37

Gustafson, Ralph (Barker) 1909-1995 .... **CLC 36**
See also CA 21-24R; CANR 8, 45, 84; CP; DLB 88; RGEL

Gut, Gom
See Simenon, Georges (Jacques Christian)

Guterson, David 1956- .... **CLC 91**
See also CA 132; CANR 73; MTCW 2; NFS 13

Guthrie, A(lfred) B(ertram), Jr. 1901-1991 .... **CLC 23**
See also CA 57-60; 134; CANR 24; DLB 6, 212; SATA 62; SATA-Obit 67

Guthrie, Isobel
See Grieve, C(hristopher) M(urray)

Guthrie, Woodrow Wilson 1912-1967
See Guthrie, Woody
See also CA 113; 93-96

Guthrie, Woody .... **CLC 35**
See also Guthrie, Woodrow Wilson
See also LAIT 3

Gutierrez Najera, Manuel 1859-1895
See also HLCS 2; LAW

Guy, Rosa (Cuthbert) 1928- .... **CLC 26**
See also AAYA 4, 37; BW 2; CA 17-20R; CANR 14, 34, 83; CLR 13; DLB 33; JRDA; MAICYA; SATA 14, 62, 122; YAW

Gwendolyn
See Bennett, (Enoch) Arnold

H. D. .... **CLC 3, 8, 14, 31, 34, 73; PC 5**
See also Doolittle, Hilda

H. de V.
See Buchan, John

Haavikko, Paavo Juhani 1931- .. **CLC 18, 34**
See also CA 106

Habbema, Koos
See Heijermans, Herman

Habermas, Juergen 1929- .... **CLC 104**
See also CA 109; CANR 85; DLB 242

Habermas, Jurgen
See Habermas, Juergen

Hacker, Marilyn 1942- ...... **CLC 5, 9, 23, 72, 91; DAM POET**
See also CA 77-80; CANR 68; CP; CWP; DLB 120; FW; GLL 2

Haeckel, Ernst Heinrich (Philipp August) 1834-1919 .... **TCLC 83**
See also CA 157

Hafiz c. 1326-1389(?) .... **CMLC 34**
See also RGWL

Haggard, H(enry) Rider 1856-1925 .... **TCLC 11**
See also BRWS 3; BYA 4, 5; CA 108; 148; DLB 70, 156, 174, 178; FANT; MTCW 2; RGEL; RHW; SATA 16; SCFW; SFW; SUFW; WLIT 4

Hagiosy, L.
See Larbaud, Valery (Nicolas)

Hagiwara, Sakutaro 1886-1942 .... **TCLC 60; PC 18**
See also CA 154

Haig, Fenil
See Ford, Ford Madox

Haig-Brown, Roderick (Langmere) 1908-1976 .... **CLC 21**
See also CA 5-8R; 69-72; CANR 4, 38, 83; CLR 31; CWRI; DLB 88; MAICYA; SATA 12

Hailey, Arthur 1920- ..... **CLC 5; DAM NOV, POP**
See also AITN 2; BEST 90:3; BPFB 2; CA 1-4R; CANR 2, 36, 75; CCA 1; CN; CPW; DLB 88; DLBY 82; MTCW 1, 2

Hailey, Elizabeth Forsythe 1938- ..... **CLC 40**
See also CA 93-96; CAAE 188; CAAS 1; CANR 15, 48; INT CANR-15

Haines, John (Meade) 1924- .... **CLC 58**
See also CA 17-20R; CANR 13, 34; CSW; DLB 5, 212

Hakluyt, Richard 1552-1616 .... **LC 31**
See also DLB 136; RGEL

Haldeman, Joe (William) 1943- .... **CLC 61**
See also Graham, Robert
See also AAYA 38; CA 53-56, 179; CAAE 179; CAAS 25; CANR 6, 70, 72; DLB 8; INT CANR-6; SCFW 2; SFW

Hale, Sarah Josepha (Buell) 1788-1879 .... **NCLC 75**
See also DLB 1, 42, 73, 243

Halevy, Elie 1870-1937 .... **TCLC 104**

Haley, Alex(ander Murray Palmer) 1921-1992 . **CLC 8, 12, 76; BLC 2; DA; DAB; DAC; DAM MST, MULT, POP**
See also AAYA 26; BPFB 2; BW 2, 3; CA 77-80; 136; CANR 61; CDALBS; CPW; CSW; DA3; DLB 38; LAIT 5; MTCW 1, 2; NFS 9

Haliburton, Thomas Chandler
1796-1865 .... **NCLC 15**
See also DLB 11, 99; RGEL; RGSF

Hall, Donald (Andrew, Jr.) 1928- ...... **CLC 1,
13, 37, 59, 151; DAM POET**
See also CA 5-8R; CAAS 7; CANR 2, 44,
64, 106; CP; DLB 5; MTCW 1; RGAL;
SATA 23, 97

Hall, Frederic Sauser
See Sauser-Hall, Frederic

Hall, James
See Kuttner, Henry

Hall, James Norman 1887-1951 ..... **TCLC 23**
See also CA 123; 173; LAIT 1; RHW 1;
SATA 21

Hall, (Marguerite) Radclyffe
1880-1943 .... **TCLC 12**
See also BRWS 6; CA 110; 150; CANR 83;
DLB 191; MTCW 2; RGEL; RHW

Hall, Rodney 1935- .... **CLC 51**
See also CA 109; CANR 69; CN; CP

Hallam, Arthur Henry
1811-1833 .... **NCLC 110**
See also DLB 32

Halleck, Fitz-Greene 1790-1867 .... **NCLC 47**
See also DLB 3, 250; RGAL

Halliday, Michael
See Creasey, John

Halpern, Daniel 1945- .... **CLC 14**
See also CA 33-36R; CANR 93; CP

Hamburger, Michael (Peter Leopold)
1924- .... **CLC 5, 14**
See also CA 5-8R; CAAE 196; CAAS 4;
CANR 2, 47; CP; DLB 27

Hamill, Pete 1935- .... **CLC 10**
See also CA 25-28R; CANR 18, 71

Hamilton, Alexander
1755(?)-1804 .... **NCLC 49**
See also DLB 37

Hamilton, Clive
See Lewis, C(live) S(taples)

Hamilton, Edmond 1904-1977 .... **CLC 1**
See also CA 1-4R; CANR 3, 84; DLB 8;
SATA 118; SFW

Hamilton, Eugene (Jacob) Lee
See Lee-Hamilton, Eugene (Jacob)

Hamilton, Franklin
See Silverberg, Robert

Hamilton, Gail
See Corcoran, Barbara (Asenath)

Hamilton, Mollie
See Kaye, M(ary) M(argaret)

Hamilton, (Anthony Walter) Patrick
1904-1962 .... **CLC 51**
See also CA 176; 113; DLB 10, 191

Hamilton, Virginia (Esther)
1936-2002 .... **CLC 26; DAM MULT**
See also AAYA 2, 21; BW 2, 3; BYA 1, 2,
8; CA 25-28R; CANR 20, 37, 73; CLR 1,
11, 40; DLB 33, 52; DLBY 01; INT
CANR-20; JRDA; LAIT 5; MAICYA;
MAICYAS; MTCW 1, 2; SATA 4, 56, 79,
123; WYA; YAW

Hammett, (Samuel) Dashiell
1894-1961 .... **CLC 3, 5, 10, 19, 47; SSC
17**
See also AITN 1; AMWS 4; BPFB 2; CA
81-84; CANR 42; CDALB 1929-1941;
CMW; DA3; DLB 226; DLBD 6; DLBY
96; LAIT 3; MSW; MTCW 1, 2; RGAL;
RGSF

Hammon, Jupiter 1720(?)-1800(?) . **NCLC 5;
BLC 2; DAM MULT, POET; PC 16**
See also DLB 31, 50

Hammond, Keith
See Kuttner, Henry

Hamner, Earl (Henry), Jr. 1923- ...... **CLC 12**
See also AITN 2; CA 73-76; DLB 6

Hampton, Christopher (James)
1946- .... **CLC 4**
See also CA 25-28R; CD; DLB 13; MTCW
1

Hamsun, Knut .... **TCLC 2, 14, 49**
See also Pedersen, Knut
See also EW 8; RGWL

Handke, Peter 1942- .... **CLC 5, 8, 10, 15, 38,
134; DAM DRAM, NOV**
See also CA 77-80; CANR 33, 75, 104;
CWW 2; DLB 85, 124; MTCW 1, 2

Handy, W(illiam) C(hristopher)
1873-1958 .... **TCLC 97**
See also BW 3; CA 121; 167

Hanley, James 1901-1985 ..... **CLC 3, 5, 8, 13**
See also CA 73-76; 117; CANR 36; CBD;
DLB 191; MTCW 1; RGEL

Hannah, Barry 1942- .... **CLC 23, 38, 90**
See also BPFB 2; CA 108; 110; CANR 43,
68; CN; CSW; DLB 6, 234; INT CA-110;
MTCW 1; RGSF

Hannon, Ezra
See Hunter, Evan

Hansberry, Lorraine (Vivian)
1930-1965 ..... **CLC 17, 62; BLC 2; DA;
DAB; DAC; DAM DRAM, MST,
MULT; DC 2**
See also AAYA 25; AFAW 1, 2; AMWS 4;
BW 1, 3; CA 109; 25-28R; CABS 3;
CANR 58; CDALB 1941-1968; DA3;
DFS 2; DLB 7, 38; FW; LAIT 4; MTCW
1, 2; RGAL

Hansen, Joseph 1923- .... **CLC 38**
See also Brock, Rose; Colton, James
See also BPFB 2; CA 29-32R; CAAS 17;
CANR 16, 44, 66; CMW; DLB 226; GLL
1; INT CANR-16

Hansen, Martin A(lfred)
1909-1955 .... **TCLC 32**
See also CA 167; DLB 214

Hansen and Philipson eds. .... **CLC 65**

Hanson, Kenneth O(stlin) 1922- .... **CLC 13**
See also CA 53-56; CANR 7

Hardwick, Elizabeth (Bruce)
1916- .... **CLC 13; DAM NOV**
See also AMWS 3; CA 5-8R; CANR 3, 32,
70, 100; CN; CSW; DA3; DLB 6;
MAWW; MTCW 1, 2

Hardy, Thomas 1840-1928 .. **TCLC 4, 10, 18,
32, 48, 53, 72; DA; DAB; DAC; DAM
MST, NOV, POET; PC 8; SSC 2; WLC**
See also BRW 6; BRWR 1; CA 104; 123;
CDBLB 1890-1914; DA3; DLB 18, 19,
135; EXPN; EXPP; LAIT 2; MTCW 1, 2;
NFS 3, 11; PFS 3, 4; RGEL; RGSF;
WLIT 4

Hare, David 1947- .... **CLC 29, 58, 136**
See also BRWS 4; CA 97-100; CANR 39,
91; CBD; CD; DFS 4, 7; DLB 13; MTCW
1

Harewood, John
See Van Druten, John (William)

Harford, Henry
See Hudson, W(illiam) H(enry)

Hargrave, Leonie
See Disch, Thomas M(ichael)

Harjo, Joy 1951- ...... **CLC 83; DAM MULT;
PC 27**
See also CA 114; CANR 35, 67, 91; CP;
CWP; DLB 120, 175; MTCW 2; NNAL;
RGAL

Harlan, Louis R(udolph) 1922- .... **CLC 34**
See also CA 21-24R; CANR 25, 55, 80

Harling, Robert 1951(?)- .... **CLC 53**
See also CA 147

Harmon, William (Ruth) 1938- .... **CLC 38**
See also CA 33-36R; CANR 14, 32, 35;
SATA 65

Harper, F. E. W.
See Harper, Frances Ellen Watkins

Harper, Frances E. W.
See Harper, Frances Ellen Watkins

Harper, Frances E. Watkins
See Harper, Frances Ellen Watkins

Harper, Frances Ellen
See Harper, Frances Ellen Watkins

Harper, Frances Ellen Watkins
1825-1911 ...... **TCLC 14; BLC 2; DAM
MULT, POET; PC 21**
See also AFAW 1, 2; BW 1, 3; CA 111; 125;
CANR 79; DLB 50, 221; MAWW; RGAL

Harper, Michael S(teven) 1938- ... **CLC 7, 22**
See also AFAW 2; BW 1; CA 33-36R;
CANR 24; CP; DLB 41; RGAL

Harper, Mrs. F. E. W.
See Harper, Frances Ellen Watkins

Harris, Christie (Lucy) Irwin
1907- .... **CLC 12**
See also CA 5-8R; CANR 6, 83; CLR 47;
DLB 88; JRDA; MAICYA; SAAS 10;
SATA 6, 74; SATA-Essay 116

Harris, Frank 1856-1931 .... **TCLC 24**
See also CA 109; 150; CANR 80; DLB 156,
197; RGEL

Harris, George Washington
1814-1869 .... **NCLC 23**
See also DLB 3, 11, 248; RGAL

Harris, Joel Chandler 1848-1908 ... **TCLC 2;
SSC 19**
See also CA 104; 137; CANR 80; CLR 49;
DLB 11, 23, 42, 78, 91; LAIT 2; MAI-
CYA; RGSF; SATA 100; WCH; YABC 1

**Harris, John (Wyndham Parkes Lucas)
Beynon** 1903-1969
See Wyndham, John
See also CA 102; 89-92; CANR 84; SATA
118; SFW

Harris, MacDonald .... **CLC 9**
See also Heiney, Donald (William)

Harris, Mark 1922- .... **CLC 19**
See also CA 5-8R; CAAS 3; CANR 2, 55,
83; CN; DLB 2; DLBY 80

Harris, Norman .... **CLC 65**

Harris, (Theodore) Wilson 1921- ..... **CLC 25**
See also BRWS 5; BW 2, 3; CA 65-68;
CAAS 16; CANR 11, 27, 69; CN; CP;
DLB 117; MTCW 1; RGEL

Harrison, Barbara Grizzuti 1934- . **CLC 144**
See also CA 77-80; CANR 15, 48; INT
CANR-15

Harrison, Elizabeth (Allen) Cavanna
1909-2001
See Cavanna, Betty
See also CA 9-12R; CANR 6, 27, 85, 104;
YAW

Harrison, Harry (Max) 1925- .... **CLC 42**
See also CA 1-4R; CANR 5, 21, 84; DLB
8; SATA 4; SCFW 2; SFW

Harrison, James (Thomas) 1937- ...... **CLC 6,
14, 33, 66, 143; SSC 19**
See also Harrison, Jim
See also CA 13-16R; CANR 8, 51, 79; CN;
CP; DLBY 82; INT CANR-8

Harrison, Jim
See Harrison, James (Thomas)
See also AMWS 8; RGAL; TCWW 2

Harrison, Kathryn 1961- .... **CLC 70, 151**
See also CA 144; CANR 68

Harrison, Tony 1937- .... **CLC 43, 129**
See also BRWS 5; CA 65-68; CANR 44,
98; CBD; CD; CP; DLB 40, 245; MTCW
1; RGEL

Harriss, Will(ard Irvin) 1922- .... **CLC 34**
See also CA 111

Harson, Sley
See Ellison, Harlan (Jay)

Hart, Ellis
See Ellison, Harlan (Jay)

Hart, Josephine 1942(?)- .... **CLC 70; DAM POP**
See also CA 138; CANR 70; CPW

Hart, Moss 1904-1961 .... **CLC 66; DAM DRAM**
See also CA 109; 89-92; CANR 84; DFS 1; DLB 7; RGAL

Harte, (Francis) Bret(t) 1836(?)-1902 ... **TCLC 1, 25; DA; DAC; DAM MST; SSC 8; WLC**
See also AMWS 2; CA 104; 140; CANR 80; CDALB 1865-1917; DA3; DLB 12, 64, 74, 79, 186; EXPS; LAIT 2; RGAL; RGSF; SATA 26; SSFS 3

Hartley, L(eslie) P(oles) 1895-1972 ... **CLC 2, 22**
See also BRWS 7; CA 45-48; 37-40R; CANR 33; DLB 15, 139; HGG; MTCW 1, 2; RGEL; RGSF; SUFW

Hartman, Geoffrey H. 1929- .... **CLC 27**
See also CA 117; 125; CANR 79; DLB 67

Hartmann, Sadakichi 1869-1944 ... **TCLC 73**
See also CA 157; DLB 54

Hartmann von Aue c. 1170-c. 1210 .... **CMLC 15**
See also DLB 138; RGWL

Haruf, Kent 1943- .... **CLC 34**
See also CA 149; CANR 91

Harwood, Ronald 1934- .... **CLC 32; DAM DRAM, MST**
See also CA 1-4R; CANR 4, 55; CBD; CD; DLB 13

Hasegawa Tatsunosuke
See Futabatei, Shimei

Hasek, Jaroslav (Matej Frantisek) 1883-1923 .... **TCLC 4**
See also CA 104; 129; DLB 215; EW 9; MTCW 1, 2; RGSF; RGWL

Hass, Robert 1941- ... **CLC 18, 39, 99; PC 16**
See also AMWS 6; CA 111; CANR 30, 50, 71; CP; DLB 105, 206; RGAL; SATA 94

Hastings, Hudson
See Kuttner, Henry

Hastings, Selina .... **CLC 44**

Hathorne, John 1641-1717 .... **LC 38**

Hatteras, Amelia
See Mencken, H(enry) L(ouis)

Hatteras, Owen .... **TCLC 18**
See also Mencken, H(enry) L(ouis); Nathan, George Jean

Hauptmann, Gerhart (Johann Robert) 1862-1946 .... **TCLC 4; DAM DRAM; SSC 37**
See also CA 104; 153; DLB 66, 118; EW 8; RGSF; RGWL

Havel, Vaclav 1936- ..... **CLC 25, 58, 65, 123; DAM DRAM; DC 6**
See also CA 104; CANR 36, 63; CWW 2; DA3; DFS 10; DLB 232; MTCW 1, 2

Haviaras, Stratis .... **CLC 33**
See also Chaviaras, Strates

Hawes, Stephen 1475(?)-1529(?) .... **LC 17**
See also DLB 132; RGEL

Hawkes, John (Clendennin Burne, Jr.) 1925-1998 .. **CLC 1, 2, 3, 4, 7, 9, 14, 15, 27, 49**
See also BPFB 2; CA 1-4R; 167; CANR 2, 47, 64; CN; DLB 2, 7, 227; DLBY 80, 98; MTCW 1, 2; RGAL

Hawking, S. W.
See Hawking, Stephen W(illiam)

Hawking, Stephen W(illiam) 1942- . **CLC 63, 105**
See also AAYA 13; BEST 89:1; CA 126; 129; CANR 48; CPW; DA3; MTCW 2

Hawkins, Anthony Hope
See Hope, Anthony

Hawthorne, Julian 1846-1934 .... **TCLC 25**
See also CA 165; HGG

Hawthorne, Nathaniel 1804-1864 ... **NCLC 2, 10, 17, 23, 39, 79, 95; DA; DAB; DAC; DAM MST, NOV; SSC 3, 29, 39; WLC**
See also AAYA 18; AMW; AMWR 1; BPFB 2; BYA 3; CDALB 1640-1865; DA3; DLB 1, 74, 183, 223; EXPN; EXPS; HGG; LAIT 1; NFS 1; RGAL; RGSF; SSFS 1, 7, 11; SUFW; WCH; YABC 2

Haxton, Josephine Ayres 1921-
See Douglas, Ellen
See also CA 115; CANR 41, 83

Hayaseca y Eizaguirre, Jorge
See Echegaray (y Eizaguirre), Jose (Maria Waldo)

Hayashi, Fumiko 1904-1951 .... **TCLC 27**
See also CA 161; DLB 180

Haycraft, Anna (Margaret) 1932-
See Ellis, Alice Thomas
See also CA 122; CANR 85, 90; MTCW 2

Hayden, Robert E(arl) 1913-1980 . **CLC 5, 9, 14, 37; BLC 2; DA; DAC; DAM MST, MULT, POET; PC 6**
See also AFAW 1, 2; AMWS 2; BW 1, 3; CA 69-72; 97-100; CABS 2; CANR 24, 75, 82; CDALB 1941-1968; DLB 5, 76; EXPP; MTCW 1, 2; PFS 1; RGAL; SATA 19; SATA-Obit 26; WP

Hayek, F(riedrich) A(ugust von) 1899-1992 .... **TCLC 109**
See also CA 93-96; 137; CANR 20; MTCW 1, 2

Hayford, J(oseph) E(phraim) Casely
See Casely-Hayford, J(oseph) E(phraim)

Hayman, Ronald 1932- .... **CLC 44**
See also CA 25-28R; CANR 18, 50, 88; CD; DLB 155

Hayne, Paul Hamilton 1830-1886 . **NCLC 94**
See also DLB 3, 64, 79, 248; RGAL

Haywood, Eliza (Fowler) 1693(?)-1756 .... **LC 1, 44**
See also DLB 39; RGEL

Hazlitt, William 1778-1830 ...... **NCLC 29, 82**
See also BRW 4; DLB 110, 158; RGEL

Hazzard, Shirley 1931- .... **CLC 18**
See also CA 9-12R; CANR 4, 70; CN; DLBY 82; MTCW 1

Head, Bessie 1937-1986 .... **CLC 25, 67; BLC 2; DAM MULT**
See also AFW; BW 2, 3; CA 29-32R; 119; CANR 25, 82; DA3; DLB 117, 225; EXPS; FW; MTCW 1, 2; RGSF; SSFS 5, 13; WLIT 2

Headon, (Nicky) Topper 1956(?)- ..... **CLC 30**

Heaney, Seamus (Justin) 1939- ..... **CLC 5, 7, 14, 25, 37, 74, 91; DAB; DAM POET; PC 18; WLCS**
See also BRWR 1; BRWS 2; CA 85-88; CANR 25, 48, 75, 91; CDBLB 1960 to Present; CP; DA3; DLB 40; DLBY 95; EXPP; MTCW 1, 2; PAB; PFS 2, 5, 8; RGEL; WLIT 4

Hearn, (Patricio) Lafcadio (Tessima Carlos) 1850-1904 .... **TCLC 9**
See also CA 105; 166; DLB 12, 78, 189; HGG; RGAL

Hearne, Vicki 1946- .... **CLC 56**
See also CA 139

Hearon, Shelby 1931- .... **CLC 63**
See also AITN 2; AMWS 8; CA 25-28R; CANR 18, 48, 103; CSW

Heat-Moon, William Least .... **CLC 29**
See also Trogdon, William (Lewis)
See also AAYA 9

Hebbel, Friedrich 1813-1863 .... **NCLC 43; DAM DRAM**
See also DLB 129; EW 6; RGWL

Hebert, Anne 1916-2000 .... **CLC 4, 13, 29; DAC; DAM MST, POET**
See also CA 85-88; 187; CANR 69; CCA 1; CWP; CWW 2; DA3; DLB 68; GFL 1789 to the Present; MTCW 1, 2

Hecht, Anthony (Evan) 1923- ...... **CLC 8, 13, 19; DAM POET**
See also AMWS 10; CA 9-12R; CANR 6; CP; DLB 5, 169; PFS 6; WP

Hecht, Ben 1894-1964 .... **CLC 8**
See also CA 85-88; DFS 9; DLB 7, 9, 25, 26, 28, 86; FANT; IDFW 3, 4; RGAL; TCLC 101

Hedayat, Sadeq 1903-1951 .... **TCLC 21**
See also CA 120; RGSF

Hegel, Georg Wilhelm Friedrich 1770-1831 .... **NCLC 46**
See also DLB 90

Heidegger, Martin 1889-1976 .... **CLC 24**
See also CA 81-84; 65-68; CANR 34; MTCW 1, 2

Heidenstam, (Carl Gustaf) Verner von 1859-1940 .... **TCLC 5**
See also CA 104

Heifner, Jack 1946- .... **CLC 11**
See also CA 105; CANR 47

Heijermans, Herman 1864-1924 .... **TCLC 24**
See also CA 123

Heilbrun, Carolyn G(old) 1926- .... **CLC 25**
See also Cross, Amanda
See also CA 45-48; CANR 1, 28, 58, 94; CMW; CPW; FW

Hein, Christoph 1944- .... **CLC 154**
See also CA 158; CWW 2; DLB 124

Heine, Heinrich 1797-1856 .... **NCLC 4, 54; PC 25**
See also DLB 90; EW 5; RGWL

Heinemann, Larry (Curtiss) 1944- .. **CLC 50**
See also CA 110; CAAS 21; CANR 31, 81; DLBD 9; INT CANR-31

Heiney, Donald (William) 1921-1993
See Harris, MacDonald
See also CA 1-4R; 142; CANR 3, 58; FANT

Heinlein, Robert A(nson) 1907-1988 . **CLC 1, 3, 8, 14, 26, 55; DAM POP**
See also AAYA 17; BPFB 2; BYA 4, 13; CA 1-4R; 125; CANR 1, 20, 53; CLR 75; CPW; DA3; DLB 8; EXPS; JRDA; LAIT 5; MAICYA; MTCW 1, 2; RGAL; SATA 9, 69; SATA-Obit 56; SCFW; SFW; SSFS 7; YAW

Helforth, John
See Doolittle, Hilda

Hellenhofferu, Vojtech Kapristian z
See Hasek, Jaroslav (Matej Frantisek)

Heller, Joseph 1923-1999 . **CLC 1, 3, 5, 8, 11, 36, 63; DAB; DAC; DAM MST, NOV, POP; WLC**
See also AAYA 24; AITN 1; AMWS 4; BPFB 2; BYA 1; CA 5-8R; 187; CABS 1; CANR 8, 42, 66; CN; CPW; DA3; DLB 2, 28, 227; DLBY 80; EXPN; INT CANR-8; LAIT 4; MTCW 1, 2; NFS 1; RGAL; YAW

Hellman, Lillian (Florence) 1906-1984 .. **CLC 2, 4, 8, 14, 18, 34, 44, 52; DAM DRAM; DC 1; TCLC 119**
See also AITN 1, 2; AMWS 1; CA 13-16R; 112; CAD; CANR 33; CWD; DA3; DFS 1, 3; DLB 7, 228; DLBY 84; FW; LAIT 3; MAWW; MTCW 1, 2; RGAL

Helprin, Mark 1947- .... **CLC 7, 10, 22, 32; DAM NOV, POP**
See also CA 81-84; CANR 47, 64; CDALBS; CPW; DA3; DLBY 85; FANT; MTCW 1, 2

Helvetius, Claude-Adrien 1715-1771 .. **LC 26**

Helyar, Jane Penelope Josephine 1933-
See Poole, Josephine
See also CA 21-24R; CANR 10, 26; SATA 82

Hemans, Felicia 1793-1835 ...... **NCLC 29, 71**
See also DLB 96; RGEL

Hemingway, Ernest (Miller)
1899-1961 ...... **CLC 1, 3, 6, 8, 10, 13, 19, 30, 34, 39, 41, 44, 50, 61, 80; DA; DAB; DAC; DAM MST, NOV; SSC 1, 25, 36, 40; WLC**
See also AAYA 19; AMW; AMWR 1; BPFB 2; BYA 2, 3, 13; CA 77-80; CANR 34; CDALB 1917-1929; DA3; DLB 4, 9, 102, 210; DLBD 1, 15, 16; DLBY 81, 87, 96, 98; EXPN; EXPS; LAIT 3, 4; MTCW 1, 2; NFS 1, 5, 6; RGAL; RGSF; SSFS 1, 6, 8, 9, 11; TCLC 115; WYA

Hempel, Amy 1951- .... **CLC 39**
See also CA 118; 137; CANR 70; DA3; DLB 218; EXPS; MTCW 2; SSFS 2

Henderson, F. C.
See Mencken, H(enry) L(ouis)

Henderson, Sylvia
See Ashton-Warner, Sylvia (Constance)

Henderson, Zenna (Chlarson)
1917-1983 .... **SSC 29**
See also CA 1-4R; 133; CANR 1, 84; DLB 8; SATA 5; SFW

Henkin, Joshua .... **CLC 119**
See also CA 161

Henley, Beth .... **CLC 23; DC 6, 14**
See also Henley, Elizabeth Becker
See also CABS 3; CAD; CD; CSW; CWD; DFS 2; DLBY 86; FW

Henley, Elizabeth Becker 1952-
See Henley, Beth
See also CA 107; CANR 32, 73; DA3; DAM DRAM, MST; MTCW 1, 2

Henley, William Ernest 1849-1903 .. **TCLC 8**
See also CA 105; DLB 19; RGEL

Hennissart, Martha
See Lathen, Emma
See also CA 85-88; CANR 64

Henry VIII 1491-1547 .... **LC 10**
See also DLB 132

Henry, O. .... **TCLC 1, 19; SSC 5, 49; WLC**
See also Porter, William Sydney
See also AAYA 41; AMWS 2; EXPS; RGAL; RGSF; SSFS 2

Henry, Patrick 1736-1799 .... **LC 25**
See also LAIT 1

Henryson, Robert 1430(?)-1506(?) ...... **LC 20**
See also BRWS 7; DLB 146; RGEL

Henschke, Alfred
See Klabund

Hentoff, Nat(han Irving) 1925- .... **CLC 26**
See also AAYA 4, 42; BYA 6; CA 1-4R; CAAS 6; CANR 5, 25, 77; CLR 1, 52; INT CANR-25; JRDA; MAICYA; SATA 42, 69; SATA-Brief 27; WYA; YAW

Heppenstall, (John) Rayner
1911-1981 .... **CLC 10**
See also CA 1-4R; 103; CANR 29

Heraclitus c. 540B.C.-c. 450B.C. ... **CMLC 22**
See also DLB 176

Herbert, Frank (Patrick)
1920-1986 .... **CLC 12, 23, 35, 44, 85; DAM POP**
See also AAYA 21; BPFB 2; BYA 4, 14; CA 53-56; 118; CANR 5, 43; CDALBS; CPW; DLB 8; INT CANR-5; LAIT 5; MTCW 1, 2; SATA 9, 37; SATA-Obit 47; SCFW 2; SFW; YAW

Herbert, George 1593-1633 ..... **LC 24; DAB; DAM POET; PC 4**
See also BRW 2; BRWR 2; CDBLB Before 1660; DLB 126; EXPP; RGEL; WP

Herbert, Zbigniew 1924-1998 ..... **CLC 9, 43; DAM POET**
See also CA 89-92; 169; CANR 36, 74; CWW 2; DLB 232; MTCW 1

Herbst, Josephine (Frey)
1897-1969 .... **CLC 34**
See also CA 5-8R; 25-28R; DLB 9

Herder, Johann Gottfried von
1744-1803 .... **NCLC 8**
See also DLB 97; EW 4

Heredia, Jose Maria 1803-1839
See also HLCS 2; LAW

Hergesheimer, Joseph 1880-1954 ... **TCLC 11**
See also CA 109; 194; DLB 102, 9; RGAL

Herlihy, James Leo 1927-1993 .... **CLC 6**
See also CA 1-4R; 143; CAD; CANR 2

Hermogenes fl. c. 175- .... **CMLC 6**

Hernandez, Jose 1834-1886 .... **NCLC 17**
See also LAW; RGWL; WLIT 1

Herodotus c. 484B.C.-c. 420B.C. .. **CMLC 17**
See also AW 1; DLB 176; RGWL

Herrick, Robert 1591-1674 .... **LC 13; DA; DAB; DAC; DAM MST, POP; PC 9**
See also BRW 2; DLB 126; EXPP; PFS 13; RGAL; RGEL; WP

Herring, Guilles
See Somerville, Edith Oenone

Herriot, James .... **CLC 12; DAM POP**
See also Wight, James Alfred
See also AAYA 1; BPFB 2; CA 148; CANR 40; LAIT 3; MAICYAS; MTCW 2; SATA 86

Herris, Violet
See Hunt, Violet

Herrmann, Dorothy 1941- .... **CLC 44**
See also CA 107

Herrmann, Taffy
See Herrmann, Dorothy

Hersey, John (Richard) 1914-1993 .... **CLC 1, 2, 7, 9, 40, 81, 97; DAM POP**
See also AAYA 29; BPFB 2; CA 17-20R; 140; CANR 33; CDALBS; CPW; DLB 6, 185; MTCW 1, 2; SATA 25; SATA-Obit 76

Herzen, Aleksandr Ivanovich
1812-1870 .... **NCLC 10, 61**

Herzl, Theodor 1860-1904 .... **TCLC 36**
See also CA 168

Herzog, Werner 1942- .... **CLC 16**
See also CA 89-92

Hesiod c. 8th cent. B.C.- .... **CMLC 5**
See also AW 1; DLB 176; RGWL

Hesse, Hermann 1877-1962 ... **CLC 1, 2, 3, 6, 11, 17, 25, 69; DA; DAB; DAC; DAM MST, NOV; SSC 9, 49; WLC**
See also AAYA 43; BPFB 2; CA 17-18; CAP 2; DA3; DLB 66; EW 9; EXPN; LAIT 1; MTCW 1, 2; NFS 6; RGWL; SATA 50

Hewes, Cady
See De Voto, Bernard (Augustine)

Heyen, William 1940- .... **CLC 13, 18**
See also CA 33-36R; CAAS 9; CANR 98; CP; DLB 5

Heyerdahl, Thor 1914- .... **CLC 26**
See also CA 5-8R; CANR 5, 22, 66, 73; LAIT 4; MTCW 1, 2; SATA 2, 52

Heym, Georg (Theodor Franz Arthur)
1887-1912 .... **TCLC 9**
See also CA 106; 181

Heym, Stefan 1913- .... **CLC 41**
See also CA 9-12R; CANR 4; CWW 2; DLB 69

Heyse, Paul (Johann Ludwig von)
1830-1914 .... **TCLC 8**
See also CA 104; DLB 129

Heyward, (Edwin) DuBose
1885-1940 .... **TCLC 59**
See also CA 108; 157; DLB 7, 9, 45, 249; SATA 21

Heywood, John 1497(?)-1580(?) .... **LC 65**
See also DLB 136; RGEL

Hibbert, Eleanor Alice Burford
1906-1993 .... **CLC 7; DAM POP**
See also Holt, Victoria
See also BEST 90:4; CA 17-20R; 140; CANR 9, 28, 59; CMW; CPW; MTCW 2; RHW; SATA 2; SATA-Obit 74

Hichens, Robert (Smythe)
1864-1950 .... **TCLC 64**
See also CA 162; DLB 153; HGG; RHW; SUFW

Higgins, George V(incent)
1939-1999 .... **CLC 4, 7, 10, 18**
See also BPFB 2; CA 77-80; 186; CAAS 5; CANR 17, 51, 89, 96; CMW; CN; DLB 2; DLBY 81, 98; INT CANR-17; MSW; MTCW 1

Higginson, Thomas Wentworth
1823-1911 .... **TCLC 36**
See also CA 162; DLB 1, 64, 243

Higgonet, Margaret ed. .... **CLC 65**

Highet, Helen
See MacInnes, Helen (Clark)

Highsmith, (Mary) Patricia
1921-1995 .... **CLC 2, 4, 14, 42, 102; DAM NOV, POP**
See also Morgan, Claire
See also BRWS 5; CA 1-4R; 147; CANR 1, 20, 48, 62; CMW; CPW; DA3; MSW; MTCW 1, 2

Highwater, Jamake (Mamake)
1942(?)-2001 .... **CLC 12**
See also AAYA 7; BPFB 2; BYA 4; CA 65-68; CAAS 7; CANR 10, 34, 84; CLR 17; CWRI; DLB 52; DLBY 85; JRDA; MAICYA; SATA 32, 69; SATA-Brief 30

Highway, Tomson 1951- .... **CLC 92; DAC; DAM MULT**
See also CA 151; CANR 75; CCA 1; CD; DFS 2; MTCW 2; NNAL

Hijuelos, Oscar 1951- .... **CLC 65; DAM MULT, POP; HLC 1**
See also AAYA 25; AMWS 8; BEST 90:1; CA 123; CANR 50, 75; CPW; DA3; DLB 145; HW 1, 2; MTCW 2; RGAL; WLIT 1

Hikmet, Nazim 1902(?)-1963 .... **CLC 40**
See also CA 141; 93-96

Hildegard von Bingen 1098-1179 . **CMLC 20**
See also DLB 148

Hildesheimer, Wolfgang 1916-1991 .. **CLC 49**
See also CA 101; 135; DLB 69, 124

Hill, Geoffrey (William) 1932- ...... **CLC 5, 8, 18, 45; DAM POET**
See also BRWS 5; CA 81-84; CANR 21, 89; CDBLB 1960 to Present; CP; DLB 40; MTCW 1; RGEL

Hill, George Roy 1921- .... **CLC 26**
See also CA 110; 122

Hill, John
See Koontz, Dean R(ay)

Hill, Susan (Elizabeth) 1942- .... **CLC 4, 113; DAB; DAM MST, NOV**
See also CA 33-36R; CANR 29, 69; CN; DLB 14, 139; HGG; MTCW 1; RHW

Hillard, Asa G. III .... **CLC 70**

Hillerman, Tony 1925- . **CLC 62; DAM POP**
See also AAYA 40; BEST 89:1; BPFB 2; CA 29-32R; CANR 21, 42, 65, 97; CMW; CPW; DA3; DLB 206; MSW; RGAL; SATA 6; TCWW 2; YAW

Hillesum, Etty 1914-1943 .... **TCLC 49**
See also CA 137

Hilliard, Noel (Harvey) 1929-1996 ... **CLC 15**
See also CA 9-12R; CANR 7, 69; CN

Hopkins, John (Richard) 1931-1998 .. **CLC 4**
See also CA 85-88; 169; CBD; CD

Hopkins, Pauline Elizabeth
1859-1930 ...... **TCLC 28; BLC 2; DAM MULT**
See also AFAW 2; BW 2, 3; CA 141; CANR 82; DLB 50

Hopkinson, Francis 1737-1791 .... **LC 25**
See also DLB 31; RGAL

Hopley-Woolrich, Cornell George 1903-1968
See Woolrich, Cornell
See also CA 13-14; CANR 58; CAP 1; CMW; DLB 226; MTCW 2

Horace 65B.C.-8B.C. .... **CMLC 39**
See also AW 2; DLB 211; RGWL

Horatio
See Proust, (Valentin-Louis-George-Eugene-)Marcel

Horgan, Paul (George Vincent O'Shaughnessy) 1903-1995 . **CLC 9, 53; DAM NOV**
See also BPFB 2; CA 13-16R; 147; CANR 9, 35; DLB 102, 212; DLBY 85; INT CANR-9; MTCW 1, 2; SATA 13; SATA-Obit 84; TCWW 2

Horn, Peter
See Kuttner, Henry

Hornem, Horace Esq.
See Byron, George Gordon (Noel)

Horney, Karen (Clementine Theodore Danielsen) 1885-1952 .... **TCLC 71**
See also CA 114; 165; DLB 246; FW

Hornung, E(rnest) W(illiam) 1866-1921 .... **TCLC 59**
See also CA 108; 160; CMW; DLB 70

Horovitz, Israel (Arthur) 1939- ...... **CLC 56; DAM DRAM**
See also CA 33-36R; CAD; CANR 46, 59; CD; DLB 7

Horton, George Moses
1797(?)-1883(?) .... **NCLC 87**
See also DLB 50

Horvath, Odon von 1901-1938 .... **TCLC 45**
See also von Horvath, Oedoen
See also CA 118; 194; DLB 85, 124; RGWL

Horvath, Oedoen von -1938
See Horvath, Odon von

Horwitz, Julius 1920-1986 .... **CLC 14**
See also CA 9-12R; 119; CANR 12

Hospital, Janette Turner 1942- .... **CLC 42, 145**
See also CA 108; CANR 48; CN; RGSF

Hostos, E. M. de
See Hostos (y Bonilla), Eugenio Maria de

Hostos, Eugenio M. de
See Hostos (y Bonilla), Eugenio Maria de

Hostos, Eugenio Maria
See Hostos (y Bonilla), Eugenio Maria de

Hostos (y Bonilla), Eugenio Maria de
1839-1903 .... **TCLC 24**
See also CA 123; 131; HW 1

Houdini
See Lovecraft, H(oward) P(hillips)

Hougan, Carolyn 1943- .... **CLC 34**
See also CA 139

Household, Geoffrey (Edward West)
1900-1988 .... **CLC 11**
See also CA 77-80; 126; CANR 58; CMW; DLB 87; SATA 14; SATA-Obit 59

Housman, A(lfred) E(dward)
1859-1936 .... **TCLC 1, 10; DA; DAB; DAC; DAM MST, POET; PC 2; WLCS**
See also BRW 6; CA 104; 125; DA3; DLB 19; EXPP; MTCW 1, 2; PAB; PFS 4, 7; RGEL; WP

Housman, Laurence 1865-1959 .... **TCLC 7**
See also CA 106; 155; DLB 10; FANT; RGEL; SATA 25

Howard, Elizabeth Jane 1923- ..... **CLC 7, 29**
See also CA 5-8R; CANR 8, 62; CN

Howard, Maureen 1930- .... **CLC 5, 14, 46, 151**
See also CA 53-56; CANR 31, 75; CN; DLBY 83; INT CANR-31; MTCW 1, 2

Howard, Richard 1929- .... **CLC 7, 10, 47**
See also AITN 1; CA 85-88; CANR 25, 80; CP; DLB 5; INT CANR-25

Howard, Robert E(rvin)
1906-1936 .... **TCLC 8**
See also BPFB 2; BYA 5; CA 105; 157; FANT; SUFW

Howard, Warren F.
See Pohl, Frederik

Howe, Fanny (Quincy) 1940- .... **CLC 47**
See also CA 117; CAAE 187; CAAS 27; CANR 70; CP; CWP; SATA-Brief 52

Howe, Irving 1920-1993 .... **CLC 85**
See also AMWS 6; CA 9-12R; 141; CANR 21, 50; DLB 67; MTCW 1, 2

Howe, Julia Ward 1819-1910 .... **TCLC 21**
See also CA 117; 191; DLB 1, 189, 235; FW

Howe, Susan 1937- .... **CLC 72, 152**
See also AMWS 4; CA 160; CP; CWP; DLB 120; FW; RGAL

Howe, Tina 1937- .... **CLC 48**
See also CA 109; CAD; CD; CWD

Howell, James 1594(?)-1666 .... **LC 13**
See also DLB 151

Howells, W. D.
See Howells, William Dean

Howells, William D.
See Howells, William Dean

Howells, William Dean 1837-1920 .. **TCLC 7, 17, 41; SSC 36**
See also AMW; CA 104; 134; CDALB 1865-1917; DLB 12, 64, 74, 79, 189; MTCW 2; RGAL

Howes, Barbara 1914-1996 .... **CLC 15**
See also CA 9-12R; 151; CAAS 3; CANR 53; CP; SATA 5

Hrabal, Bohumil 1914-1997 .... **CLC 13, 67**
See also CA 106; 156; CAAS 12; CANR 57; CWW 2; DLB 232; RGSF

Hroswitha of Gandersheim c. 935-c. 1000 .... **CMLC 29**
See also DLB 148

Hsi, Chu 1130-1200 .... **CMLC 42**

Hsun, Lu
See Lu Hsun

Hubbard, L(afayette) Ron(ald)
1911-1986 .... **CLC 43; DAM POP**
See also CA 77-80; 118; CANR 52; CPW; DA3; FANT; MTCW 2; SFW

Huch, Ricarda (Octavia)
1864-1947 .... **TCLC 13**
See also CA 111; 189; DLB 66

Huddle, David 1942- .... **CLC 49**
See also CA 57-60; CAAS 20; CANR 89; DLB 130

Hudson, Jeffrey
See Crichton, (John) Michael

Hudson, W(illiam) H(enry)
1841-1922 .... **TCLC 29**
See also CA 115; 190; DLB 98, 153, 174; RGEL; SATA 35

Hueffer, Ford Madox
See Ford, Ford Madox

Hughart, Barry 1934- .... **CLC 39**
See also CA 137; FANT; SFW

Hughes, Colin
See Creasey, John

Hughes, David (John) 1930- .... **CLC 48**
See also CA 116; 129; CN; DLB 14

Hughes, Edward James
See Hughes, Ted
See also DA3; DAM MST, POET

Hughes, (James) Langston
1902-1967 .... **CLC 1, 5, 10, 15, 35, 44, 108; BLC 2; DA; DAB; DAC; DAM DRAM, MST, MULT, POET; DC 3; PC 1; SSC 6; WLC**
See also AAYA 12; AFAW 1, 2; AMWR 1; AMWS 1; BW 1, 3; CA 1-4R; 25-28R; CANR 1, 34, 82; CDALB 1929-1941; CLR 17; DA3; DLB 4, 7, 48, 51, 86, 228; EXPP; EXPS; JRDA; LAIT 3; MAICYA; MTCW 1, 2; PAB; PFS 1, 3, 6, 10; RGAL; RGSF; SATA 4, 33; SSFS 4, 7; WCH; WP; YAW

Hughes, Richard (Arthur Warren)
1900-1976 .... **CLC 1, 11; DAM NOV**
See also CA 5-8R; 65-68; CANR 4; DLB 15, 161; MTCW 1; RGEL; SATA 8; SATA-Obit 25

Hughes, Ted 1930-1998 . **CLC 2, 4, 9, 14, 37, 119; DAB; DAC; PC 7**
See also Hughes, Edward James
See also BRWR 2; BRWS 1; CA 1-4R; 171; CANR 1, 33, 66; CLR 3; CP; DLB 40, 161; EXPP; MAICYA; MTCW 1, 2; PAB; PFS 4; RGEL; SATA 49; SATA-Brief 27; SATA-Obit 107; YAW

Hugo, Richard
See Huch, Ricarda (Octavia)

Hugo, Richard F(ranklin)
1923-1982 .... **CLC 6, 18, 32; DAM POET**
See also AMWS 6; CA 49-52; 108; CANR 3; DLB 5, 206; RGAL

Hugo, Victor (Marie) 1802-1885 .... **NCLC 3, 10, 21; DA; DAB; DAC; DAM DRAM, MST, NOV, POET; PC 17; WLC**
See also AAYA 28; DA3; DLB 119, 192, 217; EFS 2; EW 6; EXPN; GFL 1789 to the Present; LAIT 1, 2; NFS 5; RGWL; SATA 47

Huidobro, Vicente
See Huidobro Fernandez, Vicente Garcia
See also LAW

Huidobro Fernandez, Vicente Garcia
1893-1948 .... **TCLC 31**
See also Huidobro, Vicente
See also CA 131; HW 1

Hulme, Keri 1947- .... **CLC 39, 130**
See also CA 125; CANR 69; CN; CP; CWP; FW; INT 125

Hulme, T(homas) E(rnest)
1883-1917 .... **TCLC 21**
See also BRWS 6; CA 117; DLB 19

Hume, David 1711-1776 .... **LC 7, 56**
See also BRWS 3; DLB 104, 252

Humphrey, William 1924-1997 .... **CLC 45**
See also AMWS 9; CA 77-80; 160; CANR 68; CN; CSW; DLB 6, 212, 234; TCWW 2

Humphreys, Emyr Owen 1919- .... **CLC 47**
See also CA 5-8R; CANR 3, 24; CN; DLB 15

Humphreys, Josephine 1945- ..... **CLC 34, 57**
See also CA 121; 127; CANR 97; CSW; INT 127

Huneker, James Gibbons
1860-1921 .... **TCLC 65**
See also CA 193; DLB 71; RGAL

Hungerford, Pixie
See Brinsmead, H(esba) F(ay)

Hunt, E(verette) Howard, (Jr.)
1918- .... **CLC 3**
See also AITN 1; CA 45-48; CANR 2, 47, 103; CMW

Hunt, Francesca
See Holland, Isabelle

Hunt, Howard
See Hunt, E(verette) Howard, (Jr.)

Hunt, Kyle
See Creasey, John

Johnson, J. R.
    See James, C(yril) L(ionel) R(obert)
Johnson, James Weldon
    1871-1938 .. TCLC 3, 19; BLC 2; DAM
    MULT, POET; PC 24
    See also AFAW 1, 2; BW 1, 3; CA 104;
    125; CANR 82; CDALB 1917-1929; CLR
    32; DA3; DLB 51; EXPP; MTCW 1, 2;
    PFS 1; RGAL; SATA 31
Johnson, Joyce 1935- .... CLC 58
    See also CA 125; 129; CANR 102
Johnson, Judith (Emlyn) 1936- .... CLC 7, 15
    See also Sherwin, Judith Johnson
    See also CA 25-28R, 153; CANR 34
Johnson, Lionel (Pigot)
    1867-1902 .... TCLC 19
    See also CA 117; DLB 19; RGEL
Johnson, Marguerite (Annie)
    See Angelou, Maya
Johnson, Mel
    See Malzberg, Barry N(athaniel)
Johnson, Pamela Hansford
    1912-1981 .... CLC 1, 7, 27
    See also CA 1-4R; 104; CANR 2, 28; DLB
    15; MTCW 1, 2; RGEL
Johnson, Paul (Bede) 1928- .... CLC 147
    See also BEST 89:4; CA 17-20R; CANR
    34, 62, 100
Johnson, Robert .... CLC 70
Johnson, Robert 1911(?)-1938 .... TCLC 69
    See also BW 3; CA 174
Johnson, Samuel 1709-1784 . LC 15, 52; DA;
    DAB; DAC; DAM MST; WLC
    See also BRW 3; BRWR 1; CDBLB 1660-
    1789; DLB 39, 95, 104, 142, 213; RGEL;
    TEA
Johnson, Uwe 1934-1984 .. CLC 5, 10, 15, 40
    See also CA 1-4R; 112; CANR 1, 39; DLB
    75; MTCW 1; RGWL
Johnston, George (Benson) 1913- .... CLC 51
    See also CA 1-4R; CANR 5, 20; CP; DLB
    88
Johnston, Jennifer (Prudence)
    1930- .... CLC 7, 150
    See also CA 85-88; CANR 92; CN; DLB
    14
Joinville, Jean de 1224(?)-1317 ..... CMLC 38
Jolley, (Monica) Elizabeth 1923- ..... CLC 46;
    SSC 19
    See also CA 127; CAAS 13; CANR 59; CN;
    RGSF
Jones, Arthur Llewellyn 1863-1947
    See Machen, Arthur
    See also CA 104; 179; HGG
Jones, D(ouglas) G(ordon) 1929- ..... CLC 10
    See also CA 29-32R; CANR 13, 90; CP;
    DLB 53
Jones, David (Michael) 1895-1974 .... CLC 2,
    4, 7, 13, 42
    See also BRW 6; BRWS 7; CA 9-12R; 53-
    56; CANR 28; CDBLB 1945-1960; DLB
    20, 100; MTCW 1; PAB; RGEL
Jones, David Robert 1947-
    See Bowie, David
    See also CA 103; CANR 104
Jones, Diana Wynne 1934- .... CLC 26
    See also AAYA 12; BYA 6, 7, 9, 11, 13; CA
    49-52; CANR 4, 26, 56; CLR 23; DLB
    161; FANT; JRDA; MAICYA; SAAS 7;
    SATA 9, 70, 108; SFW; YAW
Jones, Edward P. 1950- .... CLC 76
    See also BW 2, 3; CA 142; CANR 79; CSW
Jones, Gayl 1949- ..... CLC 6, 9, 131; BLC 2;
    DAM MULT
    See also AFAW 1, 2; BW 2, 3; CA 77-80;
    CANR 27, 66; CN; CSW; DA3; DLB 33;
    MTCW 1, 2; RGAL

Jones, James 1931-1978 ...... CLC 1, 3, 10, 39
    See also AITN 1, 2; BPFB 2; CA 1-4R; 69-
    72; CANR 6; DLB 2, 143; DLBD 17;
    DLBY 98; MTCW 1; RGAL
Jones, John J.
    See Lovecraft, H(oward) P(hillips)
Jones, LeRoi .... CLC 1, 2, 3, 5, 10, 14
    See also Baraka, Amiri
    See also MTCW 2
Jones, Louis B. 1953- .... CLC 65
    See also CA 141; CANR 73
Jones, Madison (Percy, Jr.) 1925- ...... CLC 4
    See also CA 13-16R; CAAS 11; CANR 7,
    54, 83; CN; CSW; DLB 152
Jones, Mervyn 1922- .... CLC 10, 52
    See also CA 45-48; CAAS 5; CANR 1, 91;
    CN; MTCW 1
Jones, Mick 1956(?)- .... CLC 30
Jones, Nettie (Pearl) 1941- .... CLC 34
    See also BW 2; CA 137; CAAS 20; CANR
    88
Jones, Preston 1936-1979 .... CLC 10
    See also CA 73-76; 89-92; DLB 7
Jones, Robert F(rancis) 1934- .... CLC 7
    See also CA 49-52; CANR 2, 61
Jones, Rod 1953- .... CLC 50
    See also CA 128
Jones, Terence Graham Parry
    1942- .... CLC 21
    See also Jones, Terry; Monty Python
    See also CA 112; 116; CANR 35, 93; INT
    116; SATA 127
Jones, Terry
    See Jones, Terence Graham Parry
    See also SATA 67; SATA-Brief 51
Jones, Thom (Douglas) 1945(?)- .... CLC 81
    See also CA 157; CANR 88; DLB 244
Jong, Erica 1942- .... CLC 4, 6, 8, 18, 83;
    DAM NOV, POP
    See also AITN 1; AMWS 5; BEST 90:2;
    BPFB 2; CA 73-76; CANR 26, 52, 75;
    CN; CP; CPW; DA3; DLB 2, 5, 28, 152;
    FW; INT CANR-26; MTCW 1, 2
Jonson, Ben(jamin) 1572(?)-1637 .. LC 6, 33;
    DA; DAB; DAC; DAM DRAM, MST,
    POET; DC 4; PC 17; WLC
    See also BRW 1; BRWR 1; CDBLB Before
    1660; DFS 4, 10; DLB 62, 121; RGEL;
    WLIT 3
Jordan, June 1936- .... CLC 5, 11, 23, 114;
    BLCS; DAM MULT, POET; PC 38
    See also Meyer, June
    See also AAYA 2; AFAW 1, 2; BW 2, 3;
    CA 33-36R; CANR 25, 70; CLR 10; CP;
    CWP; DLB 38; GLL 2; LAIT 5; MAI-
    CYA; MTCW 1; SATA 4; YAW
Jordan, Neil (Patrick) 1950- .... CLC 110
    See also CA 124; 130; CANR 54; CN; GLL
    2; INT 130
Jordan, Pat(rick M.) 1941- .... CLC 37
    See also CA 33-36R
Jorgensen, Ivar
    See Ellison, Harlan (Jay)
Jorgenson, Ivar
    See Silverberg, Robert
Joseph, George Ghevarughese .... CLC 70
Josephus, Flavius c. 37-100 .... CMLC 13
    See also AW 2; DLB 176
Josiah Allen's Wife
    See Holley, Marietta
Josipovici, Gabriel (David) 1940- ...... CLC 6,
    43, 153
    See also CA 37-40R; CAAS 8; CANR 47,
    84; CN; DLB 14
Joubert, Joseph 1754-1824 .... NCLC 9
Jouve, Pierre Jean 1887-1976 .... CLC 47
    See also CA 65-68

Jovine, Francesco 1902-1950 .... TCLC 79
Joyce, James (Augustine Aloysius)
    1882-1941 .. TCLC 3, 8, 16, 35, 52; DA;
    DAB; DAC; DAM MST, NOV, POET;
    DC 16; PC 22; SSC 3, 26, 44; WLC
    See also AAYA 42; BRW 7; BRWR 1; BYA
    11, 13; CA 104; 126; CDBLB 1914-1945;
    DA3; DLB 10, 19, 36, 162, 247; EXPN;
    EXPS; LAIT 3; MTCW 1, 2; NFS 7;
    RGSF; SSFS 1; WLIT 4
Jozsef, Attila 1905-1937 .... TCLC 22
    See also CA 116; DLB 215
Juana Ines de la Cruz, Sor
    1651(?)-1695 ...... LC 5; HLCS 1; PC 24
    See also FW; LAW; RGWL; WLIT 1
Juana Inez de La Cruz, Sor
    See Juana Ines de la Cruz, Sor
Judd, Cyril
    See Kornbluth, C(yril) M.; Pohl, Frederik
Juenger, Ernst 1895-1998 .... CLC 125
    See also Junger, Ernst
    See also CA 101; 167; CANR 21, 47, 106;
    DLB 56
Julian of Norwich 1342(?)-1416(?) . LC 6, 52
    See also DLB 146
Julius Caesar 100B.C.-44B.C.
    See Caesar, Julius
    See also DLB 211
Junger, Ernst
    See Juenger, Ernst
    See also RGWL
Junger, Sebastian 1962- .... CLC 109
    See also AAYA 28; CA 165
Juniper, Alex
    See Hospital, Janette Turner
Junius
    See Luxemburg, Rosa
Just, Ward (Swift) 1935- .... CLC 4, 27
    See also CA 25-28R; CANR 32, 87; CN;
    INT CANR-32
Justice, Donald (Rodney) 1925- .. CLC 6, 19,
    102; DAM POET
    See also AMWS 7; CA 5-8R; CANR 26,
    54, 74; CP; CSW; DLBY 83; INT CANR-
    26; MTCW 2; PFS 14
Juvenal c. 60-c. 130 .... CMLC 8
    See also AW 2; DLB 211; RGWL
Juvenis
    See Bourne, Randolph S(illiman)
Kabakov, Sasha .... CLC 59
Kacew, Romain 1914-1980
    See Gary, Romain
    See also CA 108; 102
Kadare, Ismail 1936- .... CLC 52
    See also CA 161
Kadohata, Cynthia .... CLC 59, 122
    See also CA 140
Kafka, Franz 1883-1924 . TCLC 2, 6, 13, 29,
    47, 53, 112; DA; DAB; DAC; DAM
    MST, NOV; SSC 5, 29, 35; WLC
    See also AAYA 31; BPFB 2; CA 105; 126;
    DA3; DLB 81; EW 9; EXPS; MTCW 1,
    2; NFS 7; RGSF; RGWL; SFW; SSFS 3,
    7, 12
Kahanovitsch, Pinkhes
    See Der Nister
Kahn, Roger 1927- .... CLC 30
    See also CA 25-28R; CANR 44, 69; DLB
    171; SATA 37
Kain, Saul
    See Sassoon, Siegfried (Lorraine)
Kaiser, Georg 1878-1945 .... TCLC 9
    See also CA 106; 190; DLB 124; RGWL
Kaledin, Sergei .... CLC 59
Kaletski, Alexander 1946- .... CLC 39
    See also CA 118; 143
Kalidasa fl. c. 400-455 .... CMLC 9; PC 22
    See also RGWL

Knapp, Caroline 1959- .... **CLC 99**
See also CA 154

Knebel, Fletcher 1911-1993 .... **CLC 14**
See also AITN 1; CA 1-4R; 140; CAAS 3;
CANR 1, 36; SATA 36; SATA-Obit 75

Knickerbocker, Diedrich
See Irving, Washington

Knight, Etheridge 1931-1991 . **CLC 40; BLC
2; DAM POET; PC 14**
See also BW 1, 3; CA 21-24R; 133; CANR
23, 82; DLB 41; MTCW 2; RGAL

Knight, Sarah Kemble 1666-1727 .... **LC 7**
See also DLB 24, 200

Knister, Raymond 1899-1932 .... **TCLC 56**
See also CA 186; DLB 68; RGEL

Knowles, John 1926-2001 . **CLC 1, 4, 10, 26;
DA; DAC; DAM MST, NOV**
See also AAYA 10; BPFB 2; BYA 3; CA
17-20R; CANR 40, 74, 76; CDALB 1968-
1988; CN; DLB 6; EXPN; MTCW 1, 2;
NFS 2; RGAL; SATA 8, 89; YAW

Knox, Calvin M.
See Silverberg, Robert

Knox, John c. 1505-1572 .... **LC 37**
See also DLB 132

Knye, Cassandra
See Disch, Thomas M(ichael)

Koch, C(hristopher) J(ohn) 1932- .... **CLC 42**
See also CA 127; CANR 84; CN

Koch, Christopher
See Koch, C(hristopher) J(ohn)

Koch, Kenneth 1925- .... **CLC 5, 8, 44; DAM
POET**
See also CA 1-4R; CAD; CANR 6, 36, 57,
97; CP; DLB 5; INT CANR-36;
MTCW 2; SATA 65; WP

Kochanowski, Jan 1530-1584 .... **LC 10**
See also RGWL

Kock, Charles Paul de 1794-1871 . **NCLC 16**

Koda Rohan
See Koda Shigeyuki

Koda Shigeyuki 1867-1947 .... **TCLC 22**
See also CA 121; 183; DLB 180

Koestler, Arthur 1905-1983 ... **CLC 1, 3, 6, 8,
15, 33**
See also BRWS 1; CA 1-4R; 109; CANR 1,
33; CDBLB 1945-1960; DLBY 83;
MTCW 1, 2; RGEL

Kogawa, Joy Nozomi 1935- ..... **CLC 78, 129;
DAC; DAM MST, MULT**
See also CA 101; CANR 19, 62; CN; CWP;
FW; MTCW 2; NFS 3; SATA 99

Kohout, Pavel 1928- .... **CLC 13**
See also CA 45-48; CANR 3

Koizumi, Yakumo
See Hearn, (Patricio) Lafcadio (Tessima
Carlos)

Kolmar, Gertrud 1894-1943 .... **TCLC 40**
See also CA 167

Komunyakaa, Yusef 1947- .... **CLC 86, 94;
BLCS**
See also AFAW 2; CA 147; CANR 83; CP;
CSW; DLB 120; PFS 5; RGAL

Konrad, George
See Konrad, Gyorgy
See also CWW 2

Konrad, Gyorgy 1933- .... **CLC 4, 10, 73**
See also Konrad, George
See also CA 85-88; CANR 97; CWW 2;
DLB 232

Konwicki, Tadeusz 1926- .... **CLC 8, 28, 54,
117**
See also CA 101; CAAS 9; CANR 39, 59;
CWW 2; DLB 232; IDFW 3; MTCW 1

Koontz, Dean R(ay) 1945- .... **CLC 78; DAM
NOV, POP**
See also AAYA 9, 31; BEST 89:3, 90:2; CA
108; CANR 19, 36, 52, 95; CMW; CPW;
DA3; HGG; MTCW 1; SATA 92; SFW;
YAW

Kopernik, Mikolaj
See Copernicus, Nicolaus

Kopit, Arthur (Lee) 1937- ..... **CLC 1, 18, 33;
DAM DRAM**
See also AITN 1; CA 81-84; CABS 3; CD;
DFS 7; DLB 7; MTCW 1; RGAL

Kops, Bernard 1926- .... **CLC 4**
See also CA 5-8R; CANR 84; CBD; CN;
CP; DLB 13

Kornbluth, C(yril) M. 1923-1958 .... **TCLC 8**
See also CA 105; 160; DLB 8; SFW

Korolenko, V. G.
See Korolenko, Vladimir Galaktionovich

Korolenko, Vladimir
See Korolenko, Vladimir Galaktionovich

Korolenko, Vladimir G.
See Korolenko, Vladimir Galaktionovich

Korolenko, Vladimir Galaktionovich
1853-1921 .... **TCLC 22**
See also CA 121

Korzybski, Alfred (Habdank Skarbek)
1879-1950 .... **TCLC 61**
See also CA 123; 160

Kosinski, Jerzy (Nikodem)
1933-1991 .... **CLC 1, 2, 3, 6, 10, 15, 53,
70; DAM NOV**
See also AMWS 7; BPFB 2; CA 17-20R;
134; CANR 9, 46; DA3; DLB 2; DLBY
82; HGG; MTCW 1, 2; NFS 12; RGAL

Kostelanetz, Richard (Cory) 1940- .. **CLC 28**
See also CA 13-16R; CAAS 8; CANR 38,
77; CN; CP

Kotlowitz, Robert 1924- .... **CLC 4**
See also CA 33-36R; CANR 36

Kotzebue, August (Friedrich Ferdinand) von
1761-1819 .... **NCLC 25**
See also DLB 94

Kotzwinkle, William 1938- ..... **CLC 5, 14, 35**
See also BPFB 2; CA 45-48; CANR 3, 44,
84; CLR 6; DLB 173; FANT; MAICYA;
SATA 24, 70; SFW; YAW

Kowna, Stancy
See Szymborska, Wislawa

Kozol, Jonathan 1936- .... **CLC 17**
See also CA 61-64; CANR 16, 45, 96

Kozoll, Michael 1940(?)- .... **CLC 35**

Kramer, Kathryn 19(?)- .... **CLC 34**

Kramer, Larry 1935- .. **CLC 42; DAM POP;
DC 8**
See also CA 124; 126; CANR 60; DLB 249;
GLL 1

Krasicki, Ignacy 1735-1801 .... **NCLC 8**

Krasinski, Zygmunt 1812-1859 .... **NCLC 4**
See also RGWL

Kraus, Karl 1874-1936 .... **TCLC 5**
See also CA 104; DLB 118

Kreve (Mickevicius), Vincas
1882-1954 .... **TCLC 27**
See also CA 170; DLB 220

Kristeva, Julia 1941- .... **CLC 77, 140**
See also CA 154; CANR 99; DLB 242; FW

Kristofferson, Kris 1936- .... **CLC 26**
See also CA 104

Krizanc, John 1956- .... **CLC 57**
See also CA 187

Krleza, Miroslav 1893-1981 .... **CLC 8, 114**
See also CA 97-100; 105; CANR 50; DLB
147; EW 11; RGWL

Kroetsch, Robert 1927- . **CLC 5, 23, 57, 132;
DAC; DAM POET**
See also CA 17-20R; CANR 8, 38; CCA 1;
CN; CP; DLB 53; MTCW 1

Kroetz, Franz
See Kroetz, Franz Xaver

Kroetz, Franz Xaver 1946- .... **CLC 41**
See also CA 130

Kroker, Arthur (W.) 1945- .... **CLC 77**
See also CA 161

Kropotkin, Peter (Aleksieevich)
1842-1921 .... **TCLC 36**
See also CA 119

Krotkov, Yuri 1917-1981 .... **CLC 19**
See also CA 102

Krumb
See Crumb, R(obert)

Krumgold, Joseph (Quincy)
1908-1980 .... **CLC 12**
See also BYA 1, 2; CA 9-12R; 101; CANR
7; MAICYA; SATA 1, 48; SATA-Obit 23;
YAW

Krumwitz
See Crumb, R(obert)

Krutch, Joseph Wood 1893-1970 ..... **CLC 24**
See also ANW; CA 1-4R; 25-28R; CANR
4; DLB 63, 206

Krutzch, Gus
See Eliot, T(homas) S(tearns)

Krylov, Ivan Andreevich
1768(?)-1844 .... **NCLC 1**
See also DLB 150

Kubin, Alfred (Leopold Isidor)
1877-1959 .... **TCLC 23**
See also CA 112; 149; CANR 104; DLB 81

Kubrick, Stanley 1928-1999 .... **CLC 16**
See also AAYA 30; CA 81-84; 177; CANR
33; DLB 26; TCLC 112

Kueng, Hans 1928-
See Kung, Hans
See also CA 53-56; CANR 66; MTCW 1, 2

Kumin, Maxine (Winokur) 1925- ..... **CLC 5,
13, 28; DAM POET; PC 15**
See also AITN 2; AMWS 4; ANW; CA
1-4R; CAAS 8; CANR 1, 21, 69; CP;
CWP; DA3; DLB 5; EXPP; MTCW 1, 2;
PAB; SATA 12

Kundera, Milan 1929- . **CLC 4, 9, 19, 32, 68,
115, 135; DAM NOV; SSC 24**
See also AAYA 2; BPFB 2; CA 85-88;
CANR 19, 52, 74; CWW 2; DA3; DLB
232; EW 13; MTCW 1, 2; RGSF; SSFS
10

Kunene, Mazisi (Raymond) 1930- ... **CLC 85**
See also BW 1, 3; CA 125; CANR 81; CP
7; DLB 117

Kung, Hans .... **CLC 130**
See also Kueng, Hans

Kunikida Doppo 1869(?)-1908
See Doppo, Kunikida
See also DLB 180

Kunitz, Stanley (Jasspon) 1905- .. **CLC 6, 11,
14, 148; PC 19**
See also AMWS 3; CA 41-44R; CANR 26,
57, 98; CP; DA3; DLB 48; INT CANR-
26; MTCW 1, 2; PFS 11; RGAL

Kunze, Reiner 1933- .... **CLC 10**
See also CA 93-96; CWW 2; DLB 75

Kuprin, Aleksander Ivanovich
1870-1938 .... **TCLC 5**
See also CA 104; 182

Kureishi, Hanif 1954(?)- .... **CLC 64, 135**
See also CA 139; CBD; CD; CN; DLB 194,
245; GLL 2; IDFW 4; WLIT 4

Kurosawa, Akira 1910-1998 .... **CLC 16, 119;
DAM MULT**
See also AAYA 11; CA 101; 170; CANR 46

Kushner, Tony 1957(?)- .... **CLC 81; DAM
DRAM; DC 10**
See also AMWS 9; CA 144; CAD; CANR
74; CD; DA3; DFS 5; DLB 228; GLL 1;
LAIT 5; MTCW 2; RGAL

Laurence, (Jean) Margaret (Wemyss)
1926-1987 . **CLC 3, 6, 13, 50, 62; DAC; DAM MST; SSC 7**
See also BYA 13; CA 5-8R; 121; CANR 33; DLB 53; FW; MTCW 1, 2; NFS 11; RGEL; RGSF; SATA-Obit 50; TCWW 2

Laurent, Antoine 1952- .... **CLC 50**

Lauscher, Hermann
See Hesse, Hermann

Lautreamont 1846-1870 .. **NCLC 12; SSC 14**
See also Lautreamont, Isidore Lucien Ducasse
See also GFL 1789 to the Present; RGWL

Lautreamont, Isidore Lucien Ducasse
See Lautreamont
See also DLB 217

Laverty, Donald
See Blish, James (Benjamin)

Lavin, Mary 1912-1996 . **CLC 4, 18, 99; SSC 4**
See also CA 9-12R; 151; CANR 33; CN; DLB 15; FW; MTCW 1; RGEL; RGSF

Lavond, Paul Dennis
See Kornbluth, C(yril) M.; Pohl, Frederik

Lawler, Raymond Evenor 1922- .... **CLC 58**
See also CA 103; CD; RGEL

Lawrence, D(avid) H(erbert Richards)
1885-1930 .... **TCLC 2, 9, 16, 33, 48, 61, 93; DA; DAB; DAC; DAM MST, NOV, POET; SSC 4, 19; WLC**
See also Chambers, Jessie
See also BPFB 2; BRW 7; BRWR 2; CA 104; 121; CDBLB 1914-1945; DA3; DLB 10, 19, 36, 98, 162, 195; EXPP; EXPS; LAIT 2, 3; MTCW 1, 2; PFS 6; RGEL; RGSF; SSFS 2, 6; WLIT 4; WP

Lawrence, T(homas) E(dward)
1888-1935 .... **TCLC 18**
See also Dale, Colin
See also BRWS 2; CA 115; 167; DLB 195

Lawrence of Arabia
See Lawrence, T(homas) E(dward)

Lawson, Henry (Archibald Hertzberg)
1867-1922 .... **TCLC 27; SSC 18**
See also CA 120; 181; DLB 230; RGEL; RGSF

Lawton, Dennis
See Faust, Frederick (Schiller)

Laxness, Halldor .... **CLC 25**
See also Gudjonsson, Halldor Kiljan
See also EW 12; RGWL

Layamon fl. c. 1200- .... **CMLC 10**
See also Layamon
See also RGEL

Laye, Camara 1928-1980 ... **CLC 4, 38; BLC 2; DAM MULT**
See also AFW; BW 1; CA 85-88; 97-100; CANR 25; MTCW 1, 2; WLIT 2

Layton, Irving (Peter) 1912- .... **CLC 2, 15; DAC; DAM MST, POET**
See also CA 1-4R; CANR 2, 33, 43, 66; CP; DLB 88; MTCW 1, 2; PFS 12; RGEL

Lazarus, Emma 1849-1887 ...... **NCLC 8, 109**

Lazarus, Felix
See Cable, George Washington

Lazarus, Henry
See Slavitt, David R(ytman)

Lea, Joan
See Neufeld, John (Arthur)

Leacock, Stephen (Butler)
1869-1944 .... **TCLC 2; DAC; DAM MST; SSC 39**
See also CA 104; 141; CANR 80; DLB 92; MTCW 2; RGEL; RGSF

Lead, Jane Ward 1623-1704 .... **LC 72**
See also DLB 131

Lear, Edward 1812-1888 .... **NCLC 3**
See also BRW 5; CLR 1, 75; DLB 32, 163, 166; MAICYA; RGEL; SATA 18, 100; WCH; WP

Lear, Norman (Milton) 1922- .... **CLC 12**
See also CA 73-76

Leautaud, Paul 1872-1956 .... **TCLC 83**
See also DLB 65; GFL 1789 to the Present

Leavis, F(rank) R(aymond)
1895-1978 .... **CLC 24**
See also BRW 7; CA 21-24R; 77-80; CANR 44; DLB 242; MTCW 1, 2; RGEL

Leavitt, David 1961- ..... **CLC 34; DAM POP**
See also CA 116; 122; CANR 50, 62, 101; CPW; DA3; DLB 130; GLL 1; INT 122; MTCW 2

Leblanc, Maurice (Marie Emile)
1864-1941 .... **TCLC 49**
See also CA 110; CMW

Lebowitz, Fran(ces Ann) 1951(?)- ... **CLC 11, 36**
See also CA 81-84; CANR 14, 60, 70; INT CANR-14; MTCW 1

Lebrecht, Peter
See Tieck, (Johann) Ludwig

le Carre, John .... **CLC 3, 5, 9, 15, 28**
See also Cornwell, David (John Moore)
See also AAYA 42; BEST 89:4; BPFB 2; BRWS 2; CDBLB 1960 to Present; CMW; CN; CPW; DLB 87; MSW; MTCW 2; RGEL

Le Clezio, J(ean) M(arie) G(ustave)
1940- .... **CLC 31, 155**
See also CA 116; 128; DLB 83; GFL 1789 to the Present; RGSF

Leconte de Lisle, Charles-Marie-Rene
1818-1894 .... **NCLC 29**
See also DLB 217; EW 6; GFL 1789 to the Present

Le Coq, Monsieur
See Simenon, Georges (Jacques Christian)

Leduc, Violette 1907-1972 .... **CLC 22**
See also CA 13-14; 33-36R; CANR 69; CAP 1; GFL 1789 to the Present; GLL 1

Ledwidge, Francis 1887(?)-1917 .... **TCLC 23**
See also CA 123; DLB 20

Lee, Andrea 1953- ... **CLC 36; BLC 2; DAM MULT**
See also BW 1, 3; CA 125; CANR 82

Lee, Andrew
See Auchincloss, Louis (Stanton)

Lee, Chang-rae 1965- .... **CLC 91**
See also CA 148; CANR 89

Lee, Don L. .... **CLC 2**
See also Madhubuti, Haki R.

Lee, George W(ashington)
1894-1976 .... **CLC 52; BLC 2; DAM MULT**
See also BW 1; CA 125; CANR 83; DLB 51

Lee, (Nelle) Harper 1926- . **CLC 12, 60; DA; DAB; DAC; DAM MST, NOV; WLC**
See also AAYA 13; AMWS 8; BPFB 2; BYA 3; CA 13-16R; CANR 51; CDALB 1941-1968; CSW; DA3; DLB 6; EXPN; LAIT 3; MTCW 1, 2; NFS 2; SATA 11; WYA; YAW

Lee, Helen Elaine 1959(?)- .... **CLC 86**
See also CA 148

Lee, John .... **CLC 70**

Lee, Julian
See Latham, Jean Lee

Lee, Larry
See Lee, Lawrence

Lee, Laurie 1914-1997 .... **CLC 90; DAB; DAM POP**
See also CA 77-80; 158; CANR 33, 73; CP; CPW; DLB 27; MTCW 1; RGEL

Lee, Lawrence 1941-1990 .... **CLC 34**
See also CA 131; CANR 43

Lee, Li-Young 1957- .... **PC 24**
See also CA 153; CP; DLB 165; PFS 11

Lee, Manfred B(ennington)
1905-1971 .... **CLC 11**
See also Queen, Ellery
See also CA 1-4R; 29-32R; CANR 2; CMW; DLB 137

Lee, Shelton Jackson 1957(?)- .... **CLC 105; BLCS; DAM MULT**
See also Lee, Spike
See also BW 2, 3; CA 125; CANR 42

Lee, Spike
See Lee, Shelton Jackson
See also AAYA 4, 29

Lee, Stan 1922- .... **CLC 17**
See also AAYA 5; CA 108; 111; INT 111

Lee, Tanith 1947- .... **CLC 46**
See also AAYA 15; CA 37-40R; CANR 53, 102; FANT; SATA 8, 88; SFW; SUFW; YAW

Lee, Vernon .... **TCLC 5; SSC 33**
See also Paget, Violet
See also DLB 57, 153, 156, 174, 178; GLL 1; SUFW

Lee, William
See Burroughs, William S(eward)
See also GLL 1

Lee, Willy
See Burroughs, William S(eward)
See also GLL 1

Lee-Hamilton, Eugene (Jacob)
1845-1907 .... **TCLC 22**
See also CA 117

Leet, Judith 1935- .... **CLC 11**
See also CA 187

Le Fanu, Joseph Sheridan
1814-1873 ..... **NCLC 9, 58; DAM POP; SSC 14**
See also CMW; DA3; DLB 21, 70, 159, 178; HGG; RGEL; RGSF; SUFW

Leffland, Ella 1931- .... **CLC 19**
See also CA 29-32R; CANR 35, 78, 82; DLBY 84; INT CANR-35; SATA 65

Leger, Alexis
See Leger, (Marie-Rene Auguste) Alexis Saint-Leger

Leger, (Marie-Rene Auguste) Alexis
Saint-Leger 1887-1975 .. **CLC 4, 11, 46; DAM POET; PC 23**
See also Saint-John Perse
See also CA 13-16R; 61-64; CANR 43; MTCW 1

Leger, Saintleger
See Leger, (Marie-Rene Auguste) Alexis Saint-Leger

Le Guin, Ursula K(roeber) 1929- ..... **CLC 8, 13, 22, 45, 71, 136; DAB; DAC; DAM MST, POP; SSC 12**
See also AAYA 9, 27; AITN 1; BPFB 2; BYA 5, 8, 11, 14; CA 21-24R; CANR 9, 32, 52, 74; CDALB 1968-1988; CLR 3, 28; CN; CPW; DA3; DLB 8, 52, 256; EXPS; FANT; FW; INT CANR-32; JRDA; LAIT 5; MAICYA; MTCW 1, 2; NFS 6, 9; SATA 4, 52, 99; SCFW; SFW; SSFS 2; SUFW; WYA; YAW

Lehmann, Rosamond (Nina)
1901-1990 .... **CLC 5**
See also CA 77-80; 131; CANR 8, 73; DLB 15; MTCW 2; RGEL; RHW

Leiber, Fritz (Reuter, Jr.)
1910-1992 .... **CLC 25**
See also BPFB 2; CA 45-48; 139; CANR 2, 40, 86; DLB 8; FANT; HGG; MTCW 1, 2; SATA 45; SATA-Obit 73; SCFW 2; SFW; SUFW

Li Fei-kan 1904-
See Pa Chin
See also CA 105

Lifton, Robert Jay 1926- .... **CLC 67**
See also CA 17-20R; CANR 27, 78; INT CANR-27; SATA 66

Lightfoot, Gordon 1938- .... **CLC 26**
See also CA 109

Lightman, Alan P(aige) 1948- .... **CLC 81**
See also CA 141; CANR 63, 105

Ligotti, Thomas (Robert) 1953- ...... **CLC 44; SSC 16**
See also CA 123; CANR 49; HGG

Li Ho 791-817 .... **PC 13**

Liliencron, (Friedrich Adolf Axel) Detlev von 1844-1909 .... **TCLC 18**
See also CA 117

Lilly, William 1602-1681 .... **LC 27**

Lima, Jose Lezama
See Lezama Lima, Jose

Lima Barreto, Afonso Henrique de 1881-1922 .... **TCLC 23**
See also CA 117; 181; LAW

Lima Barreto, Afonso Henriques de
See Lima Barreto, Afonso Henrique de

Limonov, Edward 1944- .... **CLC 67**
See also CA 137

Lin, Frank
See Atherton, Gertrude (Franklin Horn)

Lincoln, Abraham 1809-1865 .... **NCLC 18**
See also LAIT 2

Lind, Jakov .... **CLC 1, 2, 4, 27, 82**
See also Landwirth, Heinz
See also CAAS 4

Lindbergh, Anne (Spencer) Morrow 1906-2001 .... **CLC 82; DAM NOV**
See also BPFB 2; CA 17-20R; 193; CANR 16, 73; MTCW 1, 2; SATA 33; SATA-Obit 125

Lindsay, David 1878(?)-1945 .... **TCLC 15**
See also CA 113; 187; DLB 255; FANT; SFW; SUFW

Lindsay, (Nicholas) Vachel 1879-1931 . **TCLC 17; DA; DAC; DAM MST, POET; PC 23; WLC**
See also AMWS 1; CA 114; 135; CANR 79; CDALB 1865-1917; DA3; DLB 54; EXPP; RGAL; SATA 40; WP

Linke-Poot
See Doeblin, Alfred

Linney, Romulus 1930- .... **CLC 51**
See also CA 1-4R; CAD; CANR 40, 44, 79; CD; CSW; RGAL

Linton, Eliza Lynn 1822-1898 .... **NCLC 41**
See also DLB 18

Li Po 701-763 .... **CMLC 2; PC 29**
See also WP

Lipsius, Justus 1547-1606 .... **LC 16**

Lipsyte, Robert (Michael) 1938- ..... **CLC 21; DA; DAC; DAM MST, NOV**
See also AAYA 7; CA 17-20R; CANR 8, 57; CLR 23, 76; JRDA; LAIT 5; MAICYA; SATA 5, 68, 113; WYA; YAW

Lish, Gordon (Jay) 1934- ... **CLC 45; SSC 18**
See also CA 113; 117; CANR 79; DLB 130; INT 117

Lispector, Clarice 1925(?)-1977 .... **CLC 43; HLCS 2; SSC 34**
See also CA 139; 116; CANR 71; DLB 113; DNFS; FW; HW 2; LAW; RGSF; RGWL; WLIT 1

Littell, Robert 1935(?)- .... **CLC 42**
See also CA 109; 112; CANR 64; CMW

Little, Malcolm 1925-1965
See Malcolm X
See also BW 1, 3; CA 125; 111; CANR 82; DA; DA3; DAB; DAC; DAM MST, MULT; MTCW 1, 2

Littlewit, Humphrey Gent.
See Lovecraft, H(oward) P(hillips)

Litwos
See Sienkiewicz, Henryk (Adam Alexander Pius)

Liu, E. 1857-1909 .... **TCLC 15**
See also CA 115; 190

Lively, Penelope (Margaret) 1933- .. **CLC 32, 50; DAM NOV**
See also BPFB 2; CA 41-44R; CANR 29, 67, 79; CLR 7; CN; CWRI; DLB 14, 161, 207; FANT; JRDA; MAICYA; MTCW 1, 2; SATA 7, 60, 101

Livesay, Dorothy (Kathleen) 1909-1996 . **CLC 4, 15, 79; DAC; DAM MST, POET**
See also AITN 2; CA 25-28R; CAAS 8; CANR 36, 67; DLB 68; FW; MTCW 1; RGEL

Livy c. 59B.C.-c. 12 .... **CMLC 11**
See also AW 2; DLB 211; RGWL

Lizardi, Jose Joaquin Fernandez de 1776-1827 .... **NCLC 30**
See also LAW

Llewellyn, Richard
See Llewellyn Lloyd, Richard Dafydd Vivian
See also DLB 15

Llewellyn Lloyd, Richard Dafydd Vivian 1906-1983 .... **CLC 7, 80**
See also Llewellyn, Richard
See also CA 53-56; 111; CANR 7, 71; SATA 11; SATA-Obit 37

Llosa, (Jorge) Mario (Pedro) Vargas
See Vargas Llosa, (Jorge) Mario (Pedro)
See also LAIT 5

Lloyd, Manda
See Mander, (Mary) Jane

Lloyd Webber, Andrew 1948-
See Webber, Andrew Lloyd
See also AAYA 1, 38; CA 116; 149; DAM DRAM; SATA 56

Llull, Ramon c. 1235-c. 1316 .... **CMLC 12**

Lobb, Ebenezer
See Upward, Allen

Locke, Alain (Le Roy) 1886-1954 . **TCLC 43; BLCS**
See also BW 1, 3; CA 106; 124; CANR 79; RGAL

Locke, John 1632-1704 .... **LC 7, 35**
See also DLB 101, 213, 252; RGEL; WLIT 3

Locke-Elliott, Sumner
See Elliott, Sumner Locke

Lockhart, John Gibson 1794-1854 .. **NCLC 6**
See also DLB 110, 116, 144

Lockridge, Ross (Franklin), Jr. 1914-1948 .... **TCLC 111**
See also CA 108; 145; CANR 79; DLB 143; DLBY 80; RGAL; RHW

Lodge, David (John) 1935- ...... **CLC 36, 141; DAM POP**
See also BEST 90:1; BRWS 4; CA 17-20R; CANR 19, 53, 92; CN; CPW; DLB 14, 194; INT CANR-19; MTCW 1, 2

Lodge, Thomas 1558-1625 .... **LC 41**
See also DLB 172; RGEL

Loewinsohn, Ron(ald William) 1937- .... **CLC 52**
See also CA 25-28R; CANR 71

Logan, Jake
See Smith, Martin Cruz

Logan, John (Burton) 1923-1987 .... **CLC 5**
See also CA 77-80; 124; CANR 45; DLB 5

Lo Kuan-chung 1330(?)-1400(?) .... **LC 12**

Lombard, Nap
See Johnson, Pamela Hansford

Lomotey (editor), Kofi .... **CLC 70**

London, Jack 1876-1916 ..... **TCLC 9, 15, 39; SSC 4, 49; WLC**
See also London, John Griffith
See also AAYA 13; AITN 2; AMW; BPFB 2; BYA 4, 13; CDALB 1865-1917; DLB 8, 12, 78, 212; EXPS; LAIT 3; NFS 8; RGAL; RGSF; SATA 18; SFW; SSFS 7; TCWW 2; TUS; WYA; YAW

London, John Griffith 1876-1916
See London, Jack
See also CA 110; 119; CANR 73; DA; DA3; DAB; DAC; DAM MST, NOV; JRDA; MAICYA; MTCW 1, 2

Long, Emmett
See Leonard, Elmore (John, Jr.)

Longbaugh, Harry
See Goldman, William (W.)

Longfellow, Henry Wadsworth 1807-1882 .. **NCLC 2, 45, 101, 103; DA; DAB; DAC; DAM MST, POET; PC 30; WLCS**
See also AMW; CDALB 1640-1865; DA3; DLB 1, 59, 235; EXPP; PAB; PFS 2, 7; RGAL; SATA 19; WP

Longinus c. 1st cent. - .... **CMLC 27**
See also AW 2; DLB 176

Longley, Michael 1939- .... **CLC 29**
See also CA 102; CP; DLB 40

Longus fl. c. 2nd cent. - .... **CMLC 7**

Longway, A. Hugh
See Lang, Andrew

Lonnrot, Elias 1802-1884 .... **NCLC 53**
See also EFS 1

Lonsdale, Roger ed. .... **CLC 65**

Lopate, Phillip 1943- .... **CLC 29**
See also CA 97-100; CANR 88; DLBY 80; INT 97-100

Lopez, Barry (Holstun) 1945- .... **CLC 70**
See also AAYA 9; ANW; CA 65-68; CANR 7, 23, 47, 68, 92; DLB 256; INT CANR-7, -23; MTCW 1; RGAL; SATA 67

Lopez Portillo (y Pacheco), Jose 1920- .... **CLC 46**
See also CA 129; HW 1

Lopez y Fuentes, Gregorio 1897(?)-1966 .... **CLC 32**
See also CA 131; HW 1

Lorca, Federico Garcia
See Garcia Lorca, Federico
See also DFS 4; EW 11; RGWL; WP

Lord, Bette Bao 1938- .... **CLC 23; AAL**
See also BEST 90:3; BPFB 2; CA 107; CANR 41, 79; INT CA-107; SATA 58

Lord Auch
See Bataille, Georges

Lord Byron
See Byron, George Gordon (Noel)

Lorde, Audre (Geraldine) 1934-1992 ... **CLC 18, 71; BLC 2; DAM MULT, POET; PC 12**
See also Domini, Rey
See also AFAW 1, 2; BW 1, 3; CA 25-28R; 142; CANR 16, 26, 46, 82; DA3; DLB 41; FW; MTCW 1, 2; RGAL

Lord Houghton
See Milnes, Richard Monckton

Lord Jeffrey
See Jeffrey, Francis

Loreaux, Nichol .... **CLC 65**

Lorenzini, Carlo 1826-1890
See Collodi, Carlo
See also MAICYA; SATA 29, 100

Lorenzo, Heberto Padilla
See Padilla (Lorenzo), Heberto

Loris
See Hofmannsthal, Hugo von

Machen, Arthur .... **TCLC 4; SSC 20**
  See also Jones, Arthur Llewellyn
  See also CA 179; DLB 156, 178; RGEL;
  SUFW

Machiavelli, Niccolo 1469-1527 ..... **LC 8, 36;
  DA; DAB; DAC; DAM MST; DC 16;
  WLCS**
  See also EW 2; LAIT 1; NFS 9; RGWL

MacInnes, Colin 1914-1976 .... **CLC 4, 23**
  See also CA 69-72; 65-68; CANR 21; DLB
  14; MTCW 1, 2; RGEL; RHW

MacInnes, Helen (Clark)
  1907-1985 .... **CLC 27, 39; DAM POP**
  See also BPFB 2; CA 1-4R; 117; CANR 1,
  28, 58; CMW; CPW; DLB 87; MSW;
  MTCW 1, 2; SATA 22; SATA-Obit 44

Mackay, Mary 1855-1924
  See Corelli, Marie
  See also CA 118; 177; FANT; RHW

Mackenzie, Compton (Edward Montague)
  1883-1972 .... **CLC 18**
  See also CA 21-22; 37-40R; CAP 2; DLB
  34, 100; RGEL; TCLC 116

Mackenzie, Henry 1745-1831 .... **NCLC 41**
  See also DLB 39; RGEL

Mackintosh, Elizabeth 1896(?)-1952
  See Tey, Josephine
  See also CA 110; CMW

MacLaren, James
  See Grieve, C(hristopher) M(urray)

Mac Laverty, Bernard 1942- .... **CLC 31**
  See also CA 116; 118; CANR 43, 88; CN;
  INT CA-118; RGSF

MacLean, Alistair (Stuart)
  1922(?)-1987 .. **CLC 3, 13, 50, 63; DAM
  POP**
  See also CA 57-60; 121; CANR 28, 61;
  CMW; CPW; MTCW 1; SATA 23; SATA-
  Obit 50; TCWW 2

Maclean, Norman (Fitzroy)
  1902-1990 .... **CLC 78; DAM POP; SSC
  13**
  See also CA 102; 132; CANR 49; CPW;
  DLB 206; TCWW 2

MacLeish, Archibald 1892-1982 ... **CLC 3, 8,
  14, 68; DAM POET**
  See also AMW; CA 9-12R; 106; CAD;
  CANR 33, 63; CDALBS; DLB 4, 7, 45;
  DLBY 82; EXPP; MTCW 1, 2; PAB; PFS
  5; RGAL

MacLennan, (John) Hugh
  1907-1990 . **CLC 2, 14, 92; DAC; DAM
  MST**
  See also CA 5-8R; 142; CANR 33; DLB
  68; MTCW 1, 2; RGEL

MacLeod, Alistair 1936- .... **CLC 56; DAC;
  DAM MST**
  See also CA 123; CCA 1; DLB 60; MTCW
  2; RGSF

Macleod, Fiona
  See Sharp, William
  See also RGEL; SUFW

MacNeice, (Frederick) Louis
  1907-1963 .... **CLC 1, 4, 10, 53; DAB;
  DAM POET**
  See also BRW 7; CA 85-88; CANR 61;
  DLB 10, 20; MTCW 1, 2; RGEL

MacNeill, Dand
  See Fraser, George MacDonald

Macpherson, James 1736-1796 .... **LC 29**
  See also Ossian
  See also DLB 109; RGEL

Macpherson, (Jean) Jay 1931- .... **CLC 14**
  See also CA 5-8R; CANR 90; CP; CWP;
  DLB 53

Macrobius fl. 430- .... **CMLC 48**

MacShane, Frank 1927-1999 .... **CLC 39**
  See also CA 9-12R; 186; CANR 3, 33; DLB
  111

Macumber, Mari
  See Sandoz, Mari(e Susette)

Madach, Imre 1823-1864 .... **NCLC 19**

Madden, (Jerry) David 1933- .... **CLC 5, 15**
  See also CA 1-4R; CAAS 3; CANR 4, 45;
  CN; CSW; DLB 6; MTCW 1

Maddern, Al(an)
  See Ellison, Harlan (Jay)

Madhubuti, Haki R. 1942- . **CLC 6, 73; BLC
  2; DAM MULT, POET; PC 5**
  See also Lee, Don L.
  See also BW 2, 3; CA 73-76; CANR 24,
  51, 73; CP; CSW; DLB 5, 41; DLBD 8;
  MTCW 2; RGAL

Maepenn, Hugh
  See Kuttner, Henry

Maepenn, K. H.
  See Kuttner, Henry

Maeterlinck, Maurice 1862-1949 ... **TCLC 3;
  DAM DRAM**
  See also CA 104; 136; CANR 80; DLB 192;
  EW 8; GFL 1789 to the Present; RGWL;
  SATA 66

Maginn, William 1794-1842 .... **NCLC 8**
  See also DLB 110, 159

Mahapatra, Jayanta 1928- .... **CLC 33; DAM
  MULT**
  See also CA 73-76; CAAS 9; CANR 15,
  33, 66, 87; CP

Mahfouz, Naguib (Abdel Aziz Al-Sabilgi)
  1911(?)- .... **CLC 153; DAM NOV**
  See also Mahfuz, Najib (Abdel Aziz al-
  Sabilgi)
  See also BEST 89:2; CA 128; CANR 55,
  101; CWW 2; DA3; MTCW 1, 2; RGWL;
  SSFS 9

Mahfuz, Najib (Abdel Aziz al-Sabilgi)
  .... **CLC 52, 55**
  See also Mahfouz, Naguib (Abdel Aziz Al-
  Sabilgi)
  See also AFW; DLBY 88; RGSF; WLIT 2

Mahon, Derek 1941- .... **CLC 27**
  See also BRWS 6; CA 113; 128; CANR 88;
  CP; DLB 40

Maiakovskii, Vladimir
  See Mayakovski, Vladimir (Vladimirovich)
  See also IDTP; RGWL

Mailer, Norman 1923- ... **CLC 1, 2, 3, 4, 5, 8,
  11, 14, 28, 39, 74, 111; DA; DAB;
  DAC; DAM MST, NOV, POP**
  See also AAYA 31; AITN 2; AMW; BPFB
  2; CA 9-12R; CABS 1; CANR 28, 74, 77;
  CDALB 1968-1988; CN; CPW; DA3;
  DLB 2, 16, 28, 185; DLBD 3; DLBY 80,
  83; MTCW 1, 2; NFS 10; RGAL

Maillet, Antonine 1929- .. **CLC 54, 118; DAC**
  See also CA 115; 120; CANR 46, 74, 77;
  CCA 1; CWW 2; DLB 60; INT 120;
  MTCW 2

Mais, Roger 1905-1955 .... **TCLC 8**
  See also BW 1, 3; CA 105; 124; CANR 82;
  DLB 125; MTCW 1; RGEL

Maistre, Joseph 1753-1821 .... **NCLC 37**
  See also GFL 1789 to the Present

Maitland, Frederic William
  1850-1906 .... **TCLC 65**

Maitland, Sara (Louise) 1950- .... **CLC 49**
  See also CA 69-72; CANR 13, 59; FW

Major, Clarence 1936- . **CLC 3, 19, 48; BLC
  2; DAM MULT**
  See also AFAW 2; BW 2, 3; CA 21-24R;
  CAAS 6; CANR 13, 25, 53, 82; CN; CP;
  CSW; DLB 33; MSW

Major, Kevin (Gerald) 1949- . **CLC 26; DAC**
  See also AAYA 16; CA 97-100; CANR 21,
  38; CLR 11; DLB 60; INT CANR-21;
  JRDA; MAICYA; SATA 32, 82; WYA;
  YAW

Maki, James
  See Ozu, Yasujiro

Malabaila, Damiano
  See Levi, Primo

Malamud, Bernard 1914-1986 .. **CLC 1, 2, 3,
  5, 8, 9, 11, 18, 27, 44, 78, 85; DA;
  DAB; DAC; DAM MST, NOV, POP;
  SSC 15; WLC**
  See also AAYA 16; AMWS 1; BPFB 2; CA
  5-8R; 118; CABS 1; CANR 28, 62;
  CDALB 1941-1968; CPW; DA3; DLB 2,
  28, 152; DLBY 80, 86; EXPS; LAIT 4;
  MTCW 1, 2; NFS 4, 9; RGAL; RGSF;
  SSFS 8, 13

Malan, Herman
  See Bosman, Herman Charles; Bosman,
  Herman Charles

Malaparte, Curzio 1898-1957 .... **TCLC 52**

Malcolm, Dan
  See Silverberg, Robert

Malcolm X .... **CLC 82, 117; BLC 2; WLCS**
  See also Little, Malcolm
  See also LAIT 5

Malherbe, Francois de 1555-1628 .... **LC 5**
  See also GFL Beginnings to 1789

Mallarme, Stephane 1842-1898 ...... **NCLC 4,
  41; DAM POET; PC 4**
  See also DLB 217; EW 7; GFL 1789 to the
  Present; RGWL

Mallet-Joris, Francoise 1930- .... **CLC 11**
  See also CA 65-68; CANR 17; DLB 83;
  GFL 1789 to the Present

Malley, Ern
  See McAuley, James Phillip

Mallowan, Agatha Christie
  See Christie, Agatha (Mary Clarissa)

Maloff, Saul 1922- .... **CLC 5**
  See also CA 33-36R

Malone, Louis
  See MacNeice, (Frederick) Louis

Malone, Michael (Christopher)
  1942- .... **CLC 43**
  See also CA 77-80; CANR 14, 32, 57

Malory, Sir Thomas 1410(?)-1471(?) . **LC 11;
  DA; DAB; DAC; DAM MST; WLCS**
  See also BRW 1; BRWR 2; CDBLB Before
  1660; DLB 146; EFS 2; RGEL; SATA 59;
  SATA-Brief 33; WLIT 3

Malouf, (George Joseph) David
  1934- .... **CLC 28, 86**
  See also CA 124; CANR 50, 76; CN; CP;
  MTCW 2

Malraux, (Georges-)Andre
  1901-1976 .... **CLC 1, 4, 9, 13, 15, 57;
  DAM NOV**
  See also BPFB 2; CA 21-22; 69-72; CANR
  34, 58; CAP 2; DA3; DLB 72; EW 12;
  GFL 1789 to the Present; MTCW 1, 2;
  RGWL

Malzberg, Barry N(athaniel) 1939- ... **CLC 7**
  See also CA 61-64; CAAS 4; CANR 16;
  CMW; DLB 8; SFW

Mamet, David (Alan) 1947- .. **CLC 9, 15, 34,
  46, 91; DAM DRAM; DC 4**
  See also AAYA 3; CA 81-84; CABS 3;
  CANR 15, 41, 67, 72; CD; DA3; DFS 2,
  3, 6, 12; DLB 7; IDFW 4; MTCW 1, 2;
  RGAL

Mamoulian, Rouben (Zachary)
  1897-1987 .... **CLC 16**
  See also CA 25-28R; 124; CANR 85

Mandelshtam, Osip
  See Mandelstam, Osip (Emilievich)
  See also EW 10; RGWL

Mandelstam, Osip (Emilievich)
  1891(?)-1943(?) .... **TCLC 2, 6; PC 14**
  See also Mandelshtam, Osip
  See also CA 104; 150; MTCW 2

Marut, Ret
See Traven, B.
Marut, Robert
See Traven, B.
Marvell, Andrew 1621-1678 .. **LC 4, 43; DA; DAB; DAC; DAM MST, POET; PC 10; WLC**
See also BRW 2; BRWR 2; CDBLB 1660-1789; DLB 131; EXPP; PFS 5; RGEL; WP
Marx, Karl (Heinrich) 1818-1883 . **NCLC 17**
See also DLB 129
Masaoka, Shiki .... **TCLC 18**
See also Masaoka, Tsunenori
Masaoka, Tsunenori 1867-1902
See Masaoka, Shiki
See also CA 117; 191
Masefield, John (Edward)
1878-1967 ..... **CLC 11, 47; DAM POET**
See also CA 19-20; 25-28R; CANR 33; CAP 2; CDBLB 1890-1914; DLB 10, 19, 153, 160; EXPP; FANT; MTCW 1, 2; PFS 5; RGEL; SATA 19
Maso, Carole 19(?)- .... **CLC 44**
See also CA 170; GLL 2; RGAL
Mason, Bobbie Ann 1940- ... **CLC 28, 43, 82, 154; SSC 4**
See also AAYA 5, 42; AMWS 8; BPFB 2; CA 53-56; CANR 11, 31, 58, 83; CDALBS; CN; CSW; DA3; DLB 173; DLBY 87; EXPS; INT CANR-31; MTCW 1, 2; NFS 4; RGAL; RGSF; SSFS 3,8; YAW
Mason, Ernst
See Pohl, Frederik
Mason, Hunni B.
See Sternheim, (William Adolf) Carl
Mason, Lee W.
See Malzberg, Barry N(athaniel)
Mason, Nick 1945- .... **CLC 35**
Mason, Tally
See Derleth, August (William)
Mass, Anna .... **CLC 59**
Mass, William
See Gibson, William
Massinger, Philip 1583-1640 .... **LC 70**
See also DLB 58; RGEL
Master Lao
See Lao Tzu
Masters, Edgar Lee 1868-1950 .... **TCLC 2, 25; DA; DAC; DAM MST, POET; PC 1, 36; WLCS**
See also AMWS 1; CA 104; 133; CDALB 1865-1917; DLB 54; EXPP; MTCW 1, 2; RGAL; WP
Masters, Hilary 1928- .... **CLC 48**
See also CA 25-28R; CANR 13, 47, 97; CN; DLB 244
Mastrosimone, William 19(?)- .... **CLC 36**
See also CA 186; CAD; CD
Mathe, Albert
See Camus, Albert
Mather, Cotton 1663-1728 .... **LC 38**
See also AMWS 2; CDALB 1640-1865; DLB 24, 30, 140; RGAL
Mather, Increase 1639-1723 .... **LC 38**
See also DLB 24
Matheson, Richard (Burton) 1926- .. **CLC 37**
See also AAYA 31; CA 97-100; CANR 88, 99; DLB 8, 44; HGG; INT 97-100; SCFW 2; SFW
Mathews, Harry 1930- .... **CLC 6, 52**
See also CA 21-24R; CAAS 6; CANR 18, 40, 98; CN
Mathews, John Joseph 1894-1979 .. **CLC 84; DAM MULT**
See also CA 19-20; 142; CANR 45; CAP 2; DLB 175; NNAL

Mathias, Roland (Glyn) 1915- .... **CLC 45**
See also CA 97-100; CANR 19, 41; CP; DLB 27
Matsuo Basho 1644-1694 .... **LC 62; DAM POET; PC 3**
See also Basho, Matsuo
See also PFS 2, 7
Mattheson, Rodney
See Creasey, John
Matthews, (James) Brander
1852-1929 .... **TCLC 95**
See also DLB 71, 78; DLBD 13
Matthews, Greg 1949- .... **CLC 45**
See also CA 135
Matthews, William (Procter III)
1942-1997 .... **CLC 40**
See also AMWS 9; CA 29-32R; 162; CAAS 18; CANR 12, 57; CP; DLB 5
Matthias, John (Edward) 1941- .... **CLC 9**
See also CA 33-36R; CANR 56; CP
Matthiessen, F(rancis) O(tto)
1902-1950 .... **TCLC 100**
See also CA 185; DLB 63
Matthiessen, Peter 1927- ... **CLC 5, 7, 11, 32, 64; DAM NOV**
See also AAYA 6, 40; AMWS 5; ANW; BEST 90:4; BPFB 2; CA 9-12R; CANR 21, 50, 73, 100; CN; DA3; DLB 6, 173; MTCW 1, 2; SATA 27
Maturin, Charles Robert
1780(?)-1824 .... **NCLC 6**
See also DLB 178; HGG; RGEL; SUFW
Matute (Ausejo), Ana Maria 1925- .. **CLC 11**
See also CA 89-92; MTCW 1; RGSF
Maugham, W. S.
See Maugham, W(illiam) Somerset
Maugham, W(illiam) Somerset
1874-1965 ... **CLC 1, 11, 15, 67, 93; DA; DAB; DAC; DAM DRAM, MST, NOV; SSC 8; WLC**
See also BPFB 2; BRW 6; CA 5-8R; 25-28R; CANR 40; CDBLB 1914-1945; CMW; DA3; DLB 10, 36, 77, 100, 162, 195; LAIT 3; MTCW 1, 2; RGEL; RGSF; SATA 54
Maugham, William Somerset
See Maugham, W(illiam) Somerset
Maupassant, (Henri Rene Albert) Guy de
1850-1893 . **NCLC 1, 42, 83; DA; DAB; DAC; DAM MST; SSC 1; WLC**
See also BYA 14; DA3; DLB 123; EW 7; EXPS; GFL 1789 to the Present; LAIT 2; RGSF; RGWL; SSFS 4; SUFW; TWA
Maupin, Armistead (Jones, Jr.)
1944- .... **CLC 95; DAM POP**
See also CA 125; 130; CANR 58, 101; CPW; DA3; GLL 1; INT 130; MTCW 2
Maurhut, Richard
See Traven, B.
Mauriac, Claude 1914-1996 .... **CLC 9**
See also CA 89-92; 152; CWW 2; DLB 83; GFL 1789 to the Present
Mauriac, Francois (Charles)
1885-1970 .... **CLC 4, 9, 56; SSC 24**
See also CA 25-28; CAP 2; DLB 65; EW 10; GFL 1789 to the Present; MTCW 1, 2; RGWL
Mavor, Osborne Henry 1888-1951
See Bridie, James
See also CA 104
Maxwell, William (Keepers, Jr.)
1908-2000 .... **CLC 19**
See also AMWS 8; CA 93-96; 189; CANR 54, 95; CN; DLB 218; DLBY 80; INT CA-93-96
May, Elaine 1932- .... **CLC 16**
See also CA 124; 142; CAD; CWD; DLB 44

Mayakovski, Vladimir (Vladimirovich)
1893-1930 .... **TCLC 4, 18**
See also Maiakovskii, Vladimir; Mayakovsky, Vladimir
See also CA 104; 158; MTCW 2; SFW
Mayakovsky, Vladimir
See Mayakovski, Vladimir (Vladimirovich)
See also EW 11; WP
Mayhew, Henry 1812-1887 .... **NCLC 31**
See also DLB 18, 55, 190
Mayle, Peter 1939(?)- .... **CLC 89**
See also CA 139; CANR 64
Maynard, Joyce 1953- .... **CLC 23**
See also CA 111; 129; CANR 64
Mayne, William (James Carter)
1928- .... **CLC 12**
See also AAYA 20; CA 9-12R; CANR 37, 80, 100; CLR 25; FANT; JRDA; MAICYA; SAAS 11; SATA 6, 68, 122; YAW
Mayo, Jim
See L'Amour, Louis (Dearborn)
See also TCWW 2
Maysles, Albert 1926- .... **CLC 16**
See also CA 29-32R
Maysles, David 1932-1987 .... **CLC 16**
See also CA 191
Mazer, Norma Fox 1931- .... **CLC 26**
See also AAYA 5, 36; BYA 1, 8; CA 69-72; CANR 12, 32, 66; CLR 23; JRDA; MAICYA; SAAS 1; SATA 24, 67, 105; WYA; YAW
Mazzini, Guiseppe 1805-1872 .... **NCLC 34**
McAlmon, Robert (Menzies)
1895-1956 .... **TCLC 97**
See also CA 107; 168; DLB 4, 45; DLBD 15; GLL 1
McAuley, James Phillip 1917-1976 .. **CLC 45**
See also CA 97-100; RGEL
McBain, Ed
See Hunter, Evan
See also MSW
McBrien, William (Augustine)
1930- .... **CLC 44**
See also CA 107; CANR 90
McCabe, Patrick 1955- .... **CLC 133**
See also CA 130; CANR 50, 90; CN; DLB 194
McCaffrey, Anne (Inez) 1926- .... **CLC 17; DAM NOV, POP**
See also AAYA 6, 34; AITN 2; BEST 89:2; BPFB 2; BYA 5; CA 25-28R; CANR 15, 35, 55, 96; CLR 49; CPW; DA3; DLB 8; JRDA; MAICYA; MTCW 1, 2; SAAS 11; SATA 8, 70, 116; SFW; WYA; YAW
McCall, Nathan 1955(?)- .... **CLC 86**
See also BW 3; CA 146; CANR 88
McCann, Arthur
See Campbell, John W(ood, Jr.)
McCann, Edson
See Pohl, Frederik
McCarthy, Charles, Jr. 1933-
See McCarthy, Cormac
See also CANR 42, 69, 101; CN; CPW; CSW; DA3; DAM POP; MTCW 2
McCarthy, Cormac .... **CLC 4, 57, 59, 101**
See also McCarthy, Charles, Jr.
See also AAYA 41; AMWS 8; BPFB 2; CA 13-16R; CANR 10; DLB 6, 143, 256; TCWW 2
McCarthy, Mary (Therese)
1912-1989 .. **CLC 1, 3, 5, 14, 24, 39, 59; SSC 24**
See also AMW; BPFB 2; CA 5-8R; 129; CANR 16, 50, 64; DA3; DLB 2; DLBY 81; FW; INT CANR-16; MAWW; MTCW 1, 2; RGAL
McCartney, (James) Paul 1942- . **CLC 12, 35**
See also CA 146

Meredith, George 1828-1909 .. **TCLC 17, 43;
DAM POET**
    See also CA 117; 153; CANR 80; CDBLB
    1832-1890; DLB 18, 35, 57, 159; RGEL

Meredith, William (Morris) 1919- .... **CLC 4,
13, 22, 55; DAM POET; PC 28**
    See also CA 9-12R; CAAS 14; CANR 6,
    40; CP; DLB 5

Merezhkovsky, Dmitry Sergeyevich
    1865-1941 .... **TCLC 29**
    See also CA 169

Merimee, Prosper 1803-1870 ... **NCLC 6, 65;
SSC 7**
    See also DLB 119, 192; EW 6; EXPS; GFL
    1789 to the Present; RGSF; RGWL; SSFS
    8; SUFW

Merkin, Daphne 1954- .... **CLC 44**
    See also CA 123

Merlin, Arthur
    See Blish, James (Benjamin)

Merrill, James (Ingram) 1926-1995 .. **CLC 2,
3, 6, 8, 13, 18, 34, 91; DAM POET; PC
28**
    See also AMWS 3; CA 13-16R; 147; CANR
    10, 49, 63; DA3; DLB 5, 165; DLBY 85;
    INT CANR-10; MTCW 1, 2; PAB; RGAL

Merriman, Alex
    See Silverberg, Robert

Merriman, Brian 1747-1805 .... **NCLC 70**

Merritt, E. B.
    See Waddington, Miriam

Merton, Thomas 1915-1968 ..... **CLC 1, 3, 11,
34, 83; PC 10**
    See also AMWS 8; CA 5-8R; 25-28R;
    CANR 22, 53; DA3; DLB 48; DLBY 81;
    MTCW 1, 2

Merwin, W(illiam) S(tanley) 1927- ... **CLC 1,
2, 3, 5, 8, 13, 18, 45, 88; DAM POET**
    See also AMWS 3; CA 13-16R; CANR 15,
    51; CP; DA3; DLB 5, 169; INT CANR-
    15; MTCW 1, 2; PAB; PFS 5; RGAL

Metcalf, John 1938- .... **CLC 37; SSC 43**
    See also CA 113; CN; DLB 60; RGSF

Metcalf, Suzanne
    See Baum, L(yman) Frank

Mew, Charlotte (Mary) 1870-1928 .. **TCLC 8**
    See also CA 105; 189; DLB 19, 135; RGEL

Mewshaw, Michael 1943- .... **CLC 9**
    See also CA 53-56; CANR 7, 47; DLBY 80

Meyer, Conrad Ferdinand
    1825-1905 .... **NCLC 81**
    See also DLB 129; EW; RGWL

Meyer, Gustav 1868-1932
    See Meyrink, Gustav
    See also CA 117; 190

Meyer, June
    See Jordan, June
    See also GLL 2

Meyer, Lynn
    See Slavitt, David R(ytman)

Meyers, Jeffrey 1939- .... **CLC 39**
    See also CA 73-76; CAAE 186; CANR 54,
    102; DLB 111

**Meynell, Alice (Christina Gertrude
Thompson)** 1847-1922 .... **TCLC 6**
    See also CA 104; 177; DLB 19, 98; RGEL

Meyrink, Gustav .... **TCLC 21**
    See also Meyer, Gustav
    See also DLB 81

Michaels, Leonard 1933- .... **CLC 6, 25; SSC
16**
    See also CA 61-64; CANR 21, 62; CN;
    DLB 130; MTCW 1

Michaux, Henri 1899-1984 .... **CLC 8, 19**
    See also CA 85-88; 114; GFL 1789 to the
    Present; RGWL

Micheaux, Oscar (Devereaux)
    1884-1951 .... **TCLC 76**
    See also BW 3; CA 174; DLB 50; TCWW
    2

Michelangelo 1475-1564 .... **LC 12**
    See also AAYA 43

Michelet, Jules 1798-1874 .... **NCLC 31**
    See also EW 5; GFL 1789 to the Present

Michels, Robert 1876-1936 .... **TCLC 88**

Michener, James A(lbert)
    1907(?)-1997 .... **CLC 1, 5, 11, 29, 60,
109; DAM NOV, POP**
    See also AAYA 27; AITN 1; BEST 90:1;
    BPFB 2; CA 5-8R; 161; CANR 21, 45,
    68; CN; CPW; DA3; DLB 6; MTCW 1,
    2; RHW

Mickiewicz, Adam 1798-1855 . **NCLC 3, 101;
PC 38**
    See also EW 5; RGWL

Middleton, Christopher 1926- .... **CLC 13**
    See also CA 13-16R; CANR 29, 54; CP 7;
    DLB 40

Middleton, Richard (Barham)
    1882-1911 .... **TCLC 56**
    See also CA 187; DLB 156; HGG

Middleton, Stanley 1919- .... **CLC 7, 38**
    See also CA 25-28R; CAAS 23; CANR 21,
    46, 81; CN; DLB 14

Middleton, Thomas 1580-1627 .... **LC 33;
DAM DRAM, MST; DC 5**
    See also BRW 2; DLB 58; RGEL

Migueis, Jose Rodrigues 1901- .... **CLC 10**

Mikszath, Kalman 1847-1910 .... **TCLC 31**
    See also CA 170

Miles, Jack .... **CLC 100**

Miles, Josephine (Louise)
    1911-1985 .. **CLC 1, 2, 14, 34, 39; DAM
POET**
    See also CA 1-4R; 116; CANR 2, 55; DLB
    48

Militant
    See Sandburg, Carl (August)

Mill, Harriet (Hardy) Taylor
    1807-1858 .... **NCLC 102**
    See also FW

Mill, John Stuart 1806-1873 .... **NCLC 11, 58**
    See also CDBLB 1832-1890; DLB 55, 190;
    FW 1; RGEL

Millar, Kenneth 1915-1983 ... **CLC 14; DAM
POP**
    See also Macdonald, Ross
    See also CA 9-12R; 110; CANR 16, 63;
    CMW; CPW; DA3; DLB 2, 226; DLBD
    6; DLBY 83; MTCW 1, 2

Millay, E. Vincent
    See Millay, Edna St. Vincent

Millay, Edna St. Vincent
    1892-1950 .... **TCLC 4, 49; DA; DAB;
DAC; DAM MST, POET; PC 6;
WLCS**
    See also Boyd, Nancy
    See also AMW; CA 104; 130; CDALB
    1917-1929; DA3; DLB 45, 249; EXPP;
    MAWW; MTCW 1, 2; PAB; PFS 3;
    RGAL; WP

Miller, Arthur 1915- ...... **CLC 1, 2, 6, 10, 15,
26, 47, 78; DA; DAB; DAC; DAM
DRAM, MST; DC 1; WLC**
    See also AAYA 15; AITN 1; AMW; CA
    1-4R; CABS 3; CAD; CANR 2, 30, 54,
    76; CD; CDALB 1941-1968; DA3; DFS
    1, 3; DLB 7; LAIT 4; MTCW 1, 2; RGAL;
    WYAS 1

Miller, Henry (Valentine)
    1891-1980 .... **CLC 1, 2, 4, 9, 14, 43, 84;
DA; DAB; DAC; DAM MST, NOV;
WLC**
    See also AMW; BPFB 2; CA 9-12R; 97-
    100; CANR 33, 64; CDALB 1929-1941;
    DA3; DLB 4, 9; DLBY 80; MTCW 1, 2;
    RGAL

Miller, Jason 1939(?)-2001 .... **CLC 2**
    See also AITN 1; CA 73-76; 197; CAD;
    DFS 12; DLB 7

Miller, Sue 1943- .... **CLC 44; DAM POP**
    See also BEST 90:3; CA 139; CANR 59,
    91; DA3; DLB 143

Miller, Walter M(ichael, Jr.)
    1923-1996 .... **CLC 4, 30**
    See also BPFB 2; CA 85-88; DLB 8; SCFW;
    SFW

Millett, Kate 1934- .... **CLC 67**
    See also AITN 1; CA 73-76; CANR 32, 53,
    76; DA3; DLB 246; FW; GLL 1; MTCW
    1, 2

Millhauser, Steven (Lewis) 1943- .... **CLC 21,
54, 109**
    See also CA 110; 111; CANR 63; CN; DA3;
    DLB 2; FANT; INT CA-111; MTCW 2

Millin, Sarah Gertrude 1889-1968 ... **CLC 49**
    See also CA 102; 93-96; DLB 225

Milne, A(lan) A(lexander)
    1882-1956 ..... **TCLC 6, 88; DAB; DAC;
DAM MST**
    See also BRWS 5; CA 104; 133; CLR 1,
    26; CMW; CWRI; DA3; DLB 10, 77, 100,
    160; FANT; MAICYA; MTCW 1, 2;
    RGEL; SATA 100; WCH; YABC 1

Milner, Ron(ald) 1938- .... **CLC 56; BLC 3;
DAM MULT**
    See also AITN 1; BW 1; CA 73-76; CAD;
    CANR 24, 81; CD; DLB 38; MTCW 1

Milnes, Richard Monckton
    1809-1885 .... **NCLC 61**
    See also DLB 32, 184

Milosz, Czeslaw 1911- ...... **CLC 5, 11, 22, 31,
56, 82; DAM MST, POET; PC 8;
WLCS**
    See also CA 81-84; CANR 23, 51, 91;
    CWW 2; DA3; DLB 215; EW 13; MTCW
    1, 2; RGWL

Milton, John 1608-1674 .... **LC 9, 43; DA;
DAB; DAC; DAM MST, POET; PC 19,
29; WLC**
    See also BRW 2; BRWR 2; CDBLB 1660-
    1789; DA3; DLB 131, 151; EFS 1; EXPP;
    LAIT 1; PAB; PFS 3; RGEL; WLIT 3;
    WP

Min, Anchee 1957- .... **CLC 86**
    See also CA 146; CANR 94

Minehaha, Cornelius
    See Wedekind, (Benjamin) Frank(lin)

Miner, Valerie 1947- .... **CLC 40**
    See also CA 97-100; CANR 59; FW; GLL
    2

Minimo, Duca
    See D'Annunzio, Gabriele

Minot, Susan 1956- .... **CLC 44**
    See also AMWS 6; CA 134; CN

Minus, Ed 1938- .... **CLC 39**
    See also CA 185

Miranda, Javier
    See Bioy Casares, Adolfo
    See also CWW 2

Miranda, Javier
    See Bioy Casares, Adolfo

Mirbeau, Octave 1848-1917 .... **TCLC 55**
    See also DLB 123, 192; GFL 1789 to the
    Present

Miro (Ferrer), Gabriel (Francisco Victor)
    1879-1930 .... **TCLC 5**
    See also CA 104; 185

Misharin, Alexandr .... **CLC 59**

Mishima, Yukio ... **CLC 2, 4, 6, 9, 27; DC 1;
SSC 4**
    See also Hiraoka, Kimitake
    See also BPFB 2; DLB 182; GLL 1; MJW;
    MTCW 2; RGSF; RGWL; SSFS 5, 12

Mistral, Frederic 1830-1914 .... **TCLC 51**
    See also CA 122; GFL 1789 to the Present

Mistral, Gabriela
  See Godoy Alcayaga, Lucila
  See also LAW; RGWL; WP
Mistry, Rohinton 1952- .... **CLC 71; DAC**
  See also CA 141; CANR 86; CCA 1; CN;
  SSFS 6
Mitchell, Clyde
  See Ellison, Harlan (Jay); Silverberg, Robert
Mitchell, James Leslie 1901-1935
  See Gibbon, Lewis Grassic
  See also CA 104; 188; DLB 15
Mitchell, Joni 1943- .... **CLC 12**
  See also CA 112; CCA 1
Mitchell, Joseph (Quincy)
  1908-1996 .... **CLC 98**
  See also CA 77-80; 152; CANR 69; CN;
  CSW; DLB 185; DLBY 96
Mitchell, Margaret (Munnerlyn)
  1900-1949 . **TCLC 11; DAM NOV, POP**
  See also AAYA 23; BPFB 2; BYA 1; CA
  109; 125; CANR 55, 94; CDALBS; DA3;
  DLB 9; LAIT 2; MTCW 1, 2; NFS 9;
  RGAL; RHW; WYAS 1; YAW
Mitchell, Peggy
  See Mitchell, Margaret (Munnerlyn)
Mitchell, S(ilas) Weir 1829-1914 .... **TCLC 36**
  See also CA 165; DLB 202; RGAL
Mitchell, W(illiam) O(rmond)
  1914-1998 .. **CLC 25; DAC; DAM MST**
  See also CA 77-80; 165; CANR 15, 43; CN;
  DLB 88
Mitchell, William 1879-1936 .... **TCLC 81**
Mitford, Mary Russell 1787-1855 ... **NCLC 4**
  See also DLB 110, 116; RGEL
Mitford, Nancy 1904-1973 .... **CLC 44**
  See also CA 9-12R; DLB 191; RGEL
Miyamoto, (Chujo) Yuriko
  1899-1951 .... **TCLC 37**
  See also CA 170, 174; DLB 180
Miyazawa, Kenji 1896-1933 .... **TCLC 76**
  See also CA 157
Mizoguchi, Kenji 1898-1956 .... **TCLC 72**
  See also CA 167
Mo, Timothy (Peter) 1950(?)- ... **CLC 46, 134**
  See also CA 117; CN; DLB 194; MTCW 1;
  WLIT 4
Modarressi, Taghi (M.) 1931-1997 ... **CLC 44**
  See also CA 121; 134; INT 134
Modiano, Patrick (Jean) 1945- .... **CLC 18**
  See also CA 85-88; CANR 17, 40; CWW
  2; DLB 83
Mofolo, Thomas (Mokopu)
  1875(?)-1948 .. **TCLC 22; BLC 3; DAM
  MULT**
  See also AFW; CA 121; 153; CANR 83;
  DLB 225; MTCW 2; WLIT 2
Mohr, Nicholasa 1938- .... **CLC 12; DAM
  MULT; HLC 2**
  See also AAYA 8; CA 49-52; CANR 1, 32,
  64; CLR 22; DLB 145; HW 1, 2; JRDA;
  LAIT 5; MAICYAS; RGAL; SAAS 8;
  SATA 8, 97; SATA-Essay 113; WYA;
  YAW
Mojtabai, A(nn) G(race) 1938- ..... **CLC 5, 9,
  15, 29**
  See also CA 85-88; CANR 88
Moliere 1622-1673 .... **LC 10, 28, 64; DA;
  DAB; DAC; DAM DRAM, MST; DC
  13; WLC**
  See also DA3; DFS 13; EW 3; GFL Beginnings to 1789; RGWL
Molin, Charles
  See Mayne, William (James Carter)
Molnar, Ferenc 1878-1952 .. **TCLC 20; DAM
  DRAM**
  See also CA 109; 153; CANR 83; DLB 215;
  RGWL

Momaday, N(avarre) Scott 1934- ...... **CLC 2,
  19, 85, 95; DA; DAB; DAC; DAM
  MST, MULT, NOV, POP; PC 25;
  WLCS**
  See also AAYA 11; AMWS 4; ANW; BPFB
  2; CA 25-28R; CANR 14, 34, 68;
  CDALBS; CN; CPW; DA3; DLB 143,
  175, 256; EXPP; INT CANR-14; LAIT 4;
  MTCW 1, 2; NFS 10; NNAL; PFS 2, 11;
  RGAL; SATA 48; SATA-Brief 30; WP;
  YAW
Monette, Paul 1945-1995 .... **CLC 82**
  See also AMWS 10; CA 139; 147; CN;
  GLL 1
Monroe, Harriet 1860-1936 .... **TCLC 12**
  See also CA 109; DLB 54, 91
Monroe, Lyle
  See Heinlein, Robert A(nson)
Montagu, Elizabeth 1720-1800 .... **NCLC 7**
  See also FW
Montagu, Mary (Pierrepont) Wortley
  1689-1762 .... **LC 9, 57; PC 16**
  See also DLB 95, 101; RGEL
Montagu, W. H.
  See Coleridge, Samuel Taylor
Montague, John (Patrick) 1929- ..... **CLC 13,
  46**
  See also CA 9-12R; CANR 9, 69; CP; DLB
  40; MTCW 1; PFS 12; RGEL
Montaigne, Michel (Eyquem) de
  1533-1592 .... **LC 8; DA; DAB; DAC;
  DAM MST; WLC**
  See also EW 2; GFL Beginnings to 1789;
  RGWL
Montale, Eugenio 1896-1981 ... **CLC 7, 9, 18;
  PC 13**
  See also CA 17-20R; 104; CANR 30; DLB
  114; EW 11; MTCW 1; RGWL
Montesquieu, Charles-Louis de Secondat
  1689-1755 .... **LC 7, 69**
  See also EW 3; GFL Beginnings to 1789
Montessori, Maria 1870-1952 ...... **TCLC 103**
  See also CA 115; 147
Montgomery, (Robert) Bruce 1921(?)-1978
  See Crispin, Edmund
  See also CA 179; 104; CMW
Montgomery, L(ucy) M(aud)
  1874-1942 .... **TCLC 51; DAC; DAM
  MST**
  See also AAYA 12; BYA 1; CA 108; 137;
  CLR 8; DA3; DLB 92; DLBD 14; JRDA;
  MAICYA; MTCW 2; RGEL; SATA 100;
  WCH; WYA; YABC 1
Montgomery, Marion H., Jr. 1925- .... **CLC 7**
  See also AITN 1; CA 1-4R; CANR 3, 48;
  CSW; DLB 6
Montgomery, Max
  See Davenport, Guy (Mattison, Jr.)
Montherlant, Henry (Milon) de
  1896-1972 ..... **CLC 8, 19; DAM DRAM**
  See also CA 85-88; 37-40R; DLB 72; EW
  11; GFL 1789 to the Present; MTCW 1
Monty Python
  See Chapman, Graham; Cleese, John
  (Marwood); Gilliam, Terry (Vance); Idle,
  Eric; Jones, Terence Graham Parry; Palin,
  Michael (Edward)
  See also AAYA 7
Moodie, Susanna (Strickland)
  1803-1885 .... **NCLC 14**
  See also DLB 99
Moody, Hiram F. III 1961-
  See Moody, Rick
  See also CA 138; CANR 64
Moody, Rick .... **CLC 147**
  See also Moody, Hiram F. III
Moody, William Vaughan
  1869-1910 .... **TCLC 105**
  See also CA 110; 178; DLB 7, 54; RGAL

Mooney, Edward 1951-
  See Mooney, Ted
  See also CA 130
Mooney, Ted .... **CLC 25**
  See also Mooney, Edward
Moorcock, Michael (John) 1939- ...... **CLC 5,
  27, 58**
  See also Bradbury, Edward P.
  See also AAYA 26; CA 45-48; CAAS 5;
  CANR 2, 17, 38, 64; CN; DLB 14, 231;
  FANT; MTCW 1, 2; SATA 93; SFW;
  SUFW
Moore, Brian 1921-1999 ... **CLC 1, 3, 5, 7, 8,
  19, 32, 90; DAB; DAC; DAM MST**
  See also Bryan, Michael
  See also CA 1-4R; 174; CANR 1, 25, 42,
  63; CCA 1; CN; DLB 251; FANT; MTCW
  1, 2; RGEL
Moore, Edward
  See Muir, Edwin
  See also RGEL
Moore, G. E. 1873-1958 .... **TCLC 89**
Moore, George Augustus
  1852-1933 .... **TCLC 7; SSC 19**
  See also BRW 6; CA 104; 177; DLB 10,
  18, 57, 135; RGEL; RGSF
Moore, Lorrie .... **CLC 39, 45, 68**
  See also Moore, Marie Lorena
  See also AMWS 10; DLB 234
Moore, Marianne (Craig)
  1887-1972 .... **CLC 1, 2, 4, 8, 10, 13, 19,
  47; DA; DAB; DAC; DAM MST,
  POET; PC 4; WLCS**
  See also AMW; CA 1-4R; 33-36R; CANR
  3, 61; CDALB 1929-1941; DA3; DLB 45;
  DLBD 7; EXPP; MAWW; MTCW 1, 2;
  PAB; PFS 14; RGAL; SATA 20; WP
Moore, Marie Lorena 1957-
  See Moore, Lorrie
  See also CA 116; CANR 39, 83; CN; DLB
  234
Moore, Thomas 1779-1852 .... **NCLC 6, 110**
  See also DLB 96, 144; RGEL
Moorhouse, Frank 1938- .... **SSC 40**
  See also CA 118; CANR 92; CN; RGSF
Mora, Pat(ricia) 1942-
  See also CA 129; CANR 57, 81; CLR 58;
  DAM MULT; DLB 209; HLC 2; HW 1,
  2; SATA 92
Moraga, Cherrie 1952- .... **CLC 126; DAM
  MULT**
  See also CA 131; CANR 66; DLB 82, 249;
  FW; GLL 1; HW 1, 2
Morand, Paul 1888-1976 .... **CLC 41; SSC 22**
  See also CA 184; 69-72; DLB 65
Morante, Elsa 1918-1985 .... **CLC 8, 47**
  See also CA 85-88; 117; CANR 35; DLB
  177; MTCW 1, 2; RGWL
Moravia, Alberto .... **CLC 2, 7, 11, 27, 46;
  SSC 26**
  See also Pincherle, Alberto
  See also DLB 177; EW 12; MTCW 2;
  RGSF; RGWL
More, Hannah 1745-1833 .... **NCLC 27**
  See also DLB 107, 109, 116, 158; RGEL
More, Henry 1614-1687 .... **LC 9**
  See also DLB 126, 252
More, Sir Thomas 1478(?)-1535 .... **LC 10, 32**
  See also BRWS 7; DLB 136; RGEL
Moreas, Jean .... **TCLC 18**
  See also Papadiamantopoulos, Johannes
  See also GFL 1789 to the Present
Morgan, Berry 1919- .... **CLC 6**
  See also CA 49-52; DLB 6
Morgan, Claire
  See Highsmith, (Mary) Patricia
  See also GLL 1

Murray, James Augustus Henry
1837-1915 .... **TCLC 117**
Murray, Judith Sargent
1751-1820 .... **NCLC 63**
See also DLB 37, 200
Murray, Les(lie Allan) 1938- .... **CLC 40;**
DAM POET
See also BRWS 7; CA 21-24R; CANR 11,
27, 56, 103; CP; DLBY 01; RGEL
Murry, J. Middleton
See Murry, John Middleton
Murry, John Middleton
1889-1957 .... **TCLC 16**
See also CA 118; DLB 149
Musgrave, Susan 1951- .... **CLC 13, 54**
See also CA 69-72; CANR 45, 84; CCA 1;
CP; CWP
Musil, Robert (Edler von)
1880-1942 .... **TCLC 12, 68; SSC 18**
See also CA 109; CANR 55, 84; DLB 81,
124; EW 9; MTCW 2; RGSF; RGWL
Muske, Carol .... **CLC 90**
See also Muske-Dukes, Carol (Anne)
Muske-Dukes, Carol (Anne) 1945-
See Muske, Carol
See also CA 65-68; CANR 32, 70; CWP
Musset, (Louis Charles) Alfred de
1810-1857 .... **NCLC 7**
See also DLB 192, 217; EW 6; GFL 1789
to the Present; RGWL; TWA
Mussolini, Benito (Amilcare Andrea)
1883-1945 .... **TCLC 96**
See also CA 116
My Brother's Brother
See Chekhov, Anton (Pavlovich)
Myers, L(eopold) H(amilton)
1881-1944 .... **TCLC 59**
See also CA 157; DLB 15; RGEL
Myers, Walter Dean 1937- ..... **CLC 35; BLC**
3; DAM MULT, NOV
See also AAYA 4, 23; BW 2; BYA 6, 8, 11;
CA 33-36R; CANR 20, 42, 67; CLR 4,
16, 35; DLB 33; INT CANR-20; JRDA;
LAIT 5; MAICYA; MAICYAS; MTCW
2; SAAS 2; SATA 41, 71, 109; SATA-
Brief 27; WYA; YAW
Myers, Walter M.
See Myers, Walter Dean
Myles, Symon
See Follett, Ken(neth Martin)
Nabokov, Vladimir (Vladimirovich)
1899-1977 .... **CLC 1, 2, 3, 6, 8, 11, 15,**
23, 44, 46, 64; DA; DAB; DAC; DAM
MST, NOV; SSC 11; WLC
See also AMW; AMWR 1; BPFB 2; CA
5-8R; 69-72; CANR 20, 102; CDALB
1941-1968; DA3; DLB 2, 244; DLBD 3;
DLBY 80, 91; EXPS; MTCW 1, 2; NFS
9; RGAL; RGSF; SSFS 6; TCLC 108
Naevius c. 265B.C.-201B.C. .... **CMLC 37**
See also DLB 211
Nagai, Kafu .... **TCLC 51**
See also Nagai, Sokichi
See also DLB 180
Nagai, Sokichi 1879-1959
See Nagai, Kafu
See also CA 117
Nagy, Laszlo 1925-1978 .... **CLC 7**
See also CA 129; 112
Naidu, Sarojini 1879-1949 .... **TCLC 80**
See also RGEL
Naipaul, Shiva(dhar Srinivasa)
1945-1985 .... **CLC 32, 39; DAM NOV**
See also CA 110; 112; 116; CANR 33;
DA3; DLB 157; DLBY 85; MTCW 1, 2

Naipaul, V(idiadhar) S(urajprasad)
1932- .... **CLC 4, 7, 9, 13, 18, 37, 105;**
DAB; DAC; DAM MST, NOV; SSC 38
See also BPFB 2; BRWS 1; CA 1-4R;
CANR 1, 33, 51, 91; CDBLB 1960 to
Present; CN; DA3; DLB 125, 204, 207;
DLBY 85, 01; MTCW 1, 2; RGEL; RGSF;
WLIT 4
Nakos, Lilika 1899(?)- .... **CLC 29**
Narayan, R(asipuram) K(rishnaswami)
1906-2001 .... **CLC 7, 28, 47, 121; DAM**
NOV; SSC 25
See also BPFB 2; CA 81-84; 196; CANR
33, 61; CN; DA3; DNFS; MTCW 1, 2;
RGEL; RGSF; SATA 62; SSFS 5
Nash, (Fredric) Ogden 1902-1971 . **CLC 23;**
DAM POET; PC 21
See also CA 13-14; 29-32R; CANR 34, 61;
CAP 1; DLB 11; MAICYA; MTCW 1, 2;
RGAL; SATA 2, 46; TCLC 109; WP
Nashe, Thomas 1567-1601(?) .... **LC 41**
See also DLB 167; RGEL
Nathan, Daniel
See Dannay, Frederic
Nathan, George Jean 1882-1958 .... **TCLC 18**
See also Hatteras, Owen
See also CA 114; 169; DLB 137
Natsume, Kinnosuke
See Natsume, Soseki
Natsume, Soseki 1867-1916 .... **TCLC 2, 10**
See also Soseki
See also CA 104; 195; DLB 180; RGWL
Natti, (Mary) Lee 1919-
See Kingman, Lee
See also CA 5-8R; CANR 2
Navarre, Marguerite de
See de Navarre, Marguerite
Naylor, Gloria 1950- . **CLC 28, 52, 156; BLC**
3; DA; DAC; DAM MST, MULT,
NOV, POP; WLCS
See also AAYA 6, 39; AFAW 1, 2; AMWS
8; BW 2, 3; CA 107; CANR 27, 51, 74;
CN; CPW; DA3; DLB 173; FW; MTCW
1, 2; NFS 4, 7; RGAL
Neff, Debra .... **CLC 59**
Neihardt, John Gneisenau
1881-1973 .... **CLC 32**
See also CA 13-14; CANR 65; CAP 1; DLB
9, 54, 256; LAIT 2
Nekrasov, Nikolai Alekseevich
1821-1878 .... **NCLC 11**
Nelligan, Emile 1879-1941 .... **TCLC 14**
See also CA 114; DLB 92
Nelson, Willie 1933- .... **CLC 17**
See also CA 107
Nemerov, Howard (Stanley)
1920-1991 .... **CLC 2, 6, 9, 36; DAM**
POET; PC 24
See also AMW; CA 1-4R; 134; CABS 2;
CANR 1, 27, 53; DLB 5, 6; DLBY 83;
INT CANR-27; MTCW 1, 2; PFS 10, 14;
RGAL
Neruda, Pablo 1904-1973 .. **CLC 1, 2, 5, 7, 9,**
28, 62; DA; DAB; DAC; DAM MST,
MULT, POET; HLC 2; PC 4; WLC
See also CA 19-20; 45-48; CAP 2; DA3;
DNFS; HW 1; LAW; MTCW 1, 2; PFS
11; RGWL; WLIT 1; WP
Nerval, Gerard de 1808-1855 ... **NCLC 1, 67;**
PC 13; SSC 18
See also DLB 217; EW 6; GFL 1789 to the
Present; RGSF; RGWL
Nervo, (Jose) Amado (Ruiz de)
1870-1919 .... **TCLC 11; HLCS 2**
See also CA 109; 131; HW 1; LAW
Nesbit, Malcolm
See Chester, Alfred
Nessi, Pio Baroja y
See Baroja (y Nessi), Pio

Nestroy, Johann 1801-1862 .... **NCLC 42**
See also DLB 133; RGWL
Netterville, Luke
See O'Grady, Standish (James)
Neufeld, John (Arthur) 1938- .... **CLC 17**
See also AAYA 11; CA 25-28R; CANR 11,
37, 56; CLR 52; MAICYA; SAAS 3;
SATA 6, 81; YAW
Neumann, Alfred 1895-1952 .... **TCLC 100**
See also CA 183; DLB 56
Neumann, Ferenc
See Molnar, Ferenc
Neville, Emily Cheney 1919- .... **CLC 12**
See also BYA 2; CA 5-8R; CANR 3, 37,
85; JRDA; MAICYA; SAAS 2; SATA 1;
YAW
Newbound, Bernard Slade 1930-
See Slade, Bernard
See also CA 81-84; CANR 49; CD; DAM
DRAM
Newby, P(ercy) H(oward)
1918-1997 .... **CLC 2, 13; DAM NOV**
See also CA 5-8R; 161; CANR 32, 67; CN;
DLB 15; MTCW 1; RGEL
Newcastle
See Cavendish, Margaret Lucas
Newlove, Donald 1928- .... **CLC 6**
See also CA 29-32R; CANR 25
Newlove, John (Herbert) 1938- .... **CLC 14**
See also CA 21-24R; CANR 9, 25; CP
Newman, Charles 1938- .... **CLC 2, 8**
See also CA 21-24R; CANR 84; CN
Newman, Edwin (Harold) 1919- ...... **CLC 14**
See also AITN 1; CA 69-72; CANR 5
Newman, John Henry 1801-1890 . **NCLC 38,**
99
See also BRWS 7; DLB 18, 32, 55; RGEL
Newton, (Sir) Isaac 1642-1727 ...... **LC 35, 53**
See also DLB 252
Newton, Suzanne 1936- .... **CLC 35**
See also BYA 7; CA 41-44R; CANR 14;
JRDA; SATA 5, 77
New York Dept. of Ed. .... **CLC 70**
Nexo, Martin Andersen
1869-1954 .... **TCLC 43**
See also DLB 214
Nezval, Vitezslav 1900-1958 .... **TCLC 44**
See also CA 123; DLB 215
Ng, Fae Myenne 1957(?)- .... **CLC 81**
See also CA 146
Ngema, Mbongeni 1955- .... **CLC 57**
See also BW 2; CA 143; CANR 84; CD
Ngugi, James T(hiong'o) .... **CLC 3, 7, 13**
See also Ngugi wa Thiong'o
Ngugi wa Thiong'o 1938- .. **CLC 36; BLC 3;**
DAM MULT, NOV
See also Ngugi, James T(hiong'o)
See also AFW; BW 2; CA 81-84; CANR
27, 58; DLB 125; DNFS; MTCW 1, 2;
RGEL
Nichol, B(arrie) P(hillip) 1944-1988 . **CLC 18**
See also CA 53-56; DLB 53; SATA 66
Nichols, John (Treadwell) 1940- .... **CLC 38**
See also CA 9-12R; CAAE 190; CAAS 2;
CANR 6, 70; DLBY 82; TCWW 2
Nichols, Leigh
See Koontz, Dean R(ay)
Nichols, Peter (Richard) 1927- .... **CLC 5, 36,**
65
See also CA 104; CANR 33, 86; CBD; CD;
DLB 13, 245; MTCW 1
Nicholson, Linda ed. .... **CLC 65**
Ni Chuilleanain, Eilean 1942- .... **PC 34**
See also CA 126; CANR 53, 83; CP; CWP;
DLB 40
Nicolas, F. R. E.
See Freeling, Nicolas

Niedecker, Lorine 1903-1970 ..... **CLC 10, 42; DAM POET**
See also CA 25-28; CAP 2; DLB 48

Nietzsche, Friedrich (Wilhelm)
1844-1900 .... **TCLC 10, 18, 55**
See also CA 107; 121; DLB 129; EW 7; RGWL

Nievo, Ippolito 1831-1861 .... **NCLC 22**

Nightingale, Anne Redmon 1943-
See Redmon, Anne
See also CA 103

Nightingale, Florence 1820-1910 ... **TCLC 85**
See also CA 188; DLB 166

Nijo Yoshimoto 1320-1388 .... **CMLC 49**
See also DLB 203

Nik. T. O.
See Annensky, Innokenty (Fyodorovich)

Nin, Anais 1903-1977 ..... **CLC 1, 4, 8, 11, 14, 60, 127; DAM NOV, POP; SSC 10**
See also AITN 2; AMWS 10; BPFB 2; CA 13-16R; 69-72; CANR 22, 53; DLB 2, 4, 152; GLL 2; MAWW; MTCW 1, 2; RGAL; RGSF

Nisbet, Robert A(lexander)
1913-1996 .... **TCLC 117**
See also CA 25-28R; 153; CANR 17; INT CANR-17

Nishida, Kitaro 1870-1945 .... **TCLC 83**

Nishiwaki, Junzaburo 1894-1982 .... **PC 15**
See also Nishiwaki, Junzaburo
See also CA 194; 107; MJW

Nishiwaki, Junzaburo 1894-1982
See Nishiwaki, Junzaburo
See also CA 194

Nissenson, Hugh 1933- .... **CLC 4, 9**
See also CA 17-20R; CANR 27; CN; DLB 28

Niven, Larry .... **CLC 8**
See also Niven, Laurence Van Cott
See also AAYA 27; BPFB 2; BYA 10; DLB 8; SCFW 2

Niven, Laurence Van Cott 1938-
See Niven, Larry
See also CA 21-24R; CAAS 12; CANR 14, 44, 66; CPW; DAM POP; MTCW 1, 2; SATA 95; SFW

Nixon, Agnes Eckhardt 1927- .... **CLC 21**
See also CA 110

Nizan, Paul 1905-1940 .... **TCLC 40**
See also CA 161; DLB 72; GFL 1789 to the Present

Nkosi, Lewis 1936- ... **CLC 45; BLC 3; DAM MULT**
See also BW 1, 3; CA 65-68; CANR 27, 81; CBD; CD; DLB 157, 225

Nodier, (Jean) Charles (Emmanuel)
1780-1844 .... **NCLC 19**
See also DLB 119; GFL 1789 to the Present

Noguchi, Yone 1875-1947 .... **TCLC 80**

Nolan, Christopher 1965- .... **CLC 58**
See also CA 111; CANR 88

Noon, Jeff 1957- .... **CLC 91**
See also CA 148; CANR 83; SFW

Norden, Charles
See Durrell, Lawrence (George)

Nordhoff, Charles (Bernard)
1887-1947 .... **TCLC 23**
See also CA 108; DLB 9; LAIT 1; RHW 1; SATA 23

Norfolk, Lawrence 1963- .... **CLC 76**
See also CA 144; CANR 85; CN

Norman, Marsha 1947- .... **CLC 28; DAM DRAM; DC 8**
See also CA 105; CABS 3; CAD; CANR 41; CD; CSW; CWD; DFS 2; DLBY 84; FW

Normyx
See Douglas, (George) Norman

Norris, (Benjamin) Frank(lin, Jr.)
1870-1902 .... **TCLC 24; SSC 28**
See also AMW; BPFB 2; CA 110; 160; CDALB 1865-1917; DLB 12, 71, 186; NFS 12; RGAL; TCWW 2; TUS

Norris, Leslie 1921- .... **CLC 14**
See also CA 11-12; CANR 14; CAP 1; CP; DLB 27, 256

North, Andrew
See Norton, Andre

North, Anthony
See Koontz, Dean R(ay)

North, Captain George
See Stevenson, Robert Louis (Balfour)

North, Milou
See Erdrich, Louise

Northrup, B. A.
See Hubbard, L(afayette) Ron(ald)

North Staffs
See Hulme, T(homas) E(rnest)

Northup, Solomon 1808-1863 ...... **NCLC 105**

Norton, Alice Mary
See Norton, Andre
See also MAICYA; SATA 1, 43

Norton, Andre 1912- .... **CLC 12**
See also Norton, Alice Mary
See also AAYA 14; BPFB 2; BYA 4, 10, 12; CA 1-4R; CANR 68; CLR 50; DLB 8, 52; JRDA; MTCW 1; SATA 91; SUFW; YAW

Norton, Caroline 1808-1877 .... **NCLC 47**
See also DLB 21, 159, 199

Norway, Nevil Shute 1899-1960
See Shute, Nevil
See also CA 102; 93-96; CANR 85; MTCW 2

Norwid, Cyprian Kamil
1821-1883 .... **NCLC 17**

Nosille, Nabrah
See Ellison, Harlan (Jay)

Nossack, Hans Erich 1901-1978 .... **CLC 6**
See also CA 93-96; 85-88; DLB 69

Nostradamus 1503-1566 .... **LC 27**

Nosu, Chuji
See Ozu, Yasujiro

Notenburg, Eleanora (Genrikhovna) von
See Guro, Elena

Nova, Craig 1945- .... **CLC 7, 31**
See also CA 45-48; CANR 2, 53

Novak, Joseph
See Kosinski, Jerzy (Nikodem)

Novalis 1772-1801 .... **NCLC 13**
See also DLB 90; EW 5; RGWL

Novis, Emile
See Weil, Simone (Adolphine)

Nowlan, Alden (Albert) 1933-1983 . **CLC 15; DAC; DAM MST**
See also CA 9-12R; CANR 5; DLB 53; PFS 12

Noyes, Alfred 1880-1958 ...... **TCLC 7; PC 27**
See also CA 104; 188; DLB 20; EXPP; FANT; PFS 4; RGEL

Nunn, Kem .... **CLC 34**
See also CA 159

Nwapa, Flora 1931-1993 .... **CLC 133; BLCS**
See also BW 2; CA 143; CANR 83; CWRI; DLB 125; WLIT 2

Nye, Robert 1939- . **CLC 13, 42; DAM NOV**
See also CA 33-36R; CANR 29, 67; CN; CP; CWRI; DLB 14; FANT; HGG; MTCW 1; RHW; SATA 6

Nyro, Laura 1947-1997 .... **CLC 17**
See also CA 194

Oates, Joyce Carol 1938- .. **CLC 1, 2, 3, 6, 9, 11, 15, 19, 33, 52, 108, 134; DA; DAB; DAC; DAM MST, NOV, POP; SSC 6; WLC**
See also AAYA 15; AITN 1; AMWS 2; BEST 89:2; BPFB 2; BYA 11; CA 5-8R; CANR 25, 45, 74; CDALB 1968-1988; CN; CP; CPW; CWP; DA3; DLB 2, 5, 130; DLBY 81; EXPS; FW; HGG; INT CANR-25; LAIT 4; MAWW; MTCW 1, 2; NFS 8; RGAL; RGSF; SSFS 1, 8

O'Brian, Patrick 1914-2000 .... **CLC 152**
See also CA 144; 187; CANR 74; CPW; MTCW 2; RHW

O'Brien, Darcy 1939-1998 .... **CLC 11**
See also CA 21-24R; 167; CANR 8, 59

O'Brien, E. G.
See Clarke, Arthur C(harles)

O'Brien, Edna 1936- ..... **CLC 3, 5, 8, 13, 36, 65, 116; DAM NOV; SSC 10**
See also BRWS 5; CA 1-4R; CANR 6, 41, 65, 102; CDBLB 1960 to Present; CN; DA3; DLB 14, 231; FW; MTCW 1, 2; RGSF; WLIT 4

O'Brien, Fitz-James 1828-1862 ..... **NCLC 21**
See also DLB 74; RGAL; SUFW

O'Brien, Flann .... **CLC 1, 4, 5, 7, 10, 47**
See also O Nuallain, Brian
See also BRWS 2; DLB 231; RGEL

O'Brien, Richard 1942- .... **CLC 17**
See also CA 124

O'Brien, (William) Tim(othy) 1946- . **CLC 7, 19, 40, 103; DAM POP**
See also AAYA 16; AMWS 5; CA 85-88; CANR 40, 58; CDALBS; CN; CPW; DA3; DLB 152; DLBD 9; DLBY 80; MTCW 2; RGAL; SSFS 5

Obstfelder, Sigbjoern 1866-1900 .... **TCLC 23**
See also CA 123

O'Casey, Sean 1880-1964 .... **CLC 1, 5, 9, 11, 15, 88; DAB; DAC; DAM DRAM, MST; DC 12; WLCS**
See also BRW 7; CA 89-92; CANR 62; CBD; CDBLB 1914-1945; DA3; DLB 10; MTCW 1, 2; RGEL; WLIT 4

O'Cathasaigh, Sean
See O'Casey, Sean

Occom, Samson 1723-1792 .... **LC 60**
See also DLB 175; NNAL

Ochs, Phil(ip David) 1940-1976 .... **CLC 17**
See also CA 185; 65-68

O'Connor, Edwin (Greene)
1918-1968 .... **CLC 14**
See also CA 93-96; 25-28R

O'Connor, (Mary) Flannery
1925-1964 ... **CLC 1, 2, 3, 6, 10, 13, 15, 21, 66, 104; DA; DAB; DAC; DAM MST, NOV; SSC 1, 23; WLC**
See also AAYA 7; AMW; BPFB 3; CA 1-4R; CANR 3, 41; CDALB 1941-1968; DA3; DLB 2, 152; DLBD 12; DLBY 80; EXPS; LAIT 5; MAWW; MTCW 1, 2; NFS 3; RGAL; RGSF; SSFS 2, 7, 10

O'Connor, Frank .... **CLC 23; SSC 5**
See also O'Donovan, Michael John
See also DLB 162; RGSF; SSFS 5

O'Dell, Scott 1898-1989 .... **CLC 30**
See also AAYA 3; BPFB 3; BYA 1, 2, 3, 5; CA 61-64; 129; CANR 12, 30; CLR 1, 16; DLB 52; JRDA; MAICYA; SATA 12, 60; WYA; YAW

Odets, Clifford 1906-1963 ..... **CLC 2, 28, 98; DAM DRAM; DC 6**
See also AMWS 2; CA 85-88; CAD; CANR 62; DFS 3; DLB 7, 26; MTCW 1, 2; RGAL

O'Doherty, Brian 1934- .... **CLC 76**
See also CA 105

O'Donnell, K. M.
See Malzberg, Barry N(athaniel)

Phillips, Caryl 1958- . **CLC 96; BLCS; DAM MULT**
See also BRWS 5; BW 2; CA 141; CANR 63, 104; CBD; CD; CN; DA3; DLB 157; MTCW 2; WLIT 4

Phillips, David Graham
1867-1911 .... **TCLC 44**
See also CA 108; 176; DLB 9, 12; RGAL

Phillips, Jack
See Sandburg, Carl (August)

Phillips, Jayne Anne 1952- .... **CLC 15, 33, 139; SSC 16**
See also BPFB 3; CA 101; CANR 24, 50, 96; CN; CSW; DLBY 80; INT CANR-24; MTCW 1, 2; RGAL; RGSF; SSFS 4

Phillips, Richard
See Dick, Philip K(indred)

Phillips, Robert (Schaeffer) 1938- .... **CLC 28**
See also CA 17-20R; CAAS 13; CANR 8; DLB 105

Phillips, Ward
See Lovecraft, H(oward) P(hillips)

Piccolo, Lucio 1901-1969 .... **CLC 13**
See also CA 97-100; DLB 114

Pickthall, Marjorie L(owry) C(hristie)
1883-1922 .... **TCLC 21**
See also CA 107; DLB 92

Pico della Mirandola, Giovanni
1463-1494 .... **LC 15**

Piercy, Marge 1936- .... **CLC 3, 6, 14, 18, 27, 62, 128; PC 29**
See also BPFB 3; CA 21-24R; CAAE 187; CAAS 1; CANR 13, 43, 66; CN; CP; CWP; DLB 120, 227; EXPP; FW; MTCW 1, 2; PFS 9; SFW

Piers, Robert
See Anthony, Piers

Pieyre de Mandiargues, Andre 1909-1991
See Mandiargues, Andre Pieyre de
See also CA 103; 136; CANR 22, 82; GFL 1789 to the Present

Pilnyak, Boris 1894-1938 . **TCLC 23; SSC 48**
See also Vogau, Boris Andreyevich

Pinchback, Eugene
See Toomer, Jean

Pincherle, Alberto 1907-1990 .... **CLC 11, 18; DAM NOV**
See also Moravia, Alberto
See also CA 25-28R; 132; CANR 33, 63; MTCW 1

Pinckney, Darryl 1953- .... **CLC 76**
See also BW 2, 3; CA 143; CANR 79

Pindar 518(?)B.C.-438(?)B.C. .... **CMLC 12; PC 19**
See also AW 1; DLB 176; RGWL

Pineda, Cecile 1942- .... **CLC 39**
See also CA 118; DLB 209

Pinero, Arthur Wing 1855-1934 ... **TCLC 32; DAM DRAM**
See also CA 110; 153; DLB 10; RGEL

Pinero, Miguel (Antonio Gomez)
1946-1988 .... **CLC 4, 55**
See also CA 61-64; 125; CAD; CANR 29, 90; HW 1

Pinget, Robert 1919-1997 .... **CLC 7, 13, 37**
See also CA 85-88; 160; CWW 2; DLB 83; GFL 1789 to the Present

Pink Floyd
See Barrett, (Roger) Syd; Gilmour, David; Mason, Nick; Waters, Roger; Wright, Rick

Pinkney, Edward 1802-1828 .... **NCLC 31**
See also DLB 248

Pinkwater, Daniel Manus 1941- .... **CLC 35**
See also Pinkwater, Manus
See also AAYA 1; BYA 9; CA 29-32R; CANR 12, 38, 89; CLR 4; CSW; FANT; JRDA; MAICYA; SAAS 3; SATA 46, 76, 114; SFW; YAW

Pinkwater, Manus
See Pinkwater, Daniel Manus
See also SATA 8

Pinsky, Robert 1940- .... **CLC 9, 19, 38, 94, 121; DAM POET; PC 27**
See also AMWS 6; CA 29-32R; CAAS 4; CANR 58, 97; CP; DA3; DLBY 82, 98; MTCW 2; RGAL

Pinta, Harold
See Pinter, Harold

Pinter, Harold 1930- .. **CLC 1, 3, 6, 9, 11, 15, 27, 58, 73; DA; DAB; DAC; DAM DRAM, MST; DC 15; WLC**
See also BRWR 1; CA 5-8R; CANR 33, 65; CBD; CD; CDBLB 1960 to Present; DA3; DFS 3, 5, 7; DLB 13; IDFW 3, 4; MTCW 1, 2; RGEL

Piozzi, Hester Lynch (Thrale)
1741-1821 .... **NCLC 57**
See also DLB 104, 142

Pirandello, Luigi 1867-1936 ...... **TCLC 4, 29; DA; DAB; DAC; DAM DRAM, MST; DC 5; SSC 22; WLC**
See also CA 104; 153; CANR 103; DA3; DFS 4, 9; EW 8; MTCW 2; RGSF; RGWL

Pirsig, Robert M(aynard) 1928- ... **CLC 4, 6, 73; DAM POP**
See also CA 53-56; CANR 42, 74; CPW 1; DA3; MTCW 1, 2; SATA 39

Pisarev, Dmitry Ivanovich
1840-1868 .... **NCLC 25**

Pix, Mary (Griffith) 1666-1709 .... **LC 8**
See also DLB 80

Pixerecourt, (Rene Charles) Guilbert de
1773-1844 .... **NCLC 39**
See also DLB 192; GFL 1789 to the Present

Plaatje, Sol(omon) T(shekisho)
1878-1932 .... **TCLC 73; BLCS**
See also BW 2, 3; CA 141; CANR 79; DLB 125, 225

Plaidy, Jean
See Hibbert, Eleanor Alice Burford

Planche, James Robinson
1796-1880 .... **NCLC 42**
See also RGEL

Plant, Robert 1948- .... **CLC 12**

Plante, David (Robert) 1940- ...... **CLC 7, 23, 38; DAM NOV**
See also CA 37-40R; CANR 12, 36, 58, 82; CN; DLBY 83; INT CANR-12; MTCW 1

Plath, Sylvia 1932-1963 ..... **CLC 1, 2, 3, 5, 9, 11, 14, 17, 50, 51, 62, 111; DA; DAB; DAC; DAM MST, POET; PC 1, 37; WLC**
See also AAYA 13; AMWS 1; BPFB 3; CA 19-20; CANR 34, 101; CAP 2; CDALB 1941-1968; DA3; DLB 5, 6, 152; EXPN; EXPP; FW; LAIT 4; MAWW; MTCW 1, 2; NFS 1; PAB; PFS 1; RGAL; SATA 96; WP; YAW

Plato c. 428B.C.-347B.C. .... **CMLC 8; DA; DAB; DAC; DAM MST; WLCS**
See also AW 1; DA3; DLB 176; LAIT 1; RGWL

Platonov, Andrei
See Klimentov, Andrei Platonovich

Platt, Kin 1911- .... **CLC 26**
See also AAYA 11; CA 17-20R; CANR 11; JRDA; SAAS 17; SATA 21, 86; WYA

Plautus c. 254B.C.-c. 184B.C. ...... **CMLC 24; DC 6**
See also AW 1; DLB 211; RGWL

Plick et Plock
See Simenon, Georges (Jacques Christian)

Plieksans, Janis
See Rainis, Janis

Plimpton, George (Ames) 1927- .... **CLC 36**
See also AITN 1; CA 21-24R; CANR 32, 70, 103; DLB 185, 241; MTCW 1, 2; SATA 10

Pliny the Elder c. 23-79 .... **CMLC 23**
See also DLB 211

Plomer, William Charles Franklin
1903-1973 .... **CLC 4, 8**
See also AFW; CA 21-22; CANR 34; CAP 2; DLB 20, 162, 191, 225; MTCW 1; RGEL; RGSF; SATA 24

Plotinus 204-270 .... **CMLC 46**
See also DLB 176

Plowman, Piers
See Kavanagh, Patrick (Joseph)

Plum, J.
See Wodehouse, P(elham) G(renville)

Plumly, Stanley (Ross) 1939- .... **CLC 33**
See also CA 108; 110; CANR 97; CP; DLB 5, 193; INT 110

Plumpe, Friedrich Wilhelm
1888-1931 .... **TCLC 53**
See also CA 112

Po Chu-i 772-846 .... **CMLC 24**

Poe, Edgar Allan 1809-1849 ..... **NCLC 1, 16, 55, 78, 94, 97; DA; DAB; DAC; DAM MST, POET; PC 1; SSC 1, 22, 34, 35; WLC**
See also AAYA 14; AMW; BPFB 3; BYA 5, 11; CDALB 1640-1865; CMW; DA3; DLB 3, 59, 73, 74, 248, 254; EXPP; EXPS; HGG; LAIT 2; MSW; PAB; PFS 1, 3, 9; RGAL; RGSF; SATA 23; SCFW 2; SFW; SSFS 2, 4, 7, 8; SUFW; WP; WYA

Poet of Titchfield Street, The
See Pound, Ezra (Weston Loomis)

Pohl, Frederik 1919- .... **CLC 18; SSC 25**
See also AAYA 24; CA 61-64; CAAE 188; CAAS 1; CANR 11, 37, 81; CN; DLB 8; INT CANR-11; MTCW 1, 2; SATA 24; SCFW 2; SFW

Poirier, Louis 1910-
See Gracq, Julien
See also CA 122; 126; CWW 2

Poitier, Sidney 1927- .... **CLC 26**
See also BW 1; CA 117; CANR 94

Polanski, Roman 1933- .... **CLC 16**
See also CA 77-80

Poliakoff, Stephen 1952- .... **CLC 38**
See also CA 106; CBD; CD; DLB 13

Police, The
See Copeland, Stewart (Armstrong); Summers, Andrew James; Sumner, Gordon Matthew

Polidori, John William 1795-1821 . **NCLC 51**
See also DLB 116; HGG

Pollitt, Katha 1949- .... **CLC 28, 122**
See also CA 120; 122; CANR 66; MTCW 1, 2

Pollock, (Mary) Sharon 1936- .... **CLC 50; DAC; DAM DRAM, MST**
See also CA 141; CD; CWD; DFS 3; DLB 60; FW

Polo, Marco 1254-1324 .... **CMLC 15**

Polonsky, Abraham (Lincoln)
1910-1999 .... **CLC 92**
See also CA 104; 187; DLB 26; INT 104

Polybius c. 200B.C.-c. 118B.C. ...... **CMLC 17**
See also AW 1; DLB 176; RGWL

Pomerance, Bernard 1940- ... **CLC 13; DAM DRAM**
See also CA 101; CAD; CANR 49; CD; DFS 9; LAIT 2

Ponge, Francis 1899-1988 . **CLC 6, 18; DAM POET**
See also CA 85-88; 126; CANR 40, 86; GFL 1789 to the Present; RGWL

Poniatowska, Elena 1933- ... **CLC 140; DAM MULT; HLC 2**
See also CA 101; CANR 32, 66; DLB 113; HW 1, 2; LAWS 1; WLIT 1

Pontoppidan, Henrik 1857-1943 .... **TCLC 29**
See also CA 170

Poole, Josephine .... **CLC 17**
See also Helyar, Jane Penelope Josephine
See also SAAS 2; SATA 5

Popa, Vasko 1922-1991 .... **CLC 19**
See also CA 112; 148; DLB 181; RGWL

Pope, Alexander 1688-1744 ...... **LC 3, 58, 60, 64; DA; DAB; DAC; DAM MST, POET; PC 26; WLC**
See also BRW 3; BRWR 1; CDBLB 1660-1789; DA3; DLB 95, 101, 213; EXPP; PAB; PFS 12; RGEL; WLIT 3; WP

Popov, Yevgeny .... **CLC 59**

Porter, Connie (Rose) 1959(?)- .... **CLC 70**
See also BW 2, 3; CA 142; CANR 90; SATA 81

Porter, Gene(va Grace) Stratton .. **TCLC 21**
See also Stratton-Porter, Gene(va Grace)
See also BPFB 3; CA 112; CWRI; RHW

Porter, Katherine Anne 1890-1980 ... **CLC 1, 3, 7, 10, 13, 15, 27, 101; DA; DAB; DAC; DAM MST, NOV; SSC 4, 31, 43**
See also AAYA 42; AITN 2; AMW; BPFB 3; CA 1-4R; 101; CANR 1, 65; CDALBS; DA3; DLB 4, 9, 102; DLBD 12; DLBY 80; EXPS; LAIT 3; MAWW; MTCW 1, 2; RGAL; RGSF; SATA 39; SATA-Obit 23; SSFS 1, 8, 11

Porter, Peter (Neville Frederick) 1929- .... **CLC 5, 13, 33**
See also CA 85-88; CP; DLB 40

Porter, William Sydney 1862-1910
See Henry, O.
See also CA 104; 131; CDALB 1865-1917; DA; DA3; DAB; DAC; DAM MST; DLB 12, 78, 79; MTCW 1, 2; YABC 2

Portillo (y Pacheco), Jose Lopez
See Lopez Portillo (y Pacheco), Jose

Portillo Trambley, Estela 1927-1998
See Trambley, Estela Portillo
See also CANR 32; DAM MULT; DLB 209; HLC 2; HW 1

Posse, Abel .... **CLC 70**

Post, Melville Davisson 1869-1930 .... **TCLC 39**
See also CA 110; CMW

Potok, Chaim 1929- ... **CLC 2, 7, 14, 26, 112; DAM NOV**
See also AAYA 15; AITN 1, 2; BPFB 3; BYA 1; CA 17-20R; CANR 19, 35, 64, 98; CN; DA3; DLB 28, 152; EXPN; INT CANR-19; LAIT 4; MTCW 1, 2; NFS 4; SATA 33, 106; YAW

Potter, Dennis (Christopher George) 1935-1994 .... **CLC 58, 86, 123**
See also CA 107; 145; CANR 33, 61; CBD; DLB 233; MTCW 1

Pound, Ezra (Weston Loomis) 1885-1972 .. **CLC 1, 2, 3, 4, 5, 7, 10, 13, 18, 34, 48, 50, 112; DA; DAB; DAC; DAM MST, POET; PC 4; WLC**
See also AMW; AMWR 1; CA 5-8R; 37-40R; CANR 40; CDALB 1917-1929; DA3; DLB 4, 45, 63; DLBD 15; EFS 2; EXPP; MTCW 1, 2; PAB; PFS 2, 8; RGAL; WP

Povod, Reinaldo 1959-1994 .... **CLC 44**
See also CA 136; 146; CANR 83

Powell, Adam Clayton, Jr. 1908-1972 .... **CLC 89; BLC 3; DAM MULT**
See also BW 1, 3; CA 102; 33-36R; CANR 86

Powell, Anthony (Dymoke) 1905-2000 .... **CLC 1, 3, 7, 9, 10, 31**
See also BRW 7; CA 1-4R; 189; CANR 1, 32, 62; CDBLB 1945-1960; CN; DLB 15; MTCW 1, 2; RGEL

Powell, Dawn 1897-1965 .... **CLC 66**
See also CA 5-8R; DLBY 97

Powell, Padgett 1952- .... **CLC 34**
See also CA 126; CANR 63, 101; CSW; DLB 234; DLBY 01

Powell, (Oval) Talmage 1920-2000
See Queen, Ellery
See also CA 5-8R; CANR 2, 80

Power, Susan 1961- .... **CLC 91**
See also BYA 14; CA 160; NFS 11

Powers, J(ames) F(arl) 1917-1999 ..... **CLC 1, 4, 8, 57; SSC 4**
See also CA 1-4R; 181; CANR 2, 61; CN; DLB 130; MTCW 1; RGAL; RGSF

Powers, John J(ames) 1945-
See Powers, John R.
See also CA 69-72

Powers, John R. .... **CLC 66**
See also Powers, John J(ames)

Powers, Richard (S.) 1957- .... **CLC 93**
See also AMWS 9; BPFB 3; CA 148; CANR 80; CN

Pownall, David 1938- .... **CLC 10**
See also CA 89-92; 180; CAAS 18; CANR 49, 101; CBD; CD; CN; DLB 14

Powys, John Cowper 1872-1963 ... **CLC 7, 9, 15, 46, 125**
See also CA 85-88; CANR 106; DLB 15, 255; FANT; MTCW 1, 2; RGEL; SUFW

Powys, T(heodore) F(rancis) 1875-1953 .... **TCLC 9**
See also CA 106; 189; DLB 36, 162; FANT; RGEL; SUFW

Prado (Calvo), Pedro 1886-1952 ... **TCLC 75**
See also CA 131; HW 1; LAW

Prager, Emily 1952- .... **CLC 56**

Pratt, E(dwin) J(ohn) 1883(?)-1964 .... **CLC 19; DAC; DAM POET**
See also CA 141; 93-96; CANR 77; DLB 92; RGEL

Premchand .... **TCLC 21**
See also Srivastava, Dhanpat Rai

Preussler, Otfried 1923- .... **CLC 17**
See also CA 77-80; SATA 24

Prevert, Jacques (Henri Marie) 1900-1977 .... **CLC 15**
See also CA 77-80; 69-72; CANR 29, 61; GFL 1789 to the Present; IDFW 3, 4; MTCW 1; RGWL; SATA-Obit 30

Prevost, (Antoine Francois) 1697-1763 .... **LC 1**
See also EW 4; GFL Beginnings to 1789; RGWL

Price, (Edward) Reynolds 1933- ... **CLC 3, 6, 13, 43, 50, 63; DAM NOV; SSC 22**
See also AMWS 6; CA 1-4R; CANR 1, 37, 57, 87; CN; CSW; DLB 2, 218; INT CANR-37

Price, Richard 1949- .... **CLC 6, 12**
See also CA 49-52; CANR 3; DLBY 81

Prichard, Katharine Susannah 1883-1969 .... **CLC 46**
See also CA 11-12; CANR 33; CAP 1; MTCW 1; RGEL; RGSF; SATA 66

Priestley, J(ohn) B(oynton) 1894-1984 ...... **CLC 2, 5, 9, 34; DAM DRAM, NOV**
See also BRW 7; CA 9-12R; 113; CANR 33; CDBLB 1914-1945; DA3; DLB 10, 34, 77, 100, 139; DLBY 84; MTCW 1, 2; RGEL; SFW

Prince 1958(?)- .... **CLC 35**

Prince, F(rank) T(empleton) 1912- .. **CLC 22**
See also CA 101; CANR 43, 79; CP; DLB 20

Prince Kropotkin
See Kropotkin, Peter (Aleksieevich)

Prior, Matthew 1664-1721 .... **LC 4**
See also DLB 95; RGEL

Prishvin, Mikhail 1873-1954 .... **TCLC 75**

Pritchard, William H(arrison) 1932- .... **CLC 34**
See also CA 65-68; CANR 23, 95; DLB 111

Pritchett, V(ictor) S(awdon) 1900-1997 ...... **CLC 5, 13, 15, 41; DAM NOV; SSC 14**
See also BPFB 3; BRWS 3; CA 61-64; 157; CANR 31, 63; CN; DA3; DLB 15, 139; MTCW 1, 2; RGEL; RGSF

Private 19022
See Manning, Frederic

Probst, Mark 1925- .... **CLC 59**
See also CA 130

Prokosch, Frederic 1908-1989 ...... **CLC 4, 48**
See also CA 73-76; 128; CANR 82; DLB 48; MTCW 2

Propertius, Sextus c. 50B.C.-c. 16B.C. .... **CMLC 32**
See also AW 2; DLB 211; RGWL

Prophet, The
See Dreiser, Theodore (Herman Albert)

Prose, Francine 1947- .... **CLC 45**
See also CA 109; 112; CANR 46, 95; DLB 234; SATA 101

Proudhon
See Cunha, Euclides (Rodrigues Pimenta) da

Proulx, Annie
See Proulx, E(dna) Annie

Proulx, E(dna) Annie 1935- .. **CLC 81; DAM POP**
See also AMWS 7; BPFB 3; CA 145; CANR 65; CN; CPW 1; DA3; MTCW 2

Proust, (Valentin-Louis-George-Eugene-)Marcel 1871-1922 . **TCLC 7, 13, 33; DA; DAB; DAC; DAM MST, NOV; WLC**
See also BPFB 3; CA 104; 120; DA3; DLB 65; EW 8; GFL 1789 to the Present; MTCW 1, 2; RGWL

Prowler, Harley
See Masters, Edgar Lee

Prus, Boleslaw 1845-1912 .... **TCLC 48**
See also RGWL

Pryor, Richard (Franklin Lenox Thomas) 1940- .... **CLC 26**
See also CA 122; 152

Przybyszewski, Stanislaw 1868-1927 .... **TCLC 36**
See also CA 160; DLB 66

Pteleon
See Grieve, C(hristopher) M(urray)
See also DAM POET

Puckett, Lute
See Masters, Edgar Lee

Puig, Manuel 1932-1990 .... **CLC 3, 5, 10, 28, 65, 133; DAM MULT; HLC 2**
See also BPFB 3; CA 45-48; CANR 2, 32, 63; DA3; DLB 113; DNFS; GLL 1; HW 1, 2; LAW; MTCW 1, 2; RGWL; WLIT 1

Pulitzer, Joseph 1847-1911 .... **TCLC 76**
See also CA 114; DLB 23

Purchas, Samuel 1577(?)-1626 .... **LC 70**
See also DLB 151

Purdy, A(lfred) W(ellington) 1918-2000 .... **CLC 3, 6, 14, 50; DAC; DAM MST, POET**
See also CA 81-84; 189; CAAS 17; CANR 42, 66; CP; DLB 88; PFS 5; RGEL

Purdy, James (Amos) 1923- .... **CLC 2, 4, 10, 28, 52**
    See also AMWS 7; CA 33-36R; CAAS 1; CANR 19, 51; CN; DLB 2, 218; INT CANR-19; MTCW 1; RGAL

Pure, Simon
    See Swinnerton, Frank Arthur

Pushkin, Aleksandr Sergeevich
    See Pushkin, Alexander (Sergeyevich)
    See also DLB 205

Pushkin, Alexander (Sergeyevich) 1799-1837 . **NCLC 3, 27, 83; DA; DAB; DAC; DAM DRAM, MST, POET; PC 10; SSC 27; WLC**
    See also DA3; EW 5; EXPS; RGSF; RGWL; SATA 61; SSFS 9

P'u Sung-ling 1640-1715 .... **LC 49; SSC 31**

Putnam, Arthur Lee
    See Alger, Horatio, Jr.

Puzo, Mario 1920-1999 .... **CLC 1, 2, 6, 36, 107; DAM NOV, POP**
    See also BPFB 3; CA 65-68; 185; CANR 4, 42, 65, 99; CN; CPW; DA3; DLB 6; MTCW 1, 2; RGAL

Pygge, Edward
    See Barnes, Julian (Patrick)

Pyle, Ernest Taylor 1900-1945
    See Pyle, Ernie
    See also CA 115; 160

Pyle, Ernie .... **TCLC 75**
    See also Pyle, Ernest Taylor
    See also DLB 29; MTCW 2

Pyle, Howard 1853-1911 .... **TCLC 81**
    See also BYA 2, 4; CA 109; 137; CLR 22; DLB 42, 188; DLBD 13; LAIT 1; MAICYA; SATA 16, 100; WCH; YAW

Pym, Barbara (Mary Crampton) 1913-1980 .... **CLC 13, 19, 37, 111**
    See also BPFB 3; BRWS 2; CA 13-14; 97-100; CANR 13, 34; CAP 1; DLB 14, 207; DLBY 87; MTCW 1, 2; RGEL

Pynchon, Thomas (Ruggles, Jr.) 1937- ...... **CLC 2, 3, 6, 9, 11, 18, 33, 62, 72, 123; DA; DAB; DAC; DAM MST, NOV, POP; SSC 14; WLC**
    See also AMWS 2; BEST 90:2; BPFB 3; CA 17-20R; CANR 22, 46, 73; CN; CPW 1; DA3; DLB 2, 173; MTCW 1, 2; RGAL; SFW; TUS

Pythagoras c. 582B.C.-c. 507B.C. . **CMLC 22**
    See also DLB 176

Q
    See Quiller-Couch, Sir Arthur (Thomas)

Qian Zhongshu
    See Ch'ien Chung-shu

Qroll
    See Dagerman, Stig (Halvard)

Quarrington, Paul (Lewis) 1953- ..... **CLC 65**
    See also CA 129; CANR 62, 95

Quasimodo, Salvatore 1901-1968 ..... **CLC 10**
    See also CA 13-16; 25-28R; CAP 1; DLB 114; EW 12; MTCW 1; RGWL

Quay, Stephen 1947- .... **CLC 95**
    See also CA 189

Quay, Timothy 1947- .... **CLC 95**
    See also CA 189

Queen, Ellery .... **CLC 3, 11**
    See also Dannay, Frederic; Davidson, Avram (James); Deming, Richard; Fairman, Paul W.; Flora, Fletcher; Hoch, Edward D(entinger); Kane, Henry; Lee, Manfred B(ennington); Marlowe, Stephen; Powell, (Oval) Talmage; Sheldon, Walter J(ames); Sturgeon, Theodore (Hamilton); Tracy, Don(ald Fiske); Vance, John Holbrook
    See also BPFB 3; CMW; MSW; RGAL

Queen, Ellery, Jr.
    See Dannay, Frederic; Lee, Manfred B(ennington)

Queneau, Raymond 1903-1976 ..... **CLC 2, 5, 10, 42**
    See also CA 77-80; 69-72; CANR 32; DLB 72; EW 12; GFL 1789 to the Present; MTCW 1, 2; RGWL

Quevedo, Francisco de 1580-1645 .... **LC 23**

Quiller-Couch, Sir Arthur (Thomas) 1863-1944 .... **TCLC 53**
    See also CA 118; 166; DLB 135, 153, 190; HGG; RGEL; SUFW

Quin, Ann (Marie) 1936-1973 .... **CLC 6**
    See also CA 9-12R; 45-48; DLB 14, 231

Quinn, Martin
    See Smith, Martin Cruz

Quinn, Peter 1947- .... **CLC 91**
    See also CA 197

Quinn, Simon
    See Smith, Martin Cruz

Quintana, Leroy V. 1944- .... **PC 36**
    See also CA 131; CANR 65; DAM MULT; DLB 82; HLC 2; HW 1, 2

Quiroga, Horacio (Sylvestre) 1878-1937 .... **TCLC 20; DAM MULT; HLC 2**
    See also CA 117; 131; HW 1; LAW; MTCW 1; RGSF; WLIT 1

Quoirez, Francoise 1935- .... **CLC 9**
    See also Sagan, Francoise
    See also CA 49-52; CANR 6, 39, 73; CWW 2; MTCW 1, 2

Raabe, Wilhelm (Karl) 1831-1910 . **TCLC 45**
    See also CA 167; DLB 129

Rabe, David (William) 1940- .. **CLC 4, 8, 33; DAM DRAM; DC 16**
    See also CA 85-88; CABS 3; CAD; CANR 59; CD; DFS 3, 8, 13; DLB 7, 228

Rabelais, Francois 1494-1553 .... **LC 5, 60; DA; DAB; DAC; DAM MST; WLC**
    See also EW 2; GFL Beginnings to 1789; RGWL

Rabinovitch, Sholem 1859-1916
    See Aleichem, Sholom
    See also CA 104

Rabinyan, Dorit 1972- .... **CLC 119**
    See also CA 170

Rachilde
    See Vallette, Marguerite Eymery

Racine, Jean 1639-1699 . **LC 28; DAB; DAM MST**
    See also DA3; EW 3; GFL Beginnings to 1789; RGWL

Radcliffe, Ann (Ward) 1764-1823 ... **NCLC 6, 55, 106**
    See also DLB 39, 178; HGG; RGEL; SUFW; WLIT 3

Radclyffe-Hall, Marguerite
    See Hall, (Marguerite) Radclyffe

Radiguet, Raymond 1903-1923 ...... **TCLC 29**
    See also CA 162; DLB 65; GFL 1789 to the Present; RGWL

Radnoti, Miklos 1909-1944 .... **TCLC 16**
    See also CA 118; DLB 215; RGWL

Rado, James 1939- .... **CLC 17**
    See also CA 105

Radvanyi, Netty 1900-1983
    See Seghers, Anna
    See also CA 85-88; 110; CANR 82

Rae, Ben
    See Griffiths, Trevor

Raeburn, John (Hay) 1941- .... **CLC 34**
    See also CA 57-60

Ragni, Gerome 1942-1991 .... **CLC 17**
    See also CA 105; 134

Rahv, Philip .... **CLC 24**
    See also Greenberg, Ivan
    See also DLB 137

Raimund, Ferdinand Jakob 1790-1836 .... **NCLC 69**
    See also DLB 90

Raine, Craig (Anthony) 1944- .. **CLC 32, 103**
    See also CA 108; CANR 29, 51, 103; CP; DLB 40; PFS 7

Raine, Kathleen (Jessie) 1908- ..... **CLC 7, 45**
    See also CA 85-88; CANR 46; CP; DLB 20; MTCW 1; RGEL

Rainis, Janis 1865-1929 .... **TCLC 29**
    See also CA 170; DLB 220

Rakosi, Carl .... **CLC 47**
    See also Rawley, Callman
    See also CAAS 5; CP; DLB 193

Ralegh, Sir Walter
    See Raleigh, Sir Walter
    See also BRW 1; RGEL; WP

Raleigh, Richard
    See Lovecraft, H(oward) P(hillips)

Raleigh, Sir Walter 1554(?)-1618 .... **LC 31, 39; PC 31**
    See also Ralegh, Sir Walter
    See also CDBLB Before 1660; DLB 172; EXPP; PFS 14; TEA

Rallentando, H. P.
    See Sayers, Dorothy L(eigh)

Ramal, Walter
    See de la Mare, Walter (John)

Ramana Maharshi 1879-1950 .... **TCLC 84**

Ramoacn y Cajal, Santiago 1852-1934 .... **TCLC 93**

Ramon, Juan
    See Jimenez (Mantecon), Juan Ramon

Ramos, Graciliano 1892-1953 .... **TCLC 32**
    See also CA 167; HW 2; LAW; WLIT 1

Rampersad, Arnold 1941- .... **CLC 44**
    See also BW 2, 3; CA 127; 133; CANR 81; DLB 111; INT 133

Rampling, Anne
    See Rice, Anne
    See also GLL 2

Ramsay, Allan 1686(?)-1758 .... **LC 29**
    See also DLB 95; RGEL

Ramsay, Jay
    See Campbell, (John) Ramsey

Ramuz, Charles-Ferdinand 1878-1947 .... **TCLC 33**
    See also CA 165

Rand, Ayn 1905-1982 ...... **CLC 3, 30, 44, 79; DA; DAC; DAM MST, NOV, POP; WLC**
    See also AAYA 10; AMWS 4; BPFB 3; BYA 12; CA 13-16R; 105; CANR 27, 73; CDALBS; CPW; DA3; DLB 227; MTCW 1, 2; NFS 10; RGAL; SFW; YAW

Randall, Dudley (Felker) 1914-2000 . **CLC 1, 135; BLC 3; DAM MULT**
    See also BW 1, 3; CA 25-28R; 189; CANR 23, 82; DLB 41; PFS 5

Randall, Robert
    See Silverberg, Robert

Ranger, Ken
    See Creasey, John

Rank, Otto 1884-1939 .... **TCLC 115**

Ransom, John Crowe 1888-1974 .. **CLC 2, 4, 5, 11, 24; DAM POET**
    See also AMW; CA 5-8R; 49-52; CANR 6, 34; CDALBS; DA3; DLB 45, 63; EXPP; MTCW 1, 2; RGAL

Rao, Raja 1909- ..... **CLC 25, 56; DAM NOV**
    See also CA 73-76; CANR 51; CN; MTCW 1, 2; RGEL; RGSF

Raphael, Frederic (Michael) 1931- ... **CLC 2, 14**
    See also CA 1-4R; CANR 1, 86; CN; DLB 14

Ratcliffe, James P.
    See Mencken, H(enry) L(ouis)

Rathbone, Julian 1935- .... CLC 41
See also CA 101; CANR 34, 73
Rattigan, Terence (Mervyn)
    1911-1977 .... CLC 7; DAM DRAM
See also BRWS 7; CA 85-88; 73-76; CBD;
    CDBLB 1945-1960; DFS 8; DLB 13;
    IDFW 3, 4; MTCW 1, 2; RGEL
Ratushinskaya, Irina 1954- .... CLC 54
See also CA 129; CANR 68; CWW 2
Raven, Simon (Arthur Noel)
    1927-2001 .... CLC 14
See also CA 81-84; 197; CANR 86; CN
Ravenna, Michael
See Welty, Eudora
Rawley, Callman 1903-
See Rakosi, Carl
See also CA 21-24R; CANR 12, 32, 91
Rawlings, Marjorie Kinnan
    1896-1953 .... TCLC 4
See also AAYA 20; AMWS 10; ANW;
    BPFB 3; BYA 3; CA 104; 137; CANR 74;
    CLR 63; DLB 9, 22, 102; DLBD 17;
    JRDA; MAICYA; MTCW 2; RGEL;
    SATA 100; WCH; YABC 1; YAW
Ray, Satyajit 1921-1992 .. CLC 16, 76; DAM
    MULT
See also CA 114; 137
Read, Herbert Edward 1893-1968 ..... CLC 4
See also BRW 6; CA 85-88; 25-28R; DLB
    20, 149; PAB; RGEL
Read, Piers Paul 1941- .... CLC 4, 10, 25
See also CA 21-24R; CANR 38, 86; CN;
    DLB 14; SATA 21
Reade, Charles 1814-1884 .... NCLC 2, 74
See also DLB 21; RGEL
Reade, Hamish
See Gray, Simon (James Holliday)
Reading, Peter 1946- .... CLC 47
See also CA 103; CANR 46, 96; CP; DLB
    40
Reaney, James 1926- .. CLC 13; DAC; DAM
    MST
See also CA 41-44R; CAAS 15; CANR 42;
    CD; CP; DLB 68; RGEL; SATA 43
Rebreanu, Liviu 1885-1944 .... TCLC 28
See also CA 165; DLB 220
Rechy, John (Francisco) 1934- ...... CLC 1, 7,
    14, 18, 107; DAM MULT; HLC 2
See also CA 5-8R; CAAE 195; CAAS 4;
    CANR 6, 32, 64; CN; DLB 122; DLBY
    82; HW 1, 2; INT CANR-6; RGAL
Redcam, Tom 1870-1933 .... TCLC 25
Reddin, Keith .... CLC 67
See also CAD
Redgrove, Peter (William) 1932- . CLC 6, 41
See also BRWS 6; CA 1-4R; CANR 3, 39,
    77; CP; DLB 40
Redmon, Anne .... CLC 22
See also Nightingale, Anne Redmon
See also DLBY 86
Reed, Eliot
See Ambler, Eric
Reed, Ishmael 1938- .. CLC 2, 3, 5, 6, 13, 32,
    60; BLC 3; DAM MULT
See also AFAW 1, 2; AMWS 10; BPFB 3;
    BW 2, 3; CA 21-24R; CANR 25, 48, 74;
    CN; CP; CSW; DA3; DLB 2, 5, 33, 169,
    227; DLBD 8; MSW; MTCW 1, 2; PFS
    6; RGAL; TCWW 2
Reed, John (Silas) 1887-1920 .... TCLC 9
See also CA 106; 195
Reed, Lou .... CLC 21
See also Firbank, Louis
Reese, Lizette Woodworth 1856-1935 . PC 29
See also CA 180; DLB 54
Reeve, Clara 1729-1807 .... NCLC 19
See also DLB 39; RGEL

Reich, Wilhelm 1897-1957 .... TCLC 57
Reid, Christopher (John) 1949- .... CLC 33
See also CA 140; CANR 89; CP; DLB 40
Reid, Desmond
See Moorcock, Michael (John)
Reid Banks, Lynne 1929-
See Banks, Lynne Reid
See also CA 1-4R; CANR 6, 22, 38, 87;
    CLR 24; CN; JRDA; MAICYA; SATA 22,
    75, 111; YAW
Reilly, William K.
See Creasey, John
Reiner, Max
See Caldwell, (Janet Miriam) Taylor
    (Holland)
Reis, Ricardo
See Pessoa, Fernando (Antonio Nogueira)
Remarque, Erich Maria
    1898-1970 ... CLC 21; DA; DAB; DAC;
    DAM MST, NOV
See also AAYA 27; BPFB 3; CA 77-80; 29-
    32R; DA3; DLB 56; EXPN; LAIT 3;
    MTCW 1, 2; NFS 4; RGWL
Remington, Frederic 1861-1909 ..... TCLC 89
See also CA 108; 169; DLB 12, 186, 188;
    SATA 41
Remizov, A.
See Remizov, Aleksei (Mikhailovich)
Remizov, A. M.
See Remizov, Aleksei (Mikhailovich)
Remizov, Aleksei (Mikhailovich)
    1877-1957 .... TCLC 27
See also CA 125; 133
Renan, Joseph Ernest 1823-1892 .. NCLC 26
See also GFL 1789 to the Present
Renard, Jules 1864-1910 .... TCLC 17
See also CA 117; GFL 1789 to the Present
Renault, Mary .... CLC 3, 11, 17
See also Challans, Mary
See also BPFB 3; BYA 2; DLBY 83; GLL
    1; LAIT 1; MTCW 2; RGEL; RHW
Rendell, Ruth (Barbara) 1930- . CLC 28, 48;
    DAM POP
See also Vine, Barbara
See also BPFB 3; CA 109; CANR 32, 52,
    74; CN; CPW; DLB 87; INT CANR-32;
    MSW; MTCW 1, 2
Renoir, Jean 1894-1979 .... CLC 20
See also CA 129; 85-88
Resnais, Alain 1922- .... CLC 16
Reverdy, Pierre 1889-1960 .... CLC 53
See also CA 97-100; 89-92; GFL 1789 to
    the Present
Rexroth, Kenneth 1905-1982 .... CLC 1, 2, 6,
    11, 22, 49, 112; DAM POET; PC 20
See also CA 5-8R; 107; CANR 14, 34, 63;
    CDALB 1941-1968; DLB 16, 48, 165,
    212; DLBY 82; INT CANR-14; MTCW
    1, 2; RGAL
Reyes, Alfonso 1889-1959 .. TCLC 33; HLCS
    2
See also CA 131; HW 1; LAW
Reyes y Basoalto, Ricardo Eliecer Neftali
See Neruda, Pablo
Reymont, Wladyslaw (Stanislaw)
    1868(?)-1925 .... TCLC 5
See also CA 104
Reynolds, Jonathan 1942- .... CLC 6, 38
See also CA 65-68; CANR 28
Reynolds, Joshua 1723-1792 .... LC 15
See also DLB 104
Reynolds, Michael S(hane)
    1937-2000 .... CLC 44
See also CA 65-68; 189; CANR 9, 89, 97
Reznikoff, Charles 1894-1976 .... CLC 9
See also CA 33-36; 61-64; CAP 2; DLB 28,
    45; WP

Rezzori (d'Arezzo), Gregor von
    1914-1998 .... CLC 25
See also CA 122; 136; 167
Rhine, Richard
See Silverstein, Alvin; Silverstein, Virginia
    B(arbara Opshelor)
Rhodes, Eugene Manlove
    1869-1934 .... TCLC 53
See also DLB 256
R'hoone
See Balzac, Honore de
Rhys, Jean 1894(?)-1979 ...... CLC 2, 4, 6, 14,
    19, 51, 124; DAM NOV; SSC 21
See also BRWS 2; CA 25-28R; 85-88;
    CANR 35, 62; CDBLB 1945-1960; DA3;
    DLB 36, 117, 162; DNFS; MTCW 1, 2;
    RGEL; RGSF
Ribeiro, Darcy 1922-1997 .... CLC 34
See also CA 33-36R; 156
Ribeiro, Joao Ubaldo (Osorio Pimentel)
    1941- .... CLC 10, 67
See also CA 81-84
Ribman, Ronald (Burt) 1932- .... CLC 7
See also CA 21-24R; CAD; CANR 46, 80;
    CD
Ricci, Nino 1959- .... CLC 70
See also CA 137; CCA 1
Rice, Anne 1941- .. CLC 41, 128; DAM POP
See also Rampling, Anne
See also AAYA 9; AMWS 7; BEST 89:2;
    BPFB 3; CA 65-68; CANR 12, 36, 53,
    74, 100; CN; CPW; CSW; DA3; GLL 2;
    HGG; MTCW 2; YAW
Rice, Elmer (Leopold) 1892-1967 ...... CLC 7,
    49; DAM DRAM
See also CA 21-22; 25-28R; CAP 2; DFS
    12; DLB 4, 7; MTCW 1, 2; RGAL
Rice, Tim(othy Miles Bindon)
    1944- .... CLC 21
See also CA 103; CANR 46; DFS 7
Rich, Adrienne (Cecile) 1929- ... CLC 3, 6, 7,
    11, 18, 36, 73, 76, 125; DAM POET;
    PC 5
See also AMWS 1; CA 9-12R; CANR 20,
    53, 74; CDALBS; CP; CSW; CWP; DA3;
    DLB 5, 67; EXPP; FW; MAWW; MTCW
    1, 2; PAB; RGAL; WP
Rich, Barbara
See Graves, Robert (von Ranke)
Rich, Robert
See Trumbo, Dalton
Richard, Keith .... CLC 17
See also Richards, Keith
Richards, David Adams 1950- .... CLC 59;
    DAC
See also CA 93-96; CANR 60; DLB 53
Richards, I(vor) A(rmstrong)
    1893-1979 .... CLC 14, 24
See also BRWS 2; CA 41-44R; 89-92;
    CANR 34, 74; DLB 27; MTCW 2; RGEL
Richards, Keith 1943-
See Richard, Keith
See also CA 107; CANR 77
Richardson, Anne
See Roiphe, Anne (Richardson)
Richardson, Dorothy Miller
    1873-1957 .... TCLC 3
See also CA 104; 192; DLB 36; FW; RGEL
Richardson (Robertson), Ethel Florence
    Lindesay 1870-1946
See Richardson, Henry Handel
See also CA 105; 190; DLB 230; RHW
Richardson, Henry Handel .... TCLC 4
See also Richardson (Robertson), Ethel Flo-
    rence Lindesay
See also DLB 197; RGEL; RGSF
Richardson, John 1796-1852 .... NCLC 55;
    DAC
See also CCA 1; DLB 99

Richardson, Samuel 1689-1761 ...... **LC 1, 44;
DA; DAB; DAC; DAM MST, NOV;
WLC**
See also BRW 3; CDBLB 1660-1789; DLB
39; RGEL; WLIT 3

Richler, Mordecai 1931-2001 .... **CLC 3, 5, 9,
13, 18, 46, 70; DAC; DAM MST, NOV**
See also AITN 1; CA 65-68; CANR 31, 62;
CCA 1; CLR 17; CWRI; DLB 53; MAI-
CYA; MTCW 1, 2; RGEL; SATA 44, 98;
SATA-Brief 27

Richter, Conrad (Michael)
1890-1968 .... **CLC 30**
See also AAYA 21; BYA 2; CA 5-8R; 25-
28R; CANR 23; DLB 9, 212; LAIT 1;
MTCW 1, 2; RGAL; SATA 3; TCWW 2;
YAW

Ricostranza, Tom
See Ellis, Trey

Riddell, Charlotte 1832-1906 .... **TCLC 40**
See also Riddell, Mrs. J. H.
See also CA 165; DLB 156

Riddell, Mrs. J. H.
See Riddell, Charlotte
See also HGG; SUFW

Ridge, John Rollin 1827-1867 ...... **NCLC 82;
DAM MULT**
See also CA 144; DLB 175; NNAL

Ridgeway, Jason
See Marlowe, Stephen

Ridgway, Keith 1965- .... **CLC 119**
See also CA 172

Riding, Laura .... **CLC 3, 7**
See also Jackson, Laura (Riding)
See also RGAL

Riefenstahl, Berta Helene Amalia 1902-
See Riefenstahl, Leni
See also CA 108

Riefenstahl, Leni .... **CLC 16**
See also Riefenstahl, Berta Helene Amalia

Riffe, Ernest
See Bergman, (Ernst) Ingmar

Riggs, (Rolla) Lynn 1899-1954 ..... **TCLC 56;
DAM MULT**
See also CA 144; DLB 175; NNAL

Riis, Jacob A(ugust) 1849-1914 ..... **TCLC 80**
See also CA 113; 168; DLB 23

Riley, James Whitcomb
1849-1916 .... **TCLC 51; DAM POET**
See also CA 118; 137; MAICYA; RGAL;
SATA 17

Riley, Tex
See Creasey, John

Rilke, Rainer Maria 1875-1926 .. **TCLC 1, 6,
19; DAM POET; PC 2**
See also CA 104; 132; CANR 62, 99; DA3;
DLB 81; EW 9; MTCW 1, 2; RGWL; WP

Rimbaud, (Jean Nicolas) Arthur
1854-1891 . **NCLC 4, 35, 82; DA; DAB;
DAC; DAM MST, POET; PC 3; WLC**
See also DA3; DLB 217; EW 7; GFL 1789
to the Present; RGWL; TWA; WP

Rinehart, Mary Roberts
1876-1958 .... **TCLC 52**
See also BPFB 3; CA 108; 166; RGAL;
RHW

Ringmaster, The
See Mencken, H(enry) L(ouis)

Ringwood, Gwen(dolyn Margaret) Pharis
1910-1984 .... **CLC 48**
See also CA 148; 112; DLB 88

Rio, Michel 19(?)- .... **CLC 43**

Ritsos, Giannes
See Ritsos, Yannis

Ritsos, Yannis 1909-1990 .... **CLC 6, 13, 31**
See also CA 77-80; 133; CANR 39, 61; EW
12; MTCW 1; RGWL

Ritter, Erika 1948(?)- .... **CLC 52**
See also CD; CWD

Rivera, Jose Eustasio 1889-1928 ... **TCLC 35**
See also CA 162; HW 1, 2; LAW

Rivera, Tomas 1935-1984
See also CA 49-52; CANR 32; DLB 82;
HLCS 2; HW 1; RGAL; TCWW 2; WLIT
1

Rivers, Conrad Kent 1933-1968 .... **CLC 1**
See also BW 1; CA 85-88; DLB 41

Rivers, Elfrida
See Bradley, Marion Zimmer
See also GLL 1

Riverside, John
See Heinlein, Robert A(nson)

Rizal, Jose 1861-1896 .... **NCLC 27**

Roa Bastos, Augusto (Antonio)
1917- .... **CLC 45; DAM MULT; HLC 2**
See also CA 131; DLB 113; HW 1; LAW;
RGSF; WLIT 1

Robbe-Grillet, Alain 1922- .... **CLC 1, 2, 4, 6,
8, 10, 14, 43, 128**
See also BPFB 3; CA 9-12R; CANR 33,
65; DLB 83; EW 13; GFL 1789 to the
Present; IDFW 3, 4; MTCW 1, 2; RGWL

Robbins, Harold 1916-1997 .... **CLC 5; DAM
NOV**
See also BPFB 3; CA 73-76; 162; CANR
26, 54; DA3; MTCW 1, 2

Robbins, Thomas Eugene 1936-
See Robbins, Tom
See also CA 81-84; CANR 29, 59, 95; CN;
CPW; CSW; DA3; DAM NOV, POP;
MTCW 1, 2

Robbins, Tom .... **CLC 9, 32, 64**
See also Robbins, Thomas Eugene
See also AAYA 32; AMWS 10; BEST 90:3;
BPFB 3; DLBY 80; MTCW 2

Robbins, Trina 1938- .... **CLC 21**
See also CA 128

Roberts, Charles G(eorge) D(ouglas)
1860-1943 .... **TCLC 8**
See also CA 105; 188; CLR 33; CWRI;
DLB 92; RGEL; RGSF; SATA 88; SATA-
Brief 29

Roberts, Elizabeth Madox
1886-1941 .... **TCLC 68**
See also CA 111; 166; CWRI; DLB 9, 54,
102; RGAL; RHW; SATA 33; SATA-Brief
27; WCH

Roberts, Kate 1891-1985 .... **CLC 15**
See also CA 107; 116

Roberts, Keith (John Kingston)
1935-2000 .... **CLC 14**
See also CA 25-28R; CANR 46; SFW

Roberts, Kenneth (Lewis)
1885-1957 .... **TCLC 23**
See also CA 109; DLB 9; RGAL; RHW

Roberts, Michele (Brigitte) 1949- ..... **CLC 48**
See also CA 115; CANR 58; CN; DLB 231;
FW

Robertson, Ellis
See Ellison, Harlan (Jay); Silverberg, Robert

Robertson, Thomas William
1829-1871 .... **NCLC 35; DAM DRAM**
See also Robertson, Tom

Robertson, Tom
See Robertson, Thomas William
See also RGEL

Robeson, Kenneth
See Dent, Lester

Robinson, Edwin Arlington
1869-1935 ..... **TCLC 5, 101; DA; DAC;
DAM MST, POET; PC 1, 35**
See also AMW; CA 104; 133; CDALB
1865-1917; DLB 54; EXPP; MTCW 1, 2;
PAB; PFS 4; RGAL; WP

Robinson, Henry Crabb
1775-1867 .... **NCLC 15**
See also DLB 107

Robinson, Jill 1936- .... **CLC 10**
See also CA 102; INT 102

Robinson, Kim Stanley 1952- .... **CLC 34**
See also AAYA 26; CA 126; CN; SATA 109;
SCFW 2; SFW

Robinson, Lloyd
See Silverberg, Robert

Robinson, Marilynne 1944- .... **CLC 25**
See also CA 116; CANR 80; CN; DLB 206

Robinson, Smokey .... **CLC 21**
See also Robinson, William, Jr.

Robinson, William, Jr. 1940-
See Robinson, Smokey
See also CA 116

Robison, Mary 1949- .... **CLC 42, 98**
See also CA 113; 116; CANR 87; CN; DLB
130; INT 116; RGSF

Rochester, Earl of 1647-1680 .... **LC 75**
See also Wilmot, John
See also RGEL

Rod, Edouard 1857-1910 .... **TCLC 52**

Roddenberry, Eugene Wesley 1921-1991
See Roddenberry, Gene
See also CA 110; 135; CANR 37; SATA 45;
SATA-Obit 69

Roddenberry, Gene .... **CLC 17**
See also Roddenberry, Eugene Wesley
See also AAYA 5; SATA-Obit 69

Rodgers, Mary 1931- .... **CLC 12**
See also BYA 5; CA 49-52; CANR 8, 55,
90; CLR 20; CWRI; INT CANR-8; JRDA;
MAICYA; SATA 8

Rodgers, W(illiam) R(obert)
1909-1969 .... **CLC 7**
See also CA 85-88; DLB 20; RGEL

Rodman, Eric
See Silverberg, Robert

Rodman, Howard 1920(?)-1985 .... **CLC 65**
See also CA 118

Rodman, Maia
See Wojciechowska, Maia (Teresa)

Rodo, Jose Enrique 1871(?)-1917
See also CA 178; HLCS 2; HW 2; LAW

Rodolph, Utto
See Ouologuem, Yambo

Rodriguez, Claudio 1934-1999 .... **CLC 10**
See also CA 188; DLB 134

Rodriguez, Richard 1944- ... **CLC 155; DAM
MULT; HLC 2**
See also CA 110; CANR 66; DLB 82, 256;
HW 1, 2; LAIT 5; WLIT 1

Roelvaag, O(le) E(dvart) 1876-1931
See Rolvaag, O(le) E(dvart)
See also CA 117; 171

Roethke, Theodore (Huebner)
1908-1963 .... **CLC 1, 3, 8, 11, 19, 46,
101; DAM POET; PC 15**
See also AMW; CA 81-84; CABS 2;
CDALB 1941-1968; DA3; DLB 5, 206;
EXPP; MTCW 1, 2; PAB; PFS 3; RGAL;
WP

Rogers, Samuel 1763-1855 .... **NCLC 69**
See also DLB 93; RGEL

Rogers, Thomas Hunton 1927- .... **CLC 57**
See also CA 89-92; INT 89-92

Rogers, Will(iam Penn Adair)
1879-1935 ... **TCLC 8, 71; DAM MULT**
See also CA 105; 144; DA3; DLB 11;
MTCW 2; NNAL

Rogin, Gilbert 1929- .... **CLC 18**
See also CA 65-68; CANR 15

Rohan, Koda
See Koda Shigeyuki

Rohlfs, Anna Katharine Green
See Green, Anna Katharine

Rohmer, Eric .... **CLC 16**
See also Scherer, Jean-Marie Maurice

Rohmer, Sax .... **TCLC 28**
See also Ward, Arthur Henry Sarsfield
See also DLB 70; MSW; SUFW

Roiphe, Anne (Richardson) 1935- .. **CLC 3, 9**
See also CA 89-92; CANR 45, 73; DLBY
80; INT 89-92

Rojas, Fernando de 1475-1541 .... **LC 23;**
HLCS 1
See also RGWL

Rojas, Gonzalo 1917-
See also CA 178; HLCS 2; HW 2; LAWS 1

Rolfe, Frederick (William Serafino Austin
Lewis Mary) 1860-1913 .... **TCLC 12**
See also Corvo, Baron
See also CA 107; DLB 34, 156; RGEL

Rolland, Romain 1866-1944 .... **TCLC 23**
See also CA 118; 197; DLB 65; GFL 1789
to the Present; RGWL

Rolle, Richard c. 1300-c. 1349 ...... **CMLC 21**
See also DLB 146; RGEL

Rolvaag, O(le) E(dvart) .... **TCLC 17**
See also Roelvaag, O(le) E(dvart)
See also DLB 9, 212; NFS 5; RGAL

Romain Arnaud, Saint
See Aragon, Louis

Romains, Jules 1885-1972 .... **CLC 7**
See also CA 85-88; CANR 34; DLB 65;
GFL 1789 to the Present; MTCW 1

Romero, Jose Ruben 1890-1952 .... **TCLC 14**
See also CA 114; 131; HW 1; LAW

Ronsard, Pierre de 1524-1585 . **LC 6, 54; PC**
11
See also EW 2; GFL Beginnings to 1789;
RGWL

Rooke, Leon 1934- . **CLC 25, 34; DAM POP**
See also CA 25-28R; CANR 23, 53; CCA
1; CPW

Roosevelt, Franklin Delano
1882-1945 .... **TCLC 93**
See also CA 116; 173; LAIT 3

Roosevelt, Theodore 1858-1919 ..... **TCLC 69**
See also CA 115; 170; DLB 47, 186

Roper, William 1498-1578 .... **LC 10**

Roquelaure, A. N.
See Rice, Anne

Rosa, Joao Guimaraes 1908-1967 ... **CLC 23;**
HLCS 1
See also Guimaraes Rosa, Joao
See also CA 89-92; DLB 113; WLIT 1

Rose, Wendy 1948- .. **CLC 85; DAM MULT;**
PC 13
See also CA 53-56; CANR 5, 51; CWP;
DLB 175; NNAL; PFS 13; RGAL; SATA
12

Rosen, R. D.
See Rosen, Richard (Dean)

Rosen, Richard (Dean) 1949- .... **CLC 39**
See also CA 77-80; CANR 62; CMW; INT
CANR-30

Rosenberg, Isaac 1890-1918 .... **TCLC 12**
See also BRW 6; CA 107; 188; DLB 20,
216; PAB; RGEL

Rosenblatt, Joe .... **CLC 15**
See also Rosenblatt, Joseph

Rosenblatt, Joseph 1933-
See Rosenblatt, Joe
See also CA 89-92; CP; INT 89-92

Rosenfeld, Samuel
See Tzara, Tristan

Rosenstock, Sami
See Tzara, Tristan

Rosenstock, Samuel
See Tzara, Tristan

Rosenthal, M(acha) L(ouis)
1917-1996 .... **CLC 28**
See also CA 1-4R; 152; CAAS 6; CANR 4,
51; CP; DLB 5; SATA 59

Ross, Barnaby
See Dannay, Frederic

Ross, Bernard L.
See Follett, Ken(neth Martin)

Ross, J. H.
See Lawrence, T(homas) E(dward)

Ross, John Hume
See Lawrence, T(homas) E(dward)

Ross, Martin 1862-1915
See Martin, Violet Florence
See also DLB 135; GLL 2; RGEL; RGSF

Ross, (James) Sinclair 1908-1996 ... **CLC 13;**
DAC; DAM MST; SSC 24
See also CA 73-76; CANR 81; CN; DLB
88; RGEL; RGSF; TCWW 2

Rossetti, Christina (Georgina)
1830-1894 . **NCLC 2, 50, 66; DA; DAB;**
DAC; DAM MST, POET; PC 7; WLC
See also BRW 5; BYA 4; DA3; DLB 35,
163, 240; EXPP; MAICYA; PFS 10, 14;
RGEL; SATA 20; WCH

Rossetti, Dante Gabriel 1828-1882 . **NCLC 4,**
77; DA; DAB; DAC; DAM MST,
POET; WLC
See also BRW 5; CDBLB 1832-1890; DLB
35; EXPP; RGEL

Rossi, Cristina Peri
See Peri Rossi, Cristina

Rossner, Judith (Perelman) 1935- . **CLC 6, 9,**
29
See also AITN 2; BEST 90:3; BPFB 3; CA
17-20R; CANR 18, 51, 73; CN; DLB 6;
INT CANR-18; MTCW 1, 2

Rostand, Edmond (Eugene Alexis)
1868-1918 .... **TCLC 6, 37; DA; DAB;**
DAC; DAM DRAM, MST; DC 10
See also CA 104; 126; DA3; DFS 1; DLB
192; LAIT 1; MTCW 1; RGWL

Roth, Henry 1906-1995 ..... **CLC 2, 6, 11, 104**
See also AMWS 9; CA 11-12; 149; CANR
38, 63; CAP 1; CN; DA3; DLB 28;
MTCW 1, 2; RGAL

Roth, (Moses) Joseph 1894-1939 ... **TCLC 33**
See also CA 160; DLB 85; RGWL

Roth, Philip (Milton) 1933- ... **CLC 1, 2, 3, 4,**
6, 9, 15, 22, 31, 47, 66, 86, 119; DA;
DAB; DAC; DAM MST, NOV, POP;
SSC 26; WLC
See also AMWS 3; BEST 90:3; BPFB 3;
CA 1-4R; CANR 1, 22, 36, 55, 89;
CDALB 1968-1988; CN; CPW 1; DA3;
DLB 2, 28, 173; DLBY 82; MTCW 1, 2;
RGAL; RGSF; SSFS 12

Rothenberg, Jerome 1931- .... **CLC 6, 57**
See also CA 45-48; CANR 1, 106; CP; DLB
5, 193

Rotter, Pat ed. .... **CLC 65**

Roumain, Jacques (Jean Baptiste)
1907-1944 ...... **TCLC 19; BLC 3; DAM**
MULT
See also BW 1; CA 117; 125

Rourke, Constance (Mayfield)
1885-1941 .... **TCLC 12**
See also CA 107; YABC 1

Rousseau, Jean-Baptiste 1671-1741 ...... **LC 9**

Rousseau, Jean-Jacques 1712-1778 ... **LC 14,**
36; DA; DAB; DAC; DAM MST; WLC
See also DA3; EW 4; GFL Beginnings to
1789; RGWL

Roussel, Raymond 1877-1933 .... **TCLC 20**
See also CA 117; GFL 1789 to the Present

Rovit, Earl (Herbert) 1927- .... **CLC 7**
See also CA 5-8R; CANR 12

Rowe, Elizabeth Singer 1674-1737 ..... **LC 44**
See also DLB 39, 95

Rowe, Nicholas 1674-1718 .... **LC 8**
See also DLB 84; RGEL

Rowlandson, Mary 1637(?)-1678 .... **LC 66**
See also DLB 24, 200; RGAL

Rowley, Ames Dorrance
See Lovecraft, H(oward) P(hillips)

Rowling, J(oanne) K(athleen)
1966(?)- .... **CLC 137**
See also AAYA 34; BYA 13, 14; CA 173;
CLR 66; SATA 109

Rowson, Susanna Haswell
1762(?)-1824 .... **NCLC 5, 69**
See also DLB 37, 200; RGAL

Roy, Arundhati 1960(?)- .... **CLC 109**
See also CA 163; CANR 90; DLBY 97

Roy, Gabrielle 1909-1983 .... **CLC 10, 14;**
DAB; DAC; DAM MST
See also CA 53-56; 110; CANR 5, 61; CCA
1; DLB 68; MTCW 1; RGWL; SATA 104

Royko, Mike 1932-1997 .... **CLC 109**
See also CA 89-92; 157; CANR 26; CPW

Rozanov, Vassili 1856-1919 .... **TCLC 104**

Rozewicz, Tadeusz 1921- ..... **CLC 9, 23, 139;**
DAM POET
See also CA 108; CANR 36, 66; CWW 2;
DA3; DLB 232; MTCW 1, 2

Ruark, Gibbons 1941- .... **CLC 3**
See also CA 33-36R; CAAS 23; CANR 14,
31, 57; DLB 120

Rubens, Bernice (Ruth) 1923- .... **CLC 19, 31**
See also CA 25-28R; CANR 33, 65; CN;
DLB 14, 207; MTCW 1

Rubin, Harold
See Robbins, Harold

Rudkin, (James) David 1936- .... **CLC 14**
See also CA 89-92; CBD; CD; DLB 13

Rudnik, Raphael 1933- .... **CLC 7**
See also CA 29-32R

Ruffian, M.
See Hasek, Jaroslav (Matej Frantisek)

Ruiz, Jose Martinez .... **CLC 11**
See also Martinez Ruiz, Jose

Rukeyser, Muriel 1913-1980 . **CLC 6, 10, 15,**
27; DAM POET; PC 12
See also AMWS 6; CA 5-8R; 93-96; CANR
26, 60; DA3; DLB 48; FW; GLL 2;
MTCW 1, 2; PFS 10; RGAL; SATA-Obit
22

Rule, Jane (Vance) 1931- .... **CLC 27**
See also CA 25-28R; CAAS 18; CANR 12,
87; CN; DLB 60; FW

Rulfo, Juan 1918-1986 ...... **CLC 8, 80; DAM**
MULT; HLC 2; SSC 25
See also CA 85-88; 118; CANR 26; DLB
113; HW 1, 2; LAW; MTCW 1, 2; RGSF;
RGWL; WLIT 1

Rumi, Jalal al-Din 1207-1273 .... **CMLC 20**
See also RGWL; WP

Runeberg, Johan 1804-1877 .... **NCLC 41**

Runyon, (Alfred) Damon
1884(?)-1946 .... **TCLC 10**
See also CA 107; 165; DLB 11, 86, 171;
MTCW 2; RGAL

Rush, Norman 1933- .... **CLC 44**
See also CA 121; 126; INT 126

Rushdie, (Ahmed) Salman 1947- .... **CLC 23,**
31, 55, 100; DAB; DAC; DAM MST,
NOV, POP; WLCS
See also BEST 89:3; BPFB 3; BRWS 4;
CA 108; 111; CANR 33, 56; CN; CPW 1;
DA3; DLB 194; FANT; INT CA-111;
MTCW 1, 2; RGEL; RGSF; WLIT 4

Rushforth, Peter (Scott) 1945- .... **CLC 19**
See also CA 101

Ruskin, John 1819-1900 .... **TCLC 63**
See also BRW 5; BYA 5; CA 114; 129; CD-
BLB 1832-1890; DLB 55, 163, 190;
RGEL; SATA 24; WCH

Russ, Joanna 1937- .... **CLC 15**
See also BPFB 3; CA 5-28R; CANR 11,
31, 65; CN; DLB 8; FW; GLL 1; MTCW
1; SCFW 2; SFW

Russell, George William 1867-1935
See A.E.; Baker, Jean H.
See also CA 104; 153; CDBLB 1890-1914;
DAM POET; RGEL

Russell, Jeffrey Burton 1934- .... **CLC 70**
See also CA 25-28R; CANR 11, 28, 52

Russell, (Henry) Ken(neth Alfred)
1927- .... **CLC 16**
See also CA 105

Russell, William Martin 1947- .... **CLC 60**
See also CA 164; DLB 233

Rutherford, Mark .... **TCLC 25**
See also White, William Hale
See also DLB 18; RGEL

Ruyslinck, Ward .... **CLC 14**
See also Belser, Reimond Karel Maria de

Ryan, Cornelius (John) 1920-1974 ..... **CLC 7**
See also CA 69-72; 53-56; CANR 38

Ryan, Michael 1946- .... **CLC 65**
See also CA 49-52; DLBY 82

Ryan, Tim
See Dent, Lester

Rybakov, Anatoli (Naumovich)
1911-1998 .... **CLC 23, 53**
See also CA 126; 135; 172; SATA 79;
SATA-Obit 108

Ryder, Jonathan
See Ludlum, Robert

Ryga, George 1932-1987 .... **CLC 14; DAC;**
DAM MST
See also CA 101; 124; CANR 43, 90; CCA
1; DLB 60

S. H.
See Hartmann, Sadakichi

S. S.
See Sassoon, Siegfried (Lorraine)

Saba, Umberto 1883-1957 .... **TCLC 33**
See also CA 144; CANR 79; DLB 114;
RGWL

Sabatini, Rafael 1875-1950 .... **TCLC 47**
See also BPFB 3; CA 162; RHW

Sabato, Ernesto (R.) 1911- .... **CLC 10, 23;**
DAM MULT; HLC 2
See also CA 97-100; CANR 32, 65; DLB
145; HW 1, 2; LAW; MTCW 1, 2

Sa-Carneiro, Mario de 1890-1916 . **TCLC 83**

Sacastru, Martin
See Bioy Casares, Adolfo
See also CWW 2

Sacastru, Martin
See Bioy Casares, Adolfo

Sacher-Masoch, Leopold von
1836(?)-1895 .... **NCLC 31**

Sachs, Marilyn (Stickle) 1927- .... **CLC 35**
See also AAYA 2; BYA 6; CA 17-20R;
CANR 13, 47; CLR 2; JRDA; MAICYA;
SAAS 2; SATA 3, 68; SATA-Essay 110;
WYA; YAW

Sachs, Nelly 1891-1970 .... **CLC 14, 98**
See also CA 17-18; 25-28R; CANR 87;
CAP 2; MTCW 2; RGWL

Sackler, Howard (Oliver)
1929-1982 .... **CLC 14**
See also CA 61-64; 108; CAD; CANR 30;
DLB 7

Sacks, Oliver (Wolf) 1933- .... **CLC 67**
See also CA 53-56; CANR 28, 50, 76;
CPW; DA3; INT CANR-28; MTCW 1, 2

Sadakichi
See Hartmann, Sadakichi

Sade, Donatien Alphonse Francois
1740-1814 .... **NCLC 3, 47**
See also EW 4; GFL Beginnings to 1789;
RGWL

Sadoff, Ira 1945- .... **CLC 9**
See also CA 53-56; CANR 5, 21; DLB 120

Saetone
See Camus, Albert

Safire, William 1929- .... **CLC 10**
See also CA 17-20R; CANR 31, 54, 91

Sagan, Carl (Edward) 1934-1996 .... **CLC 30,**
112
See also AAYA 2; CA 25-28R; 155; CANR
11, 36, 74; CPW; DA3; MTCW 1, 2;
SATA 58; SATA-Obit 94

Sagan, Francoise .... **CLC 3, 6, 9, 17, 36**
See also Quoirez, Francoise
See also CWW 2; DLB 83; GFL 1789 to
the Present; MTCW 2

Sahgal, Nayantara (Pandit) 1927- .... **CLC 41**
See also CA 9-12R; CANR 11, 88; CN

Said, Edward W. 1935- .... **CLC 123**
See also CA 21-24R; CANR 45, 74; DLB
67; MTCW 2

Saint, H(arry) F. 1941- .... **CLC 50**
See also CA 127

St. Aubin de Teran, Lisa 1953-
See Teran, Lisa St. Aubin de
See also CA 118; 126; CN; INT 126

Saint Birgitta of Sweden c.
1303-1373 .... **CMLC 24**

Sainte-Beuve, Charles Augustin
1804-1869 .... **NCLC 5**
See also DLB 217; EW 6; GFL 1789 to the
Present

Saint-Exupery, Antoine (Jean Baptiste
Marie Roger) de 1900-1944 .... **TCLC 2,**
56; DAM NOV; WLC
See also BPFB 3; BYA 3; CA 108; 132;
CLR 10; DA3; DLB 72; EW 12; GFL
1789 to the Present; LAIT 3; MAICYA;
MTCW 1, 2; RGWL; SATA 20

St. John, David
See Hunt, E(verette) Howard, (Jr.)

St. John, J. Hector
See Crevecoeur, Michel Guillaume Jean de

Saint-John Perse
See Leger, (Marie-Rene Auguste) Alexis
Saint-Leger
See also EW 10; GFL 1789 to the Present;
RGWL

Saintsbury, George (Edward Bateman)
1845-1933 .... **TCLC 31**
See also CA 160; DLB 57, 149

Sait Faik .... **TCLC 23**
See also Abasiyanik, Sait Faik

Saki .... **TCLC 3; SSC 12**
See also Munro, H(ector) H(ugh)
See also BRWS 6; LAIT 2; MTCW 2;
RGEL; SSFS 1; SUFW

Sakutaro, Hagiwara
See Hagiwara, Sakutaro

Sala, George Augustus 1828-1895 . **NCLC 46**

Saladin 1138-1193 .... **CMLC 38**

Salama, Hannu 1936- .... **CLC 18**

Salamanca, J(ack) R(ichard) 1922- .. **CLC 4,**
15
See also CA 25-28R; CAAE 193

Salas, Floyd Francis 1931-
See also CA 119; CAAS 27; CANR 44, 75,
93; DAM MULT; DLB 82; HLC 2; HW
1, 2; MTCW 2

Sale, J. Kirkpatrick
See Sale, Kirkpatrick

Sale, Kirkpatrick 1937- .... **CLC 68**
See also CA 13-16R; CANR 10

Salinas, Luis Omar 1937- ..... **CLC 90; DAM**
MULT; HLC 2
See also CA 131; CANR 81; DLB 82; HW
1, 2

Salinas (y Serrano), Pedro
1891(?)-1951 .... **TCLC 17**
See also CA 117; DLB 134

Salinger, J(erome) D(avid) 1919- .. **CLC 1, 3,**
8, 12, 55, 56, 138; DA; DAB; DAC;
DAM MST, NOV, POP; SSC 2, 28;
WLC
See also AAYA 2, 36; AMW; BPFB 3; CA
5-8R; CANR 39; CDALB 1941-1968;
CLR 18; CN; CPW 1; DA3; DLB 2, 102,
173; EXPN; LAIT 4; MAICYA; MTCW
1, 2; NFS 1; RGAL; RGSF; SATA 67;
WYA; YAW

Salisbury, John
See Caute, (John) David

Salter, James 1925- .... **CLC 7, 52, 59**
See also AMWS 9; CA 73-76; DLB 130

Saltus, Edgar (Everton) 1855-1921 . **TCLC 8**
See also CA 105; DLB 202; RGAL

Saltykov, Mikhail Evgrafovich
1826-1889 .... **NCLC 16**
See also DLB 238:

Saltykov-Shchedrin, N.
See Saltykov, Mikhail Evgrafovich

Samarakis, Antonis 1919- .... **CLC 5**
See also CA 25-28R; CAAS 16; CANR 36

Sanchez, Florencio 1875-1910 .... **TCLC 37**
See also CA 153; HW 1; LAW

Sanchez, Luis Rafael 1936- .... **CLC 23**
See also CA 128; DLB 145; HW 1; WLIT
1

Sanchez, Sonia 1934- .... **CLC 5, 116; BLC 3;**
DAM MULT; PC 9
See also BW 2, 3; CA 33-36R; CANR 24,
49, 74; CLR 18; CP; CSW; CWP; DA3;
DLB 41; DLBD 8; MAICYA; MTCW 1,
2; SATA 22; WP

Sand, George 1804-1876 ..... **NCLC 2, 42, 57;**
DA; DAB; DAC; DAM MST, NOV;
WLC
See also DA3; DLB 119, 192; EW 6; FW;
GFL 1789 to the Present; RGWL

Sandburg, Carl (August) 1878-1967 . **CLC 1,**
4, 10, 15, 35; DA; DAB; DAC; DAM
MST, POET; PC 2; WLC
See also AAYA 24; AMW; BYA 1, 3; CA
5-8R; 25-28R; CANR 35; CDALB 1865-
1917; CLR 67; DA3; DLB 17, 54; EXPP;
LAIT 2; MAICYA; MTCW 1, 2; PAB;
PFS 3, 6, 12; RGAL; SATA 8; WCH; WP;
WYA

Sandburg, Charles
See Sandburg, Carl (August)

Sandburg, Charles A.
See Sandburg, Carl (August)

Sanders, (James) Ed(ward) 1939- ... **CLC 53;**
DAM POET
See also Sanders, Edward
See also CA 13-16R; CAAS 21; CANR 13,
44, 78; CP; DLB 16

Sanders, Edward
See Sanders, (James) Ed(ward)
See also DLB 244

Sanders, Lawrence 1920-1998 .... **CLC 41;**
DAM POP
See also BEST 89:4; BPFB 3; CA 81-84;
165; CANR 33, 62; CMW; CPW; DA3;
MTCW 1

Sanders, Noah
See Blount, Roy (Alton), Jr.

Sanders, Winston P.
See Anderson, Poul (William)

Sandoz, Mari(e Susette) 1900-1966 .. **CLC 28**
See also CA 1-4R; 25-28R; CANR 17, 64;
DLB 9, 212; LAIT 2; MTCW 1, 2; SATA
5; TCWW 2

Saner, Reg(inald Anthony) 1931- .... **CLC 9**
See also CA 65-68; CP

Sankara 788-820 .... **CMLC 32**

Sannazaro, Jacopo 1456(?)-1530 .... **LC 8**
See also RGWL

Spengler, Oswald (Arnold Gottfried)
1880-1936 .... **TCLC 25**
See also CA 118; 189

Spenser, Edmund 1552(?)-1599 ..... **LC 5, 39;**
DA; DAB; DAC; DAM MST, POET;
PC 8; WLC
See also BRW 1; CDBLB Before 1660;
DA3; DLB 167; EFS 2; EXPP; PAB;
RGEL; WLIT 3; WP

Spicer, Jack 1925-1965 .... **CLC 8, 18, 72;**
DAM POET
See also CA 85-88; DLB 5, 16, 193; GLL
1; WP

Spiegelman, Art 1948- .... **CLC 76**
See also AAYA 10; CA 125; CANR 41, 55,
74; MTCW 2; SATA 109; YAW

Spielberg, Peter 1929- .... **CLC 6**
See also CA 5-8R; CANR 4, 48; DLBY 81

Spielberg, Steven 1947- .... **CLC 20**
See also AAYA 8, 24; CA 77-80; CANR
32; SATA 32

Spillane, Frank Morrison 1918-
See Spillane, Mickey
See also CA 25-28R; CANR 28, 63; DA3;
DLB 226; MTCW 1, 2; SATA 66

Spillane, Mickey .... **CLC 3, 13**
See also Spillane, Frank Morrison
See also BPFB 3; CMW; DLB 226; MSW;
MTCW 2

Spinoza, Benedictus de 1632-1677 .. **LC 9, 58**

Spinrad, Norman (Richard) 1940- ... **CLC 46**
See also BPFB 3; CA 37-40R; CAAS 19;
CANR 20, 91; DLB 8; INT CANR-20;
SFW

Spitteler, Carl (Friedrich Georg)
1845-1924 .... **TCLC 12**
See also CA 109; DLB 129

Spivack, Kathleen (Romola Drucker)
1938- .... **CLC 6**
See also CA 49-52

Spoto, Donald 1941- .... **CLC 39**
See also CA 65-68; CANR 11, 57, 93

Springsteen, Bruce (F.) 1949- .... **CLC 17**
See also CA 111

Spurling, Hilary 1940- .... **CLC 34**
See also CA 104; CANR 25, 52, 94

Spyker, John Howland
See Elman, Richard (Martin)

Squires, (James) Radcliffe
1917-1993 .... **CLC 51**
See also CA 1-4R; 140; CANR 6, 21

Srivastava, Dhanpat Rai 1880(?)-1936
See Premchand
See also CA 118; 197

Stacy, Donald
See Pohl, Frederik

Stael
See Stael-Holstein, Anne Louise Germaine
Necker
See also EW 5; RGWL

Stael, Germaine de
See Stael-Holstein, Anne Louise Germaine
Necker
See also DLB 119, 192; FW; GFL 1789 to
the Present; TWA

Stael-Holstein, Anne Louise Germaine
Necker 1766-1817 .... **NCLC 3, 91**
See also Stael; Stael, Germaine de

Stafford, Jean 1915-1979 .. **CLC 4, 7, 19, 68;**
SSC 26
See also CA 1-4R; 85-88; CANR 3, 65;
DLB 2, 173; MTCW 1, 2; RGAL; RGSF;
SATA-Obit 22; TCWW 2

Stafford, William (Edgar)
1914-1993 .. **CLC 4, 7, 29; DAM POET**
See also CA 5-8R; 142; CAAS 3; CANR 5,
22; DLB 5, 206; EXPP; INT CANR-22;
PFS 2, 8; RGAL; WP

Stagnelius, Eric Johan 1793-1823 . **NCLC 61**

Staines, Trevor
See Brunner, John (Kilian Houston)

Stairs, Gordon
See Austin, Mary (Hunter)
See also TCWW 2

Stairs, Gordon 1868-1934
See Austin, Mary (Hunter)

Stalin, Joseph 1879-1953 .... **TCLC 92**

Stancykowna
See Szymborska, Wislawa

Stannard, Martin 1947- .... **CLC 44**
See also CA 142; DLB 155

Stanton, Elizabeth Cady
1815-1902 .... **TCLC 73**
See also CA 171; DLB 79; FW

Stanton, Maura 1946- .... **CLC 9**
See also CA 89-92; CANR 15; DLB 120

Stanton, Schuyler
See Baum, L(yman) Frank

Stapledon, (William) Olaf
1886-1950 .... **TCLC 22**
See also CA 111; 162; DLB 15, 255; SFW

Starbuck, George (Edwin)
1931-1996 .... **CLC 53; DAM POET**
See also CA 21-24R; 153; CANR 23

Stark, Richard
See Westlake, Donald E(dwin)

Staunton, Schuyler
See Baum, L(yman) Frank

Stead, Christina (Ellen) 1902-1983 ... **CLC 2,**
5, 8, 32, 80
See also BRWS 4; CA 13-16R; 109; CANR
33, 40; FW; MTCW 1, 2; RGEL; RGSF

Stead, William Thomas
1849-1912 .... **TCLC 48**
See also CA 167

Stebnitsky, M.
See Leskov, Nikolai (Semyonovich)

Steele, Sir Richard 1672-1729 .... **LC 18**
See also BRW 3; CDBLB 1660-1789; DLB
84, 101; RGEL; WLIT 3

Steele, Timothy (Reid) 1948- .... **CLC 45**
See also CA 93-96; CANR 16, 50, 92; CP;
DLB 120

Steffens, (Joseph) Lincoln
1866-1936 .... **TCLC 20**
See also CA 117

Stegner, Wallace (Earle) 1909-1993 .. **CLC 9,**
49, 81; DAM NOV; SSC 27
See also AITN 1; AMWS 4; ANW; BEST
90:3; BPFB 3; CA 1-4R; 141; CAAS 9;
CANR 1, 21, 46; DLB 9, 206; DLBY 93;
MTCW 1, 2; RGAL; TCWW 2

Stein, Gertrude 1874-1946 .... **TCLC 1, 6, 28,**
48; DA; DAB; DAC; DAM MST, NOV,
POET; PC 18; SSC 42; WLC
See also AMW; CA 104; 132; CDALB
1917-1929; DA3; DLB 4, 54, 86, 228;
DLBD 15; EXPS; GLL 1; MAWW;
MTCW 1, 2; RGAL; RGSF; SSFS 5; WP

Steinbeck, John (Ernst) 1902-1968 ... **CLC 1,**
5, 9, 13, 21, 34, 45, 75, 124; DA; DAB;
DAC; DAM DRAM, MST, NOV; SSC
11, 37; WLC
See also AAYA 12; AMW; BPFB 3; BYA 2,
3, 13; CA 1-4R; 25-28R; CANR 1, 35;
CDALB 1929-1941; DA3; DLB 7, 9, 212;
DLBD 2; EXPS; LAIT 3; MTCW 1, 2;
NFS 1, 5, 7; RGAL; RGSF; RHW; SATA
9; SSFS 3, 6; TCWW 2; WYA; YAW

Steinem, Gloria 1934- .... **CLC 63**
See also CA 53-56; CANR 28, 51; DLB
246; FW; MTCW 1, 2

Steiner, George 1929- .. **CLC 24; DAM NOV**
See also CA 73-76; CANR 31, 67; DLB 67;
MTCW 1, 2; SATA 62

Steiner, K. Leslie
See Delany, Samuel R(ay), Jr.

Steiner, Rudolf 1861-1925 .... **TCLC 13**
See also CA 107

Stendhal 1783-1842 .... **NCLC 23, 46; DA;**
DAB; DAC; DAM MST, NOV; SSC
27; WLC
See also DA3; DLB 119; EW 5; GFL 1789
to the Present; RGWL

Stephen, Adeline Virginia
See Woolf, (Adeline) Virginia

Stephen, Sir Leslie 1832-1904 .... **TCLC 23**
See also BRW 5; CA 123; DLB 57, 144,
190

Stephen, Sir Leslie
See Stephen, Sir Leslie

Stephen, Virginia
See Woolf, (Adeline) Virginia

Stephens, James 1882(?)-1950 .... **TCLC 4;**
SSC 50
See also CA 104; 192; DLB 19, 153, 162;
FANT; RGEL; SUFW

Stephens, Reed
See Donaldson, Stephen R(eeder)

Steptoe, Lydia
See Barnes, Djuna
See also GLL 1

Sterchi, Beat 1949- .... **CLC 65**

Sterling, Brett
See Bradbury, Ray (Douglas); Hamilton,
Edmond

Sterling, Bruce 1954- .... **CLC 72**
See also CA 119; CANR 44; SCFW 2; SFW

Sterling, George 1869-1926 .... **TCLC 20**
See also CA 117; 165; DLB 54

Stern, Gerald 1925- .... **CLC 40, 100**
See also AMWS 9; CA 81-84; CANR 28,
94; CP; DLB 105; RGAL

Stern, Richard (Gustave) 1928- ... **CLC 4, 39**
See also CA 1-4R; CANR 1, 25, 52; CN;
DLB 218; DLBY 87; INT CANR-25

Sternberg, Josef von 1894-1969 .... **CLC 20**
See also CA 81-84

Sterne, Laurence 1713-1768 .. **LC 2, 48; DA;**
DAB; DAC; DAM MST, NOV; WLC
See also BRW 3; CDBLB 1660-1789; DLB
39; RGEL

Sternheim, (William Adolf) Carl
1878-1942 .... **TCLC 8**
See also CA 105; 193; DLB 56, 118; RGWL

Stevens, Mark 1951- .... **CLC 34**
See also CA 122

Stevens, Wallace 1879-1955 ...... **TCLC 3, 12,**
45; DA; DAB; DAC; DAM MST,
POET; PC 6; WLC
See also AMW; AMWR 1; CA 104; 124;
CDALB 1929-1941; DA3; DLB 54;
EXPP; MTCW 1, 2; PAB; PFS 13; RGAL;
WP

Stevenson, Anne (Katharine) 1933- .. **CLC 7,**
33
See also BRWS 6; CA 17-20R; CAAS 9;
CANR 9, 33; CP; CWP; DLB 40; MTCW
1; RHW

Stevenson, Robert Louis (Balfour)
1850-1894 . **NCLC 5, 14, 63; DA; DAB;**
DAC; DAM MST, NOV; SSC 11, 51;
WLC
See also AAYA 24; BPFB 3; BRW 5;
BRWR 1; BYA 1, 2, 4, 13; CDBLB 1890-
1914; CLR 10, 11; DA3; DLB 18, 57,
141, 156, 174; DLBD 13; HGG; JRDA;
LAIT 1, 3; MAICYA; NFS 11; RGEL;
RGSF; SATA 100; SUFW; WCH; WLIT
4; WYA; YABC 2; YAW

Stewart, J(ohn) I(nnes) M(ackintosh)
1906-1994 .... **CLC 7, 14, 32**
See also Innes, Michael
See also CA 85-88; 147; CAAS 3; CANR
47; CMW; MTCW 1, 2

Stewart, Mary (Florence Elinor)
1916- .... **CLC 7, 35, 117; DAB**
See also AAYA 29; BPFB 3; CA 1-4R;
CANR 1, 59; CMW; CPW; FANT; RHW;
SATA 12; YAW

Stewart, Mary Rainbow
See Stewart, Mary (Florence Elinor)

Stifle, June
See Campbell, Maria

Stifter, Adalbert 1805-1868 .. **NCLC 41; SSC 28**
See also DLB 133; RGSF; RGWL

Still, James 1906-2001 .... **CLC 49**
See also CA 65-68; 195; CAAS 17; CANR
10, 26; CSW; DLB 9; DLBY 01; SATA
29; SATA-Obit 127

Sting 1951-
See Sumner, Gordon Matthew
See also CA 167

Stirling, Arthur
See Sinclair, Upton (Beall)

Stitt, Milan 1941- .... **CLC 29**
See also CA 69-72

Stockton, Francis Richard 1834-1902
See Stockton, Frank R.
See also CA 108; 137; MAICYA; SATA 44;
SFW

Stockton, Frank R. .... **TCLC 47**
See also Stockton, Francis Richard
See also BYA 4, 13; DLB 42, 74; DLBD
13; EXPS; SATA-Brief 32; SSFS 3;
SUFW; WCH

Stoddard, Charles
See Kuttner, Henry

Stoker, Abraham 1847-1912
See Stoker, Bram
See also CA 105; 150; DA; DA3; DAC;
DAM MST, NOV; HGG; SATA 29

Stoker, Bram .... **TCLC 8; DAB; WLC**
See also Stoker, Abraham
See also AAYA 23; BPFB 3; BRWS 3; BYA
5; CDBLB 1890-1914; DLB 36, 70, 178;
RGEL; SUFW; WLIT 4

Stolz, Mary (Slattery) 1920- .... **CLC 12**
See also AAYA 8; AITN 1; CA 5-8R;
CANR 13, 41; JRDA; MAICYA; SAAS
3; SATA 10, 71; YAW

Stone, Irving 1903-1989 . **CLC 7; DAM POP**
See also AITN 1; BPFB 3; CA 1-4R; 129;
CAAS 3; CANR 1, 23; CPW; DA3; INT
CANR-23; MTCW 1, 2; RHW; SATA 3;
SATA-Obit 64

Stone, Oliver (William) 1946- .... **CLC 73**
See also AAYA 15; CA 110; CANR 55

Stone, Robert (Anthony) 1937- ... **CLC 5, 23, 42**
See also AMWS 5; BPFB 3; CA 85-88;
CANR 23, 66, 95; CN; DLB 152; INT
CANR-23; MTCW 1

Stone, Zachary
See Follett, Ken(neth Martin)

Stoppard, Tom 1937- ... **CLC 1, 3, 4, 5, 8, 15, 29, 34, 63, 91; DA; DAB; DAC; DAM DRAM, MST; DC 6; WLC**
See also BRWR 2; BRWS 1; CA 81-84;
CANR 39, 67; CBD; CD; CDBLB 1960
to Present; DA3; DFS 2, 5, 8, 11, 13; DLB
13, 233; DLBY 85; MTCW 1, 2; RGEL;
WLIT 4

Storey, David (Malcolm) 1933- . **CLC 2, 4, 5, 8; DAM DRAM**
See also BRWS 1; CA 81-84; CANR 36;
CBD; CD; CN; DLB 13, 14, 207, 245;
MTCW 1; RGEL

Storm, Hyemeyohsts 1935- ..... **CLC 3; DAM MULT**
See also CA 81-84; CANR 45; NNAL

Storm, Theodor 1817-1888 .... **SSC 27**
See also RGSF; RGWL

Storm, (Hans) Theodor (Woldsen)
1817-1888 .... **NCLC 1; SSC 27**
See also DLB 129; EW

Storni, Alfonsina 1892-1938 . **TCLC 5; DAM MULT; HLC 2; PC 33**
See also CA 104; 131; HW 1; LAW

Stoughton, William 1631-1701 .... **LC 38**
See also DLB 24

Stout, Rex (Todhunter) 1886-1975 ..... **CLC 3**
See also AITN 2; BPFB 3; CA 61-64;
CANR 71; CMW; MSW; RGAL

Stow, (Julian) Randolph 1935- ... **CLC 23, 48**
See also CA 13-16R; CANR 33; CN;
MTCW 1; RGEL

Stowe, Harriet (Elizabeth) Beecher
1811-1896 .... **NCLC 3, 50; DA; DAB; DAC; DAM MST, NOV; WLC**
See also AMWS 1; CDALB 1865-1917;
DA3; DLB 1, 12, 42, 74, 189, 239, 243;
EXPN; JRDA; LAIT 2; MAICYA; NFS
6; RGAL; YABC 1

Strabo c. 64B.C.-c. 25 .... **CMLC 37**
See also DLB 176

Strachey, (Giles) Lytton
1880-1932 .... **TCLC 12**
See also BRWS 2; CA 110; 178; DLB 149;
DLBD 10; MTCW 2

Strand, Mark 1934- .... **CLC 6, 18, 41, 71; DAM POET**
See also AMWS 4; CA 21-24R; CANR 40,
65, 100; CP; DLB 5; PAB; PFS 9; RGAL;
SATA 41

Stratton-Porter, Gene(va Grace) 1863-1924
See Porter, Gene(va Grace) Stratton
See also ANW; CA 137; DLB 221; DLBD
14; MAICYA; SATA 15

Straub, Peter (Francis) 1943- . **CLC 28, 107; DAM POP**
See also BEST 89:1; BPFB 3; CA 85-88;
CANR 28, 65; CPW; DLBY 84; HGG;
MTCW 1, 2

Strauss, Botho 1944- .... **CLC 22**
See also CA 157; CWW 2; DLB 124

Streatfeild, (Mary) Noel
1897(?)-1986 .... **CLC 21**
See also CA 81-84; 120; CANR 31; CLR
17; CWRI; DLB 160; MAICYA; SATA
20; SATA-Obit 48

Stribling, T(homas) S(igismund)
1881-1965 .... **CLC 23**
See also CA 189; 107; CMW; DLB 9;
RGAL

Strindberg, (Johan) August
1849-1912 .... **TCLC 1, 8, 21, 47; DA; DAB; DAC; DAM DRAM, MST; WLC**
See also CA 104; 135; DA3; DFS 4, 9; EW
7; IDTP; MTCW 2; RGWL

Stringer, Arthur 1874-1950 .... **TCLC 37**
See also CA 161; DLB 92

Stringer, David
See Roberts, Keith (John Kingston)

Stroheim, Erich von 1885-1957 ..... **TCLC 71**

Strugatskii, Arkadii (Natanovich)
1925-1991 .... **CLC 27**
See also CA 106; 135; SFW

Strugatskii, Boris (Natanovich)
1933- .... **CLC 27**
See also CA 106; SFW

Strummer, Joe 1953(?)- .... **CLC 30**

Strunk, William, Jr. 1869-1946 ...... **TCLC 92**
See also CA 118; 164

Stryk, Lucien 1924- .... **PC 27**
See also CA 13-16R; CANR 10, 28, 55; CP

Stuart, Don A.
See Campbell, John W(ood, Jr.)

Stuart, Ian
See MacLean, Alistair (Stuart)

Stuart, Jesse (Hilton) 1906-1984 ... **CLC 1, 8, 11, 14, 34; SSC 31**
See also CA 5-8R; 112; CANR 31; DLB 9,
48, 102; DLB 84; SATA 2; SATA-Obit
36

Stubblefield, Sally
See Trumbo, Dalton

Sturgeon, Theodore (Hamilton)
1918-1985 .... **CLC 22, 39**
See also Queen, Ellery
See also BPFB 3; BYA 9, 10; CA 81-84;
116; CANR 32, 103; DLB 8; DLBY 85;
HGG; MTCW 1, 2; SCFW; SFW; SUFW

Sturges, Preston 1898-1959 .... **TCLC 48**
See also CA 114; 149; DLB 26

Styron, William 1925- .... **CLC 1, 3, 5, 11, 15, 60; DAM NOV, POP; SSC 25**
See also AMW; BEST 90:4; BPFB 3; CA
5-8R; CANR 6, 33, 74; CDALB 1968-
1988; CN; CPW; CSW; DA3; DLB 2,
143; DLBY 80; INT CANR-6; LAIT 2;
MTCW 1, 2; NCFS 1; RGAL; RHW

Su, Chien 1884-1918
See Su Man-shu
See also CA 123

Suarez Lynch, B.
See Bioy Casares, Adolfo; Borges, Jorge
Luis

Suassuna, Ariano Vilar 1927-
See also CA 178; HLCS 1; HW 2; LAW

Suckling, Sir John 1609-1642 .. **LC 75; DAM POET; PC 30**
See also BRW 2; DLB 58, 126; EXPP;
PAB; RGEL

Suckow, Ruth 1892-1960 .... **SSC 18**
See also CA 193; 113; DLB 9, 102; RGAL;
TCWW 2

Sudermann, Hermann 1857-1928 .. **TCLC 15**
See also CA 107; DLB 118

Sue, Eugene 1804-1857 .... **NCLC 1**
See also DLB 119

Sueskind, Patrick 1949- .... **CLC 44**
See also Suskind, Patrick

Sukenick, Ronald 1932- .... **CLC 3, 4, 6, 48**
See also CA 25-28R; CAAS 8; CANR 32,
89; CN; DLB 173; DLBY 81

Suknaski, Andrew 1942- .... **CLC 19**
See also CA 101; CP; DLB 53

Sullivan, Vernon
See Vian, Boris

Sully Prudhomme, Rene-Francois-Armand
1839-1907 .... **TCLC 31**
See also GFL 1789 to the Present

Su Man-shu .... **TCLC 24**
See also Su, Chien

Summerforest, Ivy B.
See Kirkup, James

Summers, Andrew James 1942- .... **CLC 26**

Summers, Andy
See Summers, Andrew James

Summers, Hollis (Spurgeon, Jr.)
1916- .... **CLC 10**
See also CA 5-8R; CANR 3; DLB 6

**Summers, (Alphonsus Joseph-Mary
Augustus) Montague**
1880-1948 .... **TCLC 16**
See also CA 118; 163

Sumner, Gordon Matthew .... **CLC 26**
See also Police, The; Sting

Surtees, Robert Smith 1805-1864 .. **NCLC 14**
See also DLB 21; RGEL

Susann, Jacqueline 1921-1974 .... **CLC 3**
See also AITN 1; BPFB 3; CA 65-68; 53-
56; MTCW 1, 2

Su Shi
See Su Shih
See also RGWL

Su Shih 1036-1101 .... **CMLC 15**
See also Su Shi

Suskind, Patrick
   See Sueskind, Patrick
   See also BPFB 3; CA 145; CWW 2

Sutcliff, Rosemary 1920-1992 .... **CLC 26; DAB; DAC; DAM MST, POP**
   See also AAYA 10; BYA 1, 4; CA 5-8R; 139; CANR 37; CLR 1, 37; CPW; JRDA; MAICYA; MAICYAS; RHW; SATA 6, 44, 78; SATA-Obit 73; WYA; YAW

Sutro, Alfred 1863-1933 .... **TCLC 6**
   See also CA 105; 185; DLB 10; RGEL

Sutton, Henry
   See Slavitt, David R(ytman)

Suzuki, D. T.
   See Suzuki, Daisetz Teitaro

Suzuki, Daisetz T.
   See Suzuki, Daisetz Teitaro

Suzuki, Daisetz Teitaro
   1870-1966 .... **TCLC 109**
   See also CA 121; 111; MTCW 1, 2

Suzuki, Teitaro
   See Suzuki, Daisetz Teitaro

Svevo, Italo .... **TCLC 2, 35; SSC 25**
   See also Schmitz, Aron Hector
   See also EW 8; RGWL

Swados, Elizabeth (A.) 1951- .... **CLC 12**
   See also CA 97-100; CANR 49; INT 97-100

Swados, Harvey 1920-1972 .... **CLC 5**
   See also CA 5-8R; 37-40R; CANR 6; DLB 2

Swan, Gladys 1934- .... **CLC 69**
   See also CA 101; CANR 17, 39

Swanson, Logan
   See Matheson, Richard (Burton)

Swarthout, Glendon (Fred)
   1918-1992 .... **CLC 35**
   See also CA 1-4R; 139; CANR 1, 47; LAIT 5; SATA 26; TCWW 2; YAW

Sweet, Sarah C.
   See Jewett, (Theodora) Sarah Orne

Swenson, May 1919-1989 ...... **CLC 4, 14, 61, 106; DA; DAB; DAC; DAM MST, POET; PC 14**
   See also AMWS 4; CA 5-8R; 130; CANR 36, 61; DLB 5; EXPP; GLL 2; MTCW 1, 2; SATA 15; WP

Swift, Augustus
   See Lovecraft, H(oward) P(hillips)

Swift, Graham (Colin) 1949- ...... **CLC 41, 88**
   See also BRWS 5; CA 117; 122; CANR 46, 71; CN; DLB 194; MTCW 2; RGSF

Swift, Jonathan 1667-1745 ..... **LC 1, 42; DA; DAB; DAC; DAM MST, NOV, POET; PC 9; WLC**
   See also AAYA 41; BRW 3; BRWR 1; BYA 5, 14; CDBLB 1660-1789; CLR 53; DA3; DLB 39, 95, 101; EXPN; LAIT 1; NFS 6; RGEL; SATA 19; WCH; WLIT 3

Swinburne, Algernon Charles
   1837-1909 .... **TCLC 8, 36; DA; DAB; DAC; DAM MST, POET; PC 24; WLC**
   See also BRW 5; CA 105; 140; CDBLB 1832-1890; DA3; DLB 35, 57; PAB; RGEL

Swinfen, Ann .... **CLC 34**

Swinnerton, Frank Arthur
   1884-1982 .... **CLC 31**
   See also CA 108; DLB 34

Swithen, John
   See King, Stephen (Edwin)

Sylvia
   See Ashton-Warner, Sylvia (Constance)

Symmes, Robert Edward
   See Duncan, Robert (Edward)

Symonds, John Addington
   1840-1893 .... **NCLC 34**
   See also DLB 57, 144

Symons, Arthur 1865-1945 .... **TCLC 11**
   See also CA 107; 189; DLB 19, 57, 149; RGEL

Symons, Julian (Gustave)
   1912-1994 .... **CLC 2, 14, 32**
   See also CA 49-52; 147; CAAS 3; CANR 3, 33, 59; CMW; DLB 87, 155; DLBY 92; MSW; MTCW 1

Synge, (Edmund) J(ohn) M(illington)
   1871-1909 . **TCLC 6, 37; DAM DRAM; DC 2**
   See also BRW 6; BRWR 1; CA 104; 141; CDBLB 1890-1914; DLB 10, 19; RGEL; WLIT 4

Syruc, J.
   See Milosz, Czeslaw

Szirtes, George 1948- .... **CLC 46**
   See also CA 109; CANR 27, 61; CP

Szymborska, Wislawa 1923- .... **CLC 99**
   See also CA 154; CANR 91; CWP; CWW 2; DA3; DLB 232; DLBY 96; MTCW 2

T. O., Nik
   See Annensky, Innokenty (Fyodorovich)

Tabori, George 1914- .... **CLC 19**
   See also CA 49-52; CANR 4, 69; CBD; CD; DLB 245

Tagore, Rabindranath 1861-1941 ... **TCLC 3, 53; DAM DRAM, POET; PC 8; SSC 48**
   See also CA 104; 120; DA3; MTCW 1, 2; RGEL; RGSF; RGWL

Taine, Hippolyte Adolphe
   1828-1893 .... **NCLC 15**
   See also EW 7; GFL 1789 to the Present

Talese, Gay 1932- .... **CLC 37**
   See also AITN 1; CA 1-4R; CANR 9, 58; DLB 185; INT CANR-9; MTCW 1, 2

Tallent, Elizabeth (Ann) 1954- .... **CLC 45**
   See also CA 117; CANR 72; DLB 130

Tally, Ted 1952- .... **CLC 42**
   See also CA 120; 124; CAD; CD; INT 124

Talvik, Heiti 1904-1947 .... **TCLC 87**

Tamayo y Baus, Manuel
   1829-1898 .... **NCLC 1**

Tammsaare, A(nton) H(ansen)
   1878-1940 .... **TCLC 27**
   See also CA 164; DLB 220

Tam'si, Tchicaya
   See Tchicaya, Gerald Felix

Tan, Amy (Ruth) 1952- .... **CLC 59, 120, 151; AAL; DAM MULT, NOV, POP**
   See also AAYA 9; AMWS 10; BEST 89:3; BPFB 3; CA 136; CANR 54, 105; CDALBS; CN; CPW 1; DA3; DLB 173; EXPN; FW; LAIT 3, 5; MTCW 2; NFS 1, 13; RGAL; SATA 75; SSFS 9; YAW

Tandem, Felix
   See Spitteler, Carl (Friedrich Georg)

Tanizaki, Jun'ichiro 1886-1965 ... **CLC 8, 14, 28; SSC 21**
   See also CA 93-96; 25-28R; DLB 180; MJW; MTCW 2; RGSF; RGWL

Tanner, William
   See Amis, Kingsley (William)

Tao Lao
   See Storni, Alfonsina

Tarantino, Quentin (Jerome)
   1963- .... **CLC 125**
   See also CA 171

Tarassoff, Lev
   See Troyat, Henri

Tarbell, Ida M(inerva) 1857-1944 . **TCLC 40**
   See also CA 122; 181; DLB 47

Tarkington, (Newton) Booth
   1869-1946 .... **TCLC 9**
   See also BPFB 3; BYA 3; CA 110; 143; CWRI; DLB 9, 102; MTCW 2; RGAL; SATA 17

Tarkovsky, Andrei (Arsenyevich)
   1932-1986 .... **CLC 75**
   See also CA 127

Tartt, Donna 1964(?)- .... **CLC 76**
   See also CA 142

Tasso, Torquato 1544-1595 .... **LC 5**
   See also EFS 2; EW 2; RGWL

Tate, (John Orley) Allen 1899-1979 .. **CLC 2, 4, 6, 9, 11, 14, 24**
   See also AMW; CA 5-8R; 85-88; CANR 32; DLB 4, 45, 63; DLBD 17; MTCW 1, 2; RGAL; RHW

Tate, Ellalice
   See Hibbert, Eleanor Alice Burford

Tate, James (Vincent) 1943- ..... **CLC 2, 6, 25**
   See also CA 21-24R; CANR 29, 57; CP; DLB 5, 169; PFS 10; RGAL; WP

Tauler, Johannes c. 1300-1361 ...... **CMLC 37**
   See also DLB 179

Tavel, Ronald 1940- .... **CLC 6**
   See also CA 21-24R; CAD; CANR 33; CD

Taviani, Paolo 1931- .... **CLC 70**
   See also CA 153

Taylor, Bayard 1825-1878 .... **NCLC 89**
   See also DLB 3, 189, 250, 254; RGAL

Taylor, C(ecil) P(hilip) 1929-1981 .... **CLC 27**
   See also CA 25-28R; 105; CANR 47; CBD

Taylor, Edward 1642(?)-1729 ..... **LC 11; DA; DAB; DAC; DAM MST, POET**
   See also AMW; DLB 24; EXPP; RGAL

Taylor, Eleanor Ross 1920- .... **CLC 5**
   See also CA 81-84; CANR 70

Taylor, Elizabeth 1932-1975 ..... **CLC 2, 4, 29**
   See also CA 13-16R; CANR 9, 70; DLB 139; MTCW 1; RGEL; SATA 13

Taylor, Frederick Winslow
   1856-1915 .... **TCLC 76**
   See also CA 188

Taylor, Henry (Splawn) 1942- .... **CLC 44**
   See also CA 33-36R; CAAS 7; CANR 31; CP; DLB 5; PFS 10

Taylor, Kamala (Purnaiya) 1924-
   See Markandaya, Kamala
   See also CA 77-80; NFS 13

Taylor, Mildred D(elois) 1943- .... **CLC 21**
   See also AAYA 10; BW 1; BYA 3, 8; CA 85-88; CANR 25; CLR 9, 59; CSW; DLB 52; JRDA; LAIT 3; MAICYA; SAAS 5; SATA 15, 70; WYA; YAW

Taylor, Peter (Hillsman) 1917-1994 .. **CLC 1, 4, 18, 37, 44, 50, 71; SSC 10**
   See also AMWS 5; BPFB 3; CA 13-16R; 147; CANR 9, 50; CSW; DLB 218; DLBY 81, 94; EXPS; INT CANR-9; MTCW 1, 2; RGSF; SSFS 9

Taylor, Robert Lewis 1912-1998 .... **CLC 14**
   See also CA 1-4R; 170; CANR 3, 64; SATA 10

Tchekhov, Anton
   See Chekhov, Anton (Pavlovich)

Tchicaya, Gerald Felix 1931-1988 .. **CLC 101**
   See also CA 129; 125; CANR 81

Tchicaya U Tam'si
   See Tchicaya, Gerald Felix

Teasdale, Sara 1884-1933 .... **TCLC 4; PC 31**
   See also CA 104; 163; DLB 45; GLL 1; PFS 14; RGAL; SATA 32

Tegner, Esaias 1782-1846 .... **NCLC 2**

Teilhard de Chardin, (Marie Joseph) Pierre
   1881-1955 .... **TCLC 9**
   See also CA 105; GFL 1789 to the Present

Temple, Ann
   See Mortimer, Penelope (Ruth)

Tennant, Emma (Christina) 1937- .. **CLC 13, 52**
   See also CA 65-68; CAAS 9; CANR 10, 38, 59, 88; CN; DLB 14; SFW

Tenneshaw, S. M.
   See Silverberg, Robert

Tennyson, Alfred 1809-1892 ... **NCLC 30, 65; DA; DAB; DAC; DAM MST, POET; PC 6; WLC**
  See also BRW 4; CDBLB 1832-1890; DA3; DLB 32; EXPP; PAB; PFS 1, 2, 4, 11; RGEL; WLIT 4; WP

Teran, Lisa St. Aubin de .... **CLC 36**
  See also St. Aubin de Teran, Lisa

Terence c. 184B.C.-c. 159B.C. ...... **CMLC 14; DC 7**
  See also AW 1; DLB 211; RGWL

Teresa de Jesus, St. 1515-1582 .... **LC 18**

Terkel, Louis 1912-
  See Terkel, Studs
  See also CA 57-60; CANR 18, 45, 67; DA3; MTCW 1, 2

Terkel, Studs .... **CLC 38**
  See also Terkel, Louis
  See also AAYA 32; AITN 1; MTCW 2

Terry, C. V.
  See Slaughter, Frank G(ill)

Terry, Megan 1932- .... **CLC 19; DC 13**
  See also CA 77-80; CABS 3; CAD; CANR 43; CD; CWD; DLB 7, 249; GLL 2

Tertullian c. 155-c. 245 .... **CMLC 29**

Tertz, Abram
  See Sinyavsky, Andrei (Donatevich)
  See also CWW 2; RGSF

Tesich, Steve 1943(?)-1996 .... **CLC 40, 69**
  See also CA 105; 152; CAD; DLBY 83

Tesla, Nikola 1856-1943 .... **TCLC 88**

Teternikov, Fyodor Kuzmich 1863-1927
  See Sologub, Fyodor
  See also CA 104

Tevis, Walter 1928-1984 .... **CLC 42**
  See also CA 113; SFW

Tey, Josephine .... **TCLC 14**
  See also Mackintosh, Elizabeth
  See also DLB 77; MSW

Thackeray, William Makepeace
  1811-1863 ...... **NCLC 5, 14, 22, 43; DA; DAB; DAC; DAM MST, NOV; WLC**
  See also BRW 5; CDBLB 1832-1890; DA3; DLB 21, 55, 159, 163; NFS 13; RGEL; SATA 23; WLIT 3

Thakura, Ravindranatha
  See Tagore, Rabindranath

Thames, C. H.
  See Marlowe, Stephen

Tharoor, Shashi 1956- .... **CLC 70**
  See also CA 141; CANR 91; CN

Thelwell, Michael Miles 1939- .... **CLC 22**
  See also BW 2; CA 101

Theobald, Lewis, Jr.
  See Lovecraft, H(oward) P(hillips)

Theocritus c. 310B.C.- .... **CMLC 45**
  See also AW 1; DLB 176; RGWL

Theodorescu, Ion N. 1880-1967
  See Arghezi, Tudor
  See also CA 116

Theriault, Yves 1915-1983 .... **CLC 79; DAC; DAM MST**
  See also CA 102; CCA 1; DLB 88

Theroux, Alexander (Louis) 1939- .... **CLC 2, 25**
  See also CA 85-88; CANR 20, 63; CN

Theroux, Paul (Edward) 1941- ..... **CLC 5, 8, 11, 15, 28, 46; DAM POP**
  See also AAYA 28; AMWS 8; BEST 89:4; BPFB 3; CA 33-36R; CANR 20, 45, 74; CDALBS; CN; CPW 1; DA3; DLB 2, 218; HGG; MTCW 1, 2; RGAL; SATA 44, 109

Thesen, Sharon 1946- .... **CLC 56**
  See also CA 163; CP; CWP

Thevenin, Denis
  See Duhamel, Georges

Thibault, Jacques Anatole Francois
  1844-1924
  See France, Anatole
  See also CA 106; 127; DA3; DAM NOV; MTCW 1, 2

Thiele, Colin (Milton) 1920- .... **CLC 17**
  See also CA 29-32R; CANR 12, 28, 53, 105; CLR 27; MAICYA; SAAS 2; SATA 14, 72, 125; YAW

Thomas, Audrey (Callahan) 1935- .... **CLC 7, 13, 37, 107; SSC 20**
  See also AITN 2; CA 21-24R; CAAS 19; CANR 36, 58; CN; DLB 60; MTCW 1; RGSF

Thomas, Augustus 1857-1934 .... **TCLC 97**

Thomas, D(onald) M(ichael) 1935- . **CLC 13, 22, 31, 132**
  See also BPFB 3; BRWS 4; CA 61-64; CAAS 11; CANR 17, 45, 75; CDBLB 1960 to Present; CN; CP; DA3; DLB 40, 207; HGG; INT CANR-17; MTCW 1, 2; SFW

Thomas, Dylan (Marlais)
  1914-1953 ...... **TCLC 1, 8, 45, 105; DA; DAB; DAC; DAM DRAM, MST, POET; PC 2; SSC 3, 44; WLC**
  See also BRWS 1; CA 104; 120; CANR 65; CDBLB 1945-1960; DA3; DLB 13, 20, 139; EXPP; LAIT 3; MTCW 1, 2; PAB; PFS 1, 3, 8; RGEL; RGSF; SATA 60; WLIT 4; WP

Thomas, (Philip) Edward
  1878-1917 .... **TCLC 10; DAM POET**
  See also BRW 6; BRWS 3; CA 106; 153; DLB 19, 98, 156, 216; PAB; RGEL

Thomas, Joyce Carol 1938- .... **CLC 35**
  See also AAYA 12; BW 2, 3; CA 113; 116; CANR 48; CLR 19; DLB 33; INT CA-116; JRDA; MAICYA; MTCW 1, 2; SAAS 7; SATA 40, 78, 123; WYA; YAW

Thomas, Lewis 1913-1993 .... **CLC 35**
  See also ANW; CA 85-88; 143; CANR 38, 60; MTCW 1, 2

Thomas, M. Carey 1857-1935 .... **TCLC 89**
  See also FW

Thomas, Paul
  See Mann, (Paul) Thomas

Thomas, Piri 1928- .... **CLC 17; HLCS 2**
  See also CA 73-76; HW 1

Thomas, R(onald) S(tuart)
  1913-2000 . **CLC 6, 13, 48; DAB; DAM POET**
  See also CA 89-92; 189; CAAS 4; CANR 30; CDBLB 1960 to Present; CP; DLB 27; MTCW 1; RGEL

Thomas, Ross (Elmore) 1926-1995 .. **CLC 39**
  See also CA 33-36R; 150; CANR 22, 63; CMW

Thompson, Francis (Joseph)
  1859-1907 .... **TCLC 4**
  See also BRW 5; CA 104; 189; CDBLB 1890-1914; DLB 19; RGEL; TEA

Thompson, Francis Clegg
  See Mencken, H(enry) L(ouis)

Thompson, Hunter S(tockton)
  1939- ... **CLC 9, 17, 40, 104; DAM POP**
  See also BEST 89:1; BPFB 3; CA 17-20R; CANR 23, 46, 74, 77; CPW; CSW; DA3; DLB 185; MTCW 1, 2

Thompson, James Myers
  See Thompson, Jim (Myers)

Thompson, Jim (Myers)
  1906-1977(?) .... **CLC 69**
  See also BPFB 3; CA 140; CMW; CPW; DLB 226; MSW

Thompson, Judith .... **CLC 39**
  See also CWD

Thomson, James 1700-1748 ... **LC 16, 29, 40; DAM POET**
  See also BRWS 3; DLB 95; RGEL

Thomson, James 1834-1882 .... **NCLC 18; DAM POET**
  See also DLB 35; RGEL

Thoreau, Henry David 1817-1862 .. **NCLC 7, 21, 61; DA; DAB; DAC; DAM MST; PC 30; WLC**
  See also AAYA 42; AMW; ANW; BYA 3; CDALB 1640-1865; DA3; DLB 1, 183, 223; LAIT 2; RGAL

Thorndike, E. L.
  See Thorndike, Edward L(ee)

Thorndike, Edward L(ee)
  1874-1949 .... **TCLC 107**
  See also CA 121

Thornton, Hall
  See Silverberg, Robert

Thucydides c. 455B.C.-c. 395B.C. . . **CMLC 17**
  See also AW 1; DLB 176; RGWL

Thumboo, Edwin Nadason 1933- .... **PC 30**
  See also CA 194

Thurber, James (Grover)
  1894-1961 .... **CLC 5, 11, 25, 125; DA; DAB; DAC; DAM DRAM, MST, NOV; SSC 1, 47**
  See also AMWS 1; BPFB 3; BYA 5; CA 73-76; CANR 17, 39; CDALB 1929-1941; CWRI; DA3; DLB 4, 11, 22, 102; EXPS; FANT; LAIT 3; MAICYA; MTCW 1, 2; RGAL; RGSF; SATA 13; SSFS 1, 10; SUFW

Thurman, Wallace (Henry)
  1902-1934 .... **TCLC 6; BLC 3; DAM MULT**
  See also BW 1, 3; CA 104; 124; CANR 81; DLB 51

Tibullus c. 54B.C.-c. 18B.C. .... **CMLC 36**
  See also AW 2; DLB 211; RGWL

Ticheburn, Cheviot
  See Ainsworth, William Harrison

Tieck, (Johann) Ludwig
  1773-1853 .... **NCLC 5, 46; SSC 31**
  See also DLB 90; EW 5; RGSF; RGWL; SUFW

Tiger, Derry
  See Ellison, Harlan (Jay)

Tilghman, Christopher 1948(?)- .... **CLC 65**
  See also CA 159; CSW; DLB 244

Tillich, Paul (Johannes)
  1886-1965 .... **CLC 131**
  See also CA 5-8R; 25-28R; CANR 33; MTCW 1, 2

Tillinghast, Richard (Williford)
  1940- .... **CLC 29**
  See also CA 29-32R; CAAS 23; CANR 26, 51, 96; CP; CSW

Timrod, Henry 1828-1867 .... **NCLC 25**
  See also DLB 3, 248; RGAL

Tindall, Gillian (Elizabeth) 1938- ...... **CLC 7**
  See also CA 21-24R; CANR 11, 65; CN

Tiptree, James, Jr. .... **CLC 48, 50**
  See also Sheldon, Alice Hastings Bradley
  See also DLB 8; SCFW 2; SFW

Tirso de Molina
  See Tirso de Molina
  See also RGWL

Tirso de Molina 1580(?)-1648 ..... **LC 73; DC 13; HLCS 2**
  See also Tirso de Molina

Titmarsh, Michael Angelo
  See Thackeray, William Makepeace

Tocqueville, Alexis (Charles Henri Maurice Clerel Comte) de 1805-1859 .. **NCLC 7, 63**
  See also EW 6; GFL 1789 to the Present

Waruk, Kona
See Harris, (Theodore) Wilson
Warung, Price .... **TCLC 45**
See also Astley, William
See also DLB 230; RGEL
Warwick, Jarvis
See Garner, Hugh
See also CCA 1
Washington, Alex
See Harris, Mark
Washington, Booker T(aliaferro)
1856-1915 ...... **TCLC 10; BLC 3; DAM
MULT**
See also BW 1; CA 114; 125; DA3; LAIT
2; RGAL; SATA 28
Washington, George 1732-1799 .... **LC 25**
See also DLB 31
Wassermann, (Karl) Jakob
1873-1934 .... **TCLC 6**
See also CA 104; 163; DLB 66
Wasserstein, Wendy 1950- .. **CLC 32, 59, 90;
DAM DRAM; DC 4**
See also CA 121; 129; CABS 3; CAD;
CANR 53, 75; CD; CWD; DA3; DFS 5;
DLB 228; FW; INT CA-129; MTCW 2;
SATA 94
Waterhouse, Keith (Spencer) 1929- . **CLC 47**
See also CA 5-8R; CANR 38, 67; CBD;
CN; DLB 13, 15; MTCW 1, 2
Waters, Frank (Joseph) 1902-1995 .. **CLC 88**
See also CA 5-8R; 149; CAAS 13; CANR
3, 18, 63; DLB 212; DLBY 86; RGAL;
TCWW 2
Waters, Mary C. .... **CLC 70**
Waters, Roger 1944- .... **CLC 35**
Watkins, Frances Ellen
See Harper, Frances Ellen Watkins
Watkins, Gerrold
See Malzberg, Barry N(athaniel)
Watkins, Paul 1964- .... **CLC 55**
See also CA 132; CANR 62, 98
Watkins, Vernon Phillips
1906-1967 .... **CLC 43**
See also CA 9-10; 25-28R; CAP 1; DLB
20; RGEL
Watson, Irving S.
See Mencken, H(enry) L(ouis)
Watson, John H.
See Farmer, Philip Jose
Watson, Richard F.
See Silverberg, Robert
Waugh, Auberon (Alexander)
1939-2001 .... **CLC 7**
See also CA 45-48; 192; CANR 6, 22, 92;
DLB 14, 194
Waugh, Evelyn (Arthur St. John)
1903-1966 .. **CLC 1, 3, 8, 13, 19, 27, 44,
107; DA; DAB; DAC; DAM MST,
NOV, POP; SSC 41; WLC**
See also BPFB 3; BRW 7; CA 85-88; 25-
28R; CANR 22; CDBLB 1914-1945;
DA3; DLB 15, 162, 195; MTCW 1, 2;
NFS 13; RGEL; RGSF; WLIT 4
Waugh, Harriet 1944- .... **CLC 6**
See also CA 85-88; CANR 22
Ways, C. R.
See Blount, Roy (Alton), Jr.
Waystaff, Simon
See Swift, Jonathan
Webb, Beatrice (Martha Potter)
1858-1943 .... **TCLC 22**
See also CA 117; 162; DLB 190; FW
Webb, Charles (Richard) 1939- .... **CLC 7**
See also CA 25-28R
Webb, James H(enry), Jr. 1946- ...... **CLC 22**
See also CA 81-84
Webb, Mary Gladys (Meredith)
1881-1927 .... **TCLC 24**
See also CA 182; 123; DLB 34; FW

Webb, Mrs. Sidney
See Webb, Beatrice (Martha Potter)
Webb, Phyllis 1927- .... **CLC 18**
See also CA 104; CANR 23; CCA 1; CP;
CWP; DLB 53
Webb, Sidney (James) 1859-1947 .. **TCLC 22**
See also CA 117; 163; DLB 190
Webber, Andrew Lloyd .... **CLC 21**
See also Lloyd Webber, Andrew
See also DFS 7
Weber, Lenora Mattingly
1895-1971 .... **CLC 12**
See also CA 19-20; 29-32R; CAP 1; SATA
2; SATA-Obit 26
Weber, Max 1864-1920 .... **TCLC 69**
See also CA 109; 189
Webster, John 1580(?)-1634(?) ... **LC 33; DA;
DAB; DAC; DAM DRAM, MST; DC
2; WLC**
See also BRW 2; CDBLB Before 1660;
DLB 58; IDTP; RGEL; WLIT 3
Webster, Noah 1758-1843 .... **NCLC 30**
See also DLB 1, 37, 42, 43, 73, 243
Wedekind, (Benjamin) Frank(lin)
1864-1918 .... **TCLC 7; DAM DRAM**
See also CA 104; 153; DLB 118; EW 8;
RGWL
Wehr, Demaris .... **CLC 65**
Weidman, Jerome 1913-1998 .... **CLC 7**
See also AITN 2; CA 1-4R; 171; CAD;
CANR 1; DLB 28
Weil, Simone (Adolphine)
1909-1943 .... **TCLC 23**
See also CA 117; 159; EW 12; FW; GFL
1789 to the Present; MTCW 2
Weininger, Otto 1880-1903 .... **TCLC 84**
Weinstein, Nathan
See West, Nathanael
Weinstein, Nathan von Wallenstein
See West, Nathanael
Weir, Peter (Lindsay) 1944- .... **CLC 20**
See also CA 113; 123
Weiss, Peter (Ulrich) 1916-1982 .. **CLC 3, 15,
51; DAM DRAM**
See also CA 45-48; 106; CANR 3; DFS 3;
DLB 69, 124; RGWL
Weiss, Theodore (Russell) 1916- ... **CLC 3, 8,
14**
See also CA 9-12R; CAAE 189; CAAS 2;
CANR 46, 94; CP; DLB 5
Welch, (Maurice) Denton
1915-1948 .... **TCLC 22**
See also CA 121; 148; RGEL
Welch, James 1940- ..... **CLC 6, 14, 52; DAM
MULT, POP**
See also CA 85-88; CANR 42, 66; CN; CP;
CPW; DLB 175, 256; NNAL; RGAL;
TCWW 2
Weldon, Fay 1931- . **CLC 6, 9, 11, 19, 36, 59,
122; DAM POP**
See also BRWS 4; CA 21-24R; CANR 16,
46, 63, 97; CDBLB 1960 to Present; CN;
CPW; DLB 14, 194; FW; HGG; INT
CANR-16; MTCW 1, 2; RGEL; RGSF
Wellek, Rene 1903-1995 .... **CLC 28**
See also CA 5-8R; 150; CAAS 7; CANR 8;
DLB 63; INT CANR-8
Weller, Michael 1942- .... **CLC 10, 53**
See also CA 85-88; CAD; CD
Weller, Paul 1958- .... **CLC 26**
Wellershoff, Dieter 1925- .... **CLC 46**
See also CA 89-92; CANR 16, 37
Welles, (George) Orson 1915-1985 .. **CLC 20,
80**
See also AAYA 40; CA 93-96; 117
Wellman, John McDowell 1945-
See Wellman, Mac
See also CA 166; CD

Wellman, Mac .... **CLC 65**
See also Wellman, John McDowell; Well-
man, John McDowell
See also CAD; RGAL
Wellman, Manly Wade 1903-1986 ... **CLC 49**
See also CA 1-4R; 118; CANR 6, 16, 44;
FANT; SATA 6; SATA-Obit 47; SFW;
SUFW
Wells, Carolyn 1869(?)-1942 .... **TCLC 35**
See also CA 113; 185; CMW; DLB 11
Wells, H(erbert) G(eorge)
1866-1946 . **TCLC 6, 12, 19; DA; DAB;
DAC; DAM MST, NOV; SSC 6; WLC**
See also AAYA 18; BPFB 3; BRW 6; CA
110; 121; CDBLB 1914-1945; CLR 64;
DA3; DLB 34, 70, 156, 178; EXPS;
HGG; LAIT 3; MTCW 1, 2; RGEL;
RGSF; SATA 20; SCFW; SFW; SSFS 3;
SUFW; WCH; WLIT 4; YAW
Wells, Rosemary 1943- .... **CLC 12**
See also AAYA 13; BYA 7, 8; CA 85-88;
CANR 48; CLR 16, 69; CWRI; MAICYA;
SAAS 1; SATA 18, 69, 114; YAW
Welsh, Irvine 1958- .... **CLC 144**
See also CA 173
Welty, Eudora 1909-2001 .... **CLC 1, 2, 5, 14,
22, 33, 105; DA; DAB; DAC; DAM
MST, NOV; SSC 1, 27, 51; WLC**
See also AMW; AMWR 1; BPFB 3; CA
9-12R; CABS 1; CANR 32, 65; CDALB
1941-1968; CN; CSW; DA3; DLB 2, 102,
143; DLBD 12; DLBY 87, 01; EXPS;
HGG; LAIT 3; MAWW; MTCW 1, 2;
NFS 13; RGAL; RGSF; RHW; SSFS 2,
10
Wen I-to 1899-1946 .... **TCLC 28**
Wentworth, Robert
See Hamilton, Edmond
Werfel, Franz (Viktor) 1890-1945 ... **TCLC 8**
See also CA 104; 161; DLB 81, 124;
RGWL
Wergeland, Henrik Arnold
1808-1845 .... **NCLC 5**
Wersba, Barbara 1932- .... **CLC 30**
See also AAYA 2, 30; BYA 6, 12, 13; CA
29-32R, 182; CAAE 182; CANR 16, 38;
CLR 3; DLB 52; JRDA; MAICYA; SAAS
2; SATA 1, 58; SATA-Essay 103; WYA;
YAW
Wertmueller, Lina 1928- .... **CLC 16**
See also CA 97-100; CANR 39, 78
Wescott, Glenway 1901-1987 .. **CLC 13; SSC
35**
See also CA 13-16R; 121; CANR 23, 70;
DLB 4, 9, 102; RGAL
Wesker, Arnold 1932- ... **CLC 3, 5, 42; DAB;
DAM DRAM**
See also CA 1-4R; CAAS 7; CANR 1, 33;
CBD; CD; CDBLB 1960 to Present; DLB
13; MTCW 1; RGEL
Wesley, Richard (Errol) 1945- .... **CLC 7**
See also BW 1; CA 57-60; CAD; CANR
27; CD; DLB 38
Wessel, Johan Herman 1742-1785 .... **LC 7**
West, Anthony (Panther)
1914-1987 .... **CLC 50**
See also CA 45-48; 124; CANR 3, 19; DLB
15
West, C. P.
See Wodehouse, P(elham) G(renville)
West, Cornel (Ronald) 1953- .... **CLC 134;
BLCS**
See also CA 144; CANR 91; DLB 246
West, Delno C(loyde), Jr. 1936- .... **CLC 70**
See also CA 57-60
West, Dorothy 1907-1998 .... **TCLC 108**
See also BW 2; CA 143; 169; DLB 76

West, (Mary) Jessamyn 1902-1984 ... CLC 7, 17

See also CA 9-12R; 112; CANR 27; DLB 6; DLBY 84; MTCW 1, 2; RHW; SATA-Obit 37; YAW

West, Morris L(anglo) 1916-1999 ..... CLC 6, 33

See also BPFB 3; CA 5-8R; 187; CANR 24, 49, 64; CN; CPW; MTCW 1, 2

West, Nathanael 1903-1940 .... TCLC 1, 14, 44; SSC 16

See also AMW; BPFB 3; CA 104; 125; CDALB 1929-1941; DA3; DLB 4, 9, 28; MTCW 1, 2; RGAL

West, Owen

See Koontz, Dean R(ay)

West, Paul 1930- .... CLC 7, 14, 96

See also CA 13-16R; CAAS 7; CANR 22, 53, 76, 89; CN; DLB 14; INT CANR-22; MTCW 2

West, Rebecca 1892-1983 ... CLC 7, 9, 31, 50

See also BPFB 3; BRWS 3; CA 5-8R; 109; CANR 19; DLB 36; DLBY 83; FW; MTCW 1, 2; RGEL

Westall, Robert (Atkinson) 1929-1993 .... CLC 17

See also AAYA 12; BYA 2, 6, 7, 8, 9; CA 69-72; 141; CANR 18, 68; CLR 13; FANT; JRDA; MAICYA; MAICYAS; SAAS 2; SATA 23, 69; SATA-Obit 75; WYA; YAW

Westermarck, Edward 1862-1939 . TCLC 87

Westlake, Donald E(dwin) 1933- .... CLC 7, 33; DAM POP

See also BPFB 3; CA 17-20R; CAAS 13; CANR 16, 44, 65, 94; CMW; CPW; INT CANR-16; MSW; MTCW 2

Westmacott, Mary

See Christie, Agatha (Mary Clarissa)

Weston, Allen

See Norton, Andre

Wetcheek, J. L.

See Feuchtwanger, Lion

Wetering, Janwillem van de

See van de Wetering, Janwillem

Wetherald, Agnes Ethelwyn 1857-1940 .... TCLC 81

See also DLB 99

Wetherell, Elizabeth

See Warner, Susan (Bogert)

Whale, James 1889-1957 .... TCLC 63

Whalen, Philip 1923- .... CLC 6, 29

See also CA 9-12R; CANR 5, 39; CP; DLB 16; WP

Wharton, Edith (Newbold Jones) 1862-1937 .... TCLC 3, 9, 27, 53; DA; DAB; DAC; DAM MST, NOV; SSC 6; WLC

See also AAYA 25; AMW; AMWR 1; BPFB 3; CA 104; 132; CDALB 1865-1917; DA3; DLB 4, 9, 12, 78, 189; DLBD 13; EXPS; HGG; LAIT 2, 3; MAWW; MTCW 1, 2; NFS 5, 11; RGAL; RGSF; RHW; SSFS 6, 7; SUFW

Wharton, James

See Mencken, H(enry) L(ouis)

Wharton, William (a pseudonym) . CLC 18, 37

See also CA 93-96; DLBY 80; INT 93-96

Wheatley (Peters), Phillis 1753(?)-1784 ...... LC 3, 50; BLC 3; DA; DAC; DAM MST, MULT, POET; PC 3; WLC

See also AFAW 1, 2; CDALB 1640-1865; DA3; DLB 31, 50; EXPP; PFS 13; RGAL

Wheelock, John Hall 1886-1978 .... CLC 14

See also CA 13-16R; 77-80; CANR 14; DLB 45

White, Babington

See Braddon, Mary Elizabeth

White, E(lwyn) B(rooks) 1899-1985 . CLC 10, 34, 39; DAM POP

See also AITN 2; AMWS 1; CA 13-16R; 116; CANR 16, 37; CDALBS; CLR 1, 21; CPW; DA3; DLB 11, 22; FANT; MAI-CYA; MTCW 1, 2; RGAL; SATA 2, 29, 100; SATA-Obit 44

White, Edmund (Valentine III) 1940- .... CLC 27, 110; DAM POP

See also AAYA 7; CA 45-48; CANR 3, 19, 36, 62; CN; DA3; DLB 227; MTCW 1, 2

White, Hayden V. 1928- .... CLC 148

See also CA 128; DLB 246

White, Patrick (Victor Martindale) 1912-1990 ...... CLC 3, 4, 5, 7, 9, 18, 65, 69; SSC 39

See also BRWS 1; CA 81-84; 132; CANR 43; MTCW 1; RGEL; RGSF; RHW

White, Phyllis Dorothy James 1920-

See James, P. D.

See also CA 21-24R; CANR 17, 43, 65; CMW; CN; CPW; DA3; DAM POP; MTCW 1, 2

White, T(erence) H(anbury) 1906-1964 .... CLC 30

See also AAYA 22; BPFB 3; BYA 4, 5; CA 73-76; CANR 37; DLB 160; FANT; JRDA; LAIT 1; MAICYA; RGEL; SATA 12; SUFW; YAW

White, Terence de Vere 1912-1994 ... CLC 49

See also CA 49-52; 145; CANR 3

White, Walter

See White, Walter F(rancis)

White, Walter F(rancis) 1893-1955 ...... TCLC 15; BLC 3; DAM MULT

See also BW 1; CA 115; 124; DLB 51

White, William Hale 1831-1913

See Rutherford, Mark

See also CA 121; 189

Whitehead, Alfred North 1861-1947 .... TCLC 97

See also CA 117; 165; DLB 100

Whitehead, E(dward) A(nthony) 1933- .... CLC 5

See also CA 65-68; CANR 58; CD

Whitemore, Hugh (John) 1936- .... CLC 37

See also CA 132; CANR 77; CBD; CD; INT CA-132

Whitman, Sarah Helen (Power) 1803-1878 .... NCLC 19

See also DLB 1, 243

Whitman, Walt(er) 1819-1892 .. NCLC 4, 31, 81; DA; DAB; DAC; DAM MST, POET; PC 3; WLC

See also AAYA 42; AMW; AMWR 1; CDALB 1640-1865; DA3; DLB 3, 64, 224, 250; EXPP; LAIT 2; PAB; PFS 2, 3, 13; RGAL; SATA 20; WP; WYAS 1

Whitney, Phyllis A(yame) 1903- ...... CLC 42; DAM POP

See also AAYA 36; AITN 2; BEST 90:3; CA 1-4R; CANR 3, 25, 38, 60; CLR 59; CMW; CPW; DA3; JRDA; MAICYA; MTCW 2; RHW; SATA 1, 30; YAW

Whittemore, (Edward) Reed (Jr.) 1919- .... CLC 4

See also CA 9-12R; CAAS 8; CANR 4; CP; DLB 5

Whittier, John Greenleaf 1807-1892 .... NCLC 8, 59

See also AMWS 1; DLB 1, 243; RGAL

Whittlebot, Hernia

See Coward, Noel (Peirce)

Wicker, Thomas Grey 1926-

See Wicker, Tom

See also CA 65-68; CANR 21, 46

Wicker, Tom .... CLC 7

See also Wicker, Thomas Grey

Wideman, John Edgar 1941- ...... CLC 5, 34, 36, 67, 122; BLC 3; DAM MULT

See also AFAW 1, 2; AMWS 10; BPFB 4; BW 2, 3; CA 85-88; CANR 14, 42, 67; CN; DLB 33, 143; MTCW 2; RGAL; RGSF; SSFS 6, 12

Wiebe, Rudy (Henry) 1934- .. CLC 6, 11, 14, 138; DAC; DAM MST

See also CA 37-40R; CANR 42, 67; CN; DLB 60; RHW

Wieland, Christoph Martin 1733-1813 .... NCLC 17

See also DLB 97; EW 4; RGWL

Wiene, Robert 1881-1938 .... TCLC 56

Wieners, John 1934- .... CLC 7

See also CA 13-16R; CP; DLB 16; WP

Wiesel, Elie(zer) 1928- .... CLC 3, 5, 11, 37; DA; DAB; DAC; DAM MST, NOV; WLCS

See also AAYA 7; AITN 1; CA 5-8R; CAAS 4; CANR 8, 40, 65; CDALBS; DA3; DLB 83; DLBY 87; INT CANR-8; LAIT 4; MTCW 1, 2; NFS 4; SATA 56; YAW

Wiggins, Marianne 1947- .... CLC 57

See also BEST 89:3; CA 130; CANR 60

Wiggs, Susan .... CLC 70

Wight, James Alfred 1916-1995

See Herriot, James

See also CA 77-80; CPW; SATA 55; SATA-Brief 44; YAW

Wilbur, Richard (Purdy) 1921- ..... CLC 3, 6, 9, 14, 53, 110; DA; DAB; DAC; DAM MST, POET

See also AMWS 3; CA 1-4R; CABS 2; CANR 2, 29, 76, 93; CDALBS; CP; DLB 5, 169; EXPP; INT CANR-29; MTCW 1, 2; PAB; PFS 11, 12; RGAL; SATA 9, 108; WP

Wild, Peter 1940- .... CLC 14

See also CA 37-40R; CP; DLB 5

Wilde, Oscar (Fingal O'Flahertie Wills) 1854(?)-1900 .... TCLC 1, 8, 23, 41; DA; DAB; DAC; DAM DRAM, MST, NOV; SSC 11; WLC

See also BRW 5; BRWR 2; CA 104; 119; CDBLB 1890-1914; DA3; DFS 4, 8, 9; DLB 10, 19, 34, 57, 141, 156, 190; EXPS; FANT; RGEL; RGSF; SATA 24; SSFS 7; SUFW; TEA; WCH; WLIT 4

Wilder, Billy .... CLC 20

See also Wilder, Samuel

See also DLB 26

Wilder, Samuel 1906-

See Wilder, Billy

See also CA 89-92

Wilder, Stephen

See Marlowe, Stephen

Wilder, Thornton (Niven) 1897-1975 .. CLC 1, 5, 6, 10, 15, 35, 82; DA; DAB; DAC; DAM DRAM, MST, NOV; DC 1; WLC

See also AAYA 29; AITN 2; AMW; CA 13-16R; 61-64; CAD; CANR 40; CDALBS; DA3; DFS 1, 4; DLB 4, 7, 9, 228; DLBY 97; LAIT 3; MTCW 1, 2; RGAL; RHW; WYAS 1

Wilding, Michael 1942- ...... CLC 73; SSC 50

See also CA 104; CANR 24, 49, 106; CN; RGSF

Wiley, Richard 1944- .... CLC 44

See also CA 121; 129; CANR 71

Wilhelm, Kate .... CLC 7

See also Wilhelm, Katie (Gertrude)

See also AAYA 20; CAAS 5; DLB 8; INT CANR-17; SCFW 2

Wilhelm, Katie (Gertrude) 1928-
See Wilhelm, Kate
See also CA 37-40R; CANR 17, 36, 60, 94;
MTCW 1; SFW
Wilkins, Mary
See Freeman, Mary E(leanor) Wilkins
Willard, Nancy 1936- .... **CLC 7, 37**
See also BYA 5; CA 89-92; CANR 10, 39,
68; CLR 5; CWP; CWRI; DLB 5, 52;
FANT; MAICYA; MTCW 1; SATA 37,
71, 127; SATA-Brief 30
William of Ockham 1290-1349 ..... **CMLC 32**
Williams, Ben Ames 1889-1953 ..... **TCLC 89**
See also CA 183; DLB 102
Williams, C(harles) K(enneth)
1936- .... **CLC 33, 56, 148; DAM POET**
See also CA 37-40R; CAAS 26; CANR 57,
106; CP; DLB 5
Williams, Charles
See Collier, James Lincoln
Williams, Charles (Walter Stansby)
1886-1945 .... **TCLC 1, 11**
See also CA 104; 163; DLB 100, 153, 255;
FANT; RGEL; SUFW
Williams, (George) Emlyn
1905-1987 .... **CLC 15; DAM DRAM**
See also CA 104; 123; CANR 36; DLB 10,
77; MTCW 1
Williams, Hank 1923-1953 .... **TCLC 81**
Williams, Hugo 1942- .... **CLC 42**
See also CA 17-20R; CANR 45; CP; DLB
40
Williams, J. Walker
See Wodehouse, P(elham) G(renville)
Williams, John A(lfred) 1925- ..... **CLC 5, 13;**
BLC 3; DAM MULT
See also AFAW 2; BW 2, 3; CA 53-56;
CAAE 195; CAAS 3; CANR 6, 26, 51;
CN; CSW; DLB 2, 33; INT CANR-6;
RGAL; SFW
Williams, Jonathan (Chamberlain)
1929- .... **CLC 13**
See also CA 9-12R; CAAS 12; CANR 8;
CP; DLB 5
Williams, Joy 1944- .... **CLC 31**
See also CA 41-44R; CANR 22, 48, 97
Williams, Norman 1952- .... **CLC 39**
See also CA 118
Williams, Sherley Anne 1944-1999 . **CLC 89;**
BLC 3; DAM MULT, POET
See also AFAW 2; BW 2, 3; CA 73-76; 185;
CANR 25, 82; DLB 41; INT CANR-25;
SATA 78; SATA-Obit 116
Williams, Shirley
See Williams, Sherley Anne
Williams, Tennessee 1914-1983 . **CLC 1, 2, 5,**
7, 8, 11, 15, 19, 30, 39, 45, 71, 111; DA;
DAB; DAC; DAM DRAM, MST; DC
4; WLC
See also AAYA 31; AITN 1, 2; AMW; CA
5-8R; 108; CABS 3; CAD; CANR 31;
CDALB 1941-1968; DA3; DFS 1, 3, 7,
12; DLB 7; DLBD 4; DLBY 83; GLL 1;
LAIT 4; MTCW 1, 2; RGAL
Williams, Thomas (Alonzo)
1926-1990 .... **CLC 14**
See also CA 1-4R; 132; CANR 2
Williams, William C.
See Williams, William Carlos
Williams, William Carlos
1883-1963 .... **CLC 1, 2, 5, 9, 13, 22, 42,**
67; DA; DAB; DAC; DAM MST,
POET; PC 7; SSC 31
See also AMW; AMWR 1; CA 89-92;
CANR 34; CDALB 1917-1929; DA3;
DLB 4, 16, 54, 86; EXPP; MTCW 1, 2;
PAB; PFS 1, 6, 11; RGAL; RGSF; WP
Williamson, David (Keith) 1942- ..... **CLC 56**
See also CA 103; CANR 41; CD

Williamson, Ellen Douglas 1905-1984
See Douglas, Ellen
See also CA 17-20R; 114; CANR 39
Williamson, Jack .... **CLC 29**
See also Williamson, John Stewart
See also CAAS 8; DLB 8; SCFW 2
Williamson, John Stewart 1908-
See Williamson, Jack
See also CA 17-20R; CANR 23, 70; SFW
Willie, Frederick
See Lovecraft, H(oward) P(hillips)
Willingham, Calder (Baynard, Jr.)
1922-1995 .... **CLC 5, 51**
See also CA 5-8R; 147; CANR 3; CSW;
DLB 2, 44; IDFW 3, 4; MTCW 1
Willis, Charles
See Clarke, Arthur C(harles)
Willy
See Colette, (Sidonie-Gabrielle)
Willy, Colette
See Colette, (Sidonie-Gabrielle)
See also GLL 1
Wilmot, John
See Rochester, Earl of
See also BRW 2; DLB 131; PAB
Wilson, A(ndrew) N(orman) 1950- .. **CLC 33**
See also BRWS 6; CA 112; 122; CN; DLB
14, 155, 194; MTCW 2
Wilson, Angus (Frank Johnstone)
1913-1991 . **CLC 2, 3, 5, 25, 34; SSC 21**
See also BRWS 1; CA 5-8R; 134; CANR
21; DLB 15, 139, 155; MTCW 1, 2;
RGEL; RGSF
Wilson, August 1945- ... **CLC 39, 50, 63, 118;**
BLC 3; DA; DAB; DAC; DAM
DRAM, MST, MULT; DC 2; WLCS
See also AAYA 16; AFAW 2; AMWS 8; BW
2, 3; CA 115; 122; CAD; CANR 42, 54,
76; CD; DA3; DFS 3, 7; DLB 228; LAIT
4; MTCW 1, 2; RGAL
Wilson, Brian 1942- .... **CLC 12**
Wilson, Colin 1931- .... **CLC 3, 14**
See also CA 1-4R; CAAS 5; CANR 1, 22,
33, 77; CMW; CN; DLB 14, 194; HGG;
MTCW 1; SFW
Wilson, Dirk
See Pohl, Frederik
Wilson, Edmund 1895-1972 .. **CLC 1, 2, 3, 8,**
24
See also AMW; CA 1-4R; 37-40R; CANR
1, 46; DLB 63; MTCW 1, 2; RGAL
Wilson, Ethel Davis (Bryant)
1888(?)-1980 .... **CLC 13; DAC; DAM**
POET
See also CA 102; DLB 68; MTCW 1;
RGEL
Wilson, Harriet
See Wilson, Harriet E. Adams
See also DLB 239
Wilson, Harriet E. Adams
1827(?)-1863(?) .... **NCLC 78; BLC 3;**
DAM MULT
See also Wilson, Harriet
See also DLB 50, 243
Wilson, John 1785-1854 .... **NCLC 5**
Wilson, John (Anthony) Burgess 1917-1993
See Burgess, Anthony
See also CA 1-4R; 143; CANR 2, 46; DA3;
DAC; DAM NOV; MTCW 1, 2
Wilson, Lanford 1937- .... **CLC 7, 14, 36;**
DAM DRAM
See also CA 17-20R; CABS 3; CAD; CANR
45, 96; CD; DFS 4, 9, 12; DLB 7
Wilson, Robert M. 1944- .... **CLC 7, 9**
See also CA 49-52; CAD; CANR 2, 41; CD;
MTCW 1
Wilson, Robert McLiam 1964- .... **CLC 59**
See also CA 132

Wilson, Sloan 1920- .... **CLC 32**
See also CA 1-4R; CANR 1, 44; CN
Wilson, Snoo 1948- .... **CLC 33**
See also CA 69-72; CBD; CD
Wilson, William S(mith) 1932- .... **CLC 49**
See also CA 81-84
Wilson, (Thomas) Woodrow
1856-1924 .... **TCLC 79**
See also CA 166; DLB 47
Wilson and Warnke eds. .... **CLC 65**
Winchilsea, Anne (Kingsmill) Finch
1661-1720
See Finch, Anne
See also RGEL
Windham, Basil
See Wodehouse, P(elham) G(renville)
Wingrove, David (John) 1954- .... **CLC 68**
See also CA 133; SFW
Winnemucca, Sarah 1844-1891 .... **NCLC 79;**
DAM MULT
See also DLB 175; NNAL; RGAL
Winstanley, Gerrard 1609-1676 .... **LC 52**
Wintergreen, Jane
See Duncan, Sara Jeannette
Winters, Janet Lewis .... **CLC 41**
See also Lewis, Janet
See also DLBY 87
Winters, (Arthur) Yvor 1900-1968 .... **CLC 4,**
8, 32
See also AMWS 2; CA 11-12; 25-28R; CAP
1; DLB 48; MTCW 1; RGAL
Winterson, Jeanette 1959- .... **CLC 64; DAM**
POP
See also BRWS 4; CA 136; CANR 58; CN;
CPW; DA3; DLB 207; FANT; FW; GLL
1; MTCW 2; RHW
Winthrop, John 1588-1649 .... **LC 31**
See also DLB 24, 30
Wirth, Louis 1897-1952 .... **TCLC 92**
Wiseman, Frederick 1930- .... **CLC 20**
See also CA 159
Wister, Owen 1860-1938 .... **TCLC 21**
See also BPFB 3; CA 108; 162; DLB 9, 78,
186; RGAL; SATA 62; TCWW 2
Witkacy
See Witkiewicz, Stanislaw Ignacy
Witkiewicz, Stanislaw Ignacy
1885-1939 .... **TCLC 8**
See also CA 105; 162; DLB 215; EW 10;
RGWL; SFW
Wittgenstein, Ludwig (Josef Johann)
1889-1951 .... **TCLC 59**
See also CA 113; 164; MTCW 2
Wittig, Monique 1935(?)- .... **CLC 22**
See also CA 116; 135; CWW 2; DLB 83;
FW; GLL 1
Wittlin, Jozef 1896-1976 .... **CLC 25**
See also CA 49-52; 65-68; CANR 3
Wodehouse, P(elham) G(renville)
1881-1975 .... **CLC 1, 2, 5, 10, 22; DAB;**
DAC; DAM NOV; SSC 2
See also AITN 2; BRWS 3; CA 45-48; 57-
60; CANR 3, 33; CDBLB 1914-1945;
CPW 1; DA3; DLB 34, 162; MTCW 1, 2;
RGEL; RGSF; SATA 22; SSFS 10; TCLC
108
Woiwode, L.
See Woiwode, Larry (Alfred)
Woiwode, Larry (Alfred) 1941- ... **CLC 6, 10**
See also CA 73-76; CANR 16, 94; CN;
DLB 6; INT CANR-16
Wojciechowska, Maia (Teresa)
1927- .... **CLC 26**
See also AAYA 8; BYA 3; CA 9-12R, 183;
CAAE 183; CANR 4, 41; CLR 1; JRDA;
MAICYA; SAAS 1; SATA 1, 28, 83;
SATA-Essay 104; YAW
Wojtyla, Karol
See John Paul II, Pope

Literary Criticism Series
Cumulative Topic Index

This index lists all topic entries in Gale's *Classical and Medieval Literature Criticism, Contemporary Literary Criticism, Drama Criticism, Literature Criticism from 1400 to 1800, Nineteenth-Century Literature Criticism,* and *Twentieth-Century Literary Criticism.*

Topic Index

TCLC Cumulative Nationality Index

AMERICAN

Adams, Andy **56**
Adams, Brooks **80**
Adams, Henry (Brooks) **4, 52**
Addams, Jane **76**
Agee, James (Rufus) **1, 19**
Allen, Fred **87**
Anderson, Maxwell **2**
Anderson, Sherwood **1, 10, 24**
Anthony, Susan B(rownell) **84**
Atherton, Gertrude (Franklin Horn) **2**
Austin, Mary (Hunter) **25**
Baker, Ray Stannard **47**
Bambara, Toni Cade **116**
Barry, Philip **11**
Baum, L(yman) Frank **7**
Beard, Charles A(ustin) **15**
Becker, Carl (Lotus) **63**
Belasco, David **3**
Bell, James Madison **43**
Benchley, Robert (Charles) **1, 55**
Benedict, Ruth (Fulton) **60**
Benét, Stephen Vincent **7**
Benét, William Rose **28**
Bierce, Ambrose (Gwinett) **1, 7, 44**
Biggers, Earl Derr **65**
Bishop, John Peale **103**
Black Elk **33**
Boas, Franz **56**
Bodenheim, Maxwell **44**
Bok, Edward W. **101**
Bourne, Randolph S(illiman) **16**
Boyd, James **115**
Boyd, Thomas (Alexander) **111**
Bradford, Gamaliel **36**
Brennan, Christopher John **17**
Bromfield, Louis (Brucker) **11**
Broun, Heywood **104**
Bryan, William Jennings **99**
Burroughs, Edgar Rice **2, 32**
Cabell, James Branch **6**
Cable, George Washington **4**
Cahan, Abraham **71**
Caldwell, Erskine (Preston) **117**
Cardozo, Benjamin N(athan) **65**
Carnegie, Dale **53**
Cather, Willa (Sibert) **1, 11, 31, 99**
Chambers, Robert W(illiam) **41**
Chandler, Raymond (Thornton) **1, 7**
Chapman, John Jay **7**
Chesnutt, Charles W(addell) **5, 39**
Childress, Alice **116**
Cobb, Irvin S(hrewsbury) **77**
Coffin, Robert P(eter) Tristram **95**
Cohan, George M(ichael) **60**
Comstock, Anthony **13**
Cotter, Joseph Seamon Sr. **28**
Cram, Ralph Adams **45**
Crane, (Harold) Hart **2, 5, 80**
Crane, Stephen (Townley) **11, 17, 32**
Crawford, F(rancis) Marion **10**
Crothers, Rachel **19**

Cullen, Countée **4, 37**
Darrow, Clarence (Seward) **81**
Davis, Rebecca (Blaine) Harding **6**
Davis, Richard Harding **24**
Day, Clarence (Shepard Jr.) **25**
Dent, Lester **72**
De Voto, Bernard (Augustine) **29**
Dewey, John **95**
Dreiser, Theodore (Herman Albert) **10, 18, 35, 83**
Dulles, John Foster **72**
Dunbar, Paul Laurence **2, 12**
Duncan, Isadora **68**
Dunne, Finley Peter **28**
Eastman, Charles A(lexander) **55**
Eddy, Mary (Ann Morse) Baker **71**
Einstein, Albert **65**
Erskine, John **84**
Faust, Frederick (Schiller) **49**
Fenollosa, Ernest (Francisco) **91**
Fields, W. C. **80**
Fisher, Dorothy (Frances) Canfield **87**
Fisher, Rudolph **11**
Fitzgerald, F(rancis) Scott (Key) **1, 6, 14, 28, 55**
Fitzgerald, Zelda (Sayre) **52**
Fletcher, John Gould **35**
Foote, Mary Hallock **108**
Ford, Henry **73**
Forten, Charlotte L. **16**
Freeman, Douglas Southall **11**
Freeman, Mary E(leanor) Wilkins **9**
Fuller, Henry Blake **103**
Futrelle, Jacques **19**
Gale, Zona **7**
Garland, (Hannibal) Hamlin **3**
Gilman, Charlotte (Anna) Perkins (Stetson) **9, 37, 117**
Glasgow, Ellen (Anderson Gholson) **2, 7**
Glaspell, Susan **55**
Goldman, Emma **13**
Green, Anna Katharine **63**
Grey, Zane **6**
Griffith, D(avid Lewelyn) W(ark) **68**
Griggs, Sutton (Elbert) **77**
Guest, Edgar A(lbert) **95**
Guiney, Louise Imogen **41**
Hall, James Norman **23**
Handy, W(illiam) C(hristopher) **97**
Harper, Frances Ellen Watkins **14**
Harris, Joel Chandler **2**
Harte, (Francis) Bret(t) **1, 25**
Hartmann, Sadakichi **73**
Hatteras, Owen **18**
Hawthorne, Julian **25**
Hearn, (Patricio) Lafcadio (Tessima Carlos) **9**
Hecht, Ben **101**
Hemingway, Ernest (Miller) **115**
Henry, O. **1, 19**
Hergesheimer, Joseph **11**
Heyward, (Edwin) DuBose **59**
Higginson, Thomas Wentworth **36**
Holley, Marietta **99**

Holly, Buddy **65**
Holmes, Oliver Wendell Jr. **77**
Hopkins, Pauline Elizabeth **28**
Horney, Karen (Clementine Theodore Danielsen) **71**
Howard, Robert E(rvin) **8**
Howe, Julia Ward **21**
Howells, William Dean **7, 17, 41**
Huneker, James Gibbons **65**
Ince, Thomas H. **89**
James, Henry **2, 11, 24, 40, 47, 64**
James, William **15, 32**
Jewett, (Theodora) Sarah Orne **1, 22**
Johnson, James Weldon **3, 19**
Johnson, Robert **69**
Kerouac, Jack **117**
Kinsey, Alfred C(harles) **91**
Kornbluth, C(yril) M. **8**
Korzybski, Alfred (Habdank Skarbek) **61**
Kubrick, Stanley **112**
Kuttner, Henry **10**
Lardner, Ring(gold) W(ilmer) **2, 14**
Lewis, (Harry) Sinclair **4, 13, 23, 39**
Lewisohn, Ludwig **19**
Lewton, Val **76**
Lindsay, (Nicholas) Vachel **17**
Locke, Alain (Le Roy) **43**
Lockridge, Ross (Franklin) Jr. **111**
London, Jack **9, 15, 39**
Lovecraft, H(oward) P(hillips) **4, 22**
Lowell, Amy **1, 8**
Mankiewicz, Herman (Jacob) **85**
March, William **96**
Markham, Edwin **47**
Marquis, Don(ald Robert Perry) **7**
Masters, Edgar Lee **2, 25**
Matthews, (James) Brander **95**
Matthiessen, F(rancis) O(tto) **100**
McAlmon, Robert (Menzies) **97**
McCoy, Horace (Stanley) **28**
Mead, George Herbert **89**
Mencken, H(enry) L(ouis) **13**
Micheaux, Oscar (Devereaux) **76**
Millay, Edna St. Vincent **4, 49**
Mitchell, Margaret (Munnerlyn) **11**
Mitchell, S(ilas) Weir **36**
Mitchell, William **81**
Monroe, Harriet **12**
Moody, William Vaughan **105**
Morley, Christopher (Darlington) **87**
Morris, Wright **107**
Muir, John **28**
Nabokov, Vladimir (Vladimirovich) **108**
Nash, (Frediric) Ogden **109**
Nathan, George Jean **18**
Neumann, Alfred **100**
Nisbet, Robert A(lexander) **117**
Nordhoff, Charles (Bernard) **23**
Norris, (Benjamin) Frank(lin Jr.) **24**
O'Neill, Eugene (Gladstone) **1, 6, 27, 49**
Oppen, George **107**
Osbourne, Lloyd **93**
Oskison, John Milton **35**

Nationality Index

ISBN 0-7876-5862-6